Buying Social Justice

*Equality, Government Procurement,
and Legal Change*

CHRISTOPHER McCRUDDEN

*Professor of Human Rights Law and Fellow of Lincoln College,
University of Oxford*

OXFORD
UNIVERSITY PRESS

OXFORD
UNIVERSITY PRESS

Great Clarendon Street, Oxford OX2 6DP

Oxford University Press is a department of the University of Oxford.
It furthers the University's objective of excellence in research, scholarship,
and education by publishing worldwide in

Oxford New York

Auckland Cape Town Dar es Salaam Hong Kong Karachi
Kuala Lumpur Madrid Melbourne Mexico City Nairobi
New Delhi Shanghai Taipei Toronto

With offices in

Argentina Austria Brazil Chile Czech Republic France Greece
Guatemala Hungary Italy Japan Poland Portugal Singapore
South Korea Switzerland Thailand Turkey Ukraine Vietnam

Oxford is a registered trade mark of Oxford University Press
in the UK and in certain other countries

Published in the United States
by Oxford University Press Inc., New York

© C. McCrudden, 2007

British Library Cataloguing in Publication Data

Data available

Library of Congress Cataloging in Publication Data

McCrudden, Christopher.
Buying social justice : equality, government procurement, and legal change /
Christopher McCrudden
p. cm.
Includes bibliographical references and index.
ISBN-13: 978-0-19-923242-0
ISBN-13: 978-0-19-923243-7
1. Government purchasing—Law and legislation—Political aspects.
2. Public contracts—Political aspects. 3. Social justice. 4. Social policy.
I. Title.
K.M33 2007
346.7302'—dc22

2007020812

Typeset by Newgen Imaging Systems (P) Ltd., Chennai, India
Printed in Great Britain
on acid-free paper by
Biddles Ltd., King's Lynn

ISBN 978–0–19–923242–0
ISBN 978–0–19–923243–7 (Pbk)

1 3 5 7 9 10 8 6 4 2

To my wife, Caroline, and my children, Joseph and
Kathleen, with my love

AMDG

Acknowledgements

Many people and institutions have contributed to the writing of this book, in addition to those mentioned in the Preface. I am grateful to the Faculty of Law, Oxford University, and to Lincoln College, Oxford for providing excellent facilities, stimulating students, congenial colleagues, several grants from research funds, and permission to take sabbatical leave at opportune moments. I am also grateful to the Arts and Humanities Research Council for funding an extra term's sabbatical to facilitate completion of a draft of the manuscript. Versions of various parts of the book were presented in early forms at University of Michigan Law School seminars, as well as at workshops and lectures at the University of Texas Law School, Yale Law School, the National University of Ireland (Galway), Kingston University, Leeds University, Nottingham University, University College, London, and at the International Training Centre of the ILO in Turin; thanks are due to participants at these events for useful comments.

In Oxford, several colleagues helped with particular aspects of the book, particularly Simon Whittaker, Dan Sarooshi, Stephen Weatherill, and Paolisa Nebbia. Colleagues at the University of Michigan Law School have also been unfailingly helpful, particularly Brian Simpson, Rob Howse, Don Regan, Daniel Halberstam, Michael Barr, Ted St Antoine, Don Herzog, Sallyanne Payton, Catharine MacKinnon, Evan Caminker, Jim Hathaway, Joseph Vining, Grace Tonner, Carl Schneider, Steven Ratner, and Nina Mendelson. Mark Freedland and Ted St Antoine conspired together to shame me into finally publishing. Sir Bob Hepple's work on integrating the social and economic aspects of globalization in the legal context gave me confidence that the project was worthwhile. Several colleagues read and commented on drafts of the complete manuscript, particularly Mark Freedland, Christine Bell (who also suggested the title of the book), William Twining, and Sue Arrowsmith (who gave unstintingly of her prodigious knowledge of procurement law). Many excellent research assistants in Oxford and Michigan helped with various aspects of the research; Jürgen Adam was particularly helpful with WTO materials. Many other people helped with parts of the book, but I must thank in particular: Gherado Bonini, of the Historical Archives of the European Communities in Florence, and Mary-Ann Grosset, Head of the OECD Records Management and Archives Service in Paris for their help in gaining access to the OEEC and OECD archives, Phoebe Bolton for providing a copy of her thesis and advice on South Africa, and both Gabrille Marceau and Professor John Jackson for wise advice on the WTO.

I have drawn freely and frequently on my previously published work, although often in a significantly amended and updated form. 'Using Public Procurement to

Achieve Social Outcomes' (2004) 28 Natural Resources Forum 257 is drawn on in chapter 1. 'Advice to a legislator on problems regarding the enforcement of anti-discrimination law and strategies to overcome them' in T Loenen, and P Rodrigues, *Non-discrimination law: comparative perspectives* (Kluwer Law International, 1999) 295 is drawn on in chapter 3. 'Human Rights Codes for Transnational Corporations: What Can the Sullivan and MacBride Principles Tell Us?' (1999) 19 Oxford Journal of Legal Studies 167 is drawn on in chapters 3 and 9. 'Mainstreaming Equality in the Governance of Northern Ireland (1999) 22 *Fordham International Law Journal* 1696 is drawn on in chapters 3 and 13. 'National Remedies for Racial Discrimination in European and International Law' in S Fredman (ed), *Discrimination and Human Rights* (OUP 2001) 251 is drawn on in chapters 3 and 16. 'Theorising European Equality Law' in C Costello and E Barry (eds), *Equality in Diversity* (Irish Centre for European Law, 2003) 1 is drawn on in chapters 3 and 16. Work that I did whilst on secondment to the Policy Studies Institute, 'Groups versus Individuals: the Ambiguity behind the Race Relations Act, (1991) 12 Policy Studies 26; and *Racial Justice at Work: The Enforcement of the Race Relations Act 1976 in Employment* (PSI, 1991) (both with David Smith, and Colin Brown), is drawn on in chapters 3 and 16. 'International Economic Law and the Pursuit of Human Rights: A Framework for Discussion of the Legality of "Selective Purchasing" Laws under the WTO Government Procurement Agreement, (1999) 2 (1) Journal of International Economic Law 3 is drawn on in chapters 4, 9, and 15. 'Property Rights and Labour Rights Revisited: International Investment Agreements and the "Social Clause" Debate', in M Irish (ed), *The Auto Pact: Investment, Labour and the WTO* (Kluwer, 2004) 300 is drawn on in chapters 4, 12, 16, and 17. 'The Constitutionality of Affirmative Action in the United States: A Note on Adarand Constructors Inc. v Pena' (1996) 1 International Journal of Discrimination and the Law 369 is drawn on in chapter 6. Chapter 16 draws extensively on 'Equality and Non-Discrimination' in D Feldman (ed), *English Public Law* (OUP 2004).

Several previous articles on which I have drawn were written with other people. In chapters 3 and 16, the discussion of the development of European Community law relating to equality and human rights draws on the article Christopher McCrudden and Haris Kountouros, 'Human Rights and European Equality Law' in H Meenan (ed), *Equality Law for an Enlarged Europe: Towards a Greater Understanding of the Article 13 Directives* (Cambridge University Press, in press), to which the reader is referred for more extensive discussion. I am grateful to Haris Kountouros for permission to draw on this article.

In chapters 4 and 9, the discussion of Malaysian practices and the controversy involving the negotiation of a new Transparency in Government Procurement Agreement draws substantially on the article Christopher McCrudden and Stuart G Gross, 'WTO Government Procurement Rules and the Local Dynamics of Procurement Policies: A Malaysian Case Study' (2006) 17(1) European Journal of International Law 151. I am most grateful to Stuart Gross for permission to use this article as part of that chapter but more generally I am particularly grateful to him for so significantly advancing my understanding of the Malaysian situation regarding procurement preferences in favour of the Bumiputera.

In chapters 12 and 18, the discussion draws on the article Christopher McCrudden and Anne Davies, 'A Perspective on Trade and Labour Rights' (2000) 3(1) European Journal of International Law 43. I am most grateful to Anne Davies for permission to draw on this article for these chapters. More generally I am particularly grateful to her for commenting on a previous draft of the book and for co-teaching with me a graduate seminar on 'Globalization and Labour Rights' for several years at Oxford, a seminar that provided a stimulating forum for exploring many of the ideas fleshed out in this book.

I have also drawn on several pieces of unpublished work. A study carried out for the United Nations Department of Economic and Social Affairs, 'Integration of Social Policy into Sustainable Public Procurement: A Study for the United Nations, Department of Economic and Social Affairs' (2004), is drawn on in chapters 4, 5, and 18. A study carried out for the European Commission, Directorate General Social Affairs, 'Public Procurement and Equal Opportunities in the EC: a study of "contract compliance" in the Member States of the European Community and under European Community Law' (1995), is drawn on in chapters 5, 10, 11, and 17. A study carried out for the ILO, 'Public Procurement: How effective is it in combating discrimination?' (May 2006), is drawn on in chapter 18.

Several chapters of the book will be published elsewhere: 'Buying Social Justice: Equality and Procurement' [2007] Current Legal Problems (in press) forms the basis of chapter 5, and is drawn on in chapter 18. 'Corporate Social Responsibility and Public Procurement' in D McBarnet, V Voiculescu, and T Campbell (eds), *The New Corporate Accountability: Corporate Social Responsibility and the Law* (Cambridge University Press, in press) forms the basis for chapter 12. A version of chapter 15 is published as 'EC Public Procurement Law and Equality Linkages: Foundations for Interpretation' in S Arrowsmith and P Kunzlik (eds), *Social and Environmental Policies under the EC Procurement Rules: New Directives and New Directions* (provisional title) (Cambridge University Press, in press).

My colleagues in the Central Procurement Directorate (particularly John McMillan), on the Procurement Board for Northern Ireland, and in the Department of Finance and Personnel (particularly Brian Doherty) provided valuable insights into procurement policy and practice, as did Professor Andrew Erridge when we both sat on the committee reviewing Northern Ireland procurement policy mentioned in the Preface. Inez McCormack, Maggie Beirne, Tim Cunningham, and Martin O'Brien saw the point. My daughter, Kathleen, suggested the cover illustration.

At OUP, John Louth combined a faith that the book would eventually be worthwhile with immense tolerance for missed deadlines. The staff responsible for the production process at OUP were consistently superb, particularly

Fiona Stables, Alison Floyd, Rachel Kemp, Alex Flach, and Carolyn Fox. The book could not have been produced without their thorough professionalism.

Finally, my gratitude for putting up with so much, even including reading parts of an early draft, goes to Caroline, Joseph, and Kathleen. This book is dedicated to them, with my love.

Christopher McCrudden

Preface

It used to be fashionable in certain circles in legal scholarship to link the author's personal experiences with the problem that he or she is writing about. Sometimes, I have to confess that this approach often leaves me rather embarrassed for the author. It often seems either too forced or too personal, but perhaps that is merely because I have lived and worked in England for too long. Sceptical though I am of such approaches to legal scholarship, I will nevertheless introduce the topic of this book with a more personal account than I usually give of why I became involved with the issue, and my modest non-scholarly contribution to the political and legal debate on the questions we will be pursuing at greater length later in the book. I do this not to be fashionable, but to give the reader a sense of how my involvement may have coloured the way I have approached the topic and my conclusions. It is an attempt to be, in the jargon of European Community law, as open and transparent as possible.

The relationship between public procurement and social policy has intrigued me for many years. My first encounter with it was while I was working on my doctorate at Nuffield College, Oxford in 1976, under the supervision of Paul Davies. The thesis was a study of anti-discrimination law in employment, involving a comparison between the United States, Britain, and Northern Ireland, and I was looking at the legislative history of legal provisions in each of these jurisdictions. I had recently returned from the United States, where I had been a graduate student at Yale Law School, intrigued by the possibility of linking 'the power of the public purse' with equality policy, and I was considering how far such a development was possible in the United Kingdom. I had been much influenced by professors at Yale, such as Burke Marshall, Owen Fiss, and Guido Calabresi. Both Professors Fiss and Marshall had been involved in various ways in devising and implementing anti-discrimination law in the United States. Professor Calabresi inspired me to consider the economics of law more seriously, an approach that I have been conscious of in writing this book. Among those I interviewed when I returned to the United Kingdom was an interesting civil servant in Northern Ireland who raised a potential problem with such an approach, due to the possible constraints of the European procurement directive, which I had never heard of. This began a thirty-year consideration of the problem of linking social policy with public procurement.

That is not to say that every waking moment was spent considering the issue, but the issue kept popping up from time to time, each time more insistently than previously. In 1984, the Secretary of State for Northern Ireland asked me to join the Standing Advisory Commission of Human Rights. We soon embarked on a major reconsideration of employment discrimination law in Northern Ireland, and eventually published a report that served as a basis for the debates surrounding the development and subsequent enactment of the Fair Employment (Northern Ireland) Act 1989. One of the major issues we considered was how to supplement traditional anti-discrimination law enforcement techniques by drawing on other mechanisms to make the law more effective. Among the mechanisms we considered in some detail, was the linkage of public procurement to anti-discrimination goals, and again the issue was raised of how far such a linkage would raise legal problems under European Community law. The British government did not accept the approach we advocated and this led to a continuing debate during the passage of the legislation about the preferable method of linkage. By that time I was an informal adviser to Kevin McNamara MP, Labour's Shadow Secretary of State for Northern Ireland, (the Labour Party was then in Opposition) and he pushed the issue in Parliament with determination and skill, if unsuccessfully.

At that time, various groups in the United States took up the issue of equality in Northern Ireland. This resulted in the development of the MacBride principles, a set of weak affirmative action commitments that United States corporations with subsidiaries in Northern Ireland were asked to sign up to. The campaign had been inspired by similar campaigns opposing apartheid in South Africa during the 1970s and 1980s. One of the methods used by the MacBride activists was to secure support from state and local governments in the United States, and one of the methods used by these governments to encourage corporations to adopt the Principles was to require corporations with which they had contracts to sign up. The use of public procurement as a transnational anti-discrimination weapon was firmly on the agenda. Another method adopted by campaigners was to use shareholder activism to pressure corporations. When one of the corporations subject to the latter pressure sought to contest the legality of the MacBride Principles, I was asked to supply expert evidence to the United States federal district court trying the issue.

More recently still, the issue arose in another forum in which I became involved. In 1986, the European Commission Directorate General responsible for social policy (DGV) re-established a committee of experts in anti-discrimination law to advise it on how to move forward on the issue of women's equality. This committee (named the Network of Experts on the Application of Equality Directives) was a fascinating experiment in applied comparative law, since it was composed of both academics and practitioners from each Member State of the European Community. One of the issues that tended to arise from time to time at meetings of the Network, and conferences which Network members attended, was how far public procurement could be used in pursuit of the goal of women's equality throughout Europe—an issue which we soon discovered was a hot topic in Germany where several Länder (states) had developed such mechanisms, in part because of American influence, as had many Labour-controlled local authorities in Britain. Several conferences recommended this mechanism as a preferred technique, and the European Parliament attempted to create such a linkage in amendments it proposed to the procurement directives, which in the late 1980s were being substantially revised and expanded.

In the early 1990s, we became aware, however, of significant opposition to the linkage being suggested. Not only were governments becoming uneasy (Britain being the primary example) but so too was the European Commission's internal market Directorate General responsible for the development and enforcement of the procurement directives. On each occasion it seemed to oppose linkage. The European Parliament's amendments were rejected; and in the early 1990s the Commission held that one of the German Länder's use of procurement for equality purposes was contrary to Community law. It was becoming clear that there would be little movement towards increased use of what appeared a powerful weapon, at least based on the American experience, unless a modus vivendi could be worked out between the social policy and the public procurement directorates of the Commission. It was at this point that I was drawn more directly into the debate.

The conclusions of one of these periodic conferences on women's equality (I was the rapporteur) recommended that the Commission conduct a study of the problem. Unlike most of the other suggestions of this and similar conferences, this recommendation was acted on, and DG employment and social affairs commissioned me to undertake the study, over a two-year period. The study was completed in August 1995, making several recommendations. After a period in which the Commission considered whether to release the report, permission was given in 1997 for it to be published.

Much was to happen, however, between delivery of the report, and production of this book. Two developments, in particular, drew me further into the issue. The first was the development in the United Kingdom of compulsory competitive tendering, the government policy which sought to ensure greater competition in the delivery of services by local authorities and other public bodies by requiring that services be open to tendering by private sector companies. The implications of this policy were of considerable concern to many of the big public sector trade unions, and to the equality commissions in Britain and Northern Ireland. Eventually, both the British Equal Opportunities Commission and the Northern Ireland Equal Opportunities Commission undertook research into the effects of the policy on women in particular. The Northern Ireland EOC went one step further in turning its research into a formal investigation, a legal procedure that gave it the power to issue formal recommendations to government. I was invited to act as a consultant in developing their recommendations.

During the course of the study I undertook for the European Commission, I was struck by the extent to which public procurement was increasingly becoming an issue of global (and not just European) legal significance, resulting in a proliferation of international and regional agreements which sought to open up public procurement markets to international competition. The most significant of these developments are the Government Procurement Agreements. First in 1979, and later in 1994, several governments concluded agreements liberalizing procurement as part of the negotiations aimed at lowering tariff and non-tariff barriers to international trade, under the auspices of the General Agreement on Tariffs and Trade (GATT). The 1994 Agreement resulted not only in significantly enhanced coverage of the Agreement, but also in more effective dispute resolution mechanisms based on the World Trade Organization (WTO). I had raised the issue of the significance of these developments in my report for the Commission, but had neither the time, nor the knowledge at that stage, to do more than touch on the relevant issues.

By a pure coincidence, however, I was able to develop my interest in this aspect of procurement because of a sabbatical I was granted by my College, and University. During the academic year 1996–97, my family and I were based in the United States, first at the University of Texas at Austin School of Law, then at Michigan University's Law School where I had the good fortune to be able to draw on the expertise of the United States' foremost scholar on GATT and the WTO, Professor John Jackson. He not only pointed me in the right direction as regards basic raw material. He was also a source of unfailing enthusiasm and encouragement on the project. As luck would have it, while I was in the United States, a major controversy arose between the Europe, Japan, and the United States over the use of so-called 'selective purchasing' by several states, which sought to use 'the power of the purse' in the pursuit of human rights goals. I was able to talk to several of the participants, and gain a sense of powerful forces at play.

On returning to the United Kingdom, I was almost immediately involved in activities surrounding the emergence of the Belfast (or Good Friday) Agreement in Northern Ireland. Part of my involvement was in attempting to secure the incorporation of a strong equality and human rights dimension to the Agreement. I was invited by the premier human rights NGO in Northern Ireland, the Committee on the Administration of Justice, and Unison, the public sector union, to work on proposals to put the 'mainstreaming' of equality on a statutory footing. This eventually developed into Section 75 of the Northern Ireland Act 1998 (the legislation implementing the Agreement). This required that equality of opportunity should become an integral part of all governmental decision-making in Northern Ireland. This included the integration of equality considerations into public procurement.

When the new local administration was established in Northern Ireland, I was invited by the then Minister of Finance, Mark Durkan, to become a member of a group that he established to review procurement policy in Northern Ireland. Part of the brief given to the group was to consider how to integrate equality issues into procurement. The report considered the issue in depth, made several recommendations on how to do so, and these were accepted by the Executive. I was then asked to become a member of the Procurement Board, the body established to oversee procurement policy following the report. As a member of the Board, the integration of equality issues into procurement has been a recurring issue.

More recently, I have been involved with United Nations bodies in ways that are particularly relevant to this book. First, I have acted as a consultant over the past few years for the Department of Economic and Social Affairs. The Department was given responsibility, as is related subsequently in the book, to work with countries interested in developing 'sustainable procurement' initiatives, bringing the economic, environmental, and social dimensions of procurement together in a workable way. This involved preparing a lengthy study on the social dimensions of procurement for the Department. Second, the Office of the High Commissioner for Human Rights involved me in commenting on work they were undertaking on the relationship between the concept of non-discrimination in international human rights law and international economic law. The issue of procurement became a good illustration of the problematic relationship between them.

Not surprisingly, my involvement in these various initiatives, domestic, European, and international, has profoundly affected my approach to the issues discussed in the book. It has required me, above all, to be aware of the different expectations that those involved have of public procurement, the tensions between social and economic approaches to the area, the role of law, and the interrelationships between the different layers of governance in addressing these issues. Whether it has enabled me to capture fully the complexity of the issues, and (as importantly) whether I have explained the tensions generated in a way that makes them understandable and (as I argue) able to be resolved, readers must decide. The research on which this book is based was substantially completed by the summer of 2006, although some (few) developments since that time have been included.

Christopher McCrudden

May 2007

Contents

PART II. THE WORLD TRADE ORGANIZATION AND PROCUREMENT LINKAGES

PART III. EQUALITY LINKAGES AND THE EUROPEAN COMMUNITY

10. Procurement Linkages and the 1980s Reform of EC Procurement Regulation

11. Domestic Procurement Linkages During the 1990s and the Chilling Effect of European Procurement Regulation

PART IV: INTERPRETATION

Table of Cases

FRANCE

Conseil Constitutionnel

Conseil d'Etat

GERMANY

MALAYSIA

UNITED KINGDOM

UNITED STATES

WORLD TRADE ORGANIZATION

Table of National Legislation

UNITED STATES

Federal

Presidential Executive Orders

Massachusetts

Table of International and Regional Treaties and Conventions

INTERNATIONAL LABOUR
ORGANIZATION:
CONSTITUTION, CONVENTIONS,
DECLARATIONS

INTERNATIONAL ECONOMIC
LAW TREATIES, AGREEMENTS,
AND INSTRUMENTS

Bilateral Trade Agreements

List of Abbreviations

General

AFL-CIO	American Federation of Labor and Congress of Industrial Organizations
AGBG	Gesetz zur Regelung des Rechts der Algemeinen Geschäftsbedingungen (General Terms and Conditions Act, Germany)
AIT	Agreement on Internal Trade (1994) (Canada)
ASEAN	Association of South-East Asian Nations
ASIST	Advisory Support Information Services and Training for Employment-Intensive Infrastructure (ILO)
B-BBEE	Broad-Based Black Economic Empowerment
B-BBEE Act	Broad-Based Black Economic Empowerment Act, 2003
BCIC	Bumiputera Commercial and Industrial Community (Malaysia)
BEE	Black Economic Empowerment (SA)
BetrVG	Betriebsverfassungsgesetz (Works Constitution Act, Germany)
BGB	Bürgerliches Gesetzbuch (German Civil Code)
BGH	Bundesgerichtshof (Federal Supreme Court, Germany)
BHO	Bundeshaushaltsordnung (Federal Budgetary Regulations, Germany)
BSI	British Standards Institute
BverfG	Bundesverfassungsgericht (German Constitutional Court)
CAJ	Committee on the Administration of Justice
CBI	Confederation of British Industry (UK)
CCEOU	Contract Compliance Equal Opportunities Unit (UK, GLC/ILEA)
CCT	compulsory competitive tendering
CDU	Christian Democratic Union (Germany)
CEEP	Centre européen des entreprises à participation publique et des entreprises d'intérêt économique général (European Centre of Enterprises with Public Participation and of Enterprises of General Economic Interest)
CHRC	Canadian Human Rights Commission
CITT	Canadian International Trade Tribunal
CLCAs	comprehensive land claims agreements (Canada)
CLCSA	comprehensive land claims settlement area (Canada)
COREPER	Committee of Member States' Permanent Representatives (EC)
COSATU	Congress of South African Trade Unions
CPB	Central Procurement Body (UK)
CPN	Contracting Policy Notice (Canada)
CPRS	Central Policy Review Staff (UK)
CRE	Commission for Racial Equality (UK)
CSD	Commission on Sustainable Development
CSR	corporate social responsibility

DDR	Deutsche Demokratische Republik (former East Germany)
DEFRA	Department for Environment, Food and Rural Affairs (UK)
DfES	Department for Education and Skills (UK)
DG	Directorate General (EC)
DGB	German Trades Unions Federation
DIAND	Department of Indian Affairs and Northern Development (Canada)
DIO	designated Inuit organization (Canada)
DRP	domestic review procedure
DSU	Dispute Settlement Understanding
DTI	Department of Trade and Industry (UK and Malaysia)
DWP	Department of Work and Pensions (UK)
EC	European Community
ECJ	European Court of Justice
EEC	European Economic Community
EEF	Engineering Employers' Federation (UK)
EEOC	Equal Employment Opportunities Commission (US)
EFTA	European Free Trade Association
EMAS	Environmental Management and Audit Scheme
EOC	Equal Opportunities Commission (UK)
ETUC	European Trades Union Congress
EU	European Union
Euratom	European Atomic Energy Community
FAR	Federal Acquisition Regulations (US)
FCP	Federal Contractors Program (Canada)
FDP	Federal Democratic Party (Germany)
FEC	Fair Employment Commission (Northern Ireland)
FEPC	Fair Employment Practices Committee (US)
FETO	Fair Employment and Treatment Order 1998 (Northern Ireland)
GATS	General Agreement on Trade in Services
GATT	General Agreement on Tariffs and Trade
GG	Grundgesetz (German Basic Law)
GLC	Greater London Council
GPA	Government Procurement Agreement
GWB	Gesetz gegen den Wetbewerbsbeschränkungen (Act Against Restraint of Trade (Germany))
HDIs	historically disadvantaged individuals (SA)
HGrG	Haushaltsgrundsatzgesetz (Principles of Federal and States Budgetary Law Act, Germany)
HRDC	Human Resources Development Canada
IBRD	International Bank for Reconstruction and Development
ICLEI	International Council for Local Environmental Initiatives
IDA	International Development Association

IGOs	international governmental organizations
ILEA	Inner London Education Authority
ILO	International Labour Organization
IMF	International Monetary Fund
IPP	National Industrial Participation Programme (SA)
ITC	International Trade Commission (US)
JORF	Journal Officiel de la Republique Française (France)
LCC	London County Council
LEAP	Local Environment Management Systems and Procurement
LHO	Landeshaushaltsordnung (Budget Code for the Land, Germany)
MCCM	Malay Chamber of Commerce of Malaysia
MFN	most favoured nation
MITI	Ministry of International Trade and Industry (Malaysia)
MNE	multinational enterprise
NAACP	National Association for the Advancement of Colored People (US)
NAALC	North American Agreement on Labor Co-operation
NAFTA	North American Free Trade Agreement
NDP	National Development Policy (replaced the NEP) (Malaysia)
NEP	New Economic Policy (Malaysia)
NFTC	National Foreign Trade Council (US)
NGO	non-governmental organization
NIC ICTU	Northern Ireland Committee, Irish Congress of Trade Unions
NIO	Northern Ireland Office
OECD	Organisation for Economic Co-operation and Development
OEEC	Organisation for European Economic Co-operation (precursor to the OECD)
OEED	Office of Employment, Equity, and Diversity
OFCC(P)	Office of Federal Contract Compliance (Programs) (US)
OGC	Office of Government Commerce (UK)
PAFT	Policy Appraisal and Fair Treatment
PCEEO	President's Committee on Equal Employment Opportunity (US)
PFMA	Public Finance Management Act, 1999 (SA)
PIU	Performance and Innovation Unit (Cabinet Office, UK)
PPMs	Process and Production Methods
PPPFA	Preferential Procurement Policy Framework Act, 2000 (SA)
PPPs	Public Private Partnerships
PSAB	Procurement Strategy for Aboriginal Business (Canada)
PSI	Policy Studies Institute (UK)
RDP	Reconstruction and Development Programme (SA)
RRB	Race Relations Board (UK)

SABS	South African Bureau of Standards
SACU	Southern African Customs Union
SACHR	Standing Advisory Commission on Human Rights (UK)
SBA	Small Business Administration (US)
SEA	Single European Act 1986
SGB	Sozialgesetzbuch (Federal Code of Social Law, Germany)
SMEs	small and medium-sized enterprises
SMMEs	small, medium and micro enterprises (SA)
SPD	German Social Democratic Party
SPV	Special Purpose Vehicle
TCLs	Treasury Circular Letters (Malaysia)
TEU	Treaty on European Union
TGP	transparency in government procurement
TIs	Treasury Instructions (Malaysia)
TRIMS	Trade-Related Investment Measures
TRIPS	Trade Related Aspects of Intellectual Property Rights
TUC	Trades Union Congress (UK)
UMNO	United Malays National Organisation
UNCED	United Nations Conference on Environment and Development
UNCITRAL	United Nations Commission on International Trade Law
UNICE	Union of Industrial and Employers' Confederations of Europe
UNICEF	United Nations Children's Fund
USC	United States Code
USCRC	United States Civil Rights Commission
UWG	Gesetz gegen den unlauteren Wettbewerb (Anti-trust Act, Germany)
VOB	Verdingungensordnung für Bauleistungen (tendering ordinance for services, Germany)
VOL	Verdingungensordnung für Leistungen (tendering ordinance for building contracts, Germany)
VwVfG	Verwaltungsverfahrensgesetz (Administrative Procedures Acts on the federal and Land level, Germany)
WGTGP	Working Group on Transparency in Government Procurement
WHO	World Health Organization
WTO	World Trade Organization

Publications

AJIL	American Journal of International Law
BYU LR	Brigham Young University Law Review
CMLR	Common Market Law Review
Col HRLR	Columbia Human Rights Law Review

Col J Env L	Columbia Journal of Environmental Law
Col J Eur L	Columbia Journal of European Law
Col JTL	Columbia Journal of Transnational Law
EJIL	European Journal of International Law
ELR	European Law Review
EOR	Equal Opportunities Review
EPL	European Public Law
GW JILE	George Washington Journal of International Law and Economics
Harv ILJ	Harvard International Law Journal
ICLQ	International and Comparative Law Quarterly
IDS Bulletin	Institute of Development Studies Bulletin
ILJ	Industrial Law Journal
IRRR	Industrial Relations Review and Report
JEPP	Journal of European Public Policy
JIEL	Journal of International Economic Law
JWTL	Journal of World Trade Law
LPIB	Law and Policy in International Business
LQR	Law Quarterly Review
Maas JEL	Maastricht Journal of European Law
MLR	Modern Law Review
NYU JILP	New York University Journal of International Law and Politics
NYU LR	New York University Law Review
OJLS	Oxford Journal of Legal Studies
PPLR	Public Procurement Law Review
UP JIEL	University of Pennsylvania Journal of International Economic Law
UP LR	University of Pennsylvania Law Review
Van JIL	Vanderbilt Journal of International Law
Van JTL	Vanderbilt Journal of Transnational Law
Virg JIL	Virginia Journal of International law
Virg JTL	Virginia Journal of Transnational Law
Yale JIL	Yale Journal of International Law

1

What is This Book About?

The title of this book is provocative, deliberately so. The idea of 'buying social justice' may strike you as paradoxical, even as deeply problematic. Perhaps you think that we simply should not subject some values to the market place of buying and selling. Just as we would regard selling love as a contradiction in terms, and selling votes as perhaps the ultimate in political corruption, justice should not be bought or sold either. Judges, surely, should not be able to sell a favourable decision to the highest bidder. Bribing juries is, and should be, a serious criminal offence and regarded as the antithesis of justice. Some have termed this as 'commodification', which Stark has defined as 'the transformation of something which is not commonly sold, traded or otherwise alienated—love, water . . . —into something that is—mail order brides, bottled water . . . '.[1]

But what about *social* justice? Governments often consider it not only appropriate but also desirable to purchase social justice from employers, universities, and service providers, in somewhat similar ways that governments buy computers for their schools, buildings for their citizens, weapons for their armies, and paper for their bureaucrats; and sometimes at the same time as making these purchases. How should we react to this?

Many ideas jostle to dominate the public imagination and popular discourse of this new century. One has to do with a collective commitment to markets as one of the most efficient ways of optimizing the use and distribution of scarce resources. Another has to do with social justice, particularly with equality, often traditionally assumed to be the sphere of action outside the market, particularly by governmental institutions. In this book, I aim to probe the relationship between the market and social justice, and consider how (or whether) they converge and how they diverge in the context of government 'buying social justice'.

There are, of course, many different ways in which governments pursue several different aspects of social justice: using direct and indirect taxation as a means of collecting from the rich to give to the poor in the form of welfare payments, giving grants of aid internationally to developing regions, allocating departments of government the funds necessary to operate preferred labour market policies, and giving grants to private bodies in order to support them in activities that are considered to

---

[1] B Stark, 'After/word(s): "Violations of Human Dignity" and Postmodern International Law' (2002) 27 Yale JIL 315, 322.

be in the public interest. Common to each of these is the 'power of the purse', the use of government funds, usually raised through taxation, to achieve social goals. This is a pervasive aspect of modern government and one of the principal ways in which social justice is advanced. Daintith has distinguished between the implementation of policy through 'imperium', meaning the use of instruments involving the use, or threatened use, of force, and 'dominium', meaning the use of instruments involving the use of wealth by the state, such as the use of grants to deliver particular policies.[2] This book is primarily about the use of 'dominium', in this sense.

But the use of imperium is also pervasive in modern government, of course. Most developed countries operate a mixed economy, where markets operate within a regulatory structure that seeks to encourage them when it is desirable, and control their failures and excesses when necessary. So, governments are usually given powers to prevent the growth of monopolies where they would be likely to be able to abuse their power to the detriment of consumers, or prevent factories from spewing out dangerous chemicals, or require that they provide their workers with appropriate wages, or prevent them from discriminating on the basis of race in delivering their services to consumers.

Sometimes, governments combine the 'power of the purse' with this regulatory function. This is often controversial because the conditions on which grants, for example, are given involve a balancing of considerations: supporting what is good, whilst not supporting what is considered objectionable. Let us take two examples to illustrate this use of the power to fund being used in this way, both taken from the United States. Grove City College, a private, coeducational, liberal arts college enrolled students who received direct federal government grants to enable them to study. When the College refused to promise not to discriminate on grounds of sex, it was deprived of its ability to take federally assisted students until it agreed not to discriminate.[3] More recently, several law schools in the United States restricted the access of military recruiters to their students because of the law schools' disagreement with the federal government's policy prohibiting self-identified homosexuals in the military. Congress responded by enacting the Solomon Amendment,[4] a provision that specified that if any part of an institution of higher education denies military recruiters access equal to that provided to other recruiters, the entire institution would lose certain federal funds.[5]

Modern governments spend taxpayers' money in supporting appropriate programmes and they regulate by establishing controls on the use of private institutions. But governments also engage in another activity. They also *buy* things. They buy computers, clothing for the military, buildings, advertising space in newspapers, and

---

[2] T Daintith, 'Regulation by Contract: The New Prerogative' [1979] Current Legal Problems 41.
[3] In *Grove City College v Bell* 465 US 555 (1984), the US Supreme Court upheld the restriction in most respects.   [4] See 10 USCA §983 (Supp 2005).
[5] In *Rumsfeld v Forum for Academic and Institutional Rights, Inc* 126 S Ct 1297 (2006), the US Supreme Court upheld this restriction.

warships. This function of government, long something of a cinderella area of academic study, goes under various terms, sometimes being called government purchasing, sometimes government contracting, sometimes public procurement. The differences between these terms need not detain us, for the moment. Public procurement involves the purchasing by government from private sector contractors, usually on the basis of competitive bidding, of goods and services that government needs. In this context, rather than government regulating the market, it is participating in it as a market actor. It is, in each of these situations, purchasing from the private sector. It might, of course, decide to obtain these items in another way. Government has a range of alternative methods that it can use, including obtaining such goods or services by employing people to produce them directly (such as by direct labour organizations in the case of construction, or nationalization in the case of utility services); it might produce the desired items itself, building its own factories. But modern governments have increasingly moved away from these methods. Instead, governments now generally purchase from the market. Indeed, governments play an increasingly important role as an active participant in the market, purchasing public works, supplies, and services.

My particular interest in this book is examining how governments use *government contracting* to produce social justice results. The particular issue that is the focus of this book is how government attempts to combine the three functions of government distinguished up to now: *participating* in the market but *regulating* it *at the same time*, by using its *purchasing* power to advance conceptions of social justice, particularly equality and non-discrimination. The term 'linkage' is used throughout this book to describe this use of procurement.[6]

Concentrating on 'social justice' is problematic. There is a rich literature on the political philosophy of social justice but, for the purposes of this book, my concern is not to explore that literature. Nor am I concerned with possible theoretical differences between social justice and social policy. I shall merely stipulate that my concern is to concentrate on a particular instance of what has been conceived as an example of a concern with social justice: the attempt to eradicate unjust discrimination and advance status equality. There is an important set of questions about what that body of laws and norms actually consists of, and this will be explored subsequently, but the reader should not assume that any particularly technical meaning is being adopted when the idea of 'social justice' is used. Let us explore briefly some examples of the type of linkages that this book is concerned with. Several of these examples will be considered in some depth later in the book.

---

[6] 'Linkage' is used in preference to the concept of 'conditionality', with which it shares certain similarities, because the diversity of ways in which procurement and social justice have been brought together goes beyond simply awarding contracts on certain conditions, and extends to include, for example, the definition of the contract, the qualifications of contractors, and the criteria for the award of the contract. 'Linkage' is also used in preference to 'secondary criteria' because we shall see subsequently that social justice isues can be (part of) the subject matter of the contract. For a discussion of the concept of 'linkage' generally see DW Leebron, 'Linkages' (2002) 96 AJIL 5.

I. Introducing Procurement Linkages

Disabled workers

After the First World War, government contracting came to be seen as an important mechanism for addressing the needs of disabled workers. In particular, the British government introduced a significant programme for providing work to disabled ex-servicemen, using the mechanism of government contracting.[7] After the Second World War, this approach spread beyond ex-servicemen and was generalized to the rest of the disabled working population. A popular approach was the establishment of 'sheltered workshops' for disabled workers, where limited types of goods were manufactured, and these products were given preference in government purchasing.

The approach also spread beyond Britain. In 1938, the United States passed an act 'to create a Committee on Purchases of Blind-made Products, and for other purposes'.[8] The Committee was composed 'of a private citizen conversant with the problems incident to the employment of the blind' and representatives from the main Cabinet Departments, appointed by the President. The Committee was 'to determine the fair market price of all brooms and mops and other suitable commodities manufactured by the blind and offered for sale to the Federal Government by any non-profit-making agency for the blind organized under the laws of the United States or of any State'. The Act required that 'all suitable commodities...procured...by or for any Federal department or agency shall be procured from such non-profit-making agencies for the blind'. The legislation remained in this restrictive form until the Act was revised in 1971, extending it to include 'other severely handicapped' among the beneficiaries of the legislation, and 'services' as well as 'commodities' that should be given priority in procurement by the federal government from non-profit agencies employing disabled workers.[9]

More recently, several countries have developed the use of government procurement to try to improve the availability of new technology, particularly for those who are disabled workers. In 1998, the United States Congress passed legislation requiring the buying of accessible information and communication technology by government agencies.[10] Ontario has a similar, if weaker, requirement,[11] and there has been an active debate on the issue in Australia.[12]

---

[7] Official Report, HC, vol 191, col 1830 (16 February 1926). The House of Lords Resolution: Official Report, HL, vol 63, col 129 (16 February 1926).

[8] Public Law No 739, commonly called the Wagner-O'Day Act.

[9] Public Law 92-28, commonly called the Javits-Wagner-O'Day Act.

[10] Rehabilitation Act 1973, s 508.   [11] Ontarians with Disabilities Act 2001, s 5.

[12] Australian Government, Productivity Commission, 'Review of the Disability Discrimination Act 1992', Report No 30, 30 April 2004, vol 1, para 15.5; Human Rights and Equal Opportunity Commission, 'People with Disability in the Open Workplace: Final Report of the National Inquiry into Employment and Disability' (December 2005).

Civil rights movement in the United States and contract compliance

The growth of the movement for an end to discrimination against black Americans (the 'civil rights movement' as it was called) galvanized the development of the anti-discrimination principle both in the United States and in several other countries. Successive Presidents issued 'executive orders' requiring non-discrimination by federal government contractors by virtue of their inherent powers to control the operation of government contracts.[13] The importance of the issue of race in the United States, its intractability, and the intensity of the legal effort brought to bear in the 1950s and 1960s gave rise to 'affirmative action', the meaning of which is considered in chapter 3 below. Beginning from the mid to late 1960s, the term came to be used to describe approaches to dealing with discrimination that went beyond simply enforcing a prohibition of discrimination, and came to encompass a wide variety of pro-active measures seeking to achieve greater equality for the disadvantaged group. One of the central regulatory pillars of this strategy was attaching conditions requiring affirmative action in employment in government contracts. This continues to be an important source of government regulation in the area.

The Executive Order is enforced by the Secretary of Labor through the Office of Federal Contract Compliance Programs (OFCCP). The obligations are set out both in the Executive Order itself and in several sets of regulations. The Order applies to federal contractors and subcontractors[14] who have government contracts which exceed US $10,000 in aggregate and which are performed in the United States. All workplaces of the contractor are required to meet the non-discrimination obligations whether or not they are directly involved in carrying out the contract. In addition, written affirmative action plans must be devised by non-construction contractors with one or more contracts or subcontracts in excess of US $50,000, employing fifty or more employees. The written affirmative action plan is to be based on a statistical analysis of all major job categories, and must in addition contain goals and timetables aimed at redressing any under-utilization of the protected groups. Contractors who have a single contract of US $50,000 or more and fifty employees are required to submit a report[15] in which the workforce composition of the firm, broken down by race and sex, is analysed. The OFCCP uses this to see if contractors are accomplishing the goals of their affirmative action

---

[13] ME Reed, *Seedtime for the Modern Civil Rights Movement: The President's Committee on Fair Employment Practice, 1941–1946* (Louisiana State University Press, 1991); L Kesselman, *Social Politics of FEPC* (University of North Carolina Press, 1948); L Ruchames, *Race, Jobs and Politics: The Story of FEPC* (Columbia University Press, 1953).

[14] These terms are defined broadly in the regulations to include any agreement between the contracting agency and any other person for the furnishing of supplies or services or for the use of real or personal property, including lease arrangements. A subcontract is defined as any agreement between a government contractor and any other person for the furnishing of supplies or services, or for the use of real or personal property, including lease arrangements, which are necessary to the performance of any one or more contracts or under which any portion of the contractor's obligation under any one or more contracts is performed, undertaken, or assumed.   [15] Termed an EEO-1 report.

programmes. It is used as a device to determine which contractors to schedule for compliance evaluations. The OFCCP conducts compliance reviews to evaluate the contractors' compliance with the obligations. Where a contract exceeds US $10,000,000, the OFCCP must conduct a pre-award review. In other cases, the compliance review occurs after the award of the contract. Construction contractors must comply with contract terms and conditions specifying affirmative action requirements applicable to specific geographical areas or projects.[16]

Failure to comply with the obligations, which government agencies are required to insert in contracts, may lead to the imposition of a range of sanctions: a determination that the contractor is 'nonresponsible'; administrative proceedings, after negotiations have failed, leading to cancellation of the government contract or debarment from future contracts; judicial proceedings for enforcement of the Order through the Department of Justice; and a recommendation to the Equal Employment Opportunities Commission (EEOC) or Department of Justice that proceedings be begun.[17]

Procurement and anti-discrimination law: the United Kingdom, Canada, Australia, and the EU

From the 1960s onwards, anti-discrimination law developed significantly in other countries, often influenced by developments in American law. The influence of the US civil rights movement in other countries is well known, and that influence was not confined to campaigning around the anti-discrimination principle itself. It extended also to the import of some of the legal strategies that the United States developed to tackle the problem of discrimination against black Americans. This was true in particular throughout the common law world, where anti-discrimination legislation, based on variations of the American state or federal approaches, was widely adopted from the 1960s onwards.

This spread of American influence appears to have its first tangible legislative results in the United Kingdom, where limited legislation to tackle the growing problem of discrimination on the grounds of race against black and Asian immigrants from the Commonwealth was finally enacted in 1965. Once enacted, however, further anti-discrimination law to tackle such discrimination was not long in coming, and additional legislation prohibiting racial discrimination in employment and housing was passed in 1968 and 1976. In 1969, the British government introduced anti-discrimination conditions into central government contracts. Northern Ireland adopted procurement linkage as one of the techniques of enforcement of anti-discrimination legislation from 1977 and this was continued in 1989

---

[16] FAR 22.804–2.

[17] For a discussion of the procedural aspects of enforcement of the Order, see WF Leimkuhler, 'Enforcing Social and Economic Policy Through Government Contracts' [1980] Annual Survey of American Law 539, 552–9.

and 1998 in revised legislation, which provides that consistent failure to follow the legislative requirements could lead to deprivation of the opportunity to contract with government.

In turn, other Commonwealth countries adopted anti-discrimination legislation drawing on American experience, with the Canadian provinces enacting 'human rights' statutes (in practice anti-discrimination legislation) from the early 1960s. The adoption of anti-discrimination legislation was also often accompanied by the adoption of modified forms of linkage of non-discrimination to government contracting. The Canadian government instituted a Federal Contractors Programme, which came into effect on 1 September 1986.[18]

By the late 1960s, affirmative action requirements were extended in the United States to benefit women in employment under federal government contracts. This, too, has spread to other jurisdictions. The Australian government adopted a policy in 1993 to use procurement to support the Affirmative Action (Equal Employment Opportunity for Women) Act 1986. Failure to submit an affirmative action annual report or failure to provide evidence of an affirmative action programme could lead to being 'named' in Parliament, which then led to the employer becoming ineligible for government contracts.[19] The Australian Capital Territory also adopted a policy of not dealing with suppliers who did not comply with the requirements of Commonwealth anti-discrimination law.[20] There is a continuing debate in Australia over whether to introduce an equivalent contract compliance policy to tackle discrimination against disabled workers.[21]

One of the features of the approach to compliance with European Community (EC) equality norms at the national level is the extent to which governmental authorities in some countries adopted linkages with procurement as a regulatory tool of enforcement. For example, Italian legislation prohibiting discrimination on grounds of gender linked enforcement with the procurement tool. This was particularly the case at the levels of government below the national level of governance. So we see, during the 1980s, the adoption by several Länder in Germany, several local authorities in the United Kingdom, and many local authorities in the Netherlands, of linkage between procurement and non-discrimination requirements. This approach has spread to near neighbours. Switzerland has introduced

---

[18] Directive 3055 of 30 September 1986, replacing Directive 3055 dated 29 August 1986, Supply and Services Canada, Supply Policy Manual.

[19] See Australian Government, 'Guidance on Complying with Legislation and Government Policy in Procurement', available at <http://www.finance.gov.au/procurement/complying_with_legislation.html>. A review in 1998 concluded that this should be retained, see Australian Government, 'Unfinished Business: Equity for Women in Australian Workplaces: Final Report of the Regulatory Review of the Affirmative Action (Equal Employment Opportunity for Women) Act 1986' June 1998, 69–70.

[20] Australian Capital Territory, Government Procurement Board, 'Equal Employment Opportunity for Women in the Workplace: Procurement Circular', December 2002.

[21] Australian Government, Productivity Commission, 'Review of the Disability Discrimination Act 1992', Report No 30, 30 April 2004, vol 1, 456 *et seq.*

a requirement that equal pay between men and women be a condition for the performance of public contracts within Switzerland.[22]

'Set-asides' in the United States, Malaysia, South Africa, Canada, and Australia

The use of procurement to advance equal status policies in the United States is not confined to advancing equality in employment. It goes much further in attempting to restructure the economy more broadly. Subsequent to the introduction of anti-discrimination law, the United States federal government introduced additional provisions to ensure that certain proportions of government contracts would be secured by black-owned businesses. This was an attempt to stimulate the growth of an entrepreneurial black middle class. An early example was the Public Works Employment Act of 1977, which provided that at least 10 per cent of each grant for local work projects under that Act be expended for minority business enterprises. Federal agencies and state and local government authorities that administered public works construction projects created equivalent programmes. These came to be known in the United States as 'set-asides'. Although different terms were used, similar programmes were adopted in several other countries.

The likelihood of serious instability led the Malaysian government, for example, to introduce a similar set of economic policies designed to encourage economic growth at the same time as ensuring redistribution designed to lift the native Malays (Bumiputera). One of the important elements in that strategy was the use of procurement contracts structured in such a way as to generate over time an entrepreneurial Malay middle class. Malaysian Bumiputera companies benefited from price preferences. Contracts below certain thresholds were reserved for Bumiputera suppliers.

After the collapse of apartheid, it was not surprising that procurement was also seen as one of the regulatory techniques that should be used to redress the effects of the institutional discrimination and inequality in South Africa. The new Constitution for South Africa specifically provided that procurement should serve the aims of efficiency and equity. The South African Constitution provides that when an organ of state in the national, provincial, or local sphere of government, or any other institution identified in national legislation, contracts for goods or services, it must do so in accordance with a system that is fair, *equitable*, transparent, competitive, and cost-effective.[23] An extensive system of 'targeted procurement', somewhat similar to that established in Malaysia with regard to the native Malays, has been established.[24]

---

[22] C Bock, 'An Overview of Swiss Federal Procurement Policy' (1998) 7 PPLR CS134, CS135.
[23] Section 217.
[24] Preferential Procurement Policy Framework Act, 2000 (Act 5, 2000) provides for the framework for implementation of national procurement policy, in this respect.

The United States, Malaysia, and South Africa are not the only states with extensive programmes giving preferences to certain businesses defined by race or ethnic ownership in the award of procurement contracts. In Canada, the Minister of Indian Affairs and Northern Development announced in March 1996 that measures would be adopted designed to increase the participation of Aboriginal businesses in bidding for federal government contracts. Mandatory set-asides in procurements above a threshold were introduced to benefit the Aboriginal populations, and further provisions encouraged non-Aboriginal firms to subcontract with Aboriginal firms. These were developed with the aim of achieving increased representation of Aboriginal business in contract awards by individual departments and agencies.[25]

Since 2001, the Australian state of Queensland has operated an Indigenous Employment Policy for Queensland government building and civil construction projects, which requires contractors to ensure that employment and accredited training occurs on sites carrying out such work, and that a minimum of 20 per cent of the total labour hours on any such site in specified Indigenous comunities be undertaken by Indigenous people recruited from the local community.[26] At the federal level, the Australian government adopted a policy that where individual projects involve expediture over A\$5 million (A\$6 million for construction projects) and are sited in places where there are significant Indigenous populations with limited employment and training opportunities, procurement officials should at least consider opportunities for training and employment on the projects for these local communities.[27] Other countries, such as Taipei, have adopted legislation permitting similar preferences.[28]

Selective purchasing and local activism in the United States

Thus far, we have looked at examples of 'linkages' where the goal linked to public procurement is one of securing greater equality within the jurisdiction awarding the contract. There are several examples, however, in which the goal is to secure policy aims *outside* the jurisdiction. Local communities in North America and Europe adopted procurement linkages to signal their support for defeating apartheid and protesting against the coup in Chile. In the Netherlands, several cities threatened to cancel their contracts with Stevin, a dredging and building firm, after the company concluded a contract with Chile. 'Afraid of losing the more than fifty percent of its business dependent on Dutch local governments, Stevin

---

[25] Contracting Policy Notice on Aboriginal Business Procurement Policy and Incentives 1996–2, para 4.

[26] Queensland Government, Department of Employment and Training, 'Indigenous Employment Policy for Queensland Government Building and Civil Construction Projects', January 2004.

[27] Australian Government Department of Finance and Administration, 'Commonwealth Procurement Guidelines and Best Practice Guidance' (February 2002).

[28] Chinese Taipei, Government Procurement Law, 1998, art 22(12).

cancelled its Chilean work.'[29] A similar technique adopted in several states in the
United States was to put pressure on companies operating in South Africa and
Northern Ireland by threatening them with loss of state government contracts.
Another controversial example of this approach was the legislation enacted by the
state of Massachusetts. In 1996 the Commonwealth of Massachusetts adopted leg-
islation limiting the ability of state agencies to sign new contracts or renewals of con-
tracts with companies doing business with or in Myanmar (formerly called
Burma).[30]

These examples of selective purchasing illustrate the development of an
important new role that linkage has been given, in the global as opposed to the
national economy. The links between procurement and such initiatives as those
relating to South Africa, Northern Ireland, and Burma involve the use of procurement to secure human rights *transnationally*.[31] This use of procurement helps to
produce an increasing convergence between private business and government in
some contexts. Private contractors, particularly larger multinationals, stress the
need to consider their reputational interests, and their corporate social responsibilities, requiring subcontractors to behave responsibly or lose their opportunity
to contract with the company.

Changing role of procurement and linkages

Not only has the role of procurement linkages expanded, the role of procurement
itself is changing dramatically as well. There were several major changes in the
world of public procurement after the 1980s.[32] There was, first, a significant
change of attitude in public opinion regarding the role of the state in the economy
in particular countries. Particularly with the introduction of much tighter budgetary constraints, methods of government delivery of services were placed under
more intense scrutiny, particularly with a view to reducing costs and increasing
efficiency. One effect of this was that government withdrew to a considerably
greater extent than at any time since the beginning of the Second World War from
areas of public services that they considered would be more efficiently delivered by
the private market. Where public services continued to be delivered by public
bodies, they should at least emulate the methods of commercial organizations in
the methods they used to deliver those services. A second, related, element was a
belief that public spending was massively in excess of what was necessary to deliver
public services, and that issues of cost and efficiency should become much more

---

[29] MH Shuman, 'GATTzilla v Communities' (1994) 27 Cornell International Law Journal 527, 534.

[30] An Act Regulating Contracts with Companies Doing Business with or in Burma (Myanmar),
ch 130, 1996 Session Laws, Mass Gen Laws Ann, ch 7, 223.

[31] See SH Cleveland, 'Norm Internalization and US Economic Sanctions' (2001) 26 Yale JIL 1, 47–8.

[32] See G O' Brien, 'Envisaged Change in the Procurement Regime: the Point of View of the
European Commission', Paper to seminar on 'Legal Aspects of EC Public Procurement', Luxembourg,
29–30 October 1998.

firmly embedded in the public sector ethos than previously. At least in part, these developments were thought to be necessary in order to make the national economy better able to compete in the world economy.

Accompanying these developments was a new emphasis on a notion of 'contract' as the basis for relationships between the citizen and the state, and indeed between different parts of the state, although the idea of contract used was often hazy in the extreme. Another key element in the ideological package was an increasing emphasis on 'competition', which was conceived to be an important element in reducing costs and controlling the power of vested interests. Privatization of state-run industries, liberalization of utilities regulation, and the introduction of concessions and various forms of Public Private Partnerships(PPPs) providing for a larger injection of private funding into public service delivery, increased significantly the role of procurement in many countries. Some jurisdictions saw procurement as a method of delivering public services, whilst at the same time subjecting these to the disciplines of the market. Procurement was also used as the instrument for partnerships between the public sector and the private sector, through such mechanisms as PPPs, using the private sector to provide funds for the operation of public services.

Where procurement contracts were used, as they increasingly were, as the basis for delivering these public services, 'value for money' was proclaimed as the basis on which contracts should be allocated. This reflected a desire to secure the 'biggest bang for the least bucks', but also a belief that government procurement should emulate the procurement practices of the private sector that was (assumed to) operate entirely on the basis of narrow commercial considerations. Such policies were introduced into both central government and, with considerably greater difficulty, local government spending. Where public services, such as health and education, were delivered directly by government, 'contracting-out' was developed. 'Contracting-out' involved government injecting a competitive element into the process of deciding how to deliver the public service in issue. Disbanding the part of government that had previously provided the service directly and organizing a competition between private sector bidders that wished to provide the service was the most radical option. Retaining a capacity within government to deliver the service directly, but introducing open bidding between that in-house group and the private sector contractor was another possibility, termed 'market-testing'.

These developments stimulated interest in procurement linkages. Of particular importance was the inclusion of such services as cleaning and catering in contracting-out, areas that were substantially female dominated. Research increasingly showed that women, in particular, were less well off when they were transferred from the public sector to the private sector under pressures of contracting-out. Several different approaches have been adopted to address these side-effects. Some, particularly public sector trade unions, have sought to call a halt to the expansion of public procurement. Some have sought to require private sector employers taking over the functions of public sector service delivery to adopt equivalent terms and conditions for transferred workers—an approach favoured in the countries of the European Community, where EC legislation requires undertakings to accord equivalent terms and conditions to transferred workers, whether they be transferred from the public or private sector. These approaches are not the focus of this book. Instead we shall focus on a third approach where, in order to deal with these problems, countries introduce conditions into their contracts to attempt to address equality issues. Contractors working on projects related to the Olympic Games to be held in London in 2012, for example, will be subject to requirements regarding equality, as well as employment conditions and ethical sourcing.[33]

II. Themes

Those are some particular examples of the phenomenon of linkage that I am interested in exploring in this book. There is no claim that the book tackles the phenomenon from all possible perspectives. One of the purposes of this book, indeed, is to encourage more research to be carried out on the phenomenon from different perspectives. I have sought to examine the use of procurement linkages using four main themes: (1) equal status law and social policy; (2) 'economic' versus 'social' approaches to public procurement law and policy; (3) debates about adaptation to globalization; and (4) the role of law.

Equal status law and social policy

We have seen that the considerably expanded role of government in furthering status equality since the Second World War gave rise to a new area of opportunities to link domestic social policies and domestic procurement policy. In several jurisdictions, the development of efforts to tackle status discrimination and provide greater status equality since the War were significantly linked to the procurement tool. We can begin to systematize the examples given in the previous pages somewhat. Five relatively distinct types of linkage may be particularly emphasized at this stage of the discussion: the use of procurement as a method of enforcing anti-discrimination law in the employment context; the use of procurement to advance a wider conception of distributive justice, particularly affirmative action in employment; the use of procurement as a method to help stimulate increased entrepreneurial activity by disadvantaged groups defined by ethnicity or gender; the inclusion in procurement contracts of requirements to ensure fairness and equality when services are transferred from the public sector to the private sector;

---

[33] See KD Ewing, *Global Rights in Global Companies: Going for Gold at the UK Olympics* (Institute of Employment Rights, 2006).

and the use of procurement as a means of putting pressure on companies operating in other countries to conform to equality norms.

In the light of this preliminary taxonomy, subsequent chapters of the book consider the development of procurement linkages, in particular jurisdictions, in considerably more detail. Although considered to be at the cutting edge of current regulatory policy in achieving status equality, there is a longer history of the use of procurement for achieving social justice goals more generally. The more closely we look at the instrument choices adopted to further many of the most important social policies of the nineteenth and twentieth centuries, the more public procurement seems to crop up. In the past, public procurement was seen much more frequently as an instrument intimately involved in securing national economic and social policies. It is not too much of an exaggeration to say that modern procurement systems developed alongside the development of the welfare state, and it is hardly surprising that the former was used in part to underpin the latter's goals. The early beginnings of procurement linkages, considering issues of fair wages, unemployment, and disabled workers, are not only worthy of study in their own right but also because when equality linkages are introduced, the approaches taken are, unsurprisingly, affected by what has gone before.

I shall be primarily concerned, however, not with the past social policy linkages but with the development of current equality linkages. In this context, the general development of anti-discrimination and status equality is considered. In particular, the variety of approaches that may be adopted in enforcing equal status requirements is detailed. The types of mechanisms that are thought to be appropriate are likely to be strongly influenced by the aim that the policy maker wants to achieve in adopting such policies in the first place. While this may seem a relatively straightforward task, it turns out not to be so, and the choice of enforcement instruments thus requires political choices of considerable significance. These choices raise the difficult and important issue of what is meant by 'status equality' and the extent to which different (and conflicting) ideas of status equality operate in these different contexts. In particular, there is a significant difference between approaches aiming to achieve individual justice and approaches aiming to advance group justice. These two approaches are not only different, in some circumstances they may actually conflict. In countries where both individual and group justice approaches are to be found, such as the United States, there is an ever present debate about which has priority. If the individual justice approach has priority, then procurement linkages aiming to further group justice goals may be challenged as contrary to individual justice constraints, and thus one important source of legal debate about the acceptability of procurement linkages arises from debates *within* equal status law and policy. In practice, this debate has (so far at least) taken place at the domestic level, as a matter of domestic equality law and policy. The first important theme, therefore, *is the influence of social and, particularly, equality policy on the development of procurement linkages.*

'Economic' versus 'social' approaches to public procurement law and policy

The second theme that is reflected in the book is the *importance of public procurement law and policy in influencing the development of procurement linkages*. One of the attractions that procurement linkage has for governments that wish to regulate is the sheer weight of economic muscle that procurement decisions involve.

The OECD has estimated the size of government procurement markets, expressed as a percentage of 1998 GDP data and in billions of US dollars.[34] For the OECD countries as a whole, the ratio of total procurement (consumption and investment expenditure) for all levels of government is estimated at 19.96 per cent of GDP or US$4,733 billion, and for the non-OECD countries it is estimated at 14.48 per cent of GDP or US$816 billion. Total government procurement worldwide is estimated to be roughly equivalent to 82.3 per cent of world merchandise and commercial services exports in 1998. The ratios of government procurement markets that are potentially competitive are estimated at 7.57 per cent of GDP or US$1,795 billion for OECD countries and at 5.10 per cent of GDP or US$287 billion for non-OECD countries. The value of potentially competitive government procurement markets worldwide is estimated at US$2,083 billion, which is equivalent to 7.1 per cent of world GDP or 30.1 per cent of world merchandise and commercial services exports in 1998. Procurement by sub-central governments is larger than procurement by central governments by an estimated margin of two to three times, depending on the ratios measured. These aggregate estimates mask considerable differences between and within countries, of course, but the point is a simple one. Public procurement is a huge market.

Although we shall see subsequently that it is too crude a distinction, we can distinguish (following Trepte)[35] between two broad sets of objectives that regulation of procurement markets can be seen as serving: a set of political objectives, and a set of economic objectives. The political objectives may well be broad, from serving as a tool for promoting a country's industrial policy, to serving as a way of promoting human rights in other countries. However, one of the most important developments in the last fifty years in procurement regulation has been the push for reform of public procurement to make it more efficient, less expensive, and more transparent. In a time of pressure on government budgets, these economic considerations have become increasingly important as a factor motivating procurement regulation. A major choice in constructing or reforming a system of procurement regulation is what is the appropriate balance between the political and the economic objectives

---

[34] OECD, 'The Size of Government Procurement Markets', OECD Journal on Budgeting, vol 1, No 4 Country-specific procurement estimates are detailed for 28 OECD countries and for 106 non-OECD countries.

[35] P Trepte, *Regulating Procurement: Understanding the Ends and Means of Public Procurement Regulation* (OUP, 2004) 8.

of that procurement regulation. Procurement regulation is now frequently seen as attempting to lessen the political and to increase the economic.

The relationship between the movements for status equality and economically-driven public procurement regulation aiming at achieving greater economic efficiency is complex and multi-faceted. Almost inevitably, the relationship is often characterized as involving two 'sides', antagonistic and suspicious of each other. Reconciliation has not been helped by the relative degree of ignorance of many on each side of the histories, concerns, and aspirations of the other. Often, debates between the two seem more like two cultures talking past each other rather than real engagement. This is as true of those coming from an economically-driven procurement perspective, who are often sceptical (at best) of social movements seeking to use public procurement to further their ends, as it is of those coming from an equality perspective, who frequently view public procurement professionals as barriers to the use of a legitimate public policy tool to help achieve important political (even moral) ends. Too often, one side characterizes the other in ways that bear little relationship to its own perception of itself. So, public procurement professionals are stereotyped as unreconstructed free-market liberals, whilst equality movements are seen either as closet protectionists, or their 'useful fools'.

In some ways, the antagonism between movements for status equality and those advocating the support of economically-based procurement regulation might seem puzzling, because superficially they have much in common. Both movements essentially developed at around the same time. Important aspects of the ideology of both appear strikingly similar: both are concerned with discrimination, equal treatment, and fair competition. Whilst procurement refers to 'value for money' and status equality often refers to 'merit', for example, these concepts share many common elements in practice. Both movements place a high degree of importance on legal and regulatory structures. Both movements have been highly dependent on international and European Community patronage. But these apparent similarities camouflage real differences.

The book considers in detail the legal relationships between linkages and the reform of public procurement to accomplish economic goals (what, for the sake of brevity, will be termed the 'liberalization' of public procurement markets). The appropriate extent and functions of such liberalization has become a persistent issue of debate.[36] The second issue that arises throughout the book, therefore, is the issue of the tension between 'social' and 'economic' motivations for procurement policy. On occasion, as we shall see, this policy debate has generated significant legal conflict at the domestic level, for example in Britain during the 1980s and 1990s.

---

[36] To a considerable extent, this debate is part of a much larger one about the relationship between domestic labour law and global trade. For an excellent introduction, see B Hepple, *Labour Laws and Global Trade* (Hart, 2005), to which the reader is referred for a comprehensive overview of the issues.

Debates about adaptation to globalization

The references in the previous paragraphs to international and European developments provide a hint of the third major theme of the book: *the interplay of domestic
and international influences on the trajectory of procurement policy*. The choice as to
where the balance is to be struck between the political and the economic in
procurement regulation can be made in several different venues. Crudely, it can be
determined anywhere along a continuum between the purely local, and the international. Increasingly, choices are influenced, if not determined, by decisions
taken internationally. We shall see that one of the recurring issues in procurement
regulation is the question of the legality of such uses of procurement linkages, not
only domestically, but also under the various international trade agreements that
these states have entered into.

As if this were not complex enough, there is a yet further complexity because
there is not only extensive international procurement regulation but also a significant number of regional and bilateral procurement agreements that regulate procurement activity. For the purposes of this book, we can group international and
regional procurement regulation into two significantly different approaches: the
'World Trade Organization (WTO) model' and the 'European Community (EC)
model'. Thus in addition to national legal provisions governing public procurement, there are two additional sets of legal requirements that we shall be primarily
concerned with: those arising under EC law (in particular, but not exclusively,
arising from a series of Directives on public procurement that began in the 1970s),
and those arising under international law (in particular, but not exclusively, arising from the WTO Government Procurement Agreement). Fortunately, these
share many common assumptions as well as much common language. They developed in close relationship with each other and each cross-fertilized the other. In
subsequent chapters, I consider the principles that underpin the reform of public
procurement (from an international and regional perspective): is it about achieving greater market access for foreign firms, or reducing barriers, or ensuring non-
discrimination between foreign and domestic firms tendering for contracts, or
securing more efficient and cheaper public procurement, or advancing good governance goals? These moves towards regional and international procurement
reform are examined historically, together with how these reforms took into
account national procurement linkages.

Role of law

This is a book about law, and law provides the fourth theme. First, I shall be interested in exploring *the understanding and internal coherence of legal concepts and
legal reasoning*, how legal concepts fit together, the consistency of the use of concepts in different areas of law, the extent to which general principles can be
extracted from legal reasoning that can be used to predict or guide future legal

decision-making. This will involve, in part, an assessment of the legality or otherwise of procurement linkages. Second, I consider *the ethical and political acceptability of public policy delivered though the relevant legal instruments*, involving the consideration of issues such as whether specific legal interventions are acceptable when assessed against external political and economic principles. This will involve, in part, an articulation and evaluation of the rationales made for and against linkages. Third, I am interested in *the effect of law*. What effect, if any, does law have on human behaviour, attitudes, and actions? How does it have these effects? Are some institutional mechanisms for delivering legal outcomes more appropriate or effective than others? This will involve a consideration, where possible, of the effects of procurement linkages (including tracing how these effects have played into the complex international and national webs that now shape policy in this area).

III. Outline of the Book

What emerges is an intense debate about the appropriate relationship between procurement and social policy linkages around four different themes: an equal status theme, a procurement policy theme, and the theme of the interplay between the domestic and the international. I shall also explore the complex role that *law* has played in these debates. On the one hand, the complexity of the legal provisions in play, and the uncertainty as to whether particular linkages are permissible, acts as a constraint on risk-averse public authorities adopting procurement linkages.[37] On the other hand, legal sites have proven particularly useful in addressing the conflicts and attempting to resolve them because adaptation can be eased through the manipulation of various concepts, sometimes resulting in process adaptations, sometimes in substantive adaptations. Law provides a language in which these tensions are often addressed. A range of legal adaptations has been developed that aim to make the relationship between, for example, the social and the economic uses of procurement less fraught.

Part I: Preliminaries

In Part I, the next three chapters, I sketch out in more detail each of the themes discussed previously. In chapters 2 and 3, I set out what might be called the 'social' theme. In chapter 2, there is an extensive discussion of the origins of the social use of procurement prior to its use in the equal status context. In chapter 3, I discuss

---

[37] See eg finding of a survey into determinants of green public procurement, L Brander and X Olsthoorn, 'Three scenarios for Green Public Procurement', December 2002, Institute for Environmental Studies, Vrije Universiteit, 20ff. See also J Morgan and J Niessen, 'Immigrant and Minority Businesses: Making the Policy Case' (2003), 4 European Journal of Migration and Law 329, 332, 334.

the development of equal status law and policy. There are two main functional models to which anti-discrimination law conforms: an individual justice model, and a group justice model.[38] More recently, however, two additional approaches have become apparent: an attempt to secure the implementation of equality norms extraterritorially, and the introduction of 'mainstreaming'. In chapter 4, I provide an introduction to the international and European procurement regimes. This chapter attempts to do for procurement regulation what chapter 3 does for equal status regulation: to provide a map of the relevant law and policy in such a way as to to make the subsequent discussion of the role of procurement linkages to promote equal status more understandable. In chapter 5, I turn to consider the relationship between equal status and procurement more directly. Rather than jump into the detail of any particular jurisdiction, however, chapter 5 stands back and asks what are the arguments that might be made for and against linking the two systems. My conclusion is that whether one considers procurement linkages beneficial or not is highly dependent on how procurement linkages work out in practice, but that the potential for benefits to accrue from such linkages is worth experimentation and engagement.

Part II: Role of the World Trade Organization and procurement linkages

In Part II, I introduce the reader to more detail of the development of procurement linkages in several non-European countries. Chapters 6 to 8 consider the development of procurement linkages at the domestic level in four jurisdictions: the United States, Canada, Malaysia, and South Africa. These jurisdictions are not chosen at random, but represent four of the most prominent examples of the use of procurement linkages to achieve equal status goals. They are linked in various ways. The United States has influenced Canada. Malaysia has influenced developments in South Africa. There are, however, significant differences, most notably between the United States and Canada, being developed countries that are parties to the Government Procurement Agreement (GPA), and Malaysia and South Africa, being developing countries that are not party to the GPA. In this Part, as in the next Part, an attempt will be made to identify the reasons for adopting procurement linkages, and any legal issues that arose in domestic law in doing so. Readers will see, however, that the coverage of particular issues is often uneven. In some jurisdictions, for example the United States, there has been extensive litigation surrounding the use of procurement linkages; in others, notably Malaysia, there has been practically none.

These jurisdictions also illustrate the differing uses of procurement linkages, particularly the difference between using procurement linkages in the employment

---

[38] These models are discussed more fully in C McCrudden, DJ Smith, and C Brown, *Racial Justice at Work: The Enforcement of the Race Relations Act 1976 in Employment* (PSI, 1991).

context, in contrast to the use of linkage to increase supplier diversity by using 'set-asides'. Chapter 6 considers the development of employment-related equal status linkages in the United States and Canada (sometimes referred to as 'contract compliance'). Chapter 7 discusses the use of set-asides in the United States and Canada.

In Part II, I also concentrate on one important aspect of the third of the themes identified above: the role of the *WTO* and procurement linkages. In particular, I examine the operation of procurement linkages under the GPA, the most prominent of the international agreements attempting to regulate public procurement. In chapter 8, I consider, in particular through a close examination of the early OECD negotiations that paved the way for the GPA, the way in which procurement linkages were considered in the early days of international procurement regulation, and consider further the mechanisms that were developed to address these linkages in the GPA itself. These negotiations took place against a background of domestic use of procurement linkages. What effect did these domestic developments have on the discussion of how to address procurement linkages in the international procurement reform debates that took place during the 1960s through to the end of the 1990s? In chapter 8, I examine the negotiation of state-specific exceptions as part of the accession negotiations. I consider the United States' negotiations at the time of joining the 1979 WTO GPA, and then the Canadian approach to accession to the 1994 GPA.

Chapter 9 considers the relationship between international procurement regulation and procurement linkages in the context of developing countries. First, the development of procurement linkages in South Africa since the fall of apartheid and South Africa's decision not to join the GPA are discussed. Second, the approaches adopted by Malaysia, especially the defeat of a proposed multilateral agreement on transparency in government procurement are considered. The use of domestic constitutional law to avoid tensions caused by the use of procurement linkages to bring about changes in other countries is considered in the context of the United States Supeme Court's decision relating to the constitutionality of the Massachussetts legislation concerning Myanmar.

Part III: European equality developments and the European Community

In Part III, the development of procurement linkages in the European context is considered. The relationship between the 'economic' and the 'social' is central to the debate about the future of European integration, and crucial to the issues discussed in this book. One vision of Europe sees the existing functions of the Community, and the future role of the Union, as one determined largely by the need to secure the economic integration of the Member States. For some this role is in itself the goal; achieving such integration would increase efficiency, bring economic growth, and lead to increased standards of living for the citizens of the

Member States. Several of the fundamental policies of the Community, it is said, reflect this approach, in particular competition policy and public procurement policy. Indeed, it might be argued, the EC Treaty has given the economic approach priority.[39] There is, on the other hand, an approach to Europe which sees the integration of the Member States as necessarily also involving the development of a social dimension at Community level. Community social policy is a reflection of an approach which views the process of integration as properly involving a concern for the citizens of the Community, not merely as economic actors, but also as social beings. On this view, whether for reasons of social justice, or for more pragmatic political reasons, it would be wrong to neglect the need to counter-balance the economic with the social.[40] One of the most developed of Community social policy approaches is that relating to status equality.

The legal and political debate about the appropriate relationship between public procurement and equality is a classic example of where the tension between the two approaches is most in evidence.[41] It is this tension, and how to resolve it, which is considered in Part III. From the point of view of (some) equal status advocates, the use of procurement for these purposes is a natural consequence of moves to 'mainstream' equality throughout governmental decision-making. From the point of view of (some) European procurement practitioners, this use of procurement threatens to undermine the transparency and fairness of procurement systems, thus delaying the achievement of the single market in Europe.

Unlike the position in those countries outside the EC, such as the United States, Canada, Malaysia, and South Africa, where international procurement regulation has had relatively little effect on shaping the use of procurement linkages, in many countries within the EC, domestic procurement regulation and procurement linkages have been intimately shaped by the overarching EC procurement regime. Chapter 10 considers the development of EC approaches to procurement linkages in the 1980s alongside the emergence of significant developments in linkage at the domestic level in Northern Ireland, Ireland, Italy, Germany, and the Netherlands. It sketches the legislative reform of EC procurement regulation during the 1980s and early 1990s. Chapter 11 then turns to examine the chilling effect of EC law on the adoption of domestic procurement linkages in Germany, the United Kingdom, the Netherlands, and France during the early 1990s. Although pervasive, EC procurement regulation was not the only or even the dominant element affecting the development of domestic procurement linkages. There were, of

---

[39] A starting point for such an argument would probably lie in an interpretation of the history of the Treaty of Rome, and in the predominance of economic issues in Art 3 of the pre-Maastricht version of the Treaty.

[40] Textual support for the need to balance social and economic approaches could derive from the presence of Arts 117–122 in the original Treaty, as well as the insertion of para (i) into Art 3 of the EC Treaty by the Treaty on European Union.

[41] For a discussion of how the tension is reflected in ECJ judgments in several other areas, see P Davies, 'Market Integration and Social Policy in the Court of Justice' (1995), 24 ILJ 49.

course, continuing purely domestic reasons for not adopting procurement link-ages in particular countries and this is illustrated through an exploration of the limits on the use of procurement linkages in Britain during the 1980s and 1990s.

Chapter 12 considers how approaches to procurement linkages changed during the 1990s. Several particular developments occurred that altered the discussion of procurement linkages in the equality context. There was, first, the development of a renewed emphasis on corporate social responsibility (CSR). The importance of the use by both national governments and international organisations of procure-ment linkages as part of a raft of incentives to encourage corporate social responsi-bility is examined. Second, the development of 'green procurement' policies was nothing short of dramatic, at the national but particularly at the European and international levels. The development of 'green procurement' came to be seen as one part of a raft of initiatives to promote the general goal of sustainable develop-ment. Given that sustainable development has taken on an important social dimension, it is unsurprising that there is now a growing interest in the social aspects of procurement. More recently, therefore, there has been growing debate about how aspects of social procurement can be combined with green procure-ment to produce 'sustainable procurement', which addresses both social and envi-ronmental issues. The linkage of both social and environmental purchasing under the umbrella of sustainable procurement appears to be leading to a renewed inter-est in exploring the applicability of social linkages with procurement. Third, there has been a significant shift towards the use of public procurement to stimulate 'fair trade' initiatives, particularly aiming to increase the consumption of products, such as coffee or chocolate, that are produced by enterprises that, for example, pay 'fair' wages.

This growing interest in the 'social' use of procurement linkages in turn led to a growing sympathy to linking procurement with equal status goals, both at the Community level and in the Member States. Chapter 13 traces this development, concentrating on the growth of interest in procurement linkages in Italy, Spain, Austria, Belgium, Sweden, Denmark, the Netherlands, and the United Kingdom. By 2000, the development of 'equality mainstreaming' was beginning to have a marked effect on approaches to procurement linkages at both the Community and at some national levels. These developments in the 'social' use of procurement link-ages both reacted to and contributed to a major rethinking of the procurement Directives that made European procurement regulation considerably more sympa-thetic to procurement linkages. Initially, this was accomplished through interpreta-tion of the existing Directives by the European Court of Justice (ECJ), which took upon itself the task of interpreting the Directives in a way that would decrease the tensions between the economic and social approaches to procurement. The chang-ing policy context of European procurement contributed in turn to further, legisla-tive, reform of EC procurement regulation, building on the approach adopted by the ECJ. This is considered in Chapter 14.

Part IV: Interpretation

Parts II and III consider the development of domestic procurement linkages and the relationship between these and the development of global procurement regulation, both international and regional. In the light of these developments, Part IV considers how far domestic procurement linkages are legal. Despite their common history, concepts, and structure, it is necessary to distinguish between two significantly different approaches: the approach adopted in the WTO context and that adopted in the EC. Chapter 15 considers in detail how far the GPA restricts the use of procurement linkages. Chapters 16 and 17 then discuss in detail the legality of procurement linkages under the reformed EC Directives. Chapter 16 lays the foundations for a new interpretation of the Directives. Chapter 17 considers the detail of the Directives in regulating the government as consumer, and structuring the role of government as regulator.

Part V: Conclusions

It will become clear that, although the GPA and EC systems have grown apart to some extent, with the EC adopting a considerably more detailed regulatory approach so far as procurement linkages are concerned, they share several elements in common. One of these common elements is the extent to which judgments of legality under the two legal regimes are informed by how far particular procurement linkages are deemed to be 'proportional' policy responses. Making this judgement requires empirical information. Chapter 18 brings together information on the empirical effects of domestic procurement linkages in those jurisdictions considered in the earlier parts of the book: the United States, Malaysia, Canada, South Africa, and the EC. It will be seen that in some jurisdictions, particularly Canada and the United States, there have been sustained attempts to identify the effects of different types of procurement linkages, but that in many jurisdictions there has been relatively little empirical research conducted, thus rendering judgments of proportionality more difficult in the interpretative legal context, as well as reducing the extent to which public policy decisions on whether or not to adopt procurement linkages can be evidence-based. Chapter 18 also reflects on the four themes of the book that this opening chapter has identified, and brings together some conclusions.

PART I

PRELIMINARIES

2
Roots

This book concentrates on procurement as an instrument of social justice in a fairly narrow sense, as concerned with anti-discrimination and status equality goals. This is, however, merely one example of the social justice uses of procurement, which in turn is merely one of several several social and economic uses of procurement linkages. It is important to understand that these uses of procurement are merely one of several socio-economic goals that have been pursued because of the effect that the other uses have had in affecting attitudes towards the narrower examples. Based on the analyses of Jeanrenaud[1] as supplemented by Fernández Martín,[2] five principal domestic (as distinguished from foreign policy) socio-economic or political goals which public procurement has been used to achieve may be identified: to stimulate economic activity; to protect national industry against foreign competition; to improve the competitiveness of certain industrial sectors; to remedy regional disparities; and to help to realize particular social policy goals. The first four goals may usefully be distinguished from the last.[3] In this chapter, we turn first to look at the use of procurement linkages as part of national industry policy (comprising the first four goals). We then examine its use by government to achieve certain more narrowly social policy functions (comprising the last goal), in particular to foster the creation of jobs to relieve unemployment, to promote fair labour conditions, and to promote the increased utilization of the disabled in employment.

I. National Industry Policy Procurement Linkages

In this section, we consider the use of procurement to promote various differing aspects of national industrial policy: protecting national industry against foreign competition, the promotion and restriction of the use of prison labour, improving

---

[1] C Jeanrenaud, 'Marchés publics et politique économique' in C Jeanrenaud (ed), *Regional Impact of Public Procurement* (Saint-Saphorin, 1984) 151.

[2] JM Fernández Martín, *The EC Public Procurement Rules: A Critical Analysis* (OUP, 1996) 46–8.

[3] Some of the best illustrations of the attempt to use public procurement to achieve the first four goals come from the US. See DP Arnavas and WJ Ruberry, *Government Contract Guidebook* (2nd edn, Federal Publications Inc, 1994) ch 6, from which this section draws extensively. Indeed the

the competitiveness of certain industrial sectors, remedying regional disparities, and serving as an instrument of general economic policy.

Protecting national industry against foreign competition

Perhaps the best known example of these types of policies are the United States preferences, contained in the Buy American Act of 1933,[4] for the purchase of American-made materials and domestically-manufactured goods by government. At least since 1844 there has been federal legislation that has required some federal agencies and departments to purchase domestically, where to do so would not be more expensive than to buy from outside the United States.[5] Though the modern legislation is complex, and subject to important limitations, the basic legal requirement on federal purchasers since 1933 has been that materials, supplies, articles, or (since 1990)[6] services that are acquired for public use should be substantially American.[7] It was the onset of the Depression in the late 1920s that significantly enhanced such protectionism in procurement. The reasons underlying the passage of the Buy American Act have been considered by Gantt and Speck.[8] They identify three primary factors at work.

First, there was a desire to relieve domestic unemployment. One of the supporters of the measure, Senator Vandenberg, described the legislation as 'primarily...an employment measure conceived in the notion that American tax money should maintain American labor in a moment of American crisis and exigency'.[9] Senator Davis expanded on the argument:

Why we permit these competitive imports or products from other lands to be dumped into the United States while our own workmen are in the breadlines is beyond my comprehension. As long as we maintain the American standard of living there is not the slightest hope of America's competing with the cheap labor of Europe and Asia unless we give ample protection to American industry and agriculture. Our Government, through contractors, is buying foreign products while our workers are idle. It is bad enough for us to refuse legislation which will bar these products, but when it comes to the Government of the United States' levying a tax on the American people and using that tax money to buy foreign-made products while its own are idle, I have not words to describe my opposition to it.[10]

Federal Acquisition Regulation, 48 CFR ch 1, subchs A–H, which contains the basic set of regulations relating to federal procurement and establishes uniform policies and procedures for procurement of supplies, services, and public works, includes 'Socioeconomic Programs' as one of its eight principal parts. 48 CFR ch 1, subch D.

  [4] 47 Stat 1520 (codified at 41 USC §10a *et seq*).
  [5] PH Gantt and WH Speck, 'Domestic v. Foreign Trade Problems in Federal Government Contracting: But American Act and Executive Order' (1958) 7 Journal of Public Law 378, 379; M Pomeranz, 'Toward a New International Order in Government Procurement' (1979) 11 Law and Policy in International Business 1263, 1267 fn 13.
  [6] Omnibus Trade and Competitiveness Act of 1988, PL 100-418, title VII (amending the Buy American Act).   [7] See Arnavas and Ruberry (n 3 above) paras 6-17–6-19.
  [8] ibid.   [9] 76 Cong Rec 3,254 (1933), quoted in Gantt and Speck (n 5 above) 379.
  [10] 76 Cong Rec 2,985 (1933), quoted ibid 380.

Such general arguments often need a focus of attention before they become accepted. Protests about the award of contracts for the Hoover Dam provided that focus of attention and were thus the second important factor leading to Congressional action. The issue concerned the purchase of hydraulic apparatus for the power plant at the Dam. There was much concern that the contract might be awarded to a German manufacturer after a German firm had almost success-fully been awarded the contract for the supply of turbines for one of the dams for the Panama Canal. The bids for the Hoover contract were due to be opened on 3 February 1933, but 'in view of the introduction of . . . legislation [the Buy American Act] by Senator Hiram Johnson [of California] on February 2, 1933, bid opening was postponed until March 10, 1933'.[11] The legislation was passed and signed by President Hoover on his last day in office, 3 March 1933.

Retaliation against other countries was the third motivating factor. The British government, from 1920, had required that all materials to be used for construc-tion funded by the Treasury 'will be of British origin and all manufactured articles of British manufacture'.[12] For Senator Bingham (Connecticut): 'There is only one way to meet a perfectly reasonable national movement of that kind and that is the so-called "buy American" movement'.[13]

The essential requirements of the Buy American legislation were that there 'shall be acquired for public use', 'only such manufactured articles, materials and supplies as have been mined or produced in the United States' and 'only such manufactured articles, materials, and supplies as have been manufactured in the United States substantially all from articles, materials, or supplies mined, pro-duced, or manufactured, as the case may be, in the United States'. There were sev-eral exceptions, however, the most important of which were that the prohibitions did not apply where 'the head of the department or independent establishment concerned shall determine it to be inconsistent with the public interest'. A second exception related to cost. The requirements of the Act did not apply where 'the head of the department or independent establishment concerned shall deter-mine . . . the cost to be unreasonable'. In practice, instructions were given to depart-ments as to how 'unreasonable' should be interpreted. In 1934, for example, the Treasury Department fixed the test at a differential of 25 per cent in favour of domestic supplies. The interpretation of 'unreasonable' changed with economic conditions. Executive Order 10582 issued in 1954, for example, provided that if a bid tendered by a domestic firm was more than 6 per cent higher than the offer price of an eligible foreign bidder, that bid should be deemed to be unreasonable and the contract awarded to the foreign firm. The preference granted to domestic firms was increased from 6 to 12 per cent if the low domestic bidder undertook to produce substantially all of the procurement in a 'labor surplus area', ie an area which had high unemployment.

---

[11] ibid 380–1.   [12] 76 Cong Rec 3,175, 3,262 (1933), quoted ibid 381.
[13] 76 Cong Rec 3175 (1933), quoted ibid 381.

Goods made by prison labour

More specific attempts to prevent 'unfair' competition from particular sources
have been introduced. The use of goods made by prison labour has had a long and
controversial history.[14] By the end of the nineteenth century, several countries had
adopted legislation prohibiting the import of goods made in prisons abroad. In
the United States, in 1890, the McKinley Tariff Act banned the import of goods,
wares, articles, and merchandise manufactured by convict labour. In 1930, the
Smoot-Hawley Tariff Act (section 307) banned the import of goods produced,
mined, or manufactured by convict, forced, or indentured labour. In 1897, the
United Kingdom, in the Foreign Prison Made Goods Act, had done the same.
Similar arguments about the need to exclude 'unfair' competition contributed to
the development of limits on the use of *domestic* prison labour working on federal
contracts. In the United States, Executive Order No 325A, which was originally
issued by President Theodore Roosevelt in 1905, prohibited the employment, in
the performance of federal contracts, of any person serving a sentence of imprison-
onment 'at hard labor' imposed by a court of a state, territory, or municipality.[15]

Improving the competitiveness of certain industrial sectors

There have been several examples in the recent past of the use of procurement to
improve the competitiveness of particular industrial sectors.[16] French law, for
example, provided for certain preferences for *workers' and artisans' co-operatives*
in the award of public contracts.[17] (Equivalent schemes applied to groupings of
agricultural producers. Other preference schemes applied to artist's cooperatives.)
Where the contract was defined as capable of being carried out by such groups, a
price preference of up to a quarter of the total value operated; where works of an
artistic nature were concerned the price preference was up to half of the total value
of the contract. In another preference scheme, a percentage of contract lots (one in
four) was set aside for beneficiaries of the scheme, including for worker's cooperatives. The reserved lots were awarded to such beneficiaries at the average price
obtained for the rest of the contracts in the lot. Where equivalent prices or offers
were received from several tenderers and one of them was a cooperative, the tender
was awarded to the cooperative.[18]

---

[14] SP Garvey, 'Freeing Prisoners' Labor' (1998) 50 Stanford Law Review 339.

[15] Until amended by President Nixon's Executive Order which permitted the employment of
non-Federal prison inmates in the performance of Federal contracts under terms and conditions that
are comparable to those now applicable to inmates of Federal prisons. Executive Order 11755, 29
December 1973.

[16] See, P Geroski, 'Procurement Policy as a Tool of Industrial Policy' (1990) 4(2) International
Review of Applied Economics 182.   [17] Code des marchés publics, Arts 61–65 and 69–74.

[18] Originally these preferences only applied to French nationals, but from 1985 (and as a result of
intervention by the European Commission) it was applied to nationals of EC Member States, Journal
Officiel de la Republique Française (JORF), 13 juillet 1985, 7911, Loi no 85-703 du juillet 1985.

Small business preferences constitute one of the largest categories of procurement preferences in the United States.[19] Small business concerns have been given a special place in government contracting under the Small Business Act.[20] This was enacted in 1953 and established the Small Business Administration, which was made permanent in 1958.[21] A government-wide goal has been set of awarding 20 per cent of the total value of all prime[22] contracts in each year to small businesses.[23] In addition, each contract for supplies or services that has an anticipated value between US$2,500 and $100,000 is reserved exclusively for small businesses.[24] A small business is defined as one 'which is independently owned and operated and which is not dominant in its field of operation',[25] as determined by the Small Business Administration.

The Federal Government of (West) Germany passed guidelines in 1976 for involving small and medium-sized companies and craftsmen in the process of awarding public sector contracts.[26] At the heart of these guidelines was the facility for small and medium-sized companies to 'step in' once the cheapest bid was submitted. The actual competitive tender process might be over but small and medium-sized companies still had the chance of being awarded the contract provided they could match the terms and conditions offered by the cheapest bidder. But, in contrast to the truly preferential regulations already mentioned, this procedure did not allow such a company to be awarded the contract if the bid was more expensive than the bid submitted by a competitor.

Remedying regional disparities

The remedying of regional disparities has also been, in the past, a particularly popular use of public procurement. Greek law operated preference schemes to avoid over-concentration of economic activity in the area around the capital, Athens. Act 2176/1952 'on measures for the protection of provincial industry' granted provincial industrial enterprises (ie enterprises outside the prefecture of Attica, which encompasses the area around Athens) a price advantage of up to 8 per cent over the lowest tender submitted by a firm based in the Attica prefecture area.[27] The percentages for each particular category of industrial product were fixed by

See eg the decision to extend the preference scheme to an Italian cooperative, JORF, 20 janvier 1993, 1003, Arrêté du 30 decembre 1992.

[19] For a general account of federal small business policies, see JJ Bean, *Beyond the Broker State: Federal Policies Towards Small Business, 1936–1961* (University of North Carolina Press, 2002).

[20] Small Business Act of 1953, 83rd Congress, 1st Session, PL 85-536, 72 Stat 384, as amended (codified at 15 USC §§631 *et seq*).

[21] See VA Mund, *Government and Business* (Harper and Row, 1965) 263.

[22] Prime contracts are those contracts which are not subcontracts.

[23] Office of Federal Procurement Policy, Policy Letter 91-1, 56 Fed Reg 11796 (20 March 1991).

[24] 15 USC §644(j).   [25] 15 USC §632(a).

[26] P Weissenberg, 'Öffentliche Aufträge—Instrumente neutraler Beschaffung oder staatlicher Steuerung?', Der Betrieb 1984, p 2285.   [27] Act 2176/1952, Art 3.

decree. Act 3213/1955 provided for these percentages to be increased by 50 per cent as regards industrial enterprises based in the Greek islands. In addition, small and medium-sized enterprises and urban producer cooperatives also benefited from certain other preferential measures.[28] There were, for example, less stringent requirements placed on them regarding the provision of guarantees.[29]

German law has frequently used public procurement for such purposes. Several statutory provisions were designed in particular to address the problems of Nazism and a divided Germany.[30] Before the Berlin Wall fell, these regulations contained specific provisions for preferential consideration to be given to refugees, evacuees, persons suffering persecution from the National Socialists, and companies operating in areas bordering East Germany (the DDR) when public sector contracts were awarded. Guidelines were developed for preferential treatment for companies based in the border area with the DDR and based in Berlin. In order to compensate them for their disadvantageous locations, a state sector customer granted such companies competitive advantages in the form of graded financial preferences.[31] Following the unification of Germany, the federal government decided that the preferences in public procurement in favour of persons and enterprises in the former eastern frontier areas should cease to apply on 1 January 1991. It decided, however, that preferences introduced in the new Länder should be continued until 31 December 1992 in a limited form. The preference regime consisted of a decree which gave all enterprises located in the new Länder certain advantages in access to tender procedures and to subcontracting; and a circular provided for preferential treatment for small and medium-sized businesses established in the new Länder.

In the United Kingdom, regional preference schemes were first introduced in the 1930s. A General Preference Scheme and a Special Contract Preference Scheme were introduced in the 1950s to assist 'development areas'. Later a Northern Ireland Contract Preference Scheme was added.[32] The general scheme 'required that government departments (and certain other public bodies) had to give preference to a tender received from a firm based in one of the eligible areas in cases where such a tender was equal in terms of price, quality, delivery and other relevant criteria to a tender made by a firm located in a non-qualifying area'.[33] In addition, '25 per cent

[28] Act 1797/1988, Art 8.

[29] All these provisions have now been repealed by Act 2286/1995, Art 10. According to the Explanatory Memorandum accompanying the legislation, the repeal was due to infringement proceedings against Greece by the European Commission, alleging that the provisions constituted a breach of the EC Treaty, Art 30. Letter from Sophia Spiliotopolis to the author, 18 July 1995.

[30] Law Governing Refugees and Displaced Persons, para 74 *Federal Law Gazette* 1964 (Part I) 571; Law Governing Federal Evacuees, para 12a *Federal Law Gazette* 1961, 1866; Law for the Promotion of Zonal Border Areas, para 2, s 3 *Federal Law Gazette* 1971, 1237.

[31] OECD, Working Party of the Trade Committee, Government Purchasing, Replies to Questionnaire on Derogations, Note by the Secretariat, TFD/TD/616, 25 January 1971, reply by UK, 12.

[32] UK Government, Department of Industry and the Central Office of Information, 'Government Contracts Preference Schemes' (1976).   [33] (1992) PPLR C3.2.

of an available contract may be offered to firms in Development Areas in cases where, if the lowest tender were accepted, such firms would not otherwise receive this proportion' provided 'it will not increase the total cost of a contract above that of the lowest tender submitted'.[34] In the United States, a system of contracting preferences was established (primarily by setting aside a proportion of contracts) which favoured contractors who perform work in a 'labor surplus area', defined as 'a geographical area identified by the Department of Labor . . . as an area of concentrated employment or underemployment or an area of labor surplus'.[35]

Serving as an instrument of general economic policy

An example of an even more general use of procurement as an instrument of economic policy arose in the United Kingdom. The White Paper, 'The Attack on Inflation',[36] developed the use of government contracts, among other techniques,[37] as a mechanism for fighting wage inflation during the 1970s. This led to the blacklisting of firms that had breached the government's pay guidelines.[38] During the 1960s to 1980s 'enlightened public sector purchasing policies' were developed to stimulate industrial efficiency and technological innovation, including a renewed commitment by government to this policy at the beginning of the 1980s.[39]

II. Public Works and Unemployment

Some distinctions

Although some have traced the use of public works as a method of employment creation back to the building of the pyramids in Egypt and the building of the great cathedrals of Europe in the Middle Ages, historians often concentrate on the nineteenth century as one of the most important periods for this use of public works. Before discussing this in more depth, however, some important distinctions need to be made. The first is that when we speak of the use of public works as an employment creation method, we need to realize that two broad methods of financing were available, only one of which brings these schemes within the purview of this book.[40] One method used was direct funding of the project by

---

[34] ibid.   [35] FAR 20.101.

[36] UK Government, White Paper, Cmnd 6151, HMSO, (1975).

[37] Including the placing of government contracts, the consideration of industrial assistance, export credit guarantees, withdrawal of diplomatic assistance in commercial ventures abroad, withdrawal of government aid in development areas.

[38] For discussions see, RB Ferguson and AC Page, 'Pay Restraint: The Legal Constraints' (1978) 127 New Law Journal 515; G Ganz, 'Comment' [1978] Public Law 333; HC vol 960, cols 799–810 (13 December 1978).

[39] See R Williams and R Smellie, 'Public Purchasing: An Administrative Cinderella' (1985) 63 Public Administration 23–39.

[40] I leave to one side a third method involving the allocation of concessions.

government, and the use of direct labour employed by government on the project. A second method brings the topic more directly within our sphere of interest: where government contracted with a private sector contractor to build the public work and employ the labour. When public works were developed during the nineteenth century to try to deal with the consequences of the famine in Ireland, for example, both methods of funding were used.[41] Often historians do not distinguish between these two different sources of funding.[42]

A second distinction is also usefully introduced at this point: between public works simply being used to create work for the unemployed and nothing else, and public works being used to produce something else valuable and useful to government but being planned to take place at a time or in circumstances when it would have the most effect in dealing with unemployment. The primary objective of the first type of public works programme was to provide relief to the unemployed: 'It was socially unacceptable that able-bodied men should receive direct relief during long periods of time for doing nothing; at the same time, there was the feeling that an effort should be made to preserve, and if necessary rehabilitate, the moral fibre of the individual who was unemployed. Much of the motive power behind these programmes derived from philanthropic concerns. The orientation was social rather than economic.'[43] Projects of these types were more often than not poorly funded, with minimal expenditure on materials and equipment, with subsistence wages, and concentration on the unemployed as the target class. It was essentially work relief.

Examples to illustrate this use of procurement are too numerous to list, let alone detail. Some flavour of the way in which it was used, however, can be gleaned by looking more closely at the way in which the city of Birmingham, one of the largest metropolitan areas in Britain, used this tool in the nineteenth and early twentieth centuries.[44] The official history of municipal public works in Birmingham, up to the early 1970s, illustrates the close connection between public works and unemployment relief when it states that the 'Public Works Department by reason of its wide interest in constructional work was one of the first choices when members of the City Council looked round to see which Committee might be expected to provide work to relieve unemployment'.[45] By 1879, the borough surveyor was instructed to give employment to not more than 500 of the able bodied poor of the borough.[46] Off and on throughout the next fifty years, various unemployment relief schemes were developed to relieve chronic unemployment.

---

[41] See eg the Acts of Parliament passed to deal initially with the Famine in Ireland: contrast 9 Vict c 1 (direct funding) with 9 Vict c 2 (execution of works by contractors).

[42] An honourable exception is C Woodham-Smith, *The Great Hunger: Ireland 1845–1849* (Penguin, 1991) 78.

[43] EJ Howenstein, 'Contemporary Public Works Policy: An International Comparison of its Role in Economic Stabilization and Growth', OECD Archives, OECD 166, MS/S/65.214, 8.

[44] The following details are taken from JL Macmorran, *Municipal Public Works and Planning in Birmingham* (City of Birmingham Public Works Committee, 1973) 73–4.   [45] ibid 73.

[46] ibid.

In 1920, the city council agreed to the public works and the parks committees increasing their budgets by £5,000 to provide work for the unemployed for three months during the winter.

By the beginning of the twentieth century, however, the second conception of the public works project was gradually emerging. Essentially, the purpose behind this second use of public works was to use them as a way of meeting unemployment that was thought to be *cyclical*. The first session of the International Labour Conference held in 1919 recommended that 'each Member of the International Labour Organisation co-ordinate the execution of all work undertaken under public authority, with a view to reserving such work as far as practicable for periods of unemployment'.[47] Under this approach, whilst the purpose of the *timing* of the public works was to relieve unemployment indirectly, there would not be the creation of artificial demand for labour. The unemployed would not be the target group but rather those who would ordinarily have been employed on such projects, and the wages paid would not be kept particularly low, but would be paid on an ordinary commercial basis. Public works became part of economic policy planning to provide greater stability in economic conditions. Public works should be planned and executed on an anti-cyclical basis: 'In prosperity years when employment was full, public works reserves should be built up by deferring postponable projects... then in depression years the reserves should be spent in order to take up the slack. In this way public authority could efficiently compensate for the ups and downs of the business cycle'.[48] So, for example, in Birmingham, the city surveyor reported in 1916 to the Public Works Committee 'with a list of roads and sewage works which could be put in hand immediately after the end of the war to provide work for a large number of men'.[49]

Public works in this second sense were to be distinguished from relief works in the first sense. In its 1931 report on Unemployment and Public Works, the International Labour Office explained the differences as follows:

This [the second use of public works] is an entirely different thing from the institution of relief works the main purpose of which is to give work to unemployed persons, and it involves more than merely deciding to put public works in hand after the crisis has already developed. The object of such a policy is to provide a definite stimulus to the economic system as a whole in periods of depression by concentrating the economic demand of public authorities as far as possible in such periods, and thus providing employment for labour which would otherwise be idle—providing it, be it noted, through ordinary economic channels, not through relief organisations.[50]

A subsequent study for the OECD expanded on this analysis:

Relief works provided jobs because men were unemployed; public works employed men because they were fitted for the job. Relief works adopted a relay system so as to employ as

---

[47] International Labour Office, 'Unemployment and Public Works: Studies and Reports', Series C, No 15 (ILO, Geneva, 1931) (hereafter ILO, 1931 Report) 1.   [48] ibid 9–10.
[49] Macmorran (n 44 above) 73.   [50] ILO, 1931 Report (n 47 above) 2.

many men as possible; public works aimed at continuous full employment of the workers in the construction industry. On public works customary wage rates were paid; relief work wages were, however, normally below the customary rate. Finally, because of the special circumstances attached to relief works, in practice they proved to be more costly than public works carried out under normal circumstances.[51]

However clear the distinction in theory, in practice it is likely that any particular scheme may well have veered between these two models. In Birmingham, for example, the work that was started in 1920 on public works that were in abeyance during the war (thus the second model) appears to have operated substantially as outdoor relief work for the unskilled unemployed (the first model): 'Queries were raised in Committee and also by a Trade Union suggesting that the Department was getting the benefit of cheap labour, but the Surveyor pointed out that although most of the men were doing their best, they were in no way fit to be compared with navvies; it was not cheap labour but dear and the cost of excavation per cubic yard worked out at 75% in excess of the navvy rate.'[52]

By the 1930s, with the onset of the Depression in many countries, the idea that public works should be regarded as a reserve to be drawn on in times of cyclical unemployment was not regarded as sufficient to meet the severe unemployment then existing. Indeed, the explanation for unemployment had undergone a marked shift in thinking: 'By the end of the decade the generally accepted diagnosis of persistent unemployment of resources was that there was a deficiency of aggregate demand; consequently, the solution lay in raising total spending to a level that would employ all resources.'[53] For public works, this meant that low priority projects should be held in readiness for when aggregate demand needed to be stimulated.

The New Deal marks, in the United States, a significant ratcheting-up of this use of public works as an instrument of public policy. President Roosevelt's use of procurement was particularly important. Federal expenditure on public works projects, he believed, should be significantly increased in order to 'prime the pump' of business recovery and, more immediately, create jobs for the growing number of unemployed, in short to 'provide for the immediate reemployment of labor'.[54] In other words, government spending on public works would be one route to recovery through extensive public works projects. We can see this approach to the use of procurement reflected in the National Industrial Recovery Act, which was one of the key legislative initiatives in Roosevelt's first term. Specifically, it established a Federal Emergency Administration of Public Works, under the direction of a powerful administrator.[55] The administrator was required to 'prepare a comprehensive program of public works'.[56] The President was authorized, 'with a view to increasing employment quickly', to construct or finance public works projects, and to make grants to states and cities enabling them to engage in public works.[57]

---

[51] ibid 10.   [52] Macmorran (n 44 above) 73.   [53] ibid 14.
[54] S Vittoz, *New Deal Labor Policy and the American Industrial Economy* (University of North Carolina Press, 1987) 79.   [55] National Industrial Recovery Act, s 201(a).
[56] ibid s 202.   [57] ibid s 203.

The President was authorized to engage in public highway construction.[58] We can also see the effect of the New Deal in the other extensive public works projects that continued to be generated in various ways at the federal, state, and local levels throughout the 1930s.

The National Industrial Recovery Act attached significant conditions in the 'contracts let for construction projects and all loans and grants pursuant to [the provisions discussed above]'. Section 206 provided that such contracts, loans and grants 'shall contain such provisions as are necessary to ensure' certain social policy objectives. These are extensive, but the section is worth quoting in full:

(1) that no convict labor shall be employed on any such project; (2) that (except in executive, administrative, and supervisory positions), so far as practicable and feasible, no individual directly employed on any such project shall be permitted to work more than thirty hours in any one week; (3) that all employees shall be paid just and reasonable wages which shall be compensation sufficient to provide, for the hours of labor as limited, a standard of living in decency and comfort; (4) that in the employment of labor in connection with any such project, preference shall be given, where they are qualified, to ex-service men with dependents, and then in the following order: (A) To citizens of the United States and aliens who have declared their intention of becoming citizens, who are bona fide residents of the political subdivision and/or county in which the work is to be performed, and (B) to citizens of the United States and aliens who have declared their intention of becoming citizens, who are bona fide residents of the State, territory, or district in which the work is to be performed: Provided, That these preferences shall apply only where such labor is available and qualified to perform the work to which the employment relates; and (5) that the maximum of human labor shall be used in lieu of machinery wherever practicable and consistent with sound economy and public advantage.[59]

As a 1935 study by the International Labour Office details, other countries used public works to address unemployment in somewhat similar ways.[60] For our purposes, the details of the conditions used by states to target the benefits of public works employment are of particular interest. The report details, for example, how France's Decree of 26 July 1934 required contractors to make known their labour requirements to the public employment exchanges so that vacancies might be filled at least partly from that source. In addition, the 'proportion of foreign workers who can be taken on . . . should not exceed 10 per cent. of the total number of workers'.[61] But perhaps the most chilling details are those provided on developments in Germany following the election of the new National Socialist government in 1933:

Under the German Decree of 28 June 1933, containing administrative regulations under the Act of 1 June 1933 for the development of employment, the only persons who may be engaged for the work prescribed under that Act are unemployed persons and, in the first

---

[58] ibid s 204.   [59] ibid s 206.
[60] International Labour Office, Public Works Policy: Studies and Reports, Series C, No 19 (ILO, Geneva, 1935).   [61] ibid 121.

instance, those who have a family to support and who have been unemployed for a long time. At the same time, preference was to be given to members of National Socialist or Stahlhelm organisations belonging to the occupations concerned.[62]

The post-Second World War world differed from the pre-war world in several respects that impacted on the use of public works. First, to the extent that the previous use of public works was an attempt to stimulate demand, by the 1960s the economic problem had become the opposite and one of the most difficult economic problems was how to curb excess demand and the inflationary pressures to which this gave rise. Skilled labour for work on construction was particularly difficult to obtain, and with this shortage came increased wage demands. In this situation, the role of public policy was not to use public works as a way of reducing unemployment, but rather to attempt to limit public works in order to reduce skill shortages in the construction industry, thus reducing wage demands, and the danger of creating a chain effect through the economy generally.

A second major difference was the emergence of economic growth as a major economic and political objective of post-war governments. With this emphasis on growth, the function of public policy was no longer simply the provision of employment and enough resources to keep body and soul together, but also the creation of economic conditions that would lead to faster growth in order to satisfy increased expectations. In this context, at least in the most developed economies, public works lost their attraction as a way of tackling unemployment, which had, in any event, declined significantly from the worst days of the 1930s. Instead, public policy was directed at creating an environment where growth could be generated. To the extent possible, this involved attracting external investment. Policies that hitherto would have been attractive in an era of economic planning were now seen as creating an unattractive climate for external investment of the type that was necessary for increased economic growth. Investors liked free-market rhetoric and reduced centralized control and economic planning of the type that the 1930s had seen. The proportion of national wealth devoted to public expenditure came to be seen as a factor in judging the attractiveness of a country for external investment, with lower public expenditure being seen as a plus. Income and property taxes became politically unpopular. Public expenditure needed to be used ever more efficiently.

Both because of the need to tackle inflation, and because of the importance of investment-led growth, and declining tax revenue, public procurement became a potential economic problem. Costs had to be controlled and external investment encouraged; direct use of public works for philanthropic purposes came to be seen increasingly as an anomaly from long ago, particularly when other economic and policy levers were developed to achieve the full-employment goals that public works procurement had been used to achieve before the war.

---

[62] ibid 122.

III. Fair Wages and Procurement

The origins

The relationship between public procurement and labour relations issues begins in the United States in the 1830s. At that time the emerging organized labour movement was campaigning intensely for the acceptance by employers, private and public, of a 'ten-hour day'. This campaign was patchily successful. At the local level, where employees succeeded in securing acceptance by private employers of the ten-hour day, municipal governments tended to accept also. However, this was not true of the federal government. In particular, the federal navy yards 'were most stubborn in holding on to the old system'.[63] In 1835 the 'mechanics' in New York and Brooklyn 'petitioned the Secretary of the Navy and the Board of the Navy Commissioners to reduce the hours to ten',[64] but this was refused. They turned to Congress for redress but were again unsuccessful. In 1836, shipwrights, joiners, and others employed in the navy yard in Philadelphia went on strike claiming the ten-hour day, and successfully appealed to the President of the United States, who 'ordered the system established'.[65] From that time on, it was clear that the President would prove more amenable than Congress on the issue: 'The President could be more effectively reached through the ballot-box than could Congress.'[66]

On 31 March 1840, President Van Buren issued an executive order establishing the ten-hour day on all government works. This read:

> The President of the United States, finding that different rules prevail at different places as well as in respect to the hours of labor by persons employed on the public works under the immediate authority of himself and the Departments as also in relation to the different classes of workmen, and believing that much inconvenience and dissatisfaction would be removed by adopting a uniform course, hereby directs that all such persons, whether laborers or mechanics, be required to work only the number of hours prescribed by the ten-hour system.[67]

For Kelly, this Executive Order was 'model regulation', since 'it established the ten-hour system for laborers and mechanics on federal public works at a time when private employers were successfully combating the pressures of organized labor, begun in the ten-hour movement of the 1830s, for shortening the workday'.[68]

Whilst the trade unions were pressing successive Presidents and the Congress to regulate private employers: 'The enactment of maximum hours regulations for private employment by federal law was deemed to be unconstitutional, and labor's primary efforts at reducing hours of work by law were directed towards the state legislatures.'[69] During the 1840s and 1850s, individual states increasingly passed

[63] JR Commons *et al*, *History of Labor in the United States, volume 1* (Macmillan, 1926) 393.
[64] ibid.   [65] ibid 395.   [66] ibid.
[67] A Compilation of the Messages and Papers of the Presidents, Vol IV, 1819.
[68] M Kelly, 'Early Federal Regulation of Hours of Labor in the United States' (1950) 3 Industrial and Labor Relations Review 362, 368.   [69] ibid 368.

legislation adopting the ten-hour day generally, with New Hampshire being the first in 1847.[70] However, such legislation was often merely declaratory, with no mechanism for effective enforcement. By the end of the American Civil War in 1865, the unions were claiming not a ten-hour day, but an eight-hour day, and doing so with increased vigour. Alongside this general movement, there existed a parallel movement led by the trade union movement urging protection against long hours on public works more specifically. In 1853, the New York State legislature had decided that ten hours would be the maximum hours of work on all New York State public works.

By 1866, '[organized] labor was certain that Congress believed itself bound by the Constitution to refrain from enacting an eight-hour law for private employment, and, since it lacked the strength to secure the shorter workday by collective bargaining, it advocated an eight-hour law for public employment with the expectation that it would encourage its introduction in private establishments'.[71] In 1868, the United States Congress enacted legislation that eight hours constituted 'a day's work for all laborers, workmen, and mechanics . . . employed by or *on behalf of* the government of the United States',[72] thus appearing to include those employed by government contractors. As Kelly noted, 'the inclusion of employees of government contractors in federal hours regulations was an innovation'.[73] By 1896, eight states had enacted eight-hour laws for men employed on public works. And cities also 'were beginning to enact ordinances establishing an eight-hour day for public works within their jurisdictions'.[74] Five more states and three other jurisdictions passed equivalent laws by 1902. Brandeis explained the thinking behind this movement:

Special protection for this group was sought, not because of any special hazard either for the public or for the workers involved, but because of the belief that where the government was the employer, its establishment of maximum hours would be more readily approved by the public and by the courts than would laws for other groups. These public works laws, it was believed, would then serve as an entering wedge for more legislation and as an example to private employers.[75]

By 1914, however, according to Brandeis, the union movement had 'lost interest in this method of securing shorter working hours'.[76]

The hours that could be worked on public works were not the only focus of attention. In some states, wages were also the subject of regulation, with some requiring contractors to pay 'the prevailing wage' to workers on the project. The prevailing wage generally meant the wage that had been agreed by the unions in the locality for such work. In several states, trade unions also succeeded in persuading legislatures to pass legislation requiring that only union labour could be employed on public

---

[70] E Brandeis, 'Labor Legislation' in JR Commons (ed), *History of Labor in the United States, 1896–1932, volume III* (Macmillan, 1935) 542–3.   [71] Kelly (n 68 above) 369.
[72] Act of June 25, 1868, US Statutes at Large, XV, 77, quoted in D Montgomery, *Beyond Equality: Labor and the Radical Republicans 1862–1872* (Alfred A Knopf, 1967) 318 (emphasis added).
[73] Kelly (n 68 above) 370.   [74] Brandeis (n 70 above) 542.   [75] ibid.
[76] ibid 547.

works, as in Illinois, Nebraska, Michigan, and Montana, but these too were struck down as unconstitutional by the state courts.[77] Several states went further in limiting competition in various ways. A Louisiana statute limited employment on public works to those who had paid their poll tax. Oregon and California laws prohibited the employment of Chinese labourers on public works projects. A New York law prohibited the employment of aliens on such projects, followed by Illinois.

Enforcing these laws was another matter, however, not least because of the antagonistic attitude taken by the public officials whose responsibility it was to enforce the laws, with many either ignoring them, or interpreting them so narrowly that they were rendered ineffective.[78] Equally, the attitude the courts took to these laws often 'eviscerated' them.[79] Eventually, the United States Supreme Court held, in 1877, that employment 'on behalf of' the government did not include employment by government contractors.[80] This, and similarly restrictive decisions, contributed to the law becoming effectively a dead letter.

Protection from competition and the Davis-Bacon Act of 1931

Whilst protection from 'foreign' competition was an important element in some union thinking before the First World War, reflected in restrictions on who could work on public works projects, this ceased to be as important following that war, and particularly after the Immigration Act of 1924, which 'substantially limited the influx of southern- and eastern-European immigrants'.[81] Instead, the new 'threat' came from southern black workers moving to the mid-western and the north-eastern states, which increased significantly after the war. The challenge this population movement posed was particularly keenly felt in the construction trades. Black workers were substantially excluded from joining the construction unions, and hence were often restricted in the work that they could do. One of the ways in which such workers made themselves more attractive to employers was by accepting work at less than the rates of pay that were paid to union members. Indeed, not infrequently, employers imported black workers from the South to work at lower wages. Not surprisingly, this competition became entangled in state regulation of public works construction projects, particularly when, in the late 1920s, the Depression began and with it an even more intense competition for jobs.

---

[77] *Fiske v People, ex p Raymond* 188 Ill 206 (1900); *Adams v Brennan* 177 Ill 194 (1898); *Wright v Hoctor* 95 Neb 342 (1914); *Lewis v Board of Education*, 139 Mich 306 (1905); *State v Toole* 26 Mont 22 (1901).

[78] DB Robertson, *Capital, Labor, and State: The Battle for American Labor Markets from the Civil War to the New Deal* (Rowman and Litttlefield Publishers, 2000) 44–5.

[79] ibid 45. For a comprehensive listing of cases during this period dealing with public works hours laws, see WE Forbath, *Law and the Shaping of the American Labor Movement* (Harvard University Press, 1991) 180–1.   [80] *United States v Driscoll* 96 US Rep 421 (1877).

[81] DE Bernstein, *Only One Place of Redress: African-Americans, Labor Regulations, and the Courts from Reconstruction to the New Deal* (Duke University Press, 2001) 70.

'Prevailing wage' legislation had, as we have seen, been introduced into several states during the 1890s, but by the 1920s New York was one of the few to have retained it.[82] The Great Depression hit the construction industry hard at a much earlier stage than it affected the rest of the economy. By the end of the 1920s, the availability of surplus labor had reduced construction wages by 50 per cent.[83] In 1927, a contractor from Alabama was awarded a federal government contract to build a Veterans' Bureau hospital on Long Island, New York. 'The firm imported a crew of African American construction workers from Alabama to work on the project. Because this was a federal project, New York's prevailing wage law did not cover it. Besieged with constituent complaints, Bacon [the local Congressman for the district] submitted a bill that would require contractors working on federal public works projects to comply with state prevailing wage laws.' This Bill, which after several significant changes became the Davis-Bacon Act of 1931, required contractors to pay local prevailing wage rates on construction projects in excess of two thousand dollars when the United States or the District of Columbia was a party to the construction contract.[84] The supporters of Davis-Bacon argued that the legislation would protect local contractors and workers from construction workers who would come into the area in which there was a federal construction project and take those jobs for lower wages than the local workforce. Without such protections, the effect of awarding government contracts to the lowest bidder would be to depress the local wages; contractors would lower wages in order to win federal contracts. The Act therefore required that the local 'prevailing wage' should be paid by all contractors on federal construction projects. 'When Congress enacted the Davis-Bacon Act, the federal government funded sixty per cent of new construction in the country.'[85] Disputes regarding the prevailing wage were to be settled by arbitration mediated by the Secretary of Labor. In 1935, the law was amended to provide that the Department of Labor would determine the 'prevailing wage' at the beginning of the contract and the Department issued regulations requiring that wages be paid at the union rate in any locality in which at least 30 per cent of those working in construction were union members.[86]

David Bernstein has argued, convincingly, that part of the motivation of some of those supporting the Bill in Congress was a desire to exclude black workers competing with the local white workers.[87] That was not the only motivation, however:

Besides playing to racist sentiment at a time of economic hardship, the legislative history of Davis-Bacon reveals that the law appealed to pro-union legislators, to congressmen who shared the popular (but foolish) view that unemployment could be lowered by the imposition

---

[82] ibid 72.

[83] C Tracey, 'Comment: An Argument for the Repeal of the Davis-Bacon Act' (2001) 5 Journal of Small and Emerging Business Law 285, 286.   [84] ibid.

[85] ibid.   [86] Pub L No 403, 74th Cong.

[87] Bernstein (n 81 above). See also, DE Bernstein, 'Roots of the "Underclass": the Decline of Laissez-Faire Jurisprudence and the Rise of Racist Labor Legislation' (1991) 43 American University Law Review 85; RA Levy, 'An Equal Protection Analysis of the Davis-Bacon Act' (1995) Detroit College of Law Review 973.

of high wages in a deflationary environment, and to congressmen who sought to ensure that pork barrel projects brought to their district in a time of mass unemployment benefited local constituents, not itinerant workers.[88]

Whatever the motivation, the effect was significantly to exclude black workers from competing with union (largely white) workers and to give a significant incentive to employers to hire union workers since there was now no competitive advantage in hiring black workers.[89] Davis-Bacon 'effectively eliminates cost penalties associated with unionization within the construction industry', allowing 'unionized firms to be more competitive in bids for federal construction contracts, thus lowering employer resistance to unions and collective bargaining for wages'.[90]

The New Deal and the social uses of procurement

This approach adopted the indirect use of public procurement as a tool of social policy, through attaching conditions to public contracts that aimed to use the purchasing power of government to exert pressure on the contractor to adopt particular social policies that the contractor might (probably, would) not otherwise adopt. The Davis-Bacon Act, signed by Herbert Hoover in 1931, and the other provisions we have seen arising from 1839, were examples of this.

What marks out the administration of Franklin D Roosevelt as different was the *extent* to which it used federal government procurement as a mechanism to deliver socio-economic goals, particularly in the employment field, to which it attached central importance politically and economically. In the previous examples we have considered, governments (federal, state, and local) have more often been seen as succumbing to external (often trade union) pressure to use procurement. In the case of the Roosevelt Administration, however, it was an instrument of choice.

The use of the contracting power had one marked advantage over other policy instruments that the President had at his disposal: the United States Supreme Court appeared to have accepted that the use of the federal public procurement power to achieve social goals was constitutional. Earlier in the century there had been significant debate over the whether the federal, state, and local legislation was unconstitutional under both the state or federal constitutions. As early as 1868, the California Supreme Court had limited the extent to which a city could impose penalties on a contractor for failure to comply with these requirements.[91] In 1890, the Supreme Court of California held invalid a Los Angeles city ordinance on hours of work on public works.[92] In Illinois and Louisiana, the state courts had held city ordinances unconstitutional; in New York and Ohio, the state courts held state legislation unconstitutional.[93] In 1903, however, the United States Supreme

---

[88] Bernstein (n 81 above) 78–9.   [89] ibid 84.   [90] Tracey (n 83 above) 286.
[91] *Drew v Smith* 38 Cal 325 (1869).   [92] *Ex p CJ Kuback* 85 Cal 274 (1890).
[93] *Fiske v People, ex p Raymond* 188 Ill 206 (1900); State v McNally 48 La Ann 1450 (1896); *People v Orange County Road Construction Co* 175 NY 84 (1903); *Cleveland v Clements Bros Construction Co* 67 Ohio St 197 (1902).

Court upheld a similar Kansas law under the federal constitution.[94] Following this, state courts sometimes followed this lead and upheld the statutes; in those cases where they did not, as in New York, amendments were introduced into the state constitutions to permit such legislation. In 1907, the Court upheld an equivalent federal eight-hour requirement.[95] In 1915, the US Supreme Court upheld a state law prohibition on the employment of aliens on public works.[96] By 1940,[97] the Court would say that: 'Like private individuals and businesses, the Government enjoys the unrestricted power . . . to determine those with whom it will deal, and to fix the terms and conditions upon which it will make needed purchases.'[98]

In contrast, the use of other traditional sources of federal power for social policy purposes, such as the Commerce Power, was viewed within the Roosevelt Administration, rightly as it turned out, as likely to be held by the Supreme Court to be unconstitutional. In the face of such doubts,[99] the use of the procurement power was thus doubly attractive: it packed considerable economic punch, and it was pretty clearly constitutional. After the Supreme Court did hold much of the New Deal's social and labour legislation unconstitutional, the attractiveness of the procurement power was further confirmed. After the *Schechter* decision, for example, Congress passed the Walsh-Healey Public Contracts Act in 1936 which 'kept alive government regulation of labor standards'.[100] Along with the Davis-Bacon Act, the Walsh-Healey Act was the second major federal prevailing wage law of the Depression, extending prevailing wage rates beyond construction contracts to goods-producing industries.[101] The Walsh-Healey Act provided that all government contractors should pay the prevailing wage as determined by the Secretary of Labor, should observe the eight-hour day and the forty-hour week, and prohibited the use of child labour and convict labour by government contractors. The subsequent change of approach by the Supreme Court to the use of the Commerce Power as a basis for social legislation, provided an expanded source of constitutional authority, but, as we shall see, the procurement power remained to be used when convenient alongside these other sources of authority.

Origins of the linkage: fair wages in Britain

The origins of the fair wages movement in Britain date from the 1880s, when complaints began to be made that those working on government contracts were being paid less than the rate that private employers had agreed with trade unions

---

[94] *Atkin v Kansas* 191 US 207 (1903).   [95] *Ellis v United States* 206 US 246 (1907).
[96] *Heim v McCall* 239 US 175 (1915).
[97] *Perkins v Lukens Steel Co* 310 US 113, 125–32 (1940).   [98] ibid 127.
[99] See GE Paulsen, *A Living Wage for the Forgotten Man* (Susquehanna University Press, 1996) ch 3 'Horse and Buggy Days'.   [100] ibid 59.
[101] A third major piece of such legislation, the Services Contract Act of 1965, extended prevailing wage protection to all workers on federal service contracts except executive, administrative, and professional employees.

on equivalent jobs. These complaints, particularly from the building and printing trades unions, focused initially on government printing contracts, but spread relatively quickly to a range of government contract work, becoming closely connected to the trade union campaign against 'sweating', ie the system where cheap labourers, working in unacceptable conditions and paid a pittance, were used to produce manufactured goods.

A report to the Board of Trade in 1887 by a Mr HG Calcraft, the labour correspondent of the Board, described the competition that had developed in various trades in London's East End.[102] In particular, the report identified sweating as arising in a context where the division of labour was developed, with individual workers concentrating on only one task in the production process, replacing the traditional process where one worker was responsible for the product from beginning to end. Those who organized this new process were termed 'sweaters'. When this division of labour was combined with the influx of foreign workers, the reduction of wages followed in a relatively brief period of time. 'Foreigners coming here absolutely ignorant of the language fall into the hands of these sweaters, and not only give free labour but pay small premiums to learn this trade, the premiums being paid out of their earnings as soon as they become entitled to receive wages.'[103] A Select Committee was established by the House of Lords, which took extensive evidence that tended to echo the findings of the Report to the Board of Trade on the importance of subcontracting and the division of labour as essential components of the problem. One civil service witness from the War Office (the Director of Contracts, Mr Nepean) described the problem for government contracting as follows:

... our contracts have been used for some years as a vehicle for sweating, ... the work has been handed down from contractor to gangmaster, and ... the gangmasters [have] prices given them by the contractors, of which we knew nothing, and which necessitated the grant of low wages to the actual worker, and ... the whole of the sweating business has been carried out almost under the protection of the War Office.[104]

The Report by the Select Committee was, however, more cautious. 'When we come to consider the causes of and the remedies for the evils attending the conditions of labour which go under the name of sweating, we are immediately involved in a labyrinth of difficulties.'[105] The Report considered some of the arguments put to it, including the use of subcontractors, the effect of foreign immigration, the development of machinery, and the division of labour, but found none to be wholly convincing. The Committee had another explanation: 'With more truth it may be said that the inefficiency of many of the lower class of workers, early marriages, and the tendency of the residuum of the population in large towns to form

---

[102] Copy of report to the Board of Trade on the Sweating System at the East End of London by the Correspondent of the Board, 12 September 1887, HC 331 (1887) LXXXIX, 253 (hereafter 1887 Sweating Report). [103] ibid 19.

[104] Select Committee on the Sweating System, Fourth Report (1889) HC 331, para 14, Q 24655.

[105] Select Committee on the Sweating System, Final Report (1890) HC 257, para 181 (hereafter 1890 Report).

a helpless community, together with a low standard of life and the excessive supply of unskilled labour, are the chief factors in producing sweating.'[106] To these factors, however, the Committee added another: 'Moreover, a large supply of cheap female labour is available in consequence of the fact that married women working at unskilled labour in their homes, in the intervals of attendance on their domestic duties and not wholly supporting themselves, can afford to work at what would be starvation wages to unmarried women.'[107]

Whatever the reasons considered by the Select Committee, the growing trade union movement focused primarily on the undercutting of wages as the evil they wished to see addressed. At this time, of course, collective bargaining between unions and employers was becoming more accepted.[108] The threat posed by sweating to the continued growth of such collective bargaining seemed pressing. Sidney and Beatrice Webb identify Mr CJ Drummond, then Secretary to the London Society of Compositors, as having been responsible for first attempting to link government contracts with fair wages.[109] In 1884, Drummond was involved in a dispute over the scale of wages to be paid on a printing contract to be awarded by the Stationery Office. The Parliamentary Committee of the Trades Union Congress had raised the issue with the Financial Secretary to the Treasury and the Controller of the Stationery Office. The Committee complained that the schedule of prices prevented firms employing union labour from competing for tenders. The wages to be paid should, instead, have been based on the London Scale of Prices, which would have permitted such firms to remain competitive.

The issue became a central focus of concern for the Compositors, and particularly for Drummond. A circular of the London Society of Compositors in June 1886 proposed that candidates standing in the General Election of that year be questioned on their willingness to support 'fair wages'. Concern about the low wages paid on government contracts spread swiftly, with concern growing over wages on government contracts for clothing for the army and navy, and maintenance contracts for the repair of government buildings. By 1887, the Report to the Board of Trade identified several 'remedies' for these problems as having been proposed by 'workers and their friends'.[110] Among these were the extension of the Factory Acts to men as well as women, restrictions on the immigration of foreigners, the government doing all its own work, the holding of a commission of inquiry into 'the general working of the system and the condition of the workers',[111] and 'making it a condition of all Government clothing contracts that they must not be worked out under the sweating or sub-contract system'.[112]

George Dew, of the carpenters' and joiners' union, claimed to be the originator of the idea of linking fair wages to government contract terms in 1888. As we have

---

[106] ibid para 185.
[107] ibid.   [108] B Bercusson, *Fair Wages Resolutions* (Mansell, 1978) 11–13.
[109] S and B Webb, *The History of Trade Unionism, 1666–1920* (Longmans, Green, 1920) at 398 (hereafter Webbs, History of Trade Unionism).
[110] 1887 Sweating Report (n 102 above) 19.   [111] ibid.   [112] ibid.

seen, the Webbs gave Drummond the honour. Whatever the truth, it is clear that Dew also took a close interest in the issue, concentrating initially on the wages paid on public works maintenance contracts. 'After closely examining the question', he later explained in a pamphlet, 'I thought I had found a remedy which was "that the workman's wages and his recognised limit of working hours should form a part of every contract, and to be strictly observed by any person who may obtain a contract"'.[113] He approached Mr H Broadhurst MP, then Secretary to the Trades Union Congress Committee, who promised his support. A conference of delegates from the building trades was held in April 1888, which approved the plan, and a deputation appointed to lobby the government. The proposal was that 'clauses shall be inserted in all Government contracts to the following effect: (1) That all contractors be required to pay the Trade Union or standard rate of wages. (2) The working hours to be in accordance with the rules and customs of the various trades. (3) That as far as possible overtime should be abolished. (4) Sub-letting to be strictly prohibited'.[114] The delegation met the Rt Hon DR Plunket, First Commissioner of Works, who promised a response. Four months later, the reply came. According to Dew, it 'was a marvellous piece of circumlocution, occupying no fewer than nine pages of foolscap. They stated that they could not undertake to introduce such an infringement of the principle of Freedom of Contract, that their sole and only duty was to look at the solvency of the contractor, and that the question of the payment of Fair Wages was a matter in which they had no concern.'[115] As Bercusson describes: 'Another deputation was dispatched by the delegates, who had meanwhile formed themselves into a Committee to promote the campaign—known as the London Building Trades' Committee. This time the main plea of the government was that it had to be guided by public opinion. The Committee thereupon resolved to get the question tested by a Resolution in the House of Commons.'[116]

There had been a history of problems associated with government contract work carried out for other public bodies as well as central government. A contract awarded by the London School Board in October 1886 had attracted the ire of the London Society of Compositors 'and led to a futile deputation from the London Trades Council'.[117] The Board had also attracted the attentions of the Building Trades Committee. Dew describes how, 'through unrestricted competition, the work had passed into the hands of a gang of jerry builders, and the scamping and inferior work done for the Board had become a public scandal'.[118] The government rebuff in 1888 led to the proponents of the measure seeking more hospitable forums, and the London School Board was chosen. During the elections to the School Board in November 1888,

...the question of Fair Contracts was brought to the front, and many candidates pledged themselves to support the principle if returned to the Board. Several of those elected

---

[113] G Dew, *Government and municipal contracts: fair wages movement: a brief history* (2nd edn, 1896) 4.   [114] ibid 5.
[115] ibid 6.   [116] Bercusson (n 108 above) 7.   [117] ibid 6.   [118] ibid.

supported the movement and the Board became the first public body to adopt the policy. The resolution adopted by the Board was that all contractors should be required to sign a declaration, that they paid the minimum standard rate of wages in each branch of their trade.[119]

After further lobbying, the Board agreed that the trade union rate should be paid, 'and a schedule of wages was printed in the terms of the contract'.[120] Soon after, other public bodies began to adopt similar provisions, beginning with Nottingham Corporation, followed by the London County Council,[121] where the issue again had featured in the election. According to the Webbs, by 1894, 150 local authorities had adopted some kind of fair wages resolution.[122]

Attention focused again on the central government authorities. One issue, of course, was how to ensure that appropriate contract terms would be inserted, when the government was so clearly opposed. The procedures of the House of Commons, at that time,[123] provided that individual backbench MPs had some limited opportunities to present issues for debate at regular intervals, and these opportunities were allocated by ballot. The origin of these occasions derived from the 'ancient constitutional doctrine, that redress of grievances should be considered before the grant of supply'.[124] The Commons had the opportunity to adopt Resolutions that expressed the opinion of the House on a matter of topical importance, without formalizing this expression of opinion into legislation. The Resolution, therefore, was not a source of law, but indicated what the Commons thought the government should do.

Nor was a Commons Resolution necessary to change the conditions included in government contracts, which were substantially left to individual departments to determine. The Office of Works, for example, had a detailed procedure requiring the submission of schedules of wages,[125] and other departments had a 'factory clause' inserted into government contracts providing that the work contracted for should be done on the premises of the contractor. This appears to have been introduced into War Office contracts in 1888.[126] The penalty for breach of this clause was £100. The House of Lords Select Committee reported in 1890, however, 'in no case did it appear that the penalty had been enforced previous to the investigation of this Committee'.[127] In his evidence to the Committee, the Superintendent of Army Clothing at Pimlico was asked whose duty it was to ensure that the clause was enforced. He replied: 'I do not know whether we consider it anybody's duty.'[128] Indeed, the Department had never taken steps to find out whether the contractors had complied with the clause. When Mr. Nepean, the Director of Contracts for the

---

[119] ibid.   [120] ibid 7.
[121] See W Saunders, *History of the First London County Council, 1889–1890–1891* (National Press Agency, 1892) 31 (Resolution adopted 12 March 1889).
[122] Webbs, History of Trade Unionism (n 109 above) 399.
[123] TL Webster, *Erskine May, A Treatise on the Law, Privileges, Proceedings and Usage of Parliament* (11th edn, William Clowes, 1906) 608–9.   [124] ibid 608.
[125] Bercusson (n 108 above) 54.
[126] Select Committee on the Sweating System, 1889, Q 24676.
[127] Select Committee on the Sweating System, 1890 Report, para 144.   [128] ibid Q 10859.

War Office, was asked whether anyone was responsible for ensuring that the clause was adhered to, he replied: 'Not at present.'[129]

Although not legally necessary, a Resolution was clearly politically required. A Resolution was developed which supporters of the policy asked Mr Broadhurst to bring before the House of Commons, 'but he was unsuccessful in obtaining a day to bring the matter before the House'.[130] In 1890, Broadhurst's illness led to Mr Sydney Buxton, MP for Poplar, being asked to take up the issue, which he did, apparently 'with great tact and energy, and by questions and letters to the various Government officials kept the business well to the front'.[131] The government appointed a departmental committee to report on the issue, including officials from the Mint, the Board of Trade, the Office of Works, and the Treasury. Their favourable report was published in November 1890. But there was hardly a consensus on the issue. The House of Lords report, published in April 1890, was fairly lukewarm, preferring to rely on departments to include such provisions themselves:

We are glad to find that efforts are being made to put an end to the grave scandal of sweating in the making up of Government contracts for clothing and accoutrements . . . Municipal and other public bodies will, we hope, observe with care these efforts to content with the evils of sweating, and take, as we are aware some of them have already taken, every precaution in their power to ensure fair and reasonable terms to the worker. *We think that practical experience alone can determine how this result may best be effected.*[132]

Buxton was not deterred, however, and when he secured the first place in the orders of the day for February 13th, 1891, he moved the following resolution:

That clauses be inserted in all Government contracts requiring that the contractor shall, under penalty, observe the recognised customs and conditions as to rates of wages and working hours that prevail in each particular trade; and that the contractor should, under penalty, be prohibited from sub-letting any portion of his contract, except where the department concerned specially allows the sub-letting of such special portions of the work as would not be produced or carried out by the contractor in the ordinary course of his business.[133]

In something of a reversal of its previously stated position, the government proposed an alternative Resolution, which was adopted by the House:

That, in the opinion of this House, it is the duty of the Government in all Government contracts to make provision against the evils recently disclosed before the Sweating Committee, to insert such conditions as may prevent the abuse arising from sub-letting, and to make every effort to secure the payment of such wages as are generally accepted as current in each trade for competent workmcn.[134]

This remained in force until 1909.

---

[129] ibid Q 10986.   [130] ibid 8.   [131] ibid 8.
[132] 1890 Report, para 203 (emphasis added).
[133] *Hansard*, vol CCCL, col 626 (13 February 1891).   [134] ibid col 647.

Why the emphasis on government contracts?

Several reasons appear in the contemporary literature for the emphasis on government contracting by reformers. Buxton, for example, advanced several reasons in support. Permitting unregulated competition in wages, he argued, was 'unfair to the good employer, hard on the good workman, and injurious to the community'.[135] The good employer 'either gives up tendering for contracts; or if it is necessary for him to continue tendering, he is seduced into imitating the example of his bad competitor—to follow that broad road which leads to the destruction of the workmen'.[136] Contractors are 'not able to obtain the services of the most skilled workmen, and [have] to put up with an inferior class of labour'[137] with a tendency to substitute unskilled for skilled labour. The contractor is encouraged to employ foreign pauper labour which is then encouraged to come into the country in greater numbers, 'which many of us regard as a very great social curse, labour which not only helps to reduce the rate of wages, but . . . lowers the standard of living among our working classes'.[138] So too, the public would save in the longer term if, for example, work was produced which was better in the first place, needing less expenditure in the future on costs of repair.

In his defence of the London County Council's fair wages policy, published in 1898, Sidney Webb advanced an essentially economic argument in favour of the policy, although the section of the pamphlet is headed 'The Moralization of the Contractor'. He considered, first, the argument against the policy that was made by its critics:

It is, say such critics, no concern of the Council how a contractor manages his business; and if he can get his workmen at less than the ordinary price of the best men, so much the better for him, and, in the long run, for his customers. The very object of industrial competition, they would add, is to keep the cost of production down to the lowest possible point, and any interference with the contractor's freedom to do his business in his own way tends to increase that cost.[139]

For Webb, however, this argument confused what he called the 'cost of production' with 'expenses of production'.

What the community has at heart is a reduction of the cost of production—that is, of the efforts and sacrifices involved in getting the object desired. This is of no concern to the contractor. What he wants is to diminish the expenses of production to himself—that is, the sum which he has to pay for materials and labor [sic]. This object he may effect in one of two ways. He may, by skilful management, ingenious invention, or adroit manipulation of business, get the work accomplished with less effort and sacrifice on the part of those concerned, allowing for the reduction of the out-of-pocket payments by himself; or he

---

[135] *Hansard*, vol CCCL, col 618 (13 February 1891).   [136] ibid.
[137] ibid.   [138] ibid col 619.
[139] S Webb, *The Economics of Direct Employment, with an account of the fair wages policy* (Fabian Tract No 84, 1898) 5.

may, on the other hand, without diminishing the effort and sacrifices induce those concerned to accept a smaller remuneration for their labor. Either way will equally serve his profit, but either way will not equally serve the community. In the first case, a real economy in the cost of production has been effected, to the gain of all concerned. In the second case, no economy in the cost of production has taken place; but the pressure of competition has been used to depress the standard of life of some of the workers. The one result is a real and permanent advantage to the community; the other is a serious economic calamity bringing far-reaching secondary evils in its train.[140]

For Webb the justification for the Fair Wages Resolution was to prevent contractors lowering wages, and hence increase their incentive to compete with each other on the basis of 'industrial efficiency'. 'The speeding up of machinery, the better organization of labor, the greater competency of manager, clerk, or craftsman, are all stimulated and encouraged by the deliberate closing up to the contractor of other means of making profit.'[141]

Following the success of the Parliamentary Resolution, 'the policy came to be advocated with renewed fervour in the country at large'.[142] By 1898, 'there had been an enormous proliferation of Fair Wages clauses of all varieties'[143] adopted in particular by local government. The administration of the 1891 Resolution itself, however, appears to have been patchy at best. For Bercusson, the authoritative source for discussion of the issue, 'it seems that a contractual condition upon which the departments looked with disfavour, was discarded on the flimsiest of grounds'.[144] Perhaps the most flagrant recalcitrance was shown by the Irish administration, which issued a 'flat refusal to comply' in 1892.[145] Sydney Buxton, in particular, was scathing about the response of Departments. Here is his analysis in 1897: 'The novel duties cast upon the Departments... have been considerably more arduous, and probably more distasteful, than the old simpler process of acceptance of the lower tender with no responsibility for the conditions of employment that might subsequently prevail under the contract.'[146] Five years later, his assessment was hardly more favourable: 'He knew from personal experience in office in many Departments what an extraordinary amount of deadweight there was in regard to this question; there was a tendency to take the lowest contract, and not to inquire too closely into the wages paid.'[147]

Subsequent history

Complaints about the way in which the Resolution was being interpreted and administered led to the establishment of several committees to examine whether improvements were necessary. However, probably the most important event was the election of a reforming Liberal government in 1906. It established an inter-departmental committee (the Murray Committee) in 1907, which reported in

[140] ibid. [141] ibid 6. [142] Bercusson (n 108 above) 15. [143] ibid 16.
[144] ibid 58. [145] ibid 76. [146] ibid 80. [147] ibid.

1908.[148] Of particular interest was the issue of how women were to be treated in the interpretation of the requirement that wages paid should be those 'generally accepted as current in each trade for competent workmen'. The Committee interpreted this as requiring 'that the wages paid for Government work were those ordinarily paid by good employers to competent workmen in each trade *in the district where the work was carried out*'.[149] In order to prevent the undercutting of the men's wages by cheaper women, several unions objected to the employment of women at all in their trades, although most 'agreed in asking that when women are employed they should be paid the same rates of wages as men',[150] and sought to have the Committee recommend that the men's wages should be required as part of the Fair Wages Resolution. The Committee, however, did not accede to this suggestion: 'There would seem little doubt that the effect of any regulation providing that women employed on Government work, in which they enter more or less into competition with men, should be paid the same rates of wages as men, would tend to deprive the women of employment. In most cases they are employed because they are cheaper...'[151] The Committee concluded: 'The competition of female labour is viewed with considerable alarm in certain trades by the representatives of the men, but we do not see any ground on which the Government can on general principles restrict the employment of women on work which they can do efficiently, and no such intention is apparent in the Fair Wages Resolution.'[152]

By 1909, sufficient pressure had been generated for a revised Resolution to be proposed, attempting to address several of the interpretative difficulties that had plagued the administration of the 1891 Resolution. This resulted in the adoption of a new Resolution on 10 March 1909. The material part of this stated:

> That in the opinion of this House, the fair wages clauses in government contracts should be so amended to provide as follows: The contractor shall under penalty of a fine or otherwise, pay rates of pay and observe hours of labour not less favourable than those recognised by employers and trade societies (or in the absence of such recognised wages and hours, those which in practice prevail amongst good employers) in the trade in the district where the work is carried out.

Thereafter, the idea of the clause spread rapidly. In 1911, for example, the Local Government Boards of England, Wales, and Scotland recommended that the fair wages policy should be followed by local authorities, and subsequently the Local Government Act of 1933 provided that all contracts entered into by a local authority should include a fair wages clause. Fair wages policy was also incorporated into several other Acts of Parliament, for example, the Sugar (Subsidy) Act 1925, the Sugar Industry (Reorganisation) Act 1936, and the Road Traffic Act 1930.[153]

---

[148] Report of the Fair Wages Committee, Cd 4422, HC vol XXXIV, col 551 (1908).
[149] ibid para 7 (emphasis added).   [150] ibid para 75.   [151] ibid para 77.
[152] ibid 79.
[153] International Labour Conference, 31st Session, Report VI (b)(1): Wages: (b) Fair Wages Clauses in Public Contracts (ILO, Geneva, 1947) 12.

An advisory committee (the Fair Wages Advisory Committee) was established, but primary responsibility was left with individual departments to oversee the obligation and deal with any complaints over its application. Shortly before the Second World War, a review of the Resolution was initiated. Agreement with both sides of industry on the text of a revised resolution was reached in 1942 and published in a White Paper, and a new Resolution was passed by the House of Commons in 1946.

Fair Wages Resolution and free trade

Before turning to consider the spread of this type of procurement linkage to other countries, we should pause briefly to observe a particularly important aspect of the British debate on fair wages procurement linkages: the relationship between such linkages and free trade.

The debate on the issue in the House of Commons in 1909 is remarkable, not because it rehearsed the various problems of interpretation and administration that had been exposed since 1891, but for the intervention of FE Smith, who made the connection between the Fair Wages Resolution and the issue of tariff reform and free trade more broadly, an issue that had previously been raised by the Secretary of the London Chamber of Commerce in evidence to the Select Committee on fair wages.[154] Although he expressed himself in favour of a revised Resolution, Smith echoed the views of the Chamber of Commerce that 'unless it were found possible to impose similar conditions upon foreign competitors, any extension of the Fair Wages Clause must inevitably cause hardship amongst English contractors and unemployment amongst English working men'.[155] 'If a sempstress [sic] at the East End of London works under hideous conditions of labour she is deprived of doing that work in order that a foreign sempstress working under worse conditions may send her goods here.'[156] The essential question he posed was whether those in favour of the Resolution were willing to let the government 'place contracts with foreigners who outbid us by employing standards which you will not allow in this country'.[157]

Smith linked the debate on the Resolution to 'tariff reform' (a more politically acceptable term for 'protectionism'), and in doing so tried to persuade trade unions and the Labour Party to support tariff reform. His proposal was to keep the Fair Wages Resolution, but to combine it with a price preference for English contractors, or a duty on the foreign-made goods, that reflected the increased costs that adherence to the Resolution involved.

If you achieve the object by either of those means you have a real Fair Wages Clause. You have a national Fair Wages Clause. You have the one advantage, which is comparatively unimportant, of protecting one branch of English workmen against another, but you also have a Fair Wages Clause which will protect your artisans and your trade unionists in this country

---

154 *Hansard*, vol 2, Session 1909 col 443 (10 March 1909).   155 ibid col 444.
156 ibid col 447.   157 ibid col 449.

against the unfair competition of men who are not paid that standard of wages, and who do not work those hours which you acknowledge to be necessary for decent subsistence.[158]

He ended with the following prediction: 'that the Labour party will ultimately, and within the Parliamentary memory of those who are listening to me, drift towards Protection, because they are committed to principles which are essentially Protectionist in their character'.[159]

To understand the context of this intervention, and its subsequent significance, it is necessary to understand that 'tariff reform' or 'protectionism' was a major element in Conservative and Unionist policy from the 1890s. This meant, in effect, the adoption of a system of preferences for British and Empire goods by means of taxing imports from other countries. Joseph Chamberlain, who was one of the principal advocates of tariff reform, 'believed that duties on goods would not only deter foreign competition but would contribute towards financing of social reform and municipal enterprise which in their turn would help ensure national efficiency'.[160] However, he went further in also advocating more local preferences, at the level of local government, on the basis of the same logic. Since he advocated significant locally-financed social provision, there needed to be municipal protectionism as well as national protectionism. 'Applying local preference policies was, in his view, the only way of ensuring certain standards of living and employment for British workers.'[161]

As we have seen, some supporters of the Fair Wages Resolution used arguments that had a distinctly protectionist flavour to them, but in general the progressives who supported the Resolution 'did not reflect a protectionist bias'.[162] Indeed, Sidney Webb 'was a convinced free trader'.[163] However, a Tariff Reform League was established in 1903 and was 'committed to the task of converting the British working class to protectionism and away from their traditional allegiance to free trade'.[164] As the First World War approached, anti-German sentiment was an additional source of protectionist pressures. Although the Conservative Party formally abandoned protectionism under Baldwin, in practice it continued to operate. By 1920, Lloyd-George, then Prime Minister, was reassuring Members of Parliament that: 'General instructions are already in force to give preference in contracts for British Government Departments to products of the Empire.'[165] In the 1920s, the government 'dispatched a series of government circulars, directing local authorities as far as possible to place their contracts in Britain'.[166] By 1929, as FE Smith predicted, 'the Labour Party nationally expressed considerable sympathy for protectionism. Arthur Greenwood, the Minister of Health, issued a circular echoing those dispatched by previous administrations, drawing the attention of

---

[158] ibid col 451.   [159] ibid.

[160] S Laurence, 'Moderates, Municipal Reformers, and the Issue of Tariff Reform 1894–1934' in Andrew Saint (ed), *Politics and the People of London: The London County Council 1889–1965* (Hambledon Press, 2003) 94.   [161] ibid 95.

[162] ibid 96.   [163] ibid.   [164] ibid 98.

[165] *Hansard*, vol 135, col 1713 (6 December 1920).   [166] Laurence (n 160 above) 100.

local authorities to the necessity of pursuing protectionist policies when purchasing goods and materials'.[167]

At the local level, the ability to play up the protectionist aspects of the Fair Wages Resolution was taken advantage of by the so-called municipal reformers in local government, who took over the London County Council (LCC) in 1907. The LCC developed a reputation as a model of good practice in its use of outside contractors. The wages paid to those working under LCC contracts were 30 per cent higher than the national rates established in 1909 with the introduction of the trade boards, and higher too than the wages of those who worked under central government contracts.[168] This was accompanied by increasing protectionism. Soon after taking over in 1907, 'they passed a resolution directing the committees of the Council when buying goods to give ten per cent preference to goods manufactured in Britain'.[169] Interestingly, this policy was justified 'by arguing that approximately 70 per cent of the money spent on British contracts represented the wages to the British workman'.[170] In 1910, the Council established a London preference, requiring 'all men under LCC contracts to have previously been employed in the County of London or else be resident within a twenty-mile radius of Charing Cross'.[171] But the mixture of local protectionism and national protectionism led to some tensions arising as to which should have priority. In another decision prior to the onset of the First World War, the Council decided 'to purchase furniture at a more inflated price from the provinces rather than supporting the London furniture trade at half the cost'.[172] This was explained on the basis that 'since the London cabinet-making trade was largely in the hand of aliens, a contract with them was tantamount to purchasing a product abroad'.[173]

Procurement and labour clauses in France

The pattern of explanation for the use of procurement to achieve social policies is similar in France to that we have seen emerging in Great Britain and in the United States. There was, in France, a similar strong connection with local government (as in Britain), there was a similar problem with the legislature (as in the United States), there was a similar mixture of localism and social welfare, and the key period was the latter part of the nineteenth century.

The role of Alexandre Millerand is crucial to the story of the emergence of the linkage between procurement and social policy. Millerand, a socialist who became Minister of Commerce in 1899, came to the position with a reputation as a social reformer. In office, one of his most famous achievements were the 'epochal'[174] Millerand Decrees of 10 August 1899. These relied on the contracting power of the state to enact far-reaching standards of employment. The Decrees 'gave workers

---

[167] ibid.   [168] ibid 98.   [169] ibid 97.   [170] ibid.   [171] ibid 98.
[172] ibid.   [173] ibid 99.
[174] CW Pipkin, *The Idea of Social Justice: A Study of Legislation and Administration and the Labour Movement in England and France between 1900 and 1926* (Macmillan, 1927) 372.

a day off each week, set salary and work hours normal for the region... and required authorization for subcontracting'.[175] The interpretation of the Decrees was essentially based on the unions (syndicates) in the areas where the work would be carried on. The collective agreements of the employers and the syndicates 'were the basis of the decisions and agreements'.[176] 'Where such groups did not exist the mixed syndicates of employers and workers were to determine the basis for contracts of work. This gave the syndicates a new power and importance, not only in their bargaining capacity, but most important of all, gave the authority which the Government recognition of their function of representation in trade interests had made possible.'[177] The Decrees were overtly nationalistic in limiting 'the proportion of the foreign workers to between 5 and 30 percent of the employees [on state contracts], depending on regions, so that French workers did not suffer unfair foreign competition. Previously, the entrance and employment of foreign manpower had been virtually uncontrolled.'[178] They thus, in the view of Farrar, 'satisfied the working-class demand to shield national labor from foreign competition, as tariffs had protected French markets'.[179]

These Decrees need to be seen in context. First, the Decrees were part of a general reform of the Ministry of which he was now Minister. On 1 August, he had reorganized the Ministry to form a new Department of Labour, and empowered it with rights of inspection to ensure minimum standards of health and safety. He had also created a Department of Insurance and Social Welfare to apply the then recently enacted worker's compensation law.[180] Second, although similar proposals had been debated in the Chamber of Deputies from 1894, 'it had still not passed one when Millerand became Minister of Commerce'.[181] Although he believed he would have the support of the Chamber of Deputies if he proposed legislation, Millerand suspected that the Senate would oppose his reform efforts.[182] In addition, the government of which he was a part was split on his reforms, and legislation would require a debate that would reveal this. These political considerations resulted in his use of a decree rather than attempting to secure legislation. The effect of enacting the requirements as decrees rather than as laws was, however, to limit them in significant ways. 'Because... they were decrees and not laws, no court could penalise employers failing to comply. The government could take punitive action only by refusing to associate itself with the offending firms.'[183]

The idea of using the contracting power also appears to have derived from a long-held belief of a group of socialists that the state should 'set standards and so provide an example to private industry' and that this required the regulation of state contracts.[184] Millerand will also have had detailed knowledge of developments in

---

[175] MM Farrar, *Principled Pragmatist: The Political Career of Alexandre Millerand* (Berg, 1991) 59–60.   [176] Pipkin, Idea of Social Justice (n 174 above) 373.
[177] ibid 373–4.   [178] Farrar (n 175 above) 60.   [179] ibid 60–1.
[180] L Derfler, *Alexandre Millerand: The Socialist Years* (Mouton, 1977) 168.
[181] Farrar (n 175 above) 60.
[182] CW Pipkin, *Social Politics and Modern Democracies* (Macmillan, 1931) 55.
[183] Derfler (n 180 above) 169.   [184] ibid.

the Paris Municipal Council. In 1882, 'some of its members attempted to give the city "the right to fix a minimum wage and maximum hours for all city contracts"'.[185] In May 1888, Edouard Vaillant had succeeded in introducing a minimum wage provision in public contracts. 'Although at first annulled by the Ministry of Interior, by the late 1890s it had become accepted practice in Paris and in several large towns.'[186] It is likely that Millerand drew some inspiration from the equivalent developments that were occurring in England around the same time, resulting in the Fair Wages Resolution, given the increasingly close contacts that were developing between socialists in France and in England.[187] George Dew records that in July 1889, the London branches of the Amalgamated Carpenters and Joiners delegated him 'to attend the International Congress, held in Paris, to submit the policy to that body, who gave it their unanimous approval, thereby placing the matter on International lines'.[188] Other countries adopted similar approaches, for example the Netherlands.[189]

International Labour Organization and procurement

The International Labour Organization (ILO), since its inception, had been interested in the use of public works for tackling unemployment. By the 1930s it was also considering the issue of labour standards in public works. In 1936, the Conference adopted the Reduction of Hours of Work (Public Works) Convention. This applied to 'persons directly employed on building or civil engineering works financed or subsidised by central Governments'. It provided for a normal working week of 40 hours, overtime work up to a limit of 100 hours in any year, and overtime wage rates of not less than 25 per cent in excess of normal rates. This Convention was more concerned with the ILO's perception that a reduction in the hours of work should help to reduce unemployment than with any general concern with labour conditions on government contracts as such. Public contracts were a focus of attention because, in the case of public contracts, the 'decision is a matter for administrative action, and there is no occasion for legislation or protracted negotiations with employers' and workers' organizations or any other procedure such as might delay the establishment of a shorter working week in an employment not directly under the control of the Government'.[190] In 1937, the Conference adopted the Public Works (National Planning) Recommendation, which included provisions regarding the rates of wages of workers on public works. Rates of pay 'should be not less favourable than those commonly recognised by workers' organizations and employers for work of the same character in the district where the work is carried out'.

---

[185] ibid.   [186] ibid.

[187] Pipkin, Idea of Social Justice (n 174 above) 77–9.

[188] G Dew, *Government and municipal contracts: fair wages movement: a brief history* (2nd edn, 1896) 13.

[189] B Hepple (ed), *The Making of Labour Law in Europe: A Comparative Study of Nine Countries up to 1945* (Mansell, 1986) 237.

[190] International Labour Conference, 19th Session, Report VI (vol 1): Reduction of Hours of Work (ILO, Geneva, 1935) 20.

After the Second World War, the ILO focused on ensuring that government contractors would not undermine collectively-agreed pay rates adopted by other employers not engaged in government contracting. By then, the ILO had identified a 'tendency towards the internationalisation of the fair wages clause'.[191] For example, during the War, the United States had inserted labour clauses in contracts for the procurement of strategic material from other countries.[192] The British Colonial Development and Welfare Act 1940, for example, made approval of certain grants conditional on the maintenance of certain labour standards.[193] After the usual procedure of reports and comments, the International Labour Conference adopted the Labour Clauses (Public Contracts) Convention (Convention No 94) in 1949.[194] This provided that workers employed under contracts issued by a central public authority were to be protected. States which were parties to the Convention were required to include clauses in the public contracts ensuring them wages (including allowances), hours of work, and other conditions of labour which were not less favourable than those established for work of the same character in the trade or industry concerned in the district where the work was carried on.[195] This, in turn, contributed to several states adopting such provisions in their domestic legislation.

IV. Disability and Procurement

Disabled ex-servicemen and procurement in Britain

The fourth area where there has been an extensive history of linkage between procurement and social policy relates to disabled workers. In Britain, following the end of the First World War, a Royal Proclamation of 1919 introduced a scheme to assist the re-employment of disabled ex-servicemen by appealing to employers to employ a specified quota, normally 5 per cent of the existing workforce.[196] Employers who responded to the appeal and satisfied the conditions were enrolled on the King's National Roll, and were entitled to use the special emblem of the scheme. There were three distinctive features to the King's Roll scheme. The first was that the scheme was limited to ex-servicemen who were awarded disability

---

[191] International Labour Conference, 31st Session, Report VI (b)(1): Wages: (b) Fair Wages Clauses in Public Contracts (ILO, Geneva, 1947) 5.

[192] See further International Labour Conference, 31st Session, 1948, Wages: (b) Fair Wages Clauses in Public Contracts, Reports: VI(b)(1) and (2) and Supplement (ILO, Geneva, 1947 and 1948) (hereafter ILO, 1948).

[193] International Labour Conference, 31st Session, Report VI (b)(1): Wages: (b) Fair Wages Clauses in Public Contracts (ILO, Geneva, 1947) 5.

[194] See further ILO, 1948, n 192 above for discussions leading to the adoption of this Convention.

[195] Art 2(1) and (2). See HK Nielsen, 'Public Procurement and International Labour Standards' (1995) 4 PPLR 94.

[196] Royal Proclamation of 18 August 1919 *London Gazette* 16 September 1919, 1.

pensions. The second was that it was limited to men who had served in HM Forces. Third, 'the appeal for voluntary action is reinforced by a substantial inducement in the form of a preference for enrolled firms in the allocation of Government contracts'.[197] This third feature was originally introduced in 1921 and confirmed by Resolution of both Houses of Parliament in 1926. It is the origins of this third element that are of particular interest to our study.

In August 1920, an Interim Report of the Committee on Re-Employment of Ex-Service Men was published.[198] It recommended, amongst other things, that:

... proposals should be submitted to Parliament, that after a further interval to enable employers to join the Scheme, Government contracts should contain a condition that contractors should be on the King's Roll. We make this recommendation on the assumption that it shall not act to the detriment of any employer who is debarred from fulfilling his obligations under this clause by reasons beyond his control. We understand that arrangements have now been made that employers on the King's Roll should receive a preference in the distribution of Government contracts, and that this arrangement should be reviewed after three months.[199]

In August 1921, the Minister of Labour announced that, as from that June 'save in very exceptional circumstances, all firms contracting for Government contracts to whom the conditions for membership of the King's Roll are applicable must be on the Roll'.[200] As subsequently detailed, this meant that 'where there is equality in price and in the quality of the product, without question, the contract goes to the firm that is on the King's Roll, and in cases where things are much of a muchness, the fact that a firm is on the King's Roll is taken into account, and weight is given to it'.[201]

In August 1922, the Select Committee on Training and Employment of Disabled Ex-Service Men reported.[202] 'It is obvious', reported the Select Committee, 'that the sentiment in favour of preferential treatment and general sympathy towards the disabled ex-service man is on the decline'.[203] The issue was whether a compulsory system where employers would be required to employ a 'reasonable percentage of disabled ex-service men' should now be adopted to replace the existing voluntary system. Instead they recommended the establishment of a King's Roll National Council and local King's Roll Committees to promote the scheme. The Committee concluded that a compulsory system should not be introduced at that time. There were several reasons against this: the 'traditional national dislike of any form of compulsion', the 'danger of industrial trouble resulting from bad feeling arising between employer, employed and disabled men, and between the Government and the various trades in the application of compulsion', the 'possible diminution of the spirit of good will', the 'possibility that some of these concerns which now employ more than the compulsory percentage ... would get rid of the surplus, thereby causing hardship', and the existing economic difficulties existing at the time would mean

---

[197] 1943, Cmd 6415, para 68.   [198] (1920) vol XIX, 503, Cmnd 951.   [199] ibid 10.
[200] *Hansard*, vol 145, col 1691 (4 August 1921); see also *Hansard*, vol 152, col 1372 (29 March 1922) (written answer).   [201] *Hansard*, vol 180, col 1041 (17 February 1925).
[202] (1922) vol vi, 389 (HC 170).   [203] ibid p. vii.

that other workers would probably have to be dismissed to make way for disabled workers.[204] However, if the voluntary scheme did not show results, some form of compulsion should be introduced.

The General Election in the autumn of 1922 delayed the adoption of the Committee's recommendations, and the local committees were established in January 1923. The National Council, under the chairmanship of Field Marshall Earl Haig, met for the first time in February 1923. In July 1923, the National Council produced an interim report that agreed with the system of decentralized voluntary effort, but considered that more effort should be made to use government contracts as a way of encouraging more firms to join the King's Roll.[205] The Council regarded it as 'obvious that one of the most powerful inducements to firms to go on the Roll is the restriction or preference in letting contracts to enrolled firms'.[206] It found that where firms employed twenty-five employees or more, 'the restriction on the part of [central] Government Contracting Departments is almost absolute'.[207] Departments, suggested the Council, 'might find it practicable to extend preference even in the case of smaller firms'.[208] As regards local government, the Council found that 'only 208 restrict their contracts, and only 167 give a preference, out of a total of 2,821 in all'.[209] The Council considered 'the present position to be far from satisfactory'. Indeed, the Council considered that where local authority services are financed in part by Exchequer grants, 'the State Department responsible for the control of the Exchequer grant should bring further pressure upon the Local Authorities to give preference for all contracts let in performance of the Authorities' services to firms on the Roll'.

The preference was well publicized, it would seem, but there was no formal Parliamentary support for it until 1926. A general resolution was passed in 1925 that the 'House desires to leave no avenues unexplored which may lead to a permanently satisfactory solution of the question of employment of disabled ex-service men',[210] but although the preference was clearly thought to be included as one of these avenues, one would hardly call such a motion a clear endorsement. In 1926, however, five years after the preference was announced, there were resolutions presented in both the House of Commons and the House of Lords supporting the preference explicitly. These stated: 'That in the opinion of this House, it is the duty of the Government in all Government contracts to make provision for the employment to the fullest possible extent of disabled ex-service men, and to this end to confine such contracts, save in exceptional circumstances, to employers enrolled on the King's National Roll.'[211] The resolution was welcomed by the government. The Minister

---

[204] ibid pp vii–viii.
[205] Interim Report of the King's Roll National Council on the employment of disabled ex-service men, Session 1923, vol xii, Part 1, 517, Cmd 1919 (July 1923).   [206] ibid p 9.
[207] ibid.   [208] ibid.   [209] ibid.
[210] *Hansard*, vol 180, col 1042 (17 February 1925).
[211] ibid vol 191, col 1830 (16 February 1926). HL Res: *Hansard*, HL, vol 63, col 129 (16 February 1926).

of Labour said: 'it is not a revolutionary Motion by any manner of means. It expresses what is in fact the existing practice of the Government, but it does two things. It gives that practice the quite deliberate endorsement of the House [and it] states that policy in a clear and definite and easily imitable form, so that it may be made a standard for local authorities and other bodies to follow.'[212]

Second World War

During the Second World War, in January 1943, the Report of the Inter-departmental Committee on the Rehabilitation and Resettlement of Disabled Persons reported.[213] This prepared the way for the Disabled Persons (Employment) Act 1944 which replaced the King's National Roll. The Act authorized the provision of vocational training and industrial rehabilitation courses for 'disabled persons' and of facilities enabling the most severely disabled to obtain employment or undertake work on their own account. In addition, the Act provided for the establishment of a register of disabled persons and imposed on larger employers the obligation to employ a quota of these registered disabled persons, and enabled vacancies in certain suitable employment to be given to registered persons only.

The Committee envisaged that the workshops established for the severely disabled would be funded by government, and would produce goods particularly suitable for supply to the government and other public bodies. The Committee recognized that this scheme would have distributional consequences for others as it:

... will cause a corresponding reduction in the demand ordinarily made upon competitive industry for the articles in question, but this will have to be recognised as an essential feature of any national scheme to secure satisfactory employment for disabled persons who cannot find a place in ordinary industry; the private employer must be prepared for work of this kind to be undertaken by disabled persons on a non-competitive basis and able bodied workers who might otherwise have found employment in this field must realise that they will have to seek their livelihood in some other way. Although the cost of the articles in question to the Government will be higher than the ordinary cost of production by able-bodied workers, there will be a saving to national funds in respect of unemployment or other maintenance expenditure.[214]

After the establishment of the scheme, in 1950, the Treasury issued a circular which 'sought to ensure that a due proportion of Government contracts should be placed with disabled workers' organisations and Her Majesty's prisons and it listed so-called priority suppliers to whom, under certain conditions, preference should be given in the placing of Government orders'.[215]

After a review of the relationship between government departments and priority suppliers, 'in light of a report by the National Advisory Council on the Employment

---

[212] ibid vol 191, col 1859 (16 February 1926).   [213] 1943, Cmd 6415.
[214] ibid para 91.
[215] *Hansard*, vol 579, col 1640 (13 December 1957) (Mr Collins) citing Treasury Circular 8/50, 6 October 1950.

of Disabled People', the government issued revised guidance to departmental pur-chasing officers in April 1979. This guidance was reported by the Chancellor of the Exchequer as laying 'greater emphasis on the desirability of increasing the amount of work available on long-run contracts', but the guidance was not published. 'It has not been the practice to publish guidance of this sort since it is for internal use.'[216]

A 'Priority Suppliers Scheme' was in existence between 1979 and 1994.[217] Priority Suppliers was the name given to a network of more than 120 factories and workshops approved by the Department of Employment under the Disabled Persons (Employment) Acts 1944 and 1958, for the provision of employment under special (sheltered) conditions for severely disabled persons. In addition, the Priority Suppliers Scheme included the major firm employing disabled people (Remploy), and the Prison Services Industries and Farms. Where a priority sup-plier could provide the goods or services needed by the government purchaser, it should be given every opportunity to compete for the contract. Government buyers should award contracts for the supply of goods or services to a priority supplier if the cost was no greater than the most economically advantageous commercial trade tender. If a priority supplier's tender was unsuccessful on price alone the contract should be 'offered back' to the priority supplier if everything else in the tender document was acceptable. If on 'offer back' the priority supplier was able to match the lowest tender, its revised tender should then be accepted. If only part of a requirement was met by a priority supplier, the unit price paid to the priority supplier should be no lower than that paid to the trade supplier. Certain restric-tions applied to the ambit and use of the scheme. Government buyers could not use 'offer back' as a means of subsequent negotiations with trade suppliers in order to reduce tender prices further. Government buyers were not required to transfer existing contracts from satisfactory commercial suppliers to priority suppliers or to cease placing orders with commercial suppliers where the maintenance of suitable outside manufacturing capacity was necessary for strategic reasons, even if a Priority Supplier was able to match the commercial supplier's tender.

Disabled workers and federal procurement in the United States

In the United States, in the rush of legislation emanating from the Congress on employment and labour issues during the New Deal, we have seen that resort to procurement powers was useful for several reasons. Perhaps not surprisingly, therefore, we find one of the principal architects of modern United States labour law, Senator Wagner, co-sponsoring a small but significant piece of legislation to benefit disabled workers, and utilizing the procurement power. We have seen that

---

[216] ibid vol 967, col 198 (24 May 1979) (written answer).

[217] As publicized through the Treasury's Public Procurement Committee papers PPC(79)5 and PPC(79)8 and subsequent reminders. See Sheltered Employment Procurement and Consultancy Service, The Priority Suppliers Scheme: A Guide for Public Sector Buyers (nd).

in Britain, the problems of disabled ex-servicemen had led to the establishment of a system of preferences in awarding government contracts. This system was known and studied in the United States by those concerned to construct a federal government programme for assisting disabled workers during the New Deal period.[218] However, a somewhat different approach was adopted in the United States, utilizing the growth of 'sheltered workshops', usually run by private, non-profit agencies and employing disabled workers who were thought at the time to be otherwise not able to be employed in regular employment.

It is an easy piece of legislation to miss in the statute book for the year 1938, taking up less than one page, with three sections in all. The Act 'to create a Committee on Purchases of Blind-made Products, and for other purposes',[219] commonly called the Wagner-O'Day Act after its two principal sponsors, established a committee 'to be composed of a private citizen conversant with the problems incident to the employment of the blind' and representatives from the main Cabinet departments, to be appointed by the president.[220] As we saw in chapter 1 above, the Act required the committee 'to determine the fair market price of all brooms and mops and other suitable commodities manufactured by the blind and offered for sale to the Federal Government by any non-profit-making agency for the blind organized under the laws of the United States or of any State' to revise these prices periodically, and to organize the distribution of these materials to the relevant government departments.[221] Of most importance, for our purposes, the Act required that 'all brooms and mops and other suitable commodities ... procured ... by or for any Federal department or agency shall be procured from such non-profit making agencies for the blind'. The major limits set on this obligation were availability and price. The articles were to be procured from this source where 'available within the period specified at the price determined by the committee to be the fair market price for the article or articles so procured'.[222] In part because of this incentive, in part because of other types of government support, by 1950 there were about 400 workshops employing about 35,000 disabled workers daily.[223] The legislation remained in this restrictive form until Senator Javits (Republican, New York) succeeded in substantially revising the Act in 1971, extending it to include 'other severely handicapped' amongst the beneficiaries of the legislation, and 'services' as well as 'commodities' that should be given priority in procurement by the federal government from non-profit agencies.[224] By 1976, there were more than 3,000 shops and the daily employment of disabled workers had grown to about 155,000.[225]

---

[218] See eg HH Kessler, *The Crippled and the Disabled: Rehabilitation of the Physically Handicapped in the United States* (Columbia University Press, 1935) 190.

[219] PL 739 (hereafter Wagner-O'Day Act).   [220] Wagner-O'Day Act, s 1.

[221] ibid s 2.   [222] ibid s 3.

[223] RV Burkhauser and RH Haveman, *Disability and Work: The Economics of American Policy* (The Johns Hopkins University Press, 1982) 35.

[224] PL 92-28, commonly called the Javits-Wagner-O'Day Act.

[225] Burkhauser and Haveman (n 223 above) 35.

Procurement and sheltered workshops for disabled workers in Germany

Other countries adopted similar schemes, giving certain preferences to such 'sheltered workshops' in bidding for particular government contracts. In Germany, for example, the Law on Disabled Persons[226] stated that public sector contracts which could be implemented by workshops employing disabled persons should be offered on a preferential basis to these workshops. The workshops offered disabled persons who, as a result of their disability or its gravity were not able to fulfil a role on the general employment market or who were not yet able to return to such a role, a place of work in which to exercise a form of work appropriate to them. The Federal Minister of Economics in conjunction with the Federal Minister of Labour and Social Affairs issued guidelines on the award of public sector contracts to workshops for disabled persons. This preferential award treatment also applied to workshops employing blind people. If contracts were suitable for companies employing disabled persons, these companies must be given 'preferential tendering conditions'. The contract was awarded to a bidder from among the circle of people defined in the guidelines even if the bidder quoted a price that, within certain margins, was greater than the cheapest bid from a competitor. In other words, the social policy objective (for example compensation for physical infirmities or the desire to integrate the disabled into the labour market) was given greater weight than the mere satisfaction of the product requirement, and was seen as justifying an increased call on budgetary resources.[227]

Länder were also active in this area. In 1979, for example, the Hamburg District Parliament decided that when public sector contracts were awarded, the only companies to be considered for such awards were those which could prove that they had a works council and a body representing young people, as provided for in the Works Constitution Act (BetrVG), paid their employees at least the agreed minimum wage for their sector, paid men and women equal pay, complied with all relevant health and safety at work regulations, provided for vocational training, and employed the number of severely disabled people specified in the Law on Disabled Persons.[228]

---

[226] Law on Disabled Persons, para 56.

[227] See OECD, Working Party of the Trade Committee, Government Purchasing, Replies to Questionnaire on Derogations, Note by the Secretariat, TFD/TD/616, 25 January 1971, reply by Germany, 4.   [228] Letter from Prof U Rust to the author.

3

Status Equality Law and Policy

In the previous chapter, it was seen that there have been significant developments at the national level regarding the development of social justice as a concern of government. By the end of the nineteenth century, a relatively limited set of social policies (particularly labour standards) had been developed and came to be regarded as a stable, if controversial, part of the public procurement system of several countries during the twentieth century. In this chapter, we consider the development of status equality law and policy, domestically, internationally, and in the European context. This discussion of the development of status equality law and policy will, however, only be as detailed as is necessary to enable the reader to follow the subsequent, more detailed, discussion of linkages between procurement and equal status in particular jurisdictions.

There is a close connection between the *function* that we attribute to equal status law and policy, and the compliance institutions that are thought to be both appropriate and effective. Since there are different instrumental functions which equal status law is frequently thought to serve, which function, or which combination of functions, are chosen has important implications for the enforcement mechanisms that will be appropriate. There are two main functional models to which anti-discrimination laws conform: an individual justice model, and a group justice model.[1] More recently, however, two additional approaches are apparent: an attempt to secure the implementation of equality norms extraterritorially, and the introduction of 'mainstreaming'. In this chapter, we consider these important dimensions of equal status law and policy before setting out the different ways in which equality-based procurement linkages aim to advance one or more of these functional models.

I. Ethical Dimensions of Equal Status Law and Policy

The problem of securing status equality often raises issues very similar to the enforcement of social and economic policy requirements more generally. As Karen

[1] These models are discussed more fully in C McCrudden, D J Smith, and C Brown, *Racial Justice at Work: The Enforcement of the Race Relations Act 1976 in Employment* (Policy Studies Institute, 1991).

Yeung has written: 'The aim of any form of regulation is to modify the behaviour of those subject to regulation in order to generate a desired outcome'[2], and this is no less true in the context of equal status law and policy than it is in the regulation of monopolies. There are, however, several respects in which the development of equal status law and policy give rise to approaches that are somewhat particular. For a start, those advocating equal status law have usually seen the creation of a system of individual rights as one of the most important arrows in the quiver of regulatory instruments, whilst other attempts at enforcing social and economic policy requirements (such as antitrust regulation) have sometimes not done so. As importantly, anti-discrimination law has eschewed some regulatory instruments that have proven popular in other areas of regulation. So, for example, as far as I am aware, corrective taxation (in which the disapproved conduct has not been legally constrained, but if an actor chooses to behave in this undesired way, he or she must pay a tax, thus forcing the internalization of negative externalities) has never been adopted in the context of anti-discrimination enforcement,[3] whilst it has been widely discussed as a means of controlling environmental pollution, and has been introduced in several countries.[4] What distinguishes the regulation of status equality from some other areas of regulation is the heavily ethical aspect of the status equality issue.

As a result, legislators often think that the purpose of equality law is at least partly symbolic, an unequivocal declaration of public policy, aiming to change hearts and minds through making clear what the representative institutions of the society thinks is inappropriate behaviour. In some contexts, this symbolic function may be the primary function that non-discrimination requirements in some national constitutions often seem to serve. And the symbolic power of such law should not be underestimated. We need only think of the powerful argument that Gunnar Myrdal made in his classic book *The American Dilemma* (where he pointed to the difference between the constitutional ideal of equality, and the reality of segregation in the United States) to understand the power of symbols, and their potential in bringing about change. But, not surprisingly, legislators are unlikely to be satisfied with this limited symbolic approach and, indeed, jurisdictions increasingly become dissatisfied with equal status law that is 'merely' symbolic, considering that the gap between reality and the ideal is something that they should actively seek to bridge.

---

[2] K Yeung, 'The Private Enforcement of Competition Law' in C McCrudden (ed), *Regulation and Deregulation: Policy and Practice* (OUP, 1999) 37.

[3] Although Derrick Bell has discussed the issue in the US context. See D Bell, 'The Racial Preference Licensing Act' in D Bell, *Faces at the Bottom of the Well: The Permanence of Racism* (Basic Books, 1992) 47.

[4] See A Ogus, 'Corrective Taxation as a Regulatory Instrument' in C McCrudden (ed), *Regulation and Deregulation: Policy and Practice* (OUP, 1999) 15.

II. Market and Non-Market Enforcement

There is another important feature of the political landscape of countries that adopt equal status law and policy: a tacit acceptance that market forces alone will not result in sufficient change. This is not a conclusion that all would agree with. Some argue that the most effective way in which to get rid of adverse discrimination, for example, may be to create and maintain a fully functioning free market. Only where that is not possible, for example where there is discrimination by governmental entities that are not subject to market pressures, or there are market failures such as the inadequate provision of information, should legal enforcement be contemplated. Creating and maintaining a free market would involve reducing informational barriers, dealing with market imperfections, and reducing discrimination by natural monopolies; but that is all.

But there are considerable difficulties with this approach. First, market-oriented approaches have often failed in the past to achieve even the limited result desired. More significantly, the concept of discrimination involved in such analysis is limited. To equate non-discrimination only with efficiency implies that there should be no 'efficient discrimination' which is also unlawful. Yet, in many instances, national anti-discrimination law rightly restricts just such efficient discrimination. Examples are where membership of the protected group may well be an accurate indicator of some importance, and yet the law refuses to permit that indicator to be used—the prohibition on the use of actuarial tables based on gender in the United States for computing pension contributions and payouts is an illustration. Legislators aiming for equal status assume, in other words, that organizations will only modify disapproved-of behaviour if faced with sufficient incentives. Where an organization expects to benefit from infringing the law by continuing to act in a certain way, it is unlikely to change its behaviour unless the costs of doing so outweigh the anticipated benefits. To that extent, we should assume that organizations subject to anti-discrimination regulation are amoral pragmatists. Therefore the system of incentives and disincentives put in place to secure compliance is crucial to both the effectiveness and efficiency of equal status law and policy.

III. Individual Justice Model

I suggested in chapter 1 above, that a distinction should be made between two models of status equality law and policy: an individual justice model and a group justice model. The individual justice model generally aims to secure the reduction of discrimination by eliminating from decisions illegitimate considerations based on race or other prohibited considerations that have harmful consequences for individuals. This approach concentrates on cleansing the process of decision-making, and is not concerned with the general effect of decisions on groups, except as an indication of a flawed process. It is markedly individualistic in its orientation: concentrating on securing fairness for the individual. It is generally expressed in universal and symmetrical terms: blacks and whites are equally protected, for example. It reflects respect for efficiency, 'merit',[5] and achievement and, given the limited degree of intervention permitted, it preserves and possibly enhances the operation of the market. It is 'manageable' in that its aims can be stated with some degree of certainty, and its application does not depend on extensive enquiries and judgments on complex socio-economic facts. The individual justice model is particularly associated with law and policy that aims to prohibit discrimination, rather than aiming to advance a wider conception of equality.

Anti-discrimination law at the domestic level

This individual justice model of status equality is often particularly associated with the development of anti-discrimination law. Anti-discrimination law at the domestic level is classically illustrated by the use of law during the 1940s through to the 1960s in the United States to counter discrimination against black Americans. There were three somewhat different approaches. The first involved the application of United States Constitutional guarantees, in particular the Equal Protection Clause of the fourteenth Amendment. Over time, this was interpreted as a rather limited anti-discrimination provision countering discrimination in legislation or in actions taken by public bodies, where such discrimination was intentional, based on a 'suspect classification' (such as race), and could not be shown to be justified by an overriding state interest. A second approach was the enactment of anti-discrimination legislation, such as Title VII of the Civil Rights Act of 1964, which prohibited discrimination on the grounds of race in private employment. Third, there was the use of the President's executive powers to introduce anti-discrimination requirements in the federal public service and in government contracting, which we considered briefly in chapter 1 above, and shall consider in more detail in chapter 6 below.

Although anti-discrimination law in the United States was orginally used against racial discrimination, one of the most important developments from the 1960s was what has been referred to as the 'proliferation of the protectorate',[6] ie the extension of the coverage of anti-discrimination law beyond the original prohibition of discrimination on the basis of race or colour. The extent to which grounds other than race should come within the purview of anti-discrimination law has been the subject of considerable debate. The most common, and now most firmly

---

[5] For different conceptions of 'merit', see C McCrudden, 'Merit Principles' (1998) 18 OJLS 543–79.
[6] O Fiss, 'The fate of the idea whose time has come: Anti-discrimination Law in the Second Decade after Brown v. Board of Education' (1974) 41 University of Chicago Law Review 742.

accepted, extension of the protectorate, relates to gender. In 1963, the United States statutory requirement of equal pay for the same or similar work, irrespective of sex, was enacted. In 1964, the prohibition of race discrimination in employment was extended to include sex discrimination in the Civil Rights Act 1964. Increasingly, too, there was litigation to extend the coverage of the Equal Protection Clause to prohibit government-sponsored sex discrimination, on the analogy of the use of the Fourteenth Amendment against race discrimination, and this met with some success from the early 1970s.

The Ontario Human Rights Code[7] also provides a good example of the basic - anti-discrimination statute, influenced by developments in the United States. It prohibits discrimination across a range of areas, including employment, and on several grounds, including gender. It entrusts the enforcement of the legislation to the Ontario Human Rights Commission, and an Ontario Human Rights Tribunal. The Commission investigates complaints of discrimination, endeavours to settle complaints between parties, and litigates cases at the Human Rights Tribunal of Ontario and higher courts. The approach taken to enforcement is essentially one based on complaints and investigation of discrimination.

Another example of domestic anti-discrimination legislation was the Northern Ireland Constitution Act 1973, which introduced clear, if limited, legislative anti-discrimination requirements for the first time in Northern Ireland. The 1973 Act made it unlawful for a public authority carrying out functions relating to Northern Ireland to discriminate, or to aid or incite another person to discriminate, against a person or class of person on the ground of religious belief or political opinion. Two features of the Act's approach were important. First, although a constitutional anti-discrimination provision, its protection was confined to protection from discrimination only in the religio-political context. Second, the conception of discrimination that it incorporated was one that was largely confined to direct discrimination, ie discrimination that usually arises from an intentional act. The provisions of the 1973 Act were reincorporated, substantially untouched, in the Northern Ireland Act 1998.

International Labour Organization and status equality

These are all examples of anti-discrimination law at the domestic level. The International Labour Organization (ILO) is also a significant source of international provisions on non-discrimination reflecting an approach based on the individual justice model. The ILO Constitution, 1919, was one of the first multilateral international treaties to recognize the right to equal treatment. The Preamble to the ILO Constitution refers to the need for 'recognition of the principle of equal remuneration for work of equal value'. Article 1 of the Declaration

---

[7] Human Rights Code, RSO 1990, c H.19.

of Philadelphia 1944, subsequently incorporated in the Constitution, affirms the principle that 'all human beings, irrespective of race, creed or sex, have the right to pursue both their material well-being and their spiritual development in conditions of freedom and dignity, of economic security and equal opportunity'. Together with the other principles set out in the Declaration, most notably that 'labour is not a commodity', the principle of non-discrimination is intended to be 'fully applicable to all peoples everywhere'.

The elimination of discrimination in employment and occupation remains a key issue for the ILO. Two of the ILO Conventions in this area have been identified by the Organization's governing body as 'fundamental'. These are the Equal Remuneration Convention 1951 (No 100) and the Discrimination (Employment and Occupation Convention) 1958 (No 111). The principle of non-discrimination is also found in Article 1 of the Employment Policy Convention 1964 (No 122), which is a 'priority' Convention, while other relevant instruments include Convention No 156, on Workers with Family Responsibilities, 1981, the Maternity Protection Convention 2000 (No 183), the Vocational Rehabilitation and Employment (Disabled Persons Convention) 1981 (No 159), the Equality of Treatment (Accident Compensation) Convention 1925 (No 19), and the Equality of Treatment (Social Security) Convention 1962 (No 118). Since the mid-1990s, the ILO has adopted a policy of emphasizing a limited set of the 180+ Conventions as 'core' to its mission, and has designated them as 'fundamental rights at work' in order to provide a better focus for its work.[8] Among these fundamental rights are the right to non-discrimination.

Enforcement issues

One of the classic ways of enforcing the individual justice model is by using individual grievances as a tool for enforcement, not surprisingly given its individualistic orientation. Private action can play a valuable dual role in the regulation of discrimination. Not only is it valuable in empowering those harmed by discrimination to seek compensation for injury to themselves, it *may* contribute to deterring discriminatory behaviour more generally. An individual complaints procedure may, therefore, make a general, strategic impact as well as providing a remedy for an individual complainant. Individual complaints machinery can operate to clarify and refine the meaning of discrimination by applying this legal concept to the particular circumstances of different cases. The nature of discrimination and the circumstances in

---

[8] The importance of these Conventions is also reflected by their basic principles being incorporated in the ILO Declaration on Fundamental Principles and Rights at Work, 1998, in which the International Labour Conference declared that 'all Members, even if they have not ratified the Conventions in question, have an obligation arising from the very fact of membership in the Organization to respect, to promote and to realize, in good faith and in accordance with the Constitution, the principles concerning the fundamental rights which are the subject of those [fundamental] Conventions'.

which it occurs may, as a result, be better and more generally understood. Becoming aware of the concept of discrimination and recognition of the risk of further litigation and the imposition of remedies, can encourage other employers and service providers to recognize, review, and end discriminatory practices. In this way the complaints process may have a major and beneficial impact beyond the resolution of a particular complaint. This impact will be enhanced to the extent that the complaints machinery facilitates decisions on important issues of principle.

In several jurisdictions, the mechanism for resolving private complaints is by way of an application to an *enforcement agency* to investigate and resolve the complaint, rather than to the courts. The argument in favour of this approach is often that an investigatory approach is preferable for the complainant, who will not be put to the difficulty of proving discrimination. Over time, however, this approach has somewhat fallen out of fashion in several jurisdictions, and the preferred approach has been to allow the individual to sue directly in some form of judicial forum. Direct private enforcement in courts and tribunals has been thought to have several advantages over agency adjudication. In practice, public enforcement bodies are often underfunded, resulting in regulatory failure, and this has resulted in an 'enforcement gap'. As importantly, direct access to courts or tribunals has been thought to protect the autonomy of complainants to a greater extent, giving them more control and ownership of the complaint.

Research has demonstrated in many jurisdictions, however, the difficulties of remedying discrimination that has occurred through such methods.[9] We can point to several recurring complaints: the inadequacy of institutional assistance to individual litigants; the need to pay extensive costs to commence and complete litigation successfully; the lack of trained and motivated lawyers and other representatives; the inadequacy of remedies provided, either to compensate the individual fully in financial terms, or to ensure that the individual victim secures the benefit denied due to discrimination; the inadequate knowledge of anti-discrimination law principles by judges leading to victims not securing redress to which they are entitled; the absence of adequate information being made available to an actual or potential plaintiff; and delays in the operation of the judicial process leading effectively to denial of individual justice. These limitations of traditional enforcement of individual justice approaches to status equality encouraged several jurisdictions to adopt procurement linkages as an additional enforcement mechanism.

IV. Group Justice Model

Despite its obvious attractions, the individual justice model of status equality has been criticized as deeply flawed, and not just at the level of enforcement. Various

---

[9] C McCrudden, 'The Effectiveness of European Equality Law: National Mechanisms for Enforcing Gender Equality Law in the Light of European Requirements' (1993) 13 OJLS 320–67.

arguments tend to recur. The individual justice model is said to misconceive the deep structure of discrimination. Such discrimination is as often institutional as individual, it is argued, and therefore there is little likelihood that a highly individualistic model of enforcement will work. The problem, it is said, is misconceived as being one of intention rather than effect. The individual justice model is said not to take adequately into account the surrounding and enforcing nature of disadvantage and membership of certain groups. The individual justice model is seen as emphasizing the eradication of discrimination, rather than securing a broader conception of equal status.

Out of these criticisms come various alternative approaches. Some have argued for an approach which is concerned with results, not just process, and which seeks to redistribute resources from the advantaged group to the disadvantaged group. Common to such approaches is a view that the aim of equal status regulation should be to concentrate on the outcomes of the decision-making processes. The basic aim is the improvement of the relative position of particular groups, whether to redress past subordination and discrimination, or out of a concern for distributive justice at the present time. The approaches tend to be redistributive and to be concerned with the relative position of groups or classes, rather than individuals. The principle is often expressed in asymmetrical terms as focusing on the betterment of disadvantaged groups and is less concerned than the individual justice model with symmetrical protection for non-disadvantaged groups.[10]

Limits of litigation

If achieving individual justice by way of private litigation is problematic, achieving group justice by such means faces even greater difficulties. Recurring complaints include: the lack of involvement by unions in addressing equality; the absence of mechanisms for tackling institutional discrimination directly; settlements which do not adequately ensure that equivalent discrimination against others in addition to the individual victim is adequately dealt with; remedies and sanctions which are addressed only to the individual plaintiff and not generalized to any class affected; the absence of adequate aggregate information on employers' pay or workforce composition making proof of discriminatory practices extremely difficult; concentration, where litigation does take place, on the individual victim rather than the institutional problem; the absence of public bodies with a specific equality mandate to adopt a strategic approach to enforcement rather than an ad hoc reactive approach; understaffed, ill-equipped, badly resourced, or poorly led strategic enforcement bodies; and inadequate opportunities to challenge discriminatory collective agreements. Individual complaints of discrimination in themselves are unlikely to secure the much more far-reaching

---

[10] C McCrudden, D Smith, and C Brown, 'Groups versus Individuals: the Ambiguity behind the Race Relations Act' (1991) 12 Policy Studies 26.

changes which are necessary to further significantly a group justice model. In particular, courts often consider the extent to which they can engage in redistribution to be limited. More often courts attempt to limit such redistribution, ameliorating what would be seen as disruptive social change, rather than engaging in it.[11]

Jurisdictions that have adopted a group justice perspective (such as the United States, Canada, Northern Ireland, and South Africa) tend to provide mechanisms for promoting more widespread change throughout different spheres of economic and social life, adopting specifically tailored group justice mechanisms. This is particularly the case where the uses to which equal status law and policy have been put have involved situations in which quasi-constitutional problems are being addressed: attempts to address racial inequality in the United States, or attempts to resolve the issue of native Bumiputera in Malaysia, for example. More recent and more explicit use of equal status policy in the settlement of major constitutional disputes is apparent in Northern Ireland, relating to the respective positions of the two religiously-defined communities, and in South Africa relating to the end of apartheid and the development of democratic government. In each of these situations equal status policy has become part of these constitutional settlements, although in somewhat different ways.

United States and 'affirmative action'

'Affirmative action' is the term used in the United States to refer to actions taken to promote a group justice perspective. The term is to be found in at least two important employment discrimination law contexts: in Title VII of the Civil Rights Act 1964[12] where it is used to describe the power given to judges to remedy unlawful discrimination, and in Executive Order 11246[13] where it is used to describe the obligations of a federal government contractor in a situation where minority or women workers are underrepresented in the workforce of the contractor.

Canada

At the federal government level,[14] the Canadian Human Rights Act 1977 made discrimination unlawful on several grounds, including gender, in various situations, including employment. However, by the early 1980s the Act appeared to be achieving insufficient effect, and the government appointed a Royal

---

[11] C McCrudden and J Black, 'Achieving Equality between Men and Women in Social Security: Some Issues of Costs and Problems of Implementation' in C McCrudden (ed), *Equality Between Women and Men in Social Security* (Butterworths, 1994) 215.

[12] 42 USC §2000e *et seq*, s 706(g).

[13] 3 CFR 339 (1964), reprinted in 42 USC 2000e (1982).

[14] See in general C Raskin, *Equal Opportunity for Women: Affirmative Action: A Canadian Perspective* (ILO, unpublished, October 1992).

Commission, chaired by Judge Abella, to report. In 1984, the Abella Report[15] recommended that stronger legislation was necessary and, in particular, that 'employment equity' (the term preferred over the more American-sounding 'affirmative action') be required throughout the federal jurisdiction. Crucial to the recommendation was the argument that it was necessary to move beyond an approach to compliance that concentrated on individualized enforcement of anti-discrimination requirements to an approach that used sustained, active governmental efforts to ensure that employers engaged in efforts to change the composition of their workforces.

As a response to this report, new legislation was introduced.[16] The Employment Equity Act 1986, which operates additional requirements to those in the 1978 Act, required organizations of 100 or more employees under federal jurisdiction to introduce systematic monitoring of workforces, to submit an annual report, and to introduce 'employment equity programmes'[17] where this would reduce underrepresentation of certain groups, including women. The legislation applies, however, only to federally regulated industries, such as banking, communications, and transport. In 1992, a Parliamentary Review Committee, chaired by Alan Redway MP, reviewed the impact of the Act. In 1994, the Minister of Human Resources tabled Bill C-64, a new Act to replace the 1986 Act. The new Act received Royal Assent in 1995 and came into force in 1996.

Northern Ireland

A similar move from an individual justice towards a more group justice perspective occurred in Northern Ireland, where what was thought of as the American approach was emulated much more closely than in the rest of the United Kingdom, in the specific context of an attempt to tackle the inequality that persisted between Catholics and Protestants. Legislation was introduced by the British government in 1976 prohibiting discrimination on grounds of religious belief and political opinion, using the New York state legislation as a model. This legislation had little effect on employers' practices. Research carried out by the Policy Studies Institute (PSI) in 1987 showed that the vast majority of employers believed that the Act had made little, if any, impact on their behaviour.[18] This research also confirmed the startling dimensions of the economic

[15] RS Abella, 'Equality in Employment: A Royal Commission Report' (Ottawa, Supply and Services Canada, 1984).

[16] A useful overview of the Canadian legislation and its interpretation is provided by C Sheppard, 'Challenging Systematic Racism in Canada: Affirmative Action and Equity for Racialized Communities and Aboriginal Peoples' in E Dubordieu (ed), *Race and Inequality: World Perspectives on Affirmative Action* (Ashgate, 2006).

[17] See in general Canadian Government, Employment and Immigration Canada, 'Employment Equity: A guide for employers' (1991).

[18] D Smith and G Chambers, *Inequality in Northern Ireland* (Clarendon Press, 1991).

inequality between the two communities in Northern Ireland. According to the PSI study, for example, Catholic male unemployment, then at 35 per cent, was two and a half times that of Protestant male unemployment, and continued at this level despite there being over 100,000 job changes a year.

The 1976 legislation, which had adopted the individual justice model, was deemed substantially unsuccessful and was reformed in 1989, following extensive discussion of the advantages and disadvantages of adopting elements of the American approach, and following pressure on American businesses with subsidiaries in Northern Ireland to adopt the MacBride Principles, which are discussed below in section VI of this chapter. In the late 1980s, as part of an overall reassessment of anti-discrimination law, the Northern Ireland Department of Economic Development proposed a new model but this still fell short of what was likely to be effective.[19] The report did, however, succeed in concentrating the minds of others. The Standing Advisory Commission on Human Rights (SACHR) published a major report in October 1987.[20] This report provided the most comprehensive and authoritative analysis of the problem and a detailed set of proposals for legislation and other government initiatives. Most crucially the report shifted the terms of the debate from concentrating on the eradication of prejudiced discrimination, to reducing unjustified structural inequality in the employment market, whether caused by discrimination or not. In December 1988 the government responded by publishing new legislation. After significant amendments this was passed in July 1989.[21] The 1989 legislation went beyond anything that had hitherto operated in Northern Ireland or the rest of the United Kingdom, and introduced a variant of affirmative action.[22] Employers were required to take steps to ensure 'fair participation' by both religious communities in Northern Ireland, and set out various steps to achieve this, including introducing compulsory monitoring and self-assessment. This was reformed again in 1998, but the essential characteristics of the 1989 legislation were retained.

Malaysia

The development of an approach to equality that emphasized the need to address disadvantages based on particular statuses became closely linked with the movement for decolonization, ie the movement for independence in countries that

---

[19] Northern Ireland Government, Department of Economic Development, 'Equality of Opportunity in Northern Ireland: Future Strategy Options' (HMSO, 1986).

[20] Standing Advisory Commission on Human Rights, 'Religious and Political Discrimination and Equality of Opportunity in Northern Ireland: Report on Fair Employment', Cm 237 (HMSO, 1987).

[21] See C McCrudden, 'The Fair Employment Bill in Parliament', in J Hayes and P O'Higgins, *Lessons from Northern Ireland* (SLS, 1990) 57.

[22] C McCrudden, 'Affirmative Action and Fair Participation: Interpreting the Fair Employment Act 1989' (1992) 21 ILJ 170.

were then British, French, and Belgian colonies in Asia and Africa. Given the status discrimination that so often accompanied colonial rule, independence movements often stressed the need for non-discrimination, and, on independence, supported international moves to secure equality. Preferences in favour of the indigenous Malays or Bumiputera, for example, had existed in colonial Malaya. In the run-up to independence, they took on an even more important political salience.[23] The Constitutional Commission established to recommend the structure and content of an independence constitution reported in 1957.[24] Its terms of reference had required it to include provisions 'safeguarding... the special position of the Malays and the legitimate interests of other Communities'.[25] It recommended that existing preferences should be retained, but that they should ultimately cease, and that no new preferences should be created.[26]

These recommendations were implemented in Article 153 of the new Constitution, as part of a package of measures aimed at securing multi-ethnic support for the new Constitution. The Constitution imposed the responsibility 'to safeguard the special position of the Malays'[27] on the Yang di-Peruan Agong (the King or presiding Sultan), who should 'exercise his functions under this Constitution and federal law in such a manner as may be necessary' to safeguard that special position.[28] There were specific provisions permitting preferences for Malays in employment in the public service, in education, in land distribution, and in the granting of permits and licences required for trade and business operations. These provisions were, however, only part of the package. First, the provisions were explicitly limited by other provisions in the Constitution.[29] Second, they would remain in place only for a period of fifteen years from the date of independence; they would be repealed in 1972. Third, in exchange for agreeing to these special rights, non-Malays 'would be granted favourable revisions in citizenship regulations... after independence'.[30] Finally, these constitutional provisions were set in the political context whereby the government would be formed by an alliance of the three main ethnically-based political parties representing the Malays, the Chinese, and the Indians.

After independence, a 'laissez-faire economic model' was developed that 'guided development'[31] in which the emphasis was on growth rather than redistribution.

---

[23] On the background, see S Abbas, 'Traditional Elements of the Malaysian Constitution' in FA Trindade and HP Lee (eds), *The Constitution of Malaysia: Further Perspectives and Developments* (1986) 1; D Nesiah, *Discrimination With Reason?: The Policy of Reservations in the United States, India and Malaysia* (OUP, 2004) 74–88.

[24] UK Government, Colonial Office, Report of the Federation of Malaya Constitutional Commission 1957, Colonial No 330 (HMSO, 1957).   [25] ibid para 163.

[26] ibid paras 163–168.   [27] Constitution of Malaysia, Art 153(1).

[28] ibid Art 153(2).

[29] See generally LA Sheridan and HE Groves, *The Constitution of Malaysia* (3rd edn, Malayan Law Journal, 1979) 382–6.

[30] E Phillips, 'Positive Discrimination in Malaysia: A Cautionary Tale for the United Kingdom' in B Hepple and EM Szyszczak (eds), *Discrimination: the Limits of Law* (Mansell, 1992) 349.

[31] J van der Westhuizen, *Adapting to Globalization: Malaysia, South Africa, and the Challenges of Ethnic Redistribution with Growth* (Praeger, 2002) 19.

Growth plus an ethnic balance of power would, it was assumed, satisfy 'Malay aspir-ations for progress towards parity... [and] non-Malay desires to protect and enhance their existing living standards', and thus secure a stable 'political founda-tion' of endorsement from Malays and non-Malays.[32] The importance of tackling these deep-seated inequalities was brought home when, in the late 1960s, serious rioting broke out between the native Malays (Bumiputera) and the Chinese Malaysians. This resulted in the adoption of extensive preferences in favour of Bumiputera, which have become a central policy plank in Malaysian approaches to dealing with status inequalities.

South Africa

With the end of apartheid and the election of a new government in 1994, the South African government saw the need for an extensive programme of economic redistribution, whilst at the same time retaining a liberal economic system that would be attractive to investors.[33] Clearly, one of the major problems facing the government was how to tackle the massive economic inequality between black and white South Africans. The government's main plank for addressing these problems was the Reconstruction and Development Programme (RDP).[34] This was soon followed by the Growth, Employment and Redistribution policy that emphasized as well the need for a competitive and fast growing economy that would create the growth that would enable redistribution to take place without massive upheaval.

Following extensive consultation on earlier proposals,[35] in 1998, the Employment Equity Act[36] was introduced to address discrimination and imbal-ances in the workplace, and is said to have been modelled on the Canadian legisla-tion.[37] The legislation provides for both non-discrimination requirements and extensive programmes of affirmative action, enforced in various ways. A broader approach is adopted in equality legislation adopted in 2000.[38] In 2003, the Broad-Based Black Economic Empowerment Act (B-BBEE Act) was enacted, setting out the government's strategy. The purpose of the Act[39] was, *inter alia*, to transform South Africa's economy to allow meaningful participation by black people, and

---

[32] ibid 27.   [33] ibid passim.

[34] South African Government, Reconstruction and Development Programme (Government Printers, Pretoria, 1994).

[35] Department of Labour, Employment and Occupational Equity *Government Gazette*, vol 373, No 17303, 1 July 1996; White Paper on Affirmative Action *Government Gazette*, vol 394, No 18 800, 23 April 1998.

[36] Employment Equity Act (No 55 of 1998), as amended by the Employment Equity Act 2006.

[37] A Thomas and HC Jain, 'Employment Equity in Canada and South Africa: Progress and Propositions' (2004) 15 International Journal of Human Resource Management 36.

[38] Act No 4, Promotion of Equality and Prevention of Discrimination Act 2000, and subsequent Regulations implementing the legislation: No R 764, 13 June 2003.

[39] B-BBEE Act 2003, No 53 of 2003, s 2. See also 'Codes for better BEE' <http://www.southafrica.info>.

substantially change the racial profile of ownership and management in the private sector. It established a Black Economic Empowerment Advisory Council, chaired by the President, to advise the government and review progress.

Enforcement issues

Several jurisdictions have considered that powerful, respected, and effective enforcement agencies are necessary to achieve the more widespread organizational change that a group justice approach requires. There are considerable variations as to how such bodies operate in practice to achieve such change.[40] Complex issues arise relating to regulatory capture, the adequacy of resources, the membership of such agencies, and the extent of the agency's investigatory and remedial powers.

There is a persistent problem of what has been called 'creative compliance' where organizations subject to regulatory requirements, '[f]aced with regulations they do not like . . . find imaginative ways to . . . interpret rules such that their activities can be claimed to *comply* with regulations at the same time as avoiding any disadvantageous impact they would otherwise have had'.[40a] How best can this be overcome? In part, this involves a choice on whether primarily to use sanctions or persuasion in seeking compliance. It is commonly assumed, in the regulatory literature, that persuasion is preferable to the imposition of sanctions, not only in preserving cooperation between regulators and firms, and because of that in being more effective in securing compliance. One of the crucial roles that an enforcement agency can play is that of negotiating with organizations to bring about structural change. The imposition of sanctions has been said to undermine cooperation and lessen the likelihood of successful compliance through negotiation.

In practice, however, the situation is often considerably more complex. An empirical study by Anne Davies in another area of regulation appears to confirm that sanctions are not invariably unsuccessful, nor does their use invariably cause a breakdown in cooperation.[40b] She concludes that the application of sanctions is sometimes more effective than previous studies have argued it is likely to be. In addition, from experience in other areas, we may say that, for successful negotiations to take place, there is a need to give adequate strength to the negotiating hand of an enforcement agency, and that often means giving the agency the ultimate power to impose effective sanctions.

---

[40] See eg, C McCrudden, 'The Commission for Racial Equality: Formal Investigations in the Shadow of Judicial Review' in R Baldwin and C McCrudden (eds), *Regulation and Public Law* (Weidenfeld, 1987) 222–66; C McCrudden, D J Smith, and C Brown, *Racial Justice at Work: The Enforcement of the Race Relations Act 1976 in Employment* (Policy Studies Institute, 1991); C McCrudden, 'Law Enforcement by Regulatory Agency: the Case of Employment Discrimination in Northern Ireland' (1982) 45 MLR 617.

[40a] D McBarnet and C Whelan, 'Challenging the Regulators: Strategies for Resisting Control' in C McCrudden, *Regulation and Deregulation* (OUP, 1999) 67, 68 (emphasis in original).

[40b] ACL Davies, 'Using Contracts to Enforce Standards: The Case of Waiting Times in the National Health Service' in McCrudden, n 40a above, 79.

The implementation of a group justice approach is likely to mean that organizations will have to change established practices and there may be varying degrees of resistance to this. In part, this resistance may result from a belief that what is required is uncertain, and in part, from a belief that the introduction of group justice may mean additional expenditure. Organizations may be more inclined to make the necessary changes if there is a clear understanding of the nature and implications of changes sought. Some jurisdictions have also considered that there should, in addition, be provision for organizations to receive financial or non-financial benefits in order to offset some or all of the costs that may arise from introducing equality of opportunity practices. The issue is whether organizations should be expected to bear the entire burden of providing equality of opportunity. Different measures have been adopted in various jurisdictions: the provision of technical advice to organizations about the implementation of monitoring and the remedial measures most appropriate to an organization's circumstances; providing grants for initial start-up costs associated with monitoring and other affirmative action measures; and financial assistance towards the provision of equality of opportunity courses for personnel managers, or as part of professional education. Not surprisingly, procurement linkage has been adopted in several jurisdictions as an additional mechanism to secure group justice.

V. Mainstreaming

There is growing concern in many countries about the extent to which traditional mechanisms of securing status equality, whether individual justice or group justice, are adequate. In particular, there have been attempts to go further by requiring that government and public bodies should attempt to weave policies of equality into the fabric of decision-making across *all* spheres of government—in short, to 'mainstream' fairness issues in public policy.[41] This is a particularly important issue if the problem is defined, as it increasingly is, as involving not only the problem of 'discrimination' but also the larger issue of unacceptable inequalities affecting women and particular disadvantaged groups, whether caused by discrimination or not. Mainstreaming concentrates attention on government decision-making across the board, attempting to stimulate government proactively to take equality into account. Mainstreaming approaches are intended to be *anticipatory* (rather than essentially retrospective, or relatively late insertions into the policy-making process), to be *participatory* (rather than limited to small groups of the knowledgeable, and to be *integrated* into the policy-making of those primarily involved (rather than add-ons perceived to be exogenous by policy makers).

---

[41] C McCrudden, *Mainstreaming Fairness* (CAJ, 1996); C McCrudden, *Benchmarks for Change: Mainstreaming Fairness in the Governance of Northern Ireland* (CAJ, 1998).

Underlying these attempts at mainstreaming is a common perception: that unless special attention is paid to the equality issue within government, it will become too easily submerged in the day-to-day concerns of policy makers who do not view that particular policy preference as central to their concerns. The motivation for mainstreaming fairness and equality lies in the perception that questions of equality and non-discrimination may easily become *sidelined*. A specific agency, or other enforcement mechanism, dedicated to equality issues, may be viewed as satisfying concern about inequality, yet have little effect on the large decisions of government which have the greatest impact on the life chances of women and minorities. Mainstreaming attempts to address this problem of sidelining directly, by requiring all government departments to engage directly with equality issues.

There are various methods by which such mainstreaming could take place, but it is arguable that all would require significant input of information and analysis of the impact of proposed policies from sources external to government. Non-governmental organizations (NGOs) such as community groups, pressure groups, and unions may wish to assist in supplying such information. This is not to say, of course, that the involvement of such groups is unproblematic, raising issues of the competence of such groups in this field, due to lack of information and lack of resources. In principle, however, a major argument in favour of mainstreaming is that it may contribute to increased participatory democracy—what the European Commission has termed 'civil dialogue'.

There are several sources from which the idea of equality mainstreaming has emerged. One early 1980s source was the attempt to integrate gender issues into policy-making in the area of development assistance, such as lending by the World Bank,[42] decision-making in the United Nations Development Programme,[43] and decision-making processes in developing states themselves.[44] Mainstreaming was seen as 'a means of promoting the role of women in the field of development and of integrating women's values into development work'.[45] The European Community was instrumental in having the concept adopted more widely with other governments.[46] The idea of mainstreaming was adopted as a major policy for future action

[42] See JL Murphy, *Gender Issues in World Bank Lending* (World Bank, 1995); J Cock and EC Webster, 'Environmental and Social Impact Assessments' in JM Griesgraber and BG Gunter, *The World Bank: Lending on a Global Scale* (Pluto Press, 1996) 81.

[43] S Razavi and C Miller, 'Gender Mainstreaming: A Study of Efforts by the UNDP, The World Bank and the ILO to Institutionalize Gender Issues' (Occasional Paper No 4, UN Research Institute for Social Development, 1995).

[44] AM Goetz, 'The Politics of Integrating Gender into State Development Processes' (Occasional Paper No 2, UN Research Institute for Social Development, 1995). For an interesting discussion of mainstreaming women's equality in the Philippines, see VO del Rosario, 'Mainstreaming Gender Concerns: Aspects of Compliance, Resistance and Negotiation' (1995) 26(3) IDS Bulletin 102.

[45] Council of Europe, Rapporteur Group on Equality Between Women and Men, Gender Mainstreaming, GR-EG (98) 1, 26 March 1998, 10 (hereafter Rapporteur Group).

[46] P Flynn, Address at the Fourth World Conference on Women, Reuter Textline, 8 September 1995 (presenting European Community view); S Dale, Canada Seeks Gender Impact Assessments at Beijing, Inter Press Serv, 15 August 1995 (discussing Canada's view).

at the Fourth United Nations World Conference on Women, which took place in Beijing in September 1995. Strategic Objective H.2 calls for the integration of gender perspectives in legislation, public policies, programmes, and projects.[47] The Strategic Objective has been a major influence in stimulating governments, and the United Nations system itself, to address the issue systematically.

The European Commission's Third Action Programme stressed the importance of integrating equality issues into government decision-making. More recently, the Commission became involved in attempting to develop such approaches in Europe more systematically.[48] Mainstreaming is a feature of the Community's development cooperation policy.[49] Mainstreaming was central to the Fourth Action Program on Equal Opportunities for Men and Women (1996–2000).[50] The Council Decision establishing this action programme reinforced this idea further.[51] The Commission should integrate equality issues into its decision-making as should the Member State governments.[52] A group of Commissioners, chaired by President Santer,[53] produced a communication on mainstreaming of equality in all appropriate Community policies.[54] In 1996, the Commission urged the mainstreaming of equality for people with disabilities in policy formulation.[55] The Amsterdam Treaty[56] amended the Treaty on European Union[57] ('EC Treaty') to

[47] Report of the Fourth World Conference on Women, UN Doc A/Conf.177/20 (1995). For a general discussion, see VA Dormady, 'Note, Women's Rights in International Law: A Prediction Concerning the Legal Impact of the United Nations' Fourth World Conference on Women' (1997) 30 Van JTL 97.

[48] European Commission, Equal Opportunities for Women and Men in the European Union 1996 (1997) 15–20 (hereafter Equal Opportunities); see T Rees, *Mainstreaming Equality in the European Union* (Routledge, 1998).

[49] European Commission, 'Communication from the Commission and Council and the European Parliament on Integrating Gender Issues in Development Cooperation' COM(95)423 final (1995).

[50] European Commission, 'Proposal for a Council Decision on the Fourth Medium-term Community Action Programme on Equal Opportunities for Women and Men (1996–2000)', COM(95)381 final (1995).   [51] Council Decision No 95/593/EC [1995], OJ L335/1, 37.

[52] See EU Commissioner Padraig Flynn, Reuter Textline, 28 November 1995 ('The global objective of the Fourth Programme is to contribute to the integration of the equality dimension into all relevant policies and actions.... Mainstreaming is one of the leitmotifs of the Fourth Programme...').

[53] European Commission, 'Progress Report from the Commission on the Follow-up of the Communication, "Integrating Equal Opportunities for Women and Men in All Community Policies and Activities"', COM(98)122 final (1998) 8.

[54] European Commission, 'Communication from the Commission "Incorporating Equal Opportunities for Women and Men into All Community Policies and Activities"', COM(96)67 final (1996). A report critical of the lack of impact of this initiative was completed in 1998. See 18 CREW Reports No 2/3, at 3.

[55] European Commission, 'Communication of the Commission on Equality of Opportunity for People with Disabilities' COM(96)406 final (1996) 12.

[56] Treaty of Amsterdam amending the Treaty on European Union, the Treaties establishing the European Communities and certain related acts, 2 October 1997 [1997] OJ C340/1 (hereafter Treaty of Amsterdam).

[57] Treaty establishing the European Community, 7 February 1992 [1992] OJ C224/1, [1992] 1 CMLR 573 (hereafter EC Treaty), incorporating changes made by Treaty on European Union,

incorporate gender equality as a principle of Community law.[58] The regulations governing the Structural Funds were revamped to include greater recognition of the importance of women's equality issues.[59]

There were several examples of 'mainstreaming' policies at the national level during the 1990s. Such initiatives had been in place in the Netherlands for some years.[60] The Nordic Council of Ministers developed a project to develop methods of mainstreaming gender into labour market and youth policy.[61] In Sweden, gender issues were considered in the formulation of government legislation and other policies prior to discussion by Cabinet.[62] Mainstreaming initiatives were developed in Denmark, Flanders, Portugal, and Finland as well.[63] In Ireland, the National Economic and Social Forum produced a report on equality proofing issues in 1996.[64] Local governments in several European countries also had experience in attempting to mainstream equality.[65]

The Council of Europe convened a group of specialists on mainstreaming in February 1996 in the context of the activities of the Steering Committee for Equality Between Women and Men. The resulting report, in March 1998, presented a conceptual framework, a methodology for conducting mainstreaming, and a discussion of 'good practice' in the area.[66] In a useful intervention into the debate, mainstreaming was defined as 'the reorganization, improvement, development and evaluation of policy processes, so that a gender equality perspective is incorporated in all policies at all levels and at all stages, by the actors normally involved in policy-making'.[67] The Committee of Ministers subsequently recommended that the governments of the Member States of the Council 'encourage decision-makers

---

7 February 1992 [1992] OJ C224/1, [1992] 1 CMLR 719 (hereafter TEU). The Treaty on European Union ('TEU') amended the Treaty establishing the European Economic Community, 25 March 1957, 298 UNTS 11 (hereafter EEC Treaty), as amended by Single European Act [1987] OJ L169/1, [1987] 2 CMLR 741 (hereafter SEA). The Treaty establishing the European Community ('EC Treaty') was amended by the Treaty of Amsterdam (n 55 above) [1997] OJ C340/1. These amendments were incorporated into the EC Treaty, and the articles of the EC Treaty were renumbered in the Consolidated version of the Treaty establishing the European Community [1997] OJ C340/3, 37 ILM 79 (hereafter Consolidated EC Treaty), incorporating changes made by the Treaty of Amsterdam.

[58] Consolidated EC Treaty, Art 3(2) [1997] OJ C340/3, 182, 37 ILM 80 (ex Art 3(2)).

[59] Proposal for a Council Regulation (EC) laying down general provisions on the Structural Funds (98/0090 (AVC)).

[60] Emancipatieraad, Van Marge Naar Mainstream: Adviesgrief Onderzoek Over Het Mainstreamen Van Emancipatie, in Algemeen Beleid (Adv Nr IV/51/96, 1997); see Mieke Verloo, 'Planning for Public Space: A Gender Impact Assessment Analysis, Paper for the International Conference on Women and Public Policy: The Shifting Boundary Between the Public and Private Domains', 8–10 December 1994. The author is grateful to Elizabeth Meehan for supplying a copy of this paper. Rapporteur Group, 38–9.　　　　　　[61] Rapporteur Group (n 45 above) 38–9.

[62] ibid 39.　　　[63] ibid Part III.2.

[64] See National Economic and Social Forum, 'Equality Proofing Issues National Economic and Social Forum' (February 1996); see also Equality Studies Centre, 'A Framework for Equality Proofing: A Paper Prepared for the National Economic and Social Forum' (April 1995).

[65] Equal Opportunities Commission, 'Mainstreaming Gender in Local Government' (1997).

[66] Rapporteur Group (n 45 above) 34, 38.　　　[67] ibid 6.

to take inspiration from the report in order to create an enabling environment and facilitate conditions for the implementation of gender mainstreaming in the public sector'.[68]

For the purposes of this book, however, the development of mainstreaming in Canada and the United Kingdom (examining Northern Ireland and Britain separately) is particularly important because it led to increasing emphasis being placed on procurement linkages in advancing equality goals. It is to the development of mainstreaming in these jurisdictions that we now turn.

Aboriginal self-government in Canada

The history of the relationship between Aboriginal peoples in Canada and the various federal and provincial governments is lengthy and complex.[69] Suffice it to say, for the purposes of this chapter, that from the 1970s there have been several particularly significant developments growing from the continuing land disputes between various groups of Aboriginal peoples and others. Litigation involving these claims was relatively favourably received in the Canadian courts, resulting in pressure on the federal and provincial governments to develop comprehensive settlements of such claims, rather than attempting to deal with them in a piecemeal and expensive fashion through the courts. This in turn led, from the 1970s, to negotiations resulting in various agreements, such as the James Bay and Northern Quebec Agreement in 1973, the Inuvialuit Final Agreement in 1984, and the Agreement Between the Inuit of the Nunavut Settlement Area and Her Majesty the Queen in Right of Canada in 1993.[70]

Each of these agreements had a common core: that in exchange for extinguishing their rights to traditional lands and waters, the Aboriginal group involved would receive financial compensation, land ownership, participation in government, and assistance with economic development. In 1984, for example, the Government of Canada and Inuvialuit reached agreement on the Inuvialuit Final Agreement. This provided financial compensation and ownership of about 35,000 square miles of land, including a proportion with valuable sub-surface rights to oil, gas, and minerals. An Inuvialuit Regional Corporation was created to receive the lands and the financial compensation. The Agreement also contained

[68] Council of Europe, Committee of Ministers, Recommendation No R(98)14 of the Committee of Ministers to Member States on Gender Mainstreaming (7 October 1998).

[69] See Report of the Royal Commission on Aboriginal Peoples, five volumes, Ottawa. Available online at <http://www.ainc-inac.gc.ca/ch/Rcap/sg/sgmm_e.html>.

[70] See the excellent article by KR Gray, 'The Nunavut Land Claims Agreement and the Future of the Eastern Arctic: The Uncharted Path to Effective Self-Government' (1994) 52 University of Toronto Faculty of Law Review 300 to which I am indebted. See also C J Marecic, 'Nunavut Territory: Aboriginal Governing in the Canadian Regime of Governance' (1999–2000) 24 American Indian Law Review 275.

measures to help Inuvialuit development. These included a commitment from the federal government to use its best efforts to 'overcome any institutional prejudices that may exist against the Inuvialuit'[71] and to 'take the measures it considers reasonable to afford economic opportunities to Inuvialuit with respect to employment and projects within the Inuvialuit Settlement Region.'[72]

Perhaps the most far-reaching of such agreements was concluded between the Canadian federal government and the Inuit of Nunavut. Both ratified the Agreement, the Inuit by a vote and the federal government by enactment of the Nunavut Land Claims Agreement Act 1993. The Agreement was the largest Aboriginal land claim settlement then negotiated in Canada. The territory covered by the Agreement amounted to about two million square kilometres, nearly one-fifth the size of Canada. The Agreement gave title to Inuit-owned lands measuring over 350,000 square kilometres, of which about 35,000 square kilometres included mineral rights. Capital transfer payments of Can$1.148 billion were payable to the Inuit over fourteen years, together with a share of federal government royalties for Nunavut Inuit from oil, gas, and mineral development on Crown lands. In addition, and in contrast to the provisions of the other agreements discussed previously,[73] this Agreement also created a new regionally-based government and established a new territory, Nunavut, coming into existence in 1999, and carved out from the Northwest Territories. The new territory was established with its own legislature and government. Given that the Inuit were a clear majority within the new territory, this had the effect of producing a government that was likely to be dominated by Inuit concerns.[74]

In addition to land claims, another important element in the growing Aboriginal self-identity was the development of claims to self-government. The new Canadian Constitution of 1982 recognized the inherent right of self-government.[75] From that time, there were efforts to amend the Constitution to include explicit references to the right to *Aboriginal* self-government. These efforts were initially unsuccessful, but resulted in the development in 1995 of a policy by the incoming Liberal government, elected in 1993. The government recognized 'the inherent right to self-government as an existing Aboriginal right under section 35 of the Constitution Act, 1982.'[76] The meaning of self-government was recognized as open to significantly different interpretations, and as potentially raising issues of enforceability in the courts, and so the government proposed instead to set in train a series of tripartite negotiations between the federal government, the relevant provincial government, and the Aboriginal groups, leading to agreements. Existing treaties, such as those dealing with land claims, would remain in existence, but could be supplemented by

---

[71] Inuvialuit Final Agreement, 1984, s 16(6)(b).   [72] ibid s 16(6)(c).
[73] Gray (n 70 above) 320.   [74] ibid 302.   [75] Constitution Act 1982, s 35.
[76] Federal Policy Guide, 'Aboriginal Self-Government: The Government of Canada's Approach to Implementation of the Inherent Right and the Negotiation of Aboriginal Self-Government' (1995) 3.

further agreements. Where the parties to such negotiations agreed, the federal government was prepared 'to constitutionally protect rights set out in negotiated self-government agreements as treaty rights' within the meaning of section 35 of the Constitution Act.[77] No one model of agreement was proposed, allowing various possible approaches to be explored in negotiations, although the federal government recognized that Inuit groups in various parts of Canada 'have expressed a desire to address their self-government aspirations within the context of larger public government arrangements, even though they have, or will receive, their own separate land base as part of a comprehensive land claim settlement'.[78] The creation of the new territory of Nunavut was recognized as one example of such an arrangement. This new approach has resulted in the conclusion of a considerable number of agreements.[79]

Mainstreaming equality in Northern Ireland

Although necessary, anti-discrimination law was gradually perceived in Northern Ireland as insufficient to achieve the substantial change that was defined as necessary. The 1987 SACHR Report was clear that anti-discrimination legislation could only be part, though a necessary part, of the process of government addressing the problem of employment inequality.[80] In 1990, a circular was issued giving advice to all Northern Ireland departments about the need to consider discrimination in relation to religious affiliation, political opinion, and gender.[81] (This was coordinated with an initiative launched in the United Kingdom by the ministerial group on women's issues that encouraged all government departments to develop basic guidance on the importance of considering equality in policy-making throughout the United Kingdom.) There were several years of continuing controversy over their content, according to an internal Northern Ireland Office (NIO) briefing, 'on the grounds that they did not match the expectation that they would unambiguously set out and establish a positive and pro-active approach to equality of opportunity'. The guidelines were finally issued in December 1993, to come into effect in 1994.[82] 'Equality and equity' the guidelines said, 'are central issues which must condition and influence policy making in all spheres and at all levels of Government activity'. This indicated an important shift from non-discrimination to equality.

---

[77] ibid 5.   [78] ibid 9.

[79] These are collected together on the website of the Department of Indian Affairs and Northern Development, http://www.ainc-inac.gc.ca>.

[80] Standing Advisory Commission on Human Rights, Religious and Political Discrimination and Equality of Opportunity in Northern Ireland: Report on Fair Employment (Cm 237, 1987, HMSO) ch 13.

[81] Equal Opportunity Proofing: Guidelines, Central Secretariat, CSC1/90. See Northern Ireland Information Service, Equal Opportunity Proofing of Policy Making, 9 March 1990.

[82] Policy Appraisal and Fair Treatment, Central Secretariat Circular 5/93, 22 December 1993.

The Policy Appraisal and Fair Treatment (PAFT) Guidelines, as they were called, were an attempt to establish a procedure within government decision-making by which this shift could be made effective. The groups coming within the scope of the guidelines went beyond the two religious communities, and included people of different gender, age, ethnic origin, marital and family status, and sexual orientation, and those who were disabled. As importantly, the final guidelines marked a substantial shift towards equality and away from a narrow preoccupation solely with discrimination. However, little detailed guidance was given to departments or other public bodies as to how to accomplish this task. A commitment was subsequently given that the Annual Report on PAFT implementation would be published, providing a degree of transparency to the process,[83] but no coordination. Most importantly, there was little, if any, legal sanction supporting these requirements.

The Northern Ireland Act 1998 introduced a revised approach. Section 75 provided that each 'public authority' is required, in carrying out its functions relating to Northern Ireland, to have due regard to the need to promote equality of opportunity between certain different individuals and groups. The relevant categories between which equality of opportunity is to be promoted are persons of different religious belief, political opinion, racial group, age, marital status, or sexual orientation; between men and women generally; between persons with a disability and persons without; and between persons with dependants and persons without. Without prejudice to these obligations, a public authority in Northern Ireland is also, in carrying out its functions, to have regard to the desirability of promoting good relations between persons of different religious belief, political opinion, or racial group. Schedule 9 to the Act makes detailed provisions for the enforcement of these duties.

All public authorities are required to submit an equality scheme to the Equality Commission.[84] Only where a public authority has been notified in writing by the Commission that it does not need to, is it exempted from producing such a scheme. An equality scheme must show how the public authority proposes to fulfil the duties imposed by section 75 in relation to the relevant functions,[85] and specify a timetable for measures proposed in the scheme.[86] Schedule 9 specifies particular elements that an equality scheme must contain in order to be in compliance, without being exhaustive.[87] It must state the authority's arrangements for: assessing its compliance with the duties under section 75;[88] consulting on matters to which a duty under that section is likely to be relevant (including details of the persons to be consulted);[89] assessing and consulting on the likely impact of

---

[83] CCRU, Policy Appraisal and Fair Treatment, Annual Reports, 1994, 1995, 1996, 1997.

[84] Northern Ireland Act 1998, Sch 9, para 2(1).

[85] ibid Sch 9, para 4(1). 'The relevant functions' means the functions of the public authority or, in the case of a scheme submitted in response to a request which specifies particular functions of the public authority, those functions. Sch 9, para 4(4).   [86] ibid Sch 9, para 4(3)(b).

[87] ibid Sch 9, para 4(2).   [88] ibid Sch 9, para 4(2)(a).   [89] ibid Sch 9, para 4(2)(a).

policies adopted or proposed to be adopted by the authority on the promotion of equality of opportunity;[90] monitoring any adverse impact of policies adopted by the authority on the promotion of equality of opportunity;[91] publishing the results of such assessments and such monitoring;[92] training staff;[93] and ensuring, and assessing, public access to information and to services provided by the authority.[94]

In addition, an equality scheme must conform to any guidelines as to form or content which are issued by the Equality Commission. These guidelines are subject to the approval of the Secretary of State.[95] Before submitting a scheme to the Equality Commission, a public authority must consult, in accordance with any directions given by the Commission, with representatives of persons likely to be affected by the scheme,[96] and with such other persons as may be specified in the directions.[97] What happens after a scheme is submitted for approval to the Equality Commission depends on what type of public body is involved. A distinction is made between Northern Ireland departments and public bodies, and United Kingdom-wide public bodies.

In the former case, regarding Northern Ireland bodies, on receipt of a scheme the Commission must approve it,[98] or refer it to the Secretary of State.[99] Where the Commission refers a scheme to the Secretary of State, the Commission is required to notify the Northern Ireland Assembly in writing that it has done so and send to the Assembly a copy of the scheme.[100] Where a scheme is referred to the Secretary of State, he or she has three options: to approve it, to request the public authority to make a revised scheme, or to make a scheme for the public authority.[101] A public authority must respond to a request to make a revised scheme by submitting a scheme to the Commission before the end of the period of six months beginning with the date of the request.[102] Where the Secretary of State requests a revised scheme, or makes a scheme himself or herself, he or she must notify the Assembly in writing that he or she has done so. Where the Secretary of State has made a scheme for the public authority, he or she is required also to send the Assembly a copy of the scheme.[103]

Certain of these provisions do not apply in the case of United Kingdom-wide departments. On receipt of a scheme submitted by a United Kingdom government department, the Commission must approve it, or *itself* request the department to make a revised scheme.[104] A public authority must respond to this request by submitting a scheme to the Commission before the end of the period of

---

[90] ibid Sch 9, para 4(2)(b). 'Equality of opportunity' means such equality of opportunity as is mentioned in s 75(1). Sch 9, para 4(4).

[91] ibid Sch 9, para 4(2)(c).   [92] ibid Sch 9, para 4(2)(d).

[93] ibid Sch 9, para 4(2)(e).   [94] ibid Sch 9, para 4(2)(f).   [95] ibid Sch 9, para 4(3)(a).

[96] ibid Sch 9, para 5(a).   [97] ibid Sch 9, para 5(b).   [98] ibid Sch 9, para 6(1)(a).

[99] ibid Sch 9, para 6(1)(b).   [100] ibid Sch 9, para 6(2).   [101] ibid Sch 9, para 7(1).

[102] ibid Sch 9, para 7(2).   [103] ibid Sch 9, para 7(3).   [104] ibid Sch 9, para 12(2).

six months beginning with the date of the request.[105] Where such a request is made, the government department must, if it does not submit a revised scheme to the Commission before the end of the period of six months beginning with the date of the request, send to the Commission a written statement of the reasons for not doing so.[106] The provisions relating to notification of the Assembly do not apply.[107] Nor do the provisions apply that empower the Secretary of State to make schemes for the public body directly.[108] These modifications are intended to 'avoid a situation where the Secretary of State must reach a decision or issue a direction in a case involving her Department or that of a Cabinet colleague'.[109]

An equality scheme is required to state the authority's arrangements for publishing the results of such assessments.[110] The legislation details with some specificity what is required. In publishing the results of such an assessment, a public authority is required to state the aims of the policy to which the assessment relates.[111] It is also required to publish details of any consideration given by the authority to measures which might mitigate any adverse impact of that policy on the promotion of equality of opportunity,[112] and alternative policies which might better achieve the promotion of equality of opportunity.[113] In making any decision with respect to a policy adopted or proposed to be adopted by it, a public authority is required take into account any such assessment and consultation carried out in relation to the policy.[114] The government made clear that it expected consultation 'to embrace those directly affected by a policy as well as non-governmental organisations and relevant statutory bodies'.[115]

If the Commission receives a complaint, made in accordance with certain formalities,[116] of failure by a public authority to comply with an equality scheme approved by the Commission or made by the Secretary of State, it is required to investigate the complaint,[117] or give the complainant reasons for not investigating.[118] The complaint must be made in writing by a person who claims to have been directly affected by the failure.[119] A complaint must also be sent to the Commission during the period of twelve months starting with the day on which the complainant first knew of the matters alleged.[120] Before making a complaint, the complainant must bring the complaint to the notice of the public authority,[121] and give the public authority a reasonable opportunity to respond.[122]

In addition to investigating on the basis of a complaint, it appears that the Equality Commission itself has power to carry out an investigation into the

---

[105] ibid Sch 9, para 3(2).   [106] ibid Sch 9, para 12(4).   [107] ibid Sch 9, para 6(2).
[108] ibid Sch 9, para 7(1).
[109] House of Commons, Official Report, 18 November 1998, col 1068 (Mr Murphy).
[110] Northern Ireland Act 1998, Sch 9, para 4(2)(d).   [111] ibid Sch 9, para 9(1).
[112] ibid Sch 9, para 9(1)(a).   [113] ibid Sch 9, para 9(1)(b).   [114] ibid Sch 9, para 9(2).
[115] House of Lords, Official Report, 11 November 1998, col 810 (Lord Dubs).
[116] Northern Ireland Act 1998, Sch 9, para 10(2)–(4).   [117] ibid Sch 9, para 10(1)(a).
[118] ibid Sch 9, para 10(1)(b).   [119] ibid Sch 9, para 10(2).   [120] ibid Sch 9, para 10(3).
[121] ibid Sch 9, para 10(4)(a).   [122] ibid Sch 9, para 10(4)(b).

compliance by a public authority with a scheme without having received a valid complaint. Although not without doubt, the power to carry out such an investigation appears to be derived from the Equality Commission's general duty to keep under review the effectiveness of the duties imposed by section 75. Paragraph 11 of Schedule 9, in addition, provides explicitly for the same conditions to be applied to investigations which arise from complaints as investigations which are 'carried out by the Commission where it believes that a public authority may have failed to comply with a scheme . . . '.[123]

What happens to the results of these investigations again depends on the type of public authority involved. Again, a distinction is drawn between Northern Ireland and United Kingdom-wide public bodies. In the case of the former, the Commission is required to send a report of both types of investigation to the public authority concerned,[124] the Secretary of State,[125] the Assembly,[126] and the complainant (if any).[127] If a report recommends action by the public authority concerned and the Commission considers that the action is not taken within a reasonable time, the Commission may refer the matter to the Secretary of State.[128] Where a matter is referred to the Secretary of State, he or she may give directions to the public authority in respect of any matter referred to him.[129] Where the Commission refers a matter to the Secretary of State it shall also notify the Assembly in writing that it has done so.[130] Where the Secretary of State gives directions to a public authority, he or she shall notify the Assembly in writing that he or she has done so.[131] Somewhat different provisions again apply in the case of United Kingdom-wide bodies. The provisions empowering the Secretary of State to give directions to the public authority in respect of a public authority's failure to present a scheme do not apply.[132] Instead, the Commission may lay before Parliament and the Assembly a report of any investigation regarding compliance with an equality scheme by such a department.[133]

Mainstreaming equality in Britain

Mainstreaming equality as a legal concept came later to Britain than to Northern Ireland. To some extent, the Northern Ireland experience moulded the way in which the issue was approached in Britain, although that aspect of its origin is seldom adverted to in British discussions. Clearly one of the other main sources of mainstreaming was the Race Relations Act 1976 duty on local authorities. Between 1976 and 2000, when the first large-scale mainstreaming provision was introduced, there were other broadly similar equality duties legislated for. In some

---

[123] ibid Sch 9, para 11(1)(b).
[124] ibid Sch 9, para 11(2)(a).
[125] ibid Sch 9, para 11(2)(b).
[126] ibid Sch 9, para 11(4)(a).
[127] ibid Sch 9, para 11(2)(c).
[128] ibid Sch 9, para 11(3)(a).
[129] ibid Sch 9, para 11(3)(b).
[130] ibid Sch 9, para 11(4)(b).
[131] ibid Sch 9, para 11(5).
[132] ibid Sch 9, para 11(3)(b).
[133] ibid Sch 9, para 12(5).

cases, legislation applying to specific public authorities imposed a broad duty of equality of opportunity applying to several different groups. The Broadcasting Act 1990, for example, provided that certain television and sound broadcasting licences should include conditions requiring the licence holder 'to make arrangements for promoting, in relation to employment by him, equality of opportunity between men and women and between different racial groups'.[134]

It was after the success of Labour in the election of 1997, however, that this approach flourished. The Greater London Authority was required to 'make appropriate arrangements with a view to securing that' in the exercise of its powers, in the formulation of its policies and proposals, and in their implementation, 'there is due regard to the principle that there should be equality of opportunity for all people'.[135] In addition, the Greater London Authority Act 1999 placed the Greater London Authority, the Metropolitan Police Authority, and the London Fire and Emergency Planning Authority under a duty, in exercising their functions, 'to have regard to the need to promote equality of opportunity for all persons irrespective of their race, sex, disability, age, sexual orientation or religion', 'to eliminate unlawful discrimination', and 'to promote good relations between persons of different racial groups, religious beliefs and sexual orientation'.[136] The Learning and Skills Council for England was required, in exercising its functions, to 'have due regard to the need to promote equality of opportunity' between persons of different racial groups, between men and women, and between persons who are disabled and persons who are not.[137] Childcare providers needed to provide information on their commitment to equality of opportunity.[138] The members of particular public bodies were placed under specific personal obligations to 'carry out their duties and responsibilities with due regard to the need to promote equality of opportunity for all people, regardless of their gender, race, disability, sexual orientation, age or religion, and show respect and consideration for others'.[139]

By far the most important mainstreaming provision in Britain for the purposes of this study was the Race Relations (Amendment) Act 2000, which was passed in the wake of the murder of a black teenager, Stephen Lawrence, and the subsequent McPherson Report into the handling of the murder investigation by the

---

[134] Broadcasting Act 1990, ss 34, 38, and 68.
[135] Greater London Authority Act 1999, s 33.   [136] ibid s 404.
[137] Learning and Skills Act 2000, s 14.
[138] Tax Credit (New Category of Child Care Provider) Regulations 2002, SI 2002/1417, Sch 2, Pt I, para 1.
[139] Conduct of Members (Principles) (Wales) Order 2001, SI 2001/2276, Sch, para 7; Conduct of Members (Model Code of Conduct) (Wales) Order 2001, SI 2001/2289, Sch, Pt II, para 4; Local Government Act 2000 (Model Code of Conduct) (Amendment) Order 2002, SI 2002/1719; Relevant Authorities (General Principles) Order 2001, SI 2001/1401, Sch, para 7; Local Authorities (Model Code of Conduct) (England) Order 2001, SI 2001/3575, Sch 1, para 2 and Sch 2, para 2; Parish Councils (Model Code of Conduct) Order 2001, SI 2001/3576); National Parks and Broads Authorities (Model Code of Conduct) (England) Order 2001, SI 2001/3577; Police Authorities (Model Code of Conduct) Order 2001, SI 2001/3578.

Metropolitan Police.[140] The Act provided for an equivalent duty applying to a wide group of public authorities, but with the narrower focus of only applying in the racial context. The Act came into effect in December 2001. In particular, the Act required that each of a specified list of public bodies must, in carrying out its functions, have due regard to the need to eliminate unlawful racial discrimination, and to promote equality of opportunity and good relations between persons of different racial groups.[141] These positive duties applied only to public sector bodies and not directly to the private sector. All public authorities bound by the general duty had more particular duties regarding employment. They were required to monitor, by ethnic group, their existing staff, and applicants for jobs, promotion and training, and they must publish the results every year. Authorities with at least 150 full-time staff were also required to monitor grievances, disciplinary action, performance appraisals, training, and dismissals.

The Secretary of State made an Order that imposed certain more specific duties on certain bodies and other persons subject to the general duty.[142] The duties were imposed for the purpose of ensuring the better performance of the general duty. The Order imposed on the main public authorities specified a duty to publish a Race Equality Scheme by 31st May 2002.[143] Such a scheme must show how the public body intended to fulfil the general duty and its specific duties under this Order. Specifically, the schemes must show how the designated public authority would assess whether its functions and policies were relevant to racial equality; how it would monitor its policies to see how they affected race equality; how it would assess and consult on policies it proposed to introduce; how it would publish the results of these consultations, monitoring, and assessments; how it would make sure that the public had access to the information and services it provided; and how it would train its staff regarding the new duties. The Secretary of State subsequently approved the Commission for Racial Equality's Code of Practice relating to these statutory duties, and this was published in its final form on 27th May 2002, four days before the racial equality schemes were due to be delivered.[144]

As regards enforcement of the duty, the Commission for Racial Equality (CRE) was given the central role. If the CRE is satisfied that a person has failed to comply with, or is failing to comply with, any duty, it may serve on that person a compliance notice, which requires the person concerned to comply with the duty concerned and to inform the CRE of the steps that the person has taken, or is taking, to comply with the duty. It may also require the person concerned to furnish the CRE with written information as may be reasonably required by the notice in order to

---

[140] Mainstreaming duties have also been introduced more recently regarding gender equality and disability. These will be considered further in ch 14 below, but the race duty has so far had the most impact on procurement.   [141] Race Relations (Amendment) Act 2000, s 71.

[142] Race Relations Act 1976 (Statutory Duties) Order 2001.

[143] There are also specific duties for schools and further education and higher education institutions.   [144] CRE Code of Practice on the Duty to Promote Race Equality, 2002.

verify that the duty has been complied with. The CRE may apply to a designated county court for an order requiring the authority to furnish any information required by a compliance notice if the person fails to furnish the information to the CRE in accordance with the notice, or if the CRE has reasonable cause to believe that the person does not intend to furnish the information. If the CRE considers that a person has not, within three months of the date on which a compliance notice was served on that person, complied with any requirement of the notice for that person to comply with a duty imposed by an order, it may apply to a designated county court for an order requiring the person to comply with the requirement of the notice. In establishing whether there was a breach of the duty, a court or tribunal should take into account the CRE Code of Practice.

VI. Extraterritorial Regulation of Equality

So far, I have portrayed the development of equal status law or policy as essentially a domestic debate, in which international actors are marginal, although we have seen in several contexts there was significant learning from other jurisdictions and borrowing of regulatory techniques. The United States experience has been particularly important in Canada, Germany, and the United Kingdom. The ILO has been influential more broadly.

There is now, however, an increasingly complex web of international, and regional human rights law relating to discrimination, equality and socio-economic rights, both treaty-based legal requirements, 'soft-law' standards, and customary international law.[145] Following the typology articulated by Henry Shue, we may distinguish three somewhat different obligations on the state that may arise in the human rights context: the duty to *respect* human rights; the duty to *protect* human rights; and the duty to *fulfil* human rights.[146] Although often used in the context of discussions of social and economic rights,[147] the typology is as useful in identifying various state human rights obligations generally, including equality rights. The obligation to *respect* human rights requires that a state refrain from infringing a human right directly through its own actions. Thus, it would be contrary to this obligation for the state to authorize the torture of individuals by its police or armed forces. The obligation to *protect* human rights places the state under a duty to

---

[145] Such norms include the International Convention on the Elimination of all Forms of Racial Discrimination, 1966; the International Covenant on Civil and Political Rights, 1966; the International Covenant on Economic, Social and Cultural Rights, 1966; the Refugee Convention, 1951; the Convention on the Rights of the Child (1989); the International Convention on the Protection of the Rights of Migrant Workers and Members of their Families (1990); and many more.

[146] H Shue, *Basic Rights: Subsistence, Affluence, and US Foreign Policy* (2nd edn, Princeton University Press, 1996).

[147] C Scott and P Macklem, 'Constitutional Ropes of Sand or Justiciable Guarantees? Social Rights in a New South African Constitution' (1992) 141 UP LR 1.

prevent a right from being infringed by actors other than the state. This obligation requires a state to prohibit others from torturing or murdering. The obligation on the state to *fulfil* human rights requires states to facilitate access to these rights, or even to provide these rights directly through the use of state power.

Why should such positive obligations stop at the border? One of the effects of globalization is vastly to improve communication across the world. This, in turn, has the effect of increasing awareness of the conditions, for example, under which goods are made. It is at this point that an argument deriving from solidarity comes into play. The argument is that it is legitimate for a group in one country, by collective action, to express its sense of common humanity or common interests with a group in another country by attempting to help them to secure their rights.[148] That might be achieved by NGOs organizing collective boycotts, for example. Indeed, where the human rights abuse targeted is contrary to *jus cogens*, it is arguable that states may be under a legal obligation not to 'assist' in maintaining that breach through investing in those in breach.[149]

The worldwide campaign to ensure the removal of apartheid in South Africa was one manifestation of this seuse of solidarity. This campaign operated continuously from the 1960s through to the release of Nelson Mandela, and the subsequent development of a democratic South Africa. The anti-apartheid movement developed techniques for bringing external pressure to bear on South Africa that owed something to the techniques that had been developed to tackle racial discrimination within the United States, most notably the attempt to ensure political progress by applying economic sanctions, including the application of consumer and investor boycotts of businesses based in Europe and North America with subsidiaries in South Africa. Activists sought to have these companies leave South Africa, or at least uphold certain principles in their employment practices if they remained.

Although the South African anti-apartheid campaign is probably the best known, there have been numerous other examples. A campaign in the United States was begun during the 1980s to bring pressure to bear on American corporations, state legislatures, and municipal governments with investments in Northern Ireland to adopt a set of anti-discrimination principles called the 'MacBride Principles'.[150] These sought to encourage employers to adopt affirmative action. This American campaign began to fill, however partially and inadequately, the political vacuum caused by the failure of Northern Ireland's political institutions to address the issue adequately. One of the key mechanisms for the enforcement of these principles was through procurement linkages.

---

[148] C Barnard, 'Labour Market Integration: Lessons from the European Union' in JDR Craig and SM Lynk, *Globalization and the Future of Labour Law* (Cambridge University Press, 2006) 225.

[149] International Law Commission (ILC) Articles of Responsibility of States for Internationally Wrongful Acts, Art 41(2). See also Resolution of the International Labour Conference on Myanmar, 88th Session (2000).

[150] For an extensive discussion, see C McCrudden, 'Human Rights Codes for Transnational Corporations: What Can the Sullivan and MacBride Principles Tell Us?' (1999) 19 OJLS 167.

VII. Procurement Linkages, Equal Status Law, and Policy

The function of this chapter has been to provide an introduction to several of the most important developments in equal status law and policy that have helped to stimulate the development of equality-based procurement linkages. Seen from the perspective of equal status law and policy, several issues will be particularly relevant in understanding the ways in which we shall see subsequently that equality-based procurement linkages differ.

What groups are included?   The content of the requirements differs from country to country in terms of the protected groups involved. Procurement is used in different countries to pursue equality between racial and ethnic groups, and between men and women, but also to promote equality between religious groups, and between disabled workers and the able-bodied. There are often subtle differences in approach to the use of procurement depending on which area of equality is the primary focus of attention. Thus, for example, in the context of government policy relating to disabled persons, there is more likely to be a use of technical specifications in the tender, and more likelihood that set-asides will be used, than in the use of procurement for other grounds. In addition, however, several countries also use public procurement as a technique for dealing with social disadvantage and social exclusion, in ways which indirectly tackle inequality on the basis of gender, race, etc because these groups are more likely to be among the socially excluded and socially disadvantaged. Several countries that use procurement to tackle long-term unemployment, for example, view this as part of their policies for tackling ethnic disadvantages in the labour market.

Equality of what?   The way in which public procurement linkages have been thought of traditionally has to do with employment. So, equal pay, fair recruitment, and equality within employment contexts, have tended to be the focus of attention. The use of public procurement may go well beyond that, and the diversity of suppliers is becoming an important issue. In the future, it is likely that public procurement may well become as important in many other contexts going well beyond these into the use of procurement for other kinds of social policy delivery mechanisms. So, for example, public procurement is already being used in contexts as diverse as housing and the provision of public services more generally.

Aiming at individual or group justice?   Programmes also differ, crucially, in the content of the requirement or preference. In some it consists of an obligation not to discriminate on status grounds, in others of much more. For some programmes, the additional requirements are to monitor their workforce; in others to allow the contracting authority to inspect or notify statistics to the contracting authority; in others more extensive forms of affirmative action are required.

Inward or outward directed? There are two different focuses of equality-based linkages: where procurement linkages are used to produce effects *outside* the jurisdiction, and where procurement linkages are used to produce effects *inside* the jurisdiction. The former is illustrated where equality is being used as part of 'fair trade' policies abroad, for example attempting to ensure that coffee producers do not discriminate on grounds of gender in their employment conditions. That is essentially an attempt to use procurement power to affect issues abroad. The use of procurement to produce external equality outcomes is often part of a larger human rights agenda.

Supporting existing or going beyond legal equality obligations? One way of viewing the relationship between equality requirements and procurement is by seeing to what extent such procurement requirements *go beyond the existing equality law*, requiring companies to take action under their procurement contracts that they would not otherwise have been required to take. The extent to which public procurement requires corporations with which government is contracting to go beyond what is otherwise legally required or to merely comply with the law depends crucially on how far particular legal systems incorporate into law requirements that in other jurisdictions are left to the private sector to deal with on a voluntary basis. Different jurisdictions draw the lines between what is legally required and what is not in the social field very differently. Until recently, for example, most European countries did not have extensive prohibitions on racial discrimination. These requirements also differ considerably from country to country, in terms of their relationship to the legal obligations of employers generally. In some countries, these requirements are already required of all or most employers, whether they contract with the government or not; in others the requirements are additional to those imposed on employers generally.

How to ensure compliance? There are also crucial differences between procurement linkages as to what, if any, institutional mechanisms are established within the administration to support and monitor the policy. For those that have such institutional support, there are further differences in the function that it plays. In some, the mechanism established is responsible for the enforcement of requirements in the contract; in others merely for monitoring; in others for negotiating with potential or actual contractors; in others for setting the standards that contractors should comply with; and in others for certifying that potential contractors have reached that standard. The status of the machinery vis-à-vis the administration also differs. In some, it is centralized within the administration of the contracting authority; in some, it is situated outside the administration of the contracting authority; and in some, it is an independent public body. In others, the social partners (particularly the unions) are relied on to enforce the provisions. Lastly, programmes differ as to what extent contractors are supposed to bear any costs of implementing the requirements, and how much support is available to contractors to enable them to meet the requirements. In some, financial subsidies are available; in some, merely advice; and in some others, state resources are made available for identifying relevant members of the protected group(s). The penalty for breach differs from programme to programme: in some it can include cancellation of the contract; in others contractual penalties; and in some breach is used to evaluate the bidder's reliablility in the award of future contracts. In some, the programme considers the policy to be adopted during the course of pre-award negotiations. In some the issues are of relevance at the award stage.

4

International and European Procurement Regulation

In the previous chapter I explored some features of equal status law and policy that have stimulated procurement linkages in several jurisdictions. I turn in this chapter to introduce two further themes outlined in chapter 1 above: the context of procurement regulation and the context of globalization. From the 1960s, but particularly during the 1980s and 1990s, attempts were made in the European Community, and in the international trade rounds under the General Agreement on Tariffs and Trade (GATT), to introduce procurement reforms that have impacted significantly on the use of procurement linkages at the national level.

I. The Origins of International and European Procurement Regulation

Until the Second World War, attempts to limit the type of exclusion of foreign suppliers from the domestic government procurement market, detailed in chapter 2 above, were dealt with, if at all, by way of diplomatic, ad hoc, and (mostly) bilateral agreements. Following the Second World War, however, the issue of public procurement was increasingly considered as an important element in international and regional attempts to reduce barriers to international trade. The most important developments, for the purposes of this discussion, were those that took place in the European Economic Community, and in the multilateral trade negotiations (or 'rounds') resulting in international trade agreements. Though often considered separately in the academic literature discussing the development of government procurement reforms, there was a significant cross-fertilization between the international and the regional, as would be expected. The map is a complex one, and so an initial brief survey in this chapter of the interrelations between the various developments should help in understanding the more detailed subsequent discussion of the approaches that emerged as to how to treat domestic socio-economic policy linkages.

Post-Second World War international economic architecture

During the Second World War, it was clear to the Allies that a substantial restructuring of the institutional basis of international economic policy would be necessary after the war and this led to the establishment of the Bretton Woods institutions (the World Bank and the International Monetary Fund (IMF)). The opening up of international trade was also seen as a necessity. This led to negotiations that resulted in the Havana Charter establishing an International Trade Commission (ITC) and a detailed set of rules aiming to dismantle tariff and non-tariff barriers to trade. American congressional opposition to the Havana Charter led to it being still-born, and as a 'provisional' measure that was to last until 1994, the part of the Charter that dealt with tariffs and trade (GATT) was separated from the rest and came into effect without the other parts of the Charter, in particular without the institution of the ITC. Subsequently, periodic trade rounds took place leading to agreements to expand the coverage of the GATT in various respects, and to conclude agreements covering additional areas. Of these rounds, the most important for our purposes were the Tokyo Round in 1979, and the Uruguay Round that led, in 1994, to a substantial restructuring of the previous agreements, and the establishment of the World Trade Organization (WTO).

The Uruguay Round agreement retained the old GATT 1947, incorporated via Article 1(a) of the General Agreement on Tariffs and Trade 1994, which did not itself contain substantive provisions of general importance. References to GATT generally mean GATT 1947 as incorporated in GATT 1994. New dispute settlement provisions were elaborated on in a Dispute Settlement Understanding (DSU).[1] The DSU was one of the crucial achievements of the Uruguay Round: GATT contracting parties, each with a veto over the adoption of panel reports (quasi-judicial determinations of GATT disputes), suddenly became WTO members who had to agree unanimously in order to *block* the adoption of panel reports. The possibility of an appeal to a new Appellate Body of the WTO was also instituted, partly as a trade-off in return for the surrender of the veto. The members of the Appellate Body may be seen as more impartial and as having better legal training than the members of the panels (who are largely selected by the trade-oriented WTO Secretariat). The creation of the Appellate Body may therefore increase the legitimacy of the WTO dispute settlement system, especially where conflicting values are involved in a dispute, and particularly where trade liberalization may come into conflict with other policies, such as environmental protection.

At the same time as these developments were taking place, the European enterprise of economic integration was proceeding apace. This is a complicated story, only the bare bones of which can be sketched out here. There are several institutions of relevance. Following the Second World War, the Marshall Plan for economic reconstruction in Europe brought large amounts of American aid to a devastated

---

[1] Final Act of the Uruguay Round, Annex 2.

continent. One of the institutions established in the wake of the Marshall Plan was the Organisation for European Economic Co-operation (OEEC). This consisted of a group of western European countries and its role, as its name makes clear, was to seek economic cooperation within Europe. Based in Paris, it provided an important forum for the evolving discussions concerning closer economic integration in Europe. In 1951, the Six (France, Germany, Italy, Belgium, Luxembourg, and the Netherlands) formalized discussions that had been taking place around economic cooperation by signing the treaty of Paris establishing the European Coal and Steel Community. In March 1957, the treaties establishing the European Atomic Energy Community (Euratom) and the European Economic Community (EEC) were signed in Rome, establishing a common market among the Six. Since 1957, of course, the EEC has grown, both in numbers of Member States (now twenty-seven) and in the scope of its activities, increasingly incorporating social and political issues into its remit.

The establishment of the EEC led to two major developments of importance for our analysis. First, several European states that were unwilling to commit themselves to an EEC-model of closer economic integration decided in July 1959 to establish a somewhat looser free-trade agreement, the European Free Trade Association (EFTA). Second, the OEEC was re-established in December 1960 with a new mandate as the Organisation for Economic Co-operation and Development (OECD) and expanded to include several non-European major economic powers, in particular Japan.

Development of international and regional norms regulating procurement

After the Second World War, domestic procurement was often seen, rightly or wrongly, as characterized by corruption, inefficiency, political capture, rent seeking, protectionism, inflated costs, and the development of cartels. Many saw procurement reform as necessary to limit these features of unreformed procurement markets, but how this should be achieved remained controversial. An interesting analysis of the problems of reforming public procurement just before the onset of the international and European reform period is provided by the report of a consultant employed by the OECD to examine the role of public works and presented to the OECD's Directorate of Manpower and Social Affairs in 1965. This report, contemporary with the beginnings of discussions within the OECD on procurement reform, identified several problematic aspects of the administration of public works. Perhaps the greatest difficulty, the report said, lay 'in introducing modern management principles into relationships between various units of governments, particularly in countries with a federal system of government'.[2] There

---

[2] EJ Howenstein, 'Contemporary Public Works Policy: An International Comparison of its Role in Economic Stabilization and Growth', OECD Archives, OECD 166, MS/S/65.214, 241.

were several reasons. In the first place, 'this is an area in which there are fundamental differences in political philosophy. On the one hand, are those wanting to preserve local rights, independence and autonomy; on the other hand, are those wishing to centralise more and more functions in the hands of the national government.'[3] Second, 'are the complexities of party politics, and as a corollary, the conflicts of individual ambition':[4]

If different parties control legislative bodies of the three different layers of government—local, provincial and national—this will immediately inject elements of conflict which have no place in an objective consideration of the requirements of effective full employment and economic growth policy. Even if all three layers of government are controlled by the same political party, sectional interests and individual rivalries may, nevertheless, inject non-rational elements into the political scene.[5]

Third, effective implementation is:

. . . enormously complicated by the multiplicity of public authorities which have responsibilities in this domain. The amount of public works directly controlled by the national government is less than a half—and often more nearly a quarter—of total public works . . . Provincial and municipal governments and many different types of special public or quasi-public authorities have their own sources of revenue and their own special responsibilities.[6]

As Blank and Marceau perceptively note, there is considerable sensitivity in negotiating procurement liberalization. Not only is the value of government procurement enormous, thus giving the government considerable buying power, there is also 'the fact that in this area states are negotiating about their own actions and are binding themselves as trade actors and consumers. In most other areas, although states are the relevant negotiators in the GATT forum, their actions are concerned with rights of firms and rights of consumers'.[7]

Early beginnings

No doubt due to the complexity of the interests involved, none of the aspects of procurement linkages sketched out earlier in this book was touched by the international regulation of trade that emerged at the end of the Second World War. The otherwise wide-ranging Havana Charter excluded public procurement from coverage.[8] Although the United States Administration had proposed in its draft treaty that procurement should be included, there was insufficient support and active opposition by the United Kingdom and several other major countries. An explicit provision was included in GATT which had the effect of excluding procurement

---

[3] ibid 241.   [4] ibid.   [5] ibid.   [6] ibid 242.
[7] A Blank and G Marceau, 'The History of the Government Procurement Negotiations Since 1945' (1996) 5 PPLR 77, 78.
[8] Final Act and Related Documents, United Nations Conference on Trade and Employment, Havana, Cuba, 21 November 1947–24 March 1948, UN Doc ICITO/1/4 (1948).

from the ambit of the agreement. Although Article III(4) of GATT 1947, concerning national treatment on internal taxation and regulation, would have covered procurement, paragraph 8(a) stated: 'The provisions of this Article shall not apply to laws, regulations or requirements governing the procurement by governmental agencies of products purchased for governmental purposes and not with a view to commercial resale or with a view to use in the production of goods for commercial sale'. Paragraph 8(b) provided further: 'The provisions of this Article shall not prevent the payment of subsidies exclusively to domestic producers, including payments to domestic producers derived from the proceeds of internal taxes or charges applied consistently with the provisions of this Article, and subsidies effected through government purchases of domestic products.'[9]

Why procurement reform?

The subsequent movement at the regional and international levels to reform the practice of public procurement was part of a wider move to reduce non-tariff barriers to international trade. International trade law increasingly sought to limit non-tariff barriers, including domestic regulation, that may appear to be neutral from a trade point of view but intentionally or unintentionally had the same or an equivalent effect as tariffs, excluding products from other countries entirely, or making their import more expensive. It is because of this important shift in thinking about the ambit of international economic law that the question arose as to how far procurement reform principles should be applied not only between countries, to ensure that the methods chosen for the allocation of contracts were not intentionally protectionist, but also within a particular country to ensure that domestic social regulation was not unintentionally protectionist. There were, however, several additional reasons why this movement occurred, and some controversy over what it hoped to achieve,[10] an issue we return to consider in chapter 5 below.

EFTA and procurement

Beginning in the 1960s, procurement regulation underwent a significant change domestically, regionally, and internationally.[11] As we have seen, EFTA developed

---

[9] The argument that procurement was included to some extent, however, derives from the provisions of Art XVII, concerning state trading. Para 1 provides that state trading shall be carried out on the basis of the General Agreement. Para 2 states that with respect to imports involving government procurement, 'each contracting party shall afford to the trade of the other contracting parties fair and equitable treatment'. In so far as procurement was included in this minimal way in GATT, the general exceptions provided in Art XX and the national security provisions in Art XXI were applicable.

[10] See S Arrowsmith, J Linarelli, and D Wallace, Jr, *Regulating Public Procurement: National and International Perspectives* (Kluwer Law International, 2000) 15 *et seq.*

[11] See in general A Reich, *International Public Procurement Law: The Evolution of International Regimes on Public Purchasing* (Kluwer Law International, 1999); S Arrowsmith, *Government Procurement in the WTO* (Kluwer Law International, 2003).

out of the breakdown in 1958 of negotiations within the OEEC to establish a European-wide free trade agreement. In the summer of 1959, Austria, Denmark, Norway, Portugal, Sweden, Switzerland, and the United Kingdom agreed to establish a free trade agreement among themselves. The Stockholm Convention establishing EFTA was signed in January 1960, coming into force in May 1960.[12] Article 14(1) of the Convention provided for the elimination, in the practices of public undertakings, of (a) measures the effect of which was to afford protection to domestic production which would be inconsistent with this Convention 'if achieved by means of a duty or charge with equivalent effect, quantitative restriction or government aid, or (b) trade discrimination on grounds of nationality in so far as it frustrates the benefits expected from the removal or absence of duties and quantitative restrictions on trade between Member States'. The wording of this Article was sufficiently broad to cover the procurement activities of public undertakings. In February 1964, the EFTA Council commissioned the EFTA Committee of Trade Experts to undertake a study of the operation of Article 14. A sub-committee was established to undertake a study of the procurement aspects. In June 1966, a report was produced. At a meeting of the EFTA Council in Lisbon in October 1966, an 'authoritative interpretation' of Article 14 was agreed and published, based on the report.

OECD discussions

At the OEEC, and then subsequently at the OECD, discussions also took place in the 1960s and 1970s on the possibility of international regulation of procurement, which resulted in no formal agreement.[13] Yet these discussions were vital in paving the way for discussions in the Tokyo Round. The fruits of the OECD discussions were transferred to the multilateral negotiations in the Tokyo Round, leading to the conclusion of the Government Procurement Agreement (GPA) in 1979.[14] The GPA 1979, though limited, was, in the words of one participant, 'an outstanding reversal of more than fifty years of international trade and economic history'.[15]

---

[12] 370 UNTS I, No 5266. In 1961 Finland and the other members of EFTA signed an association agreement.

[13] I am grateful to Gherado Bonini, of the Historical Archives of the European Communities in Florence, and Mary-Ann Grosset, Head of OECD Records Management and Archives Service in Paris, for their help in gaining access to the OEEC and OECD records of these discussions.

[14] See ML Jones, 'The GATT-MTN System and the European Community as International Frameworks for the Regulation of Economic Activity: The Removal of Barriers to Trade in Government Procurement' (1984) 8 Maryland Journal of International Law 53; JHJ Bourgeois, 'The Tokyo Round Agreements on Technical Barriers and on Government Procurement in International and EEC Perspective'(1982) 19 CMLR 5.

[15] M Pomeranz, 'Toward a New International Order in Government Procurement' (1979) 11 LPIB 1263.

II. Government Procurement Agreement

The GPA 1979 required each party to accord the products and suppliers of each other party 'treatment no less favourable' than that accorded to its own or any other party's products and suppliers, together with a significant array of administrative requirements relating to the process of procurement including requirements as to technical characteristics, qualifications of suppliers, the criteria for the award of the contract, and mechanisms for dispute settlement essentially building on and reflecting the GATT panel procedures and remedies.[16] However, coverage was limited. Only procurement of products was covered. The Agreement did not cover military and arms procurement. The value of the purchase was required to be at least SDR 150,000[17] before it was covered by the Agreement. Only central government-controlled purchasing entities were included in coverage, excluding local and (in federal systems) state purchasing. In addition, only those purchasing entities listed by a state party in an Annex to the Agreement were covered; which were included and which were not was the subject of multilateral negotiations in which states attempted to arrive at a rough balance of procurement value commitments offered by each state party.[18] There was a general exception similar to that contained in Article XX of GATT. There was a detailed set of provisions on special and differential treatment for developing countries, including permitting developing countries to request derogations from the non-discrimination requirement when conditions warranted, and a grudging acceptance of tied-aid arrangements where governments granted aid to developing countries on condition that aid-financed procurements must originate in the donor state. The GPA came into force on 1 January 1981.[19]

International procurement reform after 1979

Although amended somewhat in the late 1980s,[20] it was not until the 1990s that any significant extension of coverage was introduced. A new Agreement on Government Procurement (GPA 1994) was concluded as part of the Uruguay Round multilateral trade negotiations on 15 December 1993, and signed in Marrakesh in

---

[16] 1979 Agreement, Art II.   [17] At that time, around US$190,000.

[18] 1979 Agreement, Art I.

[19] For background on GPA 1979 see E Goldstein, 'Doing Business Under the Agreement on Government Procurement: The Telecommunications Business—a Case in Point' (1980) 55 St John's Law Review 63; DJ Peterson, 'The Trade Agreements Act of 1979: The Agreement on Government Procurement' (1980) 14 GW JILE 321; ALC De Mestral, 'The Impact of the GATT Agreement on Government Procurement in Canada' in J Quinn and P Slayton (eds), *Non-Tariff Barriers After the Tokyo Round* (Institute for Research on Public Policy, 1982) 171; RA Horsch, 'Eliminating Nontariff Barriers to International Trade: The MTN Agreement on Government Procurement' (1979) 12 NYU JILP 315.

[20] The Agreement was amended in 1987, but only relatively minor changes were made to its text.

April 1994, entering into force in January 1996.[21] The GPA 1994 extended coverage beyond goods to construction works and other services specified in Annexes to the Agreement.[22] It further included procurement by those sub-national governmental authorities (such as states within federations and municipalities) and public utilities specified in positive lists included in Annexes. Coverage by the GPA 1994 still depended on whether the value of the procurement was above a threshold, which varied depending on the type of procurement and the level of government involved in purchasing; the applicable thresholds were specified by each state party.[23] Access to procurement by sub-central governments, public utilities, and for services was contingent on other parties making acceptable reciprocal offers. Not all have done so, and so commitments do not, therefore, apply uniformly to all parties. In addition, as in the GPA 1979, General Notes are included at the end of most states' schedules and these provide for a number of additional exceptions. The GPA 1994, like the GPA 1979 but unlike GATT, remained plurilateral in nature rather than multilateral. All Members States of the European Community are parties, as are the other major industrialized countries in North America and the Far East.[24] The membership of the GPA 'club', with thirty-seven members in January 2007, is considerably smaller than the membership of GATT, with 150. The GPA has proven relatively unpopular with other countries, particularly developing countries, despite the GPA 1994 continuing and somewhat expanding the provisions for special treatment of developing countries that were included in GPA 1979.

A brief outline of some of the more relevant provisions of the agreement applying to procurement above the specified thresholds will be useful at this point.[25] A basic non-discrimination provision requires parties to the GPA 1994 to accord

[21] Agreement on Government Procurement, contained in Proposal for a Council Decision Concerning the Conclusion of the Results of the Uruguay Round of Multilateral Trade Negotiations (1986–1994), COM(94)143 final/2, Brussels, 25 April 1994. The full Agreement, including the Annexes, is contained in Agreement Establishing the World Trade Organization: Plurilateral Trade Agreements: Agreement on Government Procurement, Cm 2575, HMSO, May 1994. For discussion of the background to the Agreement, see C Barshevsky, A Sutton, and A Swindler, 'Developments in EC Procurement Under the 1992 Program' (1990) 4 BYU LR 1269, 1326–36; PA Messerlin, 'Agreement on Public Procurement', in *OECD, The New World Trading System: Readings* (OECD,1995) 65; BM Hoekman and PC Mavroidis (eds), *Law and Policy in Public Purchasing: The WTO Agreement on Government Procurement* (University of Michigan Press, 1997), in addition to the literature cited below.
[22] See the useful article, M Low, A Mattoo, and A Subramanian, 'Government Procurement in Services' (1996) 20 World Competition 5, 6.
[23] The GPA 1994 threshold is 130,000 SDR (1 SDR = US$1.45 (2005)) for procurements of goods and services (except construction services) by central government entities. Thresholds for purchases by sub-central entities vary by country (usually around 200,000 SDR), as do purchases by government-related enterprises (usually around 400,000 SDR). In general, the threshold is 5,000,000 SDR for procurement of construction services by all of these entities. Government Procurement Agreement, Appendix 1.
[24] For a detailed discussion of EC implementation of the 1994 GPA, see P Didier, 'The Uruguay Round Government Procurement Agreement: Implementation in the European Union' in B Hoekman and P Mavroidis (eds), *Law and Policy in Public Purchasing* (1997) ch 7.
[25] See in general Arrowsmith (n 11 above).

the covered products, services, and suppliers of any other party treatment 'no less favourable' than that given to their domestic products, services, and suppliers. It also requires that parties should not discriminate amongst goods, services, and suppliers of other parties.[26] Each party is required to ensure that its contracting bodies do not treat a locally established supplier less favourably than another locally established supplier on the basis of degree of foreign affiliation or ownership.[27] Each party is also required not to discriminate against a locally established supplier on the basis of country of production of the goods or service being supplied.[28]

In addition to this basic set of non-discrimination requirements, there is a detailed set of obligations which procuring entities are required to follow in respect of covered procurements. Regarding qualification of suppliers, for example, the Agreement provides that 'any conditions for participation shall be limited to those which are essential to ensure the firm's capability to fulfil the contract in question',[29] and that such conditions may not discriminate between national and foreign suppliers, or among foreign suppliers. In the case of selective tendering procedures, entities maintaining permanent lists of qualified suppliers are required to publish 'the conditions to be fulfilled by suppliers with a view to their inscription on those lists'.[30] Tender documentation must in general contain all information necessary to permit suppliers to submit responsive tenders, 'the criteria for awarding the contract',[31] and 'any other terms and conditions'.[32] In particular, the documentation must include, 'the criteria for awarding the contract, including any factors other than price that are to be considered in the evaluation of tenders'.[33] To be considered for the award of a contract the tender 'must . . . conform to the essential requirements of the notices or tender documentation and be from a supplier which complies with the conditions for participation'.[34] Under the Agreement, the public body may decide not to issue the contract to anyone. If it does award the contract, the public body 'shall make the award to the tenderer who has been determined to be fully capable of undertaking the contract and whose tender . . . is either the lowest tender or the tender which in terms of the specific criteria set forth in the notices or tender documentation is determined to be the most advantageous'.[35]

An entity which has received a tender which is abnormally lower than other tenders may enquire with the tenderer to ensure that it can comply with the conditions of participation and be capable of fulfilling the terms of the contract.[36] Regarding the award of contracts, awards 'shall be made in accordance with the criteria and essential requirements specified in the tender documentation'.[37] Except in the case of developing countries, procuring entities 'shall not, in the qualification of suppliers, products, or services, or in the evaluation of tenders and award

---

[26] GPA 1994, Art III. [27] ibid Art III(2)(a). [28] ibid Art III(2)(b).
[29] ibid Art VIII (b). [30] ibid Art IX(9)(b). [31] ibid Art XIII(2)(h).
[32] ibid Art XIII(2)(j). [33] Art XII(2)(h). [34] ibid Art XIII(4)(a).
[35] ibid Art XIII(4)(b). [36] ibid Art XIII(4). [37] ibid Art XIII(4)(d).

of contract, impose, seek or consider offsets'.[38] Article XXIII of the GPA 1994 provides a general exception to the provisions of the Agreement:

Subject to the requirement that such measures are not applied in a manner which would constitute a means of arbitrary or unjustified discrimination between countries where the same conditions prevail or a disguised restriction on international trade, nothing in this Agreement shall be construed to prevent any Party from imposing or enforcing measures: necessary to protect public morals, order or safety, human, animal or plant life or health or intellectual property; or relating to the products or services of handicapped persons, of philanthropic institutions or of prison labour.[39]

The GPA 1994 also provided stronger enforcement procedures and new remedies for breach.[40] Disputes between parties under the Agreement are subject, with a few modifications, to the procedures of the WTO Understanding on Rules and Procedures Governing the Settlement of Disputes (DSU).[41] The GPA 1994 also introduces a mechanism for firms to use if they consider that there has been a breach of the agreement affecting them, the so-called bid challenge system.[42] The GPA 1994 requires each party to establish a procedure whereby a supplier has a right of challenge to an independent domestic tribunal.[43] As Messerlin has written, this is a 'unique innovation in the GATT system; it is the first time that direct access to enforcement procedures under the regulations of the importing country has been granted to foreign firms within the context of a GATT text'.[44]

III. Early Activities Relating to Procurement by the European Community

Slow beginnings

None of the three original treaties establishing, the European Coal and Steel Community, the European Economic Community, or the European Atomic Energy Community included any reference to procurement. As Reich has observed, 'this was not as a result of a simple omission by the drafters of the Treaty, but of a failure to reach agreement on a set of principles, because of the complexity of the subject

---

[38] ibid Art XVI(1). According to a footnote to this Article, included in the text of the Agreement, offsets are regarded as 'measures used to encourage local development or improve the balance-of-payments accounts by means of domestic content, licensing of technology, investment requirements, countertrade or similar requirements'.   [39] ibid Art XXIII(2).

[40] A Davies, 'Remedies for Enforcing the WTO Agreement on Government Procurement from the Perspective of the European Community: A Critical View' (1996–7) 20 World Competition 113; B Hoekmann and P Mavroidis, 'The WTO's Agreement on Government Procurement: Expanding Disciplines, Declining Membership?' (1995) 4 PPLR 63.   [41] GPA 1994, Art XXII(1).

[42] ibid Art XX.   [43] ibid Art XX(6).

[44] PA Messerlin, 'Agreement on Public Procurement' in OECD, *The New World Trading System: Readings* (OECD, 1995) 65.

matter and the highly sensitive nature of preference policies'.[45] Several articles of the Treaty of Rome were relevant, however, to procurement, at least potentially, in particular Article 7 (prohibiting discrimination on grounds of nationality), Article 30 (free movement of goods), Article 48 (free movement of workers), and Articles 52 to 66 (freedom to provide services and freedom of establishment). Particularly important was Article 30, which prohibited quantitative restrictions on imports from other Member States 'and all measures having an equivalent effect thereto'.

From the point of view of the history of procurement regulation, these provisions were particularly important since they provided a basis for future legislative action. Articles 52 to 66 of the EEC Treaty required Member States progressively to abolish restrictions on the freedom of establishment of nationals of other Member States. The Council of Ministers was authorized to issue directives to further that end. On 25 October 1961, the Council adopted two General Programmes[46] setting out how restrictions on access to government contracts were to be reduced over time, 'in essence action plans for Community institutions', as Reich describes them.[47] In 1971, the Council adopted two further directives regarding public works contracts.[48] The first, Directive (EEC) 71/304 was effectively a Directive implementing the General Programmes agreed in 1962. More important for our purposes, is Directive (EEC) 71/305 'concerning the co-ordination of procedures for the award of public works contracts' (the Works Directive). This second Directive effectively began the regulation of procurement under Community law. Many of the concepts in current use in EC procurement law derive from this instrument. In 1976, a further directive was adopted, coordinating procedures for the award of public supply contracts, which was essentially similar to the Works Directive.[49]

We shall be considering aspects of this legislative programme in detail subsequently, but, for the moment, two aspects of the Community's approach need to be made clear. The first vital aspect of Community policy is one of non-discrimination between national and non-national tenderers; the second is the transparency of the process of decision-making in the area. The thrust of Community policy has been, in essence, to decrease the former and to increase the latter. Although riddled with limitations and exceptions, the basic structure of the Works Directive, for example, was clear. There were essentially four important elements established in order to free the public procurement markets from discrimination against tenderers from other Member States. First, provisions were introduced to attempt to limit the extent to which technical specifications restricted participation in contracts,

---

[45] A Reich, *International Public Procurement Law: The Evolution of International Regimes on Public Purchasing* (Kluwer, 1999) 71–2 .

[46] General Programme for the abolition of restrictions on freedom of establishment [1962] OJ No 2, 36/62.   [47] Reich (n 43 above) 75.

[48] Council Directive (EEC) 71/304 of 26 July 1971 [1971] JO 1971 L185/1; Council Directive [EEC] 71/305 [1971] JO L185/5.

[49] Council Directive (EEC) 77/62 of 21 December 1976, [1977] OJ L13/1.

Preliminaries

particularly the use of specifications that referred to products of a specific make or source. Second, there were provisions setting out rules to require advertising of the availability of contracts, thus helping to make the process more open and transparent. Third, criteria were established for the selection of tenderers, permitting exclusion of contractors only for specified reasons, for example excluding those who were bankrupt, guilty of grave professional misconduct, and so forth. In addition, rules were established providing criteria by which technical capacity and financial standing were to be assessed. Finally, two alternative criteria for the award of contracts were set out, either the lowest price, or 'the most economically advantageous tender'. 'Abnormally low tenders' might be examined before an award of the contract was made, and the results of that examination taken into account in the award of the contract.

The Community approach to procurement reform is important, not only because it regulates an increasingly large area of the European continent, but also because of the close relationship between the approach developed in the EC and the approach developed in the WTO Government Procurement Agreement. We shall see that the two processes of reform, the international and the European, went hand in hand. In the negotiation of the GPA 1979 and 1994, this was facilitated by the fact that: 'From the outset the entire negotiations were . . . conducted by the Community and by the Community alone', rather than by each Member State individually.[50] Pomeranz has asked whether 'the close resemblance between the EC goods procurement Directive and the [1979 GPA Agreement] was the result of initiatives in one or the other forum or of the Directive and the Code feeding upon each other'[51] but the answer probably matters only to historians. What is crucial is the fact that they do resemble each other so closely, at least in so far as the substantive rules are concerned.

IV. The Growth of Neo-Liberalism and Further European Procurement Reform

The 1979 GPA and the 1970s EEC procurement directives demonstrated a high degree of acceptance by those agreeing to these measures that national public procurement was used to secure important national social policy goals (such as increasing social welfare) and that these social goals were not subject to international or Community restrictions. After the Community directives of the 1970s and 1980s and the first Government Procurement Agreement were finalized, this general policy position began to change, however. The consensus around what Ruggie has termed 'embedded liberalism'[52] disappeared 'both because it was no longer apparent that one could avoid trade offs between domestic interventionism

---

[50] Bourgeois (n 14 above) 20.   [51] Pomeranz (n 15 above) 1275.

[52] JG Ruggie, 'International Regimes, Transactions, and Change: Embedded Liberalism and the Postwar Economic Order', (1982) 36(2) International Organization 379.

and open global markets, and also because large numbers of countries were welcomed as members of the multilateral trading system, without any attention to whether they shared even a minimalist conception of appropriate domestic public interest regulation'.[53] In its place emerged an alternative neo-liberal consensus, later known as the Washington Consensus, and this continued as the dominant paradigm until at least the mid-1990s. This considered that it was appropriate to separate the economic forces of globalization from the social and political realm. 'On this view', according to Langille:

...the economic...is prior to and separate from the social (including basic issues of democracy, human rights, equality concerns, etc.), the latter being conceived as a set of luxury goods which might be purchased with the fruits of economic progress generated elsewhere. All this is reflected in an institutional division of labour, both domestically and internationally, between the financial institutions and ministries on the one hand...and the social ones...on the other.[54]

In this context, the 'narrative of globalisation' 'puts in question the normative floor and indeed views it as antithetical to economic development'.[55] This fundamental change in ideology is reflected in important changes in procurement policy, particularly in the Community, during the 1980s.

Procurement and internal market reforms

In the mid-1980s, the Commission developed a major programme of opening up the public procurement market. The Commission's White Paper, 'Completing the Internal Market',[56] set out a legislative programme for achieving this, involving a tightening of then existing provisions and a substantial expansion of measures bringing legal regulation into areas hitherto excluded from coverage. Given the increasing significance of public procurement in the economic activity of the Member States, the Community considered that it had a legitimate role in opening up procurement markets if a single European market was to be made a reality. Protectionist public procurement policies by national public bodies would delay the achievement of the single market more generally. The Community had long had an interest in breaking down such protectionist approaches and in stimulating further cross-border activity. Competitive tendering would reduce 'the burden on the public purse but also enhance[ ] macro-economic growth, since it promotes restructuring and adjustment'.[57] The Cechinni report developed a projection that

---

[53] R Howse and B Langille, with J Burda, 'The World Trade Organization and Labour Rights: Man Bites Dog' in VA Leary and D Warner (eds), *Social Issues, Globalisation and International Institutions: Labour Rights and the EU, ILO, OECD and WTO* (Brill Academic, 2005) 158.

[54] B Langille, 'Globalization and the Just Society—Core Labour Rights, the FTAA, and Development' in JDR Craig and SM Lynk, *Globalization and the Future of Labour Law* (Cambridge University Press, 2006) 278.   [55] Howse and Langille, with Burda (n 53 above) 158.

[56] Commission of the European Communities, White Paper, 'Completing the Internal Market' (Office for Official Publications of the European Communities, Luxembourg, 1985).

[57] JM Fernández Martín, *The EC Public Procurement Rules: A Critical Analysis* (OUP, 1996) 42.

extensive savings could be expected from a competitive regime in the area of public contracts.[58] Achieving efficiency in public procurement was thus considered to be of considerable importance to the economic health of the Community.[59]

There followed a period of sustained legislative reform of the Directives from 1986 to 1992. The Commission proposed a draft of a revised Supplies Directive in June 1986.[60] This was subsequently amended by the Commission, largely to take account of GPA requirements.[61] Following Parliamentary consideration, in October 1987, the Commission produced a revised proposal.[62] On 5 October 1987, the Council of Ministers adopted a 'Common Position'.[63] On 16 December 1987, following the report from its Economic Committee, the Parliament in its second reading adopted further amendments.[64] A new proposal was published by the Commission in February 1988.[65] On 22 March 1988, the Council adopted the Directive. In December 1986, the Commission had sent the Council a proposal for a directive amending Directive (EEC) 71/305 concerning the coordination of procedures for the award of public works contracts.[66] Following Parliamentary consideration, the Commission adopted some amendments in its amended proposal of June 1988.[67] The Council Common Position was adopted on 4 November 1988.[68] Parliament adopted several amendments at second reading stage in February 1989.[69] A new Commission proposal was presented in April 1989.[70] On 18 July 1989, the Council adopted a revised common position. The initial proposal of the Commission for a Services Directive was presented to the Council in December 1990.[71] Following Parliamentary consideration, the Commission adopted an amended proposal.[72] In October 1988, the Commission sent to the Council two proposals for directives in the utilities sectors, one relating to water, energy, and transport,[73] and the second relating to telecommunications.[74] Modified Commission proposals were presented following the Parliamentary debate.[75] The

---

[58] European Commission, 'The Cost of Non-Europe in Public Sector Procurement' in *The Cost of Non-Europe, Basic Findings*, Vols 5A and 5B.

[59] European Commission, Public Procurement: Regional and Social Aspects, COM(89)400, paras 9 and 10.　　　　　　　　　　　　　　[60] COM(86)297 final [1986] OJ C173/4.

[61] COM(87)233 final, 27 May 1987 [1987] OJ C161/10.

[62] Second alteration of the Proposal for a Council Directive amending Directive (EEC) 77/62 relating to the coordination of procedures on the award of public supply contracts and deleting certain provisions of Directive (EEC) 80/767, COM(87)468 final, 2 October 1987.

[63] Doc C 2-184/87.　　　　　[64] [1988] OJ C13/62.

[65] Re-examined proposal for a Council Directive amending Directive (EEC) 77/62 relating to the coordination of procedures on the award of public supply contracts and deleting certain provisions of Directive (EEC) 80/767, COM(88)42 final/2, 17 February 1988 [1988] OJ C65/5.

[66] COM(86)679 final of 23 December1986.　　　　[67] COM(88)354 final of 21 June 1988.

[68] Doc C2-193/88.

[69] Second Reading by the Parliament, 15 February 1989 [1989] OJ C69/69.

[70] COM(89)141 final of 4 April 1989 [1989] OJ C115/4.

[71] COM(90)372 of 6 December 1990 [1991] OJ C23.

[72] COM(91)322 final of 30 August 1991 [1991] OJ C250/4.

[73] COM(88)377 final of 11 October 1988.

[74] COM(88)378 final of 11 October 1988 [1989] OJ C40.

[75] COM(89)380 final of 31 August1989 [1989] OJ C267.

Council's Common Position was arrived at on 28 March 1990. A revised Commission proposal was submitted in July 1990.[76] The Council adopted the Directive as proposed by the Commission on 17 September 1990. In 1992, the Commission proposed a consolidation of the Supplies Directive.[77] Following Parliamentary consideration,[78] the proposal was subsequently adopted by the Council.

V. European Procurement Reforms of 2003

By the end of the 1990s, however, the political context of European procurement regulation had undergone yet another sea-change and was significantly different than it had been during the 1980s. Despite the promise of economic benefits from the procurement reforms of the 1980s, changes in the practice of procurement at the national level were slow in appearing. This was partly seen as a result of slow implementation by Member States of their obligations under the directives, leading to Commission decisions to increase infringement action, and partly as a result of entrenched attitudes among purchasers and suppliers. To the extent, for example, that the procurement reforms of the 1980s were intended to increase cross-border flows of procurement, by the mid-1990s little appeared to have changed. Hence, there was a sense that the economic benefits that were expected had been imperfectly realized. This led to a view that a further streamlining of the procurement directives, with alterations to reflect changes in the economy, would be beneficial. Particular attention was given to the potential benefits of electronic procurement in achieving radical reductions in transaction costs.

There was a significant debate emerging within procurement circles as to whether the highly regulated, rule-based, centralized approach to procurement regulation that increasingly characterized EC procurement law was the appropriate approach, or whether alternative more deregulatory approaches would be preferable. In part, this debate was one about methods of regulation; but in significant part, it was also a debate about the function of EC law in the procurement area. Was the function of EC procurement law 'fundamentally economic'? For some, promoting value for money and efficient allocation of resources was a primary function of the directives, leading them either to disapprove the integration of other policies into procurement as fundamentally opposed to these basic functions, incompatible with the basic aims of Community law in this area, and thus to be rejected almost out of hand, or to seek to balance this primary economic function with other Community policies such as social or environmental considerations. For others, however, an approach based on the primacy of the economic function of the directives was flawed because, in their view, the concern of Community law was not with securing these economic aims, nor with balancing these aims with other policies at

---

[76] COM(90)301 of 12 July 1990.   [77] COM(92)346 final OJ C 277/1.
[78] [1993] OJ C72/73.

the European level.[79] This led Arrowsmith, for example, to consider that the best option might be for Community law to abandon the detailed rule-based restrictions on award procedures, including even the principle of transparency, and 'to allow entities to focus solely on compliance with the Treaty. If an entity can positively show that it procures in a non-discriminatory manner and does not otherwise impose unjustified access restrictions, there is no justification to subject it to transparency requirements as a means for securing these ends.'[80] It is unclear how far similar approaches were being developed in the European Commission during this period, but there is some evidence that radical deregulation was contemplated by some, particularly perhaps the emphasis given to attempting to develop general principles from the then emerging Court of Justice jurisprudence.[81]

The Commission's Green Paper, 'Public Procurement in the European Union: Exploring the Way Forward', was adopted in November 1996.[82] One of the principal themes of the Green Paper was the need to simplify the legal framework, whilst maintaining the stability of the basic structure already in place. In March 1998, the Commission published its Communication, 'Public Procurement in the European Union'.[83] The Lisbon Economic Council in March 2000 stated that reform of procurement was a key element in the Community's programme to boost the European economy. On 11 July 2000, the Commission submitted to the Council its proposals for reform of the three public sector directives regarding works, supplies, and services,[84] and a separate proposal regarding utilities.[85] The Communication also figured among the actions announced in the Social Policy Agenda adopted by the European Council of Nice in December 2000.[86] On 17 January 2002, the European Parliament delivered its Opinion at first reading on both proposals, broadly approving the Commission proposal, but subject to 103 amendments.[87] In early May 2002, the Commission issued its amended proposal on both the public sector[88] and utilities directives,[89] commenting on the amendments made by the Parliament. Of the 103 amendments proposed by the

[79] S Arrowsmith, 'The EC Procurement Directives, National Procurement Policies and Better Governance: The Case for a New Approach' (2002) 27 ELR 3, 7–8.   [80] ibid 21–2.
[81] P Braun, A Matter of Principle(s)—The Treatment of Contracts Falling Outside the Scope of the European Public Procurement Directives, (2000) 9 PPLR 39.
[82] COM(96)583 final of 27 November 1996.
[83] COM(98)143, 11 March 1998. For discussion, see S Arrowsmith, 'The Community's Legal Framework on Public Procurement: "The Way Forward" at Last?'(1999) 36 CMLR 13–49.
[84] COM (2000)275 final/2 [2001] OJ C29/11.
[85] ibid.
[86] Social Policy Agenda, COM(2000)379 of 28 June 2000.
[87] Works etc. proposal: 17 January 2002; PE-T5(2002)0010, [2002] OJ C271/62. Only adopted text with amendments highlighted available, no listing of amendments. Amendments regarding social aspects are identified in COM (2002)236 final. Utilities proposal: 17 January 2002, PE-T5(2002)0011 [2002] OJ C271/293. Only adopted text with amendments highlighted available, no listing of amendments. Amendments regarding social aspects are identified in COM(2002)235 final.
[88] COM(2002)236 final, 6 May 2002.
[89] COM(2002)235 final, 6 May 2002.

Parliament, the Commission felt able to accept 63 in full or in part. On 21 May 2002, the Council had reached a political agreement on the public sector proposals.[90] On 30 September 2002, the Council had reached a political agreement on a common position on the utilities proposals.[91] However, the Council's Common Position was not published until 20 March 2003.[92] The Commission's assessment of the Council's Common Position was published in March 2003.[93] On 2 July, the European Parliament adopted a legislative resolution, under the Second Reading of the co-decision procedure, amending the common position.[94] The directives could only be adopted without further negotiations between the Commission, the Council, and the Parliament, if the Council accepted all the amendments tabled by the Parliament. However, the Council did not do so, and the conciliation process was initiated as a result. The Council working group and the Committee of Member States' Permanent Representatives (COREPER) met to discuss the amendments before the summer break. The first informal 'trilogue' meeting of Parliament, Council, and Commission met on 2 September 2003. The power of the Parliament at this stage was considerable. Any compromise agreed on in conciliation must be agreed to by a majority of the votes cast in Parliament. 'This procedure makes it easier for the Directives to be thrown out than in the second Reading stage where an "absolute majority" (314 votes) is needed.'[95] A compromise was agreed, leading to final approval by a plenary vote of the Parliament on 29 January 2004.

VI. Procurement Linkages, International and European Procurement Regulation

The function of this chapter has been to provide a brief introduction to several of the most important developments in international and European procurement regulation that affect the development of equality-based procurement linkages. We shall see in subsequent chapters that procurement linkages are now encountering 'economic globalization', by which I mean those international economic developments that have been spurred on by a type of economic liberalism. Economic globalization has developed an institutional face, particularly with the growth of international and supranational organizations like the World Bank, the WTO, and the EC. Economic globalization has affected procurement linkages through the attempts by these organizations to further economic liberalism by regulatory means, particularly regulation designed to address protectionism by states using non-tariff measures. Some aspects of the use of procurement linkages of the type discussed in previous chapters were bound to come into conflict with the thrust of regulation designed to address protectionist state measures because we have seen that some, but my no means all,

---

[90] Doc 9270/02.   [91] Doc 12204/02.   [92] [2003] OJ C147/001E.
[93] SEC(2003)0366, 25 March 2003.   [94] T5-0312/2003, 2 July 2003.   [95] ibid.

of the former were explicitly linked to the protection of domestic producers and suppliers, and that the potential for procurement linkage that was not explicitly protectionist to facilitate protectionism was in practice ever present.

The effect of economic liberalization on procurement linkages has been complex and multifaceted. Seen from the perspective of procurement law and policy, several issues will be particularly relevant in understanding the ways in which equality-based procurement linkages differ.

Which governmental entities?   It is important to understand that the level of government involved in using public procurement linkages to produce equality outcomes will often be significant, both politically and legally, depending on the particular jurisdiction concerned. Levels of government below the national government may or may not be constrained by legal or policy requirements relating to the use of public procurement in these circumstances. Different levels of government may have different policy tools available to them to bring about preferred policy outcomes; one level of government may have a greater preference for the use of public procurement than others simply because those other levels of government have additional tools that they do not. Equality-based linkages also vary depending on which public bodies' contracts are involved. In some, the programme is applicable to the contracts of central government departments; in some, regional governments are involved; and in some, local governments are included. Sometimes, other public bodies are involved, sometimes not.

Linked to local development policies?   Although the use of public procurement involves the furtherance of social objectives in seeking to address status inequality and in encouraging local economic development, there are sometimes crucial differences between them. First, whilst linkages to encourage local development often depend on protectionism and discrimination against foreign contractors in order to effectuate their social objective (and are presumptively the types of measure that international trade law and EC procurement law are likely to want to tackle), linkages addressing status inequality do not necessarily do so. Failure to distinguish between these two groups of measures results in all (unfairly) being treated as protectionist and presumptively invalid under international and EC procurement law disciplines. As importantly, as Estivill argues, it 'is important to distinguish between local development and combating exclusion...Local development can have a positive impact on exclusion but not always.... [E]stablished powers... can be stronger at the local than at other levels'.[96]

Which types of contract?   The types of contracts covered by the procurement linkages differ significantly. Some cover supplies, others works, others services. Some

---

[96] J Estivill, *Concepts and Strategies for Combating Social Exclusion* (ILO, 2003) 114.

programmes are limited to contracts above a threshold amount, others not; for some the threshold amount is relevant for the type of requirement imposed—the larger the contract, the greater the set of obligations. The type of firm is sometimes specified; sometimes the programme only affects firms employing a certain minimum number of employees; sometimes subcontractors are covered, sometimes not. In some programmes, all the activities of the contractor, whether involved in carrying out the contract or not, are subject to the requirements; in others, only those activities of the contractor directly involved in carrying out the contract are affected.

5

Buying Social Justice?

This part of the book has attempted to provide a basic introduction to some of the more salient background factors necessary for a better understanding of what follows in the remainder of the book. In chapter 2, we considered the roots of current equality-based procurement linkages in previous socio-economic or political goals that public procurement has been used to achieve from the early nineteenth century. In chapters 3 and 4, we examined respectively the equal status law and policy context, and then the international and EC public procurement law and policy context. These provide the vital contexts in which equality-based procurement linkages operate. We have seen that the use of linkages between public contracting and social regulation, what I termed 'buying social justice' in chapter I above, has been in the past a deeply controversial strategy, legally and politically. We have seen in chapter 2 that, historically, there have been real dangers in exploiting the clout of the state's power in this way. We have seen in chapter 4 how, increasingly, international and regional procurement reforms have addressed some of these problems. And yet for all its complexity and risks, we have also seen that the presence of the state in the market does present unique opportunities for it to influence market behaviour. Are sceptics of procurement linkages right to be so sceptical? Or is there a way of harnessing or exploiting the presence of the state in the market for social purposes without causing unacceptable political harms or detriment to the market as the primary means of generating wealth in society? Can the two be brought into alignment to achieve optimum economic, political, and social results? In this chapter, I want to present a relatively full preliminary exploration of the pros and cons of the use of procurement linkages to advance status equality, from an economic and political perspective initially.

I. Objections to Linkage

It is possible to identify seven broad arguments that suggest that linkages between procurement and social policies may be ill advised. These are based as much on my own experience as they are on the politics and economics literature. Each of these arguments has several aspects.

Irrelevance to the appropriate functions of purchasing

Here is an attempt to articulate the first argument. According to Miller, the only 'mission of the contracting agency ... [is] to obtain what is needed, in both quantity and quality, at the time when it is needed, at a decent price, and under circumstances which are fair to both the Government and the contractor'.[1] Private contracting is subject to market disciplines to ensure that this is achieved. Government would truly be acting in the public interest if it were to act just like another commercial organization motivated by commercial considerations.[2] There should be no significant difference between what private actors do in contracting, and what governments do in contracting.[3] The benefits of using contract are more likely to be dissipated when essentially regulatory policies creep in. Government should be restrained from acting in this way, in the public interest. The contractual relationship should be kept 'pure' and uncomplicated by social and political concerns. Decisions should be made on the basis of 'value for money', interpreted largely as lowest price. In public contracting, the market does not provide an effective discipline to achieve this, therefore there are legal and policy constraints that attempt to ape these market disciplines.

This approach to procurement is one that is seen not only as justified in its own terms, but also as one that is particularly suited to the new public sector management approach stressing the need for a less bureaucratic form of government, one that is revenue driven and competitive, and one that seeks to take a more commercial approach to government operations.[4] In this form of government, the public sector manager should be encouraged to act as if he or she were a private sector manager. Procurement linkages, it is argued, cut in exactly the opposite direction and should therefore be resisted.

Costs of linkage

Here is the second argument. There are, it is said, extra financial costs that result from procurement linkages. Let us assume that equality linkages seek to distinguish 'good' buyers from 'bad' buyers, using 'good' and 'bad' loosely. Based on the analysis of procurement linkages in chapters 2 and 3 above, and anticipating the descriptions of national practice in subsequent chapters, we can identify at least four basic models of how equality issues are currently addressed in public procurement.

[1] AS Miller, 'Government Contracts and Social Control: A Preliminary Inquiry' (1955) 41 Virginia Law Review 27, 54.

[2] cf PM Risik, 'Federal Government Contract Clauses and Forms' (1954) 23 GWLR 125, 134 'the contract become[s] cluttered with impediments which are not encountered in commercial contracting'.

[3] cf HR Van Cleve, Jr, 'The Use of Federal Procurement to Achieve National Goals' (1961) Wisconsin Law Review 566, describing such requirements as 'slightly absurd' in the private business context.

[4] P Trepte, *Regulating Procurement: Understanding the Ends and Means of Public Procurement Regulation* (OUP, 2004) 14–15.

In the first model, there is a prohibition on obtaining government contracts as a penalty for previous wrongdoing, or to prevent public bodies contracting with those who are currently failing to achieve a particular standard of behaviour relating to equality. Where this '*tenderer qualification*' model is adopted, it is most likely that the tender (or general legislation) will specify that a person will be disqualified from tendering for the contract if they have been found to have failed to comply with anti-discrimination or equality requirements. The point of this use of procurement is, essentially, to add the deprivation of government contracts to the other penalties to which the contractor may be subject.

The second model focuses its attention on the stage *after* the contract has been awarded. It does not attempt to exclude potential contractors on the basis of their previous activities or current behaviour, as does the first model. Instead, it requires that whoever is awarded the contract must comply with certain conditions in carrying out the contract once it is awarded. In this second '*contract conditions*' model, there is no attempt to build the ability of the contractor to comply with such conditions into the award of the contract. This model presents all contractors with the same boilerplate requirement that the contractor must sign up to. The simplest approach includes a straightforward non-discrimination clause as a contract condition.

The third model attempts to get tenderers to commit to equality norms and have their success in doing so taken into account in the *award* of the contract. The form in which this third 'award criteria' approach can be found in practice is where the public body takes conformity to certain equality issues into account as an award criterion. This approach differs enormously, however, between different programmes. In some, the approach taken is to establish a quota of contracts that is set aside for contractors of a particular type. In others there is a price preference for certain types of contractors. In others the approach taken is that the willingness or ability or past practice of the bidder is taken into account as a tie-break where otherwise equal tenders are in competition. (Here too, however, in some programmes the social criterion is one among many to be taken into account where tenders are equal; in others the social criterion is determinative.) In others, the procedure is to offer-back to preferred tenderers to allow them to match the lowest bid of their non-preferred competitors.

The fourth model arises where the tender lays down the *technical specifications* that must be met by successful contractors in a way that includes equality criteria. When combined with the award approach this may enable the most flexibility, combined with a clear constraint, where the specifications may be linked to the subject matter of the contract. One example of this 'technical specifications' model is where the specifications specify that computer equipment must conform to certain accessibility criteria.

Using the studies of international procurement economics as our guide,[5] particularly the helpful analysis of Evenett, we can construct three types of effects that

---

[5] These are usefully summarized in SJ Evenett, 'Multilateral Disciplines and Government Procurement' in P English, BM Hoekman and A Matto (eds), *Development, Trade and the WTO* (WTO, 2002) 417–27.

may arise in using equality linkages. First, there are linkages (for example qualification criteria, set asides at the award stage) that directly or indirectly reduce the number of 'bad' bidders, sometimes referred to as 'entry discrimination'. Second, there are linkages that reduce price competition for 'good' bidders, for example giving price preferences for preferred bidders such as black-owned corporations at the award stage (termed 'price discrimination'). Third, there are types of linkages that directly or indirectly increase the cost of bidding for 'bad' bidders, such as using the contract conditions model to require those awarded the contract to introduce equality policies subsequently ('cost discrimination').

We are interested in the effect of the three types of 'discrimination' against 'bad' bidders'. There are various types of effects that we should be interested in: what effect do these linkages have in increasing the number of 'good' firms and reducing the number of 'bad' firms in particular procurements, or in particular markets? But we should also be interested in what the effect on national welfare is more broadly. Based on economic studies of discrimination against foreign buyers in auction-type procurements, we might predict several effects. First, 'entry discrimination' approaches are likely, according to Evenett, to 'reduce the competition faced by each [good] bidder, which then all submit higher bids. The government then finds itself choosing from a range of higher bids, and the overall cost of the contract rises.'[6] Second, 'cost discrimination' measures similarly increase the costs of one group of bidders, raising its bid, and the other bidders 'facing less competition, raise their bids, too. Again government's procurement costs rise',[7] although less than in the case of entry discrimination where there are outright prohibitions on certain bidders participating. Third, 'price discrimination' does not necessarily lead to higher procurement costs because 'bad' firms may 'make their bids knowing that a price preference will be used to inflate those bids. They respond to high price preferences by lowering their bids and reducing their profit margins. If the probability of a [bad] firm being the low bidder is high, raising price preferences might actually reduce procurement costs.'[8] However, cost reductions are likely to be small, and if the government chooses the 'wrong' rate of price preference, these cost reductions become cost increases. In addition, the profitability of the 'good' firms is considerably enhanced.

Procurement linkages that advance status equality will, if these predictions are accurate, by increasing the costs of procurement, indirectly lead to a smaller economic pie, and a consequential reduction in what can be redistributed through social welfare measures.[9] To the extent that the social requirement also discriminates against foreign contractors, then the cost implications may be even greater. Higher costs for contractors may also mean higher prices for some consumers. Procurement linkage could result in the loss of jobs. Such measures introduce an additional level of uncertainty for contractors and this will affect investment decisions adversely.

---

[6] ibid 422.   [7] ibid.   [8] ibid.
[9] A key objection which Epstein raises, see R Epstein, *Forbidden Grounds: The Case Against Employment Discrimination Laws* (Harvard, 1992) 435–6.

Linkage makes it harder to encourage growth and, in the absence of new jobs, it is more difficult to provide social justice. The policy implications are clear. It is better to keep the two policy areas (equality and procurement) separate, otherwise public procurement will be less effective in doing what it should, which is ensuring that the goods necessary for government are purchased at the best price.[10]

Fairness and discrimination arguments

Here is the third argument against procurement linkages. A requirement that contractors should deliver social policies along with the goods or services they were primarily contracted to deliver is unfair to those who will bear the burdens. Linkages may disadvantage contractors dependent on public contracts who are in competition with others not dependent on government contracts. To this extent, procurement linkages are unfair because they inflict a particular set of social costs on only one group. The more complex and costly the requirements that linkages impose, the more they will constitute barriers to entry which may reduce the number of competitors, contributing to greater concentration in carrying out public contracting.[11] It is the larger companies that are primarily able to satisfy complex social requirements.

Once we include the global effects of procurement linkages that make access to government contracts more difficult, then the risks of adverse distributional effects increase considerably. Howse and Langille have made the point that

> ... the integration of the world economy ... has the potential, at least, to provide developing countries with access to markets and capital, which are the required preconditions to economic and social progress. From the point of view of global equity it is important that open trade and investment rules be directed to these nations. At the same time it is in the self interest of workers and firms in the developed world to resist this competition and potential exit of capital and jobs.[12]

Procurement linkages facilitate this type of protectionist behaviour, thus risking a conflict with principles of global, as well as domestic, equity.

Direct regulation preferable to procurement linkages

Underlying many of the suspicions about linkages between social policies and public procurement is the view that such uses of public procurement are, quite simply, unnecessary. This is the fourth argument supporting scepticism. If government

---

[10] Risik (n 2 above) 133.

[11] See D Biggar, Background Note, in 'Procurement Markets' (1999) 1(4) OECD Journal of Competition Law and Policy 6, 14.

[12] R Howse and B Langille, with J Burda, 'The World Trade Organization and Labour Rights: Man Bites Dog' in VA Leary and D Warner (eds), *Social Issues, Globalisation and International Institutions: Labour Rights and the EU, ILO, OECD and WTO* (Brill Academic, 2005) 165.

believes that one practice is not acceptable, or that another is desirable, then it should act directly rather than through procurement. Direct legislation, for example, and not the use of indirect financial incentives or sanctions that have unacceptable or unpredictable distorting effects, are seen as the best way of enforcing required norms without unacceptable side-effects. If procurement linkages are unnecessary, then the suspicion grows there is a less benign explanation of such linkages.

So far, we have identified scepticism regarding linkage between equality and procurement as arising primarily from the procurement side of the relationship. However, some might see such involvement as problematic from the social policy perspective also; linkage may be a poor way to deliver the social policy desired. Here is one way of articulating the argument. General social policy problems cannot be resolved through the medium of public procurement because, as we have seen, only some sectors of the economy, which happen to be particularly dependent on government contracts and can therefore be subjected to particular burdens, will be affected. The desired influence can only be achieved where the state is a major customer. The desired objective can therefore only be achieved patchily using public sector contracts as an instrument. This may contribute to aggravating what Maupain has called the 'dualization'[13] of working conditions, for example improving the lot of only those fortunate enough to be employed under government contracts. If the government believes that employers should adopt certain forms of practice, it should make this a legislative requirement for all employers. Direct legislation, and not the use of discretionary financial incentives or sanctions, is the proper way of indicating the desired form of action. Why should procurement be used as the policy tool for the delivery of the social policy preferred? Other regulatory tools are often available, including transfer payments directly to the beneficiary group, for example.

Regulatory capture

Here is the fifth argument. Linkage, to be successful, essentially depends on a benign theory of regulation, a public interest theory. But an alternative (less benign) regulatory theory is more convincing, based on public choice. In the latter theory, government is not thought to be operating in the public interest, but rather in the interest of powerful groups that put pressure on government to act in their narrow sectional self-interest, or in the interest of politicians. The discretion and absence of transparency that linkage brings with it contributes to the risk that those awarding the contract will succumb to corruption, vote-buying, or protectionist pressures. Consumers and taxpayers who would otherwise benefit from decreased costs and increased efficiency are poorly organized and ineffective watchdogs of

---

[13] F Maupain, 'Is the ILO effective in Upholding Workers' Rights? Reflections on the Myanmar Experience', in P Alston (ed), *Labour Rights as Human Rights* (OUP, 2005) 139.

the public interest, whereas those who gain from procurement linkages are likely to be well organized.[14]

Public choice theories identify an important feature of government regulation. McChesney has identified the power of regulation to 'create benefits that were unavailable other than through politics, or were more cheaply available through politics'.[15] These benefits are termed 'rents'. Government's ability, through procurement linkages, to restrict entry into markets 'can often perform rent-creating functions',[16] in ways unavailable to private parties. Where rents are created or maintained through 'the mechanism of law, including bureaucratic administration of law' they will be even more desirable.[17] The ability to legislate by establishing these rents makes them more durable and therefore more valuable than private sector rents.

Some procurement linkages can be seen as creating rents for those groups that have persuaded politicians to favour them. Government procurement, then, is a prime site for rent-seeking behaviour by people who 'hardly care about its overall welfare-economic implications as long as they gain personally'.[18] The benefits (rents) that result may be in the form of greater financial profits, or simply in the increased political clout that will accrue to an NGO which is seen to have lobbied successfully for its own constituency. Consumers, taxpayers, or other special interest groups may pay the losses. This basic model has been extended to predict that politicians may themselves benefit (whether financially or in terms of votes) not only by creating such rents that benefit particular groups, but even by threatening to regulate and then being 'paid' for *not* doing so (so called 'rent-extraction').[19] All in all, public procurement linkages seem tailor made for extensive rent-seeking, rent creation, and rent-extraction. They benefit politically organized groups at the cost of politically unorganized groups.[20]

Good governance objections

Here is the sixth argument. One of the features of procurement markets, as Trepte has argued,[21] is that principal-agent problems arise to a significant extent. The government (the principal) relies on purchasing officers (the agent) to ensure that the government's procurement policy is put into effect. This has often given rise to

---

[14] This argument is derived from J-J Laffont and J Tirole, *A Theory of Incentives in Procurement and Regulation* (MIT, 1993) 9.

[15] FS McChesney, *Money for Nothing: Politicians, Rent Extraction, and Political Extortion* (Harvard University Press, 1997) 11. [16] ibid 11.

[17] ibid 13. [18] ibid. [19] ibid 19.

[20] Different national jurisdictions have sought legal methods to restrict rent extraction. In the US, this has taken the form of the doctrine of unconstitutional conditions under which the government may not selectively threaten to deny certain privileges (licences, for example) in order to extract benefits from others, see *Nollan v California Coastal Commission* 483 US 825 (1987), and see generally R Epstein, *Bargaining with the State* (Princeton University Press, 1993).

[21] Trepte, Regulating (n 4 above) 13.

a complex web of regulation to ensure that the agent does what the principal wants. The process of government purchasing is, as Miller has observed, 'a complex, often tediously detailed operation'.[22] The more policies extraneous to the main purpose of the contract are taken into account, the more the process of awarding the public sector contract will have to become bureaucratized in order to deal with this problem. All of this tends to impede the procurement process and goes against the goal of trying to decrease bureaucratic constraints on business. 'To some extent', says Miller, 'delays in procurement occur as a result of these non-buying requirements'.[23] They place the 'burden of insuring adherence to their terms on Government personnel not trained to enforce statutes, and whose job it is to do something entirely unrelated to law enforcement'.[24]

The use of linkage to achieve some social policies may also result in overwhelming pressure to adopt more and more extraneous social policy requirements, over-burdening the procurement system, and thus defeating the primary purpose of procurement, which is to obtain the best goods for the lowest price.[25] The greater the number of social policy objectives incorporated into the process by which tenders are awarded, the more the process is likely to generate requirements that are contradictory, or at least in tension with each other. The larger the number of extraneous criteria taken into account, the less easy it is to predict the decision made on the award of a contract, and the more the problem arises of how to balance all of those considerations so that all of these legitimate considerations can be taken into account effectively. In the absence of government as a whole setting priorities, this will be left to the particular procuring entity, or (even worse) to the individual procurement officer. If social policy objectives are incorporated into the process by which tenders are awarded, the process may thus no longer be transparent. The larger the number of extraneous criteria which are taken into account, the less easy it is to predict the decision made on the award of a tender.

Abuse of power

Here is a seventh reason for scepticism about procurement linkages. Procurement is more likely to be harnessed by a public body to further a social goal in situations where that public body's ability to use other tools to further the social policy is limited for political, constitutional, or legal reasons. This illustrates the reason why linkage has been particularly popular in situations, for example in the United States, where, as we shall see in chapter 6 below, civil rights *legislation* proved difficult to achieve but the use of procurement was possible by *executive* action. Where different levels of government adopt different values on particular issues, or significantly differ on the means of delivering these values, then procurement is also likely to be used as a tool for the implementation of the contested value by the

---

[22] Miller (n 1 above) 54. [23] ibid. [24] ibid 55.
[25] PF Hannah, 'Government by Procurement' *The Business Lawyer*, July 1963, 997.

'lower' tier of government, because it may be one of the relatively few ways in which the lower tier can exercise regulatory power.

As a matter of good governance, however, sceptics see something rather distasteful in using a mechanism that seems so closely associated with evading democratic and constitutional controls. However valid the purpose, evading these controls by using linkage is in principle wrong and should not be encouraged. To the extent that there is a constitutional division of power within a country, between local authorities and central government, or between federal and state government, then evasion of this division of responsibilities by using procurement is unacceptable.

II. Arguments in Favour of Linkage

Can a positive theoretical case be made *for* procurement linkages? I believe, on balance, that it can. Again, these arguments derive from the theoretical literature and from my own experience.

Inadequacy of other methods of compliance with equality legislation

We saw in chapter 3 above that there is a growing concern in many countries that traditional mechanisms of securing status equality are not adequate. Orthodox legal methods of combating discrimination in employment, for example, have proved to be of limited effectiveness. The purpose of using linkage is, then, to bring an influence to bear indirectly on the exercise of business decisions. Its power lies in the firm's economic interest in obtaining orders from public authorities and linkage seeks to use this economic interest for the promotion of social policy objectives, usually in addition to the use of other regulatory approaches.[26]

Procurement linkages have been used as an additional mechanism of enforcement to secure both individual justice and group justice aims. Some types of procurement linkage are more associated with one, and some more with the other. Thus, for example, tender qualification approaches are more often associated with individual justice models, and set-asides or price preferences are more associated with jurisdictions that have adopted a group justice model. Where procurement linkages are used in the context of securing individual justice, the dominant emphasis of linkage is on a more traditional *prohibitory* approach to anti-discrimination enforcement. In the context of group justice approaches, procurement linkages often provide a more *incentive-based* method of anti-discrimination law enforcement.

The use of procurement is not usually the sole or even the primary method adopted to enforce equality. More frequently, it is but one of several other methods of enforcement that mutually reinforce each other. 'Contract compliance' measures

---

[26] L Osterloh, 'Rechtsgutachten zu Fragen der Frauenförderung im Rahmen der öffentlichen Mittelvergabe' (June 1991).

of the type made popular in the United States are combined with agency-type regulation and individual litigation to produce a raft of incentives for compliance with employment equality laws. When more orthodox command and control regulation seems of limited effectiveness, it is unsurprising, perhaps, that states resort to public procurement as one weapon in their armoury. The explanation for the popularity of linkage lies in part, then, in the comparative strength of procurement and, in part, in the comparative weakness of other regulatory mechanisms. The greater the public perception of a *compliance gap* between the aspirations towards equality incorporated in public policy, and its delivery in practice, the more likely it is that equality will be linked to public procurement.

Mainstreaming requires linkage

Second, the argument that linkage is unnecessary because other instruments are available runs directly counter to the recent major development in equality regulation discussed in chapter 3 above, ie that government and public bodies are increasingly required to weave equality into the fabric of decision-making across *all* spheres of government—in short, to 'mainstream' equality issues in public policy.[27] We have seen that underlying these attempts at mainstreaming is a common perception: that unless special attention is paid to the equality issue within government, it will become too easily submerged in the day-to-day concerns of policy makers who do not view that particular policy preference as central to their concerns. The increasing adoption of 'mainstreaming' equality issues into government policy increases the likelihood that public procurement becomes subject to equality disciplines. The argument is simply put: one area of government policy (procurement) should not cut across, and should where possible assist, the pursuit of other government policies (equality). An organization can hardly be said to be mainstreaming equality if it neglects to do so in its procurement functions, often leading to the adoption of procurement linkages.

Limits of a 'commercial' model of government contracting

We have seen that those who are sceptical of procurement linkages quite frequently assert the importance of ensuring that a 'commercial' approach should be taken by government in its contracting. There are several assumptions in this argument that those in favour of linkage challenge.

To begin with, it is clear that in some respects the difference between private contracting and public contracting has narrowed considerably regarding the use of linkages. Part of the corporate social responsibility (CSR) agenda is, as we shall see subsequently, to urge private firms to engage with their contractors in such a

---

[27] C McCrudden, *Mainstreaming Fairness* (CAJ, 1996); C McCrudden, *Benchmarks for Change: Mainstreaming Fairness in the Governance of Northern Ireland* (CAJ, 1998).

way as to gain the greatest possible social benefits, whether in terms of employment conditions or environmental benefits. We shall see examples in chapter 12 below of *private* firms aping *government's* incorporation of social issues in procurement. The idea has been widely promoted by government, indeed, that there are 'commercial' benefits to be gained from CSR. All this undermines the argument that following private sector procurement practices requires linkages to be avoided.

More importantly, the assumption of commonalities between public and private contracting is challenged at a more fundamental level. Selznick has made the perceptive point that 'governmental authority has an irreducibly comprehensive character. That is so because government (unlike the private sector) has inherent responsibility, and at least a minimum of implied authority', to protect the welfare of its citizens.[28]

Applied to government contracting, this implies that governments award public contracts on behalf of the communities that they serve. It is not unreasonable that these communities expect that public contracts should go to contractors who do not violate the basic norms of that community. The award of public contracts is not simply an economic activity by the administration, in which the administration can consider itself simply as equivalent to a private sector organization. This makes it difficult for a public purchaser to appear as an entirely neutral actor in the market place. Public purchasing activity can only to a limited extent be a separate area, one in which social criteria are ignored that are considered politically self-evident in other areas of state activity. It is unacceptable that government should allow those acting in its place to behave in ways in which government itself would not wish or be permitted to act, and in this context it seems not only permissible but an act of good government that social and political considerations should enter into the award of government contracts. Those acting at the behest of government, in its stead, and with its financing should at least uphold the norms that government would be held to, acting directly.[29] One important justification for linkages, then, relates to their signalling effect on the public. As Justice Brandeis said in *Olmstead* v *United States*: 'For good or ill, [government] teaches the whole people by its example.'[30]

Assisting the internalization of externalities

Such arguments are controversial, of course. Can arguments be articulated that are based less on any moral function for government and more on the economics of procurement? Two different sources of inequality are in issue: status inequality caused directly or indirectly by the government itself, and status inequality caused directly or indirectly by the private sector. Procurement linkages have a justified role to play in

---

[28] P Selzick, *Law, Society and Industrial Justice* (Russell Sage Foundation, 1969) 61.
[29] See in general BLR Smith (ed), *The New Political Economy: The Public Use of the Private Sector* (Macmillan, 1975).   [30] *Olmstead v United States*, 277 US 438, 485 (1928) (in dissent).

dealing with each of these sources of inequality. For the moment, I want to concentrate on the former issue: status inequality caused directly or indirectly by government itself. Sceptics of linkage appear to assume that the function of contracting is largely, from the point of view of status equality, a neutral activity. With the growth of governmental purchasing throughout the developed world, there have been many voices that have, however, seen the expansion of the use of public procurement as being far from neutral in its effects.[31] This is the starting point for a fourth positive argument for linkage.

During the 1980s and 1990s, extensive changes occurred in the delivery of public services, in part under pressures from global economic developments. This involved a combination of privatization, and contracting-out. The contractual method came to be seen by some as an important instrument of deregulation. It was argued by some, particularly trade unions, that procuring services from the private sector had distributional consequences for employees and consumers that needed to be taken into account in the initial decision on whether or not to use procurement. An important example of this was the proposal to contract out the delivery of services that had previously been delivered by government itself through its own directly employed workforce to private sector service deliverers employing workers not in public employment. It was argued that there was a significantly adverse effect on status equality in using procurement as the chosen method of delivery where wage rates in the private sector were significantly lower than in the private sector, and where those employed on procurement contracts were more likely to be women and ethnic minorities.

We can put this in more 'economic' language. One of the traditional justifications for government intervention in markets is the need to address market failures. One traditional category of market failure is where there are externalities. These arise when one person's production or consumption decision affects another person's production or consumption decision, without that effect being reflected in the market price. The spill over may be either to the benefit or detriment of the other person. The crucial point is that in neither case is the price related to the spill over: the person benefiting does not pay for the benefit; the person damaged is not compensated through a lower price. The classic externality is pollution from a factory affecting a neighbouring village. The cost of the pollution is not reflected in the price of the good sold by the factory. The role of government regulation is to require that the cost be internalized by the factory owner, for example by taxing the factory for polluting, or requiring that new technology be introduced to stop the pollution from occurring.

If the use of government contracting is more likely to produce reductions in status equality than other methods of delivering public services, procurement linkage may operate as a method of government intervention to internalize unacceptable externalities.[32] From this point of view, they are a means of assigning obligations to those

---

[31] See eg J D Hanrahan, *Government by Contract* (Norton, 1983) 21–6.
[32] Trepte, Regulating (n 4 above) 9–10 on externalities in procurement regulation.

best able to perform them.[33] Where procurement itself is thought likely to be the cause of status inequality or discrimination, the linkage between procurement and social policy is justified to limit or control the perceived damage.[34] The argument that this is not only justified but required is strengthened when one takes into account that the move to procurement may lead to a diminution of accountability because such contracts are often beyond more traditional administrative law controls, and are often negotiated in secret, in the absence of democratic political controls. Thus the role of procurement linkages in some contexts, is to reinsert what might be thought of as public values into a contractual context that would otherwise ignore or underestimate them.

Sustaining and increasing competition

What of the cost arguments against procurement linkages? They appear to underestimate significantly the costs of *not* intervening. To the extent that *in*equality results in reduced competition and, possibly, increased costs in any particular contract, there is a clear narrowly financial justification for government intervening to require, for example, non-discrimination in public procurement markets where this would result in lower costs to government in delivering that contract. There is, however, a broader economic argument for such linkages. A fifth argument in favour of linkage derives from the belief that exclusion of some from the market is damaging to everyone in that it deprives society of the benefits that would derive from their involvement and the greater competition that this would bring. Government regulation is necessary to ensure that significant groups in society (women, minorities) are included in important market activities in order for there to be an effective market in the first place.[35] Certain types of procurement linkages, such as set-asides or bidding preferences for minority-owned businesses, may be justified, therefore, on the basis that they have a 'market-creating function' which may reduce the cost of the procurement to the government by increasing the competition among bidders.[36]

Ian Ayres and Frederick Vars have developed arguments in support of the broader use of procurement linkages. Their argument is that the government has a role in addressing status discrimination by private actors where this has the effect of

---

[33] cf M Seidenfeld, 'An Apology for Administrative Law in "The Contracting State"' (2000) 28 Florida University Law Review 215.

[34] See eg in Scotland, STUC/Scottish Executive, PPP Employment Protocol, to be found at <http://www.unison-scotland.org.uk/briefings/protocolapp1.html>.

[35] S Deakin, 'Social Rights in a Globalized Economy' in P Alston (ed), *Labour Rights as Human Rights* (OUP, 2005) 55.

[36] Ayres and Crampton have provided some empirical support for this, based on a case study of a 1994 auction of licences by the Federal Communications Commission. I Ayres and P Crampton, 'How Affirmative Action at the FCC Auctions Decreased the Deficit' in I Ayres (ed), *Pervasive Prejudice?: Unconventional Evidence of Race and Gender Discrimination* (Chicago University Press, 2001) 315, 316.

reducing the number of minority firms that are able to contract with government, using its procurement power to address the discrimination in the private market by purchasing 'as much from minority firms as it would but for private discrimination'.[37] Government purchasing can be used, then, 'to correct shortfalls in government purchasing caused by private discrimination'.[38] Going further still, however, they argue that it is justified 'to correct shortfalls in private purchasing caused by private discrimination' in an even more extensive way.[39] If analysis suggests 'that minority businesses are selling less [in a particular market] than one would expect [without] discrimination, then the government may ... increase its purchases of that product from minority businesses to off set the private discrimination'.[40]

Supplying the 'public good' of equality

As we have seen, one of the traditional justifications for intervention by government in markets is the idea of market failure and, as argued above, a classic example of this relates to externalities. Market failure has also been identified in the supply of so-called 'public' goods.[41] This is the basis for a sixth argument in favour of linkages.

Public goods are those that 'even if consumed by one person can still be consumed by other people',[42] such as clean air. Since everyone can benefit if they are available, then it is in no one's interest to buy them, if they can simply free ride on someone else's purchase. Since the providers of the public good will not profit from the consumption of the good by those who consume it, public goods will not be provided through the market. The solution is for the government to intervene and establish a mechanism whereby the public good is supplied. We can conceptualize status equality as a public good that will not be adequately supplied in the absence of government intervention. Assuming that providing equality would cost more than the benefits it would produce to the individual firm, but that others in that society want more equality, then the market itself will not produce equality sufficient to satisfy that demand since everyone could consume it without paying for it, or it would be prohibitively expensive for any single individual to do so—a classic public good.

Procurement linkages are sometimes attempts by government to ensure the supply of this public good by 'buying' it from the employer, but on behalf of the public. As Trepte put it: 'the government is to be seen as disposing of the financial means ... as well as the material means and facilities necessary to render the service for the benefit of society as a whole and for which no private market exists or could exist at a reasonable price'.[43] The volume of public procurement and the limits

---

[37] I Ayres and FE Vars, 'When Does Private Discrimination Justify Public Affirmative Action?' (1998) 98 Columbia Law Review 1577, 1586.   [38] ibid 1587.
[39] ibid.   [40] ibid.   [41] Trepte, Regulating (n 4 above) 9–10.   [42] ibid 10.
[43] ibid 11.

placed upon direct social intervention by budgetary stringency make this an attractive area for buying these public goods. The greater the emphasis placed on the importance of the efficient use of tax expenditure, the more likely that the argument will be made that if it is possible to use procurement to deliver on necessary social policies, by piggybacking on other purchases, the more efficient that will be. A European Parliamentary Committee, for example, argued that 'the limits placed upon direct social expenditure by budgetary stringency make [procurement] an attractive area for the promotion of socially desirable outcomes'.[44]

III. Theoretical Issues and Legal Form

Achieving social change through regulation is immensely complex and uncertain. There is no consensus on what makes for an effective regulatory scheme. The wise policy maker, therefore, will not want to put all her eggs in one basket, and will want instead to keep a range of tools available with which to attempt to achieve the desired changes in behaviour. Achieving the benefits of the use of a particular regulatory instrument, whilst avoiding the pitfalls, is a complex policy challenge. What I have attempted in this chapter is to bring together largely theoretical arguments both for and against linking procurement with the goal of increased status equality. What emerges is a complex picture of apparently competing considerations that seem to be starkly at odds with each other. One of the aims of the remainder of the book is to describe in some detail how countries have attempted to deal with these issues, and assess the limited experience that we now have worldwide on the development and effects of procurement linkage, including the successes of such engagement, as well as its limits.

I have said nothing so far about the legal form in which procurement linkages are best presented. Nor have I said much about the legal limits on the use of linkages. A major argument against linkages is that they are frequently of questionable *legality*, whether under domestic law or under supranational legal obligations that states have accepted. Another task in the book is to engage in a detailed analysis of the relevant provisions in WTO, European, and domestic law. What emerges is, I think, a fascinating story in which law becomes a site for the working out of many of the arguments that I have presented as theoretical issues. In my experience, there are profound political and economic conflicts underlying the legal debates, and it is these that I wanted to identify in this chapter. This chapter, indeed the whole of Part I of this book, should be seen as an attempt to explore the deeper underpinnings of the policy debate than has been attempted in the past. Understanding these underpinnings, I argue, will help us to understand the way the law has evolved and should be interpreted.

---

[44] European Parliament, Committee on Employment and Social Affairs, Response to the Green Paper on Procurement Reform.

PART II

THE WORLD TRADE ORGANIZATION AND PROCUREMENT LINKAGES

6

Contract Compliance in the United States and Canada

In this chapter, we explore what are often considered to be the origins of procurement linkage as a tool for tackling employment discrimination on the basis of race, beginning in the United States during the Second World War, and continuing during the 1950s and 1960s, mutating into a mechanism for securing affirmative action. We trace the development of this approach up to the early 1990s. The expansion of this approach to cover other groups in the United States is then considered, in particular the use of procurement to encourage the development of access by disabled workers to information technology. We also consider the development of a type of procurement linkage in Canada that mirrors that of the United States: schemes that link the award of government contracts with attempts to secure 'employment equity' in employment for various groups—what we have called 'contract compliance' in our discussion of the United States in chapter 1 above, although the terminology is somewhat different in the Canadian context. Finally, we see how the International Labour Organization (ILO) has adopted this contract compliance approach.

I. Procurement Linkages and Equality for Black Americans

In chapter 2 above, it was shown that the use of procurement as a social policy tool in the United States was largely authorized through state legislatures or the federal Congress. We saw, however, some major exceptions to this, perhaps significantly its first use in the early nineteenth century, where the President of the United States used his powers to issue executive orders regulating the contracting power. We saw that, at least in part, the President used his executive powers because of the difficulty at that time of securing the type of reforming legislation that was necessary. At the beginning of the 1940s, another major use of Presidential powers arises, and for similar reasons.[1]

---

[1] In addition to the sources cited below, see L Ruchames, *Race, Jobs and Politics: The Story of FEPC* (Columbia University Press, 1953) 10–21.

Second World War and employment discrimination against black Americans

With the outbreak of the Second World War in 1939, and the consequent military mobilization and increased government expenditure on defence in the United States, the spectre of unemployment that had haunted the nation during the Depression appeared to be at an end, at least for white Americans. 'Unemployment rapidly decreased from over 8 million in 1940 to five and a half million in 1941 to 2 and a half million in 1942.'[2] With the decline in unemployment, the New Deal emergency employment measures were wound up, as workers found jobs in regular industry. The disbandment of these programmes was, however, a substantial problem for black Americans who (although still unequally) had benefited from these programmes. Only if they could also secure jobs in the sectors of the economy that were expanding so rapidly could they survive. Yet they were subject to substantial segregation in the armed forces, and substantial exclusion from defence industries. And when they were hired, they were relegated to the worst jobs. The War, then, presented black Americans with further evidence of their second-class status. Blacks, as usual, were last hired, first fired.[3]

However, the War also, paradoxically, presented black Americans with an opportunity to advance their long-advocated position that the federal government should act to prohibit discrimination in employment. The reason was simple: the War was loudly trumpeted as being fought against totalitarianism and for democracy, yet how could this be other than hypocritical given the status of black Americans?[4] One of the most important black American leaders at that time, A Philip Randolph, a leader of one of the main black trade unions, the Brotherhood of Sleeping Car Porters, brilliantly capitalized on this tension between reality at home and idealism abroad. Initially, Randolph focused on securing the desegregation of the armed forces, and thought, indeed, after meeting with President Roosevelt in September 1940 that he had secured the agreement of the President to intervene, but this proved to be illusory. Randolph determined that, in the future, more militant action would need to be taken, and that reliance on the goodwill of the President alone would not secure his goals. He upped the ante, deciding that the goal should henceforth not only be the desegregation of the armed forces, but also the opening up of defence industry jobs to black Americans. His tactics were equally radical. He proposed 'to have done with the tactics of entreaty and petition and to force the government's hand with a massive display of Negro strength'.[5]

---

[2] A E Kersten, *Race, Jobs, and the War: The FEPC in the Midwest. 1941–1946* (University of Illinois Press, 2000) 10.   [3] H Garfinkel, *When Negroes March* (The Free Press, 1959) 17–21.
[4] H Sitkoff, *A New Deal for Blacks: The Emergence of Civil Rights as a National Issue, Volume 1: The Depression Decade* (OUP, 1978) 298–9.
[5] D M Kennedy, *Freedom from Fear: the American People in Depression and War, 1929–1945* (OUP, 2001) 766.

That the pressure was put on the President rather than Congress was highly significant. The New Deal had, after all, largely been authorized by Congress rather than by the President acting without Congressional authorization. But whilst Southern Democrats were willing to vote in favour of the New Deal, they would not vote in favour of civil rights legislation, as was made embarrassingly clear when, in 1938, Senator Wagner failed to secure enough votes in favour of a cloture vote to end a Southern Democratic filibuster directed against his anti-lynching bill. The pattern established then was to be repeated for the next twenty-five years in the Senate: a civil rights Bill was presented, a filibuster was launched to delay it coming to a vote, the rest of the business of the Senate was stalled as the filibuster continued, and the two-thirds vote necessary to end the filibuster was defeated, ending the prospects of the Bill being enacted. In the case of the anti-lynching Bill, the filibuster lasted from January 1938 until the end of February and not one but two cloture votes failed to secure the requisite majority.[6]

Consequently, by the end of the 1930s, Congressional action against racial discrimination was seen as impossible. 'Southern Democrats and conservative Republicans blocked all legislative attempts to deal with the issue, including the first two federal fair employment practice bills introduced in early 1941. . . . If the [movement for racial equality] were to affect national policy, pressuring [the President] was its only practical course of action.'[7] But that would be no easy task. On the one hand, the President feared that taking too favourable a stand on racial issues, and thus antagonizing Southern senators, risked the defeat or delay of other legislation that he regarded as vital; the President 'would not risk the alienation of Southern Democrats and others upon whom the success of his programs rested for the chance of racial reforms'.[8] Yet there were political pressures from the other direction too. The increasing defection to the Republican Party of parts of the coalition that had kept him in power, made the votes of the increasingly urban, and increasingly Northern-based black voters more and more important to Roosevelt. Before the election of 1940, then, Roosevelt made various moves to garner black votes by issuing various policy statements against discrimination. That did little to placate the black leadership but rather contributed to their sense that the White House could be pressured to go further. 'His concessions had proved both the potential of black voting power and the possibility of utilizing the White House as an agency for racial reforms, stimulating the hopes of African-American leaders for further steps by the Chief Executive toward their goal of ending discrimination.'[9]

So too, the demands that Randolph and others were making were increasingly gaining ground in the state legislatures. We have seen in chapter 2 above that the states were effectively social laboratories, and that moves made in the states regarding

---

[6] JJ Huthmacher, *Senator Robert F Wagner and the Rise of Urban Liberalism* (Atheneum, 1968) 239–43.   [7] Kersten (n 2 above) 16.
[8] ibid 301.   [9] Sitkoff (n 4 above) 309.

the use of government contracts for social purposes often presaged subsequent federal action, and this proved to be the case in this context too. In 1933, 'the Chicago branch of the NAACP [National Association for the Advancement of Colored People, the main black civil rights organisation at that time] had African-American State Representative Charles J. Jenkins of Cook County'[10] introduce a Bill to prohibit discrimination in employment under contracts for public buildings and public works.[11] Subsequently, New Jersey and Pennsylvania 'adopted the Illinois model'.[12] In 1941, New York made 'discrimination by public officials or by defense contractors because of race, color, or creed a misdemeanor punishable by fines'.[13] Subsequently, a New York Committee on Discrimination in Employment was established to receive complaints.

In 1941, Randolph decided to organize a demonstration by 10,000 black Americans in the heart of Washington, DC, and established a broadly based March on Washington Committee. The President 'feared the possibility of an outbreak of violence by Washington whites and police against the demonstrators. He wanted to avoid the embarrassment of a racial protest in the nation's capital.'[14] He invited Randolph and Walter White, head of the NAACP, to a meeting at the White House two weeks before the planned demonstration. The black leadership's demand was simple and direct: unless the President issued executive orders prohibiting discrimination in the defence industries, government employment, and the armed forces, the march would go ahead. Eventually, the President agreed to appoint a committee headed by the Mayor of New York, Fiorello LaGuardia, to work on the issue. During these negotiations, the White House was initially unwilling to concede anything other than restrictions on discrimination in defence industry employment. Eventually, the black leadership agreed, provided that the order included government employment as well.[15] On 25 June 1941, seven days after the White House meeting, the President issued Executive Order 8802. It provided that there 'shall be no discrimination in the employment of workers in defense industries or government because of race, creed, color or national origin'. Contracting agencies of government were required to include in all contracts a provision requiring the contractor not to discriminate on grounds of race. Both employers and unions had a duty 'to provide for the full and equitable participation of all workers in defense industries'. A President's Committee on Fair Employment Practice was established and given powers to investigate complaints and impose remedies where the grievances were found to be valid. The March on Washington was called off.

The Committee was both politically and legally a weak creature. 'Initially the Committee had a part-time staff of eleven and a modest yearly budget of eighty

---

[10] Kersten (n 2 above) 25.

[11] Approved 8 July 1933, 58th General Assembly, Illinois Laws 1933, 296.

[12] ME Reed, *Seedtime for the Modern Civil Rights Movement: The President's Committee on Fair Employment Practice, 1941–1946* (Louisiana State University Press, 1991) 16.   [13] ibid 16

[14] Sitkoff (n 4 above) 317.   [15] Sitkoff (n 4 above) 321.

thousand dollars'.[16] When it was clear that there was substantial violation of the Order, the President issued a second Executive Order in 1943,[17] which increased its budget to half a million dollars, and replaced the part-time staff with a full-time staff distributed in regional offices.[18] But opposition from sections of Congress grew. The 'funds of the reconstituted FEPC [Fair Employment Practices Committee] were brought under congressional control by a measure forbidding the use of appropriations for agencies created by executive order after one year unless specifically authorized by statute. Thus the hope that Congress could be by-passed, with appropriations drawn from the President's general emergency funds, was shattered.'[19] This provision (the so-called Russell amendment) effectively killed off the FEPC.

Following the Second World War

Despite these restrictions, however, the political attractiveness of regulating by executive order continued for subsequent presidents, given the absence of other federal regulatory tools that could be used. Between 1943 and 1961, a considerable number of similar executive orders were issued by successive presidents regarding employment discrimination.[20] Of particular relevance for our purposes, several took the Roosevelt approach of using the government's contracting power as the principal means of addressing private industry practices. In February 1951, President Truman issued Executive Order 10210 authorizing the Secretaries of the Department of Defence and the Department of Commerce to require nondiscrimination in employment on government contracts, but without any equivalent to the FEPC. After pressure, Truman issued another executive order in December 1951, creating the President's Committee on Government Contract Compliance, although it was advisory only.[21] President Eisenhower reconstituted this Committee in August 1953, giving Vice President Nixon the role of chairing it.[22]

The greatest importance of the Roosevelt fair employment committee lay, perhaps, in the stimulus it gave to the movement for permanent legislation authorizing a more broadly based and more powerful FEPC. As the Committee's reputation grew, the opinion that legislation could help to eliminate discrimination gained support. Civil, religious, labour, and black American organizations demanded increasingly that the Committee's lessons be applied on state and municipal levels and that Congress enact employment discrimination legislation. When it again became clear that efforts in the federal Congress were unlikely to be successful, civil rights organizations increased their pressure on the state legislatures. The first such state FEPC

---

[16] Kersten (n 2 above) 19.   [17] Executive Order No 9346 (1943).
[18] Kennedy (n 5 above) 774.   [19] Garfinkel (n 3 above) 149.
[20] Executive Orders Nos 9980 (1948), 9981 (1948), 10210 (1951), 10308 (1951), 10479 (1953), 10590 (1955), 10925 (1961), 10988 (1962).   [21] Executive Order 10308 (1951).
[22] Executive Order 10479 (1953).

legislation was enacted in New York in 1945. Other state legislatures were soon flooded with similar Bills. At least twenty state legislatures, and Congress, considered some form of equal employment opportunity law during the spring of 1945 alone, and the New York legislation served as a precedent for many of these. By the end of 1959, sixteen states had fair employment laws substantially modelled on the New York Act. So too, between 1945 and 1965, at least twenty large cities adopted similar FEPC ordinances.[23]

In the federal Congress, however, legislation against employment discrimination did not pass until 1964. Effective legislation was impossible in a Congress where Southern Democrats and conservative Republicans were sufficiently powerful to resist any significant breach in segregation.[24] Though far from constituting a majority, the organization and procedures of the Congress enabled them to block legislation of which they disapproved and this continued until the early 1960s.[25]

President Kennedy, on election, faced the same major problems in securing civil rights legislation as had his predecessors: the Congressional procedural roadblocks of legislative committees, the House Rules Committee and Senate filibusters. In addition, like Roosevelt, Kennedy wanted to preserve the possibility of other social and economic legislation that would have been damaged if the Administration had forced the issue of civil rights legislation. The combination of these factors led to a decision early in the life of the Administration not to press for civil rights legislation, preferring litigation and executive action.[26] He too, followed the route of his predecessors in issuing executive orders, including one relating to government contracts.

Approaches to enforcement

President Kennedy's Committee on Equal Employment Opportunity (PCEEO) placed considerable emphasis on voluntary compliance, despite its ability to operate sanctions against defaulting contractors. In 'Plans for Progress', as these voluntary agreements were called, businesses agreed to carry out certain actions in order to further equal opportunity. Within a year of the Lockheed Agreement, the first of these Plans for Progress, 'dozens of defense contractors as well as labor unions followed suit'.[27] George Reedy, Vice President Johnson's full-time assistant on racial matters, privately attributed two great virtues to Plans for Progress: 'It was

---

[23] JP Witherspoon, *Administrative Implementation of Civil Rights* (University of Texas Press, 1968).

[24] See eg R Kluger, *Simple Justice: The History of Brown v. Board of Education and Black America's Struggle for Equality* (Alfred A Knopf, 1976) 166.

[25] RW Bolling, *House Out of Order* (Dutton, 1966) 201–2. See also JA Robinson, 'The Role of the Rules Committee in Arranging the Program of the U.S. House of Representatives' (1959) 12(3) Western Political Quarterly 653. Very limited action was taken in the Civil Rights Acts of 1957 and 1960. Neither of these Acts touched on employment discrimination.

[26] HC Fleming, 'The federal executive and civil rights: 1961–1965' (1965) 94(Fall), Daedalus 921–48.

[27] CM Brauer, *John F. Kennedy and the Second Reconstruction* (Columbia University Press, 1979) 81.

"more likely than any other approach to really do something for Negroes" who needed jobs and were victimized by discrimination and it so involved PCEEO "in constructive activities that the temptation to the committee staff to become a cop with a nightstick chasing down individual cases would be held to a minimum" '.[28]

Plans for Progress did, no doubt, create a climate in which it became acceptable for some firms to desegregate plants and employ black Americans in what had hitherto been closed positions. Voluntary acceptance of the need to improve the economic position of the black worker did take place in individual companies.[29] But in terms of achieving an overall improvement in the employment situation of blacks it was later seen to be largely unsuccessful,[30] and because of this it came under increasing criticism both within and outside the Committee, and was quietly dropped.[31]

Civil rights legislation and contract compliance

It was not until the political climate changed dramatically in the middle of 1963 that effective federal legislation became a real possibility. Demonstrations and rioting in Birmingham, Alabama during April and May 1963 precipitated a major volte-face in Administration policy. Black demonstrators demanding access to restaurants, lunch counters, and jobs were subjected to mass arrests by state authorities. After the bombing of the motel in which the leader of the demonstrators, Martin Luther King, was staying, rioting broke out and the Birmingham police reacted with violence to suppress it. Pictures of snarling police dogs set on black demonstrators were seen throughout the nation. And Birmingham was only the most publicized of a growing number of demonstrations against segregation. During the week of 25 May 1963, according to the Justice Department, demonstrations took place in thirty-three Southern and ten Northern communities.[32] Birmingham and these other demonstrations presented both the excuse and the spur for a major change in Administration policy. President Kennedy asked his brother, Robert, to prepare a legal response to avert further Birminghams.[33] By mid-May, a firm decision to seek legislation to deal with the type of problem that had generated Birmingham appears to have been made by the President. At a press conference on 22 May, the President spoke of the need to develop a 'legal outlet' as an alternative to demonstrations.[34]

---

[28] ibid.

[29] See L Ferman, *The Negro and Equal Employment Opportunities: A Review of Management Experiences in Twenty Companies* (Praeger, 1968) 39.

[30] cf JC Harvey, *Civil Rights During the Kennedy Administration* (University and College Press of Mississippi, 1971) 47–8; DF Sullivan, *Civil Rights Programs of the Kennedy Administration* (University Microfilms International, 1986) 281.

[31] AM Schlesinger, Jr, *Robert Kennedy and His Times* (Reissue edn, Ballantine Books, 1996) 335–7.

[32] See JL Sundquist, *Politics and Policy: the Eisenhower, Kennedy, and Johnson years* (The Brookings Institution, 1968) 260–1.   [33] Brauer(n 27 above) 239.

[34] ibid 249.

The political and procedural restrictions that had previously prevented an effective Civil Rights Bill from passing continued to make themselves felt in the form and content of the Civil Rights Bill. Of overriding importance was the necessity of securing passage in the Senate. To achieve this, Republican cooperation, (particularly that of Senator Dirksen), was necessary, and the price paid was the resulting comparatively weak compromise package.[35] After much revision and debate, and the intervening death of President Kennedy in November 1963, the Civil Rights Act, including Title VII prohibiting employment discrimination by many private employers and establishing an enforcement agency the Equal Employment Opportunities Commission (EEOC), was passed in the summer of 1964.

Not surprisingly, in view of the weaknesses of Title VII and in view of the deteriorating racial situation in the South and increasingly in the North, focusing on employment discrimination issues among other grievances, President Johnson kept the executive order tool. Indeed, he strengthened and expanded it. In September 1965, Executive Order 11246 abolished the President's Committee on Equal Employment Opportunity and established a new administrative and enforcement structure for contract compliance.[36] Partly in response to Congressional pressure, the 1965 Order placed the Secretary of Labor rather than the Vice-President in charge of the contract compliance programme. He was authorized to investigate compliance with the requirements of the order, exempt contractors from its requirements when the national interest so required, and invoke a variety of sanctions for non-compliance. These included cancelling contracts, conditioning their continuance upon a programme of future compliance, barring contractors from future contracts if found in violation of the order, and recommending that enforcement action be commenced against a violator by the Department of Justice or the EEOC. The order further allowed the Secretary of Labor to delegate his functions or duties, 'except authority to promulgate rules and regulations of a general nature'.[37]

The Secretary of Labor delegated most of his duties to the Office of Federal Contract Compliance (OFCC), which was set up in the Labor Department in 1966.[38] The OFCC in turn sub-delegated its task of enforcement to the various federal agencies and departments that placed the contracts.[39] Those agencies and departments had the primary responsibility for securing compliance with the

---

[35] Several features of Title VII reflect this compromise: the anti-quota rule; the stipulation that professionally developed tests were acceptable; the acceptance of bona fide seniority systems; the enforcement provisions which did not provide the EEOC with enforcement powers; the deferral by Title VII agencies to state FEPCs; the limitations on the power of the EEOC to require the keeping of records by employers. See further FJ Vaas, 'Title VII: Legislative History' (1966) 7 Boston College Industrial & Commercial Law Review 431.   [36] Executive Order 11246, 3 CFR 169 (1965).

[37] Executive Order 11246, s 401.

[38] RP Nathan, *Jobs and Civil Rights: The role of the Federal Government in promoting equal opportunity in employment and training* (US Govt Printing Office, 1969) 101.

[39] 41 CFR, para 60-1, 60-1.20(c).

order. The OFCC 'retained essentially only the functions of providing guidance, co-ordination, standardization and review',[40] and giving approval to the use of sanctions in particular cases.

Affirmative action under the Executive Order

Of most importance for our understanding of the role procurement linkage played in the context of United States racial equality is an appreciation of how significant the contract mechanism was (and is) in enforcing an approach that goes beyond what was required under the statutes authorized by Congress. There is, therefore, a continuation of the theme already identified, that the contracting power is used in circumstances where the Executive cannot, or does not wish to, get statutory authority for the approach it prefers to adopt. In the United States, under Executive Order 11246, first promulgated by President Johnson,[41] but still the basis of the programme, government contractors have the obligation (a) not to discriminate against any employee or applicant for employment on the basis of race, colour, religion, sex, or national origin, *and* (b) to take *affirmative action* measures to ensure equality of opportunity. It is the affirmative action obligation that takes the executive order beyond what Title VII requires.

In the late 1950s, the Nixon Committee had drawn attention, in its reports and in its operations, to the need to go beyond the goal of simple non-discrimination. What was later to be termed 'affirmative action' in employment has its roots in this period, and in this institutional context. The Committee's compliance officers were directed to use 'every means of persuasion, conciliation and mediation' to have contractors, for example, 'select qualified minority group personnel for apprenticeship and on-the-job training'.[42] In negotiations with employers, the United States Civil Rights Commission (USCRC) reported that: 'The Committee often attempted to foster minority group employment by urging the hiring of Negroes on a limited preferential basis, i.e. of giving preference to a Negro applicant where he and a white applicant were equally qualified.'[43] As the Committee observed: 'Administration of the compliance program was designed not only to provide a measure of the effectiveness of the non-discrimination program and to permit corrective action in the absence of specific complaints, but to foster fuller utilization of minority group manpower.'[44]

At least one agency, the Public Housing Administration, went further by setting quotas, until 1958, in the construction projects financed under it by federal grants. These quotas 'were based upon the number of Negro skilled and unskilled workers, respectively employed in construction work in the locality of the projects

---

[40] J de J Pemberton, Jr, (ed), *Equal employment opportunity: responsibilities, rights, remedies* (New York: Practising Law Institute, 1975) 52.   [41] 30 Fed Reg 12319 (24 September 1965).
[42] USCRC, 1961 Report, 61–2.   [43] ibid 62.   [44] ibid 68.

in relation to the total number of skilled and unskilled workers so employed, as reflected by the latest Federal Census and other relevant data'.[45]

To some extent, such policies met a need for administrative convenience because they were easier to apply and monitor, but a more compelling reason lay in the realization of the type of problem that it was necessary to combat. In its 1961 Report, the USCRC observed:

Part of the problem is sometimes an unwillingness on the part of Negroes to apply for jobs that have always been closed to them, coupled with lack of information as to jobs that have in fact been opened on a non-discriminatory basis. Affirmative recruitment may be necessary during a transitional period to overcome past discriminatory employment practices. But even this initial recruitment may not be sufficient to counteract the feeling on the part of many Negroes that it is futile to apply for non-traditional jobs.[46]

Another report noted that 'by 1960, the view was developing that passive non-discrimination was not enough'.[47]

The term 'affirmative action' was itself adopted explicitly as an additional requirement in President Kennedy's Executive Order.[48] An example of what was meant by it was provided by the May 1961 agreement with the Lockheed Corporation concerning their Marietta, Georgia plant. In the agreement,[49] Lockheed, which had been found to have discriminated in the past, agreed that they would 'aggressively seek out more qualified minority group candidates in order to increase the number of employees' in many job categories. This 'Plan for Progress' was to be implemented, *inter alia*, by recruiting at black colleges, by publicizing the commitment, by re-analysing its openings for salaried jobs 'to be certain that all eligible group employees had been considered for placement and upgraded', by re-examining personnel records of minority group employees to make certain that employee skill and potential beyond current job requirements had been properly identified for use in filling job openings, and by making a commitment to non-discriminatory admission to apprenticeship training.

A growing emphasis on results became apparent in the Department of Labor's emforcement of the Executive Order issued by President Johnson. Results were increasingly stressed by OFCC administrators, although how employers were to bring these results about was initially left largely undefined. Executive Order 11246 required 'affirmative action' to accomplish its aims, but this was as undefined in

---

[45] US Housing and Home Finance Agency, Terms and Conditions, Form No PHA—3001, s 304(B) (1956).   [46] USCRC, 1961 Report, 61.

[47] Potomac Institute, Affirmative Action: The Unrealized Goal. A decade of opportunity (The Potomac Institute, Inc, 1973) 6–7. See also, 'Note: The Philadelphia Plan: A Study in the Dynamics of Executive Power' (1972) 39 University of Chicago Law Review 723, 726.

[48] The term was originally used in the National Labor Relations Act 1935, s 10(c) to define the powers of the NLRB to fashion remedies in labor disputes.

[49] USCRC, 1961 Report, 78–9.

the new order as it was in the old. The statement in January 1967 by the Director of the OFCC illustrates the approach that was taken at that time:

Affirmative action is going to vary from time to time, from day to day, place to place, from escalation to escalation. It depends upon the nature of the area in which you are located, it depends upon the kinds of people who are there, it depends upon the kind of business that you have. There is no fixed and firm definition of affirmative action. I would say that in a general way affirmative action is anything that you have to do to get results. But this does not necessarily mean preferential treatment. The key word here is 'results'.[50]

A new toughness of approach, a growing emphasis on results, and a consequent fear that the programme would be labelled as one of preferential treatment for black Americans, are the dominant characteristics of the enforcement of the executive order during the 1960s after the enactment of Title VII. However, with the growing unrest in the major urban centres, culminating in the Watts riots of 1967, a new urgency overcame the fear of controversy. With Northern cities burning, action was needed quickly. The Kerner Report provided both a diagnosis of the problem and a proposed remedy, urging in part increased enforcement of both Title VII and the executive order.

A more explicit approach to what affirmative action required developed first in the OFCC's approach to the construction industry. The NAACP had focused on the problems of discrimination in construction for nearly two decades and had made it 'the central symbol for our time of the quest for equality in employment opportunity'.[51] For black workers, access to construction jobs was, according to Herbert Hill, the Labor Director of the NAACP, 'of unique importance'.[52] Construction was a huge industry with considerable growth potential. Wages in the industry were amongst the highest in the nation. The building trade represented a major area of the economy that could provide new job opportunities at high wages for large numbers of unemployed or underemployed black workers. In addition, jobs in the building trade were also highly visible. Much new construction at that time (including urban renewal, the Model Cities programme, and the construction of roads and public housing) was in, or very near, large black communities. The construction industry was also highly dependent on public funds in that the federal government was directly responsible for at least one-third of all money spent on construction throughout the country at that time.

From its inception, the OFCC handled construction contracts differently from other government contracts subject to the executive order. Construction employment was temporary and no fixed site of operations existed; nor did construction contractors maintain regular workforces. The demand for labour in the construction industry was characterized by sharp peaks and troughs, as contractors hired labour for specific jobs and then laid them off when the job was over. In addition,

---

[50] Nathan (n 38 above) 93.
[51] A Fletcher, *The Silent Sell-Out: Government Betrayal of Blacks to the Craft Unions* (Third Press, 1974) 64.   [52] H Hill, *Racism and Organized Labor* (NAACP, 1971).

the demand for labour was affected by problems of seasonality (in that not all work could be done in all weathers) and by the general level of business in the construction industry.[53] Job selection was usually based on a combination of union membership and seniority. Labour was usually referred to contractors by the relevant union. The OFCC was never given enforcement authority over the practices of construction unions.

For these reasons, OFCC officials developed a new method of ensuring compliance with the requirements of the order.[54] Beginning in 1965, area coordinators were established in more than a dozen metropolitan areas to try to improve minority construction employment within the entire labour market of that metropolitan area. Special area programmes were developed in some of these areas. These plans, in their most comprehensive form, attempted to establish a coordinated approach by all the federal contractors operating in that area to tackle discrimination in construction jobs. All federal agencies in selected areas with construction in progress or pending were expected to participate and the same rules and guidelines were to be used on all contracts.[55]

The first such special area plan was developed in St Louis in January 1966. It resulted apparently from local minority group agitation against job discrimination on a large, federally funded construction job. This work might have provided job opportunities for many black workers, but did not. Some of the trade unions were importing white craftsmen rather than hiring local black craftsmen. Eventually, a compromise was agreed, permitting some minority group contractors to receive sub-contracts on the job.[56] In March 1967, a 'Cleveland Plan' required affirmative action programmes to assure black representation 'in all trades and in all phases of the work'.[57] The subsequent development of the content of this 'affirmative action' requirement was heavily influenced by *Ethridge v Rhodes*,[58] a federal district court case decided in May 1967. Originally sponsored by the NAACP, the plaintiffs sought to enjoin the state of Ohio from entering a contract for the construction of part of Ohio State University on the ground that it was in breach of the Fourteenth Amendment. Such a contract, it was argued, represented state participation in racial discrimination. In particular, discrimination by craft unions was alleged. An injunction was granted. In *Ethridge*, the NAACP proposed the principle that: 'Government agencies [should] require a contractual commitment from building contractors to employ a specific number of black and other minority workers in each craft at every stage of construction.'[59]

In June 1967, during pre-award negotiations, a contractor proposed that he adopt a table specifying the number of skilled workers he would use on the job

[53] Fletcher (n 51 above) 63.
[54] USCRC, Federal Civil Rights Enforcement Effort 1971, 53.   [55] ibid.
[56] ibid 54.   [57] Nathan (n 38 above) 109.   [58] 268 F Supp 83 (SD Ohio 1967).
[59] H Hill, 'Labor union control of job training: A critical analysis of apprenticeship outreach programs and the hometown plans' (Occasional paper—Institute for Urban Research, Howard University; Vol 2, No 1) 15.

and the number in each trade who would be members of the minority group. Shortly after that, a decision was made by the federal agencies involved to require similar 'manning tables' for all the federal construction contractors in the seven-county Cleveland area. The agencies required that at a pre-award conference (ie a meeting between prospective contractors and federal officials held prior to the acceptance of the winning bid) contractors should agree to a set of minority manning tables for the construction contract.[60] Awards on federal construction contracts worth US$80 million were delayed pending compliance with these new requirements. By mid-November, Cleveland contractors had committed themselves to hiring 110 minority craftsmen out of total crews of 474 in the mechanical trades and for operating engineers.[61]

A similar approach was taken in the original 'Philadelphia Plan' initiated in November 1967. It, too, required a pre-award commitment on a detailed affirmative action plan which would result in an increase in minority employment in eight technical trades. The Plan was based on a finding that there was significant discrimination by building trade unions in the Philadelphia metropolitan area and that voluntary efforts to change the situation had been ineffectual.[62] These manning tables came under strong attack from the organized labour movement. Secretary of Labor, W Willard Wirtz, in a speech to the AFL-CIO building and construction trades department in November 1967, stressed the exceptional nature of the Philadelphia and Cleveland circumstances and indicated that the approach adopted in those Plans would not be repeated. In those cases, he said:

> . . . the Government contract situation had gotten so bad with antagonism and recrimination piled on top of each other to the point where symbolism was more important than substance, evidence more important than equity that there was probably no effective alternative to that kind of ruling. But it isn't right as a general principle and it won't work. Even if it drags someone who worships his prejudice into line it demeans somebody who has done the right thing for the right reason.[63]

Organized labour opposition to 'quotas' was supplemented by the intervention of the United States Comptroller General. In an opinion issued in May 1968, he ruled that companies could not be asked to bid on federally assisted construction contracts unless they were first informed about the specific affirmative action obligations which would run with the contract. Since the manning table requirement was not in the bid specification but rather was later negotiated between the contractor and the federal contracting official, the Comptroller General found it unlawful.[64] In a further opinion issued in November 1968, the Comptroller General held that the Philadelphia Plan was in violation of competitive bidding

---

[60] USCRC, Federal Civil Rights Enforcement Effort, 1971, 54.
[61] Nathan (n 38 above) 109.
[62] USCRC, Federal Civil Rights Enforcement Effort, 1971, 54–5.
[63] Nathan (n 38 above) 110–11.
[64] USCRC, Federal Civil Rights Enforcement Effort, 1971, 54.

principles in that it required affirmative action requirements to be determined after bids had been made:

...where Federally assisted contracts are required to be awarded on the basis of publicly advertised competitive bidding, award may not properly be withheld...on the basis of an unacceptable affirmative action program until provision is made for informing prospective bidders of definite minimum requirements to be met by the bidders' program and any other standards or criteria by which the acceptability of such program would be judged.[65]

After the 1968 election in which Richard Nixon was elected President, George Schultz was appointed Secretary of Labor and Arthur Fletcher Assistant Secretary of Labor. According to Fletcher, shortly after he took office, the OFCC staff proposed that 'specific percentage targets for minority employees in several trades be set forth in Philadelphia and incorporated in the bid specification in all Government contracts issued in that area. OFCC wished to be specific with respect to numbers and then impose a "good faith" obligation to achieve the numerical result.'[66] This was designed, on the one hand, to counter the argument that the numbers constituted quotas and violated the 'no quota' provision of Title VII. On the other hand, it was also intended to satisfy the requirement of the Comptroller General that bid specifications be specific and notified to bidders prior to their bids.

In March 1969, black groups in Philadelphia began another series of mass demonstrations at major federal contractors' construction sites. Demonstrations were also held to protest against the discriminatory practices of the operating engineers' union at several state highway construction projects. These and other demonstrations protested in particular about the failure of federal agencies to enforce the law as well as the continued exclusion of black workers from jobs in large-scale public contractor construction programmes. Subsequently, three days of public hearings were held by the OFCC about the exclusion of non-whites from jobs in the construction industry in Philadelphia. With the support of Secretary Schultz, a revised Philadelphia Plan was issued in June 1969. The Plan contained Department of Labor documentation of the virtually total exclusion of black Americans from seven crafts. It stated that the small number of black workers employed in these trades was due to the practices of unions in excluding black workers from membership in the union or from apprenticeship programmes.

Contractors on federal or federally-assisted construction in the Philadelphia area exceeding US$500,000 were required to submit acceptable affirmative action programmes including specific 'goals' or 'ranges' of minority employment in the form of minimum percentage requirements established by the Department of Labor in these trades. These goals were taken to express the contractor's commitment to the percentage of minority personnel who would be working in each specified craft or trade during the term of the contract. In the event that contractors failed to meet their goals, they were given an opportunity to demonstrate that they had

---

[65] 48 Comptroller General 666 (1968).   [66] Fletcher (n 51 above) 64–5.

made every 'good faith effort' to meet them. Only in the event that this 'good faith effort' was not demonstrated would a contractor be declared in breach of the executive order.

Despite the Revised Plan ostensibly taking into account the objections that had rendered the first Plan invalid, on 5 August 1969 the Comptroller General ruled that the Philadelphia Plan violated the prohibition on quotas in the Civil Rights Act. The distinction advanced by the OFCC between 'goals' and 'quotas' was rejected as largely a matter of semantics, since the purpose of both these was to have contractors commit themselves to considering race in hiring new employees.[67] In response, Secretary of Labor Schultz said that the Plan would go ahead, basing his authority on the opinions of both the Attorney General and, separately, of the Solicitor of Labor. The Comptroller General did not have the authority to interpret the Civil Rights Act and therefore ruling against the Plan was outside his powers. Nor did the Civil Rights Act require obliviousness or indifference to the racial consequences of alternative courses of action that involved the application of outwardly neutral criteria. Indeed, in a reference to *Ethridge v Rhodes*, in some circumstances the Philadelphia Plan approach might even be required and not just permitted.[68]

The second part of the revised Philadelphia Plan was issued in September 1969. It affirmed the June 1969 Plan, amending it to establish minority group employment ranges for the next four years. The September order made findings that minority group participation in the trade unions ranged from a high of 1.76 per cent (electricians) to a low of 0.15 per cent (plumbers and pipe fitters) and that minority craftsmen were available but were not admitted into the unions. It required contractors to commit themselves to hire from 4 to 9 per cent minority workers in 1970, 9 to 15 per cent in 1971, 14 to 20 per cent in 1972, and 19 to 26 per cent in 1973. Ranges were given to each of the six skilled trades that had virtually no black members or referrals in 1969, with the aim of increasing minority participation to 20 per cent over a four-year period. The significance of the Plan, as Herbert Hill pointed out, was that 'for the first time the concept of mandatory minimum percentage requirements for the employment of black workers in specific job classifications was included in government procedure for enforcing civil rights laws in the building trades'.[69]

On 29 September 1969, the Department of Labor announced that similar plans would become effective in New York, Seattle, Boston, Los Angeles, San Francisco, St Louis, Detroit, Pittsburgh, and Chicago.[70] The extension of the Philadelphia Plan approach seems to have been not unconnected with the mass protests against racial bias in construction jobs in the latter two cities during the summer (Pittsburgh) and autumn (Chicago).[71]

---

[67] 49 Comptroller General 59 (1969).   [68] Hill, Labor Union Control (n 59 above) 21.
[69] ibid 22.   [70] Congressional Quarterly Almanac, 1969, 418.
[71] LA Sobel, *Job bias* (Facts on File, 1976) 26–29.

Due to a combination of administrative need and union pressure, the OFCC developed and encouraged what became known as 'home-town' plans.[72] These voluntary agreements between unions, construction contractors, and representatives of the minority community were negotiated for a particular metropolitan area and usually contained employment and training goals and timetables for specific skilled trades. The OFCC 'assisted' the groups during negotiations. The first such 'home-town' plan was developed in Chicago in 1970.[73] The Chicago Plan sought to increase, over five years, minority participation in the industry proportionate to their percentage in the Community. It covered all construction in the Chicago area; it established an overall planning committee representing the three parties (a coalition of minority groups, contractors, and unions); and it laid the foundation of the sub-committees to be established for each participating construction craft union to develop actual details of the plan.[74] George Meany, head of the AFL-CIO, praised the Chicago Plan as 'truly a home town product . . . vastly superior to any government-imposed quota system—which is, of course, artificial and discriminatory'.[75] Shortly after the Chicago Plan was developed, the OFCC issued a model area-wide agreement for the guidance of communities seeking to develop other similar local plans.[76] Dissatisfaction with these voluntary plans increased, however. The OFCC announced that if a 'hometown solution' to the problem of the exclusion of minorities was not reached in eighteen selected cities, it was prepared to install a federal Plan similar to that imposed in Philadelphia in each of the cities. This was later done in several cities.[77] Subsequently, even in Chicago, the hometown plan collapsed and a plan was imposed by the OFCC.[78]

Legal challenges unsuccessful

The Sub-committee on Separation of Powers of the Senate Judiciary Committee held hearings in October 1969 to determine whether the Executive Branch (the Attorney General) had breached the principle of the separation of powers by his action. Subsequently, the Appropriations Committee of the Senate introduced a rider to the 1970 Supplementary Appropriations Bill which would have forbidden the use of any federal funds as direct aid or through contracts or agreements which the Comptroller General 'holds to be in contravention of any Federal Statute'.[79] This would have barred funds for the contracts in which the Philadelphia Plan requirements were incorporated. In December, the Bill passed the Senate with the rider included. In the House, the Bill was passed without the rider. The House-Senate Conference Committee then convened and the House conferees agreed to the Senate rider and the Bill was returned to both chambers for a second

---

[72] USCRC, Federal Civil Rights Enforcement Effort, 1971, 65–6.   [73] ibid.
[74] ibid.   [75] Quoted in Hill, Labor Union Control (n 59 above) 71.
[76] USCRC, 1971 Report, 64.   [77] ibid 66.
[78] Hill, Labor Union Control (n 59 above) 75–7.   [79] HR 15209 (1970).

vote. However, following 'enormous pressure' from President Nixon, the House rejected the rider. The Senate then voted again and passed the Bill without the rider.[80]

Opposition to the Plan in the federal courts was equally unsuccessful. Contractors filed suit in the federal district court in Philadelphia against the Secretary of Labor. The plaintiffs contended, first, that the minimum requirements for minority hiring constituted a racial preference which violated the Constitution and, second, that the imposition of 'quotas' required them to violate Title VII by taking race into account in hiring. District Judge Harold Weiner rejected the contractors' contentions.[81] The third circuit court of appeals subsequently affirmed the lower court's decision,[82] Judge Gibbons holding that it was proper for the government to impose goals and timetables for the employment of minority workers in federally assisted construction as a condition for contract awards. For the court of appeals this was justified by vital government interests in cost and performance factors where federal funds were used. The court termed as 'pure sophistry' the union's argument that the Philadelphia Plan imposed on contractors contradictory duties impossible to attain. The fulfilment of the racial employment goals was found to be compatible with a requirement that, at the same time, they operate non-discriminatory hiring practices. Nor did the imposition of quotas to redress the racial imbalance violate the Fifth Amendment. The contractors appealed to the United States Supreme Court which, in denying *certiorari*, let the decision stand.[83]

Revised Order No 4

In May 1968, the OFCC had issued its first regulations relating to non-construction contractors.[84] The new regulations included a section on affirmative action requirements. It stipulated that:

A necessary pre-requisite to the development of a satisfactory affirmative action program is the identification and analysis of the problem areas inherent in minority employment and an evaluation of opportunities for utilisation of minority group personnel. The contractor's program shall provide in detail for specific steps to guarantee equal employment opportunity keyed to the problems and needs of members of minority groups including, when there are deficiencies, the development of specific goals and timetables for the prompt achievement of full and equal employment opportunity ... The evaluation of utilisation of minority group personnel shall include the following: (1) an analysis of minority group representation in all job categories. (2) analysis of hiring practices for the past year including recruitment sources and testing to determine whether equal employment opportunity is being afforded in all job categories. (3) analysis of upgrading, transfer and promotion for the past year to determine whether equal employment opportunity is being afforded.[85]

---

[80] See Note, The Philadelphia Plan: A Study in the Dynamics of Executive Power (n 47 above).
[81] *Contractors Association of Eastern Pennsylvania v Schultz* 311 F Supp 1002 (DC Pa 1969).
[82] 442 F 2d 159 (CA-3 1971). [83] 404 US 854 (1971).
[84] 41 CFR 60-1. See USCRC, Federal Civil Rights Enforcement Effort, 1971, 55.
[85] 41 CFR 60-1.40

As Nathan Glazer pointed out, 'the affirmative action requirement is not based on a finding that a contractor has unlawfully discriminated: rather it imposes upon the contractor the duty to make his own determination of the need for affirmative action'[86] without a prior finding that he has committed an unlawful act.

A draft of a new order was sent to the heads of all agencies in November 1969. However, because of Congressional criticism, this draft was not adopted formally. Order No 4, as finally issued, differed from the original draft in assuring the contractors that their acceptability would not be dependent upon whether they met the targets set out in affirmative action plans. It stated that the detailed criteria represented only guidelines for action, whereas the earlier draft had indicated that the contractor was expected to meet the goals in order to be found to be in compliance. The emphasis on results, however, can still be seen from the statement in the order that: 'An affirmative action programme is a set of specific and result oriented procedures to which a contractor commits himself to apply every good faith effort. The objective of these procedures plus such efforts is equal employment opportunity. Procedures without effort to make them work are meaningless; and effort undirected by specific and meaningful procedures is inadequate.'[87]

Revised Order No 4, similar in most respects to Order No 4 and replacing it, was issued in December 1971.[88] Written programmes to comply with the Order were to comprise three main parts. One part required that procedures be developed to ensure that the programme would be widely disseminated, enforced internally in the firm, and reviewed periodically so as to keep it up to date. Second, an analysis was to be carried out to determine areas within which the contractor was deficient in the utilization of minority groups and women. Underutilization was defined as 'having fewer minorities or women in a particular job classification than would reasonably be expected by their availability'. Third, and most controversially, goals and timetables were required to be developed to correct any deficiencies found in the analysis. The goals should be 'significant, measurable and attainable . . . specific for planned results with timetables for completion' and should take into account 'the anticipated expansion, contraction and turnover of and in the workforce'. They should not be 'rigid and inflexible quotas which must be met' but must be targets reasonably attainable by means of 'applying every good faith effort to make all aspects of the entire affirmative action program work'.

The order stressed that no contractor's compliance status would be judged solely on whether or not he reached his goals and met his timetable. Rather, each contractor's compliance would be determined by reviewing the contents of his programme, the extent of his adherence to this programme, and 'his good faith efforts to make his program work towards the realization of the program's goals within the timetables set for completion'.

---

[86] N Glazer, *Affirmative Discrimination: Ethnic Inequality, and Public Policy* (Basic Books, 1975) 47.
[87] 41 CFR 60-2.10 (1970).   [88] 41 CFR 60-2 (1972).

The influence of the Philadelphia Plan is apparent in the emphasis on correcting abuses on the demand side of the labour market, in the emphasis on 'goals and timetables', and in the assessment of 'underutilization'. The major differences between Revised Order No 4 and the Philadelphia Plan were that in the Revised Order the contractor, not the government, determined the existence and extent of deficiency and set the achievement goals himself. Second, under the revised Philadelphia Plan the contractor had to commit himself to comply with government-imposed goals before the contract was awarded.

In 1971, a Bill seeking to reform the employment discrimination provisions of the Civil Rights Act 1964 was introduced into the House of Representatives. This included provisions transferring the responsibilities of the OFCC to the EEOC.[89] The House Education and Labor Committee reported this Bill in June, including the transfer provisions. On the floor of the House in September, John H Dent, the floor manager of the Bill tried to win additional support for the Bill, by proposing a package of additional Committee supported amendments which would have, *inter alia*, banned the EEOC from imposing quotas or requiring preferential treatment for minority group citizens. However, the Bill eventually passed by the House omitted the transfer provision and the suggested anti-quota amendments. On 28 January, the Senate also rejected an amendment, proposed by Senator Ervin, that no federal department, agency, or official could require an employer to practise reverse discrimination by employing persons of a particular race, religion, national origin, or sex in order to meet a quota. Another Ervin amendment designed to expand the ban on preferential treatment of minority group employees and forbid such action not only under Title VII of the 1964 Act, but also under Executive Order 11246 and any other executive order or laws, was similarly rejected.[90]

Nixon Administration support

The Nixon Administration's support for the Philadelphia Plan and for affirmative action in general in the early years of the Administration might seem paradoxical. President Nixon himself was unpopular with many black politicians, and he was not beholden to the black electorate for his election to the Presidency. The Administration had attempted to slow up the desegregation of Southern schools. The 'Southern strategy', of which this slowing up of desegregation was a part (it also included developing an alliance with Southern politicians in return for congressional support), required a low profile on other pro-black actions as well, at least in the South.[91]

Several explanations have been advanced for the undoubted support the Nixon Administration did give to the Philadelphia Plan. For some, it was an aspect of the liberal side of the Administration. According to Safire: 'Nixon showed his pride

---

[89] Congressional Quarterly Almanac, 1972 (hereafter CQA) 250–1.
[90] CQA (n 89 above) 254.   [91] See LE Panetta, *Bring Us Together* (Lippincott, 1971) 182–8.

at this liberal side of his administration. "The Democrats are token-oriented", he pointed out, "we're job oriented".'[92] To an extent, support for this type of programme might be seen as deriving also from Nixon's period as Vice-President when he headed the President's Committee. Nor did any significant opinion in his Administration publicly oppose the Plan. Indeed, there was Cabinet-level representation in favour of it, since the Secretary of Labor actively supported it[93] and he in turn 'won over' the Attorney General, John Mitchell. To both, according to Safire, the aim of the Plan was 'to show blacks that the Administration would help them gain the opportunity for economic advancement, now far more important than new laws or more welfare, the thrust of which was consistent with a spirit of self reliance'.[94] In addition, precisely because of Nixon's low popularity with blacks, and perhaps also because he had to do something specific as a counter-balance to the slowing up of Southern school desegregation, supporting the Plan was an acceptable way in which to derive some such benefit. It did not involve civil rights enforcement primarily directed against the South, after all.

A rather different explanation was put forward mainly by Bayard Rustin, an old associate of A Philip Randolph, who is referred to above. The explanation he advanced saw the Plan as 'part and parcel of the general Republican attack on Labor.[95] For Rustin, the:

... advantages to the Republicans for this kind of strategy should be obvious. Nixon supports his friends among the corporate elite and hurts his enemies in the unions. He also gains a convenient cover for his anti-Negro policies in the South and, above all, he weakens his political opposition by aggravating the differences between its two strongest and most progressive forces—the Labor movement and the civil rights movement.

Nixon's support for the Plan was 'also part of the administration's attempts to pin onto Labor the blame for inflation in construction costs'. Increasing the supply of labour that could be drawn on should lessen the wage costs, and reduce wage inflation.

A third explanation would appear to be that a greater redistribution of resources to the urban black population was recognized as necessary in order to stave off the possibility of the repetition of black riots in the cities which, as noted above, had erupted each summer since 1963. Given the financial costs of the Vietnam War and Nixon's conservative fiscal policies, much of the spending which President Johnson had begun and the Kerner Commission had recommended be expanded, was cut back. The Philadelphia Plan was, in effect, indirect redistribution. Thus, the *New York Times* reported in January 1970 that 'the Administration is promoting means of putting more wealth into the hands of minorities while reducing to a minimum the structural urban and poverty program instituted by the Democrats. In that regard, informed sources said, it was likely that contract compliance might

[92] W Safire, *Before the Fall* (Tower Publications, 1975) 317.
[93] TH Anderson, *The Pursuit of Fairness: A History of Affirmative Action* (OUP, 2004) 118.
[94] Safire(n 92 above) 266.   [95] B Rustin, *Down the Line* (Quadrangle Books, 1971) 343–5.

be utilized more than it has been in the past.'[96] Whatever the reason (or reasons) for the Administration's support of the Philadelphia Plan, it proved to be of fundamental importance for the development of the requirements of affirmative action whether adopted 'voluntarily' by construction contractors in 'hometown' plans, required of construction contractors in 'imposed plans', or required of non-construction contractors under the OFCC orders.

Supreme Court and 'private' affirmative action

The Supreme Court also proved to be a willing ally of the strategy in an important respect. It was open to those who considered that they had 'lost out' in the enforcement of affirmative action to argue that the employer was acting unlawfully, being in breach of Title VII's prohibition on race and sex discrimination in employment. The cases that considered 'voluntary' (ie not court ordered) affirmative action by 'private' employers (ie not public employers who were held to the Constitutional standards) were therefore of critical importance to the operation of affirmative action under the executive order. Two cases were of particular importance.

In *United Steelworkers of America, AFL-CIO-CLC v Weber*[97] the Court adopted a position that was broadly supportive of affirmative action. An affirmative action plan was adopted to eliminate racial imbalances in Kaiser's almost exclusively white craft workforce. On the basis of this plan, Kaiser established a programme at one of the plants to train its production workers to fill craft openings, selecting trainees on the basis of seniority, with the proviso that at least 50 per cent of the trainees were to be black until the percentage of black skilled craft workers in the plant approximated the percentage of blacks in the local labour force. During the plan's first year of operation, seven black and six white craft trainees were selected from the plant's production workforce, with the most senior black trainee having less seniority than several white production workers whose bids for admission were rejected. The majority of the Supreme Court held that Title VII's prohibition of racial discrimination did not condemn all private, voluntary, race-conscious affirmative action plans. An interpretation that forbade all race-conscious affirmative action was seen as bringing about an end at variance with the purpose of the statute, and was rejected.

The Court did not consider it necessary to define the line of demarcation between permissible and impermissible affirmative action plans. It held, however, that the challenged actions fell on the permissible side of the line. The purposes of the plan mirrored those of the statute, being designed to break down old patterns of racial segregation. It did not unnecessarily trammel the interests of white employees. It did not require the discharge of white workers and their replacement with new black hirings, nor did it create an absolute bar to the advancement of white employees, since half of those trained in the programme would be white. Moreover, the plan

[96] *New York Times*, 25 January 1970, 71.   [97] 443 US 193 (1979).

was a temporary measure, not intended to maintain racial balance, but simply to eliminate an existing clear racial imbalance.

Eight years later, in *Johnson v Santa Clara County Transportation Agency*,[98] the Court returned to consider the relationship between 'voluntary' affirmative action and Title VII and gave an equally generous interpretation of the legislation to permit the contested affirmative action in favour of women as it had in the case of racial preferences in the *Weber* case. An affirmative action plan for hiring and promoting minorities and women was voluntarily adopted by the Santa Clara County Transportation Agency. Applying the affirmative action plan, a male employee was passed over for a particular appointment and a woman was appointed instead, although both were rated as well qualified for the job. The Supreme Court held that the Agency appropriately took into account the woman's sex as one factor in determining that she should be promoted. Assessment of the legality of the Agency's plan was guided by the *Weber* decision. Consideration of the sex of applicants for skilled craft jobs was justified by the existence of a 'manifest imbalance' that reflected underrepresentation of women in 'traditionally segregated job categories'. The Agency plan did not unnecessarily trammel male employees' rights or create an absolute bar to their advancement. The plan set aside no positions for women, and expressly stated that its goals should not be construed as 'quotas' that must be met. Denial of the promotion unsettled no legitimate, firmly rooted expectations, since the Agency director was authorized to select any of the seven applicants deemed qualified for the job.

President Reagan's challenge

The principal problems for the executive order came from the Administration itself, not from the Supreme Court. Reports on the process of implementation of the contract compliance programme during the 1970s tended to emphasize the lack of rigour in enforcement activity. Studies of the operation of the programme by the United States Commission on Civil Rights and the United States General Accounting Office blamed weak enforcement and a reluctance to apply sanctions for what they considered the relative ineffectiveness of the programme.[99] One of the weaknesses in enforcement was due to the lack of power that the OFCC had over other departments. Formally, the OFCC only 'had overview responsibilities while each department had responsibility for the compliance of their own contractors with uneven results'.[100] In 1978, President Carter issued Executive Order 12067 restructuring the responsibility for administration of the programme, centralizing

[98] 480 US 616 (1987).

[99] US Commission on Civil Rights, The Federal Civil Rights Enforcement Effort—1974, Vol 5, To Eliminate Employment Discrimination (Washington, July 1975); US General Accounting Office, The Equal Employment Opportunity Program for Federal Nonconstruction Contractors Can be Improved, 29 April 1975.

[100] RA Johnson, 'Affirmative Action Policy in the United States: its impact on women' (1990), 18(2) Policy and Politics 77, 80.

the contract compliance programmes in the (renamed) Office of Federal Contract Compliance Programs (OFCCP). In the last days of his Administration, a complete overhaul of the contract compliance regulations was drawn up to take effect at the beginning of 1981.[101]

The Carter Administration's regulations were, however, frozen by the incoming Reagan Administration.[102] The new Administration published its own proposals to amend the regulations implementing the order in August 1981 and April 1982.[103] These included raising the threshold for the requirement to have a written affirmative action plan, eliminating pre-award reviews, providing for back-pay remedies, and reducing the requirement to set goals and timetables. All major civil rights groups and the relevant House of Representatives Sub-Committee, were opposed to these changes.[104] The changes were not implemented, possibly to avoid controversy before the November 1982 Congressional elections,[105] nor were further changes to these proposals published in 1983.[106] These would also have established higher thresholds for written affirmative action plans, sanctioned back-pay as a remedy but limited it to identifiable victims, eliminated pre-award reviews, simplified the method of analysing underrepresentation, and reduced the affirmative action required of construction contractors. Again, these proposals were strongly opposed by all of the major civil rights groups at Congressional hearings held to consider them during April and June 1983,[107] and subsequently by the chairman of the relevant House Sub-Committee.[108] In 1985, the Attorney General drafted a further proposed amendment to the executive order which would have prohibited federal contractors from using goals and timetables, barred the use of statistical evidence, and (possibly) limited the coverage of the prohibition of discrimination to overt and intentional acts.[109] The amendments were not adopted. They were, apparently, opposed by the Secretary of Labor, and internecine squabbling continued intermittently for several years thereafter.[110] In addition, predictably, civil rights groups and trade unions mobilized against the changes. More surprisingly, so too did business groups.[111] On 20 November 1991, just

---

[101] 45 Fed Reg 86215 (1980), corrected at 46 Fed Reg 7332, 23 January 1981.

[102] Executive Order 12291, 28 January 1981, 46 Fed Reg 9084 (1981).

[103] 46 Fed Reg 42968 (1981); 47 Fed Reg 17770 (1982).

[104] US Congress, House of Representatives, Committee on Education and Labor, Sub-Committee on Employment Opportunities, 'Record of Oversight Hearings on Affirmative Action and the Federal Enforcement of Equal Opportunity Laws' (US GPO, 1981); Report on Affirmative Action and the Federal Enforcement of Equal Employment Opportunity Laws (US GPO, 1981).

[105] BNA DLR No 160, 18 August 1982, A-1.

[106] BNA DLR No 54, 18 March 1983, A-10.

[107] US Congress, House of Representatives, Committee on Education and Labor, Sub-Committee on Employment Opportunities, Oversight Hearings on the OFCCP's proposed affirmative action regulations (US GPO, 1983).   [108] BNA DLR No 27, 9 February 1984, A-7.

[109] CCH, *Employment Practices Guide, New Developments*, (CCH, 1985) ¶5138.

[110] See BNA DLR No 205, 23 October 1985, A-11; BNA DLR No 241, 16 December 1985, A-7; BNA DLR No 64, 3 April 1986, A-7.

[111] Including the Association of Manufacturers and Time Inc. The US Chamber of Commerce was in favour of the changes. See US Congress, House of Representatives, Committee on Education and Labor,

before President Bush was due to sign the Civil Rights Bill into law, the White House counsel issued a directive on the President's behalf, ordering termination of 'any regulation, rule, enforcement practice . . . that mandates, encourages, or otherwise involves the use of quotas, preferences, set-asides, or other similar devices, on the basis of race, color, religion, sex, or national origin'.[112] However, after pressure was brought, the President rescinded the directive.

Although the programme as a whole survived, significant administrative changes in OFCCP policy were made during the Reagan Presidency and these, combined with substantial budget cuts, have been seen by some commentators[113] as having undermined the effectiveness of OFCCP enforcement during the 1980s.[114] Six months after President Reagan came into office, the *New York Times* reported a 'virtual paralysis' of civil rights enforcement at the OFCCP.[115] The Senate Committee on Labor and Human Resources in 1982 compared the OFCCP's administration of the programme to 'a rudderless ship: unpredictable, erratic, and thoroughly susceptible to the political attitudes and presumptions of those responsible for its direction'.[116] A report for the United States House of Representatives found in 1987 that enforcement of the scheme had been afflicted by self-paralysis.[117] The report characterized the OFCCP as having 'come to a virtual standstill since 1980'. Much of the decline in enforcement activities was attributed to the 'political and ideological turmoil' that existed, in part because of the proposed regulations issued by the Reagan Administration. The report found that although the revisions had not been finalized and approved, in practice several of the elements of the proposals were implemented by the OFCCP through internal policy-making changes. In addition, the agency had suffered 'substantial and unjustified reductions' in personnel since 1978, losing around one-third of its workforce.[118] Analyses of enforcement activity over the period 1980–93 showed consistent patterns of declining activity by the OFCCP.[119]

The approach to enforcement within the OFCCP was significantly affected by the hostility that was growing in some circles towards affirmative action.[120]

Sub-Committee on Employment Opportunities, Oversight Review of the Department of Labor's Office of Federal Contract Compliance Programs and Affirmative Action Programs (US GPO, 1986).

[112]   TRB, 'Race unconscious' *The New Republic*, 16 December 1991, 4.

[113]   See eg AW Blumrosen, *Modern Law: The Law Transmission System and Equal Employment Opportunity* (University of Wisconsin Press, 1993) 274.

[114]   V du Rivage, 'The OFCCP Under the Reagan Administration: Affirmative Action in Retreat' (1985), 36 Labor Law Journal 360. For a review of the literature confirming this view, see A Kalev and R Wood Johnson, Enforcement of Civil Rights Law in Private Workplaces: The Effects of Compliance Reviews and Lawsuits Over Time, December 2005 available at <http://www.wjh.harvard.edu/~dobbin/cv/working_papers/eeopractice2.pdf>, p. 8.   [115]   Quoted in Anderson (n 93 above) 169.

[116]   BNA DLR No 82, 28 April 1982, A-8.

[117]   US House of Representatives, Committee on Education and Labour, A Report on the Investigation of the Civil Rights Enforcement Activities of the Office of Federal Contract Compliance Programs, US Department of Labour (1987).

[118]   See BNA DLR, No 15, 25 January 1988, A-12.

[119]   See eg BNA DLR, 2 December 1993.

[120]   Information in this paragraph is drawn from J Dubray, 'Use of Public Procurement Policies in the United States to Combat Discrimination and to Promote Equal Employment Opportunities', paper prepared for the ILO, 2006.

Increasingly, the OFCCP downplayed those aspects of its work (such as compliance reviews directed at ensuring increased participation rates of minorities and women in hiring and promotions) that were based on implementing affirmative action going beyond what was required under the federal anti-discrimination law that applied to most employers. Instead, it shifted its activity to its other principal mandate, challenging discrimination, increasingly using its powers to investigate such discrimination and take action against it, including securing monetary remedies for those discriminated against.

The development of contract compliance during the 1990s was significantly affected by legal challenges to affirmative action set-asides, considered in chapter 7 below. Before turning to these developments, however, the expansion of contract compliance beyond race in the United States, and to other countries, will be considered.

Expanding the groups covered

The importance of the expansion of the 'protectorate' of status equality law and policy in many jurisdictions was noted in chapter 3 above. This trend is illustrated by the expansion of the groups covered by contract compliance in the United States. Executive Order 11375 expanded the coverage of Executive Order 11246 to include women in 1967.[121] Despite this, women were originally excluded from the regulations detailing the requirements. However, following the 1972 amendments to Title VII, and because of publicity and pressure by women's groups, by April 1973, women were finally included as full beneficiaries in Revised Order No 4.[122] Other legislation imposed requirements to be inserted in government contracts for the benefit of other groups, in particular the Rehabilitation Act 1973,[123] and the Vietnam Era Veterans' Readjustment Assistance Act of 1974.[124]

Disability

Section 503 of the Rehabilitation Act of 1973, as amended, provided that any contract worth in excess of US$10,000 entered into by any federal department or agency for the procurement of personal property and non-personal services (including construction) for the United States must contain a provision requiring that the party contracting with the United States shall take 'affirmative action' to employ and advance in employment qualified individuals with disabilities. The provisions of this section also applied to any subcontract in excess of US$10,000 entered into by a principal contractor in carrying out any equivalent contract for the United States. If any individual with a disability believed that any contractor had failed or refused to comply with these provisions, the individual could file a complaint with

---

[121] Executive Order 11375, 32 Fed Reg 14303 (1967).   [122] Johnson (n 100 above) 79.
[123] PL 101-336, 104 Stat 327 (codified at 29 USC Sec 791 (1994).
[124] PL 92-450, 86 Stat 1074 (codified at 38 USC §2012).

the Department of Labor, which was required to investigate the complaint and 'shall take such action thereon as the facts and circumstances warrant, consistent with the terms of such contract and the laws and regulations applicable thereto'.

More recently, however, a rather different approach has been adopted: to use public procurement as a mechanism for stimulating the information technology industry to enable those with disabilities to gain access to this new technology. The Rehabilitation Act of 1973 had included a broad prohibition against discrimination on the basis of disabilities, barring discrimination against an 'otherwise qualified individual'. A new section 508 was added in 1986 as an amendment to the Rehabilitation Act 1973. The original section 508 dealt with electronic and information technologies. The enactment of the Americans with Disabilities Act 1990 was intended to create a more effective anti-discrimination statute. The 1990 Act broadened the coverage of the prohibition of discrimination safeguards to include within its protection persons with disabilities in private sector employment, those who used public services, and those who sought to gain access to public accommodations and use telecommunications. In 1998, Congress amended the Rehabilitation Act of 1973 to require federal agencies to make their electronic and information technology accessible to people with disabilities.[125] Section 508 was enacted to eliminate barriers in information technology, to make available new opportunities for people with disabilities, and to encourage the development of technologies that will help to achieve those goals. The law applied to all federal agencies when they developed, *procured*, maintained, or used electronic and information technology. An exception existed if such access would impose an undue burden on the agency.

In April 2001, a rule was issued that made the standards part of the government procurement process. From 25 June 2001, federal agencies were required to buy only the most accessible products on the market unless doing so would be an undue burden on the agency.[126] The electronic and information technology purchased must enable individuals with disabilities who were federal employees to have access to and use of information and data that was comparable to the access to and use of the information and data by federal employees who were not individuals with disabilities. Individuals with disabilities who were members of the public seeking information or services from a federal department or agency must have access to and use of information and data that is comparable to the access to and use of the information and data by such members of the public who are not individuals with disabilities. Individuals with a disability might file a complaint alleging that a federal department or agency had failed to comply. Civil remedies were also provided for.

Vietnam veterans

The Vietnam Era Veterans' Readjustment Assistance Act of 1974, as amended, provided that any contract of US$25,000 or more (subsequently changed to

---

[125] Rehabilitation Act, s 508 (29 USC 794d), as amended by the Workforce Investment Act of 1998 (PL 105-220), 7 August 1998.

[126] Final FAR Rule For Implementing Section 508 of the Rehabilitation Act Electronic and Information Technology Accessibility for Persons with Disabilities, 66 Fed Reg 20894 (25 April 2001).

US$100,000 or more after December 2003) entered into by any department or agency for the procurement of personal property and non-personal services (including construction) for the United States, should contain a provision requiring the party contracting with the United States to take 'affirmative action' to employ and advance in employment qualified disabled veterans, veterans of the Vietnam era, and any other veterans 'who served on active duty during a war or in a campaign or expedition for which a campaign badge has been authorized'. The provisions of this section also applied to any subcontract entered into by a prime contractor in carrying out any contract for the procurement of personal property and non-personal services (including construction) for the United States.

II. Contract Compliance in Canada

The development of anti-discrimination law in Canada was noted in chapter 3 above. Just as the substance of Canadian legislation was influenced by developments in the United States, so too were the enforcement techniques adopted, including contract compliance. We consider first the development of contract compliance in Canada at the federal level and then look at two important provincial developments.

Federal government equality legislation and contract compliance

The Canadian Human Rights Act 1978 permitted the federal government to make regulations requiring that any contract or grant should include provisions prohibiting discrimination.[127] Abella had recommended that employers who did business with the federal government, and would otherwise not be required to do so, should be required to implement employment equity programmes to ensure that the designated groups achieved employment representation consistent with their presence in the labour force. In 1985, the Parliament of Canada ordered the Standing Committee on Justice and Legal Affairs to report on equality rights in the Charter of Rights and Freedoms.[128] The Committee recommended that legislation requiring contract compliance at the federal level be adopted. The Employment Equity Act was passed in June 1986. To accompany the legislation, the Canadian government instituted a Federal Contractors Program (FCP), which came into effect on 1 September 1986.[129] The Employment Equity Act covered *federally* regulated employers. The FCP applied to *provincially* regulated employers with a total national resident workforce in Canada of 100 or more permanent full- or part-time employees that received federal government goods or services contracts of Can$200,000 or more. As a condition for bidding on large federal

---

[127] Canadian Human Rights Act, s 23.
[128] P Boyer, *Equality for All: Report of the Parliamentary Committee on Equality Rights* (Queen's Printer for Canada, 1985).
[129] Directive 3055 of 30 September 1986, replacing Directive 3055 dated 29 August 1986, Supply and Services Canada, Supply Policy Manual.

contracts, such contractors, domestic or foreign, were required to certify in writing their commitment to employment equity. The objective was to ensure that suppliers of goods and services to the federal government achieved a fair and representative workforce for women, visible minorities, aboriginal peoples, and people with disabilities. Contractors were to eliminate barriers to the integration of these four groups, a continuing obligation that extended beyond the end date of the contract. The programme was therefore 'an initiative which complements the federal Employment Equity Act, and which extends the basic ideals expressed in that law into areas that would otherwise fall within provincial jurisdiction'.[130]

Several changes were introduced by legislation in 1995, including an expansion in the coverage of employers (the federal public service was now included). Employers covered by the legislation were subject to compliance audits by the Canadian Human Rights Commission and a tribunal was given authority to enforce compliance. The Federal Contractors Programme requirements were to be made equivalent to those under the new legislation.[131] Employers subject to the Employment Equity Act were required to report annually.[132]

In December 2001, the Standing Committee on Human Resources and the Status of Persons with Disabilities began a review of the 1995 Act, including the operation of the FCP, producing a report in June 2002 that suggested improvements. The Committee reported that according to 'several witnesses . . . the lack of a legislative basis for the FCP, no requirement to report annually, inadequate program support and guidance, and the absence of a meaningful monitoring mechanism, have all created the impression that employment equity in workplaces covered under the FCP is in a state of disarray'.[133] The Committee was 'totally convinced that this program needs to be strengthened'. It recommended that the Department do more to ensure that federal contractors complied with the requirements of the FCP. In particular, it recommended an even greater degree of equivalence in employers' obligations between those covered by the Act and those covered by the FCP. In anticipation of this review, the government had initiated its own review of the legislation and an evaluation of the FCP had been commissioned and was subsequently published.[134] This concluded that there was 'still a need for such a program', that 'there is positive evidence of the value of the program model

---

[130] WS Tarnopolsky, *Discrimination and the Law*, 7th Cumulative Supplement, 1991, 37.

[131] Employment Equity Act 2003, s 42(2).

[132] C Agócs, 'Canada's employment equity legislation and policy, 1987–2000', (2002) 23(3), International Journal of Manpower 256, 260. See also C Agócs and C Burr, 'Employment Equity, Affirmative Action and Managing Diversity: Assessing the Differences' (1996) 17 (4–5), International Journal of Manpower 30.

[133] Standing Committee on Human Resources Development and the Status of Persons with Disabilities, Judi Longfield, MP, Chair, Promoting Equality in the Federal Jurisdiction: A Review of the Employment Equity Act: Committee Report (Public Works Canada, 2002, June 2002) Chapter IV, at Recommendation 7, available at <http://cmte.parl.qu.ca/CMTE/CommitteePublication.aspx?com=220&Lorg=1&Sourceld=37258>.

[134] Evaluation of the Federal Contractors Program, Evaluation and Data Development, Strategic Policy, Human Resources Development Canada, Final Report, SP-AH183-04-02E, April 2002.

as many employers report they are only engaging in employment equity activities because of the FCP', but that the success of the FCP 'is limited by the way in which it has been implemented. Weaknesses in the organization, resourcing and delivery of the program suggest that changes in the FCP could allow for improved effectiveness and more positive impacts.'[135] Following these reviews, a restructuring of the programme took place in the latter part of 2002[136] to streamline activities, accelerate the audit process across Canada, and maintain consistency and unifomity in the application of the programme among employers in various regions of the country.[137] The revised policy included measures to strengthen employer compliance by ensuring that firms declared ineligible could not bid for contracts. Reporting requirements were streamlined. Subsequently, a new audit framework similar to the one used by the Canadian Human Rights Commission (CHRC) was introduced to enable workplace equity officers to work closely with the employer to achieve compliance with the FCP requirements of the Act.[138]

Requirements of the Federal Contractors Program[139]

We can turn now to examine the details of the scheme. Provincially-regulated employers[140] which employ 100 or more permanent full-time and permanent part-time employees and wish to bid on contracts of Can$200,000 or more to supply goods and services to the federal government, are required to commit themselves to implementing employment equity and to demonstrate this commitment by signing a Certificate of Commitment to Employment Equity. All suppliers, including offshore or foreign suppliers, with a resident workforce of a hundred or more employees in Canada are covered by the programme. In 2004, the FCP covered approximately 936 contractors with a combined workforce of 1,121,965 employees. The criteria for implementation of employment equity to which those signing the certificate commit themselves are set out in detail. The certificate is a prerequisite to the qualification of bids, rather than a condition of

---

[135] ibid, Executive Summary, v.

[136] Treasury Board, Contract Policy Notice 2003–4, Strengthened Federal Contractors Program for Employment Equity, 2 July 2003.

[137] Human Resources and Skills Development Canada, 2003 Annual Report: Employment Equity Act 2003 (Government of Canada, 2004) 11.

[138] Human Resources and Skills Development Canada, 2004 Annual Report: Employment Equity Act (Government of Canada, 2005) 77–8.

[139] This section is based on: HRSDC Internet site at <http://www.hrsdc.gc.ca/en/lp/lo/lswe/we/programs/fcp/criteria/index-we.shtml>. The following Guides operated under the pre-2004 FCP: Employment and Immigration Canada, Federal Contractors Program: Information for Suppliers and Organizations (1991) 3–6; Employment and Immigration Canada, Employment Equity: Federal Contractors Program: Questions and Answers (1987) 1.

[140] Contracting organizations that are federally regulated and have 100 or more employees are subject to the Employment Equity Act and do not need to certify their commitment under the Federal Contractors Program.

the contract per se. A bid that does not include a signed certificate is considered non-responsive. Wherever there is only one source capable of performing a contract subject to the programme, and the vendor does not conform to the requirements, the matter is referred to the Minister for resolution. The certificate commits the entire organization named in the certificate, and all of its component parts, except where otherwise stated. Contracts relating to construction, the purchase of real property, and contracts for legal services entered into under the authority of the Minister of Justice are exempted from the programme. All federal suppliers, including offshore or foreign suppliers, with a resident work force of 100 or more employees in Canada are covered by the programme. It does not apply to offshore suppliers who conducted and executed the work outside Canada, to contracts with provincial governments, or to subcontracts.

After a certified employer is awarded a contract of Can$200,000 or more, it is then required to develop and implement an 'employment equity programme' consistent with eleven criteria. The essential components of this are the development and implementation of a plan of action involving the removal of discriminatory barriers to the employment and promotion of designated groups, improvement in the participation of designated group members throughout the contractor's organization, the introduction of special measures and the establishment of internal goals and timetables towards the achievement of employment equity for designated group members, and the retention of records regarding the employment equity implementation process. The commitment to employment equity is not made just for the 'life of the contract'. Each organization must make a continuing commitment to employment equity. The signed certificate also commits the entire Canadian workforce of the organization named in the certificate, including all of its components (divisions, branches, sales offices, etc). The terms and conditions of the commitment, therefore, require contractors to fulfil several criteria satisfactorily. These include determining and analysing the internal workforce; eliminating policies and practices that have an adverse impact on designated groups; identifying areas for change; establishing goals and timetables for the hiring and promotion of designated group members; and developing an action plan to achieve the stated goals. Designated groups, as we have seen, are women, aboriginal peoples, persons with disabilities, and 'visible' minorities (ie those who are identifiable as such by virtue of skin colour, for example).

Contractors must also agree to allow 'workplace equity officers' from Human Resources Development Canada, the relevant department, to conduct on-site compliance reviews to determine whether compliance is taking place and the results achieved, at any point after the award of a contract. The selection of contractors for review is conducted by periodic random sampling. However, the FCP administration may give priority to contractors that have not yet received a first review or have gone more than five years since their last review. Compliance reviews are conducted by Workplace Equity Officers from Human Resources Development Canada (HRDC)-Labour. A review consists of inspection of the records and documents kept by the contractor; an assessment of compliance with the programme criteria and the results obtained; a determination of the extent of efforts made by contractors on behalf of designated groups; and a measurement of the performance levels attained by contractors. Particular consideration is given to an organization's 'good faith efforts' to reach its objectives. Should a compliance review indicate a failure to respect the commitment to implement employment equity, negotiation is likely to take place in order to achieve improvements, followed by a further review at the end of a negotiated period. After another unsatisfactory review, sanctions can be applied which can include the exclusion of the employer from future government business. This decision is subject to review by the Minister of Labour, who appoints an independent assessor to review the case. If the government debars an employer, a new Certificate of Commitment must be signed. The next time a contractor bids on a contract, it would be required to attach a summary of employment equity measures instituted since the last review, and present a form outlining the present representation of designated groups. The contractor would not be considered for further contracts until satisfactory improvement is demonstrated.

Provincial programmes

Somewhat similar approaches have been developed at the provincial level. In Ontario, the basic anti-discrimination statute is the Ontario Human Rights Code.[141] The Code itself provides for a limited use of contract compliance. Section 26 provides that: '[I]t shall be deemed to be a condition of every contract entered into by or on behalf of the Crown or any agency thereof and of every sub-contract entered into in the performance thereof that no right under section 5 [the basic non-discrimination obligation] will be infringed in the course of performing the contract.' An equivalent provision applies to grants. The Code further provides that: 'Where an infringement of a right under section 5 is found by the Tribunal upon a complaint and constitutes a breach of a condition under this section, the breach of condition is sufficient grounds for cancellation of the contract, grant, contribution, loan or guarantee and refusal to enter into any further contract with or make any further grant, contribution, loan or guarantee to the same person'.[142]

In 1990, the government of Ontario promised to introduce employment equity legislation, thus going beyond the substantially individual justice approach adopted in Ontario as discussed in the previous paragraph. In 1991, it appointed an Employment Equity Commissioner to conduct consultations and to advise the government. In 1991, a framework paper was produced to facilitate consultations in the context of a decision that employment equity would be a legislative requirement. In that context, one of the questions raised by the paper was the type of

---

141 Human Rights Code, RSO 1990, c H.19.
142 RSO 1990, c H.19, s 26(3); 2002, c 18, Sch C, s 5.

contract compliance policy that should be adopted. It raised the possibility that 'government could also promote compliance through preferential contract awards similar to the contract compliance program in the United States. Compliance could also be considered as a factor in determining eligibility for government grants or financial assistance.'[143] On the basis of consultations, a further report was published in June 1992 on the structure and implementation of employment equity legislation. The paper pointed out that: 'The public consultations showed widespread support for contract compliance. It was seen as an effective way of introducing and reinforcing an existing employment equity program.'[144] The paper argued that 'a contract compliance program can be useful when employment equity legislation does not cover all companies'.[145] In addition, the public consultations raised the issue of whether set-asides should be introduced.[146] In a paper produced in 1992, the Ontario government pointed out that:

The Ministry of Government Services . . . has employment equity requirements in some of its contracts and funding programs. However, a relatively small proportion of the government's total budget is spent on contracts, and government contracts are a fairly small proportion of the total sales of private companies. In addition, the current process of awarding contracts within the government is decentralized with each ministry awarding the majority of its contracts.[147]

In June 1992, the government proposed its legislation in Parliament. This included a significantly enhanced set of obligations on employers. In Part III of the Bill, employers were required to prepare and implement an employment equity plan in accordance with prescribed requirements and to review and revise it periodically. In addition to other enforcement methods, the Bill provided a similar set of requirements and sanctions to that found in the earlier Act relating to government contracts and grants for breach of these obligations. The effect, however, was significantly greater because of the greater breadth of the statutory obligations.[148] After considerable debate, the legislation was passed and came into effect in September 1994.

However, following a General Election in 1995, the previous government party failed to be returned to power, and the incoming government announced that it would repeal the legislation at the earliest opportunity, replacing it with a new law, the Job Quotas Repeal Act.[149] This 'was introduced in the aftermath of a political campaign in Ontario which relied heavily on the incitement of fears and anxieties

[143] Ontario Government, 'Working Towards Equality: The Discussion Paper on Employment Equity Legislation' (Office of the Employment Equity Commissioner, Ministry of Citizenship, 1992, Queen's Printer for Ontario) 43.
[144] Ontario Government, 'Opening Doors: A report on the Employment Equity Consultations' (Office of the Employment Equity Commissioner, Ministry of Citizenship, 1992, Queen's Printer for Ontario) 61.   [145] ibid.
[146] ibid.   [147] ibid.
[148] Bill 79: An Act to provide for Employment Equity for Aboriginal People, People with Disabilities, members of Racial Minorities and Women (25 June 1992).
[149] Repealed by the Statutes of Ontario, 1995, ch 4, s 1(1).

during a time of high unemployment and extensive corporate downsizing and lay-offs'.[150] Among its many effects was that it repealed the contract compliance elements in the Employment Equity Act, leaving only the provisions of the Human Rights Code as linkage between equality and public procurement.

In Quebec, on the other hand, contract compliance has been retained to serve a substantially group justice approach. In a decision of the Council of Ministers on 23 September 1987, the government of Quebec announced the establishment of a contract compliance programme.[151] The programme applies to businesses or organizations located in Quebec with more than 100 employees, bidding for contracts for goods or services of an amount of Can$100,000 or more, and subcontractors with more than 100 employees for subcontracts of Can$100,000 or more. The government contracts included are those for services and supplies (contracts for moveable property and contracts for services) that are subject to tender, including permanent tender. The Quebec Department of Supply and Services is responsible for establishing the rules to be followed by departments and bodies responsible for awarding contracts, and for managing the information relating to the undertakings given in the awarding of the contracts. No such contract or subcontract may be awarded unless the supplier has made a commitment to implement an affirmative action programme conforming to the Quebec Charter of Human Rights and Freedoms,[152] and holds an attestation issued by the Minister of Supply and Services.[153]

There are several important elements in the Quebec experience. First, the programmes in Quebec tend to support the view that contract compliance is legally compatible with a civil law legal system. Second, there is a clear recognition in Quebec of the problem of out-of-province contractors being unable to satisfy provincial requirements; the attempt in Quebec to develop an approach of equivalence of contractor obligations in different provinces, through the ability of such a contractor to supply an attestation, is of interest. If such a contract or subcontract must be awarded to a supplier who is located outside Quebec but inside Canada and whose business has more than 100 employees, that supplier is required to provide in advance an attestation that he has committed himself to the equal opportunity programme of his province or territory, where applicable, or failing that, to a federal equal opportunity programme.[154] In addition the programme applies to Quebec profit-making businesses, associations, and bodies with more than 100 employees, applying for grants of Can$100,000 or more. Other government departments are responsible for the application of the requirements relating to grants.

---

[150] Agócs and Burr (n 132 above) 34.

[151] The following description is taken, unless otherwise stated, from Quebec Government, 'Contract Compliance: One More Step Towards Employment Equity: Information for Organizations' (Government of Quebec, 1989).   [152] Charter of Human Rights and Freedoms (RSQ, c C-12).

[153] General Regulation Respecting the Conditions of Contracts of Government Departments and Public Bodies under the Public Administration Act (RSQ, C A-6.01) ch 2. Conditions for Validity of Contracts, Division 1. General, OC 1166-93, 18 August 1993, *Gazette officielle du Québec*, Vol 125, 1 September 1993, No 37: Part 2: Laws and regulations, 4923, Art 5; Art 6.   [154] ibid Art 5.

The undertaking to comply with the programme is evidenced by signing an *engagement au programme* (programme undertaking). Following this, an *attestation d'engagement* (confirmation of undertaking) is supplied to the business or undertaking following signature of the undertaking. The official number entered on the attestation must be noted on any subsequent tender or grant application. The *engagement au programme* stipulates the terms and conditions to which the organization commits itself. These include a requirement to inform employees of the undertaking, the appointment of senior managers to carry out the programme, the identification of underrepresented groups, and the setting of goals and time-tables for reducing underrepresentation. The duration of the undertaking extends for as long as the objectives of the affirmative action programme remain to be fulfilled. Any business that omits or neglects to implement an affirmative action programme is liable to have its attestation cancelled and may not be awarded either a services or supply contract, or subcontract, or a grant, until such time as the business is issued with a new attestation.[155]

III. Procurement Linkages, the ILO, and Equality

We have seen in chapter 3 above that the International Labour Organization (ILO) adopted several conventions dealing specifically with status discrimination, including two that the ILO came to regard as central to its mission, drawing heavily on emerging national developments.[156] The utility of 'contract compliance' approaches at the national level, particularly in the United States, has been important in influencing the ILO's approach to the relationship between procurement and equality. Article 2 of the 1957 ILO Convention on employment discrimination provided that a member of the ILO for which the Convention is in force 'undertakes to declare and pursue a national policy designed to promote, by methods appropriate to national conditions and practice, equality of opportunity and treatment in respect of employment and occupation, with a view to eliminating any discrimination in respect thereof'. Article 3 is more specific, providing that a member undertakes, 'by methods appropriate to national conditions and practice', to take various actions. These are: to seek the cooperation of employers' and workers' organizations and other appropriate bodies in promoting the acceptance and observance of this policy; to enact such legislation and to promote such educational programmes as may be calculated to secure the acceptance and observance

---

[155] ibid Art 7.

[156] The first was the Equal Remuneration Convention, 1951 (Convention 100), which introduced the principle of equal pay for men and women for work of equal value. The second was the Discrimination (Employment and Occupation) Convention, 1958 (Convention 111), and its associated Recommendation (R111), which prohibits discrimination in employment on grounds of race, colour, sex, religion, political opinion, national extraction, or social origin.

of the policy; to repeal any statutory provisions and modify any administrative instructions or practices which are inconsistent with the policy; to pursue the policy in respect of employment under the direct control of a national authority; to ensure observance of the policy in the activities of vocational guidance, vocational training, and placement services under the direction of a national authority; and to indicate in its annual reports on the application of the Convention the action taken in pursuance of the policy and the results secured by such action.

The accompanying Recommendation R111 is more explicit still, although its status is one of soft law at most. Regarding the formulation and application of the policy referred to in Article 2, the Recommendation states that the policy 'should be applied by means of legislative measures, collective agreements between representative employers' and workers' organisations or in any other manner consistent with national conditions and practice'.[157] Clearly drawing on contract compliance approaches developed in the United States up to that time, the Recommendation further provides that each member should promote the observance of the principles of non-discrimination 'where practicable and necessary' by such methods as *making eligibility for contracts involving the expenditure of public funds dependent on observance of the principles*, and making eligibility for grants to training establishments and for a licence to operate a private employment agency or a private vocational guidance office dependent on observance of the principles.[158]

More broadly, the ILO Committee of Experts subsequently stressed the desirability of the use of government contracts for securing equal pay and equal opportunities: 'Guaranteeing equal remuneration in contracts awarded by the public authorities can be an extremely effective tool in ensuring respect for the principles contained in the Convention.'[159] The Committee considered that 'the possibility of resort to this method of application of the principle of equality of opportunity and treatment should be given careful examination'.[160] The ILO's 2003 Global Report under the Follow-up to the ILO Declaration on Fundamental Principles and Rights at Work[161] also discussed the issue of the use of public procurement policies as a mechanism to complement legislation, pointing to the growth in the use of such policies in Europe, North America, and South Africa under the Preferential Procurement Policy Framework Act of 2000.[162] Subsequently, the InFocus

---

[157] Recommendation R111, Art 2.   [158] ibid Art 3.

[159] International Labour Conference, 72nd Session 1986, Equal Remuneration: General Survey by the Committee of Experts on the Application of Conventions and Recommendations (ILO, Geneva, 1986) 123, para 158.

[160] International Labour Conference, 75th Session 1988, Equality in Employment and Occupation: General Survey by the Committee of Experts on the Application of Conventions and Recommendations (ILO, Geneva, 1988) para 177.

[161] International Labour Office, Report of the Director-General, 'Time for Equality at Work: Global Report under the Follow-up to the ILO Declaration on Fundamental Principles and Rights at Work, 2003', (International Labour Conference, 91st Session 2003), Report I(B), (ILO, Geneva, 2003).   [162] ibid para 186.

Programme within the ILO, which is responsible for the reporting processes and technical cooperation activities associated with the Declaration, has focused on procurement as a channel for affirmative action, and included discussion of United States, Malaysian, and South African procurement policies in a study on affirmative action arising out of the first Global Report.[163]

[163] M. Tomei, 'Affirmative Action for Racial Equality: Features, impact and challenges', InFocus Programme, Working Paper 44 (May 2005) especially 15–16.

7

Set-asides in the United States and Canada

In chapter 6 above, we considered how procurement linkages have been developed to assist in tackling discrimination and securing greater status equality in the employment context. In this chapter, we examine somewhat different schemes that link the award of contracts to programmes that advantage particular status groups that are considered to be economically disadvantaged by giving preferences to *businesses* that are owned or controlled by such groups in the award of contracts, what we have termed 'set-asides' in chapter 1 above. After examining the development of set-asides in the United States, including the significant legal challenges to such schemes under the United States Constitution, we consider the development in Canada of set-asides favouring Aboriginal-owned businesses.

I. Origin and Development: United States

In the United States, set-asides involve preferences in contracting for small businesses owned by women, and small businesses owned and controlled by socially or economically disadvantaged individuals, particularly ethnic minority groups. There had been growing concerns during the 1960s about the problems of black businesses in the United States.[1] Following the urban riots of the 1960s, there was increasing concern to stimulate the growth of 'black capitalism' in order to help bring growth and stability to the ghettoes.[2] We saw in chapter 2 above, how the United States used procurement set-asides to support small businesses generally. Not surprisingly, then, the Small Business Administration (SBA) began the first programmes to give limited procurement preferences to firms owned by minorities. Without explicit Congressional authority, the SBA adopted regulations requiring federal contracts to be allocated to firms owned by 'socially or economically disadvantaged' persons.[3] In practice, members of minority groups were presumed

---

[1] See eg N Fitzhugh (ed), *Problems and Opportunities Confronting Negroes in the Field of Business* (National Conference on Small Business, 1961).

[2] See eg AF Brimmer and HS Terrell, 'The economic potential of black capitalism' (Paper presented before the 82nd meeting of the American Economic Association 1969). Brimmer was a member of the Board of Governors of the Federal Reserve System.

[3] G La Noue, 'Split Visions: Minority Set-Asides' in H Orlans and J O'Neill (eds), *Affirmative Action Revisited Annals of the American Academy of Political and Social Science*, Vol 523, September 1992, 104, 105.

to be disadvantaged and they received the bulk of such preferences. President Nixon established an Office of Minority Business Enterprise and required the SBA to 'consider the needs and interests of... members of minority groups seeking entry into the business community', leading eventually to the SBA '8(a) programme'.[4] In 1978, this programme was codified for the first time.[5] However, rather than retain the criterion of 'social *or* economically disadvantaged', the legislation required that both conditions be satisfied.[6] The standard of economic disadvantage adopted was an owner's net worth of US$250,000. Participants in the programme were required to establish business development plans and were eligible for technical assistance. The eligible firms were able to benefit from sole source contracting and sheltered competition but, from the 1980s, only for a limited time before 'graduating' from the programme. Eligibility to participate in the programme was certified by the SBA.

All federal agencies were required to set percentage goals for procurement contract awards to such businesses, and required contractors with contracts worth over US$500,000 (or US$1 million in certain construction contracts) to set percentage goals for the use of subcontractors with these characteristics. From 1991, there was a government-wide goal of awarding 5 per cent of the total value of all contracts and subcontracts in each fiscal year to small business concerns owned and controlled by socially and economically disadvantaged individuals.[7] The SBA consulted with each agency to set annual agency-level goals to ensure progress towards the overall goal. In 1994, Congress authorized agencies to apply a 10 per cent price evaluation preference for such businesses.[8]

Regarding small businesses owned by women, contractors were required to use their 'best efforts to give women-owned small business the maximum practicable opportunity to participate in the subcontracts it awards to the fullest extent consistent with the efficient performance of its contract'.[9] In 1994, Congress added women-owned small businesses to the set-aside programme discussed previously, and established a government-wide goal of 5 per cent participation by such businesses in contracts and subcontracts for each year.[10]

In addition, there were numerous other similar programmes authorized by Congress, most notably, during the Carter Presidency, the Public Works Employment Act of 1977. This provided that at least 10 per cent of each federal grant for public work projects under that Act should be allocated to minority business enterprises. A minority business enterprise was defined to mean a business half or more of which was owned by minority group members, defined to include black Americans, but also 'Spanish-speaking, Orientals, Indians, Eskimos, and Aleuts'. A waiver of the set-aside requirement could be obtained if it could not be filled by

---

[4] TH Anderson, *The Pursuit of Fairness: A History of Affirmative Action* (OUP, 2004) 119.
[5] PL 95-507, 15 USC, s 637.   [6] ibid s 637(a)(1), (4).
[7] Office of Federal Procurement Policy, Policy Letter 91-1, 56 Fed Reg 11796 (20 March 1991).
[8] PL 103-355, 108 Stat 3243.   [9] FAR 52.219-13, para (c).
[10] 15 USC §644(g), 637(d).

minority businesses located within a reasonable trade area. Equivalent programmes were created by federal agencies and state and local government authorities that administered other public works construction projects.

In addition to government-wide programmes, several programmes specific to particular federal government agencies were developed. Congress established goals and granted authority to promote the participation of small disadvantaged businesses in procurement to the Department of Defense, NASA, and the Coast Guard. A particular emphasis was placed on procurement in the area of transport. For example, the Department of Transportation was authorized to encourage business with minority- and women-owned firms through its grants to state and local bodies.[11] One estimate established that, by 1989, at least 234 jurisdictions had a minority business set-aside programme, and most of these also included a set-aside programme for women-owned business.[12] In the 1994 Federal Acquisition Streamlining Act, Congress extended to federal agencies equivalent authority to use race conscious measures in procurement. Federal programmes were also 'widely copied by state and local government'.[13]

There were many criticisms of such programmes.[14] It was alleged that minority-ownership was not closely enough defined, nor enforced in practice, with persistent stories of fraud where white businesses simply used a minority business as a front in order to gain the preferences. There were allegations that only small numbers of minority-owned firms actually benefited, so that in 1990 it appeared that 'only 50 firms, just 2 per cent of those eligible, received 40 per cent of the $4 billion awarded'.[15] Some local programmes seemed misguided. 'In Dade County, Florida, for example, Cubans could apply for set-asides although almost all of them were middle class or professionals.'[16] In Richmond, Virginia, the set-aside included preferences for natives of the Aleutian Islands. A large proportion of the firms that benefited were not owned by black Americans, but by Hispanic, Asian, or other groups, leading to criticism that the programmes had lost their original rationale.

Constitutionality of affirmative action set-asides

The constitutionality of these provisions was heavily litigated at the federal level. The Supreme Court had, for well over a decade, handed down decisions on the constitutionality and legality of various types of affirmative action in varying contexts. In these cases, an important distinction was made between the standard the federal government was required to satisfy, and the standard which local and state governments were required to satisfy. (Constitutional limitations do not apply to

---

[11] First by the Surface Transportation Assistance Act of 1982, PL 97-424, 96 Stat 2100 (6 January 1983), and then by the Surface Transportation and Uniform Relocation Assistance Act of 1987, PL 100-17, 101 Stat 132, and the Intermodal Surface Transportation Efficiency Act of 1991.
[12] ibid.   [13] La Noue (n 3 above) 111.
[14] Information from Anderson (n 4 above) 200–1, 238–41.   [15] ibid 200.
[16] ibid 237.

affirmative action carried out by non-governmental entities.) Three different standards of scrutiny have been developed by the Supreme Court to indicate how severely government action will be scrutinized for unconstitutionality under the Equal Protection Guarantee of the Fourteenth Amendment. (1) The first standard, the 'rational basis' test, was easily satisfied by government. This test is not applied in the affirmative action context. (2) A second standard, 'strict scrutiny', required a clear and convincing demonstration by the governmental entity concerned. Under strict scrutiny a racial or ethnic classification must serve a 'compelling interest' and must be 'narrowly tailored' to serve that interest. The application of such a test was commonly thought to be fatal in practice, demonstrating the distaste that the modern Supreme Court showed to racial classifications. (3) A third standard, so-called 'intermediate scrutiny' (ie intermediate between the first and the second types of scrutiny above), was adopted in cases challenging the use of gender-based classifications.

The first case challenging racial set-asides in the procurement context under the Fourteenth Amendment arose in the late 1970s. At issue in *Fullilove v Klutznik*[17] was the federal statutory programme which required that 10 per cent of certain federal construction grants under the Public Works Employment Act of 1977 be awarded to minority contractors. This programme was challenged as unconstitutional as in violation of the equal protection principle. The Supreme Court upheld the programme as constitutional under paragraph 5 of the Fourteenth Amendment, which empowered Congress to act to further the principles of the Fourteenth Amendment, including removing the effects of society-wide discrimination. The Court regarded this as granting additional remedial powers to the federal government.

In the subsequent case of *City of Richmond v JA Croson Co*[18] the issue involved the constitutionality of a local government programme that allocated a portion of public contracting opportunities exclusively to minority-owned businesses. The plan required prime contractors to whom the City of Richmond awarded construction contracts, unless they were themselves minority owned, to subcontract at least 30 per cent of the dollar amount of the contract to enterprises which were at least 51 per cent owned and controlled by minority group members. A contractor argued that the programme was unconstitutional under the Fourteenth Amendment and the majority of the Supreme Court agreed. The Court applied a strict scrutiny analysis to the provision, holding that the standard of review was not dependent on the race of those burdened or benefited by a particular classification. This was the first time that the Court had held, by a majority, that all racial classifications by a state or local authority, including benign classifications, were subject to strict scrutiny under the equal protection clause.

The programme did not survive this scrutiny. Merely asserting that the city was attempting to redress societal discrimination against black entrepreneurs could

---

[17] 448 US 448 (1980).   [18] 109 SCt 706 (1989).

not justify the rigid racial quota in this case. It was 'sheer speculation' how many minority firms there would be in the city in the absence of past societal discrimination. So too, evidence of nationwide discrimination in the construction industry was of limited usefulness in demonstrating discrimination in Richmond. The city had to demonstrate sufficient evidence of discrimination in the past within its own jurisdiction. None of the evidence presented pointed to any identified discrimination in the Richmond construction industry. The city had therefore failed to demonstrate a compelling interest in apportioning public contracting opportunities on the basis of race. Had it been necessary, there were clear indications that the Court would also have decided that it was not sufficiently narrowly tailored: there did not appear to have been any consideration of the use of race-neutral methods to achieve the same ends. The fixing of the quota at 30 per cent could not be said to be tailored to any goal, except perhaps outright racial balancing. The decision gave rise to considerable controversy.[19]

In *Metro Broadcasting Inc v FCC*[20] the issue concerned the practice of the Federal Communications Commission, as authorized by Congress, to award a preference to those firms bidding for the award of new broadcasting licences which were minority owned in order to increase the diversity of programme making. The Supreme Court held that the programme did not violate the Equal Protection Clause of the Fourteenth Amendment. The policy had been continually approved by Congress, and therefore a strict scrutiny review was not required. The policy was substantially related to the achievement of a legitimate governmental interest in broadcasting diversity. It was a legitimate purpose even though it was not directed at remedying specific racial discrimination in the past. It did not impose impermissible burdens on non-minorities. Essentially, the Court adopted the third, intermediate, scrutiny for affirmative action by federal government bodies.

In *Adarand Constructors Inc v Pena, Secretary of Transportation*[21] the Supreme Court overturned this third approach, applying the full rigours of 'strict scrutiny' to *federal* affirmative action, as well as state and local government affirmative action. By a five-four vote, in an opinion written by O'Connor J, the Supreme Court held that strict scrutiny was now the standard of constitutional review for federal affirmative action programmes using racial or ethnic classifications (whether mandated by Congress or not). Of the five in the majority, two (Scalia J and, more ambiguously, Thomas J) took a more stringent position, in effect ruling out the use of race for any governmental decision-making purposes. O'Connor J, however, went out of her way to stress (and in this she was joined by Rehnquist CJ, Kennedy J, and Thomas J) that the federal government may have a compelling interest to act on the basis of race to overcome the 'persistence of both the practice and lingering effects of racial discrimination against minority groups

---

[19] See exchanges between several scholars and the former Solicitor General, Yale Law Journal, vol 98, 1711, vol 99, 155, and vol 99, 163. [20] 497 US 547 (1990).

[21] 515 US 200 (1995).

in this country'. The four dissenters (Stevens, Souter, Ginsburg, and Breyer JJ) would have reaffirmed the intermediate scrutiny standard of review for Congressionally authorized affirmative action measures.

Reviewing procurement linkages after *Adarand*

Following the 1995 judgment of the Supreme Court in the *Adarand* case, the Department of Justice issued a lengthy memorandum setting out the Administration's interpretation of the decision.[22] In it, the Justice Department advised that the decision made it necessary to re-evaluate federal programmes that use race or ethnicity as a basis for decision-making, but stressed that no programme should be suspended prior to such an evaluation. Moreover, the Department pointed to the uncertainty of the implications of the case in some respects, and its limited scope in others. The detailed requirements of 'strict scrutiny' were unclear; the Court had left open how far deference should be given to Congressional determinations of the need for affirmative action to remedy discrimination. It was unclear what constituted sufficient evidence of discrimination to justify affirmative action as a remedial tool. The Court did not address whether goals other than the remedying of discrimination could justify affirmative action (such as promoting diversity and inclusion of racial minorities). The appropriate standard of review to be applied to gender classifications was not addressed. The decision did not apply to limit outreach and special recruitment efforts designed to expand the pool of applicants and bidders even if that involved race-conscious action.

In terms, then, of the practical effect of the reviews to be undertaken following *Adarand*, much would depend on the rigour with which departments and agencies reviewed their programmes. In March 1995, President Clinton announced a review of federal affirmative action policies, including those contract compliance programmes discussed in chapter 6 above, following successful attempts during the winter by the Republican leadership in Congress to make affirmative action a central domestic political issue. George Stephanopoulos (Special Adviser to the President) and Christopher Edley, Jr (the President's special counsel) were given the task of carrying out the review. The White House review report, together with the President's speech announcing it in July 1995, signalled the political and policy stand the President would take in the future.[23] The speech in particular was a forthright support of the basic principles underlying affirmative action. Though it had sometimes given rise to unfairness and inefficiency, it should be 'mended' rather than 'ended'. Against some expectations, no programmes were suspended or revoked. Instead, in an accompanying memorandum, the President instructed all federal bodies to review their policies using the interpretation of the constitutional requirements laid

---

[22] US Justice Department, Office of Legal Counsel, Memorandum to General Counsels, 28 June 1995.
[23] Affirmative Action Review Report to President Clinton, 19 July 1995, BNA, DLR, 20 July 1995.

down in *Adarand*, together with four policy principles. The policy principles were that any programme must be eliminated or reformed if it: (1) created a quota; (2) created preferences for unqualified individuals; (3) created reverse discrimination; or (4) continued even after its equal opportunity purposes had been achieved.

The immediate political reaction was predictable: strong support from civil rights groups and unions (and some business leaders), and opposition from the Republican leadership in Congress and beyond. Senators Dole and Gramm, both Republican Presidential hopefuls, announced that legislation would be introduced the following week to limit affirmative action much more radically. Crucially, the President's chances of holding off this challenge depended on conservative Democrats. Legislation was introduced by Senator Dole (amongst others) which would have prohibited the use of racial and gender 'preferences' in all federal government programmes, including 'any use of a quota, set-aside, numerical goal, timetable, or other numerical objective',[24] but this was easily defeated, on a bipartisan basis, as were all the other attempts in the federal Congress to rein in the use of set-asides by legislation.[25]

At the state level, however, there were some successful efforts to stop state and local set-asides modelled on the federal programmes. A well-organized campaign in California succeeded in persuading Governor Pete Wilson to sign an executive order requiring the state department of transportation to reduce the proportion of state money set aside for contracts to be awarded to women and minority businesses. In 1996, a proposition was included on the California ballot (a form of referendum) that would prevent the state government from using race or gender as a factor in hiring and contracting. Proposition 209, as it was called, passed easily with over 54 per cent of the vote.[26] An equivalent referendum held in the state of Washington resulted in 58 per cent of the voters approving a ban on preferential treatment in hiring, contracting, and admissions to college.[27] In order to head off a similar move in Florida, Governor Jeb Bush issued an executive order limiting the State's set-aside programme.[28]

At the federal level, the main focus was on the results of President Clinton's review of affirmative action. Taken together, the various internal reviews resulted in some significant scaling back of programmes that set aside proportions of government contracts for business contractors from racial or ethnic minority groups.[29] Race-neutral alternatives were to be used to the maximum extent possible. Race would be relied on only when research indicated that minority contracting fell below the level that would be anticipated had there not been discrimination. Race would not be relied on as the sole factor in procurement decisions. In most cases,

---

[24] BNA DLR, No 144, 27 July 1995, d3.   [25] Anderson (n 4 above) 245–51.

[26] ibid 256. An attempt to have it declared unconstitutional under the federal Equal Protection Clause failed, *Coalition for Economic Equity v Wilson* 122 F 3d 692, cert denied 522 US 963 (1997).

[27] ibid 261.   [28] idid 262.

[29] Information in this paragraph is taken from Department of Justice Proposed Reform to Affirmative Action in Fderal Procurement, 1996 *Daily Labor Report* 100 d22. See also Anderson (n 4 above) 252–8.

set-asides would not be used; instead, credits would be used which would ensure that all firms had an opportunity to compete. Reliance on race would be closely tied to an analysis of the relative capacity of minority firms to perform the work in question, or what their capacity would be in the absence of discrimination. As minority firms became more successful in obtaining federal contracts, reliance on race would decrease automatically.

The application of these principles led to certain significant changes. The Defense Department suspended a rule that had the effect that if at least two qualified small, disadvantaged buinesses expressed an interest in bidding, only those firms could compete for the contract. The Energy Department, the Federal Highway Administration, and the Commerce Department, among others, cut back their set-aside programmes. Eligibility would need to be certified for participation in all programmes. The review of the 8(a) program resulted in several changes. Race-conscious set-asides would only be permitted where a study had found credible evidence of discrimination. A certification process was introduced to ensure that companies were minority owned. Disadvantaged businesses would only be given preferences in particular areas and industries where they were underrepresented and not generally. There would be a crackdown on fraud in the award of such contracts; in particular, new requirements were introduced to ensure that those who were disadvantaged retained control of firms receiving preferences.

Set-asides and equivalent preferences were more limited, therefore, but were far from dead.[30] In 2000, for example, the Equity in Contracting for Women Act was passed.[31] This was intended to allow for greater representation of women-owned small businesses in certain historically underrepresented industries in federal contracting. Under the Act, the SBA was required to establish a preferential procurement programme for 'small business concerns owned and controlled by women'. The Act provided, in part, that the SBA may restrict competition for any contract for the procurement of goods or services by the federal government to small business concerns owned and controlled by women under certain conditions. The concerns must be not less than 51 per cent owned by one or more women who are economically disadvantaged, and must be certified as (or capable of being certified as) small business concerns owned and controlled by women. There must be a reasonable expectation that two or more small business concerns owned and controlled by women will submit offers for the contract. The anticipated award price of the contract (including options) must not exceed US$5 million in the case of a contract assigned an industrial classification code for manufacturing, or

---

[30] Also in May 1996, the Department of Labor announced changes in the operation of the requirements under Executive Order 11246, the contract compliance programme. The OFCCP Proposed Rule on Affirmative Action Requirements for Federal Contractors: Implementation of Executive Order 11246, 1996 *Daily Labor Report* 98 d25. These were much less significant than those announced for the set-aside programmes. The proposed changes related to relatively mundane issues such as record retention, complaince monitoring, and paperwork concerning segregated faciltities.

[31] Pub Law No 106-554, 114 Stat 2763A-708 (2000) (codified, as amended, at 15 USC §637(m)).

US$3 million in the case of all other contracts. The contract award could be made at a fair and reasonable price.

II. Aboriginal Set-asides in Canada

Role of procurement linkage in the Aboriginal agreements

In chapter 3 above, the development of Canadian approaches to equal status for Aboriginal peoples in Canada was examined. A common element in both the pre- and post-1995 agreements between the Aboriginal peoples and the Canadian government was the role of procurement linkage. The earliest modern agreement, the James Bay and Northern Quebec Agreement, provided that the Cree would have a 'preferential status for employment arising from remedial works and programs' of the body set up to administer the agreement. As far as possible, Cree bands and Cree enterprises should get a fair opportunity to tender on such contracts. Cree bands and enterprises were to 'enjoy a 10% price preferential'.[32] The Inuvialuit Final Agreement required the federal government to 'notify the Inuvialuit [of] all Government contracts subject to public tender that relate to activities in the Inuvialuit Settlement region and the Inuvialuit communities'.[33] In addition, where the Inuvialuit 'submit the best bid having regard to price, quality, delivery and other stipulated conditions, the contract shall be awarded to the Inuvialuit'.[34] Commentators also considered that the agreement allowed the federal government to award contracts to Inuvialuit contractors, or to 'impose compliance with [social] objectives . . . on those with whom it contracts for supplies and services within the Settlement Region'.[35]

The Nunavut Land Claims Agreement provided much more extensively for the regulation of government contracts. Article 26 of the agreement provided that the Government of Canada agreed to develop procurement policies respecting Inuit firms for all federal government contracts required in support of its activities in the Nunavut Settlement Area. The objectives of the article were subject to an overriding limitation, that they should be achieved through the allocation or re-allocation of government expenditures without imposing additional financial obligations on the Government of Canada or the territorial government.[36] Within these limits, the Government of Canada and the territorial government agreed to undertake various obligations.

Both governments would provide reasonable support and assistance to Inuit firms to enable them to compete for government contracts.[37] The Government of

---

[32] James Bay and Northern Quebec Agreement, s 8, para 8.9.2.
[33] Inuvialuit Final Agreement, s 16(8)(b).   [34] ibid.
[35] JM Keeping, 'The Inuvialuit Final Agreement' (Canadian Institute of Resources Law, October 1989) 229.   [36] Nunavut Land Claims Agreement, art 24.9.1.
[37] ibid art 24.2.1.

Canada would develop, implement, or maintain procurement policies respecting Inuit firms for all Government of Canada contracts required in support of its activities in the Nunavut Settlement Area.[38] It would develop or maintain its procurement policies in close consultation with designated Inuit organizations (DIOs), and would implement the policies through legislative, regulatory, or administrative measures.[39] The territorial government would maintain preferential procurement policies, procedures, and approaches for all territorial government contracts required in support of territorial government activities in the Nunavut Settlement Area and would consult with the DIO when developing modifications to its preferential policies, procedures, and approaches in order that the provisions of the agreement might be met.[40] However, the territorial government agreed only to carry out the terms of the article through the application of territorial government preferential contracting policies, procedures, and approaches intended *to maximize local, regional, and northern employment and business opportunities*.[41] The difference between the commitments lies in the omission in the obligations undertaken by the territorial government to adopt preferential policies specifically targeted on Aboriginal business development. Procurement policies and implementing measures would be carried out in a manner that responded to the developing nature of the Nunavut Settlement Area economy and labour force. In particular, the policies would take into account the increased ability, over time, of Inuit firms to compete for and to successfully complete government contracts.[42]

Procurement policies and implementing measures would reflect, to the extent possible, several objectives:[43] increased participation by Inuit firms in business opportunities in the Nunavut Settlement Area economy; improved capacity of Inuit firms to compete for government contracts; and the employment of Inuit at a representative level in the Nunavut Settlement Area workforce. To support these objectives, both governments would develop and maintain policies and programmes in close consultation with the DIO which were designed to achieve particular objectives:[44] increased access by Inuit to on-the-job training, apprenticeship, skill development, upgrading, and other job-related programmes; and greater opportunities for Inuit to receive training and experience to successfully create, operate, and manage Northern businesses.

In cooperation with the DIO, both governments would assist Inuit firms to become familiar with their bidding and contracting procedures, and encourage Inuit firms to bid for government contracts in the Nunavut Settlement Area.[45] In inviting bids on government contracts, both governments would provide all reasonable opportunities to Inuit firms to submit competitive bids, and, in doing so, would take, where practicable and consistent with sound procurement management, certain measures:[46] set the date, location, and terms and conditions for bidding so that Inuit firms may readily bid; invite bids by commodity groupings to

---

[38] ibid art 24.3.1.   [39] ibid art 24.3.2.   [40] ibid art 24.3.4.   [41] ibid art 24.9.2.
[42] ibid art 24.3.5.   [43] ibid art 24.3.6.   [44] ibid art 24.3.7.   [45] ibid art 24.4.1.
[46] ibid art 24.4.2.

permit smaller and more specialized firms to bid; permit bids for goods and services for a specified portion of a larger contract package to permit smaller and more specialized firms to bid; design construction contracts in such a way as to increase the opportunity for smaller and more specialized firms to bid; and avoid artificially inflated employment skills requirements not essential to the fulfilment of the contract.

Where either government intended to invite bids for government contracts to be performed in the Nunavut Settlement Area, that government would take all reasonable measures to inform Inuit firms of such bids, and provide Inuit firms with a fair and reasonable opportunity to submit bids.[47] Where either government solicited bids for government contracts to be performed in the Nunavut Settlement Area, it would ensure that qualified Inuit firms were included in the list of those firms solicited to bid.[48] Where an Inuit firm had previously been awarded a government contract, and had successfully carried out the contract, that Inuit firm would be included in the solicitation to bid for contracts of a similar nature.[49] In the absence of competitive bidding for government contracts, qualified Inuit firms would be given fair consideration.[50]

Whenever practicable, and consistent with sound procurement management, and subject to Canada's international obligations, particular criteria, or as many as may be appropriate with respect to any particular contract, would be included in the bid criteria established by both governments for the awarding of government contracts in the Nunavut Settlement Area:[51] the existence of head offices, administrative offices, or other facilities in the Nunavut Settlement Area (for the federal government contracts) or to the area where the contract would be carried out (for territorial government contracts);[52] the employment of Inuit labour, engagement of Inuit professional services, or use of suppliers that are Inuit or Inuit firms in carrying out the contracts; or the undertaking of commitments, under the contract, with respect to on-the-job training or skills development for Inuit. The DIO would prepare and maintain a comprehensive list of Inuit firms, together with information on the goods and services that they would be in a position to furnish in relation to government contracts. This list would be considered by both governments in meeting their obligations under the agreement.[53]

Finally, both governments and the DIO would conduct a review of the effect of the procurement aspects of the agreement within twenty years of its implementation. If the DIO and either government agreed after the review that the objectives had been met, the obligations of the Government of Canada or the Territorial Government would cease within one year of the completion of the review. If the obligations of either under the Article remained in effect after the initial review, the Parties would review the requirement to continue such provisions every five years or at such other times as they may agree.[54]

---

47 ibid art 24.4.3.
51 ibid art 24.6.1.
48 ibid art 24.5.1.
52 ibid art 24.6.2.
49 ibid art 24.5.2.
53 ibid art 24.7.1.
50 ibid art 24.5.3.
54 ibid art 24.9.3.

Procurement Strategy for Aboriginal Business

There is an additional preferential procurement programme outside the ambit of the Aborigonal agreement. During the early 1990s, the Department of Indian Affairs and Northern Development (DIAND) found that federal procurement with Aboriginal business was generally problematic. In 1993, the Liberal government, in 'Creating Opportunities', called for the adoption of procurement policies that would address the issue. The report of the Royal Commission on Aboriginal Peoples supported similar proposals.[55] In March 1996, new procurement measures were announced by the Minister of Indian Affairs and Northern Development that were designed to increase the participation of Aboriginal businesses in bidding for federal government contracts. This Procurement Strategy for Aboriginal Business was to apply throughout the federal government.[56] This was achieved without the need for new primary legislation specifically addressing Aboriginal procurement issues. The Treasury Board, which is a committee of the Privy Council (Cabinet), had authority to formulate federal government procurement policy under the Financial Administration Act. The Act required all departments and agencies to adhere to all policies and guidelines issued by the Treasury Board. The Board issued Government Contracts Regulations under the Act, and the Treasury Board's Contracting Policy.[57]

In March 1996, a Contracting Policy Notice was issued concerning Aboriginal Business Procurement Policy and Incentives, which formally notified federal departments and agencies that the government had approved a strategy to promote Aboriginal business development through the federal government procurement process. The initiative consisted of several different elements: a greater emphasis on Aboriginal economic development when planning procurements; and mandatory set-asides in procurements above a threshold which were destined for Aboriginal populations; selective set-asides for specific procurements.[58] These supplier development activities aimed to achieve increased representation of Aboriginal business in contract awards by individual departments and agencies.[59] These have remained substantially the same since that time, and the following paragraphs set out the bare bones of these requirements.[60]

The programme is wide ranging. It is, however, regarded as 'consistent with the current Treasury Board contracting policy, requiring among other objectives the goal of best value in relation to other national objectives'.[61] However, where the

---

[55] See NL Vertes, DMH Connelly, and BAS Knott, 'Five year Review 1993 to 1996, Implementation of the Nunavut Land Claims Agreement: An Independent Review' (Nortext Multimedia Inc, October 1999) 1.

[56] The current policy set out at <http://www.ainc-inac.gc.ca/saea-psab/cpn/pol_e.html>.

[57] This description draws on A Van Dyk, 'Recent Changes in the Canadian Government's Contracting Policy' (1998) 7 PPLR CS110, CS110-1.

[58] Contracting Policy Notice 1996-2 on Aboriginal Business Procurement Policy and Incentives, para 4.   [59] ibid.

[60] The current PSAB—Guidelines for Buyers/Government Officials, Revised December, 2005, is available at <http://www.ainc-inac.gc.ca/saea-psab/cpn/glindex_e.html>.

[61] Contracting Policy Notice 1996-2, para 11.

requirement to use Aboriginal business would cause 'severe economic dislocation', departments and agencies are permitted to request authority of the Treasury Board to exclude specific contracts or classes of contracts from the mandatory requirements of the policy.[62]

The first phase, which became effective on 1 April 1996, requires all contracting Authorities, where a procurement is valued in excess of Can$5,000, and for which Aboriginal populations are the primary recipients, to restrict this procurement to qualified Aboriginal suppliers where operational requirements, best value, prudence and probity, and sound contracting management can be assured. Contracts valued at less than Can$5,000 may also be set aside for qualified Aboriginal suppliers if it is practical to do so. All departments and agencies are authorized and encouraged to voluntarily set aside other procurements under the set-aside programme for Aboriginal business, where practical and cost-effective. There is no upper limit for these types of procurements, but procurements over Can$2.0 million in value continue to be subject to the procurement review process. In addition, in other procurements, the participation of Aboriginal businesses as subcontractors to the prime contractors should be encouraged. However, where a procurement is subject to one of the international trade agreements, an issue considered in chapter 8 below, any consideration of, or requirement to use Aboriginal subcontractors was considered to be inconsistent with those agreements.[63] The principal relevant agreements are the Government Procurement Agreement and the procurement aspects of the North American Free Trade Agreement.

An Aboriginal person for the purposes of the set-aside programme is an Indian, Metis, or Inuit who is ordinarily resident in Canada. Evidence of being an Aboriginal person consists of such proof as: Indian registration in Canada; membership in an affiliate of the Metis National Council or the Congress of Aboriginal Peoples, or other recognized Aboriginal organizations in Canada; acceptance as an Aboriginal person by an established Aboriginal community in Canada; enrolment or entitlement to be enrolled pursuant to a comprehensive land claim agreement, or membership or entitlement to membership in a group with an accepted comprehensive claim.

An 'Aboriginal business' is defined in detail.[64] It consists of a band (as defined by the Indian Act), a sole proprietorship, a limited company, a cooperative, a partnership, or a not-for-profit organization, in which Aboriginal persons have at least 51 per cent ownership and control. In addition, however, an Aboriginal business could also consist of a joint venture consisting of two or more Aboriginal businesses or an Aboriginal business and a non-Aboriginal business, provided that the Aboriginal business has at least 51 per cent ownership and control of the joint venture. When an Aboriginal business has six or more full-time employees at the date of submitting the bid, at least 33 per cent of them must be Aboriginal persons, and this ratio must be maintained throughout the duration of the contract. The bidder must certify in its submitted bid that it is an Aboriginal business or a joint venture

---

[62] ibid para 10.   [63] ibid para 9.   [64] Appendix B of CPN 1996-6.

constituted in this way. It is not necessary to provide evidence of eligibility at the time the bid is submitted. However, the business should have evidence of eligibility ready in case it is audited.

There are three other requirements attached to bidders in the set-aside programme for Aboriginal business. First, in respect of a contract (goods, service, or construction) on which a bidder is making a proposal which involves subcontracting, the bidder must certify in its bid that at least 33 per cent of the value of the work performed under the contract would be performed by an Aboriginal business. The value of the work performed is considered to be the total value of the contract, less any materials directly purchased by the contractor for the performance of the contract. Therefore, the bidder must notify and, where applicable, bind the subcontractor in writing with respect to the requirements that the Aboriginal set-aside programme may impose on the subcontractor or subcontractors. Ownership of an Aboriginal business refers to 'beneficial ownership', ie to the individual who is the real owner of the business. The federal authorities may consider a variety of factors to satisfy whether Aboriginal persons have true and effective control of an Aboriginal business.

Where an Aboriginal business has six or more full-time employees at the date of submitting the certification and is required by the federal government to substantiate that at least 33 per cent of the full-time employees are Aboriginal, the business must, upon request by the federal authorities, immediately provide a completed Owner/Employee Certification form for each full-time employee who is Aboriginal. Evidence as to whether an employee is or is not full-time and evidence as to the number of full-time employees may include payroll records, written offers of employment, and remittance and payroll information maintained under federal obligations, as well as information related to pension and other benefit plans.

A full-time employee, for the purpose of this programme, is one who is on the payroll, is entitled to all benefits that other full-time employees of the business receive, such as pension plan, vacation pay, and sick leave allowance, and works at least thirty hours a week. It is the number of full-time employees on the payroll of the business at the date of bid submission that determines the ratio of Aboriginal to total employees of the business for the purpose of establishing eligibility under the programme. Owners who are Aboriginal and full-time employees who are Aboriginal must be ready to provide evidence in support of such status. The Owner/Employee Certification to be completed by each owner and full-time employee who is Aboriginal must state that the person meets the eligibility criteria and that the information supplied is true and complete. This certification provides the person's consent to the verification of the information submitted.

Second, the bidder's contract with a subcontractor must also, where applicable, include a provision in which the subcontractor agrees to provide the bidder with information substantiating its compliance with the Program, and to authorize the bidder to have an audit performed by the federal authorities to examine the subcontractor's records to verify the information provided. Failure by the bidder to exact or enforce such a provision is deemed to be a breach of contract and subject to the civil consequences discussed below. Evidence of the proportion of work done by subcontractors may include contracts between the contractor and subcontractors, invoices, and paid cheques. Evidence that a subcontractor is an Aboriginal business (where this is required to meet minimum Aboriginal content of the contract) is the same as evidence that a prime contractor is an Aboriginal business. Eligibility certification is subject to audit by Consulting and Audit Canada through an arrangement with Indian and Northern Affairs Canada.

Third, as part of its bid, the bidder must complete the Certification of Requirements for the Set-Aside Program for Aboriginal Business, stating that it meets the requirements for the programme and will continue to do so throughout the duration of the contract; that it will, upon request, provide evidence that it meets the eligibility criteria; that it is willing to be audited regarding the certification; and that it acknowledges that if it is found not to meet the eligibility criteria, it is subject to one or more civil consequences. The civil consequences of making a false statement in the bid documents, or of not complying with the requirements of the programme, or failing to produce satisfactory evidence to the federal authorities regarding the requirements of the programme, may include: forfeiture of the bid deposit; retention of the holdback; disqualification of the business from participating in future contracts under the programme; and termination of the contract. In the event that the contract is terminated because of an untrue statement or non-compliance with the requirements of the programme, the federal authorities may engage another contractor to complete the performance of the contract and any additional costs incurred by the federal authorities are borne by the business, if the federal authorities so request.

Under phase two of the initiative, each department and agency with an annual contracting budget in excess of Can$1.0 million was required to develop multi-year performance objectives for contracting with Aboriginal businesses. The performance objectives phase of this policy took effect on 1 January 1997.[65] This requires all departments and agencies with a contracting budget in excess of Can$1 million to develop objectives relating to procurements from aboriginal businesses and related reporting mechanisms.[66] Performance objectives are required of them on a calendar year basis, in the following areas:

(a) Estimated number of contract awards to Aboriginal business: departments and agencies must develop a performance objective specifying the number of contracts and subcontracts to be awarded to Aboriginal firms and outlining the means to be used to increase the number of contracts.[67]

---

[65] PSAB—Guidelines for Buyers/Government Officials (n 60 above).
[66] Contracting Policy Notice 1996-6 on Aboriginal Business Procurement Policy Performance.
[67] Contracting Policy Notice 1996-6, para 7(a).

(b) Estimated dollar value of contract awards to Aboriginal business: a combination of approaches may be used to develop this objective. First, a total value of contracts and subcontracts to be awarded to Aboriginal businesses should be specified. In addition, specific contracts, or sectors and regions in which increased contract values will be sought, may be specified.

(c) Estimated representation of Aboriginal business in supplier development activities: in the context of ongoing supplier development activities in departments and agencies, the department or agency must describe the means that it intends to take to increase representation of Aboriginal businesses, with specific references to regional activities where they exist.[68]

(d) Estimated representation of Aboriginal business in supplier inventories:[69] objectives must be set on a calendar year basis, for a rolling three-year period, commencing 1 January 1997.

It is acknowledged that the creation and maintenance of inventories of Aboriginal suppliers is a responsibility shared by DIAND with each department and agency. Each department and agency must describe what means it will take to increase its inventory, again with specific reference to regional activities.[70] Initial proposals were reviewed by DIAND and confirmed in an exchange of letters between DIAND and the department or agency. Agreements would be adjusted or extended annually within thirty days of the anniversary date of the agreement.[71]

---

[68] ibid para 7(c).   [69] ibid para 5.   [70] ibid para 7(d).   [71] ibid para 6.

8

Evolution of the Government Procurement Agreement Model and Procurement Linkages

In chapters 6 and 7 above, the extensive use of procurement linkages in the United States and Canada was considered and the two main forms that these procurement linkages take were identified, ie contract compliance and set-asides for businesses particularly associated with the disadvantaged group. It has been seen, too, that in discussing Canadian set-asides for Aboriginal businesses, it was necessary to refer to both the Government Procurement Agreement (GPA) and the North American Free Trade Agreement (NAFTA), which the Canadian government clearly regarded as setting limits to its programmes. In this chapter and the next, the connections between the GPA, NAFTA, and the types of domestic procurement linkages considered in chapters 6 and 7 above are explored more systematically. This chapter begins by examining the original discussions in the OECD that preceded the development of the GPA, before turning to examine the approach that the GPA itself took to such linkages. We shall see that the type of procurement linkages discussed in chapters 6 and 7, were largely ignored and that the primary focus of attention in these early drafting discussions related only to the types of linkages discussed in chapter 2 above.

I. Procurement Linkages in the Context of OECD Procurement Reform Discussions

Initial approach to linkages in the OEEC

In July 1954, the Executive Committee of the Organisation for European Economic Co-operation (OEEC) set out the terms of reference for an enquiry into technical and administrative regulations that hampered the operation of intra-European trade.[1] The OEEC had established various 'Vertical Technical Committees' covering iron and steel, timber, textiles, chemical products, and

---

[1] OEEC, CE(54)30. The terms of reference were subsequently amended in July 1956 by the Council OEEC, C(56)255 (final).

machinery. These committees reported to the Steering Board for Trade. The Machinery Committee reported in July 1956 on the regulations that it considered hampered trade in machinery.[2] Among its findings, the Committee pointed to various examples of regulations in central government purchasing that excluded or deterred foreign suppliers. It referred to 'administrative regulations designed to eliminate or handicap makers or users of foreign equipment when public tenders are invited', giving as examples the use of different criteria for judging domestic and foreign tenders, and the issuing of instructions to national buying departments to deal only with domestic suppliers.[3] The Committee recommended that Member countries should be 'requested to review their procedure and inform the OEEC of any changes introduced'.[4]

In its report to the Council of the OEEC, in January 1958, the Steering Board took up this issue, but regarded it as more complex that the Machinery Committee apparently did.[5] The Steering Board for Trade therefore asked the Machinery Committee for 'information in regard to regulations, procedure or practice concerning public tenders and government contracts, insofar as such regulations, procedure or practices are likely to hamper intra-European trade'.[6] Effectively, the issue was referred back to the Machinery Committee, but whilst the issue was still in the specific context of machinery, it had been effectively broadened to include the *practices* of government, at whatever level, rather than simply formal regulations issued at the national level. The Machinery Committee carried out a further detailed enquiry based on questionnaires sent to the member countries, reporting back to the Steering Board in December 1960.[7]

The Committee distinguished between three categories of national practice that were clearly discriminatory. It identified preferences given to domestic tenders as compared with equivalent or lower-priced foreign tenders, preferences given to certain categories of domestic bidder, which entailed discrimination against all other bidders, whether domestic or foreign, and cases in which foreign tenders were rejected for security reasons. In the second category, it identified several West German and United States practices. In West Germany two practices were singled out for comment.[8] First, there was a requirement that the contract must be awarded to persons expelled from East Germany, persons and enterprises from distressed regions, those who had suffered under Nazism, and those who had been evacuated, provided their bid was as economical as (or even slightly above) the most economical bid submitted by a non-privileged applicant. A second practice which was identified involved the Department of Defence setting aside a certain percentage of the total value of the contract for German 'medium-sized' firms.

---

  [2] OEEC 485, EQ(56)7.   [3] OEEC, EQ(56)7, Annex 4, paras A and B.
  [4] OEEC, EQ(56)7, para 30(1).   [5] OEEC, C(58), 13 January 1958.
  [6] Note from the Steering Board for Trade to the Machinery Committee, adopted on 14 November 1958, Annex to EQ(58)7.   [7] OEEC 124, EQ(60)13, 22 December 1960.
  [8] ibid para 6.

Regarding the United States, the report identified the ability of department heads to set aside procurements exclusively for domestic small businesses. As importantly, however, the results of the Committee's research demonstrated that, even leaving these practices to one side, the 'tendering procedure...sometimes includes requirements with which it would be difficult for foreign suppliers to comply, and although, a priori,...the conditions governing the final choice are not necessarily more favourable to the domestic manufacturer than the foreign supplier, in practice the liberty left to the buying department is wide and may open the door to discrimination'.[9]

The group considered that the report 'clearly shows the existence of a problem which has been receiving attention not only in the OEEC but in other international organisations also',[10] mentioning the developments in the European Free Trade Association (EFTA), by the Benelux countries, and within the EEC. However, it was clear that the problem applied well beyond the purchase of machinery and existed with regard to 'other goods purchased by government departments also'.[11] Further study would therefore be necessary and the OECD would be likely to take up the issue. In the interim, the material that the Committee had collected should be 'derestricted', meaning that it could be published by member countries, provided that the material 'should be limited to a description of the regulations and of the procedure followed...to eliminate any comment by the Machinery Committee'.[12]

OECD negotiations on procurement begin

With the establishment of the OECD, there was a reconsideration of how best to take further action to address administrative and technical regulations that hampered the expansion of trade. In 1961, the Trade Committee established a working party to consider the issues which required priority and to consider the methods that the OECD should adopt. The working party reported in May 1962.[13] As regards issues that should be given priority, 'regulations regarding government buying' were identified along with import licensing procedures and customs procedures.[14] The working party considered that the work completed to date within the OEEC, together with the work that was then being undertaken with the EEC 'may well provide a starting point for a general confrontation on government buying aimed at abolishing discrimination resulting from public laws and regulations, to be carried out by the Trade Committee',[15] and this was endorsed by the Trade Committee itself in its report to the Council.[16]

---

[9] OEEC 485, SBC(61)5, 4 November 1961, para 2.   [10] ibid para 3.   [11] ibid para 4.
[12] ibid para 5.   [13] OECD 124, TC(62)18, 24 May 1962.   [14] ibid para 10.
[15] ibid para 13.   [16] OECD 124, C(62)108, 12 June 1962.

More generally, the Trade Committee recommended that the Council should adopt a:

... specific procedure in this field [ie in the field of administrative and technical regulations which hamper the expansion of trade], combined with a general recommendation to reduce the detrimental effect on trade of administrative and technical regulations to the absolute minimum. This would have the advantage of focusing attention on problems which exist in this particular field and would provide a firm basis for efficient action by the Organisation.[17]

This recommendation was accepted by the Council, which issued a formal Recommendation on 3 July 1962.[18] The Council recommended 'that Member Governments keep under review their administrative and technical regulations in order to eliminate those provisions which are not essential for the purpose of the regulation and which hamper trade'.[19] In addition, the Council decided to establish a procedure whereby any member government which considered that an administrative or technical regulation enforced in another member country 'hampers its exports to that country, or has the effect of directly or indirectly discriminating against its trade, may refer the case to the Organisation', although it went on to provide that: 'As a general rule cases should be referred only when direct negotiations between the Governments concerned have proved unsuccessful.'[20] The Trade Committee was given the responsibility of examining any such case and reporting to the Council if necessary.

The Trade Committee, in turn, established a working party on procedures for government purchasing, with two mandates: to bring up to date the information collected by the OEEC Machinery Committee, supplementing it where necessary, and to carry out an inquiry into any cases 'where Member countries considered that regulations, procedures, administrative practices, etc. had in law or in fact hampered one of their nationals in tendering for or obtaining a government contract in another Member country'.[21] From this point, the work on procurement divided into two streams. One stream was the general work on investigating domestic practices and engaging in a 'general confrontation'. The other stream arose from the possibility of submitting a case under the specific complaints procedure just discussed.

Belgian complaint against the Buy American Act

In October 1962, the Belgian government referred to the OECD a complaint against the United States arising from the 'Buy American Act' of 1933 discussed in chapter 2 above. The precipitating event was a significant change in policy adopted

---

[17] ibid para 4.
[18] Council Recommendation of the Council on Administrative and Technical Regulations which Hamper the Expansion of Trade, OECD 124, C(62)108 (final), 11 July 1962.   [19] ibid para I.
[20] ibid para II(1).   [21] OECD, TC/M(62)3(Prov) item 11C.

by the United States Department of Defense in August 1962. The Belgian complaint was against the Act in general, but specifically drew attention to the change of policy in the following terms:

In the case of purchases of products intended for use outside United States territory, the preference given to national suppliers has been increased [from 6 and 12 per cent in favour of national suppliers] to 50 per cent . . . Further, the Secretary of Defence has ordered that the documentation relating to the purchase of foreign goods should be submitted to his office for individual examination. As a result of these directives, various offers of foreign products have been ruled out, either because the preferential margin was increased to the detriment of foreign suppliers, or because of the considerable delay involved in the allotment of the contracts.[22]

The issue was referred to a working party of the Trade Committee. The United States replied to this complaint in June 1963, explaining in more detail the operation of its regulation of federal government procurement. Two parts of the response are of particular interest. First, the sudden hike in the domestic preference in Department of Defense contracts was defended on the basis of the United States' need to address balance of payments problems.[23]

The other interesting aspect of the United States memorandum relates to its treatment of the plethora of other socio-economic provisions in the United States federal government procurement requirements. Federal government procurement was governed 'principally by the Buy American Act'.[24] Other legislation affecting federal procurement 'is of comparatively minor importance'.[25] In addition to the Buy American Act, 'heads of United States Government agencies may set aside procurement exclusively for small business and reject any offers of imported materials for security reasons or because it would be inconsistent *with the public interest*' (emphasis added), but 'these additional exceptions have not been important factors limiting United States Government use of imported goods'.[26] In a separate note, the United States Delegation proposed to the working group of the Trade Committee that, as part of a general study of the procurement practices of member governments, the Secretariat should be authorized to collect information from member governments including 'the extent to which bidding is open to international competition . . . and . . . other requirements operating to discourage foreign bidders'.[27]

The United Kingdom Delegation subsequently joined the debate, submitting a detailed memorandum in November 1963 essentially joining the Belgian complaint.[28] The bulk of the submission dealt with the legal basis of public procurement

---

[22] Belgian Delegation to the OECD, memorandum on United States Legislation and Regulations Regarding Government Contracts, 25 October 1962, OECD 143, TC(62)30, 29 October, 1962.

[23] US Delegation, United States Legislation and Regulations Applicable to the United States Government Procurement: Memorandum by the United States Delegation, OECD 143, TFD/TD/142, 11 June 1963.   [24] ibid.

[25] ibid.   [26] ibid.   [27] OECD 124, TFD/TD/144, 11 June 1963.

[28] OECD 143, TFD/TD/193, 30 November 1963.

in the United States and the adverse effects of the Buy American Act. In addition, directly challenging the assertion to the contrary by the United States delegation, the United Kingdom considered that the labour surplus area preference and the small business set-aside operated by the Department of Defense, and discussed in chapter 2 above, 'may be important factors limiting United States Government use of imported goods'.[29] Apart from these restrictions, the United Kingdom also listed a further eight provisions which 'directly or indirectly restrict the purchase of foreign goods by the United States Government'.[30] Interestingly, however, the complete list does not contain any which 'indirectly' restrict; all are direct, explicit domestic preference provisions. Finally, complaints were also made about the adoption by United States state authorities of domestic preference rules. All in all, concluded the United Kingdom, 'the restrictions have substantially impaired concessions granted by the United States in past tariff negotiations'.[31]

The United States responded to the United Kingdom memorandum in March 1964.[32] Again making a connection to the Trade Committee's ongoing general work on public procurement, the United States restricted itself to dealing with issues that were of bilateral concern between the United States and the United Kingdom, noting that 'several issues... will be covered in the United States' contributions to that general work. It was particularly careful to rebut the argument arising from the impairment of tariff concessions. Not surprisingly, the United States relied on the exception in Article III 8(a) of GATT:

> Tariff concessions granted by the United States in past tariff negotiations have not been impaired by the procurement practices of the Defense department. These tariff concessions have been granted in the context of the general provisions of the General Agreement on Tariffs and Trade (GATT). Article III 8(a) of GATT specifically exempts from the general application of national treatment, laws, regulations or requirements governing the procurement by governmental agencies of products purchased for governmental purposes and not with a view to commercial resale. Under these circumstances whatever may have been the actual adverse effect of Defense department practices on potential United Kingdom exports of products on which the United States has granted concessions, the regulation of government purchases for governmental use is so expressly excepted from the provisions of GATT as to prevent such practices from forming the basis of formal complaints under the appropriate provisions of the GATT.

Pomeranz points to the paradox of the conflicting positions on this application of the GATT agreement to procurement:

> ... in the early days of the negotiations that produced the GATT, the United States had argued *for* national treatment. It was only after opposition to this position by the United Kingdom and several other major countries that the GATT exception was created. Thus, at least one of the parties in the OECD case was in the anomalous position of complaining about an action taken by the United States, when that action was consistent with the GATT

---

[29] ibid.   [30] ibid, Annex, para 12.   [31] TFD/TD/193 (see above) para 11.
[32] OECD 143, TFD/TD/215, 24 March 1964.

because that same complaining country had succeeded in defeating the earlier U.S. proposal which, if adopted, would have provided a GATT basis for the OECD complaint.[33]

The working party of the Trade Committee reported on the case in July 1964.[34] It focused entirely on increased preferences introduced by the Department of Defense, ignored the issue relating to paragraph 8(a) of Article III, and left alone the issue of the Buy American Act preferences more generally: 'the question of United States Government procurement practices in general are [sic] dealt with in the framework of the overall examination of Members' procurement regulations and practices'.[35] Even confining itself to that issue, the working group was unable to reach a consensus, and was able only to put the competing views of the United States and 'several members of the Working Party'. The latter 'expressed their Government's concern not only with the sharp increase in the preference margin but also with the uncertainty created by the present procurement practices of the Department of Defence'. The same group expressed 'regret... that the United States Government had chosen to impose a restrictive trade measure as a means for helping to resolve its balance of payments problem [and] did not consider a measure which was restrictive of trade as an appropriate one for the United States in present circumstances'.[36]

Not surprisingly, when the working party reported to the Trade Committee, the Belgian delegation 'regretted that the Working Party's conclusions had not been accepted unanimously'.[37] The Committee approved the report, and (as the United States had clearly been advocating) rolled up the specific issue of United States practices into the Working Party's general review of government procurement procedures applied by the member countries.[38] Pomeranz, reporting from the United States position, describes how 'the U.S. Delegate, while agreeing to a further study of the case against the United States, was successful in shifting the focus of the investigation to a general review of government procurement procedures in all of the member countries'.[39]

The OECD's general work on government procurement

Whilst the Belgian complaint was under consideration by the working group of the Trade Committee, the same group was undertaking the much larger task of preparing documentation on the procurement practices of all the member countries of the OECD. The general approach adopted by the Secretariat of the working party was first to update the information collected in 1960 by the Machinery Committee of the OEEC on the regulations and procedures applicable to government purchases of engineering products in member countries, and to supplement it to cover all products. This was issued to the working party members.[40] A set of

---

[33] M Pomeranz, 'Toward a New International Order in Government Procurement' (1979) 11 Law and Policy in International Business 1263, 1271–2.
[34] OECD 143, TC(64)18, 3 July 1964.   [35] ibid para 4.   [36] ibid para 11.
[37] OECD, TC/M(64) 2 (Prov).   [38] ibid.   [39] Pomeranz (n 33 above) 1272.
[40] OECD, TFD/TD/190, 2 December 1963.

clear recommendations as to how the work might best be continued was also circulated by the Secretariat. The Secretariat did not play down the difficulty of the project and argued for the work to be completed in stages:

It must be borne in mind that there are no commonly accepted standards by which a government's procurement policy and practices can be judged as to restrictiveness or liberality. While it may be argued that a difference in the treatment accorded domestic and foreign suppliers is *ipso facto* restrictive of international trade, the complexity of the problem suggests that our future work should be carried out in stages involving firstly a full appreciation and understanding of the policy and practices of member Governments in this field and subsequently the development of the possible criteria which might apply with respect to government buying.[41]

Member governments and the Secretariat would prepare written questions to be answered by the member countries. These answers would be circulated and opportunities given to comment on the responses 'to assure that there is a full understanding of the procedure, policy and practices of member governments in the field of government buying'.[42] The Note prepared by the Secretariat further suggested that this could be followed by an analysis by the Secretariat of the information showing the similarities in practices as well as the divergences. 'The emphasis would be on the differences in treatment afforded national and foreign suppliers'.[43] The 'final stage would be an examination of this analysis by the Working Party, perhaps at this time calling on experts from capitals who are knowledgeable on the commercial policy aspects of the problem. The Working Party might seek to culminate this examination with the establishment of some minimum standards regarding participation of foreign suppliers in government procurement.'[44]

There were several major limits built into the shape and scope of the inquiry. There was a major issue relating to the scope of coverage of the examination of procurement procedures, in particular how far the inquiry should include procurement by local authorities as well as the central government and its agencies. The original Secretariat Note suggested, in an important move that was to have major repercussions, that 'it would probably be desirable, at this time, to limit the scope of the study to the central government and its agencies'. Subsequently, this was agreed by the working party and the Trade Committee, with the additional clarification that 'purchases by regional and local authorities and nationalised or semi-nationalised enterprises would not be considered either'.[45] A second major limit on the scope of the inquiry was that it was limited to purchases of supplies, and that public works contracts and procurement for public services would not be covered. 'Consequently, while the information obtained applies partly to government contracts in general, those aspects of the question which relate only to contracts for work or services have not been studied in detail.'[46]

---

[41] OECD 124, TFD/TD/191, 2 December 1963.   [42] ibid para 1.   [43] ibid para 2.
[44] ibid para 3.   [45] OECD, TFD/TD/243, 6 October 1964, para 5.   [46] ibid para 6.

Much of the work of the working party between 1964 and 1966 consisted of the tedious task of collecting, summarizing, and agreeing the information on national procurement practices from the Member countries. This was subsequently published in 1966 by the OECD in the form of chapters on each member country under common headings.[47] The booklet was later updated and republished in 1976, incorporating some changes that had occurred over the ten years since the first edition.[48] (In the following discussion, reference will be made to the 1976 publication.)

In addition to the United States preferences in the form of the Buy American legislation, other countries identified particular examples of social policy linkages with procurement many of which have been discussed in chapter 2 above. In Denmark, certain goods produced by particular public undertakings were given a certain preference by public authorities 'if they meet the need of their purchasing agencies'. The particular public authorities included goods produced 'in protected workshops, in prisons and in social welfare institutions for training purposes'.[49] Finland reported that account was taken 'of the requirements of promoting domestic production and the use of domestic labour'.[50] In France, preferences were given to particular types of French suppliers. Where there was equality of tenders, the procurement code gave preference to 'the producers' co-operatives and agricultural producers' societies' and to 'workers' co-operatives and artists' co-operatives', although 'in practice these preferences are seldom applied'.[51] In West Germany, tenders from a range of sources were accorded a price preference: 'expelled people, refugees from the Soviet zone, victims of persecution, evacuees, workshops for disabled persons and workshops for the blind'.[52] Further, an additional margin of preference was given to bids made 'by persons or enterprises in the peripheral regions bordering on the German Democratic Republic and in West Berlin'.[53] Finally, there were set-aside provisions for Ministry of Defence contracts for 'medium-sized' firms employing up to fifty people.[54] In Italy, a proportion of government buying was set aside for goods produced in Southern Italy and the Islands, and the National Agency for the Work of Blind People. Such preferential treatment 'affects Italian as well as foreign products'.[55] In the United Kingdom, preferences were given to firms situated in Development Areas and Northern Ireland. A measure of preference was also given to 'selected non-profit making bodies such as prison workshops and organisations for the employment of incapacitated and disabled workers'.

Frankly, the more interesting and important work of the working party consisted in considering what should be done with such information, and in particular whether an attempt should be made to seek agreement on limiting some or all

---

[47] OECD, Government Purchasing in Europe, North America and Japan: Regulations and Procedures (OECD, 1966).

[48] Government Purchasing: Regulations and Procedures of OECD Member Countries (OECD, 1976).   [49] ibid 29.

[50] ibid 34.   [51] ibid 40.   [52] ibid 44.   [53] ibid 45.   [54] ibid.

[55] ibid 63.

of these practices, and if so on what grounds. By October 1964, the Secretariat was already putting forward an analysis that it had drawn from the information supplied by the Member countries that had responded by that time under various headings, including the nature and scope of national regulations, the procedures of tendering adopted, the circumstances in which tenders were opened, the time allowed for tendering, requirements laid down for possible suppliers, criteria for assessing bids and awarding contracts, post-award publicity concerning the details of the contract awarded, and discrimination between suppliers. The Note ended with some general observations to take discussion further. With regard to the issue of socio-economic criteria, the information available was thin, but the approach taken by the Secretariat was conciliatory and sympathetic to such linkages where they were not discriminatory. This paper set the general approach that the Secretariat was to follow, with modifications, for the next few years and it is therefore of some importance to examine the approach it takes to socio-economic factors.

The procedures in the member countries were seen to be varied and that was in part because considerations other than economic considerations applied, 'such as the requirements of national defence, the effects of government purchases on the general economic situation or on that of certain branches or areas, the speed and regularity of deliveries, etc'.[56] The paper identified the use of social linkages as arising in several different elements of the procurement decision: in the requirements laid down for possible suppliers, and in the award criteria that give privileges for certain categories of suppliers. With regard to the requirements for suppliers, the Note observed that some countries:

... have reported that they require suppliers to submit to certain checks, especially before they are entered on lists of approved suppliers, to establish their financial and technical capacity ... or verify that they have complied with the fiscal and social legislation (France). For some contracts suppliers may also be required to put up financial guarantees, to ensure that the contract will be carried out (Canada, France). In no case do these requirements seem to be excessive or discriminatory.[57]

With regard to the privileged categories of suppliers, the Note discussed the German preferences for expatriates and refugees, evacuees, victims of Nazism, and firms in critical areas, who benefited from preferences. The Note continued:

In France, other things being equal, priority must be given to certain organisations (craftsmen's co-operatives, agricultural co-operatives). In Italy, 25 per cent of State purchases must be made from firms in the South of Italy. In addition, for purchases for the railways, priority must be given to Italian suppliers if their bids are comparable with those of other suppliers. In the United Kingdom, 25 per cent of official purchases must benefit suppliers in economically depressed areas, provided that their bids are not higher than those of other competitors.[58]

---

[56] ibid para 7(b).   [57] ibid para 7(e).   [58] ibid para 7(h).

These examples were distinguished from preferences for domestic suppliers such as those adopted in the Buy American Act.

In its general comments, the Note appeared to accept that such linkages between procurement and socio-economic objectives were a part of the existing functions that procurement had in the various member countries. With regard to the rules for participation in contracts and requirements to be met by suppliers, the Note struck a tone of moderation:

It does not seem unreasonable that the authorities should require their suppliers to meet certain conditions enabling their technical, commercial, and financial capacity to be assessed. On the other hand it seems that as a general rule such conditions should not extend to legal or technical requirements, the effect of which is in law or in fact to exclude certain categories of suppliers, and in particular foreign suppliers, from participation in tenders. Where there are exceptions for reasons of national defence or national interest such exceptions should follow rules laid down in advance and made public. In cases where limited invitations are addressed to certain suppliers in accordance with lists of suppliers approved by the purchasing authority, such lists should not be immutable but should be revised periodically, and new suppliers should have the opportunity to be included in them if they have the necessary qualifications.[59]

As regards the criteria for the award of the contracts, the Note reminded the working party that 'in a number of countries preferences, privileges or priority are granted to certain categories of suppliers for reasons of national interest or economic, regional or social policy'. The Note continued:

It would be unreasonable to condemn these practices as a whole, and it is normal for governments to use the powerful economic lever represented by official purchasing to support certain aims of their general policy. On the other hand, it seems legitimate to ask that these practices should not be left to the arbitrary choice of purchasing authorities and should in any case not be prohibitive in regard to non-privileged or foreign suppliers. It would therefore seem desirable that they be channelled along certain lines which could not be changed at the sole discretion of purchasing authorities and could be to some extent harmonized internationally.[60]

In a crucially important paragraph, paragraph 10, the Note set out what the aim of the Trade Committee should be in this area:

To this end [ie the expansion of international trade], it is desirable that agreement should be reached on a number of criteria or norms to which the Member countries should endeavour to adapt their procedures. These criteria should, it seems, aim at limiting discrimination against foreign suppliers and products and, more generally, should limit the possibilities of arbitrary decision on the part of purchasing authorities.[61]

The working party essentially adopted this approach at its meeting on 16 and 17 February 1965, with the subsequent Note drawing attention to the 'particular emphasis given to [the aims] expressed in paragraph 10'.[62]

---

[59] ibid para 16.   [60] ibid para 16.   [61] ibid para 10.
[62] OECD 95(1), TFD/TD/322, 12 May 1965, para II.4.

The close connections between the various regional and international actors are visible in the approach made by the Secretariat of the OECD to the EEC Commission during 1962 to find out what it was planning to do.[63] Contacts between the OECD and the EEC continued at official level throughout the period described. So, for example, an EEC representative reported to the working party meeting on 16 and 17 February 1965 on the activities of the EEC Commission on procurement, including an introduction to the content of the draft directives being developed by the Commission during that period.[64] Two points emerged at that meeting that were of particular importance. First, as reported subsequently by the OECD Secretariat, the Commission representative argued that the aim of the EEC was to establish 'the most satisfactory conditions possible for competition in the public contract sector and, notably, bring about the abolition, by the contracting authorities of any de jure or de facto discrimination within the frontiers of the community, between nationals or firms of the EEC Member States'.[65] However, to achieve this 'it is not enough to lay down that the principle of non-discrimination is applicable to public contracts. It is indispensable to abolish or at least to limit as far as possible the discretionary powers available to the administration in all countries. This entails harmonization of national regulations.'[66]

A second important point to emerge was the relationship between what the Community was doing in public procurement and developments in third countries outside the Community. Asked by various delegations what regime would be applied to third countries, the EEC representative said that no decision had been made, but that there were essentially two options:

Either the Community decides to apply the inter-Community regime to third countries; if this particularly liberal solution is to have any chance of being adopted, these countries will have to supply equivalent counterparts. Or the EEC would favour restrictive legislation similar to that applied by some of its main trading partners, although this solution is obviously not the best since it is clearly very protectionist in character.[67]

The preferred solution, as perceived by the EEC representative:

...would be for the main countries to reach agreement, either within the OECD or other international forums where these questions are also dealt with, so as to abolish, in the first place, the most flagrant restrictive practices and, secondly, to elaborate a sort of international code to govern the conclusion of contracts. It would be these rules that could then be generally adopted by the EEC in its relations with non-member countries; the Community would certainly be ready to take an active part in negotiations or enable its partners to benefit from its own experience in this field.

---

[63] OECD 124, TC/WP1(62)9, 14 September 1962.
[64] OECD 95(1), TFD/TD/315, 15 April 1965. The working party was subsequently circulated with the Commission's proposal for a directive on public works, OECD 95(1), TFD/TD/315, 7 May 1965.   [65] ibid.
[66] ibid.   [67] ibid.

The working party agreed to discuss at its next meeting 'whether the Community's plans could be adopted in a broader sphere'.[68]

By August 1965, the Secretariat felt able to circulate a Note on 'Possible harmonization in the field of government purchasing'.[69] The aim should be to try to achieve harmonization 'by agreeing on a number of criteria or norms to which Member countries should endeavour to adapt their procedures'.[70] The 'basic aim underlying the criteria should be the aim *to ensure maximum fairness* in the field of public tendering through limiting discrimination against foreign suppliers and products and, more generally, eliminating the possibilities of arbitrary decisions on the part of the purchasing authorities'.[71] The 'paragraph 10' aims were, therefore, somewhat broadened to focus more on fairness and the elimination of arbitrariness in decision-making, as well as non-discrimination. The Note identified specific aspects of the procurement process for which criteria might be developed, in particular the publication of general rules and procedures applied to government contracts, publicity for issuing tenders and the period of time allowed for tendering, the provisions governing participation in tenders and the requirements for tenderers, the awarding of contracts, and information on awarded contracts.[72]

Several of the areas where criteria might be developed were seen as involving implications for the socio-economic use of procurement. Regarding provisions governing participation in tenders, the Note observed that 'it appears normal that the authorities required their suppliers to meet certain conditions enabling their technical, commercial and financial capacity to be assessed and the view appears to be generally accepted that the basis of operation for all *these* rules should be economic and commercial considerations'.[73] The Note recognized, however, that other requirements might be used and considered how best to treat these. The aim in dealing with these, it said, should be to ensure that they were 'not . . . construed in a way which would unjustifiably exclude, de facto or de jure, certain categories of suppliers, and in particular, foreign suppliers, from participation in tenders'. Even then, it was accepted that some countries would want to seek exceptions where these were deemed 'necessary for reasons of national security or national interest'.[74] Several solutions were put forward: 'such exceptions should follow rules laid down in advance and made public; such exceptions would be admissible only with regard to products included on an agreed list, or with regard to a category or kind of product which corresponds to an agreed definition; such exceptions would be dealt with under an agreed consultation procedure'.[75]

As regards the possible criteria governing the awarding of contracts, the Note recognized that in a number of member countries, 'preferences, privileges or priorities are granted to certain categories of suppliers for reasons of national interest or economic, regional or social policy'.[76] Indeed, repeating a point made earlier, it

---

[68] OECD 95(1), TFD/TD/322, 12 May 1965.
[69] OECD 95(1), TFD/TD/345, 4 August 1965.   [70] ibid para 1.
[71] ibid para 3 (emphasis added).   [72] ibid para 4.   [73] ibid para 7 (emphasis added).
[74] ibid para 7.   [75] ibid.   [76] ibid para 8.

'is normal for governments to use the powerful economic lever represented by offi-cial purchasing to support certain aims of their general policy, and some of these reasons (e.g. regional or social difficulties) are internationally recognised as justify-ing requests for waivers from certain obligations'.[77] However, it was clear that it would not be enough just to follow this approach in the procurement context, given the resistance to such policies where they were thought to be protectionist. The Note continued:

... any comprehensive exercise aiming at ensuring fair conditions of competition in the field of government purchasing will have to deal with these practices, which are not announced, or even clearly defined, in all cases. Without general agreement on certain lines or proced-ures which would preclude these policies from being left to the arbitrary choice of purchas-ing authorities and being prohibitive in regard to non-privileged or foreign suppliers, Member countries might have to draw the conclusion that their own efforts with regard to other aspects of government purchasing would not be adequately rewarded.[78]

What might be called the EEC approach (although its advocacy was not confined to the EEC Member States) of harmonizing procedures with the aim of eliminat-ing the use of 'arbitrary' elements in procurement processes, and reducing the dis-cretion available to procurement entities in order to ensure a fair level playing field, was not without criticism. Indeed the United States' approach to how best to secure the paragraph 10 aims differed considerably from this approach. The difference in view appears most clearly in the progress report submitted by the working party to the Trade Committee in October 1965.[79] In paragraph 9, the working party reported a consensus on the expanded paragraph 10 aims, but with the important omission of the need to limit arbitrariness. As now reformulated, the aim became one of '*ensuring fairness* in the field of government purchasing *through limiting discrimination* against the suppliers of foreign products'.[80] It was also agreed that guidelines 'could' be elaborated to achieve these aims. Henceforth, this paragraph 9 became the touchstone for the analysis of domestic procedures and practices. Beyond that, however, the progress report detailed the divergence of views:

In the view of some delegations [ie the United States], particular emphasis should be placed on the examination of preferential arrangements laid down in the national rules of Member countries or inherent in their procurement practices. They do not, however, object to discussing—at the same time—the merits of harmonising certain formal proce-dures. Other delegations, however, are of the opinion that guidelines to be respected on procedural aspects are a prerequisite for limiting discrimination and ensuring the achieve-ment of maximum fairness in the field of government purchasing.[81]

The Trade Committee itself, at its meeting of 21 and 22 October, essentially instructed the working party to continue on both tracks: 'account is to be taken

---

[77] ibid.   [78] ibid.   [79] OECD 95(1), TC(65)27, 11 October 1965, paras 9–11.
[80] ibid para 9 (emphasis added).   [81] ibid para 11.

of the need to examine the interrelated problems both of the procedural aspects and the existing preferential rules and practices applied by Member countries in this field'.[82]

During 1966, the activities of the working group became more focused on attempting to structure the information received from the Member countries in a way that grouped the information into categories that might be used as the basis for deciding how far such practices were acceptable. In January 1966, the Secretariat prepared a first attempt at such a classification, drawing up an analysis of the Member country responses for the use of the working party.[83] Of particular relevance for our purposes was a table setting out 'preferential regulations or practices', under eight headings: (1) 'prison labour and products of handicapped persons' (under which Denmark and Italy were listed); (2) 'national defence' (Canada, Denmark, Switzerland, United States); (3) 'regional or sectoral development' (France, Germany, Greece, Italy, Turkey, United Kingdom, United States); (4) 'economic situation, employment' (Belgium, Canada, Luxembourg, United States); (5) 'balance of payments position' (Canada, United Kingdom, United States); (6) 'obligations to investigate first if domestic goods available' (Canada, France, Greece, Italy, Luxembourg, Portugal, Spain, Switzerland, United Kingdom); (7) 'general recommendation to grant a preference to domestic goods or suppliers in certain circumstances' (Austria, Ireland, Italy, Norway, United States); and (8) 'preferences expressed in precise percentages' (Canada, Germany, Greece, Norway, United States). In a subsequent paper, in February 1966, these eight categories were amalgamated by the Secretariat, after discussion in the working party, to: 'prison labour; products of handicapped persons; goods manufactured by certain categories of persons (artists, small handicraft, co-operatives); development of certain industrial sectors)'; 'regional development'; 'general economic situation; employment; balance of payments position'; 'general preferences in favour of domestic goods'.[84]

By June 1966, a paper was produced by the Secretariat for the working party suggesting a 'tentative list of issues for discussion'. This included a section on the 'degree of compatibility of preferential rules and practices with the aims of paragraph 9', and consisted of comments on the whole range of preferences. Of particular relevance for our discussion were the comments on the categories of preferences detailed earlier. It is at this point that the categories of preferences listed come to look remarkably like the general exception provision of the Government Procurement Agreement ultimately agreed in 1979. Regarding 'products of prison labour and of handicapped persons', the comment suggested that 'such preferences are not of real significance for international trade'. Regarding 'considerations of national security, public health, public order, etc' (which includes 'considerations

---

[82] OECD 95(2), TFD/TD/370, 12 January 1966.   [83] ibid.
[84] OECD 95(2) 'Government Purchasing: Tentative List of Issues for Discussion' (Draft by the Secretariat) (no OECD number listed).

of secrecy, of the safety of supply of military, strategic, medical or other emergency supplies, compliance with certain standards, etc'), the comment reads: 'such considerations are not in themselves incompatible with paragraph 9 . . . However, as they might easily be applied in such a way as to afford preferential treatment to a greater extent than would be strictly necessary to serve the legitimate purposes mentioned above, Member countries should stand ready to justify any specific cases of this kind if complaints or doubts are raised by other Member Governments.' Regarding 'regional or sectoral development considerations' (which included preferences for 'goods manufactured by certain categories of persons (artists, small handicraft, co-operatives); development of certain industrial sectors (small business, etc.)'), the suggested comment is:

. . . government preferences for these purposes do not make it easier to achieve the aims set out in paragraph 9 . . . The Working Party might consider that government preferences are hardly the best possible way of dealing with such development problems. Member Governments might therefore be invited to consider other better ways of furthering regional or sectoral development, taking into account the advisability of assisting only enterprises which are or may become competitive in the long run, and of assisting them only by means which would increase their competitive ability.

Regarding 'considerations concerning the economic situation including employment problems' (which included 'preferences accorded domestic products in order to fight unemployment or economic recession'), the suggested comment is that

. . . if government preferences are accorded to domestic products in order to fight unemployment or economic recession, the aims of paragraph 9 . . . cannot be pursued at the same time. It might be added that although government expenditure is an important element in economic policy, it seems doubtful whether preferential arrangements with regard to government purchases would be a very effective weapon and whether it should be desirable to use it, taking into account the prejudicial effects thereof on the competitive ability of domestic industry and the risk of inducing other countries to take similar steps.

Restrictions on government purchasing to deal with balance of payments issues were such as to be 'impossible' to reconcile with the aims of paragraph 9. Prior control of public purchases abroad by some central government body 'could easily be at variance' with those aims. Arrangements of a 'clearly preferential nature' 'cannot possibly be reconciled' with those aims 'and Member countries should, therefore, be urged to abolish such rules or practices, or to modify them in order to ensure that they cannot be practiced in such a way that they would be incompatible with paragraph 9'.

    This paper, somewhat amended, was circulated to delegations in early July 1966.[85] Whilst the comments detailed above were retained, virtually unamended, the paper restructured the way in which the comments were presented. The preferences discussed above and the comments were re-categorized into three basic

---

[85] OECD 96, TFD/TD/401, 11 July 1966.

types: 'national security considerations,' 'general economic and social considerations', and 'exceptional financial and economic problems'. Although this structure had been included in the previous paper, it now dominated the new paper.
National security considerations included 'defence contracts' but also 'contracts
involving considerations of national security (other than strictly defence security),
public health, public order, etc.'. General economic and social considerations
included: 'products of prison labour and of handicapped persons', 'goods manufactured by certain categories of persons (artists, small handicraft co-operatives)',
'sectoral development considerations' (for example small business), as well as the
other preferences discussed above. The category of 'exceptional financial and economic problems' included: 'balance of payment considerations', 'considerations
concerning the economic situation including employment problems', and 'regional
considerations'. The separation of regional considerations from sectoral development policies allowed a more qualified comment to be made regarding regional
policies than in the previous paper: 'the comments of the Working Party with
regard to regional development, might differ slightly from those formulated with
regard to preferential treatment granted for sectoral development considerations'.

Meetings of the working group in October and November discussed this paper,
'with the assistance of experts from capitals'.[86] These were clearly important meetings, exploring the possibilities for agreement on guidelines. The subsequent
report of the meeting by the Secretariat reflects debate over the essential question
of what the guidelines were supposed to be for. The ritual incantation of the 'paragraph 9' aim was included, but, as we have seen, this had been followed in the
previous paper by a clear description of the differences in approach different delegations took as to how best to implement these aims. In the Secretariat's Note, the
purpose of the guidelines was again considered and agreement reached on what
they were *not* for, rather than attempting to resolve the differences between the
Europeans and the Americans. 'The purpose of the guidelines is not to change the
purchasing systems in force in the various Member countries but to propose
means of limiting the risks of discrimination inherent in the various procedures
where such risks are shown to exist. They should also lay down the scope of preferential rules and practices and the extent to which these are compatible with the
aims being pursued.'[87]

The working party agreed that attention should be focused on 'promoting
international competition for participation in tenders', and 'limiting discrimination in the awarding of contracts'.[88] Essentially, the first issue was addressed by
emphasizing the need for transparency, publicity, and non-discriminatory procedures and requirements. Regarding the conditions that might be required of suppliers in order to participate in contracts, there was a clear difference of opinion
between delegations. On the one hand, 'a number of Delegations consider that
equitable treatment is ensured for suppliers of foreign products when the terms of

---

[86] OECD 96, TFD/TD/419, 13 December 1966.   [87] ibid para 4.   [88] ibid para 7.

their participation in public contracts are the same as those for domestic suppliers'.[89] Other delegations, however, 'consider that it must not be more difficult for foreign firms to comply with the normal conditions of a country than it is for domestic firms'.[90] As regards the criteria for the awarding of contracts, the 'Working Party recognised that in principle, bids should be assessed on the basis of commercial considerations only. They ought to be judged objectively and the same criteria should apply to domestic and foreign bids.'[91]

As regards what should be done about 'preferential rules and practices', the discussions accepted that in 'all the Member countries there may be considerations *other* than purely commercial ones which decide the award of a contract to certain suppliers in preference to others'.[92] The working party had 'paid great attention to these preferential rules and practices to find out to what extent and on what terms such rules and practices could be reconciled with the ideal of non-discrimination'.[93] Again the issue of how to classify the various 'preferences' became pressing. One way of moderating opposition to limiting these preferences would have been to apply any restrictions to new preferences introduced in the future rather than to existing preferences and, not surprisingly, it 'was suggested that, while seeking to avoid the introduction of further discrimination in the future, allowance might be made when examining existing preferences for situations that had given rise to measures of this kind, and it might be kept in mind that some time would no doubt be needed to change them'.[94] It is unclear what the status of this 'suggestion' was and there is no record of agreement on it.

It does appear, however, that the working party agreed on another important limiting factor on the extent to which such preferences would be challenged. The Note recounts that the working party 'agreed that the preferences with which this exercise was concerned were those which had, or could have, a real effect from the point of view of international trade. Some very limited preferences could in practice be reconciled with the objectives, or could be tolerated even if they could not be accepted in principle.'[95] Explicit preferences for domestic products were generally disapproved of although delegations clearly wanted to hold off any agreement until 'the results of the work of the Working Party can be assessed as a whole'.[96] More specific preferences of the type we have been considering above generated considerably more disagreement among the delegations. Recalling that the 'safeguarding of health, security and public order' were among the derogations in the GATT, the Treaty of Rome, and the EFTA Convention of Stockholm, the working party recognized that such requirements 'are legitimate'.[97] However, 'the Working Party thought that considerations of national defence or security should not be an excuse for discrimination or preference going beyond what is strictly necessary'. Some delegations 'expressed the view that the Member countries should be ready

---

[89] ibid para 28.   [90] ibid para 29.   [91] ibid para 31.
[92] ibid para 38 (emphasis added).   [93] ibid.   [94] ibid.   [95] ibid para 39.
[96] ibid para 42.   [97] ibid para 44.

to give their reasons in cases where doubts were expressed by other Governments as to whether the procedure adopted was justified or not'. Other Delegations, however, 'feel that such a requirement would be too binding'.[98]

Preferences for economic and social reasons were treated separately in the discussion. The sense that the treatment of such issues was taking the working group into significant areas of government policy well beyond the narrow issue of procurement was now accepted. Beginning its recounting of the discussion on such preferences in the working group, indeed, the Note recalled that the 'Working Group found that the granting of preference in government purchases for economic or social reasons was only one aspect of more general policies, which often went beyond its competence'.[99] In a statement of very considerable importance, the Note then says that the working group *therefore expressed no final opinion on such measures*.[100] The group confined itself to suggesting criteria by which preferences could be judged 'as far as the trade policy aspect is concerned'.[101] From that point of view, three general considerations were suggested, which then were applied to specific examples of particular types of preference. First, 'it was suggested' that a distinction should be drawn between permanent measures and those taken to meet temporary difficulties. 'Permanent preferences would be tolerable only if they affected sectors very restricted from the point of view of international trade. Preferences which might have an effect over wider sectors in international trade could be tolerated only temporarily and it would be necessary to be able to ensure that they were not prolonged unduly.'[102] Some delegations suggested another distinction: between those preferences that discriminated against foreign suppliers and products, and 'those that discriminated not only against foreign suppliers and products, but also against classes of domestic products, or suppliers other than a favoured group'.[103] For those who wished to see this distinction accepted, 'the question should be whether any damage that might be suffered would be the same for all, independent of their nationality', with the implication that if this was the case, then the latter preferences should be acceptable.[104] A third consideration related to the effectiveness of such preferences in achieving the aims that they were intended to further. 'As this depends on the individual case it cannot always be dealt with by the Working Party. It was thought desirable in any event to examine whether more appropriate measures than preferences for government purchases might be found, at least in some cases.'[105]

Turning to the specific examples of preferences detailed earlier, the working party concluded, 'permanent preferences for goods manufactured in prisons or by handicapped persons, which are partly subsidised by the State, are very limited in volume and may be tolerated'.[106] As regards preferences given for certain classes of producers such as cooperatives and small craftsmen, these were seen by some delegations as

---

[98] ibid.   [99] ibid para 46.   [100] ibid (emphasis added).   [101] ibid.
[102] ibid para 47.   [103] ibid para 48.   [104] ibid.   [105] ibid para 49.
[106] ibid para 51.

having 'very limited effects', whilst other delegations 'disapprove of them in principle, as in their opinion government purchases should not be used as a permanent means of aid'.[107] Preference for products manufactured in a certain structure of production such as small and medium-sized firms was seen as raising the issue of whether 'the amount of the resulting discrimination is not felt more severely by foreign firms than by other domestic firms'.[108] Preferences in favour of products manufactured in development areas, as part of regional development policies, 'weakened the position of products manufactured in other parts of the country as well as of foreign products'. The duration of such measures 'should in all cases be limited'.[109] As regards preferences granted as part of policies to encourage the growth of certain domestic industries as part of a country's industrial development policy, the working party split. Some delegations 'considered that systems of preferential rules should not be set aside until Governments had considered whether they could find better methods. Other delegations thought that preferences were not a good method and that other more suitable instruments ought to be used.' It was uncertain whether preferences for domestic products for reasons of protecting employment were effective, whilst such preferences in cases of balance of payments difficulties 'should not be maintained beyond a limited time'.[110] By the end of the discussions, 'most delegations' considered that an agreement might be reached on general guidelines 'constituting a kind of "code of good behaviour" '[111] and that a recommendation to the governments of the Member countries 'progressively to eliminate discrimination would logically form part of such a code'.[112]

In late 1967, the Secretariat was asked to prepare a set of 'guidelines' on government procurement. A draft text, of less than two and a half pages, was distributed in December 1967,[113] followed in January by a set of explanatory notes to the guidelines.[114] The guidelines were 'drafted along the lines of two 1965 EEC Directives then in force'.[115] There were essentially four sets of provisions. The first set of provisions established the principle that government purchasing policy and practices 'should be based on the principle of non-discrimination against foreign products and suppliers of foreign products'.[116] This general principle was then supplemented by a second set of provisions setting out particular procedures that would be applicable to the tendering process to ensure that the process was open, transparent, and non-discriminatory. What the prohibition of discrimination covered, however, was contested. One delegation argued that 'any measure designed to give preference to certain domestic products or suppliers over other domestic products or suppliers, and similar foreign products or suppliers of such products, should not be considered

---

[107] ibid para 52.   [108] ibid para 53.   [109] ibid para 54.   [110] ibid para 57.
[111] ibid para 59.   [112] ibid para 62.   [113] OECD, TFD/TD/466, 20 December 1967.
[114] Addendum to TFD/TD/466, 4 December 1968, Draft Explanatory Notes to the Guidelines (hereafter Explanatory Notes).
[115] A Blank and G Marceau, 'The History of the Government Procurement Negotiations Since 1945' (1996) 5 PPLR 77, 89.
[116] Annex II, Draft of Guidelines on Government Purchasing, para 1.

as contrary to the principle of non-discrimination'.[117] It is probable that this was the position of the United Kingdom as this precise argument was used some months later to defend the United Kingdom's contracts preference scheme relating to purchases from firms in Development Areas, in respect of which the United Kingdom 'does not consider that any derogation from the guidelines is necessary' because they were not discriminatory against foreign firms any more than firms in non-development areas of the United Kingdom.[118]

The third set of provisions set out various 'derogations' (what were later to be termed 'exceptions') to that principle. The issue of 'derogations' raised what was clearly a fundamental issue for the negotiations: should government purchasing be seen as legitimately an instrument of general economic policy, or should such purchases 'not be made on other than a commercial basis'?[119] Since the Secretariat considered that 'it would be impossible entirely to exclude taking other considerations into account', this 'might imply certain derogations from the principle of non-discrimination'.[120] These included measures taken 'to meet legitimate aims of national defence or national security, or the maintenance of public health and public order,'[121] which were 'similar in their aims' to Articles XX and XXI of GATT, Article 36 of the EEC Treaty of Rome, and Articles 12 and 18 of the EFTA Stockholm Convention. They should 'not be interpreted extensively'.[122] Included also were measures taken 'as part of the implementation of regional development policies, assistance to new and ailing enterprises, or the defence of small and medium sized enterprises,'[123] and 'preferences ... maintained in specific cases of very limited importance to trade (for example, products made in prison or by handicapped persons)'.[124] The latter preferences clearly raised problems for several delegations. On the one hand, some considered that, since they affected 'other suppliers of domestic products as well as suppliers of foreign products', they 'could therefore not be considered entirely as discrimination against foreign products'.[125] Others considered that alternative methods might be used that 'would not directly affect international trade' and they ought to be limited in duration and scope 'to avoid withdrawing a large purchasing sector entirely from competition (domestic and foreign)'.[126]

Lastly, there was a provision dealing with the award of contracts. 'Bids should be judged objectively, in the light of the specifications laid down in the invitations

---

[117] Explanatory Notes (n 114 above) para (1)(1)(c).

[118] OECD, Working Party of the Trade Committee, Government Purchasing, Replies to Questionnaire on Derogations, Note by the Secretariat, TFD/TD/616, 25 January 1971, reply by UK, 13.   [119] Explanatory Notes (n 114 above) para 3.

[120] ibid.   [121] Guidelines (n 116 above) para 3.

[122] Explanatory Notes (n 114 above) para 2.

[123] Guidelines (n 116 above) para 5, although these preferences 'should be limited in time and in scope, and should not affect suppliers of foreign products more severely than suppliers of similar domestic products which do not benefit from those measures'.

[124] Guidelines (n 116 above) para 6.   [125] Explanatory Notes (n 114 above) para 5.

[126] ibid.

to tender, and on the basis of commercial considerations (price, quality, delivery terms, after-sales service, etc.)'.[127] The reasons for rejecting a bid should be made available to rejected bidders. The provision on the award of contracts sought to strike a balance between the need for limits on the discretion of those awarding contracts, and the impossibility of determining in advance everything that could be taken into account. The Explanations noted that 'it did not seem possible to envisage that the commercial considerations . . . should be determined in advance. The purchasing service should remain free in its assessment of bids.'[128] On the other hand, the award of the contract 'should be based on ordinary commercial considerations'.[129]

Whilst the 'European countries were prepared to accept [these] in the form of a Recommendation',[130] the United States 'took the position that the draft was unsatisfactory because the guidelines . . . would require the elimination of specifically stated preferences, such as those in the U.S. system, [for] domestic suppliers [presumably the Buy American Act requirements], and . . . would not adequately ensure open bidding and award procedures by other countries'.[131] In June 1968, at the Trade Committee, the United States Delegation proposed 'that the Working Party continue its efforts at drafting non-discriminatory procurement guidelines'[132] by focusing on only one sector of procurement, the heavy electrical equipment sector, harkening back to the original discussions in the OEEC. In February 1969, the United States circulated its own proposal for a draft procurement guidelines text to the working party.[133] Pomeranz recounts how the 'draft proposal was produced by the leading procurement and trade experts in the U.S. government, building on an original effort by counsel from the principal U.S. electrical manufacturers'.[134] It soon became apparent that the limited focus on heavy electrical equipment would not work, and negotiations continued on a more general code.

It is worth remembering that the context in which the work of OECD was progressing changed significantly due to the progress being made in the EEC on the public procurement directives. As seen in chapter 4 above, in August 1971, the EEC had adopted the Works Directive. Perhaps not surprisingly, Member States that were also members of the working party frequently put forward proposals from that time that reflected what the EEC had agreed to.[135] During 1972, the Supplies Directive was well under way and a draft was in the process of being adopted. By June 1972, in its report to the Trade Committee, the OECD working party felt the need to draw the Committee's attention to the consequences of the EEC developments. On the one hand, the EEC's work was 'of considerable use to the Working Party'.[136] On the other hand, these developments gave rise 'to a number of questions concerning the exercise undertaken at the OECD'.

---

[127] Guidelines (n 116 above) para 16.   [128] Explanatory Notes (n 114 above) para 16.
[129] ibid.   [130] Blank and Marceau (n 115 above) 89.
[131] Pomeranz (n 33 above) 1273.   [132] ibid 1275.
[133] TFD/TD/521, 19 February 1969.   [134] Pomeranz (n 33 above) 1275.
[135] [1971] OJ L185/5.   [136] TC(72)13, 28 June 1972.

In the first place, the Member States of the enlarged European Coomunities [sic] are hardly able to take up a position with regard to the OECD provisions before they have laid down their common regulations. Another question is how much the two systems might really differ; in fact, the thinking behind the Guidelines considered at the OECD is close to that behind the provisions being drafted in the European Communities...A major difficulty would arise, if stronger obligations in respect of items common to both sets of regulations were envisaged at OECD.[137]

In October 1971, the working party of the Trade Committee returned to examine various aspects of the draft guidelines first circulated in February 1969.[138] There were three issues of particular interest raised, all reflecting to some extent the EEC Directives. The first related to the issue of thresholds, and there was general agreement on the principle that the detailed provisions relating to procedures should only apply to purchases of a relatively high value.

The second issue related to 'derogations'. A distinction was accepted between 'exceptions' and 'derogations'. By 'exceptions', the working party meant those exclusions from coverage that would be permanent. Most of what had previously been termed 'derogations' in previous meetings became 'exceptions'. Henceforth, the term 'derogations' was reserved for the non-acceptance by a particular country of the guidelines for purchases in respect of one of more specific contracts to which the guidelines would ordinarily apply. There was disagreement both on what particular exceptions were justified, and whether any derogation would be acceptable. Exceptions such as those for national security, and the purchase of products made in prisons or 'in philanthropic institutions' were agreed, but beyond that there was no agreement. In particular, there was disagreement as to whether general exceptions such as those in GATT were sound, with the EEC states among others proposing language that reflected GATT (and the Treaty of Rome) and the United States and Canada objecting that exceptions such as those for 'public health, public order, etc.' left 'too much uncertainty'.[139] The delegate for the United States 'stressed that what he wanted was a set of precise rules'.[140] As regards 'derogations', in an intervention that presaged the unease that developing countries would take to international procurement liberalization measures, Spain, Greece, and Turkey stressed the need for developing countries 'to be able to avail themselves of a general derogation in view of their special economic situation'. This position met considerable opposition and in response the possibility was raised that developing countries would simply not subscribe to the guidelines.

The third issue related to the award criteria that could be used. In a paper circulated by the Danish delegation after the October meeting but arising from it,[141] it was proposed that 'the award shall be made to the domestic or foreign bidder...found to be fully capable of undertaking the contract and whose bid is either the lowest bid or the bid which after evaluation has been found to be the

---

[137] ibid 1.   [138] TFD/TD/662, 26 November 1971.   [139] ibid 4.   [140] ibid 5.
[141] Addendum to TFD/TD/662, 26 November 1971.

economically most advantageous bid for the contract in question'. In addition, 'abnormally low' bids would not be excluded before the bidder had an opportunity to justify the bid. Both of these provisions were in the recently adopted EEC Directive.

By September 1973, the working group considered that the preparation of a possible instrument prohibiting discrimination in government purchasing was sufficiently advanced for it to be possible to submit it to the Trade Committee for consideration.[142] There were several points of importance that emerged from the text. The first related to the general exceptions; the text included a provision very similar to that ultimately included in the 1979 Government Procurement Agreement (GPA).[143] Second, there was included a provision that permitted purchasing entities to exclude suppliers 'on grounds, such as bankruptcy, false declarations etc., which a purchasing entity considers to be serious enough to justify such a measure, provided that the purchasing entity does not apply such a measure in a more severe or strict fashion to foreign than to domestic suppliers'.[144]

Of most interest, perhaps, was the working group's inability to supply an agreed text setting out the award criteria. The conflict arose, in part, because of a dispute over how far purchasing entities could or should be obliged to award a contract only on the basis of criteria previously set out in the tender documents. Some delegations considered that it was impractical 'to provide an exhaustive list of the criteria it would apply for the evaluation of bids'.[145] These different positions are reflected in the alternative versions of two sets of provisions presented to the Committee in the draft text, an issue arising again in chapter 15 below, which deals with the interpretation of the GPA.

There was nothing in the draft specifying what might be included as 'derogations'. In a separate paper presented to the Trade Committee, the Secretariat set out the possibilities. The question posed was whether in addition to thresholds, and exceptions, 'governments would still be able, in certain cases or circumstances, to use government purchasing as an instrument of internal policy in such a way as to entail some protection of national production'.[146] The working party had been unable to agree whether there should be any possibility of derogations ever being permitted, if so what they might consist of, or what other alternative approaches might be adopted.

The question of permitted exceptions and derogations remained a point of considerable disagreement. During 1974, two papers by the Secretariat identified

---

    [142] TC(73)15, 27 September 1973.

    [143] The draft text provided, in ibid, Draft, para 6: 'Subject to the requirement that such measures are not applied in a manner which would constitute a means of arbitrary or unjustified discrimination between countries where the same conditions prevail or a disguised restriction on international trade, nothing in this instrument shall be construed to prevent any signatory government to impose or enforce measures necessary to protect public morals, order or safety, necessary to protect human and animal health and life and plant life, necessary to protect industrial and commercial property, or relating to the products of handicapped persons, of philanthropic institutions or of prison labour'.

    [144] ibid Draft, para 25.   [145] ibid Add 18(g)(i).
    [146] TC(73)16, 27 September 1973, para 2.

the major sticking points on reaching agreement on a draft instrument. Some delegations continued to argue that permitting exceptions such as those included in GATT was desirable, whilst others continued to argue that exceptions for public health and public order were unacceptable as constituting 'too wide a loophole'.[147] As regards allowing derogations, again there were radically different positions taken. In particular, for some delegations 'any possibility of derogation would constitute a danger for the effective application of the Instrument and for the reciprocity of advantages, because of the difficulty of strictly limiting its use'.[148] On the other hand, other delegations argued that 'it would be difficult to exclude totally and finally the use of government purchasing, in certain circumstances, as an instrument of various policies, and it would therefore be preferable to provide certain possibilities for derogations. These latter would however remain limited and temporary, and invocations of them would be subject to control'.[149] Several grounds were suggested as possible candidates for such derogations: 'balance of payments; cyclical or employment difficulties; aid for the development of advanced technology industries, for regional development, small businesses, *underprivileged social categories*, etc'.[150] Yet others were developing a position that linked the level of the threshold with the need for derogations. Would some of the difficulties caused by such policy instruments be reduced if higher thresholds were introduced, below which the non-discrimination principle would not apply?[151]

So too, the criteria for the award of contracts was an area of considerable divergence. There was divergence over 'how much information must be given at the time of invitation to tender: must it cover all the criteria, or only the most important criteria, and must it also classify them according to their relative importance?'[152] More serious still, there was a lack of agreement concerning how much 'freedom of judgment . . . the procurement entity may retain in its choice, after application of the various criteria adopted' at the bid evaluation stage.[153] There was also a growing rift over how much information those failing to be awarded contracts could expect to be given about the reasons for their failure, and whether there should be a requirement that each state establish a national bid protest mechanism to receive and adjudicate disputes.

Lastly, a new concern with the implications of a general prohibition on discrimination was raised. The existing draft instrument established national treatment for foreign suppliers and products. The working party had not considered previously the issue of whether the instrument should also prohibit discrimination between foreign suppliers or between foreign products. This involved two somewhat different concerns: discrimination between one signatory country and another

---

[147] TFD/TD/773, 29 March 1974, Annex, para 19.
[148] TC(74)(1), 11 January 1974, para 7.   [149] ibid para 7.
[150] ibid fn (1) (emphasis added).
[151] TFD/TD/773, 29 March 1974, Annex, paras 17, 23.   [152] ibid para 12.
[153] ibid.

signatory country; and the application of the instrument to suppliers in non-signatory countries.[154]

Meanwhile the Multilateral Trade Negotiations under the auspices of GATT had been launched in September 1973 in Tokyo.[155] A Trade Negotiations Committee was subsequently established 'to elaborate and put into effect detailed trade negotiating plans and establish appropriate negotiating procedures'.[156] That Committee in turn set up several specialized groups and sub-groups which were to deal with the issues set out for negotiation in the Tokyo Declaration. However, the EEC needed assurances that the United States 'would implement into U.S. domestic law any agreement that might be concluded'[157] without unpicking any deals that had been agreed. The Trade Act of 1974, signed by President Ford in January 1975, required Congress either to accept or reject a trade agreement submitted by the President in its entirety without having the opportunity to amend it. Government procurement was dealt with in a specialized sub-group of the group dealing with non-tariff measures. The procurement sub-group was established in July 1976, holding its first meeting in October 1976. It appears that the establishment of the sub-group 'was pressed by the developing countries—in particular some of the more advanced—who believed that government procurement held out possibilities for the expansion of their trade and provided scope for special and differential treatment in their favour'.[158]

The sub-group 'undertook the collection of relevant data which would assist it in identifying the main issues and problems'.[159] This work 'led to the conclusion that the objectives on government procurement should be to provide for greater international competition and the application of commercial considerations'.[160] The expansion of world trade was clearly an important factor in driving the negotiations forward, but we should remember that the mid- to late 1970s was also a period of significant inflationary pressures. Not surprisingly, therefore, 'many countries also stressed the need, inter alia, to make more efficient use of tax revenues allocated to government procurement and also through competition to undertake purchases at the most favourable price, thus providing an additional instrument in the battle against inflation'.[161]

In October 1976, 'a carefully drafted note—all countries made sure that this note would in no way detrimentally affect their respective position at the beginning of the GATT negotiations—was transmitted from the OECD to the GATT negotiations for the first meeting' of the sub-committee.[162] This document detailed the

---

[154] ibid para 19.
[155] The Tokyo Round of Multilateral Trade Negotiations: Report by the Director General of GATT (GATT, 1979–80, Geneva) 1. The Secretary General was Mr Olivier Long. Except where otherwise indicated, the following account is based on this source. See also JHJ Bourgeois, 'The Tokyo Round Agreements on Technical Barriers and on Government Procurement in International and EEC Perspective' (1982) 19 CMLR 5, 12.   [156] ibid 6.
[157] R A Horsch, 'Eliminating Nontariff Barriers to International trade: The MTN Agreement on Government Procurement' (1979) 12 NYU JILP 315, 317.   [158] ibid 77.
[159] ibid.   [160] ibid.   [161] ibid.   [162] Blank and Marceau (n 115 above) 96.

results that had been achieved up until that time in the OECD negotiations.[163] In December 1976, the OECD transmitted the 'Draft Instrument on Government Purchasing Policies, Procedures and Practices' to GATT.[164] Article 6 provided:

Subject to the requirement that such measures are not applied in a manner which would constitute a means of arbitrary or unjustifiable discrimination between countries where the same conditions prevail or a disguised restriction on international trade, nothing in this instrument shall be construed to prevent any signatory government to impose or enforce measures necessary to protect public morals, order or safety, necessary to protect industrial and commercial property, or relating to the products of handicapped persons, or philanthropic institutions or of prison labour.

Regarding the criteria for award of the contract, the draft instrument provided: 'Any factors other than price that are to be considered in the evaluation of bids' must be included in the tender documents. The paragraph on award criteria provided:

Unless in the public interest all bids are rejected, the purchasing entities shall make the award to the bidder who has been determined to be fully capable of undertaking the contract and whose bid, whether for domestic or foreign products is either the lowest bid or the bid which in terms of the specific evaluation criteria set forth in the tender documentation . . . is determined to be the most advantageous bid for the contract in question.[165]

A domestic bid protest mechanism was also required.[166] There was no agreement as to whether or not to include derogations.

II. Tokyo Round Negotiations and the GPA's Approach to Linkage

In December 1977, the GATT Secretariat prepared and circulated a 'Draft Integrated Text for Negotiations on Government Procurement'. This was revised in March 1978. The negotiations that took place between these two dates have been examined in detail by others.[167] The text of the final Agreement was established in early April 1979 and sent to the Trade Negotiations Committee, with the results sketched out in chapter 4 above.

From the point of view of the effect of the Agreement on procurement linkages, the Agreement was complex. Although Blank and Marceau have stated that the 'information was rearranged but the logic of the OECD draft was however maintained', this is questionable when it comes to the effect of the Agreement on socioeconomic linkages.[168] The problem of potential conflict was addressed, but largely

---

[163] TC(76)20, 15 October 1976.   [164] TC(76)27, 8 December 1976.
[165] ibid para 30.   [166] ibid para 34.
[167] Blank and Marceau (n 115 above); Pomeranz (n 33 above).
[168] Blank and Marceau (n 115 above) 97.

by side-stepping the issue rather than dealing with it directly as the OECD negotiations had (partially) tried and failed to do. Most of the devices adopted to limit
conflict between the Agreement and the use of socio-economic linkages were indirect. The limits on the coverage of the Agreement were important in limiting the
extent to which conflict might arise between the Agreement and socio-economic
linkages. Only purchases over a threshold were covered, and procurement linkages
often operated in practice below that threshold. Procurement by regional and
local governments was not covered by the Agreement and, as seen in earlier chapters, much of the use of procurement linkages was undertaken at that level. So too,
the exclusion of public works contracts from coverage by the Agreement meant
that many procurement linkages in construction were not covered. The exclusion of
particular central government entities, such as the Department of Transportation in
the United States, further reduced the likelihood that linkages would come into
conflict with the Agreement. The status of the Agreement as plurilateral rather than
multilateral meant that the extensive socio-economic preferences used by developing countries were never addressed.

Those countries that have ratified the GPA are overwhelmingly from the developed world.[169] The original small group of parties to the GPA has become larger,
due in part to the requirement from some existing members of the GPA that if they
were to agree to other states becoming members of the WTO generally, they would
be expected also to become members of the GPA (thus bringing China, for
example, into the fold), and in part due to the EC's requirement that states becoming members of the EC will also become members of the GPA.[170] However, very
few developing countries are members, and in part that seems to be because of a
perception that the GPA would be too restrictive of their use of procurement linkages.[171] It is clear that some states have made assessments of what would need to be
changed in that area if they were to become members of the GPA.[172]

There were several direct methods provided in the GPA for lessening conflict
with procurement linkages. The GPA 1979 contained a general exception for certain types of procurement preferences, including 'measures necessary to protect
public morals, order or safety; human, animal or plant life; intellectual property;
or the products of handicapped persons, or philanthropic institutions or of prison
labour'. This was no general 'public welfare exception', however, and it has been

---

[169] Parties to the Agreement: Canada, European Communities (including its 25 Member States:
Austria, Belgium, Cyprus, Czech Republic, Denmark, Estonia, Finland, France, Germany, Greece,
Hungary, Ireland, Italy, Latvia, Lithuania, Luxembourg, Malta, the Netherlands, Poland, Portugal,
Slovak Republic, Slovenia, Spain, Sweden, the UK), Hong Kong, China, Iceland, Israel, Japan,
Korea, Liechtenstein, the Netherlands with respect to Aruba, Norway, Singapore, Switzerland, the
US. Negotiating accession: Albania, Bulgaria, Georgia, Jordan, the Kyrgyz Republic, Moldova,
Oman, Panama, Chinese Taipei. (Information from the WTO website at <http://www.wto.org/
english/tratop_e/gproc_e/memobs_e.htm> last visited January 2007).
[170] For the details, see S Arrowsmith, 'Reviewing the GPA: The Role and Development of the
Plurilateral Agreement After Doha' (2002) 5(4) JIEL 761, 768.   [171] ibid 769.
[172] Australian Government Department of Foreign Affairs and Trade, WTO Agreement on
Government Procurement: Review of Membership Implications (AGPS, 1997).

noted that: 'Some of the more common public interest justifications for trade barriers are noticeably missing from this part of the Agreement. For example, no exemption on balance of payments grounds is allowed, and neither aiding growth in underdeveloped regions of a nation nor assisting small and minority-owned businesses are exempt from coverage under this paragraph.'[173] In addition, however, parties to the Agreement were able to specify particular additional limitations in coverage. Several parties to the Agreement specified additional limits to coverage of the Agreement in respect of certain national procurement linkages involving socio-economic preferences. In most cases, these reflected issues that had long been discussed in the OECD. The West German government, for example, included a limit to the coverage that it accepted on the basis that there was an obligation under German law to 'award contracts in certain regions which, as a consequence of the division of Germany, are confronted with economic disadvantages'. Contracts that attempted 'to remove the difficulties of certain groups caused by the last war' were similarly exempted.[174] We are more interested, however, in the extent to which the parties used the ability to specify particular exceptions to immunize *status equality* procurement linkages from the disciplines of the GPA. We shall see that the United States and Canada did so regarding small business and minority set-asides.

Set-asides and the United States reaction to the 1979 Agreement

During the negotiation of the 1979 Agreement, United States Congressional pressure was exerted to insert a specific exception for the United States' labour surplus set-aside programmes (which targeted procurement on those areas with the highest unemployment), and (most particularly) the small business and minority set-aside programmes. The issue first became public in March 1979, when an article in the *Washington Post* stated that the small and minority business set-aside programmes would be 'overturned' by the United States' ratification of the Agreement.[175] An authoritative study of the issue has described how: 'Representatives of those businesses, and congressional supporters, particularly members of the House Small Business Subcommittee and a study group on minority enterprises, quickly rallied to apply pressure on the administration to protect the set-asides'.[176] Congressional pressure that was critical of the Administration built quickly, resulting in Congressional hearings. Initially, Ambassador Robert Strauss, the chief United States negotiator for the Tokyo Round, argued that the set-aside programmes

---

[173] DJ Peterson, The Trade Agreements Act of 1979: The Agreement on Government Procurement (1980) 14 GW JILE 321, 337.

[174] GATT, Practical Guide to the GATT Agreement on Government Procurement (Revised), February 1989, 64.

[175] 'US Would Relax Preferences to Small and Minority Firms; Small and Minority Firms Face Loss of Preference' *The Washington Post*, 14 March 1979.

[176] JE Twiggs, *The Tokyo Round of Multilateral Trade Negotiations: A Case Study in Building Domestic Support for Diplomacy* (University Press of America, 1987) 66.

would not be adversely affected by ratification of the Agreement. This was because of the exclusion of contracts valued at under US$190,000 and the exclusion of particular types of contracts from the coverage of the Agreement, such as construction and service contracts, and state and local government contracts.[177] In addition, it was argued, any loss of federal contracts to these businesses would be made up by the greater access these businesses would have to contracts in other countries. By the end of March, however, the Administration announced that it would seek a specific exemption for these United States set-aside programmes in the Agreement.[178] The rapid change in the Administration's position reflected its perception that it could not risk the possibility that small business and minority votes could stop congressional approval of the Agreement, 'or worse, the whole Geneva trade package'.[179] The United States succeeded in renegotiating the draft Agreement to have such an exemption included in its Annex to the Agreement, 'in return for inclusion of NASA on the entity list'.[180] The Canadian government included a similar exemption in its Annex. The European Community did not seek similar exceptions for small business or minority set-aside programmes. On 12 April 1979, an agreed text emerged.

Further Congressional hearings were held in April 1979.[181] These hearings, significantly, raised the issue of the effect of the Agreement not only on the labour surplus preferences, but on the whole area of socio-economic preferences in United States procurement. Detailed evidence was given by the Administrator for Federal Procurement Policy of the Office of Management and Budget. This evidence described how there were at that time over forty such programmes. These ranged 'from prison inmates supplies to handicapped, to preferential veterans' hiring programs, to equal employment opportunity, to humane slaughter of animals, to preferences for domestically made twine, speciality metals, jewel bearings from Indian reservations', as well as anti-inflation conditions.[182] The evidence given strongly argued that United States procurement policy at that time was attempting to 'serve two masters'[183]—buying high-quality goods at reasonable prices, and trying to bring about social and economic change—and that these were contradictory policies. The administrator did not argue that either role should

[177] Hearings before the Subcommittee on General Oversight and Minority Enterprise of the Committee on Small Business, House of Representatives, Multinational Trade Negotiations, 96th Congress, 1st Session, 20 March 1979, 19.

[178] 'Set-Aside Restored by Carter; White House Gives in on Minority Trade Plan' *The Washington Post*, 23 March 1979, F1.

[179] R Lawrence, 'Defenders of Smaller US Firms Force Strauss to Amend Negotiating Plans on Procurement Practices Code' *Journal of Commerce*, 29 March 1979, 171.

[180] US Senate, United States International Trade Commission, MTN Studies 6, Pt 3; Agreements Being Negotiated at the Multilateral Trade Negotiations in Geneva, Analysis of Non-tariff Agreements, Agreement on Government Procurement, A Report prepared at the request of the Committee on Finance, United States Senate, 96th Congress, 1st Session, CP 96-27 (Washington 1979, US GPO) (hereafter ITC Committee Print) 268.

[181] Hearings before the Subcommittee on General Oversight and Minority Enterprise of the Committee on Small Business, House of Representatives, Multinational Trade Negotiations, 96th Congress, 1st Session, 4 April 1979, 81.   [182] ibid 118.

[183] ibid 117.

be given up, but conceded that it was a difficult combination to manage. The potential for each of these socio-economic schemes to be in violation of the GPA was hinted at,[184] rather than spelled out, and the hearings focused on the labour surplus programme. Despite pressure, the Administration did not agree to seek an exemption, indicating instead that it would waive the requirements of the set-aside programme where it would conflict with the Agreement.[185]

An extensive study of the relationship between United States socio-economic preferences and the Agreement was published in August 1979. This is a valuable account because it gives a clear indication of what one of the major negotiating parties thought it was agreeing to at the time, and what the implications of the Agreement were thought to be for United States domestic law. The study was undertaken by the United States International Trade Commission (ITC) at the request of the Senate Committee on Finance.[186] Of particular interest is the discussion of which particular United States laws and regulations the ITC thought likely to be affected by the Agreement.[187] Without exception, those laws and regulations which were identified as potentially contrary to the Agreement were those which intentionally, and indeed facially, discriminated against foreign bidders and suppliers. The Buy American Act and its equivalents 'clearly cannot stand in light of Part II of the Code, which requires national treatment to be accorded foreign goods and suppliers'.[188] The preferences for small businesses 'establish a prohibited form of national treatment discrimination because for the purposes of these laws small businesses are defined to include only American enterprises fitting the pertinent criteria'.[189] The preferences for minority businesses 'by definition include only American firms; thus, this preference program triggers the national treatment principles'.[190] The labour surplus area set-aside programme provided that 'preference be given to bids which, if executed, would benefit areas of persistent unemployment or underemployment in the United States'[191] and would fall foul of the non-discrimination requirement.

It is interesting to observe the absence of any apparent consideration of a broader approach to the meaning of discrimination that concentrated on provisions that had a discriminatory *effect* irrespective of intent. Instead, much attention is given to whether there are any exceptions which would permit the *intentionally* discriminatory programmes identified as otherwise contrary to the Agreement, in particular the small and minority business set-asides, and the labour surplus area set-aside. But in general the report concluded that, without the type of specific exception negotiated for small and minority set-asides, these programmes would contravene the Agreement. The report dismissed with little discussion any suggestion that

---

[184] ibid 119.

[185] This discussion is taken from the Hearings before the Subcommittee on International Trade of the Committee on Finance, Oversight on Government Procurement Code and Related Agreements, United States Senate, 97th Congress, 2nd Session, 9 June 1982, 24.

[186] ITC Committee Print (n 180 above).   [187] ibid 233–7, 264–78.   [188] ibid 264.

[189] ibid 266.   [190] ibid 269.   [191] ibid 270 (emphasis added).

the socio-economic policy behind these programmes would save them: 'the strong social and economic policies underlying [the small business] set-aside programs find no safe harbour in the code';[192] 'strong economic and social policies also underlie the minority business set-asides, but again there exists no textual provision which would allow it to continue for covered procurements';[193] 'programs to ameliorate economically distressed areas find no shelter in the code'.[194] The report concluded that the various exceptions in the GPA 1979 were inapplicable in the case of any of these programmes: 'Policies discriminating in favour of minority-owned businesses, labour surplus areas, or small enterprises do not fit within the ambit of these exceptions, neither literally nor in intent.'[195]

Only in the case of the labour surplus area set-aside programme was any real hope offered using the general exceptions provided in the Agreement. An argument was considered in detail that the programme might be defended under Article VIII(1), relating to national security. This argument was raised because the programme was 'part of the overall defense preparedness plan, and can be construed to satisfy the language of Part VIII excepting from the code procurement indispensable to national defense or security'.[196] It was 'designed to ensure a wide and stable distribution of the labour force consistent with the need for quick mobilisation in time of war'.[197] But the report concluded that this argument was likely to fail: 'This argument assumes the parties to the code agree that a stable, dispersed labour force is an "action . . . necessary for the protection of . . . essential security interests"'. But the labour surplus area programme in reality reflected the type of economic-based preference that the code was envisioned as prohibiting. It seemed unlikely that the United States would be able to point to the demonstrable defence-related origins and goals of the programme as sufficient to justify an exception under Part VIII.[198]

III. GPA 1979 Model as the Basis of Further Regional, International, and Bilateral Procurement Regulation

North American Free Trade Agreement and procurement linkages

The approach adopted to procurement linkages in the GPA 1979 became the model for other bilateral agreements in the 1980s and early 1990s, the most important of which was the procurement chapter of the North American Free

---

[192] ibid 266.   [193] ibid 269.   [194] ibid 270.   [195] ibid 359.
[196] ibid 270.   [197] ibid 366.
[198] ibid 272. '[T]he program does not appear to comport with the intent or language of the exception. The essence of paragraph (1) is expressed by the modifiers "essential" and "indispensable", words which the United States will find difficult to argue as appropriately applying to the labor surplus program. Although any conclusion is dependent upon the attitude adopted by other signatories regarding their own similar programs, it seems unlikely that Part VIII could be used to shelter the Labor Surplus Area Concerns program from the code.' ITC Committee Print (n 180 above) 366.

Trade Agreement (NAFTA). A Free Trade Agreement had been reached by Canada and the United States in October 1987 and had included a chapter (Chapter 10) on procurement.[199] NAFTA, which was agreed in October 1992 and replaced the US-Canada Agreement, united Mexico, Canada, and the United States in one free trade area. The main text of the procurement chapter (Chapter 10) followed closely the text of the 1979 Agreement.[200] It was in its market access element that NAFTA differed from the GPA. The procurement chapter of NAFTA used a negative list method to designate what was covered by that aspect of the Agreement, ie all services were included, except those that were explicitly excluded in the annex referred to in 1001.1b-2 of NAFTA. As it had under the United States-Canada Free Trade Agreement, in which the United States' General Notes provided that the government procurement provisions 'will not apply to set asides on behalf of small and minority businesses',[201] the United States sought and gained an equivalent exclusion in NAFTA.[202]

There had also been increasing attention paid by Canada to the relationship between the Canadian programmes devised for aboriginal preferences and trade agreements regulating procurement, beginning with Article 1802 of the Agreement on Internal Trade (AIT), which was an internal trade agreement between the Canadian provinces. This provided: 'This agreement does not apply to any measure adopted or maintained with respect to Aboriginal peoples.'[203] Under the procurement chapter of the AIT, therefore, the government of Nunavut was excepted from obligations to grant contractors from other Canadian provinces the same conditions as those accorded to in-province contractors. Canada followed what might be called the United States approach in NAFTA.[204] Canada's NAFTA Annex was in rather different terms from those of the AIT, excluding 'set-asides for small and minority businesses'. Bona fide set-asides for Aboriginal procurement were, therefore, exempt from the application of these trade agreements.

The fact that such a traditional GATT-type of approach was taken to the issue of procurement linkages in NAFTA might seem, at first sight, surprising. After all, in other respects NAFTA has been seen as innovative in dealing with the tensions between social standards and globalization. An agreement was concluded much at the same time as NAFTA, the North American Agreement on Labor Co-operation (NAALC), also known as the NAFTA side agreement.[205] NAALC is essentially an

---

[199] For an assessment from a Canadian perspective, see Canadian Government, Minister of Supply and Services, 'The Canada-U.S. Free Trade Agreement and Government Procurement: An Assessment' (1989).

[200] C Muggenberg, 'The Government Procurement Chapter of NAFTA' (1993) 1 United States-Mexico Law Journal 295.

[201] United States-Canada Free Trade Agreement, Annex 1304.3, United States Schedule.

[202] NAFTA, Annex 1001.2b, General Notes, Schedule of the United States, para 1.

[203] Agreement on Internal Trade, Art 18.0.2.

[204] NAFTA, Annex 1001.2b General Notes, Schedule of Canada, para 1(d).

[205] 'North American Agreement on Labour Co-operation, 13 September 1993, Can.-Mex.-US' (1993) 32 ILM 1499.

elaborate social clause for NAFTA. NAALC was negotiated to address the concerns of United States organized labour over free trade with Mexico. But NAALC's enforcement mechanisms are subject to expansive exceptions and have been heavily criticized. The regional model's efficacy depends heavily on its design: critics of NAFTA's labour side agreement have blamed its limited effectiveness on weak dispute resolution mechanisms and a failure to set minimum standards applicable to the three member states.[206] NAALC may have been more window dressing than substance and so it is not surprising, perhaps, that an apparently innovative approach had little effect on the rest of the negotiations in NAFTA.

Linkages and the 1994 GPA

The reason for stressing the development of the 1979 Government Procurement Agreement and its approach to the use of socio-economic preferences is also because the 1994 Agreement also basically adopted the same approach despite some concerns at the way the 1979 Agreement operated. In practice, complaints under the GPA 1979 involving the impact of socio-economic policies on procurement were more likely to arise against the United States, than from the United States. For example, the European Community was concerned at the exclusion for small and minority business set-asides. It claimed in 1981, for example, that 'since the enactment of the Agreement, US government agencies have markedly increased their use of small-business set-asides'.[207] A continuing source of complaint, relevant to the use of socio-economic policies, was the continued existence of the federal, as well as the state, Buy American preferences.[208] Indeed, it was the application of the provisions of the federal Buy American Act to the purchase of a US$2.5 million sonar mapping system for use in the United States Antarctic Survey that led to one of the few rulings by a GATT panel under the 1979 Agreement.[209] An article in *The Economist* in January 1981 identified growing 'protectionism' among state and local governments in the United States, and the increase in restricting purchases to American goods, partly as a way of counteracting growing local unemployment.[210] Socio-economic programmes in other countries were

---

[206] For discussion, see RJ Adams and P Singh, 'Early Experience with NAFTA's Labour Side Accord' (1997) 18 Comparative Labor Law Journal 161; K van Wezel Stone, 'Labour in the Global Economy: Four Approaches to Transnational Labour Regulation' in W Bratton, J McCahery, S Picciotto, and C Scott (eds), *International Regulatory Competition and Co-ordination* (OUP, 1996).

[207] US GAO, The International Agreement on Government Procurement: An Assessment of Its Commercial Value and US Government Implementation (GAO/NSIAD-84-117, 16 July 1984) 17.

[208] P Tate, 'Breaking into the US market; It's Rough Sailing for Europeans Trying to Cross the Atlantic with Their DP Wares' (1983) 29 Datamation 162; 'Buy America Actions Concern Allies' *Aviation Week and Space Technology*, 22 March 1982, 27.

[209] United States, Procurement of a Sonar Mapping System, GPR. DS1/R, not adopted, 23 April 1992.

[210] 'Government Procurement; Free Trade Stops at City Hall' *The Economist*, 17 January 1981, 63. For a discussion of the legality of state Buy American Laws under US constitutional Law, see Note, 'State Buy American Laws in a World of Liberal Trade' (1992) 7 Connecticut Journal of International Law 311.

seldom raised, however, as problems during the course of the implementation of the 1979 Agreement by the United States.[211] Reviews conducted by the United States General Accounting Office in 1984[212] and 1990[213] did not identify such programmes in other countries as raising any substantial barrier to the entry of United States firms into foreign procurement markets.

Even if it had been contemplated, the likelihood of an approach to linkages being taken in the 1994 GPA that was any more sympathetic was slim. In the context of the Uruguay Round discussions more generally, a tough line was being taken to any proposals to link GATT to social policy issues. This question of linkage between trade and social issues came to a head in the final stages of the negotiations leading to the establishment of the World Trade Organization regarding the issue of labour rights.[214] It was clear that the World Trade Organization (WTO) was set to be one of the most important legal institutions in the management of the global economy. Engaging the WTO with labour rights issues had two dimensions. First there was an issue concerning whether the WTO would be used as an instrument of labour rights enforcement (especially by the proposed addition of a 'social clause' to the General Agreement on Tariffs and Trade, or GATT). Second, rules on free trade may restrict many of the mechanisms, public and private, for the monitoring and enforcement of labour standards. By the early 1990s, NGOs were identifying the detailed rules of the GATT as presenting an impediment to international labour regulation and private labour rights initiatives, in the same way that they had identified problems with NAFTA. The fear was that the Godzilla of the WTO would overwhelm the Bambi of labour regulation, particularly given the radical new dispute settlement procedures of the WTO and the monitoring and enforcement procedures of those other institutions and mechanisms.

Several western countries (the United States and France were both prominent) sought explicitly to build labour rights into the new architecture of world trade, partly at least to lessen concerns at home that globalization could undercut social standards in the developed world. This led to a stand-off with some important states in the developing world. The latter perceived attempts to link further liberalization of free trade to adherence to certain labour standards as protectionist or neo-colonial in their motivation or effect. At Marrakesh, all that was agreed was that the issue would be kept under review until the Ministerial meeting following the conclusion of the Uruguay Round.[215] At this meeting, in Singapore in 1996,

---

[211] See eg MT Janik, 'A US Perspective on the GATT Agreement on Government Procurement' (1987) 20(3) GW JILE 491, 502–12.

[212] US GAO, The International Agreement on Government Procurement: An Assessment of Its Commercial Value and US Government Implementation (GAO/NSIAD-84-117, 16 July 1984).

[213] US GAO, International Procurement: Problems in Identifying Foreign Discrimination Against US Companies (GAO/NSIAD-90-127, 5 April 1990).

[214] For an account, see F Weiss, *Public Procurement in European Community Law* (Athlone Press, 1993) 81–3.

[215] See para 8(c)(iii) of the 'Decision on the Establishment of the Preparatory Committee for the WTO' (1994) 33 ILM 1270, 1272.

the issue was discussed again. Starkly divergent opinions were expressed, and tensions between those countries that supported further work on the issue within the WTO, and those that opposed it, increased significantly.[216] An invitation to the head of the International Labour Organization (ILO) to address the Ministerial meeting was withdrawn at the last moment, due to pressure from several developing countries. Finally, a compromise statement was issued saying that, although those who were present all agreed that core labour standards should be upheld, the WTO was not the place to deal with them. The ILO was, and should remain, the body with responsibility.[217] Clearly, the Uruguay Round negotiations would have been against any substantially different approach to social issues in the GPA also.

However, there were two major increases in the coverage of the Agreement that meant that the 1994 Agreement would have much greater effect on the operation of socio-economic linkages than the 1979 Agreement did: construction works and services were now included, and procurement by states (in federally organized countries) and local administrations was also included. In the context of the WTO negotiations, a somewhat different approach was taken to what was covered and what was excluded than under NAFTA. All parties, except the United States, had recourse to a positive list approach, and financial thresholds for contracts subject to the Agreement were higher than in the case of NAFTA. From an examination of the public documents, the effect of these extensions on the use of procurement linkages was not, however, considered during the negotiations.

As under the GPA 1979, several countries sought exemptions from the coverage of the Agreement for particular social policies. The United States continued to seek an exemption. The Agreement would not apply 'to set asides on behalf of small and minority businesses'.[218] Canada was 'unable to persuade the United States to moderate the terms'[219] of these programmes. 'Consequently', according to an official Canadian Government report, 'the Canadian federal government is not required to open up to Code members its procurement of high-technology communications, transportation-related construction and specified services'.[220] Canada also included a minority and small business exception in its own Annex.[221] Korea and Japan included restrictions excluding coverage of small business preferences. Regarding sub-central government entities, covered for the first time in the 1994 Agreement, the United States also required that a provision be inserted which provided that the Agreement 'shall not apply to preferences or restrictions associated with programs promoting the development of distressed areas and businesses owned by minorities, disabled veterans and women'.[222] The exemptions taken by the United States in the

---

[216] For an account, see R Howse, 'The World Trade Organization and the Protection of Workers' Rights' (1999) 3 Journal of Small and Emerging Business Law 131, 166.

[217] WTO, Singapore Ministerial Declaration (13 December 1996), WT/MIN(96)/DEC (1997) 36 ILM 218, para 4.   [218] United States Annex to Appendix 1, General Notes, Note 1.

[219] Canadian Government, Industry Canada, 'Industry and the Uruguay Round, vol 1-Results of the Negotiations' (March 1995).   [220] ibid.

[221] Canadian Annex to Appendix 1, General Notes, 1(d).

[222] United States, Annex 2, Sub-Central Government Entities, Notes to Annex 2, para 2.

GPA 1994 applied both in relation to the provisions forbidding discrimination on the basis of nationality and to the rules on award procedures.[223]

The European Community (as the EEC became known after the Maastricht Treaty in 1992) was opposed to these United States exceptions. It responded, not by including a general exception of an equivalent kind, but by providing that bid challenge provisions of Article XX 'shall not apply to suppliers and service providers of . . . Japan, Korea and the USA in contesting the award of contracts to a supplier or service provider of Parties other than those mentioned, which are small or medium sized enterprises under the relevant provisions of EC law, until such time as the EC accepts that they no longer operate discriminatory measures in favour of certain domestic small and minority businesses'.[224] An equivalent Note was included by Switzerland, Lichtenstein, Iceland, and Norway. Since the conclusion of the 1994 Agreement, there have been two trade policy reviews of the United States, each of which has been the occasion for critical questioning of the United States by Canada and the EC, particularly on the need for these preferences to continue.[225]

Procurement agreements and Aboriginal set-asides

Canada has agreed to three principal plurilateral free trade agreements covering public procurement: the Agreement on Internal Trade (1994) agreed to by the federal government, all ten of the provinces and the two territories, Chapter 10 of NAFTA, replacing the previous Canada-US Free Trade Agreement,[226] and the WTO Government Procurement Agreement. All have been ratified by federal implementing legislation.[227] It was hardly coincidental that less than two years after the GPA was agreed, in March 1996, new procurement measures were announced by the Minister of Indian Affairs and Northern Development that were designed to increase the participation of Aboriginal businesses in bidding for federal government contracts. We saw in chapter 7 above, that a Contracting Policy Notice was issued on Aboriginal Business Procurement Policy and Incentives in March 1996. This noted specifically that NAFTA and the GPA:

. . . provide for procurements to be 'set aside' for minority and small businesses. This means any procurement set aside under this policy for Aboriginal businesses is excluded from the

---

[223] GPA 1994, United States Annexes to Appendix 1, General Note 1.

[224] They were notified by the European Community to the WTO in a communication dated 22 December 1995 (WTO, Interim Committee on Government Procurement, Modifications to Appendix I of the European Communities and the United States, GPA/IC/10 of 16 January 1996, 8).

[225] See eg WT/TPR/M/56/Add.1, 9 March 2000, Trade Policy Review Body, 12 and 14 July 1999, Trade Policy Review, United States, Minutes of Meeting, Addendum, Outstanding Responses to Questions (Government procurement).

[226] For an interesting 'insiders'' account of the negotiations, including those on government procurement in the Canada-US negotiations, see M Hart, *Decision at Midnight: Inside the Canada-US Free-Trade Negotiations* (UBC Press, 1994) passim.

[227] See further A Van Dyk, 'Recent Changes in the Canadian Government's Contracting Policy' (1998) 7 PPLR CS110.

provisions of these two international trade agreements. These agreements do not permit *subcontracts* to be reserved for Aboriginal businesses. Participation of Aboriginal business as subcontractors to the prime contractors was generally to be encouraged. However, where procurement is subject to one of the international trade agreements, any consideration of, or requirement to use Aboriginal subcontractors would be inconsistent with those agreements unless the primary requirement is outside of the NAFTA and WTO Agreements.[228]

Finally, it announced that (for the purposes of Canadian law, presumably) 'Comprehensive Lands Claims Agreements take precedence over the trade agreements and the Aboriginal business set aside program.'[229] Procurements subject to any of the current and future Comprehensive Land Claims take precedence over this policy.

The Canadian International Trade Tribunal (CITT) is responsible for dealing with complaints from local and foreign contractors that concern the signing and awarding of government procurement contracts. The CITT can hear complaints under the GPA and NAFTA. Section 7(1) of the Canadian International Trade Tribunal Procurement Inquiry Regulations (the Regulations) sets out conditions that must be satisfied before the Tribunal may conduct an inquiry in respect of a complaint. One of these conditions is that the complaint be in respect of a 'designated contract' (ie a contract to which the trade agreements apply).

In two decisions, the CITT has considered whether the exceptions for Aboriginal set-asides exclude the CITT from proceeding with a complaint, because such set-asides are exempted in the various agreements under which the CITT is able to receive complaints. In one case, the CITT held that the complaint did relate to an Aboriginal set-aside.[230] In the second case, the CITT held that it did not constitute an Aboriginal set-aside.[231] One of the evaluation reports concerning the Procurement Strategy for Aboriginal Business (PSAB) has noted that one effect of the programme, identified by federal procurement managers, was that it freed federal personnel from NAFTA constraints, and some federal personnel themselves regarded this as a positive, if unintended, impact.[232] It is clear that the Tribunal realized the problem and sought to fire a warning shot across the bows, indicating that the PSAB and comprehensive land claims exceptions would not be allowed to undermine the overall thrust of the Agreements' reform implications.

The Department submitted that, since the services being procured were to be provided in a comprehensive land claims settlement area (CLCSA), the procurement constituted a set-aside for small and minority businesses and was, therefore, excluded from Chapter Ten of NAFTA. The Department submitted that the

---

[228] Contracting Policy Notice 1996-2, para 9 (emphasis added).   [229] ibid para 1.

[230] *Re Rosemary Trehearne and Associates and Bud Long and Associates Inc.*, 25 April 2005.

[231] *Re a complaint filed by Conair Aviation, a division of Conair Aviation Ltd.*, 8 August 1996.

[232] Canadian Government, Department of Indian Affairs and Northern Development Corporate Services, Departmental Audit and Evaluation Branch, 'Evaluation of the Procurement Strategy for Aboriginal Business' (August 2002) 31.

granting of contracting priority to beneficiary groups in CLCSAs was required pursuant to Canada's treaty obligations under the various comprehensive land claims agreements (CLCAs). These agreements, where concluded, had been sanctioned by statutes of the federal parliament and had quasi-constitutional status by virtue of the Constitution Act 1982. As such, they were considered to take precedence over the laws of Canada and Canada's international obligations, and had to be complied with. The Department stated that, prior to the implementation of NAFTA, it consulted with the Department of Foreign Affairs and International Trade and concluded that the CLCAs constituted set-asides for minority businesses under NAFTA and that procurements affected by these CLCAs were excluded from NAFTA. The Department further stated that it had consistently applied these standards to procurements where the goods were to be delivered into or provided within a CLCSA. The Tribunal did not agree. If the Tribunal were to accept the Department's position, the Department or any contracting authority could avoid the provisions of Chapter Ten of NAFTA simply by stating that a solicitation was subject to a CLCA, even though, as was the case here, the procurement only related, in part, to territories covered by a CLCA and the contract awardee was only to employ or subcontract 'where possible' to Aboriginals. Moreover, to accept the Department's position could, in the Tribunal's view, lead to an abuse of the contracting process and create an unpredictable commercial environment, circumstances which NAFTA expressly set out to eliminate.

Procurement agreements and the Federal Contractors Program

Canada appears to have been conscious of the need for caution in dealing with the relationship between trade agreements covering procurement and its domestic contract compliance programmes in the context of negotiating the texts of the agreements. Under the AIT, procurement measures that were discriminatory or trade restrictive with regard to another party to the Agreement may nevertheless be permissible (Article 504) if the purpose of the measure was to achieve a 'legitimate objective', if it was proportionate, and was not a disguised restriction on trade. Article 200 of the AIT provided that 'legitimate objectives' included 'affirmative action programmes for disadvantaged groups', among other objectives.[233] This caution has manifested itself in, perhaps, two other ways. First, the Canadian government has drawn attention to its employment equity provisions on several occasions in WTO committees since the conclusion of these agreements.[234]

---

[233] A 'legitimate objective means any of the following objectives pursued within the territory of a Party: (a) public security and safety; (b) public order; (c) protection of human, animal or plant life or health; (d) protection of the environment; (e) consumer protection; (f) protection of the health, safety and well-being of workers; or (g) affirmative action programs for disadvantaged groups'.

[234] WTO, Working Party on GATS Rules, S/WPGR/W/11/Add.7, 4 October 1996, (96-4054), Communication from Canada, drawing attention to the fact that 'additional standards have to be

Consistency with the trade agreements appears to have contributed to certain limits being introduced. As regards the Federal Contractors Program (FCP), we have seen that it applies to all suppliers, including offshore or foreign enterprises, with a resident workforce of 100 or more employees in Canada. That means, of course, that it exempts those businesses that submit bids and provide goods and services to Canadian public bodies from a territorial point outside Canada, unless they have a resident workforce of 100 or more, from the requirement of obtaining an employment equity certificate.[235]

Beyond these scattered pieces of evidence, however, the procurement agreements appear to have had relatively little effect on devising, operating, or reforming the FCP at the federal level, or at the provincial or municipal levels. In a study conducted for Status of Women Canada on the effect of trade agreements on this and other employment equity programmes,[236] Lamarche argues that this lack of attention is in part because of the lack of effect such programmes have at the moment. The implication is that if they were made more effective, then more attention to the effect of the procurement agreements would follow. There was no reason to believe, based on her analysis of the agreements that employment equity regulations were, however, necessarily incompatible with Canada's international commitments.

Bilateral procurement agreements

The main developments regarding international procurement regulation now occur in bilateral trade negotiations, which frequently include chapters on procurement as part of the final agreement.[237] The approach adopted in these negotiations is, almost without exception, to regard the GPA as the basic model for the procurement aspect of the bilateral agreement, and for negotiation to be concentrated around the market access aspects of procurement, resulting in all cases in extensive annexes in which the parties specify their agreed sets of offers. It is in these annexes, as occured in the context of the GPA, that countries now routinely specify what procurement linkages they want to protect. This generalization of the GPA approach has important consequences. Usually, there are no attempts made to specify in the main text of the procurement chapter anything about procurement linkages, and so no attempt, for example, to expand the exceptions in the

met by Canadian firms, such as health and safety or employment equity considerations'. WTO, Working Party on GATS Rules S/WPGR/W/20, 7 July 1997 (97-2833), Synthesis of the Responses to the Questionnaire on Government Procurement of Services, Note by the Secretariat: 'In some Members, tenderers have to comply with health, safety and employment equity considerations (Canada, Switzerland).'

[235] A point made by L Lamarche, *et al*, 'Retaining Employment Equity Measures in Trade Agreements' (Status of Women Canada, February 2005): 'Canada seems to have been cautious about the requirements posed by government procurement trade agreements.'

[236] ibid Executive Summary.

[237] For an overiew, see JH Grier, 'Recent Developments in International Trade Agreements Covering Government Procurement' (2006) 35 Public Contract Law Journal 385.

GPA text beyond what they currently contain.[238] All the 'work', as it were, is done in the annexes. This is apparent, for example, in all of the agreements negotiated between the United States and other countries since 1994. There is another important aspect of these agreements. In all of them, the United States has specified almost exactly the same procurement linkages as are excluded from coverage of the agreement.[239] In general, the procurement agreement 'does not apply to set-asides on behalf of small or[240] minority-owned[241] businesses'. Since the changes in the set-aside programme discussed above, following the Supreme Court decision in the *Adarand* case discussed in chapter 7 above, set-asides have been defined to include 'any form of preference, such as the exclusive right to provide a good or service and price preferences'.[242] In addition, in those agreements covering sub-federal entities, as in the GPA, there is an additional restriction. In the United States-Australia Agreement, the United States exempted practices of regional entities involving 'preferences or restrictions associated with programs promoting the development of distressed areas or businesses owned by minorities, disabled veterans, or women'.[243]

The major variation has been in the annexes of *other* countries in their bilateral Agreements with the United States.[244] Many have taken reservations for programmes equivalent to those adopted by the United States.[245] These developments have been influenced by what we might call 'social' globalization, in which ideas of social justice are spread by a combination of international and regional

---

[238] The main exception to this statement might have been the proposed Free Trade Area of the Americas (FTAA) Agreement. The third Draft of the Agreement (FTAA.TNC/w/133/Rev.3, 21 November 2003) included in the main text of the procurement chapter of the Agreeement (Ch XVIII, Art 3.2(i), on the scope of application of the procurement provisions) a proposal to exclude from the coverage of procurement 'any measure adopted or maintained with respect to Aboriginal peoples', but a note to this proposal indicates that the negotiation committee 'agreed it would be appropriate to consider this item as a market access issue or as an exception'.

[239] US-Bahrain FTA, Annex 9-E, General Notes, Schedule of the United States; US-Australia FTA, Annex 15-A, Section 7: General Notes, Schedule of the United States, para 1; US-Oman FTA, Annex 9, Section F: General Notes, Schedule of the United States, para 1; Chile-US FTA, 2003, Annex 9.1, Section H: General Notes, Schedule of the United States, para 1: CAFTA, Annex 9.1.2(b)(i)-48, Section G: General Notes, Schedule of the United States, para 1; Peru-US TPA, 2006, Annex 9.1, Section G: General Notes, Schedule of the United States, para 1: Columbia-US TPA, 2006, Annex 9.1, Section H: General Notes, Schedule of the United States, para 1.

[240] In some cases the word 'and' is used instead.

[241] In some cases, the US specifies 'minority businesses', in others 'minority-owned businesses'. The difference does not appear to have been material to the negotiation, although it may be significant legally.

[242] The provision specifying that set-asides 'include...' appears in the more recent agreements, probably to reflect the changes in US domestic law regarding minority set-asides' (see ch 7 above).

[243] US-Australia, Annex 15-A, Section 7: General Notes, Schedule of United States, para 2. This is the same as the Notes attached to the US-El Salvador and US-Chile Agreements, General Notes, Schedules of the United States, paras 2, 6.

[244] Equality-based restrictions in coverage are not confined to Agreements with the United States, see eg that between Chile and Costa Rica, see WTO, WT/REG136/5, 27 August 2004, Committee on Regional Trade Agreements, Free Trade Agreement Between Chile and Costa Rica (aboriginal and minorities provisions).   [245] eg Costa Rica, Dominican Republic, Oman, Australia.

governmental actors, and NGOs. This is an example of what de Souza Santos has termed 'globalized localism' in which a local practice becomes successfully globalized.[246] An interesting example of this is provided by the development of procurement reform policies in China, where Fuguo Cao describes how industrial, social, and environmental policies, including preferences for supplies from 'minority populated areas' were incorporated into their new procurement law 'not as a result of economic analysis, but rather [as] a result of the learning process. These policies have been imported along with the very concept of government procurement.'[247]

Some countries go further in their annexes. Columbia has retained its ability in road construction services to hire 'local personnel in rural areas in order to promote employment and improve living conditions in such areas'.[248] It has also negotiated that the procurement provisions do not apply 'to programs of reintegration to civil life as a result of peace processes, to aid persons displaced due to violence, to support those living in conflict zones, and general programs resulting from the resolution of the armed conflict'.[249] Relatively few include protections for equality purposes. The Dominican Republic, Guatemala, and Austrilia do, however. The Dominican Republic specifies in its Annex that the procurement provisions do not apply 'to government procurement programs to promote the alleviation of poverty, or to protect women, the disabled, or children and adolescents, including at the border with Haiti...or in other rural or impoverished areas'.[250] Australia specifies that the procurement agreements do not apply to measures for the 'health and welfare' and measures for the 'economic and social advancement' of indigenous people.[251] In each case, however, the United States position in negotiations has been that, since specifications of coverage and non-coverage are matters of market access, each 'protected' procurement linkage must be negotiated, and be 'paid' for by offering market access in other areas of the procurement activity of that country, or paid for by additional restrictions being imposed in terms of what the United States is prepared to offer. In the case of Guatemala, this need for negotiation carried on even after the Agreement was concluded. If Guatemala wished to implement a procurement measure in the future that was intended to promote its minority-owned enterprises, it needed to negotiate with the United States. Only if the two countries agreed was Guatamala

---

[246] B de Sousa Santos, *Toward a New Legal Common Sense: Science and Politics in the Paradigmatic Transition* (Routledge, 1995) 262–3.

[247] F Cao, 'China's Government Procurement Reform: From the Bidding Law to the Government Procurement Law' in S Arrowsmith and M Trybus, *Public Procurement: The Continuing Revolution* (Kluwer, 2003) 78–9.

[248] Columbia-US, Annex 9.1, Section G: Construction Services, Schedule of Columbia.

[249] ibid Section H: General Notes, Schedule of Columbia, para 4.

[250] CAFTA, Section G: General Notes, Schedule of the Dominican Republic, para 3.

[251] US-Australia, Annex 15-A, Section 7: General Notes, Schedule of Australia. The narrowness of this exemption has been criticized by some, see J Malbon, 'The Australia-United States Free Trade Agreement: Trade Trumps Indigenous Interests' (2004) 111 Media International Australia (incorporating Culture and Policy) 34.

permitted to implement the measure.[252] This puts pressure on a country with a less-developed economy wanting to get access to United States markets not to put additional barriers on what the country is willing to offer in exchange.

IV. Assessment of the 'GPA Model'

Although the work of the OECD was undoubtedly important in preparing the ground for the work of negotiating what became the 1979 GPA, it is worth reflecting on how the work of the OECD in this respect stands up to subsequent scrutiny. Most of the domestic procurement linkages discussed in the previous chapters, and the entirety of the ILO developments, were not considered in the context of the OECD negotiations. There was no mention of 'fair wages' linkages, by far the most widely used form of linkage at that time. There was no mention of 'contract compliance'-type linkages, such as those that had been at the centre of political controversy in the United States for all of the time during which the negotiations continued. There was no mention of *minority* set-asides, despite their introduction in the United States and Canada in the 1960s. There was one reference in over ten years of work to linkages addressing 'underprivileged social categories'. Why the absence of consideration of these measures?

Epistemic communities

Different explanations are possible. One set of explanations relates to the limits of international diplomacy, and the effect of critical choices during those negotiations that had the indirect effect of excluding otherwise relevant examples from consideration. When information about national practices was sought, it was sought in areas that severely limited its utility in dealing in a fully informed way with the complete range of procurement linkages. Given the extent to which the collection of information concentrated on supplies rather than public works, and given the extent to which it concentrated on central government rather than local government, and given the extent to which it concentrated on explicit preferences for domestic products, it is not surprising that when it came to the formulation of policy at the OECD, the extent and the range of socio-economic linkages was not fully appreciated. Indeed, were one intentionally to have constructed a profile to exclude as many as possible of the socio-economic linkages discussed in chapters 6 and 7 above, one could hardly have done a better job.

In general, then, the conclusions reached by the negotiators were grounded in ignorance of what their own countries were actually doing in the area of status equality at first. At this point it will be useful to draw on the concept of an 'epistemic community'.[253] An epistemic community consists of a network of professionals with

---

[252] CAFTA, Schedule of Guatemala, para 3.
[253] There is now an extensive literature, see eg PM Haas, 'Introduction, Epistemic Communities and International Policy Coordination' (1992) 46 International Organization 1; A Wendt, *Social*

recognized expertise in a particular domain and an authoritative claim to knowledge within that domain who have a shared set of normative beliefs, shared causal beliefs, shared notions of validity, and a common policy enterprise. In the procurement negotiations in the OECD, the epistemic community consisted initially of a relatively small group of national civil servants who specialized in trade. We see in this period the growth of an international community of trade policy negotiators. They were seldom procurement practitioners; they were seldom experts in the social justice dimensions of government policy.[254] Communication between the international negotiators often appears to have been considerably better than that between the same negotiators and their own national policy community. NGOs had no role to play, and the 'social' (as opposed to the 'economic') departments of government seldom appear to have been consulted. Developing countries were largely excluded from the process and when the delegations of Spain, Portugal, Greece, and Turkey sought to raise concerns from a developing country perspective that sufficient attention had not been given to the effect on development of doing away with some of the social preferences, these were brushed aside.

Embedded liberalism

There is another possible explanation, however, for the approach taken in the early OECD negotiations regarding status equality procurement linkages: that these procurement linkages were known to negotiators but were regarded by some as so accepted, or at least so unchallengeable, as to be uncontroversial, and therefore not even worth bringing to the table. The view that certain types of procurement linkage were outside the scope of consideration is strengthened by an awareness of the then dominant policy consensus of what Ruggie has termed 'embedded liberalism'.[255] At that time, reducing tariff protectionism went hand in hand with an acceptance of the legitimacy of progressive domestic social regulation, and a view that 'the trading regime should be based on deference of states to each other's different approaches to, or cultures of, domestic regulation',[256] including, for example,

---

Theory of International Politics (Cambridge University Press, 1999); MN Barnett and M Finnemore, 'The Politics, Power and Pathologies of International Organizations' (1999) 53 International Organization 699; AM Slaughter, *et al*, 'International Law and International Relations Theory: A New Generation' (1998) 92 AJIL 367.

[254] For a similar critique of a more recent set of trade negotiations, see A Taylor, 'Trade, Human Rights, and the WHO Framework Convention on Tobacco Control: Just What the Doctor Ordered?' in T Cottier, J Pauwelyn, and E Bürgi (eds), *Human Rights and International Trade* (OUP, 2005) 322.

[255] JG Ruggie, 'International Regimes, Transactions, and Change: Embedded Liberalism and the Postwar Economic Order' (1982), 36(2) International Organization 379.

[256] R Howse and B Langille, with J Burda, 'The World Trade Organization and Labour Rights: Man Bites Dog' in VA Leary and D Warner (eds), *Social Issues, Globalisation and International Institutions: Labour Rights and the EU, ILO, OECD and WTO* (Brill Academic, 2005) 157.

the advancement of social policy at the domestic level. For Howse and Langille, this 'broad overlapping consensus on the post-New Deal regulatory and welfare state',[257] lasted until the economic pressures and changes of the 1970s and 1980s. It was in this policy context, therefore, that the OECD and early EEC negotiations on procurement took place. In the light of this, it is, again, not surprising that nothing other than the most explicitly trade discriminatory procurement linkages were addressed and even then considerable efforts were made to accommodate most with exceptions. Fernández Martín has explicitly linked the widespread acceptance of 'Keynesian doctrines which claimed that an increase in public spending could galvanize a relaunching of the general economy' with the frequent use of public procurement 'to further general economic, regional or social policies'.[258]

What is procurement reform for, again?

As regards the purpose of international procurement reform, there was no real resolution of several key questions that were crucial to addressing procurement linkages in an analytically sophisticated way, and this may also have affected what were thought by different delegations to be relevant examples of linkage to bring to the table. There are two different models of what procurement reform might be for.

In the first model, the point of international procurement reform is to bring procurement markets into the international trade agreement context and the fundamental purpose of such agreements is increased market access, meaning the increased flow of goods and services from one country to another. 'At the heart of trade negotiations is the exchange of market access concessions.'[259] This can be done bilaterally, plurilaterally, or multilaterally. The negotiation is usually merchantilist in nature. What is given away and what is retained is up to each party, which will make its own calculations of benefits and costs resulting from its offer. Those costs and benefits may be economic or political. For example, the gains may include encouraging deep integration of the economies concerned in order to limit the possibility of political conflict in the future. Provided each party sees what it is getting from the other side as, at least, acceptable compensation for what it gives up, then there will be an agreement. Once the agreement has been reached, it is then vital to ensure that the market access that has been negotiated is implemented, and the basic technique for ensuring this is seen to be the concept of 'discrimination'. A procurement process operated by one party to the agreement would be discriminatory if it treated differently a bid from a company under the

---

[257] ibid 158.

[258] JM Fernández Martín, *The EC Public Procurement Rules: A Critical Analysis* (OUP, 1996) 45.

[259] SJ Evenett and BM Hoekman, 'Transparency in Government Procurement: What Can We Expect from International Trade Agreements?' in S Arrowsmith and M Trybus, *Public Procurement: The Continuing Revolution* (Kluwer, 2003) 271. cf the Ministerial Declaration of Ministers of Trade, FTAA, 19 March 1998 stating that the 'broad objective of negotiations in government procurement is to expand access to the government procurement markets of the FTAA countries'.

protection of the other party. Reforming domestic procurement as such, from this perspective, is of no interest to either party; what is important is to ensure that covered procurements that are of commercial interest to potential bidders from each party are treated equally. Transparency is important to ensure opportunities for contracting and increase the chances that discrimination will be exposed.

In the second model, the point of international procurement reform is rather different. It is to achieve an efficient procurement market. This will be achieved by ensuring greater competition, with a resulting reduction in costs 'which will therefore produce savings for the public exchequer and the maximization of operating efficiency'.[260] It also 'enhances macro-economic growth, since it promotes restructuring and adjustment'.[261] The purpose of international agreements, from this perspective, is to maximize this approach to procurement reform so that the world economy will grow. It is essentially non-mercantilist and would see benefits of procurement reform resulting for those states adopting it irrespective of whether other countries did so, although the benefits will be greater, the more states implement these reforms. Although prohibiting discrimination against foreign bidders is important, it is not the only objective. Rather, the purpose is to ensure that strict commercial criteria are used when awarding contracts. In this context, preferences, set-asides, and other social aspects of procurement are merely examples of 'wasteful rent seeking activities', which are simply 'designed to protect or promote the interests of special groups' within the economy.[262] In this model, a procurement process is 'discriminatory' 'if any of its provisions are such that it treats differently any two potential bids that are identical in every commercially-relevant respect; that is, in those factors which have a bearing on a bid's price, and likely quality and timeliness of delivery'.[263] From this point of view, increasing trade flows may not be that important, provided the procurement process is efficient. Transparency, however, is vital to ensure that divergencies from a commercial approach are exposed.

The OECD and subsequent GATT and WTO negotiations did not arrive at a clear view of which of these purposes an international instrument concerning procurement was meant to further. On the one hand, some delegations considered that the purpose of such an instrument was to address market access, whilst others considered that the purpose was to ensure that an instrument should require that 'commercial considerations' would become the general principle for the award of government contracts. Again, which approach is taken is crucial for assessing which socio-economic uses of procurement are relevant for discussion. From the latter perspective, all socio-economic uses were 'unhelpful' in this regard, and should have been discussed, even if not positively protectionist. From the former perspective, they were problematic only where they were protectionist. In practice,

---

[260] Fernández Martín (n 258 above) 41.   [261] ibid.

[262] J Linarelli, 'The WTO Transparency Agenda: Law, Economics and International Relations Theory' in S Arrowsmith and M Trybus, *Public Procurement: The Continuing Revolution* (Kluwer, 2003) 256, 266.   [263] Evenette and Hoekman (n 259 above) 272.

the two perspectives were illustrated by the early differences between the United States and the European approaches, with the United States favouring the market access approach, and the EEC favouring the 'commercial' approach. Given that most of the experience of procurement linkages that would have been adversely affected by the commercial approach were in the United States, it is not surprising that they were not brought to the table by the United States, which considered that the function of the instrument should in any case be to deal with discriminatory practices, which they would not have considered contract compliance programmes to be.

The GPA and, as we shall see, the EC procurement directives of the 1970s and 1980s are an uneasy compromise between the two approaches, with the GPA edging closer to the former model with its inclusion of the annexes, and the EC procurement directives coming closer to the latter. Linarelli's characterization of the GPA closely fits the elements of the first model. He notes how those negotiating 'acted rationally to maximise their own interests by transforming the GPA into an umbrella arrangement for bilateral negotiations between contracting parties. Each contracting party negotiates with each of the other contracting parties to agree on market access.'[264] The function of the detailed rules in the GPA is simply to:

. . . reduce[ ] transaction costs for governments to agree bilaterally to concessions . . . As an international regime, the GPA facilitates political management in that it allows contracting parties to take politics into account and to distribute government benefits through procurement. If their markets are large enough a WTO member can still be a GPA contracting party, yet refuse to give concessions that would have serious adverse distributional effects on important constituencies within its borders.[265]

The actions of the United States on how to deal with minority set-asides after the 1979 GPA is a classic illustration of this approach. In 'exchange' for allowing the protection of set-asides, NASA was included in the coverage.

On the other hand, leaving aside the annexes, and the 'concessions' approach, the substantive rules of the GPA seem to come closer to the second model and, indeed, to the 1970s and 1980s European directives. All of these texts ban preferences and other forms of discrimination, but go beyond that in specifying detailed rules on how procurement should be carried out. And these rules, at least on one reading of them, appear to be pushing a model of economic efficiency. From this perspective, the annexes are merely examples of incomplete agreement on how far the economic efficiency approach should be taken, rather than the essence of the agreement, as the first model would view them. Procurement linkages were acceptable as a necessary part of getting agreement, but only as exceptions and (hopefully) not for very much longer. The action of the EC in not seeking to emulate the United States in excluding preferences from coverage seems to indicate an acceptance of this second approach.

---

[264] Linarelli (n 262 above) 252.   [265] ibid 252–3.

Beyond that, however, the principal uncertainties generated by the failures of the OECD process remained. It was unclear precisely what the exception for 'public order' included, as the American delegation had continuously stressed. It was unclear what precisely was meant by 'discrimination', as the United Kingdom delegation had demonstrated. It was unclear how far the procedural requirements of the Agreement excluded the use of 'non-commercial' considerations from the award process. The effect was to leave the dispute settlement process to cope. But therein lay a risk, as Bourgeois observed soon after the conclusion of the 1979 GPA:

The risk of overtaxing the machinery is real, especially in the non-tariff area where, on the one hand, recourse to vague language is technically unavoidable and consequently multilateral enforcement requires an assessment of the economic merits or the reasonableness of the contracting party's action; on the other hand, the international disciplines the [Agreement] seek[s] to establish touch on domestic policy issues.[266]

---

[266] JHJ Bourgeois, 'The Tokyo Round Agreements on Technical Barriers and on Government Procurement in International and EEC Perspective' (1982) 19 CMLR 5, 18.

9

Procurement Linkages and Developing Countries

The previous chapters in this part of the book have all related primarily to developed countries that are members of the GPA. What of *developing* countries that are *not* members of the GPA? We saw in chapters 4 and 8 above, that there was discussion and agreement as to how to treat developing countries which wanted to join the GPA. There are, in particular, provisions allowing developing countries specifically to become members of the GPA, whilst retaining certain preferences. Article V specifies that parties 'shall, in the implementation and administration of this Agreement', 'take into account the development, financial and trade needs of developing countries, in particular least-developed countries, in their need' to 'promote the establishment or development of domestic industries including the development of small-scale and cottage industries in rural or backwater areas; and economic development of other areas of the economy'. These objectives should be 'taken into account in the course of negotiations with respect to the procurement of developing countries to be covered by the provisions of this Agreement'.[1] Further, a developing country 'may negotiate with other participants . . . mutually acceptable exclusions from the rules on national treatment with respect to certain entities, products or services that are included in its coverage lists' taking these objectives into account.[2]

One issue we have not seen being considered so far is the problem of 'offsets' being used in the context of procurement linkages.[3] The GPA 1994 forbids offsets, which it defines as 'measures used to encourage local development or improve the balance of payments accounts by means of domestic content, licensing of technology, investment requirements, counter-trade or similar requirements'.[4] This prohibition on offsets prevents both direct and indirect offsets. The former arises when the offset is directly related to the procurement contract, for example requiring a company to subcontract a proportion of this contract to domestic companies; the latter arises when the requirement is unrelated to the specific contract

---

[1] GPA, Art V(3).   [2] ibid Art V(4).
[3] See, generally, RF Dodds, 'Offsets in Chinese Government Procurement: The Partially Open Door' (1995) 26 Law and Policy in International Business 1119.   [4] GPA, Art XVI.

under consideration, for example where the government requires foreign bidders to purchase unrelated goods in order to win the contract. The GPA is wide-ranging in its prohibition, not just in terms of the range of offsets prohibited, but also in terms of the type of actions forbidden to governments. The GPA states that procuring entities may not 'impose, seek or consider offsets'.[5] There is, however, an exception for developing countries. A developing country may at the time of accession 'negotiate conditions for the use of offsets, such as requirements for the incorporation of domestic content. Such requirements shall be used only for qualification to participate in the procurement process and not as criteria for awarding contracts. Conditions shall be objective, clearly defined and non-discriminatory.'[6] So far, only Israel has successfully negotiated such offset exceptions.

We have also seen, despite these provisions, that, in the main, developing countries have not sought to join the GPA. In this chapter, we consider the use of procurement linkages aiming to further status equality in two developing countries, Malaysia and South Africa, and reactions to these policies at the international level. In the third part of the chapter, we turn to look at the use of procurement linkages by a developed country (the United States), not for the purpose of addressing discrimination and inequalities within that country but in a developing country (Burma/Mayanmar). The theme of this chapter, therefore, is the relationship between procurement linkages and the developing world. In the final part of chapter, we consider the relationship between there developments and international procurement disciplines.

I. Bumiputera and National Stability in Malaysia

In chapter 3 above we considered the development of Malaysian governments' policies seeking to reduce the disadvantages associated with the indigenous Malays (Bumiputera). We now turn to consider how procurement preferences fit into this development. The scale of government procurement in Malaysia is considerable. In 2003, Malaysian governmental entities, state and federal, spent over RM100 billion (roughly US$26 billion) on procurement, the equivalent to over a quarter of Malaysia's nominal GDP.[7] As has been the case since 1974, a large percentage

---

⁵ ibid Art XVI(1).   ⁶ ibid Art XVI(2).

⁷ This figure was reached by adding the total federal government expenditure for supplies and services with the development expenditure of local governments, state governments, statutory bodies and 'non-financial public enterprises' (the government's term for government-owned companies not involved in banking or other financial business). Finance Ministry, Economic Report 2003/2004, Annex tables 2.2, 4.4, 4.6, 4.10, 4.11, 4.12, and 4.13, available at <http://www.treasury.gov.my/index.php?ch=22&pg=165&ac=232&lang=eng> (last visited 21 December 2003). For an analogously based analysis of Malaysian government procurement expenditure see, Report by the Secretariat, Trade Policy Review-Malaysia WT/TPR/S/92, table 111-4 (5 November 2001) (hereafter Malaysia TPR (2001)). As this figure does not include the non-development related procurement of supplies and services by non-federal governmental bodies, it can be assumed that the true total figure including these elements would be significantly higher.

of this total was allocated to two particular types of providers through two sets of interlinked preferences: one set involving preferences for indigenous Malays, and another set of preferences for other domestic providers.[8]

Preferences for Bumiputera have developed into a complex arrangement of set-asides and price preferences that vary in form and size depending on a number of factors. Their complexity and variety reflect the Malaysian government's periodic efforts to make the preferences more effective at delivering enhanced status policy goals of amongst the most important equality, Malaysia's rulers for the last three and half decades, while at the same time decreasing well-documented abuses of the system.[9] Preferences for other domestic providers, on the other hand, consist of relatively straightforward set-asides, operating in most cases to limit procurement to domestic sources unless one is not available.[10] Why does Malaysia operate such an extensive system of preferences?

History and economic context of preferences

Malaysia is a paradigmatic example of what Amy Chua has characterized as the problem of the 'market-dominant minority.'[11] Malaysian Chinese, in particular, conform to the pattern she identifies of 'ethnic minorities who . . . tend under market conditions to dominate economically . . . the 'indigenous' majorities around them'.[12] For Chua, such situations are particularly problematic where the countries in which these market dominant minorities live are being pressed by powerful economic and political forces to adopt more democracy *and* free-market economic policies.

Markets concentrate wealth, often spectacular wealth, in the hands of the market-dominant minority, while democracy increases the political power of the impoverished majority. In these circumstances the pursuit of free market democracy becomes an engine of potentially catastrophic ethno-nationalism, pitting a frustrated 'indigenous'

---

[8] See Surat Pekeliling Perbendaharaan Bil 7 Thn 2002 (Treas Circ Let No 7/2002), Penggunaan Bahan/Barangan/Perkhidmatan Tempatan Dalam Perolehan Kerajaan (Use of Domestic Materials/ Goods/Services in Government Procurement) §2 (5 June 2002) (hereafter Treas Circ Let No 7/2002); Surat Pekeliling Perbendaharaan Bil 4 Thn 1995 (Treas Circ Let No 4/1995), Dasar dan Keutamaan Kepada Syarikat Bumiputera Dalam Perolehan Kerajaan (Policy and Preferences for Bumiputera Firms in the Context of Government Procurement) (12 April 1995) (hereafter Treas Circ Let No 4/1995); Surat Pekeliling Perbendaharaan Bil 2 Thn 1995 (Treas Circ Let No 2/1995), Tatacara Penydiaan, Penilaian dan Penerimaan Tender (Tender Preparation, Evaluation and Acceptance) §4.1.3 (10 April 1995) (hereafter Treas Circ Let No 2/1995). According to the Midterm Review of the Eighth Malaysia Plan 2001–2005, already large preferences for Bumiputera would be scrapped in favour of a set-aside of 60% of government procurement spending for Bumiputera providers. Midterm Review of the Eighth Malaysia Plan 2001–2005 §3.53 (30 October 2003) (hereafter Midterm Review of the Eighth Malaysia Plan).

[9] See Treas Circ Let No 4/1995 (n 8 above) §§5.1–5.5, 6–7; see also, Midterm Review of the Eighth Malaysia Plan, (n 8 above) §1.57; Third Malaysia Plan 1976–1980 §§599–600 (5 July 1976) (hereafter Third Malaysia Plan).

[10] Treas Circ Let No 7/2002 (n 8 above) §2 ; Treas Circ Let No 2/1995 (n 8 above) §4.1.1; see also, eg, Midterm Review of the Eighth Malaysia Plan, (n 8 above) foreword, §§1.33, 1.67, 5.76, 8.09.

[11] A Chua, *World on Fire: How Exporting Free Market Democracy Breeds Ethnic Hatred and Global Instability* (new edn, Arrow, 2004) 6.

[12] ibid 6.

majority, easily aroused by opportunistic vote-seeking politicians, against a resented, wealthy ethnic minority.[13]

For Chua, where 'free market democracy is pursued in the presence of a market-dominant minority, the almost invariable result is backlash'.[14] This backlash will either be against free-market ideology, or against democracy. Managing such situations is, therefore, particularly problematic. The place of preferences for particular ethnic groups in government contracting in assisting Malaysia to handle this problem is therefore of particular interest.

Central to the development of extensive preferences for Bumiputera in the allocation of government contracts were the riots that broke out in Kuala Lumpur in May 1969. The riots were seen as resulting from Malay dissatisfaction with economic distribution since independence from the British in 1957 and were 'mainly against the Chinese'.[15] Whilst the Chinese were gaining ground economically, Malays perceived themselves to be losing out economically despite the preferences. When the government which Malays dominated politically lost ground in the General Election of 1969, Malay sensitivities were heightened further, leading to increasing tensions with the Chinese community and, ultimately, ferocious attacks by Malays on Chinese and Chinese business. As Stafford says: 'Having already lost control of much of the economy to Chinese-Malaysians and foreigners, the weakening of the Alliance, the Malay-dominated coalition, frightened many Malays by highlighting the possibility that political control might also be in jeopardy.'[16] In an influential book, *The Way Forward*,[17] by Mahathir bin Mohamad (a future Prime Minister), the 1969 riots were explained as being the result of the Malays and the Chinese 'not knowing each other' because of the divide and rule policy of the British colonial government. As a result, he said, the Alliance leaders and some of the opposition came to realize that 'economic imbalances between the races were an important contributory factor to poor race relations'.[18] A less generous assessment is that the Bumiputera aristocratic elite had, since independence, maintained an implicit deal with Malaysia's ethnic Chinese, which allowed the former to retain political power in exchange for their acceptance of the latter's economic dominance, a deal which the riots proved to be unsustainable.[19]

Riots and the introduction of procurement set-asides

We saw in chapter 3 above, that there was a relatively modest programme of preferential treatment in favour of the Malays, particularly in government employment,

[13] ibid 6–7.　　[14] ibid 10.

[15] D Nesiah, *Discrimination With Reason? The Policy of Reservations in the United States, India and Malaysia* (OUP, 2004) 90.

[16] DGSD Stafford, 'Malaysia's New Economic Policy and the Global Economy: The Evolution of Ethnic Accommodation' (1997) 10 Pacific Review 556.

[17] M Mahathir, *The Way Forward: Growth, Prosperity and Multiracial Harmony in Malaysia* (Weidenfeld and Nicholson, 1998).　　[18] ibid.

[19] ET Gomez, *Political Business: Corporate Involvement of Malaysian Political Parties* (Centre for South-east Asian Studies, James Cook University of North Queensland, 1994) 1–2.

prior to the riots in 1969. Despite these provisions, however, the economic position of the Malays had hardly improved by the late 1960s.[20] After the riots, 'they were given added political muscle',[21] and the system of preferences was considerably increased, in the award of loans and licences, in admissions to higher education, and in government employment (in the police and the armed forces particularly). After a period of emergency rule, elections were held in 1971, after which a new government was formed in which non-Malay parties were significantly weaker. The new government was aggressively in favour of preferences, which became key to the government's stated goal to create social harmony and stability by ensuring 'that within one generation [Bumiputera] can be full partners in the economic life of the nation'.[22] Affirming this commitment, when Parliament was restored, the Constitution was amended to strengthen the system of preferences, remove their time-limited nature, and make questioning the special privileges a criminal offence under the Sedition Act 1948.[23]

There are several contrasts between the systems of preferences adopted in other countries (particularly in the United States and Canada, discussed in chapters 6 and 7 above), and those adopted in Malaysia. First, unlike in the United States, in Malaysia these preferences 'remained outside the area of constitutional litigation'.[24] Why this should be the case, remains unclear. Harding comments: 'It may be that the lack of litigation is a function of the designation of special privileges as sensitive issues: in practice the challenge of special privileges, even through litigation, is

[20] In 1969, 65% of Bumiputera still lived in poverty, and though they represented 62% of the populations they owned only 2.3% of the nation's commercial equity. Ganguly, 'Ethnic Policies and Political Quiescence in Malaysia and Singapore' in ME Brown and S Ganguly (eds), *Government Policies and Ethnic Relations in Asia and the Pacific* (MIT Press, 1997) 234 (citing 1995 Malaysian Government Census figures). Second Outline Perspective Plan 1991–2000, tables 2-1, 2-6 (17 June 1991) (hereafter Second Outline Perspective Plan). The situation of the Chinese, though better, was not good; 26% of Chinese also lived in poverty. Ganguly (above) 234 (again, citing 1995 Malaysian Government Census figures). However, their per capita and absolute share of the nation's commercial equity was quite a bit better: representing just 27% of the population, they held 22.8% of its commercial equity. Second Malaysia Plan, 1971–1975, table 3-1 (25 June 1971) (hereafter Second Malaysia Plan). That said, in reality it was foreign interests rather than the Chinese that dominated Malaysia's economy; they owned 63.3% of Malaysia's commercial equity, Second Outline Perspective Plan (above) table 2-1, and with the exception of those parts controlled by the Chinese, continued to 'control large-scale commercial agriculture and all forms of non-agricultural enterprises' as they had during colonial times. Ganguly (above) 261.

[21] A Harding, *Law, Government and the Constitution in Malaysia* (Brill Academic, 1996) 230.

[22] See Second Malaysia Plan (n 20 above) foreword, §§20, 26, 26, 27, 126, 135, 147, 149, 155(1), 155(iv), 25; ET Gomez and KS Jomo, *Malaysia's Political Economy* (Cambridge University Press, 1999) 29–32.

[23] See Sedition Act 1948 (Act 15) §§ 3(1)(a), 3(1)(f) (amended 1969). For a general discussion of the various laws enacted by the government in this period to pacify the country and the important role they have played in defending subsequent regimes from political attack see W Case, *Politics in Southeast Asia: Democracy or Less* (Routledge Curzon, 2002) 108–11.

[24] RH Hickling, 'An Overview of Constitutional Changes in Malaysia: 1957–1977', in TM Suffian, HP Lee, and FA Trindade (eds), *The Constitution of Malaysia: Its Development: 1957–1977* (OUP, 1978) 23.

likely to involve the inflaming of public feeling on the issue, thereby discouraging the litigant, who might be held responsible for any adverse consequences. It could also be that litigants view these issues as beyond the willingness of the judiciary to intervene.'[25] Second, unlike in some other jurisdictions, the public services in Malaysia identified much more closely with the recipient of the preferences leading some to comment, 'in Malaysia, the public services tend to be over-zealous in implementing Bumiputera policies'.[26]

The new, heightened system of preferences was set in the context of a significantly revised economic policy. A New Economic Policy (NEP) was developed over time after the 1969 riots. Its aim was poverty reduction and ethnic redistribution accomplished in part by means of economic growth.[27] Two inter-linking policies that rose to considerable prominence in the 1970s as part of the NEP are of particular importance for our purposes. The first was the policy of increasing Bumiputera share ownership in Malaysian companies. The Second Malaysia Plan adopted the objective of increasing Bumiputera ownership of publicly quoted equity to 30 per cent by 1990, up from an estimated 4 per cent in 1971.[28] The Industrial Co-ordination Act 1975 furthered the policy by requiring the restructuring of equity ownership in manufacturing industry as a condition for the award of a government licence. All qualifying companies were required to submit a plan for the achievement of a 30 per cent Bumiputera share by 1990. New manufacturing companies of a particular size were required to have Bumiputera equity of at least 30 per cent of the total.[29]

The second, and the primary focus of this chapter, is the use of the government procurement power to bolster the system of preferences by institutionalizing preferences for majority Bumiputera-controlled companies in the award of government contracts. Together, these two policies can be seen as attempts to achieve, as the Malaysian government put it, the goal of 'eliminating the present identification of race with economic function'.[30] To do so it was necessary to go beyond merely rectifying imbalances in income between Bumiputera and non-Bumiputera and attempt to equalize equity ownership. This was seen as contributing to wealth equalization in the longer term. It was also necessary to achieve a significant cultural shift within the Malay population, from conceiving of themselves not only as rural agricultural workers but also as (potential) urban entrepreneurs. In addition,

---

[25] Harding (n 21 above) 231–2; see also AH Othman *et al*, 'Social Change and National Integration', in J Yahaya *et al* (eds), *Sustaining Growth, Enhancing Distribution: The NEP and NDP Revisited* (Proceedings of CEDER Conference) (2003) 141, 145 ('The logic of the exercise is simple enough: if the questioning of these "sensitive issues" had led or paved the way to serious social discord, its prohibition could help ensure, if not guarantee, societal harmony.')

[26] Nesiah (n 15 above) 231.

[27] See Second Malaysia Plan (n 20 above) foreword; Othman *et al* (n 25 above) 141, 145; Gomez 1994 (n 19 above) 3.   [28] Second Malaysia Plan (n 20 above) §135.

[29] See Gomez and Jomo (n 22 above) 29–32.

[30] Third Malaysian Plan (n 9 above) para 567. See also I Emsley, *The Malaysian Experience of Affirmative Action: Lessons for South Africa* (Human & Rousseau Tafelberg, 1996) 49.

it was likely that companies that were majority Bumiputera owned would be more likely to increase the proportion of Bumiputera employees. Although he claims that the NEP was formulated independently, and without knowledge of steps towards 'affirmative action' in the United States, Mahathir states in his 1998 book that it was 'roughly an embodiment of the affirmative action approach formulated in the USA'.[31] The NEP was essentially about the creation of the same class structure in the Bumiputera community as existed in the non-Bumiputera communities.

What marks out the policy context in which these redistributive policies developed, is the extent to which the Malaysian government situated them within an overall economic policy of substantially investment-led economic growth. Economic growth, it was made clear, provided the resources which could then be redistributed. The two went hand-in-hand. Without racial stability, investors would be scared away; without investment, racial stability could not be financed.[32] From the government's point of view at least, redistributive policies were necessary to provide a stable political context in which to attract investment. Equally, for redistribution to achieve the goal of greater stability, it had to be financed from growth, rather than squeezing the Chinese and Indian populations, because to do so would increase ethnic tensions rather than lessen them. No particular group should feel that it was losing out.[33] Without external investment, in other words, everything was at risk. This meant that redistributive policies were, to an extent, affected by the external economic climate affecting Malaysia, as well as the internal domestic political climate.[34] This made the government more sensitive than some to the problems that were thrown up by its redistributive policies. As a result, the NEP was 'continually amended to take account of changing external conditions as well as the program's own successes and failures'.[35]

Subsequent development of set-asides

Subsequently, the National Development Policy (NDP) replaced the New Economic Policy:

While the NDP maintains the basic strategies of the NEP, its new dimensions will be to: (a) shift the focus of the anti-poverty strategy towards eradication of hard-core poverty while at the same time reducing relative poverty; (b) focus on employment and the rapid development of an active Bumiputera Commercial and Industrial Community (BCIC) as a more effective strategy to increase the meaningful participation of Bumiputera in the modern sectors of the economy; (c) rely more on the private sector to be involved in the restructuring objective by creating greater opportunities for its growth; and (d) focus on human resource development as a fundamental requirement for achieving the objectives of growth and distribution.[36]

---

[31] ibid 81. [32] See Second Malaysia Plan (n 20 above) §3. [33] ibid.
[34] This is essentially Stafford's argument (n 16 above) 75. [35] ibid 559.
[36] Second Outline Perspective Plan (n 20 above) foreword.

Growth and redistribution were both seen as key elements, but redistribution was seen as dependent on growth even more than before. 'The emphasis will be on managing the success already achieved and enhancing the growth momentum to bring about a better distribution of income opportunities...'[37] The process of creating the BCIC 'will take into account the need for Bumiputera to participate in an environment of competition and efficiency'. Government policies and programmes 'will continue to provide the necessary support to Bumiputera entrepreneurs' but they would 'be expected to develop their business activities increasingly on their own efforts and be less dependent on Government subsidies and assistance'.[38] The system of preferences would be implemented to 'ensure that only Bumiputera with potential, commitment and good track records will be accorded access so that the objectives of creating a viable and resilient BCIC under the NDP are achieved'.[39] Edmund Gomez has termed this approach Mahathir's 'pick a winner' strategy.[40] This strategy involved a self-conscious favouritism, whereby Mahathir and/or other top officials individually chose to bestow advantages upon only those Bumiputera entrepreneurs who, in their minds, were most promising and thus most capable of using the advantages to their benefit.[41]

From the 1990s, a considerably reduced role for the government in the economy was adopted. Privatization was heavily promoted. It was, however, privatization with a redistributive aspect, with preferences for Bumiputera in the distribution of shares.[42] In this context, government contracting became even more important since many of the activities that had been carried out directly by government-owned business were now to be carried out by private enterprise under contract to government. Preferences for Bumiputera companies therefore became even more important than in the past. The combination of share-preference and contract-preference lessened opposition from Malays to the NEP. At the same time, however, the increased opportunities for investment in the newly privatized sectors of the economy led to an expansion of foreign direct investment.

Operation of preferences in Malaysia

We shall concentrate on the organization of preferences for Bumiputera operating between 1995 and Mahathir's retirement as prime minister in 2003.[43] The Finance Ministry exercised a broad grant of rule-making authority through Treasury regulations in two basic forms: *Arahan Perbendaharaan*, Treasury Instructions (TIs), and

---

[37] Sixth Malaysia Plan, 1991–1995 §§1.99, 1.30 (10 July 1991) (hereafter Sixth Malaysia Plan).
[38] Second Outline Perspective Plan (n 20 above) para 4.51.   [39] ibid para 4.53.
[40] ET Gomez, 'Capital Development in Malaysia' in J Yahaya *et al* (eds), *Sustaining Growth, Enhancing Distribution: The NEP and NDP Revisited* (Proceedings of CEDER Conference) (2003) 71, 81 (hereafter Gomez 2003).   [41] ibid.
[42] Stafford (n 16 above) 573.
[43] See Treas Circ Let No 4/1995 (n 8 above); Treas Circ Let No 2/1995 (n 8 above) §4.1.3.

Surat Pekeliling Perbendaharaan, Treasury Circular Letters (TCLs).[44] The system established by TCL No 4/1995 roughly divides into five categories: (1) generally applicable preferences for Bumiputera *suppliers* of goods and services; (2) generally applicable preferences for Bumiputera *producers* of goods; (3) generally applicable preferences for Bumiputera works providers; (4) special preferences for Bumiputera providers administered by the Finance Ministry and/or state financial officials; and (5) special preferences for members of the Malay Chamber of Commerce of Malaysia (MCCM).[45] The last established that, if all other things were equal between the bid of a Bumiputera tenderer which was an MCCM member, and the bid of a Bumiputera tenderer which was not, the member should be awarded the contract over the non-member.[46] While TCL No 4/1995 provided specific details with regard to the first three categories,[47] the fourth was stated in only the most general of terms.[48]

Preferences for Bumiputera providers in government procurement were focused principally on contributing to the restructuring of Malaysian society through the creation of a viable BCIC, and in particular the development of Bumiputera-owned small and medium-sized enterprises (SMEs). Over the years, this focus was maintained with preferences consistently concentrated in lower value tenders where small and medium-scale Bumiputera business could best compete.[49] However, the system of preferences also reflected government efforts to control abuse of the system by Bumiputera acting as front-men for non-Bumiputera businesses,[50] as well furthering the policy's secondary purposes of contributing to the NEP's poverty eradication goals.[51] The latter included encouraging the movement of Bumiputera into the upper levels of company hierarchies and creating opportunities for Bumiputera to shift from low-paying rural,

---

[44] Arahan Perbendaharaan [Treas Instr] §§166 *et seq.* (1997); Treas Circ Let No 7/2002 (n 8 above); Treas Circ Let No 4/1995 (n 8 above); Treas Circ Let No 2/1995 (n 8 above). In addition to these provisions, government procurement is also regulated by the very brief Government Contracts Act 1949 (Act 67) (amended 1973), which grants to Ministers the authority to contract directly or by delegation on behalf of the Federal Government, §2, and to Chief Ministers of States the authority to contract directly, or by delegating, on behalf of their respective states.

[45] See Treas Circ Let No 4/1995 (n 8 above) §§5–6. In addition to establishing/reaffirming these preferences, Treas Circ Let No 4/1995 eliminates preferences for providers from other ASEAN nations that had been in effect since 1984. ibid §10.1(v) (cancelling Surat Pekeliling Perbendaharaan Bil 7 Thn 1984 [Treas Circ Let No 7/1984], Peraturan-Peraturan Untuk Melaksanakan Artikal 7, Perjanjian Istimewa Perdagangan Di Kalangan Negara-Negara ASEAN: Indonesia, Filipina, Singapura, Thailand, Brunei dan Malaysia [Special Trading Provisions for ASEAN Nations: Indonesia, Philippines, Singapore, Thailand, Brunei and Malaysia] §3 (19 December 1984). Whilst there does not appear to be any official document confirming that this is the case, additional evidence suggests that Article 7 of the 1977 ASEAN Preferential Trading Arrangements (PTA) is no longer in force.

[46] Treas Circ Let No 4/1995 (n 8 above) §5.6.   [47] ibid §§5–6.

[48] ibid §§5.2.1, 5.3.3.

[49] ibid §§5, 7, 8; see also Midterm Review of the Eighth Malaysia Plan (n 8 above) §1.57; Third Malaysia Plan (n 9 above)§§599–600.

[50] Treas Circ Let No 4/1995 (n 8 above) §§2, 5–7; Sixth Malaysia Plan (n 37 above) §§1.99, 1.109.

[51] See Third Perspective Plan, 2001–2010 foreword (3 April 2001); Second Outline Perspective Plan (n 20 above) foreword; Second Malaysia Plan (n 20 above) foreword.

agricultural, low-skilled jobs to higher-paying urban, industrial, semi-skilled jobs,[52] and, arguably, indirectly reducing poverty by increasing the money circulating within Bumiputera communities.[53]

The other major preference programme in Malaysian government procurement was one that favoured domestic providers.[54] For many years, the programme focused mainly on aiding the development of domestic SMEs, by concentrating preferences in lower-value contracts where SMEs could best compete.[55] This had a particular importance in the light of the NEP's underlying goal of creating national unity.[56] Whilst the two major prongs of the NEP's strategy to achieve national unity focus on improving the socio-economic position of the Bumiputera majority, the government recognized that to be successful in creating unity they must be 'implemented in such a manner that no one [is] deprived of his rights, privileges, income, job, or opportunity'.[57] Thus, the NEP and its successors always predicated their distributive strategies on 'increasing opportunities for *all* Malaysians', from which an increased portion could be allocated to Bumiputera without a corollary decrease in the welfare of other groups.[58] Chief among the strategies for achieving this condition was a 'rapidly expanding economy' made possible by the peace and stability bought by the NEP's two-prong distributive strategy.[59] However, programmes, like preferences for *all* domestic providers, also played a role: first, by mitigating some of the negative impact of Bumiputera preferences on other domestic providers and, second, if successful in their stated goal, by 'promot[ing] of domestic industry', which would benefit all Malaysians.[60]

Internal controversy about preferences in Malaysia

There has clearly been significant internal political debate within Malaysia as to how these preferences are operated in practice. The redistribution arising from the preferences has increasingly been seen as bringing some unacceptable costs.[61] One problem continually identified is political corruption arising from the process of

---

[52] See Treas Circ Let No 4/1995 (n 8 above) §§2.1.1.2–2.1.1.6; Second Malaysia Plan (n 20 above) §§122–124.

[53] See Second Malaysia Plan (n 20 above) foreword; Midterm Review of the Eighth Malaysia Plan (n 8 above) §1.57.

[54] See Treas Circ Let No 7/2002 (n 8 above) §2; Treas Circ Let No 2/1995 (n 8 above) §4.

[55] See Treas Circ Let No 11 Year 1965, Preference in the Purchase of Domestically Made Articles (14 August 1965) (referencing a General Circular Memorandum No 5 of 1963); Arahan Perbendaharaan [Treas Instr] §169.2 (1997).

[56] See Second Malaysia Plan (n 20 above) foreword.   [57] ibid §3.

[58] ibid §3 (emphasis added); see also ibid, §§20, 140 ('The strategy is founded on the philosophy of active participation not on disruptive redistribution.').   [59] ibid §3 (emphasis added).

[60] Datuk Seri Dr Mahathir Bin Mohamad (then Prime Minister of Malaysia), The 2004 Budget Speech ¶ 99 (12 September 2003 at Dewan Rakyat) (official translation).

[61] Thomas Sowell also criticizes these policies as not achieving a reduction in income differences between the races, but that does not appear to have been their purpose. T Sowell, *Preferential Policies: An International Perspective* (William Morrow, 1990) 45–9.

preference in the award of contracts. This has been seen as due to the 'rent that exists in protected contracts ... [, which] has been a feature of Malaysian 'money politics' at the highest levels'.[62] In December 2000, Abdul Rahman Yusof (Keadilan-Kemaman) during the Committee stage debate on the Supply Bill, for example, accused the government of blacklisting Bumiputera contractors who supported the opposition.[63] Entrepreneur Development Minister Datuk Mohamed Nazri Abdul Aziz, said that the award of government contracts was based on the capability of Bumiputera contractors, regardless of whether they are government supporters. 'There is no truth to allegations that contracts are given based on political consideration ... '[64]

However, the *New York Times* reported in 2002,[65] Prime Minister Mahathir Mohamad

... appears to have ostracized a clique of tycoons once extolled as role models for an emerging Malay bourgeoisie. Entrusted with national assets and lavished with government contracts, they expanded their reach, only to find themselves drowning in debt when the Asian financial crisis erupted in 1997. After a series of controversial bailouts that deepened foreign investors' cynicism about Malaysia, Dr. Mahathir began to purge his tarnished champions last year.

Their downfall, reported the *Times*:

... coincided with a new emphasis here on meritocracy and, with it, a re-evaluation of affirmative action policies for Malaysia's native races, known as Bumiputera. Recently Dr. Mahathir has repeated publicly what many here have said privately for years: that policies intended to help give the Bumiputera a fairer stake in an economy once dominated by foreigners and ethnic Chinese have succeeded in creating a Malay middle class but have also created a culture of entitlement, complacency and mediocrity.

The *New York Times* continued: 'The removal of the best-known beneficiaries of crony capitalism has undoubtedly helped restore confidence in Malaysia's corporate integrity.'

A second common problem that has been identified is the potential that such policies lead to a decline in entrepreneurial activity among the target group. Entrepreneur Development Minister Datuk Mohamed Nazri Abdul Aziz, was reported to have said that Bumiputera contractors were too dependent on government contracts for business. 'We try to make them competitive in acquiring outside contracts, but it seems, year in year out, they still continue to depend on the government.'[66] In May 2001, Datuk Seri Abdullah Ahmad Badawi, the Deputy

---

[62] Emsley (n 30 above) 65.

[63] BERNAMA (Malaysian National News Agency), 'Award of Government Contracts Based on Contractors' Capability' *Malaysia General News*, 5 December 2000.   [64] ibid.

[65] W Arnold, 'Scandal Lets Malaysia Prove Its Mettle', *The New York Times*, 16 October 2002, sec W, p 1, col 4.

[66] BERNAMA (Malaysian National News Agency), 'Award of Government Contracts Based on Contractors' Capability' *Malaysia General News*, 5 December 2000.

Prime Minister, said[67] that the affirmative action policy must go straight to those who needed the help and this would mean that special privileges for the Bumiputeras would be channelled to those who deserved them either through need or merit. 'Poor Bumiputeras and brilliant Bumiputeras must be the first recipients of special privileges. We must cut the vicious cycle of mediocrity perpetuated by those who deserve no help but keep receiving it,' Abdullah said. In August 2002, Dr Mahathir Mohamad said that Bumiputera entrepreneurs must stop depending solely on the government to buy their goods because such a market is limited and it is not the way to do business.[68] The prime minister said that Bumiputera entrepreneurs must focus on the open market, which is the real market and which can help them to improve the quality of and demand for their goods. 'The entrepreneurs must avoid being too dependent on the government to buy their products. Instead, they should try to market their goods to the public within and outside the country,' he added. Later, at a media conference, he said that 100 per cent of the Bumiputera contractors depended on government contracts and in the absence of government contracts 'they are not competitive enough'.

This concern is particularly important in view of a third problem: the increased competition from contractors outside Malaysia that is likely to arise with the implementation of the Association of South-East Asian Nations (ASEAN) Free Trade Area. Malaysia increasingly saw itself as benefiting from liberalized trade, particularly among Asian trading countries. The development of the ASEAN Free Trade Area was considered to be an important opportunity, but also one that would impose increased market disciplines on domestic entrepreneurs. To be successful, increased international competitiveness was necessary. For one observer, 'efficiency-decreasing policies such as the NEP have become costly luxuries'.[69] The government 'has been forced to promote overall competitiveness at the expense of continued ethnic restructuring. In other words, it is no longer possible for growth *and* equity to continue in tandem to the same degree as they had in the 1970s.'[70]

A fourth problem continually adverted to is the tendency of Bumiputera contractors to become commission agents by subcontracting the contracts offered to them to others. This was a recurring criticism, not least from Dr Mahathir himself. In September 2002,[71] he returned yet again to the problem of those who sell such contracts to obtain quick profits. 'This irresponsible action has jeopardised the government's efforts to create a Bumiputera Commercial and Industrial Community,' he said. As a result, the government would be more cautious in awarding contracts only to those who are committed, responsible, have proper organization, and adequate

---

[67] BERNAMA (Malaysian National News Agency), 'M'sians Urged Not to Recoil into Own Racial Cocoons' *Malaysia General News*, 18 May 2001.
[68] BERNAMA (Malaysian National News Agency), 'Dr Mahathir Tells Bumi Entrepreneurs to Stop Depending on Govt' *Malaysia General News*, 6 August 2002.
[69] Stafford (n 16 above) 572.   [70] ibid 573.
[71] BERNAMA (Malaysian National News Agency), 'Contract Value of All Class Bumi Contractors Increased' *Malaysia General News*, 20 September 2002.

capital and who strive hard to become successful entrepreneurs in the construction industry. Those who sell contracts and do not actively manage the contracts would be blacklisted, he warned.

The 'administrative law' of government procurement in Malaysia

These controversies, whilst lively and public, do not translate into the development of any effective administrative law controls of the type that would be recognized in most developed countries. At all stages in the procurement process, including the administration of preferences, the Finance Ministry and, to a lesser extent, the Contractor Service Centre of the Ministry of Entrepreneur Development, maintain firm control. Further, this power is wielded virtually free from accountability to other entities in the federal or state governments, aggrieved providers, or interested citizens. The Treasury Division of the Finance Ministry enjoys almost complete discretion to make rules, which govern government procurement by all federal, state, and local governmental entities.[72] These rules delegate some authority to procuring entities at various stages of the process and to the Contractor Service Centre in specific instances. However, the Finance Ministry retains varying levels of authority at different stages of the process that, in combination with the absence of effective accountability mechanisms discussed below, leave it free to conduct as much of the process as it sees fit.

Significant mechanisms exist, which allow the Finance Ministry to monitor and control the government procurement activities of other governmental entities to ensure that they obey Treasury-issued government procurement regulations. However, remedies for aggrieved tenderers who believe that the Finance Ministry or another governmental entity has wronged them at any of the various stages of the tendering process (registration, tendering, award) are practically non-existent. Further, the more general controls, which ensure in a liberal democracy that the actions of an administrative agency will be contained within the bounds of the powers granted to it by democratically elected bodies, are similarly absent. Thus, the Finance Ministry is practically free to rule government procurement in Malaysia according to its discretion, whilst the government procurement activities of other governmental entities are subject, for the most part, only to its control.[73]

There are virtually no means for an aggrieved provider or other interested citizen to challenge either Treasury rules governing government procurement or specific decisions made under those rules, whether by the Finance Ministry or another governmental entity. There are no complaint procedures established specifically to deal with problems that arise in the context of government procurement generally, or applicable preference systems specifically, and the only generally available

---

[72] See Financial Procedures Act 1957 (Act 61) §4 (amended 1972).

[73] The minor exception is the monitoring role of procurement boards, which play a role in some types of procurement but which are themselves significantly controlled by the Finance Ministry. See Arahan Perbendaharaan [Treas Instr] §191 (1997).

mechanism for non-judicial resolution of complaints lacks teeth and is of questionable independence.

Judicial challenge of both Treasury government procurement rules and actions taken pursuant to them is also limited. The broad grant of power, under which the Treasury issues government procurement rules, in combination with other elements of the Malaysian legal system, make challenging the legality of government procurement rules almost impossible and,[74] in the case of challenges to rules applicable to Bumiputera preferences, potentially dangerous to one's freedom. (Treasury rules promulgating preferences for Bumiputera in government procurement are protected from legal challenge (and even open criticism) by provisions of the Sedition Act, which, *inter alia*, makes questioning privileges granted to Bumiputera a seditious act, a strict liability offence punishable by up to three years in jail and/or a fine of RN5000 (equivalent to US$1,300)).[75] Neither interested citizens nor participating providers appear to have access to courts to challenge specific contract decisions.[76] In grievances based on *status* decisions, such as general sector registration and preference-related registrations, the grounds for challenge are extremely limited. There are significant obstacles to compiling the necessary information to prevail, and the court's decision on whether to grant any remedy is discretionary.[77] Further, whilst some have noted 'a heartening surge in judicial activism',[78] there are still questions about how truly independent the judiciary is, especially in situations where it is up against a powerful element of the executive, like the Finance Ministry.[79] Finally, in Malaysia, government contracting is dealt with as

---

[74] See Financial Procedures Act 1957 (Act 61) §4 (amended 1972). Jain calls the Malaysian judiciary's role in determining whether administrative agencies have overstepped their rule authority under laws such as the Financial Procedures Act, 'almost symbolic'. MP Jain, 'Administrative Law in Malaysia', in MB Hooker (ed), *Malaysian Legal Essays* (Malaysian Legal Journal, 1986) 213, 214, 222–3; see also Interpretation Act 1948 (Act 81) §§20, 25 (amended 1967); MP Jain, *Administrative Law of Malaysia and Singapore* (Butterworths Asia, 1997) 91, 105–6.

[75] Sedition Act 1948 (Act 15) §§3(1)(a), 3(1)(f) (amended1969).

[76] See Jain (1997) (n 74 above) 568–9; *Lim Kit Sang v United Engineers of Malaysia* [1988] 1 SCR 22; [1988] 2 MJL 25.

[77] No cases in which a provider has challenged his status in Malaysian courts have been discovered. Some cases, which deal with other status type administrative decisions, appear to indicate that such a claim could be entertained by the courts. See eg *Ketua Pengarah Kastam v Ho Kwan Seng* [1977] 2 MJL 152; *Metal Industry Employees v Registrar of Trade Unions* [1992] 1 MLJ 46; *Keith Sellar v Lee Kwang* [1980] 2 MJL 191; *Au Kong Weng v Bar Committee Pahang* [1980] 2 MJL 89; *DK Gudgeon v Professional Engineers Board* [1980] 2 MJL 181; *Tann Boo Chee, David v Medical Council of Singapore* [1980] 2 MJL 116; *Tan Choon Chye v Singapore Society of Accountants* [1980] 1 MLJ 258; *Lim Ko v Board of Architects* [1966] 2 MLJ 80. However, in order for a provider to prevail, it is likely that it would have to show that it had a legitimate expectation of the status which it was denied, Jain 1997 (n 74 above) 273–4, which might be difficult given the 'private law' perspective from which government contracting decisions are viewed by Malaysia's courts, ibid 568–9. See also ibid 606–10 (for a discussion of some of the obstacles to gathering evidence that a challenger to a decision by an administrative agency might have); 655–7 (for a discussion of the discretion courts have to hear or refuse to hear challenges of administrative agency decisions).

[78] SCKG Pillay, 'The Changing Faces of Administrative Law in Malaysia' (1999) 1 Malayan Law Journal cxl, cxli; See also Jain 1997 (n 74 above) 255.

[79] The dangers posed for judges who take on the executive was powerfully demonstrated in 1988, when a High Court ruling, which nullified for registration irregularities UMNO party elections that

part of private law, and therefore the government is largely free to contract however, and with whomever, it pleases. Those who feel they have been wronged in this process only have access to the judicial remedies that would apply in a contractual dispute between private parties.[80] In other words, a provider which has not been awarded a government contract has no more right to challenge that decision than it would have in the context of a rejection by a private party.

II. Procurement Reform in South Africa

The end of apartheid in South Africa at the beginning of the 1990s provided an equivalent galvanizing event to the 1969 Malaysian riots. As in Malaysia, the new government was faced with a market-dominant minority and an impoverished majority. As in Malaysia, public procurement was identified as an opportunity for advancing redistributive policies. Unlike in Malaysia, this was accompanied by significant reform of the public procurement system. The dual-faceted nature of the necessary changes in public procurement that were identified as necessary reflects the dual-faceted nature of the problem facing the government. Procurement reform was necessary not only to promote good governance in public procurement, leading to greater efficiencies, but also so that it could be used effectively to deliver socio-economic objectives.[81]

   As part of this reform, an ambitious two-prong strategy was developed to address public procurement.[82] One prong was the development of an appropriate legislative basis for a reformed public procurement system. The second was an attempt to use the existing, if flawed, public procurement regulatory structure to begin the task of reform. The aim was not only to introduce principles of good governance into procurement but also to harness its redistributive potential. The Reconstruction and Development Programme (RDP) stated that 'tenders must be

had narrowly left Mahathir in power, precipitated the removal of, first, the Lord President of Supreme Court (principally for criticizing moves by Mahathir to consolidate the executive's power against the judiciary), and then five other Supreme Court judges, who rose to the Lord President's defence. See Gomez 1994 (n 19 above) 62–3; K Marks, 'Judicial Independence' (1994) 68 Australian Law Journal (1994) 173, 177–9 (stating, *inter alia*, that these events 'resulted in a judiciary stripped of whatever independence it formerly had'); W Case, *Politics in Southeast Asia: Democracy or Less* (Routledge Curzon, 2002) 116–17.

   [80] See Jain 1997 (n 74 above) 568–9.
   [81] S Gounden, 'The Impact of the National Department of Public Works's Affirmative Procurement Policy on the Participation and Growth of Affirmable Business Entrerprises in the Construction Sector', unpublished PhD thesis (2000), available at <http://www.targetedprocurement .co.za/papers/SG/SGpapers.html>. This thesis has been exceptionally useful in tracing the history of the development of policy in this area in South Africa. P Bolton, 'The Legal Regulation of Government Procurement in South Africa' (PhD thesis, 2005) was also an important source of background information for this chapter.
   [82] For an insider's overiew, see D Letchmiah, 'The Process of Public Sector Procurement Reform in South Africa' (1999) 8 PPLR 15.

utilized to encourage stakeholder participation in the RDP, to promote workers rights, human resource development and job creation'.[83] The interim Constitution provided that no persons were to be unfairly discriminated against, but that this did not preclude measures designed to achieve the adequate protection and advancement of persons or groups or categories of persons disadvantaged by unfair discrimination, in order to enable their full and equal enjoyment of all rights and freedoms.[84] The Ministry of Public Works and the Ministry of Finance developed the initiative.

During 1995, acting under legislation enacted under apartheid,[85] an interim ten-point strategy for procurement reform in South Africa was developed. Within the constraints of the existing system, the aim was to develop policies that would begin to address the perceived tendency of the existing policies and procedures to 'tend to favour the larger and better established entrepreneurs', which did not 'create an environment that allows easy access for small, medium and micro enterprises into the mainstream procurement activities'.[86] Amongst the ten points were that government should assist more with access to tendering information, establish tender advice centres, incorporate smaller businesses into databases of suppliers, waive financial sureties, package tenders into smaller contracts, shorten the time of payment, simplify the tender submissions, appoint a procurement ombudsman to receive and resolve complaints, and open up the building and engineering procurements.

In addition, however, a detailed additional strategy was included to address previous disadvantage and unfair discrimination, particularly on racial grounds. A price preference system was adopted to target a specific group, those 'persons disadvantaged by unfair discrimination' (so-called HDIs, or Historically Disadvantaged Individuals) within the emerging small, medium and micro enterprise (SMME) sector. The policy was based on a percentage preference and would usually apply to contracts worth less than R2 million. The threshold was adopted in order 'to control the possibility of any undue expenditure resulting from this preference policy during the untested period of implementing these interim strategies. In addition, this limit targets the emerging SMME sector rather than the better established businesses.'[87] The tenderers to benefit from this preference were those businesses 'controlled by such [disadvantaged] persons or to businesses where such [disadvantaged] persons have an equity shareholding'. A disadvantaged person was defined as 'a South African citizen disadvantaged by unfair racial discrimination in the previous political dispensation'.[88] The contract would be awarded using a combination of lowest price, with additional preferences for firms with equity owned by women and disadvantaged persons thus defined. The tender selected was the one with the highest

[83] RDP, 1994, para 4.8.11.   [84] Interim Constitution, s 8.
[85] State Tender Board Act (Act 86) 1968, and Government Notice R 1237, 1988.
[86] Public Sector Procurement Reform in South Africa: Interim Strategies: A 10-point Plan, 29 November 1995, Introduction.   [87] ibid 7.
[88] ibid 13.

number of points, out of 100. Of these 100 points, up to 10 could be gained depending on the proportion of equity in the business owned by disadvantaged persons, and up to 2 points could be gained depending on the proportion of equity owned by women, thus leaving 88 points to be gained on the basis of price.

A variation on this was adopted for construction contracts, in which a wider range of socio-economic factors (including the use of labour-intensive construction methods, use of local resources, use of contractors engaged in development programmes, equity shareholding, and adoption of affirmative action principles in employment) could contribute up to 15 points in the case of larger contracts. The focus on construction contracts was in part because much of the local and international strategies 'for using public sector procurement as a socio-economic instrument are well developed within the construction sector', not least in Malaysia and the United States.[89] The 10 Point Plan was adopted by the National Cabinet, endorsed by the State Tender Board and put into operation in pilot projects from June 1996, with some apparent success in increasing the proportion of black firms involved in subcontracting on public contracts at a relatively low level of extra costs.[90] In 1997, the government published its Green Paper on public sector procurement reform,[91] which took forward the work on preferential procurement that had been developed earlier. The operational systems largely drew from experience in the United States.[92]

Socio-economic functions of public procurement in South Africa

In its General Procurement Guidelines, the government summed up the variety of different types of socio-economic policies that it seeks to promote through procurement. Its aim is to: '(a) advance the development of SMMEs and HDIs; (b) promote women and physically handicapped people; (c) create new jobs; (d) promote local enterprises in specific provinces, in a particular region, in a specific local authority, or in rural areas; and (e) support the local product'.[93] This chapter concentrates primarily on categories (a) and (b), but it would be misleading not to set out, at least to some extent, some features of three other policies that the government currently adopts, as they set the context for the discussion of the more limited aspects of procurement policy that this chapter primarily considers.

---

[89] Gounden thesis (n 81 above) 3.16–3.17.

[90] Presentation by Mr. Sipho Shezi, Director-General of the National Department of Public Works, Republic of South Africa at the 9th International Public Procurement Association Conference in Copenhagen, Denmark, 8 June 1998 'Public Sector Procurement as an Instrument of Government Policy', 3. See also Address by the Minister of Public Works, Mr Jeff T Radebe, to the Black Economic Empowerment Conference, 15 July 1997. The most extensive discussion is to be found in the Gounden thesis (n 81 above) discussed subsequently.

[91] Green Paper on Public Sector Procurement Reform in South Africa: An Initiative of the Ministry of Finance and the Ministry of Public Works, April 1997 (*Government Gazette*, Vol 382, No 17928, 14th April 1997) (hereafter Green Paper).   [92] Gounden thesis (n 81 above) 3.9.

[93] Government of the Republic of South Africa, General Procurement Guidelines.

The first relevant policy involves preferences for local industry. These policies were first initiated under apartheid, and have been continued by post-apartheid governments, having been considered as still necessary by the Green Paper on procurement reform.[94] As set out in the current conditions governing state contracts, certain tender price preferences are taken into account when calculating the price of tenders. These price preferences are aimed at promoting local manufacturing. The following preferences are considered:[95] a preference based on the local content of the entire local process, use of the South African Bureau of Standards (SABS) mark, and of locally manufactured electronic systems and components. In addition, such other preferences are permitted, as may be determined by the Minister of Finance. The preference is up to 10 per cent if local content is more than 80 per cent; up to 10 per cent for the use of locally manufactured electronic systems and components, plus a minimum of 5 per cent for local design, provided that the two together do not exceed 10 per cent; and 2.5 per cent for the use of products that carry the SABS mark.[96] These have attracted the attention of successive WTO Trade Policy Reviews.[97] If the combination of local protectionism and ethnic redistribution, within a liberal economic framework, seems remarkably like some of the developments in Malaysia that have been examined previously, that is not coincidental, as there is evidence that Malaysia had some effect in the development of targeted procurement as part of a general policy of redistribution in favour of the majority, but economically dispossessed, indigenous population.[98]

The second specific socio-economic policy that merits attention is more particularly associated with Africa than with Malaysia. There has, for several years, been a sustained attempt to establish methods of public infrastructure development that use labour-intensive methods of construction. During the 1970s and 1980s, the International Labour Organization (ILO) developed an important role in assisting in the establishment of labour-intensive methods of road building and other infrastructure development in developing countries, often as part of World Bank or other international donor-provided funding for such provision. The interest of the ILO in developing such labour-(as opposed to equipment-) intensive methods was so that developing countries put their large labour forces to productive use, reducing the substantial pool of long-term unemployed, and reducing the extent to which the developing country needed to spend scarce foreign reserves to import expensive foreign equipment. The role of the ILO in these programmes has developed significantly in recent years, and with it a more clearly

---

[94] Green Paper (n 91 above) 96–7.

[95] State Tender Board, General Conditions and Procedures (ST 36) para 25.

[96] See Preference Certificate, <http://www.treasury.gov.za/organisation/ostb/docs/st11.pdf>.

[97] WTO, Trade Policy Review—Republic of South Africa—Report by the Secretariat, WT/TPR/S/34, 06/04/1998, paras 79–80; WTO, Trade Policy Review: Southern African Customs Union: report by the Secretariat, Annex: South Africa, WT/TPR/S/114/ZAF, 24 March 2003, para 37.

[98] Gounden thesis (n 81 above) 3.16–3.17; PM Madi, 'The Malaysian Connection' in *Black Economic Empowerment in the New South Africa: The Rights and the Wrongs* (Knowledge Resources, 1997) 45–7.

defined policy that infrastructure development in developing countries should bene-fit local people, not just in the provision of the road or building, but in the course of its construction as well. The ILO's Employment-Intensive Investment Branch cur-rently runs a programme called the Advisory Support Information Services and Training for Employment-Intensive Infrastructure (ASIST).

This approach has been taken up in both Namibia[99] and in South Africa, for example in the programmes that had developed during the apartheid era to address development needs in Soweto.[100] The Green Paper had recommended that procure-ment could facilitate the creation of jobs in South Africa by promoting employment-intensive construction practices.[101] Most recently, under the 'Expanded Public Works Programme', one of the government's programmes aimed at alleviating and reducing unemployment, opportunities for implementing the programme have been identified in several sectors of the economy. In the infrastructure sector the emphasis has been on creating additional work opportunities through the introduc-tion of labour-intensive construction methods. All public bodies involved in infra-structure provision are expected to attempt to contribute to the programme. As part of this initiative, the national government has required provinces and municipalities to use the 'Guidelines for the implementation of labour intensive infrastructure projects under the EPWP'[102] for the identification, design, and construction of projects financed through the national government.

The third use of procurement for socio-economic purposes is the national Industrial Participation Programme (IPP), which is designed to stimulate local economic development. The IPP became an obligation on 1 September 1996, and the Cabinet endorsed the policy and operating guidelines in April 1997.[103] All purchases by government and parastatals (ie, state-owned enterprises) or lease contracts (goods, equipment, or services) with an imported content equal to or exceeding US$10 million (or the equivalent thereof) are subject to the IPP obliga-tion. Those supplying the contract are required to participate in some additional respects in the South African economy. The total of this extra commercial or indus-trial activity must equal or exceed 30 per cent of the imported content, and must be carried out within seven years from the effective date of the Industrial Participation Agreement. So, for example, suppose a state-owned enterprise purchases goods to the

---

[99] Namibian Government, Department of Transport, 'Green Paper on Labour Based Works' (February 1997).

[100] RB Watermeyer, G Nevin, S Amod, RA Hallet, 'An evaluation of projects within Soweto's con-tractor development programme' (Second Quarter 1995) SAICE Journal 17.

[101] Green Paper (n 91 above) 71–5. For sustained arguments in favour of such programmes, see R Watermeyer, 'Mobilising the Private Sector to Engage in Labour-Based Infrastructure Works: A South African Perspective', Sixth Regional Seminar for Labour-Based Practitioners, 29 September–3 October 1997, Jinja, Uganda.

[102] <http://www.epwp.gov.za/downloads/legal/guidelines.pdf>.

[103] DTI, South Africa into the Future: The National Industrial Participation Programme (nd), available from <http://www.google.com/search?q=cache:AOPgmhjSmkIJ:www.dti.gov.za/uploads/offerings/files/127_46.pdf+%22south+africa%22+2B+future+%2B+%22national+industrial+participation+programme%22&hl=en&ct=clnk&cd=2&client=safari>. The details of the programme in this paragraph are taken from this publication.

value of US$100 million, and the imported content of these goods amounts to US$80 million. The seller of such goods would incur an Industrial Participation obligation to the value of US$24 million (30 per cent). The seller would be obliged to submit and implement within seven years business projects that would generate Industrial Participation credits equalling or exceeding US$24 million. The Industrial Participation obligation is not to result in an increase in the price of the purchase, and all industrial participation proposals must reflect incremental or new business. IPP is a precondition but not a factor in the adjudication, unless all bids are relatively close.

Constitutionalizing linkage in South Africa

We can return now to consider procurement initiatives directed specifically at ensuring status equality. The final South African Constitution of 1996 aimed to empower government even more clearly with substantial tools to address the task of reconstruction. The first tool was the inclusion of broad anti-discrimination provisions,[104] permitting extensive affirmative action.[105] A second of these tools was the power of the purse in the shape of procurement. The Interim Constitution of 1993, although it included a reference to the arrangements for the management of public procurement, had not included any reference to linkages.[106] The inclusion of explicit references to preferences in the final Constitution has been attributed by Gounden 'to the work done by the procurement Task Team during the intervening period'.[107] During that period, the Team had reviewed the United States experience and, on the basis of this experience, had concluded that a system of price preferences rather than set-asides should be adopted in South Africa. As importantly, however, it had also concluded, given the legal challenges to the United States system of set-asides, that there was 'a need for a national legislative framework to define such preferencing and targeting'.[108] It 'was, primarily, on the basis of this work that changes were proposed for inclusion in the final version of the Constitution'.[109]

The final Constitution provided, in section 217, the first example of a national constitution incorporating linkage.[110] It is a culmination in its drafting of two themes: the need for procurement reform, and the need for linkage. The procurement reform message is given by the first clause of the section: 'When an organ of state in the national, provincial or local sphere of government, or any other institution identified in national legislation, contracts for goods or services, it must do so in accordance with a system which is fair, equitable, transparent, competitive and cost-effective.' The need for linkage is provided in the next subsection: 'Subsection (1) does not prevent the organs of state or institutions referred to in that

---

[104] Constitution of the Republic of South Africa 1996, Act 109 of 1996, s 9 (3) and (4).
[105] ibid s 9 (2).   [106] Interim Constitution, Act No 200 of 1993, s 187.
[107] Gounden, thesis (n 81 above) 3.14.   [108] ibid.   [109] ibid 3.15.
[110] Final Constitution, n 104 above, s 217.

subsection from implementing a procurement policy providing for (a) categories of preference in the allocation of contracts; and (b) the protection or advancement of persons, or categories of persons, disadvantaged by unfair discrimination.' The third subsection makes clear that the second subsection was not self-executing and needed legislation for it to be operationalized: 'National legislation must prescribe a framework within which the policy referred to in subsection (2) may be implemented.' Following the coming into effect of the Constitution, the Employment Equity Act was passed in 1998, and the Preferential Procurement Policy Framework Act in 2000. In 2001, section 217(3) was amended to provide that 'organs of state who implement a preferential procurement policy are also obliged to do so *in accordance with* the national legislation referred to in section 217(3)'.[111]

Equality legislation

Following extensive consultation on earlier proposals,[112] in 1998, the Employment Equity Act[113] was introduced to address discrimination and imbalances in the workplace, and is said to have been modelled on the Canadian legislation.[114] The legislation provides for both non-discrimination requirements and extensive programmes of affirmative action, enforced in various ways, including by linkage to procurement. This linkage of procurement to employment equity was not uncontroversial. The Green Paper on procurement reform, published in April 1997, had been sceptical, concluding that 'the practicalities associated with the implementation of employment equity by means of such routes needs to be established'. Despite this, the 1998 legislation provided that every employer 'that makes an offer to conclude an agreement with any organ of state for the furnishing of supplies or services to that organ of state or for the hiring or letting of anything'[115] must comply with particular aspects of the Employment Equity Act, depending on whether the employer is a 'designated employer' or not. A designated employer includes[116] those with fifty or more employees, those with fewer than fifty but whose annual turnover is larger than that of a small business, municipalities, most organs of the state, and employers bound by collective agreements. If the employer is a designated employer in this sense, then the employer must comply with both the affirmative action and the non-discrimination requirements of the legislation.

---

[111] P Bolton, 'An Analysis of the Preferential Procurement Legislation in South Africa', in S Arrowsmith and P Kunzlik, *Social and Environmental Policies under the EC Procurement Rules: New Directives and New Directions* (provisional title) (Cambridge University Press, in Press) (emphasis added) citing The Constitution of the Republic of South Africa Second Amendment Act, No 61 of 2001.

[112] Department of Labour, 1996, Employment and Occupational Equity, *Government Gazette*, Vol 373, No 17303, 1 July 1996; White Paper on Affirmative Action, *Government Gazette*, Vol 394, No 18 800, 23 April 1998.

[113] Employment Equity Act (No 55 of 1998) as amended by the Employment Equity Act 2006.

[114] A Thomas and HC Jain, 'Employment Equity in Canada and South Africa: Progress and Propositions' (2004) 15 International Journal of Human Resource Management 36.

[115] Employment Equity Act 1998, s 53(1).   [116] ibid s 53(1)(a).

If the employer is not a designated employer, then only the non-discrimination requirements must be complied with for these purposes. An employer may request a certificate from the Director General of the Department of Labour 'confirming compliance [by that employer] with the non-discrimination and/or affirmative action requirements of the legislation'. When making a procurement offer to the organ of state, the employer is required to attach to that offer this certificate, or a declaration by the employer that it complies with the relevant chapters. The certificate and the declaration, when verified by the Director General, are 'conclusive evidence of compliance'.[117] This certificate is valid for one year from the date of issue or until the next date on which the employer is required to submit an affirmative action report, whichever is the longer. The point of all these requirements, legally, is to create a link between compliance with the Employment Equity Act, and the award of public contracts. Section 53 provides that a 'failure to comply with the relevant provisions of [the] Act is sufficient ground for rejection of any offer to conclude an agreement . . . or for cancellation of the agreement'.[118]

A broader approach is adopted in equality legislation adopted in 2000.[119] This provides, in section 26, that it is 'the responsibility of any person directly or indirectly contracting with the State or exercising public power to promote equality' by 'adopting appropriate equality plans, codes, regulatory mechanisms and other appropriate measures for the effective promotion of equality in the spheres of their operation', by 'enforcing and monitoring the enforcement of the equality plans, codes and regulatory mechanisms developed by them', and by 'making regular reports to the relevant monitoring authorities or institutions as may be provided in regulations, where appropriate'. It would appear that no regulations have yet been made under this provision. However, this provision seldom features in discussions about procurement in the South African context, and questions must therefore be raised about its effectiveness in practice. Instead, the focus of attention has shifted out of the realm of equality legislation strictly defined, and into specific legislation relating to procurement.

Preferential procurement legislation

The preferential procurement policy aspects of the Green Paper were later given partial legislative force in the Preferential Procurement Policy Framework Act (PPPFA), enacted in 2000.[120] It had been envisaged that the Act would be preceded by a White Paper setting out the government's collective views on the issues,

---

[117] ibid s 53(1)(b).   [118] ibid s 53(4).

[119] Act No 4, Promotion of Equality and Prevention of Discrimination Act 2000, and subsequent Regulations implementing the legislation: No R 764, 13 June 2003.

[120] No 5 of 2000. For commentary on the legislation and its regulations, see Bolton (n 111 above); G Penfold and P Reyburn, 'Public Procurement' in S Woolman *et al* (eds), *Constitutional Law of South Africa* (loose leaf)(2nd edn, 2003) Vol 1. See also P Bolton, 'The Use of Government Procurement as an Instrument of Policy' (2004) 121 South African Law Journal 619, 624–32.

but this did not occur, probably because the two major departments dealing with the issue, the Department of Public Works and the National Treasury, fought over which was to be the lead Department. This inauspicious start to the legislation has been identified by the Congress of South African Trade Unions (COSATU) as having contributed to subsequent difficulties, which will be considered below.[121] The Act, together with the regulations made under the Act,[122] provide for the approach that must be adopted by those organs of the state to which the Act applies. It establishes that a preference points system must be followed. This continues the policies developed earlier, but attempts to rationalize the somewhat ad hoc arrangements that had preceded it. The legislation sets out a non-exhaustive list of several social policy goals, although the Regulations appear to restrict preferential procurement to the achievement of these goals. The inclusion of these in the contract will attract preference points.

For contracts with an estimated Rand value above a prescribed amount (R500,000), a maximum of 10 points may be allocated for the specific social policy goals, provided that the lowest acceptable tender scores 90 points for price. For contracts with an estimated value of between R30,000 and R500,000, a maximum of 20 points may be allocated for the specific social policy goals, provided that the lowest acceptable tender scores 80 points for price. Any other acceptable tenders which are higher in price must score fewer points, on a pro rata basis, calculated on their tender prices in relation to the lowest acceptable tender, in accordance with a prescribed formula. Any specific social policy goal for which points may be awarded, and what system of points is to be used, must be clearly specified in the invitation to submit a tender. Such goals must be measurable, quantifiable, and monitored for compliance. The contract must be awarded to the tenderer who scores the highest points, unless objective criteria justify the award to another tenderer. There are severe penalties, including the cancellation of the contract, and debarment from future contracts, for obtaining contracts by fraud. Thus, although securing equality goals is an important function of the regulation of procurement in South Africa, it is not the only goal. The PPPFA sets out the minimum that a state organ to which it applies must do, but it also establishes the maximum that it may do as well.

The legislation and the Regulations contemplate public procurement being used to advance various socio-economic policies. These policy goals include: contracting with persons, or categories of persons, historically disadvantaged by unfair discrimination on the basis of race, gender, or disability, having black equity ownership, and implementing the programmes of the RDP. An HDI is defined as a South African citizen who, due to apartheid, 'had no franchise in national elections',

[121] Congress of South African Trade Unions (COSATU), Mr E Paulus, Finance Select Committee, 9 September 2003, Preferential Procurement Policy Framework Act, Public Hearings, available <http://www.pmg.org.za>.

[122] Preferential Procurement Regulations, Government Notice R725, *Government Gazette* No 22549, 10 August 2001. These regulations are currently being redrafted, see below.

and/or is female, and/or has a disability.[123] A maximum of 20 points may be awarded to a tenderer for being an HDI, and/or subcontracting with an HDI, and/or achieving any of a set of other specified goals. The tendering conditions may stipulate that specific goals be attained. The stipulation must include the method to be used to calculate the points scored for achieving specific goals. Over and above the awarding of preference points in favour of HDIs, the following activities are regarded as a contribution towards achieving the RDP goals: the promotion of South African-owned enterprises; the promotion of export-orientated production to create jobs; the promotion of SMMEs; the creation of new jobs or the intensification of labour absorption; the promotion of enterprises located in a specific province for work to be done or services to be rendered in that province; the promotion of enterprises located in a specific region for work to be done or services to be rendered in that region; the promotion of enterprises located in a specific municipal area for work to be done or services to be rendered in that municipal area; the promotion of enterprises located in rural areas; the empowerment of the workforce by standardizing the level of skill and knowledge of workers; the development of human resources, including by assisting in tertiary and other advanced training programmes, in line with key indicators such as percentage of wage bill spent on education and training and improvement of management skills; and the improvement of communities through, but not limited to, housing, transport, schools, infrastructure donations, and charity organizations.

Separately, however, in the adjudication of tenders, an organ of state may give particular consideration to procuring locally manufactured products, and preferences in this regard may be accommodated within the ambit of the Act's 80/20 or 90/10 point systems. For specific industries (identified by the Department of Trade and Industry), where the award of tenders to local manufacturers is of critical importance, such tenders may be advertised with a specific tendering condition that only locally manufactured products will be considered. Should preference points be awarded for local manufacturing and/or content, the award of such points must be clearly specified in the tendering conditions.

Thus far, the use of preferences for advancing these goals is permissive. If the public body does award preferences, then the Act sets down how this is to be done. However, the Regulations set out that preference points stipulated in respect of a tender *must* include preference points for equity ownership by HDIs, equated to the percentage of an enterprise or business owned by individuals or, in respect of a company, the percentage of a company's shares that are owned by individuals, who are actively involved in the management of the enterprise or business and exercise control over the enterprise, commensurate with their degree of ownership at the closing date of the tender. In the event that the percentage of ownership changes after the closing date of the tender, the tenderer must notify the relevant organ of state and such tenderer will not be eligible for any preference points.

---

[123] ibid 1(h).

Preference points may not be claimed in respect of individuals who are not actively involved in the management of an enterprise or business and who do not exercise control over an enterprise or business commensurate with their degree of ownership.

Recent government initiatives

The Regulations made under the PPPFA came into effect in 2001. Within two years, criticisms of the way in which it was being operated were made by most sections of the South African political establishment. Several criticisms of the operation of preferential procurement policies recurred during this period. Mostly, the criticisms related to policy incoherence, close-to-chaotic administration, corruption, and the absence of adequate monitoring of outcomes. Initiatives by government recognized these problems and sought to introduce mechanisms to address them, not least in attempting to establish a national system of administration of procurement. During 2001–02, to assist the National Treasury in adopting a more uniform implementation approach, the Supply Chain Management unit of the National Treasury conducted a Joint Country Procurement Assessment Review with the World Bank, which assessed procurement practices throughout the public sector. The Review identified certain deficiencies in current practices relating to governance aspects and the interpretation and implementation of the PPPFA and its associated Regulations that reflected the criticisms discussed above.[124] During 2002 and the early part of 2003, a Treasury team developed a strategy to increase uniformity in the procurement reform process in government in conjunction with provincial treasuries. Hearings before the national Parliament's Finance Select Committee in September 2003 enabled criticisms of the system to be aired publicly, by groups as diverse as the National Treasury, Business South Africa, and COSATU.[125] On 10 September 2003, the Cabinet approved the 'Policy Strategy to Guide Uniformity in Procurement Reform Processes in Government'.[126] With regard to the deficiencies associated with the current PPPFA and its Regulations, the Strategy accepted that amendments to the Act and Regulations would be necessary, particularly in respect of the need to more effectively achieve government's Black Economic Empowerment (BEE) policy objectives. This aspect would be addressed as part of the process associated with

---

[124] World Bank, Report No 25751-SA, South Africa Country Procurement Assessment Report, Refining the Public Procurement System, Vol I: Summary of Findings and Recommendations, February 2003, <http://www-wds.worldbank.org/external/default/WDSContentServer/IW3P/IB/2003/05/13/000094946_03042504054534/Rendered/PDF/multi0page.pdf> para 4.7.

[125] Finance Select Committee, 8 September 2003, Preferential Procurement Policy Framework Act, Public Hearings, available at <http://www.pmg.org.za>.

[126] National Treasury, 2003, Policy Strategy to Guide Uniformity in Procurement Reform Processes in Government (07-04/2003).

the promulgation of the Broad-Based Black Economic Empowerment Bill and implementing its supporting strategy document.

Broad-based black economic empowerment

A Black Economic Empowerment Commission had been established by black business organizations as an independent initiative in 1998. Its function was to work out a comprehensive strategy that would lead to a significant transfer of economic ownership in South Africa to the majority of the population. The Commission's report was published in 2001.[127] It concentrated on setting targets relating to ownership of productive land, black equity participation throughout the economy, participation as non-executive and executive directors of companies, increased black ownership of private companies, and increased participation of black South Africans as managers of private sector companies. In addition, however, and particularly relevant for the purposes of this chapter, it argued that the preferential procurement legislation had proved inadequate to the task, and it made sweeping recommendations for reform of the process, including the redrafting of the regulations under the legislation, to ensure that procurement would be used more effectively in the future to hasten significant redistribution of resources towards the black population. During March 2003, the Cabinet adopted a Strategy on Black Empowerment and also the Broad-Based Black Economic Empowerment Bill, 2003, building on these recommendations.

Together with the effects of the procurement legislation, it had been clear long before this that government was prepared to use its significant purchasing power to place 'additional pressure on certain industries to review their approach to empowerment'.[128] One effect of this was that several industrial sectors 'began negotiations on voluntary "Charters" between established business, government and black representatives'.[129] The first such charter to be concluded, in 2000, was the charter in the liquid fuels business. According to Fiona Thompson, this charter included several 'ground-breaking' aspects,[130] 'such as 25% of the industry throughout the value chain to be in the hands of previously disadvantaged South Africans' within ten years, and recognition of empowerment efforts by companies other than in ownership such as procurement, employment and social programmes'.

Separately, several parastatals were actively involved in using their procurement power. Of these, the most successful has been Eskom, the state-owned company that generates, transmits, and distributes electricity in South Africa. Eskom generates in

---

[127] BEE Commission Report (Skotaville Press, 2001).

[128] F Thompson, 'Black Economic Empowerment in South Africa: the role of parastatals and choices for the restructuring of the electricity industry', Paper presented at the ICS/CAS International Conference 'Looking at South Africa Ten Years On', London, 10–12 September 2004.

[129] ibid.   [130] ibid 4.

the region of 95 per cent of the electricity used in South Africa. By 2003, the company had increased its procurement spend on small businesses and large black-owned businesses by 40 per cent to nearly half of the company's direct costs.[131] Those companies wishing to do business with Eskom must supply statements of BEE performance, 'not just on ownership but also on control, employee statistics and procurement and Eskom scores them on a points system'.[132] The effect has been to encourage 'a major trickle-through effect to the wider economy as each of its suppliers in turn is under pressure to apply similar empowerment criteria to its own purchasing procedures'.[133] There were other indirect effects as 'companies with an approved Eskom supplier number are often automatically accredited as empowerment companies by other purchasers'.[134]

In 2003, the Broad-Based Black Economic Empowerment Act was enacted, setting out the government's strategy. The purpose of the Act[135] was, *inter alia*, to transform South Africa's economy to allow meaningful participation by black people, and substantially change the racial profile of ownership and management in the private sector. It made provision for the establishment of a Black Economic Empowerment Advisory Council, chaired by the President, to advise the government and review progress. The Act was preceded by a Department of Trade and Industry strategy document, which outlined a BEE 'balanced score card', and weightings (of which more later), but did not detail how these were to be applied. (In part, this approach followed the earlier approach developed in the Minerals and Petroleum Development Act of 2002.) The Broad-Based Black Economic Empowerment Act provided, in section 9, that Codes of Good Practice may be issued to promote the functions of the Act, and covered compliance issues in more detail. The first phase of the Codes was released for public consultation in December 2004, and finalized in November 2005. A second phase of Codes was released in December 2005, and was expected to be finalized during 2006.

Once 'Gazetted', ie published in the official government journal, the Codes are binding on organs of the state and public entities. They are required to use the Codes when engaging with companies and organizations in relation to procurement, licensing and concessions, public private partnerships, and the sale of state-owned assets or business.[136] Public bodies are required to evaluate the BEE status of these companies, using these Codes. Companies that do not adopt the Codes will be less successful in interactions with government in these areas than those that do adopt the Codes. The Codes set out the various areas where BEE measurement is to take place, including ownership, management control, employment equity, skills development, enterprise development, and procurement. The Codes also deal with how the different elements are to be weighted, and how BEE compliance is to be regulated.

[131] ibid 10.　　[132] ibid.　　[133] ibid 11.　　[134] ibid.
[135] B-BBEE Act 2003, No 53 of 2003, s 2. See also 'Codes for better BEE' at <http://www.southafrica.info>.　　[136] B-BBEE Act 2003, No 53 of 2003, s 10.

In addition to these Codes, particular sectors of the economy can draw up sectoral 'charters' that apply to companies in that sector, such as the financial sector, the mining sector, and the tourism sector, amongst others. Until these sectoral charters are adopted, the general Codes will apply. These sectoral charters, in order to be accepted by government, must comply with the Codes. These provisions are intended to allow the government to exercise a degree of control over the development of the Charters. As we have seen, around the time of the development of the 2003 legislation, several sectors of the economy were developing voluntary Charters on BEE. These varied considerably in terms of what industry was willing to commit to. The development in the Codes of criteria for approval of Charters 'will ensure that even when different gazetted charters are applied to different entities... no entities will be unfairly disadvantaged because of the application of a more stringent industry charter. The intention of the Codes... is thus to level the playing field by providing clear and comprehensive criteria for the measurement of broad-based BEE'.[137]

The BEE status of a business is crucial to the way the system works. A business is assessed, using a 'generic scorecard', giving points to compliance with each of the core components of empowerment. Equity ownership, consisting of the percentage of shares owned by black South Africans, amounts to 20 per cent of the total, the proportion of black persons in executive management amounts to 10 per cent, compliance with employment equity amounts to 10 per cent, the proportion of skills development expenditure as a proportion of total payroll amounts to 20 per cent, the proportion of procurement from black-owned and 'empowered' enterprises amounts to 20 per cent, investment in black-owned and empowered enterprises as a proportion of total assets amounts to 10 per cent. A residual 10 per cent is left to sectors and enterprises themselves to develop, for example including labour-intensive production methods, or spending on workers' housing. The enterprise is evaluated, based on its overall performance in terms of the generic scorecard, and is accorded a BEE status. The BEE status attained in turn determines the BEE procurement recognition level that the enterprise will obtain for the purposes of measurement of the preferential procurement element contemplated in Code 500 (and discussed below). The BEE status of an enterprise must be raised to the next highest BEE status level to the one at which it is evaluated, when: black people hold more than 50 per cent of the exercisable voting rights and more than 50 per cent of the economic interest in that enterprise; and that enterprise has achieved the full seven points under the net equity interest component of the ownership scorecard. For the purposes of the operation of the Codes, a Verification Certificate based upon a BEE balanced scorecard provided for in the Codes must record the individual element score, where applicable, and overall BEE status of an enterprise and other relevant information regarding the identity of the measured enterprise.

[137] See 'Codes for better BEE' at <http://www.southafrica.info>.

BEE Status	Qualification	BEE procurement recognition level
Level One Contributor	≥ 100 points on the Generic Scorecard	135%
Level Two Contributor	≥ 85 but <100 points on the Generic Scorecard	125%
Level Three Contributor	≥ 75 but <85 on the Generic Scorecard	110%
Level Four Contributor	≥ 65 but <75 on the Generic Scorecard	100%
Level Five Contributor	≥ 55 but <65 on the Generic Scorecard	80%
Level Six Contributor	≥ 45 but <55 on the Generic Scorecard	60%
Level Seven Contributor	≥ 40 but <45 on the Generic Scorecard	50%
Level Eight Contributor	≥ 30 but <40 on the Generic Scorecard	10%
Non Compliant Contributor	< 30 on the Generic Scorecard	0%

The issue of procurement, then, comes into focus in two ways: first, public procurement is used as a point of pressure on companies to adopt the Codes and as a reward mechanism for following them but, second, as part of their responsibilities under the Codes, private companies will be expected to use their own procurement decisions as a pressure point on other private companies with which they themselves do business. As a private sector guide to the system of regulation established under the Act points out: 'As the Codes will be enforced from the government or first-tier suppliers down the supply chain, some aspects of the Codes such as preferential procurement are eventually expected to impinge on most private companies.'[138]

The Codes set out a compliance target that 70 per cent of total measurable procurement spend should be procured from companies that are BEE-compliant, of which 15 per cent would go to qualifying small enterprises and at least 5 per cent to micro enterprises. The record of particular companies is assessed on a scorecard against this target, and the company is assessed as being at one of eight levels of compliance, ranging from non-compliant to fully compliant. Compliance with the preferential procurement aspects of the Codes leads to a maximum of 15 points being awardable to that company in deciding on its BEE status.

The Codes also attempt to set up a system of how BEE compliance is to be regulated. How, exactly, is the detailed administration of the system of BEE-status designation to work? Effectively, the Codes provide for a system of regulated, mostly privatized, measurement and assessment. The Codes provide that BEE status will be assessed by setting out regulations for the approval, accreditation, and regulation of BEE verification agencies, whose role it is to award BEE status to companies, a status that will be accepted by government bodies with which the company deals, thus enabling the government body to escape having to do the BEE assessment itself. In exercising their powers, organs of state and public entities are required to rely on the validity of a Verification Certificate issued by an accredited Verification Agency in respect of any enterprise. Private sector enterprises are

---

[138] Empowerdex, Guide to the Codes of Good Practice; An Empowerdex Guide (2006) Pt 1, p 7.

strongly encouraged to rely on the validity of a Verification Certificate issued by an accredited Verification Agency, as failure to do so may impact upon their own Verification Certificates if used in relation to organs of state and public entities.

The Minister, through the South African National Accreditation System (the Accreditation Body),[139] or any other body authorized by the Minister to undertake accreditation of verification agencies, must ensure the development and implementation of Verification Standards in consultation with the Industry Body, a collection of private sector-based verification agencies recognized by the Minister. All Verification Certificates must comply with the requirements set out in the Verification Standards.

In order to obtain accreditation as a verification agency, a person or entity must apply in writing to the Minister; and provide evidence of compliance with the requirements of the Code. Upon receiving an application, the Minister must accredit the applicant as a verification agency if the applicant is qualified and has been accredited by the Accreditation Body. To qualify for accreditation as a verification agency, applicants must be Superior Contributors to BEE, ie they must themselves have been recognized as a Level One to Level Four BEE Contributor. An applicant must be a member of an Industry Body, ensure that its personnel are sufficiently qualified and competent to undertake the preparation of Verification Certificates, and ensure that it complies with the Verification Standards. The applicant must also have implemented sufficiently robust internal controls to ensure that it operates on an independent and impartial basis, to identify and manage potential conflicts of interest, and to protect the confidential and proprietary information of its clients. It must ensure that none of the personnel involved in preparing a Verification Certificate for any client has provided any other services to that client for a period of at least twenty-four months preceding the date upon which a Verification Certificate is issued. It must maintain appropriate levels of professional indemnity and other applicable insurance, have implemented a standard form of verification agreement for use with its clients that meets the minimum requirements set out in the Verification Standards, and demonstrate that it has substantial operational capacity to undertake the provision of Verification Certificates without undue reliance on any other enterprise. It must provide the Minister with the required statistical information concerning the progress of the BEE compliance efforts of clients in accordance with the Verification Standards. Nothing precludes any enterprise, organ of state, or public entity from applying for accreditation as a verification agency. Organs of state and public entities as well as private sector enterprises undertaking significant volumes of procurement are strongly encouraged to seek accreditation. Accreditation as a verification agency is for an indefinite period, but may be reviewed and withdrawn by the Minister for good cause.

---

[139] The South African National Accreditation System is a company registered under the Companies Act of 1973, s 21 and affiliated to the DTI.

This description, it must be emphasized, is based on the draft Codes of Good Practice. We have seen that the second phase of the codes was released in December 2005, with the deadline for public comment being 31 March 2006. The Department of Trade and Industry (DTI) received almost 180 submissions from big business, black business, the government, and state-owned enterprises. Following a meeting with Business Unity South Africa, the Trade and Industry Minister, Mandisi Mpahlwa, is reported to have conceded that the draft black economic empowerment codes of good practice were 'too complex', and resolved to ensure that the finalized codes are 'easier to understand and implement'. 'We acknowledge that when you look at all the indicators to measure black economic empowerment, there is a lot to review.' 'We will try for more simplicity without affecting the intended objectives of the codes.'[140] The DTI would reduce the number of indicators on the scorecard to make compliance quicker and easier. The department would make BEE compliance easier for small businesses by giving them a special dispensation in the codes of good practice. The BEE Advisory Council would be established after Cabinet's approval of the codes.[141]

Public private partnerships and black econmic empowerment

The central legislation governing Public Private Partnerships (PPPs) for national and provincial government is Treasury Regulation 16, issued under the Public Finance Management Act, 1999 (PFMA).[142] The PFMA provides, in section 76, that the National Treasury must make regulations for a range of matters to do with the effective and efficient management and use of financial resources. Many of these matters are relevant to PPPs, and National Treasury Regulation 16 provides precise and detailed instructions for PPPs. The 'National Treasury's PPP Manual' and 'Standardised PPP Provisions' are based on the PFMA and Treasury Regulation 16. The PPP Manual consists of several 'modules'. Each module of 'National Treasury's PPP Manual', together with 'Standardised PPP Provisions',[143] is issued by the National Treasury as a PPP Practice Note, under section 76(4)(g) of the PFMA. The 'instructions' contained in 'National Treasury's PPP Manual' are presented in the form of detailed best practice guidance, based on the National Treasury's PPP Unit's experience with PPPs. An institution to which Treasury Regulation 16 applies which seeks materially to deviate from this guidance should

---

[140] Minister of Trade and Industry gives update on Broad-Based Black Economic Empowerment Codes of Good Practice, <http://www.dti.gov.za/article/articleview.asp?current=1&arttypeid=1&artid=1163>; BEE codes to be simplified, 12 July 2006, <www.southafrica.info>.

[141] After this book had gone to press, the draft Codes of Good Practice (as amended) were approved by the Cabinet on 6 December 2006, and were gazetted on 9 February 2007, *Government Gazette*, Vol 500, No 29617.

[142] PPP Manual Module 1: South African Regulations for PPPs, issued as National Treasury PPP Practice Note, No 02 of 2004.

[143] National Treasury PPP Practice Note, No 01 of 2004, issued as National Treasury Standardised PPP Provisions, 11 March 2004.

inform the relevant treasury of this intention prior to execution, and justify its reasons for such material deviation in the relevant application(s) for treasury approvals.

Treasury Regulation 16 states that the procurement procedure for a PPP 'must include a preference for the protection or advancement of persons, or categories of persons, disadvantaged by unfair discrimination'.[144] National Treasury PPP Practice Note No 03 of 2004 'Code of Good Practice for Black Economic Empowerment in Public Private Partnerships' was issued in March 2004. It was the National Treasury's intention that BEE be contractually binding in all PPP Agreements. The provisions of the 'Code for BEE in PPPs' are therefore reflected in all modules of 'National Treasury's PPP Manual', and in 'Standardised PPP Provision'. The Code thus constituted the National Treasury's official framework for black economic empowerment in public private partnerships. Following public consultation and incorporation of comments, the Code of Good Practice was also submitted by the Minister of Finance to the Minister of Trade and Industry to be issued in terms of the Broad-Based Black Economic Empowerment Act, 2003.

The BEE policy is applied by institutions in the two distinct procurements of the regulated PPP project cycle: first, in the selection of its Transaction Advisor; and second, in the selection of a Private Party for the PPP itself. In compliance with the Preferential Procurement Policy Framework Act, the BEE component of a Transaction Advisor bid will constitute 10 per cent of the bid evaluation weighting, with the price and technical elements constituting the remaining 90 per cent. BEE in the Transaction Advisor bid will be evaluated against a balanced scorecard for PPP Transaction Advisor appointments. The balanced scorecard contains four sub-elements to the BEE element of the Transaction Advisor bid evaluation, making up 100 points, 60 of which constitute the minimum threshold; bidders must achieve a minimum threshold of 60 per cent of the total BEE points. If a Transaction Advisor bid fails to pass this BEE threshold, it should not be evaluated further. The technical and price elements are each also scored out of 100 points. The BEE score achieved (if it meets or betters the minimum threshold) by each bidder will be calculated into the bidder's overall score. The Transaction Advisor bids must show how black people are included in all professional aspects of the work (legal, financial, and technical and at all phases of the PPP project cycle), and must specifically indicate those aspects where black people are designated to play leading roles. Fronting of black people for the purpose of winning contracts could lead to contract termination. Black people are therefore expected to perform the work they were assigned to, and the fee-sharing structure must reflect the actual work, risk, and responsibility assumed by each of the team members. The cash flow earmarked for each member of the consortium must therefore also be shown, indicating how black people will benefit. The bids must show the percentage of black equity in the companies making up the Transaction Advisor

---

[144] Treasury Reg 16.5.3(b).

consortium, with a weighted average calculated on the percentage of the work to be performed by each company. The bids must also demonstrate that the member(s) of the consortium responsible for structuring BEE in the PPP can demonstrate insights into how to apply the 'Code for BEE in PPPs'. References should be provided to substantiate claims of skills and experience in structuring BEE in PPPs. Finally, the bids must show that the skills transfer plan allows the institution to see success in this respect throughout the Transaction Advisor assignment.

The National Treasury requires that all PPPs issued to the market by an institution must contain a BEE balanced scorecard for the project containing a clear and appropriate set of BEE elements, targets, minimum thresholds, and weightings, duly approved as part of the feasibility study for Treasury approval. Bids received are evaluated by the institution, including the private party's BEE commitments. The quality of the BEE component of the preferred bid forms part of the value-for-money report to be submitted by the institution for Treasury approval, prior to the commencement of negotiations. Negotiations that follow must seek to maximize BEE benefits in the final terms of the deal. The BEE commitments are taken into account in final Treasury approval, allowing the parties to sign the PPP Agreement. The PPP Agreement binds the parties to their BEE commitments for the duration of the PPP, stipulating the consequences of default. Reporting obligations are substantively on the private party for all its contractual commitments, including BEE. The institution must, however, establish, in its service delivery management arrangements, and contract administration system, the ability to check and verify such reporting, manage remedy periods that may be provided for, effect contractual penalties in the event of poor performance, and manage termination should this arise. In large projects, it may be necessary for the parties to establish a joint independent monitor specifically for BEE. Above all, the quality of the PPP partnership management, and the parties' ability to identify impediments to BEE and to resolve disputes effectively, are paramount to the PPP's success, not least in respect of BEE. The penalty regime should be deployed only after genuine efforts have been made by the parties to address the impediments to compliance.

While PPP projects differ, and the BEE elements identified are not exhaustive, several elements must be incorporated in the structure of PPP projects governed by the terms of Treasury Regulation 16 to the PFMA. BEE must be reflected in the percentage of black equity in the private party SPV(Special Purpose Vehicle).[145] An indicative target of 40 per cent is set out in the Code. The actual percentage set will vary from project to project. There will be a lock-in provision for a specified period, to contractually bind the agreed percentages and conditions of black equity, requiring the private party not to effect changes in its capital structure that will dilute black equity during this period. The black equity commitment sought

---

[145] A Special Purpose Vehicle is an 'entity, usually a limited liability company, created to act as the legal form of a project consortium', as defined by the New Zealand Controller and Auditor-General <http://www.oag.govt.NZ/2006/public-private/glossary.htm>.

by the institution must be costed in its feasibility study, presented to the private sector in the bid documentation, identifiable in the financial models presented by bidders, demonstrated in the private party's shareholders' agreement, and included as a commitment in the PPP Agreement. The source of the committed black equity must be substantiated by bidders and verified by the institutions during bid evaluation.

The PPP should also encourage black South Africans to take responsibility and operational risk in the project and secure direct benefits in management. This so-called 'active equity' may be achieved in a variety of ways, determined on a project-by-project basis, but must show black people and/or black enterprises participating directly in the day-to-day management and operations of the project, either in the private party only, or in the subcontractors only, or in a combination of private party and subcontractors. The Code establishes an active equity indicative target of 55 per cent of black equity in the private party SPV. Advisors, sponsors, banks and the black enterprises in PPPs are also encouraged to find innovative ways of unlocking value in project cash flow, particularly in structuring early cash flows for black shareholders. How this is to be achieved is not prescribed, but bids should show how their funding structures effectively unlock value for black shareholders early and throughout the project term. Bidders' proposals on this element must be clearly demonstrated in their financial models and reflected in their shareholders' agreements. The commitment agreed between the parties become a contractual obligation in the PPP Agreement.

All PPP Agreements bind the private party to minimum commitments to increase the number of black people in the executive and senior management of enterprises and the number of black-engendered enterprises, and to increase income levels of black people, and reduce income inequalities. Human resource development and employment equity are also targeted elements. The percentage of management control by black people in the private party SPV should be at least commensurate with the black equity (passive and active) in the SPV. An initial percentage may be designed to grow over the project term. The percentage of black women in management control in the private party must be targeted and committed appropriately. An initial percentage may be designed to grow over the project term. The private party must be in compliance with the Employment Equity Act, 1998, and produce a comprehensive employment equity plan as part of its bid. Bidders must present a clear skills development plan and targets for the private party's managers and employees, and must commit a minimum percentage of their payroll for expenditure on meeting these targets each year of the project. This sum is additional to the skills development levy prescribed in other legislation,[146] and must be applied to the skills development of staff employed in the PPP itself. The Code encourages those structuring PPPs to take advantage of the subcontracting arrangements of the PPP to secure BEE benefits. Institutions

---

[146] Skills Development Levies Act, 1999.

may adjust these elements on a project-by-project basis, but their effect should be achieved in all PPP projects. Although the Code is not prescriptive about how the participation is to be structured, the extent of such participation must be measurable as a percentage participation in the total capital expenditure cash flows and operating expenditure cash flows to the subcontractors.

Every PPP must be designed, and proactively seek, to produce a positive local socio-economic impact in any way that is appropriate to the project and its location. The targets that may be set in this element need not be limited only to black people or black enterprises, but in targeting local communities must directly benefit the poor and the marginalized, and must effect local socio-economic improvement. This set of PPP BEE elements must be: determined by the institution on a project-by-project basis during the feasibility study phase; communicated with bidders during procurement; proposed by bidders in their plans, with costs reflected in their financial models; negotiated with the preferred bidder; and committed to in the PPP Agreement. The Code gives indications of the type of beneficial local socio-economic impacts that may be targeted, including involvement of, and direct benefits to, NGOs, religious institutions, civics, clinics, child-care centres, and the like; employment preferences for youth in a targeted geographical area; employment targets for disabled people; employment preferences for women; preferences for contracting with SMMEs as suppliers of materials and/or services in a targeted geographic area; initiatives that will support HIV and Aids education; and other local socio-economic impacts appropriate to the project and its location. Such elements may be itemized individually or, on larger projects, incorporated under a requirement that the private party devise and implement an innovative and effective social responsibility programme as part of its operations.

Redrafting preferential procurement regulations

We have seen that the process of drawing up the Broad-Based Black Economic Empowerment (B-BBEE) Act and its Strategy Document highlighted the deficiencies of the Preferential Procurement Policy Framework Act and its associated regulations to effectively achieve government's BEE objectives, and that the Strategy had accepted that the Preferential Procurement Regulations needed to be aligned with the B-BBEE Act and the related Strategy.[147] The National Treasury, in consultation with the DTI, was still in the process of reviewing the regulations by the end of 2006. Draft new Regulations were issued for public comment in October 2004.[148] The effect of these would be to tighten up some of the aspects of preferential procurement alleged to be problematic, impose tighter uniformity, and realign the regulations with BEE.

---

[147] BEE, National Treasury, Strategic Plans 2004–2007, 53.
[148] 2174 Preferential Procurement Policy Framework Act (5/2000): Draft Preferential Procurement Regulations, 2004 *Government Gazette*, Vol 472, 4 October 2004, No 26863.

First, the draft Regulations recognize changes in the procurement environment more generally. The draft Regulations, for example, change the thresholds where the 10 and 20 point preferences apply. Instead of R500,000 being the critical point, the draft Regulations provide that the critical point would be R1,000,000. Thus competitive bids/price quotations with a value equal to, or above R30,000 and up to a value of R1,000,000 would attract a 20 point preference, whilst those above R1,000,000 would attract a 10 point preference. So, contracts with a value between R500,000 and R1 million, which previously would only have had 10 point preferences, would now attract 20 point preferences, increasing the overall effect of preferences in the public procurement market.

Second, in an attempt to align the draft Regulations with B-BBEE legislation, all mention of 'historically disadvantaged' individuals is dropped, as is all mention of the Reconstruction and Development Programme goals. Instead of these, the Regulations refer instead to the B-BBEE goals. 'Broad-based black economic empowerment' is defined as:

... the economic empowerment of all black people through diverse but integrated socio economic strategies that include, but not limited to: increasing the number of black people that manage, own and control enterprises and productive assets; facilitating ownership and management of enterprises and productive assets by communities, workers, cooperatives and other collective enterprises; human resources and skills development; achieving equitable representation in all occupational categories and levels in the workforce; preferential procurement; and investment in enterprises that are owned or managed by black people.

That is not to say that preferences cannot be given for advancing other socio-economic goals, but such preferences would be granted within relatively tight limits. The draft Regulations, for example, continue to give a specific regulatory authority to the operation of local preferences. For specific industries (identified by the DTI), where the award of bids to local manufacturers is of critical importance, such bids may be advertised with a specific bidding condition that only locally manufactured products will be considered. The draft Regulations specify that a maximum of 20 or 10 points, depending on the value of the tender, may be awarded to a bidder for achieving *all* of Government's procurement-related socio-economic objectives. Achieving B-BBEE goals will, therefore, be calculated within that total. The total percentage scored for B-BBEE will be converted to a point score out of a maximum of 20 or 10 points. Presumably, therefore, other socio-economic preferences, such as for local goods, or promoting small enterprises, when combined with BEE preferences, must not be greater than 10 or 20 points. The draft Regulations do not appear to specify, however, what the minimum level of BEE preferences should be, out of the 10 or 20 points.

In a further attempt to integrate the application of the preferential procurement legislation with the B-BBEE strategy, the balanced scorecard measuring B-BBEE prescribed by the National Treasury must form part of the evaluation criteria of all bids. With regard to those procurements priced below R1,000,000, a maximum of 20 points may be awarded to a bidder for achieving the government's procurement-related socio-economic objectives. The total percentage scored for B-BBEE would be converted to a point score out of a maximum of 20 points. This would be calculated by multiplying the total percentage scored by 20. No points would be awarded for achieving the government's B-BBEE objectives if the total percentage scored for B-BBEE is less than the prescribed minimum. The points scored by a bidder in respect of these objectives must be added to the points scored for price. Only the bid with the highest number of points scored may be selected.

With regard to those procurements with a value above R1 million, a balanced scorecard measuring B-BBEE must also form part of the evaluation criteria of all bids. There is an additional measure of integration, however. Where the Minister of Trade and Industry has Gazetted a code of good practice for a particular sector, the scorecard contained in the Gazetted code of good practice must be utilized in the evaluation process. In the absence of such a code of good practice for a particular sector, the balanced scorecard prescribed by the National Treasury must form part of the evaluation criteria. A maximum of 10 points may be awarded to a bidder for achieving the government's procurement related socio-economic objectives. The total percentage scored for B-BBEE would be converted to a score out of a maximum of 10 points. This would be calculated by multiplying the total percentage scored by 10. No points would be awarded for achieving the government's B-BBEE objectives if the total percentage scored for B-BBEE is less than the prescribed minimum. Only the bid with the highest number of points scored may be selected.

Fourth, there are various mechanisms included to attempt to address the problem of 'fronting'. Some reflect what is in the existing Regulations. An organ of state may require a bidder to substantiate claims it has made with regard to preference. In the event that the percentage equity ownership by a black person changes after the closing date of the bid, the bidder must notify the relevant organ of state of the changes. The bidder would, if the percentage ownership by a black person increased, not be eligible for any additional preference points. Should the percentage equity ownership by a black person decrease, the preference points for equity ownership would be reduced accordingly. There is, however, a new provision that is also relevant. A person awarded a contract as a result of preference for B-BBEE (and not just as a result of HDI equity ownership preferences, as under the existing Regulations) may not subcontract more than 25 per cent of the value of the contract to a person who does not qualify for such preference.

III. Selective purchasing in the United States Relating to Myanmar

In this third part of the chapter, we turn to look at the use of procurement linkages not for the purpose of addressing discrimination and inequalities within a developing country but by individual states in the United States which have developed procurement linkages to influence conditions *outside* the United States, particularly in developing countries. Some background is necessary. From 1990, when the Soviet Union began to disintegrate and the Cold War effectively ended, American foreign policy was no longer clear on its priorities and aims.[149] This encouraged more active participation by a wider range of groups and interests seeking to claim an American interest in particular foreign policy issues. At the federal level, Congressional involvement in foreign policy became manifest in ways which were more apparent than during the Cold War. In particular, Congress passed legislation requiring the imposition, on a range of countries, of a range of economic sanctions, for a range of reasons, but particularly focused on issues of human rights.[150] For example, the United States took action with respect to Myanmar.[151] On several occasions, these sanctions provisions attempted to bring economic pressures to bear on a disapproved-of foreign government by penalizing corporations which were involved with these countries. A well-known example was the Helms-Burton law regarding Cuba.[152] Another was the Iran and Libyan Sanctions Act, which contained restrictions on the award of federal government contracts to companies operating in Libya and Iran.[153] This 'extra-territoriality', if that is what it is, caused particular irritation to other industrialized countries.[154]

Sullivan and MacBride Principles and selective purchasing

In parallel with these *federal* developments, but going beyond them on occasion, *state and local governments* in the United States also saw the use of economic instruments as a method of demonstrating their concern with aspects of foreign affairs, in particular human rights.[155] State and local involvement in international human rights issues long pre-dated the end of the Cold War, however. State and local governmental action was first taken in support of a set of principles, the Sullivan Principles, relating to South Africa during the apartheid era. These

---

[149] R Haass (ed), *Economic Sanctions and American Diplomacy* (Council on Foreign Relations, 1998) 1–3.

[150] See The President's Export Council, Unilateral Economic Sanctions: A Review of Existing Sanctions and their Impacts on US Economic Interests with Recommendations for Policy and Process Improvement (June 1997). See also, 'Converting the Dollar into a Bludgeon', *New York Times*, 20 April 1997.

[151] Omnibus Consolidated Appropriations Act 1997, Pub L No 104-208, §570(c), 110 Stat 3009-166, 3009-167 (1997); Executive Order 13047, §3, 62 Fed Reg 28, 301 (20 May 1997).

[152] Cuban Liberty and Democratic Solidarity (Libertad) Act 1996, Pub Law No 104-114, 110 Stat 785 (1996).

[153] Iran and Libya Sanctions Act of 1996, Pub Law No 104-172 (1996), §6(6).

[154] See eg P Glossop, 'Recent US Trade Restrictions Affecting Cuba, Iran and Libya—a View from Outside the US' (1997) 15 Journal of Energy and Natural Resources Law 212.

[155] See KA Rodman ' "Think Globally, Punish Locally": Nonstate Actors, Multinational Corporations, and Human Rights Sanctions' (1998) 12 Ethics and International Affairs 19. For a more general discussion of the reaction of local US communities to globalization, see SE Clark and GL Gaile, 'Local Politics in a Global Era: Thinking Locally, Acting Globally' (1997) 551 Annals of the American Academy of Political and Social Science 28. Individual US states have also shown an increasing tendency to develop their own approaches to a variety of social issues, see J Donahue, *Disunited States* (Basic Books, 1997).

Principles incorporated non-discrimination requirements and (weak) affirmative action requirements. American corporations with subsidiaries were pressed to sign up to these Principles by NGOs. Added weight was given to the Principles by the activities of church groups, human rights groups, institutional investors, college and university students, and several state and local governments in the United States, which used the Sullivan Principles as benchmarks against which to assess corporations with which they were involved.

State and local governments sought to add whatever economic weight they had available to bolster NGO activity supporting the Sullivan Principles, and one of the economic instruments they had available was the use of procurement linkages. The history of state and local activity on South Africa involved considerable recourse to the use of what was called 'selective purchasing' as a tool to bring pressure for change. Indeed, the first recorded economic initiative at a state or local level involved the adoption of a binding resolution by the city council of Madison, Wisconsin, to seek purchasing contracts only with companies that did not have 'economic interests in South Africa'.[156] Many more localities and states were to follow suit, particularly during the mid-1980s. According to research carried out by the Investor Research Responsibility Centre, at the height of such activity, six states had adopted selective purchasing laws or policies.[157] In addition, fifty-three cities and fourteen other localities had adopted similar legislation or policies.[158] In many cases, there was a simple ban imposed on contracting with companies that had business relations with South Africa, subject on occasion to exceptions, such as in the case of the non-availability of other suppliers. In other cases a price preference was given to companies that were not engaged in South Africa. In yet other cases, constructive engagement by companies was deemed permissible and the legislation gave price preferences to companies complying with the Sullivan Principles.[159] The purpose of the reference to the Principles in the Maryland legislation, for example, was to provide a basic set of minimum requirements, compliance with which the purchasing authority was to regard as a necessary condition for state purchasing from that company. The Maryland law, for example, required any bidder for state contracts with a value of more than US$100,000 to certify either that it did no business in South Africa, or that it complied with specified parts of the Sullivan Principles.[160] The ordinances also differed as to whether they applied only to the bidder, or also encompassed the activities of subsidiaries and subcontractors. How far these selective purchasing requirements were symbolic or actually operated in practice is unclear.[161] In most cases, selective purchasing laws

---

[156] WF Moses, *A Guide to American State and Local Laws on South Africa* (IRRC, 1993) 29.

[157] P De Simme and WF Moses, *A Guide to American State and Local Laws on South Africa* (IRRC, 1995) 17–22.

[158] David Caron identified 36 such laws as having been adopted up to 1988. See DD Caron, 'The Structure and Pathologies of Local Selective Procurement Ordinances: A Study of the Apartheid-Era South Africa Ordinances' (2003) 21 Berkeley Journal of International Law 159.   [159] See ibid.

[160] Moses (n 156 above).

[161] Caron (n 158 above) considers that several were symbolic only.

were merely one part of a much larger range of economic pressures which the state or locality sought to bring to bear, such as divestment of holdings in South Africa-related companies, restriction on which financial institutions a state or locality was able to use, and the ban on the purchase of South African-made goods. A survey in 1993 found that twenty-four states had restrictions on South African investments by their public pension funds either by statute or by pension fund board policy.[162]

There is some indication that the Sullivan Principles had several positive effects: first, that corporations found them useful in that they provided a focus for their social and political activities in South Africa; second, that the Principles brought about some changes in conditions for black workers which may not otherwise have occurred; third, that the Principles led to increased funding by companies of social causes in the South African community, and fourth, that they may have increased pressure on government for the recognition of black trade unions, an important factor in the development of organized black politics.[163] It is difficult, however, for the effect of the Principles to be distinguished from the effect of other similar activity outside the context of the Principles, such as that undertaken by other countries, or from larger political and economic forces operating at that time in South Africa. Nor is there evidence as to how far selective purchasing requirements played a part in helping the Principles to achieve what success they did. On the other hand, Caron has argued that there were costs that arose from implementing the selective purchasing laws. One involved allegations of companies selling assets in South Africa but maintaining an indirect interest through which business was chanelled, introducing a degree of fraud and double dealing. There were also compliance costs incurred both by the locality administering the requirements, and by companies seeking to satisfy monitoring requirements. Finally, there is some evidence that local protectionism crept into decisions as to whether to adopt such laws: '[T]o the extent that it is the foreign or large US bidder that is more likely to have the specified relationship with South Africa and thereby be tainted, small local suppliers will benefit from such ordinances.'[164]

Selective purchasing and Myanmar

The selective purchasing approach to the use of procurement, which developed first in the context of the Sullivan Principles, burgeoned during the 1990s, in part because of increased United States press and consumer interest in human rights in other parts

---

[162] R Romano, 'Public Pension Fund Activism in Corporate Government Reconsidered' (1993) 93 Columbia Law Review 795, 809.

[163] For assessments, see Note, 'US Labor Practices in South Africa: Will a Mandatory Fair Employment Code Succeed where the Sullivan Principles Have Failed?' (1983–4) 7 Fordham International Law Journal 358, 363–5; DC Campbell, 'US Firms and Black Labor in South Africa: Creating a Structure of Change' (1986) VII (1) Journal of Labor Research 1; JM Klein, *Intenational Codes and Multinational Business* (Westport, 1985) 95; RT de George, *Competing with Integrity in International Business* (OUP, 1993) 57.   [164] Caron (n 158 above) 182.

of the world.[165] During the 1980s and 1990s, there was a considerable increase in the popularity of state and local policies designed to restrict the award of government contracts to companies that dealt with other countries regarded as breaching human rights standards. As discussed in chapter 3 above, selective purchasing was part of the range of instruments adopted in the late 1980s to put pressure on American companies with subsidiaries in Northern Ireland to sign up to the MacBride Principles, like the Sullivan Principles, a set of (weak) affirmative action requirements. Although selective purchasing based on the Sullivan and MacBride Principles was thought by some to be legally dubious, it was never challenged in a sustained way.

In 1996, the Commonwealth of Massachusetts enacted legislation limiting state agencies from signing new contracts or renewals of contracts with companies doing business with or in Myanmar (formerly Burma).[166] The legislation was based directly on previous legislation regulating state contracts with companies that had South African links. Indeed, the state legislator responsible for introducing the Myanmar legislation, state Representative Byron Rushing,[167] had previously been responsible for introducing the state legislation on South Africa and Northern Ireland. The Myanmar legislation provided for the establishment of a restricted purchase list, which included persons doing business with Myanmar. Most state agencies were only able to procure goods or services from persons on the restricted purchase list if the procurement was essential and if elimination of the person from bidding would have resulted in inadequate competition among bidders. Even then, it would seem that where any procurement included bidders who were on the restricted purchase list, the state authority would award the contract to a person on the list only if there was no 'comparable low bid or offer' by a person not on the list. A bid by a person not on the list could be up to 10 per cent higher than a bid submitted by a person on the restricted list and still remain comparably low. Exceptions were provided for news organizations operating in Myanmar, and for the procurement of medical supplies.

Myanmar was not the only target of such selective purchasing policies at the state and local levels. Actual or proposed measures were developed to restrict the award of public contracts to businesses involved with Nigeria, Switzerland, China, Egypt, Kuwait, Turkey, Saudi Arabia, and Indonesia.[168] The motivation behind the

---

[165] 'Advocacy Group's 1997 World Report Shows Heightened Interest in Labour Rights', *BNA International Trade Daily*, 6 December 1996, reporting a study by Human Rights Watch, which is reported as saying that 'perhaps the most potent force in support [of] labour rights is the growing consumer interest on guarantees that the good[s] being purchased are not the products of abusive labour conditions'.

[166] An Act Regulating Contracts with Companies Doing Business with or in Burma (Myanmar) ch 130, 1996 Session Laws, Mass Gen Laws Ann, ch 7, 223 (West 1997). See IRRC, US Business in Burma (Myanmar), Social Issues Service, 1998 Background Report E:2 (IRRC 1998).

[167] 'States, Cities Increase Use of Trade Sanctions Troubling Business Groups and US Partners' *Wall Street Journal* 1 April 1998.

[168] K Whitelaw, 'The Very Long Arm of the Law. Is the World Ready for 7,284 Secretaries of State?' *US News and World Report*, 14 October 1996, 57; P Blustein, 'Thinking Globally, Punishing Locally; States, Cities Rush to Impose Their Own Sanctions, Angering Companies and Foreign

adoption of these policies included a concern with Indonesian activities in East Timor, the persecution of Christians in several Islamic states and China, and the unwillingness of Swiss banks to deal effectively with their Holocaust-related deposits.[169]

The growth of the use of economic sanctions at the federal level and the proliferation of state and local measures had long given rise to increasing concern among some academic commentators.[170] The selective purchasing approach by United States state and local governments had been seen as raising a host of domestic legal issues involving federalism questions.[171] It had been argued by some that the imposition of such requirements was unconstitutional under the United States Constitution on the ground that it involved an impermissible entry by a state into an area of federal responsibility.[172] Although, as we have seen, similar laws were in operation from the late 1970s and throughout the 1980s, beginning with protests against apartheid in South Africa, and then discrimination in Northern Ireland, no major challenges were mounted on constitutional grounds, although there was some commentary contesting their constitutionality.[173] After 1990, however, the American business community in particular increasingly called for a reassessment of these sanctions within the Executive Branch.[174] This resulted in the development of lobbying efforts designed to head off the growth of

Affairs Experts' *Washington Post*, 16 May 1997, G01; G de Jonquieres, 'Business Worried by US States' Sanctions' *Financial Times*, 24 April 1997, 9; GG Yerkey, 'Administration Still Has No Policy on State, Local Government Sanctions' *International Trade Reporter*, 14, No 28, 9 July 1997, 1176–7; 'A State's Foreign Policy: the Mass that Roared' *The Economist*, 8 February 1997, 32; P Magnusson, 'A Troubling Barrage of Trade Sanctions from All Across America' *Business Week*, 24 February 1997, 59. For a survey of the status of state and local selective purchasing, see IRRC, State and Local Selective Purchasing Laws As of September 1997 (IRRC, 1997).

[169] The settlement between several Swiss banks and Holocaust survivors appears to have included a commitment by several US states not to proceed with selective purchasing laws directed against Switzerland. See 'Are State Sanctions Legal?' *Washington Times*, 14 September 1998.

[170] See eg JE Garten, 'Destination Unknown' *Foreign Affairs*, May–June 1997; GC Hufbauer, KA Elliott, T Cyrus, and E Winston, 'US Economic Sanctions: Their Impact on Trade, Jobs, and Wages', Working Paper, Institute for International Economics, 1997.

[171] L Henkin, *Foreign Affairs and the United States Constitution* (2nd edn, OUP, 2002) ch 6; Note, 'State Buy America Laws in a World of Liberal Trade' (1992) 7 Connecticut Journal of International Law 311; JD Southwick, 'Binding the States: A Survey of State Law Conformance with the Standards of the GATT Procurement Code' (1992) 13 UP JIBL 57; Note, 'To Compel or Encourage: Seeking Compliance with International Trade Agreements at the State Level' (1993) 2 Minnesota Journal of Global Trade 143.

[172] eg PJ Spiro, 'Note: State and Local Anti-South African Action as an Intrusion upon the Federal Power in Foreign Relations' (1986) 72 Virginia Law Review 813.

[173] ibid. However, in 1986 an opinion from the Office of Legal Counsel of the Department of Justice concluded that the selective purchasing laws relating to South Africa were probably constitutional, 10 US Op. Office of Legal Counsel 49 (9 April 1986).

[174] See the President's Export Council Report, 'Unilateral Economic Sanctions: A Review of Existing Sanctions and their Impacts on U. S. Economic Interests With Recommendations for Policy and Process Improvement' (PEC, June 1997) note 2.

economic leverage of this type at the federal and state levels,[175] the threat of constitutional challenges being mounted against state and local initiatives, and the use of the WTO dispute resolution procedures.[176]

IV. The GPA Model and Procurement Linkages: Reacting to Malaysia, South Africa, and Myanmar

As non-members of the GPA, neither South Africa or Malaysia are directly subject to its disciplines and so their procurement linkages are immune from direct scrutiny. As a non-member of the GPA, Myanmar was not able to invoke the GPA disciplines against the United States with regard to selective purchasing policies. That does not mean, however, that Malaysia, South Africa, or the United States (in relation to Myanmar) are immune from the *indirect* influence of the GPA or of the WTO, and it is to these issues that we now turn, beginning with South Africa, then turning to Malaysia, and finally considering the treatment of selective purchasing by Massachussetts relating to Myanmar.

Is opting out feasible? South Africa as a test case

As regards membership of the GPA, there have long been influential voices against membership in South Africa. The issue seems to have been more on the agenda during the late 1990s and early part of the new century than it appeared to be by 2006. Frequently, the issue of preferential procurement related to black empowerment was seen as part of a larger policy of protection and advancement of local interests through procurement that would be adversely affected by GPA membership. For example, COSATU, the major trade union confederation, was historically opposed to South Africa joining the WTO GPA. 'Particularly those aspects of the . . . agreement[ ] which will require foreign investors to be treated the same way as local firms with regard to government procurement should be strongly rejected, as it is vitally important that procurement policy be used to promote domestic industry.'[177] An influential civil servant sketched out the government's position in 1998:[178]

---

[175] See eg the National Association of Manufacturers, 'A Catalog of New US Unilateral Economic Sanctions for Foreign Policy Purposes 1993–96' (NAM, 1997). In addition, a coalition of business interests formed a pressure group specifically on the issue named USA*ENGAGE.

[176] See 'Businesses Battle State Sanctions' *Journal of Commerce*, 28 August 1997, 1.

[177] COSATU's Submission on the Preferential Procurement Policy Framework Bill, Submitted to the Joint Committee on the Preferential Procurement Policy Bill, 15 December 1999, para 4.6.

[178] Presentation by Mr Sipho Shezi, Director-General of the National Department of Public Works, Republic of South Africa at the 9th International Public Procurement Association Conference in Copenhagen, Denmark, 8 June 1998 'Public Sector Procurement as an Instrument of Government Policy', 8.

Our standpoint on this matter is that the preferencing mechanism utilised by the South African government via the Affirmative Procurement Policy should not merely be viewed as protectionism of domestic industries, but rather as a mechanism to promote more equitable spread of work and entrepreneurial opportunities amongst all sectors of South Africa's population. Compliance with the Affirmative Procurement Policy places the same compliance conditions on domestic contractors and foreign contractors. It is also important to note that the direct preference in mechanisms [for preferential procurement] have contract thresholds which are much lower than the procurement thresholds specified in any of the bilateral or multilateral trade agreements and therefore focus on domestic markets with very little bearing on international trade liberalisation.

The Green Paper largely followed this line of argument,[179] recommending in addition, that the preference system for local content should be continued and somewhat expanded.

The Green Paper also recognized, however, that pressure would grow for South Africa to engage with international negotiations on procurement, that 'the issue will not disappear from the multilateral trade agenda', and that while it may 'be opportune to resist accession to the Agreement at this time, it is important that South Africa begins to engage the issue directly and to define its interest empirically', in part by researching the scope for retaining its socio-economic preferences.[180]

In practice, however, during the 1990s South Africa appears to have been under somewhat less pressure internationally than might have been supposed. The EC-South Africa Agreement on Trade, Development and Co-operation, 1999,[181] provided, for example, that the Parties 'agree to cooperate to ensure that access to the Parties' procurement contracts is governed by a system which is *fair, equitable* and transparent' echoing the provisions of the Constitution.[182] So too, although it appears that there had been discussions concerning the implications of black economic empowerment (BEE) policy for public procurement in talks between South Africa and EFTA negotiators,[183] the public procurement provisions of the final agreement were bland. Article 29 of the South Africa-EFTA Free Trade Agreement, signed in 2006, provides that the Parties 'agree on the importance of co-operation to enhance the mutual understanding'[184] of their respective procurement systems. They undertake to make the relevant legal provisions publicly available, and to respond to questions about them. Within five years after the agreement comes into force, they agree to hold consultations 'to consider *possible* steps to be taken with a view to mutually liberalizing their procurement markets'.[185]

---

[179] Green Paper on Public Sector Procurement Reform in South Africa: An Initiative of the Ministry of Finance and the Ministry of Public Works, April 1997 (*Government Gazette*, Vol 382, No 17928, 14 April 1997), 96–101.   [180] ibid 100.

[181] EC-South Africa Agreement on Trade, Development and Co-operation, 1999, OJEU, L311/3, 4.12.1999.   [182] ibid Art 45 (emphasis added).

[183] J Fraser, 'Free trade talks cover black empowerment' *Business Day*, 23 May 2003.

[184] South Africa-EFTA Free Trade Agreement, Art 29(1).

[185] ibid Art 29(3) (emphasis added).

These agreements with European trade partners may not be representative, however, of an ability for South Africa to negotiate acceptance of preferential procurement. Negotiations with the United States have been unsuccessful, and there is some debate over to what extent, if at all, preferential procurement played a role in preventing agreement. During the, now stalled, negotiations several commentators identified BEE as a potential difficulty.[186] The Trade Law Centre for Southern Africa Trade Brief in November 2003 noted how any US-Southern African Customs Union (SACU) Free Trade Agreement (FTA) 'may severely limit the circumstances under which the procurement entities can give preferences to locals. It is, therefore, vital for the negotiators to make sure that some of the objectives of . . . s217 of the constitution[,] the [preferential procurement] Act and the broad based Black Economic Empowerment are not undermined by the FTAA.'[187] Some senior South African politicians have also identified BEE procurement as a problem in the negotiations.[188] On the other hand, a senior United States negotiator is quoted as having denied that black empowerment was a problem in the negotiations. This was 'absolutely not true', 'procurement rules in the US include "minority set-asides", which are loosely comparable to black economic empowerment efforts'.[189]

The effect of black empowerment initiatives on foreign multinationals has also come into contention outside the context of trade negotiations. Section 3 of the Preferential Procurement Act, as we have seen, provides that an organ of the state is entitled to submit a request to the Minister of Finance to be exempted from the application of the Act, if the likely tenderers are international suppliers, but it was in the context of developing the BEE Codes of Good Practice that the issue came most into the debate. In the development of the draft Codes, there were concerns among those representing foreign business interests that a foreign company hoping to win South African government procurement would have a more difficult task in gaining such contracts because of the criteria that made up the scorecard, and the weightings of those elements. Among the highest priorities in the scorecard was likely to be the ownership of the potential tenderer by black South Africans. If a foreign company was unwilling or unable to transfer ownership of its South African subsidiary, for instance, that would mean it would have to engage in enhanced efforts in other areas that were less highly weighted. For example, promoting a greater proportion of black people into top management, better

---

[186] D Langton, 'United States-Southern African Customs Union (SACU) Free Trade Agreement Negotiations: Background and Potential Issues', <http://www.nationalaglawcenter.org/assets/crs/RS21387.pdf>; C Ryan, 'No to free trade with US' *Mail & Guardian*, South Africa, 28 February 2006.

[187] G Zanamwe, 'Transparency in government procurement', TRALAC Trade Brief, No 7/2003, November 2003, 13.

[188] D Pressly, 'BEE "an obstacle to free trade"', Tuesday, 23 August 2005 <http://business.iafrica.com/news/475158.htm> quoting Tony Leon, the Democratic Alliance leader, as arguing that this 'appeared to be one of the stumbling blocks in the way of the Southern African Customs Union signing a Free Trade Agreement (FTA) with the United States'.

[189] T Cohen and C Lourens, 'New impetus behind a deal', *Business Day*, South Africa, 31 August 2005.

training for black employees, or purchasing a greater proportion of supplies from black-owned companies would be necessary in order to make up the deficit, or it would be at a severe disadvantage in winning the contract. Initially, the government indicated that the requirements would be the same for foreign as for local companies.[190] After further discussions with business interests, however, this position was reversed and a draft additional code of good practice was proposed in order to accommodate the argument that treating the firms the same would lead to unfairness for foreign firms.[191] The method chosen was to devise a system of 'equity equivalent' contributions made by multinational companies. In order to qualify for equity equivalents, the multinational enterprise (MNE) must own and control the entire equity in the local subsidiary, the MNE must operate a global and uniformly applied policy against the sale of shares in or ownership of such subsidiaries, and the MNE would suffer substantial commercial harm if it were to implement the equity ownership requirements that applied locally. What the MNE would have to do to secure these 'equity equivalents' was, however, left to Ministers to decide. It appears, therefore, that (with some flexibility on the South African side, heading off individual problems that may arise ad hoc) South Africa has considered that it is able to prosper without joining the GPA, retain its extensive procurement linkages, and that the costs have not been too high.

World Bank procurement policy, development, and linkage

There is, however, increasing pressure from the IMF, the World Bank and the EC on developing countries to reform their domestic procurement, often by adopting a variation of the United Nations Commission on International Trade Law (UNCITRAL) model procurement legislation,[192] in order to secure access to loans and other technical assistance. In some developing countries, the role of international financial institutions is of vital importance in funding development projects. Frequently, the method adopted for the dispersal of funds is for the lending institution to lend to a government or private body (depending on the financial institution involved), which then in turn contracts with another party to deliver works, supplies, or services to the loan recipient. The question is what, if anything, the lending institution requires to be included in contracts that are financed by loans from the financial institution.[193]

---

[190] C Mortished, 'Black empowerment hurdle for government contracts', *The Times*, 26 April 2003.

[191] Code 100: Measurement of the Ownership Element of Broad-Based Black Economic Empowerment: Statement 103: The recognition of Ownership Contributions Made by Multinational Companies, Draft, 2005.

[192] UNCITRAL Model Law on the Procurement of Goods, Construction and Services, adopted 15 June 1994, available at <http://www.uncitral.org>.

[193] After the manuscript of this book was completed, my attention was drawn to M de C Meireles, 'The World Bank Procurement Regulations: A Critical Analysis of the Enforcement Mechanism and of the Application of Secondary Policies in Financial Projects' (PhD thesis, University of Nottingham, 2006).

It is clear that these financial institutions, because of their role, have had (and will continue to have) an important role in furthering procurement liberalization in these countries. Countries that are not subject to EC procurement rules, and are not members of the GPA, are nevertheless likely to come under considerable pressure from international financial institutions to liberalize their public procurement practices. A report in 2003 described how an incentive-based approach had been adopted initially.[194] The report acknowledged, however, that this work 'has proceeded with limited success. It received a major boost in the late 1990's when the international donor community decided to tackle the question of corruption head on.' However, progress 'in the development of public procurement systems worldwide, that can deliver on the basic principles of a well functioning system, contribute to better governance and reduce the opportunity for corruption, has been slow'.[195] Efforts are now being made to ensure that greater progress will be made in future in securing procurement reform.[196] Under the auspices of the joint World Bank/OECD Development Assistance Committee, developing countries and bilateral and multilateral donors developed a set of tools and standards to provide guidance for improvements in procurement systems. This culminated in the adoption, in December 2004, of the 'Johannesburg Declaration', and the adoption of a 'Baseline Indicators Tool' as the agreed international standards for assessment of national procurement systems.[197] It remains to be seen whether moves to further harmonize the procurement requirements of these financial institutions result in development of further guidance on the social aspects of procurement.[198]

The World Bank's Articles of Agreement[199] establish the Bank's responsibility to ensure that the proceeds of its loans are used only for specified purposes, with due attention to economy and efficiency and without regard to political and other non-economic influences or considerations. For this purpose, the Bank has established procurement rules to be followed by borrowers for the procurement of goods, works, and services required for the projects financed by the Bank, and procedures for Bank review of the procurement decisions made by borrowers. The rules that apply to the procurement of goods, works, and services financed out of the proceeds of Bank loans are detailed in a set of procurement guidelines. Those that apply to the selection and employment of consultant services are detailed in

---

[194] 'International Benchmarks and Standards for Public Procurement Systems', paper presented to the OECD/DAC World Bank Round Table, Strengthening Procurement Capacities in Developing Countries, Paris, 22–23 January 2003 (hereafter International Benchmarks) paras 2–3.

[195] ibid.

[196] ibid. And see also, RC Hernandez, 'Harminization [sic] of Procurement Policies and Practices of Public International Financial Institutions: Report on the Progress of Work by Heads of Procurement', November 2002, Presentation made at the High Level Forum on Harmonization, Rome, 24–25 February 2003.

[197] This tool was incorporated into the Preliminary DAC Guidelines and Reference Series, Harmonising Donor Practices for Effective Aid Delivery: Volume III (Strengthening Procurement Capacities in Developing Countries). This was tabled during the High level Forum on Aid Effectiveness in Paris in March 2005.   [198] International Benchmarks (n 194 above).

[199] See IBRD Articles of Agreement, Art III, ss 4 and 5, and IDA Articles of Agreement, Art V, s 1.

the consultant guidelines.[200] These guidelines have been endorsed by the Bank's executive directors. They are incorporated by reference in the loan agreement in the manner specified in the project appraisal document for that project, and are binding on the borrower. In the case of a conflict between the loan agreement and the borrower's national regulations, therefore, the loan agreement takes precedence.[201] Additional instructions and guidance material on procurement are provided in the Procurement Manual and the Consultants Manual.

Four basic principles guide the Bank's procurement requirements, the third of which has considerable significance for the application of social linkages: (1) ensuring economy and efficiency in the procurement of goods, works, and services, as mandated by the Articles; (2) giving eligible bidders from developed and developing countries a fair opportunity to compete in providing goods, works, and services financed by the bank; (3) encouraging the development of domestic industries—contracting, manufacturing, and consulting industries—in borrowing countries; and (4) providing for transparency in the procurement process.[202]

The procurement guidelines indicate that the crucial issue in many cases is the precise purpose for which the loan is provided, and that this is regarded as setting the boundaries for what the contracts arising out of that loan may contain.[203] Apart from this issue, of most significance for the purposes of this study are the provisions dealing with domestic preferences. To encourage the development of domestic industries, the Bank permits each borrower to give preference to bids offering goods manufactured within its country, and those countries below a specified per capita threshold, to give preference to bids for works contracts from eligible domestic contractors.[204] These appear to allow some scope for social policy linkages, under certain tightly controlled conditions. Procurement guidelines for procurement under World Bank loans and credits, for example, provide that with regard to procurement involving international competitive bidding (the procedure

---

[200] Guidelines: Procurement under IBRD Loans and IDA Credits (Washington, DC: World Bank, May 2004); and Guidelines: Selection and Employment of Consultants by World Bank Borrowers (Washington, DC: World Bank, May 2004) (hereafter World Bank Guidelines).

[201] See s 10.01 of the relevant General Conditions Applicable to Loan and Guarantee Agreements, or General Conditions Applicable to Development Credit Agreements.

[202] World Bank, Guidelines (n 200 above) para 1.2.

[203] eg World Bank Operational Directive, OD 4.15, December 1991, para 43 states: 'When projects include social objectives, the procurement procedures and contract packaging should be adapted, as appropriate, within the framework of the Procurement Guidelines. For example, projects can be designed for labor-intensive construction, where it is consistent with economic cost minimization, and contracts can be packaged to encourage small firms and NGOs to participate. Use of simple contract documents and expeditious payment procedures can also facilitate the involvement of small firms and NGOs. In the procurement of simple goods—such as school/hospital furniture, agricultural tools, school uniforms, textbooks, and street cleaning equipment—appropriate specifications may be used to promote small-scale, labor-intensive production methods, where such methods are consistent with minimizing economic cost.'

[204] See OP 3.10, Annex D, IBRD/IDA Countries: Per Capita Incomes, Lending Eligibility, and Repayment Terms, which sets forth which borrowing countries are eligible to give preference to bids for works contracts.

where international competition is likely) 'a margin of preference may be provided in the evaluation of bids for: (a) goods manufactured in the country of the Borrower when comparing bids offering such goods with those offering goods manufactured abroad; and (b) works in member countries below a specified threshold of GNP per capita, when comparing bids from eligible domestic Contractors with those from foreign firms'.[205] With regard to National Competitive Bidding (where international competition is unlikely), the procurement guidelines for procurement under International Bank for Reconstruction and Development (IBRD) loans and International Development Association (IDA) credits, goes somewhat further.[206] The World Bank might, as a result, have been a source of a developing interpretation of what linkages might be acceptable, but this likelihood is reduced by the fact that the World Bank Inspection Panel has no jurisdiction to deal with complaints concerning procurement.[207]

In addition to the World Bank using procurement linkages as an aid in developing the local economy in developing countries, other donor countries adopt similar policies. The United States included requirements in reconstruction contracts in Iraq that prime contractors use Iraq subcontractors and employ Iraqi workers to the maximum extent practicable, although whether these types of conditions were driven more by counter-insurgency than development concerns is a moot point.[208]

The World Bank has been cautious, but not overly hostile, to South African preferential procurement policies. The country assessment report it undertook, as described above, appeared to accept that there was a tension between international procurement principles and targeted procurement policy: 'International procurement principles underscore equal access to bids and equal treatment in bid-evaluation and contract award. These principles would seem to conflict with

---

[205] World Bank Guidelines (n 200 above) para 2.55.

[206] ibid para 3.17: 'Where, in the interest of project sustainability, or to achieve certain specific social objectives of the project, it is desirable in selected project components to (a) call for the participation of local communities and/or nongovernmental organizations (NGOs) in the delivery of services, or (b) increase the utilization of local know-how and materials, or (c) employ labor-intensive and other appropriate technologies, the procurement procedures, specifications, and contract packaging shall be suitably adapted to reflect these considerations, provided these are efficient and are acceptable to the Bank. The procedures proposed and the project components to be carried out by community participation shall be outlined in the Loan Agreement and further elaborated in the Procurement Plan or the relevant project implementation document approved by the Bank.'

[207] Para 14(b) of the Panel's Resolution and its subsequent 1996 and 1999 Clarifications; The 1996 Clarifications state: 'No procurement action is subject to inspection by the Panel, whether taken by the Bank or by a borrower. A separate mechanism is available for addressing procurement related complaints.' See also Request No 35, Public Works and Employment Creation Project in Burundi, Inspection Panel, Annual Report, 2004–05 (2005), 24, in which the Inspection Panel rejected a complaint on these grounds.

[208] For a discussion of the issues and a detailed account, see M Likosky, *Infrastructures* (Cambridge University Press, 2006), ch 4.

applying preferences in national procurement to target groups for domestic socio-economic purposes.' However, it then went on to argue that:

...the preferential system in South Africa may be defended in the same manner as, for example, the World Bank defines domestic preferences for procurement of works and goods in international bids, which give an advantage to domestic manufacturers or contractors of developing nations over competitors from industrial nations, or in the case of South Africa's dual economy, competition of 'established enterprises' with 'emerging historically disadvantaged enterprises'.

It essentially adopted, therefore, a policy of cautious concern. If such a policy was to be retained, however, at least there should be close monitoring of the policy: 'Nonetheless, progress with achieving the goal of merging the two economies should be measurable in order to continuously assess whether the policy is meeting the desired goals and, more importantly, that it is not causing undesirable distortions in overall competitiveness and other undesirable consequences.'[209]

At least some of the pressure on South Africa to adopt international procurement approaches has been lessened due to the acceptance by South Africa that international donors would not be required to use South African procurement requirements. In 1998, the Reconstruction and Development Programme Fund Act 1994[210] was amended to allow procurement carried out using foreign assistance not to use South African procurement procedures but such procedures as were stipulated in any agreement between South Africa and the donors. The EC-South Africa Agreement on Trade, Development and Co-operation provides that procedures for procurement or contracts financed by the Community are laid down in general clauses to be adopted by decision of the Cooperation Council (and by implication not under procedures laid down for procurement generally under South African law).[211]

Malaysia and international procurement disciplines

The GPA, as we have seen, is a plurilateral instrument, ie one that members of the WTO are not required to accept as part of the package of measures to which all members are committed. For some time, the WTO has had on its agenda revisions to international public procurement regulation that would expand considerably the geographical coverage of such regulation, including (in some contexts) making a commitment to such regulation one of the basic requirements for all WTO members.

---

[209] World Bank, Report No 25751-SA, South Africa Country Procurement Assessment Report, Refining the Public Procurement System, Volume I: Summary of Findings and Recommendations, February 2003, <http://www-wds.worldbank.org/external/default/WDSContentServer/IW3P/IB/2003/05/13/000094946_03042504054534/Rendered/PDF/multi0page.pdf> para 4.7.
[210] Reconstruction and Development Programme Fund Act, 1994, No 7 of 1994; Reccontruction and Development Programme Fund Act 1998, No 79 of 1998, s 4 amending s 4 of the 1994 Act.
[211] EC-South Africa Agreement on Trade, Development and Co-operation, Arts 75 and 76.

Several developments within the WTO may yet produce a revised regime governing public procurement at the international level.[212] The first is that a working group on Transparency in Government Procurement was established by the WTO Ministers at their meeting in Singapore in December 1996.[213] This is a multilateral exercise, and its mandate is to conduct a study on transparency and develop elements for inclusion in an appropriate agreement. This work is now on hold, as a result of the failure to agree to include these negotiations in the current trade round negotiations, an issue we consider in detail below. Second, also on a multilateral level, a working party has been set up, pursuant to Article XIII of the General Agreement on Trade in Services, to carry out negotiations on government procurement in the area of services, but it appears that these discussions are not proceeding with any speed.[214] Third, the Government Procurement Committee that oversees the GPA has agreed to undertake an early review of the GPA, aiming at simplification, expansion of coverage, and the removal of exceptions from the Agreement. The latter may, in particular, be an appropriate forum in which to consider these issues, although progress has been slow, in part because of the EU's 'desire to complete its internal programme of procurement reform before committing to GPA revisions'.[215] The work of the Committee focused primarily on simplification and improvement of the Agreement. In June 2003, the various proposals from member countries were consolidated into a single revised draft text.[216]

In this section we focus on the failure to persuade developing countries to agree to the inclusion of the issue of a multi-lateral 'transparency' in government procurement (TGP) agreement as part of the Doha Round negotiations. We look, in particular, at the approach taken by Malaysia to the issue of the proposed TGP agreement. Malaysia regarded the elements of the proposed agreement as having the potential to increase resort to legal challenges to its procurement policies, and as tantamount to stripping it of its ability to use procurement as part of its development agenda, particularly in the context of redistributive policies directed at increasing the economic empowerment of the native Malays or 'Bumiputera'.

Although a member of the WTO, Malaysia has consistently refused to become a party to the GPA, although it has not escaped scrutiny entirely. The WTO Trade Policy Report commented:

Government procurement preferences accorded to Malaysian firms constitute government assistance to these firms. Selected state-owned enterprises are required by public procurement

[212] V Kulacoglu, 'An Overview of Developments within the WTO since the Singapore Ministerial Conference', Paper delivered to the Conference 'Public Procurement: Global Revolution', University of Wales, Aberystwyth, 11–12 September 1997.

[213] See S Arrowsmith, 'Towards a Multilateral Agreement on Tranparency in Government Procurement' (1997) 47 ICLQ 793.

[214] S Arrowsmith, 'Reviewing the GPA: The Role and Development of the Plurilateral Agreement After Doha' (2002) 5(4) JIEL 761, 764.   [215] ibid 772.

[216] After this book went to press, a revised draft was published in December 2006, GPA/W/297, 11 December 2006.

regulations to follow similar practices. These preferences not only restrict competition among suppliers, thereby impairing economic efficiency, but also raise the cost to the Government and state-owned enterprises of procuring goods and services. The competitiveness of state-owned enterprises is, in turn, hampered insofar as they are forced by preferential procurement regulations to purchase their inputs from relatively high-cost local suppliers.[217]

Although subject to international scrutiny, Malaysia is a relatively wealthy member of the group of developing countries, and thus not subject to the type of pressure that requiring loans from the World Bank and the IMF would entail.[218] This degree of immunity from the international procurement rules was threatened, however, by the establishment of a Working Group on Transparency in Government Procurement (WGTGP) by the WTO Ministers at its meeting in Singapore in December 1996. Members agreed to establish the WGTGP to *study* the issues involved, 'taking into account national policies, and based on this study . . . [to] develop elements for inclusion in an appropriate multilateral agreement'.[219] This was a *multilateral* exercise, and its mandate was to conduct a study on transparency and develop elements for inclusion in an appropriate agreement. However, a movement developed among several developing countries that resisted further development of international procurement disciplines, particularly any that would be multilateral, and would thus result in an obligation for all members of the WTO to comply with them.

At the Ministerial Meeting in Doha in November 2001, setting in motion a new Round of trade liberalization negotiations, it was decided that multilateral negotiations would take place after the Fifth Ministerial Meeting 'on the basis of a decision to be taken, by explicit consensus, at that session on the modalities of negotiations'.[220] These negotiations would include consideration of whether to include transparency in government procurement in the future negotiating agenda.[221] Due to the divisiveness of the work at the WGTGP there was no negotiating text, but only a 'List of Issues and Points Raised', the ambiguous name of which reflects its amorphous contents.[222] As a result the draft agreements respectively submitted by

[217] WTO Trade Policy Review: Malaysia, WT/TPR/S/31, 3 November 1997, para 122.

[218] Interestingly in this regard, however, Malaysia has consistently drafted in exceptions to its various preferences programmes for procurement paid for by international development organizations, such as the IMF and World Bank. See eg Surat Pekeliling Perbendaharaan Bil 7 Thn 1974 [Treas Circ Let No 7/1974], Keutamaan Kepada Bumiputra Dalam Perolehan Barang-Barang, Perkhidmatan Dan Kerja-Kerja [Preferences for Bumiputera in the Procurement of Goods Services and Works] §11 (1 June 1974). Current regulations simply require that any such procurement should be done in accordance with requirements established by the funding organization. Treas Circ Let No 2/1995 (n 8 above) §§2.2.3, 4.3ff, 8.4.

[219] Singapore Ministerial Declaration (Adopted 13 December 1996), WT/Min(96)/DEC ¶21(18 December 1996); see also F Abbott, 'Rule-Making in the WTO: Lessons from the Case of Bribery and Corruption' (2001) 4 JIEL 275, 287.

[220] WTO, Ministerial Declaration, Ministerial Conference Fourth Session, 14 November 2001 (WT/MIN(01)DEC/W/1) (Doha Declaration) para 26.

[221] Doha Declaration (n 220 above) para 26.

[222] See Note by the Secretariat, Work of the Working Group on the Matters Related to the Items I-V of the List of Issues Raised and Points Made, WT/WGTGP/W/32 (23 May 2002); Note by the Secretariat, Work of the Working Group on the Matters Related to the Items VI-XII of the List of

the EU (EU draft agreement) and a coalition of countries led by the US (US draft agreement) provided the most accurate and complete picture of the sort of agreement which proponents of a TGP agreement sought.[223] There were several features of these drafts that were of particular importance for our purposes.

Both draft agreements would have required that members 'maintain fair and transparent judicial, arbitral, or administrative bodies or procedures for the purpose of prompt review' of disputes arising out of the procurement process. These were the so-called 'domestic review procedure' (DRP) requirements.[224] Both agreements shared the requirement that whatever domestic institution was established for this purpose, it must operate independently of the procuring entity, but the drafts differed somewhat from one another in terms of scope of review and standing requirements.[225] This DRP requirement would have been in addition to requiring parties to accept that *inter-state* complaints under a transparency agreement would be able to be taken through the WTO dispute settlement procedures, otherwise known as 'linkage' to the DSU.

Closely related to the DRP requirements (in the case of the EU draft agreement, explicitly related) were obligations in the two draft agreements regarding the provision of information.[226] Both would have required procuring entities not only to inform unsuccessful bidders of their failure but also to respond to requests for information from such bidders concerning the reason for the rejection of their bids and, in the case of the EU draft agreement, also the reasons why the successful bid was chosen.[227] Further, each would have required that procuring entities keep, and with some differences in manner make available, a record of the process by which they reached award decisions.[228] The United States draft agreement would have required that such information be 'available upon request by another Member' (a provision which was actually contained within brackets).[229] The EU draft agreement, on the other hand, included within the same article which details other DRP requirements, a clause stating that 'Members shall ensure that each procuring entity is able to respond to requests for information on the way the procurement was carried out', apparently making the receipt of such information a matter of right, at least for every provider involved in a covered challenge.[230]

Issues Raised and Points Made, WT/WGTGP/W/33 (3 October 2002); see also Abbott (n 219 above) 289 (noting the passively named 'List of the Issues Raised and Points Made').

[223] See Elements for an Agreement on Transparency in Government Procurement, Communication from the European Communities, WT/WGTGP/W/26 (5 November 1999) (hereafter EU Draft Agreement); Communication from Hungary, Korea, Singapore, and the United States, Preparations for the 1999 Ministerial Conference, The WTO's Contribution to Transparency in Government Procurement, WT/GC/W/384, WT/WGTGP/W/27 Annex, Draft Text for an Agreement on Transparency in Government Procurement Articles X, XII (9 November 1999) (hereafter US Draft Agreement).

[224] US Draft Agreement, Art X(2)–(3); EU Draft Agreement, Art 8(1)–(2).   [225] ibid.

[226] US Draft Agreement, Arts VIII(2.2)–VIII(3), IX(1); EU Draft Agreement, Arts 7(2), 8(3).

[227] US Draft Agreement, Art VIII(2); EU Draft Agreement, Art 7(2).

[228] US Draft Agreement, Art IX(1); EU Draft Agreement, Art 8(3).

[229] US Draft Agreement, Art IX(1).   [230] EU Draft Agreement, Art 8(3).

Despite arguments that a proposed multilateral agreement on transparency in public procurement would be beneficial for developed and developing countries,[231] several developing countries strongly objected to the proposals on the basis that they could undermine the ability of such states to use procurement for social policy purposes. In Malaysia's case in particular, notwithstanding the statements of developed countries (embodied in the Doha Declaration's mandate regarding the transparency issue) that domestic preferences were off the table,[232] a TGP agreement such as that envisioned by the United States and the EU was seen as threatening the preferences granted to Bumiputera and other domestic providers. Apart from the provisions of the draft agreements themselves, there were strong suspicions that a transparency agreement was intended by its developed country proponents to be an initial step on the way to a multilateral GPA, which was seen as requiring Malaysia to abandon its preference programmes, unless it negotiated a specific exception in its Annex.[233] The transparency agreement was seen as a step towards more open access—that was seen as the ambition of those pressing for it—therefore the Agreement should be resisted.[234] This argument was particularly associated with Malaysia.[235]

Provisions requiring DRPs and linkage to the DSU were of particular concern to Malaysia and other developing country members in this context.[236] The strength of this concern appears to derive from two sources: (1) the worry that

---

[231] World Trade Organization, WT/WGTGP/W/41, 17 June 2003, Working Group on Transparency in Government Procurement, Positive effects of transparency in government procurement and its implementation: Communication from the European Communities.

[232] See eg Communication from the European Communities, Positive Effects of Transparency in Government Procurement, WT/WGTGP/W/41 ¶10 ('It is not the case, as it is often claimed, that new multilateral TGP rules will open DC procuring markets to suppliers from developed countries.') (17 June 2003); Communication from the United States, Proposal for a Work Plan to Build on the Progress of the Working Group WT/WGTGP/W/35 ¶ 9 ('The Doha Ministerial Declaration has narrowed scope by limiting its parameters to "transparency aspects, and explicitly providing that an agreement will neither restrict domestic preferences nor require market access commitments."') (30 September 2002); Doha Declaration (n 220 above) 154, ¶ 26.

[233] See eg Note by the Secretariat, Report of the Meeting of 6 October 1999, WT/WGTGP/M/9, ¶ 11 (9 November 1999) (relating suspicions voiced by Malaysia's representative on behalf of itself and other developing country members that in the view of developed country members 'an agreement on transparency in government was merely a building block towards the establishment of a multilateral framework for government procurement'.); cf Abbott (n 219 above) 290 (stating on the basis of interviews with trade officials from the US and EU that: 'The whole aim of the [TGP] exercise from the US and EU perspectives, was to multilateralize the GPA.').

[234] For opposition to the Transparency Agreement from a developing country perspective, see M Khor, 'WTO "Singapore Issues": What's at Stake and Why it Matters', in TWN Briefings for Cancun, No 3 <www.twnside.org.sg>. See also United Nations Development Programme *et al, Making Global Trade Work for People* (UNDP, 2003) ch 15, noting the extent to which a new agreement on transparency in procurement may reduce domestic policy space for linkages and give rise to extra implementation costs for developing countries.

[235] For Malaysian opposition to Transparency agreement, see Rafidah Aziz, Minister of International Trade and Industry, Malaysia, 'Doha Development Agenda—The Way Forward', in The Federal Trust, 'Where Next for the WTO? After Cancun: Views, ideas and proposals by trade ministers' (2003) 31.

[236] See eg Note by Secretariat, Report of the Meeting of 18 June 2003, WT/WGTGP/M/18 ¶ 12 (relating comments by the Malaysian representative 'In addition there were two elements that his

powerful providers from wealthy countries would use these mechanisms in combination with other provisions as a way to challenge decisions in the procurement process and thus coerce greater market access;[237] and (2) the perception that these sorts of challenge mechanisms made no sense in the structure of an agreement which did not purport to guarantee market access and thus might, by implication, create such a guarantee.[238] A particularly litigious provider could use challenges as a way to harass procuring entities, and thus place pressure on the entity to treat it favourably.[239] The same was true in regard to non-discrimination provisions, which could give rise to harassing, amorphous claims that domestic or other foreign providers were granted better treatment at some stage in the tendering or contract award process.[240]

Leaving this objection aside, in the Malaysian context, the provisions of the draft agreements, particularly those provisions dealing with the DRP and information requirements, would appear to have required a radical reversal of current Malaysian approaches to procurement award processes, leading to a radical shift of power within the Malaysian system. In order for Malaysia to comply with either draft agreement's DRPs requirements, it would have been required either to establish a *sui generis* administrative structure that was independent of all other procuring entities to hear provider claims, or it would have had to widen considerably the scope of judicial review of government contractual decisions generally.[241] The issues raised in this context echo similar debates over the implications for domestic regulation of other international economic law agreements, such as in the area of intellectual property. Since obligations arising from these agreements 'involve domestic regulatory structures embedded in the institutional infrastructure of the economy', they are potentially expensive and may well affect sensitive areas of national sovereignty.[242] According to World Bank estimates, creating the regulatory

delegation—together with those of other developing countries—had repeatedly emphasized, namely domestic review procedures as well as linkage to the WTO's DSU. In his view, these elements were not concerned with transparency and should never be a part of an agreement on transparency in government procurement.') (7 July 2003); Report of the Meeting of 7 February 2003, Working Group on Transparency, WT/WGTGP/M/17 ¶ 22 (15 April 2003); Working Group on Transparency, WT/WGTGP/M/15 ¶ 13 (relating statement by Malaysian representative, 'Developing countries ha[ve] difficulties with essentially two elements, namely domestic review procedures and the application of WTO dispute settlement procedures.') 47, 78, 83 (9 January 2003); Report of the Meeting of 25 September 2000, Working Group on Transparency, WT/WGTGP/M/11 ¶¶ 31, 33 (19 December 2000); Report of the Meeting of 7 June 2000, Working Group on Transparency, WT/WGTGP/M/10 ¶ 16 (1 August 2000).

[237] See eg WT/WGTGP/M/17 (n 236 above) ¶ 23.   [238] See eg ibid ¶ 16.

[239] See eg ibid ¶ 36 (relating comments by the Brazilian representative: '. . . his authorities experience has been that suppliers who lost a procurement would use each and every possible recourse, administratively and judicially, to delay the procurement, perhaps even feel that if they could protract the whole bidding process long enough the whole bidding process could be declared null and void and they could get a second chance.').   [240] ibid.

[241] Courts of Judicature Act 1964 (Act 91); see also nn 72–79 above and accompanying text.

[242] S Ostry, 'The World Trading System: In Dire Need of Reform' (2003) 109 Temple International and Comparative Law Journal (2003) 109–11.

structure required by TRIPS had cost some developing countries an entire year's development budget.[243] These experiences influenced developing countries' evaluations of developed country TGP agreement proposals and their ultimate decision to oppose the process.[244]

Obligations in both draft agreements, regarding the provision of information in the post-contract award context, would also have required a significant transformation of the current system in Malaysia, which conflicts with these requirements in several ways. First, while current rules require that unsuccessful bidders be notified of their failure, there are no provisions to allow them to request reasons why their bids were rejected, let alone why the successful bid was chosen.[245] Second, while individual procuring entities and their respective procurement boards and committees are required to keep a record of the process by which they reach a contract award decision, no similar provision applies when the decision is made by the Finance Ministry or state financial officials, as it often is.[246] Finally and most significantly, under Malaysian law, not only is that information, if produced, not freely and easily available, but it is subject to the discretion of ministry officials to deem it confidential, making its possession, receipt, or distribution a serious crime.[247] In order to comply with either draft agreement, Malaysia would have needed to restructure not only how information was collected and distributed by governmental entities in the context of contract award decisions, but also

[243] JM Finger and P Schuller, 'Implementation of Uruguay Commitments: The Development Challenge', in The World Bank Research Department, Policy Research Working Paper (World Bank 1999).

[244] In a statement posted on the Malaysian Ministry of International Trade and Industry (MITI) website soon after the collapse of the Cancun Ministerial, MITI Minister, YB Dato'Seri Rafidah Aziz made this explicit: 'The developing countries do not want a repeat of earlier experiences where they had signed on to agreements such as Trade-Related Investment Measures (TRIMS) and Trade-Related Aspects of Intellectual Property Rights (TRIPS) which are seen to be imbalanced as they restrict their ability to pursue development objectives. The price for developing countries to pay would be too high.' Cancun WTO Ministerial Conference: The Malaysian Perspective, available at <http://www.miti.gov.my/wto-cancun.html> (accessed 12 January 2004).

[245] See Treas Circ Let No 2/1995 (n 8 above) §13.2.3.

[246] See Arahan Perbendaharaan [Treas Instr] Nos 170.3, 198.1(b), 198.3 (1997).

[247] See Official Secrets Act 1972 (Act 88) §§2(1) (defining 'official secrets' to include, *inter alia*, 'Cabinet documents, records of decisions and deliberations including those of Cabinet committees' and 'any other official document, information and materials as may be classified as "Top Secret", "Secret", "Confidential" or "Restricted" as the case may be, by a Minister . . . or such public officer appointed under section 2B.') §8 (making unauthorized distribution (even inadvertent) or knowing receipt of designated documents punishable by a prison sentence of one to seven years) (26 September 1972). See also Jain, 1997 (n 74 above) 611–19 (discussing, *inter alia*, *Lim Kit Siang v Public Prosecutor* [1979] 2 MJL 37 (upholding designation of purely administrative material: 'Broadly speaking, it may be said that secret official information within the meaning of section 8 of the Act is really the government information the confidentiality and secrecy of which depends upon the manner in which the government treats the information.'), *Datuk Haji Dzulkifli v Public Prosecutor* [1981] 1 MJL 112, 113 ('[A] document does not lose its status as a secret document merely because . . . [it] happens to contain information which is already known to the public.'). According to KS Jomo, in operation this has meant that: 'Almost everything has become confidential. As far as the government is concerned when in doubt, chop it as secret.' A Reyes, 'The War Against Cronies' *Asiaweek*, Vol 26, No 43 (3 November 2000) 1.

the way in which it had chosen to balance the government's need for privacy and the public's need for information.

An additional effect that a TGP agreement in the form of either of the two drafts could have had on the Malaysian political system (though not one generally publicized by Malaysian officials) was disruption of the existing system of patrimonial power exercised by the Malaysian federal executive via the procurement system.[248] It appears that for much of Malaysia's modern history the political structure of, and the distribution of power within, the ruling United Malays National Organisation (UMNO) (which dominates the coalition of parties that has, in turn overwhelmingly dominated Malaysian politics since 1969) has been based to a very large degree on patrimonial political relationships.[249] Within that context, government contracts have circulated like currency: providing candidates with a means to generate support as well as punish those who fail to support them, creating incentives for party politicians to move up in the hierarchy and curry favour with those above them, and giving politicians a means to distribute wealth to donors that can later be funnelled back to the politicians as campaign contributions.[250] Eliminating the Finance Ministry's discretionary contract award authority, making it subject to record-keeping requirements, and constraining the availability of negotiated tenders, would make it much more difficult for the officials at the highest level in the federal government to distribute contracts to political allies to secure future support.[251] The same requirements in combination with the elimination, or strict limitation of, exceptions would disrupt the practice of allowing district level

---

[248] Not surprisingly, this type of effect is amongst those which the US has cited in favour of concluding a strong TGP agreement. See United States Trade Representative, Annual Report on Discrimination in Foreign Government Procurement §III (30 April 1996) (hereafter USTR Annual Report (1996)).

[249] See Case (n 79 above) 99 ('Politics in Malaysia can be conceptualized in terms of a steep pyramid . . . [a]t its apex looms a national leader . . . tightly concentrating power in his prime ministerial office, then dispensing benefits to elites in patrimonialist ways.') 111–14; Gomez (1994) (n 19 above) 6–26, 35, 60–1; D Horowitz, *Ethnic Groups in Conflict* (University of California Press, 1985) 666–9; Gomez (2003) (n 40 above) 77–80.

[250] ibid; see also, eg, 'Leaders Support PM's Stand on Government Contracts' *New Straits Times*, 4 April 2002, 2; 'Con-fusing' *Malay Times*, 30 March 2002, 3; S Zain, 'Reform: Questioning our Feudal Loyalty; Malaysians are New People' *Asiaweek*, Vol 26 No 43, 3 November 2000, 1; Reyes (n 247 above) 1; 'No Corruption in Pularek Project, Says Agency' *New Straits Times*, 5 July 2000, 1; 'Shahrir to be UMNO "Postman"', *New Straits Times*, 22 May 2000, 2; 'Government Agencies Rapped for not Doing Enough for the Poor' *New Straits Times*, 14 May 2000, 14; S Jayasankaran, 'Revenge Attack' *Far Eastern Economic Review*, 30 March 2000, 25; S Jayasankaran, 'Regional Briefing', *Far Eastern Economic Review*, 30 March 2000, 16; 'Malacca Takes Action Against Civil Servants', *New Straits Times*, 26 March 2000, 4; 'Bank Submits List of Errant Staff', *New Straits Times*, 22 March 2000, 4; 'Preparations to be Made for Sanggang By-Election', *New Straits Times*, 7 March 2000, 2; 'UMNO Divisions Must Nominate all Posts' *New Straits Times*, 7 March 2000, 18; 'Malacca Takes Steps to be Fair to Supporters' *New Straits Times*, 6 March 2000, 4; 'Unity Versus Choice as UMNO Polls *New Straits Times*, 9 January 2000, 13; 'Caterers Fear Losing Contracts' *New Straits Times*, 28 February 2000, 10; Funston, 'Malaysia's Tenth Elections: Status Quo, Reformasi, or Islamization?' (2000) 22(1) Contemporary Southeast Asia 32.

[251] See US Draft Agreement (n 223 above) Arts V(2), VIII(1), IX(1); EU Draft Agreement (n 223 above) Arts 5(4), 7(1), 8(3); Gomez 2003 (n 40 above) 78–80.

UMNO officials to award themselves government contracts as a way to pay for party activities at that level.[252] Rules that limit qualification factors to preset criteria and that give providers a way to challenge their treatment, either directly through *sui generis* DRPs or in the courts, would make it less likely that officials could use procurement decisions to punish those who failed to support them and/or their party.[253]

In short, many of the processes currently used by the Finance Ministry and others would have had to be replaced with processes that in most cases would have reduced the flexibility and discretion that the Finance Ministry and others currently enjoy, transferring authority away from the Finance Ministry and out of the Malaysian political system. Given the 'hegemony of the executive' in the procurement context,[254] most of these changes would have brought about, at least in part, a diminution of that hegemony, changing the balance of rights and review authority within the operation of the procurement system, subjecting Treasury-issued rules to unprecedented review, and being likely to disrupt informal patrimonial relationships of political power exercised by the Executive.

In discussions of the working group that followed Doha, consensus (or, at least, grudging acceptance) emerged on some issues, but on the key points of domestic review DRPs and linkage to the DSU, the developing and developed country members remained far apart.[255] Following the collapse of the September 2003 Ministerial Meeting of the WTO at Cancun, the then Malaysian Prime Minister launched an attack on the potential effect of the draft texts on transparency in

---

[252] US Draft Agreement, Arts IV, V(2), VIII(1), IX(1); EU Draft Agreement, Arts 5(4), 7(1), 8(3); 'Leaders Support PM's Stand on Government Contracts' (n 250 above) 2 ('If Umno does not want division heads to expect government awards, then the party should perhaps increase the allocation given to each division to carry out activities.' quoting Marang UMNO deputy head Datuk Dr Bdul Latiff Awang.)

[253] US Draft Agreement, Arts VII(2), X; EU Draft Agreement, Arts 7(1), 8; Jaysankaran, 'Revenge Attack' (n 250 above) 25 (describing actions of the Chief Minster of the state of Malacca, who sought to punish those who had voted for the opposition Islamic party in the 2000 by issuing an order to the various governmental entities located in his state, placing 'private clinics, architects, a property valuer and several providers on a blacklist where they [were] excluded from government contracts.'; See also Jayasankaran, 'Regional Briefing' (n 247 above) 16 (reporting that 20 contractors and professionals were banned as part of the action); 'Malacca Takes Steps to be Fair to Supporters' (n 250 above) 4 (quoting the Malaccan Minister as saying, 'It is only right that we replace [those who voted for other parties] with supporters who "swim and sink" with the government.' 'Bank Submits List of Errant Staff' (n 250 above) 4 (detailing actions by Bank Islam against errant employees and contractors done to appease state and get funds back, and actions taken in compliance by federal government-owned companies such as Petronas and Telekom to blacklist any doctors or lawyers who sided with opposition candidates).

[254] Jain 1986 (n 74 above) 214.

[255] See eg WT/WGTGP/M/15 (n 236 above) ¶ 13 (relating statement by Malaysian representative: 'Developing countries ha[ve] difficulties with essentially two elements, namely domestic review procedures and the application of WTO dispute settlement procedures. Although the details of some other elements might also cause some difficulties, by and large, they were acceptable.'); 42 (relating comments by the Singapore representative: '...a bid challenge mechanism was an integral part of national procurement systems.'); WT/WGTGP/M/17 (n 236 above) ¶ 65 (relating comments by the US representative: 'Without a link to the DSU, an agreement could not be effective.').

public procurement discussed during the meeting, accusing supporters of these texts of undermining Malaysian attempts to ensure greater economic equality for native Malays:

…We strongly oppose the agenda to open up markets for Government procurement, which is being discussed at the WTO forum in Cancun. Once again, the West is using the WTO to push forward their agenda for economic colonisation. If we do not oppose this agenda, our efforts to implement the National Development Policy, which safeguards the interests of domestic entrepreneurs, including Bumiputera as well as the objective of promoting domestic industries, will not be achieved.[256]

On 16 December, 2003, meetings held to overcome the impasse of the Cancun Ministerial also ended in failure.[257] Among the issues still dividing WTO Members was whether discussions regarding a potential TGP agreement should move into actual negotiations on a multilateral agreement.[258] The official position of a group of developing countries (including, *inter alia*, Malaysia, India, Pakistan, and China) was that 'all further work' on the subject, apparently including even work at the WGTGP, 'should be dropped'.[259] There seems to have been some willingness to compromise on the part of developed country members demonstrated by concessions made in the interim between submission of the original and the revised daft ministerial texts at Cancun, but it was not enough. Suspicion that an agreement on TGP was to be 'a stalking horse for the expansion of the GPA' continued,[260] as did general developing country unhappiness with the proposed TGP texts themselves and the possible expansion of 'behind-the-border' rule-making, which it and companion initiatives on other Singapore Issues represented.[261]

A deal was subsequently struck between developed and developing country members to restart Doha Round negotiations that had floundered in Cancun.[262] The highlight of the deal was the establishment of a framework according to which members would negotiate an agreement, which would ultimately eliminate agricultural export subsidies and significantly reduce domestic agricultural support.[263] The framework also contained a provision that suspended indefinitely all work on

---

[256] M Mahatir, 'The 2004 Budget Speech' (12 September 2003) para 99 (official translation).

[257] See '16 December 2003 General Council: Follow-up to the Cancun Ministerial Conference: Chair wraps up: groups can restart, but still no deal on tough issues', WTO News, available at <http://www.wto.org/english/news_e/news03_e/stat_gc_chair_16dec03_e.htm> (hereafter WTO News: 16 December 2003).   [258] ibid.

[259] Joint Communication for Bangladesh (on behalf of the LDC Group), Botswana, China, Egypt, India, Indonesia, Kenya, Malaysia, Nigeria, the Philippines, Tanzania, Uganda, Venezuela, Zambia, and Zimbabwe; Singapore Issues: The Way Forward, WT/GC/W/522 ¶ 6 (12 December 2003).   [260] Abbott (n 219 above) 287.

[261] ibid.

[262] 'Round-the-Clock Meeting Produces Historic Breakthrough', WTO News—2004, available at <http://www.wto.org/english/news_e/news04_e/dda_package_sum_31july04_e.htm> (visited 15 August 2004).

[263] See Decision Adopted by the General Council on 1 August 2004, Doha Work Programme, WT/L/579 ¶ 1(a)–(b) (2 August 2004) (hereafter Doha Work Programme).

negotiating an agreement on TGP.[264] The need to achieve a consensus among the members had resulted in the ability of those hostile to the development of a multi-lateral agreement dealing with transparency in government procurement to prevent it being put on the agenda for further trade liberalization negotiations. Or, put differently, those in support of an agreement on TGP had failed to convince all those whose support was necessary for its acceptance, that the benefits it could offer outweighed what it could cost.

The story of the failure of the TGP agreement is one of complexity and uncertainty, particularly regarding the role that Malaysia played. We can regard it either as the story of a self-interested elite attempting to hold on to the tools of political patronage, or as the story of a country strong enough to hold out against the imposition of principles that are unsuitable. Such policies as preferences for less economically powerful members of society could be made much more difficult to handle in the context of a full panoply of administrative law controls of the type included in the draft TGP agreements. Should we see the administrative law controls in the draft agreements as merely part of a strategy to open market access to powerful Western economic interests, underpinning an 'Economic constitutionalism . . . [which] . . . attempt[s] to treat the market as a constitutional order with its own rules, procedures and institutions, operating to protect the market order from political influence',[265] and threatening the types of programmes that had allowed Malaysia to become one of the most successful countries in Southeast Asia? For Janis van der Westhuizen, without the maintenance of networks of influence sustained by programmes such as the contract preferences, 'Malaysia's adaptation to the competition state model would have been even more difficult, complex and unstable.'[266]

Nor is it clear whether this is a story of a temporary stalling in the movement towards global procurement regulation by a small group of countries that are *sui generis*, or whether it indicates a much greater scepticism among a larger group of countries that is only slowly beginning to build. For example, in the case of Malaysia, the retirement by Prime Minister Mahathir and his replacement by Abdullah Ahmad Badawi may have created a shift in attitudes within the Malaysian executive that would be more favourable towards an agreement on TGP.[267] It is too early to tell, but this indicates the need for any theorizing about

---

[264] ibid ¶ 1(g) ('Relationship between Trade and Investment, Interaction between Trade and Competition Policy and Transparency in Government Procurement: the Council agrees that these issues, mentioned in the Doha Ministerial Declaration in paragraphs 20–22, 23–25 and 26 respectively, will not form part of the Work Programme set out in that Declaration and therefore *no work towards negotiations on any of these issues will take place within the WTO during the Doha Round.*') (emphasis added).

[265] See K Jayasuriya, 'Governance, Post-Washington Consensus and the New Anti-Politics' in T Lindsey and H Dick (eds), *Corruption in Asia: Rethinking the Governance Paradigm* (Federation Press, 2002) 24, 31.

[266] J van der Westhuizen, Adapting to Globalization: Malaysia, South Africa, and the Challenges of Ethnic Redistribution with Growth (Praeger, 2002) 91.

[267] See S Jayasankaran, 'The New Way: Thinking Small', Far Eastern Economic Review (6 November 2003) 14. Since taking office Badawi has publicly made cleaning up governmental

the development of global public procurement regulation to take into account the development dimension in a way that accommodates this complexity.

European Commission, the United States, and Myanmar

We turn, finally, to examine the response to the use by states in the United States of procurement to influence events in Burma. The European Commission was active in protesting against United States federal, state, and local sanctions measures when they had purported extraterritorial effect. The best-known dispute involved the application of the Helms-Burton legislation to European companies.[268] As part of its strategy of putting pressure on the United States to modify this legislation, the EU threatened to ask a WTO disputes panel to adjudicate on a complaint by the EC that the legislation was contrary to WTO disciplines, and in October 1996 officially did so.[269] As part of these general concerns about the extraterritoriality of such laws, the European Commission also formally complained to the United States in January 1997, regarding the Massachusetts legislation, and threatened to invoke the WTO dispute settlement procedure if the issue was not resolved satisfactorily.[270] The Commission's concern had been heightened by the likelihood of similar legislation being enacted by Massachusetts and other states regarding other countries with dubious human rights records. Legislation was pending in Massachusetts prohibiting the award of contracts to those doing business in or with Indonesia.

The issue was not settled diplomatically, despite consultations organized under the auspices of the WTO between the United States, the EC and Japan, another concerned party. Following this lack of success, the EC formally requested consultations with the United States under Article 4(4) of the Dispute Settlement Understanding (DSU) in June 1997,[271] despite a resolution of the European Parliament opposing such a move.[272] Japan requested to join these consultations under Article 4(11) of the DSU.[273] In a subsequent communication of July 1997, Japan independently requested consultations on the same matter,[274] which the

---

corruption, particularly in the area of government procurement, a focus of his administration. S Jayasankaran, 'Tycoons in Trouble', Far Eastern Economic Review (15 January 2004) 50.

[268] See E Vermulst and B Driessen, 'The Choice of a Switch: The European Reaction to the Helms-Burton Act' (1998) 11 Leiden Journal of International Law 81.

[269] United States—The Cuban Liberty and Democratic Solidarity Act, WTO Doc WT/DS 38/2 (1996).

[270] EU, Amicus Curiae Brief in Support of Plaintiff National Foreign Trade Council, Appendix 4 (hereafter EC Brief).

[271] United States—Measure Affecting Government Procurement; Request for Consultations by the European Communities, WT/DS88/1; GPA/D2/1, 26 June 1997.

[272] C 200 [1997] OJ 0174.

[273] United States—Measure Affecting Government Procurement; Request to Join Consultations; Communication from Japan, WT/DS88/2; 2 July 1997.

[274] United States—Measure Affecting Government Procurement; Request for Consultations by Japan, WT/DS95/1; GPA/D3/1, 21 July 1997.

EC in turn requested to join.[275] In addition, the issue was the topic of 'intensive discussions between the European Union and the United States at the highest levels, including at the bi-annual EU-US Summit'.[276]

The discussions on state and local government selective purchasing laws, such as the Massachusetts legislation, took place in the context of wider-ranging negotiations on US extraterritorial economic sanctions generally. The EU and the United States agreed at the EU-US Summit on 18 May 1998 on a set of principles covering the future use of sanctions in the context of the Transatlantic Partnership on Political Co-operation.[277] This included agreeing that the EU and the United States 'will not seek or propose, and will resist, the passage of new economic sanctions legislation based on foreign policy grounds which is designed to make economic operators of the other behave in a manner similar to that required of its own economic operators'. Such sanctions will be targeted 'directly and specifically against those responsible for the problem'.[278] It was also agreed that it was in the interests of both the EU and the United States 'that the policies of governmental bodies at other levels should be consonant with these principles and avoid sending conflicting messages to countries engaged in unacceptable behaviour'.[279] As a result of this agreement, the EU formally withdrew its complaint to the WTO against the United States regarding Helms-Burton.[280] However, the discussions failed to resolve the Massachusetts legislation issue, and in September 1998, the Japanese government asked the WTO to establish a dispute panel on the issue,[281] followed by the European Commission.[282] International and European trade union federations immediately denounced the EU's action.[283] The United States blocked the establishment of a panel at that time, but following a renewed request[284] a panel was established on 21 October 1998.[285]

The European Commission was of the opinion that the Myanmar legislation was in breach of the GPA in three respects.[286] First, it was alleged to violate Article VIII(b) of the GPA, on the basis that it imposed conditions on a tendering company which were not essential to ensure the firm's capability to fulfil the contract. Second, it was alleged to infringe Article X of the GPA because it imposed qualification criteria based on political rather than economic considerations. Third, it was

[275] United States—Measure Affecting Government Procurement; Request to Join Consultations, Communication from the European Communities, WT/DS96/2; 30 July 1997.

[276] EC Brief, (n 270 above) 6–7.

[277] See 'Brussels and US End Sanctions Dispute' *Financial Times*, 19 May 1998.

[278] EU-US Summit, London, 18 May 1998, 'Transatlantic Partnership on Political Co-operation'.

[279] EC Brief, 9.

[280] 'EU Drops WTO Helms-Burton Suit' (1998) 12 Export Practitioner 5.

[281] 'Japan Seeks WTO Panel to Repeal Massachusetts Law' *Japan Economic Newswire*, 9 September 1998.   [282] *Bulletin Quotidien Europe*, No 7306, 23 September 1998, 11.

[283] 'EU Accused of Condoning "Pariah" Burma with WTO Action', Agence Fr Presse, 21 September 1998 (objection by the International Confederation of Free Trade Unions and the European Trade Union Confederation).   [284] WT/DS88/3, 9 September 1998.

[285] WT/DS88/4; WT/DS95/4, 11 January 1999.

[286] WT/DS88/1; GPA/D2/1.

to honour international commitments it has entered into in the framework of the World Trade Organisation'.[310]

In response, Massachusetts made several arguments but one was of general importance in the context of this discussion, as it related specifically to the fact that the challenged law related to public procurement. Essentially, the state argued that the use of the state's procurement power turned the state into a 'market participant', and in doing so enabled the state to rely on an exception that the Supreme Court had recognized in the domestic Commerce Clause context. If this argument were to be successful, the Supreme Court would have had to accept that the use of procurement brought the state within the market participant doctrine. Second, the Supreme Court would have had to accept that the 'market participant' defence was still applicable in the domestic Commerce Clause context. Third, the Court would have had to be willing to apply the doctrine to the Foreign Commerce Clause. Fourth, the Court would have had to consider whether a similar doctrine would apply in the context of the Foreign Affairs Clause. In expressly declining to address either the foreign affairs power or the Foreign Commerce Clause issues, and instead deciding on the statutory pre-emption issue, the Supreme Court took the narrowest approach it could, leaving the broader issues to another day. Controversy continued, however, on how broad or narrow the statutory pre-emption decision should be interpreted as being.[311] The success of the constitutional challenge meant that the EC and Japan considered that it did not need to pursue its WTO challenge. In February 1999, it had requested the Panel to suspend its work.[312] The Panel was not asked by the EC or Japan to resume its work, and the authority for the Panel lapsed as of 11 February 2000.[313]

---

[310] ibid 2.

[311] For a discussion of the literature, see eg Symposium: 'Whither Zschernig?' (2001) 46 Villanova Law Review 1259.   [312] WT/DS88/5; WT/DS95/5, 12 February 1999.

[313] WT/DS88/6; WT/DS95/6, 14 February 2000.

PART III

EQUALITY LINKAGES AND THE EUROPEAN COMMUNITY

10

Procurement Linkages and the 1980s Reform of EC Procurement Regulation

In Part II of this book, we examined the detailed discussions that took place during the 1950s and 1960s, leading to the development of the Government Procurement Agreement (GPA) 1979. We then considered the effects, direct and indirect, on procurement linkages of the 'GPA model' on members of the GPA (in particular the United States and Canada) and non-members (in particular Malaysia, South Africa, and in relation to Myanmar). In this third part of the book, we turn to examine the development of European approaches to procurement linkages aimed at securing greater status equality. We shall see that, of the two models of procurement regulation discussed in chapter 8 above, the EC has tended to pursue the second (efficient procurement) model, whilst the GPA has tended to pursue the first (market access) model, with important consequential effects on the approach that Community law has taken to procurement linkages. However, this general orientation has been significantly modified to accommodate (some) domestic procurement linkages. In this chapter, the approach taken to domestic procurement linkages during the fist wave of European procurement reforms of the 1980s is examined. We begin, however, by examining the extent of equality-promoting domestic procurement linkages in EC Member States just prior to these reforms. We shall see that such linkages were particularly in play in Britain, Northern Ireland, and Germany.

I. United Kingdom Initiatives in the 1960s and 1970s

Developing linkages in Britain in the 1960s

The use of the British government's contracting power to counter racial discrimination was increasingly advocated by equality campaigners from 1966.[1] In February 1966, the employment panel of the National Committee for Commonwealth Immigrants proposed that a provision should be included in the contract of anyone supplying goods or services to the government, committing the contractor not to practice or condone discrimination on the grounds of colour, race, religion, ethnic, or

---

[1] See B Hepple, *Race, Jobs and the Law in Britain* (2nd edn, Penguin, 1970) 276.

national origin in engaging, training, promoting, or discharging any persons in his employment, or when fixing any terms or conditions of employment.[2] In July 1966, James Callaghan, the Home Secretary and responsible for race relations, announced to the House of Commons that consultations were taking place between government departments and those outside government on whether the principle of non-discrimination should be introduced 'in a particular contract or in government contracts generally'.[3] The government approached the Confederation of British Industry (CBI) and the Trades Union Congress (TUC) separately, and each had reservations.[4] In 1967, the Street Report, unofficial but highly influential, recommended that a non-discrimination clause should be embodied in a resolution of the House of Commons as the Fair Wages Resolution (examined in chapter 2 above) had been.[5] It was proposed that the clause should then be included in all government contracts. (Other public bodies, including nationalized industries and local authorities, would be left to decide for themselves whether to incorporate a similar provision.) Contractors should be required, however, not merely to refrain from discrimination but also to take 'affirmative action' to ensure that minority group persons were employed. Little more was heard in public about this use of the government's procurement power until 1969, following the enactment of the first legislation tackling racial discrimination in employment, the Race Relations Act 1968.

In October 1969, Roy Jenkins, the Chancellor of the Exchequer and responsible for procurement, announced in Parliament that a non-discrimination clause would be included in United Kingdom government contracts, requiring 'contractors in the United Kingdom to conform to the provisions of the Race Relations Act 1968 relating to discrimination in employment. Government departments will be required to withhold contracts from firms practising racial discrimination in employment.'[6] The Race Relations Board, a government enforcement body for race equality, was subsequently given an extra-statutory (and very limited) role. A procedure was introduced whereby the contracting department would be notified in cases where the Board, after finding discrimination by the contractor, had been unable to resolve the matter through the provisions of the Act, and had decided not to take proceedings. The British scheme was developed, then, without explicit Parliamentary approval, but in the context of, and arising out of, the development of the Race Relations Act 1968.

Attempts to reform the British scheme 1968–85

Assessments of the separate British scheme adopted in 1968 were uniformly sceptical that it had had any significant effect. The Race Relations Board continually

---

[2] ibid.   [3] Official report, vol 731 HC, 5 July 1966, cols 238–239 (5 July 1966).
[4] TUC Report, 1967, 267–8 from which the following account of discussions between the Government and the TUC is taken.
[5] H Street *et al, Street Report on Anti-Discrimination Legislation* (Political and Economic Planning, 1967) paras 192–194.
[6] Official Report, vol 788 HC, 22 October 1969, cols 296–297 (written answer).

stressed the inadequacy of the British scheme set up in 1969 in comparison with that envisaged by the Street Report.[7] In its report on British race relations policy, the Central Policy Review Staff (CPRS), a unit within the central civil service, noted in the early 1970s that there had been no attempt to enforce the provisions of the anti-discrimination clause in British government contracts.[7a] The terms of the clause, and the cumbersome machinery for enforcing it, appeared to reinforce the widespread impression inside and outside government that contracting departments regarded convenience in contracting as more important than equal employment opportunity, and the CPRS recommended substantial changes. The CPRS proposed that contractors for business worth more than £100,000 should be required at the time of tender to furnish evidence of the steps they had taken to introduce equal employment policies within their own organization. In the absence of such evidence, contracts should be withheld. Regular reports should be furnished during the contract period. The CPRS also recommended that responsibility should be laid on the Race Relations Board, or its successor, to survey the employment policies and practices of such contractors. Later, a Select Committee of the House of Commons put forward similar proposals drawing on United States experience.[8]

During the parliamentary discussions on the Sex Discrimination Bill in 1975, an attempt was made to include a provision requiring government contractors to adhere to a non-discrimination clause.[9] This was rejected. In the second chamber, the House of Lords, a similar attempt was made to include a mandatory disqualification of contractors found to have been discriminating, from tendering for public contracts of central and local government for a period to be determined by a county court judge. Again this was rejected.[10] There were several objections put forward. First, this involved a 'double penalty only for certain types of persistent offender; namely the one who has an interest in public contracts'.[11] Second, it was likely to be unworkable: 'Let us take a case involving an important new defence contract where one of the sub contractors is one of these persistent offenders. However—and this is where I suspect that the parallel with the United States is not a particularly strong one—he may well be involved in supplying a part for, let us say, an armoured fighting vehicle, or a radar installation, he may be the only person capable of supplying that part.'[12]

In 1975, in the White Paper 'Racial Discrimination', the government did put forward plans for a limited revision of the non-discrimination contract clause with regard to race. It stated that it intended, when new legislation was enacted, to require contractors to give a similar undertaking to comply with its provision as

---

[7] Race Relations Board (RRB) Report for 1971–2, para 95; RRB Report for 1972, para 60; RRB Report for 1973, para 64.   [7a] Central Policy Review Staff, *Report on Race Relations* (1973).
[8] See UK Parliament, HC, Select Committee on Race Relations and Immigration, 'Organisation of Race Relations Administration, Report' (HMSO, 1975) paras 54–59.
[9] Official Report, 893 HC, 18 June 1975, cols 1478–1482.   [10] ibid col 1390.
[11] Official Report, 362 HL, 17 July 1975, cols 1478–1482 (Lord Harris).
[12] ibid col 1389.

had previously been required regarding the 1968 Act. The government had, however, also considered 'whether [the government's] duty to take an active role to eliminate discrimination requires something additional'. Thenceforth, 'it should be a standard condition of Government contracts that the contractor will provide on request to the Department of Employment such information about its employment policies and practices as the department may reasonably require'. It would be an 'unacceptable burden', however, to require all contractors 'to supply as a matter of form full particulars of their employment policies'.[13]

Both the Confederation of British Industry (CBI) and the Engineering Employers' Federation (EEF) opposed even these limited proposals.[14] The CBI objected to the principle of enforcing government policy through contracts, and doubted the effectiveness of such a policy. The EEF believed that it would place an intolerable burden on companies. In addition, the EEF did not believe that the termination of a contract should depend on a requirement to produce information. On the other hand, the Race Relations Board criticized the proposals, in particular, for not requiring that contractors take 'affirmative action' of any kind. 'There are undoubtedly legal problems associated with the formulation of contractual terms but it should be possible at least to establish minimum requirements such as those contained in Federal Government contracts in the U.S.'[15] Nor did the proposals contain any indication what (if any) sanctions would be imposed on contractors. Though there would be circumstances where the ultimate sanction of refusal to grant contracts would be difficult to apply (especially in monopoly or near monopoly situations), the Board argued that many contractors operated in competitive conditions where the sanction of debarment could be effective. Even without the use of debarment, a system of graduated sanctions might be developed: for example the publication of the names of contractors who refused to comply; reference by the Department to the Commission for Racial Equality (the CRE, the enforcement body which was the successor of the Race Relations Board) for investigation; or a recommendation of criminal proceedings if false information is supplied.[16] The enforcement mechanism chosen was also criticized by the Board: 'We find it remarkable that the [CRE] is given no role at all. It remains our view that the main policing role should be given to the Commission with contracting departments having the ultimate responsibility for determining what action should be taken against a defaulting contractor.'[17]

Although there were proposals, during the parliamentary stage of the Race Relations Bill in 1976, that equivalent provisions be included,[18] the government rejected all such attempts with the assurance that discussions with the CBI and the Trades Union Congress (TUC) would continue after the Bill was passed.[19] There

[13] UK Government White Paper, 'Racial Discrimination' (Cmnd 6234, HMSO, 1975) para 20.
[14] See IRRR No 121, February 1976, 14.   [15] RRB Comments on the White Paper, para 9.
[16] ibid para 10.   [17] ibid para 11.
[18] See eg Runnymede Trust, 'Race Relations Bill Briefing Group', Brief No 1, Government Contracts and their Role in Promoting Equal Opportunity in Employment (nd).
[19] Official Report, Standard Committee, 24 June 1976, col 755 (Mr Grant).

were periodic reviews of central government policy between then and 1985, but these did not lead to the limited contract provision described above being strengthened, or being extended to include sex discrimination.

Procurement and Northern Ireland anti-discrimination policy

The situation was different in Northern Ireland. In Britain, it was as part of the limited set of reforms introduced in 1969 that linkage between procurement and anti-discrimination legislation first appeared, but in Northern Ireland it arose in the absence of anti-discrimination legislation and to some extent instead of such legislation.

A commitment was first given in October 1969 that Northern Ireland government contracts would contain an anti-discrimination provision prohibiting religious discrimination. Contractors were to be required to complete an undertaking not to practise religious discrimination in hiring or terminating employment during the performance of the contract.[20] Departments were not to consider a tender from a contractor who failed to complete the undertaking. The contractor was to commit himself to taking all reasonable steps to secure the observance of the terms of the undertaking by all subcontractors employed in the execution of the contract. Where a nominated subcontractor was to be employed, the contracting department was required to procure an undertaking in similar terms from the subcontractor. Where there was no nominated subcontractor, this was to be the responsibility of the main contractor. In turn the subcontractor was to agree to take all reasonable steps to secure the observance of the terms of the undertaking by all subcontractors employed by the first subcontractor. Any person who considered himself to have been discriminated against in his employment or intended employment on a government contract might complain to the contracting department. The department would refer the complaint to the Northern Ireland Parliamentary Commissioner for Administration who would investigate on an extra-statutory basis, and, if he found the case proven, try to achieve a settlement. If the Commissioner was unsuccessful in his efforts to achieve a settlement, the department concerned would then consider the action which should be taken. This would normally involve the debarring of the contractor from tendering for any government contract for a stipulated period.[21]

Procurement linkage in Northern Ireland 1973–80

Although originally introduced instead of anti-discrimination legislation, when such legislation was eventually introduced in the 1970s, procurement linkages

---

[20] Undertaking not to practise Religious Discrimination. Explanatory note to tenders (MF 79/1 and 2); Main Contractor Undertaking (MF 79); Subcontractor Undertaking (MF 80A).

[21] cf Northern Ireland Parliamentary Commissioner for Administration, 1971 Annual Report, para 15.

were retained. A government committee established to consider the issue of employment discrimination legislation (the van Straubenzee Working Party)[22] recommended that new anti-discrimination legislation should be enacted, but it also considered that the procurement tool should be retained. It advised that the Fair Employment Agency (the government body responsible for enforcing the legislation) should take over the function of the Parliamentary Commissioner in enforcing the Northern Ireland government contract provisions,[23] and the government accepted this. An additional scheme was also recommended and incorporated in the legislation enacted in 1976. The Fair Employment Act 1976 provided[24] that the Fair Employment Agency was to invite such organizations as appeared to it to be representative of employers, of organizations of workers, and of persons engaged in occupations in Northern Ireland to subscribe to a declaration of commitment to the principle of equality of opportunity[25] and to encourage their members to subscribe to it. The Agency was also to use its best endeavours to encourage all employees and all vocational organizations to subscribe to the declaration. The Agency was to keep a register of those who subscribed to the declaration, and each employer or organization whose name was on this register was entitled to receive from the Agency and to hold a certificate describing her, him, or it as an equal opportunity employer or organization.[26]

The published list of those who had signed the declaration was to be distributed to all public authorities.[27] The Minister in the debates noted that he assumed that government departments 'will take into account those who are and those who are not registered'.[28] Enoch Powell, MP, rather more directly stated that there was 'a clear implication in the body of the clause that the public service in deciding between two contractors or two persons who may offer their services or sell their goods or services to a public authority should prefer the persons who were on the list of declarants to those who were not'.[29] This appears to have been assented to by those on the government front bench. At the end of 1981, the government announced that from April 1982, tenders for government contracts would not normally be accepted from firms within the scope of the Act unless they held an equal opportunity certificate issued by the Agency.[30]

The Fair Employment Agency was empowered under the Act to require a declarant, as a condition of remaining on the register, to reaffirm at such intervals and in such manner as the Agency might determine, an intention to adhere to the declaration. More importantly, the Agency was empowered to remove from the

---

[22] Northern Ireland Government, 'Report and Recommendations of the Working Party on Discrimination in the Private Sector of Employment' (HMSO, 1973).   [23] ibid para 141.
[24] Fair Employment Act 1976, s 6.
[25] Known as the Declaration of Principle and Intent, Sch 3.
[26] Fair Employment Act 1976, s 7.   [27] ibid s 9.
[28] Official Report, Standing Committee on the Fair Employment Bill, 5th day, col 222.
[29] ibid cols 219–220.
[30] Official Report, HC, 10 December 1981, col 473 (written answer).

alleged to be contrary to Article XIII(4)(b) to the extent that the statute allowed the award of contracts to be based on political instead of economic considerations.[287] Fourth, it was alleged that Article III, prohibiting discrimination, had been breached. 'The Law', it was said, 'does not provide to the suppliers of other Parties offering products or services of the Parties immediate and unconditional treatment no less favourable than that accorded to domestic services and suppliers and that accorded to services and suppliers of any other Party.'[288] Finally, there was an argument that even if there was no breach of these provisions, the actions of the state constituted a nullification or impairment of the concessions that the United States accepted in the Agreement, 'particularly as it limits the access of EC suppliers to procurement by a sub-federal authority covered by the [Agreement] in such a way so as to result in a de facto reduction of the US sub-federal offer under the GPA'.[289] In its request for consultations in July 1997, Japan formally complained to the United States, citing Articles III(2), VIII(b), X, and XIII(4) of the GPA.[290]

There was extensive publicity about these provisions in the specialist press in the United States and Europe. Much of it focused on the desirability of selective purchasing as a tool of public policy;[291] the extent to which the individual states were subject to federal foreign policy; the compatibility of the Massachusetts law with American constitutional law;[292] and the political implications of intervention by the WTO. There was much less discussion of the compatibility of such legislation with the GPA. Where compatibility with the GPA was discussed, discussion tended to focus on whether Massachusetts was bound by the GPA. The issue involved two interlinked questions: first, did the United States include Massachusetts in its offer to other countries as to what was included as a sub-federal entity,[293] and second, if the United States did so, did it do so legitimately

---

[287] The request for the establishment of the Panel did not state the point quite so baldly. Instead it says that 'by imposing a 10% price increase on the basis of whether or not a company does business in or with Myanmar, the Law violates the basic GPA requirement embodied inter alia in Article XIII.4(b)'.   [288] EC Request for Establishment of a Panel.

[289] EC Request for Consultations.

[290] WT/DS95/1; GPA/D3/1. See also *Inside US Trade*, 25 July 1997, 14.

[291] See, in particular, the testimony by various individuals, companies and groups on the proposed Massachusetts Indonesia legislation. Those against included: the Institute for Training and Development, Associated Industries of Massachusetts, the Alliance for the Commonwealth, United Parcel Service, the American Indonesian Chamber of Commerce. Those in favour included Professor Richard Falk, the Robert F Kennedy Memorial Center for Human Rights. See MS Lelyveld, 'Corporate giants take on state in sanctions fight' *Journal of Commerce*, 3 March 1997, 1A.

[292] GG Yerkey, 'Administration Still Has No Policy on State, Local Government Sanctions' (1997) 14(28) International Trade Reporter 1176–7.

[293] The modifications to the Annex submitted by the United States and the European Community following the bilateral agreement reached between the EC and the US in Marrakesh in April 1994 (see G de Graaf and M King, 'Towards a More Global Government Procurement Market: The Expansion of the GATT Government Procurement Agreement in the Context of the Uruguay Round' (1995) 29(2) The International Lawyer 435, 448–51) specifically included Massachusetts. They were notified to the WTO in a communication dated 22 December 1995 (WTO, Interim Committee on Government Procurement, Modifications to Appendix I of the European Communities and the United States, GPA/IC/10, 16 January 1996), p 8).

under United States law?[294] In contrast, the legality of the legislation under the GPA 1994 if the state was bound by it received little academic or public attention. On this issue, many commentators assumed the legislation to be incompatible with the GPA, but without detailed analysis of why that might be the case.[295]

The EU's complaint to the WTO drew opposition from some members of the United States Congress. As a sign of its displeasure, in September 1997, the House of Representatives passed an amendment to a 1998 appropriations Bill. This diverted US$1 million from the Department of Commerce's budget to the United States Trade Representative's Office in order to fund it to report to Congress, state, and local governments whenever a foreign government initiated an action in the WTO that could affect United States laws.[296] In August 1998, the House narrowly defeated an amendment to an appropriations Bill that would have barred the federal government from spending money to challenge any state or local law on the ground that the measures were inconsistent with international agreements. This would have limited the federal government's ability to litigate against a state that was found by a WTO disputes panel to violate WTO disciplines. In the discussions prior to the vote, the USTR indicated that the federal government had never sued a sub-national body in the fifty years in which GATT had issued rulings but stopped short of a commitment not to sue Massachusetts.[297] It seemed unlikely that the United States government would take legal action against Massachusetts (or indeed any other state enacting similar legislation) under its authority under United States law to enforce the WTO Agreements. The indication was that the federal government supported Massachusetts in the complaint made by the EC in Geneva.[298] More generally, however, the Administration had now moved to a position that state and local legislation of this type would cause more harm than good, due in part to its effect on United States trade agreements.

---

[294] This issue, involving the authority of the US to put Massachusetts forward as part of its proposals, arose because of the way in which the US chose to deal with the tricky political issue of how best to involve the separate states in the WTO process. The US asked the states to agree to be included under the GPA. Thirty-seven states agreed to be covered by the GPA 1994. Of the 37, however, there was considerable variation in the extent to which their executive branch agencies were covered. Several 'only agreed to coverage of selected executive branch agencies, or excepted significant sectors', C Tiefer, 'The GATT Agreement on Government Procurement in Theory and Practice' (1997) 26 University of Baltimore Law Review 31, 39 (1997). A letter from Massachusetts Governor William Weld to the then United States Trade Representative Mickey Kantor stated that he had reviewed the terms of the Agreement and that Massachusetts 'has no present intention of going against it'. In the controversy surrounding the Myanmar legislation, an argument was made that this was both ambiguous and in any event an inadequate legal basis on which to regard the state as legally committed to the Agreement. See MS Lelyveld, 'Weld letter a new wrinkle in EU-Massachusetts spat' *Journal of Commerce*, 13 March 1997, 5A. See further A Carvajal, 'State and Local "Free Burma" Laws: The Case for Sub-national Trade Sanctions', 29 Law and Policy in International Business 257, 265.

[295] K A Elliott, 'Backing Illegal Sanctions' *Journal of Commerce*, 6 August 1997, 8A.

[296] HR 2267.

[297] J Lobe, 'Clinton Manages to Avert Blow to WTO's Power', Inter Press Service, 7 August 1998; MS Lelyveld, 'Anti-sanctions Forces Win Key Vote' *Journal of Commerce*, 7 August 1998, 1A.

[298] 'US Vows to Defend Sanctions by State' *Journal of Commerce*, 11 September 1998, 3A.

This could be seen, in particular, in the State Department's opposition to state legislation on Nigeria.[299]

Restructuring the Myanmar legislation in order to bring it within the provisions of the GPA 1994—by applying the legislation only to those contracts below the GPA thresholds, excluding the application of the law to tenderers from states which are party to the GPA—appears to have been explored in negotiations between the EC and the United States, and between the United States and Massachusetts. The federal government advocated that states should avoid the potential legal problems under the GPA by attaching such policies to contracts below the thresholds for the GPA. Indeed, after intervention by the State Department, the Massachusetts legislature amended the Indonesia legislation to apply the conditions to contracts below the GPA threshold.[300] Essentially, this approach avoided a conflict on the point of principle.[301] Prior to the filing by the European Commission of its *amicus curiae* brief in the constitutional challenge (discussed below), it seemed possible that the Massachusetts Myanmar issue might be similarly resolved. Reportedly, the chief sponsor of the legislation, state Representative Byron Rushing, proposed an amendment that would have exempted contracts above the GPA 1994 threshold from the 10 per cent penalty on procurement imposed on companies doing business in Burma in order to resolve the US-EU WTO dispute.[302] However, it was subsequently reported that state Representative Rushing had made clear that amending the Myanmar legislation to apply it only below the threshold would be more difficult following the European Commission's intervention.[303]

United States Constitutional arguments

Instead, however, the National Foreign Trade Council (NFTC), which represented about 580 United States companies, challenged the constitutionality of the Myanmar legislation under the United States Constitution.[304] The arguments on the question of the constitutionality of the Massachusetts law under United States

---

[299] See Testimony of Deputy Assistant Secretary David Marchick before the Maryland House of Delegates Committee on Commerce and Government Matters, 25 March 1998. See also 'Sanctions Bid Against Nigeria Stirs Ire' *Washington Post*, 27 March 1998.

[300] cf House Bill 3730, An Act regulating state contracts and investments with companies doing business with or in Indonesia, with House Bill 4575, An Act regulating state contracts and investments with companies doing business with or in Indonesia. The latter, which was the Bill favourably reported out of the Committee on State Administration in July 1997, inserted a provision limiting coverage of the legislation to contracts below the GPA thresholds in cases where the state agency is subject to the GPA.

[301] When President Clinton promulgated this executive order prohibiting the acquisition of products produced by forced or indentured labour, Executive Order 13126 of June 12, 1999, it covered only those purchases not covered by the GPA or NAFTA, see Executive Order 13126, s 5(b).

[302] 'NFTC Files Suit Contesting State and Local Sanctions' (1988) 12 Export Practitioner 5.

[303] 'EU in Burma Law Protest' *Financial Times*, 13 July 1998.

[304] The text of the complaint can be found at <http://usaengage.org.archives/background/lawsuit/nftcindex.html>.

constitutional law were complicated and controversial.[305] The NFTC argued that the legislation was unconstitutional on three broad grounds. The first argument, and the one that eventually succeeded before the Supreme Court, was that federal Congressional action against Burma in 1996, some three months after the enactment of the Massachusetts legislation, pre-empted states from enacting laws of the Massachusetts type. The state argued that there was no express pre-emption by Congress of such legislation. Indeed, Congress had given implicit permission to such legislation, since Congress knew when it acted that Massachusetts had already acted as it had and did nothing to stop it. The Supreme Court held that the law was indeed pre-empted by the actions of Congress, because it stood as 'an obstacle to the accomplishment of Congress's full objectives under the federal Act'.[306]

The other two arguments that were made by the NFTC were much broader, essentially posing the problem as one between 'our desire to speak with one voice on international trade and our desire to have a federal system', a conflict 'exacerbated by the increasing need to engage in international relations, to cover more areas in international trade'.[307] The first of these broader arguments was that by enacting this type of legislation, with the implications it had for foreign relations, the state hindered the ability of the United States to speak with 'one voice' on issues of foreign relations, and also discriminated against foreign commerce, contrary to the Foreign Commerce Clause of the Constitution. The second of these broader arguments was, somewhat similarly, that the Foreign Affairs Clause of the Constitution prohibited the state from unduly interfering with the ability of the United States government to conduct foreign affairs. The United States District Court for the District of Massachusetts had, indeed, held the legislation to be unconstitutional because it impermissibly impinged on the federal government's power to regulate foreign affairs.[308] The EU had submitted an *amicus curiae* brief in support of the NFTC's action in July 1998. The brief set out the 'concrete and negative ramifications that the Massachusetts Burma law is having on the EU's dealings with the United States, in terms of both foreign policy and commercial relations'.[309] In particular, the brief stressed that the law 'has created a significant issue in EU-US relations, including raising questions about the ability of the US

---

[305] More extensive discussions on the constitutionality of the Massachusetts Myanmar law can be found in D Schmahmann and J Finch, 'The Unconstitutionality of State and Local Enactments in the United States Restricting Business Ties with Burma (Myanmar)' (1997) 30 Van JTL 2; A Carvajal, 'State and Local "Free Burma" Laws: The Case for Sub-national Trade Sanctions' (1998) 29 LPIB 257; DM Price and JP Hannah, 'The Constitutionality of United States State and Local Sanctions' (1998) 39 Harv ILJ 443. For a discussion of the constitutionality of proposed legislation by Massachusetts relating to Indonesia, see DR Schmahmann, J Finch, and T Chapman, 'Off the Precipice: Massachusetts Expands Its Foreign Policy Expedition from Burma to Indonesia' (1997) 30 Van JTL 1021.   [306] *Crosby v National Foreign Trade Council* 530 US 363 (2000) 374.
[307] Prof Joel Trachtman, quoted in Symposium: New York Law School Centre for International Law: 'States' Rights vs International trade: The Masschusetts Law' (2000) 19 New York Law School Journal of International and Comparative Law 347, 353.
[308] *NFTC v Baker and ors* 26 F Supp 2d 287 (D Mass, 1998).   [309] EU Brief, 2.

register the name of any person who, amongst other things, was found by the Agency, in consequence of an investigation under the 1976 Act, to have acted in a manner inconsistent with adhering to the declaration.[31] When an employer's name was removed from the register, the Agency was required as soon as reasonably practicable to notify the removal to all the relevant public authorities. In addition, the published list of those who signed the declaration was distributed to all public authorities[32] and where a public authority formed the opinion that a contractor had acted in the course of performing a contract entered into with the authority in a manner inconsistent with the term of the declaration and his name had not already been removed from the register, the authority was required to inform the Agency of this opinion stating the reasons for it.[33] A person aggrieved by the removal of his name from the register could appeal to an Appeals Board against the removal.[34]

In its subsequent assessment of the operation of the Northern Ireland arrangements at the end of the 1980s, the Standing Advisory Commission on Human Rights (SACHR) found that these previous attempts to promote equality of opportunity through the award of contracts and grants had proved ineffective. What was lacking was an adequate mechanism to ensure that those who received contracts had actually fulfilled their commitment to refrain from discrimination and to provide equality of opportunity. Originally, as we have seen, the Northern Ireland Parliamentary Commissioner for Administration was given responsibility for overseeing this undertaking on an extra-statutory basis. It was envisaged that the Parliamentary Commissioner would be able to receive a complaint from an employee, or an applicant for employment, about a contractor's actions, and would investigate that complaint. This arrangement had little impact. For whatever reason, the Parliamentary Commissioner was seldom, if ever, asked to use his extra-statutory power to oversee the effectiveness of a contractor's commitment not to discriminate. Subsequently, under the arrangements introduced to run in parallel with the 1976 Act, possession of a certificate was also little guarantee that an employer was providing equality of opportunity, or even attempting to. This meant that government contracts were awarded to those employers who had made a commitment on paper to the declaration, not necessarily to those who actually attempted to provide equality of opportunity. The mechanism had not been an effective way of promoting compliance with the contractual undertaking.[35]

Reformed fair employment legislation and procurement linkage

In the late 1980s, as part of an overall reassessment of anti-discrimination law, the Northern Ireland Department of Economic Development proposed in its Consultative Document that the principle of linking the receipt of contracts to the provision

---

[31] Fair Employment Act 1976, s 7.   [32] ibid s 9.   [33] ibid s 9(4).   [34] ibid s 8.
[35] Standing Advisory Commission on Human Rights, 'Report on Fair Employment' (Cm 237, 1987, HMSO) (hereafter SACHR, Fair Employment) ch 9.

of equality of opportunity should be continued.[36] It proposed that the government should only accept tenders for contracts from employers who had been certified as equality of opportunity employers.

SACHR also recommended that public contracts and grants should normally only be awarded to employers who subscribed to a new declaration of practice and possessed a new certificate. However, a revised mechanism was set out which would allow the new Agency to assess whether those subscribing to the declaration were following the key elements of equality of opportunity contained in it. Improved opportunity for oversight was recommended, and only employers who carried out the declaration of practice would be allowed to retain an Equal Opportunity Employer Certificate. SACHR recommended that all public authorities should be subject to equivalent requirements.

SACHR specifically warned that it would be necessary to ensure that employers who normally operated outside Northern Ireland would not be prevented from tendering for contracts by the new arrangements. In an early indication of issues to come, it warned that in particular it would be important to avoid any conflict with the provisions of the EEC Treaty. Such companies would usually only begin to employ workers in Northern Ireland after the receipt of a contract. It would therefore be unreasonable to expect them to be reviewed before the award of the contract so that they might receive a certificate and thereby qualify for access to the list of tenderers. SACHR recommended that employers normally operating outside Northern Ireland but who tendered for contracts which entailed the employment of labour within Northern Ireland should be required to subscribe to the declaration only upon receipt of that contract and they would be granted a certificate if they did so. Certificates would have to be renewed in the ordinary way during the period in which the employer was operating in Northern Ireland.[37]

The approach recommended by the Department of Economic Development and by SACHR was a system of pre-award certification for most employers. This was not, however, the system finally adopted in the Fair Employment (Northern Ireland) Act 1989. Instead, a system was adopted which used government contracts and grants as a final sanction against an employer that was acting contrary to the provisions of the legislation in a recalcitrant way. The legislation imposed significant duties on employers to take 'affirmative action' where the employer's workforce did not accord 'fair participation' to either religious community in Northern Ireland. The legislation provided that both government contracts and government grants may be withdrawn in cases of persistent and recalcitrant behaviour (where the respondent was deemed to be 'in default'), thus placing contract

---

[36] Northern Ireland Government, Department of Economic Development, 'Equality of Opportunity in Employment in Northern Ireland' (1986) 29–31.

[37] SACHR, Fair Employment (n 35 above) para 9.95.

compliance on a statutory footing.[38] An employer was regarded as 'in default', for example, where the employer had failed within the time allowed to serve a monitoring return and he or she had been convicted of an offence in respect of that failure, or where the employer had failed to comply with an order of the Fair Employment Tribunal (for example to engage in 'affirmative action') and a penalty had been imposed.[39]

Where an employer was in default, the Fair Employment Commission (the body replacing the Fair Employment Agency) could serve notice on him stating that he was not 'qualified'. The Commission was required to take all such steps as it considered reasonable to bring the fact that a person was an unqualified person, or had ceased to be an unqualified person, to the attention of public authorities. An application could be made by the person on whom the notice was served to have it revoked, but such an application could not be made sooner than six months after the notice was served, or more frequently than at six-monthly intervals. The applicant could appeal to the Fair Employment Tribunal against the refusal. Where a public authority entered into a contract either made by the public authority accepting an offer made by any person, being an offer made in response to an invitation by the public authority to submit offers, or falling within a class or description for the time being specified in an order made by the Department, the public authority was required to take all steps as were reasonable to secure that no work was executed or goods or services supplied for the purposes of the contract by any unqualified person. A public authority could not enter into any such contract with an unqualified person.

These restrictions did not apply to the execution of any work, or the provision of any goods or services, by any person, which was certified in writing to be necessary or desirable by the Secretary of State for the purpose of safeguarding national security or protecting public safety or public order, or by the Secretary of State, by the Department of Economic Development or, after consultation with that department, by any other Northern Ireland department (1) for the purpose of securing works, goods or services which could not otherwise be secured without disproportionate expense, or (2) in the public interest.

Although nothing in these provisions affected the validity of any contract, there were other specific enforcement procedures. The Fair Employment Commission (FEC) could require any person to give it such information as it specified for the purpose of determining whether a contract of either of the two kinds specified above had been made or was likely to be made, or whether any person had executed any work or supplied any goods or services for the purposes of any such contract, or was likely to do so. The FEC could apply to the High Court for an injunction restraining a public authority from contravening the prohibition on contracting with an unqualified person and requiring the authority to comply

---

[38] Fair Employment Act (Northern Ireland)1989, ss 38–43.
[39] For an earlier discussion of this system, see R Fee and A Erridge, 'Contract Compliance in Canada and Northern Ireland: A Comparative Analysis', 8th International Annual IPSERA Conference, 1999.

with that prohibition in two circumstances. First, it could take such action if it appeared to the FEC that the public authority had taken any action in contravention of the prohibition stated above or had, in neglecting to take any action, failed to comply with that prohibition, and that, unless an injunction was granted, the authority was likely again to contravene or fail to comply with that section. Second, the FEC could take such action where any public authority proposed to take any action in contravention of the prohibition. In addition, any contravention of or failure to comply with the prohibition was actionable by any person who, in consequence, suffered loss or damage, but the amount recoverable in any such action could not exceed any expenditure reasonably incurred by him before the date of the contravention or failure in question.

The legislation further provided that Northern Ireland departments could refuse to give to any unqualified person specific types of financial assistance or, where it had given or agreed to give such assistance to any unqualified person, refuse or cease to make any payments to him in pursuance of the assistance. This provision applied to any financial assistance by way of grant or otherwise which could be given at the discretion of a Northern Ireland department, if the moneys required for giving the assistance were payable out of the Consolidated Fund of Northern Ireland or were appropriated by Measure of the Northern Ireland Assembly.

These enforcement provisions of the legislation were seldom operated. The FEC disqualified only one employer who defaulted from obligations under the legislation. Following the conviction of the employer for failing to submit a monitoring return with the prescribed period, and his subsequent refusal to make a proper return, an FEC notice disqualifying him was issued, with the consequences described above.[40] Within a month, the employer complied with the legislation by completing a monitoring return, and as a result the Commission lifted the disqualification notice.[41] The British government viewed the provisions as 'working well': 'indeed there is every reason to suppose that their very existence was a major factor in achieving the high level of compliance by employers with the new registration and monitoring duties in the Act'.[42]

II. Developing Procurement Linkages in Germany

Overview of German procurement law up to the mid-1990s

Germany had no special government procurement code until it was effectively required to have one by EC law. Even that was relatively late in coming, really only coming into existence by the late 1990s.[43] Prior to that, the private law of

---

[40] FEC Press Release, 24 October 1991.   [41] FEC press release, 25 November 1991.

[42] Letter from N Robinson, Department of Economic Development, to T Carlin, NIC ICTU, 3 August 1992.

[43] This paragraph relies heavily on the following articles: N Cleesattel, 'Government procurement in the Federal Republic of Germany' (1987) 21 GW JILE 59 and C Lamm, 'Vergaberecht in Deutschland' (1992) 2/3 Europäisches Vergaberecht 90.

contract contained in the German Civil Code (Bürgerliches Gesetzbuch—BGB) applied. Above this in the hierarchy of legal requirements lay the German Basic Law (Grundgesetz—GG). In addition, several other Acts imposed relevant constraints on public bodies fulfilling public tasks: the Administrative Procedures Acts on the federal and Länder level (Verwaltungsverfahrensgesetz—VwVfG); the General Terms and Conditions Act (Gesetz zur Regelung des Rechts der Allgemeinen Geschäftsbedingungen—AGBG); the Unfair Competition Act (Gesetz gegen den unlauteren Wettbewerb—UWG); the Anti-trust Act (Gesetz gegen Wettbewerbsbeschränkungen—GWB); and (possibly) the Works Constitution Act (Betriebsverfassungsgesetz—BetrVG).

The Principles of Federal and States Budgetary Law Act (Haushaltsgrundsatzgesetz—HGrG)[44] established rules for state and federal government spending and authorized the Ministries to issue regulations. The supervision of awarding public sector contracts came within the jurisdiction of the Ministries of Finance, which were required to draw up a budget under the terms of the Basic Law and the constitutions of the individual Länder.[45]. This 'entitles the Administration to spend monies and incur commitments'.[46] The Principles of Federal and States Budgetary Law Act (HGrG), the Budgetary Codes governing the Federal Authorities and the Länder (Budget Code for the Land (Landeshaushaltsordnung— LHO), and the Federal Budget Code (Bundeshaushaltsordnung—BHO)) included provisions on the procedures to be followed. For example, the BHO (Federal Budgetary Regulations)[47] required in principle that a public tender procedure be implemented before contracts should be concluded for the supply of goods and services, and that it 'must be on uniform lines'.[48] Construction work, major procurements, and development expenditure could not be implemented or commenced until adequate documentation was available.[49] In addition, the award of public sector contracts was subject to the governing principle of 'compliance with the basic criteria of economy and value for money',[50] given that this is all part of the budgetary plan.

A uniform series of administrative provisions concerning both tendering procedures and contract conditions were promulgated for use by public authorities. These regulations included the Verdingungsordnung für Leistungen (VOL) and the Verdingungsordnung für Bauleistungen (VOB). The VOL was the tendering ordinance for services. The VOB was the tendering ordinance for building contracts. VOL was divided into two parts: Section A contained the terms of procurement; Section B contained contractual regulations. All government contracts at the federal level were subject to the procedures set out in the VOL/A and VOB/A,[51]

---

[44] Gesetz über die Grundsätze des Haushaltsrechts des Bundes und der Länder (1969), BGB1.I 1273.   [45] cf Basic Law, art 110, s 1.
[46] Federal Budget Regulations, para 3, s 1.   [47] HGrG, para 30 and para 55, s 1.
[48] BHO, para 55, s 2.   [49] HGrG, paras 16 and 29.   [50] BHO, para 7, s 1.
[51] VOL was originally developed before the Second World War, and VOL/A was amended in 1984 and 1990. VOL/B was amended in 1992.

which in turn contained a binding recommendation that the purchasing agency include in its requests for tender the general conditions of contract provided in the VOL/B and VOB/B, which set out the general conditions of contract for government sponsored contracts. These provisions 'had the legal character of merely internal rules of good administration only. Thus they bound the executive powers only, but gave no legal right to aggrieved tenderers.'[52] In a major change brought about by EC law, at the end of 1992 a new legal provision was enacted,[53] which 'requires the application of VOL/A and VOB/A by all awarding authorities listed whenever the contract in question is above the threshold value for the application of the E.C. procurement rules. Due to this incorporation into the regulation, VOL and VOB become legally binding with effect erga omnes.'[54]

The most important provisions in the context of this discussion were briefly as follows: contracts were to be awarded to professional, competent, and reliable tenderers at appropriate prices.[55] The basic rule was competition: improper or unsavoury concomitant practices must be resisted. All competitors must be treated equally.[56] Other sections provided justification for excluding an applicant or tenderer from a competitive tender process or from having his tender appraised if certain personnel-related characteristics or features were present. Competitors in default of certain statutory obligations, such as the obligation to pay social security contributions, could be excluded from the tender process.[57] The supplier bore sole responsibility for compliance with all statutory, official, and trade association responsibilities in respect of his employees.[58] Bids from tenderers who were not members of the relevant trade association would be excluded.[59] If there were several bids that met the specifications in every respect, the award should be made to the bid which seemed to be the most acceptable taking into account all the technical and economic aspects.[60] The award should be made to the bid which met the terms and conditions and the principles outlined and which was the most economical taking due account of all circumstances.

The most economical bid was determined not only on the basis of the lowest bid. According to Lamm, the most favourable bid was the bid that achieved the most favourable relationship between the contract work desired and the price offered. The contract work encompassed all circumstances relating to the contract. Some social policies could also be taken into consideration in the valuation, but only when this had been expressly stated in the performance specifications, since only then could all bidders make allowances for it. For this reason, appropriate

[52] A Niedzela, 'Recent Legislation on Public Procurement in Germany: Measures for Implementing the E.C. Procurement Rules' (1994) 3 PPLR CS44, CS45.
[53] Verdingungsordnung für Bauleistungen Teil A—VOB/A.
[54] Niedzela (n 52 above) CS45.
[55] VOB/A, para 2, s 1; VOL/A, para 2, s 1 is drafted in identical terms to VOB/A, para 2, s 1.
[56] VOB/A, para 8, s 1, cl 1.   [57] VOB/A, para 8, s 4, sub-s 1, lit d.
[58] VOB/D, para 4, s 2, sub-s 2; VOL/B, para 5, s 1, cls 3 and 4 is drafted in identical terms to VOB/B, para 4, s 2, sub-s 2.   [59] VOB/A, para 25, section 1, sub-s 1, lit c.
[60] VOB/A, para 25, section 2, sub-s 2, cls 2 and 3.

notification should be included in the performance specifications to permit the contracting agency to fulfil particular responsibilities, such as in the area of environmental protection.[61]

Use of procurement linkages other than for equal status goals

According to Menzel,[62] any company that paid its employees, as a whole or only female employees, a lower wage than the compulsory minimum wage agreed industry-wide for that sector, or any company which failed to make a financial outlay on prescribed measures to promote health and safety at work, was easily able to submit a lower bid than a competitor which was complying with all such regulations. This gave him or her a competitive advantage in the bidding process, but at the cost of the employees. This should be assessed as an 'improper or unsavoury subsidiary effect',[63] if one understood this somewhat dated expression to mean an infringement of the practices followed by a proper and orderly business. He pointed out that the German Supreme Court (Reichsgericht) had stated before the Second World War that a low bid which was based on wages below the industry-wide agreed levels was improper and unfair. According to Menzel, the construction industry forbade contractors in the rules governing competition to adopt a pricing policy 'which consciously prevents the upholding of commitments to . . . the workforce'. A working group at the Federal Ministry of Construction decided accordingly in 1978 in its new Guidelines on the Assessment of Tender Offers that prices calculated by bidders should be scrutinized so as to ensure that wage costs were shown at industry-wide agreed levels and that general site costs included adequate provision for measures to ensure health and safety at work and accident prevention.[64]

In an article published in 1988, Strohs[65] singled out North Rhine-Westphalia as best known of all the Länder for its policy of awarding public sector contracts with labour market and employment policy aims in mind. For example, companies that trained apprentices were given preferential consideration when public sector contracts were awarded. Depending on the value of the order, the tender price submitted by such companies could be between 0.5 and 6 per cent more than the otherwise cheapest tender. When contracts were awarded it was also permissible to specify that environmentally friendly products should be offered whenever possible (particularly those bearing the environmental logo) or that environmental friendliness would be taken into account when the various bids were assessed. The award of public sector contracts was also used to fight illegal

---

[61] C Lamm, 'Vergaberecht in Deutschland' (1992) 2/3 Europäisches Vergaberecht 90,100.

[62] H-J Menzel, 'Berücksichtigung sozialpolitischer Kriterien bei der öffentlichen Auftragsvergabe', 6 *Der Betrieb* (DB) 6 February 1981, 303.   [63] VOB/A and VOL/A, para 2, s 1.

[64] in accordance with VOB/A, para 25.

[65] M Strohs, 'Die Berücksichtigung vergabefremder Kriterien bei der Vergabe von Bauaufträgen durch die öffentliche Hand' 2 BauR 2/88, (1988) 144.

employment practices and black market labour on government building contracts. Illegal employment practices included circumstances in which an employer made employees available to a third party for professional, paid work without having the requisite licence under the terms of the Supply of Employees Law. Black market labour was defined in the Law for the Prevention of Black Market Labour as including a situation in which a person pursues a trade as an 'established profession' on an independent basis without being registered on the Roll of Craftsmen.

Several other Länder adopted environmental clauses in their government contracts. The Land government of Lower Saxony set as its objective the improvement of environmental protection by means of an environmentally aware policy of public procurement. The Lower Saxony Economics Ministry issued a Circular Order[66] which instructed public sector purchasing and procurement bodies to make an exemplary contribution to the achievement of the objectives of the reduction of waste materials, the minimization of pollutants or dangerous materials in waste, the recycling of unavoidable waste materials, and a reduction in the use of energy and water.

The award of public sector contracts was also used to limit the extent of employment which was not subject to social security contributions. The Federal Code of Social Law (Sozialgesetzbuch—SGB) excluded certain activities from compulsory social security contributions. These rules stated that a certain level of remuneration (in the old Länder, DM560; in the new Länder, DM440 (1994 figures)), and a certain period of time (15 or 18 hours a week), must not be exceeded. In particular, when cleaning contracts were awarded in the public sector, some local authorities and Länder provided that companies which were to receive cleaning contracts must only employ persons for whom compulsory social security contributions must be paid or must employ a certain percentage of such persons. Administrative regulations of this sort existed, for example, in Hamburg and Berlin. In Hamburg, office cleaning firms had to agree in any cleaning contracts they concluded with the City of Hamburg that they were prepared to be monitored by a special inspection centre set up at Guild Headquarters, and to submit all requisite documents to this centre. It was therefore possible to check whether the agreed ratio of employees paying compulsory social security contributions was actually observed in practice when the cleaning contract was carried out. Any infringements might mean that no new contract was signed in future with that particular company.

The federal Law on Disabled Persons stated that public sector contracts which could be implemented by workshops employing disabled persons should be offered on a preferential basis to these workshops.[67] Workshops for disabled persons were institutions designed to bring disabled persons into employment. They offered

---

[66] Öffentliches Auftragswesen: Berücksichtigung des Umweltschutzes, Niedersächsisches Ministerialblatt, No 32, 30.9.92.   [67] Federal Law on Disabled Persons, para 56.

disabled persons who, as a result of their disability or its gravity were not able to fulfil a role on the general employment market or who were not yet able to return to such a role, a place of work or opportunity to exercise a form of work appropriate to them. The Federal Minister of Economics, in conjunction with the Federal Minister of Labour and Social Affairs, issued guidelines on the award of public sector contracts to workshops for disabled persons. This preferential award treatment also applied to workshops employing blind people along the lines of the Law on the Sale of Goods made by the Blind. If contracts were suitable for companies employing disabled persons, these companies must be given 'preferential tendering conditions'. The contract was awarded to a bidder from amongst the circle of people defined in the guidelines even if the bidder quoted a price that, within certain margins, was greater than the cheapest bid from a competitor. In other words, the social policy objective (for example compensation for physical infirmities or the desire to integrate the disabled into the labour market) was given greater weight than the mere satisfaction of the subject matter of the contract, and justified an increased call on budgetary resources.

Länder were also active in this area. In 1979, for example, the Hamburg District Parliament decided that when public sector contracts were awarded, the only companies to be considered for such awards were those which proved that they: had a Works Council and a body representing young people, as provided for in the Works Constitution Act (BetrVG); paid their employees at least the agreed minimum wage for their sector; paid men and women equal pay; complied with all relevant health and safety at work regulations; provided for vocational training; and employed the number of severely disabled people specified in the Law on Disabled Persons.[68]

Use of procurement linkages for equal status goals

In the late 1970s, the German Social Democratic Party (SPD) and trades union circles increasingly advocated that public sector contracts should be awarded to private companies on the basis of greater awareness of the way in which they treated their employees (with rewards for those which treated them well).[69] A DGB (German Trades Unions Federation) Draft Declaration of Principles included the following: 'public sector contracts and subsidies for the economy must be linked to employment policy criteria and compliance with protective social provisions'. These pressures were particularly directed at the Länder that were controlled by the SPD or by SPD/Green coalitions. During the period in which the SPD, on the federal level, was in a coalition government with the Federal Democratic Party (FDP), the Federal Ministry of the Interior developed a

---

[68] Letter from Prof U Rust to the author.   [69] Menzel (n 62 above) 303.

draft anti-discrimination law which included a provision making the award of government contracts and grants conditional on the development of equal opportunity plans.[70] A Committee of Enquiry of the federal German Parliament which considered the issue in 1980 recommended: 'if public funds are being expended ... voluntary aims and objectives or initiatives by companies to improve the professional opportunities open to women at work should be made compulsory; ... the obligation to develop plans on these lines [should be included] in guidelines governing the award of public sector contracts ...'.

Draft Bills were placed before the federal German Parliament specifying a linkage between the award of public sector contracts and measures to promote equality of opportunity and treatment for women. These included a draft equality law put forward by the SPD on equality for men and women in 1988,[71] and a 1994 draft for an equality law also contained similar proposals,[72] although these draft laws were not passed. Equivalent initiatives were more successful in the Länder, influenced partly by developments in Britain and the United States.[73]

Conditions designed to promote equality of treatment and opportunity for women were introduced in North Rhine-Westphalia. A circular from the North Rhine-Westphalian Minister of Economics in 1983[74] required that where equivalent bids were submitted, preferential treatment should be accorded companies training apprentices when public sector contracts were awarded. The requirement was renewed until 31 December 1988 by a circular of 18 December 1986. Special preferential treatment was introduced at the same time for those businesses which, compared with other companies, offered a higher ratio of apprentice and trainee places to young women in trades, with a training period of at least three years. Various other additional provisions relating to this requirement were introduced in a further circular of 8 October 1987. The order of 29 November 1983 was extended indefinitely, by a circular of 21 November 1988.

The Berlin Equality Law of 1990[75] included a provision on the promotion of equality for women by means of the contract award process.[76] This stated that when contracts were concluded for goods and services costing more than DM 10,000, if several bidders were similarly qualified, preference should be given to the bidder who could prove that he or she had implemented a special scheme for

---

[70] HM Pfarr and L Eitel, 'Equal Opportunity Policies for Women in the Federal Republic of Germany' in G Schmid and R Weitzel (eds) *Sex Discrimination and Equal Opportunity: The Labour Market and Employment Policy* (Gower, 1984) 174.

[71] BT-Drucksache 11/3728, 13 December 1988. This contained clauses linking public procurement with equality for women. Modifications were proposed (in Arts 20 and 21) of the Haushaltsgrundsätzegesetz and the Bundeshaushaltsgesetz.

[72] BT-Drucksache 12/5717, also published in Recht der Arbeit 1994, 34 *et seq.*

[73] U Knapp, 'Betriebliche Frauenförderpläne und Strukturpolitik', WSI Mitteilungen 11/1990, 738.

[74] Nordrhein-Westfalen: Bevorzugte Berücksichtigung von Lehrlingsausbildungsbetrieben bei der Vergabe öffentlicher Aufträge.

[75] Landesgleichstellungsgesetz (formerly: Landesantidiskriminierungsgesetz, 31 December 1991, GVBl 1991, 8 of 18.1.1991, as amended) GVBl 1993, 184 of 13.4.1993.

[76] 31 December 1990, para 13.

the promotion of equality of treatment and opportunity for women in professional life. This positive action programme ('positive action' was increasingly the term used in Europe instead of 'affirmative action') must contain a fixed timetable for increasing the number of women. The person letting the contract must establish which organizational measures should generally be taken by the tenderer in order to increase the number of women in areas in which they were underrepresented. A tenderer was to be considered as comparably well qualified with another even if the price of the first tender was above the price of another within a range prescribed in a Schedule to the Act. Someone who had a positive action plan was regarded as equal to someone who did not, even though the price they were offering to complete the tender exceeded that of the company without the positive action plan, within limits prescribed by the Schedule. For example, a person with a positive action plan putting in a tender price of DM5,000 could be 6 per cent higher than another tender and still be regarded as equal; up to DM1 million, it was up to 0.5 per cent. In addition, contracts were generally not to be awarded to bidders who employed persons for whom social security contributions were not payable. The legislation provided, however, that a special law would subsequently be passed regulating in detail the type of companies involved, the content of the equality plans that should be introduced, and the control of the implementation of the plans.

III. Legislative Reform of the Procurement Directives 1986–92

We now consider the development of the European public procurement directives during the late 1980s and early 1990s from the perspective of the debate on whether such linkages as we have seen being developed in the United Kingdom and Germany should be permitted by European public procurement rules.[77] The debates on the reform of the procurement directives in the 1980s were the first time that issues of status equality were raised directly in the context of international or regional procurement reform efforts.

Some context

The period of EC legislative activity between the mid-1980s and the early 1990s was primarily focused on making concrete the overall strategy of reform in public procurement, a daunting task given the considerable political complexities. It was, therefore, a period of great uncertainty in which the philosophy underpinning the reform programme was struggling to be accepted. Speed was perceived to be of

---

[77] For general discussions of the background to and the development of these directives, see F Weiss, *Public Procurement in European Community Law* (Athlone Press, 1993), and JA Sohrab, 'The Single European Market and Public Procurement' (1990) 10 OJLS 522.

the essence, otherwise the momentum would be halted. Partly because of this, the issue of how far to allow a linkage between public procurement and equality considerations was very much a 'sideshow' to the main performance, which was how to operationalize competitive tendering.

The dichotomy between the social and the economic approaches to public procurement issues, did, however, come strongly to the fore during the period of legislation. The difference of approach taken by the Council of Ministers and the Parliament is a paradigm illustration of the dichotomy influencing policy-making in public procurement discussed in chapter 8 above, with the Commission attempting to reach an uneasy compromise between the two. The European Parliament tended to adopt a strongly instrumental view of the role of public procurement, advocating strong links between public procurement and achieving social policy objectives. The Council of Ministers, on the other hand, tended to adopt a strong, though in some cases tempered, 'purity principle', whereby the economic function of competition in public procurement should not be tainted by social policy diversions. The greatest pressure to include social issues came from the majority of the Parliament that, together with a loosely organized group of trade unions and others, sought to persuade the Commission and the Council of Ministers to incorporate them. It is important for what follows, however, to understand that, at that time, the Parliament had no effective power to require the Commission or the Council to adopt its viewpoint, even when the majority of the Parliament agreed that they should. Although the social policy of the Community was developing rapidly at the time these procurement debates were taking place, the perceived need for trade-offs between the social and the economic was still weak in this period.

An important additional concern reflected in the legislative history of the directives adopted in the 1980s is the issue of subsidiarity. A clear difference emerges between an approach that concentrates on the *Community* setting mandatory requirements regarding the linkage between social policy and public procurement, and the Community permitting *Members States* to adopt such a linkage if they wished. Connected to this was the issue of power relations between central and local (or regional) government in some states. Giving a discretion to the Member State might increase the power of the central government over sub-central government.

It will make the following account of the debates surrounding social linkages somewhat easier to understand if it is appreciated that for much of the period under consideration three types of social linkages were in issue: first, a provision designed to guarantee that all contractors, ie both domestic contractors and those from another Community country (or non-Community country), respect the existing terms and conditions of workers in the place where the work is carried out; second, a provision designed to allow public authorities to discriminate in favour of contractors who give preference in their hiring to certain categories of workers, such as the long-term unemployed, young people, the disabled, women, and ethnic minorities; and, third, a provision designed to allow public authorities to continue to exempt some regions or parts of them from the full opening of public procurement in order to assist their development. Of the social issues in contention, the issues of regional preferences in particular tended to be seen as politically the most important. Indeed, it seems likely that failure to resolve this issue would have resulted in failure to pass the directives.

Much the greatest controversy from the Commission's perspective arose, then, from the third category, concerning the regional preference clause. The debate on this issue markedly affected the acceptability of the second, and to some extent the first. The debate on regional preferences was highly polarized. One other factor is particularly relevant, before we turn to the details of the debate. The negotiations for a new Government Procurement Agreement (GPA) within the WTO framework were taking place during this period.[78] The Community found itself under pressure on preferences in the context of these negotiations. Reactions to the types of clauses listed above were to some extent affected by a view that any preferences set out in the directives were likely to create greater negotiation difficulties for Commission negotiators.

Status equality and the Supplies Directive

The debate on the inclusion of an equality clause in the Supplies Directive was crucial. It largely determined the approach adopted by the Council in the context of the other directives. The Commission proposed a draft of a revised Supplies Directive in June 1986.[79] This was subsequently amended by the Commission, largely to take account of GPA requirements.[80] Neither included any new provisions relating to social issues. After referral by the Commission to the Parliament, the Committee on Economic and Monetary Affairs and Industrial Policy reported, and the Committee on Legal Affairs and Citizens' Rights produced an opinion.[81] No social provisions were mentioned in either report.

In July 1987, however, the Parliament recommended, after the first reading of the draft directive, that the draft be amended to include social linkages. The legislative resolution of the Parliament stated that the Parliament: 'Recognizes that public purchases and contracts may constitute an important part of a government's policy of job creation and regional assistance; emphasizes therefore, that any system regulating the placing of public supply contracts must take into account the need to reduce regional disparities and to create jobs and industries in those areas which are either underdeveloped or experiencing acute industrial decline.' It also recognized 'that public purchases and contracts may constitute an

---

[78] See A Halford, 'An Overview of E.C.-United States Trade Relations in the Area of Public Procurement' (1995) PPLR 35.   [79] COM(86)297 final [1986] OJ C173/4.

[80] COM(87)233 final, 27 May 1987 [1987] OJ C161/10.

[81] Doc A2-100/87 (rapporteur Mr B Beumer), 25 June 1987.

important part of a government's policy of promoting equal opportunities at the workplace; [it] emphasizes therefore that any system regulating the placing of public supply contracts must take into account the need to reduce discrimination against women, ethnic minorities and the disabled at work'.[82]

Following this, in October 1987, the Commission produced a revised proposal.[83] The Commission's amendment provided that contracts could be refused where the contractor bidding 'does not fulfil obligations relating to employment rights and protection of equal opportunities in accordance with the statutory provisions of the country in which he/she is established'. It would also have inserted an article dealing with regional preferences that permitted 'until 31 December 1992, the application of existing national provisions which have as their objective the reduction of regional disparities and the promotion of job creation in regions whose development is lagging behind and in declining industrial regions, on condition that the provisions concerned are compatible with the Treaty and with the Community's international obligations'.

On 5 October 1987, however, the Council of Ministers adopted a 'Common Position'[84] which disagreed with the proposal of the Commission, and did not include the Commission's amendments. Opposition to such measures appeared to be on two grounds: the inappropriateness of a social provision in an economically-related directive, and the difficulty of interpretation and implementation of such a provision. In its Communication to the Parliament, however, the Commission stated that it understood that the Council had 'indicated readiness to continue examination' of the issue. The Commission made clear its view that 'given the link between respect for employment and equal opportunities obligations and the competitive position of bidders, a provision similar to that contained in its proposal constitutes a necessary part of the directive'.

At the end of November 1987, the Parliament's Economic Committee reported on its recommendation for the second reading.[85] This report recommended the inclusion of a provision linking status inequality with the distortion of economic advantage, and a provision on regional preferences. In addition, it included a further provision which would have allowed a restricted procedure to be adopted if 'there is a need to promote equal opportunities in order to combat discrimination against women, ethnic minorities and the disabled at the workplace'. On 16 December 1987, following the report from its Economic Committee, the Parliament in its second reading adopted proposals including a regional preferences provision, and, most importantly, one which drew a link between status

---

[82] [1987] OJ C246/84.

[83] Second alteration of the Proposal for a Council Directive amending Directive 77/62/EEC relating to the coordination of procedures on the award of public supply contracts and deleting certain provisions of Directive (EEC) 80/767, COM(87)468 final, 2 October 1987.

[84] Doc C 2-184/87.

[85] Recommendation for the second reading drawn up by the Committee on Economic and Monetary Affairs and Industrial policy (rapporteur, Mr B Beumer), Doc A2–228/87.

equality and market distortion.[86] The latter would have amended the draft Directive to provide that a tenderer could be excluded where he or she 'is distorting his/her economic advantages by failure to comply with the statutory obligations relating to health and safety at work and equal opportunities for the women, handicapped and racial or religious minorities of the country in which he/she is established'.

A new proposal was published by the Commission in February 1988.[87] The approach taken was largely to follow that adopted by the Parliament. With regard to the equal opportunities issue, the Commission proposed to insert two new preliminary recitals, and a revised article. The recitals attempted to link equality issues with free market arguments. One argued that 'the principle of equal pay for men and women is established by the Treaty; and . . . the directives on equal pay and equal treatment for men and women contribute to ensuring fair competition'. Another stated that 'failure to comply with statutory obligations regarding health and safety at work and equal opportunities for the handicapped and racial or religious minorities can enable a supplier, in certain circumstances, to derive unfair economic advantage'. The revised article provided that suppliers could be excluded where the supplier 'is distorting competition to its economic advantage by its failure to comply with the statutory obligations of the country in which it is established, relating to health and safety at work and equal opportunities for women, the handicapped and racial or religious minorities'. The Commission also proposed an article equivalent to that discussed before on regional preferences. On the 22 March 1988, the Council adopted the Directive, including the regional preferences provision, but refused to adopt the Commission's other proposals regarding status equality.

Status equality and the Works Directive

In December 1986, the Commission had sent the Council a proposal for a directive amending Directive (EEC) 71/305 on public works contracts.[88] In May 1988, the Parliament gave its opinion on the proposal, in which it suggested a number of amendments.[89] These included a provision requiring notification of employment and working conditions to contractors, and a provision permitting contracting authorities to require as a condition for participation in a contract measures aiming to alleviate youth and long-term unemployment, among others. Equal opportunities issues were not included directly.

---

[86] [1988] OJ C13/62.
[87] Re-examined proposal for a Council Directive amending Directive (EEC) 77/62 relating to the coordination of procedures on the award of public supply contracts and deleting certain provisions of Directive (EEC) 80/767, COM(88) 42 final/2, 17 February 1988 [1988] OJ C65/5.
[88] COM(86)679 final of 23 December 1986.   [89] 18 May 1988 [1988] OJ C167/64.

The Commission adopted some of the suggested amendments in its amended proposal of June 1988.[90] The Commission proposed: to include a provision allowing contracting authorities to take account in awarding contracts of attempts to tackle problems of long-term and youth unemployment; and to include a provision to ensure transparency with regard to the conditions of employment which contractors would have to observe in the country in which the project is to be carried out. Since the Directive amending the Supplies Directive had, as we have seen, been adopted on 22 March 1988, the Commission considered that the amendments introduced into the Works Directive needed to be aligned with those of the new Supplies Directive, and in particular that the use of regional preferences would need to be aligned. The Commission proposed, therefore, to include a provision on preferential treatment of contractors on regional policy grounds. The Commission also proposed that a provision should be included which would create an exception to the mandatory application of the normal award criteria (lowest price/most economically advantageous tender), where the Member State based the award of contracts on other criteria whose aim was to give preference to certain tenderers.

The Beentjes *case*

It is at this point that the first major European Court of Justice (ECJ) intervention occurred. In Case 31/87, *Beentjes*,[91] the ECJ considered a request for a preliminary ruling made by a Dutch court.[92] The proceedings before the Dutch court concerned a decision to award a public works contract. Beentjes had submitted the lowest bid, but the contract had been awarded to another bidder. Several reasons were given for preferring the other bid, including that Beentjes was not able to employ long-term unemployed persons. The awarding authority had stated this as a necessary condition. Beentjes challenged the decision contending that the Works Directive precluded the contracting authorities from taking account of this consideration. The ECJ was asked whether the ability of contractors to provide work for the long-term unemployed could be taken into account by the national awarding authority under the Works Directive (Directive (EEC) 71/305), if in the invitation to tender no criteria of this type had been stipulated. The European Court interpreted this question as raising two different issues: first, could such considerations be taken into account at all; and second, if they could be taken into account, was the awarding authority required to notify them to bidders in advance?

The ECJ emphasized in its decision that the directive was not intended to regulate procurement exhaustively in the Member States. The Court concluded that the condition relating to long-term unemployed persons was not precluded by the

---

[90] COM(88)354 final of 21 June1988.   [91] [1988] ECR 4635.

[92] For a discussion of this case, see S Arrowsmith, *A Guide to the Procurement Cases of the Court of Justice* (Earlsgate Press, 1992) 73–82.

directive. However, the Court held further that the policy could only be lawful if it was transparent and otherwise consistent with Treaty principles, which excluded practices operating in a discriminatory manner. The Court did not itself decide on whether the conditions taken into account did or did not discriminate, which was left to the national court.

Legislative activity following Beentjes

The Council Common Position of 4 November 1988[93] did not accept the Commission's suggested amendments permitting conditions relating to the long-term unemployed and youth unemployment, and adopted a modified provision regarding notification of employment and working conditions which did not make it mandatory on the Member States, but optional. The Council, in explaining its decision on the former issue, stated:

The Council and the Commission consider that, in certain circumstances, public-works contracts can help find solutions to the problems raised by long-term unemployment and the employment of young people. In this context they take into account the judgment of the Court of Justice in Case 31/87 [*Beentjes*, which had been decided on 20 September, two months before] ... The Council invites the Commission to monitor the forms and circumstances in which measures to encourage the employment of the long-term unemployed and young persons are applied, in particular so as to avoid any discrimination. If it sees fit, the Commission will make specific proposals in this respect.[94]

The Report of the Parliament's Economic Committee[95] on the long-term unemployed and youth unemployment issues stated, however, that: 'The Commission takes the view that a specific provision would nevertheless still be useful so as to facilitate monitoring of these measures in the context of public sector markets.' Regarding the provision on working conditions, the Committee reported against the voluntary approach of the Council Common Position and in favour of a mandatory approach previously preferred by the Parliament and the Commission:

One of Parliament's amendments makes it incumbent upon the contracting authorities to include in the notice of tender requirements relating to the conditions of employment that exist in the Member States, the region or commune where the work is to be carried out, and that will consequently be applicable to the job in hand. This provision was intended to ensure transparency and fairness in terms of the working conditions applicable to all parties tendering. The Council however takes the view that any attempt to implement this provision would encounter considerable difficulties, in particular in countries where working conditions are not codified, but arise out of case law or [collective agreements]. The Council's chosen solution, that the contracting authority be given the option of specifying where tenderers can acquire such information, does not, as the Commission likewise affirms, meet with the set objective of transparency and fairness to tenderers. [Parliament should seek] to replace this optional provision with an obligation on the contracting authority. In relation to this provision Parliament has also stipulated that the tenderer should submit

---

[93] Doc C2-193/88.   [94] Quoted in Doc A2-361/88, 13.   [95] Doc A2-361/88, 13.

a declaration of adherence to working conditions…Requiring such a declaration to be included in the invitation to tender should forestall any later problems of interpretation as to the requirements with which such a declaration is intended to secure compliance.

Following this, the Parliament adopted the following amendment[96] at the second reading stage in February 1989:

Without prejudice to the provisions of the Treaties and to measures adopted in accordance with them, the contracting authority shall set out, in the contract documents, the obligations relating to employment conditions which exist in the Member State, region or locality where the work is to be carried out and which will, in consequence, be applicable for work executed on site during the execution of the contract.

[Contractors when submitting tenders shall submit] a statement concerning compliance with the wage agreements and other provisions of labour law applicable to the undertaking.

[Furthermore,] in the contract documents, the contracting authority shall ask the tenderer to indicate in his tender any share of the contract he may intend to sub-contract to third parties. For each sub-contract the principal contractor shall retain full responsibility.

The Parliament also amended the text of the draft directive to include a clause permitting the inclusion of measures to assist the unemployed:

The contracting authorities may in the award of contracts have regard to the desirability of encouraging responses to the problems of the long-term unemployed and young people particularly in the regions, employment areas and urban communities affected by levels of unemployment structurally higher than the average for the Community within the context of operational programmes presented by the competent authorities in the Member States and agreed by the Commission.

The new Commission proposal of April 1989[97] largely agreed with the Parliament, including equivalent provisions to those adopted by the Parliament on compulsory notification of working conditions, and permissive conditions relating to unemployment. However, in adopting the directive on 18 July 1989, the Council returned to its common position on most issues. The directive as adopted contained a non-mandatory provision relating to working conditions. In addition, it contained a regional preference provision, a provision creating an exception to the mandatory application of the normal award criteria of lowest price/most economically advantageous tender, where the Member State bases the award of contracts on other criteria whose aim is to give preference to certain tenderers. The Council rejected the provision relating to unemployment conditions.

Status equality and the Services Directive

Much of the debate around the Supplies and Works Directives, as we have seen, centred on the issue of regional preference schemes. In July 1989 the Commission

---

[96] Second Reading by the Parliament, 15 February 1989 [1989] OJ C69/ 69.
[97] COM(89)141 final of 4 April1989 [1989] OJ C115/4.

had proposed two alternative approaches to such schemes: progressive abolition, in which case greater use would be made of other types of scheme to meet some similar objectives, or modification, in which case they would be narrowed in scope and made more transparent. However, in March 1990, the ECJ's second major intervention occurred. It decided in *Du Pont de Nemours* that an Italian regional preference scheme was unlawful despite the apparent exemptions in the directive, due to the overriding effect of Article 30 of the Treaty.[98] On the assumption that procurement decisions could constitute aid,[99] the Court held that an Italian provision that all public and semi-public bodies were required to obtain at least 30 per cent of their purchases from companies operating in the Mezzogiorno region of Italy was unlawful. The possible classification of the measure as aid did not exempt it from the Treaty restrictions requiring non-discrimination regarding the movement of goods under Article 30.[100]

The initial proposal of the Commission for a Services Directive was presented to the Council in December 1990.[101] This proposal contained the original regional and general exceptions from the requirement that awards of contracts be made on the basis of lowest price or most economically advantageous tender. The Commission's proposal included a provision which provided for optional requirements on notification of working conditions.

In 1991, the Committee on Economic and Monetary Affairs and Industrial Policy of the Parliament produced its report on the Commission's proposal. The Committee report[102] did not include recommendations for any social linkages to be included. It recommended the exclusion of regional and general preferences in the light of the decision by the ECJ in *Du Pont de Nemours*.[103] This recommendation was subsequently agreed to by the Parliament. However, the Committee on Legal Affairs and Citizens' Rights recommended several amendments, including one specifically relating to status equality. In particular, the following was proposed:

The Directive shall not prevent the application of existing or future national provisions on the award of public supply or works contracts which have as their objective the promotion and protection of equal rights and opportunities for women, the disabled, members of minority ethnic groups, migrant workers, religious groups, on condition that the provisions are compatible with the Treaty and with the international obligations of the Member States, in particular ILO Convention 94.

Various Members of the Parliament tabled a series of amendments when this report reached the Parliament in May 1991. In particular, one amendment obliged the tenderer to indicate that the firm had already met its legal obligations in respect of equal opportunities for men and women in employment. Other

---

[98] Case 21/88 *Du Pont de Nemours Italiana SpA v Unitè Sanitaiia Locale No 2 di Carrara*, [1990] ECR I-889.   [99] The ECJ did not pronounce on the question.
[100] The law ceased to apply on 31 December 1993.
[101] COM(90)372 of 6 December 1990 [1991] OJ C23.   [102] Doc A3-111/91.
[103] *Du Pont de Nemours* (n 98 above).

amendments called on Member States which had not yet done so to ratify ILO Convention No 94 (which we discussed in chapter 2 above), and provided for the possibility of excluding firms which had failed to meet legal requirements on environmental protection.

Responding to these amendments, Mr Bangemann, vice-president of the Commission, rejected many of the social clause amendments, on the basis that 'Tenders cannot be appraised on the basis of the tenderer's social attitude. Provided that he acts lawfully, his tender may be assessed only by its objective quality, and I cannot therefore accept [the social linkage amendments].'[104] Despite the objections of the Commission, the Parliament accepted three relevant social policy amendments. One provided for contracting authorities to be able to place 'restrictions on sources of supplies, works and services on environmental grounds or in pursuance of UN resolutions, provided that such restrictions are compatible with the Treaty', and two others amending the working conditions notification provision. As amended, the provision would have made notification compulsory. In addition, the provision would also have contained the following additional provision:

The directive shall not prevent the application of existing or future national, regional or local provisions on the award of public supply or works contracts which have as their objective the promotion and protection of equal rights and opportunities for the most vulnerable social categories on the labour market (women, the disabled, members of minority ethnic groups, migrant workers and religious groups, the long-term unemployed, persons in receipt of benefit, etc.) on condition that the provisions are compatible with the Treaty and with the Community's international obligations.

The Commission did not accept these amendments. The reason given in the explanatory memorandum, which accompanied the amended proposal,[105] included the following passage:

The Commission has not retained a number of amendments which were adopted by Parliament and which seek a closer supervision of the respect by bidders of their obligations under social and environmental legislation. In the Commission's view the supervision of such obligations is better carried out in the context of the relevant social or environmental legislation. To use EC procurement rules for this purpose would reduce their effectiveness in meeting their principal goal of ensuring the non-discriminatory award of public contracts.[106]

Regarding the regional preference award criteria, the Commission explained why it was accepting the Parliament's amendments: 'These deletions are in line with Parliament's amendments, recent decisions of the European Court of Justice [*Du Pont de Nemours*] and the Commission's views regarding the compatibility of preference systems with Article 30 of the Treaty. Further, it is now clear that the directive will not enter into force before 31 December 1992, the date on which the provisions of Article 35 would have ceased to apply.'

---

[104] Debates of the European Parliament, 14 May 1991, No 3-405/107-8.
[105] COM(91)322 final of 30 August 1991 [1991] OJ C250/4.   [106] ibid para 7.

Status equality and the Utilities Directive

In October 1988, the Commission had sent to the Council two proposals for directives in the utilities sectors, one relating to water, energy, and transport,[107] and the second relating to telecommunications.[108] These proposals included articles covering regional and award preferences, but did not include any provision on employment and working conditions, or on status equality.

The Parliament, in its First Reading Resolution in May 1989, amended the Commission's draft to include a compulsory requirement to notify terms and conditions of employment and a requirement that tenderers must indicate that these have been taken into account in the preparation of the bid. In addition, Amendment No 34 would have amended the draft to provide that the Directive 'shall not prevent the application of existing national provisions on the award of public supply or works contracts which have as their objective the promotion of equal rights and opportunities for women, the disabled and migrant workers, on condition that the provisions are compatible with the Treaty and with the Community's international obligations'.[109] The Commission in the Parliamentary debates appeared to indicate that it had no objection to the spirit of the amendments.[110] However, the modified Commission proposals following the Parliamentary debate did not include either of these provisions.[111]

A third ECJ judgment influenced the debates on the content of the Utilities Directive. The issue in *Rush Portuguesa*, decided on 27 March 1990, arose not under the procurement directives, but under the Treaty, in particular the Treaty provisions protecting the freedom to provide services (then Articles 59 and 60). An undertaking established in Portugal, specializing in construction and public works, entered into a subcontract with a French undertaking for the carrying out of works for the construction of a railway line in the west of France. For that purpose, it brought its Portuguese employees from Portugal. However, the French Labour Code only permitted the *Office national d'immigration* to recruit in France the nationals of third countries. The director of the Office attempted to levy the payment that an employer employing foreign workers in breach of the provisions of the Labour Code was liable to pay. The question that the Court formally answered was relatively narrow. In the situation in which the company found itself, the authorities of the Member State in whose territory the works are to be carried out may not, consistent with Articles 59 and 60, impose on the supplier of services conditions that manpower be recruited from the host state, or requiring the Portuguese workforce to obtain work permits. However, the Court addressed

---

[107] COM(88)377 final of 11 October 1988.
[108] COM(88)378 final of 11 October 1988 [1989] OJ C40.
[109] [1989] OJ C158/258, 271.
[110] Pandolfi, Vice President of the Commission, Debates of the European Parliament, 25 May 1989, No 2-378/136.   [111] COM(89)380 final of 31 August 1989 [1989] OJ C267.

the question of the application of host country labour law to such workers more broadly.

Earlier case law of the Court, notably the *Seco* case,[112] had addressed the issue of the application of labour provisions to cross-border workers of this type. The Court had held that Community law did not preclude Member States from applying their labour legislation, or collective labour agreements, to any person who was employed, even temporarily, within their territory, no matter in which country the employer was established, just as Community law did not prohibit Member States from enforcing those rules by appropriate means. However, Articles 59 and 60 required the abolition of all discrimination against a person providing a service on the grounds of his nationality or the fact that he was established in a Member State other than that in which the service must be provided. The prohibition of discrimination prohibited 'not only overt discrimination . . . but also all forms of covert discrimination which, although based on criteria which appear to be neutral, in practice lead to the same result'.[113] On the basis of this analysis, the Court held that Community law precluded a Member State from requiring an employer who was established in another Member State and temporarily carrying out work in the host Member State, using workers who were nationals of non-member countries, to pay the employer's share of social security contributions in respect of such workers, when the employer was already liable under the legislation of the state in which he was established for similar contributions in respect of the same workers and the same period of employment. The social security contributions paid in the host state did not entitle those workers to any social security benefits. Nor would such a requirement be justified if it were intended to offset the economic advantages which the employer might have gained by not complying with the legislation on minimum wages in the host state. In *Rush Portuguesa*, the Court largely repeated these statements: 'Community law', held the Court, drawing on the judgment in *Seco*, 'does not preclude Member States from extending their legislation, or collective labour agreements entered into by both sides of industry, to any person who is employed, even temporarily, within their territory, no matter in which country the employer is established; nor does Community law prohibit Member States from enforcing those rules by appropriate means.'[114]

The Council's Common Position arrived at on 28 March 1990 included an optional working conditions article for the sake of bringing the directive into line with the Works Directive. The Commission subsequently made it clear that this was introduced to align the Directive with the Works Directive and was consistent with the ECJ's decision in the *Rush Portuguesa* case.[115] It also included a new provision that specified that 'any other special condition for participation in the contract' should be notified to prospective tenderers.

---

[112] Joined cases 62 and 63/81 *Seco SA* [1982] ECR 223.   [113] ibid para 8.
[114] Case C-113/89 *Rush Portuguesa Ld v Office national d'immigration* [1990] ECR I-1417, point 18.
[115] COM(90)301 of 12 July 1990, para 11(f).

The Parliament's Committee on Economic Affairs examined the position prior to second reading and recommended against continuing to insist on Amendment 34 regarding equal opportunities: 'Although the Council has not explicitly incorporated this amendment, the new provision introduced [by the Council] ... — "any other special condition for participation in the contract"—will provide a response to the legitimate concern expressed by Parliament. There is, therefore, no need to retable Amendment No. 34, as it is covered by the general provision'.[116]

Nevertheless, the Parliament, in its Second Reading debate on 13 June 1990, although it did not press Amendment 34, passed another amendment, Amendment 16, which modified the award preferences provision to read:

Article 27(1) shall not apply where a Member State bases the award of contracts on other criteria within the framework of rules in force at the time of the adoption of this Directive whose aim is *to promote or safeguard equal rights and opportunities for women, the disabled or workers from minority groups or* to give preference to certain tenderers, provided the rules invoked are compatible with the Treaty.[117]

Other amendments made the notification of employment conditions compulsory, and omitted the time limit to regional preferences while extending them to the 'renewal of urban areas'.[118]

The Commission made it clear that it would not accept these amendments. Regarding the latter amendments, the vice-president of the Commission, Mr Bangemann, explained:

... we must not forget what the European Court of Justice decided in the Bentjes [sic] case. We are a Community based on the rule of law and cannot simply ignore that decision. These amendments would greatly reduce the scope for action to promote social objectives, because we cannot, of course, simply ignore the Court's recent disapproval of regional preferences. The Court was interpreting the treaties of Rome [sic] in this case, not some regulation or directive that we could amend ourselves ... and this quite apart from the fact that we would never get the Council to accept this amendment, and I would ask you to sympathize with the Council's position, which I personally share: if we prescribe this in a sector such as this, a large part of the Community will remain uncompetitive. We would never see—let's not beat about the bush—a Portuguese undertaking successfully tendering in the exempted water or electricity or telecommunications sector in West Germany if we insist on all the social provisions applicable in West Germany being observed in the tender ... You will achieve precisely the same as many others who have tried to use unreasonable social provisions to balance out something that can only be balanced out in the market. Although you have seen justice done on paper, you have in fact achieved nothing.[119]

Not surprisingly, then, none of these amendments were included in the re-examined Commission proposal submitted in July 1990.[120] Instead of the compulsory

[116] A3-129/90.   [117] Emphasis added.   [118] [1990] OJ C175/78.
[119] Debates of the European Parliament, 12 June 1990, No 3-391/93-4.
[120] COM(90)301 of 12 July 1990.

notification of working conditions, an optional clause was included.[121] The Council finally adopted the directive as proposed by the Commission on 17 September 1990.

Status equality and the consolidated Supplies Directive

In 1992, the Commission proposed a consolidation of the Supplies Directive.[122] In its Explanatory Memorandum, the Commission proposed to amend and rearrange the provisions on award criteria. The amended provisions would no longer contain any references to preferential award criteria. Neither regional preferences under Article 26 nor the more generally expressed preferences exception in Article 25(4) would be included in the consolidated directive. 'The provisions of the old Article 26 expire on 31 December 1992. Reports from the Member States show that there are no schemes eligible to benefit from the provisions of the old Article 25(4)... These provisions are therefore superfluous. The deletion of the former Article 27, which provided for reporting systems as regards preferential schemes, is a consequence of the deletion of the reference to the preference schemes as such.'[123] The Parliamentary Committee that considered the proposal agreed,[124] as did the Parliament.[125] The proposal was subsequently adopted by the Council in this form.

---

[121] Commission Proposal, Art 29.   [122] COM(92)346 final [1992] OJ C277/1.
[123] COM(92)346 final [1992] OJ C277/30.   [124] A3-0039/93, 29 January 1993.
[125] [1993] OJ C72/73.

11

Domestic Procurement Linkages During the 1990s and the Chilling Effect of European Procurement Regulation

I. Growing European Commission Scepticism Regarding Procurement Linkages

The discussion in the previous chapter of the relationship between the legislative reforms of the procurement directives during the 1980s and procurement linkages aiming to promote equal status goals appears confusing. On the one hand, the Council of Ministers rejected the substantial majority of Parliamentary and Commission proposals to amend the draft directives to explicitly permit or require such procurement linkages. On the other hand, we have seen that procurement linkages were operating in several Member States and there was no indication from the Commission or the Council during the legislative debates that these were or should be made unlawful. Indeed, following the *Beentjes* case,[1] the Commission issued a Communication interpreting the case, and discussing its implications for the issue of linkage.[2] The Commission stated that the Court of Justice had upheld the legitimacy under the Public Works Directive of attaching a condition to the award of a public works contract under which the contractor was required to engage a given number of long-term unemployed registered with a regional employment office. Such a condition was nevertheless subject to the Treaty of Rome, particularly those provisions on freedom to provide services, freedom of establishment, and non-discrimination on grounds of nationality.[3] In the Commission's view, there was 'no reason to suppose' that other social objectives any more than the reduction of long-term unemployment fell outside 'the area of liberty left to the Member States by Directive 71/305':[4]

The same probably applies to a broad range of social matters including, for example, professional training, health and safety, labour relations and the suppression of racial, religious

---

[1] *Beentjes* Case 31/87 [1988] ECR 4635, see further the discussion in ch 8 above.
[2] European Commission, Public Procurement: Regional and Social Aspects, COM(89)400 final [1989], OJ C311/11–14.   [3] ibid para 45.
[4] ibid para 46.

discrimination or discrimination on the grounds of sex. In these areas too, the procurement Directives neither forbid nor expressly authorise Member States to regulate the matter. Accordingly, they and procuring entities are free under Community law to pursue such objectives, provided they respect the Directives' provisions and the constraints of the Treaty. It also follows that Member States are free under Community law to restrict the capacity of procuring entities to pursue objectives of this kind.[5]

In the area of equal opportunities, an obligation to employ a given number or proportion of women or persons from some other category not based on nationality would also not appear to give rise to difficulty, though of course a definitive judgement necessarily depends on an appreciation of all the material facts of a particular case.[6]

Far from clarifying the relationship between Community law and procurement linkages, then, the position was left ambiguous and uncertain because it was left to case-by-case assessment. Although the Commission stated that an obligation on contractors 'to employ a given number or proportion of women ... not based on nationality would ... not appear to give rise to difficulty', the Commission had also stated clearly that 'a definitive judgment necessarily depends on an appreciation of all the material facts of a particular case'.

The decade of the 1990s was the period of greatest difficulty for procurement linkages promoting equal status goals. Separate but interconnected developments contributed to an apparently irresistible pressure against such procurement linkages. The European Commission became one of the most prominent critics of such linkages and used its legal enforcement powers to create significant legal risks for public bodies in the Member States that wished to use such linkages. The prospect for linking status equality to procurement in the Community looked anything but easy, faced with the scepticism of the Council of Ministers throughout the legislative process of the 1980s, and now faced with the hostility in practice of the Commission.

We have seen that the Commission's reactions to many of the Parliament's proposals on social issues were flexible. This relatively tolerant approach[7] changed gradually, however, between the mid-1980s and the early 1990s to become one of almost implacable hostility within the Commission service tasked with implementing the directives, a change in position that José Fernández Martín attributed, 'probably ... to the development among the Commission services of [an] "economic rationale"' view of the directives.[8] Writing in the early 1990s, Fernández Martín argued that the 'result has been the withdrawal of a policy instrument such as public procurement from Member States and the imposition of a "buy efficient" approach as regards public contracting'.[9] In particular, the Commission interpreted strictly the requirement that, if the purchasing body did not use lowest

---

    [5] ibid para 46.   [6] ibid para 57.
    [7] Although as José M Fernández Martín points out (at 57 fn 64), the Commission had begun taking infringement actions against Member States for use of local labour clauses from 1987. *The EC Public Procurement Rules: A Critical Analysis* (OUP, 1996) 46–8.   [8] ibid 56.
    [9] ibid 39.

price for the award of the contract, it should use the criterion of 'most economically advantageous offer'. This was interpreted as meaning that tender evaluation
was limited to economic or commercial grounds only. 'Other noncommercial . . .
considerations should not play a role in the award decision.'[10] In 1997, the
Commission stated: 'There is widespread agreement that social policy and public
procurement should not overlap. Social objectives should be pursued through
adequate social legislation and not by using the power to award procurement
contracts.'[11]

The tide appeared to be turning against the use of procurement linkages. To
ensure that the tide would continue in this direction, from the mid-1990s, the
Commission embarked on a sustained strategy of launching infringement proceedings for alleged violations of the public procurement directives. The Commission
was less complaint-driven, and more proactive in seeking to prevent infringements,
particularly in major infrastructure projects, 'itself taking the initiative in launching proceedings and being more systematic in attacking a given abuse or malprac-
tice, once drawn to its attention'.[12] In December 1995 the Commission referred
its complaint against France (over the construction of a school building in Wingles,
Nord-Pas-de-Calais) to the European Court of Justice (ECJ). The Portuguese
government was sent a reasoned opinion complaining about award of a contract
for processing solid hospital waste.[13] The Commission sent reasoned opinions
against France (three cases), Germany, Italy (two cases), the United Kingdom,
Ireland (three cases), Belgium and Portugal, alleging violation of the directives. Of
particular importance among these was the expansion of the earlier complaint
against the school building contract in Wingles to include a general complaint
about public works contracts for school buildings in the Nord-Pas-de-Calais
region and in the Nord département. This complaint included the Commission's
objection to an additional criterion relating to unemployment, arising from an
interministerial circular (to be discussed later in this chapter), which was alleged
to be discriminatory.[14] In July 1997, there was a new wave of infringement proceedings against Member States relating to public procurement. France was
referred to the ECJ over the *Nord-Pas-de-Calais* case. Reasoned opinions were sent
to Italy (over a contract relating to the Messina Straits bridge), Spain (cleaning services for the National Library), and Austria. The reasoned opinion to Austria was
particularly relevant because it concerned the inclusion of ecological-points for

[10] ibid 44.

[11] European Commission, 'Public Procurement in the EU: Special Sectoral Report No 1' (1997).

[12] See G O' Brien, 'Envisaged Change in the Procurement Regime: the Point of View of the
European Commission', (Contribution of George O'Brien, DG XV—Internal Market and Financial
Affairs, Commission of the European Communities, at the seminar on 'Legal Aspects of EC Public
Procurement', Luxembourg, 29–30 October 1998, 7–8.

[13] European Report, 20 December 1995, No 2094, 'Public Procurement: Legal Action Against
France and Portugal'.

[14] Commission of the European Communities, RAPID, Press Release IP: 96-761 (1 August 1996).

lorries, to which the Commission objected.[15] In 1998, during the first half of the year, the Commission announced twenty-five cases of alleged infringements of the procurement directives.[16] In January 2000, the Commission opened eleven infringement proceedings.[17]

Several of the infringement proceedings during the 1990s involved challenges to social and environmental linkages. At the national level too, there was a growing scepticism about procurement linkages, reflecting a similar preference for an economic approach to be adopted to procurement. In several Member States, the 'embedded liberalism' of the 1960s and 1970s was increasingly challenged, contributing to scepticism of policies such as procurement linkages. In several EC countries[18] this also contributed to an increasingly hostile national legal environment for such linkages. In some cases this legal scepticism appears to have been given a helping hand by European legal developments. We illustrate these developments in the remainder of this chapter, with a detailed discussion of debates on procurement linkages in the United Kingdom, Germany, the Netherlands, and France during the 1990s.

II. British Public Sector Management Reform: Contracting Out, Privatization, and Procurement Linkages

The election of Margaret Thatcher as British Prime Minister in 1979, and the rise of 'Thatcherism' in Britain had profound effects on the debate about the appropriate relationship between procurement regulation and procurement linkages. Thatcherism was a complex phenomenon. For the purposes of this chapter, there were several interlinked elements. One element was that government should withdraw to a considerably greater extent than at any time since the beginning of the Second World War from areas of public services that could be more efficiently delivered by the market; where public services were to continue to be delivered by public bodies, they should at least emulate the methods of commercial organizations in the methods they used to deliver those services. A second, related, element was a belief that public spending was massively in excess of what was necessary to deliver public services, and that issues of cost and efficiency should become much more firmly embedded in the public sector ethos than previously. These two policies led, during the 1980s, to substantial privatization of publicly-owned enterprises,

---

[15] European Report, 26 July 1997, No 2244, 'Public procurement: New Wave of Infringement Proceedings against Member States'.   [16] Oxford Analytica, Daily Brief, 24 July 1998, 15.

[17] *Financial Times*, 14 January 2000.

[18] Not only in EC countries. In Norway, although not a Member of the Community but under the equivalent procurement disciplines as a member of the European Economic Area, a national Committee established in 1995 to revise Norwegian procurement legislation, produced a report in June 1997 that was hostile to the inclusion of social considerations in procurement, in part on the basis of uncertainty as to whether particular conditions were contrary to the EEA Agreement and the WTO GPA. AD Gjnnes, 'Proposed New Norwegian legislation on the Award of Public Procurement Contracts' (1997) 6 PPLR CS189, CS191.

deregulation of utilities, and either the market testing of public services previously delivered by public bodies, or their contracting-out to private sector organizations. Such policies were introduced into both central government spending and, with considerably greater difficulty, local government spending.

Compulsory competitive tendering

The role of public procurement linkages became, probably for the first time since the late nineteenth century, a significant element in the national political debate. These developments were of particular concern to two institutions that had been regarded as central to political life in Britain: local government, and (at least since the Second World War) the trade union movement.

Since the beginning of the twentieth century, local government in England and Wales had developed considerable public service delivery functions. Often, these services were delivered directly by the local authority itself, by directly employed council employees, and this contributed to local government becoming a major employer in its own right. After 1979, although the Conservatives controlled central government, they did not, in the main, control the local governments of the largest metropolitan areas, such as London and Birmingham. When local government in Britain came to be regarded as hostile to the ideological basis of central government policy, and continued to use its resources to challenge aspects of the government's economic liberalism, central government controls were introduced to restrict their ability to further challenge central government. Beginning in 1980 and continuing through to 1996, a system of compulsory competitive tendering (CCT) was progressively applied to an increasingly wide range of local authority services.[19] The aim was to ensure that competition was introduced into the process of deciding who should carry out these services. Local authorities would only be able to carry out particularly defined activities using their own employees (such as by so-called Direct Labour Organizations, or Direct Service Organizations) if the work had been put out to tender and the contract had been awarded to that group of employees on the basis of an open competition. These requirements were introduced first for construction, maintenance, and highways work in 1980.

Increasingly, those controls were legal controls. CCT was extended substantially in the Local Government Act 1988 to cover a wide range of blue-collar services, such as refuse collection and ground maintenance. The 1988 Act provided that in reaching a decision as to who should be awarded a contract, the local authority should not act in a manner having the effect, or intended or likely to have the effect of restricting, distorting, or preventing competition. After a subsequent White Paper,[20] further services were brought under CCT disciplines, and competitive

---

[19] Local Government, Planning and Land Act 1980. CCT was not introduced into the Civil Service; instead, a 'market testing' process was introduced, which resulted in a somewhat more flexible approach being adopted in practice.

[20] UK Government White Paper, 'Competing for Quality' (HMSO, 1991).

tendering for some professional services was included in the Local Government Act 1992. By 1996 CCT was beginning to be applied to some local authority professional services, involving legal, property, and personnel services.[21]

There was, however, another feature to the relationship between local government and central government that should not be underestimated. Not only was the central government perceived by local government as hostile to its interests, it was also perceived as pursuing policies that were adversarial and confrontational in other respects as well. Indeed, the 1970s and the 1980s is generally recognized as seeing the end of the post-Second World War consensus on social and economic matters that accepted a mixed economy, and relatively progressive social policies. On all fronts, the Conservative government pursued a radically confrontational agenda, perhaps particularly in areas such as race relations and equality between men and women, which the Labour Party had so recently espoused. Since it was clear that Labour was unlikely significantly to challenge the Conservative government at the national level, local government came to be seen as in some respects a Labour government in exile, attempting to pursue policies that would be seen to challenge the government on all fronts.

For the trade union movement, especially the large unions representing public sector workers, changing the basis on which public services were delivered, particularly the contracting-out of the delivery of these services to the private sector, threatened their membership directly. Their fears were that public service employees would be laid off, or, if transferred to the private sector employer, that their pay and conditions of work would be adversely affected, or that public authorities would reduce the pay and conditions of their employees in order to be able to compete with the private sector. Of particular importance was the inclusion of such services as cleaning and catering in CCT, areas that were substantially female dominated. Research increasingly showed that women, in particular, were less well off when they were transferred from the public sector to the private sector under CCT pressures.[22]

But these concerns were only part of a general hostility that quickly emerged between the government and the organized trade union movement. Among those groups regarded by the government as most likely to derail its policies was organized labour. Those who came to power in 1979 remembered the conflicts between the previous Conservative government of Edward Heath in the early 1970s, and the more recent 'winter of discontent' in 1978–79 with its substantial disruption which had contributed to the undermining of the previous Labour government,

---

[21] These objectives were accomplished by a mixture of primary legislation, regulations, and circulars (with statutory force). The principal legislation providing for CCT in local government was: Local Government, Planning and Land Act 1980, Local Government Act 1988, Local Government Act 1992, Local Government (Direct Service Organisations) (Competition) Regulations 1993 (SI 1993/848) and Amendment regulations (SI 1995/1336); Departmental Circular 5/96.

[22] Equal Opportunities Commission, 'The Gender Impact of CCT in Local Government' (EOC, 1995); Equal Opportunities Commission for Northern Ireland, 'Report on Formal Investigation into Competitive Tendering in Health and Education Services in Northern Ireland' (NIEOC, 1996).

and resolved to constrain trade union power as much as was necessary to deliver the government's agenda. Unlike the Heath government, however, the Thatcher government played a much more cautious game in putting all these policies into place. Nevertheless, over time, a radical shift in the balance of power between management and the unions was introduced.

Contract compliance and local authorities

We saw in chapter 2 above, that British local government had been in the forefront in the later nineteenth century of developing methods to constrain those that they contracted with, namely in the promulgation of the Fair Wages Resolution. The use of this method to constrain CCT had, however, been anticipated by government and was swiftly closed off. At the same time as the introduction of CCT, there was a review of the Fair Wages Resolution and its statutory equivalent. On 20 September 1982, the government denounced ILO Convention No 94.[23] On 16 December 1982, the House of Commons was asked by Norman Tebbit, the Secretary of State for Employment on behalf of the government, to rescind the Fair Wages Resolution as from 21 December 1983, and this it did, after an acrimonious debate.[24] One of the Labour MPs opposing the motion said:

I believe that the only reason for the proposal is that the Government are going in for wide scale privatisation. They wish to contract out many of the jobs that are now carried out by Government and local authority employees. They do not want fair wages. They want a scramble of undercutting. We have begun to see that in the National Health Service and in some local authorities. I am sure that some Conservative members are only too keen to see the privatisation of catering, cleaning, refuse collection and building maintenance. Conservative members are nodding their heads gleefully. That is what it is all about.[25]

However, although the Fair Wages Resolution route was closed off, other opportunities for challenging the implications of contracting out and other Conservative policies presented themselves, particularly contract compliance policies aiming to advance *equality*, and other social and political objectives. Using local authority contracts in the service of equal opportunities became a controversial part of the general debate over contract compliance, and indeed over the role of local government generally. Contract compliance became a prominent part of local government activity in England and Wales during the 1980s, particularly, if not exclusively, among Labour Party controlled local authorities. Research has indicated that approximately 20 per cent of local authorities adopted formal contract compliance policies during that period.[26] Contract compliance consisted of three different types of policy, which were sometimes combined.

---

[23] Hansard, vol 29, col 485 (28 October 1982) (written answer).
[24] ibid vol 34, cols 499–576 (16 December 1982).
[25] ibid vol 34, col 524 (16 December 1982) (Mr Leighton).
[26] Report cited in PE Morris, 'Legal Regulation of Contract Compliance: An Anglo-American Comparison' (1990) 19 Anglo-American Law Review 87, 93.

The first type of contract compliance programme involved attaching conditions to the contract which sought to reinforce statutory prohibitions, in particular in the areas of race and sex discrimination,[27] and health and safety at work. The second type of condition involved attempts to resist the deregulatory drift of government policy with regard to the contracting-out of local service provision, and the deregulation of the labour market; conditions addressing these goals sought, for example, to limit the extent to which competition between in-house direct labour organizations and outside contractors would lead to the latter being awarded the contract. The third type of policy related more to achieving general political aims, such as opposition to apartheid in South Africa, or the abolition of nuclear weapons. Local government contracts were tied in to achieving these aims by, for example, rejecting contractors who had contacts with South Africa or who were also defence contractors.

One of the most popular types of provision related to the hiring of local labour. During the 1980s, several local authorities required firms tendering for council work to demonstrate that, where possible, employment under the contract would be given to those living within the council area. The conditions were operated by a wide variety of councils, including Leicester, Lewisham, Birmingham, Chesterfield, Durham, Gwynned, and Liverpool. Chesterfield specified that 20 per cent of a contractor's workforce must be local residents. Liverpool City Council required that contractors 'shall where practical give preference to Merseyside residents' and in 1985 added a new requirement on employers to prove that 'all reasonable steps have been taken to recruit local labour through job centres and/or trade unions'. In Glasgow, the authority had the discretion to accept a higher tender by a local contractor if the tender was within 5 per cent of a lower price from a non-local contractor.[28]

The policy adopted by the Greater London Council and the Inner London Education Authority served as a model for many others. In March 1983, the GLC/ILEA adopted a policy of contract compliance.[29] Companies which were invited to tender for GLC/ILEA contracts were kept on an 'Approved List'. A clause was added to the Council's Code of Practice on Tenders and Contracts (amended in 1985) to require companies to abide by the Council's requirement to comply

---

[27] For a general discussion of the growth of equal opportunities concerns in local government, and policy implementation in one large local authority, see B Bagilhole, 'Managing to be Fair: Implementing Equal Opportunities in a Local Authority' (1993) 19(2) Local Government Studies 163–75. Support for legislative provision linking public procurement with either race or gender equality conditions: S Robarts with A Coote and E Ball, *Positive Action for Women: the next step* (NCCL 1981) 94.

[28] See J Stephenson, *New Society*, 3 July 1987, 5.

[29] Publications by GLC/ILEA: GLC Contract Compliance Equal Opportunities Unit, 'Contract Compliance and Trade Unions' (nd); GLC Contract Compliance Equal Opportunities Unit, 'The ILEA/GLC is one of the largest equal opportunities employers . . . but that's not enough . . . ' (nd); GLC Contract Compliance Equal Opportunities Unit, 'Contracting for Equality: First Annual Report of the GLC-ILEA Contract Compliance Equal Opportunities Unit' (1985–86) (GLC, 1986); 'GLC, Ethnic Minority/Contract Compliance Conference Report' (May 1984) (GLC, 1984); J Carr, 'Background Paper on Contract Compliance in the UK' (January 1986).

with the legislative provisions on race, sex, and disability, and to provide such information as required so that the Council could satisfy itself that the firms did comply with those provisions. The Council required all companies engaged in providing goods and services to take all reasonably practical steps to follow specific recommendations in the Codes of Practice produced by the two anti-discrimination enforcement bodies: the Commission for Racial Equality (CRE) and the Equal Opportunities Commission (EOC). Companies on the Approved List were asked to supply the Council with information on their employment practices. This was requested on an application form for retention/inclusion on the Council's Approved List. Not all companies were investigated in detail. A smaller number were selected for detailed review, primarily on the basis of size and the amount the Council spent with the company. A Contract Compliance Equal Opportunities Unit (CCEOU) was established to monitor the operation of the policy and conduct the employer reviews. While the ultimate sanction was to remove the company from the Approved List, the preferred approach was to work with the company to ensure that the company came into compliance. The review procedure primarily involved the drawing up by the company and CCEOU of a programme of action. The programme was set out in a letter of agreement between the Unit and the company, and retention on the approved list was conditional on the agreement being carried out in practice. The company was regularly asked for information on its progress in implementing the agreement.[30]

Policies such as those adopted by the GLC/ILEA were strongly supported by the Trades Union Congress (TUC), by several individual trade unions, by the Labour Party, by the Liberal Party, and by the Social Democratic Party.[31] Not only were they politically popular among the opposition to the Conservatives, they also seemed to deliver results.[32] These developments were, however, strongly opposed by the Confederation of British Industry (CBI), and by several other organizations representing contractors and employers. Opposition was particularly strong to the second and third types of contract compliance policies identified above. Two routes were adopted to try to limit them, one legal, the other political and both were largely successful.

[30] For descriptions of the development of the policy, see 'Contract compliance assessed', EOR No 31, May/June 1990, 26; 'Equal opportunities and contract compliance' EOR No 8 July/August 1986, 9; 'Contract compliance and equal opportunities', IRRR 381, 2 December 1986, 2.

[31] TUC Race Relations Advisory Committee, 'Guidance Note on Contract Compliance and Equal Opportunities' (May 1986), reprinted in the Report for 1985–6 of the TUC Women's Advisory Committee (1986), para 9; TUC Consultative Document, 'Industrial Relations Legislation', 18; COHSE's comments on the TUC document, February 1986, para 22; Labour's Programme 1982, 32–3; R Evans and F Bridger for the Social Democratic Campaign for Racial Justice, Racial Justice: 'An SDP Approach to Equal Opportunities' (July 1985, SDP Open Forum, No 12) 27–9, 36–7; SDP, 'Policy for Women' (Green Paper No 16) 37–8; SDP, 'The Only Way to a Fairer Britain', para 4.18; The Alliance Charter for Women, 4; Report of the Commission of Inquiry into Ethnic Minority Involvement in the Liberal Party, 'Promoting Greater Involvement' (1986) 15

[32] See ch 18 below.

Judicial intervention against linkage

As regards legal challenge, the issue was whether the adoption of such policies was legal under the existing powers of local authorities. Not only did the common law not oblige public authorities actively to promote equality in this way, it placed some obstacles in the way of particular authorities that chose to do so. In general, public authorities in Britain are prevented from doing anything not specifically authorized, particularly where it may be in tension with other more specific obligations. Local authorities, however, frequently argued that they had statutory authorization to pursue such policies, at least in the context of racial equality, and pointed to section 71 of the Race Relations Act, which provided that 'Without prejudice to their obligation to comply with any other provision of this Act, it shall be the duty of every local authority to make appropriate arrangements with a view to securing that their various functions are carried out with due regard to the need (a) to eliminate unlawful racial discrimination and (b) to promote equality of opportunity, and good relations between persons of different racial groups.'

In *Wheeler v Leicester City Council*,[33] this argument proved to be of little support. The council had banned a rugby football club from using city recreation grounds for twelve months for its failure to take sufficient action to persuade its members not to play in South Africa, then enforcing a policy of apartheid. The House of Lords held that the council had power under section 71 to consider the best interests of race relations when exercising its statutory discretion in the management of the recreation ground. However, in the absence of any infringement of the law or any improper conduct by the club, the ban was unreasonable, and a misuse of its statutory powers. Subsequently, in *R v Lewisham LBC, ex p Shell UK Ltd*,[34] it was held, on the basis of the *Wheeler* judgment, that 'though the scope of s. 71 of the 1976 Act is wide and embraces all the activities of the council, a council cannot use its statutory powers in order to punish a body or person who has done nothing contrary to English law'.[35] The Court held, given the multiracial character of the borough, that the duty permitted the council to decide that trade with a particular company should cease because of that company's links with South Africa. However, since the purpose of the boycott of the company by the council was broader, exerting pressure to sever all trading links between the company and South Africa, and was not therefore restricted to a wish to improve race relations in the borough, the actions of the council were unlawful.

Political intervention: the Local Government Act 1988

By 1988, the second (political) route of challenging these policies had also been successful. The Local Government Act 1988[36] substantially restricted the use of

---

[33] [1985] AC 1054.   [34] [1988] 1 All ER 938.   [35] *Per* Neill LJ.
[36] The equivalent in Northern Ireland was the Local Government (Miscellaneous Provisions) (Northern Ireland) Order 1991.

public procurement for social policy purposes by local authorities. Section 17 provided that it was the duty of every relevant public authority (in practice local authorities)[37] to exercise its functions in relation to its public supply or works contracts 'without reference to matters which are non-commercial matters for the purposes of this section'. Among the matters defined as non-commercial were 'the terms and conditions of employment by contractors of their workers or the composition of the arrangements for the promotion, transfer or training of or the other opportunities afforded to, their workforces.'[38]

There was a difficult issue, however, of how to deal with the race relations duty that was imposed on local authorities by section 71 of the Race Relations Act 1976. Eventually it was decided that, rather than repeal section 71, there would be a limited exception made to accommodate it. Section 18(2) provided that:

> ... nothing in section 17 shall preclude a local authority from (a) asking approved questions seeking information or undertakings relating to workforce matters and considering the responses to them, or (b) including in a draft contract or draft tender for a contract terms or provisions relating to workforce matters and considering the responses to them, if ... [this] is reasonably necessary to secure compliance with section 71 [of the Race Relations Act 1976, which requires local authorities to promote equality of opportunity for people of different racial groups.]

The Local Government Act 1988 further provided, in section 18(4), that where it was permissible to ask a question under section 18(2), it was also permissible to make an approved request for evidence in support of an answer to the question. Section 18(5) authorized the Secretary of State to specify approved questions for the purposes of section 18(2)(a) and approved descriptions of evidence for the purposes of section 18(4). The Secretary of State subsequently approved several questions which focused on whether a firm had adopted an equal opportunities policy relating to race relations and whether the firm was observing the relevant Code of Practice issued by the Commission on Racial Equality.[39] In the view of Joe Charlesworth and Véronique Voruz, however, the local authorities' scope for action was 'marginal' and did not 'allow for much effective implementation of a racial equality policy through a contracts scheme'.[40]

---

[37] As regards public bodies not subject to the Local Government Act 1988, the major legal constraints on their ability to insert procurement linkages into their contracts lay in EC law. To what extent did these bodies use their powers to insert such linkages? The CRE published an extensive list of equal opportunity conditions that it recommended that health authorities, for example, insert in their contracts. Commission for Racial Equality, 'NHS Contracts and Racial Equality: A Guide' (1991). An assessment of the activities of District Health Authorities in 1994 disclosed that some had adopted similar approaches in attaching conditions to their contracts with Health Service Trusts: 'Equal Opportunities in the Health Service: a survey of NHS trusts' (1994) 53 Equal Opportunities Review 24, 26.   [38] Local Government Act 1988, s 17(5)(a).

[39] 'Local Government Act 1988—Public Supply and Works Contracts: Non-Commercial Matters', Joint Circular 8/88 from the Department of the Environment and the Welsh Office, 6 April 1988.

[40] J Charlesworth and V Voruz, 'The Contract Compliance Policy: An Illustration of the Persistence of Racism as the Failure of Modernity' (1998) 7 Social and Legal Studies, 193, 198.

Even this limited approach was the subject of intense debate as to how far a wider or narrow approach to the interpretation of the Act was legitimate, and councils were faced with decisions that they had to be told involved some legal risks. Concern came to be focused on the meaning, implications, and compatibility with EC law of several of these questions. The practice of asking approved questions was open to the objection that it put contractors from other Member States at a disadvantage. They were less likely than their British competitors to have an established policy on race relations of the kind envisaged, and less likely to be familiar with the CRE Code of Practice, on which several of the permitted questions were based. It might be argued that the wording of the questions did not afford to tenderers from other Member States the opportunity of stating that they maintained a policy on race relations which conformed with the law of the state in which they were established (notwithstanding that it was not set out in instructions, documents, or advertisements of the kind mentioned in the approved questions) or that they observed an acceptable code of practice designed for another Member State (notwithstanding that it was not precisely the same as the CRE's Code).

Although, in 1994, the government indicated to the CRE that it saw no need to amend the specification made by the Secretary of State, it went on to emphasize that local authorities should use the questions specified with full knowledge of the requirements of the EC directives. The CRE issued further guidance to local authorities,[41] which recommended that:

... in their evaluation of responses to the approved questions authorities should take account of the obvious differences in the circumstances of companies and other bodies which have no establishment in the UK. Provided that is done, it is our view that the likelihood of a credible legal challenge is very remote. To give effect to this proviso, authorities would be well advised to append a note when they put the approved questions to potential contractors to the effect that companies and other bodies with no UK establishment should frame their response in the context of the anti (race) discrimination law and codification of good practice (if any) in force in the member state from which application is being made.

Much time was spent subsequently on attempting to develop schemes that would meet the need to comply with Community law, comply with the terms of the Local Government Act 1988, and achieve some results in terms of contributing to the achievement of racial equality.[42] An influential amendment of the CRE's suggested contract terms was adopted by Newcastle-upon-Tyne City Council during 1993.[43] Three modifications were of particular significance in this set of conditions: first the conditions applied not only to contractors but also to any subcontractors employed by the Contractor. Second, the Newcastle conditions specified more precisely that the contractor and subcontractor will not 'discriminate directly

---

[41] Letter 25 April 1994, 'Promoting Racial Equality through Supply and Works Contracts'.

[42] See eg the collection of initiatives up to June 1995 in Local Authorities Race Relations Information Exchange, 'Race Equality and the Contracting Process: Larrie Survey' (June 1995).

[43] See Newcastle City Council, 'Can We Do Business? Racial Equality in a Competitive Environment' (1993).

or indirectly'. Third, and by far the most significant divergence, the Newcastle conditions required the contractor and any subcontractor to 'observe as far as possible and at least in accordance with the Council's published criteria [included as an appendix to the contract] the Commission for Racial Equality's Code of Practice'. The appendix adopted the approach of setting out basic minimum criteria relating to equality of opportunity, which all firms must adopt, ranging from a requirement of a statement of the firm's equal opportunities policy (criterion 1) through to compulsory monitoring (criterion 6). Depending on the size of the firm, certain additional criteria must be adopted, including, for firms with more than 250 employees, the taking of positive action to encourage greater representation of underrepresented ethnic minority groups. The tender price submitted should then include any costs to that firm of compliance with the racial equality contract conditions.

Authorities might request information and evidence from contractors to ascertain ability to comply with the contract conditions. However, a local authority might not determine a contract for breach of any such contract conditions.[44] Legal advice also indicated that it would be difficult to assess what if any financial detriment an authority suffered if a contractor breached a condition, and so the remedy of damages or their equivalent would not seem available. The remedy for breach of the contract conditions in this context seems limited primarily to refusing to award further work to a contractor in breach of the conditions.

In 1995, the Local Government Management Board and the Local Authority Associations, in consultation with the CRE and the EOC, produced guidance on how and why equality issues could be considered in the context of procurement, and CCT in particular.[45] Also in 1995, the CRE, the Association of Metropolitan Authorities, and the Local Government Management Board produced an extensive set of guidlines for local authorities on how to incorporate racial equality issues into their contract procedures.[46] The CRE suggested model criteria for observance of the CRE Code of Practice by contractors.[47] Based on this, a consortium of West Midlands local authorities adopted a 'common standard' for racial equality to be adopted by council service providers, adopting an approach that distinguished between different contractors based on their size, requiring smaller firms to do less than larger firms.[48]

Other varieties of equality linkage

The limited protection afforded to race relations did not apply in other areas. In particular no equivalent exception was made with respect to sex equality issues

[44] Local Government Act 1988, s 18(3).
[45] 'Equalities and the Contract Culture' (Local Government Management Board, 1995).
[46] 'Racial Equality and Council Contractors' (CRE, 1995).
[47] Commission for Racial Equality, 'Racial Equality means Quality: A Standard for Racial Equality for Local Government in England and Wales' (CRE, 1995).
[48] West Midlands Forum, 'Racial Equality: Common Standards for Council Contracts' (July 1998).

and attempts to do so during the course of the passage of the 1988 legislation failed. The effect of this failure to include an equality exception for sex equality was highlighted by the 1989 decision in *R v London Borough of Islington, ex p Building Employers' Confederation*.[49] The Court held that the inclusion of a contract clause that the contractor should comply with certain provisions of the Sex Discrimination Act 1975 was unlawful, since it related to non-commercial matters in the Local Government Act 1988. The Court did not accept that the definition of non-commercial matters contained in section 17(5)(c) related only to matters which went directly to the composition of the workforce, such as a provision that it should include a certain number of women. The EOC recommended that the Local Government Act 1988 restrictions on what constituted a noncommercial consideration should be amended to allow terms and conditions to be regarded as a commercial matter. 'This would enable local authorities to ask potential contractors questions under the Sex Discrimination Act, as well as the Race Relations Act, as a means to assess their terms and conditions of service and their equal opportunities policies in relation to gender, race and disability.'[50] The rules for tendering 'under [CCT] and under European law should be amended, so that equal opportunities 'becomes one of the core criteria in the selection of tenderers and the evaluation of bids'.[51] An equivalent to section 71 of the Race Relations Act 1976 should be enacted which would provide that local authorities would be placed under a similar duty with regard to equality of opportunity between the sexes.[52] These recommendations were not adopted.

European Commission and disability

We have seen in chapter 2 above that a British Priority Suppliers Scheme allowed government departments to give workshops for the disabled and prison workshops the opportunity to match the best bid by others. According to Rosemary Boyle, the Treasury, as the guardian of public procurement legality, 'was conscious that the scheme's limitation to UK workshops might be questionable under the Treaty and that the offer-back process might be considered to breach the rules' of the Supplies Directive:[53] 'Officials therefore sought an informal understanding with [the Supported Employment Procurement Advice and Consultancy Service, the government body responsible for running the scheme] that departments should be advised that, for contracts above the threshold', the Supplies Directive should 'take precedence'.[54] In particular, the Treaty requirements of non-discrimination between the contractors of different Member States might have made the Priority

---

[49] [1989] IRLR 382.

[50] EOC, *The Gender Impact of CCT in Local Government: Summary report* (EOC, 1995) 28.

[51] ibid 28–9.   [52] ibid 29.

[53] R Boyle, 'Disability Issues in Public Procurement' in S Arrowsmith and P Kunzlik (eds), *Social and Environmental Policies under the EC Procurement Rules: New Directives and New Directions* (Provisional title) (Cambridge University Press, in press).   [54] ibid.

Suppliers Scheme difficult to justify. In 1992, Member States were asked by the Commission 'if they had any preference schemes they would like to list in the Supplies Directive when it was consolidated', but because the Treasury 'had doubts about the Priority Suppliers Scheme', it did not notify the Commission.[55] When a British company running these workshops sought to use the Scheme to protect itself against competition from central and eastern Europe, it found that 'it was not listed as an exception to the Supplies Directive'.[56] The company 'complained to [the] then Secretary of State for Employment [who] expressed concern to the press that the [European] Commission had intervened',[57] which in fact it had not done.

The Commission had, however, been involved in challenging a somewhat equivalent Italian scheme. In Italy, Law No 381 of 8 November 1991 on social cooperatives, enabled contracting authorities, by way of derogation from the law on public procurement, to enter into agreements to purchase supplies and services from certain cooperatives employing physically and mentally disabled workers and certain other categories of disadvantaged persons, such as ex-alcoholics and drug addicts. Such cooperatives had to be registered in the appropriate 'Albo' for their region, thus qualifying them for selection for public contracts. The European Commission considered that these arrangements breached the procurement direct-ives in that contracts were effectively negotiated outside the procedures laid down in the directives, and were discriminatory since only Italian cooperatives bene-fited.[58] Following Commission intervention in August 1994, the Italian law was amended in several respects.[59] First, the preference would be limited to contracts below the thresholds of the procurement directives; second, the preferences would be extended to comparable establishments in other Member States of the Com-munity; third, the conditions for access to the benefits and the list of those eligible would be published in the Official Journal; and fourth, as regards contracts above the thresholds in the directives, an obligation to use a workforce which included at least 30 per cent of persons from the categories of disadvantaged could be included in the conditions of execution of the contract and this would be specified in the tender notice and in specifications.

When asked by the British government about the legality of the British scheme, the Commission advised that such a scheme was legal provided it operated on an EU basis. 'This raised the prospect of having to give preferential treatment to low-cost/state-aided workshops in other Member States.'[60] During the summer of 1994, the British government announced that it was withdrawing the scheme. Changes in the Consolidated Supplies Directive were given as the reason for doing so.[61] The British government, it was said, had relied on the exception allowing already established award preferences, and considered that after its omission from the Consolidated Supplies Directive, the scheme was contrary to Community law.

---

[55] ibid.   [56] ibid.   [57] ibid.   [58] Fernández Martín (n 7 above) 45.
[59] Law No 52 of 6 February 1996, Art 20.   [60] ibid.
[61] See ch 10 above; see S Arrowsmith, *The Lawyer*, 27 September 1994, 25.

However, rather than withdraw the scheme for purchases above the threshold limit of the directive, the scheme was withdrawn entirely.[62]

In November 1994, however, the British government announced that a new scheme would be introduced under a different title, the 'special contracts arrangement', with several changes designed to comply with Community law, but also to reduce the extent to which any replacement scheme would support non-British workshops in practice. These changes extended eligibility under the special contracts arrangements to all comparable workshops in other Community and European Economic Area countries (ie those with more than 50 per cent of severely disabled workers), but contracts subject to the scheme would be confined to those below the thresholds of the procurement directives[63] (happily, for the Treasury, with the indirect effect that the purchases would be 'less likely to be suitable for cross-border bidding').[64] The scheme no longer applied to prison workshops. A list of eligible establishments would be maintained by the Employment Service, and conditions of eligibility and invitations to apply for inclusion would be published annually in the Official Journal.

III. Revisiting the Development of Procurement Linkages in Germany

Controversial nature of procurement linkages under German law

Procurement linkages also became increasingly controversial in Germany, legally as well as politically, during the late 1980s and early 1990s. Strohs argued in 1988 that the VOB/A provisions did not allow for the inclusion of additional assessment criteria when tenders were awarded, for example by means of supplementary terms and conditions for such awards additional to those set out in VOB/A.[65] Provisions and regulations of this sort represented, in his view, an infringement of VOB/A, which stipulated that all tenderers must be afforded equal treatment. The contract must be awarded to the most acceptable tender. The only criteria that might be taken into account were those relating to performance, in particular economic and technical aspects. This meant that awarding authorities may only take additional criteria into account in accordance with existing preferential criteria, other specialized administrative regulations taking precedence over the VOB, or on the basis of higher-ranking legislation.

Strohs noted that North Rhine-Westphalia provisions regarding apprenticeships, discussed in chapter 10 above, had been taken up by the Federal Cartel

---

[62] See further S Arrowsmith, 'Abolition of the United Kingdom's Procurement Preference Scheme for Disabled Workers' (1994) 3 PPLR CS225.   [63] *Financial Times*, 30 November 1994.

[64] Boyle (n 53 above) 16.

[65] M Strohs, 'Die Berücksichtinung vergabefremder Kriterien bei der Vergabe von Bauaufträgen durch die öffentliche Hand', BauR 2/88, 144.

Office in 1984. The Cartel Office stated that authorities would be infringing domestic antitrust law if they gave preference to companies employing trainees and apprentices when awarding contracts for construction works. The Cartel Office justified its point of view in the following way: Public sector contracting authorities must comply with the antitrust legislation. The public sector either held a dominant market position or at least a strong market position. To the extent that a dominant market position or at least a strong market position existed, anything that public sector principals did which conflicted with the provisions of the VOB would normally be counted as discrimination or unfair restraint of trade, and in the case of market domination as improper or abusive conduct. Because of this, the Federal Cartel Office reserved the right to intervene in future if complaints were made to it in this respect.

The government of Lower Saxony, took an even more restrictive view.[66] It stated that the award of a public sector contract could only be made to the bidder that offered the best value for money, taking account of the principles of economic efficiency and good value. The definition of the bid offering the best value for money was the bid which had the most favourable relationship between the goods and services on offer and the price requested for them. When the contract was awarded it was not permitted to take account of criteria that were of no direct relevance to the contract in question. Neither EC law nor German budgetary law had any provisions for preferential treatment for contracts to enforce social policy requirements, whether they concerned employment policy, training policy, environmental policy, or whether they served to promote equality of treatment and opportunity for women. If political criteria were taken into account when awarding public sector contracts, it would no longer be possible to award contracts on the basis of value for money offered by the bid but only on the basis of the number or importance of the various criteria being taken into consideration. Competition in the public sector market place, one of the vital objectives for achieving the single internal market, supported by Germany, would thus be abandoned.

Other assessments differed. Hans-Joachim Menzel concluded that the introduction of such contract award criteria was neither 'entirely natural',[67] as the German Trades Union Federation had argued, because of the restrictions placed on the state's contractual powers by constitutional law, nor was it an infringement of the law and the market economy, as claimed, for example, by the Hamburg Chamber of Trade Craftsmen. The welfare state principle and the equality of treatment injunction, deriving from article 3 of the Basic Law (Grundgesetz—GG) and designed to ensure competition, provided adequate justification in principle for taking due account of social policy criteria when public sector contracts were awarded.

---

[66] Letter to the author, on file.
[67] Dr H-J Menzel, 'Berücksichtigung sozialpolitischer Kriterien bei der öffentlichen Auftragsvergabe', DB Heft 6 vom 6.2.1981, 303.

Commission infringement action

In 1990, the European Commission began Article 169 infringement proceedings by asking the government of Germany to submit its observations on the legality under Community law of the North Rhine-Westphalia circular discussed above.[68] The Commission noted that, under the procurement directives, a public sector body should apply the criteria of the lowest price, or most economically advantageous tender. The Commission's preliminary view was that the requirement that, in the case of public sector contracts financed from Land funds where the tenders are of the same standard, contracts should be awarded to those businesses which train apprentices—and particularly female apprentices—therefore constituted a breach of the directives, as the condition was one which lay outside the objective requirements of the various contracts.

In reply, the federal government submitted to the Commission a circular issued by the appropriate Minister of the State of North Rhine-Westphalia, dated 4 April 1990, cancelling the previous circular, including the amendments made to it on 8 October 1987 and 21 November 1988. However, an additional circular was also included. That had been issued by the same Minister on 5 April 1990 introducing a rule similar to the previous one, but now just in favour of women apprentices. The authorities of North Rhine-Westphalia took the view, in connection with the passing of the new Circular of 5 April 1990, that special efforts were necessary to encourage young women, and that requirements such as these were fully in accordance with the Commission's objectives set out in the Commission's Communication on 'Public Procurement—Regional and Social Aspects'[69] issued after the *Beentjes* case and were in accordance with the Equal Treatment Directive ((EEC) 76/207).

The Commission decided that the new circular continued to be in breach of the directives. The only criteria which a public sector body could apply when placing a contract were either the criterion of the lowest price or that of the most economically advantageous tender. The criteria allowed to be considered in this context must be objective, apply to all offers, and be related to the objective of the contract. The contract criterion that was applicable in the Land was the most advantageous tender. This criterion related to the quality of the work, not to the quality of the firm. However, the circular in question sought to give preferential treatment to those firms which provided training places for young women. This was not an objective criterion related to the objective of the contract. The German government subsequently notified the Commission that the Land had withdrawn the contested circular.

---

[68] This section is based on information contained in a report prepared for North Rhine-Westphalia by Prof Dr L Osterloh, 'Rechtsgutachten zu Fragen der Frauenförderung im Rahmen der öffentlichen Mittelvergabe' (June 1991).

[69] EC Commission, Public Procurement: Regional and Social Aspects, COM(89)400.

It was widely expected, however, that a revised mechanism of contract compliance would be introduced by the Land. An inter-ministerial working group was established which considered a plan outlined by the Women's Ministry which would have imposed as conditions for the award of all public contracts, *inter alia*, a requirement that the federal anti-discrimination law must be obeyed, and that gender neutral job advertising must take place. In addition, in the case of a contract valued at more than DM50,000 and a firm employing more than twenty people, the company awarded the contract would have been required to monitor the composition of its workforce by gender, and select from a list of measures at least three ways to promote women, which it would be obliged to implement. If the contract was worth at least DM1 million, then it would have had to have selected at least five ways from the list. Monitoring of the operation of these requirements would have been carried out by employee representatives, to whom the company would have been under a duty to report. In the event of serious blameworthy violations of these contractual obligations, firms awarded contracts could have been required to pay a contractual penalty of a sum amounting to 5 per cent of the contract value. This plan was not, however, adopted by the Land government. Instead, the government undertook a campaign for voluntary measures in the private sector.[70]

One effect of the Commission's intervention was to stimulate considerable debate in Germany on the national and Community law basis of these types of procurement linkages, particularly regarding women, adopted by the Länder. At least three such studies were completed. The first was a report for North Rhine-Westphalia (by Prof Dr L Osterloh).[71] The second was a report for Brandenburg (also by Osterloh).[72] The third was a report for Hessen.[73] According to Osterloh, European Community procurement directives ruled out the use of special preference rules for companies that had been shown to implement measures for the promotion of women's interests. This was not the case, on the basis of the *Beentjes* judgment, with regard to the insertion of contractual requirements. Contracting authorities were entitled to make the award of a contract subject to additional conditions that must be satisfied by the successful bidder. This instrument was substantial because it completely ruled out all bidders who were either unwilling or unable to satisfy the additional conditions, regardless of whether they should or should not have been considered according to the selection and award criteria set out in the directives. The effect of this was that whereas German law left relatively broad scope for the operation of preferences in the selection between more or less identical bids, the directives ruled out the use of such additional selection criteria.

---

[70] See *Suddeutsche Zeitung*, 9 March 1995.   [71] Osterloh (n 68 above).

[72] Prof Dr L Osterloh, 'Kurzgutachten über die Möglichkeiten der Frauenförderung im Rahmen der Vergabe öffentlicher Mittel, insbesondere in Form öffentlicher Aufträge' (October, 1993).

[73] Dr M Sudhof, 'Rechtsgutachten zur Frage der Vereinbarkeit einer Kopplung der Vergabe öffentlicher Aufträge des Landes Hessen mit frauenfördernden Auftragsvergabebedingungen' (nd).

On the other hand, whereas European law allowed a broad use of additional contractual terms and conditions, under German law these were permitted only when they did not result in considerable additional expense on the contractor's part that is not covered by the agreed price. This last objection would, however, be met if the costs of implementing the requirements were included in the payments for the contract, or could be covered by additional grants or subsidies from the awarding authority.[74]

New domestic legislation and procurement linkages

New federal legislation was passed in 1998 to reform the whole procurement process and to bring German law into compliance with EC law, the Act coming into force on 1 January 1999. The Act was a compromise between the Bundestag (the 'main' chamber of Parliament, at the time led by the conservative CDU, favouring the draft prepared by the government) and the Bundesrat (the generally weaker, but for this kind of legislation almost equally powerful chamber of Parliament, representing the 16 Länder, at this time mainly led by the left-leaning SPD). This 1998 Act transferred the legal regulation of public procurement from the States Budgetary Law Act, where it was fragmentarily laid down before, as we saw in chapter 10 above, to the Anti-trust Act (Gesetz gegen Wettbewerbsbeschränkungen, GWB).[75] The inclusion of the procurement reform in this Act was seen as indicating 'a remarkable shift of perspective', since previously public procurement requirements 'were intended only to safeguard correct and economic administration of public money, not to protect competitors or competition'.[76] In addition, the Act laid down several principles for awarding public sector contracts, which until then were only either included in the VOL and VOB or deemed to be valid but unwritten. One set of rules, which was upgraded from the level of VOL and VOB to the level of formal legislation, concerned the substantive criteria according to which the public administration had to award its contracts.[77] These provided that the public body primarily procured goods, buildings, and services by way of competition and in a transparent procurement procedure. The participants in the procurement process were to be treated equally, unless a prejudicial treatment was explicitly required or allowed by virtue of this statute. The interests of the Mittelstand (the class of small businesses, in contrast to large-scale industry) were to be regarded appropriately, primarily by dividing the contract into smaller parts. Paragraph 7 provided that tenderers were entitled to claim conformity by the public body with the procurement rules. Paragraph 7 has been seen as the crucial part of the reform over all, because this provision and the additional system of judicial

---

[74] Osterloh (n 68 above).   [75] GWB, §§97–129.

[76] B Spiesshofer and M Lang, 'The New German Public Procurement Law: Commentary and English Translation of the Text' (1999) 8 PPLR CS103.

[77] It is located in the first paragraph of the part of the GWB regarding public procurement, §97.

remedies for the protection of this claim made this whole field of law judiciable, whereas before it was in the unsupervised discretion of the administration.[78]

For the purposes of our discussion, however, it was paragraph 4 that is most important. Paragraph 4 provided that contracts were to be awarded to professional, competent, and reliable companies (other or further requirements were only allowed if they were provided for by federal or Länder legislation). The best bid must be accepted. This provision was one of those that were the result of a compromise between the Bundesrat and the Bundestag.[79] The original draft prepared by the federal government was initiated by the controversy about secondary aims in procurement procedures described earlier in this chapter. The draft contained the authorization to implement secondary aims only on the basis of federal statutes, not Länder statutes. The Länder argued, through their representative at the federal level, the Bundesrat, that secondary aims should be allowed to be determined and implemented by Länder statutes as well. And the Bundesrat succeeded, as can be seen in §97(4) of the GWB. The federal government, when it originally drafted a competence only for the federal state, not for the Länder, may have been afraid that the Länder would be less willing to comply with EC standards, and that EC law-compliance would be easier to ensure if only one jurisdiction (the federal one) were competent. The Bundesrat managed to achieve another goal. In the original federal government draft of §97(4), the second part of the sentence, read: '*Further* requirements are only allowed, if they are provided for by federal statute'. As enacted it read: '*Other or further* requirements . . .'. By this wording, the Act allowed the general replacement, not merely the supplementation of the requirements and criteria mentioned in §97(4) (first part of the sentence) GWB.

However, the purpose of §97(4) (second part of the sentence) GWB, was, in general, a restrictive one. In contrast to the former legal situation, promoting procurement linkages by public procurement required a formal Act of Parliament (either at the federal or Länder level), and could not be done, as so often in the past, by internal circular, ordinance, oral order, or just custom. In order to protect public administration and its practice from too speedy an alteration of the legal situation, the Bundesrat did, however, manage to install a transitional provision for §97(4) (last part of the sentence) GWB. Until June 2000, promoting social policy through public procurement was allowed even without statutory provisions. From June 2000, these measures could not be undertaken by the administration alone, but had to be based on an Act of Parliament.[80]

The discussion about particular social policy linkages in public procurement at the time of the enactment of the federal law mainly focused on two issues: first, the issue of whether public sector contracts should be given only to companies

---

[78] Spiesshofer and Lang (n 76 above) CS104.

[79] The history of the legislation of this provision is described by C Benedict, *Sekundärzwecke im Vergabeverfahren* (Springer, 2000) 4 and 107 *et seq.*

[80] See in general M Kling, *Die Zulässigkeit vergabefremder Regelungen* (Schriffenreihe des Forum Vergabe, 2000); Benedict (n 79 above).

that declared that they paid wages according to the collectively agreed rates (tariff) in the area in which they carried out the contract. Public authorities did not want to be required to award contracts to tenderers who were not bound to the collectively agreed rate for the area, for example because they were based in other areas (mostly abroad) where there was a tariff regime of a lower standard. Given that these tenderers were able to offer lower prices, they were then able to destroy the local employers' competitiveness, since the local employers were bound by the high tariff regime. The purpose of the 'loyalty declaration' (as it was called) was to ensure that only those bidders were allowed to take part in the procurement procedure who, no matter where they were from, declared that all the employees involved in the performance of the contract, and all employees of possible subcontractors, were paid and treated in accordance with the local tariff system. At least twelve Länder required such declarations, some of them on the basis of circulars, ordinances, regulation, or custom, as was legally possible until June 2000. Some of them subsequently transferred this requirement to the level of a formal Act of Parliament.

These requirements encountered considerable legal difficulty on other grounds. Prior to the federal reform legislation, equivalent requirements were held unlawful by the Federal procurement Supervisory Committee and the Federal Cartel Office.[81] In July 1999, Berlin was the first Land to pass an Act of Parliament on public procurement after the reform legislation. This included a requirement that tenderers agreed to pay the tariff. The newly installed judicial review provided a basis for challenging this and in January 2000 the Federal Supreme Court (Bundesgerichtshof— BGH) decided a case concerning this Berlin procurement legislation.[82] The BGH was of the opinion that it was crucial for the case whether or not the new Berlin procurement Act was valid. It was invalid if it violated the Basic Law or other federal law, but only the German Constitutional Court (Bundesverfassungsgericht—BverfG) was allowed to decide this question, and for that reason the BGH submitted the case to the BVerfG. At the time of writing, the decision of the BVerfG was still awaited. In its decision, the BGH gave as one of several reasons why it held the new Berlin procurement Act to be invalid, that it violated §97(4) of the GWB. In addition, however, it also held that the Land had no jurisdiction over collective bargaining issues. Before the decision was given by the BGH, the Federal Ministry for Economy and Technology and the Federal Ministry for Family and Women had announced that they were planning to include, in a planned law on gender equality, preferences for firms that promoted women's employment.[83] The legal uncertainty over the Berlin

---

[81] H-J Priess and C Pitschas, 'Recent German Public Procurement Case Law: Bodies Governed by Public Law and Social Criteria Unrelated to Public Procurement Rules' (1999) 8 PPLR CS120, CS121.   [82] The decision is published in *Der Betrieb 2000*, 465 *et seq.*

[83] 'Court rules against linking the award of public sector contracts to observance of collectively agreed wages', European Industrial Relations Observatory on-line, <http://www.eiro.eurofound.ie/print/2000/01/feature/DE0001235F.html>. For a general overview, see E Gurlit, 'Vergabe öffentlicher Aufträge als Instrument der Frauenförderung' in M Koreuber and U Mager (eds), *Recht und Geschlecht* (Nomos Verlagsgesellschaft, 2004) 153–70.

law appears to have contributed to this federal proposal not being acted on. In July 2002, a law proposed by the federal government, which obliged companies seeking to obtain public contracts to pay their employees the collectively agreed rate, was rejected by the Bundesrat.[84]

The second issue that raised considerable debate was the issue of Scientology: 'the German Ministers of the Interior recommended in 1997 that the Federal Government and the German Länder take measures in order to protect state activities against the influence of psychological methods' based on Scientology 'when awarding public contracts'.[85] A specific clause to be included in government contracts was then adopted in June 1998 by a ministerial working group, which required a declaration by prospective tenderers that they rejected Scientology, and in an administrative circular of September 1998 the Federal Ministry of Economics 'stressed that a company refusing to sign the Scientology Declaration must be deemed unreliable'. Whatever the domestic and EC legal position was, and there was much legal argument that it was unlawful,[86] the protests from the United States that it was potentially discriminatory against their companies,[87] threatened to make it an issue of international significance, and the requirement was subsequently removed.[88]

IV. Deciding Against Procurement Linkages in the Netherlands

The debate over whether contract compliance should be developed in the Netherlands for securing women's equality was begun in the early 1970s by a women's pressure group, which advocated affirmative action on the model of that developed in the United States, including that of Executive Order 11246, considered in detail in chapter 6 above.[89] Affirmative action was put on a legal basis in 1980 when the Dutch Equal Opportunities Act was passed, which established affirmative action as legally permissible, but not obligatory. The debate concerning contract compliance specifically emerged as an important political issue in

---

[84] European Industrial Relations Observatory on-line, <http://www.eiro.eurofound.ie/2000/08/inbrief/DE0208201N.html>.

[85] H-J Priess and C Pitschas, 'Secondary Policy Criteria and Their Compatibility with EC and WTO Procurement Law: The Case of the German Scientology Declaration' (2000) 9 PPLR 171.

[86] ibid.

[87] Office of the United States Trade Representative, 'Annual Report on Discrimination in Foreign Government Procurement', 30 April 2000. See also John Burgess, 'U.S. Challenges Germany on Scientology; Trade Office Says Government Contracting Policy Discriminates Against Members' *Washington Post*, 4 May 2000, A19.

[88] United States Trade Representative, 'Foreign Trade Barriers: European Union' (2003) 120, available at <http://www.ustr.gov/assets/Document_Library/Reports_Publications/2003/2003_NTE_Report/asset_upload_file752_6193.pdf>.

[89] CE van Vleuten, 'Fact Sheet, Research on Contract Compliance, problems and possibilities' (undated, unpublished).

the mid-to-late 1980s, when the issue of contract compliance in the context of women's equality became combined with the issue of contract compliance in the context of equality for ethnic minority groups in the Netherlands. In 1986, the Minister of Social Affairs asked the Emancipation Council for advice on government policies supporting affirmative action for women. This resulted in the commissioning of a study by the Council on contract compliance policies particularly in the United States. This was published in January 1989,[90] and recommended, with the support of the Council, that equivalent policies should be developed in the Netherlands.[91]

In 1988, a majority within the Second Chamber of Parliament asked the Minister for Social Affairs to study the possibility of using contract compliance policies as a method of reducing the levels of high unemployment among ethnic minorities. In March 1989, the Ministry of Social Affairs published a consultative document exploring the legal and policy implications of contract compliance measures. The Memorandum was entitled 'Meer Kansen Afdwinghen?' (Enforcing More Opportunities?),[92] but a translation of the sub-title gives a better indication of the scope of the discussion: 'An exploration of the judicial opportunities and administrative desirability of the application of the position of the authorities as a granter of licences, subsidies and contracts on behalf of the administration with regard to groups which occupy a disadvantaged position in the labour market.' This Memorandum became a key document in the debate, as it provided the focus for much of the subsequent political and policy discussion, generating a significant number of responses from employers, unions, and other interested parties. The position it took was relatively restrictive on the legal scope for such policies without further legislation, and relatively sceptical as to their policy desirability.

An influential comment on this Memorandum by the Regeringscommissaris voor de toetsing van wetgevingsprojecten (Commission for the Examination of Legislative Projects)[93] supported the Memorandum's reservations on the use of several of these policies without a further legal base. Other groups were critical of the conservative tone and conclusions of the Memorandum. The Emancipation Council, for example, reiterated its support for contract compliance, arguing that contract compliance policies were legitimate, and that a further legal base should be established for it.[94] A detailed report was also published advocating

[90]   CE van Vleuten, *Contract Compliance in de Verenigde Statten, in Emancipatieraad, Positive Actie: Advies en onderzoek* (Emancipatieraad, 1989). See also CE van Vleuten, 'Contract Compliance 1: De situatie in de Verenigde Staten', Nemesis, Tijdschrift voor Vrouw en Recht, No 5, September/October 1989, 169.

[91]   Emancipatieraad, Advies over de nota positieve actieprogramma's voor vrouwen in arbeidssorganisaties, adv nr II/75/89; 21 March 1989, published in *Emancipatieraad, Positive Actie: Advies en onderzoek* (Emancipatieraad, 1989).

[92]   Ministry of Social Affairs and Employment, 'Meer Kansen Afdwinghen?', March 1989.

[93]   Interimadvies van de Commissie voor de toetsing van wetgevingsprojecten over de Nota 'Gelijke Kansen Afdwinghen?', CTW 89/21, 18 September 1989.

[94]   Emancipatieraad, adv nr III/02/89, 4 September 1989.

contract compliance with regard to ethnic minorities by the Landelijk Bureau Racismebestrijding.[95]

Policy at national level

In January 1991, the Dutch government issued its final position on the issue of contract compliance at national level, preceded by a letter from the Minister of Social Affairs and Employment.[96] The Cabinet's paper pointed out that, in its opinion, the agreement reached between the social partners by the Stichting van de Arbeid at the so-called 'Autumn Consultations' on 2 October 1990 on the main outlines of a package of measures to ameliorate the position of ethnic minorities in the labour market had created a new, and important, dimension to the debate on contract compliance measures. Although several instruments may be employed simultaneously in removing disadvantages of groups in the job market, the Cabinet considered it desirable to direct attention to the implementation and guidance of the approach proposed by the Trade Union Federation, which it characterized as 'self-regulation'. The introduction of other types of instruments, or even the threat of them, would be likely to interfere with the approach proposed and could entail the risk of a breakdown in the success of this approach.

As regards improving the position in the job market of other groups (in addition to ethnic minorities), the Cabinet's preference was for an approach—concentrated on the different target groups—in which the responsibilities of employers and employees were central. The Cabinet's attitude was that it was not opportune at that time to set another kind of additional requirement for licences (such as the promotion of job market opportunities for groups), which was outside the actual objective of the licensing system. The Cabinet was also of the opinion that it did not appear desirable to develop a policy for introducing qualifications on subsidies for accomplishing policy objectives which were quite separate. However legitimate the policy aim of overcoming the disadvantaged positions of certain groups on the job market might be, the setting of supplementary requirements in the case of subsidies was not consistent in general with the nature and content of existing subsidies. In any case, most subsidies did not have an objective which could be regarded as contributing to lessening the disadvantaged position of some groups in the job market.

As regards the legal admissibility of contract compliance in the case of government contracts, the Cabinet considered that setting supplementary requirements in the sense of positive action was legally permitted in principle. Because of the heterogeneity of the phenomenon, however, a general verdict as to the admissibility

[95] Landelijk Bureau Racismebestrijding—Reeks nr 7, 'Positieve Actie Bedingen: Contract compliance in Nederland' (Landelijk Bureau Racismebestrijding, 1989).

[96] Brief van de Minister van Sociale Zaken en werkgelegenheid, 14 January 1991, and Kabinetsstandpunt inzake Contract Compliance, 18 December 1990, Tweede Kamer, vergaderjaar 1990–91, 21 800 XV, nr 57.

of contract compliance as such was impossible. Consequently, the legal acceptability of supplementary requirements was not unconditional. Acceptability depended on the actual form and content of the requirements; the way in which they were made known to contractors/suppliers, as well as the relationship with the objective and the disadvantages for other interests. The authority concerned would also have to find a statutory/legal basis for its transactions. There was no conflict with Community law, if the supplementary requirements did not lead to discriminatory consequences for persons and businesses of other Member States who were in a similar position. Rather, this non-discrimination requirement only placed restrictions on possible forms of contract compliance. No restriction of free competition need occur, if the supplementary requirements were applied to all prospective tenderers in the same way and at an initial stage.

However, although the introduction of contract compliance for contracts was, legally speaking, permissible, however qualified that statement needed to be with regard to form and content, the Cabinet did not consider there was any reason at present for any movement towards any large-scale introduction of contract compliance. Apart from the legal difficulties concerning the actual introduction of the instrument, there were other arguments against such an initiative: the possible adverse consequences for the purchasing functions of government institutions; problems relating to the organization and control of such a policy; and complications for employers, who in their relations with the authorities would possibly be confronted with a variety of requirements and inspections. The Cabinet considered the merits of the instrument to be limited, therefore. Taking into account the wider context, especially the approach as proposed by the Trade Union Federation, the Cabinet was of the opinion there were no reasons at that time for introducing the instrument of contract compliance.

Policy at the provincial and local levels

As regards the use of contract compliance policies at the provincial and local levels, in a circular issued in November 1985, the Minister of Home Affairs had asked local communities to introduce preferential treatment of minorities.[97] In June 1991, the Minister of Home Affairs issued a circular which set out the cabinet's position regarding contract compliance at the local and provincial levels.[98] Although the Cabinet considered that, at that time, there were no reasons for it to introduce the contract compliance instrument itself, the Minister considered it a prime responsibility of local councils to reflect how far the instrument of contract compliance could make a contribution in reducing unemployment among members of minority groups at local and regional level. However, despite this position, provincial and local authorities seldom introduced contract compliance policies.

---

[97] Circulaire van de minister van Binnenlandse Zaken, 14 November 1985, nr CM85/U1472.
[98] Circulaire van de minister van Binnenlandse Zaken, 25 June 1991, nr DCM91/189.

V. Difficulties for Procurement Linkages in France

The French law on public procurement is to be found in the general principles of administrative law, but chiefly in the Code des Marchés Publics.[99] This codifies most laws and decrees relating to public procurement and is periodically updated. The Code requires that contract conditions must be set out in contract documents and must be divided into general and particular conditions. The Book of General Administrative Clauses (Cahier des Clauses Administratives Générales) sets out the general administrative conditions applicable. Until the mid-1990s, three types of social linkages were commonplace.

As seen in chapter 2 above, for some time French law provided certain preferences for workers', artists', and artisans' cooperatives in the award of public contracts.[100] (Equivalent schemes applied to groupings of agricultural producers.) Where the contract was defined as capable of being carried out by such groups, a price preference of up to a quarter of the total value operated; where works of an artistic nature were concerned, the price preference was up to half of the total value of the contract. In another preference scheme, a percentage of contract lots (one in four) was set aside for beneficiaries of the scheme, including for worker's cooperatives. The reserved lots were awarded to such beneficiaries at the average price obtained for the rest of the contracts in the lot. Where equivalent prices or offers were received from several tenderers and one of them was a cooperative, the tender had to be awarded to the cooperative. Originally these preferences only applied to French nationals, but from 1985 (and as a result of intervention by the European Commission) they were applied to nationals of EC Member States.[101]

Second, exclusion from the right to conclude public sector contracts was a sanction if particular penal provisions were broken. This was the case, for example, where a person was convicted of infringing any provision of the General Taxation Code (Code Général des Impôts) which provided for penal sanctions, and for which the court may include as part of the sentence a prohibition on obtaining public contracts. (Every three months the Budget Minister compiled a list of all such prohibitions pronounced by the courts and communicated it to all contracting authorities.) Law 91-1383 of 31 December 1991, for example, inserted an equivalent sanction in respect of the use of clandestine labour in the Code du Travail.[102]

---

[99] See also L Digings, *Competitive Tendering and the European Communities: Public Procurement, CCT and Local Services* (AMA, 1991) 58–72, and C Goldman, 'An Introduction to the French Law of Government Procurement Contracts' (1987) 20 GW JILE 461.

[100] Code des marchés publics, Arts 61–65 and 69–74.

[101] Journal Officiel de la République Française, 13 July 1985, 7911, Loi no 85-703 of July 1985. See eg the decision to extend the preference scheme to an Italian co-operative, JORF, 20 January 1993, 1003, Judgment of 30 December 1992.

[102] JORF, 1 January 1992, 15, Art 9, amending the Code du Travail. See also the Circulaire relevant for the interpretation of the law, JORF, 18 November 1992, 15846. The provision is now contained in the Code, Law No 362-4, as amended by Law No 93–313 of 20 December 1993, Art 33, JORF, 21 December 1993, 17769.

The Code de la Santé Publique provided a similar sanction.[103] The Code Pénal provided for the same sanction more generally.[104]

The third approach was to provide for conditions to be incorporated in the contract. For those public contracts not governed by the Code, it was both legal, and usual for public sector contracts to contain clauses relating to the status of personnel, health and safety at work and security on site, and the professional qualifications of the workforce.[105] France ratified ILO Convention No 94 in 1951. France initially referred to a Decree of 10 April 1937 as fulfilling the requirements of the Convention. Subsequently Decrees 55–256, 55–257, and 55–258 of 12 February 1955 gave fuller effect to the Convention.[106] Several further amendments and revisions were made between then and 1964, when these provisions were codified in Articles 117 to 121 of the Code.[107] These required the contracting authority to include clauses regarding the working conditions of the contractor's employees. Article 121 specifically envisaged powers for the administrative authority to exclude a contractor from public sector contracts if the contractor broke the rules. The general administrative code for purchasing included a similar set of requirements.[108]

The French debate over the use of procurement linkages as award criteria in the 1990s originated from attempts in the early 1990s to address the problem of unemployment. Two inter-ministerial circulars were of particular importance.[109] In 1993, an inter-ministerial circular[110] introduced additional criteria relative to employment in the award of public contracts. It encouraged those responsible for the award of public contracts by central and local government, and other public bodies, to allow additional employment conditions to guide their choice of contractor. These additional criteria regarded the reduction of unemployment, in particular by recourse to the services of l'ANPE (the national service for job placement for the unemployed), amongst the previously unemployed and other hard-to-place groups, as an objective to be encouraged. The circular limited the use of these additional criteria, however. It stipulated that a local labour requirement was not permissible, nor was the use of any criteria that would discriminate against contractors in other Community countries.[111]

According to the second inter-ministerial circular in 1995, public bodies had two ways to use procurement linkages. Under the first approach, the social policy to be furthered was included as a contract condition. This meant that in carrying

---

[103] Art 209-19-1 (nouveau), JORF, 23 December 1992, 17568.

[104] Art 131–134, Law No 92-683, JORF, 23 July 1992, 9864.

[105] See A de Laubadère, F Moderne, and P Delvolvé, *Traité des Contrats Administratifs* (2ème éd, 2 vol, LGDJ, 1984) 79–81.   [106] JO 15–2-55.

[107] See also ILO File No ACD 8-2-22-94, Art 22—General reports, Convention No 94, Labour clauses (Public Contracts) 1949: France.   [108] CCAG, 31.4.

[109] 29/12/1993 and 14/12/1995.

[110] Circulaire interministérielle CAB-TEFP 14/93 du 29 décembre 1994 sur la prise en compte de critères additionnels relatifs à l'emploi dans l'attribution des marchés publics, Législation sociale, No 6970, 14 janvier 1994, D4.

[111] The Conseil d'Etat in its decision of 10 May 1996 was asked to rule on the lawfulness of this Circular, but not against the clause itself.

out of the contract, the contractor was under an obligation, for example, to create new jobs (possibly in association with l'ANPE), or provide training to employees. This was a contractual term with social consequences but was not a criterion guiding the choice of contractor. It would be set out in the Cahier des Charges (conditions of the contract). Under a second approach, a social policy requirement could also be additional criteria guiding the choice of contractor. The contractor would have to show in his or her offer how he or she intended to implement this social requirement, in the same way as he or she had to show how he or she intended to carry out the work in question. The result he or she intended to achieve concerning this social requirement *must* appear in the règlement de consultation (where the promoter's requirements for the intended contract work were set out).

Realizing that the use of social criteria, particularly integration measures, were legally contestable, there was an attempt to give a statutory basis for such award criteria in 1998.[112] An amendment to the Code provided that when a public authority considered that a public contract could be used as a means for furthering the integration of people with difficulties in entering the labour market (for example young people or the long-term unemployed), the public authority could impose the taking into account of this objective, according to one of two methods. Either it could be made a condition for implementation of the contract, in which case it had to be included in the preliminary documents and be made clear that such a condition would be imposed. Or the need to engage in activities furthering integration could be included as an object of the contract, and be used as an award criterion, in which case the documents regarding the tender had to state precisely the objectives that were to be reached, and had to state the degree of importance that would be attached to this criterion at the award stage. Before it became part of the legislation, however, the Conseil Constitutionnel declared it to be unconstitutional, although the grounds of annulment were procedural rather than substantive.[113]

The sense that social award criteria were vulnerable under French domestic law was further confirmed by the Administrative Court of Strasbourg in 1999.[114] The local authority of Strasbourg had entered into a contract with an association for the cleaning and sweeping of a local area. The association had as its purpose the integration of disadvantaged people into work. Among the criteria for selection used by the local authority was an additional criterion regarding the role of the company awarded the contract in the promotion of such integration. Only firms and associations that had such integration as its purpose were able to bid. The Administrative Court was asked to cancel the contract. It held that the Code des Marchés Publics provided that additional criteria (ie criteria other than those relating to the price of

---

112 Statute No 98-657, 19 July 1998, Art 17.
113 Decision of the Conseil Constitutionnel, 29 July 1998, Decision No 98-43-DC.
114 See P Loquet, 'L'utilisation de la clause du mieux-disant social dans les marchés publics: une simple affaire de volonté politique et d'ingénierie sociale', Droit Social, 9/10, 1999, 759–61.

the work, the period of execution of the work, etc specifically listed in the Code's provision dealing with award criteria) could be included as award criteria only if these criteria were justified by the purpose of the contract, or the methods of execution of the contract. In this case, neither the purpose of the contract nor the methods of execution of a contract dealing with cleaning and sweeping justified an additional criterion related to the successful firm's function in promoting integration. This criterion may also have prevented some firms from bidding for the contract and was also, therefore, contrary to the freedom guaranteed by the Code to contractors to submit such bids. The contract was contrary to the Code and must be cancelled.

12

Changing Approaches to Procurement Linkages in the Community and Beyond

The previous chapter argued that it was in the new policy context of neo-liberalism that national governments and EC procurement officials increasingly developed and interpreted procurement regulation. In the EC context, the Commission's actions were, from the latter part of the 1980s and during much of the 1990s, hostile to the incorporation of social aspects into procurement. The demise of the social use of procurement was widely predicted, and EC legal instruments were indeed used initially as a reason to limit or suppress the social uses of procurement in several jurisdictions.[1]

By the mid-1990s, the development of European procurement regulation had, indeed, profoundly affected the issue of the role of equality in procurement regulation in several negative ways. These effects are examples of Harry Arthurs' observation of how globalization's influence is 'formative', meaning that it 'transform[s] the institutions, structures and processes through which those rules are made and administered'.[2] Those encouraging linkage at the national level were now much more on the defensive than previously; linkage was seen as an exception, as something that needed to be justified, rather than as an accepted part of procurement policy. We saw in the previous chapter the growth of legal challenges to linkage using procurement legislation under domestic law and under European Community law. The virtual disappearance of linkage in British local authorities by the mid-1990s is one of the clearest, but by no means the only example of the negative effect of procurement reform on social linkages. These examples, which can be multiplied,[3] are evidence of the well-known, even trite, argument that 'globalization strengthens the hand of social, economic, and political forces that erode the social protections that once characterized welfare capitalism'.[4] They are also an

---

[1] Consider the debates recounted in chapter 11 above on race and disability linkages in the UK; on gender linkages in Germany; and on unemployment linkages in France.

[2] H Arthurs, 'Who's Afraid of Globalization?' in JDR Craig and SM Lynk (eds), *Globalization and the Future of Labour Law* (Cambridge University Press, 2006) 56.

[3] M Lemke, 'The Experience of Centralized Enforcement in Poland' in S Arrowsmith and M Trybus (eds), *Public Procurement: The Continuing Revolution* (Kluwer, 2003) 108.

[4] Alston (ed), *Labour Rights as Human Rights* (OUP, 2005) 11.

illustration of what Boaventura de Souza Santos has termed 'localized globalism' where local conditions, structures, and practices 'change in response to trans-national influences'.[5]

If we see the linkages between socio-economic issues and public procurement as driven substantially by interest groups external to government, whose demands government accede to because they are popular but which government was never really committed to, international or regional procurement regulation which is not subject to such organized interest groups and which results in the setting of constraints on national governments, could be quite attractive. From this per-spective, we can see Community procurement law during this period as a wonderful alibi. We may even want to go further, seeing some of the more restrictive interpretations of European procurement requirements at the national level as handy excuses, providing cover for what administrators and politicians wished to do anyway.[6]

Yet, despite these developments, procurement linkages have not gone away. On the contrary, we shall see in chapter 13 below, the growth of new equality linkages in several Member States, and the strengthening of existing linkages in others. All of these have developed since the neo-liberal interpretation of procurement regu-lation discussed in chapter 11 above appeared to have become embedded. Perhaps surprisingly, efforts to suppress the social use of procurement met with only limited success so that by 2006 procurement linkages for equality purposes were firmly back on the political agenda of several Member States to an extent that would have seemed unthinkable ten years earlier.

In the remaining chapters of this Part of the book, we aim to document the claim that procurement linkages have become more popular since the EC procure-ment reforms of the 1980s and early 1990s, and explain why that has happened. It is a complex story. Before turning to consider, in chapter 13 below, the expanding role of equality linkages in the European context during the 1990s, several inter-linking reasons are offered in this chapter to explain the increasing popularity of procurement linkages generally in some countries. Two significant developments since the early 1990s are identified that affected the policy context in which pro-curement linkages came to be reassessed, both globally and in the EC: the growth of corporate social responsibility (CSR), and the increasing importance of environ-mental issues. Procurement linkages came to be seen as a useful tool for helping to deliver both these policies. Clarification of the legal position of procurement link-ages under EC law was a third important additional factor contributing to such linkages. The more the procurement directives and EC law in general were seen as

---

[5] B de Sousa Santos, *Toward a New Legal Common Sense: Law, Science and Politics in the Paradigmatic Translation* (Routledge, 1995).

[6] See eg C Hanley, 'Avoiding the Issue: The Commission and Human Rights Conditionality in Public Procurement' (2002) 27(6) ELR 714, 727.

legally compatible with such linkages, the less the justification for not adopting them at the national level.

I. Integrating the Social, Environmental, and Economic: Some Relevant International Developments

Since the late 1980s and early 1990s, there has been a sustained attempt at the international level to establish a new rapprochement between social development, economic liberalization, human rights, and world trade. One of the major issues to be resolved is how to achieve respect for social and environmental goals whilst at the same time allowing economic globalization to prosper. A multilateral approach has the potential to address one of the most significant problems confronting nation states and regional blocs as they grapple with the issues of globalization. This problem has been termed the 'paradox of globalisation'.[7] On the one hand, the dangers globalization posed for some in both developed and developing economies, such as increased job insecurity, seemed to lead to an increased demand for social protection measures, including equality rights. On the other hand, globalization may constrain the ability of governments to respond effectively to that demand due to the need to remain competitive. These issues came to a head after the seismic political events of the late 1980s, with the end of the Cold War, the collapse of Communism, the expansion of market capitalism, and the consequent growth of international trade and investment.

International public policy

Several major world conferences during the early 1990s, held under the auspices of the United Nations, sought to establish linkages between progress on human rights (often including equality), protection of the environment, and global economic liberalization.[8] The United Nations Conference on Environment and Development (UNCED) held in Rio de Janerio, Brazil in 1992 (the so-called 'Earth Summit') was a turning point for environmental issues, for example. More than 178 Governments adopted the Rio Declaration on Environment and Development. Agenda 21, as it came to be called, was a plan of action to be taken globally, nationally, and locally by organizations of the United Nations, governments, and others in the many areas in which humans impact on the environment. A Commission on Sustainable

---

[7] See E Lee, 'Globalisation and Employment: Is the Anxiety Justified?' (1996) 135 International Labour Review 485, 496. See also D Rodrik, 'Sense and Nonsense in the Globalisation Debate' (Summer 1997) Foreign Policy 19, 26.

[8] Notably the 1995 World Summit for Social Development in Copenhagen, and also conferences on environment and development (Rio 1992), population and development (Cairo 1994), and women (Beijing 1995).

Development (CSD) was created in December 1992 to ensure effective follow-up of UNCED, and to monitor and report on implementation of the agreements at the local, national, regional, and international levels.

So, too, there were significant developments in the social policy context. After the Singapore Declaration at the WTO Ministerial in 1996, discussed in chapter 4 above, the then Director-General appeared to embrace the role identified for the International Labour Organization (ILO) in Singapore with enthusiasm. He proposed two strategies to increase the effective enforcement of labour standards.[9] First, he proposed that the ILO should identify a set of core labour rights to which members of the ILO should be regarded as being committed simply by virtue of their membership of the organization. A second strategy involved a scheme for increasing the effectiveness of consumer choice by labelling goods as having been produced in conditions that conformed to these core labour standards. The ILO would monitor the operation of this scheme. After considerable debate within the ILO, the core labour rights approach was accepted, as we saw in chapter 3 above, leading to the important Declaration on the issue in 1998.[10] This marked a renewed universal commitment among members, even if they had not ratified the Conventions in question, to respect, promote, and realize certain principles regarded as fundamental. The Declaration identified the issues of child labour and forced labour, the establishment of freedom of association and collective bargaining, and freedom from discrimination as the core of international labour rights. In the wake of the ILO's 1998 Declaration, both the Tripartite Declaration and the OECD Guidelines were revised.

Measures such as these were never wholly successful in demonstrating that economic globalization was being balanced effectively by respect for social and environmental protections. The derailing of proposals within the OECD for an agreement on multilateral investment in 1998,[11] and the continuing opposition of non-governmental organizations (NGOs) to the World Bank, the IMF, and the WTO were signs that economic globalization might yet be significantly constrained by political actions.

Not surprisingly, the demand grew for global companies themselves to assume responsibility for managing their global supply chains to ensure that their products met the social and environmental preferences of their consumers. The recent explosion of the corporate social responsibility movement is in part a function of

---

[9] The ILO, *Standard Setting and Globalisation: Report of the Director-General* (1997), International Labour Conference, 85th Session, available on the ILO website <http://www.ilo.org>.

[10] *Declaration on Fundamental Principles and Rights at Work* (1998), International Labour Conference, 86th Session, available on the ILO website <http://www.ilo.org>. See also H Kellerson, 'The ILO Declaration of 1998 on Fundamental Principles and Rights: A Challenge for the Future' (1998) 137 International Labour Review 223.

[11] C McCrudden, 'Property Rights and Labour Rights Revisited: Intellectual Investment Agreements and the "Social Clause" Debate' in M Irish (ed), *The Auto Pact: Investment, Labour and the WTO* (Kluwer, 2004) 300.

globalization.[12] In this context, the consumer is a key player. If consumers were to exercise their market power to buy goods and services from companies that complied with international and regional social and environmental norms, then firms would be forced to comply or suffer from a decline in profits, particularly in markets where the reputation of the firm was a significant part of the brand image. When a person buys a Nike shoe, he or she is not just buying a shoe, but a brand which sends subtle signals to others who see the 'swoosh'.

Matters came to a head at the WTO Ministerial meeting in Seattle at the end of November 1999. This was expected, but failed, to agree an agenda for a new round of trade liberalization negotiations. In preparation for the meeting, NGOs urged that the WTO should take this opportunity to tackle the appropriate limits of economic liberalization in a more sustained way than it had done previously. Both the United States and the EC proposed greater cooperation between the ILO and the WTO.[13] In addition, the United States called for a WTO working party to examine possible links between trade and labour rights issues.[14] The United States, indeed, made labour rights a highly visible part of its negotiating position, in public at least. In particular, President Clinton devoted a significant part of a speech in Seattle to the issue. He also appeared to go beyond the then United States position by suggesting that core labour rights should be incorporated into trade agreements with sanctions to enforce them.[15] Trade unions were a highly visible presence on the streets of Seattle during the Ministerial meeting. However, developing countries strongly opposed all these proposals, and concern was voiced too by the Secretary-General of the United Nations who argued that trade was seldom an appropriate way to tackle concerns about labour issues.[16]

Davos deal

What could be done? Some months earlier, in his address to the World Economic Forum in Davos, Switzerland, on 31 January 1999, the Secretary-General of the United Nations, Kofi Annan, presented a deal to multinational business.[17] This had been emerging in practice for some time but had not been expressed so clearly and powerfully before at such a high level. Responsible capitalism was in the interests of

---

[12] P Kletz and Y Pesqueux, 'Globalization: Towards a Cross-National Model of Corporate Social Responsibility' in J Allouche (ed), *Corporate Social Responsibility, volume 1* (Palgrave Macmillan, 2006) 99. See also the Comments by D O'Connor, 29 September 2005, Report on the Third Expert Meeting on Sustainable Public Procurement, United Nations Headquarters, New York, 15–17 July 2005.

[13] See, respectively, G de Jonquières 'WTO Set for Showdown on Labour Rights' *Financial Times*, 1 November 1999, and European Commission, 'The EU and the Millennium Round: More Trade Based on Better Rules' (26 October 1999), available on the Commission website <http://europa.eu .int/comm/dg01/mren.pdf>.

[14] See the article by Lawrence Summers (US Treasury Secretary), 'A Trade Round That Works for People' *Financial Times*, 29 November 1999.

[15] 'Clinton's Demands Threaten Turmoil at WTO Summit', *Financial Times*, 2 December 1999.

[16] 'Clinton Acknowledges Concerns' *Financial Times*, 1 December 1999.

[17] United Nations Press Release SG/SM/6881, 1 February 1999.

business, he argued. Unless business became socially and environmentally responsible, particularly in the three core areas of human rights, labour standards, and environmental practices, where there was most popular pressure, it risked policy interventions generated by interest groups that would put a substantial brake on business's ability to profit from the increasing market opportunities that international market liberalization was bringing. Short-term greed would damage longer-term sustainable international markets. 'There is enormous pressure from various interest groups', he said, 'to load the trade regime and investment agreements with restrictions aimed at preserving standards in the three areas I have just mentioned. These are legitimate concerns. But restrictions on trade and investment are not the right means to use when tackling them. Instead, we should find a way to achieve our proclaimed standards by other means.' If business put its own house in order, the United Nations would try to ensure a business-friendly international policy environment: 'what [the United Nations] can do in the political arena', he stressed, '[is] to help make the case for and maintain an environment which favours trade and open markets'.[18] Corporate social responsibility (CSR) was in everyone's interests.

The definition of CSR is contested but Jeremy Moon's definition will suffice: 'In essence CSR refers to business responsiveness to social agendas in its behaviour and to the performance of these responsibilities.'[19] The 'integration of social and environmental concerns in business operations', as CSR has sometimes been defined, is nothing new. That business has an important role in the wider community in which it is situated is hardly a novel proposition. Traditionally, however, this role was regulated by governments at the national or local level by traditional command and control regulation (think of the advent of laws against child labour in the United States Fair Labor Standards Act in 1938), or addressed by philanthropic individuals (think of Cadbury and the provision of social housing for his workers).[20] Seen from the historical perspective, then, modern discussion of CSR might seem to be simply the old debate about the proper role of government and the limits of the market dressed in new clothes. However, the recent debate over CSR has aspects that mark it out from previous debates.

The 'Davos deal', as we might call it, envisaged a role for government at both the international, regional, and national levels, but it was a restricted role. Government should encourage CSR, facilitate it, and enable it, where appropriate, but *instead* of regulating. Governments also stand to gain if business adopts CSR principles.[21]

---

[18] He continued: 'I believe what I am proposing to you is a genuine compact, because neither side of it can succeed without the other. Without your active commitment and support, there is a danger that universal values will remain little more than fine words—documents whose anniversaries we can celebrate and make speeches about, but with limited impact on the lives of ordinary people. And unless those values are really seen to be taking hold, I fear we may find it increasingly difficult to make a persuasive case for the open global market.'

[19] J Moon, 'Government as a Driver of Corporate Social Responsibility', ICCSR Research Paper Series, No 20-2004, 2.   [20] T Cannon, *Corporate Responsibility* (Pearson Education, 1994).

[21] Moon has argued that there are three reasons for government to encourage CSR: 'it can substitute for government effort; it can complement government effort; and it can legitimise government policies', (n 15 above) 2.

Dirk Matten and Jeremy Moon, for example, have argued that CSR 'encourage[s] companies to assume more responsibilities as most welfare states in Europe are increasingly facing limits to their capacities of tackling social issues in the way they traditionally did'.[22] If welfare states (particularly in Europe) are in decline, then there will be pressure from governments and others on business to fill the gap of welfare provision. It is therefore in the interests of government that the CSR project is not seen to fail.

At the international level, the result has been the development of several initiatives that are intended to facilitate, enable, and complement voluntary initiatives by business. Perhaps the highest profile event was that launched by the Secretary-General himself, a year after the Davos speech. In July 2000, Kofi Annan launched a Global Compact. This was, in part, a mechanism for sharing good voluntary practice and, in part, a recognition of existing good practice. The ten principles of the Global Compact covered the areas of human rights, labour, environment, and anti-corruption. By 2005, over 2,000 companies were participating, compared to just 50 at the launch. They covered all business sectors and were from both developed and developing countries. In addition to the business sector, global labour federations, international and local NGOs, governments, and UN agencies were involved.

The OECD Guidelines and the Global Compact both deal with environmental questions and general human rights questions as well as labour rights, whereas the Tripartite Declaration deals only with labour rights and social protection. All three instruments can be considered, however, as general guidelines for good corporate behaviour, on which corporations might model their conduct. In addition, the OECD Guidelines and the Tripartite Declaration (though not the UN Global Compact) make provision for definitive interpretations of the guidelines they contain in the course of dispute resolution procedures (without sanctions). However, and this is the crucial point these standards are not legally binding. For business, that was seen as an advantage, being preferable to legal regulation. The chief legal counsel for Shell put it well in 2000, when he contrasted legal regulation with self-regulation. 'The rigidity of mandatory rules of law', he said, 'would stifle activity, mute communications and create strife rather than prosperity.'[23]

Corporate social responsibility and the rise of corporate codes of conduct

Out of the business case for CSR emerged a variety of other initiatives, particularly the rise of voluntary 'codes'. Such codes vary considerably in their origin, their content, their coverage, and the methods of compliance associated with them.

---

[22] D Matten and J Moon, ' "Implicit" and "Explicit" CSR: A conceptual framework for understanding CSR in Europe', ICCSR Research Paper Series, No 29-2004, 24.

[23] Quoted in S Macleod and D Lewis, 'Transnational Corporations: Power, Influence and Responsibility' (2004) 4(1) Global Social Policy 77, 78.

Methods of making such voluntary codes more effective in practice have been developed, consistent with the underlying assumption that market-based methods should be preferred: for example, the development of social and environmental labelling schemes, seeking to reassure consumers that the company complies with certain environmental or social norms; and the use of codes of practice as the basis of shareholder initatives, seeking to require companies to practise what they preach through shareholder resolutions. Such market-based approaches have, indeed, produced some significant changes in corporate practices. Seen from this perspective, CSR arises 'as a demand made by others upon corporations, and then . . . as an assertion made by companies themselves that is designed to reassure their critics that their complaints have been heard and that the corporate household has now been put in order'.[24] There was a flurry of such activity by corporations themselves during the 1990s, with the production of codes aimed at self-regulation.

More recently, in a new development, codes have resulted from negotiations between corporations and other interests, whether trade unions, NGOs, or governments. A Code of Practice was negotiated, for example, between a trade union coalition and FIFA (the international soccer regulatory body) regarding the production of goods licensed by FIFA.[25] During the late 1990s, governments also became increasingly involved in joint initiatives with companies and NGOs. In 1998, a US presidential taskforce that included human rights groups, labour unions, and clothing industry representatives reached an agreement to create a code of conduct on wages and working conditions in factories that American companies used throughout the world.[26] In the United Kingdom, the government launched an 'Ethical Trading Initiative' 'supporting collaboration between business and the voluntary sector in promoting ethical businesses, including the development of codes of conduct and ways of monitoring and verifying these codes'.[27] Codes, therefore, in different guises, and with varying degrees of approbation and criticism, have become the subject of increasing attention worldwide.

Compliance gap

However, the problem of lack of compliance with all these voluntary measures remained. The expectations of high standards, partly generated by NGOs and international organizations, but also by business itself, are all too frequently not met. As

---

[24] Allouche (ed), *Corporate Social Responsibility: Volume 1: Concept, Accountability and Reporting* (Palgrave Macmillan, 2006) xxiii.

[25] Code of Labour Practice for Production of Goods Licensed by the Federation Internationale de Football Association (1997).

[26] See TA Hemphill, 'The White House Apparel Industy Partnership Agreement: Will Self-Regulation be Successful?' (1999) 104(2) Business and Society Review 121.

[27] <http://www.ethicaltrade.org>.

David Vogel has written, 'there remains a substantial gap between discourse and practice with respect to virtually all codes and voluntary standards'.[28] For Vogel, and for many others: 'In order for corporations to make sustainable improvements in their social and environmental performance, the role of government must change.'[29] There is, of course, a multiplicity of differing ways in which government may play a role in encouraging CSR.[30] Tom Fox, Halina Ward, and Bruce Howard have identified how public sector bodies encourage CSR by 'using any one or a combination of various … tools'; *mandating* ('governments at different levels define minimum standards for business performance embedded within the legal framework');[31] *facilitating* ('public sector agencies enable or incentivize companies to engage with the CSR agenda or to drive social and environmental improvements');[32] *partnering* ('public sector bodies may act as participants, convenors, or facilitators');[33] and *endorsing* (taking 'various forms', including the 'demonstration effect … of public sector management practices').[34] As a recent report for the World Bank put it: 'Government action has the benefit of rationalizing market forces by creating a "level playing field"; it spreads costs across the breadth of society, [and] provides a formal and public means of recourse.'[35]

We can see various approaches aiming to reduce the compliance gap multiplying. Although the Global Compact is purely voluntary, participating companies need to submit a report on their activities in implementing the principles of the Compact. This 'Communication on Progress' policy was introduced in January 2003. After a grace period of two years, a company will be removed from the list and classified as 'non-communicating' if no report is received. But other, more legally-based approaches are also being adopted. Just as nature abhors a vacuum, law tends to fill compliance gaps. Sandra Waddock has identified 'signs emerging in the early 2000s that accountability will be enforced through an array of new laws and regulations that are slowly beginning to emerge around the world'.[36] At the national level, the United States Federal Sentencing Guidelines of 1991 have been used as an incentive for compliance, by offering reduced penalties. In Britain, the Occupational Pensions Schemes (Investment) Regulations 1996 required pensions funds, from 2000 onwards, to report how they take account of social, environmental, and ethical factors in making investment decisions. In 2002, France introduced requirements for all firms listed on the stock exchange to report on

---

[28] D Vogel, *The Market for Virtue: The Potential and Limits of Corporate Social Responsibility* (Brookings Institution, 2005) 164. [29] ibid 166.
[30] For a survey, see C Bichta, 'Corporate Social Responsibility: A Role in Government Policy and Regulation?' (University of Bath School of Management, 2003).
[31] T Fox, H Ward, and B Howard, *Public Sector Roles in Strengthening Corporate Social Responsibility: A Baseline Study* (World Bank, October 2002) 3. [32] ibid 3–4.
[33] ibid 4. [34] ibid 6.
[35] H Bank Jørgensen, PM Pruzan Jørgensen, M Jungk, and A Cramer, *Strengthening Implementation of Corporate Social Responsibility in Global Supply Chains* (World Bank, IFC, October 2003) 39.
[36] S Waddock, 'Rhetoric, Reality and Relevance for Corporate Citizenship: Building a Bridge to Actionable Knowledge' in J Allouche (ed) (n 12 above) 20, 31.

their performance in various areas of CSR.[37] There have also been attempts to harden up the 'soft law' of environmental and social standards applicable to business. The OECD Guidelines have been used to supply legally binding standards in export credit guarantees in the Netherlands.[38] The EC has incorporated the soft law ILO standards into its Generalized System of Preferences. Consumer protection laws have been used to 'enforce' voluntary codes.[39] Parent companies of multinational corporations have become subject to domestic principles of civil liability where they breach international legal norms, such as under the Alien Tort Claims Act in the United States, and equivalent principles in France and Belgium.[40] Bilateral and plurilateral trade treaties have increasingly incorporated social and environmental requirements for business. There are currently attempts in the United States to argue that corporations failing to enforce contractual obligations they place on their subcontractors abroad, for example prohibiting the use of child labour, are in breach of contract.[41] Yet, each of these approaches has clear problems that lessen their effectiveness in practice.[42]

It is in this context that public procurement linkages began to gain renewed popularity. Is the role of public procurement in CSR something new, or simply a new label for an old phenomenon? In chapter 2 above, I sketched out the historical development of the use of public procurement for social policy purposes, tracing its origins to the nineteenth century. I argued that public procurement is an extraordinarily adaptable tool, which has often been used to meet a regulatory need when other methods of regulation are not considered acceptable, available, or effective. In the CSR context, a similar development appears to be happening: governments often seem to be unwilling to regulate business using traditional command and control regulation.[43] Procurement appears to be seen again to be one of several useful regulatory mechanisms.

---

[37] J Allouche, F de Bry, I Huault and G Schmidt, 'The Institutionalization of CSR in France: the State Injunction' in J Allouche (ed) (n 12 above) 284, 299.

[38] S Macleod and D Lewis, 'Transnational Corporations: Power, Influence and Responsibility' (2004) 4(1) Global Social Policy 77, 81.

[39] Unfair Commercial Practices Directive of 11 May 2005 [2005] OJ, L149/22; *Kasky v Nike Inc* (2002) 27 Cal. 4th 939, 45 P3d 243, California Supreme Court.

[40] K Medjad, 'In Search of the "Hard Law": Judicial Activism and International Corporate Social Responsibility' in Allouche (ed), *Corporate Social Responsibility: Volume 1: Concept, Accountability and Reporting* (Palgrave Macmillan, 2006) 181.

[41] *Doe v Nestlé*, Class Action Complaint for Injunctive Relief and Damages (dist Ct Cent Dist of Calif 2005); *Doe v Wal-Mart Stores, Inc*, Class Action Complaint for Injunctive Relief and Damages (Superior Ct of Calif for the County of Los Angeles 2005), both available at <http://www.laborrights.org>.

[42] For a discussion of the difficulties with private actions based on tort, for example, see Medjad (n 40 above) 185 *et seq.*

[43] For a discussion of the failure to pass legislation in Australia, the US, and the UK to enforce standards of good practice for MNEs based in those countries in respect of their overseas operations, see A McBeth, 'A Look at Corporate Code of Conduct Legislation (2004) 33(3) Common Law World Review 222–54.

II. Realigning the Economic, Social, and Environmental Goals of the European Community

Before considering this in detail, however, we need to be aware that in the EC, there has been a similar attempt to rebalance Community policy, bringing its social, environmental, and economic aspects into greater alignment. In chapter 13 below, we shall see that an important element of this rebalancing was the significant expansion of equal status guarantees. Here, we concentrate on two other elements: EC CSR developments and EC environmental policy.

Corporate social responsibility

The field of corporate social responsibility (CSR) grew considerably during the 1990s in the European context, first as part of domestic policy in several countries, then increasingly as part of EC policy.[44] The movement for CSR was actively pursued in several Member States during the 1990s. This included, in some states, the use of public procurement in this context.[45] However, CSR was relatively slow in being recognized and incorporated into EC policy.[46] The EC's framework for CSR began to be developed soon after the Lisbon Council appealed to companies' sense of social responsibility in March 2000. A Green Paper was published by the Commission in 2001, and a Communication followed in 2002. This established the EU Multi-Stakeholder Forum on CSR, which deliberated and published a report in 2004. In 2006, the Commission published a further Communication on CSR. In the Community context, CSR includes promoting responsible production, promoting responsible consumption, promoting the transparency and credibility of CSR practices, and promoting responsible investment.

CSR, according to the European Commission, is 'a concept whereby companies integrate social and environmental concerns in their business operations and in their interaction with their stakeholders on a voluntary basis'.[47] The European Commission's approach was as clear as Kofi Annan's in Davos in stressing that linking regulation to CSR was not on their agenda: 'Because CSR is fundamentally about voluntary business behaviour, an approach involving additional obligations and administrative requirements for business risks being counter-productive and

---

[44] For a description of the development of CSR in the EU, see KK Herrmann, 'Corporate Social Responsibility and Sustainable Development: The European Union Initiative as a Case Study' (2004) 11(2) Indiana Journal of Global Legal Studies 205–32.

[45] See eg A Rosdahl, 'The Policy to Promote Social Responsibility of Enterprises in Denmark', paper prepared for the European Commission-DG EMPL Peer Review Programme (September, 2001) 9.

[46] For discussion of earlier initiatives at the EU level, see MacLeod and Lewis (n 38 above) 85.

[47] Commission Green Paper, 'Promoting a European Framework for Corporate Social Responsibility', COM(2001)366 final.

would be contrary to the principles of better regulation.'[48] What does 'voluntary' imply in this context? What role, in particular, does this imply for public policy and law? Whether CSR should be undertaken only on a voluntary basis or can be complemented with a governmental regulatory framework is, of course, a central issue in the debates surrounding CSR more generally.[49]

The European Commission's approach to CSR, as a *voluntary* engagement by business with social and environmental concerns, was, then, strikingly similar to that of Kofi Annan, and was most clearly demonstrated in its 2006 Communication.[50] For the Commission, CSR 'is about enterprises deciding to go beyond minimum legal requirements and obligations stemming from collective agreements in order to address societal needs'.[51] So, in return for a business-friendly regulatory environment in Europe, the European Commission expected business to act responsibly, otherwise popular trust in capitalism would decline. Such trust was vital for businesses because they operated in a political environment. As with Kofi Annan, the unspoken warning was clear: adopt CSR or regulation will be more likely in the future.

Growth of European environmental regulation

The growth of environmental policy during the 1990s was also highly significant, increasingly moving from the margins of policy in a few states to become an issue of significant electoral salience in many states and of central policy importance in the EC. The Single European Act, which entered into force in June 1987, provided in Article 130r(2) EC that environmental protection requirements 'shall be a component of the Community's other policies'. The Maastricht Treaty, adopted in 1993, went further in providing that environmental protection requirements 'must be integrated into the definition and implementation of other Community policies'.[52] In the Amsterdam Treaty, the objective of a 'high level of protection and improvement of the quality of the environment' was incorporated into Article 2 EC. Article 6 EC provided that environmental protection requirements 'must be integrated into the definition and implementation' of Community policies and activities 'in particular with a view to promoting sustainable development'.[53] The Amsterdam Treaty therefore reinforced the principle of the integration of

---

[48] Commission Communication, 'Implementing the Partnership for Growth and Jobs: Making Europe a Pole of Excellence on Corporate Social Responsibility', COM(2006)0136, 1.

[49] For a recent review of some of the academic literature, see M de la Cuesta González and C Valor Martinez, 'Fostering Corporate Social Responsibility Through Public Initiative: From the EU to the Spanish Case' (2004) 55 Journal of Business Ethics, 275–93.

[50] In a brief document of some 13 pages, the term 'voluntary' was used 11 times.

[51] Commission Communication, 'Implementing the Partnership for Growth and Jobs: Making Europe a Pole of Excellence on Corporate Social Responsibility', COM(2006)0136, 1.

[52] Art 130r(2) TEU.

[53] For a discussion of the implications of this in general see, M Wasmeier, 'The Integration of Environmental protection as a General Rule for Interpreting Community Law' (2001) 38 CMLR 159.

environmental requirements into other policies, recognizing that it is key in order to achieve sustainable development.[54]

The idea of such integration has long been Commission policy, reflected in a succession of environmental action programmes, with the fifth action programme in particular placing considerable emphasis on the need to integrate environmental issues into other sectoral policies.[55] In 1993, a new integration unit was created within DG XI, and each Directorate-General designated an official to liaise between that DG and DG XI to ensure that environmental issues were properly considered. Changes were introduced in 1998, following a critical assessment of these processes, in particular with the designation of the European Council (the heads of state or government, meeting in periodic summits) as the body that would thereafter adopt the role of activating the integration process.[56] Increased efforts were made to facilitate dialogue between sectoral and environmental policy makers.

III. Growth of Procurement Linkages

A perception grew that procurement linkages were potentially quite useful as a tool for securing compliance with these developing areas of policy. We have seen that procurement linkages have a tendency to be developed to meet the challenges of securing compliance with new policy goals. As chapter 2 above demonstrated, there have been consistent attempts to link public procurement with the government policy of the day, in areas as diverse as national industrial policy, reducing unemployment, improving employment conditions, support for small businesses, local development, employment of disabled workers, to mention only a few. Public procurement has proven to be a dedicated follower of political fashion. Given this, it was entirely predictable, with the increasing popularity of 'corporate social responsibility' and environmentalism, that procurement linkages would be increasingly advocated to further the new agendas. In this section we consider several examples. Individual states adopted procurement linkages in the context of dealing with problems associated with the changing global labour market. Some older forms of linkage that had been dropped were resuscitated to address the problems brought about by global economic liberalism. We shall see, for example, that use of government contracting that developed in the late nineteenth century to deal with sweated labour reappeared at the end of the twentieth century. Increasingly, the development of CSR-driven corporate codes of conduct, together with the activities of

---

[54] Article 6 of the consolidated version of the Treaty establishing the European Community states that 'environmental protection requirements must be integrated into the definition and implementation of the Community policies and activities referred to in Article 3, in particular with a view to promoting sustainable development'.

[55] European Commission, 'Towards Sustainability. A European Community Programme of Policy and Action in Relation to the Environment and Sustainable Development', COM(92)23 final (Brussels, 1992).

[56] See A Lenschow, 'New Regulatory Approaches in "Greening" EU Policies' (2002) 8 European Law Journal 19, 25–7.

NGOs, contributed to the development of procurement linkage. In at least two respects, the development of CSR has markedly expanded the types of policies that are now commonly linked to public procurement: increasing the role of public procurement in addressing environmental issues, and increasing the role of public procurement in addressing social conditions in other countries. Issues such as fair trade, reducing the use of child labour, and sustainable development are increasingly featuring on the public procurement agenda.[57] As CSR became more and more associated with sustainable development, so too did public procurement, leading to the evolution of the concept of sustainable procurement, incorporating both social and environmental goals. There has been a growing interest in integrating aspects of social policy into continuing work on eco- or green procurement in order to achieve sustainable public procurement.

Reacting to developments in the labour market

There have been several recent examples of the use of procurement to address changes in the international labour market. In the United States President Clinton promulgated an executive order prohibiting the acquisition of products produced by forced or indentured labour.[58] There is a continuing debate over whether government contracts should be able to be performed offshore by non-United States citizens, and some limited action has been taken by both state and federal legislatures to limit this practice.[59] At the local level, too, activism has grown. In the United States, several municipalities have developed so-called 'living wage' ordinances. These require certain businesses with contracts from these cities to pay a 'living wage' that is higher than the federal minimum wage. This development has grown substantially since the mid-1990s, and been adopted in many major cities, including Chicago, Detroit, San Francisco, Boston, Los Angeles, and New York.[60] Melborne City Council joined the Global Compact and required corporations

[57] See eg, A Nicholls and C Opal, *Fair Trade: Market-Driven Ethical Consumption* (Sage, 2004).

[58] Executive Order 13126 of 12 June 1999, it covered only those purchases not covered by the GPA or NAFTA, see s 5(b).

[59] Federal: Treasury, Transportation and Independent Agencies Appropriations Act 2005, Pub Law No 108–199, Div F, sect 647, 118 Stat 361 (FY 04) (stipulates various conditions before an agency can contract out an activity or function that is being performed by more than 10 federal employees; requires report on competitive sourcing activities; prohibits performance by a contractor outside the US unless the activity or function was previously performed by Federal Government employees outside the US); New Jersey: Public Law No 2005, ch 92 (requires services under state contracts or subcontracts to be performed in the US).

[60] There is now a considerable quantity of information arising from these initiatives, both academic studies of their operation, and impacts, and more locally-based studies by particular municipalities. See eg J Bernstein, The Living Wage Movement: What is it, Why is it, and What's Known about its Impact (October 2003). A good source for the reports is to be found on the websites of the City of Atlanta, which has been considering such an initiative for several years and brought together the research reports: <http://www.atlantaga.gov/mayor/lwc_relevant.aspx>.

tendering for council contracts to comply with the Compact's terms and conditions.[61] The growth of human rights in the international context has further stimulated the growth of linkages with procurement.[62]

One of the events that stimulated further use of procurement linkages in Belgium is a good illustration of the way that public procurement linkages have become intimately linked with globalization. In 1997, the general manager of Renault, the French car maker, announced that its plant near Brussels would close, although the works council had not discussed this. Several courts in both France and Belgium found against the company under both civil and criminal law. Several public authorities, from local to national, also retaliated against the company by cancelling orders for vehicles already under contract with the company, amid controversy as to the legality of these measures.[63]

Public procurement and CSR

We have seen that one important driver for the introduction of CSR requirements into public procurement is the desire to narrow the gap between aspiration and practice by firms: procurement came to be seen by some governments as a method of providing (market-based) incentives to firms to adopt and fulfil CSR obligations, by linking these obligations with access to government contracts.[64] Public procurement has become one of a range of initiatives, a 'portfolio approach',[65] in which different initiatives support each other.[66] At the international level, this approach is usefully illustrated by the use of public procurement as a mechanism for achieving compliance with the draft Norms on the Responsibility of Transnational

---

[61] Parliament of Australia, *Hansard*, 17 September 2001, 30, 827.

[62] See eg General Recommendation XXVII on discrimination against Roma adopted in 2000, in which the Committee for the Elimination of Racial Discrimination, encourages the States Parties to the Convention on the Elimination of Racial Discrimination to 'take special measures to promote the employment of Roma in the public administration and institutions, as well as in private companies' (para 28), and to 'adopt and implement, whenever possible, at the central or local level, special measures in favour of Roma in public employment such as public contracting and other activities undertaken or funded by the Government...' (para 29). Committee for the Elimination of Racial Discrimination, General Recommendation XXVII, adopted at the 57th Session (2000) in Compilation of the General Comments of General Recommendations adopted by Human Rights Treaty Bodies, UN Doc HRI/GEN/1Rev. 7, 12 May 2004, 219, paras. 28–29.

[63] See eg the responses to questions in the Belgian Parliament, Questions No 618 du mai 1997, No 130 du 20 juin 1997, Questions et Réponses, Chambre des Représentants de Belgique, pp 13468, 12217 (SO 1996–1997, DO 969701731, DO 969701730).

[64] eg 'Promoting Global Corporate Social Responsibility: The Kenan Institute Study Group Consensus' (September 2003) recommended the use of US government procurement policies as tools to promote global CSR, <http://www.csrpolicies.org>.

[65] S Zadek, S Lingayah, and M Forstater, *Social Labels: Tools for Ethical Trade: Final Report* (European Commission, 1998) 10, 58, 75.

[66] cf O de Schutter, 'The Accountability of Multinationals for Human Rights Violations in European Law' in P Alston (ed), *Non-State Actors and Human Rights* (OUP, 2005); O de Schutter, 'Transnational Corporations as Instruments of Human Development' in P Alston and M Robinson, *Human Rights and Development: Towards Mutual Reinforcement* (OUP, 2005) 403.

Corporations and Business Enterprises with Regard to Human Rights.[67] The Norms were drafted by the United Nations Subcommission on the Promotion and Protection of Human Rights. The use of procurement was commended by the Subcommission during the course of the discussions on the drafting of the Norms.[68] The Commentary to the Norms,[69] stated that 'The U.N. and its specialized agencies should ... monitor implementation by using the Responsibilities as the basis for procurement determinations as to which products and services to purchase'. The Norms have proven extremely contentious, however, and it appears at the time of writing to be unlikely that they will become the basis for international consensus.[70]

Public procurement as equivalent to private procurement

Although important, the relationship between public procurement and CSR cannot *only* be seen as a compliance gap-filling measure. The relationship between procurement and CSR is more complex than this suggests. In practice, public procurement is to be found as a tool in each of the 'mandating', 'facilitating', 'partnering', and 'endorsing' roles identified earlier.[71]

It is necessary to step back a little and look at the relationship between procurement and CSR more broadly. Increasingly, the distinction between public and private in general, and public procurement and private procurement in particular, is becoming blurred. There are several aspects to these developments.

First, with tightening public sector budgets and the increasing emphasis on efficiency and 'value for money', public bodies were urged (in some cases required) to become more like those in the private sector. Private sector values, ethos, and management styles were increasingly incorporated into public sector management. This was strikingly so in several countries with regard to public procurement activities, contributing to the dramatic extent of reform in the management of public procurement in developed countries over the past twenty years.

Second, with the advent of privatization and contracting-out, functions that would traditionally have been carried out by government are now increasingly carried out under contract, by the private sector. When this happens, however some of the 'public sector ethos' has sometimes carried over to the private sector.

---

[67] See D Weissbrodt and M Kruger, 'Norms on the Responsibilities of Transnational Corporations and Business Enterprises with Regard to Human Rights' (2003) 97 AJIL 901, footnote 108.

[68] Sub-Commission on Human Rights Resolution 2002/8 (2002), para 4(a): 'Recommends that the working group and the Sub-Commission continue their efforts to explore possible mechanisms for implementing the draft norms ... such as: (a) The use of those human-rights related norms as a basis for determining the purchases of goods and services from and the partnerships developed with transnational corporations and other enterprises ...'.   [69] Commentary, para 16b.

[70] The Interim report of the Special Representative of the Secretary-General on the issue of human rights and transnational corporations and other business enterprises, 22 February 2006, E/CN.4/2006/97, was a damning critique and was seen in many quarters as indicating the swift demise of the Norms.

[71] T Fox, H Ward, and B Howard, *Public Sector Roles in Strengthening Corporate Social Responsibility: A Baseline Study* (World Bank, 2002) 3: 'some public sector activities, such as procurement, have multiple linkages with the contemporary CSR agenda'. See also at 4.

This is, perhaps, most strikingly the case in the context of utilities privatization, where certain 'public' values have been transferred over to the private providers.[72] The 'growth of CSR activity in the 1990s occurred in response to widespread concerns about increases in corporate power through privatization and globalization'.[73]

Given the increasing sensitivity of business to reputation issues, it is not surprising that private sector firms increasingly incorporate CSR principles into their procurement. According to the United Kingdom-based Chartered Institute of Purchasing and Supply, 'Corporate Social Responsibility is currently seen by many in procurement as the number one "Hot Topic"'.[74] As CSR grew as a set of expectations on business, the responsibilities of a firm for what occurred in its supply chain became the focus of greater attention. Companies were held responsible in the court of public opinion for what happened in factories in developing countries that supplied them with products. Two examples must suffice: in Canada, the Canadian Auto Workers pressed Coca-Cola Canada to stop sourcing Coke-branded garments produced in Burma, and the company agreed.[75] In Britain, utility companies have significantly stepped up their scrutiny of their supply chains to prevent any loss of reputation that would arise were suppliers found to be involved in unacceptable practices.[76] In order to be seen to meet this responsibility, firms increasingly incorporated CSR requirements into their supply contracts.[77] 'Companies with long supply chains, such as footwear, clothing, sporting goods and toy companies, have been in the forefront of implementing ... voluntary responsibility management approaches.'[78] Contracting became a method by which firms could 'enforce' their own (voluntary) codes of practice.[79]

If private sector firms do so, why should public sector bodies not also? CSR suggests to the private sector that business should go beyond purely economic considerations, and go beyond strictly legal obligations, appreciating the social

---

[72] See C McCrudden, 'Social Policy and Economic Regulators: Some Issues for the Reform of Utility Regulation' in C McCrudden (ed), *Regulation and Deregulation: Policy and Practice* (OUP 1998) 275–94. [73] Allouche (ed) (n 12 above) xxiv.

[74] <http://www.cips.org>.

[75] 'Canadian Coca-Cola Workers Show Solidarity with Burma', 2 September 2005 <http://www.iuf.org>.

[76] 'Increasing globalisation puts unlikely sectors in the line of fire' *Financial Times*, 28 November 2005 (FT Report: Responsible Business, 2); M Ram and D Smallbone, 'Supplier Diversity Initiatives and the Diversification of Ethnic Minority Businesses in the UK' (2003) 24(4) Policy Studies 187, 195 (study of British Telecom's supplier diversity programme).

[77] See, ER Pedersen and M Andersen, 'Safeguarding Corporate Social Responsibility (CSR) in Global Supply Chains: How Codes of Conduct are Managed in Buyer-Supplier Relationships' (2006) (3–4) Journal of Public Affairs 228.

[78] S Waddock, 'Rhetoric, Reality and Relevance for Corporate Citizenship: Building a Bridge to Actionable Knowledge', in Allouche (ed) (n 12 above) 20, 26. See also Pedersen and Andersen (n 77 above).

[79] See eg discussion of Statoil and BP in G Smith and D Feldman, *Implementation Mechanisms for Codes of Conduct* (World Bank, IFC, November 2004) 36; E Rigby, 'Topshop to sell clothes by Fairtrade companies' *Financial Times*, 2 March 2006, 3; Discussion of Boots, BT, and Ricoh UK, in M Scott, 'Responsibility goes all down the line', Financial Times Survey: Business in the Community Awards, 6 July 2005, 16; Buying Matters, 'Consultation: Sourcing fairly from developing countries' (February 2006), <http://www.responsible-purchasing.org>.

and environmental externalities involved in its operations, including its supply chain. Incorporation of social and environmental concerns into *public* procurement appears to involve a similar acceptance of responsibility by government.[80]

Government service providers are increasingly to be viewed as having a broader mandate, including safeguarding the environment and the social fabric, and protecting the interests of vulnerable members of society and of future generations. On this view, government is a social welfare optimizer, seeking to internalize in its policies and practices all relevant externalities. This calls for a more activist role on the part of government with respect to its procurement decisions. The sheer size of the public procurement market, for example, might be used to encourage the development of 'green' products at an affordable price for the general market, simply by guaranteeing a sufficient number of public purchases to create viability. For example, 'Japan has successfully used green procurement of low emission cars to stimulate technological innovation in the motor industry'.[81] Efforts such as these contributed to the adoption by the OECD Council of a recommendation advocating green public procurement.[82] From this viewpoint, public bodies have CSR responsibilities themselves as purchasers, and public procurement is not just a mechanism for ensuring compliance by others with their CSR responsibilities but an important element in how the public sector can satisfy its own CSR responsibilities.[83]

Responsible public procurement as 'leading by example'

If we equate the relationship between private firms and their consumers with the relationship between public bodies and their citizens, it would be strange indeed if public bodies did not react similarly to CSR issues. Indeed, some see the role of government as being in part to represent the collective preferences of citizens. The inclusion of social and environmental conditions should not only be seen as being about the consequences of procurement decisions and the leverage those consequences give us on policy. When the government makes purchases, it acts in the name of its citizens and ought to uphold certain standards. 'We' do not want 'our' public goods purchased from companies that discriminate or pollute because it is sordid, it would dirty our hands, and not (only) because we are hoping to use government spending to alter the social landscape.[84]

Government increasingly encouraged the private sector to ensure that its supply chains were in CSR compliance. Governments also acted to facilitate such initiatives.[85] The British government, as we saw above, supported the creation of the

[80] This paragraph draws substantially on comments by D O'Connor, Third Expert Meeting on Sustainable Public Procurement, United Nations Headquarters, New York, 14–17 June 2005.

[81] R Cowe and J Porritt, *Government's Business: Enabling corporate sustainability* (Forum for the Future, 2002) 33.   [82] OECD Press Release, 23 January 2002, <http://www.oecd.org>.

[83] This is the message, for example, of such studies as that of L Mastny, 'Purchasing Power: Harnessing Institutional Procurement for People and the Planet' (Worldwatch Paper 166, July 2003).

[84] Don Herzog, personal communication.

[85] T Loew, K Ankele, S Braun, J Clausen, 'Significance of the CSR debate for sustainability and the requirements for companies: Summary', 8 (an example of the German federal government's encouragement of codes of practice in private sector procurement).

Ethical Trading Initiative, which brings together companies, NGOs, and trade unions in order to help purchasers to secure goods that are produced in conditions in developing countries that meet environmental and social standards. Not surprisingly, the result of this is also to shine a spotlight on the procurement practices of those that advocated that firms should use their procurement operations in this way. Governments, in other words, operate both as regulators of the market, and as participants in the market. When principles they espouse for others are not applied to their own actions, the government appears to lack coordination, or to be simply hypocritical. An important driver, then, for the incorporation of CSR standards in public procurement is the need to be seen to be leading by example:[86] if government expects firms to ensure that their supply chains are clean, then the least government can do is to ensure that its own house is in order too.

UN procurement policy and linkage

Leading by example developed as a key reason, for example, for UN procurement policy increasingly considering procurement linkages. In May 1995, UNICEF announced a new procurement policy on child labour, pledging to purchase materials and supplies only from companies that did not exploit child labour. The UNICEF representative in each country was required to assess the local situation and evaluate the child labour practices of local companies.[87] This approach was subsequently generalized throughout the UN system, and expanded to include restrictions on landmines. In its General Conditions for the Procurement of Goods, the UN included provisions on both children's rights and land mines. As regards child labour, the UN required the supplier to 'warrant that neither it nor any of its affiliates' is engaged in any practice inconsistent with the rights set out in the Convention of the Rights of the Child, including Article 32 of the Convention which requires that a child shall be protected from performing any work that is likely to be hazardous or to interfere with the child's education, or to be harmful to the child's health or physical, mental, spiritual, moral or social development.[88] The UN reserved the right to terminate any contract unconditionally and without liability in the event that the supplier was discovered to be in non-compliance. As regards landmines, the UN required each supplier to guarantee that neither the supplier's company, 'nor any of its affiliates, nor any subsidiaries controlled' by the supplier's company, was engaged in the sale or manufacture of anti-personnel mines or components utilized in the manufacture of anti-personnel mines.[89] The supplier was required to accept that a breach of this provision would entitle the UN to terminate its contract with the supplier. Some of the UN agencies are more

---

[86] Cowe and Porritt (n 81 above) 32; G Zappalà, 'Corporate Citizenship and the Role of Government: the Public Policy Case', Information and Research Services, Department of the Parliamentary Library, Research Paper No 4 2003 (2003) 2, 17.

[87] United Nations Background Note, Children's Rights, <http://www.un.org/rights/dpi1765e.htm>.

[88] United Nations, General Business Guide—General conditions for the Procurement of Goods, para P, available at <http://www.iapso.org/supplying/general_conditions.asp>.   [89] ibid para Q.

forthright about these requirements than others. The procurement policies website of UNICEF specifically warns that it includes restrictions on purchasing from companies that employ child labour, and manufacture land mines or their components.[90]

Subsequently, after shocking reports of sexual exploitation of women by UN personnel, a further provision was added requiring a contractor to warrant that it had taken 'all appropriate measures' to prevent the sexual exploitation or abuse of anyone by its employees 'or by any other persons who may be engaged by the Contractor to perform any services' under the contract. Sexual exploitation and abuse was defined to include 'sexual activity with any person less than eighteen years of age, regardless of any laws relating to consent'. The contractor was also obliged to prohibit 'exchanging any money, goods, services, offers of employment or other things of value, for sexual favors or activities, or from engaging in any sexual activities that are exploitative or degrading to any person'. Breach of the warranty entitles the UN to terminate the contract.[91]

The potential for embarassing the UN was clearly high on the list of reasons why these issues were dealt with in the contracts. This, indeed, has contributed to a growth of popularity in procurement linkages among IGOs generally.[92] IGOs are as likely as the governments of states to be scrutinized for hypocrisy. A prominent example was the reaction of some NGOs to the UN launch of the Global Compact. Did the UN itself comply with the principles of the Global Compact in its procurement practices? When the answer was 'not yet', a degree of embarrassment was apparent.[93] 'After the Compact's launch, United Nations management considered whether changes in administrative practice would be necessary and it was concluded that only a limited number of steps were feasible—primarily consisting of an awareness raising approach directed toward potential suppliers of the UN.'[94] This position led to continued criticism from NGOs.

The Secretary-General was directly challenged on this point by Oded Grajew, President of Instituto Ethos, at a Global Compact Advisory Council meeting that took place in July, 2003.

[90] UNICEF Procurement policies, available at <http://www.unicef.org/supply/index_procurement_policies.html>.   [91] United Nations General Conditions of Contract, 24 June 2005, para 20.
[92] See eg Cowe and Porritt (n 81 above) 46 (where the British government is encouraged to apply the same standards in its procurement as it is commending to others); EU Accused of Using Illegally Logged Timber, <http://www.tendersdirect.co.uk>, in which Greenpeace alleged that illegal timber was being used in new EU buildings in Brussels. 'If true, the allegations would be an acute embarrassment for the EU. Last year the Commission launched its own action plan to combat illegal logging and the trade in illegal timber.'
[93] Role of UN Global Compact, Human Rights and Business Matters Spring/Summer 2001, including the correspondence between Kenneth Roth, Executive Director of Human Rights Watch and John G Ruggie, Assistant Secretary-General <http://www.amnesty.org.uk/business>; P Utting, 'The Global Compact and Civil Society: Averting a Collision Course', UNRISD News, No 25. For subsequent developments, see Report on the Third Expert Meeting on Sustainable Public Procurement, United Nations Headquarters, New York, 15–17 July 2005.
[94] The United Nations Working to Internalize the Global Compact Principles: Background, February 2005, from which the details of this paragraph are drawn.

At that meeting Mr. Grajew asked the Secretary-General to ensure that the UN itself 'walks the talk' and the Secretary-General agreed to consider how the UN could find ways to translate the Compact's principles into practice. Following the meeting, the Secretary-General requested that a review be carried out to 'explore the extent to which the UN can embrace the Compact's principles in its own procurement, human resources and pension fund policies'.[95]

In February 2004, the consultant engaged to develop an assessment of the policies of the UN and to provide recommendations for future action, reported.[96] The report concluded that: 'No logical, ethical or legal bars exist to managing the Organization's staff and service functions to be consistent with' the principles of the Global Compact.[97] It became 'increasingly apparent', in the words of a UN publication, that the UN 'could no longer be asking [Global Company] participants to follow practices that the UN itself did not fully observe. Thus, to preserve the UN's credibility as the initiator of the Global Compact, the Organization could no longer do less than what it was asking of others.'[98]

It was unwilling, however, to move much beyond the 'voluntary' nature of the Global Compact.

One of the strengths of the Global Compact is its voluntary nature and its recognition of the value of continuous improvement. An important objective of the Global Compact is to foster organizational change. Thus, participants should embrace and enact policies and procedures aimed at advancing the principles of the Compact and annually communicate their progress to stakeholders—an important tool to demonstrate implementation through public accountability. The Global Compact has not adopted a compliance-based approach, but rather stresses that participants demonstrate a commitment to real organizational change.[99]

The approach that the UN became committed to amounted primarily to awareness-raising activities to inform potential UN vendors and UN procurement staff about the Global Compact and its principles. However, in addition, the UN Office of Internal Oversight Services recommended that the UN draft a 'Code of Conduct' for UN suppliers. The UN Procurement Department drafted a 'UN Supplier Code of Conduct'. It was agreed that this 'should be an "aspirational" document containing a set of standards that the UN expects its suppliers to abide by but not a "compliance based" code. It would not be mandatory or of a contractual nature. However, at the same time there should be some mechanism that could allow the UN to reserve the right not to do business with a particular vendor if the UN has knowledge that it violates these principles.'[100] In 2005, this approach

[95] ibid.
[96] Judge Karen Burstein, 'The Right Road' A Report to the Under-Secretary-General for Management on the Global Compact and the Practice of Administration in the United Nations, February 2004. [97] ibid.
[98] The United Nations Working to Internalize the Global Compact Principles: Background, February 2005. [99] ibid.
[100] ibid.

gained the acceptance of the General Assembly.[101] In June 2006, the Secretary-General reported to the General Assembly on procurement reform generally in the UN organization, following high profile problems in procurement at the UN.[102] The Secretary-General's report focused primarily on strengthening internal control measures, reducing costs of acquisition, and strategic management of UN procurement. In that context, however, the Secretary-General also announced that the UN Procurement Service had finalized a Supplier Code of Conduct.[103] This would 'further support the Organization's effort to promote the voluntary principles of corporate social responsibility'.[104]

CSR and procurement in Europe

There were two linked aspects to the idea of corporate responsibility as it developed at the European level. One related to the practices of European enterprises operating outside the EC, particularly in developing countries. A second related to the activities of enterprises operating within the EC. In both, though to somewhat differing degrees, whether to use public procurement was an element of the debate. The first of these issues was initially considered by the European Parliament.[105] In 1999, the Parliament adopted a resolution on EC standards for European enterprises operating in developing countries. The principal element of the wide-ranging resolution was a request to the Commission and the Council to make proposals 'to develop the right legal basis for establishing a European multilateral framework governing companies' operations worldwide'.[106] Among the other actions, the resolution called on the Commission 'to bring forward proposals for a system of incentives for companies complying with international standards developed in close consultation and cooperation with consumer groups and human rights and environmental NGOs—such as in procurement, fiscal incentives, access to EU financial assistance and publication in the Official Journal'.[107] In 1999 a Commission publication on codes of practice considered possible methods of making social labels more effective through public policy

---

[101] GA Res 59/288. Procurement reform, para 15: 'Notes the promotion by the Procurement Service of the voluntary principles of the corporate social responsibility initiative, the Global Compact, within the United Nations procurement framework, and requests the Secretary-General, as appropriate, to report to the General Assembly for further consideration . . .'

[102] Investing in the United Nations: for a stronger Organization worldwide: detailed report: Report of the Secretary-General: Addendum: Procurement reform, 14 June 2006, A/60/846/Add.5.

[103] ibid para 15.   [104] ibid.

[105] The European Parliament had a long history of prior involvement in this issue. For example, its Resolution on the Commission's Action Programme relating to the implementation of the Community Charter of Fundamental Social Rights for Workers, A3-175/90, 13 September 1990, it insisted that in the trade agreements and cooperation treaties 'social clauses should be incorporated under which the contracting parties would undertake to abide by ILO standards', para 10, 'international treaties and conventions on working conditions and the rights of workers', para 22, and that they should also take 'environmental considerations into account and that penalties should be imposed for failure to comply with contractual arrangements', para 23.

[106] Resolution of 15 January 1999, Code of conduct for European enterprises operating in developing countries [1999] OJ C104/180, para 11.   [107] ibid para 28.

interventions. Among the methods listed was the use of 'public procurement in promoting labelled products'.[108]

The Commission's Green Paper 'Promoting a European Framework for Corporate Responsibility'[109] published in 2001, responded to the Parliament's recommendations regarding procurement. The Green Paper was intended to launch a debate on the promotion of corporate social responsibility within the EU. In the context of a discussion on social and environmental labelling, the Green Paper accepted that there is 'increasingly a need for a debate regarding the value and desirability—in the context of the Internal Market and international obligations—of public actions aimed at making social and eco labels more effective'.[110] The Commission gave several examples of such action, including the 'use of public procurement and fiscal incentives in promoting labelled products'.[111]

The responses to the Green Paper varied considerably.[112] Sorcha MacLeod and Douglas Lewis have, however, described 'the remarkable homogeneity between individual corporate responses as well as the responses of industry representatives'.[113] They characterize these as involving 'a definite emphasis on self-regulation, a lack of enthusiasm for enforcement mechanisms, temporization of implementation requirements, the voluntary nature of CSR, good practice and a general abhorrence of a "one-size fits all" approach to CSR'.[114] Although welcoming the Commission's initiative, the Council fired a warning shot, asking the Commission to 'query carefully the added value of any new action proposed at European level'.[115] The Committee of the Regions, however, in its response to the Green Paper accepted 'that local and regional authorities can give a lead in relation to promoting good CSR practices by ensuring that their purchasing and procurement strategies are CSR compliant'.[116] The Parliament, perhaps unsurprisingly, took an even stronger position. A report from the Committee on Employment and Social Affairs[117] urged the Council to 'take into account the Parliament's position on the principle of corporate social responsibility in the directive on public procurement'[118] and called on the Commission to bring forward proposals:

... to promote the contribution of EU companies towards transparency and good-governance world-wide, including through the setting up of a blacklist to prevent the tendering for public contracts by EU companies ... for non-compliance with minimum applicable international standards (ILO core labour standards, OECD Guidelines for multinational

---

[108] Quoted in C Hanley, 'Avoiding the Issue: The Commission and Human Rights Conditionality in Public Procurement' (2002) 27 ELR 714, 714.

[109] European Commission, Green Paper: Promoting a European framework for Corporate Social Responsibility, 18 July 2001, COM(2001)366 final.   [110] Ibid para 83.

[111] ibid.   [112] For a discussion, see MacLeod and Lewis (n 38 above) 85.   [113] ibid 86.

[114] ibid.

[115] Council Resolution on the follow-up to the Green Paper on corporate social responsibility [2002], OJ C86/3.

[116] Opinion of the Committee of the Regions on the Green Paper on Promoting a European Framework for Corporate Social Responsibility [2002] OJ C192/1.

[117] 30 April 2002, A5-0159/2002.   [118] Draft Resolution, para 32.

companies); and to establish a compliance panel to ensure that companies awarded contracts in the context of EC public procurement... comply with EU human rights obligations and development policies and procedures as well as minimum standards according to the... ILO and OECD Guidelines in the execution of those contracts; companies on the blacklist would be ineligible for EU contracts or awards for a period of three years.[119]

The Parliamentary Resolution reflected these recommendations closely.[120]

The European Commission produced its Communication on corporate social responsibility in July 2002.[121] The Commission's treatment of procurement needs to be seen in the context of the developments in procurement reform then underway. By the time of its response, the Commission had issued its Interpretative Communications on the possibilities for integrating social and environmental considerations into public procurement, which are considered later in this chapter. As regards the integration of social considerations into the directives, the Commission was essentially unwilling to go beyond what it had said in these Communications. In the section dealing with external relations policy, however, the Commission was more forthcoming. Where:

> ... public support is provided to enterprises, this implies co-responsibility of the government in those activities. These activities should therefore comply with the OECD guidelines for multinational enterprises, and, inter alia, not involve bribery, pollution of the environment or child or forced labour. Making access to subsidies for international trade promotion, investment and export credit insurance, *as well as access to public procurement*, conditional on adherence to and compliance with the OECD guidelines for multinational enterprises, while respecting EC international commitments, could be considered by EU Member States and by other States adherent to the OECD Declaration on International Investment.[122]

In addition, the Commission announced its intention to 'integrate further social and environmental priorities within its management, including its own public procurement'.[123] The Council, in its Resolution responding to the Commission, whilst welcoming the general thrust of the Commission's approach, did not discuss procurement issues explicitly, and restricted itself to supporting 'the intentions of the Commission, in particular to focus its strategy on... integrating CSR

---

[119] ibid para 59.

[120] European Parliament Resolution on the Commission Green Paper on promoting a European framework for corporate social responsibility, P5-TA(2002)0278, paras 28, 54.

[121] European Commission, Corporate Social Responsibility: A business contribution to Sustainable Development, 2 July 2002, COM(2002)347 final.

[122] Ibid para 7.6. The reference to respecting international commitments presumably refers to the WTO Government Procurement Agreement, *inter alia* (emphasis added).

[123] Ibid para 7.7. As regards the formal legislative provisions governing Commission procurement, however, the Commission took the position that they should reflect the procurement directives and that any changes in the existing Regulations (Commission Regulation (EC, Euratom) No 2342/2002 of 23 December 2002 laying down detailed rules for the implementation of Council Regulation (EC, Euratom) No 1605/2002 on the Financial Regulation applicable to the general budget of the European Communities [2002] OJ L357/1) should await the completion of the legislative package, discussed in ch 13 below.

into Community policies', and calling on the Member States 'to integrate, where appropriate, CSR principles into their own management'.[124]

CSR and procurement in the United Kingdom

Since 1997, public procurement in the United Kingdom was linked more explicitly to a CSR agenda than in most other Member States.[125] During the 1980s and 1990s, as we saw in chapter 11 above under successive Conservative governments, public procurement had been significantly reformed, in part by reducing the use of public procurement for social policy purposes. This was in part due to the need to cut public budgets; more efficient public procurement was thought to require a concentration on economic elements predominating in the idea of 'value for money'. Local authorities, for example, which had experimented with incorporating social issues into their procurement, were substantially stripped of their ability to do so in 1988. However, alongside this increasing emphasis on an economically driven conception of 'value for money', the other most significant development was the expansion of contracting as a method of governance. Public bodies were increasingly required to contract out several basic services. In local government, as we saw, a regime of 'compulsory competitive tendering' (or CCT) required a market-driven element to be introduced to service provision that resulted in work previously done in-house by council employees now being done by employees of private sector firms operating under contract to the public body. The election of a Labour government in 1997, however, led to significant changes in this approach to procurement that enabled it to be incorporated into the new government's increasingly strong CSR agenda.

The Local Government Act 2000 gave local authorities general powers to promote the economic, social, and environmental 'well-being' of its population.[126] In 2002, a Joseph Rowntree Foundation report[127] appears to have set the ball rolling on procurement linkages. In 2003, as part of the overall strategy for local authorities procurement, the Office of the Deputy Prime Minister[128] highlighted how procurement could support local economic development. The Office of Government Commerce (OGC) and Department for Education and Skills (DfES) set out the scope for using procurement to address workforce skills in a 2005 guidance note[129]

[124] Council Resolution of 6 February 2003 on corporate social responsibility [2003] OJ C39/3.

[125] D Ford, 'Public-sector procurement and corporate social responsibility' in CS Brown, *The Sustainable Enterprise: Profiting from Best Practice* (Kogan Page, 2005) 49.

[126] See <http://www.opsi.gov.uk/acts/acts2000/20000022.htm>.

[127] R MacFarlane and M Cook, 'Achieving community benefits through procurement' (Joseph Rowntree Foundation, 2002). A report credits this report with triggering the 'recent wave of interest in the potential to deliver wider social benefits through procurement'. Haringey SME Procurement Pilot: Community Benefit Clauses in Tenders and Contracts (5 April 2005) 4.

[128] Office of the Deputy Prime Minister and the Local Government Association, 'National Procurement Strategy for Local Government in England' (2003).

[129] OGC and DfES, 'Approaches to support workforce skills through public procurement: The policy and legal framework' (2005) available at <http:// www.ogc.gov.uk/embedded_object.asp ?docid=1004393>.

building on 2003 guidance that focused on basic skills.[130] In 2005, in a report to government, an Apprenticeship Task Force recommended that public procurers do more to include apprenticeship requirements in contracts, particularly in the construction sector.[131] In March 2006, the Department of Trade and Industry (DTI) published a report it had commissioned to explore the potential for using public sector procurement as a lever to drive up private sector employers' demand for skills and stimulate innovation in the economy.[132] In 2004, DTI 2004 guidance had focused on how public sector organizations could encourage suppliers to proffer innovative goods and services.[133] The DTI developed a five-year programme of work to use public procurement to stimulate innovation.[134] In 2005, a review of creativity in UK business by Sir George Cox, highlighted the proposition that public procurement could be an important driver of innovation and creativity.[135] A report in 2003, by the Better Regulation Task Force and Small Business Council, emphasized that SMEs and ethnic minority businesses face a number of barriers to accessing public sector contracts.[136] Increasingly, the Office of Government Commerce (OGC), the main UK government procurement policy body, became involved in giving advice on socio-economic aspects of procurement. In December 2002, it had published an information note on the procurement of sustainable timber,[137] and in 2005, it issued guidance on fair and ethical trading.[138] In 2006, the OGC developed guidance on how to include 'social issues' in procurement.[139]

The Labour government's approach to CSR has been seen in the academic literature as part of an approach to governance based on partnership between business and the public sector, which aimed to meet the need for better public services without the tax and spend approach that had traditionally been associated with previous Labour governments. This led, for example, to considerably increased use of public private partnerships (PPPs) in areas as diverse as the provision of housing, the building and running of schools, and the provision of social transfer payments. This use of the private sector resulted in 'business . . . assum[ing] a far greater profile in social life than hitherto'.[140] However, it also brought additional political risks to

---

[130] DfES and OGC, 'The policy and legal framework for using public procurement to enable contracted in staff to access basic skills training within government departments' (2003).

[131] Apprenticeship Task Force, 2005, 'The Business Case for Apprenticeships' (2005).

[132] J Binks, 'Using Public Procurement to Drive Skills and Innovation: A Report for the Department of Trade and Industry' (DTI, March 2006).

[133] OGC, 'Capturing Innovation: Nurturing Suppliers' Ideas in the Public Sector' (2004).

[134] DTI, 'Five Year Programme: Building Wealth from Knowledge' (HM Government, 2004).

[135] 'Cox review of creativity in business: Building on the UK's strengths' (HM Treasury, 2005).

[136] Better Regulation Task Force and Small Business Council, 'Government: Supporter and Customer?' (2003).

[137] OGC, Information Note 9/2002, 'Timber Procurement by Government Departments' (December 2002); OGC, Information Note 5/2004, 'New Guidance and Revised Model Contract Specification Clause', May 2004.   [138] OGC, 'Guidance on Fair and Ethical Trading' (2005).

[139] OGC, 'Social issues in purchasing' (2006).

[140] J Moon, 'Government as a Driver of Corporate Social Responsibility', ICCSR Research Paper Series, No 20-2004, 7.

government, increasing the likelihood that the government would be seen as being no different to the Conservative administrations that they replaced, and would be 'punished for the irresponsibility of business'.[141] Together with this partnership approach to business came greater use of the rhetoric of CSR, leading to the United Kingdom being seen as one of the leading exponents of CSR in Europe.

One of the tools that government has used in helping to ensure that CSR is being delivered in the United Kingdom is the use of public procurement. It is by way of procurement, rather than increased use of traditional command and control regulation through legislation, that CSR has often been encouraged. There has, as a result, been a significant shift in approach in policy on the use of procurement to deliver social and environmental outcomes in the United Kingdom. There have been two significant changes apparent. The first is that some of the most aggressively economically driven legislation on procurement introduced by the Conservative governments has been significantly changed, most notably the shift from CCT to a 'best value' approach, and the amendment of the 1988 restrictions on the use of procurement for social purposes in local government.[142] This led to a significantly increased interest in the use of social and green procurement by major local government purchasers, not least in London. We can see this as one of the 'initiatives [taken] to adjust the regulatory environment for CSR'.[143] The second identifiable change is the extent to which public procurement has been referred to in policy pronouncements since 2000, as we have seen in the previous few pages, as a method of helping to deliver particular social or environmental goals, and the extent to which this is justified by using CSR influenced language.[144] The third identifiable change is the extent to which there have been attempts to put CSR procurement into practice. The more high profile attempts, for example, have been the Public Sector Sustainable Food Procurement Initiative,[145] the purchasing of sustainable timber products,[146] the purchase of 'green' electricity,[147] and the incorporation of 'fair trade' into some procurement.[148]

---

[141] ibid 18.

[142] See P Badcoe, 'Best Value - A New Approach in the UK' in S Arrowsmith and M Trybus (eds), *Public Procurement: The Continuing Revolution* (Kluwer, 2003) 197.

[143] Moon (n 140 above) 14.

[144] Strategy Unit, 'Ethnic Minorities in the Labour Market' (March 2003); CRE, 'Guidance on equality and procurement' (July 2003); 'National Procurement Strategy for Local Government' (October 2003); OGC/DEFRA, 'Joint Note On Environmental Issues' (October, 2003); 'National Employment Panel Report to Chancellor' (March 2005); Office of Deputy Prime Minister, 'Code of Practice on Workforce Matters' (September 2005); Women and Work Commission, 'Shaping a Fairer Future' (February 2006); OGC, 'Social Issues in Purchasing' (February, 2006); 'The Equalities Review: Interim Report for Consultation' (March 2006).

[145] D Ford, 'Public-sector procurement and corporate social responsibility' in CS Brown, *The Sustainable Enterprise: Profiting from Best Practice* (Kogan Page, 2005) 49, 52.

[146] OGC, Information Note 9/2002, 'Timber Procurement by Government Departments' (December 2002); OGC, 'Timber Procurement by Government Departments: New Guidance and Revised Model Contract Specification Clause' (September 2003).

[147] DEFRA, 'Changing Patterns: The UK Government Framework for Sustainable Consumption and Production' (September 2003).

[148] OGC, 'Guidance on Fair and Ethical Trading' (2005).

Interestingly, in contrast with the debate at the EU level over the use of public procurement as an instrument of CSR, there has been relatively little opposition by business in Britain to these developments, and in some of these cases representatives of business have been involved directly in urging the use of public procurement.[149] Indeed, delivery of social outcomes through public procurement has become increasingly seen as a business advantage in tendering for future government contracts.[150]

Opposition to CSR in European public procurement

It would be misleading to suppose that attempts to use public procurement for CSR purposes in the rest of Europe are unopposed. There are two, rather different, objections. The first arises more specifically in the context of CSR. The use of public procurement has led to objections that CSR should, as we have seen from the European Commission's definition, be 'voluntary'. We have seen that 'voluntary' in this context does not necessarily mean 'motivated by philanthropy' but rather that it should not be legally required. Several of the mechanisms used to promote CSR are based on the 'business case' argument in which consumers play a major role. The European Commission's 2002 Communication, after defining CSR as set out at the beginning of this chapter, went on to say that: 'Despite the wide spectrum of approaches to CSR, there is large consensus on its main features [including that] CSR is behaviour by businesses over and above legal requirements, voluntarily adopted because businesses deem it to be in their long-term interest.'

The second objection is based on a more general concern about the use of procurement for social policy purposes. This objection derives from a concern that the adverse effects of such linkages outweigh any good that may come of them. As we saw in chapter 5 above, common general objections are: that such linkage increases the costs of procurement; that linkage leads to a reduction in the transparency of the procurement process; that linkage leads to greater bureaucratization of procurement; or that it increases the opportunity for corruption. In the EC context, a particular concern—given that one of the primary functions of the organization is to reduce barriers to the creation of a vibrant internal market—is that such linkages increase the opportunity for, or have the effect of, reducing competition.

One of the main features of the Commission's CSR proposals, as we have seen, was the establishment of a European Multi-Stakeholder Forum—to include social partners, business networks, consumers, and investors—to exchange best practice, to establish principles for codes of conduct, and to seek consensus on evaluation methods and tools such as social labels. The acceptability of the use of procurement came to the fore in this Forum, hosted by the European Commission between 2002 and 2004, which provided an opportunity for the various interested

---

[149] One example is the CBI membership of the Women and Work Commission. There may be several reasons. Moon has sought to explain why, in general, business may urge governments to be a driver of CSR: 'This could be for reasons either of wishing to increase competitors' costs or of wishing to penalise free riders which enjoy the reputational goods and propitious governance systems that CSR may generate for business in general.' Moon (n 40 above) 19.

[150] See eg Accord, 'Corporate Social Responsibility Report' (2004).

groups (such as representatives of business, trade unions and NGOs) to discuss future European CSR policy, and help to shape the Commission's future approach.[151] As regards the use of public procurement to encourage business to adopt CSR, it quickly emerged that the representatives of business were adamantly opposed, whereas the trade unions and NGOs were in favour. The three 'round tables' in which discussions took place could simply report the disagreement. In the Round Table on the diversity, convergence, and transparency of CSR Practices and Tools: 'It was suggested by NGOs and trade unions that public authorities could play a number of roles in driving CSR and related activities, through actions in the areas of procurement policies, export credit schemes, trade policies and eligibility for subsidies and taxes.' Business and employer organizations, however, 'stressed the view that linking public policy or funding sources with CSR could have damaging consequences for SMEs, could distort competition and would involve disregarding the voluntary nature of CSR'.[152] In the Round Table on fostering CSR among SMEs, participants 'had fundamentally different views on the issue'. Some supported further analysis, 'looking particularly at how SMEs might benefit from calls for tender with social and environmental criteria', whilst others 'argued that the practical problems of introducing... social and environmental criteria into public procurement (particularly if those are built on what is accepted as voluntary practice) are too great'.[153] The emphasis on CSR being voluntary was also stressed during the course of the third Round Table, as well as the argument that it 'would amount to discrimination against other bidders'.[154] In the light of this, it was not surprising that the Final Report of the Forum merely recorded disagreement on the issue and set out the arguments for and against. Nor, given the extent to which the Commission had committed itself to going forward with CSR initiatives on the basis of a voluntary approach, was it surprising that mention of public procurement was entirely absent from the 2006 Commission Communication on CSR, much to the disappointment of trade unions and NGOs.[155]

Environmental protection, sustainable development, and procurement linkages

International developments

Another significant factor influencing the international and EC debate on procurement linkages has been the growth of policies on sustainable development. The debate on how to take the environment into account in public procurement

---

[151] M Capron, 'Forum plurilatéral européen sur la RSE: la raison d'une déconvenue' (2006) available at <http://www.lux/pdf/capron.pdf>.

[152] Round Table on 'The diversity, convergence and transparency of CSR Practices and Tools', Final Report (2004) para 3.5.

[153] Round Table on 'Fostering CSR among SMEs', Final Version (3 May 2004) para 3.1.

[154] Round Table on 'Improving Knowledge about CSR and Facilitating the Exchange of Experience and Good Practice', Final Version 29 April 2004, 12.

[155] See European Parliament Socialist Group statement.

is relatively recent.[156] An OECD report described the Danish strategy for the promotion of sustainable procurement policy from 1991 'as the starting point of several political initiatives in various countries'.[157] The growth of 'green procurement' soon became, however, a significant feature of the policy landscape by the late 1990s, at the national, regional, and international levels, with encouragement being given to such initiatives by a wide variety of different international organizations, including the OECD.[158] The United Nations Conference on Environment and Development (UNCED) held in Rio de Janerio, Brazil in 1992 (the so-called 'Earth Summit') was a turning point for the development of the use of public procurement for green purchasing. Agenda 21[159] called for governments to exercise leadership through government purchasing.[160] The 1997 Programme for the Further Implementation of Agenda 21 further encouraged governments to take the lead in changing consumption patterns by improving their own environmental performance with action-oriented policies and goals on procurement, the management of public facilities and the further integration of environmental concerns into national policy-making.

UNCED had the effect of encouraging national developments and further initiatives in various forums. In 1995, the G7 Environmental ministers, meeting in Hamilton, Canada, agreed that their own government operations should be 'greened', including public purchasing. In 1996, an OECD Council Recommendation called on members to establish and implement policies for the procurement of environmentally preferable products and services for use by government.[161] In 1996, a 'Green Purchasing Network' was founded in Japan. The International Council for Local Environmental Initiatives (ICLEI) launched a European Eco-Procurement Initiative in 1996. In 1997, the International Council for Local Environmental Initiatives and the European Partners for the Environment founded the 'European Network for Environmentally Friendly Procurement'. In 1998, municipal purchasers and others met for an EcoProcura '98 Forum for Economic and Green Purchasing. In 1998, President Clinton

---

[156] See generally DB Marron, 'Buying Green: Government Procurement as an Instrument of Environmental Policy' (1997) 25(3) Public Finance Review 285; C Erdmenger (ed), *Buying into the Environment* (Greenleaf Publishing, 2003), L Brander and X Olsthoorn, *Three Scenarios for Green Public Procurement* (Institute for Environmental Studies, December 2003).

[157] T Westphal, 'Greening Procurement: An Attempt to Reduce Uncertainty' (1999) 8 PPLR 1, 2 fn 12, citing OECD Secretariat issue paper, 'Sustainable Product and Life Cycle Management, Greener Public Procurement', 1997. The Westphal article is the source for much of the rest of this paragraph.

[158] OECD, 'Greener Public Purchasing: Issues and Practical Solutions' (OECD, 2000). See also, OECD, 'The Environmental Performance of Public Procurement: Issues of Policy Coherence' (OECD, 2003). See also J Earley, 'Green Procurement in Trade Policy: Background Paper prepared for the Commission for Environmental Cooperation' (Commission for Environmental Cooperation, 2003), available at <http://www.cec.org>.   [159] Agenda 21, ch 4, para 4.23.

[160] Procurement was addressed in element C of the CSD Work Programme on Changing Consumption and Production Patterns, adopted at the third session of the CSD in 1995.

[161] OECD Council Recommendation 1996.

issued an executive order encouraging federal agencies to buy environmentally preferable products.[162] In Taiwan, also in 1998, new legislation was introduced that included provisions to promote an eco-labelling scheme through public procurement.[163] At the 1999 EcoProcura Forum, the 'Bilbao Steps' indicated ways to implement green purchasing programmes. In February 2000, 250 European municipal leaders included their commitment to green purchasing in their 'Hanover Call'. In October 2000, the participants at the EcoProcura Forum, in Lyon, issued the 'Lyon Declaration', which included an extensive call for eco-responsible purchasing by government.[164] In 2001, the multilateral deveopment banks, United Nations organizations, and a variety of NGOs created an Interagency Sustainable Procurement Group to encourage the use of sustainable procurement by these institutions and others.[165]

A Programme for Further Implementation of Agenda 21, and the Commitments to the Rio principles, were reaffirmed at the World Summit on Sustainable Development held in Johannesburg, South Africa in 2002. Changing consumption and production patterns was, indeed, seen as one of the overarching objectives of and essential requirements for sustainable development, as recognized by the heads of state and governments in the Johannesburg Declaration. The Johannesburg Plan of Implementation called for the development of 'a 10-year framework of programmes in support of regional and national initiatives to accelerate the shift towards sustainable consumption and production'.[166] The framework should strengthen international cooperation and increase the exchange of information and best practices to facilitate the implementation of national and regional programmes to promote sustainable consumption and production. '[R]elevant authorities at all levels', were encouraged 'to take sustainable development considerations into account in decision-making, including on national and local development planning, investment in infrastructure, business development and public procurement'.[167] This would include actions to: 'Promote public procurement policies that encourage development and diffusion of environmentally sound goods and services.'[168]

Since then, the United Nations has sponsored the Marrakech Process, as it is called, to develop the ten-year framework. This has resulted in two international expert meetings on sustainable consumption and production (in Marrakech in

---

[162] Executive Order 13101 (1998).

[163] T Fox, H Ward, and B Howard, *Public Sector Roles in Strengthening Corporate Social Responsibility: A Baseline Study* (World Bank, 2002) 13.

[164] Lyon Declaration: Enhancing the Framework, Enforcing the Action for Greening Government Operations, Lyon, 17–18 October 2000.

[165] <http://www.sustainableprocurement.net/home2.html>.

[166] Johannesburg Plan of Implementation, 3.   [167] ibid ch 3, para 19.

[168] ibid ch 3, para 19(c). For further developments, see Overview of progress towards sustainable development: a review of the implementation of Agenda 21, the Programme for the Further Implementation of Agenda 21 and the Johannesburg Plan of Implementation, Report of the Secretary-General, E/CN.17/2006/2, 15 February 2006, para 46.

June 2003, and in San José, Costa Rica in September 2005), regional meetings, and three expert meetings specifically on public procurement, supported by the UN's Department of Economic and Social Affairs' Division for Sustainable Development, resulting in the sharing of information and the creation of a database of national measures on sustainable public procurement.[169] Since then, the OECD has taken particular interest in the issue at the international level, holding conferences and commissioning research.[170] New laws requiring the purchase of environmentally-friendly products by government have been enacted, for instance in Korea.[171]

An important aspect of this work has been the interpretation of 'sustainable procurement' as encompassing a significant social dimension. At least since 2003, sustainable development has been interpreted as involving three pillars, the social, the environmental, and the economic, and efforts have been made to ensure that the social is included in discussions about the meaning and implementation of sustainable procurement.[172] The term has now expanded considerably beyond a narrower environmental agenda to encompass labour rights, and human rights principles as well. Guides have been produced for major cities wanting to engage in 'responsible procurement',[173] which is interpreted to include environmental, social, and ethical purchasing, and the European Fair Trade Association has produced guidance for 'sustainable procurement', concentrating on purchasing 'fair trade' products, which aim 'to guarantee that producers in less developed countries receive a fair price that not only reflects the true costs of their production and work, but also makes socially just and environmentally sound production possible'.[174]

Green procurement in Europe

By 2001, the Commission proposal for the Sixth Environmental Action Programme, covering the years 2001–2010, identified public procurement as an area that had considerable potential for 'greening' the market through public purchasers using environmental performance as one of their purchase criteria.[175] The Commission Communication of May 2001 on 'A Sustainable Europe for a Better World: A European Union Strategy for Sustainable Development' presented to the meeting of the European Council in Gothenburg in June 2001, proposed that

---

[169] <http://www.un.org/esa/sustdev/sdissues/consumption/cpppr01.htm>.

[170] See eg OECD, 'The Environmental Performance of Public Performance: Issues of Policy Coherence' (OECD, 2003).

[171] Act on the Promotion of the Purchase of Environment-Friendly Products 2004, <http://www .kela.or.kr/english/info/view.asp?board_idx=8>.

[172] See eg C Takase, 'Integrating Social Aspects in Public Procurement', 14 June 2005, paper prepared for 3rd Expert Meeting on Sustainable Public Procurement, New York, 15–17 June 2005.

[173] EuroCities, 'CARPE Guide to Responsible Procurement' (Eurocities, 2004).

[174] EFTA, 'Fair Procura: Making Public Authorities and Institutional Buyers Local Actors of Sustainable Development' (EFTA, 2005).

[175] Communication from the Commission to the Council, the European Parliament, the Economic and Social Committee and the Committee of the Regions on the sixth environment action programme of the European Community: 'Environment 2010: Our future, Our choice'—adopted by the Commission on 24 January 2001, COM(2001)31 final.

Member States should consider how to make better use of public procurement to favour environmentally-friendly products and services. A Commission White Paper explained how 'public procurement rules could be explicitly tailored to sustainable objectives'.[176]

The relationship between three environmental policies and procurement is of particular importance. The first relates to the relationship between labelling and procurement. 'Eco-labels', as they are sometimes called, certify products that are deemed to be more environmentally sound than similar products in the same product group. The labels aim at informing consumers about environmentally sound products. Different types of eco-labels have been developed. A European eco-label was first devised at the Community level in 1992.[177] Over the decade, however, the number and type of eco-labels proliferated, with national eco-labels, plurinational eco-labels, and private eco-labels. There has been increasing use of such labels as part of procurement technical specifications.[178]

The second development relates to environmental impact assessment. For a specific category of works contracts, Community law imposes an obligation to make, prior to the decision of having the work executed, an environmental impact assessment.[179] This obligation, which originates from environmental legislation and not from the public procurement directives, influences the choice of the purchasing entity. The obligation for the competent authorities to take into account the results of the environmental impact assessment in the decision of whether or not to give authorization or consent for development, tends to lead to more environmentally sound requirements for the execution of the works.

A third European environmental development that links into procurement is the development of an Environmental Management and Audit Scheme (EMAS) in 1993.[180] This established a voluntary scheme for the 'evaluation and improvement of the environmental performance of industrial activities and the provision of the relevant information to the public'. It aims to 'promote continuous improvements in the environmental performance of industrial activities'. Companies may obtain a certificate confirming that they comply with the standards set out. The linkage to public procurement is clear: public authorities may require tenderers to 'introduce an internal policy to reduce the environmental impact of their production activity'.[181]

We can also point to significant developments in the practice of procurement, although these changes in practice are very uneven across the Community. The

[176] White Paper on Growth, Competitiveness and Employment: The challenges and ways forward into the 21st Century, COM(93)7000.

[177] Council Regulation (EEC) 880/92 of 23 March 1992 on a Community eco-label award scheme [1992] OJ L099/1–7. This regulation was repealed and replaced by Council Regulation No 1980/2000 of 17 July 2000 on a revised Community Eco-label Award Scheme [2000] L237/1.

[178] T Westphal, 'Greening Procurement: An Attempt to Reduce Uncertainty' (1999) 8 PPLR 1, 12.

[179] Projects covered by Directive (EEC) 85/337 [1985] OJ L175/40, amended by Directive (EEC) 97/11 [1997] OJ L073/5.

[180] Council Regulation (EEC) 1836/93 of 29 June 1993 [1993] OJ L168.

[181] Westphal (n 178 above) 13.

2005 European Commission survey on the state of play on green public procurement in the Member States found that seven Member States (Austria, Denmark, Finland, Germany, the Netherlands, Sweden, and the UK) were practising a significant amount of green public procurement. In these countries 40 to 70 per cent of all tenders published on Tenders Electronic Daily during the past year included environmental criteria. However in the remaining eighteen countries, this figure was below 30 per cent.[182]

IV. Addressing Legal Uncertainties

The development of CSR-related and 'green' procurement significantly affected the policy context in which procurement linkages were discussed by the late 1990s. In practice, the most effective single intervention of the Community in advancing the use of public procurement for social and environmental purposes, however, was the clarification of the legal position of social linkages under EC law. If there were a risk of being sued, some public authorities would prefer not to act.[183] Indeed, for the Commission, the clarification of the legal position was identified as part of the Commission's strategy for encouraging CSR, as it meant removing an existing barrier to the further adoption of CSR policies in the Member States.[184] The Community had a role to play, therefore, if only in improving legal clarity. The fourth major development since the early 1990s that changed the policy context for procurement linkages, therefore, was the extent to which legal uncertainties were addressed. This occurred through the intervention of the European Court of Justice (ECJ) and of the European Commission.

Judicial adaptation: the ECJ adapts EC law to social justice linkages

Given the changing political and policy context, the increased use of procurement linkages at the national level, and the increased advocacy of the use of procurement linkages at the European and international levels, a narrow 'economic' interpretation of the procurement directives that had been adopted during much of the 1990s, as we saw in chapter 11 above, came increasingly under pressure.

---

[182] M Bouwer, K de Jong, M Jonk, T Berman, R Bersani, H Lusser, and P Szuppinger, 'Green Public Procurement in Europe 2005', <http://portal.aragob.es/pls/portal30/docs/FOLDER/MEDIOAMBIENTE/CALIDAD_AMBIENTAL/COMVERD/GUIAS/GPP+REPORT+WORKKING.PDF>.

[183] See, eg finding of a survey into determinants of green public procurement, L Brander and X Olsthoorn, 'Three scenarios for Green Public Procurement', December 2002, Institute for Environmental Studies, Vrije Universiteit, The Netherlands, 20 *et seq*. See also, J Morgan and J Niessen, 'Immigrant and Minority Businesses: Making the Policy Case' (2003) 4 European Journal of Migration and Law 329, 332, 334.

[184] Report on the Expert Meeting on Sustainable Public Procurement, Copenhagen, Denmark, 2–3 December 2002, <http://www.un.org/esa/sustdev/sdissues/consumption/SPP-Report-rev.pdf> European Commission view by Herbert Aichinger.

Interpretations of Community law by the ECJ sought to accommodate this changing context, not least in demonstrating that a careful reading of the directives showed them to be less hostile to procurement linkages than had hitherto been assumed to be the case. We turn now to consider the development of a judicial strategy to adapt the procurement directives to accommodate certain forms of linkage.

The Nord-Pas-de-Calais *case*

We saw in chapter 11 above, that the Commission took infringement proceedings against France over the award of school building contracts by the region of Nord-Pas-de-Calais and the Départment du Nord. There were many grounds of complaint, but the most important for the purpose of this discussion related to the linkage between the procurement and various actions being taken to reduce unemployment. The notices in the *Official Journal* stated that the tenders would be assessed by taking account of various award criteria, including an 'additional' criterion related to employment. This derived from the circular of 29 December 1993, discussed in chapter 11 above, 'in which the French Government had suggested the use of social criteria in the award of public contracts. This Circular was issued by Ministers holding responsibilities in the field of social policy or procurement.'[185] It 'expressly set[ ] forth as an award criterion . . . a condition relating to employment linked to a local project to combat unemployment'. The Commission considered that the French authorities had infringed the Directive's restrictive terms relating to award criteria. The Commission's complaint was narrow, but important. It related only to the link with unemployment as an award criterion, viewing the *Beentjes* case, discussed in chapter 10 above, as relating only to contract conditions concerning performance. In the *Nord-Pas-de-Calais* case, however, the link to the campaign against unemployment was 'characterized as an award criterion in the contract notices in question', and, according to the Commission, award criteria must be based either on the lowest price or on the most economically advantageous tender. The French government, however, interpreted the *Beentjes* case rather differently. The Court in that case had, in the French view, permitted 'an additional award criterion'. In any event, the French government continued, 'the award criterion in question in this case does not constitute a primary criterion . . . the purpose of which is to make it possible to determine which is the most advantageous tender, but a secondary criterion which is not decisive'. Such a secondary criterion was admissible 'where several tenders of equal value have been submitted'.[186]

The Opinion of Advocate General Alber in the *Nord-Pas-de-Calais* case, delivered on 14 March 2000, accepted the Commission's argument, holding the French authorities to have infringed the Directive. *Beentjes* should be interpreted as

---

[185] J Arnould, 'A Turning Point in the Use of Additional Award Criteria?: The Judgment of the European Court in the French Lycées case' (2001) 10 PPLR NA13–14.
[186] Case C-225/98 *Commission v France, Nord-Pas-de-Calais* [2000] ECR I-7445, Advocate General's Opinion, para 45.

having ruled out criteria other than lowest price or most economically advantageous as separate award criteria. The directive would not have been infringed 'if the requirements to promote employment were expressed as a condition—as in *Beentjes*—and in that respect assumed the character of a performance criterion, as was stated by the Commission'.[187] In response to the French government's argument that the secondary criterion was used only where several tenders of equal value had been submitted, Advocate General Alber held:

> However, in such cases that would result in the employment criterion ultimately being granted the status of the sole, decisive award criterion, a possibility which is specifically ruled out in the light of *Beentjes*. The employment criterion does not serve to determine the most economically advantageous tender. Otherwise, in certain circumstances, it would have even greater importance than the criteria referred to in . . . the Directive, since the employment aspect alone could be decisive.[188]

The Court, with qualifications, sided, however, with the French government. The Court disagreed with the Commission's view that the *Beentjes* case concerned a condition of performance of the contract and not a criterion for the award of the contract, holding that 'the condition relating to the employment of long-term unemployed persons, which was at issue in that case, had been used as the basis for rejecting a tender and therefore necessarily constituted a criterion for the award of the contract'. To the argument that the award criteria specified in the directives were exhaustive, after describing the provision relating to award criteria, the Court continued: 'that provision does not preclude all possibility for the contracting authorities to use as a criterion a condition linked to the campaign against unemployment provided that that condition is consistent with all the fundamental principles of Community law, in particular the principle of non-discrimination flowing from the provisions of the Treaty on the right of establishment and the freedom to provide services'.[189] In addition, the criterion must be applied in conformity with all the procedural rules, in particular the rules on advertising. It must also be 'expressly mentioned in the contract notice so that contractors may become aware of its existence'.[190]

The judgment was difficult to interpret and subject to some criticism in academic journals.[191] The Commission's response was to interpret the decision as narrowly as possible, drawing on the arguments that the French government had made to limit the decision of the Court. In the General Report on the Activities of the European Communities for 2000,[192] the Commission described the case as follows:

> [The Court] held that the awarding authorities could apply a condition relating to the campaign against unemployment, provided that this condition was in line with all the

---

[187] ibid para 48.   [188] ibid para 45.   [189] ibid para 50.   [190] ibid para 51.
[191] See eg Arnould (n 185 above) NA15, where the reasoning of the Court is described as 'rather odd'.
[192] See the General Report on the Activities of the European Union, 2000, point 1119, 407 (emphasis added).

fundamental principles of Community law, *but only where the said authorities had to consider two or more economically equivalent bids.* Such a condition could be applied as an accessory criterion once the bids had been compared from a purely economic point of view. Lastly, as regards the criterion relating to the campaign against unemployment, the Court made it clear that this criterion must not have any direct or indirect impact on those submitting bids from other Member States of the Community and must be explicitly mentioned in the contract notice so that potential contractors were able to ascertain that such a condition existed.

The Oy Liikenne *case*

Further (oblique) support for a restricted interpretation of the procurement directives where they came into conflict with other values came from the ECJ in the *Oy* case,[193] in which the Court considered the relationship between the procurement directives and the Transfer of Undertakings Directive (Directive 77/187). Following a tender procedure, the Greater Helsinki Joint Board awarded the operation of seven local bus routes, previously operated by one company, to another company. The first company, which operated those bus routes with twenty-six buses, then dismissed forty-five drivers, thirty-three of whom were re-engaged by the second company. The second company also engaged eighteen other drivers. The drivers previously employed by the first company were, however, re-engaged on the conditions laid down by the national collective agreement in the sector, which were less favourable than those that they had previously worked under. There was no contract between the two companies. No vehicles or other assets connected with the operation of the bus routes were transferred. The national court referred several questions to the ECJ concerning whether a transfer of an undertaking could be regarded as having taken place. In its observations, however, the national court specifically observed that it considered that there might be a conflict between the procurement directive governing the tendering process in this case (the Services Directive (Directive 95/50))[194] and the Transfer of Undertakings Directive. 'Application of Directive 77/187 in such a context, while protecting the rights of employees, may obstruct competition between undertakings and prejudice the aim of effectiveness pursued by Directive 92/50. The [national court] is uncertain as the interrelationship of the two directives in those circumstances.'[195] The ECJ provided a robust response, denying the conflict:

22. The fact that the provisions of Directive 77/187 may in certain cases be applicable in the context of a transaction which come under Directive 95/50 cannot be seen as calling into question the objectives of the latter directive. Directive 92/50 is not intended to exempt contracting authorities and service providers who offer their services for the contracts in question from all the laws and regulations applicable to the activities concerned,

---

[193] Case C-172/99 *Oy Liikenne Ab v Pekka Liskojärvi and Pentti Juntunen* [2001] ECR I-745.

[194] Council Directive (EEC) 92/50 of 18 June 1992 relating to the co-ordination of procedures for the award of public service contracts [1992] OJ 1992 L209/1.

[195] *Oy Liikenne* (n 193 above) para 13.

in particular in the social sphere or that of safety, so that offers can be made without any constraints. The aim of Directive 92/50 is that, in compliance with those laws and regulations and under the conditions it lays down, economic operators may have equal opportunities, in particular for putting into practice their rights of establishment and freedom to provide services.

23. In such a context, operators retain their room to manoeuvre and compete with one another and submit different bids... An operator who makes a bid must also be able to assess whether, if his bid is accepted, it will be in his interests to acquire significant assets from the present contractor and take over some or all of his staff, or whether he will be obliged to do so, and, if so, whether he will be in a situation of a transfer of an undertaking within the meaning of Directive 77/187.

Nor was the ECJ prepared to accept that applying the Transfer of Undertakings Directive in the context of a public procurement process was an infringement of the principle of legal certainty:

24. That assessment, and that of the costs involved in the various possible solutions, are also part of the workings of competition and... cannot be regarded as disclosing an infringement of the principle of legal certainty. Any action in the field of competition will be subject to some uncertainty in relation to a number of factors, and it is the responsibility of operators to make realistic analyses. Admittedly, unlike its competitors, the undertaking which formerly had the contract knows precisely the costs it incurs in order to provide the service which is the subject of the contract; but this is inherent in the system and cannot justify not applying the social legislation, and that advantage is probably offset in most cases by the greater difficulty for that undertaking of changing its operating conditions in order to adapt them to the new conditions of the call for tenders, compared with competitors who make a bid from scratch.

The Concordia Bus *case*

The issue of award criteria was highlighted in another major ECJ intervention, in the *Concordia Bus* case, which the Court decided on 17 September 2002.[196] The Helsinki city council decided on 27 August 1997 progressively to introduce tendering for the entire bus transport network of the city of Helsinki, in such a way that the first route to be awarded would start operating from the autumn of 1998. By a letter of 1 September 1997 and a notice published in the *Official Journal* on 4 September 1997, the purchasing unit of the city of Helsinki called for tenders for operating the urban bus network within the city of Helsinki in seven lots, in accordance with routes and timetables described. The main proceedings concerned lot 6 of the tender notice. According to the tender notice, the contract would be awarded to the undertaking whose tender was most economically advantageous overall to the city. That was be assessed by reference to three categories of criteria: the overall price of operation, the quality of the bus fleet, and the operator's quality and environment management. As regards the operator's quality

---

[196] Case C-513/99 *Concordia Bus Finland Oy Ab* [2002] ECR I-7213.

and environment programme, additional points were to be awarded for various certified quality criteria and for a certified environment protection programme. The purchasing office of the city of Helsinki received eight tenders for lot 6, including those from HKL and from Swebus Finland Oy Ab ('Swebus', subsequently Stagecoach Finland Oy Ab ('Stagecoach'), then Concordia). Swebus' tender comprised two offers, designated A and B. The commercial service committee decided to choose HKL as the operator for the route in lot 6, as its tender was regarded as the most economically advantageous overall. Concordia (as it was now named) was not awarded the contract. Concordia made an application to the Kilpailuneuvosto (Finnish Competition Council) for the decision of the commercial service committee to be set aside, arguing, *inter alia*, that the award of additional points to a fleet with nitrogen oxide emissions and noise levels below certain limits was unfair and discriminatory. It submitted that additional points had been awarded for the use of a type of bus which only one tenderer, HKL, was in fact able to offer. The Kilpailuneuvosto dismissed the application. It considered that the contracting entity was entitled to define the type of vehicle it wanted to be used. The selection criteria and their weight had to be determined objectively, however, taking into account the needs of the contracting entity and the quality of the service. The contracting entity had to be able, if necessary, to give reasons to justify its choice and the application of its criteria of assessment. The decision to give preference to low-pollution buses was an environmental policy decision aimed at reducing the harm caused to the environment by bus traffic. That did not constitute a procedural defect. If that criterion was applied to a tenderer unfairly, it was possible to intervene. The Kilpailuneuvosto found, however, that all the tenderers had the possibility, if they so wished, of acquiring buses powered by natural gas. It therefore concluded that it had not been shown that the criterion in question discriminated against Concordia. Concordia appealed to the Korkein hallinto-oikeus to have the decision of the Kilpailuneuvosto set aside.

The Korkein hallinto-oikeus decided to stay the proceedings and referred several questions to the ECJ for a preliminary ruling. The most important was the second question:

Are the Community provisions on public procurement . . . to be interpreted as meaning that, when organizing a tender procedure concerning the operation of bus transport within the city, a city which is a contracting entity may, among the criteria for awarding the contract on the basis of the economically most advantageous tender, take into account, in addition to the tender price and the quality and environment programme of the transport operator and various other characteristics of the bus fleet, the low nitrogen oxide emissions and low noise level of the bus fleet offered by a tendering undertaking, in a manner announced beforehand in the tender notice, such that if the nitrogen oxide emissions or noise level of the individual buses are below a certain level, extra points for the fleet may be taken into account in the comparison?[197]

---

[197] ibid para 35.

The ECJ decided in favour of the public body. On the one hand, the Court held that the criteria that may be used for the award of a public contract to the economically most advantageous tender were not listed exhaustively in the Directive. There was no requirement that each of the award criteria used by the contracting authority to identify the economically most advantageous tender must necessarily be of a purely economic nature. 'It cannot be excluded that factors which are not purely economic may influence the value of a tender from the point of view of the contracting authority.'[198] That conclusion was supported by the wording of the provision, which expressly referred to the criterion of the aesthetic characteristics of a tender. Since the purpose of the procurement directives was to eliminate barriers to the free movement of services and goods, and since the EC Treaty provided that environmental protection requirements must be integrated into the definition and implementation of Community policies and activities, 'it must be concluded that Article 36(1)(a) of Directive 92/50 does not exclude the possibility for the contracting authority of using criteria relating to the preservation of the environment when assessing the economically most advantageous tender'.[199]

On the other hand, that did not mean that any criterion of that nature might be taken into consideration by the contracting authority. There were several constraining factors. First, despite the conclusions of the Advocate General on the point, the Court held that the additional award criteria must be 'linked' to the subject matter of the contract:

While Article 36(1)(a) of Directive 92/50 leaves it to the contracting authority to choose the criteria on which it proposes to base the award of the contract, that choice may, however, relate only to criteria aimed at identifying the economically most advantageous tender . . . Since a tender necessarily relates to the subject-matter of the contract, it follows that the award criteria which may be applied in accordance with that provision must themselves also be linked to the subject-matter of the contract.[200]

This approach had already found favour with the Conseil d'Etat in France. In its ruling on the challenge to the circular that featured in the *Nord-Pas-de-Calais* case, the Conseil held that under French law additional criteria were permitted only in so far as they were related to the object of the contract.[201]

Second, the procedural requirements of the Directive continued to apply. The criteria adopted to determine the economically most advantageous tender 'must be applied in conformity with all the procedural rules laid down in Directive 92/50, in particular the rules on advertising. It follows that, in accordance with Article 36(2) of that directive, all such criteria must be expressly mentioned in the contract documents or the tender notice, where possible in descending order of importance, so that operators are in a position to be aware of their existence and scope.'[202]

---

[198] ibid para 55.	[199] ibid para 57.	[200] ibid para 59.
[201] Conseil d'Etat, 10 May 1996, Fédération nationale de travaux publics, Rec, 164. See the discussion by Joël Arnould (n 185 above) NA17.	[202] *Concordia Bus* (n 196 above) para 52.

Third, the criteria must also comply with all the fundamental principles of Community law, in particular the principle of non-discrimination as it followed from the provisions of the Treaty on the right of establishment and the freedom to provide services.

> . . . where the contracting authority decides to award a contract to the tenderer who submits the economically most advantageous tender, in accordance with Article 36(1)(a) of Directive 92/50, it may take criteria relating to the preservation of the environment into consideration, provided that they are linked to the subject-matter of the contract, do not confer an unrestricted freedom of choice on the authority, are expressly mentioned in the contract documents or the tender notice, and comply with all the fundamental principles of Community law, in particular the principle of non-discrimination.[203]

As regards the application of these principles to the facts of this case, the Court held that the criteria relating to the level of nitrogen oxide emissions and the noise level of the buses, 'must be regarded as linked to the subject-matter of a contract for the provision of urban bus transport services'.[204] Awarding additional points to tenders which meet certain specific and objectively quantifiable environmental requirements 'are not such as to confer an unrestricted freedom of choice on the contracting authority'.[205] The criteria were expressly mentioned in the tender notice published by the purchasing office of the city of Helsinki. Finally, the criteria complied with the principle of non-discrimination.

The Wienstrom case

In *EVN AG and Wienstrom GmbH v Republik Österreich*[206] the issue also related to the legality under the procurement Directives of the use of ecological criteria by a contracting authority as award criteria for determining the most economically advantageous tender. In the *Concordia Bus* case, the ECJ held that such award criteria must, *inter alia*, be linked to the subject matter of the contract. In the *Wienstrom* case, the Court determined that the subject matter of the contract consisted of a service which was 'the supply of an amount of electricity *to the contracting authority* corresponding to its expected annual consumption as laid down in the invitation to tender'.[207] The award criteria, however, consisted in allotting points for the amount of electricity generated from renewable energy sources, which the tenderer would be able to supply to a larger group of consumers, account being taken only of the supply volume exceeding the consumption to be expected in the context of the invitation to tender. As the Court held, the award criterion related, therefore, 'to the amount of electricity that the tenderers have supplied, or will supply, to *other* customers'.[208] The Court continued: 'An award criterion that relates solely to the amount of electricity produced from renewable

---

[203] ibid para 64.   [204] ibid para 65.   [205] ibid para 66
[206] Case C-448/01 *EVN AG and Wienstrom GmbH v Republik Österreich* [2003] ECR I-14527.
[207] *Concordia Bus* (n 196 above) para 67 (emphasis added).   [208] ibid.

energy sources in excess of the expected annual consumption, as laid down in the invitation to tender, cannot be regarded as linked to the subject-matter of the contract.'[209] As with the *Beentjes* case, this does not prevent a future contracting authority from specifying that the subject matter of the contract consists of the supply of renewable energy beyond the needs of the contracting authority itself, provided it would otherwise comply with the Treaty requirements; the contracting authority in the *Wienstrom* case had not made the supply of renewable energy beyond the needs of the contracting authority part of the subject matter of the contract.

Clarification from the European Commission

The European Commission developed a strategy for clarification of the scope for procurement linkages that comprised two major elements. First, the Commission produced Interpretative Communications of the existing directives. In 2001, the Commission published an Interpretative Communication that set out the Commission's view on the use of public procurement for *environmental* purposes. In October 2001, an equivalent Communication was published relating to the pursuit of *social policy* in public procurement. At the same time, the Community was pursuing a general legislative reform of these directives. In the EC context, an approach to the issue appears to have developed in the form of an enabling model of law. This involved legal regulation enabling the relationship between CSR and public procurement to flourish, for example by explicitly setting out a common standard of what public bodies may do in the use of procurement for achieving CSR goals, but not requiring it, and in reducing legal uncertainties that might lead to unwillingness to use public procurement for CSR purposes. In this context, then, the Community fulfils one traditional function of government, which is to create the conditions for market mechanisms to operate effectively.

A second element in the strategy of the Commission to clarify the legality of linking social and environmental goals with public procurement was the use of the Commission's ability to muster 'soft power'[210] through the provision of information, and the attempt to guide the production of better coordinated standards, in the hope that public bodies will see the adoption of public procurement as a method of ensuring compliance in particular circumstances. This strategy, in particular, attempted to address the problem of the more permissive regime that emerged out of the legal strategy: the proliferation of different standards and requirements to which any particular firm may be subject. Anna Diamantopoulou, when she was Commissioner responsible for Employment and Social Affairs in the European Commission, argued that the plethora of different standards applicable

---

[209] ibid para 68.
[210] JS Nye, Jr, *Soft Power: The Means to Success in World Politics* (Public Affairs, 2004).

to CSR, not least in the public procurement context, 'carries the risk of "accidental" new barriers to trade in the EU's internal market'.[211]

Good examples of this approach in practice are to be found in the development of approaches to linking public procurement with policies for green public procurement and policies for disabled workers. As regards green procurement, there have been several interlinking elements to the strategy, in addition to clarifying the law.[212] The Commission has encouraged Member States to draw up publicly available action plans for greening their public procurement.[213] The review of the Lisbon Strategy in 2004 again stressed the need for national and local authorities to set up action plans for greening public procurement by the end of 2006.[214] In January 2005, the Commission urged that such plans should establish objectives and benchmarks for enhancing green public procurement as well as guidance and tools for public procurers.[215] The Commission also worked with other groups (such as ICLEI and Eurocities) to spread and clarify the message. For example LEAP (Local Environmental Management Systems and Procurement) is a project co-funded by the European Commission and ICLEI that aims to provide a series of practical tools for assisting public authorities in implementing sustainable procurement and its integration with existing environmental management systems.[216] The Commission also established an environmental database containing basic environmental information, refering to national and EU eco-labels where appropriate.[217] A Handbook on Green Public Procurement was published in August 2004, giving further explanations and best practice examples.[218]

As regards the use of procurement for meeting the needs of those who are disabled, the Commission supported the establishment of a Pilot Project ('Build for All') to mainstream disability policies, in particular promoting accessibility to the built environment. The Commission had established an Expert Group on Full Accessibility, which delivered its conclusions at the end of 2003, the European Year of People with Disabilities. The report[219] identified a lack of awareness as one

---

[211] Anna Diamantopoulou, Commissioner responsible for Employment and Social Affairs, European Commission, The role of public policies in promoting CSR, Address at the Presidency Conference on Corporate Social Responsibility, Venice, 14 November 2003, 6. See also: EDF Seminar Series: Can Procurement be used to promote equality? Lessons from experiences at home and abroad: Summary note of seminar on Thursday 2 March 2006. See also D O'Connor's identification of 'the risk of proliferation of sustainable procurement criteria and the need for harmonization across jurisdictions', Report on the Third Expert Meeting on Sustainable Public Procurement, United Nations Headquarters, New York, 15–17 July 2005.

[212] <http://europa.eu.int/comm/environment/gpp/index_en.htm>. See further C Day, 'Buying green: the crucial role of public authorities' (2005) 10(2) Local Environment: The International Journal of Justice and Sustainability 201.

[213] Communication on Integrated Product Policy (IPP) of June 2003.

[214] Report by the High Level Group headed by Mr Wim Kok (November 2004).

[215] Communication on the Report on the implementation of the Environmental Technologies Action Plan (January 2005).   [216] <http://www.iclei-europe.org/leap>.

[217] <http://ec.europa.eu/environment/gpp/index.en.htm>.

[218] SEC(2004) 1050.

[219] '2010 A Europe Accessible for All', October 2003, available at <http://www.eca.lu/upload/egafin.pdf>.

of the most important obstacles to achieving accessibility in the built environment. The report also recommended that guidelines should be produced that would help tenderers to comply with the new provisions of the reformed directives. In January 2005, the Commission helped launch the 'Build for All Reference Manual', as part of a public consultation. The Manual gave guidance in the establishment of essential accessibility criteria, and a methodology for step-by-step implementation of accessibility as provided for by the EU Public Procurement directives. According to the Manual, CSR was one of the reasons why the issue needed to be addressed.[220]

The concept of Corporate Social Responsibility is increasingly pressed for by political decision makers at all levels of Government and, as a result, is increasingly being highlighted as an important criterion in Public Procurement decisions. That is to say that there is a growing tendency to require that companies who are entrusted with the execution of large public works contracts are actively engaged in pursuing Corporate Social Responsibility within their structures.

[220] 'Build for All Reference Manual' (January 2005) 8.

13

Expansion of Equality Linkages in the Member States

In the previous chapter, we considered several developments since the early 1990s that combined to make the European political and legal environment more favourable to procurement linkages in general. In this chapter, we consider how, at the level of the Community and in Member States, advantage has been taken of this greater policy space to develop procurement linkages specifically addressing equal status issues. In addition, during the 1990s and early 2000s, there was a significant growth of EC social legislation in general, and equal status legislation in particular. With the expansion of equal status policy, both Member States and the Community institutions saw status equality as a matter of Community interest, leading to an understanding that methods of enforcement of status equality law adopted by Member States, such as procurement linkages, supported Community law. The stronger the Community interest in status equality, the stronger the claim that procurement linkages designed to further status equality should be seen as acceptable to the Community institutions. In particular, the stimulus to the use of procurement linkages following the introduction of *equality mainstreaming*, considered in chapter 3 above, has been significant.

I. Community Equal Status Law and Procurement Linkages

We have seen in chapter 12 above that the political context in which the procurement directives operated subtly shifted during the 1990s. At the level of Community policy development, we saw that additional areas of broadly 'social' concern came increasingly to the fore. Of particular interest in the context of our study of equality linkages was the development of Community law and policy in the area of equal status. The requirement that men and women receive equal pay in the Treaty of Rome was originally included in order to prevent what would now be termed social dumping. The Community did not begin to act on this requirement, nor extend the prohibition of sex discrimination more broadly until the mid-1970s, when further sex discrimination legislation was enacted. Since then the Community has developed a significant body of legislation addressing status discrimination across a wide range of grounds.

Growth of Community equal status law

As the EC developed its 'social face' in the 1970s and the 1980s, gender equality in employment was taken up as one of the main planks of an emerging EC social policy, and the adoption of a raft of gender equality directives by the Community led to the enactment of domestic legislation dealing with gender equality in employment for the first time in many Member States, and the strengthening of already existing legislation in several others. Of particular importance was the fact that the gender equality directives defined status equality in terms of 'rights', and empowered individual women to use legal remedies, whilst at the same time recognizing that such remedies were merely part of the raft of measures that would be necessary to address what were seen as systemic or institutional failures requiring action beyond the individual case.

The set of legislative provisions addressing gender inequality that created a legal framework for women's equality in employment and working conditions initially comprised three directives: one on equal pay (which incorporated the International Labour Organization (ILO) concept of 'equal pay for work of equal value'),[1] one on equal treatment in other aspects of employment (such as hiring, promotions, and dismissals),[2] and the third on equal treatment in a limited number of social security matters.[3] During the 1980s, only two of several proposed directives on gender equality were adopted, both in 1986, and both of relatively minor importance: one on equality in occupational social security, and one on equality between self-employed men and women (the Occupational Social Security Directive[4] and the Self-Employed Directive).[5] It was not until the late 1980s, when the Council accepted the development of a new social dimension to complement the single market initiative, and the voting system in Council was modified to permit qualified majority voting in some areas, that further equality legislation was forthcoming.

Several pieces of legislation adopted since then are of importance. The first was the acceptance by the Council in 1992 of a directive providing certain rights to pregnant women, and those who are breast feeding (Pregnant Workers Directive).[6]

---

[1] Council Directive (EEC) 75/117 on the approximation of the laws of the Member States relating to the application of the principle of equal pay for men and women [1975] OJ L45/198.

[2] Council Directive (EEC) 76/207 on the implementation of the principle of equal treatment for men and women as regards access to employment, vocational training and promotion, and working conditions [1976] OJ L39/40.

[3] Council Directive (EEC) 79/7 on the progressive implementation of the principle of equal treatment for men and women in matters of social security [1979] OJ L6/24.

[4] Council Directive (EEC) 86/378 on the implementation of the principle of equal treatment for men and women in occupational social security schemes [1986] OJ L225/40.

[5] Council Directive (EEC) 86/613 on the application of the principle of equal treatment between men and women engaged in an activity, including agriculture, in a self-employed capacity, and on the protection of self-employed women during pregnancy and motherhood [1986] OJ L359/56.

[6] Council Directive (EEC) 92/85 on the introduction of measures to encourage improvements in the safety and health at work of pregnant workers who have recently given birth or are breastfeeding [1992] OJ L348/1.

The second was the passage of the Working Time Directive in 1993.[7] The third was the agreement under the Social Protocol (and excluding the United Kingdom initially) of the Parental Leave Directive, providing for periods of time off work for mothers and fathers in certain circumstances.[8] The fourth was the acceptance of an Occupational Social Security Directive, amending the 1986 Occupational Social Security Directive).[9] Fifth, in 1997, the Council adopted the Burden of Proof Directive under the Social Protocol.[10] This included a legislative definition of indirect discrimination for the first time, and provisions aiming to adjust the rules on the burden of proof in sex discrimination cases. Sixth, the Part-time Workers Directive prohibited discrimination between part-time and full-time workers in certain circumstances.[11] Significant amendments to the 1976 Equal Treatment Directive were introduced in 2002.[12]

During the 1990s, concern with equality increasingly expanded into other grounds beyond gender. The 1990s saw the flowering of an extraordinarily diverse set of social movements each articulating their concerns in status equality terms, and often seeing the European women's movement as a model for their own activism. By the late 1990s, there were active social movements addressing issues of age, disability, race, and sexual orientation in many states, and with these pressure grew for similar legislative approaches, in particular anti-discrimination legislation, to be adopted in these areas as they had been for women. The articulation of their claims in terms of rights was particularly important for disability rights campaigners, leading to a significant shift away from the previous medicalized model of disability, which had contributed to the significant levels of segregation of disabled individuals from the able-bodied, to a model of integration and rights claims. After a long period of uncertainty, the Community eventually adopted an additional set

---

[7] Council Directive (EC) 93/104 concerning certain aspects of the organization of working time [1993] OJ L307/18.

[8] Council Directive (EC) 96/34 on the framework agreement on parental leave concluded by UNICE, CEEP, and the ETUC [1996] OJ L145/11, eventually agreed to by the UK in Council Directive (EC) 97/75 amending and extending, to the United Kingdom of Great Britain and Northern Ireland, Directive (EC) 96/34 on the framework agreement on parental leave concluded by UNICE, CEEP, and the ETUC [1997] OJ L10/24.

[9] Council Directive (EC) 96/97 amending Directive (EEC) 86/378 on the implementation of the principle of equal treatment for men and women in occupational social security schemes [1997] OJ L14/13.

[10] Council Directive (EC) 97/80 on the burden of proof in cases of discrimination based on sex [1998] OJ L14/6, eventually accepted by the UK in Council Directive (EC) 98/52 on the extension of Directive (EC) 97/80 on the burden of proof in cases of discrimination based on sex to the United Kingdom of Great Britain and Northern Ireland [1998] OJ L205/66.

[11] Council Directive (EC) 97/81 concerning the Framework Agreement on part-time work concluded by UNICE, CEEP, and the ETUC—Annex: Framework Agreement on part-time work [1998] OJ L14/9.

[12] Council Directive (EC) 2002/73 of the European Parliament and of the Council of 23 September 2002 amending Council Directive (EEC) 76/207 on the implementation of the principle of equal treatment for men and women as regards access to employment, vocational training and promotion, and working conditions [2002] OJ L269/15.

of directives addressing these newer status equality concerns, introducing individual remedies for employment discrimination on grounds of race, religion, age, disability, and sexual orientation on lines similar to the approach adopted in the earlier gender equality directives. In the context of racial discrimination, the Community went even further, adopting legislation that addressed discrimination in areas other than employment, such as goods, facilities, and services. And this approach was subsequently adopted in the gender discrimination context as well.[13]

The Race Discrimination Directive[14] prohibits racial and ethnic origin discrimination in access to employment, vocational training, employment and working conditions, membership of and involvement in unions, and employer organizations, social protection, including social security and health care, 'social advantages', and education, as well as goods and services, including housing. The Employment Discrimination Directive[15] prohibits discrimination primarily in the employment context (access to employment, self-employment, and occupations; vocational guidance and training; employment and working conditions, including dismissals and pay; membership of organizations). It applies to discrimination on grounds of disability, age, sexual orientation, religion, and belief. These directives lay down minimum requirements and give Member States the option of introducing or maintaining more favourable provisions. The directives may not be used to justify any regression in the situation that already prevailed in each Member State. Member States were required to implement the Race Directive by July 2003. The provisions in the Employment Discrimination Directive in relation to religion or belief and sexual orientation were to be implemented by November 2003, and those on age and disability by November 2006. Implementation of the Employment Discrimination and Race Directives has resulted in extensive legislation at the national level. Prior to 2000, most Member States lacked legislation on one or more of the grounds covered by the two directives.

Increasingly, anti-discrimination norms moved beyond their roots in European *social* policy, and came to be seen as an important part of other European policy developments. Perhaps of most importance, they became part of *human rights* policy, a point further emphasized by the prominent place given to status equality in the EU Charter of Fundamental Rights.[16] In part, this document sets out more systematically the fundamental rights already considered by the European Court of Justice (ECJ) as arising from the general principles of EC law. The Charter goes further, however, in setting out a wider catalogue of rights that are considered to be fundamental in the Community.

---

[13] Council Directive (EC) 2004/113 of 13 December 2004 implementing the principle of equal treatment between men and women in the access to and supply of goods and services [2004] OJ L373/37.

[14] Council Directive (EC) 2000/43 implementing the principle of equal treatment between persons irrespective of racial or ethnic origin [2000] OJ L180/22.

[15] Council Directive (EC) 2000/78 establishing a general framework for equal treatment in employment and occupation [2000] OJ 303/16.   [16] [2000] OJ C364/1.

Procurement linkages and European equal status law and policy

Growing sympathy for procurement linkages at the Community level

As early as 1987, the potential of procurement linkages (often termed 'contract compliance' and drawing particularly on US developments) was being sympathetically discussed at the European level as a way of promoting positive action strategies for women.[17] However, a turning point in the debate occurred when, as part of the European Commission's Third Action Programme, a Conference on 'Access to Equality between Women and Men in the European Community' was held at Louvain-la-Neuve in 1992. The focus of the 1992 Conference was on the application in practice of European equality law, rather than with the interpretation of the substantive principles and it focused primarily on the national mechanisms for enforcing European equality law, particularly the vital procedural and remedial aspects of such mechanisms. It considered issues relevant to access to justice, sanctions, and remedies. The issue which occupied much of the Conference discussions and the final report was the extent to which Community equality law could be made more 'effective' in practice.[18]

The report of the Conference, drawing on the experiences of Member States, identified several developments that were seen as useful for making equality law more effective in the Member States. Among these were contract compliance policies that either deprived a discriminator of access to government contracts, such as in Italy,[19] or acted as an incentive to employers to adopt positive action policies, such as applied in some of the German Länder.[20] The Forum on Equal Pay legislation in the Member States, held in Brussels in 1992 also called for 'contract compliance operating on a European level'.[21] The European Trade Union Confederation advocated and actively campaigned for social provisions of different types, including equality provisions, to be included in the various public procurement directives.[22] Several members of the Advisory Committee on Equal Opportunities advocated Community involvement in contract compliance.[23] The European Parliament took an active interest in the issue and, on several occasions, introduced amendments to secure contract compliance. From the perspective of equality law, then, the issue was, as we saw in chapter 10 above, one of how to make such law

---

[17] C Docksey, 'The European Community and the Promotion of Equality' in C McCrudden (ed), *Women, Employment and European Equality Law* (Eclipse, 1987) 1, 15.

[18] See M Verwilghen, *Access to Equality* (Presses Universitaires Louvain, 1993).

[19] Act No 125 of 10 April 1991, s 4(9).

[20] See eg the discussion below relating to Germany. See further, J Shaw, 'Equal Opportunities for Women in the Federal Republic: Institutional Developments' (1990) 9 Equal Opportunities International 15.

[21] Forum on Equal Pay legislation in the Member States, held in Brussels, 23–24 March 1992, 2.

[22] ETUC, 'Public Procurement: Social Clauses' (January 1990).

[23] See eg Equal Opportunities Commission for Northern Ireland, 'European Social Policy: Options for Union: Response to Green Paper' (March 1994) para 3.9; Equal Opportunities Commission, The Gender Impact of CCT in Local Government: Summary Report (EOC, 1995) 29 (see further, ch 7 above).

more effective in practice, and contract compliance increasingly appeared to be one possible mechanism for achieving that.

The Louvain-la-Neuve report noted, however, that there appeared to be a problem with such mechanisms on the basis of reports that contract compliance mechanisms developed in North Rhine-Westphalia had been challenged under Community law requirements, leaving the legality of other similar schemes in some uncertainty. There was substantial confusion in the Member States over the legality of such policies under Community law, as we saw in chapter 11 above, with proposals in the United Kingdom, Germany, and the Netherlands being subject to conflicting assessments as to the implications of Community law. The controversial political nature of contract compliance[24] had increased the need for clarification of the issue. The Louvain-la-Neuve report recommended, therefore, that a study on the potential of contract compliance mechanisms and their legality should be a priority for the Commission to undertake. Unlike most of the other recommendations of this and similar conferences, this recommendation was acted on, and DG V commissioned the author to undertake the study, over a two-year period.[25]

Equality mainstreaming and procurement linkages

The development of equality mainstreaming, discussed in chapter 3 above, was also seen increasingly as having important implications for procurement. The Committee of the Regions, in its 1999 opinion on the Commission's Action Plan Against Racism, drew attention to the implications for procurement of 'mainstreaming' racial equality issues.[26] As one speaker put it in 2002, at a public meeting in the European Parliament held by the European Disability Forum: 'Public procurement is a powerful weapon for social change . . . Imagine putting the power of 14% EC GDP behind anti-discrimination and social legislation'.[27]

In its Framework Strategy on gender equality, proposed in June 2000, and covering the period 2001–2005,[28] the Commission set out an action programme to promote equality between men and women. The programme focused on the promotion of gender mainstreaming. In this connection, it drew the connection between gender mainstreaming and procurement issues explicitly. In the section

[24] This was particularly in Germany and the UK where the issue was the subject of party political divergence. On the position in the UK, see 'Party policies on equal opportunity', EOR No 42, March/April 1992, 12, 18.

[25] See, 'Equal Opportunities for Men and Women: Third Community Action Programme 1991–1995: Mid Term Evaluation', (European Commission, 1993) 11.

[26] Opinion of the Committee of the Regions on the European Action Plan Against Racism [1999] OJ C198/48, paras 3.2.1.3, 6.1.1.

[27] European Disability Forum Press Release, Revision of public procurement rules: a testing ground for sustainable development in the EU, 17 April 2002, quoting Linda Mitchell, head of diversity of the British Broadcasting Corporation.

[28] European Commission, Towards a Community Framework Strategy on Gender Equality (2001–2005), 7 June 2000, COM(2000)335 final.

dealing with promoting gender equality in economic life, the Commission identified the need to develop strategies to encourage gender mainstreaming in all policies which have an impact on the place of women in the economy, giving as examples 'fiscal, financial, economic, educational, transport, research and social policy'.[29] Among the actions proposed were the preparation of a Communication on social issues in public procurement.[30]

II. Developments in Equality Linkages in the Member States

Stages of development

Consideration of the use of public procurement for equality purposes has followed a fairly predictable course in the Member States. We can identify five main stages.[31] In the *first* stage, there is no, or practically no, discussion of the use of public procurement for equality or non-discrimination purposes. Countries in this position have little direct experience of applying and enforcing anti-discrimination norms in practice, have had little experience with the use of public procurement for other social policy purposes, and have relatively little direct engagement between their country and other countries in which public procurement is used extensively for equality purposes. In the European context, many of the 'old' Member States have passed through this stage. In contrast, most of the 'new' Member States of the EU are still at this first stage across the whole spectrum of equality grounds. There is, practically speaking, no discussion of the use of procurement for equality purposes and, in the experience of the author, a degree of puzzlement as to why it would even be discussed.

In the *second* stage, there is a process of spotting a gap in compliance with equality norms, and attempts are made to identify additional policy levers to bring about change. Often this involves looking at North American or European experiences of using novel (for them) compliance methods, or adapting tools that have been used in that country but in other contexts. One of the policy levers often identified is the use of public procurement. In some states, there has been a history of linking public procurement with other social or environmental goals, as we saw in chapter 2 above and the issue appears understandable. In other states, public procurement has been seen as appropriately divorced from the delivery of policy goals and the theoretical debate about appropriateness is more intense.

---

[29] ibid para 3.1.3.   [30] ibid.

[31] This is partly based on an EC study, commissioned by the European Commission, 'Study of the Use of Equality and Diversity Considerations in Public Procurement: Final Report' (December 2003) (hereafter EC study).

In the *third* stage, which is frequently combined with stage two, questions are raised as to the legality of such uses of procurement. We have seen that, in Europe, in addition to national legal provisions governing public procurement, there are two additional sets of legal requirements: those arising under EC law (in particular, but not exclusively, arising from a series of directives on public procurement that began in the 1970s), and those arising under international law (in particular, but not exclusively, arising from the WTO Government Procurement Agreement). The complexity of these provisions, and the uncertainty as to whether particular linkages were permissible, has acted as a constraint on risk-averse public authorities adopting procurement linkages for equality purposes.[32]

In the *fourth* stage, the issue becomes not whether it is possible or desirable in principle to use public procurement, but *how* to do so in practice, in ways that will be effective, legal, and consistent with value for money. We have seen that, under EC law, substantial amounts of discretion are given to the Member States, and to the public authorities in the Member States, to decide whether to include equality policies in public procurement. As we shall see in chapter 14 below, this was clarified in intensive negotiations over the content of new EC procurement directives finalized in 2003. NGO activity then shifted to some Member States, since the new directives had to be incorporated into domestic law in each Member State, thus providing an ideal opportunity for public pressure to be brought to bear. The result was a blossoming of activism around the issue of social standards in national procurement practices, and the development of significant levels of political and legislative activity in some Member States.

The most detailed current assessment of the use of procurement to achieve equality policy goals in the EU was commissioned by the European Commission and reported in December 2003.[33] It found that there is no necessary relationship between whether a particular country incorporates public procurement linkages into legislation or into government policy pronouncements, and the amount of procurement linkage activity actually taking place in that country. Thus, some jurisdictions have fairly extensive sets of formal legal provisions or extensive references to procurement linkages in public policy statements, but very little activity appears to take place in practice. In other jurisdictions, exactly the reverse happens: a considerable degree of activity may be taking place without any fanfare. The extensiveness or otherwise of legal or policy pronouncements is no guide to the extent of activity. The EC study found also that the majority of EU Member States have, at best, reached stage 4, and are only beginning to operationalize procurement linkages for equality purposes.

---

[32] See eg the finding of a survey into determinants of green public procurement, L Brander and X Olsthoorn, 'Three scenarios for Green Public Procurement', December 2002, Institute for Environmental Studies, Vrije Universiteit, The Netherlands, 20 *et seq*. See also, J Morgan and J Niessen, 'Immigrant and Minority Businesses: Making the Policy Case' (2003) 4 European Journal of Migration and Law 329, 332, 334.   [33] EC Study (n 31 above).

In the *fifth* stage, procurement linkages are introduced, but there is continuing debate about their effectiveness and the use of such linkages is unstable, insecure, and likely to be questioned. Recent assessments of government commitments in the United Kingdom to sustainable procurement, point to difficulties that seem to recur at this stage. A recent National Audit office (NAO) report identified the following barriers to effective implementation in the United Kingdom: 'a conflict between sustainable procurement and the focus on reducing costs; a lack of leadership on these issues across government and within departments; a failure to integrate sustainability into standard procurement processes; decentralization of procurement within departments; and a lack of training and guidance about what sustainable procurement is and how to achieve it'.[34]

Several Member States have reached stages 4 or 5. Even in those Member States that have reached these stages, the use of procurement for equality purposes is usually quite limited, mostly adopting modified contract compliance approaches, or approaches that seek to use procurement as a method of encouraging increased employment of individuals from groups seen to have been disadvantaged in the past. What these developments demonstrate clearly, however, is that equality linkages have not succumbed to the neo-liberal interpretation of EC procurement law popularized in the early 1990s. A brief review of the use of equality linkages in several Member States since 1990 makes this clear.

Italy

In Italy, Law No 125 of 10 April 1991,[35] on positive action in the workplace, provided[36] that where discriminatory acts or conduct within the meaning of the legislation were found to have been committed by any employer who had been granted benefits as provided in national legislation, or who had been awarded tendered public works, services, or supply contracts, such acts or conduct should be reported immediately by the Labour Inspectorate to ministers responsible for the administration under whose authority the benefits had been granted or the tendered contract had been awarded. Such ministers should take any necessary action, including, if necessary, cancellation of the benefits; in more serious cases or in the event of a second offence, the employer responsible could be denied financial facilities, credits, or tendered contracts for a period of up to two years. This provision applied equally in all cases where financial facilities, credits, or tendered contracts had been awarded by public bodies, and the Labour Inspectorate should immediately inform these public bodies about all cases where discrimination had

---

[34] National Audit Office, Sustainable procurement in central government (September 2005) para 9.
[35] GU 15 April 1991, No 88.
[36] Law No 125 of 10 April 1991, art 4, para 9. The translation used is that published by the ILO, in Labour Law Documents, 1991-ITA 1.

been found, so that they could apply the penalties provided for: Law No 236 of 19 July 1993 required positive action measures in favour of women to be adopted as a requirement for the receipt of financial grants from the state.[37]

There was a substantial increase in the use of procurement for equality-related purposes since then. The 1991 Law, incorporating gender equality disciplines, was strengthened in 2000.[38] A Law relating to disabled workers was amended in 1999 to require that unless necessary certification atttesting to compliance with the Law was presented to contracting authorities, the employer would be excluded from participating in the tendering process.[39] Persisting high unemployment encouraged the introduction of legislation permitting additional preferences in favour of companies or cooperatives employing previously unemployed workers.[40] Paragraphs 1 to 3 of article 10 of Legislative Decree No 468 of 1 December 1997 provide for a number of derogations from the general law on public procurement for specific companies employing a significant number of previously unemployed workers. The purpose of these provisions is to enable the public administration, to create the necessary occupational opportunities for those workers employed in *lavori socialmente utili* (LSU, socially useful jobs), while at the same time meeting their need for the delivery of services. Article 6 of Legislative Decree No 81 of 28 February 2000, extended the duration of these rules to 31 December 2001. As a *Nota di Indirizzo*[41] of the Italian Ministry of Labour and Social Security pointed out, 'the extension of these rules that derogate from the general discipline concerning companies and public procurement is aimed at helping the employability of the LSU subjects, considered a 'disadvantaged' category and, thus, in need of special measures favouring their insertion in stable occupational activities'.

Spain

In Spain, during the early 1990s, there were several proposals for the reform of the law relating to public contracts being considered by the Spanish parliament. During the period of discussion of the new draft Bill for State Contracts,[42] according to official reports, the possibility of using or introducing 'social clauses' for positive action

---

[37] Legislative Decree No 148/93 convertito nella l n 236/93, art 1(2) and art 6(5bis). See further, S Scarponi, 'Rapporto Italiano, Parità e differenza in Europa', Bologna, 13 May 1994.

[38] Legislative Decree No 196 of 23 March 2000.

[39] Law No 68 of 12 March 1999, art 17.

[40] Legislative Decree No 468 of 1 December 1997, art 10(3), extended by Legislative Decree No 81 of 28 February 2000, art 6.

[41] Prot n 2251/06.14 of 4 August 2000. A 'nota d'indirizzo' is an internal administrative document.

[42] See, in general, Secretaria General del Congreso de los Diputados, Contratos de las Administraciones Publicas, Documentación preparada para la tramitación del Proyecto de Ley de Contratos de las Administraciones Públicas, BOCG Congreso, Serie A, No 109, de 26 de octubre de 1992, Documentación No 104, I and II.

in the specifications for the contract was suggested. There was an official proposal submitted in the draft for Spanish Plan II for Equality of Opportunity that, in spite of receiving a favourable report from the Works Inspectorate, appeared to have been rejected during the period when this was being negotiated with the rest of the government. In Spain, a new basic law on public contracts was adopted in May 1995.[43] This provided that in particular contract conditions, contracting authorities may give a preference to public or private firms whose total labour force included at least 2 per cent of disabled workers. This preference would apply only in those cases where the offers presented by these firms were equivalent to the most economically advantageous offers made by other tenderers.[44]

Austria

In Austria, there was a growing interest in the use of procurement linkages from the late 1990s. The Federal Procurement Act was amended in 1998 to provide that award criteria should take into account the employment of apprentices.[45] Coming into force in September 2002, Austria introduced a new Act regulating public procurement. This included a provision requiring certain social and ecological provisions to be included as contract conditions, one of which provided for the advancement of women in the workplace.[46]

Belgium

In Belgium, the 'Regions' were first to adopt measures in relation to social linkages in public procurement contracts. Initially, in the Walloon and Flemish regions, these measures were merely experimental. The Region of Bruxelles-Capitale adopted more permanent regulations providing for social linkages.[47] The region incorporated social linkages in its own public contracts, as well as, encouraging the incorporation of social clauses in those of the nineteen local governments (communes) it supervised. For this purpose, a ministerial circular was adopted. In 1999, a governmental decree was adopted.[48] The decree provided for social linkages to be incorporated in public contracts concerning the implementation of public interest investment. The decree also provided that a request for subsidies concerning work worth more than BFr30 million and lasting more than sixty days could only be granted if the public contract incorporated a clause under which the

---

[43] Law No 13/1995, of May 1995 de Contratos de las Adminsitraciones Públicas.
[44] Disposición adicional octava: Contratación con emperas que tengan en su plantilla minusvalidos.
[45] Bundesvergabegesetz 1997, §16(7).   [46] Bundesvergabegesetz 2002, §80(14).
[47] The material for this discussion is derived from J Noel, 'Étude relative à la possibilité d'introduire, par la voie légale, réglementaire ou administrative, une clause sociale dans les marchés publics des différents pouvoirs adjudicateurs en Belgique' Administration Publique 1/2000, 229.
[48] Governmental Decree, 22/04/1999.

contractor had to recruit unemployed persons registered with the ORBEM (the Brussels unemployment service).

As regards the Flemish region, a circular was issued in 1998 concerning the incorporation of a clause regarding employment in public procurement contracts.[49] This circular referred to provisions of an agreement between the regional and local services according to which the Flemish authorities would encourage the use of social linkages relative to employment by the local authorities in public contracts of work. The circular added that this clause must provide that contractors were required, during performance of the contract, to recruit persons unemployed for a long period of time. It further added that this contractual condition must not have any negative consequences for the contractor's regular employees. These unemployed persons could be registered with the local unemployment agency, or an unemployment agency of another region, or another Member State of the EU. Furthermore, the circular gave a definition of such a provision. The purpose was to incorporate provisions of a social character in the 'cahier spécial des charges'. The aim of incorporating social linkages was to help persons who had been unemployed for at least two years to re-enter the job market, at least for the duration of the public contract. The circular also provided that a social linkage could apply to other high-risk persons such as immigrants, the disabled, and women. The circular provided that the nature of the social linkage was that it is not a criterion of selection between contractors. The social linkage was a contract condition and in this regard the circular referred to the case law of the ECJ. The circular provided that the social linkage could only apply to works of a threshold value of BFr5 million. The provision was not limited to contracts within the construction sector. It could also apply to all contracts of work, supply, and services as long as they permitted the recruitment of persons with a low level of education.

In June 1998, a draft Bill was issued at the federal level. The purpose of the Bill was to add a provision to the then existing federal procurement legislation[50] that would have permitted public bodies to incorporate a contract condition under which the contractor would have to recruit and train underqualified persons, up to a certain percentage of the total number of persons employed. The Prime Minister forwarded this draft legislation to the Commission des Marchés Publics. The Commisssion gave an unfavourable response, and the Bill was not adopted. In November 2001, however, the Belgian government approved the introduction of a social provision for certain federal public procurement contracts favouring the inclusion of disadvantaged groups (for example, 5 per cent of the total share of

[49] On 23 December1998 a circular (circulaire) issued by the Vlaamse Regering was published in the Moniteur Belge (the reference of this circular is BA 98/10, 24/11/98).

[50] See D D'Hooghe and R Heijse, 'New Belgian Legislation on the award of Public Procurement Contracts' (1997) 6 PPLR CS90.

the contract was to be used to hire long-term unemployed people).[51] Legislation set out the opportunities to use social, environmental, and ethical considerations in public contracting. The federal government established a working group to establish policies, and created a website with substantial amounts of information about the initiative.[52]

Sweden

In Sweden, in the mid-1990s, the government appointed a committee to examine the effectiveness of Swedish legislation against racial discrimination. Their report recommended new legislation against such discrimination, which was enacted in 1999. In addition, it recommended, *inter alia*, the adoption of public procurement clauses in public contracts. It considered that, leaving aside any legal difficulties, these clauses were a convenient non-statutory tool for the prevention of discrimination.[53] It suggested, however, that there should be further research before government reached a final decision, and both the Swedish Parliament and government also took the view that further investigations were necessary. In 1999, the Committee on Public Procurement, a standing Parliament-appointed committee dealing with the broad field of public procurement, was authorized to analyse the issue within the constraints of EC law, and in the context of its other work.[54] Meanwhile, several cities were debating whether or not to include an anti-discrimination clause in their public contracts, leading to the city of Malmo adopting such a clause. The national anti-discrimination body, the National Integration Office, took a particular interest in the issue and commissioned a report to stimulate further debate, drawing on national and comparative experiences, in particular from the United Kingdom and the United States.[55] The Committee on Public Procurement reported in March 2001.[56] It supported the inclusion of anti-discrimination clauses in government contracts, but in a rather luke-warm way, and noted in particular that there would be an EC Commission interpretative statement on the issue forthcoming. This was of importance because the Committee paid particular attention to whether EC law permitted such a clause and emphasised the complexity of the issues involved. The Committee commissioned legal opinions, which diverged considerably on the legal issues. Given this divergence of views, the Committee decided to take no immediate action, awaiting the European Commission's interpretative communication.

---

[51] <http://europa.eu.int/comm/employment_social/emplweb/csr-matrix/csr_topic_allcountries_en.cfm?field=14>.   [52] See generally <http://www.guidedesachatsdurables.be>.
[53] SOU 1997:174, 266.   [54] Directive 1999 No 34.
[55] National Integration Office and P Lappalainen, 'Ingen diskriminering med skattemedel! Avtalsklausuler mot diskriminering vid offentlig upphandling' (2000:7).   [56] SOU 2001:31.

Denmark

In Denmark, an internet portal was developed and put into operation since 2001, providing advice on the drafting of social linkages, and information on experiences with the use of social linkages in practice.[57] From March 2001, for example, a Danish municipality included a requirement in public procurement contracts for contractors to draw up a policy to promote equal treatment for people of different ethnic backgrounds. As described by research commissioned by the European Commission:

> For those employed under the contract, the contractor must develop a written policy ensuring the equal treatment of persons with different ethnic backgrounds, covering hiring, dismissal, transfer, training and education, promotion, wages and working conditions. The policy must include measurable aims and cover at least the period of the contract. The contractor can be requested to substantiate the existence of such a policy, and to record the attainment of its specific goals. Lack of compliance with this condition is considered to be equivalent to non-fulfillment of the main contract.[58]

France

Since 2000, the reform of French procurement law has gone through several phases, with several different elements competing for attention. The first was the need to reform the Code in such a way as to conform to EC law. The second was the desire to use public procurement as a vehicle to further important public policies. Three were particularly important: environmental protection and sustainable development; anti-discrimination and equality; and social inclusion. As regards equality issues, there were several major legislative initiatives, including legislation on equal opportunities and rights for people with disabilities in 2004.[59] During its passage through the Senate in late October 2004, several amendments were made to the Bill on equal opportunities and rights of people with disabilities. These included a provision that companies failing to meet their quotas would henceforth be excluded from tendering for government contracts.[60] As regards social inclusion, the French government launched a major 'social cohesion plan' in June 2004, the aim of which was to take an integrated approach to tackling social exclusion, combining measures on employment (particularly tackling unemployment), housing, education, and local development.[61] Legislation setting a framework for

---

[57] EC Study (n 31 above) 78   [58] ibid 59.

[59] Law No 2005-102 of 11 February 2005 pour l'égalité des droits et des chances, la participation et la citoyenneté des personnes handicapées (arts 29 and 38).

[60] Discontent over amendments to disability bill, <http://www.eiro.eurofound.eu.int/2004/12/feature/fr0412104f.html>.

[61] Social cohesion plan presented, <http://www.eiro.eurofound.eu.int/2004/09/feature/fr0409104f.html>.

the programme was enacted in 2005, and this included amendments to the Code du Marchés Publics.[62] Sustainable development was the third major theme. In June 2003, a national strategy for sustainable development was published which included a substantial section on the need to develop public procurement as a major lever in achieving sustainable development, and set as one of its aims the reform of the Code to enable this to be achieved.[63] This led to a flurry of activity in the public procurement area, including the initiation of a legal study to ensure that the initiatives taken were legally 'safe',[64] culminating in the enactment of the new Code in the summer of 2006, incorporating several provisions on sustainable development.[65]

The twists and turns in procurement reform efforts between 2000 and 2006 were essentially an attempt to ensure that each was included in the Code in ways that did not end up with the social and environmental agendas being subordinated to the need to conform with EC law, or vice versa. It is important that the new French Code is seen as having evolved in close relationship to what was occurring at the European level. Close attention was paid to these developments, and the Code attempted to reflect these in ways that captured the new European requirements but at the same time enabled social and environmental aims to be achieved.[66] This point is neatly illustrated by article 1 of the new French Code (2006), which provides that public contracts subject to the present code should respect the principles of freedom of access to public procurement, equal treatment of candidates, and transparency of procedures. These principles seek to ensure effective public procurement and proper use of public funds. Interestingly, however, the new Code omits a sentence from article 1 of the previous Code, in which it was stated that the principles set out in article 1 called for prior definition of the procuring entity's needs (omitted because this is dealt with in another provision), and compliance with the publication and competition requirements (omitted because this is encompassed in the idea of 'transparency'). More telling for our purposes, it also omits as a general principle the selection of the economically most advantageous tender, whilst retaining it as part (but only part) of the award criteria, as we shall see in chapter 16 below.

---

[62] Law No 2005-32 of 18 January 2005 de programmation pour la cohésion sociale (art 58).

[63] Comité interministériel pour le développement durable, Stratégie nationale de développement durable:programmes d'actions, 3 June 2003.

[64] Rapport 2005, sur la mise en oeuvre de la Stratégie nationale de développement durable, <http://www.ecologie.gouv.fr/rubrique.php3?id_rubrique=1300>.

[65] Decree No 2006-975 of 1 August 2006 portant code des marchés publics [2006] JO 179/11627, texte 20.

[66] Translations are frequently adapted from the LegiFrance Website, which includes a translation of the 2004 Code by Dionysios Kelesidis, Association for Purchasing in the Public Sector (APASP), and Martin Trybus, Lecturer in Law, Deputy Director of the Public Procurement Research Group, University of Nottingham.

III. Equality Mainstreaming and Procurement in England and Wales

We saw in chapter 3 above, that an important recent development in equality law and policy has been the adoption of mainstreaming strategies in several countries. In this and the following sections the effect of mainstreaming in the United Kingdom, where mainstreaming has become a legal duty for public authorities, is considered. We begin with the position in England and Wales.

Equal opportunities and restrictions on local authorities

The election of a Labour government at the General Election in 1997 might be thought likely to have brought a sea change in thinking about the use of more competition in the provision of public services, and lessened enthusiasm for the promotion of an active role for the private sector in public service provision. But this Labour government was one that, perhaps above all, wanted to see itself become the natural party of government in Britain, and therefore was not keen to be seen to be returning to the dark days of the 1980s, when Labour was deemed unelectable, not least by Labour Party supporters. It was also committed to fiscal prudence, whilst also being committed to delivering better public services, and all within a policy framework that was strongly resistant to raising direct taxation. Not surprisingly, therefore, many of the features of Thatcherism were not dramatically done away with. Rather, over time, some of their rough edges were moulded into a more palatable form, and in ways that went well beyond the development of CSR, as discussed in chapter 12 above.

Chapter 11 above describes how the Thatcher government had introduced severe constraints on the adoption of procurement linkages in local government. The new Labour government reversed this policy, at least to some extent, in particular in the more permissive terms of an Order limiting what should be considered 'non-commercial matters' for the purposes of the Local Government Act 1988, and in Statutory Guidance that was published in 2003. This stated that local authorities '*may* take account of the practices of potential service providers in respect of equal opportunities (eg race, gender, disability, religion, age, and sexual orientation) where it is relevant to the delivery of the service under the contract'.[67]

---

[67] Statutory Guidance (2003) para 38 (emphasis added). As regards the use of local labour clauses, there is a somewhat surprising reference. In a separate note to the Guidance, which is specifically stated not to constitute part of the statutory guidance, the Deputy Prime Minister's Department's 'views on the use of social clauses' are set out. This states: 'Individual local authorities may wish to use local labour clauses in contracts particularly in the interest of wider regeneration objectives. However, this needs to be done within the scope of the EC Treaty and the European Public Procurement legislation.' Annex C, 46.

Contracting authorities could, during the pre-qualification stage, seek information 'as to the general competence, track record, details of criminal offences and acts of grave misconduct... including in relation to legislation on sex, race and disability. Contractors may be excluded from the tendering exercise if they have been convicted of a criminal offence or have committed an act of grave misconduct.'[68] The Guidance pointed to the limits of the information that local authorities might ask for.

Local authorities should not make requirements of potential contractors that exceed what is permitted under the [UK] Procurement Regulations [implementing the EC procurement directives] and they should be careful to strike a balance in their approach to seeking information. Neither will they wish to leave themselves vulnerable to the risk of poor performance during the life of the contract, but equally they should avoid making requests for information that are disproportionate to those risks and not strictly relevant to the contract.[69]

As regards race relations, the Guidance pointed out that the duty under the mainstreaming provisions of the Race Relations (Amendment) Act 2000, considered in chapter 3 above, replaced section 71 of the 1976 Act. Authorities 'will continue to be able to ask the six questions specified in Circular 8/88 although they are no longer restricted to those six questions as the sole means of taking account of racial equality. In addition, and where relevant to the contract, and for the purposes of achieving best value, the authority will be able to ask further questions in relation to racial equality.'[70]

The brief reference to the mainstreaming provisions of the Race Relations Act was, of course, the tip of a potentially large iceberg. Beyond what had been said up to that point, the Guidance was vague and unwilling to delve into the full range of possibilities. As regards the contract specifications, for example, the Guidance recognized that services:

...that involve regular contact between providers and the users of the service, or the wider community, may frequently require of providers specific attributes with regard to fair treatment and equal opportunities. Authorities should address such considerations fully in their contract specifications in a way that does not prejudice fair competition or best value considerations. For example, where the service requires particular qualities in the staff, contracting authorities should address these matters in output terms as part of the specification (i.e. how the bidder would meet the needs of a particular community group), not in terms of the composition of the contractor's workforce which in itself is no guarantee of quality of service.[71]

Beyond that, the Guidance refused to go, and any more general use of procurement to further anti-racism aims was explicitly ruled out:

In view of their duties under the legislation on equality, local authorities should also consider how they can promote good practice in equal opportunities *outside the contractual process*. For example, authorities can work with commercial partners to promote equality in employment and raise awareness of how the application of equal opportunities to staff recruitment and management can bring commercial and other benefits.[72]

---

[68] ibid para 39.   [69] ibid.   [70] ibid para 41.   [71] ibid para 42.
[72] ibid para 45 (emphasis added).

Prime Minister's Strategy Unit Report

Initially, the effect of the equality mainstreaming duty was, therefore, rather limited as regards stimulating procurement linkages. An evaluation of the effect of the public duty in England and Wales up to November 2002,[73] found, not surprisingly perhaps, that relatively few schemes and policies in a random sample of public authorities covered by the relevant duties included procurement in the coverage of the equality schemes the authorities were required to draw up under their mainstreaming obligations. Those that did were most likely to be found in local government. Even when procurement was included: 'Relatively few schemes and policies overall covered [it] in any depth.'[74] One of the possible reasons may well have been utter bewilderment as to what public bodies could or could not do.[75]

However, from March 2001, a major report was prepared by the Prime Minister's Strategy Unit, located in the Cabinet Office. This Unit was designed to provide the Prime Minister and government departments with a capacity to analyse major cross-cutting and strategic issues and to design solutions to cross-cutting problems. The report, published in March 2003, examined ways to ensure that barriers to employment success for ethnic minorities would be removed. In preparing the report, the Unit commissioned academic research reports on different aspects of relevant policy. Several of these mentioned the relative success in the United States of the use of contract compliance policies.[76] In addition, an earlier Anti-discrimination Legislation Review, published in May 1999 by the Cabinet Office Better Regulation Task Force, had offered some support to the use of procurement linkages in certain circumstances. It recommended government 'to use its purchasing and funding muscle to promote equality practices among contractors and suppliers to the public sector'. The Review continued: 'If the public sector has a duty to set high standards in ensuring equality of treatment and opportunity as an employer, we believe it has an equivalent responsibility as a purchaser of goods and services.'[77]

The Strategy Unit devoted a significant part of its report to the issue of linking racial equality to government procurement.[78] It was forthright and unequivocal.

---

[73] Commission for Racial Equality/Schneider-Ross, 'Towards Racial Equality: An evaluation of the public duty to promote race equality and good race relations in England and Wales' (CRE, 2003).

[74] ibid 11.

[75] With the publication of the CRE guidance, see below, it appears that local authorities may now be revising their approaches to linking race and procurement. For example, the influential West Midland Forum, Common Standards were revised in June 2005 to take into account the statutory racial equality duty, see West Midlands Forum, *Common Standards for Equalities in Public Procurement* (2nd edn, June 2005).

[76] See eg A Heath, 'Ethnic Minorities in the Labour Market', report to the PIU, Cabinet Office, October 2001, 13–14; P M Ong, 'Racial/Ethnic Inequality in the USA Labor Market: Empirical Patterns and Policy Options' Report of the PIU (Cabinet Office, February 2000).

[77] Cabinet Office, 'Better Regulation Task Force, Anti-discrimination Legislation Review' (May 1999) 25–26.

[78] Cabinet Office, 'Ethnic Minorities and the Labour Market, Final Report' (March 2003) 119–26.

Relevant employment and social issues could lawfully and legitimately be taken into account in public procurement, but 'Government is not at present benefiting from the full scope to do so'.[79] Drawing on evidence from the United States, and (perhaps more surprisingly given the controversial nature of the approach these bodies took), from the GLC/ILEA experience discussed in chapter 11 above, the report concluded that there was 'evidence of the potential effectiveness of achieving increased equality of opportunity through public procurement . . . when enforced properly'.[80] The report weighed up the advantages and disadvantages. On the one hand, racial equality was a government priority. Tenderers with effective race equality strategies were likely to perform their contractual duties better and therefore there was a business benefit to government. It would be unfair to disadvantage a contractor adhering to public policy goals because a competitor had cut costs by not doing so. It was reasonable for public contracts to go to employers who provided equality of opportunity, since public bodies awarded contracts, in part, on behalf of the ethnic minority communities they served.[81]

There were, however, potential costs associated with linkage. There was a regulatory burden on contracting companies and public authorities. Potential tenderers might be discouraged from competing, and fewer might be eligible to tender, thus reducing competition and possibly increasing costs. Pursuing unrelated social objectives could 'confuse and distort the process of awarding a contract to the bidder offering best value for money for the taxpayer'.[82] United Kingdom and EC law was complicated, leading to the possibility that public authorities 'might adopt an approach that is unwittingly outside the law'.[83] The report concluded, however, that the 'overall potential for using public procurement to reflect relevant race equality issues is substantial',[84] and it pointed to examples to show where race equality issues could be reflected within the policy and legal framework for public procurement. Among these, obviously following the ECJ decision in the *Nord-Pas-de-Calais* case, it suggested 'using wider social criteria at award stage, that is those beyond the subject of the contract and beyond a benefit to the contracting authority, where there are two equivalent bids on the basis of the basis of the permitted value for money criteria'.[85] A caveat was quickly included, however, that 'judging whether or not particular requirements are permissible within the existing legal framework can be complex and problematic'.[86]

What was missing, according to the report, was clear and comprehensive guidance on race equality issues in public procurement. Guidance on procurement issues had been prepared prior to the enactment of the mainstreaming duty in the Race Relations (Amendment) Act 2000, and 'further guidance is required to clarify the relevance of this legislation for procurement by central government departments'.[87] The guidance, which would be voluntary, should: 'explain what is and is not permissible at each stage of the procurement process, including sanctions or

---

[79] ibid 119.   [80] ibid 122.   [81] ibid 124.   [82] ibid 125.   [83] ibid.
[84] ibid.   [85] ibid.   [86] ibid.   [87] ibid 121.

incentives that might be available in relation to relevant race equality contract provisions; exercise use of the full extent of UK and EU law; explicitly encourage public authorities to use this scope; and include several model approaches that authorities can adopt'.[88] An alternative approach was rejected, which was to extend the approach to mainstreaming in the Race Relations (Amendment) Act 2000 to the private sector, as this 'would have far-reaching implications that go far beyond the scope of this recommendation'.[89] In presenting the Report as 'agreed Government policy', the government announced that it would establish a task force to 'help departments work in more co-ordinated ways to deliver improved labour market outcomes for ethnic minorities', and that it would issue annual reports on progress, with a full review of progress after three years.[90]

CRE guidance on procurement

Much greater attention was given to the issue of procurement during 2002 by the Commission for Racial Equality (CRE), the main public authority promoting racial equality in Britain. Guidelines for government departments issued in June 2002 recommended that departments write their race equality duty into procurement contracts as performance standards for delivering services that were relevant to the duty.[91] But it was in 2003 that the main CRE initiatives regarding procurement came to fruition, with the publication of separate procurement policy guidance for public authorities and contractors,[92] and for local authorities,[93] expanding and developing the guidance in the CRE Code of Practice, and setting out in more detail what public authorities could do to meet their responsibilities under the statutory duty. In addition, a joint Confederation of British Industry-Commission for Racial Equality brief was published on how external suppliers could respond to the public authorities' public duty requirements in the context of procurement.[94]

These guidelines carried the debate considerably further in some respects. There was, for example, discussion of whether contractors 'are representative of the local population, or of the area from which the businesses are drawn, with respect to ethnic diversity',[95] although it is emphasized that public bodies must not discriminate against potential contractors on the basis of ethnicity, race, or size. 'Public authorities cannot discriminate in favour of any particular organisation.

---

[88] ibid 126.   [89] ibid Annex on regulatory impact assessment, para 3.

[90] Official Report, Written Ministerial Statement, 21 March, 2003, col 59WS, Statement by the Minister for Social Exclusion and Deputy Minister for Women, Mrs Barbara Roche.

[91] CRE, 'The Duty to Promote Race Equality: Performance guidelines for government departments' (CRE, June 2002).

[92] CRE, 'Race Equality and Public Procurement' (CRE, 2003). See also CRE, 'Public procurement and race equality—guidelines for public authorities' (CRE, 2003).

[93] CRE, 'Race and procurement in local government' (CRE, 2003). See also CRE, 'Public procurement and race equality-guidelines for local government' (CRE, 2003).

[94] CBI-CRE, 'Public procurement and race equality—briefing for suppliers' (CRE/CBI, 2003) (hereafter CBI-CRE briefing).

[95] CRE, 'Public procurement and race equality—guidelines for public authorities (CRE, 2003).

However, the duty to promote race equality and the benefits of attracting a diverse supply base should motivate public authorities to make sure that their procurement processes do not deter [Ethnic Minority Businesses], small firms and other specialists from bidding.'[96] Creating 'local jobs' was specifically mentioned as an apparently acceptable policy to pursue,[97] although this was deemed likely to be more appropriate in the context of 'a long-term, wide ranging PPP deal for economic and social regeneration of a housing estate', than for 'a small-scale contract to perform minor housing repairs'.[98] The participation of ethnic minority representatives was contemplated in certain circumstances in the context of carrying out the contract: 'Particularly for strategic partnerships, governance arrangements could include a direct role for service users and other stakeholders, including representatives from key community groups.'[99]

A major limitation was, however, introduced in order to be seen to be complying with EC legal requirements. Racial equality 'will be of greater relevance to the procurement of some goods, services and infrastructure projects than to others. The more relevant race equality is to a particular contract, the more it must be considered at each stage of the procurement.'[100] In the guidelines, under the heading of 'relevance', it was stated that: 'Any contract that could have a different impact by racial group is relevant to your duty.'[101] The effect of these provisions was, it seems, to try to limit the ambit of the public sector duty substantially. The CRE guidance nowhere made it clear that the purpose of the contract, and how it should be defined, and how far it should be defined as including racial equality outcomes, was itself something that should be considered as an aspect of the application of the public duty in the procurement context. Equally, there appeared to be no clear statement that one of the aspects of the duty should be a decision as to whether it was appropriate for the delivery of the public service to be made subject to competitive procurement in the first place. In other words, the decision whether to use procurement contracts was itself subject to an equality analysis.

Jobcentre Plus

Despite their limitations, these initiatives linking race equality and procurement led to significant action. The Department of Work and Pensions (DWP) commissioned the National Employment Panel's Minority Ethnic Group Working Group to collaborate with the DWP and Jobcentre Plus to assess how Jobcentre Plus could meet its statutory obligation to promote race equality in its procurement policies and practices, and to test the application of linkage between race equality and procurement as a tool for wider use within the public sector. In 2006, this led to additional race equality requirements being introduced into the contracts

---

[96] CBI/CRE briefing (n 64 above).   [97] ibid.   [98] ibid.   [99] ibid.
[100] ibid.
[101] CRE, 'Public procurement and race equality—guidelines for public authorities' (CRE, 2003).

between the Department (acting through Jobcentre Plus) and service providers.[102] The new contract was applied to Jobcentre Plus New Deal contracts being re-let from July 2006. (Clauses already included in the old contracts had required compliance with the Race Relations Act 1976, and required cooperation with Jobcentre Plus to fulfil its duties under the Race Relations (Amendment) Act 2000.) The new clauses required suppliers to agree to and comply with policies on harassment, equality, diversity training, and supplier diversity. They required sub-contractors to meet the same requirements. They made it clear that failure to comply would be a breach of contract. They required suppliers to report the proportion of employees who were female, disabled, and from minority ethnic groups each year. The new clauses were included in the relevant clauses of the overall contract, and also in a separate Schedule.

Two further 'equality mainstreaming' duties were introduced in Britain after the race duty had been operational for some time, and both have potentially significant implications for procurement linkages. The Disability Discrimination Act 2005 amended the Disability Discrimination Act 1995 to include a new public sector duty relating to disability equivalent to that dealing with race.[103] This provides that every public authority must, in carrying out its functions, have due regard to the need to: eliminate discrimination that is unlawful under this Act; eliminate harassment of disabled persons that is related to their disabilities; promote equality of opportunity between disabled persons and other persons; take steps to take account of disabled persons' disabilities, even where that involves treating disabled persons more favourably than other persons; promote positive attitudes towards disabled persons; and encourage participation by disabled persons in public life. In addition to this general duty, certain public authorities are subject to 'specific' duties laid down in regulations.[104] In particular, the specific duties require these public authorities to produce a Disability Equality Scheme, and state what must be included within that Scheme. The Disability Rights Commission issued a Code of Practice on Disability Equality Duty (England and Wales) on 4 December 2005.[105] This includes several pages of guidance on the need to take disability considerations into account in procurement.[106]

The Equality Act 2006, among other things, introduced a new statutory duty on public bodies to further gender equality. The Sex Discrimination Act 1975 was amended to provide that a public authority 'shall in carrying out its functions have regard to the need to eliminate unlawful discrimination and harassment and to

---

[102] Using Government Procurement to Promote Race Equality: Draft terms and conditions for Jobcentre Plus—update, 24th March 2006.

[103] Disability Discrimination Act 1995 (as amended), s 49A.

[104] Disability Discrimination (Public Authorities) (Statutory Duties) Regulations 2005, SI 2005/2966.

[105] Disability Rights Commission, 'The Duty to Promote Disability Equality: Statutory Code of Practice' (England and Wales) (2005), available at <http://www.drc.org.uk/PDF/DED_Code_Dec05_pdf.pdf>.   [106] ibid 122–4.

promote equality of opportunity between men and women'.[107] The gender equality duty comes into force in April 2007. As with the disability duty, there is also a series of 'specific duties' that apply to particular public authorities.[108] Among these is the obligation for many public authorities to have gender equality schemes in place by the end of April 2007. The Equal Opportunities Commission Gender Equality Duty Code of Practice was laid before Parliament at the beginning of November 2006, and the Code came into force on 6 April 2007.[109] This provides detailed guidance on the effect of the duties. Here too, the need to consider the implications of the equality duty on procurement is emphasized.[110]

Supplier diversity

In 2002, the Performance and Innovation Unit of the Cabinet Office suggested that the use of public procurement in the area of supplier diversity had been wrongly neglected in the past, pointing to how 'public procurement has been used as a major lever overseas to improve the position of ethnic minority businesses'.[111] Monder Ram and David Smallbone have suggested that: 'Much of the impetus for the current interest in the procurement issue in the UK emanates from the USA's long-standing experience of affirmative action policies.'[112] In May 2003, a review conducted by the Better Regulation Task Force and the Small Business Council recommended government measures to address obstacles that may prevent SMEs from gaining government contracts.[113] The CRE procurement guidelines recommended measures to address how the race equality obligations impact on the selection of suppliers. The Treasury adopted an objective of increasing the number of women-owned businesses from 12 to 14 per cent in 2003 to between 18 and 20 per cent by 2006.[114] But it explicitly rejected 'quotas, targets or any sort of preferential treatment', preferring instead giving 'minority businesses a fair chance to compete'.[115] Purchaser-based initiatives included privatized utilities, local councils, and development agencies.[116]

---

[107] Equalities Act 2006, s 84. The legislation can be found at <http://www.opsi.gov.uk/acts/acts2006/ukpga_20060003_en.pdf>.

[108] Sex Discrimination Act 1975 (Public Authorities) (Statutory Duties) Order 2006.

[109] Equal Opportunities Commission, Gender Equality Duty Draft Code of Practice (November 2006), available at: <http://www.eoc.org.uk/PDF/GED_CoP_Draft.pdf>. [110] ibid 46–50.

[111] Performance and Innovation Unit, Cabinet Office, Ethnic Minorities in the Labour Market, 2002, 167, quoted in M Ram and D Smallbone, 'Supplier Diversity Initiatives and the Diversification of Ethnic Minority Businesses in the UK' 24 (2003) Policy Studies 187, 188.

[112] ibid 189.

[113] Better Regulation Task Force and Small Business Council, 'Government: Supporter and Customer' (May 2003).

[114] Speech by the Chief Secretary to the Treasury, Paul Boateng, at Migration Policy Group Seminar on Procurement and Supplier Diversity, 14 January 2004, available at <http://www.hm-treasury.gov.uk>. [115] ibid.

[116] Ram and Smallbone (n 111 above) 195 (discussing case studies of British Telecom, Haringey Council, Southwark Council, London Development Agency, among others).

Approach of the Welsh Assembly

The Government of Wales Act 1988 required the Welsh Assembly to 'make appropriate arrangements with a view to securing that its functions are exercised with due regard to the principle that there should be equality of opportunity for all people'. The duty applied to all devolved functions of government in Wales, including education, economic development, health, local government, social services, planning, transport, housing, and industry. As described in an assessment of the Welsh equality duty published in June 2002,[117] the Assembly decided to apply the equality duty to procurement issues, developing its policy and methodology over several years. A 'voluntary code' was adopted for which existing and potential tenderers were invited to register their support. A questionnaire was developed to help the Assembly to assess how much those registering had already achieved and where improvement was thought possible. Without spelling out how, the Assembly's code explained that

> ... [the] more you [firms] are doing, the more likely it is that you will win our business—particularly on large contracts ... What will be needed from you is a firm, consistent and continuing approach to improvement ... So for those of you who are prepared to work with the Assembly to help us achieve our objectives, there will be the opportunity to win our business, save money, be a good employer, a better neighbour and as a result gain competitive advantage in the wider market place.[118]

Certain workplace policies, such as status equality issues, must be upheld by the tenderer in their UK employment. More radically, the policy applied also to certain issues 'overseas'.[119]

> The Assembly respects different cultures and acknowledges that local working conditions differ from country to country but no matter where, we expect our suppliers to live up to good basic requirements and take reasonable steps to ensure that these basic requirements are met. Where possible and appropriate, products should carry the Fair Trade Mark, which guarantees a better deal for farmers, growers and small-scale producers. It is also an international guarantee that child labourers have not been used.[120]

Reform of equality legislation

More recently, the potential use of procurement linkages has become part of the debate over the reform of equality legislation in England and Wales. The opportunity to consider the role that procurement might play in reformed equality legislation began when the government initiated consultations during 2002–3 on

---

[117] P Chaney and R Fevre, 'An Absolute Duty: Equal Opportunities and the National Assembly for Wales—A Study of the Equality Policies of the Welsh Assembly Government and their Implementation: July 1999 to March 2002' (Institute of Welsh Affairs, June 2002).

[118] ibid. 99, Appendix 3; Contract Compliance: Winning Our Business—A Voluntary Code.

[119] Chaney and Fevre (n 117 above) 98.   [120] ibid.

the restructuring of the existing equality Commissions in Britain. This opportunity led to a more general debate emerging on whether there should be a 'single equality bill' which would bring together all the existing equality legislation and reform and update it. In particular, an independent review was established with funding from the Joseph Rowntree Charitable Trust and the Nuffield Foundation, under the chairmanship of Sir Bob Hepple (as he now is) to bring forward proposals for a revision of the existing legislation. The subsequent report was widely circulated and had considerable influence in shaping the public debate.[121] Included in the report were recommendations for reform of the enforcement mechanisms. Prominent among these were recommendations to incorporate provisions on deprivation from being able to tender if convicted of an offence under the legislation.[122]

Subsequently, Lord Lester introduced in the House of Lords a detailed Bill drawing extensively on these recommendations, among them the procurement provisions.[123] The government resisted the Bill, and it fell. Although the Lester Bill, broadly based on the Hepple Report, was not successful, the issue has not gone away. The Women and Work Commission (established by the Prime Minister, chaired by Baroness Prosser, a former trade union leader, and composed of representatives of unions and employers' organizations, among others) reported in February 2006.[124] It had been charged with carrying out an independent review of the gender pay gap and other issues affecting women's employment. In its report, *Shaping a Fairer Future*, the Commission recommended a considerable number of policy changes, but could not agree on the need for more legislation. There was particular disappointment by some that the Commission did not recommend compulsory pay audits. Interestingly, however, the Commission did agree to recommend that there should be more use of public procurement measures to advance women's equality at work. The Commission, indeed, proposed the use of procurement as one of the few regulatory approaches it advocated for addressing the equal pay gap.

A more wide-ranging government review of equality legislation and policy (established by the Prime Minister to consider long-term policy across the range of equality issues and chaired by Trevor Phillips, the new chair of the combined human rights and equality commission, beginning its work in October 2007) published its final report in February 2007.[125] It found that the tools available for achieving status equality in Britain were not fit for the purpose. There were limitations in the law,

---

[121] B Hepple QC, M Coussey, and T Choudhury, *Equality: A New Framework: Report of the Independent Review of the Enforcement of UK Anti-Discrimination Legislation* (Hart Publishing, 2000).
[122] ibid 79–84.   [123] Equality Bill (HL), 2003, clauses 78–85.
[124] The Women and Work Commission's report 'Shaping a Fairer Future' is available on the DTI's Women and Equality Unit website at <www.womenandequalityunit.gov.uk/women_work_ commission/shaping_fairer_future.pdf>.
[125] The Equalities Review: 'Fairness and Freedom: The Final Report of the Equalities Review' (Cabinet Office, February 2007), available at <http://www.theequalitiesreview.org.uk/upload/assets/ www.camawise.org.uk/equality_review.pdf>.

which was complex, inconsistent in the way it treated different groups, and poorly understood. In some cases the law unduly restricted action on inequality, and in others the action possible had been interpreted too narrowly, as for example with public procurement. There had also been a tendency to focus legal requirements, and the action that followed, on process rather than the outcomes sought. And problems with the form of the law had been made worse by unclear guidance and insufficient support, and by a blunt and inflexible enforcement regime. The Review made several recommendations to address these problems. It set out ten steps to greater equality, which complemented and reinforced each other, each contributing, it hoped to a systematic overall framework for creating a more equal society. These included a significant section advocating the greater positive use of public procurement linkages, as part of a more sophisticated compliance regime. The report argued that public procurement was one of the key tools that should be used to secure a reduction in status inequalities in Britain. It proposed that a new public equality sector duty 'should incorporate a specific requirement for public bodies to use procurement as a tool for achieving greater equality. Ensuring that commissioning frameworks require providers to analyse the needs of different groups, and that they monitor provision using quantitative and qualitative analysis, will also be an important element of the new duty'.[126] The Discrimination Law Review (an internal Departmental review of discrimination law reform) is, at the time of writing (March 2007), also known to be actively considering the issue.

IV. Procurement and Equality Mainstreaming in Northern Ireland

Initial discussions of implications of mainstreaming for procurement

As stated in chapter 3 above, following the passage of the Northern Ireland Act 1998, which introduced (in section 75) a legal duty of mainstreaming on public authorities in Northern Ireland, the Equality Commission for Northern Ireland was required to produce guidance on the operation of the statutory duty. One important issue was the extent to which procurement would be included within the ambit of the guidelines. The answer from the Commission was clear and unequivocal. The Commission stated that 'an authority's ... procurement policies are an integral aspect of the way in which an authority carries out its functions. Accordingly, the Scheme must cover the arrangements for assessing the impact of such policies'.[127]

---

[126] ibid 119.
[127] Equality Commission for Northern Ireland, 'Guide to Statutory Duties—A guide to the implementation of the statutory duties on public authorities arising from section 75 of the Northern Ireland Act 1998' (2000) para 2.13.

The House of Commons Northern Ireland Select Committee[128] Report recommended in 1999 that the government should 'look again at the potential contribution of contract compliance to achieving fair employment objectives'.[129] It argued that 'Government and public bodies award public contracts on behalf of the communities that they serve'.[130] It was 'not . . . unreasonable that these communities might expect that public contracts should, all other things being equal, go to contractors who further such a basic policy aim as fair employment. We do not consider the award of public contracts as simply an economic activity by the Administration, in which the Administration can consider itself as equivalent to a private sector organisation.'[131] The Committee found it 'difficult to see how public purchasing activity can in principle be regarded as a separate area of state activity in which equality criteria are ignored that are considered self-evident in other areas of state activity, such as public sector employment',[132] and it recommended that public bodies 'review the position they have taken with regard to public procurement in the context of their equality schemes' under section 75.[133]

The government response was uncompromising, however.[134] The scope for using contract compliance as a means of furthering fair employment objectives 'was carefully considered' in 1998. 'It was decided not to extend contract compliance—beyond those provisions . . . in the fair employment legislation.'[135] The government's 'long standing position [is] that all public procurement of goods and services is to be based on value for money, having due regard to propriety and regularity, and should not be used to pursue other aims'.[136] As regards the implications of section 75: 'Policy on public procurement by Departments and public bodies is determined centrally. In due course the central policy will be subject to an equality impact assessment in line with the section 75 obligation.'[137] This appeared to accept that a review of the role public procurement could play in furthering equality of opportunity would be undertaken by public bodies individually in due course. This caused considerable anxiety to some public bodies. How were they to review their public procurement policies that were, they protested, set centrally for them by the Department of Finance and Personnel, if not HM Treasury?

Adding to the headaches of government in this respect were the activities of the loose coalition of those individuals and NGOs that had campaigned for the statutory duty in the first place. After the passage of the legislation, some of these individuals and groups combined to form an 'Equality Coalition', which relatively soon established itself as an influential and authoritative voice of civil society on

---

[128] Fourth Report from the Northern Ireland Affairs Committee, Session 1998–99, 'The Operation of the Fair Employment (Northern Ireland) Act 1989: Ten Years On' (HC 95) (July 1999).
[129] ibid para 101.　　[130] ibid para 103.　　[131] ibid.　　[132] ibid para 104.
[133] For examples of such arguments by some public bodies, see Equality Commission for Northern Ireland, Report on the Implementation of the Section 75 Equality and Good relations Duties by Public Authorities, 1 January 2000–31 March 2002 (Equality Commission, 2003).
[134] Northern Ireland Affairs Committee, Fifth Special Report, Responses to the Fourth Report from the Northern Ireland Affairs Committee, HC 837 (1999).　　[135] ibid vi.
[136] ibid.　　[137] ibid vii.

issues to do with the implementation of the statutory duty. In the crucial period between January 2000 and March 2001, the Coalition organized a campaign around the development of the equality schemes that public bodies were required to produce in order to ensure that they and others were fully consulted in the development of these schemes. Prominent among the subjects that Coalition members wanted to see addressed was the issue of procurement.[138] Pressure was exerted on the individual public bodies to ensure that they committed themselves to review their procurement activities in the future but, given the central organization of procurement policy, this added to the pressure on central government to act. The mechanism for doing so was a review of procurement policy that had been bequeathed to the incoming devolved administration by the direct rule government.

Public procurement review and mainstreaming

Emulating equivalent reviews of public procurement policy in Britain, the government had commissioned a review of procurement in Northern Ireland at the end of the 1990s. This review, usually referred to as the Capita Report, was delivered in December 1999.[139] It found considerable variation in the quality of public procurement processes and recommended significant changes in procurement processes. Perhaps not surprisingly, given the then government's views, no attention was paid to equality dimensions.

A dramatic shift in policy occurred, however, with the establishment of a devolved administration in Northern Ireland. Public procurement had become a devolved responsibility of the Northern Ireland Executive and Assembly under the Northern Ireland Act 1998. By February 2001, the Programme for Government had committed the Northern Ireland Executive, 'to develop [by June 2001] proposals for implementing improvements in public procurement, ensuring that the equality dimension of cross-departmental policy and practice in relation to the procurement of goods and services by the public sector is addressed through equality impact assessment'.[140]

A Public Procurement Implementation Team was established by the Minister for Finance and Personnel in February 2001, with specific section 75 terms of reference. The terms of reference required the review team:

---

[138] See eg a typical submission by the Committee on the Administration of Justice (CAJ): Response of the Committee on the Administration of Justice to the Draft Equality Scheme relating to section 75 of the Northern Ireland Act for the Department for Environment, June 2000: 'CAJ does not believe that it is acceptable that employment and procurement issues are only dealt with substantively in the Scheme of the DFP and believes that every government departmental Scheme must address these issues directly.'

[139] Department of Finance and Personnel, 'A Strategic Review of Procurement Policy and of Purchasing Arrangements within the Northern Ireland Civil Service Departments', Final Executive Report, December 1999 (Capita Review).

[140] Northern Ireland Executive, Programme for Government (February 2001) para 2.2.1, p 16.

Having regard to commitments . . . in the Department of Finance and Personnel's Equality Scheme, to: consider the findings and recommendations of the [Capita Report]; identify the scope to use public procurement in Northern Ireland to further local social and economic objectives within the context of current EC and international law relating to procurement; and make recommendations for implementation to the Minister for submission to the Executive Committee by June 2001, including an assessment of the equality impact of the proposed policy framework for procurement to be adopted by Northern Ireland public bodies.

There were several important constraints under which the Review Team operated. The first set of constraints was legal, particularly the requirements of European Community law and the WTO Government Procurement Agreement. International relations and relations with the EC were excepted matters under the Northern Ireland Act 1998, and thus not subject to the devolved administration. A Concordat had been agreed between the Northern Ireland Executive and the United Kingdom government on Co-ordination of EC, International and Policy Issues on Public Procurement. This provided that 'the Northern Ireland Executive will seek to ensure that the policy and legal framework for public procurement in Northern Ireland complies appropriately with the UK's EU and international obligations and will not prejudice the UK's objective of seeking EU and international measures which are effective in opening procurement markets and which do not impose any unnecessary burdens or constraints on purchasers or suppliers'.[141] Although not formally legally binding, it was clearly an important factor to be considered. A constraint also arose from other provisions of the Northern Ireland Act 1998 itself. This provided that the Secretary of State for Northern Ireland may decide not to submit for Royal Assent a Bill which contains a provision which he considers 'would have an adverse effect on the operation of the single market in goods and services within the United Kingdom'.[142] If the Secretary of State considered that any subordinate legislation made, confirmed, or approved by a Minister or Northern Ireland department contained a provision which the Secretary of State considers 'would have an adverse effect on the operation of the single market in goods and services within the United Kingdom', the Secretary of State may revoke the legislation.[143]

The second set of constraints was political. The Executive to which the Review Team would report was made up of four political parties, with potentially significantly different views on economic and social policy, although these differences had yet to emerge in any stark way given that differences on issues of constitutional politics relating to the position of Northern Ireland in the United Kingdom tended to dominate political debate within the Executive. To the extent that recommendations were dealing with equality issues, however, this would be likely to be perceived as traditionally a set of interests strongly associated with the two parties most close to the Catholic/Nationalist section of the community. How far

[141] ibid para 3.3.   [142] Northern Ireland Act 1998, s 14(5)(b).   [143] ibid s 26(4)(b).

would individual Ministers, effectively uncontrolled by collective responsibility for actions taken within their departments, be prepared to assent to proposals that might constrain their discretion in public procurement within their departments? In addition, the role of the Assembly was also potentially difficult, given that a significant proportion of that body were local councillors as well, and therefore had a strong interest in local procurement issues.

Outside the formal party political structures, there were other important actors that would influence the attitudes of the political decision makers. Prominent among these actors was the business community, particularly as organized into representative bodies, such as the local Confederation of British Industry. The influential NGO sector would also need to be brought on board. Particularly important was the attitude that procurement professionals would take; if the proposals were deemed unworkable, that would be likely to damn them in the eyes of many.

The third constraint was bureaucratic, and this proved to be the most difficult. There were two fundamentally important aspects of the public finance scene that would be able to block any proposals, in practice, if not in theory. The first was the Northern Ireland Treasury Officer of Accounts, whose function was to ensure that the public finances were being safeguarded and who would be particularly concerned at any perceived move away from the 'value for money' considerations that dominated United Kingdom discussion of procurement. The second was the Office of Government Commerce (OGC), within HM Treasury. The OGC was important in so far as outright hostility to any proposals would not only be likely to stimulate objections for the Treasury Officer of Accounts, and vice versa, but also stimulate the Treasury itself into action if it was disposed to do so.

Several public finance issues were relevant. First, the Review would need to keep in mind that government in London aimed to secure extensive savings in procurement spending in England and Wales through efficiency gains, and that this should have the effect of increasing what could be purchased by any given level of spending. If equivalent gains were not secured in Northern Ireland, this would limit the extent to which improvements in public services in England funded by increased procurement efficiency could be delivered in Northern Ireland, since Northern Ireland was allocated money for particular services based on English programmes. Second, there was a tactical issue. To the extent that the Northern Ireland Executive was seen by the Treasury to be compromising on value for money, this might be seen as undermining the credibility of the case Northern Ireland would need to make for an appropriate share of public spending, in particular by threatening the formula that governed the resources allocated to the devolved administration by the Treasury (the so-called Barnett formula), the survival of which was the subject of continuing speculation. If the devolved administration was seen to be compromising 'value for money', that meant that it was misusing what resources it was being given, and the Barnett formula would need to be revisited.

The composition of the Implementation Team reflected the need to have a body that would be seen as involving the principal stakeholders. The group consisted of a senior Department of Finance civil servant as chair, the head of procurement of a large private sector manufacturing company, the Northern Ireland Director of the Confederation of British Industry, four senior procurement officers in the public sector, including the chief executives of the Construction Service and HM Treasury's Office of Government Contracts Buying Solutions, the Directors of the Equality and the Economic Policy Units within the Office of the First and Deputy First Minister, and two academics, one of whom (the author) was an informal adviser to the Equality Coalition.

In the light of these constraints, intensive discussions took place throughout the drafting of the report with the Office of Government Commerce within HM Treasury, with the Northern Ireland Treasury Officer of Accounts, with accounting officers in the Northern Ireland Civil Departments, with the Equality Commission, with Northern Ireland politicians and their advisers, with procurement professionals, and with officials from other devolved administrations. Both internal and external legal advice was obtained, particularly on issues relating to EC law.

A report was completed and sent to the Minister in July 2001.[144] This was then considered by the Executive in September 2001 and issued for consultation until January 2002. Over 400 consultees were approached, with the responses demonstrating sufficient support among all stakeholders to reassure Ministers that there would be no substantial opposition to the proposals. A revised report was completed by the Team in February 2002.[145] On 27 May 2002, the Minister of Finance and Personnel made a statement to the Assembly on public procurement policy.[146] At that time the revised report was also published. An equality impact assessment of the proposed policy was agreed by the Executive on 16 May 2002, and at the same meeting the Executive agreed to a revised public procurement policy, based on the revised report, for all Northern Ireland departments, their agencies, non-departmental public bodies, and public corporations. This paper set out the policies adopted by the Executive and the organizational structures that were established to implement them.[147] One of the bodies recommended, the Central Procurement Directorate, was established in April 2002. Another, the Procurement Board, was established in July 2002.

The recommendations of the Review Team were wide-ranging. In essence, a compromise was offered between equality and social concerns on the one hand, and efficiency on the other hand. Both were seen as important elements in any set

[144] A Review of Public Procurement: Findings and Recommendations (September 2001).

[145] A Review of Public Procurement: Findings and Recommendations (February 2002) (hereafter 'Implementation Report') <http://www.cpdni.gov.uk/pdf-main_report_rev.pdf>.

[146] Public Procurement Policy Statement to the Assembly by Dr Seán Farren, MLA, Minister of Finance and Personnel, 27 May 2002.

[147] Department of Finance and Personnel, 'Public Procurement Policy' (May 2002), <http://www.cpdni.gov.uk/pdf-public_procurement_policy.pdf>.

of procurement reforms that would be economically and politically sustainable in the longer term. The recommendations were presented as a balanced package of measures that took forward the reform of public procurement in Northern Ireland, but at the same time addressed the issue of social justice. That balance was likely to be attractive to the Executive; the need to compromise was, after all, the essence of the structure of the devolved government established by the Belfast Agreement. The tricky question was how to deliver this balance. The political compromise would only be acceptable to ministers if it could be justified legally and bureaucratically.

The report acknowledged that the concept of '*best* value for money' was central to public procurement policy. This was a central element because of the need to be seen to be following Treasury policy. It also made it clear that there was a commitment to promoting efficiency. But the report argued that the idea was often misunderstood as meaning only effectiveness or efficiency or the lowest price. The report understood the term in a wider, more encompassing sense as the summation of twelve principles: transparency, integrity, competitive supply, effectiveness, efficiency, fair-dealing, responsiveness, informed decision-making, consistency, legality, integration, and accountability. Of these, perhaps the most controversial was the principle of integration, defined as 'joined-up government, meaning that procurement should pay due regard to other Northern Ireland government economic and social policies, rather than cut across them'.[148] 'When a procurement process results in these principles being satisfied to an acceptable extent, we can say that the process has resulted in "best value for money".'[149] The concept of best value for money was defined as the 'optimum combination of whole life cost and quality (or fitness for purpose) to meet the customer's requirement'.[150] In a critical comment, the report continued: 'This definition allows for the inclusion, as appropriate, of social, economic and environmental goals within the procurement process.'[151] The team recommended that, *thus defined*, 'best value for money... should be the primary objective of procurement policy'.[152]

Several of the policy implications of adopting the twelve principles as the basis for new procurement policy were spelled out, including that 'wider economic, social and environmental strategies and initiatives of the devolved administration in Northern Ireland should be more closely integrated into procurement policy' and that 'more consultation with the wider community and with other stakeholders in the procurement system, especially members of the public who will be directly affected by the outcomes of the procurement, should become integrated into the procurement process where appropriate'.[153] The report continued: 'In particular, public bodies should be aware of the implications of the extensive public consultation requirements arising from section 75 of the Northern Ireland Act 1998, and its application to their procurement function.'[154]

---

[148] Implementation Report (n 145 above) para 2.17.   [149] ibid para 2.16.
[150] ibid para 2.16.   [151] ibid.   [152] ibid.   [153] ibid para 2.18.   [154] ibid.

As regards the thorny question of choosing *how* to introduce economic, social, and environmental policies and *which* such policies should be integrated into the process of public procurement, the report recommended that six considerations should be taken into account to ensure that the modalities of integration were appropriate: the modalities should be effective in achieving best value for money and delivering this policy; the transparency of the requirement should be ensured; the integration should be selective and targeted; the modalities must be legal; the modalities must make the policies operational and as consistent as possible with the other aspects and values of the procurement process, in particular the principles of transparency, clarity, consistency, integrity, effectiveness, and fair dealing; and the modalities should be justifiable.

Institutionally, it was recommended that there should be a high level Procurement Board, supported by a central procurement body in the Department of Finance and Personnel, and consisting of the Permanent Secretaries of Northern Ireland Departments, the Treasury Officer of Accounts, the Director of the Central Procurement Body, and two outside experts. The Procurement Board should be accountable to the Northern Ireland Executive and to the Northern Ireland Assembly and should be chaired by the Minister for Finance and Personnel. The roles and responsibilities of the Procurement Board would include ensuring that procurement policy 'pays due regard to the requirements of the Executive's wider policy commitments, including equality'.[155]

Most of the recommendations regarding the integration of social issues were uncontroversial. Legislation should provide unambiguously that direct and indirect discrimination is prohibited in relation to procurement on the grounds of religion and political belief, sex, race, or ethnic origin, or disability. Equivalent sanctions for persistent and recalcitrant breach of the other anti-discrimination laws should be enacted as were included in the Fair Employment and Treatment Order 1998, considered in chapter 10 above. Where a firm was found to be in default by a court or tribunal, then the Equality Commission should be able to serve a 'not qualified' notice on the firm, prohibiting public bodies from entering into contracts with that firm. Compliance with the anti-discrimination legislation should become a contract condition in all procurement contracts above or below the EC thresholds and appropriate arrangements for monitoring this contract condition should be developed by the Procurement Board, in consultation with the Equality Commission and business interests, to ensure that the approach was proportional. The Procurement Board should ensure that the 'Special Contracts Arrangement' to help workshops for the disabled was well publicized and that procurement staff were instructed to promote its use. The Board should review the procurement element of current environmental policy, in consultation with the Department of Environment and other interested groups. The Board should develop a database of information relevant for assessing

---

[155] ibid para 3.9.

the success or otherwise of the integration of social, economic, and environmental policies into procurement.

Most controversial, however, was the proposal that a pilot project to assist the unemployed should be instituted. We saw in chapter 3 above that the issue of unemployment had considerable status equality implications in Northern Ireland, given that for many years Catholics were more than twice as likely to be unemployed as Protestants. Addressing unemployment came to be regarded, therefore, as part of the broader fair employment agenda. Part of the explanation for why Catholics were proportionately more likely than Protestants to be unemployed lay in the concentration of Catholics in particular geographical areas that had greater unemployment. Strategies had been advocated in the past, therefore, to encourage major construction projects to recruit local labour where the project was sited close to areas of high unemployment, particularly in Belfast.[156] There were proposals, for example, on the use of local labour training and employment schemes in the construction industry.[157]

There had been a proliferation of schemes over the previous few years in Belfast. The Odyssey Trust Company encouraged the main contractors to employ local subcontractors where possible. The Training and Employment Agency established a new pre-employment training scheme to assist the unemployed to compete for job opportunities within the complex. The West Belfast Partnership Board undertook to the local community that, as far as construction was concerned, the Board would encourage successful contractors on the Springvale project to engage with local people regarding local employment. Laganside operated a voluntary scheme requiring the Belfast Corporation and the developer to encourage those involved in development to provide local people with access to any employment opportunities. The developer was required to provide the Corporation with details of an action plan for identifying employment opportunities for the local community.

The biggest scheme, however, was that involving the redevelopment of a large area of central Belfast, the Victoria Square Development. The Northern Ireland Executive had emphasized the need for the Department for Social Development to secure maximum social inclusion and equality benefits from the development. The development brief issued to developers required that 'the project must add value to the local economy by tackling unemployment particularly long-term unemployment, enhancing employability and maximising training opportunities for local people, particularly in areas of greatest social need'.[158] It required the developer to make an acceptable proposal to address these issues, not only in relation to the jobs within the developer's control, but also the jobs created by subcontractors

[156] M Sheehan and M Tomlinson, 'Long-Term Unemployment in West Belfast', in E McLaughlin and P Quirk, *Policy Aspects of Employment Equality in Northern Ireland, Volume iii Employment Equality in Northern Ireland* (SACHR, 1996) 51.

[157] C Nolan, 'Jobs on the Block: The Use of Local Labour training and employment schemes in the construction industry—a proposal for West Belfast' (West Belfast Economic Forum, August 1999).   [158] Victoria Square, Development Brief, para 9.3.

and the retailers who would be the end-users of the new development. The Department further required the developer 'to demonstrate how his proposals will promote equality of opportunity and good relations' in relation to the groups covered by section 75, and also to 'confirm that his proposals will have no negative impact on equality of opportunities and good relations'.[159] The Department would approve the developer's proposals and incorporate them into a development agreement. In 2006, this aspect of the development plan was published, setting out the objectives, actions, and targets agreed.[160]

Unemployment pilot project

The pilot project proposed by the Procurement Review took a somewhat different approach, but building on what had gone before. The pilot project would involve a condition being included in certain contracts. This condition would require suppliers to implement the plan accepted by the contracting authority on award of the contract for using the unemployed in the work on the contract, including work carried out by subcontractors. No specific proportion of unemployed to already employed should be specified, either minimum or maximum. The definition of 'unemployed' should be carefully considered, in consultation with the Equality Commission, so as not to discriminate against women, and should include unemployed from anywhere in the EC (and beyond, in the case of a tenderer from outside the EC). Bidders should be required to produce a clear, specific, and concise unemployment utilization plan showing the bidder's proposals for utilizing the unemployed on the contract, and the bidder's technical capacity to implement the proposals. Firms that had recently been recruiting from the unemployed should be able to present their approach as appropriate evidence. Failure to produce such a proposed plan should result in the bid being excluded from further consideration. The tender documentation should specify that the proposed plan should be submitted as part of the bid. The requirements should be clearly included in the bid specifications. When the bid, which included the proposed plan, was accepted, carrying out the plan should become an integral part of the contract, and become a contract condition. Failure to comply with the plan should be subject to an appropriate penalty, and it would be relevant to consider such failure in assessing future contract bids. Adherence to the contract condition should also be taken into account at the award stage, and this should be specified in the tender documentation. The feasibility and quality of the supplier's plan to utilize the unemployed should be taken into account at the award stage where otherwise equivalent tenderers who submitted a plan were in competition.

---

[159] ibid para 9.8.
[160] Multi Development UK and Department for Social Development, 'People and Place: Victoria Square Scheme—Community and Business Opportunity Plan' (May 2006), available at <http://www.dsdni.gov.uk>.

The pilot should contain a critical mass of projects, at least twenty, and at least one by each Department. The requirements of the pilot project should be confined for the first two years of operation to works contracts above £3.5 million and substantial service contracts (above £0.5 million). The Procurement Board should be tasked with drawing up a detailed set of guidance on this for departments and other public bodies within the first six months of operation. The Board should assess the operation of the unemployment strategy recommended, making recommendations for its greater effectiveness, within two years of the Board coming into operation. The requirements of the pilot project should be considered subsequently in the light of experience for inclusion in other types of contracts. Where legislation was thought likely to act as a barrier to particular public bodies being able to participate in this, it should be amended.[161]

Although there were arguments in favour of the position that public procurement policy should be the same as in United Kingdom departments, the Review considered that this was not an argument that was ultimately convincing or politically realistic. Procurement was, after all, a devolved responsibility and the logic must therefore be that it may differ in substantial respects from general United Kingdom policy (provided it complied with EC law, etc). On top of this, Northern Ireland already had different approaches in procurement even under Direct Rule, for example the provisions in the Fair Employment and Treatment Order (FETO) 1998. Most importantly, however, section 75 of the Northern Ireland Act 1998 placed a duty on public authorities regarding procurement which went beyond anything applying in the rest of the United Kingdom at that time.

Executive approval and implementing the pilot schemes

The proposals for the integration of social policy were the most controversial of the proposals, and discussions within and between departments after the final report was published were intense. In particular, the recommendation for the pilot scheme regarding the unemployed was challenged by some internally in the Civil Service as unlawful, breaching the 'value for money' principle, and generally lacking in feasibility. Eventually, the Executive reached an agreed position, largely adopting the Review's approach. In its formal policy statement, the Executive announced that it considered that 'the pilot scheme is a measured response by the Review Team to its terms of reference'. It continued: 'The Executive accepts that the pilot scheme is as forward a proposal as can be achieved within the limits of law and practicability and therefore agreed to implement it and test whether the concerns expressed by consultees are real and whether the proposal is worthwhile and workable.'[162] The pilot scheme would not proceed, however, 'until the details

---

[161] Education and Library Boards (NI) Order 1993, art 20 and the Local Government (Miscellaneous Provisions) (NI) Order 1992, art 19.

[162] Department of Finance and Personnel, 'Public Procurement Policy' (May 2002) para 23. See also the Statement to the Assembly by Seán Farren, MLA, Minister of Finance and Personnel, 27 May 2002.

have been agreed with the Procurement Board and prior to bringing forward proposals, there will be discussions with the representatives of the industries affected (namely the construction and service sectors) and the Equality Commission, to ensure that the scheme is workable'.[163] The results of the pilot scheme would be reported to the Executive at the end of a two-year pilot period 'to determine whether the policy should be mainstreamed'.[164]

The Procurement Board established in July 2002 was chaired by the Finance Minister. The membership of the Board consisted of the Permanent Secretaries of the eleven Northern Ireland departments, in order to ensure that there would be 'compliance with the agreed policies and procedures in all Departments, their Agencies, NDPBs and public corporations'.[165] Other members of the Board included the Treasury Officer of Accounts, two external experts (including the author), the head of the Central Procurement Directorate, and a representative of the Comptroller and Auditor General as an observer. The role of the Board was crucial in two particular respects. First, the Board was allocated the role of agreeing to the detailed outworking of the policy that would have to be in place before the pilot schemes could proceed. Second, for the pilot schemes to proceed, departments would have to volunteer projects to be included. If projects were not volunteered, then the pilot scheme would collapse. The Board's role was to ensure that departments did in fact propose appropriate projects. The presence of the Permanent Secretaries on the Board would be a significant feature: either they would exert pressure on each other to volunteer schemes, or they would underpin and legitimate further any refusals to participate by departments. Crucial to the politics of the Board's operation was the fact that the Northern Ireland Executive was suspended during 2003, after the failure of attempts to secure further decommissioning of arms by the IRA, and the refusal of the Ulster Unionist Party to participate in the Executive. The effect of this was to put direct rule back into operation, with the consequent lessening of local political accountability of those operating the policy.

During 2002, the identification of projects to be included, and the development of detailed guidance, went hand in hand. The Board was presented with a draft scheme to assist contracting authorities to implement the pilot scheme. This was approved by the Board in February 2003; this meeting was chaired by the new direct-rule Minister for Finance. The scheme provided that for those projects included in the pilot, it would be an objective of the contract to create opportunities to facilitate the unemployed into work. The 'unemployed' were defined as any person resident in the EC or any other country covered by the WTO Government Procurement Agreement who was not in paid employment in the three months immediately prior to being employed on the contract. Contractors wishing to be considered for a contract within the Pilot Study would be required to demonstrate clearly their commitment to the scheme. Tender documentation would

---

[163] Public Procurement Policy (n 162 above) para 23.   [164] ibid.   [165] ibid para 13.

require the contractor to provide an 'unemployment utilisation plan'. This should contain three broad elements.

The first element required the firm to set out the firm's general social policy in relation to the recruitment, training, and retention of employees from the unemployed. This should be a strategic management document signed by the managing director, chief executive, or senior partner. It should include details of any pre-qualification policy the firm operated regarding subcontractors, and any requirements imposed upon subcontractors prior to entering into contract with them. It should outline the company's pension arrangements for all employees and access rights for those employed under the scheme. It should indicate whether the firm encouraged job sharing or part-time working and the numbers of employees currently opting for these. It should indicate whether the firm operated flexible working hours, whether it operated free or subsidized transport between home and place of work, or offered any special arrangements for child minding. It should specify on what basis the remuneration package offered for those under the contract would be calculated, and specify whether employees recruited under the initiative would be employed on a full-time basis or on a short-term contract. Firms were expected to indicate whether the firm operated a mandatory probationary period that employees had to complete before particular benefits offered by the employer were available to employees. The firm's training arrangements should be set out, and the firm should indicate whether the firm would facilitate day-release for non-apprentice positions, and what training opportunities would be made available to employees recruited under the initiative. Liaison between the firm and relevant groups and bodies outside the workplace that would be relevant for the unemployment initiative should also be detailed, including examples of relationships developed with community groups, relationships developed with public sector organizations, and details of any employee support mechanisms.

The second element in the unemployed utilization plan involved the firm setting out a detailed project implementation plan, which would be specific to the contract. This would state the firm's proposals for recruitment and retention of employees from the unemployed for this contract. It would set out the mechanism for the authentication of the previous employment position of employees recruited from the unemployed for the purposes of the contract. It would propose a monitoring and reporting system for informing the contracting authority during the execution of the contract.

The third element related to previous experience. The firm was required to demonstrate its commitment, capability, and competence by providing details of any current or previous experience in this field either in partnership with other government departments or private firms or as an initiative operated directly by the firm itself, including the number of any employees recruited and their duration of employment under such initiatives.

Failure to submit an unemployed utilization plan with the tender would result in the tender being declared void and excluded from further consideration. The plan would be assessed to establish its suitability. A matrix was suggested for assessing the suitability of the proposals of individual tenderers, including a list of the items to be considered and the appropriate weightings for each of these. The overall score for the social policy elements should be 30 per cent, project implementation 50 per cent, and experience and capability 20 per cent, although specific requirements of a project might require the contracting authority to review the items included or the weightings suggested.

In the event of two or more tenders being judged by the contracting authority to be equal, the assessment of the plan would be taken into consideration to decide the award of the contract. It would be a matter for the individual contracting authority to determine the definition of when two bids were equal, in order to justify taking the plan into account at the award stage. For guidance purposes, however, where the award criteria for the contract was 'most economically advantageous', it was recommended that this should be deemed to have occurred where one or more tenders were within two points, in the overall scoring matrix (reflecting quality and price scores; scored out of 100) of the tender receiving the highest overall score. Where the award criteria for the contract was 'lowest price', then it would be when one or more tenders were within 1 per cent of the lowest satisfactory tender.

It would be a condition of the contract that the contractor would implement in full the undertakings set out in the contractor's unemployed utilization plan. Any failure to implement the plan fully would be reflected in the contractor's performance evaluation at the end of the contract. This evaluation would be taken into account in the assessment of the contractor's unemployed utilization plan in any future bid process with any Northern Ireland public body, and could give rise to a claim for damages. The contractor was required not to cause any current employee of the firm, nor permit any current employee of any subcontractor, to become unemployed, pursuant to the execution of the unemployed utilization plan.

After the award of the contract, the successful contractor would be required to satisfy the contracting authority that any persons employed under the scheme complied with the qualification requirements. Tenderers would be required to provide all reasonable assistance to the contracting authority to conduct an appraisal of the policy during or after the execution of the contract. Any employment of an individual of less than ten working days would not be included as a bona fide employment for the purposes of assessment of the contractor's compliance with the initiative. The successful contractor would be required to use his best endeavours to ensure that any person employed under the scheme would remain employed for the duration of the contract. The curtailment of any contract of employment with any person under the scheme, within the duration of the contract with the contracting authority, would be limited, with safeguards to ensure that the contracting authority was notified. Where the contractor cited the unsuitability of the employee as the reason for cessation of employment, the contractor would be required to supply details of steps taken to assist the employee to adapt to the employment environment. Details of events leading to disciplinary action must be supplied. Where the employment of any person employed under the initiative ceased, the contractor was required to advise the contracting authority of actions being undertaken to replace that person.

EC tendering procedures would be applied to all contracts. Individual Prior Indicative Notices (PIN) and the Procedural Notice to be placed in the *Official Journal* would incorporate several statements: all bona fide tenders would be required to include a project specific unemployed utilization plan in a format acceptable to the contracting authority; the contract would contain specific contract provisions that would require the implementation of the unemployed utilization plan; the unemployed utilization plan would be considered during the assessment for the award of the contract, but only in the event that two (or more) tenders were judged equal in the evaluation of the economically most advantageous; and the contracting authority would welcome the opportunity to view the firm's social policy statement if it was returned with the notice of interest, but that it would not be considered for tender short-listing purposes.

14

Procurement Linkages and the 2003
Legislative Reforms: a *Modus Vivendi* in Sight?

We saw in chapters 12 and 13 above, that significant developments affected the
political and legal context of public procurement linkages from the early 1990s and
in chapter 13 above, we saw how some Member States revised their approaches to
equality linkages in partial response to these changes. We also saw in chapter 12
that one of the significant changes in the context of European procurement law and
policy was the greater legal clarity regarding the extent to which such linkages were
legally permissible, arising from decisions of the European Court of Justice (ECJ),
and legislative reforms in 2003. In this chapter, a history of these legislative reforms
is presented. Before turning to the detail of these reforms, however, two preliminary
points relating to the political context of these reforms need to be borne in mind.

I. Political Context of Legislative Reforms

Role of unions and NGOs

As stated in chapter 12, it became increasingly apparent that governments relied
to some extent on European law as an argument to limit what local and other
authorities could do. Law became the site for political battle. Increasingly the
argument that Community law *prohibited* linkage gave way to an argument that
European law was so uncertain that local and other authorities were at significant
risk of litigation because of the *uncertainty* as to what Community law did or did
not permit. Community law became an extraordinarily useful excuse for advising
local authorities to be very careful in engaging in any such linkage beyond what
government thought appropriate. The message to those who wanted to go further
was clear. If Community law was a constraint, then Community law should be
changed either to require linkage, or to give much clearer guidance to public
authorities as to what was at least permissible, so that risk-averse bodies could
engage with linkage with somewhat greater confidence. Not surprisingly, then,
public service unions joined with non-governmental organizations (NGOs) interested in equality to form one of the main lobbying groups dedicated to reforming
EC law in this way.

Changing role of the European Parliament

In chapter 10 above, it was shown that, during the previous legislative refoms of the late 1980s, the European Parliament had been the most consistently in favour of linkage, and that the Commission and Council were much more sceptical. The Parliament was not, at that time, in any position to require that its amendments be accepted since, under the provisions of the Treaty then in force, the Parliament had the power only to give its opinion on the issue and the other institutions could, and did, largely ignore that opinion. The relative balance of power between the Institutions was changed, to some extent at least, by the 1992 Maastricht Treaty and the 1997Amsterdam Treaty. In certain areas of Community policy, most notably for our purposes in the area of internal market reforms, the Parliament was given the role of co-decision with the Council. Co-decision became the standard procedure for legislating in the Community, although important areas of Community legislation were excluded from this procedure, for example legislation dealing with anti-discrimination law under Article 13. Any further reform of the public procurement directives proposed by the Commission would, therefore, be subject to this new procedure.

The new procedure still involved the need for the Commission to submit a proposal to the European Parliament and the Council. The Council then obtained the opinion of the Parliament, which could propose amendments. The Parliament adopted this position on the basis of a report by its relevant Committee. This was the 'first reading' of the legislation in the Parliament. Having received the opinion of the Parliament, the Council had three options, acting by a qualified majority. The Council might approve all the amendments proposed by the Parliament and adopt the proposed legislation thus amended. If the Parliament did not propose any amendments, the Council could adopt the Commission's original proposal. Alternatively, the Council could adopt a 'common position' and communicate this to the Parliament, informing the Parliament of the reasons that led it to adopt this common position, including why it disagreed with the Parliament's amendments.

The Parliament then had three options at the second reading stage. On the basis of a recommendation by the relevant Committee, the Parliament could approve the common position by a simple majority, in which case the legislation as amended by the Council was adopted. It could reject the common position by an absolute majority of its component members, in which case the legislation fell. It could propose amendments to the common position by an absolute majority of its component members, in which case the amended text was forwarded to the Council and to the Commission, which delivered an opinion on those amendments. If, within three months of communicating this common position, the Parliament had not acted to adopt any of these three options, the proposed legislation was deemed to have been passed.

Where amendments had been proposed by the Parliament, and referred back to the Council, there were various possibilities available to the Council. If, within three months, the Council approved all the amendments of the Parliament, the legislation was deemed to have been adopted in the form of the common position as amended by the Parliament. Generally, the Council needed to act in approving these amendments by a qualified majority; however, where the Commission had delivered a negative opinion regarding particular Parliament amendments, the Council could only adopt these unanimously. If the Council did not approve all the amendments, the President of the Council, in agreement with the President of the Parliament was required, within six weeks, to convene a meeting of the 'Conciliation Committee'.

The Conciliation Committee was composed of the members of the Council or their representatives, and an equal number of representatives of the Parliament. The task of the Committee was to reach agreement on a joint text, starting with the common position as amended by the Parliament, by a qualified majority of the members of the Council or their representatives, and by a majority of the representatives of the Parliament. The Commission also took part in the Committee's proceedings, attempting to reconcile the positions of the Parliament and the Council. If, within six weeks of its being convened, the Conciliation Committee approved a joint text, the European Parliament, acting by an absolute majority of the votes cast, and the Council, acting by a qualified majority, each had a period of six weeks to adopt the legislation in the form of the joint text. If either of the two institutions failed to approve the joint text, or if the Conciliation Committee itself failed to approve a joint text, the legislation fell.[1] The Commission was conscious of the difficulties of achieving a successful legislative result in such a contentious area with an increasingly complex procedure. Indeed, the Commission had already seen how difficult it was to manage this procedure in the procurement context, when the Parliament threatened to derail the directives implementing the Government Procurement Agreement (GPA) agreed at the end of the Uruguay Round.[2]

We shall see, therefore, that unlike in the reform process of the 1990s, the issue of what role, if any, should be allowed to the linkage between procurement and social considerations became a central focus in the discussions that ensued. A second substantial difference was the greater importance that the Parliament had been accorded because the procurement directives proposed by the Commission were subject to the co-decision procedure, under which the Parliament had an equal role with the Council in approving the directives. A third substantial difference was the activism of a broad coalition of unions and NGOs operating in the social and environmental field in lobbying the institutions to adopt a broader role for linkage than in the past. There was, however, one major similarity in the events that unfolded

---

[1] The 3 months and 6 weeks could be extended by a maximum of 1 month and 2 weeks respectively at the initiative of the Parliament or the Council.

[2] See G O' Brien, 'Envisaged Change in the Procurement Regime: the Point of View of the European Commission', Contribution of George O'Brien, DG XV—Internal Market and Financial Affairs, Commission of the European Communities, at the seminar on 'Legal Aspects of EC Public Procurement', Luxembourg, 29–30 October 1998, 4; see also *Financial Times*, 31 January 1996, 3.

with those that had occurred in the 1990s, namely that the ECJ itself became a major, albeit distant, player in the process, with decisions in several major cases of direct relevance to the legislative discussions (a number of which we considered in chapter 12 above) being handed down in the course of those discussions.

II. Commission Procurement Reform Proposals and Linkage, 1996–99

Commission Green Paper

The Commission's Green Paper 'Public Procurement in the European Union: Exploring the Way Forward' was adopted in November 1996.[3] One of the principal themes of the Green Paper was the need to simplify the legal framework, whilst maintaining the stability of the basic structure already in place. As regards the relationship between social policy and procurement policy, there was clearly a battle about to take place within the Commission. On the one hand, the economic directorates were hostile to any significant integration of social policy into the procurement directives beyond the status quo. On the other hand the environment and social policy directorates were broadly sympathetic to linkages, at least in private. Even within the internal market Directorate, however, there were clear differences of view emerging, concerning the purposes of EC procurement policy, and how far there should be a more permissive regime of regulation adopted.

The Green Paper was already the product of a finely balanced compromise. On the one hand, it recognized and accepted that procurement would be used as a mechanism for implementing domestic and Community social policy. It was also accepted that this was compatible with the then existing directives when accomplished through the provisions enabling the exclusion of contractors or suppliers, or by requiring compliance with contract conditions. On the other hand, the Green Paper was clear that there were significant limits to what was permissible in terms of checking the suitability of tenderers more broadly, and at the award stage, except for contracts below the threshold. In particular, with regard to award criteria, the Green Paper stated that award criteria 'must relate to the economic qualities required of the supplies, works or services covered by the contract'.[4]

Reactions to the Green Paper

The Economic and Social Committee gave its opinion on the Green Paper in May 1997,[5] also taking a relatively conservative position, encouraging the Commission to:

... set out in a communication, and as part of the regional, social or environmental policies, limits on any specific conditions that might be inserted into a contract... For

---

[3] 27 November 1996, COM(96)583 final.   [4] Green Paper (n 3 above) para 5.43.
[5] 29 May 1997 [1997] OJ C 287/92.

instance, if a contracting authority wishes to favour certain types of people, such a clause should be subject to a certain number of conditions such as being limited in its duration, applying only to a given size of contract and to certain types of work, being really accessible to any firm without any discriminatory effect and being the subject, where appropriate, of a specific payment.[6]

The Committee of the Regions also gave its opinion on the Green Paper in June 1997,[7] agreeing that 'an interpretative communication is needed to clarify the opportunities public procurement law offers to the various categories concerned for implementing Community and national employment and social policy objectives'.[8]

In October 1997, the Parliament's committees took up the Green Paper.[9] The Committee on Legal Affairs and Citizens' Rights agreed that the Commission 'should . . . make it clear that the legal requirements for public procurement procedures based on Community law do not preclude contracting authorities from including into the terms of tender certain conditions relating to the fulfilment of obligations in the field of social, environmental or health policy, as long as applied in a non-discriminatory manner'.[10] The Committee on Employment and Social Affairs, perhaps not surprisingly, given its mandate, had most to say on the issue, and both the tone and detailed recommendations of its report showed the distance between at least some in the Parliament and the Commission.

It called on the Commission 'to include provisions stating to [sic] the admissibility of clauses in contracts related to social goals in future Directives on public procurement, or in the revision of existing Directives'.[11] It suggested that 'the institutions of the European Community [should] be mindful in their own procurement procedures of social policy goals, and use public procurement to the greatest possible degree as an instrument for achieving social policy objectives'. It considered that it should also be possible by means of public procurement procedures 'to increase equality of opportunity between the sexes, defend the rights of minorities and reduce the unemployment and social exclusion of citizens'.[12] It asked the Commission to 'ensure that the public authorities and public bodies do not inadvertently support contractors violating Community social legislation'. It called for public contracts 'to go to employers who provide equality of opportunity in line with obligations under international and Community law to ensure a structurally fair balance of power in the employment market between women and men'.[13] It noted 'that employers who provide for equality of opportunity and who

---

[6] Economic and Social Committee opinion on the Green Paper, May 1997, para 6.2.

[7] 12 June 1997 [1997] OJ C244/28. [8] ibid point 3.7.2.

[9] 9 October 1997, A4-0309/97: Social aspects: Committee on Economic and Monetary Affairs and Industrial Policy, resolutions 13, 15, 17, 20; Committee on Legal Affairs and Citizens' Rights, resolution 7; Committee on Employment and Social Affairs, resolutions 1–7, 10–12.

[10] Committee on Legal Affairs and Citizens' Rights, para 7.

[11] A4-0309/97, Committee on Employment and Social Affairs, Conclusion, point 3.

[12] ibid Conclusion, point 4. [13] ibid Conclusion, point 5.

respect high social standards should not be disadvantaged because competitors manage to cut costs by discriminating, by tolerating inequality or by undermining social standards'. It noted that 'contract compliance, in certain conditions, can produce change in the composition of employers' work forces and promote the status of women in the organisations in general'. It called on the Commission 'to propose an instrument regarding the use of contract compliance in public procurement'.[14] It considered that 'Member States are charged with the obligation to combat unemployment and social exclusion'. It noted that public procurement, 'which is ultimately the spending of public funds, can contribute to these goals under conditions which ensure transparency of tendering and awarding procedures'.[15] It regretted 'the absence in the Commission's Green Paper of constructive solutions aimed at giving greater prominence to labour market and social considerations in public procurement procedures'.[16] It called on the Commission to:

... take initiatives aimed at revising the public procurement Directives with a view to incorporating criteria which require the awarding body to fulfil the requirements in the areas covered by ILO Conventions 87, 98 (on the right to belong to a professional organization and the right to sign collective agreements), 29, 105 (rejecting forced labour), 111, 100 (promoting equal pay for equal work and rejecting discrimination), 138 (on child labour) and 94 (on social criteria in public procurement contracts) and in other applicable Community legislation or national legislation/collective agreements.

It called for such criteria 'to be worked out in dialogue with the European partners on the labour market'.[17]

The powerful Committee on Economic and Monetary Affairs and Industrial Policy, whose mandate included consideration of internal market reforms, was more cautious. It: 'Acknowledge[d] ... the Commission's view . . . that the procurement directives are not the place to pursue environmental or social polices, but points out that they should not be an obstacle to the promotion of best practice and the maintenance of local (high) standards if this is the wish of the contracting entity.'[18] It considered that 'contracting entities can already take into account when stipulating the qualifications of suppliers or in the drawing up of specifications, compliance with social, environmental, quality, sustainability and health legislation, and draws attention to the fact that the lowest price is only one of the alternative criteria for the awarding of a contract, together with that of the financially most advantageous tender'.[19] It encouraged the Commission 'to continue to support the social clause in the WTO and to explore how ILO convention 94 can be made an integral part of GPA'.[20] This resulted in a Resolution adopted on 22 October 1997.[21]

---

[14] ibid Conclusion, point 6.   [15] ibid Conclusion, point 7.
[16] ibid Conclusion, point 11.   [17] ibid Conclusion, point 12.
[18] A4-0309/97, Committee on Economic and Monetary Affairs and Industrial Policy, Conclusion point 13.   [19] ibid Conclusion, point 15.
[20] ibid Conclusion, point 17.
[21] 22 October 1997, A4-0309/97 [1997] OJ C339/65. Social aspects: see recital G; resolutions 13, 15, 17, 20.

Commission response

In November 1997, the Commission published its Special Sectoral Report on public procurement. The Green Paper on public procurement had provided an opportunity for actors in the EU public procurement markets to inform the Commission about their day-to-day experiences and any problems they had found with the procurement directives. The Commission was then carefully analysing the 300 contributions received, which dealt with all of the topics and issues raised in the Green Paper. In a clear reassertion of power by those in the Commission who wished to see a purely economic approach to procurement, it found general satisfaction among the Member States at the then existing position:

There is widespread agreement that social policy and public procurement should not overlap: Social objectives should be pursued through adequate social legislation and not by using the power to award procurement contracts. Finland, France, Germany, Italy, Luxembourg, the UK, Portugal and Sweden are in favour of maintaining the status quo. The introduction of social preferences seems to be envisaged only by Austria and Denmark. Belgium defends the possibility of including security and health considerations in the selection and award criteria and, like many other respondents, seeks further clarification as to what directives allow in terms of taking social considerations into account when awarding contracts.[22]

In March 1998, however, the Commission published its Communication 'Public Procurement in the European Union'.[23] Balancing economic and social goals was back in place. The Commission 're-iterates that public contracts can be a means of influencing the actions of economic operators, providing the limits laid down by Community law are respected'. The Commission went further than before, however, going so far as to 'encourage [ ] the Member States to use their procurement powers to pursue the social objectives mentioned above'. The Commission 'will act similarly in its own procurement activity'.

In May 1998, the Council of Ministers agreed a statement on the Communication.[24] As regards the social aspects of procurement, the Council agreed that 'the legislative framework for public procurement should not hinder the pursuit of other Community policies, for example on the environment or social issues, and that the provisions in the Directives for taking account of such factors should be clarified by the Commission in consultation with Member States, taking account of the priorities attached to such factors by Member States'.

Opposition was not long in building up, however. In June 1998, the Union of Industrial and Employers' Confederations of Europe (UNICE) set out its opposition to the inclusion of social criteria in public procurement tenders. While all

---

[22] European Commission, Special Sectoral report, No 1: Public procurement, Brussels, November 1997, para 4.3.
[23] COM(98)143, 11 March 1998. For discussion, see S Arrowsmith, 'The Community's Legal Framework on Public Procurement: "The Way Forward" at Last?' (1999) 36 CMLR 13–49.
[24] 18 May 1998, C/98/148.

companies should respect social legislation, inclusion of such criteria in procurement was considered to be unnecessary interference. Attempting to marry social goals with the goal of fair competition between suppliers in the internal market, would jeopardize the achievement of both goals. Procurement should not be used as a social tool.[25]

The Committee on Economic and Monetary Affairs and Industrial Policy, however, did not adopt a similar position. It: 'Remind[ed] the Commission that good procurement should facilitate and not impede best practice or choice. This is particularly important in terms of improving social, environmental and consumer standards within the framework of legal requirements not to distort competition.'[26] It: 'Note[d] the Commission's intention to interpret the basic principles for the consideration of social aspects in public procurement contracts in an interpretative communication', but 'nevertheless call[ed] urgently for binding legislation at European level to ensure compliance with social legislation in the context of procurement procedures in order to prevent unhealthy competition with regard to the price of labour or other terms and conditions of employment'. It called upon the Commission, in future directives on public procurement, 'also to include provisions permitting social clauses to be included in contracts'.[27] It argued that:

... criteria must be included in the directives on public procurement requiring the authority awarding the contract to comply with ILO Conventions 87, 98 (right to join professional organizations and to conclude collective agreements), 29, 105 (ban on forced labour), 111, 100 (equal pay for equal work and ban on discrimination), 138 (child labour) and 94 (social criteria in public procurement contracts) and with the relevant Community legislation, national legislation or collective agreements; [and it] consider[ed] that these criteria must be set by means of a dialogue with the European social partners... [28]

It called 'on the Community institutions, in their public procurement procedures, to comply in full with the obligations required by law, agreement and contract on employment protection and conditions of employment which are applicable in the place where the work is to be carried out'.

The Parliamentary Resolution[29] reflected closely the approach advocated by the Committee on Monetary Affairs. In addition, however, the Parliament began to link the Commission's proposals on the use of procurement to tackle corruption with the use of social criteria generally. If linkage could be used for these purposes, why not for social purposes? So, the Parliamentary Resolution:

... welcome[d] the Commission's initiative to explore the possibilities for black and grey lists of companies which have been accused of fraud or corruption; call[ed] on the Commission to consider the extension of these black and grey lists to cover companies accused of violations of social and environmental standards as well as corruption in

---

[25] See 'Unice rejects the inclusion of social criteria in procurement' European Industrial Relations Observatory on-line, at <http://www.eiro.eurofound.ie/1998/07/inbrief/EU9807119N.html>.
[26] 9 February 1999, A4-0394/98, Conclusion, point 7.   [27] ibid Conclusion point 10.
[28] ibid Conclusion point 11.   [29] 9 February 1999, A4-0394/98 [1999] OJ C150/64.

Member States; these lists should be made available on the Internet for consultation by Member States and local and other public authorities.[30]

It 'await[ed] with interest the Commission's investigation of the use of blacklists and other measures to combat corruption and to ensure compliance with social and environmental legislation'.[31]

III. Equality Directives and Procurement in the Parliament, 1999–2002

Race Directive

Meanwhile, the proposal for what became Directive (EC) 2000/43, implementing the principle of equal treatment between persons irrespective of racial or ethnic origin (the Race Directive), was presented by the Commission in November 1999.[32] In May 2000, the Parliamentary Committee reported, proposing various amendments relating to procurement.[33] The Committees on Citizens' Freedoms and Rights, Justice and Home Affairs and on Employment and Social Affairs proposed an identical amendment to the enforcement provisions of the draft Directive:[34]

Member States may take into account an undertaking or organisation's record of compliance with national provisions to implement this Directive, including the record of compliance with national provisions of Member States other than the State in question, when awarding contracts and grants. In public tenders authorities may include demands that intend to positively discriminate persons that fall within the scope of this directive.

The justification advanced was that:

Contract compliance is an issue of particular relevance to EU anti-discrimination policy. Whilst the single market is designed to ensure equal access to such contracts for all EU firms, concerns have been expressed that this has the unintentional effect of restricting the opportunities for contract compliance and measures to promote equal treatment This new Article intends to make it explicitly possible for authorities to include contract compliance or positive action measures in tenders for public procurement.

In late May 2000, the Parliament itself issued its opinion in which it proposed the same amendment relating to procurement.[35] The Economic and Social Committee, which also reported in May, did not, however, mention procurement issues.[36]

---

[30] ibid Conclusion, point 18.   [31] ibid Conclusion, point 22.

[32] 25 November 1999, COM(1999)566 final [2000] OJ C116 E/56.

[33] 16 May 2000, A5-0136/2000: Committee on Citizens' Freedoms and Rights, Justice and Home Affairs, amendment 46. Committee on Employment and Social Affairs, amendment 41.

[34] Amendment 46, Art 9a (new); Amendment 41, Art 9a (new).

[35] 18 May 2000 [2001] OJ C59/263. Procurement: amendment 46.

[36] 25 May 2000 [2000] OJ C204/82.

In late May, the Commission issued a revised proposal, in which procurement was not mentioned and the Parliament's amendment was rejected.[37] The Directive was agreed on 29 June 2000 without any reference to procurement.[38]

Employment Discrimination Directive

A similar fate met attempts to incorporate procurement elements in what became the Employment Discrimination Directive (EC) 2000/78, establishing a general framework for equal treatment in employment and occupation. In January 2000, the Commission published its proposal, in which procurement was not mentioned.[39] The Committee of the Regions[40] mentioned it briefly, 'regretting that no consideration has been given to contract or grant compliance with respect to funding and calls for this to be rectified'. The Economic and Social Committee[41] did not mention it in its opinion. The Parliamentary Committees made similar amendments to those suggested in the Race Directive.[42] The Committee on Citizen's Freedoms and Rights, Justice and Home Affairs, however, recommended an amendment that was somewhat different: 'In awarding contracts and subsidies, a Member State may take account of the extent to which an enterprise or organisation has abided by this directive in the past. In connection with public calls for tender, the authorities may consider bids which constitute preferential treatment of persons falling within the scope of this directive.'[43] The Committee justified this on the basis that: 'Authorities set an example, which they should also do vis-à-vis the outside world in awarding contracts and subsidies and in tendering procedures. By requiring enterprises or organisations to have abided by the spirit and letter of this directive, authorities can also provide guidance in their role as awarders of subsidies or contracts.' The Committee on Employment and Social Affairs in its report proposed several amendments of relevance: 'Public corporations [should] not conclude any contracts with undertakings which have been shown to discriminate against employees who are protected by Article 13 of the EC Treaty.'[44] This was justified on the basis that: 'As indirect representatives, public corporations should be models that show they are actively opposing discrimination by not cooperating with undertakings in which discrimination occurs.' Another amendment provided that:

Member States may take into account an undertaking's or organisation's record of compliance with national provisions implementing this directive, including the record of compliance with national provisions of Member States other than the State in question, when

---

[37] 31 May 2000, COM(2000)328 final [2000] OJ C311E/169.
[38] 29 June 2000 [2000] OJ L180/22.   [39] 6 January 2000, COM(1999)565 final.
[40] 12 April 2000 [2000] OJ C226/1, para 1.25.   [41] 25 May 2000 [2000] OJ C204/82.
[42] 21 September 2000, A5-0264/2000, Parliament Committee Opinions: Committee on Employment and Social Policy, amendment 56; Committee on Legal Affairs and Internal Market, amendment 8.
[43] ibid amendment 27, Art 10a (new).   [44] ibid amendment 55, Art 13(c) (new).

awarding contracts and grants. In public procurement tenders authorities may include demands that discriminate in favour of persons falling within the scope of this directive.[45]

This was justified on the basis that 'it is essential that Member States consider contractors' performance in adhering to or attempting to incorporate anti-discriminatory measures into employment practice. This was supported by the European Parliament in its final vote on the Directive on Racism.' The European Parliament's opinion put forward the same amendments.[46] The Commission's amended proposal did not consider procurement, except to reject the Parliament's proposal.[47] The Directive, as adopted, did not mention procurement.[48]

Equal Treatment Directive

A third attempt to insert contract compliance into equality legislation also failed. In July 2000, the Commission proposed a new directive to amend the Equal Treatment Directive 1976, bringing it into line with the race and framework employment directives.[49] There was no mention of procurement in this, nor in the opinion of the Economic and Social Committee.[50] However, perhaps predictably, the Committee on Women's Rights and Equal Opportunities, in its report to the European Parliament, recommended that an amendment be included that was broadly similar to that adopted by the Parliament for the framework discrimination directive,[51] and this was accepted by the Parliament and included in its amendment of the directive.[52] However, this amendment was rejected by the Commission in its amended proposal of the 6 June 2001.[53] Nor was there any mention of contract compliance included in the Council Common Position of 23 July 2001,[54] and the Parliament did not pursue the matter further in its recommendations for a second[55] or third reading.[56] By this time, European Parliamentary activity had moved to attempt to exploit the opportunities presented by the proposals for amended procurement directives.[57]

---

[45] ibid amendment 56, Art 13(d) (new).
[46] 5 October 2000 [2001] OJ C178/254: Procurement: amendments 55 and 56.
[47] 12 October 2000, COM(2000)652 final [2001] OJ C62E/152.
[48] 27 November 2000, Directive (EC) 2000/78.
[49] 11 July 2000, COM(2000)334, [2000] OJ C337E/204.
[50] 25 January 2001 [2001] OJ C123/81.   [51] A5-0173/2001, amendment 23.
[52] 31 May 2001, A5-0173/2002, [2002] OJ C47E.   [53] [2001] OJ C270E/9.
[54] [2002] OJ C307/5.   [55] A5-0358/2001 final, 17 October 2001.
[56] A5-0207/2002, 17 April 2002.
[57] In May 2002, the Commission issued a call for tenders for a study on the use of equality and diversity considerations in public procurement. The purpose of the study was to 'examine the extent of the use of social considerations relating to equality and non-discrimination, evaluate their effectiveness at reaching their intended objectives and highlight those seen to be both most effective and most transferable among public authorities across the Union. The intention is that . . . the report will be made available to decision-makers in contracting authorities as a source of inspiration for their activities.'

IV. Emergence of Reformed Procurement Legislation, 2000–03

Commission proposal on procurement legislation

On 11 July 2000, the Commission submitted to the Council its proposals for the amalgamations and reform of the three 'public sector' directives regarding works, supplies, and services,[58] and a separate proposal regarding utilities.[59] The following discussion concentrates on the issue in the context of the former proposal.[60] As regards the Public Sector Directive, there were several provisions that were of significance so far as social criteria are concerned, in addition to the proposal to lower the thresholds generally, thus including contracts that used linkage which were below the original thresholds. First, in Article 2, in addition to the general prohibition of discrimination, a new provision was inserted which provided that: 'Contracting authorities shall take all necessary steps to ensure compliance with the principles of equality of treatment, transparency and non-discrimination.' This was in accordance with the established case law of the ECJ. The general principle of equality of treatment, of which the prohibition of discrimination on grounds of nationality was no more than a specific expression, was one of the fundamental principles of Community law. Under this principle, analogous situations must not be treated in different ways unless the difference in treatment was justified by objective reasons.

Second, a new article (Article 23) was included as an introduction to the chapter on specifications and contract documents. Paragraph 1 provided that, for each contract, the contracting authorities should draw up a set of specifications which clarified and supplemented the information contained in the contract notices. Paragraph 2 specified that the contracting authorities could require information on the subject of subcontracting (dealt with further in Article 26) or stipulate conditions concerning obligations relating to employment protection provisions and working conditions (dealt with further in Article 27). Finally, paragraph 3 provided explicitly, following the approach adopted in the *Beentjes* case, that contracting authorities could also impose particular conditions concerning the performance of the contract. These conditions must be compatible with the applicable Community law. Recital (22) specified: 'Contract performance conditions are compatible with the Directive provided that they are not directly or indirectly discriminatory with regard to tenderers from other Member States, and provided that they are indicated in the contract notice. They may in particular be intended to favour employment of excluded or disadvantaged people or to fight against unemployment.' In addition, a new general article was added, (Article 44), providing that contracts were to be awarded after the suitability of the economic

---

[58] COM(2000)275 final/2, [2001] OJ C29E/11.

[59] COM(2000)276 final/2, [2001] OJ C29 E/11.

[60] See, in general, S Arrowsmith, 'The European Commission's proposals for New Directives on Public and Utilities Procurement' (2000) 9 PPLR NA125.

operators had been checked. With a view to making such checks more transparent, additions were made, via paragraph 2, to the operative provisions of the directives to allow the contracting authorities to determine the level of capacity and experience required for a specific contract.

Third, as regards the selection of participants in the contract, Article 46 introduced a new obligation, under which contracting authorities were obliged to exclude from a call for tenders any tenderer which had been the subject of a final judgment for membership of a criminal organization, for corruption, or for fraud against the financial interest of the Community. This obligation strengthened the Community's arsenal of weapons available to combat these phenomena. Furthermore, the cases in which competitors could lawfully be eliminated from procurement competition were extended. It was proposed to allow the exclusion of any economic operator who had been sentenced, whether or not by final judgment, on grounds of certain types of fraud or of any other illegal activity. Similarly, the right to exclude participants for an offence concerning their professional conduct was extended to cases of non-final judgments.

Fourth, there were provisions strengthening the provisions relating to award criteria, in two respects. Article 53 repeated the previous alternative of awarding the contract on the basis of either the lowest price only, or the most economically advantageous tender for the contracting authorities. However, with regard to the latter, the article specified that in deciding what constituted the most economically advantageous tender, 'various criteria directly linked to the subject of the public contract in question', might be used: 'for example, quality, price, technical merit, aesthetic and functional characteristics, environmental characteristics, running costs, cost-effectiveness, after-sales service and technical assistance, delivery date and delivery period or period of completion'. The requirement that such criteria should be 'directly linked to the subject of the public contract in question', reiterated what the Commission considered the position to be under existing Community law.

In addition, there were other important provisions regarding award criteria. The provisions concerning award criteria in the existing directives had stipulated that these criteria must be listed in the contract notice or in the contract documents, 'where possible' in descending order of the importance attached to them by the contracting authority. The Commission proposed, in Article 53, to make it compulsory to state the relative weighting of each criterion at the contract notice stage or in the contract documents. This weighting could take different forms (in particular, it could be expressed as a percentage or in terms of relative share compared with another criterion) and, to ensure a certain flexibility, could be expressed as a range within which the value attributed to each criterion should be stated. An exemption provided that the relative weighting might be stated, at the latest, in the invitation to tender (for restricted and negotiated procedures) or in the invitation to participate in the dialogue (for negotiated procedures in the case of complex contracts). In other cases—open procedures—failure to state the relative weighting right at the start of the procedure could render the procedure unlawful.

Procurement and linkage in the Parliamentary process

The extent of the divergence of opinions on the concept of linking social issues with procurement was highlighted at the public hearing in January 2001, organized by the European Parliament's Internal Market Committee, at which the issue was one of the most contentious. On the one hand, UNICE argued that the aim of procurement should be seen as primarily economic, and this should lead to considerable caution in allowing linkage of any kind. This position was echoed to some extent by the Commission's Director General for public procurement, Alfonso Mattera, and the Federation of the European Construction Industry. On the other hand, the European Trade Union Federation (ETUC), and the European Disability Forum argued for much more extensive clarification in the directives that social and environmental criteria were permitted, and urged particularly that the provisions relating to award criteria should be amended to allow this. Both the Committee of the Regions and the Economic and Social Committee adopted reports, in the latter case after much contentious debate, that included opinions in favour of greater clarification than the Commission had hitherto been willing to see incorporated in the text of the directives.

On 13 December 2000, the Committee of the Regions (COR) issued its report.[61] The COR 'consider[ed] that the Commission's plans to address a number of important topics including environmental and social considerations in procurement in non-binding interpretative documents are not appropriate and wishe[d] to see these important topics properly addressed in the directives'.[62] It 'regard[ed] it as most important that the contracting entities should be able to require suppliers to comply with national social sector regulations in the Member State concerned. A contracting entity should not have to accept suppliers which, for instance, violate rules on job protection, the working environment, minimum pay or child labour.'[63] It 'fe[lt] that it is essential for the principles established in case law to be spelt out clearly in the directive'.[64] The COR objected to the Commission proposal 'that the criteria for awarding contracts, where it is not just a matter of the lowest price, should be directly linked with the nature of the contract'.[65] The Commission's provisions dealing with contract conditions were 'restrictive in relation to the case law which it is intended to codify, since it introduces a requirement for the condition to be related to the performance of the contract'.[66] The:

... wording which provides the possibility of imposing special conditions on performance of the contract should not prejudice the contracting authorities' right to decide themselves on what shall be procured; for example, this applies to the possibility of imposing environmental requirements on production processes, and to social requirements which must of

---

[61] [2001] OJ C144/23, COR Opinion.   [62] ibid para 1.7.   [63] ibid para 2.5.4.
[64] ibid para 2.5.4.   [65] ibid para 2.6.1.   [66] ibid para 2.7.1.

course be nondiscriminatory so that the requirement can be met by suppliers of all Member States.[67]

The Economic and Social Committee reported, separately, on the public sector proposal[68] and on the utilities proposal[69] on 26 April 2001. There were a higher number of dissenters than usual for ESC Opinions and several amendments were narrowly rejected at the plenary. The report on the public sector proposal considered that it was 'legitimate for contracting authorities to take social and environmental aspects into account when assessing the quality of tenders, provided that the principle of equal treatment is respected and the current national and European social and environmental legislation is complied with'.[70] The Directive 'should state that ILO Convention 94 (Labour Clauses—Public Contracts) must be complied with'.[71] The 'absence of any social aspects among the criteria for awarding a contract' was 'remarkable'.[72] The Committee:

... recommend[ed] that the future Commission interpretative Communications dealing with environmental and social aspects are transformed into guidelines for Member States, containing the details on how these aspects could be implemented. In addition, the Commission is now working on a Green Public Procurement Handbook in order to guide public authorities on taking into account environmental characteristics when awarding a contract. The ESC recommends the drafting of a Social Procurement Handbook with a view to guiding public authorities in this field also.[73]

'There must ... be some binding provision in the directive giving ... material protection for the established rights of workers in the EU'.[74] The text of the Directive should specify 'that a tenderer could also be excluded if a serious infringement of social or environmental laws has been established. This is already possible under the current Directives but it will be reinforced and clarified by a specific mention in the text of the future Directive.'[75]

The key institutions in the legislative process (the Parliament and the Council) were very slow indeed in reaching agreement on their positions, no doubt because of the considerable complexity and sensitivity of the issues. The Parliament in particular found the issues involved to be of considerable political sensitivity and was unable to conclude its first reading until January 2002. The rapporteur for the Parliament was Stephano Zappala (European People's Party—ED, Italy). In the absence of the Parliament's opinion, the Council of Ministers had considerable difficulty in reaching its common position. High among the most contentious issues for both of these institutions was the role of social and environmental linkage. Both bodies hoped that the Commission's promised interpretative communications would help to move the debate on.

---

[67] ibid para 2.7.2.   [68] [2001] OJ C193/7; Social aspects: see para 2.6.
[69] [2001] OJ C193/1: Social aspects: see para 2.5.
[70] [2001] OJ C193/7; Social aspects: see para 2.3.   [71] ibid para 2.3.
[72] ibid para 2.6.   [73] ibid.   [74] ibid para 4.9.   [75] ibid para. 4.9.3.

Commission's Interpretative Communication

The Commission had been preparing Interpretative Communications on the possibilities for integrating environmental and social considerations into public procurement under existing Community law for some time, but the timetable had had to be altered to take into account the need to consider fully how best to integrate the Court's decision in *Commission v France* (the *Nord-Pas-de-Calais* case, discussed in chapter 12 above). The Communication on the environment was not published until 4 July 2001.[76] The separate Communication on social aspects was not published until 15 October 2001,[77] before the Parliament was due to give its first reading to the legislative proposals. The aim of the Communication was 'to clarify the range of possibilities under the existing Community legal framework for integrating social considerations into public procurement... It seeks in particular to provide a dynamic and positive interaction between economic, social and employment policies, which mutually reinforce one another.'[78]

The Communication placed greatest weight on the use of contract conditions as a means of pursuing social objectives through procurement. It was 'especially during the execution of the contract, that is, once the contract has been awarded, that public procurement can be used by contracting authorities as a means of encouraging the pursuit of social objectives'.[79] These must comply with EC law, particularly in terms of transparency and non-discrimination. Contracting authorities could require the successful tenderer to comply with contractual clauses relating to the manner in which the contract is to be performed, which may go beyond what existing national legislation required generally. Such clauses might include requirements to recruit unemployed or disabled people, set up training programmes, and devise measures to promote gender or ethnic equality, and comply with core ILO requirements. Beyond that, the Communication noted:

> ...that all relevant national rules in force in the social field, including those implementing relevant Community rules in the field, are binding on contracting authorities, insofar as they are compatible with Community law. Such rules include, in particular, provisions on workers' rights and on working conditions. Non-compliance by tenderers with certain social obligations may in some cases lead to their exclusion. It is for Member States to determine in which cases this should arise.[80]

The Communication made the important point that the existing directives 'also offer various possibilities for taking account of social considerations that relate to the products or services required, in particular when drawing up the technical specifications and selection criteria'.[81] Public purchasers were also free to pursue

---

[76] 4 July 2001, COM(2001)0274.

[77] Interpretative Communication of the Commission on the Community Law Applicable to Public Procurement and the Possibilities for Integrating Social Considerations into Public Procurement, 15 October 2001, COM(2001)566 final.   [78] ibid 3.

[79] ibid.   [80] ibid.   [81] ibid.

social objectives in respect of public procurement contracts not covered by the public procurement directives, within the limits laid down by the general rules and principles of the EC Treaty. 'It is for Member States to determine whether contracting authorities may, or must, pursue such objectives in their public procurement.'[82]

Emergence of Parliament's approach

If the purpose of the Communication was to dampen down the social argument, it was unsuccessful. Parliamentary Committees took up the Commission's proposals, reporting separately on the Public Sector Directive proposals in October 2001.[83] On 17 January 2002, the Parliament delivered its Opinion at first reading on both proposals, broadly approving the Commission proposal, subject to 103 amendments, by 370 to 82 with 26 abstentions.[84] Among these amendments were several that related to the use of social criteria. These amendments were the result of intensive discussions between the three main political groups in the Parliament, the European People's Party, the Socialists, and the Liberals.

The amendments sought to clarify that the Directive was subject to the overriding exceptions in the Treaty 'for measures necessary to protect public morality, public policy, public security or human, animal or plant life or health', to require public authorities to reject tenderers found to be in breach of employment protection provisions, to permit Member States to reserve certain contracts for sheltered employment schemes or sheltered workshops, and to require contractors to respect employment protection obligations, working conditions, and labour law obligations. Two amendments are particularly noteworthy. The first related to the scope of the provisions dealing with abnormally low tenders to include employment standards. The Parliament added to the list of explanations which had to be taken into account by the contracting authority in order to determine whether a tender was abnormally low. These additional issues concerned the fulfilment of obligations relating to health and safety at work and working conditions by the tenderer and subcontractors in performance of the contract, including, in the case of supply of products and services originating from third countries, compliance during production with international standards. A second set of amendments,

---

[82] ibid.

[83] 29 October 2001, A5-0378/2001; Social aspects: Committee. on Legal Affairs and Internal Market, amendments 11, 12, 15, 49, 50, 52, 53, 82, 86, 96, 98, 100, 116; explanatory statement at 3; Committee on the Environment, Public Health and Consumer Policy, amendments 3, 5; Committee on Economic and Monetary Policy, amendments 11, 12, 13, 25; Committee on Employment, and Social Affairs, amendments 1, 3, 5, 6, 10, 12, 20, 24, 25, 30, 33, 34, 39, 41; Committee on Industry, External Trade, Research and Energy, amendments 1, 5, 9, 13, 16, 17, 36, 41, 42, 48, 51.

[84] Public sector proposal: 17 January 2002; PE-T5(2002)0010 [2002] OJ C271E/62. Only adopted text with amendments highlighted is available, no listing of amendments. Amendments regarding social aspects are identified in COM (2002) 236 final. Utilities proposal: 17 January 2002, PE-T5(2002)0011, [2002] OJ C271E/293. Only adopted text with amendments highlighted available, no listing of amendments. Amendments regarding social aspects are identified in COM (2002) 235 final.

even more contentious from the Commission's point of view, related to the provision on award criteria. These omitted the need, in the context of the 'most economically advantageous' tender, for economic advantage to be benefiting the public authority only, extended the environmental characteristics that contracting bodies could have regard to, and included the tenderer's equal opportunities policy as a valid element at the award stage. During the debate in the Parliament, the EC Internal Market Commissioner, Frits Bolkenstein, indicated that he could not accept the amendments on social and environmental criteria as they were disproportionate.

Commission's amended proposal

In early May 2002, the Commission issued its amended proposal on both the public sector[85] and utilities directives,[86] commenting on the amendments made by the Parliament. Of the 103 amendments proposed by the Parliament, the Commission felt able to accept 63 in full or in part. The rest were rejected. As regards the issue of linkage, the strategy adopted by the Commission was to attempt to meet the Parliament's concerns by including revised recitals as far as possible, rather than issuing new substantive articles or amending existing substantive provisions.

In many cases, the revised recitals drew on the language of the Interpretative Communication. For example, the Commission included new or amended recitals on the role of the Treaty exceptions, on the relevance of the Posted Workers Directive, and on the need to comply with the social legislation of the place where the contractor is operating. The principal tactic, however, was not only to adopt more recitals, but also to play up the extent to which social issues could be dealt with through the use of contract conditions, rather than by way of award criteria. A new recital was included, in which the Commission accepted that contract conditions could be included

. . . promoting on-the-job training and the employment of people who are facing particular difficulties in finding work, at combating unemployment or at protecting the environment, and may give rise to obligations—applicable to contract performance—to, in particular, recruit the long-term unemployed or implement training schemes for the unemployed and young persons, or to comply with the substance of the provisions of the ILO core conventions, in the event that these have not been implemented in national law, to recruit a number of handicapped persons above that required under national legislation.

---

[85] 6 May 2002, COM(2002)236 final. Social aspects (in order of appearance): Commission accepts: amendment 141 (p 4), accepts with partial or substantial reformulation: amendment 127 (p 17); amendments 11 and 51 (p 17); amendments 15 and 100 (p 18); amendment 170 (p 19); amendments 93 and 95 (p 24); amendments 86, 87, 89 (p 39); amendment 110 (p 42), rejects: amendment 49 (p 46); amendment 82 (p 49); amendment 92 (p 50).

[86] 6 May 2002, COM(2002)235 final. Social aspects: Commission accepts: amendment 111 (p 3); accepts with partial or substantial reformulation: amendments 4, 33 (p 4); amendments 90, 70 (p 5); amendments 43, 47 (p 16); amendment 56 (p 31); rejects: amendment 32 (p 40); amendment 55 (p 45).

In addition, for the first time, a new article was included dealing with contract conditions: 'Contracting authorities may impose particular conditions concerning performance of the contract, provided that those conditions are compatible with Community law and provided that they are stated in the contract notice or in the contract documents. Contract performance conditions may relate in particular to social and environmental considerations.' As regards the amendment on abnormally low tenders, the Commission broadly accepted the spirit of the amendment, introducing changes into its original article dealing with the issue, although dropping the reference to ILO standards. Finally, a new article was introduced to address the issue of contracts for sheltered workshops employing disabled workers.

As regards the proposals to amend the award criteria, however, the Commission stood firm. In its view, the removal of the words 'for the contracting authorities' would enable various, often non-measurable, elements to be taken into account in relation to a possible benefit to 'society' in the broad sense of the word:

Such award criteria would no longer fulfil their function, which is to permit an evaluation of the intrinsic qualities of tenders in order to determine which one offers the purchaser the best value for money. This would completely disrupt the objective of the public contracts Directives and would amount to the institutionalisation of this legislation to the benefit of sectoral policies, while also introducing serious risks of inequality of treatment.

As regards the inclusion of references to production processes,

. . . the contract award stage is not the appropriate time at which to choose a less polluting method. Less polluting production methods can be prescribed once the subject of the contract has been defined in the technical specifications when the purchaser chooses to purchase the solution causing the least pollution. If he wishes to compare different solutions and evaluate the advantages/cost of lower- or higher-pollution solutions, he may allow or insist on the presentation of variants.

Finally, the inclusion of a reference to 'equal opportunity policies' was dismissed as confused:

. . . the concept of equality of treatment takes on a particular meaning in the context of public contracts (= treating all candidates/tenders in the same way), whereas the amendment seems to be concerned with the non-discrimination within the meaning of Article 13 of the Treaty. To the extent that this concerns a criterion relating to the policy of the enterprise and not to the qualities of a tender, it cannot be an award criterion. The introduction of criteria linked to the undertaking would lead to a situation where certain undertakings were given preference on the basis of non-measurable elements during the award phase, even if their tenders did not give the purchaser the best value for money.

The issue of award criteria was highlighted in the second major ECJ intervention in the *Concordia Bus* case (discussed in chapter 12 above), which the Court decided on 17 September 2002. The implications of the case were highly significant in several respects. First, the Commission, as we have seen, had traditionally argued for an interpretation of 'most economically advantageous' as requiring each award criterion to have a link to the subject matter of the contract, *and* to constitute an economic advantage directly benefiting the public authority. The Court upheld only the first of these, and directly rejected the second with the consequence of public authorities 'potentially referring to benefits that accrue not only directly to the public authority but also to a larger portion of society'.[87] Yet, second, the legislative reform package that the Commission had proposed reflected the Commission's traditional approach; the Commission's proposals were now more restrictive than that of the Court in requiring that the tender must be most advantageous 'for the contracting authority'. How would the Commission react? Third, the requirement of linkage might well be more problematic for social and human rights award criteria to satisfy than for environmental criteria, 'as with the latter the link to the subject matter of the product/service appears to be more tenuous'.[88] Would the broad coalition of environmental and social activists continue to adopt a common position?

Position of the Council

On 21 May 2002, the Council reached a political agreement on the Public Sector Directive.[89] It essentially maintained the Commission's basic approach, whilst integrating several of the amendments adopted by the Parliament in some form or other. A notable feature of the approach adopted by the Council was again the addition or clarification of recitals as a way of accommodating the Parliament's concerns, without amending the substantive Articles. New or amended recitals were added on the possibility for Member States to take measures according to the Treaty, on performance conditions being compatible with the Posted Workers Directive and the need to comply with national social legislation on qualification criteria. Amendments were made to the substantive articles on issues such as abnormally low tenders, and contracts for sheltered workshops.

On the issue of award criteria, the Council attempted to broker a deal between the Commission and the Parliament. On the one hand, the amendment it proposed on the substance of the relevant article largely supported the Commission's position (although with the important variations in italics):

... when award is made to the tender most economically advantageous *for the contracting authorities*, various criteria *justified* by the subject of the public contract in question: for example, quality, price, technical merit. Aesthetic and functional characteristics, environmental characteristics, running costs, cost-effectiveness, after-sales service and technical assistance, delivery date and delivery period or period of completion.

---

[87] P Charro, Case Note (2003) 40 CMLR 179, 185.   [88] ibid 187.

[89] Doc 9270/02. On 30 September 2002, the Council had reached a political agreement on a common position on the utilities proposals Doc 12204/02. However, the Council's Common Position was not published until 20 March 2003. [2003] OJ C147/ 001E.

On the other hand, the Council adopted an extensive amendment to the recitals, expanding on what was permissible at the award stage:

... Where the contracting authorities choose to award a contract to the most economically advantageous tender, they shall assess the tenders in order to determine which one offers the best value for money. In order to do this, they shall determine the economic and quality criteria which, taken as a whole, must make it possible to determine the most economically advantageous tender for the contracting authority. The determination of these criteria depends on the object of the contract since they must allow the level of performance offered by each tender to be assessed in the light of the object of the contract, as defined in the technical specifications, and the value for money of each tender to be measured.

In order to guarantee equal treatment, the criteria for the award of the contract should enable tenders to be compared and assessed objectively. If these conditions are fulfilled, economic and qualitative criteria for the award of the contract, such as meeting the needs of the public concerned, as expressed in the specification of the contract. Under the same conditions, a contracting authority may use criteria aiming to meet social requirements, in response in particular to the needs—defined in the specifications of the contract—of particularly disadvantaged groups of people to which those receiving/using the works, supplies or services which are the object of the contract belong.

Emerging compromise and the final deal

The Commission's assessment of the Council's Common Position was published in March 2003.[90] The Commission considered that the text of the Common Position was broadly in line with what the Commission had initially proposed and in line with the thrust of the European Parliament's amendments.

The Parliamentary Committee on Legal Affairs and the Internal Market adopted a report amending the Common Position under the Second Reading of the co-decision procedure.[91] It retabled a large number of amendments adopted by the Parliament at the First Reading. On 2 July 2003, the Parliament adopted a legislative resolution, under the Second Reading of the co-decision procedure, amending the common position, and taking up some of the Committee's amendments, although many of the amendments recommended by the Legal Affairs Committee were not accepted.[92] According to *European Report*:

There were three main reasons why the over 100 amendments from the Legal Affairs Committee did not pass in the plenary. Firstly, as this was a second reading phase, each amendment needed to get the support of an absolute majority of the House, i.e. at least 314 MEPs in order to be adopted. Secondly, the two main groups, EPP-ED, and Socialists, were unable to agree many compromise amendments so they both ended up tabling their own versions, neither of which had enough support to pass. Thirdly, the vote followed the long and tumultuous debate with Italian Prime Minister, Silvio Berlusconi, who was

---

[90] SEC(2003)0366, 25 March 2003.   [91] A5-0242/2003, PE332.524, 17 June 2003.
[92] T5-0312/2003, 2 July 2003.

presenting his priorities as EU Council President, and many of the MEPs did not stay for it. The result was good news for the Liberal Group, which had been arguing for minimal changes to the Council common position.[93]

Additional provisions were, however, introduced requiring a contracting authority to take into account accessibility criteria for people with disabilities when laying down technical specifications. But, the main issue related, yet again, to award criteria. Article 53, was substantially amended to provide:

(a) when award is made to the tender most economically advantageous . . . various criteria *linked to* the subject of the public contract in question: for example, quality, price, technical merit, aesthetic and functional characteristics, environmental characteristics, *including those relating to production methods*, running costs, cost-effectiveness, after-sales service and technical assistance, delivery date and delivery period or period of completion, *the tenderer's policy in relation to people with disabilities, its equal treatment policy* . . .[94]

The directives could only be adopted without further negotiations between the Commission, the Council and the Parliament, if the Council had accepted all the amendments tabled by the Parliament. However, the Council did not do so, and the conciliation process was initiated as a result. The Council working group, and the Committee of Member State's Permanent Representatives (COREPER) met to discuss the amendments before the summer break. The first informal 'trilogue' meeting of Parliament, Council, and Commission was held on 2 September 2003. The power of the Parliament at this stage was considerable. Any compromise agreed on in conciliation must be agreed to by a majority of the votes cast in Parliament. 'This procedure makes it easier for the Directives to be thrown out than in the second Reading stage where an "absolute majority" (314 votes) is needed.'[95] During conciliation, the Council argued that the Parliament's amendment could make the awarding of contracts too arbitrary, but both sides agreed that the issue should be clarified in the recitals rather than in the text of the provision on award criteria. This led to a deal, and subsequent final approval by a plenary vote of the Parliament on 29 January 2004.

[93] European Report, 5 July 2003, No 2790, Public Procurement: Parliament Moves Closer to Council Position on Legislative Package.   [94] Emphasis added.
   [95] ibid.

PART IV

INTERPRETATION

15

Interpreting the Government Procurement Agreement

Part IV of this book moves from the analysis of the interaction of domestic procurement linkages with the development of international and European procurement regulation, undertaken in Parts II and III, to consider how far domestic procurement linkages are compatible with existing European and Government Procurement Agreement (GPA) disciplines. We move from an analysis of the *development* of the current international and European provisions to their *interpretation*. In this chapter the relationship between procurement linkages and the interpretation of the existing GPA is considered. If a state subject to GPA disciplines takes action on status equality using procurement linkages, World Trade Organization (WTO) adjudicatory institutions may be called on to determine whether these actions are in compliance with trade disciplines. The issue will be the appropriate amount of legal space that states will be given to pursue such goals.[1]

We have seen that a somewhat similar issue arose in the case in the late 1990s between Europe and the United States concerning the Massachusetts procurement policies on Myanmar-Burma. As seen in chapter 9 above, the success of the constitutional challenge meant that the EC and Japan considered that they did not need to pursue their WTO challenge.

Whilst that is the most high profile example to date of a possible conflict between the GPA and procurement linkages, because it embroiled the GPA in the debate about the appropriateness of international 'sanctions', the GPA may also come into conflict with measures that are thought by those adopting them to be purely domestic. We have seen in the EC context, indeed, that domestic procurement linkages have been the type of measures most likely to be adjudicated on in Community law. We need to consider, therefore, not only the apparent conflict between the GPA 1994 and the use of procurement for achieving such social and human rights policies extraterritorially, but also domestically. We have seen a

---

[1] See in general S Arrowsmith, *Government Procurement in the WTO* (Kluwer Law International, 2002) especially ch 13; J-C Gaedtke, *Politische Auftragsvergabe und Welthandelsrecht* (Duncker und Humblot, 2006).

specific example in chapter 11 above of where this issue was raised, namely in the context of the German ban on contracting with companies that did not renounce Scientology.[2]

I. Interpreting the GPA: Some Basic Points

The inevitably compromised, often ambiguous, usually open-ended provisions of the GPA that we saw being negotiated in chapter 8 above, provide plenty of opportunity for debate over whether they enable linkage to continue, or whether they prohibit linkage completely. Some have argued that we should approach the interpretation of these provisions with a pro- or anti-linkage bias. On the one hand there is the argument that the GPA should be interpreted in such a way as to permit national social policies to operate largely unchallenged. An equivalent issue arises in the WTO with regard to other 'trade and . . .' issues. For Robert Howse and Brian Langille, the best solution is for WTO law generally to be interpreted to allow 'appropriate forebearance for trade action taken outside of the WTO itself, individually or collectively, by WTO Members'. They consider that 'there is a sound legal basis . . . that the first aim in a rational approach . . . is for the WTO to get out of the way (*by getting its jurisprudence right*)'.[3] On the other hand there is the argument that those who defend the lawfulness of such measures under the GPA 1994 are in effect arguing that countries which could have negotiated specific exceptions in their Annexes (which they would have been required to have 'paid' for with other concessions) now seek by an interpretation of the Agreement to achieve an additional advantage, without having to 'pay' for it.[4] As Frieder Rossler has argued:

From the perspective of WTO law, the issue is thus not whether domestic policy constraints should be taken into account or whether trade liberalisation entails a healthy competition or a destructive race to the bottom. Given the right of each member to adjust its market-access commitments to its perception of these issues, the real issue is whether WTO members should be able to react to the external repercussions of their own domestic policy choices by unilaterally withdrawing their market-access commitments or whether they should be able to do so only by renegotiating their commitments.[5]

Howse argues, however, that while 'such rules can be understood functionally . . . they have, nevertheless, the formal structure of general juridical norms, and therefore

---

[2] H-J Priess and C Pitschas, 'Secondary Policy Criteria and their Compatibility with EC and WTO Procurement Law' (2000) 9 PPLR 171.

[3] R Howse and B Langille, with J Burda, 'The World Trade Organization and Labour Rights: Man Bites Dog' in VA Leary and D Warner (eds), *Social Issues, Globalisation and International Institutions: Labour Rights and the EU, ILO, OECD and WTO* (Martinus Nijhoff, 2006) 157, 198 (emphasis added).

[4] In its complaint to the US, the EU called the Massachusetts legislation a 'de facto reduction of the US sub-central offer', see ch 9 above.

[5] F Roessler, 'Domestic Policy Objectives and the Multilateral Trade Order: Lessons from the Past' in AO Krueger (ed), *The WTO as an International Organisation* (1998) 213.

their validation, including through interpretation by judicial or quasi-judicial tribunals, inevitably raises the question of justice . . . The judge is inevitably concerned with justice, and seeks an interpretation that can be seen as fair *inter partes.*'[6] Interpretation of the GPA will, therefore, have to tread a fine line between the Scylla of allowing states to escape from their legal committments, and the Charybdis of imposing constraints on states that are unjust or unfair. Clearly, in resolving this tension, we should at least initially concentrate closely on the text of the GPA. The importance of the text is also emphasized not least because it reflects the approach adopted by the Appellate Body.[7] Nevertheless, in addition, where it appears to be relevant, reference is made to the negotiating history discussed in earlier chapters.[8]

Close attention to the text is also justified because it serves to counter the interpretation of the GPA based on *assumptions* as to what the GPA *should* prohibit, or an interpretation of the GPA that assumes that the approach taken in the interpretation of the basic General Agreement on Tariffs and Trade (GATT) should simply be applied to the GPA, without careful consideration.[9] Assuming that GATT and the GPA serve essentially the same purposes and should be interpreted in much the same way is questionable.[10] On some key issues, the textual language of the GPA 1994 differs from GATT in ways that appear to affect how procurement linkages should be addressed. This is not surprising. GATT can be seen as wanting to further consumer sovereignty by limiting the ability of government to impose tariff and non-tariff barriers which would prevent consumers from being able to exercise choice. In procurement, on the other hand, the 'consumer' is the government entity itself. There are significant differences between the individual consumer and the government as consumer.[11] The government procurement decision will ordinarily take into account a greater range of values, including ethical values, than the individual consumer is likely to. Public purchasers rely on highly structured and formalized processes to determine their choices. However, in the context of this discussion, the essential point to bear in mind is that GATT might be seen as trying to protect the consumer from government. Interpreting the GPA 1994 widely in order to protect the consumer (government) from the consequences of

---

[6] R Howse, 'Human Rights in the WTO: Whose Rights, What Humanity? Comment on Petersmann' (2002) 13 EJIL 651, 654.

[7] Appellate Body Report, 'United States—Standards for Reformulated and Conventional Gasoline', WT/DS2/AB/R, adopted 20 May 1996 (*Gasoline* case) IIIB (criticism of the Panel Report for its failure 'to take adequate account of the words actually used . . . ').

[8] In Appellate Body Report, 'European Communities—Conditions for the Granting of Tariff Prefences to Developing Countries', WT/DS246/AB/R, adopted 20 April 2004 (the *GSP* case), the Appellate Body referred to such preparatory work in its interpretation of the Enabling Clause.

[9] Such as the legality under customary international law of the extraterritorial assertion of jurisdiction, see RL Muse, 'A Public International Law Critique of the Extraterritorial Jurisdiction of the Helms-Burton Act (Cuban Liberty and Democratic Solidarity (Libertad) Act of 1996)' (1996–97) 30 GW JILE 207.

[10] Some significance should be attached to the fact that procurement was not dealt with simply by removing the limitation in Art III(8) of GATT.

[11] See, in general, OECD, 'Greener Public Purchasing: Issues and Practical Solutions' (OECD, 2000) 37–8.

its own preferences smacks of paternalism. Nor should the GPA 1994 be interpreted widely in order to resolve the all-too-common state versus federal, or local versus national disputes to which procurement gives rise. That is properly a task for national law.[12]

On the other hand, the disputes panels and the Appellate Body that will be called on to adjudicate on disputes under the plurilateral GPA are the same as those called on to adjudicate the multilateral WTO agreements. There are two important legal contexts, therefore, in which the discussion of the relationship between the Government Procurement Agreement and linkage must be set. The first is the context of increasing discussion within the WTO and in decisions of panels and the Appellate Body regarding the relationship between GATT requirements and domestic environmental measures. This has been seen as the closest analogy to the interpretation that might be accorded domestic social measures under WTO law, although it is also recognized that there are important differences between social issues and environmental issues that may justify a different approach to some extent.

The second legal context considers the issues that arise under the GPA as having potential implications for other WTO agreements. The Appellate Body in particular is likely to be cautious in treating the GPA as entirely *sui generis*. Approaches designed to link trade to the observance of equality may fall foul of several different sets of WTO rules. For example, some regulatory measures may have the effect of making it more difficult for market penetration to take place.[13] At the moment, this threat is more theoretical than immediate, but with the increasing number of complaints to the WTO, and the greater extent to which internal regulatory measures are being challenged, it is not at all unreasonable to expect that, in time, challenges to national equality laws may increase. More clearly, WTO rules may stop national governments using trade measures in order to enforce domestic social preferences transnationally.[14] In other words, given that the disputes panels and the Appellate Body have broader responsibilities for interpretation than simply under the GPA, we must expect them to take these into account in the interpretation of the GPA. One should not underestimate the importance to the legal mind of legal coherence and consistency leading to an approach in which fragmentation is to be avoided.[15]

Human rights treaties and the GPA

It has been seen at different points througout the book that procurement linkages have been included in international agreements (ILO Convention No 98), and

---

[12] This was, of course, the issue before the US federal courts in the *Crosby* case, see ch 9 above.

[13] In particular, they may violate GATT, Agreement on Technical Barriers to Trade (1994) <http://www.wto.org/wto/legal/finalact.htm>.

[14] See MJ Trebilcock and R Howse, *The Regulation of International Trade* (3rd edn, Routledge, 2004) passim.

[15] Introduction, in T Cottier, J Pauwelyn, and E Bürgi (eds), *Human Rights and International Trade* (OUP, 2005) 3.

have been recommended by treaty supervision bodies (the ILO and CERD). Apart from the possible effect that this has in the interpretation of the GPA provisions (for example in influencing the application of concepts such as 'necessity'), do these treaties and recommendations have any other effect on WTO law? Joost Pauwelyn has explored the argument that, under certain circumstances, WTO panels may be able to apply human rights law directly, in order to limit the potentially adverse effect of WTO agreements on human rights over and above the provisions of the agreements themselves.[16] The problem is, however, that the ILO Convention in issue pre-dates the WTO agreements, and the recommendations made by the treaty monitoring bodies are so scattered and unspecific. Until there is a more specific basis for applying this approach in the context of the GPA, the argument can be left to one side.

Basic structure of GATT

Given the importance of the legal contexts outlined above, a basic understanding of the structure of the GATT agreement is necessary at this stage. It is useful to see GATT obligations as involving a two-stage approach. First, GATT may or may not impose a prima facie obligation to uphold free trade. In relation to this issue, GATT contains four key provisions: Articles I, II, III, and XI. Articles I and III impose obligations, respectively, of most favoured nation (MFN) treatment and national treatment in internal matters. This amounts to a general prohibition of discrimination, which is, however, subject to any tariffs up to the limits determined by individual country-by-country schedules incorporated via Article II of GATT. Article XI prohibits quantitative restrictions, ie quotas. Articles I and III depend crucially on the concept of a 'like product'. It is seen as discrimination to treat products from one country differently from 'like products' from another country. This is a difficult issue: are products 'like products' despite the fact that one was produced in a labour rights-friendly way and the other by means of the most egregious breaches of fundamental labour rights? This debate relates to a more general debate over the distinction between the product itself and the process by which the product is formed: GATT orthodoxy is that processes and production methods (PPMs) cannot be taken into account in determining what constitutes a 'like product'. Second, even if there is a breach of the prima facie obligation, GATT may allow an exception from the prima facie obligations which it imposes. In relation to the exceptions allowed under GATT from a WTO member's prima facie obligations, the most important exceptions for our purposes are in Articles XX(a), XX(b), and XX(e). These relate, *inter alia*, to measures necessary for the protection of public morals, measures necessary for the protection of human life and health, and measures relating to the products of prison labour.

---

[16] J Pauwelyn, 'Human Rights in Dispute Settlement', in T Cottier, J Pauwelyn, and E Bürgi (eds) (n 15 above) 204.

The statute of the GPA can usefully be considered as taking a similar approach. In the next section, we consider the prima facie obligations of GPA members. In the section following, we consider exceptions to these prima facie obligations.

II. Prima Facie GPA Obligations

Meaning of discrimination

Article III of the GPA provides two different types of protection that, taken together, we can refer to as the protection against 'discrimination'. First, each party is required to provide 'treatment no less favourable' to the products, services, and suppliers of other parties, than 'that accorded to *domestic* products, services and suppliers'. This is referred to as the 'national treatment' requirement. Second, each party is required to provide 'treatment no less favourable' to the 'products, services and suppliers' of other Parties, than 'that accorded to products, services and suppliers of *any other Party*'. This is referred to as the MFN requirement. More specifically, each party must ensure that its procuring entities 'shall not treat a locally-established supplier less favourably than another locally-established supplier on the basis of degree of foreign affiliation or ownership' and 'shall not discriminate against locally-established suppliers on the basis of the country of production of the good or service being supplied', where the country of production is a party to the Agreement.

The meaning of 'discrimination' in the GPA is likely to be significantly affected by the approach to the interpretation of this concept in general GATT law.[17] However, since the Appellate Body places great emphasis on a close reading of the text in its decisions, one has to be careful in using GATT case law to interpret the GPA in this respect. The most notable differences regarding the non-discrimination provisions of GATT and the GPA are the following:

(1) the GPA requires non-discrimination with regard not only to goods, but also to services and suppliers;

(2) the GPA on its face does not refer to the 'likeness' of goods, services and suppliers;

(3) the national treatment obligation and the MFN obligation have exactly the same scope under the GPA but not in GATT;

(4) the GPA national treatment obligation is not further differentiated as in Article III of GATT with regard to taxation and regulation;

(5) there is no provision in the GPA comparable to Article XI of GATT, which would limit the scope of the GPA's national treatment obligation and create the necessity of a delimitation provision like Note Ad Article III of GATT; and

---

[17] See eg EA Laing, 'Equal Access/Non-Discrimination and Legitimate Discrimination in International Economic Law' (1996) 14 Wisconsin International Law Journal 246.

(6) the GPA MFN clause is more limited than Article I:1 of GATT: the latter applies to advantages extended to *any* foreign product, while Article III of the GPA applies only to advantages extended to other GPA parties.[18]

It seems to be accepted by the Appellate Body that the meaning of discrimination now includes within its prohibition those measures which have the *effect* of discriminating against tenderers from other GPA countries, and not just those measures that are *intended* to do so.[19] As interpreted by the Appellate Body, the GATT non-discrimination provisions also quite clearly apply regardless of whether discrimination takes place *de jure* or *de facto*. This seems to be true, indeed, for all three GATT non-discrimination clauses, ie Articles I:1, III:2, and III:4.[20] One can expect this jurisprudence to apply in the case of the GPA as well. If this interpretation is correct, then a procurement linkage could fall foul of the prima facie obligation if it could be shown that its effect was proportionately greater on tenderers in another state that is a party to the GPA. If, for example, 'companies of certain GPA Members are, for instance for historical or geographical reasons, much more engaged in business in a human rights violating country than others (and consequently much more exposed to the possibility of using human rights violating production methods)'[21] then discrimination against that party may arise.

It is a matter of determining whether this is the case, empirically, on a case-by-case basis. Even if this were found to be the case, that is not the end of the enquiry. Neither formally unequal treatment nor any empirically demonstrable different effect will *suffice* to constitute a GATT violation. Articles I and III:2 require that *advantages* must be extended and that taxes on imports may not *exceed* domestic taxes. Articles III:4 of GATT actually prohibits not unequal treatment, but only less favourable treatment of foreign products. In other words, as the Appellate Body has pointed out in the *Korea-Beef* case, facially or factually discriminating treatment is not prohibited per se, as long as it is equally favourable (or even more favourable for the foreign products).[22] This holding was reaffirmed in the *Asbestos* case.[23] To

---

[18] This means that if country A, member of GATT and the GPA, grants import and procurement advantage to non-member country X, it has to extend the import advantage, but not the procurement advantage, to member country B.

[19] Appellate Body Report, 'European Communities—Regime for the Importation, Sale and Distribution of Bananas', WT/DS27/AB/R, adopted 25 September 1997 (Bananas case) Report of the Appellate Body, 9 September 1997.

[20] Concerning Art I, see Appellate Body Report, 'Canada—Certain Measures Affecting the Automotive Industry', WT/DS/139/R, adopted 19 June 2000, para 78; with regard to Art III(2), see Appellate Body Report, Japan—Taxes on Alcoholic Beverages, WT/DS8/AB/R, adopted 1 November 1996 (*Japan-Alcoholic Beverages II*) 27–8; with regard to Art III(4), see Appellate Body Report, 'Korea—Measures Affecting Imports of Fresh, Chilled and Frozen Beef', WT/BS161/AB/R, adopted 10 January 2001 (*Korea-Beef*) paras 137, 144.

[21] C Spennemann, 'The WTO Agreement on Government Procurement—A Means of Furtherance of Human Rights? (2001) Zeitschrift für Europarechtliche Studien 43, 55.

[22] *Korea-Beef* (n 20 above) paras 135, 136.

[23] Appellate Body Report, 'European Communities—Measures Affecting Asbestos and Asbestos-Containing Products, WT/DS135/AB/R, adopted 5 April 2001 (*Asbestos*). See also R Howse, 'The

determine whether differential treatment is equally favourable or less favourable than the treatment accorded to national products, the Appellate Body examines 'whether a measure modifies the *conditions of competition* in the relevant market to the detriment of imported products'.[24] Since the wording of Article III of the GPA parallels that in Article III:4 of GATT, the approach of the *Korea-Beef* Appellate Body should apply to the GPA as well. Under the 'conditions of competition' test, mere (possible) disparate impacts of selective purchasing legislation should be acceptable as long as the procurement linkages do not change the conditions of competition detrimentally against foreign suppliers or products. This test should save, for example, the Massachusetts Myanmar law even if it could be shown that more foreign than domestic suppliers are affected in practice.

Process-product distinction

Debate under GATT

An important distinction has evolved, as we have seen, in the interpretation of GATT between so-called *product*-related' requirements and *process*-related' requirements in the context of determining whether there has been discrimination. The first refers to requirements that specify what product is required, the latter refers to requirements as to how the product is to be produced. The product-process distinction has two functions in GATT jurisprudence. The first function concerns the applicability of Article III:4 of GATT in relation to Article XI of GATT under the Note Ad Article III. The second function concerns the interpretation of the expression 'like products' in Article III:4.

In its first function, the product-process distinction emerges from the fact that there are two provisions in GATT under which import restrictions can be reviewed. On the one hand, there is Article XI, banning all quantitative import restrictions. On the other hand, there is the much more flexible Article III:4, requiring equally favourable treatment for foreign and imported 'like' products. Read alone, Article XI has quite a sweeping scope and outlaws any measure in the form of an import prohibition. But the Note Ad Article III states that Article XI shall yield to Article III if the import restriction is only part of an overarching scheme that only happens to be enforced at the border in case of foreign products. Under this approach, import restrictions remain prima facie under the control of Article XI, but the defending country has the possibility to invoke the Note Ad Article III.[25] The product-process distinction as employed, for example, by the panel in *United*

Appellate Body Rulings in the Shrimp/Turtle Case: A New Legal Baseline for the Trade and Environment Debate' (2002) 27 Col J Env L 491, 515.

[24] *Korea-Beef* Appellate Body Report (n 20 above) para 137, emphasis in the original.

[25] R Howse and D Regan, 'The Product/Process Distinction—An Illusory Basis for Disciplining "Unilateralism" in Trade Policy' (2000) 11 EJIL 249, 256; this entails that the burden of proof is with the defending country.

States—Restrictions on Imports of Tuna,[26] holds now that this defence is not available to import bans conditional not upon the intrinsic characteristics of the product, but solely upon the way it was produced.[27]

In contemporary academic writing, there is considerable debate surrounding the scope and operation of the distinction, with strong supporters and equally strong opponents. It is regularly pointed out by the latter that this doctrine stands on very insecure ground, as it has weak textual foundation[28] and has been consciously applied in only four Panel reports before the founding of the WTO, three of which were not even adopted.[29] Since 1994, the Appellate Body has had no opportunity to judge this theory,[30] but its text-oriented approach is commonly taken as an indication that the distinction will have to be given up.[31] We shall examine subsequently the debate in the GPA context, but it is worth pointing out at this stage that applying *this* prong of the product-process distinction in GPA cases would have the exactly opposite effects to those in GATT cases. Under GATT, it leads to application of the strict Article XI prohibition; under the GPA, as there is no provision comparable to Article XI, it would lead to a carte blanche for discriminatory process-based distinctions among products.[32] Concerning services and suppliers, one cannot even begin to make a meaningful 'service-process' or 'supplier-process' distinction.

The second function of the product-process distinction in GATT[33] is to interpret the expression 'like products' as it appears in Articles I:1, III:2, and III:4 of GATT. In this respect, the gist of the doctrine is to hold that products sharing their intrinsic properties and characteristics are 'like' without regard to differences in the production process. This distinction is of particular importance in GATT in the context of environmental requirements. Indeed two of the most famous,

---

[26] GATT BISD (39th Supp) 155, 3 September 1991.

[27] R Hudec, 'The Product-Process Distinction in GATT/WTO Jurisprudence', in M Bronckers and R Quick (eds), *New Directions in International Economic Law: Essays in Honour of John H. Jackson* (Springer, 2000) 187, 191.

[28] Howse (n 23 above) at 493; Hudec (n 27 above) 198: The holding is 'just plain wrong'.

[29] S Charnovitz, 'The Law of Environmental "PPMs" in the WTO: Debunking the Myth of Illegality' (2002) 27 Yale JIL 59, 86–8. See, however, S Gaines, 'Processes and Production Methods: How to Produce Sound Policy for Environmental PPM-Based Trade Measures?' (2002) 27 Col J Env L 383, 417 for the argument that the product-process distinction is legally sound and has been implicitly accepted by the WTO member states.

[30] cf Howse and Regan (n 25 above) 251. Charnovitz (n 29 above) 88–92 gives a detailed account of panel decisions using the distinction under WTO auspices so far.

[31] See J Jackson, 'The Limits of International Trade: Workers' Protection, the Environment and Other Human Rights' (2000) 94 Virg JIL 222, 224.

[32] Prof Joel Trachtman, quoted in 'Symposium: New York Law School Centre for International Law: States Rights vs International Trade: The Massachusetts Law' (2000) 19 New York Law School Journal of International and Comparative Law 347, 359–60. A quite similar problem arises under GATT with regard to Art III:2—there is no GATT provision that provides strict scrutiny against financial measures applied at the border, thus a consequentially applied product-process distinction would leave process-based tax differences entirely without review, see Howse and Regan (n 25 above) 256.

[33] For a thorough review of the role of this aspect in the first *Tuna* case see Hudec (n 27 above) 197 *et seq.*

and controversial, panel decisions turn on this distinction. In the *Tuna/Dolphin I*[34] and *Tuna/Dolphin II*[35] cases, GATT panels held that United States bans on the import of tuna from countries permitting fishing with purse-seine nets was contrary to Article III of GATT, which prohibits discrimination between 'like products'. In deciding the cases, the panel in *Tuna/Dolphin I* held that in determining what were 'like products' only the characteristics of the product could be taken into account, and not different production processes or methods. If this approach is taken to the interpretation of the GPA, then state concerns about the processes by which goods were made, for example in Myanmar-Burma, seem illegitimate under WTO disciplines.

It has been argued strongly, however, that the process-product distinction is generally incoherent and indefensible.[36] In general, this aspect of the distinction is not better founded in the GATT text than the first aspect and therefore should be treated with equal caution. Furthermore, the judgment of the Appellate Body in the *Asbestos* case is widely seen as an important step away from the doctrine. In *Asbestos* the Appellate Body interpreted Article III:4 in the light of the objectives contained in Article III:1 and concluded that a judgment on 'likeness' of products is essentially a judgment on whether products are in a 'competitive relationship'.[37] Following the earlier *Border Tax Adjustments*[38] case, the Appellate Body accepted the panel's approach of using four criteria for making that determination. These criteria are: '(i) the properties, nature and quality of the products; (ii) the end-uses of the products; (iii) consumers' tastes and habits—more comprehensively termed consumers' perceptions and behaviour—in respect of the products; and (iv) the tariff classification of the products.'[39] However, the Appellate Body stressed that these criteria are merely exemplary; the overall goal of coming up with a judgment on competitive relationship is to be kept in mind.[40] Each factor that can be relevant has to be taken into account. The health risk of a product, for example, has to be addressed; this can even be done as part of the evaluation of the *Border Tax Adjustments* criteria.[41] In this respect, the Appellate Body took the findings of other specialist international organizations (in that case findings of the World Health Organization) into account.[42] Consumer tastes and habits may be highly relevant to the question of a competitive relationship.[43] The minimum that can probably be said after the *Asbestos* case is that further cases will have to rely on a close reading of the GATT text and cannot simply apply the product-process distinction as an accepted doctrine.

---

[34] 'United States—Restrictions on Imports of Tuna: Report of the Panel' (*Tuna Dolphin I*), DS21/R (1991).

[35] 'United States—Restrictions on Imports of Tuna: Report of the Panel' (*Tuna Dolphin II*), DS29/R (1994).   [36] Howse and Regan (n 25 above).

[37] *Asbestos* (n 23 above) para 99.

[38] Report of the Working Party on Border Tax Adjustments, BISD 185/97, para 18.

[39] *Asbestos* (n 23 above) para 101.   [40] ibid para 102.   [41] ibid para 114.

[42] ibid para 135.   [43] ibid paras 120–122.

Theories have also been proposed which argue that process differences *should* be acceptable in any case. Robert Howse and Don Regan propose that products should be deemed to be 'like' within the meaning of Article III:4 if there are no differences between them *that justify regulation* (except for protectionist considerations); physical similarity should not be decisive.[44] Their proposal is in some ways similar to the Appellate Body's approach, as it relies strongly on the anti-protectionist objective expressed in Article III:1. However, their proposal is significantly more focused on the issue of protectionism than the Appellate Body's 'competitive relationship' test is. It remains thus to be seen whether the Appellate Body will further follow the Howse and Regan approach.[45] Driesen proposes a rather similar model by emphasizing trade free of discrimination as the guiding idea of GATT law that should be attained through provisions like Article III:4.[46] What GATT prima facie prohibits according to Driesen is 'bright-line discrimination',[47] ie explicit discrimination between domestic and foreign producers or discrimination that makes it impossible for foreign producers to comply.[48] Thus, Driesen would attack provisions that are expressly protectionist or which by their very nature have a disparate impact on foreign and domestic market participants and are therefore arguably at least suspected to be protectionist.[49]

Truly process-based measures would be admissible as long as the distinguishing criteria applied did not smack of hidden protectionism. Country-based measures, however, would still be problematic. Howse and Regan expressly pronounce that Article III forbids country-based measures and point to Article XX as the proper place to discuss their legality.[50] Under Driesen's theory, they appear as discriminating regulations because producers cannot on their own comply with them. It is, however, questionable whether this distinction between admissible process-based measures and prohibited country-based measures is really convincing. First, one can argue that if the goal of a country is really to protect certain environmental or equality 'goods' from harm that is done in another country, a process-based measure can be quite ineffective.[51] Second and more important, it seems that a country-based measure is not necessarily more protectionist than a process-based measure. If domestic shrimp producers are obliged to use costly turtle-saving technology, for example, then a process-based import restriction on shrimp harvested

---

[44] Howse and Regan (n 25 above) 260.

[45] Howse (n 23 above) 514–15 takes the Appellate Body's premises in Appellate Body Report, 'United States-Import Prohibition of Certain Shrimp and Shrimp Products, WT/DS58/AB/R, adopted 6 November 1998 (*Shrimp*) para 121 as a hint that the Appellate Body is leaning towards an anti-protectionism position.

[46] D Driesen, 'What is Free Trade?: The Real Issue Lurking Behind the Trade and Environment Debate' (2001) 41 Virg JIL 279, 329, 342, 344.   [47] ibid 346.

[48] ibid 348, 350.

[49] Therefore, it is quite confusing if Driesen, ibid 353 explicitly rejects the notion of protectionism as a guiding principle for being too unclear. It seems to me that Driesen has captured quite well a workable position of anti-protectionism.   [50] Howse and Regan (n 25 above) 252.

[51] See H Chang 'An Economic Analysis of Trade Measures to Protect the Global Environment' (1995) 83 Georgia Law Journal 2131; but see Howse and Regan (n 25 above) 270–2.

in turtle-unfriendly ways does in fact accord a certain protection to the domestic industry against competitive (not comparative)[52] advantages held by their foreign counterparts. However, since this factual protection is only a side-effect of a valid distinction aimed at a legitimate goal (protection of turtles), Howse and Regan would, correctly, not call it 'protectionist', although it might very well have been the domestic industry that lobbied for the ban.[53] Extending the import restriction to all shrimp harvested in countries which allow turtle-unfriendly fishing makes—arguably[54]—sense from an environmental viewpoint, but does not necessarily lead to a significantly higher degree of protection for the domestic industry,[55] and should therefore not be *a priori* unable to pass Howse and Regan's protectionism test.

Making a definitive statement on the admissibility of *status equality conditions* for import regulations under GATT is, for the time being, quite difficult. The brute 'product-process distinction' is quite clearly not available any more.[56] On the other side, the Appellate Body's paradigm of 'competitive relationship' could well turn against process-based measures, for one can easily argue that, in practical terms, products sharing intrinsic properties *do* compete regardless of the way in which they were produced. Also, three of the exemplary *Border Tax Adjustments* prongs (physical properties, tariff classification, and end uses) do not give much room for process-based considerations. Particularly interesting in the matter of social purposes is the fourth category, consumer tastes and habits. Here it could be argued that the way a product is produced does make a difference, especially if the conditions of production are really egregious. On the other hand, it would be hard to argue even in that respect that these differences are of such a weight as to end the competitive relationship between the products at issue. Labelling approaches, for example, rely precisely on the fact that there *is* usually a competitive relationship between 'good' and 'bad' products and try to establish a competitive advantage through labelling.

If one shifts from the Appellate Body's interpretation to the broader anti-protectionism perspective, a further problem needs to be considered. It is quite commonly accepted that process-based measures motivated by environmental concerns are not protectionist, at least if the environmental effects at issue do not entirely and exclusively take place in the country of production. Howse and Regan go even further and assume that the mere fact that inhabitants of country A like turtles and do not want them killed makes it an externality if killings take place in country B. Consequently, measures aimed by A at reducing turtle mortality in B reduce

---

[52] cf Howse and Regan (n 25 above) 280–1.

[53] See G Shaffer, 'WTO Blue-Green Blues: The Impact of U.S. Domestic Politics on Trade-Labor, Trade-Environment Linkages for the WTO's Future' (2000) 24 Fordham International Law Journal 608, 612 on the convergence of interests of environmental groups and domestic industry in such cases.

[54] Note that in the *Shrimp* case it was environmentalists who went to court twice to make the process-based measure applied by the administration a country-based one (*Shrimp* Appellate Body Report (n 45 above) para 5.

[55] That depends on the circumstances in each case. The main protective side-effect of environmental or social policy measures is to exclude imports benefiting from the ability to produce cheaply (due to a lack of internalization of costs); that effect is reached by process-based measures already.

[56] But see G Marceau, 'The WTO Dispute Settlement and Human Rights' (2002) 13(4) EJIL 753.

externalities and thus are efficient.[57] Labour laws, it is said by Howse and Regan, are 'significantly less eligible for incorporation into import restrictions', because many of them 'are primarily re-distributive in nature; few labour laws are justified on the ground that they compel the internalisation of externalities', and few are really compelled by universally binding moral standards.[58] Accordingly, there is wide consensus among commentators on the subject of 'trade and labour rights' that it is necessary to decide which labour standards deserve international recognition and which are rightly left to adapt to circumstances in individual countries. Here, the role of the ILO is widely acknowledged. Since the sum of ILO conventions is quite large, and is arguably not in every case concerned with matters of universal importance,[59] the ILO's attempts to identify 'core' labour rights are given special attention.[60] Judged from that background, internationally recognized equality rights should be an easier case for justifying trade-related measures, since moral concerns clearly play a significant role here, as seen in chapter 3 above.

One last point has to be made here. The discussion in the preceding paragraphs merely concerns the interpretation of the expression 'like products' in Article III:4 of GATT. As has been mentioned above, the Appellate Body emphasized in the *Asbestos* and *Korea-Beef* cases that a finding of likeness is not the end of the matter. If, for example, all types of running shoes are found to be 'like' regardless of the fact that some were produced under questionable labour conditions, then the next question would still have to be whether foreign shoes are treated equally or less favourably. As long as the sale of foreign and domestic shoes is equally effectively prohibited in so far as they are produced under certain conditions, Article III:4 is arguably not violated.[61]

Process-product distinction and the GPA

Irrespective of whether it survives in the GATT context, the applicability of the process-product distinction to the GPA can be independently challenged. Some have argued that the GPA does not seem to rely on this distinction.[62] First, it should be noted that the GPA prohibits discrimination not of 'like products', but of 'products'. This could possibly change the Appellate Body's approach. Sticking closely to the text, it would be possible not to bother at all with questions of the

---

[57] Howse and Regan (n 25 above) 281, 283.

[58] ibid 284. On the last point, cf R Stern, 'Labor Standards and Trade' in M Bronckers and R Quick (eds), *New Directions in International Economic Law: Essays in Honour of John H. Jackson* (Springer, 2000) 425, 428: 'diversity of working conditions between nations is the norm and is by no means in itself "unfair" '. Charnovitz (n 29 above) 64 also warns against using the arguments of the environmental debate in social contexts.

[59] V Leary, 'Workers' Rights and International Trade: The Social Clause (GATT, ILO, NAFTA, U.S. Laws' in J Bhagwati and R Hudec (eds), *Fair Trade and Harmonization* (MIT Press, 1996) 177, 214; A Blackett, 'Whither Social Clause? Human Rights, Trade Theory and Treaty Interpretation' (1999) 31 Col HRLR 1, 13–14.   [60] Leary (n 59 above) 215; Blackett (n 59 above) 14 *et seq*.

[61] See Howse (n 23 above) 515; Howse and Regan (n 25 above) 259.

[62] P Kunzlik, 'Environmental Issues in International Procurement' in S Arrowsmith and A Davies (eds), *Public Procurement: Global Revolution* (Kluwer, 1998) 199.

competitive relationship of products, and instead ask directly whether domestic and foreign products in general have been treated in an equally favourable manner. Provided it is not discriminatory, therefore, a distinction between products on the basis of non-product related production processes would be acceptable within the context of Article 3 of the GPA.

Van Calaster has argued, however, that:

... this reasoning is not convincing simply because, arguably, a non-discrimination test without benchmarks is somewhat void of legal enforceability. Indeed ... the principle of non-discrimination requires *like* situations to be treated alike, while it also implies that *unlike* situations not be treated alike. In other words, whenever discrimination is prohibited, benchmarking of like and unlike situations ... is implicit. Put differently, the inclusion in Article III of GATT of the notion of 'like products' is superfluous in that the GATT regulates trade in goods and any prohibition of discrimination between goods implies that like goods (or products) are treated alike. Given that the [GPA] covers not just goods, but also services, the *like products and services* test is inherent in its Article III.[63]

Likewise Spennemann has argued that although Article III of the GPA does not mention 'like' products or services, 'it is self-evident from the nature of non-discrimination and the objective of Art. III that only "like" products and services are to be treated equally'. He continues: 'discrimination can obviously only occur in the case of unequal treatment of something that is equal or "like"'.[64] On this reading, then, essentially the same considerations as mentioned above should apply.

However, for Griller, this approach is not convincing. 'The question is not so much whether products in one or the other way affected by human rights violations are like or unlike products', he writes, 'but whether and to what extent the contracting authority may, in awarding the contract, differentiate between like products. In fact, every decision in a procurement procedure inevitably involves a differentiation between like products. Against this background, it might well be that it is not only by chance or a result of careless drafting that the notion of "like" products does not appear in the text of the GPA.'[65]

In the case of the Massachusetts Myanmar Law, a direct text-oriented approach comes quite easily to the conclusion that foreign suppliers and domestic suppliers are treated equally favourably: both are subjected to a difference in treatment regarding their engagement in Myanmar.[66] That seems also to be a sound outcome in the light of the anti-protectionism rationale. However, it must be kept in mind that even the protagonists of this rationale, while rejecting the product-process distinction, suggest a kind of 'process-origin distinction' which would not allow *country-based* measures. The Massachusetts Myanmar Law is not a country-based

---

[63] G van Calaster, 'Green Procurement and the WTO—Shades of Gray' (2003) 11(3) RECIEL 298, 301.   [64] Spennemann (n 21 above) 55.
[65] S Griller, 'International economic law as a means to further human rights?: selective purchasing under the WTO Agreement on Government Procurement' in S Griller (ed), *International Economic Governance and Non-economic Concerns: New Challenges for the International Legal Order* (Springer, 2003) 267–88.   [66] Trachtman (n 32 above) 357.

measure in a strict sense, but it looks suspiciously close to one. Therefore, it might still be seen as an Article III violation. To the untutored observer, it is the discrimination against *Myanmar* that is the clearest effect of the legislation. However, Myanmar is not a party to the GPA and so has no standing to complain about discrimination against it under that agreement. It must be remembered that the complaint put forward by Japan and the EU is that it is *they* who were being discriminated against. However, it is equally clear that the contested legislation, on its face, applies equally to both sets of tenderers.

In addition, the GPA provides specifically for the technical specifications of the contract to include specifications 'laying down the characteristics of the products or services...or the processes and methods for their production'.[67] As Kunzlik argues: 'To this extent it seems to depart significantly from the general approach under GATT '94 taken in the Tuna/Dolphin Cases.'[68] On the other hand, it might be argued that the purpose of these provisions is very limited, essentially to prevent the specification of processes by the purchaser which are available only to specific bidders and thus discriminatory, and therefore that no broader implications should be drawn from the provision. The extent to which 'technical' specifications in the GPA can be interpreted as including social criteria is arguable (see below).[69] In addition, it is uncertain whether the specific reference to processes in this Article 'either negates, or to the contrary, enforces the conclusion, that non-product-related PPMs are within the limits of Article VI(1)'.[70] At the moment, the issue is open.[71]

Technical specifications

Article VI of the GPA provides that technical specifications may be used, 'laying down the characteristics of the products to be procured', provided they are not 'prepared, adopted or applied with a view to, or with the effect of, creating unnecessary obstacles to international trade'.[72] These technical specifications may describe the product or service itself, and the way in which the product is to be produced or the service provided. However, the technical specifications must, where appropriate, be specified in terms of performance rather than design or descriptive characteristics, and be based on international standards, where these exist. There should be no requirement or reference to a particular brand name, producer, or supplier, or to a 'specific origin' of the product or service, 'unless there is no sufficiently precise or intelligible way of describing the procurement requirements and provided that words such as "or equivalent" are included in the tender documentation'.[73] It

---

[67] GPA 1994, Art VI(1). This approach is repeated in Art VI(2).
[68] Kunzlik (n 62 above) 8.
[69] I am grateful to Peter Trepte and Christoph Benedict for pointing out these alternative arguments to me.   [70] van Calaster (n 63 above) 302.
[71] See further Spennemann (n 21 above) 60–3.   [72] GPA 1994, Art VI(1).
[73] Ibid Art VII(3).

is clear from this that some of the procurement linkages discussed previously would qualify as 'technical specifications' for these purposes, most obviously those that specify accessibility criteria for computer equipment to be used by disabled employees, or disabled members of the public. It seems equally clear that other types of linkages would not qualify as acceptable technical specifications in this sense, such as the provisions of the Massachusetts law on Burma, not only because they may be considered as creating an 'unneccesary obstacle to international trade' but primarily because they did not lay down the characteristics of the product or service to be provided, but rather the characteristics of the supplier. So, too, the Scientology ban would not appear to qualify as a technical specification for the same reason.[74]

Qualifications of suppliers

Procuring entities are entitled under the GPA to assess suppliers' qualifications for carrying out the contract. Article VIII provides certain limits on these qualifications and the way in which they are to be applied. Many relate to the processes by which the qualifications decided should be advertised and applied, rather than placing a limit on the qualifications as such: 'In the process of qualifying suppliers, entities shall not discriminate among suppliers of other Parties or between domestic suppliers and suppliers of other Parties.'[75] The qualifications must be transparent and published in good time. Foreign suppliers must be allowed to apply to be included in any permanent lists of qualified contractors. More pertinent for our consideration are the substantive requirements set out in Article VIII. There are two of particular relevance. First, '[a]ny conditions for participation required from suppliers . . . shall be no less favourable to suppliers of other Parties than to domestic suppliers and shall not discriminate among suppliers of other Parties'.[76] Second, 'any conditions for participation in tendering procedures shall be limited to those which are essential to ensure the firm's capability to fulfil the contract in question'.

Leaving aside the issue of discrimination, the major limit is that the qualifications used must only be those 'that are essential to ensure the firm's capability to fulfill the contract in question'. This appears to be a self-standing limitation that is independent of any issue relating to discrimination, and it also appears to be quite stringent: the qualification must be one that is 'essential' to fulfil the contract. Can 'minority status', 'sheltered workshop', or 'not operating in Burma' be included as a permitted qualification under Article VIII? For the European Commission, when arguing against the Massachussetts legislation, the answer would appear to be 'no'. The only qualification criteria that are allowed under this part of Article VIII are qualifications that are performance related, meaning those that relate to

---

[74] H-J Priess and C Pitschas, 'Secondary Policy Criteria and their Compatibility with EC and WTO Procurement Law' (2000) 9 PPLR 171, 187.   [75] GPA 1994, Art VIII.
[76] Art VIII(b).

financial, commercial, and technical capacity. As interpreted by Hans-Joachim Priess and Christian Pitschas, this is a justified interpretation on the basis that the references to financial, commercial, and technical capacity in Article VIII should be seen as the main focus of the Article and the ability to use other qualifications should be limited to criteria similar to those,[77] ie other performance-related qualifications. Being a minority, or a sheltered workshop, or not operating in Burma, are not related to the performance of the contract and are therefore unacceptable. However, as under EC law, discussed in chapter 16 below, there is a major question in issue. What 'the contract' is in any particular situation needs first to be determined. For example, what does 'the contract' in the case of minority set-asides in the United States context include? In the context of preferences being operated in favour of sheltered workshops, what does 'the contract' include? In the context of the Massachussetts law, what does 'the contract' include? As under EC law, there appears to be a crucial opening that allows contracting authorities to determine qualifications broadly by specifying the nature of the contract broadly. Even if we agree that the qualifications permitted are those that are performance-related, and that 'refers specifically to the capability of the bidder to supply the products or services in question',[78] that leaves open what 'the product' or 'the service' is to be, and that must be left to the contracting authority itself, provided it is non-discriminatory.

But are we required to accept the argument that qualifications must be performance related? This is cast into doubt because of the final provision of Article VIII, which specifies that the Article does not 'preclude the exclusion of any supplier on grounds such as bankruptcy or false declarations, provided that such an action is consistent with the national treatment and non-discrimination provisions of this Agreement'.[79] What are grounds '*such as* bankruptcy or false declaration'? For Priess and Pitschas 'it may be inferred from those examples that a supplier may be excluded from participating in the tendering procedure only on the basis of reasons which cast doubt on its *professional* reliability' (emphasis in the original).[80] For Priess and Pitschas the issue of professional reliability means nothing more than simply a repetition of the type of performance-related qualifications discussed previously. But the negotiating history is of some assistance on this point. We saw in chapter 8 above that the draft Instrument prepared by the OECD Working Group in 1973[81] included a provision that permitted purchasing entities to exclude suppliers 'on grounds, such as bankruptcy, false declarations etc., *which a purchasing entity considers to be serious enough to justify such a measure*, provided that the purchasing entity does not apply such a measure in a more severe or strict fashion to foreign than to domestic suppliers'.[82] From this we might conclude that the provision in the GPA is equally capable of being interpreted as similar to

---

[77] Priess and Pitschas (n 74 above) 188–9.   [78] ibid 189.   [79] GPA 1994, Art VIII(h).
[80] Priess and Pitschas (n 74 above) 189 (emphasis in original).
[81] TC(73)15, 27 September 1973.   [82] ibid draft para 25 (emphasis added).

the notion of 'professional misconduct' that we see in the EC Directives, rather than the interpretation advanced by Priess and Pitschas.[83]

Award criteria

The approach adopted by the EU to the interpretation of the GPA in its complaint regarding the Massachusetts law appears to be that non-economic criteria may not be taken into account in the award of the contract, for example by setting price preferences for certain bidders over others on non-economic criteria. Article XIII(4)(b) of the GPA sets out the award criteria that may be used. Unless the procuring entity decides not to award the contract 'in the public interest', the entity must award the contract 'to the tenderer who has been determined to be fully capable of undertaking the contract' and whose tender is either the lowest price, or is the tender 'which in terms of the specific evaluation criteria set forth in the notices or tender documentation' is determined to be the 'most advantageous'. This differs from the equivalent provisions in the EC directives that specify, as we have seen, that the award criterion other than lowest price must be that which is '*economically* most advantageous'. (Even then, as we have seen in chapter 12 above, the ECJ has broadened the meaning of this in several cases.) Some have argued, however, that although 'economically' is omitted from the GPA text, 'most advantageous' should be interpreted as meaning 'most *economically* advantageous'. Christoph Spennemann, for example, states that 'only economic considerations' are permitted.[84] Priess and Pitschas argue that since 'the award criterion of the lowest tender is unequivocally based on pure economic considerations, the other award criterion...must be of the same nature'.[85] This issue needs to be considered in somewhat greater depth.

The history of the negotiations in the OECD is of some importance in helping us to understand what an appropriate interpretation might be. We saw in chapter 8 above, how the OECD Working Group was unable to supply an agreed text to the GATT negotiators setting out how award criteria should be regulated. The debate was essentially one of how to secure the greatest transparency of award criteria. As seen above, the conflict arose, in part, because of a dispute over how far purchasing entities could or should be obliged to award a contract only on the basis of criteria previously set out in the tender documents. Some delegations considered that it was impractical 'to provide an exhaustive list of the criteria it would apply for the evaluation of bids'.[86] These different positions are reflected in the alternative versions of two sets of provisions presented to the Committee in the draft text. In both, there is a clear relationship between the text relating to award criteria and the text relating to what had to be specified in the tender documentation.

---

[83] Arrowsmith (n 1 above) 226–8, 340 also prefers the broader interpretation.
[84] Spennemann (n 21 above) 60.   [85] Priess and Pitschas (n 74 above) 190.
[86] OECD, TC(73)15, 27 September 1973. See ch 8 above.

They were clearly in both cases a package. One set of alternatives related to the information that needed to be included in the tender documentation. The paragraph on tender documentation (paragraph 18(1)(g)) provided, with the alternatives in square brackets, that the tender documentation must include 'the criteria for awarding the contract, with, in particular: (i) [*alternative 1*: <u>important</u> factors] [*alternative 2*: <u>any</u> factors] other than price that are to be considered in the evaluation of bids'.[87] The paragraph on award criteria also provided two alternatives, with the alternatives again in square brackets.

Unless in the public interest all bids are rejected, the purchasing entities shall make the award to the bidder who has been determined to be fully capable of undertaking the contract and whose bid, whether for domestic or foreign products is

[depending on what is specified in the tender, either the lowest bid, or the bid which after evaluation is determined to be the economically most advantageous bid] (*alternative 1*)

[either the lowest bid or the bid which in terms of the specific evaluation criteria set forth in the tender documentation in compliance with paragraph 18(1)(g), is determined to be the most advantageous bid] (*alternative 2*)

for the contract in question.

As can be seen from a close reading of the alternative texts, the alternatives differ essentially in how far they are willing to substitute the term 'economically most advantageous' for the specificity of all award criteria being stipulated in the tender documents. The text adopted in the GPA consisted of the second alternative proposed. The effect is, therefore, that the award criteria are not restricted to those that are 'economically most advantageous', but can include choosing the bid which is 'most advantageous' 'in terms of the specific evaluation criteria' set out in the tender documentation, which must include (under Article XII(2)(g)) 'any factors' to be used in the evaluation of the bid. Whereas in the EC directives 'economic' was used as the way of attempting to ensure objectivity and contestability at the award stage, in the GPA the approach taken to ensuring the same objective was to require a complete listing of what was to be taken into account (and these were not restricted simply to 'economic' criteria).[88] All this is subject, of course, to the additional requirement that they must not be discriminatory.

Leaving aside the textual arguments, Spennemann's argument is anyway unconvincing. We have seen that there are extensive provisions at the United States federal government level attaching social policy provisions to government contracts, and fairly extensive use of social policy requirements in the procurement regimes of the Member States of the European Community. Although

---

[87] Draft, para 18(1)(g).
[88] See JP Trachtman, 'Unilateralism and Multilateralism in US Human Rights Laws Affecting International Trade' in FM Abbott, CB Reining-Kaufman, and T Cottier (eds), *International Trade and Human Rights* (Michigan University Press, 2006) 356, 368. Arrowsmith (n 1 above) 344, takes an even broader view, that 'it seems probable that any secondary criteria can be considered at the award stage, including criteria that are not contract-specific'.

exemption was gained by the United States and Canada for the minority and small business set-aside schemes, no similar exemption was negotiated by either the United States, the EC, or Canada for those programmes under which contractors must satisfy certain procedural and substantive requirements relating to racial and gender equality before the award of the contract and during the carrying out of the contract, what we have termed 'contract compliance' approaches, such as Executive Order 11246 in the United States and similar programmes operated by both the federal and some provincial governments in Canada. We saw in chapter 6 above, that these programmes (particularly in the United States) have considerable political importance. It seems relatively clear that no substantial, if any,[89] consideration was given to the contract compliance measures issue by the parties to the negotiations.[90] The United States programme predated the original 1979 GPA by over ten years, and the 1994 GPA Agreement by over twenty-five years. More significantly, there were other, apparently more important, problems.[91] If non-economic considerations are ruled out quite so radically as the complaint by the EU to the WTO implied, these programmes would fall, and that seems a step too far.

Socio-economic considerations as contract conditions

Leaving aside the general question of whether the Massachusetts provisions were discriminatory, the essence of the complaint by Japan and the EU was that the provisions of the GPA, which lay down procedural requirements for the conduct of the procurement process, had been breached. The Massachusetts law introduced limits on who could tender and provided for price preferences on grounds of human rights. If not saved by one of the general exceptions, an issue considered below, these may be in breach of the procedural provisions of the GPA 1994 discussed above. Even if this is the case, however, the text of the GPA 1994 suggests an additional way in which, by changing its approach to the linkage, Massachusetts could have achieved its goals lawfully, without having to resort to the exceptions provisions.

To appreciate how this may be so, we need to understand that there are three rather different purposes that the GPA 1994 may be thought to serve. The first

---

[89] As opposed to the minority and small business set-asides after the conclusion of the 1979 negotiations, see ch 8 above.

[90] See eg, EC Commission, 'EC Report on United States Trade Barriers and Unfair Practices' (1990) 20–40.

[91] Bovis has written that during negotiations, the EC did raise the issue of 'protection of minorities through contract compliance'. C Bovis, 'Utilities Directive and Public Procurement Trade War' (Summer 1993) Utilities Law Review 84, 87. Greenwold and Cox have argued that the small business, and minority and women set-aside programmes restrict access to the American procurement market, S Greenwold and A Cox, 'The Legal and Structural Obstacles to Free Trade in the United States Procurement Market' (1993) 2 PPLR 237, 250. Halford, too, has written that such provisions discriminate in favour of certain US domestic businesses, A Halford, 'An Overview of E.C.-United States Trade Relations in the Area of Public Procurement' (1995) 4 PPLR 36, 44.

purpose is the establishment of a procedural regime that is intended primarily to reinforce the general anti-discrimination provision (the 'non-discrimination principle'). The second purpose is the establishment of a regime that is intended to further independently valuable notions of transparency and openness (the 'transparency principle'). The third purpose is the establishment of a system that reduces as far as possible the insertion of non-economic criteria into the procurement process (the ' "economic" principle'). If the first and second are taken as the appropriate starting points for the interpretation of these provisions, there is scope for a subtle but important shift in approach. This would allow Massachusetts to achieve its goals, without breaching the provisions of the GPA, drawing on the approach that EC law has taken to the resolution of a similar problem in the European public procurement regime.[92]

This approach would drop the price preference approach and instead focus on using contract terms. Those awarded the contract would not be able, as a condition of the contract, to operate in Myanmar during the duration of the contract. This would appear to comply with the procedural provisions of the GPA. The provisions of the GPA stipulating procedural requirements appear to envisage that any contract conditions may legitimately be imposed, provided they are non-discriminatory. Article XII is of particular importance. As we have see, this deals with tender documentation. It specifies that the tender documentation provided to suppliers 'shall contain . . . (j) any other terms or conditions' required by the procuring entity. This clearly specifies that it is open to the procuring entity to specify *any* other terms and conditions, without apparent restriction, provided they do not constitute offsets, are transparent, and are non-discriminatory.

If tenderers refuse to indicate that they will abide by this contract term in carrying out the contract, then they can legitimately be excluded from being considered for award of the contract on the basis that, under Article XIII, they are not 'fully capable of undertaking the contract'. The crucial questions, as under EC law, become whether the contract actually specifies social issues as contract conditions (to satisfy the 'transparency principle'), and whether those conditions avoid being protectionist (to satisfy the 'non-discrimination principle'). Only if it is assumed that the 'economic principle' is the primary purpose of the GPA 1994 and that all its provisions must be interpreted as intending to further this principle (and there is little evidence that this is what was intended), is this interpretation seriously challenged. It has been specifically rejected by the ECJ in the context of EC law, as we saw in chapter 10 above. If the ECJ, with its strong integrationist tendencies, considers that a public procurement regime can survive such an approach, how much more should the Appellate Body be willing to do so.

The approach suggested is, however, controversial. Sue Arrowsmith, for example, has disagreed with this approach in the past. She considered the proposition that 'the

---

[92] Case 31/87 *Beentjes* [1988] ECR 4635.

concept of "capability" to fulfil the contract covers . . . requirements imposed merely under the contract, where these are of a secondary nature and relate to contract performance'[93] not to be an acceptable argument, on the ground that it would be 'odd if contractors could not generally be excluded for non-compliance with standards set by the authority, but could be excluded when these are prescribed in a contract term'. In other words, a public authority should not be able to do indirectly what it cannot do directly. However, this argument appears to ignore the text of the Agreement,[94] which appears to be very general indeed and does not appear to prohibit 'exclusion for non-compliance with standards set by the authority'. Arrowsmith's arguments would also neglect the extent of discretion that appears to be accorded to national authorities by the GPA 1994. Pierre Didier regards the provision as leaving 'significant room for subjective evaluation'.[95] So too, as Bertrand Hoekman and Petros Mavroidis have written, 'procuring entities have substantial discretion in judging the capacity of the tenderer to fulfil the contract and determining who best meets the evaluation criteria. The main constraint on such discretion is what is specified in the notices or tender documentation.'[96] Finally, Arrowsmith's arguments ignore the important point that different provisions of the Agreement may be thought to serve different values, and thus that it may well be appropriate that achieving a goal in one way is permissible, but not in another.

What of more pragmatic, policy-based arguments against this approach that might affect the interpretation of the GPA? Two arguments predominate. First, it might be said, even if this general approach passes the test of acceptability under the GPA 1994, various detailed issues arise. Can firms be excluded for failing to comply with socio-economic policies in the past, as well as requiring that compliance be accepted during the contract? Can this only be done to the extent that past non-compliance suggests that the firm will not comply in the future?[97] More serious is the question whether this approach provides as effective a mechanism for the enforcement of the human rights provisions as would the approach currently taken to linkage under the Massachusetts legislation. The argument might be made that the 'contract conditions' approach gives too much power to government contract administrators. It would allow them to determine whether a contract condition has been breached during the term of the contract, with the likelihood that they will prefer not to find a breach because of the complications to which

[93] S Arrowsmith, 'Public Procurement as an Instrument of Policy and the Impact of Market Liberalisation' (1995) 111 LQR 235, 281. However, she has now rejected the view she previously adopted, S Arrowsmith, *Government Procurement in the WTO* (Kluwer Law International, 2003) 340, footnote 49.   [94] GPA 1994, Arts IX and XIII.

[95] P Didier, 'The Uruguay Round Government Procurement Agreement: Implementation in the European Union' in BM Hoekman and PC Mavroidis (eds), *Law and Policy in Public Purchasing* (1997) 134.

[96] BM Hoekman and PC Mavroidis, 'Basic Elements of the Agreement on Government Procurement' in BM Hoekman and PC Mavroidis (eds) (n 95 above) 14.

[97] Arrowsmith 2003 (n 93 above) considers those questions in detail at 336–7.

this is likely to give rise if such a breach is found. The Massachusetts approach, it might be said, gives more leverage to the state to achieve its purposes.

III. Exceptions

Some general considerations

Assuming that a particular procurement linkage is contrary to the substantive provisions discussed above (and, of course, in many cases they will not be contrary), we must then consider whether it is 'saved' by Article XXIII of the GPA, which provides a general exception. This provides:

1. Nothing in this Agreement shall be construed to prevent any Party from taking any action or not disclosing any information which it considers necessary for the protection of its essential security interests relating to the procurement of arms, ammunition or war materials, or to procurement indispensable for national security or for national defence purposes.

2. Subject to the requirement that such measures are not applied in a manner which would constitute a means of arbitrary or unjustifiable discrimination between countries where the same conditions prevail or a disguised restriction on international trade, nothing in this Agreement shall be construed to prevent any Party from imposing or enforcing measures: necessary to protect public morals, order or safety, human, animal or plant life or health or intellectual property; or relating to the products or services of handicapped persons, of philanthropic institutions or of prison labour.

For the purposes of this discussion, it is likely that the second paragraph would prove to be the basis for an argument that a particular procurement linkage is 'saved' by Article XXIII, rather than the first paragraph relating to national security, although as we saw in the context of Congressional discussions concerning the United States procurement linkages in chapter 6 above, national security has at times been drawn on to justify such provisions, if unconvincingly.

Although Article XXIII of the GPA has not yet been the subject of interpretation in WTO dispute settlement proceedings, guidance on its interpretation can be drawn from the GATT/WTO jurisprudence on Article XX of GATT and Article XIV of the General Agreement on Trade in Services (GATS), which are close in their structure and their preamble ('chapeau') language to the GPA exception.[98] In the *US-Gasoline* and *Shrimp* cases, the Appellate Body emphasized the importance of applying the correct sequence of steps in Article XX cases. First, it has to be asked whether one of the enumerated exceptions apply; then, special requirements like 'necessity' have to be addressed, which concentrate particularly on whether there are less trade restrictive measures available; then, the chapeau has

---

[98] And from the larger field of public international law, see D Palmeter and PC Mavroidis, 'The WTO Legal System: Sources of Law' (1998) 92 AJIL 398.

to be examined, which concentrates on whether there is unacceptable discrimination in the measure adopted.[99] This is now commonly accepted as the correct way to approach Article XX of GATT. Since the structure of Article XXIII:2 of the GPA is very similar to that of Article XX of GATT, this Appellate Body jurisprudence should apply to GPA cases as well. The effect of this approach applied to Article XIII:2 is to focus the discussion on three steps:

(1) Is the procurement linkage challenged one which involves:
  (a) public morals, order or safety, human, animal or plant life, or health or intellectual property; or
  (b) the products or services of handicapped persons, of philanthropic institutions, or of prison labour.

(2) Assuming that it is, in the case of (a), is it 'necessary' for 'protect[ing]' one or more of those aims, and in the case of (b), does it 'relate to' these products or services.

(3) Assuming that it does, are these measures 'applied in a manner which would constitute a means of arbitrary or unjustifiable discrimination between countries where the same conditions prevail or a disguised restriction on international trade'.

There is, however, an initial problem that we need to be aware of. The difficulty with arguments that take a broad interpretation of Article XXIII of the GPA permitting extensive exceptions, whether based on 'public morals' or 'public order', is that they may appear to allow such wide exceptions as to threaten to undermine the rule-based approach to the conduct of international trade that is the basis for the system.[100] In particular, it has been argued, the linkage between trade and other domestic policy objectives by use of these interpretations could 'lead to the de-legalisation of international trade relations'.[101] In addition, such an approach would 'attract protectionist forces that eventually subject that [domestic policy] objective to their ends'.[102] These fears are, of course, related. Unless such domestic policy objectives can be controlled by objective scrutiny at an international level, protectionism is more likely to flourish. Given these fears, a central question becomes whether or not the GPA's restrictions on the operation of the 'public morals' and 'public order' exceptions permit sufficient control for the adjudicatory mechanisms of the WTO. Can they ensure that the exceptions are subject to legal scrutiny and that they will not operate for protectionist ends? What basis could there be for a more concrete meaning of 'public morals' or 'public order' to be developed which does not encourage covert protectionism? The scheme of questions listed

---

[99] *Gasoline* (n 7 above); *Shrimp* (n 45 above) paras 119–120.
[100] JH Jackson, *The World Trading System: Law and Policy of International Economic Relations* (2nd edn, MIT, 1997) 25.
[101] F Roessler, 'Domestic Policy Objectives and the Multilateral Trade Order: Lessons from the Past' in AO Kreuger (ed), *The WTO as an International Organisation* (University of Chicago Press, 1998) 213. See also J Atik, 'Identifying Antidemocratic Outcomes: Authenticity, Self-Sacrifice and International Trade' (1998) 19 UP JIEL 229, 234.   [102] Roessler (n 101 above) ibid.

above indicates that there are three opportunities for controls to be built in to try to prevent Article XXIII becoming a run-away horse. Limits could be introduced into the meaning of the aims pursued, or by tightening up the 'necessity' test, or stressing the 'non-discrimination' element. We shall see that the Appellate Body has steadily been developing an interpretation of the aims pursued that takes a broad interpretation of the meaning of the aims, is quite permissive regarding what 'necessity means', but imposes quite strict requirements relating to 'non-discrimination' that states must satisfy if their measures are to be found acceptable.

Types of exceptions available

An important starting point is that there is no *express* Article XXIII provision relating to equal status, human rights, or labour rights standards. There was an explicit reference in the (failed) Havana Charter to labour standards but this provision was not included in GATT or in the GPA. However, that is not the end of the investigation. Is the equality linkage challenged one which concerns (a) protecting public morals, order or safety, human, animal or plant life or health or intellectual property; or (b) the products or services of handicapped persons, of philanthropic institutions or of prison labour? There are several exceptions in Article XXIII that might conceivably be relied on given the examples of linkages discussed in previous chapters. We have seen that, historically, 'the products or services of handicapped persons' have frequently been given preferential treatment. Some others, for example linkages similar to those adopted by the UN requiring contractors to prevent sexual aggression, would appear easily to fit within the category of measures 'promot[ing] human . . . life or health'.[103] Most procurement linkages are likely, however, to be considered instead under the category of measures concerned with 'protect[ing] public morals, order or safety'.[104] Among these enumerated exceptions, it is this set of exceptions that seem most alluring as justifications because of their apparent breadth, and this chapter will concentrate on these.[105]

We begin, first, with the 'public morals' exception. The question is not only what this exception is meant to protect, but also what (if any) constraints can be applied to limit what might otherwise be an extremely wide exception.[106] How far can one argue that certain social policy requirements are mandated by moral concerns and thus included in this exception? Should attempts to further equal

---

[103] GATT, Art XX(a). Another exception in GPA 1994, Art XXIII which I do not consider here, though it is relevant, is that relating to 'human . . . life or health'. Although earlier disputes panels suggest that this exception should not be read as applying to the 'human life or health' of those in countries other than the country claiming the exception, the text gives no clear support for this limited interpretation.   [104] GPA 1994, Art XXIII:2.

[105] For a discussion of the others, see Spennemann (n 21 above) 89.

[106] Petersmann has argued that there is a risk of interpreting the 'public morals' exception as including large areas of social policy, see E-U Petersmann, *International and European Trade and Environmental Law After the Uruguay Round* (Kluwer, 1995) 51.

status considerations, or labour standards, be seen as expressions of morality, as Bhagwati has argued?[107]

Interpretation of 'public morals' prior to US-Gambling

Until the decision in the *US-Gambling* case, the 'public morals' provision had never been subject to interpretation by a GATT Panel. Prior to that decision there was significant academic discussion of the meaning to be given to 'public morals'.[108] It was argued that the term should be limited to its 'core' meaning.[109] This would mean that the interpretation of 'moral' should be limited to allow restrictions, for example, on imports of such items as obscene, indecent, or pornographic literature or films.[110] This interpretation, it was argued, was justified on the basis of the text. Each of the exceptions in Article XX of GATT, it was argued, had its own independent meaning, and did not allow for overlap, either partial or total. Given this, it was said, the 'morals' provision could not apply to 'process' methods, because otherwise the explicit exception for the products of prison labour would be unnecessary. Since prison labour is the only 'process-related' exception to be included explicitly, this suggested that other exceptions should not be interpreted to include process-related matters. The morals exception should therefore be limited to products rather than process. Not only should the morals exception be interpreted as applying to products rather than process, it should not be regarded as encompassing a wide range of concerns about morally-based social standards, again because the only provision of Article XX which might arguably do this is the provision relating to prison labour. The explicit inclusion of this one 'social' provision argued against interpreting other apparently wide provisions as including broad social provisions within their ambit.[111]

May a state legitimately take measures under the exceptions provisions of the GPA outside its borders? Even before the decision in *US-Gambling*, there had been considerable shifts in the GATT/WTO jurisprudence. The *Tuna I* panel objected to the outward-directed dimension of the measure. In *Tuna II*, however, the panel can be taken as implying that extra territorial measures may sometimes be justified under Article XX of GATT. In the *Shrimp* case the Appellate Body left open the question of whether there is a jurisdictional limitation implied in Article XX(g) and simply noted that there was a close enough 'nexus' between the objectives pursued by the United States (the protection of sea turtles) and the extension of United States jurisdiction, since all the species of sea turtles protected were also present in United States waters.[112] The Appellate Body did not require that the

---

[107] J Bhagwati, 'The Agenda of the WTO' in P van Dijck and G Faber (eds), *Challenges to the New World Trade Organisation* (Kluwer, 1996) 27, 39: 'labour standards . . . are seen in moral terms'.

[108] C T Feddersen, 'Focussing on Substantive Law in International Economic Relations: The Public Morals of GATT's Article XX(a) and "Conventional" Rules of Interpretation' (1998) 7 Minnesota Journal of Global Trade 75; S Charnowitz, 'The Moral Exception in Trade Policy' (1998) 38 Virg JIL 689.   [109] Feddersen (n 108 above) 115.

[110] ibid.   [111] ibid 109–10.   [112] *Shrimp* (n 45 above) para 133.

protected good in its entirety be confined to the jurisdiction of the defending state. In the case of the 'public morals' defence, there are further questions to consider. Who constitutes the 'public' whose morals or order is at issue? There are principally three possible answers: the public of the targeted state, the public of the applying state, or the global public. In the first case, it would be necessary to argue that the trade measure at issue does really aim to help the public of the targeted state; in the second case, the applying state would only have to assert that its own population is concerned, which should be easy; and in the third case, one would have to make an argument that the measure is in defence of globally accepted standards. There has in the past been considerable academic support for limiting Article XX's extraterritoriality to international human and core labour rights norms.[113]

'Public order' prior to US-Gambling

Although Article XX of GATT is similar to Article XXIII of the GPA 1994, there are textual differences. In particular, there is no mention in GATT of 'public order' or 'public safety' as permitted aims in Article XX, unlike in Article XXIII of the GPA 1994. Does the inclusion of the 'public order' provision in the GPA provide an exception that is even wider than 'public morals'? To understand the full significance of the public order exception, we need to appreciate that the French text of the GPA 1994 refers to 'ordre public' in this context. 'Public order/ordre public' is now a well-established concept in many civil law jurisdictions, in EC law, and in many international treaties. In these contexts, 'public order' refers to the basic values of a domestic legal system, encompassing values that are moral, political, or economic in nature. 'Ordre public' originated in French law as a rationale for invalidating private contracts deemed to conflict with fundamental principles of domestic law.[114] In some jurisdictions, 'public order' also operates as an exception (written or unwritten) to normal choice-of-law rules where the application of a foreign law would violate fundamental values of the forum state.[115] Thus 'public order' is not a value in and of itself, but is a legal doctrine whereby existing, fundamental values of a legal system will prevail over specific laws that come into conflict with them.

Numerous international agreements contain a 'public order' exception, without precisely defining the content of that term. The language of the European Convention on Establishment suggests that 'ordre public' encompasses concerns beyond those of national security, public health, or public morality; a protocol to the Convention states that 'ordre public' is to be understood in a 'wide sense'.[116] The Treaty of Rome (in which 'ordre public' is translated as 'public policy') likewise suggests

---

[113] Feddersen (n 108 above) Charnowitz, Moral Exception (n 108 above).

[114] G Husserl, 'Public Policy and Ordre Public' (1938) 25 Virginia Law Review 27.

[115] See eg *Oppenheimer v Cattermole* [1976] AC 249, 278 (claims based on racially discriminatory foreign law will not be recognized).

[116] European Convention on Establishment, ETS No 19, Paris, 13 December 1955, Protocol, Section III(a).

that the meaning of the term extends beyond that of public security, public moral-ity, or public health. However, the ECJ has interpreted the Treaty's 'public policy' exceptions more narrowly, to cover only 'a genuine and sufficiently serious threat to one of the fundamental interests of society'.[117] The ECJ also applies 'public policy' exceptions quite narrowly by requiring that measures be 'necessary' for the maintenance of public order, an issue to which we return below. GATS contains a 'General Exceptions' article with a preamble similar to that of GATT. The subse-quent exceptions include one for measures 'necessary to protect public morals or maintain public order', along with the following explanatory footnote: 'The public order exception may be invoked only where a genuine and sufficiently serious threat is posed to one of the fundamental interests of society.'[118] The GATS footnote clari-fying the meaning of 'public order' thus mirrors the ECJ's interpretation.[119]

We saw in chapter 8 above that in the OECD negotiations some delegations objected to the breadth of terms such as 'public order' on the grounds that they left too much discretion to states to evade their obligations under any future agreement. One way of addressing that objection would be to make the meaning of 'public order' subject to the public international law of human rights. The Appellate Body has made clear that GATT 'is not to be read in clinical isolation from public international law',[120] and the same is surely the case as regards the GPA 1994. The difficulty that then arises is which human rights should inform the notion of 'public order' in this context, and that is a difficult question. One approach might be to say that peremptory norms of international human rights law (such as the prohibition of slavery) should be included. So too might those norms included in human rights treaties to which the parties in dispute have both agreed (such as the provisions of the International Covenant on Civil and Political Rights). In the context of labour rights, the International Labour Conference, as we have seen, has agreed a set of 'fundamental principles and rights at work'.[121]

All these could thus serve as an emerging 'international public policy' of human rights,[122] and help to prevent idiosyncratic local interests being regarded as 'fun-damental interests of society'. Linking the 'public order' exception to applicable

---

[117] Case 30/77 *Regina v Bouchereau* [1977] ECR 1999, 2015.   [118] GATS, Art XIV(a), n 5.

[119] It has been argued that the public order exception in the TRIPS Agreement should also be interpreted in the light of the ECJ's approach, see TG Ackermann, 'Dis"ordre"ly Loopholes: TRIPS Patent Protection, GATT, and the ECJ' (1997) 32 Texas International Law Journal 489.

[120] *Gasoline* (n 7 above) IIIB.

[121] ILO Declaration on Fundamental Principles and Rights at Work (Geneva, June 1998).

[122] Referring to the influence of the Universal Declaration of Human Rights, Schwelb wrote as long ago as 1959: 'It can be assumed, for instance, that these principles might achieve relevance, among others, in situations where public policy or ordre public governs legal relations.', S Schwelb, 'The Influence of the Universal Declaration of Human Rights on International and National Law' (1959) 53 American Society International Law Proceedings 217, 222. More recently, F Francioni, 'An International Bill of Rights: Why it Matters, How it Can be Used' (1997) 32 Texas International Law Journal 471, 481 refers to the 'international public policy' of human rights'. cf the European Court of Human Rights reference to the European Convention on Human Rights as an 'instrument of European public order ('ordre public') for the protection of individual human beings', in *Loizidou v Turkey* (1995) 20 EHRR 99, para 93.

international human rights law should also help to act as a safeguard against the use of the exception as a cover for protectionist ends. The standards used to inform the meaning of 'public order' would, after all, have been agreed explicitly on a multilateral basis, or reflect already established international norms. If this interpretation of 'public order' is correct, it is arguable that the promotion of international human rights norms, such as the prohibition of forced labour that the ILO has found Myanmar to have breached,[123] can constitute 'a fundamental interest of society'. It should be within the margin of appreciation of the state to consider whether dealing with a firm which itself engages in those practices, or depends upon an infrastructure which engages in those practices, would constitute a 'genuine and sufficiently serious threat' to that fundamental interest.

'Public order' and 'public morals' in the light of US-Gambling

The *US-Gambling* case has significantly illuminated our understanding of the meaning of 'public morals' and 'public order', and reinforced the wider interpretations of the meaning and availability of the 'public morals' defence. Although an interpretation of Article XIV of GATS, it is clearly highly relevant to the interpretation of both Article XX of GATT and Article XXIII of the GPA. There are several important aspects of the approach that the Appellate Body takes. First, the Appellate Body impliedly upheld the panel's finding that 'the term "public morals" denotes standards of right and wrong conduct maintained by or on behalf of a community or nation'.[124] It also appears to accept the panel's further finding that the definition of the term 'order', read in conjunction with footnote 5 of the GATS, 'suggests that "public order" refers to the preservation of the fundamental interests of a society, as reflected in public policy and law'.[125] It also accepted the panel's finding that 'the government of the United States consider[s] [that the Wire Act, the Travel Act, and the IGBA] were adopted to address concerns such as those pertaining to money laundering, organized crime, fraud, underage gambling and pathological gambling'.[126] On this basis, the panel had found, and the Appellate Body accepted also, that the federal statutes in issue were 'measures that are designed to "protect public morals" and/or "to maintain public order" within the meaning of Article XIV(a)'.[127] The implications of the case for the first stage in interpreting Article XXIII of the GPA are thus highly significant. There are, of course, questions left open. For example, in a federal jurisdiction, can the 'public order' or 'public morals' exception be invoked by the sub-federal entity, and justified at that level, or must it be invoked at the national level, and justified at that level as well. The better view is that, since sub-federal entities are themselves

---

[123] ILO, 'Forced Labour in Myanmar (Burma): Report of the Commission of Inquiry appointed under article 26 of the Constitution of the International Labour Organisation to examine the observance by Myanmar of the Forced Labour Convention, 1930' (No 29) Geneva, 2 July 1998.

[124] Appellate Body Report, 'United States—Measures Affecting the Cross-Border Supply of Gambling and Betting Services', WT/DS2/AB/R, adopted 20 April 2005 (*US-Gambling*) paras 296–299.

[125] ibid paras 296–299.   [126] ibid paras 296–299.   [127] ibid paras 296–299.

subject, individually, to the disciplines of the GPA 1994, the exceptions should also be interpreted as applying to them individually.

Nexus

Assuming that the procurement linkage involves one of the acceptable aims set out in the article, (which does not now seem very difficult), the second prong of the test must be examined. This requires 'that there be sufficient nexus between the measure and the interest protected'.[128] We have seen that in the case of products and services of prison labour, etc the test is whether the measure taken 'relates to' these products or services. This seems an exceptionally easy standard to satisfy and nothing more need be said about it. We have been concentrating on the public order and public morals exceptions, however, where the test is whether the measure is 'necessary' for achieving that aim.

   There are at least two starkly contrasting approaches available to the interpretation of 'necessity'. The first approach is to interpret the idea of 'necessity' narrowly, scrutinizing the justifications offered by governments strictly. Some indications were given in early GATT decisions that this approach was the one that might be taken in this context. It was the practice of GATT disputes panels in the past to interpret Article XX exceptions narrowly.[129] A WTO Appellate Body decision noted that the chapeau (the introductory clause) is animated by the principle that while the exceptions of Article XX may be invoked as a matter of legal right, they should not be so applied as to frustrate or defeat the legal obligations of the holder of the right under the substantive rules of the General Agreement.[130] Thus it would seem that 'when a particular national authority's activity or decision would undermine the effectiveness of WTO rules, or would establish a practice that could trigger damaging activities by other member countries, panels will undoubtedly show it less deference'.[131] GATT dispute settlement panels have placed the burden of proof on the party seeking to invoke an Article XX exception, holding that 'it is up to the contracting party seeking to justify measures under Article XX to demonstrate that those measures are "necessary" '.[132] GATT panels interpreting Article XX(b) and XX(d) generally followed the interpretation of 'necessary' put forward by the *Section 337* panel, which held that:

. . . a contracting party cannot justify a measure inconsistent with other GATT provisions as necessary in terms of Article XX(d) if an alternative measure which it could reasonably

---

[128] ibid para 292.
[129] *US-Measures Affecting Alcoholic and Malt Beverages* GATT BISD (39th Supp) para 5.42; (1991) *Tuna Dolphin I* (n 34 above) para 5.22.   [130] *Gasoline*, (n 7 above).
[131] SP Croley and JH Jackson, 'WTO Dispute Procedures, Standard of Review, and Deference to National Governments' (1996), 90 AJIL 193, 213.
[132] *US-Section 337* GATT BISD (36th Supp) para 5.27; see also *Canada-Administration of the Foreign Investment Review Act* GATT BISD (30th Supp) para 5.20; *Tuna Dolphin I* (n 34 above) para 5.22 (unadopted).

be expected to employ and which is not inconsistent with other GATT provisions is available to it. By the same token, in cases where a measure consistent with other GATT provisions is not reasonably available, a contracting party is bound to use, among the measures reasonably available to it, that which entails the least degree of inconsistency with other GATT provisions.[133]

However, it would be unwise to overlook the institutional pressures that point in the direction of a less strict approach. This would permit non-protectionist measures that pursue legitimate social and human rights policies where they are shown to be rational and reasonably related to the object being pursued. Where the use of the challenged instrument can be shown to further internationally accepted human rights norms, and is untainted by protectionism, a greater margin of appreciation is thus accorded to a government. The government would be required to adduce evidence 'sufficient to suggest that the choice [of instrument] is not patently unreasonable, or a grossly disproportionate adaptation of means to ends'.[134] This less strict approach to satisfying the test of 'necessity' might be seen as justified for both pragmatic and institutional reasons. One factor is the problem of making the Agreement more attractive to the large body of states that have not yet joined the GPA 1994. There is also the important consideration that 'the international system and its dispute settlement procedures, in stark contrast to most national systems, depend heavily on voluntary compliance by participating members. Inappropriate panel "activism" could well alienate members, thus threatening the stability of the GATT/WTO settlement procedure itself.'[135] A third factor is the political credibility of the WTO system more generally. As Sir Leon Brittan, the Vice President of the European Commission, said some time ago: 'There is always a risk, if the WTO appears to put big business before the interests of impoverished farmers, health, the environment or the developing world, that people will accuse it of having no heart. Yet there is already more scope for giving the world trading system a humane dimension than meets the eye.'[136]

In practice, more recent Appellate Body decisions adopt an approach somewhere between these two extremes. The *Korea-Beef* and *Asbestos* cases both contain important considerations on the meaning of 'necessity' in the context of Article XX of GATT. In the *Korea-Beef* case, the Appellate Body found on the one hand that 'necessary' is not synonymous with 'indispensable' or 'inevitable'; on the other hand, it stated that as employed in Article XX, 'necessary' should be construed as being closer to the notion of 'indispensable' than to a broad idea of 'making a

---

[133] *US-Section 337* (n 132 above) para 5.26; see also *Thailand-Restrictions on Cigarettes*, GATT BISD (37th Supp) 200 (7 November 1990), holding that 'necessary' in Art XX(b) has the same meaning as in Art XX(d)); *Tuna Dolphin I* (n 34 above) (unadopted).

[134] For an insightful discussion of the standard of review, see M Trebilcock and R Howse, 'Trade Liberalisation and Regulatory Diversity: Reconciling Competitive Markets with Competitive Politics' (1998) 6 European Journal of Law and Economics 5, 32.   [135] ibid 212.

[136] Sir Leon Brittan, 'Rough with the Smooth' *Financial Times*, 10 September 1997. For a more detailed exposition of this argument, see PM Nichols, 'Corruption in the World Trade Organisation: Discerning the Limits of the World Trade Organisation's Authority' (1996) 28 NYU JILP 711.

contribution to'.[137] An assessment of necessity under Article XX(d), the Appellate Body further stated, involves weighing and balancing three factors, namely the importance of the value protected, the degree to which the contested measure contributes to the goal of value protection, and the degree of WTO rules violation involved.[138] The values protected are explicitly included in the weighing and balancing process because Article XX(d) allows enforcement of a wide array of regulations which could serve goals of differing importance.[139] This process is 'comprehended' in the approach taken by the panel in *US-Section 337*. The *Section 337* test stated basically that a measure is only 'necessary' if there are no alternative measures 'reasonably available' which would be not—or less—GATT-inconsistent.[140] Under this approach, the decisive question becomes when a less intrusive measure is 'reasonably available'; and since it is usually not problematic to come up with available alternatives, the gist of the necessity determination is the question of 'reasonableness'.

In *Korea-Beef*, the Appellate Body proceeded in two steps. First, it asked whether any alternative, less restrictive measures were available. This was basically a factual inquiry (although it involved a normative element, since the GATT-conformity of factually possible alternatives had to be assessed). Concerning the case at issue, the Appellate Body certified that the panel in the case was correct to look at other examples of regulatory schemes comparable to the scheme that was subject to the dispute. To have a look at how Korea coped with fraud prevention with regard to, for example, different types of domestic beef,[141] was justified in the Appellate Body's eyes because it provided the panel with examples of alternative approaches. Against allegations made by Korea, the Appellate Body emphasized that if understood in this way, taking similar schemes into account did not establish a 'consistency' requirement within the necessity test.[142] The Appellate Body confirmed in this case the panel's finding that there were indeed alternative measures for fraud prevention available, and that these alternative measures were also in and of themselves GATT-consistent.[143]

The second step consisted of judging whether Korea could 'reasonably be expected' to make use of these clearly available alternatives rather than the GATT-inconsistent measure it had in fact adopted. The panel had answered this question in the affirmative. Its reasoning was that once it was shown that alternative, less restrictive measures existed concerning similar cases, the defending state had the burden to prove that they were not reasonable. In other words, the panel inferred from the existence of alternative measures a presumption that they were also reasonable[144] and thus mixed the factual and normative elements of the inquiry.

---

[137] *Korea-Beef* Appellate Body Report (n 20 above) para 161.
[138] ibid paras 162–164.   [139] ibid para 162.   [140] ibid para 166.
[141] ibid para 168.
[142] ibid para 170. A consistency requirement would find a measure necessary only if the Member State protects itself against risks for certain values from different sources in a consistent, ie equal way.
[143] *Korea-Beef* (n 20 above) para 172.   [144] ibid para 174.

Notably, the Appellate Body did not comment directly on this approach. Rather, it developed its own reasoning. The starting point was an unambiguous expression of deference: The level of protection sought is entirely up to a member state and will not be questioned by the WTO.[145] This entailed that a state may seek a higher level of protection in the case at issue than in comparable circumstances.[146] Implicitly, the Appellate Body thus rejected the panel's presumption of reasonableness for alternative measures: each measure had to be judged individually against the level of protection sought by it. The application of this test to Korea's beef retail system started by determining the level of protection. The Appellate Body concluded from the fact that Korea had not prohibited foreign beef imports entirely, that Korea did not aim at a level of protection that 'totally eliminates' fraud, but only intended to 'reduce considerably' the risk of fraud.[147] This, the Appellate Body found, could indeed also be achieved by the other methods which emerged as available and less restrictive under the first step. Finally, the Appellate Body agreed with the panel that an alternative did not cease to be reasonably available simply because it came with higher administrative costs as long as these costs were not prohibitively high.[148]

In the *Asbestos* case, the panel decision that was being appealed against had followed the framework of the *Korea-Beef* case. Both panel and Appellate Body did not see any significant differences between the appropriate approaches to necessity in Articles XX(b) (which was decisive in *Asbestos*) and XX(d) (at issue in *Korea-Beef*). Two of Canada's allegations and the respective reactions of the Appellate Body are of interest.[149] First, Canada claimed that France's ban on asbestos was not 'necessary' because France did not comparably regulate similar risks to human health, stemming not from asbestos but from other fibres. This attempt to establish a consistency requirement within the necessity test was not accepted by the Appellate Body.[150] Second, Canada argued there was a reasonably available alternative to France's ban. This was an opportunity for the Appellate Body to explain further the notion of reasonable availability. The Appellate Body rejected Canada's contention, based on its reading of the *US-Standards for Reformulated and Conventional Gasoline* case, that alternative measures could only said to be not reasonably available if they were impossible to implement.[151] The Appellate Body read the *Gasoline* case instead as only suggesting that mere administrative difficulties of an alternative measure did not exclude its reasonable availability.[152] It stated further that in any case, difficulty of implementation was only one factor to be taken into account in an inquiry into the question of reasonably available alternatives.[153]

---

[145] ibid para 176.   [146] ibid para 177.   [147] ibid para 178.
[148] ibid paras 179–180.
[149] The other allegations concerned procedural matters: whether the panel had to 'quantify' risks to human life and health in Art XX(b) cases (according to the Appellate Body, it did not, see Report, para 167), and whether the panel's findings were based on sufficient evidence (para 166).
[150] *Asbestos* (n 23 above) para 168.   [151] ibid para 169.   [152] ibid.
[153] ibid para 170.

Another factor found by the Appellate Body in the *Korea-Beef* case was the importance of the interests pursued by the measure. The Appellate Body stated:

> In this case, the objective pursued by the measure is the preservation of human life and
> health through the elimination, or reduction, of the well-known, and life-threatening,
> health risks posed by asbestos fibres. The value pursued is both vital and important in the
> highest degree. The remaining question, then, is whether there is an alternative measure
> that would achieve the same end and that is less restrictive of trade than a prohibition.[154]

The level of protection is up to the state to decide and an alternative measure must
be equally effective as the contested one to be 'reasonably' available.[155]

Perhaps even more permissive is the approach taken to 'necessity' in the
US-Gambling case. The Appellate Body held that the standard of 'necessity' was an
'objective standard'.[156] It followed *Korea-Beef* in stressing that whether a measure
is necessary should be determined through 'a process of weighing and balancing
a series of factors'[157] and that the process was one 'comprehended in the determination of whether a WTO-consistent alternative measure which the Member
concerned could "reasonably be expected to employ is available" or whether a less
WTO-inconsistent measure is "reasonably available",[158] beginning with an assessment of the 'relative importance' of the interests or values furthered by the challenged measure.[159] Having ascertained the importance of the particular interests
at stake, a panel should then turn to the other factors that are to be 'weighed and
balanced'. The Appellate Body reiterated that two factors, in most cases, would
be relevant to a panel's determination of the 'necessity' of a measure, although
not necessarily exhaustive of factors that might be considered.[160] 'One factor is
the contribution of the measure to the realization of the ends pursued by it; the
other factor is the restrictive impact of the measure on international commerce.'[161]
A comparison between the challenged measure and possible alternatives 'should
then be undertaken, and the results of such comparison should be considered in
the light of the importance of the interests at issue. It is on the basis of this "weighing and balancing" and comparison of measures, taking into account the interests
or values at stake, that a panel determines whether a measure is "necessary" or, alternatively, whether another, WTO-consistent measure is "reasonably available".'[162]
However, an alternative measure

> ... may be found not to be 'reasonably available', where it is merely theoretical in nature, for
> instance, where the responding Member is not capable of taking it, or where the measure
> imposes an undue burden on that Member, such as prohibitive costs or substantial technical
> difficulties. Moreover, a 'reasonably available' alternative measure must be a measure that
> would preserve for the responding Member its right to achieve its desired level of protection
> with respect to the objective pursued

---

[154] ibid para 172.   [155] ibid para 174.   [156] *US-Gambling* (n 124 above) para 304.
[157] *Korea-Beef* (n 20 above) para 164.   [158] *Korea-Beef* (n 20 above) para 166.
[159] *Korea-Beef* (n 20 above) para 162; *US-Gambling* (n 124 above) para 306; *Asbestos* (n 23 above)
para 172.   [160] *Korea-Beef* (n 20 above) para 164; *US-Gambling* (n 124 above) para 306.
[161] *US-Gambling* (n 124 above) para 306.   [162] *Korea-Beef* (n 20 above) para 166.

under Article XIV.[163]

Although it was ultimately for the state challenged to demonstrate that its measure satisfied the requirements of the defence, the Appellate Body stressed that:

... it is not the responding party's burden to show, in the first instance, that there are *no* reasonably available alternatives to achieve its objectives. In particular, a responding party need not identify the universe of less trade-restrictive alternative measures and then show that none of those measures achieves the desired objective. The WTO agreements do not contemplate such an impracticable and, indeed, often impossible burden.[164]

It disagreed with the panel's finding that the United States was under an obligation to explore and exhaust all reasonably available WTO-compatible alternatives, and this required the United States to have entered into consultations with Antigua: 'such consultations, in our view, cannot qualify as a reasonably available alternative measure with which a challenged measure should be compared'.[165] It also placed quite a high burden on Antigua at the stage of examining 'necessity'. Antigua should have identified what reasonable alternatives might be available if it wanted them to be considered by the panel.

In the light of this, what is the conclusion for the interpretation of 'necessary' as the term appears in Article XXIII:2 of the GPA? Assuming one follows the previous decisions examined here, the test would basically ask whether a procurement-restricting measure could be replaced by an alternative measure, to be identified by the opposing party, which would have to be less procurement-restricting, and reasonably available, in the sense that it is equally effective without (probably) imposing additional prohibitive costs. The 'reasonably available' standard requires, in other words, equally effective, but not equally efficient alternatives. A less deferential standard could be chosen, however, if the ends pursued are deemed to be of little importance.[166] The equally effective standard can also be undermined by vague and over-broad formulations of the level of protection. As applied, for example, to the Massachusetts case, there would be important issues that would need to be considered. One question that the proponents of the use of such measures would have to address is whether such measures are effective in achieving their goals (which themselves would need to be defined with some specificity). Another issue is whether there are equally effective measures open to the state which have not been taken that have a less adverse effect on open procurement. We have seen above that these issues need to be considered taking into account the point of view of

---

[163] *US-Gambling* (n 124 above) para 308. See also *Asbestos* (n 23 above), paras 172–174 and *Korea-Beef* (n 20 above) para 180.   [164] *US-Gambling* (n 124 above) para 309.

[165] ibid para 321.

[166] In the case of human rights, that could probably not easily be done. For an entirely different conception of how the necessity test would work in human rights cases, see F Garcia, 'The Global Market and Human Rights: Trading Away the Human Rights Principle' (1999) 25 Brooklyn Journal of International Law 51, III.C.3: 'the test evaluates measures favorably precisely insofar as their impact on trade is the least possible, despite the fact that more trade-impacting measures might be more effective in realizing the non-trade value'.

principle as to why public procurement has been chosen to advance the social policy, and the more pragmatic considerations relating to the inadequacy (or absence) of other means of delivering the preferred policy.

Unjustified or arbitrary discrimination

Assuming that the measure is nevertheless acceptable under the first and second prongs, are these measures 'applied in a manner which would constitute a means of arbitrary or unjustifiable discrimination between countries where the same conditions prevail or a disguised restriction on international trade'? If so, the measure will not gain the protection of the exception. Equivalent provisions are included in the 'chapeau' to Article XX of GATT. The meaning of the chapeau in Article XX has been thoroughly addressed especially in the *Shrimp* case. As in the case of Article XX in general, the Appellate Body has emphasized the importance of a structured analysis. The chapeau imposes three requirements: A measure may not constitute (1) unjustified discrimination between countries where the same conditions prevail, or (2) arbitrary discrimination between countries where the same conditions prevail, or (3) a disguised restriction on international trade.[167] If a violation of one has been shown, there is no need to address the others.[168] The arguments made by the Appellate Body in the *Shrimp* case have in some important points been clarified and refined in the subsequent *Shrimp II* report, as well as in *GSP*[169] and *US-Gambling*.[170]

In this discussion, we concentate our analysis on the issues raised in (1) and (2). As regards the meaning of (3), the traditional meaning of 'disguised restriction' was mainly to look for disguises through identifying a lack of publicity for the measures adopted, and through identifying restrictions that also constituted prohibited discrimination. The Panel Report in the *Asbestos* case, after noting that 'to disguise' usually refers to an intention, stated that 'a restriction which formally meets the requirements of Article XX(b) will constitute an abuse if such compliance is in fact only a disguise to conceal the pursuit of trade-restrictive objectives'.[171] Although the panel expressed some doubts on the workability of an inquiry into intentions, it concluded that 'the protective application of a measure can most often be discerned from its design, architecture and revealing structure' of the contested measure.[172]

As regards the question of discrimination in (1) and (2), there are several issues that arise of importance to the issue of the acceptability of procurement linkages. Country-based measures are not *a priori* condemned by Article XX of GATT.[173] Country-based measures will not per se be treated as cases of unjustified discrimination.[174] The text only prohibits discrimination between *countries* where similar

---

[167] *Shrimp* (n 45 above) para 150.   [168] ibid para 184.   [169] *GSP* case (n 8 above).
[170] *US-Gambling* (n 124 above).   [171] *Asbestos* (n 23 above) para 8.236.   [172] ibid.
[173] *Shrimp* (n 45 above) para 21.
[174] R Howse, 'The Appellate Body Rulings in the Shrimp/Turtle Case: A New Legal Baseline for the Trade and Environment Debate' (2002) Col J Env L 491, 512–13.

conditions prevail and not between *producers* working under similar circumstances. The Appellate Body in *Shrimp* followed the *Gasoline* case, interpreting 'discrimination' to encompass discrimination between foreign countries, as well as discrimination between foreign countries and the country adopting the challenged measure.[175] In the *GSP* case, India argued that the drugs regime under the EC's GSP scheme was discriminatory, in violation of one of the requirements for GSP schemes in the Enabling Clause. India interpreted the 'non-discrimination' requirement as prohibiting any unequal treatment, whereas the EC interpreted the term as aiming only to prohibit unequal treatment that was improper. The Appellate Body held that 'the ordinary meanings of "discriminate" converge in one important respect: they both suggest that distinguishing among similarly-situated beneficiaries is discriminatory' and that the 'participants disagree only as to the basis for determining whether beneficiaries are similarly situated'.[176] In the *US-Gambling* case, the Appellate Body interpreted the concept of 'discrimination' in the chapeau as requiring 'consistency' in application between domestic and foreign firms.

This conclusion is similar in many ways to the inclusion in the text of Article XXIII of the GPA of the phrase 'where the same conditions prevail'. In other words, it will not be discriminatory if a measure distinguishes between countries on the basis of relevant and acceptable differences. There should, however, be an objective standard adopted by the state using the measure, so that the distinctions drawn between states should be able to be scrutinized and tested. The standards chosen must not be applied inflexibly, following the approach adopted in the *Shrimp* case, which gave considerable weight to the inflexibility of the United States approach in deciding that it was unjustified discrimination. That becomes clear if one consults the *Shrimp II* Report. Considerable parts of the opinion deal with the improvements the United States had made to better adjust their certification procedures to the circumstances of individual countries.[177] Provisions have to be flexible enough to allow due consideration for the special situation of each country, although they do not have to be individually tailored for each country on its own.[178]

The process of application of the standard will also be important in assessing whether it is 'arbitrary'. In the first *Shrimp* Report, this gave rise to a type of due process requirement. The United States was criticized because countries adversely affected lacked the possibility to be heard or to appeal.[179] It should be possible regularly to fulfil such a due process requirement without compromising a social policy scheme. Especially in the context of procurement it might also be added that transparency and due process are valued highly by the GPA with its detailed

---

[175] *Shrimp* (n 45 above) para 150.   [176] *GSP* case (n 8 above) para 153.
[177] Appellate Body Report, 'United States—Import Prohibition of Certain Shrimp and Shrimp Products', Recourse to Article 21.5 of the DSU by Malaysia, WT/DS58/AB/RW, adopted 21 November 2001 (*Shrimp II*) paras 140–149.   [178] ibid para 149.
[179] *Shrimp* (n 45 above) paras 180, 182.

procedural provisions.[180] Judicial review must be available against decisions by procurement authorities.[181] Therefore, it must be secured that suppliers know what is expected of them and what to do if they feel that they have been treated unfairly.

To what extent are attempts to negotiate on the substantive issues with the other country to which the measures are applied relevant? The issue was clarified in the *Shrimp II* case as not involving a duty to actually conclude an agreement before trade-restricting measures could be taken[182] (in fact, any other decision would have rendered Article XX of GATT useless). Howse has further pointed out that the Appellate Body has not even created a 'duty to negotiate' before applying restrictions; he recalls that the Appellate Body's argumentation takes place within the framework of discrimination, and therefore, there is only a problem if a country negotiates with some trading partners but denies such a procedure to others.[183] A second question, then, is whether discriminatory treatment is justified. Here, the Appellate Body had recourse to other sources of international law, namely the Rio Declaration, to declare that the United States not only discriminated, but did so in an unjustified manner.[184] Finally, it is notable that a negotiating approach entails also that a failure of the targeted country to engage in good faith negotiations might justify singling out that state as a target for trade restrictions.[185]

Differentiation between countries, drawing on the approaches adopted in the *Shrimp* and in the *GSP* cases,[186] would be acceptable where there were legitimate differences between the countries, where the measures adopted responded to these differences flexibly, and where the measures were applied to all countries that were in an equivalent situation. The measures must also be transparent, objective, and rule-based. Any preferential treatment of nationals will be viewed highly sceptically. If a multilateral solution is sought, it has to be inclusive of all possible target states. Entering into a treaty with some countries and relying on unilateral measures with regard to others is only possible if there are valid reasons for doing so, especially the failure of negotiations attempted in good faith. Even country-based measures seem to be admissible under that standard, although there remains some uncertainty.

---

[180] See eg GPA 1994, Art VIII; transparency is explicitly mentioned in Art XVII.
[181] ibid Art XX.   [182] *Shrimp II* (n 177 above) paras 123–124.
[183] Howse (n 174 above) 507.   [184] ibid 508.   [185] ibid.
[186] On the *GSP* case, see L Bartels, 'Conditionality in GSP Programmes', in T Cottier, J Pauwelyn, and E Bürgi (eds), *Human Rights and International Trade* (OUP, 2006), 464, 484.

16

EC Public Procurement Law and Equality Linkages: Foundations for Interpretation

In this chapter and in the next, we turn to consider the relationship between procurement linkages and the interpretation of existing EC law, paying particular attention to the procurement directives adopted in 2003. The purpose of this chapter and the next is not to present a full analysis of the whole of EC law relating to government contracts,[1] or to speculate on what issues might arise in the future, but to try to state the position that Community law had reached by the end of 2006. This chapter and the next will concentrate primarily on the procurement directives. There are other speculative legal challenges that may be raised in the future regarding procurement linkage, such as EC state aid rules and the rules against abuse of a dominant position, but these are not discussed, in part because (in the case of state aids) they do not appear to raise any additional legal risks,[2] and in part because (in the case of competition law) the area is one of deep uncertainty[3] in respect of procurement and to do it justice would require a foray that would divert from the principal focus of the book. Nor shall we consider the intriguing issue of the extent to which government procurement that is not wholly regulated by the directives, for example procurement below the thresholds, is required to conform to procedural requirements, in addition to the requirement not to discriminate on grounds of nationality.[4] This chapter, concentrates on setting out the *foundations* for an interpretation of the procurement directives, as they apply to procurement linkages. In the next chapter, we concentrate more on the implications of this approach to the *detailed provisions* of the directives.

---

[1] The book by Sue Arrowsmith does this excellently, and the reader is referred to that: S Arrowsmith, *The Law of Public and Utilities Procurement* (2nd edn, Sweet & Maxwell, 2005) (hereafter Arrowsmith, Law).

[2] See the excellent analysis, H-J Priess and MG von Merveldt, 'The Impact of the EC State Aid Rules on Secondary Policies in Public Procurement', in S Arrowsmith and P Kunzlik, *Social and Environmental Policies under the EC Procurement Rules: New Directives and New Directions* (provisional title) (Cambridge University Press, in press).

[3] See the opaque decision of the ECJ, Case 205/03 P *Fenin* [2006] ECR I-6295.

[4] Case C-324/98 *Telaustria* [2000] ECR I-10745. See further, M Krügner, 'The Principles of Equal Treatment and Transparency and the Commission Interpretative Communication on Concessions' (2003) 12 PPLR 181. See also C-234/03, *Contse SA, Vivisol Srl, Oxigen Salud SA v Instituto Nacional de Gestión Sanitaria (Ingesa), formerly Instituto Nacional de la Salud (Insalud)*, Judgment of 27 October 2005, para 79.

I. Some Preliminary Points

It has been seen in previous chapters that the use of public procurement for social purposes has a long history. Its relationship with EC public procurement law is more recent. From at least the mid-1980s, the relationship between social linkages and EC procurement law has been seen as exhibiting a tension between the economic dimensions of the Community (encapsulated in part by the procurement direct- ives) and the social concerns of individual Member States. Although the original Community had a social dimension, of sorts, the dominant purpose of the Community was often seen as economic harmonization. Where an economically driven, EC-level approach to procurement diverged from socially driven, Member State-level use of procurement, the preference of those who saw the purpose of the Community as being to achieve 'an ever closer [economic, it was assumed] union' was to interpret Community law as limiting the use of these social linkages. This was particularly manifest in the approach to the interpretation of the Directives adopted by the European Commission's internal market directorate,[5] and some academics and procurement practitioners.[6]

We have seen in the previous chapters that several important developments have occurred that challenged an approach to the interpretation of EC procure- ment law that sees domestic procurement linkages as simply constraints on a Community policy of open markets adopted at the behest of purely national interests; in other words, a battle between Community policy (in the shape of pro- curement reform) and domestic policy (in the shape of status equality). We have seen that the Community has now developed its social dimension to a signifi- cantly greater degree. In some areas, notably in the area of social policy, the Community has adopted wide-ranging legislation. There has been an increasing emphasis in the Community on social and equality rights, particularly in the workplace. Social policy has come to play a central role in building Europe's eco- nomic strength, through the development of what came to be identified by Community institutions as a unique social model. Economic progress and social cohesion came to be regarded as complementary pillars of sustainable develop- ment and both are at the heart of the process of European integration. As sustain- able development moved beyond environmental issues into social issues, status equality was increasingly identified as an element, as it was too in the growing movement for corporate social responsibility. Increasingly, at the Community level, and also at the national level in several states, status equality became 'main- streamed', meaning that the need to further status equality came to be seen (at least

---

[5] Arrowsmith, Law (n 1 above) 1271.

[6] See eg the articles by J Arnould, 'Secondary Policies in Public Procurement: The innovations of the new directives' (2004) 13 PPLR 187; H-J Priess and C Pitschas, 'Secondary Policy Criteria and their Compatibility with EC and WTO Procurement Law: The Case of the German Scientology Declaration' (2000) 9 PPLR 171.

at the rhetorical level) as something to be integrated into a wide range of policies and institutional practices. The importance of these developments is that the tensions between the social and economic perspectives of procurement can no longer be translated as simply equating to Member State versus EC level policy clashes; the social dimension is now increasingly dominated in certain areas by EC level policy.

However much the social dimension of the Community waxes and wanes politically, *legally* there is now no reason to see the resolution of conflicts between EC social and economic policies as inevitably leading to the economic dominating the social. There is no priority given, for example, to the provisions enabling procurement legislation to be enacted over the provisions enabling status equality legislation to be enacted. Instead, three fundamental aspects of Community law relating to procurement need to be borne in mind when interpreting the procurement directives in the context of procurement linkages: the overall limits of the procurement directives deriving from the Treaty, the importance of equal treatment as the basis of both EC states' equality law and procurement law, and the importance of viewing the procurement directives as engaging with a policy instrument (public procurement) that is based on freedom of contract. The next three sections consider each of these issues.

From the point of view of interpreting EC procurement law, each of these developments is important. Taken together, they require a revised approach to the interpretation of EC procurement law as far as the use of procurement linkages is concerned. What is needed, in the light of these developments is an interpretation of the procurement directives that is true to the text of the directives, reflects the evolving ECJ case law, but crucially does not incorporate into the interpretation process other assumptions that are currently legally unsustainable. What is necessary is an interpretation of the procurement directives, in particular, that views EC law as one harmonious whole, giving appropriate weight to *all* of EC law, without assuming any particular priority or hierarchy. Is this possible? My argument in this chapter is that it is not only possible, but is now the only appropriate way of interpreting the directives. To interpret the directives otherwise is, quite simply, legally incorrect. This approach is one that is entirely consistent with the approach adopted by the ECJ. We are consistently urged by the ECJ to regard EC law as a body of law that should be interpreted as a harmonious whole. It is clear that the time has long passed when particular areas of EC law, such as procurement law, should be regarded as hermetically sealed from other areas of EC law, or indeed from international law more generally. In presenting this revised approach, I am, of course, conscious that I am building on the work of others.[7]

---

[7] There has been a stream of academic analysis that has interpreted the directives and the ECJ case law to permit significant social linkages. See eg Arrowsmith, Law (n 1 above) passim; C Tobler, 'Encore: "Women's Clauses" In Public Procurement Under Community Law' (2000) 25 ELR 618; C Hanley, 'Avoiding the Issue: The Commission and Human Rights Conditionality in Public Procurement' (2000) 27 ELR 714; K Krüger, R Nielsen, and N Bruun, *European Public Contracts in a Labour Law Perspective*

This chapter is primarily concerned with the relationship between procurement and status equality, especially when procurement is used to put into effect the principles that underpin the EC status equality directives. But those legislating the directives were also clearly willing and able to balance domestic, social, and economic considerations in deciding on coverage. First, it is instructive that the directives continue to exclude some services, 'which are especially sensitive from a cultural and social point of view',[8] allowing contracting authorities to choose the award procedure they wish to apply[9] and second, that procurement in the broadcasting context is excluded on the grounds that 'for these kinds of contracts, it must be possible to take into account aspects of cultural or social significance'.[10] Those legislating the directives were, therefore, clearly willing and able to balance social and economic considerations in deciding on coverage. It is clearly recognized that procurement decisions are affected by social considerations and the directives have accommodated that political reality also. The question is: to what extent?[11]

II. Equal Treatment as the Basis of EU Status Equality Law and Procurement Law

The principle that links and underpins each of these two sets of legal obligations (the relationship between the law of the EC governing public procurement—in particular, the new procurement directives—and the law regarding status equality) is the principle of 'equal treatment'. The ECJ has developed a jurisprudence that subjects the exercise of Community competence to the requirement that it complies with 'general principles' of EC law.[12] This has implications for equality and discrimination in several principal ways. Despite the existence of numerous provisions of the Treaty 'that provide for the principle of equal treatment with regard to specific matters',[13] the ECJ has held that the principle of equality is also one of these general principles of EC law. Within the sphere of EC law, this principle of

---

(DJØF Publishing, 1998). An extensive bibliography of academic writing on procurement linkages is included in the helpful overview: S Whitton, On the pursuit of non-economical policies in the EU law of public contracts, with special focus on case law and forthcoming Directive (EC) 2004/18, University of Warwick, unpublished paper, 22 February 2005.

 [8] Arnould (n 6 above) 192.

 [9] Public Sector Directive, Annex IIB; Utilities Directive, Annex XVIIB.

 [10] Arnould (n 6 above) 192.

 [11] In addition to the literature cited above, the following have also discussed related issues: B Bercusson and R Bruun, 'Labour law Aspects of Public Procurement in the EU' in R Nielsen and S Treumer (eds), *The New EU Public Procurement Directives* (DJØF Publishing, 2005) 97; P Kunzlik, '"Green Procurement" Under the New Regime' in R Nielsen and S Treumer (above) 117; SE Hjelmborg, PS Jacobsen and ST Poulsen, *Public Procurement Law: the EU directive on public contracts* (DJØF Publishing, 2006) 204–26; C Bovis, *Public Procurement in the European Union* (Palgrave Macmillan, 2005) 95–117.

 [12] See in general T Tridimas, *The General Principles of EC Law* (OUP, 1999) ch 2. See also 'Equality' in AG Toth, *The Oxford Encyclopaedia of European Community Law* (Clarendon Press, 1990) vol 1, 188–201.   [13] Tridimas (n 12 above).

equality precludes comparable situations from being treated differently, and different situations from being treated in the same way,[14] unless the treatment is objectively justified.[15] The ECJ has recognized, for example, that the principle that everyone is equal before the law is a basic principle of EC law.[16] Why did the Court find it necessary to hold that equality is a general principle of EC law? Takis Tridimas observes: 'It may be that those [specific] provisions do not guarantee equal treatment in all cases so that the development of a general principle is necessary to cover the lacunae left in written law.'[17]

In the public procurement context, the obvious starting point for understanding the meaning and implications of the 'equal treatment' dimension of the procurement directives is to be found in those aspects of the Treaty that protect the 'four freedoms'. There are several EC Treaty provisions in which the principles of non-discrimination or equality are expressly mentioned. These are regarded as specific enumerations of the general principle of equal treatment.[18] The principal examples are Article 12 (formerly 6) EC (discrimination on the grounds of being a national of one of the member states is prohibited), Article 18 (formerly 8a) EC (every citizen of the Union has the right to move and reside freely within the territory of the member states, subject to certain limitations), Article 34(2) (formerly 40(3)) EC (non-discrimination between producers and consumers in the context of the Common Agricultural Policy), Article 39 (formerly 48) EC (non-discrimination as between workers who are nationals of the host state and those who are nationals of another member state), Article 43 (formerly 52) EC (equal treatment as between nationals and non-nationals who are established in a self-employed capacity in a member state), Article 49 (formerly 59) EC (equal treatment for providers of services), and Article 90 (formerly 95) EC (non-discrimination in the field of taxation as between domestic and imported goods).[19] 'Probably the most obvious and central manifestation of the non-discrimination principle in EC law has been in the context of prohibiting discrimination on grounds of nationality or origin.'[20] A considerable body of secondary legislation has further supplemented these provisions.[21] One way of viewing the procurement directives is that they are instances of equal treatment in this sense.

[14] Case 106/83 *Sermide SpA v Cassa Conguaglio Zucchero* [1984] ECR 4209, para 28. See also Opinion of AG Van Gerven delivered on 15 September 1993, Case C-146/91 *Koinopraxia Enoseon Georgikon Synetairismon Diacheir iseos Enchorion Proionton Syn. PE (KYDEP) v Commission* [1994] ECR I-4199.

[15] See eg Case C-189/01 *Jippes v Minister van Landbouw, Natuurbeheer en Visserij* [2001] ECR I-5689 para 129 and Case C-149/96 *Portugal v Council* [1999] ECR I-8395 para 91.

[16] Case 283/83 *Racke* [1984] ECR 3791; Case 15/95 *EARL* [1997] ECR I-1961; Case 292/97 *Karlsson* [2000] ECR I-2737.   [17] Tridimas (n 12 above) 41.

[18] Case 1/72 *Frilli v Belgium* [1972] ECR 457, para 19; Case 145/77 *Royal Scholten-Honig (Holdings) Ltd v Intervention Board for Agricultural Produce* [1978] ECR 2037, para 26.

[19] EC Treaty, Art 18.

[20] G de Búrca, 'The Role of Equality in European Community Law' in A Dashwood and S O'Leary, *The Principle of Equal Treatment in EC Law* (Sweet & Maxwell, 1997) 20.

[21] eg Council Regulation (EEC) 1612/68 on the free movement of workers within the Community [1968] OJ L257/2.

If we are to take the approach of the ECJ seriously, however, that is too limited an interpretation. For the Court, as we have seen, equal treatment precludes comparable situations from being treated differently, and different situations from being treated in the same way,[22] unless the treatment is objectively justified.[23] This is a general principle, not limited simply to securing non-discrimination on grounds of nationality. The case in which the ECJ first articulated the idea that the principle of equal treatment 'lies at the very heart of the [procurement] directive'[24] illustrates the point. In the *Storebaelt* case[25] the Court held that 'observance of the principle of equal treatment of tenderers requires that all the tenders comply with the tender conditions so as to ensure an objective comparison of the tenders submitted by the various tenderers'.[26] It therefore considered that the principle of equal treatment precluded *Storebaelt* from taking into consideration a tender where the tender did not comply with the fundamental conditions stipulated by the authority in the tender documents.[27] This aspect of the case had nothing to do with non-discrimination on the basis of nationality. An interpretation of equal treatment that regards it as simply another way of expressing a prohibition of discrimination on grounds of nationality therefore misunderstands the complexity of the concept, as used by the Court. The question that the Court requires to be addressed is the broader one that concentrates on preventing comparable situations from being treated differently, and different situations from being treated in the same way. The issue then becomes one of determining when the situations are 'comparable'. In the *Storebaelt* case the Court emphasized the importance of 'the development of effective competition in the field of public contracts'[28] and this has led Sue Arrowsmith to suggest that tenderers are 'comparable' when the entities are in a 'comparable competitive position'.[29]

Conceptions of equality and non-discrimination

Equality and non-discrimination are complex concepts, with considerable debate about their meanings and justification. In order to better understand the variety of different ways in which legal measures advancing equal treatment currently operate, four categories[30] of, or approaches to, equality and non-discrimination may usefully be identified. Several caveats are necessary regarding these distinctions.

---

[22] Case 106/83 *Sermide SpA v Cassa Conguaglio Zucchero* [1984] ECR 4209, para 28. See also, Opinion of AG Van Gerven delivered on 15 September 1993, Case C-146/91 *Koinopraxia Enoseon Georgikon Synetairismon Diacheir iseos Enchorion Proionton Syn. PE (KYDEP) v Commission* [1994] ECR I-4199.

[23] See eg Case C-189/01 *Jippes v Minister van Landbouw, Natuurbeheer en Visserij* [2001] ECR I-5689, para 129 and Case C-149/96 *Portugal v Council* [1999] ECR I-8395, para 91.

[24] Case C-242/89, *Commission v Denmark ('Storebaelt')* [1993] ECR I-3353, para 39.

[25] ibid.   [26] ibid para 37.   [27] ibid para 43.   [28] ibid para 33.

[29] Arrowsmith, Law (n 1 above) 426.

[30] The terms 'category' 'approach', and 'meaning' are used interchangeably in this chapter. No significance should be attached to this.

First, the categories are constructed to try to make sense of a sometimes bewildering range of legal material; these categories have received no judicial approval. Second, these categories are not watertight, but porous, with developments in one category influencing approaches in others. Third, these categories attempt to describe the current approaches to equality and non-discrimination, rather than to provide a normative analysis of these approaches.

Equality as 'rationality'

The first approach is where the principle of non-discrimination (interpreted as the limited principle that likes should be treated alike, unless there is an adequate justification for not applying this principle) is a self-standing principle of general application, without specific limitation on the circumstances in which it is applicable, and without limitation on the grounds on which the difference of treatment is challengeable. In many jurisdictions, this approach to equality is particularly associated with constitutional guarantees.[31] This approach is essentially rationality-based. Under this approach, then, discrimination is merely an example of irrationality, with no greater moral or legal significance than if the government decided to allocate houses only to those with red hair. This approach is often apparent in the interpretation of constitutional provisions guaranteeing non-discrimination in general terms.

However, non-discrimination is often tied to some more specific context. There are, essentially, two methods of limiting and deepening the prohibition of discrimination, and they operate both separately and together. One method is where the prohibition of discrimination is limited to particular subject areas, such as employment, or to certain rights, such as freedom of speech. A second approach is where the right to non-discrimination is limited to certain grounds or statuses, such as sex, race, religion, disability, etc. These two different approaches give rise to important differences in methods, aims, and justifications for legal intervention, giving rise to two further approaches to equality, additional to 'equality as rationality'.

Equality as protective of other 'prized public goods'

In the second approach, the equality principle becomes an adjunct to the protection of particularly prized 'public goods', including human and other rights. The principle is essentially that such 'prized public goods' should in principle be distributed to everyone without distinction. In the distribution of the 'public good', equals should be treated on a non-discriminatory basis, except where differences can be justified. In this context, the focus is on the distribution of the public good, rather than the characteristics of the recipient. The courts will scrutinize public authorities' (less frequently, private bodies')[32] actions in a more intense way than

---

[31] See in general, the Council of Europe's Constitutional Law Bulletin, which is a good source of case law on the constitutional principle of equality.

[32] The extent to which norms applying to states give rise to state responsibility where third parties within the state act contrary to the norm is left to one side.

under the first approach, when the actions of the public authority give rise to discrimination (defined essentially as treating someone differently) in these circumstances. Under this approach, discrimination is objectionable because it is an unacceptable way of limiting access to the 'prized public good'.

Equality as preventing 'status-harms' arising from discrimination on particular grounds

In the third approach to equality, the focus of attention turns instead to the association between a limited number of particular characteristics (such as race, gender, etc) and the discrimination suffered by those who have, or who are perceived to have, those characteristics, irrespective of whether the decision might be justified as rational. The courts will scrutinize public authorities' (and others') actions in a more intense way than under the first approach where the public authorities' actions discriminate against individuals with those particular characteristics. In this context, the meaning of discrimination frequently expands beyond the principle that likes should be treated alike to embrace also the principle that unlikes should not be treated alike. This approach is essentially aimed at preventing status-harms arising from discrimination on particular grounds.

The third approach differs from the second in being less concerned with the importance of the good being allocated, and more concerned with the use of actual or imputed identity in a wide range of situations. In the second approach, the harm to be prevented lies in the arbitrary allocation of something that in principle all should have. In the third approach, the harm lies in the use made of particular statuses to affect the allocation of a wide range of opportunities, which may or may not reach the importance of rights, but where the use of those characteristics is unacceptable in such decisions. In this third approach to non-discrimination, the focus of attention shifts from the importance of the 'public good' (for example, the human right in issue) and turns instead to the association between a limited number of particular characteristics (such as race, gender, etc) and the discrimination suffered by those who have, or are perceived to have, those characteristics, where the public authorities' actions discriminate against individuals with those particular characteristics.

In several ways, the third category of discrimination and equality is more complex than the first and second categories discussed previously, and this greater complexity has resulted in the emergence of legal issues that are so far relatively underdeveloped in the context of discussions about the other categories. Unlike under the second approach, it does not apply as a penumbra of all major areas of rights (indeed many fundamental rights are not included within the coverage of anti-discrimination law). In another respect, of course, the approach taken under this third approach is considerably broader in scope, covering both public and private sector actors operating in those areas covered, whereas to a considerable extent the first and second approaches apply largely to the public sector.

*Equality as proactive promotion of equality of opportunity
between particular groups*

In the fourth approach, certain public authorities are placed under a duty actively to take steps to promote greater equality of treatment for particular groups. In that sense, it is a further development of the third ('status-based') approach. However, the concept of 'equality of opportunity' goes beyond any of the concepts of discrimination characteristic of the previous approaches. Under this fourth approach, a public authority to which this duty applies is under a duty to do more than ensure the absence of discrimination from its employment, educational, and other specified functions, and to act positively to promote equality of opportunity between different groups throughout all its policy-making and in carrying out all its activities. In the fourth approach, certain public authorities (less frequently private bodies) are placed under a duty actively to take steps to promote greater equality of opportunity (the legal meaning of which is often yet to be fully articulated) for particular groups. The concept of equal treatment here goes beyond any of the concepts of discrimination characteristic of the previous approaches and involves not only a duty on the public authority to eliminate discrimination from its activities, which is seen as merely one example of where equality of opportunity is denied, but actively to take steps to promote greater equality of opportunity through its activities. Under this approach, a public authority to which this duty applies is under a duty to do more than ensure the absence of discrimination from its employment, educational, and other specified functions, but also to act positively to promote equality of opportunity between different groups throughout all policy-making and in carrying out all those activities to which the duty applies.

Equal treatment in Community law

These various distinctions help us to understand what is going on in Community law. There are two important dimensions to the meaning of equal treatment in Community law as propounded by the ECJ. In one dimension, the non-discrimination principle is a general principle of rationality, or becomes an adjunct to the protection of particularly prized 'public goods' (the first two dimensions of equality discussed in the previous paragraphs). The principle is essentially that such 'prized public goods' should in principle be distributed to everyone without arbitrary distinction. In the distribution of the 'public good', equals should be treated on an equal basis, except where differences can be justified. In this context, the focus is on the distribution of the public good, rather than the characteristics of the recipient. Under this approach, not according equal treatment is objectionable because it is an unacceptable way of limiting access to the 'prized public good'. This is generally the view that characterizes the approach to the meaning of equal treatment in the context of the 'four freedoms' in EC law. It is also the way in which the concept of equal treatment has thus far been used in the context of procurement. The 'prized public good', in the case of procurement, being access to a competitive procurement market across Europe.

In a second dimension of EC law, however, the focus of attention of the meaning of 'equal treatment' turns instead to the association between a limited number of particular characteristics (such as race, gender, etc) and the consequences suffered by those who have, or who are perceived to have, those characteristics. This approach is essentially aimed at preventing status-harms arising from discrimination on particular grounds (the third of the approaches discussed previously). Sometimes EC law goes further, to an approach that regards the role of the Community as being to increase substantive equality for particular groups (the fourth of the approaches discussed above).

It is important, however, not to over-emphasize the differences between these dimensions of the equal treatment principle in Community law. In particular, there is a temptation to regard the first dimension as economically-based and the second dimension as socially-based. But this would be too simplistic. In the EC, rights to equality (in respect of equal pay between men and women) and non-discrimination (in respect of nationality) were both originally conceived as legal instruments to ensure the establishment and proper functioning of the common market.[33] Subsequent political and legislative developments reflect broader social considerations, leading to the recognition of new rights in a range of areas, including on gender equality as part of a strategy of building a social dimension into Community policy,[34] especially during the 1970s.[35] Simultaneously, existing rights, such as the right to equal pay, were remodelled on the basis of both economic *and* social considerations.[36] More widely still, this reflects the evolution of the Community from an economic to a markedly more wide-encompassing organization. Within this expanded scope for a broader social discourse, the right to equal treatment was gradually emancipated from the need to be formally legitimated only by economic justifications. A parallel development took place with other rights— and measures setting out such rights—in the broader social policy area.[37] Article 13

[33] See especially EEC Treaty, Arts 7, 48(2), and 119 (now EC Treaty, Arts 12, 39(2), and 141). Implicitly the principle of non-discrimination also appears in EEC Treaty, Arts 30, 52, and 59 (now EC Treaty, Arts 28, 43, and 49). cf G More, 'The Principle of Equal Treatment: From Market Unifier to Fundamental Right?' in P Craig and G de Búrca (eds), *The Evolution of EU Law* (OUP, 1999) 517, 521–35; G de Búrca, 'The Role of Equality in European Community Law' in A Dashwood and S O'Leary (eds), *The Principle of Equal Treatment in EC Law* (Sweet & Maxwell, 1997) 13–34.

[34] The adoption of Council Directive (EEC) 76/207, on the implementation of the principle of equal treatment for men and women as regards access to employment, vocational training and promotion, and working conditions [1976] OJ L39/40, is an example. cf Council Resolution of 21 January 1974 concerning a Social Action Programme [1974] OJ C13/1.

[35] J Kenner, *EU Employment Law. From Rome to Amsterdam and Beyond* (Hart Publishing, 2003) 23–69; R Nielsen and E Szyszczak, *The Social Dimension of the European Union* (3rd edn, Handelshøjskolens Forlag, 1997) 25–8.   [36] See Case 43/75 *Defrenne v Sabena (No 2)* [1976] ECR 455.

[37] cf, for instance, the Preambles to the Acquired Rights Directive and the Collective Redundancies Directive in their original and amended versions 20 or so years later. See Council Directive (EEC) 77/187 on the approximation of the laws of the Member States relating to the safeguarding of employees' rights in the event of transfers of undertakings, businesses or parts of undertakings or businesses [1977] OJ L61/26) and cf Council Directive (EC) 98/50 [1998] OJ L201/88; and Council Directive

EC appears to be part of a yet further development in Community law towards recognizing the right to equality and non-discrimination as an 'autonomous principle', ie a human right that is of value independently of the economic or social benefits that it may bring.[38] However, this development is also somewhat hesitant and halting: the limitation of the Employment Discrimination Directive to employment and occupation, ie the restriction of the material scope within which the right to non-discrimination can be exercised, shows that the right to equal treatment is still not completely autonomous.[39] Rather, its protection in Community legislation is still largely determined by the existence of a social and economic nexus. In the EC context, this issue is, in part, also related to the complex question of how far the jurisdiction of the EC extends to non-economic issues; the extension of the scope of the Race Directive is not uncontroversial from this perspective.

In its second dimension, then, several different reasons underpin the importance of equal treatment in the EC context, but one of these reasons is the importance of competition not being stifled by the use of ascriptive criteria to exclude people from being able to participate in economic relationships, such as employment. The 'business case' for status equality is, indeed, based on the argument that discrimination on the basis of race, etc is anti-competitive. In fact, there is a long tradition of viewing anti-discrimination law in this light outside the EC,[40] and in the EC the relationship of gender equality with the operation of the market goes back to the original Article 119 EEC on equal pay in the Treaty of Rome.[41] There is, therefore, some overlap between addressing status equality and promoting competitive markets.

This is not to say that the second dimension of equal treatment is simply the same as the first dimension, just that it overlaps to an extent.[42] In fact, the second dimension of equal treatment has an increasingly important role in EC law.[43] Initially, the approach of the Court was somewhat hesitant. Although in the third *Defrenne* case[44] the ECJ recognized that the elimination of sex discrimination formed part of fundamental rights, the Court declined to widen the scope of Article 119 (now 141), which provides for equal pay between men and women, to

---

(EEC) 75/129 on the approximation of the laws of the Member States relating to collective redundancies [1975] OJ L48/29; and cf Council Directive (EC) 98/59 [1998] OJ L225/16.

[38] More (n 33 above) 547–8. For interesting explorations of the relationship between social and fundamental rights in the EU context, see S Fredman, 'Transformation or Dilution: Fundamental Rights in the EU Social Space' (2006) 12 European Law Journal 41; S Prechal, 'Equality of Treatment, Non-Discrimination and Social Policy: Achievements in Three Themes' (2004) 41 CMLR 533.

[39] L Waddington, *The Expanding Role of the Equality Principle in European Union Law* (EUI, 2003) 29.

[40] C McCrudden, *Anti-Discrimination Law* (1st edn, Ashgate, 1991) Introduction.

[41] On labour law (including women's equality) having a dual economic and social aspect: ECJ in Case 43/75 *Defrenne II* [1976] ECR 455. EEC Treaty Art 119 pursues a 'double aim, which is at once economic and social', para 12.

[42] For that reason, Christine Breining-Kaufman's analysis of the differences between a trade view of equality and a human rights view is too starkly drawn. See C Breining-Kaufman, 'The Legal Matrix of Human Rights and Trade Law: State Obligations versus Private Rights and Obligations' in T Cottier, J Pauwelyn, and E Bürgi (eds), *Human Rights and International Trade* (OUP, 2005) 95, 103–4.

[43] Tridimas (n 12 above) 69.   [44] Case C-149/77 *Defrenne v Sabena* [1978] ECR I-1365.

require equality in respect of other working conditions. In the *Grant* case (regarding discrimination on grounds of sexual orientation) the Court was cautious in drawing on the apparent logic of this position to reach conclusions that were, in the Court's view, beyond the existing European political consensus.[45] In the *Razzouk* case, however, after reiterating that freedom from sex discrimination is a fundamental right, the Court held that it must, therefore, be upheld in the context of relations between the institutions and their employees. The Court held, therefore, that, in interpreting the Staff Regulations, the requirements of the principle of equal treatment 'are in no way limited to those resulting from Article 119 [now 141] of the EEC Treaty or from the Community directives adopted in this field'.[46] So too, equality as a fundamental right played an important role in *P v S and Cornwall CC*,[47] which considered whether discrimination on the grounds of gender reassignment was prohibited under EC law. For Tridimas, the case 'provides a prime example of the way the Court views the principle of equality as a general principle of EC law transcending the provisions of Community legislation'.

Perhaps the most dramatic example of this interpretation of 'equal treatment', and of its far-reaching consequences, occurred in the *Mangold* case. According to Article 1, 'the purpose of . . . [the Employment Discrimination] Directive [2000/78] is to lay down a general framework for combating discrimination on the grounds of religion or belief, disability, age or sexual orientation as regards employment and occupation, with a view to putting into effect in the Member States the principle of equal treatment'. The significance, for the operation of the equality directives, of recognizing equal treatment as a general principle can be seen in *Mangold*,[48] which involved the issue, *inter alia*, of the application of the Employment Discrimination Directive's prohibition of age discrimination in Germany. A major problem standing in the way of the application of the Directive appeared to be that the time limit for transposition of the age discrimination provisions of the Directive had not yet passed for Germany. The ECJ, however, did not find this to be an insuperable barrier. Crucially for our purposes,[49] the ECJ stated that the principle of non-discrimination on grounds of age must be regarded as a general principle of Community law (drawing on international human rights instruments, *inter alia*). This is an important aspect of Community law regarding status equality (the same reasoning would, presumably, apply to discrimination on the basis of the other statuses listed in Article 13 EC, as well as gender), and it provides a vital link with the law regarding public procurement, which the ECJ has also said is based on the concept of 'equal treatment'.

[45] Case C-249/96 *Grant v South West Trains Ltd* [1998] ECR I-621.

[46] Joined Cases 75 & 117/82 *Razzouk and Beydoun v Commission* [1984] ECR 1509, para 17. See also Case C-37/89 *Michel Weiser v Caisse Nationale des Barreaux Français* [1990] ECR I-2395.

[47] Case C-13/94 *P v S and Cornwall CC* [1996] ECR I-2143.

[48] Case C-144/04 *Mangold v Rüdiger Helm* [2005] ECR I-9981. Note, however, that the current status of *Mangold* is uncertain, following the criticism of the judgment by Advocate General Mazák in Case C-411/05 *Félix Palacios de la Villa v Cortefiel Servicios SA* of 15 February 2007.

[49] Mangold (n 48 above) paras 74–77.

Status equality and procurement law: the same principle of equal treatment?

The second dimension of equal treatment in Community law has been largely, if not entirely, ignored in current interpretations of the procurement directives by the Commission, for reasons that are not at all clear. The ECJ has made clear, after all, that the protection of fundamental rights is one of the general principles of EC law, that the requirements flowing from the protection of fundamental rights in the Community legal order are binding on the EC institutions, that they are also binding on Member States when they implement EC rules,[50] and that among the fundamental rights protected by the ECJ, particular aspects of equality have been identified. These include religious equality[51] and the prohibition of sex discrimination.[52] More broadly, the Court has held that fundamental rights 'include the general principle of equality and non-discrimination'.[53]

Although not legally binding, the Recitals to the directives are relevant to the issue.[54] Recital 2 of the Public Sector Directive and Recital 9 of the Utilities Directive both state that the directives are 'based on' several principles that 'derive' from the four freedoms set out in the Treaty, including 'the principle of equal treatment [and] the principle of non-discrimination'. Four points are immediately apparent: first, that non-discrimination appears to be a concept that is separable from equal treatment with the latter (equal treatment) being a broader concept (a point made clear in Recital 9 to the Utilities Directive, which states that 'the principle of non-discrimination is no more than a *specific expression*' of the principle of equal treatment). Second, there is no apparent limit to the scope of the principle of equal treatment as applying only to equal treatment on the basis of nationality. When the directives wish to make clear that only non-discrimination on the basis of nationality is to be included, they say so explicitly.[55] Third, the procurement directives are not a complete instantiation of the appropriate relationship between the 'equal treatment' principle and public procurement; they do not incorporate the whole of the equal treatment principle, but the equal treatment principle more broadly should be integrated into their interpretation. Fourth, there is nothing in the procurement directives that would lead anyone to suppose that equal treatment should here be seen as encompassing only equal treatment in its first dimension. As Recital 2 of the Public Sector Directive explicitly states: the provisions of the Directive 'should therefore be interpreted in accordance with both the aforementioned rules and principles and other rules of the Treaty'. The same must surely apply to the Utilities Directive.

[50] Case C-442/00 *Caballero v Fondo de Garantia Salarial (Fogasa)* [2002] ECR I-11915.

[51] Case 130/75 *Prais v Council* [1976] ECR 1589.

[52] Case C-149/77 *Defrenne v Sabena* [1978] ECR I-1365, paras 26, 27. See C Docksey, 'The Principle of Equality between Women and Men as Fundamental Right under Community Law' (1991) 20 ILJ 258.

[53] Case C-442/00 *Caballero v Fondo de Garantia Salarial (Fogasa)* [2003] IRLR 115, para 32.

[54] S Arrowsmith, Law (n 1 above) 761.   [55] eg Public Sector Directive, Art 3.

Obligations to promote status equality in the procurement directives

The analysis so far suggests that there are likely to be situations where the aim of the directives and the aim of status equality law will overlap to such an extent that they pursue the same policy objective of reducing barriers to competition, and that the concept of equal treatment goes further in promoting status equality. What are the implications for the interpretation of the directives?[56] Both Article 2 of the Public Sector Directive and Article 10 of the Utilities Directive state clearly and simply: 'Contracting authorities shall treat economic operators equally and non-discriminatorily and shall act in a transparent way.' The directives then proceed to set out various ways in which these principles should be implemented in specific situations. With the exception of Article 3 of the Public Sector Directive, these requirements to act in a non-discriminatory way, or to treat economic operators equally, are not stated only to require non-discrimination or equality on grounds of nationality,[57] or to restrict its interpretation to include only the first dimension of the meaning of equal treatment. There appears no reason, in the light of the ECJ's case law on equal treatment in the Treaty, to narrow the meaning of the directives in this way. It therefore appears that there is both a general obligation to accord equal treatment to economic operators under the directives and more specific obligations of the same kind applicable to more specific situations, and that these require non-discrimination and equality on the basis of race, gender, etc.

Indeed, to the extent that the directives require 'equal treatment' and not just 'non-discrimination', they may go further in some respects. Where do the differences between non-discrimination and equal treatment lie? The best way to consider the difference is to view non-discrimination as giving rise to a negative obligation, whereas equal treatment involves the taking of action by the Member State (as under the fourth approach to equality sketched out previously). Is there a positive obligation on Member States to further the principle of equal treatment? Mathias Krügner considers that such an obligation should be derived in part from Article 10 EC and the principle of effectiveness (effet utile) that derives from it. Article 10 provides: 'Member States shall take all appropriate measures, whether general or particular, to ensure fulfilment of the obligations arising out of this Treaty or resulting from action taken by the institutions of the Community. They shall facilitate the achievement of the Community's tasks. They shall abstain from any measure which could jeopardise the attainment of the objectives of this Treaty.' Taken together with the ECJ case law,

---

[56] I do not here discuss the issue of the implications of the principle of equal treatment for procurement outside the existing procurement Directives, see M Krügner, 'The Principles of Equal Treatment and Transparency and the Commission Interpretative Communication on Concessions' (2003) 12 PPLR 181.

[57] eg the following provisions in the Public Sector Directive: Art 29(3), Art 29(6), Art 29(7), Art 30(3), Art 42(4), Art 72.

Krüger concludes that 'Member States may have to take positive measures in order to guarantee the full scope and effect of Community law',[58] including the principle of equal treatment.

If there is a positive duty to promote equal treatment under the procurement directives (and that is unclear at the moment), then that would be an important development. Thus, we may argue that some of the voluntary initiatives in Britain, where public bodies attempt to diversify their supplier base by undertaking positive action to encourage black and minority-owned businesses to tender for public contracts, could then be seen as attempts by a Member State to fulfil its positive obligation to further the principle of equal treatment under the directives. There would, however, be limits on how far EC Member States can embrace the type of affirmative action carried out in other states in this regard, such as the United States, Malaysia, and South Africa, as EC equality law imposes limits on affirmative action that are narrower than those drawn elsewhere.[59]

Equal treatment as an interpretative principle

Beyond this context, where else would my argument that the directives be interpreted in the light of the principle of equal treatment, including both its dimensions, be of importance? It is clear from much of the legal writing on the directives that there are significant issues of interpretation that are likely to face contracting authorities and others in the next few years. With relatively few exceptions, where a question of interpretation has arisen that might go either to uphold the use of procurement linkages, or against such linkages, the interpretation advanced has more often seemed to be driven by pragmatic and policy considerations, with an absence of reference to principle. My principal suggestion is that understanding that the use of procurement linkages to advance status equality is a way of delivering a Community policy, part of the conception of equal treatment regarded by the ECJ as a fundamental interpretative principle of EC law, will allow an interpretation that is much more favourable to allowing such linkages than one that ignores such an understanding.

Conflicts between status equality linkages in procurement can come into conflict with obligations to promote competitive procurement markets in the Community. But when we recognize that both are aspects of the same fundamental principle of equal treatment, the principle enunciated by the German Constitutional Court in its interpretation of rights conflicts in German Constitutional law is of considerable relevance: 'This conflict . . . is to be resolved on the principle of practical concordancy, which requires that no one of the conflicting legal positions be preferred

---

58 Krügner (n 56 above) 194.
59 See eg Case C-319/03 *Briheche* [2004] ECR I-8807; Case C-476/99 *Lommers* [2002] ECR I-2891; Case C-407/98 *Abrahamsson* [2002] ECR I-5539; Case C-158/97 *Badeck* [2000] ECR I-1875; Case 490/95 *Marschall* [1997] ECR I-6363.

and maximally asserted, but all given as protective as possible an arrangement.'[60] It is at this point that the further principle widely utilized by the ECJ as a method of harmonizing apparently conflicting provisions, and mentioned specifically in the Recitals (Recital 2 to the Public Sector Directive; Recital 9 to the Utilities Directive) as a principle governing the interpretation of the procurement directives, comes into play, ie the principle of proportionality. This helps because it means that the procurement directives should be interpreted as not going further than is necessary to serve legitimate policies, particularly if to do so would undermine the furtherance of another fundamental EC policy, to achieve status equality.

III. Freedom of Contract and the Subject Matter of the Contract

An examination of the effect of the procurement directives on the ability of contracting authorities to incorporate procurement linkages must take into account that there is an earlier stage in contracting about which the directives have very little to say, when the contracting authority is deciding what, exactly, it is that it wants to contract for. In broad terms, a 'government contract' arises between a public body and a supplier or contractor when there is an agreement between them enforced by the law or recognized by the law as affecting the rights and duties of the parties.[61] There are many legal restrictions on the principle of freedom of contract that apply to both public contracts and private contracts; these are usually governed by domestic law.

Sometimes, for example, public contracts are subject to greater restrictions on freedom of contract than private contracts because the market disciplines that apply in the case of private contracts do not necessarily apply in the case of public contracts, and because we sometimes require public bodies to meet a higher level of ethical standards than private contractors. Do the EC procurement directives, or Community law more generally, impose restrictions on the freedom of contract of parties in a public contract? The answer is quite clearly 'yes', in that (as we have seen) both the Treaty and the directives impose an obligation that economic operators be accorded 'equal treatment', and this prohibits public authorities from discriminating against, for example, foreign contractors. As the Commission's communication on environmental matters in procurement put it:

A contracting authority, as a public body, has to observe the general rules and principles of Community law. More precisely, these are the principles regarding the free movement of goods and services as laid down in Articles 28 to 30 (formerly 30 to 36), and 43 to 55 (formerly 52 to 66) of the EC Treaty. This implies that the subject matter of a public contract

---

[60] 'Classroom Crucifix' 93 BverfGE 1 (1996), translated and reproduced in D Kommers, *The Constitutional Jurisprudence of the Federal Republic of Germany* (2nd edn, 1997).

[61] G Treitel, 'Contract: General Rules', in P Birks, *English Private Law* (OUP, 2004) Vol II, para 8.01.

may not be defined with the objective or the result that access to the contract is limited to domestic companies to the detriment of tenderers from other Member States.[62]

Does Community law go further than that in limiting freedom of contract? As we have seen, Community law is particularly concerned with the *way* in which public contracts are dealt with; is it also concerned with limiting *what* can be contracted for, beyond simply requiring that equal treatment is accorded? The question is a crucial one because if the answer is 'no', then there seems little under Community law to prevent a public body from specifying that a particular social policy goal is *that for which the public body is specifically contracting*. In its two Communications, on environmental and social considerations in procurement, the Commission made clear that, apart from the issue of equal treatment, Community law did *not* regulate what could be contracted for. 'The public procurement Directives, according to the Environmental Communication, do not prescribe in any way what contracting authorities should buy and are consequently neutral as far as the subject matter of a contract is concerned.'[63] The social Communication states: 'In general, any contracting authority is free, when defining the goods or services it intends to buy, to choose to buy goods, services or works which correspond to its concerns as regards social policy... provided that such choice does not result in restricted access to the contract in question to the detriment of tenderers from other Member States.'[64] Even more clearly, the Commission's handbook on green procurement states: 'In principle [public authorities] are free to define the subject matter of the contract in any way that meets [their] needs. Public procurement legislation is not much concerned with what contracting authorities buy, but mainly with how they buy it. For that reason, none of the procurement directives restrict the subject matter of a contract as such.'[65]

Indeed, apart from these general statements making clear the extensive freedom to contract that applies, the Communication on social issues specifically states, in an important footnote: 'Certain ... contracts targeted at a particular social category have, *by their very nature*, a social objective (for example, a contract for training for long-term unemployed persons). Another example is contracts for the purchase of computer hardware/services adapted to the needs of disabled persons.'[66] If the contracting authority defines the subject matter of the contract to be the production of widgets, then no social considerations are involved. If the subject matter of the contract is defined, however, to be the supply of food to state schools in a way that

[62] Commission interpretative communication on the Community law applicable to public procurement and the possibilities for integrating environmental considerations into public procurement, COM(2001)0274 final [2001] OJ C333/0012–0026, para 1.   [63] ibid.

[64] Interpretative communication of the Commission on the Community law applicable to public procurement and the possibilities for integrating social considerations into public procurement, COM(2001)0566 final [2001] OJ C333/0027–0041, para 1.1.

[65] European Commission, 'Buying Green!: A handbook on environmental public procurement' (OOPEC, 2004) para 3.1.1.

[66] Interpretative communication of the Commission on the Community law applicable to public procurement and the possibilities for integrating social considerations into public procurement, COM(2001)0566 final [2001] OJ C333/0027–0041, fn 15 (emphasis added).

caters to a broad mix of pupils of differing faiths (or none), then the ability to supply halal meat will be an aspect of the subject matter of the contract.

As we shall see, this broad interpretation of what can constitute the subject matter of the contract gels perfectly with, and is further borne out by, the approach taken in the directives as to what can constitute a technical specification. Of course, as the environmental Communication also makes clear, the directives kick in after the decision is made as to what it is that is being contracted for, so that:

> After having made the first choice on the subject matter of the contract, the public procurement Directives oblige contracting authorities to specify the characteristics of the subject in a manner such that it fulfils the use for which it is intended by the contracting authority. To this end, the Directives contain a number of provisions relating to common rules in the technical field, to be specified in the contract documents relating to each contract.

It is also clear that the subject matter of each contract and the criteria governing its award must be clearly defined.[67] We will be much concerned with these issues subsequently. For the moment, however, all that concerns us is whether the directives limit what can be contracted for and, apart from the issue of equal treatment and compliance with the provisions of the Treaty, the answer appears to be that the directives do not limit what can be contracted for.

Can we go further? Can we have mixed purpose public contracts, in which the contracting authority wants to achieve two objectives, rather than one, where one objective is the purchase of an everyday item (such as the supply of pencils), and the second is the achievement of a social aim (such as equal status)? Can a contracting authority, for example, say that the subject matter of the contract is (a) the supply of widgets, (b) *by a workforce made up of those drawn from the unemployed?* The answer appears to be 'yes'. Indeed, it would be surprising if contracts could not be used as such multipurpose vehicles, when we consider the complex subject matter of some Public Private Partnerships (PPP) contracts. Why might there be any argument that this is not permissible? The first response is sometimes simply disbelief that such a simple solution to such an apparently difficult and long-running issue is possible under Community law. But that is hardly an argument against the approach suggested here. Describing the incorporation of social issues into procurement as involving the use of 'secondary' considerations is potentially misleading. If the subject matter of the contract can itself be the delivery of the social policy, then social issues are no longer 'secondary' to the contract, but central to it, and the use of the term 'secondary' in this context to describe them is misleading.

Some previous commentators did, in fact, address this point.[68] Kai Krüger, Ruth Nielsen, and Niklas Bruun, argued in 1998: 'It is perfectly acceptable to award

---

[67] Case C-87/94 *Commission v Belgium* [1996] ECR I-2043, paras 51–53, and Case C-324/98 *Telaustria and Telefonadress* [2000] ECR I-10745, para 61.

[68] K Krüger, R Nielsen, and N Bruun, *European Public Contracts in a Labour Law Perspective* (DJØF Publishing, 1998) 139.

contracts for the erection or supply of facilities for more atypical functions such as bettering conditions for immigrants or national minorities, women's paid labour market participation, district areas in situations where no commercial aspects apply.'[69] They continued:

Contracts subject to procurement procedure rules could however also be aimed at national policy objectives such as . . . securing employment or aiming at environmental preservation. Or contracts could have twofold purposes with public policy objectives integrated in more conventional best value for money purchase . . . The scope of discretion left to the contracting entities in matters of objectives, purpose and aims of public contracts is wide. The object of the contract and the more specific commitments under the contract in question are to a large extent left untouched by the procurement regulations.[70]

A second objection to the approach advocated here may be that the incorporation of such considerations as primary elements of the subject matter of the contract is so liable to abuse that it should be stopped, but that argument (apart from being based on arguable empirical assumptions as we shall see in chapter 18 below) has no legal basis on which to hang its scepticism of the incorporation of such social policy considerations. There is nothing in the directives that seeks to prevent contracting authorities from doing things that, in policy terms, we might think of as stupid, or unacceptable for political reasons. Krüger, Nielsen, and Bruun pointed to a potential argument against this wide interpretation, referring to 'the underlying need for maximum transparency injected into the final award. Transparency in this rather blunt form [commercial objectives] might justify award evaluations which render otherwise acceptable Community objectives as illegal.'[71] Allowing them to be included as award criteria might 'compromise an efficient ex post review of the decisions taken at the end of the procedure'. But, provided transparency is ensured in other ways, there is no *a priori* reason to resort to the 'blunt' approach, where to do so would limit so substantially the policy space available to Member States.

A third argument against the permissive approach to the subject matter of the contract advocated here is more complex, relating to the basis on which a contact exists or not. In English law, for example, it is probably not possible to contract with someone simply to obey the law because there is no consideration by the party promising to obey the law since they are under a legal obligation to do so in any event. But that is a question of domestic law, not (at least so far) a matter of Community law. Nevertheless, to avoid such an issue arising as a matter of Community law, it may well be better therefore to require that the 'social' subject matter of the contract is one that obliges the other party to go further than simply obeying the law.

Even if the directives are not intended to operate as a mechanism of quality or price control and recognize the parties' freedom of contract with respect to the

---

[69] ibid 139.   [70] ibid 140–1.   [71] ibid 153.

essential features of their bargain, there remains an important distinction between the term or terms which express the substance of the bargain and 'incidental' (if important) terms which surround them. A fourth response may be that in most cases what a public authority is attempting to do is simply to place incidental, if important, social side constraints on the operation of a contract whose substance is primarily about something else, such as the delivery of widgets. This is, no doubt, correct but does not respond to the issue I am raising here. This is: is it *possible* for a contracting authority to specify a social objective as the subject matter of the contract? I am not addressing the empirical question of whether that is what contracting authorities are currently doing. The point does remind us, however, that if the contracting authority does want the social objective to be part of the subject matter of the contract, it will need to make clear that this is precisely what it wants to achieve, because the default position of observers may well be that, if it does not do this, the social consideration will be regarded as 'secondary', in the sense of being a mere incidental side constraint.

Does the case law of the ECJ dealing with public procurement support or challenge the permissive interpretation of the subject matter of the contract discussed above? One case in particular may seem to create problems for this interpretation: the *Beentjes* case, which has been considered previously in chapter 10. The proceedings concerned a decision to award a public works contract. Beentjes had submitted the lowest bid, but the contract had been awarded to another bidder. Several reasons were given for preferring the other bid, including that Beentjes was not able to employ long-term unemployed persons. The awarding authority had stated this as a necessary condition. Beentjes challenged the decision, contending that the Works Directive precluded the contracting authorities from taking account of this consideration. The Court concluded that the condition relating to long-term unemployed people was not precluded by the directive. However, the Court held further that the policy could only be lawful if it was consistent with Treaty principles, which excluded practices operating in a discriminatory manner.

There are several major uncertainties concerning the meaning and implications of the decision of the ECJ in the *Beentjes* case. Two major interpretations are possible. One possible interpretation is that the Court permitted the incorporation of the social policy where the authority lays down a social policy specifically as part of the *contractual conditions* which must be complied with by the contractor. An alternative interpretation would read the case as permitting the contracting authority to decide not to award a contract to a contractor for a reason *other* than failure to agree to a contractual condition. The function of the directive, on this second interpretation, is to lay down mandatory procedural requirements relating to some aspects of the contracting process, but otherwise to leave discretion to contracting authorities as to whom to award the contract. Under this interpretation, contractors could be rejected, for example, because of anticipated failure to meet a desired policy aim specified by the contracting authority. It is unclear whether the Court adopted the first or the second interpretation discussed above. On the one hand, it has been argued that Case 360/89, *Commission v Italy* implies that the first interpretation of the directive discussed above is correct. Otherwise an inconsistency between it and the *Beentjes* case would arise.[72] It should be noted also that it is the first interpretation that the Commission appears to adopt in its Communication following the *Beentjes* decision.[73]

If the first interpretation is correct, there remain several issues. First, may a contracting authority, which specifies achievement of a social policy as a contractual requirement, take agreement to comply with the contractual condition into account in deciding to whom the contract should be awarded? Second, may a contracting authority, which specifies achievement of a social policy as a contractual requirement, reject a tender where the tenderer agrees to carry out the conditions of the contract, but the contracting authority considers that the tenderer may be unable to do so? On the one hand, a limited future-oriented approach does not seem consistent with the *Beentjes* case itself. On the other hand, some have argued that the second interpretation only allows the determination of a contract once failure to comply with a contractual term is established, and not in anticipation of inability to comply. The Commission's communication stressed that the *Beentjes* approach must not be interpreted as effectively allowing the application of a criterion of award not specified in the directives.[74] As Winter argues:

... a careful analysis will be necessary to ascertain whether a contractual condition should in reality not be characterized as an unlawful criterion of award. This would be the case if the contract notice, rather than requiring the successful tenderer to employ a specific number of unemployed persons, would indicate that the contracting authority is to choose between tenders taking into account the proposals of tenderers to use unemployed persons in the performance of their contract *or their ability to employ* such persons.[75]

On this interpretation, the sanction for failure to meet the condition specified will be not to award future contracts to that contractor. Indeed, failure to meet a contractual condition might well amount to professional misconduct sufficient to refuse to consider the tenderer in future.

If the first interpretation is accepted, we need to consider also the implications of this approach for the question of what may be taken into account in the context of suitability criteria. May these contractual conditions be taken into account in *selecting* contractors? In the light of what has been said above concerning suitability criteria, the answer would seem to be that they may not be taken into account in the context of suitability. However, we have not yet considered one element in the directive relating to suitability. The Public Sector Directive clearly envisages the

---

[72] S Arrowsmith, 'Public Procurement as an Instrument of Policy and the Impact of Market Liberalisation' (1995) 111 LQR 235.   [73] COM(89)400 [1989] OJ C311/7, 12, para 47.
[74] ibid.
[75] JA Winter, 'Public Procurement' (1991) 28 CMLR 741, 774 (emphasis added). See also W van Gervan, 'General Report to the 14th FIDE Congress, in FIDE, L'Application dans les Etats Membres des Directives sur les Marchés Publics' (Madrid, 1990) 333.

rejection of contractors in the context of suitability who do not have the required 'technical capacity'. 'Technical capacity' relates to the ability to carry out the contractual conditions of the contract. If these contractual conditions include certain social policy objectives, then 'technical capacity' may include the ability to carry out these social objectives. If so, contractors may legitimately be excluded under selection criteria also for anticipated failure to meet such conditions, as well as in the context of the application of the award criteria. Otherwise, it might be said, we would be left in the position whereby it would be permissible to exclude for likely failure to meet a contractual condition when awarding the contract, but not at the stage of shortlisting potential contractors.

The major legal problem with this argument lies in the *Beentjes* case itself. For in its judgment the Court stated that the ability to comply with the condition relating to the long-term unemployed was not a matter of technical capacity.[76] It has been argued that this statement by the Court strengthens the argument that the second interpretation is the one that the Court intended to adopt. For if the Court was intending to permit such policies, however they were implemented (ie whether or not by contractual requirement), then ability to comply would not be a matter of technical capacity.[77] As Arrowsmith has observed in the past, there was a considerable degree of apparent illogicality about the legal position before the reform efforts of the late 1990s: 'to the extent that social and environmental policies may be taken into account, Member States should be permitted to call for the evidence necessary to apply these policies, and if it is to be permitted at all to include social conditions relating to the contract, it should be permitted to exclude firms that cannot meet them'.[78]

There is, however, a third interpretation of the *Beentjes* case that appears to resolve the difficulties. This interpretation distinguishes between conditions that put into effect the subject matter of the contract, and those that do not. *Beentjes* falls into the latter category. Such conditions do not need to relate to the subject matter of the contract. They operate post-award only; provided the contractor or supplier agrees to operate the condition if awarded the contract, then the ability to comply with the condition is not subject to pre-award scrutiny, and can play no part in the award of the contract itself. This is what the Court decided the local authority was able do in the *Beentjes* case. However, there is another type of condition that puts into effect the subject matter of the contract. This is not the *Beentjes* case; otherwise the Court would not have gone out of its way to stress that the condition was not a matter of technical capacity. The Court was not deciding, therefore, whether the reduction in unemployment through the use of unemployed

---

[76] *Beentjes*, judgment, para 28.

[77] S Arrowsmith, 'Restricted Awards Procedures under the Public Works Contracts Regulations 1991: A Commentary on General Building and Maintenance v Greenwich Borough Council' (1993) 4 PPLR CS92, CS100.

[78] S Arrowsmith, 'The Community's Legal Framework on Public Procurement: "The Way Forward" at Last' (1999) 36 CMLR 13, 48.

persons could be a permissible subject matter of the contract, only that it was not the subject matter of the contract *in this particular case*.[79]

Is there any better *legal* argument against the broad approach to the concept of the subject matter of the contract suggested above? Arguably, the approach that leaves open the definition of the subject matter in the way suggested might be criticized as based on a common law approach to contracts. Perhaps a different approach may be taken to this issue depending on whether the starting point is a common law or civil law approach. It is arguable that if we were to take a civil law approach, then, putting the matter simplistically, central to our understanding of the subject matter of this particular contract will have been an earlier choice made on what *general* type of contract is involved. This idea of contracts being classifiable on the basis of their general objective, an approach based on the idea of 'nominate' contracts, is then likely to lead one to consider that certain types of conditions in any particular contract are not central to that general type of contract, and therefore cannot be part of the subject matter of that contract. So, classifying a contract as one for sale of goods will generate an expectation that certain elements of the contract are central to sales contracts, whilst other terms will not. Thus, this initial classification process is a vital part of the process of understanding what will be considered by the courts to be central to assessing the subject matter of the contract. One way of describing this process might be to say that the classification of the contract as a particular type of nominate contract generates a set of abstract expectations as to what is central to that contract. In the common law, on the other hand, except where statute has intervened, the concept of nominate contracts is much less prevalent, and therefore what constitutes the subject matter of the contract is something that is much more up to the parties in any particular case to determine, rather than one affected by an earlier choice of which nominate contract is involved.

Is there any evidence that this 'civil law' approach,[80] if that is what it is, is one that should be given to the meaning of the subject matter of the contract under Community law? One argument that comes close to this approach is based on the distinction between works, supply, service, and utility contracts specified in the directives. Does this classification generate an approach akin to the nominate contracts of civil law? In other words, does the classification of contracts into works, supply, or service contracts lead to a requirement that only certain issues can be part of the subject matter of the contract? There is some support for such an approach in at least one of the Commission's communications. The environmental communication, for example says (just before referring to the distinction between works, supplies, and services contracts): 'The possibilities for the taking into account of environmental considerations differ according to the different types of contracts.'[81]

---

[79] Arrowsmith, Law (n 1 above) 1287–90, reaches a similar conclusion regarding the potential breadth of award criteria, even with an acceptance of the narrow view of *Beentjes*.

[80] See B Nicholas, *The French Law of Contract* (2nd edn, OUP, 1992), which has been a prime source of information on this.   [81] Environmental communication (n 62 above) 7.

But any sense that this means that what can be included within the agreed subject matter of a contract is limited *legally* by the nature of the contract as dealing with works, services, or supplies is rebutted by a later statement, dealing with supply contracts, which says: 'Supply contracts relate, generally, to the purchase of final or end products. Therefore, *apart from the basic and essential choice of the subject matter of the contract ("what shall I purchase?")*, the possibilities to take into account environmental considerations in addition to this choice are not as extensive as for works and service contracts.'[82] The phrase emphasized in the quotation indicates that the 'common law' approach is the one assumed to operate in this context. It is clear also from the case law of the ECJ that the subject matter of the contract determines the classification as works, supplies, or services, and not the other way round.[83]

In any event, we should be sceptical of dividing the civil from the common law approach so rigidly. It is clear that the common law approach to the subject matter of the contract suggested above is entirely consistent with the public procurement law of France, for example. The new French Procurement Code of 2006 provides various ways to integrate environmental and social agendas into procurement.[84] One approach is essentially to 'mainstream' public policy concerns into the planning process of public procurement. The Code stresses, for example, that one of the ways of addressing the goal of achieving sustainable development is to build in the issue of sustainable development right at the beginning of the project, regarding one of the purposes of the contract as being the achievement of such sustainable development. Article 5 of the Code, indeed, imposes on the public body the duty to take into account concerns of sustainable development, defined as development that meets the needs for the present without compromising the capacity of the future generations to answer theirs. Thus, it is at the first stage of the procurement process (the definition of the subject matter of the contract) that the Code envisages that the public body should consider the possibilities of integrating requirements in terms of the environment, and the cost implications of doing so.

What of the case law of the ECJ in other areas of Community law? Does this assist our understanding of what meaning we should attach to the 'subject matter of the contract' in the procurement context? The issue of what constitutes the subject matter of the contract arises in at least two other areas of Community law. It arises, first, in the context of the Unfair Terms Directive, where the 'main subject matter of the contract' is exempted from the restrictions that otherwise apply, in order to allow the retention of the freedom of contract of the parties.[85] In addition, the issue of what constitutes the subject matter of the contract arises in Article 82.

---

[82] ibid 8 (emphasis added).

[83] Case C-340/02, *Commission v France* [2004] ECR I-9845, para 35.

[84] Dècret no 2006-975 du 1er août 2006 portant code des marchés publics, JORF No 179 du 4 août 2006, 11627, available at <http://www.legifrance.gouv.fr>.

[85] See, in general, the useful discussions in Law Commission, *Unfair Terms in Contracts, A Joint Consultation Paper* (Law Com No 166, 2005) (Scot Law Com No 119, 2005); Law Commission, *Unfair Terms in Contracts* (Law Com No 292, 2005) (Scot Law Com No 199, 2005) Cm 6464.

This states that: 'Any abuse by one or more undertakings of a dominant position within the common market or in a substantial part of it shall be prohibited as incompatible with the common market in so far as it may affect trade between Member States.' Such abuse may consist in various activities: directly or indirectly imposing unfair prices or other unfair trading conditions; limiting production, markets or technical development to the detriment of consumers; or applying dissimilar conditions to equivalent transactions with other trading parties. Or, of most interest from our point of view, it may consist in making the conclusion of contracts subject to acceptance by the other parties of supplementary obligations *'which have no connection with the subject matter of such contracts'*. In neither of these contexts is there case law of the ECJ that would prevent the adoption of the broad approach to the concept of the subject matter of the contract advocated above in the context of the procurement directives.

IV. Overall Limits of the Procurement Directives: the Limits of the Treaty

In most cases the legal tensions arising out of the use of status equality linkages in procurement can be resolved within the four corners of the procurement directives, interpreted in accordance with the general principles of Community law. There is, however, an additional method of addressing the issues. The procurement directives are anyway subject to a Treaty-based exception that nothing in the directive 'should prevent the imposition or enforcement of measures necessary to protect public policy, public morality, public security, health, human and animal life or the preservation of plant life, in particular with a view to sustainable development, provided that these measures are in conformity with the Treaty'.[86] When will a measure adopted by a Member State be regarded as 'necessary' to protect 'public policy', 'public morality', or 'public security'? This is now an area of considerable activity by the ECJ and only the bare outlines of some of the issues can be discussed here. There is considerable uncertainty about the weight the Court gives respectively to economic rights and human rights where they conflict.[87]

In the *Gebhard* case[88] the Court clarified the test for justifying national requirements impacting on the right of establishment. In general, where the taking-up or the pursuit of a specific activity is subject to certain conditions in the host Member State, a national of another Member State intending to pursue that activity must

---

[86] Recital 6 to the Public Sector Directive; Recital 13 to the Utilities Directive.

[87] Craig and de Búrca (n 33 above) 347. For a more detailed discussion see JHH Weiler, 'Fundamental Rights and Fundamental Boundaries: On the Conflict of Standards and Values in the Protection of Human Rights in the European Legal Space', in JHH Weiler, *The Constitution of Europe* (Cambridge University Press, 1999) 102–29.

[88] Case C-55/94 *Reinhard Gebhard v Consiglio dell'Ordine degli Avvocati e Procuratori di Milano*, [1995] ECR I-4165.

in principle comply with them. The Court mentions 'provisions laid down by law, regulation or administrative action justified by the general good, such as rules relating to organization, qualifications, professional ethics, supervision and liability'.[89] However, national measures 'liable to hinder or make less attractive the exercise of fundamental freedoms guaranteed by the Treaty' must fulfil four conditions in order to be compatible with Community law: 'they must be applied in a non-discriminatory manner; they must be justified by imperative requirements in the general interest; they must be suitable for securing the attainment of the objective which they pursue; and they must not go beyond what is necessary in order to attain it'.[90]

What then could constitute 'imperative requirements in the general interest'? In the *Guiot* case[91] the Court considered this question in the context of national legislation that required an employer to pay employer's contributions to the social security fund of the host Member State in addition to the contributions already paid by him to the social security fund of the state where he was established. Since such legislation placed an additional financial burden on the employer—the employer was at a disadvantage compared with employers established in the host state—it was therefore liable to restrict the freedom to provide services. However, the Court held that 'the public interest relating to the social protection of workers in the construction industry may . . . because of the conditions specific to that sector, constitute an overriding requirement justifying such a restriction on the freedom to provide services'.[92] However, that was not the case where the workers in question enjoy essentially the same protection by virtue of employer's contributions already paid by the employer in the Member State of establishment.

The *Arblade* case[93] gave the Court the opportunity to re-examine the application of Articles 59 and 60 (now Articles 49EC and 50EC) to the posted worker issue, in the light of these jurisprudential developments. The issues were similar to, but went beyond, those raised in the *Guiot* case. Arblade and Leloup, two companies established in France, carried out works in connection with the construction of a complex of silos for the storage of sugar in Belgium, employing workers ordinarily employed in France. In the course of checks carried out on the site in 1993, Belgian inspectors requested the firms to produce various social documents required under French law that certified compliance with social legislation. Their failure to do so resulted in a prosecution, during which the companies argued that the legal requirements were contrary to Community law. The social legislation requirements contested were wide ranging: an obligation to pay the workers the minimum

---

[89] ibid para 35.

[90] ibid para 37. See also Case C-19/92 *Kraus v Land Baden-Wuerttemberg* [1993] ECR I-1663, para 32.　　　　　　[91] Case C-272/94 *Michel Guiot and Climatic SA* [1996] ECR I-1905

[92] ibid para 16. In Case C-222/95 *Société Civile Immobilière Parodi v Banque H Albert de Bary* [1997] ECR I-3899, the Court held that consumer protection could constitute a public interest ground for this purpose, para 32.

[93] Joined cases C-369/96 and C-376/96 *Arblade and ors* [1999] ECR I-8453.

remuneration fixed by the collective labour agreement applicable in Belgium; the obligation to pay employers' contributions to social security schemes; the obligation to draw up documents such as labour rules, a special staff register, and an individual account for each worker; the obligation to keep such documents available, throughout the period of activity within the territory of the first Member State, on site or in an accessible and clearly identified place within the territory of that State; and the obligation to retain such documentation for a period of five years after the employer has ceased to employ those workers in the first Member State at an address within that Member State.

The Court took the opportunity to give a wide-ranging judgment, upholding some elements of the legislative requirements, and condemning others. For our purposes, some general principles emerge that are of considerable importance. First, as had already happened in the *Reiseburo Broede* case, [94] the Court essentially amalgamated the two tests in *Vander Elst* and *Gebhard*, regarding the former as another way of stating some of the implications of the latter.

Second, the Court addressed the relationship between the concept of 'overriding reasons relating to the public interest' and the concept of 'public order'. The referring court had asked whether, as some of the national rules were contained in 'public order legislation', this affected the extent to which they were contestable under Articles 59 and 60. The Court understood the term 'public order' as 'applying to national provisions compliance with which has been deemed to be so crucial for the protection of the political, social or economic order in the Member State concerned as to require compliance therewith by all persons present on the national territory of that Member State and all legal relationships within that State'.[95] The Court did not consider that because the national rules were categorized as public order legislation, this meant that they were 'exempt from compliance with the provisions of the Treaty; if it did, the primacy and uniform application of Community law would be undermined'.[96] 'The considerations underlying such national legislation can be taken into account by Community law only in terms of the exceptions to Community freedoms expressly provided for by the Treaty and, where appropriate, on the ground that they constitute overriding reasons relating to the public interest.'[97]

Third, although the social protection of workers is capable of amounting to an 'overriding public interest',[98] provisions in national criminal law safeguarding this interest 'must be sufficiently precise and accessible that they do not render it impossible or excessively difficult in practice for such an employer to determine the obligations with which he is required to comply'.[99] Where they result in additional economic costs to the out-of-state service provider, because, for example, contributions are required to be paid in the host Member State and the employer

---

[94] Case C-3/95 *Reiseburo Broede v Gerd Sandker* [1996] ECR I-6511, para 28.
[95] ibid para 30.   [96] ibid para 31.   [97] ibid.   [98] ibid para 60.
[99] ibid para 43.

is already required to make equivalent contributions in the firm's state of establishment, they need to satisfy two tests: do the contributions payable in the host state 'give rise to any social advantage for the workers concerned', and second do the workers concerned already enjoy protection that is 'essentially similar' to that which the rules of the host Member State seek to ensure.[100]

This last point was of particular relevance in the *Mazzoleni* case.[101] The firm involved was established in France and employed workers as security officers in a shopping mall in Belgium. Some of the workers were employed full-time in Belgium, while others were employed there for only some of the time and also worked in France. Belgian government inspectors established that the firm was paying its workers working in Belgium below the minimum rates of pay established by the relevant collective agreement governing the private security industry. This case differed from *Arblade* in two important respects. First, it did not concern the construction industry, unlike several of the previous cases discussed already. Second, the evidence presented to the Court indicated that the firm, operating in a frontier region, was sending workers on a continuing basis to Belgium, but with some of its employees carrying out their work in the host country on a part-time basis and for very brief periods, unlike the circumstances in the previous cases, where employees were sent out of the state in which the firm was established to work on projects which were time limited. The Court accepted that these differences were important and, whilst adhering to the general principle of *Arblade* and its predecessors, and accepting also that imposing a minimum wage was for the legitimate purpose of protecting workers, it focused on the question of whether the application of those rules was 'necessary and proportionate for the purpose of protecting the workers concerned'.[102] Although leaving the determination of that issue to the national authorities in this case, the Court indicated some of the relevant factors that should be taken into account in determining the issue. It particular, it pointed to the importance of considering whether there was a disproportionate administrative burden imposed on this employer by the rules, and whether the objective of ensuring the same level of welfare protection for the employees of such service providers as that applicable in the territory of the host state to workers in the same sector 'may be regarded as attained if all the workers concerned enjoy an equivalent position overall in relation to remuneration, taxation and social security contributions in the host Member State and in the Member State of establishment'.[103]

The principle of *Arblade* was followed and applied in several cases subsequently.[104] Of these, the *Finalarte* case[105] considers an important additional point.

---

[100] ibid para 53.   [101] Case C-165/98 *André Mazzoleni and ors* [2001] ECR I-2189.
[102] ibid para 34.   [103] ibid para 35.
[104] Case C-493/99 *Commission v Germany* [2001] ECR I-8163; Joined Cases C-49/98, C-50/98 to C-54/98, and C-68/98 to C-71/98 *Finalarte Sociedade de Construção Civil Ld* [2001] ECR I-7831; Case C-164/99 *Portugaia Construções Ltd* [2002] ECR I-787; Case C-79/01 *Payroll Data Services (Italy) Srl* [2002] ECR I-8923.
[105] Joined Cases C-49/98, C-50/98 to C-54/98, and C-68/98 to C-71/98 *Finalarte Sociedade de Construção Civil Ld* [2001] ECR I-7831.

The case concerned the application of the German legislation on the posting of workers[106] in the context of entitlement to paid holidays in the construction industry. Among the many issues raised by the national court, it pointed out that it appeared from the explanatory memorandum of the law 'that the declared aim of that law is to protect German businesses in the construction industry from the increasing pressure of competition in the European internal market, and thus from foreign providers of services'.[107] The response of the Court was measured. On the one hand, the preparatory materials were relevant but not dispositive of the purpose of the legislation: 'whilst the intention of the legislature, to be gathered from the political debates preceding the adoption of a law or from the statement of the grounds on which it was adopted, may be an indication of the aim of that law, it is not conclusive'.[108] The test that should be applied is whether, 'viewed objectively, the rules in question in the main proceedings promote the protection of posted workers'.[109] To do this 'it is necessary to check whether those rules confer a genuine benefit on the workers concerned, which significantly adds to their social protection. In this context, the stated intention of the legislature may lead to a more careful assessment of the alleged benefits conferred on workers by the measures it has adopted.'[110] Do the legal requirements 'in fact pursue the public interest objective of protecting workers employed by providers of services established outside Germany'?[111]

Applying the principles that derive from these cases to measures included within public procurement by Member States that aim to further status equality, it would appear that the fact that these measures mesh with and further the principle of status equality adopted in the various status equality directives would considerably lessen the likelihood that they would be considered to be discriminatory between Member States. To the extent that they could be regarded as creating a non-discriminatory barrier to trade, the issue will be whether despite this, they are justified on the basis of the protection of an overriding public interest, especially as they further a Community objective.

What of potential conflicts between EC law on procurement and other (non-EC) sources of status equality, such as domestic legislation going beyond existing EC status equality requirements. The *Omega* case is relevant here.[112] The ECJ considered whether restrictions on a commercial activity by Germany on grounds of 'dignity' were consistent with Articles 49 to 55 EC on the freedom to provide services and Articles 28 to 30 EC on the free movement of goods. Omega, a German company, had been operating an installation known as a 'laserdrome', normally used for the practice of 'laser sport' in Bonn. The equipment used by Omega included equipment supplied by the British company Pulsar. Having

---

[106] Arbeitnehmerentsendegeseetz, 26 February 1996, BGB1 I, p 227.
[107] *Finalarte* (n 105 above) para 38.   [108] ibid para 40.   [109] ibid para 41.
[110] ibid para 42.   [111] ibid para 49.
[112] Case C-36/02 *Omega Spielhallen- und Automatenaufstellungs-GmbH v Oberbürgermeisterin der Bundesstadt Bonn* [2004] ECR I-9609.

noticed that the object of the game played in the 'laserdrome' included hitting sensory tags placed on the jackets worn by players, the Bonn police authority issued an order against Omega forbidding it from 'facilitating or allowing in its . . . establishment games with the object of firing on human targets using a laser beam or other technical devices (such as infrared, for example), thereby, by recording shots hitting their targets, "playing at killing" people', on pain of a fine for each game played in breach of the order.

In domestic proceedings, the German courts held that the commercial exploitation of a 'killing game' in Omega's 'laserdrome' constituted an affront to human dignity, a concept established in the first sentence of paragraph 1(1) of the German Basic (Constitutional) Law. The Bundesverwaltungsgericht referred the following question to the ECJ for a preliminary ruling: 'Is it compatible with the provisions on freedom to provide services and the free movement of goods contained in the Treaty establishing the European Community for a particular commercial activity—in this case the operation of a so-called "laserdrome" involving simulated killing action—to be prohibited under national law because it offends against the values enshrined in the constitution?' As interpreted by the ECJ, this involved two issues:

> . . . whether the prohibition of an economic activity for reasons arising from the protection of fundamental values laid down by the national constitution, such as, in this case, human dignity, is compatible with Community law, and, second, whether the ability which Member States have, for such reasons, to restrict fundamental freedoms guaranteed by the Treaty, namely the freedom to provide services and the free movement of goods, is subject . . . to the condition that that restriction be based on a legal conception that is common to all Member States.

Prior case law had established that where a Member State put in place obstacles to freedom to provide services on the basis of national measures which were applicable without distinction, these were permissible only if those measures were justified by overriding reasons relating to the public interest, were such as to guarantee the achievement of the intended aim, and did not go beyond what is necessary in order to achieve it. The particularly important issue that the ECJ considered in the *Omega* case was whether a common legal conception in all Member States is a precondition for one of those states being enabled to restrict at its discretion a certain category of provisions of goods or services protected by the EC Treaty.

Article 46 EC allowed restrictions justified for reasons of public policy, public security, or public health. In this case, the documents before the Court showed that the grounds relied on by the Bonn police authority in adopting the prohibition order expressly mentioned the fact that the activity concerned constitutes a danger to public policy. The ECJ considered that 'the concept of "public policy" in the Community context, particularly as justification for a derogation from the fundamental principle of the freedom to provide services, must be interpreted strictly, so that its scope cannot be determined unilaterally by each Member State without any control by the Community institutions. . . . Thus, public policy may be relied on only if there is a genuine and sufficiently serious threat to a fundamental interest of society.' However, 'the specific circumstances which may justify recourse to the concept of public policy may vary from one country to another and from one era to another. The competent national authorities must therefore be allowed a margin of discretion within the limits imposed by the Treaty.'[113] The Court:

> ... recalled in that context that, according to settled case-law, fundamental rights form an integral part of the general principles of law the observance of which the Court ensures, and that, for that purpose, the Court draws inspiration from the constitutional traditions common to the Member States and from the guidelines supplied by international treaties for the protection of human rights on which the Member States have collaborated or to which they are signatories. The European Convention on Human Rights and Fundamental Freedoms has special significance in that respect.[114]

The Court accepted that, as argued by the Advocate General in the case, 'the Community legal order undeniably strives to ensure respect for human dignity as a general principle of law'.[115] The Court accepted that: 'There can therefore be no doubt that the objective of protecting human dignity is compatible with Community law, it being immaterial in that respect that, in Germany, the principle of respect for human dignity has a particular status as an independent fundamental right.' The Court continued: 'Since both the Community and its Member States are required to respect fundamental rights, the protection of those rights is a legitimate interest which, in principle, justifies a restriction of the obligations imposed by Community law, even under a fundamental freedom guaranteed by the Treaty such as the freedom to provide services.'[116] However, 'measures which restrict the freedom to provide services may be justified on public policy grounds only if they are necessary for the protection of the interests which they are intended to guarantee and only in so far as those objectives cannot be attained by less restrictive measures'.[117]

It was not 'indispensable' for the restrictive measure issued by the authorities of a Member State 'to correspond to a conception shared by all Member States as regards the precise way in which the fundamental right or legitimate interest in question is to be protected'.[118] The 'need for, and proportionality of, the provisions adopted are not excluded merely because one Member State has chosen a system of protection different from that adopted by another State'.[119] The Court 'noted that, by prohibiting only the variant of the laser game the object of which is to fire on human targets and thus "play at killing" people, the contested order did not go beyond what is necessary in order to attain the objective pursued by the competent national authorities'.

---

[113] ibid para 31.   [114] ibid para 33.   [115] ibid para 34.   [116] ibid para 35.
[117] ibid para 36.   [118] ibid para 37.   [119] ibid para 38.

17

European Public Procurement Law and Equality Linkages: Government as Consumer, Government as Regulator

In the previous chapter, we considered three fundamental aspects of Community law relating to procurement: the importance of equal treatment as a basis of both EC status equality and procurement law, the overall limits to the procurement directives provided by the Treaty, and the importance of the subject matter of the contract. All three are relevant to the interpretation of the detailed provisions of the directives that is undertaken in this chapter. For the purposes of exposition, however, it is the third issue (the meaning of the subject matter of the contract) that proves to be of most analytical importance for assessing the legality of procurement linkages furthering equal status goals. In the first section of the chapter, we consider the implementation of the directives where equal status is part of the subject matter of the contract. In this context, government is acting as a consumer, buying social justice. In the second part of the chapter, we consider various provisions of the directives that permit procurement linkages irrespective of whether equal status is part of the subject matter of the contract. In this context, government is acting as a regulator, requiring social justice.

I. Procurement Linkages: Government as Consumer

Provisions regarding technical specifications

Can the tender lay down the technical specifications that must be met by successful contractors in a way that includes equality criteria? One example of this is where the technical specifications specify that computer equipment must conform to certain accessibility criteria and, as we shall see from the definitions of technical specifications below, these are specifically catered for. The issue that remains legally contentious under EC public procurement law, however, is how far a public body may specify other socially relevant technical specifications, for example that what it wants to purchase is a 'fair trade' product or service, or that the product should not be made with child labour, or that it should be made only by workers whose jobs have been subject to a pay audit to guarantee equal pay between men and women.

The argument that a public body is not able, lawfully, to include equality considerations appears to derive from the European Commission's interpretation of the 'old' public procurement directives as set out in its two interpretative Communications on environmental and social issues, which it continues to regard as applicable to the 'new' directives. This interpretation specifies that methods of processing and production can be requested in the technical specifications of the tender only where these help to specify the *performance* characteristics of the product or service. This includes both process and production methods that 'physically' affect the end product (for example absence of chemicals) and those that do not, but nevertheless affect the 'nature' of the end product, such as 'organically grown foodstuffs' even though this effect may not be visible.[1] Based on this interpretation, the view would be that 'fair trade' products (and the other specifications listed above) do not specify anything that affects the performance characteristics of the product (fair trade coffee delivers the same effects on the consumer of the coffee as non-fair trade coffee) and therefore it is impermissible to specify fair trade products as such. The benefits to growers (in the case of fair trade products) or to the workers (in the case of equal pay) do not affect the end product (either visibly or not).

Here is what the Commission says in its Interpretative Communication on environmental issues:

1.2. The possibility to require the use of a specific production process
The definition of technical specifications in the Directives does not explicitly refer to production processes. However, provided that this will not reserve the market to certain undertakings, the use of a specific production process may be required by contracting authorities if this helps to specify the performance characteristics (visible or invisible) of the product or service. The production process covers all requirements and aspects related to the manufacturing of the product which contributes to the characterising of the products without the latter being necessarily visible in the end-product. This implies that the product differs from identical products in terms of its manufacture or appearance (whether the differences are visible or not) because an environmentally-sound production process has been used, e.g. organically grown foodstuffs, or 'green' electricity. Contracting authorities must be careful that the prescription of a specific production process is not discriminatory. Requirements which do not relate to the production itself, like the way how the firm is run, on the contrary, are no[t] technical specifications and can therefore not be made mandatory.

Let us now turn to the details of the revised directives. In the case of the Public Sector Directive, Annex VI provides the necessary starting point for an understanding of

---

[1] Commission Communication on the Community law applicable to public procurement and the possibilities for integrating environmental considerations into public procurement COM(2001) 274, para 1.2 (hereafter 'Environmental Communication').

what elements may constitute technical specifications. In that context, technical specifications in the context of public works contracts[2] means:

> . . . the totality of the technical prescriptions contained in particular in the tender documents, *defining the characteristics required* of a material, product or supply, which permits a material, a product or a supply to be described in a manner *such that it fulfils the use for which it is intended* by the contracting authority. These characteristics shall include levels of environmental performance, design for all requirements (including accessibility for disabled persons) and conformity assessment, performance, safety or dimensions, including the procedures concerning quality assurance, terminology, symbols, testing and test methods, packaging, marking and labelling and *production processes and methods*. They shall also include rules relating to design and costing, the test, inspection and acceptance conditions for works and methods or techniques of construction and all other technical conditions which the contracting authority is in a position to prescribe, under general or specific regulations, in relation to the finished works and to the materials or parts which they involve [emphasis added].

We have seen that there are few limits to what can constitute the subject matter of the contract, provided the subject matter of the contract is otherwise acceptable under Community law. That assessment may be somewhat misleading, however, if it is taken as meaning that the technical specifications that may be required to be satisfied by the contracting authority are also unrestricted under the directives, for that is far from the case. In most respects, these other requirements in Article 23 seek to achieve three main aims: first, that the technical specifications should not reduce competition;[3] second, that they should be transparent;[4] and, third, that they should not discriminate against possible contractors from outside the Member State of the contracting authority.[5] There are various principles laid down detailing how, in particular, the second and third aims are to be achieved. The technical specifications must be formulated in one of four ways:

(1) By reference to technical specifications defined in Annex VI and some other specific standards (such as European standards). The technical specification should use European standards to define them, where possible, followed by international, and only then national standards. Where this approach is adopted, each reference shall be accompanied by the words 'or equivalent'.

(2) In terms of *performance or functional requirements*. However, these 'must be sufficiently precise to allow tenderers to determine the subject-matter of the contract and to allow contracting authorities to award the contract'.

---

[2] In the case of public supply or service contracts a technical specification means 'a specification in a document defining the required characteristics of a product or a service, such as quality levels, environmental performance levels, design for all requirements (including accessibility for disabled persons) and conformity assessment, performance, use of the product, safety or dimensions, including requirements relevant to the product as regards the name under which the product is sold, terminology, symbols, testing and test methods, packaging, marking and labelling, user instructions, production processes and methods and conformity assessment procedures'.

[3] Public Sector Directive, Art 23(2).   [4] ibid Art 23(1).   [5] ibid Art 23(3).

(3) By adopting a mixture of (1) and (2), specifying performance or functional requirements but using specifications mentioned in (1) as a means of presuming conformity with such performance or functional requirements.

(4) By adopting a different mixture of (1) and (2), by referring to the specifications mentioned in (1) for certain characteristics, and by referring to the performance or functional requirements mentioned in (2) for other characteristics.

Article 23(8) provides: '*Unless justified by the subject-matter of the contract*', technical specifications shall not refer to a specific make or source, *or a particular process*, or to trade marks, patents, types *or a specific origin or production* with the effect of favouring or eliminating certain undertakings or certain products. Such references are permitted on an exceptional basis, where a sufficiently precise and intelligible description of the subject matter of the contract is not possible. Such reference must be accompanied by the words 'or equivalent'. From the point of view of limiting process and production methods, this provision is of considerable importance. There are several elements that need some elucidation. The presumption taken is that, in general, specifications should not refer to a *particular* process, or to a *specific* production. That does not mean that process and production methods are not appropriate, simply that particular processes or specific production methods should not, in general, be used without justification. In any event, the position against only operates where the specification has the effect of favouring or eliminating certain undertakings or certain products. Even then, it is unacceptable *unless* justified by the subject matter of the contract.

In support of the Commission's position, then, we can point to the phrase '*defining the characteristics required . . . such that it fulfils the use for which it is intended*' and the preference for '*performance or functional requirements*' in the absence of European or international standards as indicating that it is performance characteristics that need to be specified. Indeed, the general position taken by the (UK) Office of Government Commerce is similarly that a public body may not specify the object of the procurement in this way. It says in its guidance: 'specifications for catering services and supplies cannot be framed in terms of fair or ethically traded requirements, as such "social" labels do not define the end product in terms of characteristics or performance as required by the EC rules'.[5a]

That does not exhaust the inquiry, however. There are several elements of the new directives (and of the Commission's interpretation) that may point in the opposite direction, permitting the inclusion of fair trade, etc specifications. The first issue relates to what the 'product' consists of.[6] This is very similar to, indeed intimately connected to, the issue of what the subject matter of the contract is, considered in

---

[5a] Office of Government Commerce, Information Note: Fair Trade and Public Procurement, 23 February 2004, Para 5.

[6] P Kunzlik, 'The Procurement of "Green" Energy', in S Arrowsmith and P Kunzlik, *Social and Environmental Policies under the EC Procurement Rules: New Directives and New Directions* (provisional title) (Cambridge University Press, in press).

chapter 16 above. If the product is conceptualized as having a defineable composition and physical existence, then the Commission's position is understandable because 'coffee', after all, is just coffee. But if that is required, then the supply of electricity, which appears to have been accepted as a 'product' for the purposes of the directives,[7] seems anomalous as it has no definable composition or physical existence. We can presume that 'goods' in this context is closer to the idea of 'product'. The very fact that there is a market for 'fair trade' products, for example, seems to indicate that from the point of view of the consumer, 'fair trade coffee' is a different product from simply 'coffee'. If what the contracting authority wants to buy includes a 'social' element in its manufacture, then the specifications can (indeed, must) specify what the characteristics of that social element are. If the 'product' that is being bought is defined in part by how it is made, then the technical specifications of the product may (indeed must) include these.

So, it is clear that if the subject matter of the contract is the supplying of 'coffee', the Commission's interpretation is correct, in that the characteristics of the product are then unaffected by whether it is 'fair trade' or not. But why cannot the public body specify *'fair trade* coffee' as the subject matter of the contract? From the public body's point of view they may well be thought to be different products. Provided that this requirement is clear, transparent, non-discriminatory, and able to be verified, what is there legally to prevent the public body from so specifying? Why cannot the object of the contract include the production process as an integral element of the definition of the product? Indeed, the Commission Communication on environmental issues in public procurement is, itself, not so clear-cut in ruling out the definition of the product in such terms. The Commission's advice, as quoted above, states after all: 'the product differs from identical products in terms of its manufacture or appearance (whether the differences are visible or not) because an environmentally-sound production process has been used, e.g. organically grown foodstuffs, or "green" electricity'.[8] It is understandable how a specified environmental process could have some identifiable effect on the product in the case of organically-grown foodstuffs, for example the absence of pesticides may have an effect on the chemical composition of the vegetable. But it is not clear how this would be the case with regard to green electricity.[9] There is, so far as I am aware, no physical or any other identifiable difference as regards *performance* between green and traditional electricity. Rather the difference lies entirely in the production methods involved. If 'green' electricity can be tendered for specifically, why cannot 'fair trade products' produced by a workforce paid 20 per cent over the minimum wage?

---

[7] Case C-448/01 *EVN AG and Wienstrom GmbH v Republik Österreich* [2003] ECR I-14527.

[8] Environmental Communication (n 1 above) para 1.2.

[9] P Kunzlik, 'International Procurement Regimes and the Scope for the Introduction of Environmental Factors in Public Procurement' (2003) 3(4) OECD Journal of Budgeting 107; S Arrowsmith, *The Law of Public and Utilities Procurement* (2nd edn, Sweet & Maxwell, 2005) 1275, fn 18.

Indeed, in a reply to a question in the European Parliament, the Commission itself stated that:

...a contracting authority *wishing to procure Fair Trade products* needs to define the technical specifications of the product in relation to the social or environmental performances underlying the label. Products which have obtained the specific label which was used as a basis may then be deemed to comply with the technical specification. However, other economic operators must be allowed to prove their compliance with the technical specifications by any other appropriate means. Which Fair Trade standard is appropriate for the respective tender needs to be established on a case by case basis.[10]

This seems to imply that specifying fair trade products is permissible. There does, however, remain the problem of specifying precisely what it is that the public body wants to buy. In that context, the convenience of using a label is clear, from the point of view of the public authority, because effectively the body authorizing the use of the label does the work, and the monitoring of compliance. Are 'social labels' permissible in this context, where a contracting authority specifies a product with a label as what it wants?

Although directly relating only to the specification of environmental characteristics, the remaining parts of Article 23 provide further insight into the thinking behind the whole of the article, and some guidance as to the way in which contracting authorities should be able to specify social characteristics using a label. Article 23(6) of the Public Sector Directive provides that where contracting authorities 'lay down environmental characteristics in terms of performance or functional requirements... they may use the detailed specifications, or, if necessary, parts thereof, as defined by European or (multi-) national eco-labels, or by any other eco-label', provided specified safeguards are present. There are four safeguards specified. The specifications must be 'appropriate to define the characteristics of the supplies or services that are the object of the contract'. The requirements for the label must be 'drawn up on the basis of scientific information'. The eco-labels must be 'adopted using a procedure in which all stakeholders, such as government bodies, consumers, manufacturers, distributors and environmental organisations can participate'. Finally, the eco-labels must be 'accessible to all interested parties'. Contracting authorities are permitted to 'indicate that the products and services bearing the eco-label are presumed to comply with the technical specifications laid down in the contract documents' but 'they must accept any other appropriate means of proof'. So far, however, the issue is somewhat theoretical in the equality context as, to the author's knowledge, there is no 'equality label' yet in existence.

Professional and technical knowledge or ability

We turn now to the assessment that the contracting authority must make of the suitability of economic operators in accordance with the criteria of professional

---

[10] Written question E-3517/03 by Baroness Sarah Ludford (ELDR) to the Commission, 17 November 2003—Answered by Commissioner Bolkestein on 8 January 2004.

and technical knowledge or ability under Article 48 of the Public Sector Directive. Article 44(2) of the Public Sector Directive provides that the contracting authorities 'may require candidates and tenderers to meet minimum capacity levels in accordance with Article[ ]...48'. In addition: 'These minimum levels shall be indicated in the contract notice.' It is clear that, as Article 48(1) provides, the 'technical and/or professional abilities of the economic operators shall be assessed and examined in accordance with' the subsequent provisions of Article 48 itself. Evidence of the economic operators' technical abilities may be furnished by one or more of several specified means, such as by providing evidence of previous contracts completed, an indication of the 'technicians' or technical bodies to be involved, a description of the technical facilities and measures used by the contractor, the educational and professional qualifications of the contractor, details of the manpower of the service provider and numbers of managerial staff, indications of the proportion of the contract that may be subcontracted, and, in certain cases, an indication of the environmental management measures that the economic operator will be able to apply when performing the contract. What links these various pieces of evidence is the need to balance an appropriate desire on the part of the contracting authority that it satisfy itself that the putative contractor will be able to deliver on what it has been contracted to do, with the need that putative contractors do not have excessive burdens placed on them by contracting authorities that may be abused for protectionist purposes, for example.[11] Article 44(2) makes this clear: 'The extent of the information referred to in Article[ ]...48 and the minimum levels of ability required for a specific contract must be related and proportionate to the subject-matter of the contract.'

So, is this at all relevant to status equality? The answer depends, again, on how the 'subject-matter of the contract' is defined. We have seen in the previous chapter that if the contracting authority defines the subject matter of the contract to be the production of widgets, then the answer must be 'no', as the technical and professional expertise required will be that related directly to widget production. To repeat a point made in chapter 16 above, if the subject matter of the contract is defined, however, to be the supply of food to state schools in a way that caters to a broad mix of pupils of differing faiths, then the technical capacity to handle halal meat will be relevant to the subject matter of the contract. In chapter 16 above, it was argued that the broad interpretation of what can constitute the subject matter of the contract gels with, and is further borne out by, the approach taken in the directives as to what can constitute a technical specification.

---

[11] Hence the inclusion of Public Sector Directive, Arts 49 and 50 requiring the use of European standards in the context of quality assurance standards and environmental management systems.

Variants

It is at this point that a new element in the regime introduced by the directives becomes important: the possibility of introducing variants. A 'variant' approach may be adopted where the public body establishes a minimal set of technical specifications for the product sought, which all tenderers must satisfy, but invites variants that add in a social dimension such as equality as well. When the bid is submitted, the public body is then able, theoretically, to compare all the bids on the basis of the same set of award criteria, with the added advantage that the public body is able to make a comparison between standard solutions and equality-friendly variants (based on the same standard technical requirements). Companies are free to provide offers based on the variant or the initial tender, unless indicated otherwise by the contracting authority.[12] An example would be the procuring of 'fair trade' products, where the public bodies invite suppliers to say how they would deliver the fair trade element without specifying that only products with a particular label will be accepted. This would involve evaluation in part on the basis of the social aspect.

The advantage of this 'variants' model appears to be that this approach is likely to reduce the costs that might otherwise be incurred in buying fair trade products in comparison with the 'award criteria' model. The disadvantages are that to conform to Community legal requirements a somewhat complicated procedure must be complied with. Article 24(1) of the Public Sector Directive[13] provides that, where the criterion for award is that of 'most economically advantageous tender' (to be considered below), then 'contracting authorities may authorise tenderers to submit variants'. The ability of the contracting authority to use variants is, however, subject to significant procedural constraints. First, contracting authorities are required to indicate in the contract notice whether or not they authorize variants. Variants are not permitted without this indication. Second, contracting authorities authorizing variants 'shall state in the contract documents the minimum requirements to be met by the variants and any specific requirements for their presentation', and only variants 'meeting the minimum requirements laid down by these contracting authorities shall be taken into consideration'. A further difficulty may arise, however, as public bodies would have to allow for 'equivalents' and this may present difficulties in judging bids objectively and thus fairly: one producer may pay excellent wages whilst another may have an excellent health plan. How would the public body choose between them? An alternative approach is that contracting authorities say that they welcome fair trade options from suppliers, to try to encourage such bids. Suppliers are given the option to offer products from fair trade sources as an addition to the minimum quality standard. A bid could not be rejected or considered non-compliant

---

[12] Based on European Commission, 'Buying Green!, Handbook on environmental procurement' (OOPEC, 2004) para 3.2.4. [13] Utilities Directive, Art 36.

simply because it did not include any desired fair trade options. Bids would then be able to be compared and the bid including the fair trade option would be compared on the basis of price, quality, etc but not the wider social considerations.

Award criteria

May contracting authorities legitimately attempt to get tenderers to commit to equality norms and have their success in doing so taken into account in the *award* of the contract? The form in which this approach can be found in practice is where the public body takes conformity to a certain equality issue into account as an award criterion. The strategy for the public body under this model is to take advantage of the greater bargaining power the public body has in the stage prior to the award of the contract. This is the most complex of the approaches examined so far but, at least under certain conditions, offers the most to the public body. This is the approach that most procurement professionals appear to prefer to use, because it enables greater flexibility to those awarding the successful tenderer to pick and choose between tenderers on the basis of the equality issue, thus promoting competition between tenderers on that issue.

The disadvantages of this model are that it depends in practice on the public body having the bargaining power that the model assumes; if the market conditions are such that it is a seller's market, then the use of this approach may produce little to satisfy the public body's equality agenda. But there may also be disadvantages even where there is significant competition. Much depends on the weight given by the public authority to the equality issue compared with the other award criteria. Depending on the extent to which equality issues are seen to be important to the public body, the award criteria approach may increase the weight that tenderers give to the issue, producing more and more elaborate ways of demonstrating that they are 'on-message', but increasing the cost of the bid. There may therefore be competition on equality, but with financial detriment to the public body. On the other hand, the weight given to the equality issue may be so negligible that little is delivered in practice.

One issue that this model confronts is how to turn equality goals into a form that 'fits' with the way public procurement works in practice. The issue in the award stage is how to commodify equality requirements in a way that makes them comparable with other (for example financial) criteria. A variation on the award criteria approach has been developed that addresses this to some extent. This takes the equality issue into account at the award stage, but only as a tie-break after the economic criteria have been assessed and two or more bids have been found to be roughly equal under these criteria. Under this alternative, the way in which the tenderers addressed equality issues is then taken into account in deciding between the otherwise equal tenderers. The way in which the Northern Ireland pilot scheme regarding unemployment was structured as discussed in detail in chapter 13 above, fits this variation.

The Public Sector Directive specifies that contracts are to be awarded on the basis of the criteria laid down in Articles 53 and 55 [abnormally low tenders], taking into account Article 24 [variants]. From the point of view of the Directive's relationship to status equality, this stage is probably the most difficult to understand, and was one of the most hard fought areas in the debates prior to the enactment of the new directives, as we saw in chapter 14 above. To what extent do these provisions permit equal status issues to be taken into account?

There are several preliminary points to bear in mind. The recitals to both directives make it clear that the intention of the legislator was to base the provisions of the directives generally 'on Court of Justice case-law' but the recitals stress that this was particularly the case in dealing with award criteria. The first recital to both directives also stress that this case law 'clarifies the possibilities for the contracting authorities to meet the needs of the public concerned, including in the environmental and/or social area, provided that such criteria are linked to the subject-matter of the contract, do not confer an unrestricted freedom of choice on the contracting authority, are expressly mentioned and comply with the fundamental principles' of Community law. It is clear, therefore, that the terms of the directives must be read with that case law in mind.

Before turning to the complexity, let us first consider the relevant texts of the relevant provisions of the directives in somewhat greater detail. Article 53 of the Public Sector Directive specifies that contracting authorities must 'base the award of public contracts' on one of two approaches, which they must choose in advance. One of the two is 'lowest price only' where the contracting authority decides that the lowest bid in strictly price terms is to be awarded the contract. In practice, this will mean that when the envelopes containing the various bids are opened by the contracting authority, the only issue that should concern the contracting authority is which bidder offered to deliver the terms of the contract at the lowest price. Only if that lowest price were considered to be 'abnormally low' (the meaning of which we consider below) should the lowest bidder not be awarded the contract. From the point of view of reducing the discretion available to the contracting authority, the lowest price approach allows the contracting authority least discretion in choosing between bidders. The author knows of no research that examines the relative frequency of contracting authorities choosing to use the lowest price approach, but personal experience seems to show that in most Member States only the least complex public contracts (which in any event would be likely to be below the thresholds) would be carried out using the lowest price. As regards including social considerations at the award stage, the use of lowest price precludes this entirely (again with the exception of abnormally low tenders, to be examined below).

The second permitted approach involves the contracting authority deciding to award the contract on the basis of the 'most economically advantageous' tender, from the point of view of the contracting authority. The reason for choosing this approach is to enable the contracting authority to award the contract to a tenderer that delivers the best deal, in the round, taking into account all the various things that the contractor wants the contract to deliver. Any sensible contracting authority, for example, in deciding to award a contract to deliver services such as providing school meals to a school, would be interested not only in the price offered by tenderers but also in the quality of the food offered, how much was wasted by not being eaten by the children, and the way in which the food was prepared and presented, among other considerations. The Public Sector Directive provides that when the award is made to the tender most economically advantageous from the point of view of the contracting authority, various criteria 'linked to the subject-matter of the public contract in question' may be used, 'for example, quality, price, technical merit, aesthetic and functional characteristics, environmental characteristics, running costs, cost-effectiveness, after-sales service and technical assistance, delivery date and delivery period or period of completion'. Making the decision in this case is clearly, therefore, a complex task in which various factors will have to be balanced. The more factors there are, the more complex the balance, and the more discretion the contracting authority will have in making the appropriate balanced decision.

In deciding how far to regulate the decision legally, there are various detailed issues to be decided but the central question is: how far should the discretion of the contracting authority be constrained, and in what ways? There are various ways in which the directives constrain the discretion of contracting authorities in making decisions on the basis of what is 'most economically advantageous'. The first is that the assessment is 'most *economically* advantageous'. What is the significance of the use of the term 'economically' in this context? The second is that the criteria that are allowed to be included are ones that are '*linked to* the subject-matter of the public contract in question'. What does 'linked to' mean? The third is the relevance of the various examples that are explicitly mentioned in the provision; is there some common feature that links these or are they simply examples of the most commonly used criteria that may be linked to the subject matter of contracts, in practice? Lastly, what are the limits of the requirement that the award of the contract must be 'based on' the 'most economically advantageous' tender? Provided that the 'most economically advantageous tender' is chosen, does this preclude additional award criteria from being used? What, if any, is the significance of the fact that unlike the provision that specifies that the lowest price may be used, the provision providing for the most economically advantageous tender does not specify that it 'alone' must be used?

Some of these issues have been addressed in the previous cases under the 'old' directives that were examined in chapter 13 above. 'Most economically advantageous' does not rule out the inclusion of award criteria that are socially and environmentally based. Even under the previous directives, the ECJ did not regard all the award criteria as having to be individually 'economic' in orientation. The criteria must be linked to the subject matter of the contract but that does not mean that the Court will prohibit an award criterion 'simply because it does not necessarily serve to achieve the objective pursued'.[14] Nor does it appear that the new directives have disallowed the approach approved in the *Nord-Pas-De-Calais* case where after the most economically advantageous tender was chosen, an additional social tie-break was used. The broad discretion allowed to contracting authorities in the *Concordia Bus* case appears to have been confirmed more generally, as the directive refers to the selection being on the basis of the most economically advantageous tender 'from the point of view of the contracting authority'.

Most other questions are not, however, clearly addressed in the substantive articles of the directives. To what extent do the recitals help in understanding the substantive articles better, in addition to making it clear that the prior case law of the ECJ remains important? The first point that emerges is that the purpose of the provisions regarding award criteria is to try to ensure transparency, 'to enable all tenderers to be reasonably informed of the criteria and arrangements which will be applied to identify the most economically advantageous tender'.[15] It is in this context that the clarity of the criteria to be adopted, and their relative weightings, is important, so that they are brought to the attention of tenderers 'in sufficient time for tenderers to be aware of them when preparing their tenders'. In other words, if the bid is to be appropriately competitive, then tenderers need to be fully informed of what it is that the contracting authority needs and wants. What the specific criteria should be is intentionally left vague because, as the recitals make clear, these depend 'on the object of the contract since they must allow the level of performance offered by each tender to be assessed in the light of the object of the contract, as defined in the technical specifications, and the value for money of each tender to be measured'.

The recitals do make clear, however, that a concern remains about the extent of discretion that is potentially involved, which is why the recitals also stress the importance of equal treatment. 'In order to guarantee equal treatment', the recitals say, 'the criteria for the award of the contract should enable tenders to be compared and assessed objectively.' So, not only must the criteria be clear in advance, and the weightings announced, but there must also be a process adopted that enables tenders to be compared with each other. The more criteria there are at the award stage, the more the comparison between the different tenderers is rendered difficult, but at least whatever comparison method is adopted, it should be 'objective'. However, this does not mean that the criteria must be expressed in quantitatively measurable terms—the criteria may also be qualitatively measurable.[16] It is in this context that the recitals address specifically environmental and social criteria. 'If *these conditions* are fulfilled', ie the requirement that the contracting authority should be able to make objective comparisons, 'economic and qualitative

---

14 *Wienstrom* (n 7 above) para 53.
15 Recital 46 to the Public Sector Directive; recital 55 to the Utilities Directive.
16 Case T-4/01, *Renco v Council* [2003] ECR II-171.

criteria for the award of the contract, such as meeting environmental requirements, may enable the contracting authority to meet the needs of the public
concerned, as expressed in the specifications of the contract', hence the inclusion
of 'environmental characteristics' as one of the examples of possible criteria
detailed above.

One important clarification provided in the text of the Public Sector
Directive is with regard to the issue of weighting. Article 53(2)[17] provides that,
where the contracting authority uses the 'most economically advantageous'
approach, it is required to specify 'the relative weighting which it gives to each of
the criteria chosen to determine the most economically advantageous tender'. It
continues: 'Those weightings can be expressed by providing for a range with an
appropriate maximum spread.' However, there are circumstances where the
Public Sector Directive envisages that weighting may not be possible: 'Where,
in the opinion of the contracting authority, weighting is not possible for
demonstrable reasons, the contracting authority shall indicate . . . the criteria in
descending order of importance.' The Court of Justice made clear in the *EVN*
case that it would not second-guess the weightings attached to each criterion,
permitting in that case a weighting as high as 45 per cent to an environmental
criterion. However, a contracting authority should not include as award criteria
requirements that it does not intend to take seriously when the contract is
awarded. The ECJ made clear that a contracting entity may not use a criterion
that 'it neither intends nor is able to verify'.[18] Nor may it include in the tendering specifications or in the evaluation criteria elements that are 'not suitable for
securing the attainment of the objective which they pursue or go beyond what is
necessary to attain it'.[19]

However, the recitals do specify that social criteria may be included as award
criteria. 'Under the same conditions', the recitals continue, 'a contracting authority may use criteria aiming to meet social requirements, in response in particular
to the needs—*defined in the specifications of the contract*—of particularly disadvantaged groups of people to which those receiving/using the works, supplies or
services which are the object of the contract belong' (emphasis added). There are
several respects in which this statement is potentially puzzling. The particular
example of a social award criterion is, to begin with, quite limited: it relates to the
use of a criterion that aims to meet the needs of a group of people to which those
standing to benefit from the contract belong. So, for example, let us say that the
contract is to deliver school meals to a number of schools that include a significant
proportion of children from an Islamic background and the specifications require
that the food, or a proportion of it, consists of halal meat, then the award criteria
may include the standard and reliability of the arrangements for providing halal

---

[17] Also Utilities Directive, Art 55. [18] *Wienstrom* (n 7 above) judgment, para 51.
[19] C-234/03, *Contse SA, Vivisol Srl, Oxigen Salud SA v Instituto Nacional de Gestión Sanitaria (Ingesa), formerly Instituto Nacional de la Salud (Insalud)* [2005] ECR I-9315, para 79.

meat, provided it is clear how the contracting authority plans to compare the claims of one tenderer with the claims of another in this respect. Although limited, this is, I would suggest, merely an *example* of what is permissible, and not an attempt to suggest that this is the only example of what is permissible. The more restricted interpretation would seem to hark back to the argument that the Commission made in the *Concordia Bus* case, which the Court did not address, let alone approve, that the award criteria must seek to provide a direct benefit to the procuring entity or its inhabitants. Provided it reflects the specifications, is transparent, and enables objective comparisons, then my interpretation is that anything could be an award criterion, as long as it is linked to the subject matter of the contract. So, there appears to be nothing preventing the subject matter of the contract being entirely altruistic, for example to benefit people in another country.

The approach taken in the French Code is interesting in this regard.[20] Article 53 of the Code now makes it possible for public purchasers to take environmental and social criteria into account alongside other criteria. To ensure that the bidder who submitted the economically most advantageous tender is awarded the contract, the public entity may rely on various criteria *which vary in accordance with the subject matter of the contract*, including the operating costs, the bid's technical merit, its innovative nature, its environmental friendliness, *its capacity in relation to the employment of disadvantaged people*, the time for completion, its aesthetic and functional features, after-sales service and technical support, the delivery time and date, and the price of the provisions. Other criteria may be taken into account if the subject matter of the contract so requires. The criteria must be set out in the contract notice or in the tender regulations. The criteria used must be weighted or, if that is not possible, prioritized. The bids should be ranked in decreasing order. The highest-ranking bid should be selected. Article 53 of the Code thus distinguishes between two types of criteria that may be taken into account. The first set of criteria is specifically listed. These environmental and social criteria must be expressly mentioned in tender documentation, must respect the general principles of the Code, and must be related to the subject matter of the contract. Other criteria may also be taken into account beyond those listed. But these other criteria must be formulated so as not to give discretion to the public body at the time of choosing the best offer, and they must be justified by the object of the contract.

There are additional provisions in the French Code relating to particular types of contracts that illustrate further the extent to which France considers that the provisions on award criteria permit broad discretion to Member States to incorporate social criteria at the award stage. Article 48 of the Code provides that in the tender documents, the public body can require candidates to indicate in their offer the share of the market that they have the intention to subcontract with third parties, in particular with small and medium-sized undertakings, or with craftsmen. Article 53(4)

---

[20] Codes des Marchés Publics was promulgated by Dècret no 2006-975 du 1er août 2006 portant code des marchés publics.

provides that in the event of corresponding prices or equivalent bids for a contract, a preferential right is granted to bids submitted by a workers' production cooperative, an agricultural producers' group, a craftsmen's or an artists' cooperative society, or a sheltered workshop. When the contracts relate, wholly or partly, to works likely to be executed by craftsmen or craft companies, or trade cooperatives or workers' production cooperatives, or sheltered workshops, the public contracting entities must, before initiating the tendering process, define the public works, services, or supplies which, within the limit of one-quarter of the amount of those provisions, will, in the event of equivalence of bids, be awarded priority to any other bidders, to craftsmen or to craftsmen's cooperative societies, or workers' production cooperatives, or adapted undertakings. When the contracts relate, wholly or partly, to works of an artistic nature and the prices correspond or the bids are similarly equivalent, priority shall be given to artists or artists' cooperative societies for up to one-half of the amount of those works.

Rejection of 'abnormally low tenders'

We are not quite finished with award criteria. There is a potentially major (from the point of view of status equality) additional feature of the directives' regime surrounding award criteria: the possibility of rejecting abnormally low tenders. The provisions regarding abnormally low tenders are, respectively, Article 55 of the Public Sector Directive and Article 57 of the Utilities Directive. The first observation to make about these provisions is that they assume that contracting authorities may reject a tender as 'abnormally low', which means that the tender is considered to be in some way aberrant and not to reflect the full cost that the tender should include. An example would be where the tenderer is being subsidized by another Member State to such an extent that it is able to reduce the cost of its tender sufficiently to be more attractive than those firms not so subsidized.

Although based on the presumption that abnormally low tenders may be rejected, the directives provide only for procedures that the contracting authority must adopt before the tender is actually rejected on the ground that it is abnormally low, hence the rather strange phrasing of the provisions in question.[21] They provide: 'If, for a given contract, tenders appear to be abnormally low in relation to the goods, works or services, the contracting authority shall, before it may reject those tenders, request in writing details of the constituent elements of the tender which it considers relevant.' The details may relate 'in particular' to 'compliance with the provisions relating to employment protection and working conditions in force at the place where the work, service or supply is to be performed', among other factors. The request for such details does not appear to be restricted to making a request from the tenderer alone, and in the case of working conditions, for

---

[21] Public Sector Directive, Art 55; Utilities Directive, Art 57.

example, it may be appropriate to request information from trade unions. Where the contracting authority does obtain information from other sources, however, the procurement directives require the contracting authority to 'verify those constituent elements by consulting the tenderer, taking account of the evidence supplied'.

So, can this provision be used to justify exclusion of contractors where, for example, a low tender is the result of discrimination against women contrary to Community law, and therefore gives rise to an unfair competitive advantage? Some have argued that this approach is debatable in the light of the restrictive approach adopted by the ECJ to an equivalent exception in the *Costanzo* case.[22] In that case Italy adopted a provision that required the automatic exclusion from procedures for the award of public works contracts of tenders which were abnormally low, judged according to a mathematical criterion. The ECJ held that these provisions were contrary to Article 29(5) of Directive 71/305 that required the contracting authority to examine each case, and to allow the tenderer to show that the bid was a genuine one. Peter Trepte has argued that the justification for the approach adopted by the Court lay in its view that the Directive's aim 'was to promote the development of effective competition in the field of public contracts'. He continues:

It is always possible that certain tenderers may benefit from exceptional or particularly advantageous economic, geographical or labour market conditions, for example, to put forward an exceptionally low bid. These bids would be genuine and to reject them, simply because they appear to be abnormally low, would not only deprive the tenderer of his right to compete fairly with other tenderers by using the legitimate advantages presented to him but would also defeat the object of the tendering game, namely to get the best deal for the awarding entity.[23]

On this interpretation, it might appear that the judgment prohibits a national authority from interpreting 'abnormally low' in a way that would permit rejection of a tender made cheaper by the sex discrimination of the tenderer. However, the *Costanzo* case hardly seems conclusive on this issue, particularly given that the ECJ stressed that what constitutes an abnormally low tender 'is for the national legislature to determine'.[24] A more limited interpretation of the case would appear more justified, that each case should be treated on its merits, that there should be no automatic exclusion, and that tenderers should have the opportunity to rebut the case against them. If these conditions are satisfied, and the condition of non-discrimination is complied with, the approach suggested seems appropriate, and is indeed more apt than that considered in the previous paragraph as a method of capturing the concerns which underlie the proposal there considered.

---

[22] Case C-103/88 *Fratelli Costanzo SpA* [1989] ECR 1839.
[23] P-A Trepte, *Public Procurement in the EC* (CCH Editions, 1993) 166–7.
[24] *Costanzo* (n 22 above) 1860, para 45(1).

The provisions of the Public Sector Directive indicate, somewhat obliquely, that this approach would be in compliance with the Directive, and specify the aspects of the tender that may give rise to an abnormally low tender. Importantly for our purposes, it indicates that the tenderer's compliance with the 'provisions relating to employment protection and working conditions in force at the place where the work, service or supply is to be performed' may be one such factor.[25] (For the reasons stated below, I will assume that this includes employment provisions relating to status equality.) This is important, as it indicates the acceptance that worsening working conditions may enable tenderers to avoid some costs that those complying with employment legislation may face, enabling those not in compliance with such legislation to submit a lower bid. In other words, the Directive adopts the idea that some methods of competition, including ignoring working conditions that are legally required, may be *unfair* competition. We saw in chapter 16 above, that there was a concern that contractors should not engage in cost-cutting to the extent of undermining employment legislation requirements. May contracting authorities go further than simply applying the 'notice and request' provisions regarding compliance with domestic employment law, to be discussed below? A key indication that they may is provided in Article 27 of the Public Sector Directive itself, which explicitly provides that the provisions regarding the giving of notice 'shall be without prejudice to the application of the provisions . . . concerning the examination of abnormally low tenders'.[26]

II. True 'Secondary' Considerations: Government as Regulator

We turn now to consider those other provisions of the directives that permit action to be taken by public bodies to link procurement with achieving status equality goals, even when status equality is *not* the subject matter of the contract. We shall see that these are substantially confined to the employment context. This is not surprising, given that, as both the Public Sector Directive and the Utilities Directive make clear in the Recitals:[27] 'Employment and occupation are key elements in guaranteeing equal opportunities for all and contribute to integration in society.'

Disability and technical specifications

Both Article 23(1) of the Public Sector Directive and Article 34(1) of the Utilities Directive provide that technical specifications set out in the contract documentation 'should be defined so as to take into account accessibility criteria for people

---

[25] Public Sector Directive, Art 55(1)(d); Utilities Directive, Art 57(1)(d).
[26] Utilities Directive, Art 39 is in similar terms.
[27] Recital 28 to the Public Sector Directive; recital 39 to the Utilities Directive.

with disabilities or design for all users'. How far does this operate as an enforceable obligation? Sue Arrowsmith has questioned what the effect of this new provision is.[28] First, she argues that the provision may be beyond the competence of the Community, as the legal basis for the provision was stated to be the internal market provisions of the EC Treaty and these may not be broad enough to permit this type of social provision. In any event, the vagueness of the requirements ('wherever possible') lessen the opportunities to contest failure to include such technical specifications provided the public body can demonstrate that it has given even minimal consideration to the issue.

Arrowsmith's reservations illustrate the type of interpretation that runs counter to the approach advocated in chapter 16 above. There seems no reason, for example, why the accessibility requirements should not be seen as contributing to achieving increased economic integration by permitting a significant group of people to participate in economic activities, and thus entirely compatible with the provisions having their legal basis in the internal market provisions. Nor is it clear why 'wherever possible' should not be interpreted to mean almost exactly the opposite of Arrowsmith's interpretation, requiring contracting authorities to be particularly assiduous in looking for opportunities to address the issue of accessibility. An interpretation that took the dual-faceted nature of the equal treatment principle fully into account would surely plump for the broader obligation, not the narrower.

Set-asides for sheltered workshops

In both the Utilities[29] and Public Sector[30] Directives, there is an explicit provision permitting Member States, as the Recitals put it, 'to reserve the right to participate in award procedures for public contracts' to sheltered workshops or to reserve performance of contracts to firms operating sheltered employment programmes.[31] The explanation provided is that 'sheltered workshops and sheltered employment programmes contribute efficiently towards the integration or reintegration of people with disabilities in the labour market. However, such workshops might not be able to obtain contracts under normal conditions of competition.' Consequently, it is appropriate to provide that Member States may accord preferences to enable them to achieve their aim without having to compete in the same way as other operators. This is another way of achieving the same effect as in the WTO GPA, which mentions such preferences as one of the listed exceptions.

The terms of the relevant articles are the same in both directives: 'Member States may reserve the right to participate in public contract award procedures to sheltered workshops or provide for such contracts to be performed in the context

---

[28]   S Arrowsmith, Law (n 9 above) 1155–6.
[29]   Utilities Directive, Art 28.
[30]   Public Sector Directive, Art 19.
[31]   Recital 28 to the Public Sector Directive; recital 39 to the Utilities Directive.

of sheltered employment programmes where most of the employees concerned are handicapped persons who, by reason of the nature or the seriousness of their disabilities, cannot carry on occupations under normal conditions.' Where Member States take advantage of these provisions, the contract notice must make reference to it, and it is also required that the scope of the preferences be included in the PIN notice.[32]

There are several important features of this provision. The first is that any such reservations must be initiated by Member States, and not simply adopted ad hoc by particular public bodies. The second is that, although there is no specific definition of a 'sheltered workshop', this has a limited meaning in practice. The third is that the provision applies not only to sheltered workshops but also to 'sheltered employment programmes'. These are defined in way that is also relatively constraining: (1) 'most of the employees concerned' in the programme must be 'handicapped persons'; (2) these 'handicapped persons' must be unable to 'carry on occupations under normal conditions' due to 'the nature and seriousness of their disabilities'. Although there is no definition of 'handicapped' or 'disabled', it would be reasonable, and entirely consistent with the principle that EC law should be read as a coherent whole, that these definitions be read as the same in all material respects to the interpretation of 'disability' that the ECJ gives to the same term in the Employment Discrimination Directive.[33]

The new French Code takes advantage of this approach and expands somewhat the circumstances in which price preferences and set-asides are available to be used. This has been achieved in various ways. First, article 15 of the Code makes it possible for public bodies to reserve certain contracts or certain lots of contracts to 'sheltered workshops', ie companies that aim to employ disabled workers. Where these set-asides are employed, the contract or the relevant part of the contract must be carried out mainly by disabled workers. The request for tender must also make clear that a set-aside is likely. Using a set-aside is not a complete exemption from the requirements of the Code. Depending on whether the contract is above or below a threshold, several provisions of the Code may apply, and publicity requirements are always applicable.

Compliance with domestic employment laws

Although somewhat badly drafted, the recitals to both procurement directives make clear that, provided that they themselves comply with EC law, and are *applied* in a way which complies with EC law, Member States may, by general legislation for example, require those carrying out a public procurement contract

---

[32] Public Sector Directive, Annex VII; Utilities Directive, Annex XIII: PIN and Contract Notices must indicate, where appropriate, 'whether the public contract is restricted to sheltered workshops, or whether its execution is restricted to the framework of protected job programmes'.

[33] Case C-13/05 *Chacón Navas* [2006] All ER (D) 132.

to comply with 'laws, regulations and collective agreements' that are in force and deal with 'employment conditions and safety at work' during the performance of the contract.[34] This reflects numerous ECJ decisions both prior to and subsequent to the enactment of the directives. The most controversial, and the most heavily litigated aspect of this jurisprudence involved the question as to how far it was consistent with EC law for Member States to require compliance with such rules where the contractor brought workers from another EC state to carry out the contract. The controversy was over whether the application of such national rules meant that the effect would be to discourage such 'posting of workers' (as it was called) from states that had a lower legal standard of employment conditions and safety at work conditions, and would thus discriminate in effect against out of state contractors.

As the same recitals make clear, Directive (EC) 96/71 of 16 December 1996 concerning the posting of workers in the framework of the provision of services lays down 'minimum conditions that must be observed by the host country in respect of such posted workers'. The substantive articles of the directives do not specifically include any reference to this legal situation, because they do not need to, as it is a matter of interpretation of the Treaty. The directives do, however, assume that this is the case and include specific provisions making clear what the contracting authorities may do to operationalize this freedom. There are four approaches the directives take to this. The first two are set out in Article 27 of the Public Sector Directive and Article 39 of the Utilities Directive. First, a contracting authority:

...may state in the contract documents, or be obliged by a Member State so to state, the body or bodies from which a candidate or tenderer may obtain the appropriate information on the obligations relating to...the employment protection provisions and to the working conditions which are in force in the Member State, region or locality in which the works are to be carried out or services are to be provided and which shall be applicable to the works carried out on site or to the services provided during the performance of the contract.[35]

Contractors might be expected to know of relevant legislation and employment rules in the country where they intend to operate, but in the interests of transparency it is clearly better if contracting authorities help contractors by informing them about where the appropriate information may be obtained.

The directives also provide, second, that a contracting authority that supplies this information 'shall request the tenderers or candidates in the contract award procedure to indicate that they have taken account, when drawing up their tender, of the obligations relating to employment protection provisions and the working conditions which are in force in the place where the works are to be carried out or

---

[34] Recital 34 to the Public Sector Directive; recital 45 to the Utilities Directive.
[35] Public Sector Directive, Art 27(1); Utilities Directive, Art 39(1).

the service is to be provided'. The purpose of this is linked to the fear that contractors may seek to reduce their levels of employment protection in order to be able to submit a lower bid. This provision requires contracting authorities at least to require tenderers to indicate that they have taken the legal requirements 'into account' when drawing up the tender. This is clearly considerably less stringent than a requirement that tenderers must cost full compliance with the legislation when drawing up the tender, or requiring contracting authorities not to award contracts to those bidders that do not comply with employment legislation. We shall see, however, that although this more stringent approach is not included, contracting authorities do have some further discretion to attempt to ensure that tenderers intend to comply with employment legislation.

Before turning to these further issues, however, there is a remaining issue that arises in the interpretation of these 'notice and request' articles. Are these provisions applicable to status equality legislation? The question is relevant because the provisions in question refer to 'employment protection' provisions. Do, for example, anti-discrimination requirements relating to employment constitute 'employment protection' rules for the purposes of these articles?

It is unclear whether, or to what extent, legislation providing for non-discrimination on the basis of sex, race, or religion is included within the meaning of legislation 'relating to employment protection . . . and working conditions'. No legal argument at the Community level appears conclusive. On the one hand, in the context of the interpretation of ILO Convention No 94, the ILO Committee of Experts considers that where national laws or regulations, arbitration awards, or collective agreements guarantee equal remuneration for workers in the trade or industry involved, the workers engaged under a public contract which is encompassed by Article 1 of the Convention should also be working under conditions of equal remuneration.[36] On the other hand, Nielsen has argued that the scope of the ILO provision is narrow. He argues that a wider definition of covered activities had been proposed, but rejected.[37] In addition, the Agreement on Social Policy attached to the Treaty on European Union appeared to distinguish between 'working conditions' and 'equality between men and women with regard to labour market opportunities and treatment at work'.[38]

If legislation providing for non-discrimination on the basis of sex, race, and religion is included within the meaning of legislation 'relating to employment protection . . . and working conditions', it would appear to be justifiable to request tenderers to provide a guarantee that their future compliance with national

---

[36] International Labour Conference, 72nd Session 1986, Equal Remuneration: General Survey by the Committee of Experts on the Application of Conventions and recommendations (ILO, Geneva, 1986) 123, fn 1.

[37] HK Nielsen, 'Public Procurement and International Labour Standards' (1995) 4 PPLR 94, 96.

[38] Agreement on Social Policy Concluded Between the Member States of the European Community with the Exception of the United Kingdom of Great Britain and Northern Ireland, Art 2(1).

anti-discrimination requirements had been included in the calculation of the cost of completing the contract. The implication of the provision goes somewhat wider, however, since it clearly envisages that contracting authorities are also permitted to require that tenderers should comply with such obligations in the first place. It would thus appear to be justifiable to request tenderers to provide guarantees regarding their future compliance with national anti-discrimination requirements, although if the contractor does so, little more can be done under this provision.

Such legislative provisions themselves, and the *methods* adopted by the contracting authorities for satisfying themselves of future conformity, must not, however, be discriminatory against contractors from other Member States, either directly or indirectly. Since, however, the directives requiring non-discrimination between women and men apply throughout the Community, any national legislation which reflects the *requirements* of the Community equality directives could hardly be regarded as discriminating against contractors in any Member State, since all are bound by these provisions already. That freedom to require a promise as to future conduct is, however, quite limited.

Disqualifying bidders

We have seen numerous instances where states have adopted an approach that involves a prohibition on obtaining government contracts as a penalty for previous wrongdoing, or prevents public bodies from contracting with those who are currently failing to achieve a particular standard of behaviour relating to equality. Where this approach is adopted, it is most likely that the tender (or general legislation) will specify that a person will be disqualified from tendering for the contract if they have been found to have failed to comply with anti-discrimination or equality requirements. In chapter 13 above, we saw an example of this approach in the United Kingdom, where six local authorities in the West Midlands developed a 'common standard' to assess whether a firm's policy on race relations met the legal requirements regarding racial equality.[39] The standard was developed for access to the councils' standing lists. The standard was introduced for building and construction in connection with the councils' approved lists.

The point of this use of procurement is, essentially, to add the deprivation of government contracts to the other penalties to which the employee is subject. In practice, it has tended to be used for narrow anti-discrimination purposes, rather than broader equality goals. This approach to the use of procurement is closely associated with the idea that the government should not have to associate itself

---

[39] See M Orton and P Ratcliffe, 'New Labour Ambiguity, or Neo-Consistency? The Debate About Inequality in Employment and Contract Compliance' (2005) 34(2) Journal of Social Policy 262–3.

with those who discriminate; that the government should be able to specify that those who deal with it have clean hands. However, Michael Orton and Peter Radcliffe observe that: 'While the *raison d' être* for such a list may be the desire to minimise the possibility of contracting unsuitably qualified or financially dubious firms, it also provides the scope for other criteria to be considered, including racial equality'.[40] They also identify several other advantages of focusing on the pre-qualification stage. 'It means that the councils ensure that all potential contractors, not just those awarded contracts, have an [equal opportunities policy] EOP thereby impacting on a larger number of firms. It also means that having an EOP is not the determining factor at award of contract stage...thereby addressing concerns...about affirmative action policies leading to failings in procurement decisions.'

The directives permit the incorporation of certain exclusions into the qualifications expected of tenderers before they are allowed to proceed to make a qualifying bid at all. These are referred to in the directives as 'criteria for qualitative selection'. Both directives specify that 'Any economic operator may be excluded from participation in a contract where that economic operator' falls into one or more categories that are regarded as unacceptable for a potential contractor with government, such as bankruptcy, non-payment of social security contributions, or non-payment of taxes. The two most relevant for our purposes, however, relate to 'professional misconduct'. Economic operators may be excluded if the operator 'has been convicted by a judgment which has the force of res judicata in accordance with the legal provisions of the country of any offence concerning his professional conduct',[41] or 'has been guilty of grave professional misconduct proven by any means which the contracting authorities can demonstrate'.[42] The important point is that these provisions are 'not concerned only with establishing technical capacity'.[43]

Member States are required to specify, in accordance with their national law and having regard for Community law, the 'implementing conditions' for this provision. The Member State's discretion in this regard is not, however, quite as open as this implies. Contracting authorities are required to accept certain material as 'sufficient evidence' that the economic operator does not fall into one of the disqualifying categories. In the case of the provisions relating to 'professional conduct', the contracting authorities must accept 'the production of an extract from the "judicial record" or, failing that, of an equivalent document issued by a competent judicial or administrative authority in the country of origin or the country whence that person comes showing that these requirements have been met'.[44] Where a particular country does not issue such documents, 'they may be

---

[40] ibid 261.

[41] Public Sector Directive, Art 45(2)(b). The Utilities Directive (in Art 54(4)) provides that selection criteria established by contracting entities 'may include the exclusion criteria listed in Article 45 of [the Public Sector Directive] on the terms and conditions set out therein'.

[42] Public Sector Directive; Art 45(2)(c).   [43] Arrowsmith, Law (n 9 above) 753.

[44] Public Sector Directive, Art 45(3)(a)

replaced by a declaration on oath or, in Member States where there is no provision for declarations on oath, by a solemn declaration made by the person concerned before a competent judicial or administrative authority, a notary or a competent professional or trade body, in the country of origin or in the country whence that person comes'.[45] Member States are required to 'designate the authorities and bodies competent to issue the documents, certificates or declarations' and also to inform the Commission of their existence.[46]

There are several important issues that arise from these provisions that are of relevance to the issue of status equality. The first is that, unlike the provisions relating to the award of contracts to economic operators who have participated in a criminal organization or who have been found guilty of corruption or of fraud to the detriment of the financial interests of the European Communities or of money laundering, these provisions merely *allow* contracting authorities to exclude economic operators, rather than require them to be excluded.

Based on the ECJ jurisprudence interpreting equivalent provisions in the former directives, the suitability criteria set out in the relevant provisions of the Public Sector Directive are 'generally exhaustive',[47] and therefore, unless the social policy which a contractor wishes to pursue comes within these provisions, the contractor may not take it into account in excluding contractors from tendering and being considered. A contractor can be excluded from participation in the contract only in the limited respects specified, and on the criteria of economic and financial standing and technical knowledge or ability,[48] using the rules for verification stipulated in the Directive. It should be added, that the means by which the contracting authority is satisfied that these criteria are met must also be non-discriminatory as between tenderers in different Member States.

To what extent do these provisions relating to suitability enable issues of equality to be taken into account? The relevant provisions are two. We have seen, first, that a contractor may be excluded from participation in the contract who 'has been convicted by a judgment which has the force of res judicata in accordance with the legal provisions of the country of any offence concerning his professional conduct'. It is unclear what constitutes a 'conviction' for the purposes of this provision. Second, a contractor may be excluded from participation in the contract who 'has been guilty of grave professional misconduct proved by any means which the contracting authorities can justify'. We have seen examples of contract compliance approaches being justified by these conditions, in particular those in the Northern

---

[45] ibid Art 45(3).   [46] ibid Art 45(4).

[47] S Arrowsmith, 'The Past and Future Evolution of EC Procurement Law: From Framework to Common Code' (2006) 35(3) Public Contract Law Journal 337, 353 (noting that the ECJ appears to have made an exception 'for exclusions made to ensure equal treatment of participants', citing case C-21/03 *Fabricom* [2005] ECR I-1559. See also H-J Priess and C Pitschas, 'Secondary Policy Criteria and Their Compatibility with EC and WTO Procurement Law: The Case of the German Scientology Declaration' (2000) 9 PPLR 171, 175–60

[48] The Supplies Directive referred to 'technical capacity', Art 15(1).

Ireland fair employment legislation considered in chapter 10 above, in which tenderers may be excluded where there has been a grave violation of legislative equality requirements. The absence of ECJ decisions on these provisions is notable, with the effect that the uncertainties have not been resolved.[49] Relating to the second clause regarding criminal offences concerning a provider's grave professional misconduct, what is sufficient to amount to 'grave' misconduct? As Elizabeth Piselli noted, 'the vagueness of this provision seems to have discouraged the recourse by purchasers to this cause for exclusion'.[50] It is particularly unclear how either of these exclusionary rules apply when another company in the same group of companies has committed an offence or been guilty of grave professional misconduct; nor is it clear whether a provider can be excluded when a proposed subcontractor has committed an offence or been guilty of grave professional misconduct.

On this issue, the recitals are clear in two respects, even if the text of the Directive is not.[51] Non-compliance with national law obligations implementing the Posted Workers Directive, for example, 'may be considered to be grave misconduct or an offence concerning the professional conduct of the economic operator concerned, liable to lead to the exclusion of that economic operator from the procedure for the award of a public contract'.[52] In addition: 'Non-observance of national provisions implementing the Council Directives (EC) 2000/78 and (EEC) 76/207 concerning equal treatment of workers, which has been the subject of a final judgment or a decision having equivalent effect may be considered an offence concerning the professional conduct of the economic operator concerned or grave misconduct'.[53] The approach taken in the French Code is to expand the list of those who are excluded from being able to tender for public contracts *ab initio*. Articles 43 and 44 of the new Code provide that persons in breach of particular legal obligations relating to employment[54] may be excluded from taking part in the tender. This now includes equal opportunities obligations, and obligations regarding disabled workers.

We can observe that all of the examples given so far involve the breach of legal standards to which the contractor is subject. In the equality context, it is likely, given the implementation of Community law obligations on equal status in Member States, that breach of legal obligations will be primarily relevant. It is a matter of dispute in the academic literature, however, whether it is a *requirement* that only breach of legal obligations can give rise to the type of professional

---

[49] E Piselli, 'The Scope for Excluding Providers who have Committed Criminal Offences under the EU Procurement Directives' (2000), 9 PPLR 267: criteria 'formulated in a rather vague way' 269.

[50] ibid 276.

[51] Recitals 34 and 43 to the Public Sector Directive; Recitals 45 and 54 to the Utilities Directive.

[52] Recital 34 to the Public Sector Directive; Recital 45 to the Utilities Directive.

[53] Recital 43 to the Public Sector Directive; Recital 54 to the Utilities Directive.

[54] Defined in Labour Code, art L 323-1.

misconduct covered by this provision.[55] The limit, if it is one, of requiring that there be a breach of a legal obligation may be somewhat overcome if, as Advocate General Gulmann has suggested,[56] this provision could also allow the exclusion of a contractor for the deliberate breach of a previous contractual obligation. Since contractual conditions may include equality conditions beyond what is legally required, this is another way in which these conditions may be given some bite, although only really effectively where contractors are repeat players, since if the contractor is a one-off supplier, the threat of exclusion for breach of a previous contract will not be very convincing.

Provisions permitting 'special' contract conditions

The use of contract conditions focuses attention on the stage *after* the contract has been awarded. It does not attempt to exclude potential contractors on the basis of their previous activities. Instead, it requires that whoever is awarded the contract must comply with certain conditions in carrying out the contract once it is awarded. Unlike those contract conditions that may be taken into account in the context of the award of the contract, discussed above, these 'special' contract conditions may not be so taken into account because they are not necessarily related to the subject matter of the contract. This approach presents all contractors with the same requirement that the contractor must sign up to. The simplest approach includes a simple non-discrimination clause as a contract condition. So, as we saw in chapter 10 above, British government contracts have, since the late 1960s, included a contract condition that the contractor will not discriminate in employment on the contract on the basis of race or ethnic origin. However, a public body may expect a great deal more from the contractor. We saw in chapter 12 above that a Danish municipality has included an extensive set of requirements in public procurement contracts for contractors to draw up a policy to promote equal treatment for people of different ethnic backgrounds. European Commission.[57]

Article 26 of the Public Sector Directive (and, with minor differences Article 38 of the Utilities Directive) provides for the inclusion of these additional contract conditions. 'Contracting authorities may lay down special conditions relating to the performance of a contract, provided that these are compatible with Community law and are indicated in the contract notice or in the specifications. The conditions governing the performance of a contract may, in particular, concern social and environmental considerations.' The recital in the Public Sector Directive (again with minor

---

[55] Contrast Priess and Pitschas (n 47 above) 175 (only legal obligations) with Arrowsmith, Law (n 9 above) 754 (ethical obligations also included).

[56] Case C-71/92, *Commission v Spain* [1993] ECR I-5923, Opinion, para 95.

[57] European Commission, 'Study of the Use of Equality and Diversity Considerations in Public Procurement: Final Report' (December 2003) 59.

differences in the Utilities Directive),[58] sets out some further indications of what is envisaged as included in the concept of a 'social consideration':

> They may, in particular, be intended to favour on-site vocational training, the employment of people experiencing particular difficulty in achieving integration, the fight against unemployment... For instance, mention may be made, amongst other things, of the requirements... to recruit long-term job-seekers or to implement training measures for the unemployed or young persons, to comply in substance with the provisions of the basic International Labour Organisation (ILO) Conventions,... and to recruit more handicapped persons...

There are several particular issues that arise, affecting the use of this approach for status equality purposes. The first is the all-important issue that arises from the use of the term 'conditions *relating to* the *performance* of the contract'. The issue that arises is what 'relating to' means in this context, and in particular whether it limits the ability of contracting authorities to include social considerations. We saw previously that a somewhat similar issue arises in the interpretation of award criteria where the term used is 'criteria *linked to the subject-matter* of the public contract in question'. This latter term appears to require a somewhat closer nexus between the 'criteria' and the 'subject-matter of the contract' than the nexus required between 'conditions' and 'performance of the contract'. The Recitals seem to bear this out, stating that 'Contract performance conditions are compatible with this Directive provided that they are not directly or indirectly discriminatory and are indicated in the contract notice or in the contract documents', concentrating on transparency and discrimination as limits, rather than emphasizing any particular degree of nexus between 'conditions' and the 'subject-matter of the contract'.[59]

It seems clear that a contract condition would not relate to the 'performance' of the contract if it required, for example, that the contractor hire a proportion of disabled workers on *another* contract. The provision requires, therefore, a clear view of what 'the contract' in question is, and in particular its boundaries, but not with a view to ensuring that the contract terms relate to the subject matter of the contract. The relevant Article refers, after all, to 'special' conditions, thus implying that the provision provides for conditions that might not ordinarily be included, and might not therefore relate to the 'subject matter' of the contract, narrowly defined. Furthermore, the distinction between the *subject matter* of the contract and the *performance* of the contract is significant.

A second possible limit that appears from a close reading of the recitals, but not the relevant Articles, relates to the use of contract conditions to require contractors to abide by legal obligations that would apply to them in any event, because they are in generally applicable legislation. This issue arises because the recitals specify that two of the possible contract conditions are relevant where they have

---

[58] Recital 33 to the Public Sector Directive; Recital 44 to the Utilities Directive.
[59] Public Sector Directive, Art 33; Utilities Directive, Art 44.

not already been made obligatory under domestic law ('to comply in substance with the provisions of the basic International Labour Organisation (ILO) Conventions, *assuming that such provisions have not been implemented in national law*, and to recruit more handicapped persons *than are required under national legislation*'). Is it contrary to the directives, then, to include contract conditions that require compliance with national status equality legislation in performing the contract? Or did the drafters of the recitals simply assume that contracting authorities would choose to use such contract conditions only where there was no generally applicable legislation? In the absence of any other indication in the drafting of the directives that the former is the preferable interpretation, the latter appears both more desirable from the perspective of leaving contracting authorities more scope for implementing the principle of equal treatment, and more sensible from a policy perspective in allowing contracting authorities to choose when using contract conditions might be a useful additional basis for enforcing already existing legal requirements.[60]

Third, the provision in the relevant Article that permits contract conditions 'provided that these are compatible with Community law' is of importance. It reminds us that, as the recitals state, direct and indirect discrimination must be avoided, in the sense that the choice of contract conditions must not be such as to disadvantage unfairly potential contractors from another state. It is also important, however, because it sets the parameters of the type of contract condition that is acceptable on human rights and status equality principles. Thus, for example, although the recital gives as an example a contract condition regarding the 'employment of people experiencing particular difficulty in achieving integration', the type of condition that would be permissible under Community law could not include a condition that required contractors to employ 20 per cent of the workforce working on the contract on the basis of racial origin, because that would be contrary to the Race Directive.

Since March 2001, the French law on public procurement has authorized the inclusion of social and environmental considerations among the clauses of public procurement contracts. This was adopted in the reform of the Code des Marchés Publics, so as to give it a firmer legal foundation.[61] Article 14 of the Code concerns social clauses. The Code provides that such social conditions may be rendered obligatory in the carrying out of the contract. These clauses must be put into the cahier des charges. The contractor chosen by the public authority will have to carry out this obligation. In terms of which conditions may be imposed, the Code has undergone some changes between 2000 and 2006. Originally, Article 14 was somewhat narrower, providing that the contract conditions of a public procurement contract in the cahier des charges may include provisions

---

[60] An interesting example that supports the latter approach is the policy of the British government, set out in detail by DEFRA and in a guidance note issued by OGC (May 2004), on the buying of timber.   [61] Dècret no 2001-210, 7 mars 2001, JORF 8.03.2001.

whose aim is to further the employment of persons who have difficulty in integrating, to act against unemployment, or to protect the environment. Article 14 now provides that such conditions can comprise elements regarding social or environmental matters that take into account the objectives of sustainable development by reconciling economic development, the protection and development of the environment, and social progress. These conditions for implementation must not have a discriminatory effect with regard to the potential candidates. They must be indicated in the public call for tender or in the public documents of the tender.

Procurement linkages and non-member states

A final significant development occurs in the more specific context of the Utilities Directive. Article 59(4) provides that Member States 'shall inform the Commission of any difficulties, in law or in fact, encountered and reported by their undertakings and which are due to the non-observance of the international labour law provisions... when these undertakings have tried to secure the award of contracts in third countries'. In these circumstances, Article 59(4) provides that:

... the Commission [on its own initiative or at the request of a Member State] may at any time propose that the Council decide to suspend or restrict, over a period to be laid down in the decision, the award of service contracts to:

(a) undertakings governed by the law of the third country in question;

(b) undertakings affiliated to the undertakings specified in point (a) and having their registered office in the Community but having no direct and effective link with the economy of a Member State;

(c) undertakings submitting tenders which have as their subject-matter services originating in the third country in question.

The Council is required to act, by qualified majority, as soon as possible. Annex XXIII specifies the international labour law provisions within the meaning of this Article, including ILO Convention No 111 on Discrimination (Employment and Occupation), and ILO Convention No 100 on Equal Remuneration.[62]

---

[62] Utilities Directive, Annex XXIII specifying International Labour Law provisions within the meaning of Art 59(4): Convention No 87 on Freedom of Association and the Protection of the Right to Organise; Convention No 98 on the Right to Organise and Collective Bargaining; Convention No 29 on Forced Labour; Convention No 105 on the Abolition of Forced Labour; Convention No 138 on Minimum Age; Convention No 111 on Discrimination (Employment and Occupation); Convention No 100 on Equal Remuneration; Convention No 182 on Worst Forms of Child Labour.

PART V
CONCLUSIONS

18

Reconciling Social and Economic Approaches to Public Procurement

Buying Social Justice has examined how governments use their purchasing power to advance conceptions of social justice, particularly equality and non-discrimination goals. Throughout the book the term 'linkage' has been used to describe this use of procurement. We began by identifying several themes and issues that we hoped to clarify. We sought: to clarify the relationship between procurement linkages and public procurement law; to examine, in particular, the relationship between equal status law, public procurement law, and procurement linkages; and to explore the interplay of domestic and international influences on the trajectory of procurement policy relating to procurement linkages. In this final chapter, the extent to which the previous chapters of the book have clarified these issues is considered, before reflecting on these themes more generally.

I. Where Have We Got To?

Preliminaries

Part I provided an introduction to some of the more salient background factors necessary for a better understanding of these issues. This book concentrates on procurement as an instrument of social justice in a fairly narrow sense, as concerned with status equality. This is, however, merely one example of the social justice uses of procurement, which in turn is merely one of several social and economic uses of procurement linkages. Chapter 2 considered the roots of current equality-based procurement linkages in socio-economic or political goals that public procurement was used to achieve from the early nineteenth century. We turned first to look at the use of procurement linkages as part of national industry policy. We then examined its use by government to achieve certain more narrowly social policy functions, in particular to foster the creation of jobs to relieve unemployment, to promote fair labour conditions, and to promote the increased utilization of the disabled in employment. We saw too that the use of linkages between public contracting and social regulation has been a deeply controversial strategy, legally and politically, and that there have been real dangers in exploiting the clout of the state's power in this way. And yet for all its complexity and risks, we saw that the presence of the state in the market does present unique opportunities for it to influence market behaviour.

In chapters 3 and 4, we examined, respectively, the development of equal status law and policy, domestically and internationally, and then the development of public procurement law and policy. Both provide vital contexts in which equality-based procurement linkages could be seen subsequently operating. As regards the development of status equality law and policy, it was shown that there is a close connection between the function that is attributed to equal status law and policy, and the compliance institutions that are thought to be both appropriate and effective. Since there were different instrumental functions which equal status law was frequently thought to serve, which function, or which combination of functions, were chosen had important implications for the enforcement mechanisms selected. There were two main functional models to which anti-discrimination law conformed: an individual justice model, and a group justice model. More recently, however, two additional approaches are apparent: an attempt to secure the implementation of equality norms extraterritorially, and the introduction of 'mainstreaming'. We saw in Parts II and III of the book how these differing functions of equal status law and regulation affected the approach to procurement linkages adopted in particular states.

We saw in chapter 4 how, from the 1960s, attempts were made in the EC, and in the international trade rounds under GATT, to introduce procurement regulation that would later impact on the use of such linkage at the national level. We saw that these efforts at procurement regulation were controversial and slow in being accepted in comparison with other trade-related policies but that procurement regulation did eventually emerge both at the international level in the shape of the Government Procurement Agreements of 1979 and 1994, and the EC procurement directives, culminating in the reformed directives of 2003.

Chapter 5 presented a relatively full exploration of the pros and cons of the use of procurement linkages to advance status equality, from an economic and political perspective initially. Several theoretical objections to procurement linkages were considered: their perceived irrelevance to the appropriate (primarily commercial) functions of purchasing; the extra costs that procurement linkages bring with them; their unfairness to particular actors; the extent to which alternative methods of regulation are better able to achieve the desired goals; the likelihood of regulatory capture by vested interests; the pressures on good governance that they bring; and the abuse of power that they provide opportunities for. On the other hand, there were several, equally theoretical, arguments that could be identified: the inadequacy of other methods of compliance; the extent to which equality mainstreaming requires procurement linkages; the limits of a commercial model of government contracting; the opportunity for procurement linkages to assist the internalization of externalities; the positive effects of linkage in sustaining and increasing competition; and the role of linkages in helping to supply the 'public good' of equality.

The World Trade Organization and procurement linkages

Part II of the book considered the evolution of the use of procurement linkages in several jurisdictions, and the relationship between these uses of procurement and the development and functioning of the Government Procurement Agreement (GPA). Chapters 6 and 7 examined the extensive use of procurement linkages in the United States and Canada. Two main forms that these procurement linkages take were discussed: contract compliance, and set-asides for businesses particularly associated with the disadvantaged group. In chapter 6 we considered how contract compliance was developed to assist in tackling discrimination and securing greater status equality in the employment context. We saw that equality linkages began as a tool for tackling employment discrimination on the basis of race, beginning in the United States during the Second World War, and continuing during the 1950s and 1960s, mutating into a mechanism for securing affirmative action. The expansion of this approach to cover other groups was then considered, in particular the use of procurement to encourage the development of the accessibility of information technology. We also considered the development of a type of procurement linkage in Canada that mirrored that of the United States: schemes that link the award of government contracts with attempts to secure 'employment equity' for various groups. We saw, too, how the International Labour Organization (ILO) has adopted this contract compliance approach.

In chapter 7, we examined schemes that link the award of contracts to programmes that advantage particular status groups that are considered to be economically disadvantaged by giving preferences to businesses that are owned or controlled by such groups in the award of contracts, what we have termed 'set-asides'. After examining the development of set-asides in the United States, including the significant legal challenges to such schemes under the United States Constitution, we considered the development in Canada of set-asides favouring Aboriginal-owned businesses.

In chapters 8 and 9, we explored the connections between the GPA and these domestic procurement linkages more systematically. Chapter 8 examined the detailed discussions that took place during the 1950s and 1960s, leading to the development of the GPA 1979. The types of procurement linkages discussed in chapters 6 and 7 were largely ignored and the primary focus of attention in these early drafting discussions related to the types of linkages discussed in chapter 2. We then considered the effect of procurement linkages of the 'GPA model' on members of the GPA (in particular the United States and Canada) and how the opportunities in the GPA to negotiate individualized country-by-country 'exceptions' were used by both Canada and the United States to protect (some of) their procurement linkages, particularly set-asides.

We saw that, in the main, developing countries have not sought to join the GPA. In chapter 9, we considered the relationship between procurement linkages aiming to further status equality and developing countries. We looked first at the use of procurement linkages by two developing countries, Malaysia and South

Africa, and we considered reactions to these policies at the international level. As non-members of the GPA, neither South Africa or Malaysia are directly subject to its disciplines and so their procurement linkages are immune from direct scrutiny. That does not mean, however, that either country is immune from the indirect influence of the GPA or of the WTO and we considered this indirect influence in the South African and Malaysian contexts. We also considered the use of procurement linkages by develop*ed* countries for the purpose of addressing status equality in develop*ing* countries, examining the treatment of selective purchasing by Massachusetts relating to Myanmar. As a non-member of the GPA, Myanmar was not able to invoke the GPA disciplines against the United States with regard to selective purchasing policies, but GPA disciplines still proved relevant, not least in the United States litigation that resulted in the Massachusetts law being held to be unconstitutional.

Equality linkages and the European Community

In Part III of the book, we turned to examine the development of EC approaches to procurement linkages aimed at securing greater status equality. We saw that the Community has tended to pursue a somewhat different approach to that adopted under the GPA, with important consequential effects on the approach taken to procurement linkages. Chapter 10 began by examining the extent of equality-promoting domestic procurement linkages in EC Member States just prior to European procurement reforms introduced during the 1980s and early 1990s. It was shown that such linkages were particularly in play in Britain, Northern Ireland, and Germany. The approach taken to domestic procurement linkages during the first wave of EC procurement reforms of the 1980s was then examined.

We saw that the decade of the 1990s was the period of greatest difficulty for procurement linkages promoting equal status goals in Europe. Separate but interconnected developments contributed to an apparently irresistible pressure against such procurement linkages. These developments were considered in chapter 11, beginning with the evolving approach of the Commission, followed by a detailed discussion of debates on procurement linkages in the United Kingdom, Germany, the Netherlands, and France. A relatively tolerant approach towards such linkages changed gradually between the mid-1980s and the early 1990s to become one of almost implacable hostility within the Commission service tasked with implementing the directives. The European Commission became one of the most prominent critics of such linkages and used its legal enforcement powers to create significant legal risks for public bodies in the Member States that wished to use such linkages. The prospect for linking status equality to procurement in the Community looked anything but easy, faced with the scepticism of the Council of Ministers throughout the legislative process of the 1980s, and then faced with the hostility in practice of the Commission. At the national level too, there was a growing scepticism about procurement linkages, reflecting a similar preference for an economic approach to be adopted to procurement. In several Member States also, the 'embedded liberalism' of the 1960s and 1970s was increasingly challenged, contributing to scepticism concerning procurement linkages. We saw that in several EC countries this contributed to an increasingly hostile national legal environment for such linkages. In some cases this legal scepticism appears to have been given a helping hand by EC legal developments.

Surprisingly, however, procurement linkages have not gone away. On the contrary, we saw in chapters 12 and 13, the growth of new linkages in several Member States, and the strengthening of existing linkages in others. All of these have developed since the neo-liberal interpretation of procurement regulation appeared to have become embedded. Efforts to suppress the social use of procurement met with only limited success, so that by 2006 procurement linkages for equality purposes were firmly on the political agenda of several Member States to an extent that would have seemed unthinkable ten years earlier. The remaining chapters of Part III explained why that happened. In chapter 12, we considered the significant developments that affected the political and legal context of public procurement linkages from the early 1990s to create greater legal space for such policies to develop. In chapter 13, we considered how Member States took advantage of this policy space to adopt such linkages for the first time or to expand those they had already adopted. In particular, the stimulus to the use of procurement linkages following the introduction of equality mainstreaming was seen to be significant. We also saw in chapter 12 that one of the significant changes in the context of European procurement law and policy was the greater legal clarity regarding the extent to which such linkages were permissible, arising from decisions of the European Court of Justice (ECJ), and legislative reforms in 2003. In chapter 14, we presented a legislative history of these reforms.

Interpretation

Part IV of the book moved from the analysis of the interaction of domestic procurement linkages with international and EC procurement regulation, undertaken in Parts II and III, to consider how far domestic procurement linkages are legally compatible with existing EC and GPA disciplines. We moved, then, from an analysis of the development of the current international and European provisions to their interpretation. In chapter 15, we considered the relationship between procurement linkages and the interpretation of the existing GPA. We considered not only the apparent conflict between the GPA 1994 and the use of procurement for achieving such social and human rights policies extraterritorially, but also domestically. We saw that the GPA was capable of being interpreted to give significant legal space to procurement linkages of the type discussed in earlier chapters.

In chapters 16 and 17, we turned to consider the relationship between procurement linkages and the interpretation of EC law, paying particular attention to the procurement directives adopted in 2003. We saw that there is now no reason to see the resolution of conflicts between EC social and economic policies as inevitably leading to the economic dominating the social. We saw that three aspects of Community law relating to procurement need to be borne in mind when interpreting the procurement directives in the context of procurement linkages: the overall limits of the procurement directives deriving from the Treaty; the importance of 'equal treatment' as the basis of both EC states' equality law and procurement law; and the importance of viewing the procurement directives as engaging with a policy instrument that is based on freedom of contract, raising the importance of what is meant by the 'subject matter of the contract'.

All three are relevant to the interpretation of the detailed provisions of the directives that was undertaken in chapter 17. For the purposes of exposition, however, it was the third issue (the meaning of the subject matter of the contract) that proved to be of most analytical importance for assessing the legality of procurement linkages furthering equal status goals in Community law. In the first section of the chapter, we considered the implementation of the directives where equal status is part of the subject matter of the contract. In this context, we saw government acting as a consumer, buying social justice. In the second part of the chapter, we considered various provisions of the directives that permit procurement equality linkages irrespective of whether equal status is part of the subject matter of the contract. In this context, we saw government acting as a regulator, requiring social justice. As with the GPA, sufficient legal space is provided under the directives to permit wide-ranging use of procurement linkages.

II. Role of Law

In retrospect, we can identify three differing relationships between procurement linkages and law.[1] One way of viewing the relationship between procurement linkages and the law is by seeing to what extent such linkages go *beyond* the existing equal status law, requiring companies to take action that they would not otherwise have been required to take. This type of analysis, whatever its merits in each particular legal system, has little utility as a comparative tool. The extent to which public procurement requires corporations with which government is contracting to go beyond what is otherwise legally required or to merely comply with the law, depends crucially on how far particular legal systems incorporate into law requirements that in other jurisdictions are left instead to the private sector to deal with on a voluntary basis. An example should make the issue clear. In the United States,

---

[1] Drawing on the helpful analytical structure developed by Doreen McBarnett: D McBarnett, 'Corporate Social Responsibility: Beyond Law, Through Law, For Law' in D McBarnett, DA Voiculescu, and T Campbell (eds), *The New Corporate Accountability: Corporate Responsibility and the Law* (Cambridge University Press, in press).

we saw that the federal government has used public procurement as one of a raft of measures to ensure compliance by government contractors with extensive legal prohibitions of employment discrimination that in any event apply to employers generally. In this case, public procurement does not go beyond the legal require-ments on business; rather it reflects them. Public procurement is used, however, to require businesses in South Africa to undertake affirmative action measures that are not otherwise applicable to businesses generally. In this case, public procure-ment goes beyond what the law otherwise requires. Different jurisdictions draw the lines between what is legally required and what is not in the social and environmen-tal fields very differently. Until recently, for example, most European countries did not have extensive prohibitions on racial discrimination. The effect of procure-ment linkages will differ significantly from jurisdiction to jurisdiction depending on the extent of social legislation otherwise applicable in that jurisdiction.

Let us turn to a second way of viewing the relationship. Most developed countries now have extensive legal regulation of the use of government procurement. The rea-sons for this are complex and multifaceted. Suffice it to say that there are often much more extensive limits on how governments can behave in undertaking procurement activity than will apply to private parties contracting together. This has given rise to considerable debate in most jurisdictions as to whether existing legal regulation of public procurement restricts the use of procurement linkages. A prominent issue, therefore, in the relationship between public procurement, procurement linkages, and the law is how far such linkages are *against the law*. This debate has involved considering the restrictions on public procurement that arise at the national level, at the regional (particularly, as we shall saw, at the EC) level, and under WTO agree-ments. One feature of the debate is the extent to which there is disagreement at each of these levels as to what the implications of the legal restrictions are for procurement linkages. The other feature of the debate is the apparent effect of this uncertainty on the willingness of public bodies to engage in procurement linkages.

One effect of this uncertainty is that some jurisdictions have attempted to clarify what public bodies are able to do to use public procurement for achieving social and environmental goals by law. Here the issue is how far procurement linkages have been *facilitated through the law*, the third way of viewing the relationship. There have been differing mixes of three basic approaches that have been adopted in different jurisdictions on different social issues. In some contexts, legislation explicitly requires public bodies not to award contracts under certain circum-stances. In other contexts, legislation requires public bodies simply to consider the use of procurement for achieving social purposes. This may be done explicitly, for example by allowing the award of contracts on a preferred basis to sheltered work-shops established to provide employment for severely disabled workers. Or it may be done impliedly, for example in the increasingly frequent requirement that pub-lic bodies 'mainstream' equality issues in their policies and practices.

Law may, therefore, require the use of procurement linkages for some purposes, permit them but not require them for other purposes, and prohibit their use for a third group of purposes. When a particular legal system does all of these at the same time (as we have seen is the case in many jurisdictions), this is likely to give at least the appearance of policy incoherence, leading to legal uncertainty. The uncertainty of the legal position regarding procurement linkages to achieve social goals is a recurrent theme. Legal uncertainty has been seen as a feature of domestic, European, and international law.[2] Uncertainty to this degree is one barrier to the further development of procurement linkages. Adopting linkages in public procurement is likely, therefore, to give rise to a continuing need to ensure policy coherence and consistency across government, ensuring that all sections of government are 'singing from the same hymn sheet'.

III. 'Economic' Versus 'Social' Approaches to Public Procurement Law and Policy

We distinguished initially between two broad sets of objectives that the regulation of procurement markets could be seen as serving: a set of political objectives, and a set of economic objectives. Procurement regulation is now frequently seen as attempting to lessen the political and to increase the economic. One of the most important developments in procurement regulation in the last fifty years has been the push for reform of public procurement to make it more efficient, less expensive, and more transparent. We saw that in a time of increasing pressure on government budgets, these economic considerations became increasingly important as a factor motivating procurement regulation. A major issue in constructing or reforming a system of procurement regulation is finding the appropriate balance between the political and the economic objectives of that procurement regulation. An important theme that arose throughout the book, therefore, was the issue of the tension between 'social' and 'economic' motivations for procurement policy. We saw that one of the difficulties of conducting this debate is the existence, hitherto at least, of largely separate spheres that those concerned with procurement, on the one hand, and equal status issues, on the other, seem to inhabit.[3] Few are expert in both, and there is often considerable difficulty in developing a common language for discussion between them. The purpose of this book has been to provide a bridge between these spheres, a framework in which such a discussion can take place in the specific context of procurement linkages.

---

[2] The confusion in the area of WTO law is well illustrated in S Zadek, S Lingayah, and M Forstater, *Social Labels: Tools for Ethical Trade: Final Report* (European Commission, 1998) 77. See also H Bank Jørgensen and PM Pruzan Jørgensen, M Jungk, and A Cramer, *Strengthening Implementation of Corporate Social Responsibility in Global Supply Chains* (World Bank, IFC, October 2003) 31.

[3] cf BA Langille, 'Eight Ways to Think about International Labour Standards'(1997) 31 Journal of World Trade 27.

Common principles

Is no compromise possible? On the basis of the preceding chapters, I think it is. The differences between the two camps may be less fundamental than at first sight appears to be the case. This is because, stripped of their complexity, many of the principles that one set of competing arguments resort to are also explicitly referred to in the other set of arguments. Even where this is not the case, there would appear to be no necessary reason why advocates of the one side cannot accommodate the principles that underpin an argument on the other side. There appear to be something like ten principles that each side accepts or could accept without jeopardizing its fundamental beliefs.[4]

One of the most important common principles is transparency, meaning openness and clarity as to what government procurement policy is and how it is delivered. Second, there is a principle of integrity, meaning that procurement regulation should ensure probity: there should be no personal or political corruption, and improper collusion between government and particular suppliers should be eliminated. Third, there appears to be agreement that procurement should be based on the concept of competitive supply; acquiring goods and services is considered as best achieved by competitive bidding unless there are convincing reasons to the contrary. Fourth, both sides are concerned to enhance the effectiveness of procurement in meeting whatever commercial or regulatory goals of government are chosen, in a manner appropriate to the requirement. Fifth, the goods, works, or services needed by government should be acquired as cost-effectively as possible. Sometimes this is termed 'value for money', redefined to ensure 'that the goods, works or services being acquired are suitable for requirements', that 'the contract itself should be concluded on the best available terms', and that 'the contractor chosen is able to provide what is required on the terms agreed'.[5] Sixth, there should be fair-dealing between government and others involved in the procurement process, which involves ensuring that suppliers and others are treated fairly and equally, without unfair discrimination. Seventh, procurement regulation should increase the responsiveness of those involved in government procurement in meeting the aspirations, expectations, and needs of the wider community served by the procurement. Eighth, there should be informed decision-making; decisions should be based on accurate information. Ninth, suppliers should, all other things being equal, be able to expect the same general procurement policy across the public sector, a principle of consistency. Tenth, accountability should be increased and effective mechanisms set in place in order to achieve such accountability.

---

[4] This part of the chapter draws heavily on Procurement Review Implementation Team, 'A Review of Public Procurement: Findings and Recommendations' (Northern Ireland Department of Finance, February 2002).

[5] S Arrowsmith, J Linarelli, and D Wallace, Jr, *Regulating Public Procurement: National and International Perspectives* (Kluwer Law International, 2000) 29.

If I am correct in my argument that most proponents and sceptics of linkage are likely to accept these general principles, then the question becomes not whether to introduce procurement linkages as a matter of principle, but how best to introduce social policies, and *which* such policies should be integrated into the process of public procurement. Here again, there appear to be several criteria that are consistent with the basic stand of each side that could guide these choices. First, linkages should be chosen that are effective in achieving the aim of the procurement and delivering the social policy. This is likely to mean concentrating procurement resources on delivering only the most important policy goals so as not to overload the system. This is a crucial point. Not every public policy can, or should, be taken into account in procurement. Second, potential suppliers should understand clearly from the outset what categories of information and service standards may be expected. They should be provided with adequate, accurate, and timely information at all the relevant stages of the procurement process. Public bodies should ensure that all stages of the procurement process can be audited satisfactorily with reference to a clear, written policy on evaluating tenders and awarding contracts, which is publicly available and made available to all suppliers. Third, choosing which government policies should be integrated into procurement will need to be carefully considered and justified, with the criteria clearly specified. Integration should be selective and targeted to achieve the best results. Integration does not mean that all such policies should be integrated, or in the same way, or to the same depth. Sometimes, integration may mean simply ensuring that public procurement decisions do not cut across other policies (ie have no negative effect); in other cases it may mean that public procurement should be harnessed to help achieve other policy objectives (ie have a positive effect). Fourth, linkages should be chosen that are as consistent as possible with the other aspects and values of the procurement process. Fifth, linkages should be chosen that are justifiable. Departments are accountable for their expenditure and, therefore, will need to determine whether any extra costs that may result (assuming that they will not be offset by savings over the longer term) are justified.

Adaptability of the procurement linkage instrument

Another important reason why the economic and social approaches to procurement are capable of being successfully managed together is because of the adaptability of the instrument. We have seen in particular the vital importance of understanding that 'government as consumer' means that status equality can become the subject matter of the contract itself, thus neatly merging the economic and social together in the concept of the government as a consumer buying social justice. Making equality a principal object of the contract can address several problems. The emphasis can be shifted from post to pre award, giving those negotiating a greater degree of leverage. The strategy for the public body under this model is to take advantage of the greater bargaining power the public body has in the stage prior to the award of the contract. This is the approach that most procurement professionals appear to prefer to use, because it enables greater flexibility to those awarding the successful tender to pick and choose between tenderers on the basis of the equality issue, thus promoting competition between tenderers on that equality issue. Much depends on the weight given by the public authority to the equality issue compared with the other award criteria. Depending on the extent to which equality issues are seen to be important to the public body, the award criteria approach may increase the weight that tenderers give to the equality issue, producing more and more elaborate ways of demonstrating that they are 'on-message', but increasing the cost of the bid. There may therefore be competition on equality, but with financial detriment to the public body. On the other hand, the weight given to the equality issue may be so negligible that little is delivered in practice. We saw that the apparent inflexibility of the instrument can be tackled in various other ways too, for example by the greater use of variations in specifying technical specifications, where the public body establishes a minimal set of technical specifications for the product sought, which all tenderers must satisfy, but also invites variants that add in a social dimension, such as equality, as well.

Post-award contract monitoring can be made more effective by giving the beneficiaries the opportunity to challenge non-compliance, and will thus be both better placed and better motivated, perhaps, to guarantee compliance. So too, the difficulties of having a secure basis for establishing breach can be tackled.[6]

Procurement regulation as beneficial for status equality

A third reason why the economic and social approaches to procurement can be reconciled is because the discipline that comes from an engagement between procurement linkages and procurement regulation can improve procurement linkages, by requiring an institutional structure to be established that increases the likely effectiveness of procurement linkages and limits the adverse side-effects that are likely to be politically damaging in the long term, thus establishing a more sympathetic and sustainable political environment. For example, the current Canadian Federal Contractors Program (FCP), Lucie Lamarche argues, is not as transparent nor as clear in its objectives nor as consistent in its operation as would be required to comply with the trade agreements. The agreements 'require an

---

[6] Swiss procurement authorities are addressing this post-award monitoring issue. Swiss procurement law obliges parties tendering for work on contract to respect, among other things, the principle of pay equity between men and women, taking current Swiss legislation and international agreements into account. But, at the same time, distortions of competition to the disadvantage of employers that abide by the rules must be avoided. The Federal Office for Equality between Women and Men (FOEWM) is assigned the task of carrying out inspections. Up to now, compliance with this provision could not be examined due to the lack of a control instrument. Recently, however, a control instrument has been developed which allows compliance with pay equity between men and women in individual companies to be examined. The instrument was successfully tested in practice and will in future be used to monitor the public procurement sector in the Confederation. It was developed and tested in practice by the Centre for Labour and Social Policy Studies BASS, commissioned by the FOEWM and the Federal Procurement Commission.

unequalled transparency and rigor from Canada in managing these programs, which, in their current state, present deficiencies in the standards that they establish'.[7] If, as she states should be the case, the FCP is to be strengthened, then Lamarche argues that those concerned to do so should pay much more attention than in the past to the implications of the trade agreements in devising these reforms. Perhaps paradoxically, the effect of the trade agreements could then be to lead to more and better regulation that would benefit the cause of gender equality. If this is to occur, however, there will be a need in the future for government to be much more conscious of the gender implications of trade agreements than in the past. In that context, she argues that gender-based analysis of trade agreements should become much more common. But she also argues that women's groups themselves should become much more conscious of, and expert in, such trade agreements, if they are not to become a barrier to progress. What is true for gender equality in Canada seems to me true more generally.

IV. Debates About Adaptation to Globalization

Another major theme of the book has been the interplay of domestic and international influences on the trajectory of procurement policy relating to procurement linkages. We saw that the choice as to where the balance is to be struck between the political and the economic in procurement regulation can be made in several different venues, along a continuum between the purely local, and the international. We saw that one of the recurring issues in procurement regulation was the question of the legality of such uses of procurement linkages, not only domestically, but also under various international trade agreements that these states have entered into. We were particularly interested in exploring the interrelationship between the domestic, regional, and international dimensions of procurement and understanding the extent to which not only the international and regional impact on the domestic, but also vice versa.

Waves of globalization analysis

The importance of the interplay between the national and the global, and how each adaptes to the other, is a common theme of much contemporary literature. Janis van der Westhuizen has usefully analysed approaches to this issue as falling into three alternative theories, which are described as constituting three 'waves'. In the first wave, global economic liberalization was regarded as constituting an unprecedented 'epocal shift in world history toward a new age in which there would be no alternative to neoliberalism'.[8] The globalization of capital, culture, and communications

---

[7] L Lamarche *et al*, 'Retaining Employment Equity Measures in Trade Agreements' (Status of Women Canada, February 2005) Executive Summary.

[8] J van der Westhuizen, *Adapting to Globalization: Malaysia, South Africa, and the Challenges of Ethnic Redistribution with Growth* (Praeger, 2002) 2.

was regarded as 'inexorable and immutable', as Colin Hay and David Marsh put it.[9] The nation state was seen as severely constrained in how to adapt to this global economic liberalism, having been deprived of the tools by which to limit its influence, and the result was that states were predicted to become increasingly homogeneous. For some of those writing in this tradition, these predicted developments were regarded as something to celebrate, for others, something to be feared and lamented. In a second wave, those writing in the first wave were criticized for exaggerating the uniqueness of what was regarded as merely the most recent in a line of similar developments, and presenting 'overblown, distorted, uncritical and seldom defended assertions'.[10] The first wave thesis, that the power of the nation state to control these developments was severely constrained, was also criticized and states were seen as able to control globalization, if they simply had the political will to do so.

A third wave attempted to mediate the first and second wave, drawing on insights from both. On the one hand, the current globalization was acknowledged as constituting 'a qualitiatively new era in the world economy, albeit one built upon a historical process of evolution since the emergence of the capitalist system'.[11] On the other hand, and this becomes a crucial point for our purposes, the 'future trajectory of globalization' was seen as 'uncertain, dynamic, and open-ended'.[12] For those in this third wave, what van der Westhuizen terms 'transformationalists', the interesting issue is how nations react to economic globalization, *and vice versa:* 'states remain resilient and adaptive creatures actively seeking and creatively producing various strategies to engage globalization'.[13] As McGrew argues, 'the power of national governments is not necessarily diminished by globalization but on the contrary is being redefined, reconstituted and restructured in response to the growing complexity of processes of governance in a more interconnected world'.[14] We can go one stage further, however, and have observed that the international and regional forces of economic globalization will then, in turn, adapt to developments at the national level. Elites at the international, regional, and state levels 'mediate structural expectations of the actors in the international political economy with often contradictory demands by domestic constituencies'.[15]

The third approach provides the most fruitful basis for understanding what we have seen happening to the issue of linkage following the international and European procurement reforms. What appears to have happened is that international and European procurement regulation, and procurement linkages, have both changed as a result of exposure to each other. A complex mediation of

[9] C Hays and D Marsh(eds), *Demystifying Globalization* (Macmillan, 2000) 4, quoted in van der Westhuizen(n 8 above) 2. It should be noted that the authors did not accept this viewpoint.
[10] ibid 4, quoted in van der Westhuizen (n 8 above) 2.
[11] van der Westhuizen (n 8 above) 2.   [12] ibid.   [13] ibid.
[14] A McGrew, 'The Globalization Debate: Putting the Advanced Capitalist State in its Place' (1998) 12(3) Global Society 299, 310, quoted in van der Westhuizen (n 8 above) 3.
[15] van der Westhuizen (n 8 above) concentrates on the role of state elites.

competing demands relating to procurement regulation and social justice is taking place. International and European procurement regulation, then, has had to interact with both old and new forms of linkage at the domestic level; procurement regulation clearly did not suppress old forms of linkage, but nor has procurement regulation been irrelevant to the evolution of new forms of procurement linkage.

A range of adaptations has been developed that make the relationship between the social and the economic uses of procurement less fraught, without sacrificing either completely. We have seen linkage weakened, but not abandoned, as a result of international and EC procurement reform measures, as was the case with linkages concerning disabled workers in Britain in the 1980s. We have seen previous linkages strengthened as a result of procurement reform measures, where a country takes advantage of approaches to linkage permitted in the reform legislation to strengthen its previous approach to linkage, as we saw occurred in Britain in the context of measures dealing with racial equality. We have seen, too, the adoption of linkage by countries that did not appear to use it previously, partly in order to be able to take advantage of gaps created by others seeking derogations for their linkages; so, for example, Canada adopted elements of linkage, partly as a result of the United States derogations to the GPA for minority and small businesses. We have seen too, in the Canadian context, procurement linkage measures carving out exceptions where they were likely to run up against GPA or NAFTA problems.[16]

Models of international and regional legal regulation of procurement linkages

Although European procurement regulation has also been significantly altered as a result of exposure to domestic procurement linkages, the legal issue concerning procurement linkages at the global level is part of a much larger continuing, and so far largely unresolved, debate about how the tensions between the social and the economic dimensions of public policy are to be addressed at the international level. In a recent assessment of the relationship between the trade and human rights regimes, the United Nations Office of the High Commissioner for Human Rights drew on tensions between the social and economic uses of procurement as a key example of an important tension between equality and economic liberalization in international public policy.[17] How these tensions are resolved will have important effects on the ability of nations, individually and collectively, to address effectively issues of social policy, equality, and human rights in the future.

---

[16] Not only in Canada, of course. When President Clinton promulgated his Executive Order prohibiting the acquisition of products produced by forced or indentured labour, Executive Order 13126 of 12 June 1999, it only applied to those purchases not covered by the GPA or NAFTA, see ibid s 5(b).

[17] United Nations High Commissioner for Human Rights, 'Analytical Study of the High Commissioner for Human Rights on the fundamental principle of non-discrimination in the context of globalization', 15 January 2004, E/CN.4/2004/40, paras 28–34.

A clear difference is emerging between two different models of how the regulation of procurement linkages is to be managed at the supranational level. In the first model,[18] an integrated or holistic approach is adopted where social policy and procurement regulation are both incorporated as prime objectives of the system, and the appropriate balance between the two is seen as a normal activity that takes place within the system itself. Social policy is seen as *endogenous*. In this context, the issue to be resolved is whether there are ways of addressing the concerns of the procurement regulation whilst still retaining linkage, but sometimes by doing both in somewhat different ways. In the second model, the role of social policy is a distinct or side issue and the bodies involved see the appropriate balance between the social and the economic as a more difficult task, not a normal activity that takes place within the system itself, but outside it, and in a more episodic manner than in the first. Social policy is seen as *exogenous*. In the first model, adaptation has proven considerably easier and resulted in more stable compromises than in the second, but at a cost (if that is what it is) to national sovereignty and the principle of subsidiarity. Which model is preferable is a complex question involving fundamental political preferences.

European Community and procurement linkages

The EC is the best-developed example of the first model at the supranational level. As Gráinne de Búrca and Joanne Scott argue, 'the multiple aspirations and tasks of the EU as a closely integrated regional organization are unquestionable. Its role and functions are wide and general and the balance struck between the imperative of free trade and its many other policy goals is complex.'[19] This type of supranational economic regulation is sometimes considered to introduce the potential for 'deep' integration. The EC experience seems to indicate that these types of problems can be dealt with by developing a holistic view of the public interest, one that recognizes the integration of the political and social, as well as the economic aspects of life. The legal resolution of these tensions is still a work-in-progress, with many uncertainties remaining, including the extent of coverage, the relationship with international legal frameworks, and the possibility of agreeing standard criteria in this area. The very broad scope of the equality agenda means that legal issues will continue to require clarification. A brief and partial list must suffice: the impact of the EC state aid rules on secondary policies in public procurement; the extent to which issues relating to employment conditions are permissible under the new directives; issues relating to the new directives' provisions on sheltered

---

[18] This has similarities to what Cottier *et al* have termed a 'constitutional model', but this terminology may have other resonances that make it a concept of doubtful value in this context, see 'Introduction', in T Cottier, J Pauwelyn, and E Bürgi (eds), *Human Rights and International Trade* (OUP, 2005) 5.

[19] G de Búrca and J Scott, 'The Impact of the WTO on EU Decision-Making', Harvard Jean Monnet Working Paper 06/00 (2000) 2.

workshops and access to disabled users; the permissibility of incorporating 'fair trade' in public purchasing; and the extent to which pursuing equality through procurement impacts differently on procurement in the utilities sector.[20] For the risk averse, there is still plenty of reason for caution, but the broad outlines of a workable compromise are there.

In the EU, a continuous adaptation of procurement regulation has progressively given greater domestic regulatory space for procurement linkages as a method of enforcement of Community social policy that seemed likely in the early 1990s. Many of the major legal concepts applicable in procurement law have been subject to extensive interpretation, leading to an adapted procurement regime that now looks substantially different in respect of the treatment of social linkages than might have been supposed when agreements including procurement reform were negotiated in the late 1980s. What we see emerging are discernible moves towards new, more coherent relationships between the social and the economic uses of procurement, in which the EC is playing a leading role. It should be noted, however, that the role of the Community and of Community law has been to give flexibility and discretion to Member States in terms of whether or not to use procurement linkages. So far, at least, there is not much prospect of EC law being used to require the use of such linkages, and (as we have seen) attempts to do this were repulsed. This is important because, in the EC, the issue is mostly concerned with the extent of policy space that will be allowed to states under Community law, not whether Community law will be used to require procurement linkages.

Role of adjudication

Adaptation of procurement regulation to accommodate procurement linkages in the EC has taken place through the manipulation of various concepts, sometimes resulting in process adaptations, sometimes in substantive adaptations. In particular, the extent to which potential contractors may be excluded from bidding on a contract on the basis of non-compliance with social standards, the extent to which social conditions may be included in contractual terms of the contract, and the somewhat greater flexibility now built into the use of social criteria at the award stage of the contract, all owe a considerable amount to the influence of the ECJ, usually in the teeth of opposition from the European Commission. Legal interpretation, particularly by the ECJ, has played a major role in mediating the tensions between the more extreme proponents of procurement reform and the equally extreme desire to continue to utilize procurement for social uses irrespective of its economic effects, leading to a modus vivendi between the two.

The role played by the ECJ in recognizing the breadth of the interests involved and broadening the epistemic community of interpretation to reflect this was crucial. In a series of cases over three decades (for example *Beentjes, Nord-Pas-de-Calais,*

---

[20] S Arrowsmith and P Kunzlik (eds), *Social and Environmental Policies under the EC Procurement Rules: New Directives and New Directions* (provisional title) (Cambridge University Press, in press).

Concordia Bus, and *Wienstrom,* discussed in chapter 12 above) the ECJ has subtly broadened the interpretative agenda on procurement beyond the economic and trade view of procurement and sought to allow a modified social agenda to be pursued as well. The Court has tended to view the issue of procurement not in isolation from, but as part of, the larger economic and social role that the Community has adopted. Effectively what the Court did was to stop the onward march of a purely commercial approach to government procurement, and allow a space for politics in which other interests could compete. Although at first extremely resistant to the Court's view, by the end of the 1990s the Commission substantially bought into the Court's approach, and in an important Communication set out its policy towards the existing directives in some detail, which (after some significant modification) was incorporated into legislation in the directives.

Regulatory competition

Simon Deakin's analysis of the concept of 'regulatory competition' helps to clarify what is happening in this context, and the tensions involved.[21] He usefully defines regulatory competition as 'a process whereby legal rules are selected and de-selected through competition between decentralized, rule-making entities'.[22] If this is applied to the selection of legal instruments of governance such as procurement linkages, which does not seem out of keeping, then the approach taken in the Community can be seen as essentially permitting, even encouraging, regulatory competition over the use of procurement for status equality purposes between the Member States. For Deakin, there are three benefits that are expected to flow from such regulatory competition:

(1) it allows the content of rules to be matched more effectively to the preferences or wants of the consumers of laws (citizens and others affected); (2) it promotes diversity and experimentation in the search for effective legal solutions; and (3) by providing mechanisms for preferences to be expressed and alternative solutions compared, it enhances the flow of information on effective law making.[23]

For Deakin, laws (and, we might add, instruments of governance such as procurement linkages) 'can be seen as products that jurisdictions *supply* through their lawmaking activities, in response to the *demands* of consumers of the laws, that is, individuals, companies, and other affected parties'.[24]

There are two roles that a higher, supervisory, body may play in this process. Put crudely, it might either see regulatory competition as an open and continuing opportunity to experiment and inform in order to enable the lower units of government to decide what approach to regulation is best for them at any given time. Deakin has termed this 'reflexive harmonization'.[25] An alternative approach is to

---

[21] S Deakin, 'Social Rights in a Globalized Economy' in P Alston (ed), *Labour Rights as Social Rights* (OUP, 2005) 25.   [22] ibid 39.
[23] ibid 40.   [24] ibid (emphasis in original).   [25] ibid 41.

see regulatory competition as encouraging experiment in order for the higher body to decide what is the best approach to take based on the results of the experiments, and then impose that solution. Deakin has called this 'comparative federalism'.[26] The current EC approach to procurement linkages (the approach may well be different in other areas of regulation) is an uneasy compromise between the two, with a degree of uncertainty as to which alternative it will end up adopting. There are elements of both at the moment.

On the one hand, the space given by the ECJ to Member States to use procurement linkages, subsequently adopted by the Commission, and then in the reformed legislation, seems strongly influenced by reflexive harmonization. For example, the role of the Commission in coordinating information in order to better enable the Member States to benefit fully from the regulatory competition within the capacious setting of corporate social responsibility, seems to fit within the first alternative. However, there are also strong elements of the second (comparative federalism) approach as well, where the role of intervention in the process of regulatory competition is one of dealing strongly with negative side-effects that are seen as arising. There may well, for example, be 'some unwanted side effects of competition ("externalities" or spill over effects of various kinds)' that may arise, 'thereby giving rise to an efficiency-related argument for some harmonization' by some higher body, 'which involves superintending the process of competition between the lower level units'.[27] Taken further, this would involve sustained attempts to generate what the European authorities would see as the most appropriate approach to procurement linkages. Again there are aspects of this approach apparent in, for example, the strong guidance that post-award contract conditions are the most suitable method of procurement linkage. In short, these two approaches to regulatory competition are in constant tension. They may remain so, or one may become dominant.

World Trade Organization and procurement linkages

If the European Community is the best developed example of the first model of supranational regulation, the WTO is a classic example of the second model, in which, as de Búrca and Scott observe, the strength of the trade rules 'effectively consign all other important policies ... to the status of exceptions which must be argued for within relatively strict constraints, rather than important competing or even co-equal policies in their own right'.[28] At the WTO, no equivalent reconciliation between the social and the economic functions of procurement has yet taken place equivalent to that in the EC. Under this second model, the social and economic functions of procurement are likely to give rise to high profile conflicts, with the potential to undermine the legitimacy of economic liberalization, at least

---

[26] ibid.   [27] ibid 40–1.

[28] G de Búrca, and J Scott, 'The Impact of the WTO on EU Decision-Making', Harvard Jean Monnet Working Paper 06/00 (2000) 2.

with regard to procurement, as we saw in the failure even to agree to begin formal talks on an agreement on transparency in public procurement, as described in chapter 8 above. We have yet to see a change in the epistemic community of interpretation in the WTO context equivalent to that which has occurred in the EC, and the resolution of the tensions between linkage and procurement reform are much less certain in that context than in the EC context, where a resolution of the tension is now far advanced. The WTO is, unlike the EC, currently embedded in an institutional context that appears ill-equipped to deal with the type of problems that deep integration brings in its wake.[29]

Deeper integration via the WTO?

One approach would be to deepen integration yet further at the international level. The WTO could move closer to the EC as a model of integration. Discussion within labour and human rights circles has frequently revolved around the question of whether labour and human rights, for example, might be promoted through 'social clauses' in international trade and investment agreements.[30] Such social clauses involve the parties promising to comply with particular labour or human rights standards, or risk trade sanctions being imposed. Such social clauses had been considered in connection, for example, with the (failed) OECD Multilateral Agreement on Investment.[31] The WTO has an elaborate system of adjudication and sanctions in order to enforce trade norms and, from the enforcement and compliance point of view, looks more attractive to some than, for example the ILO. The ILO relies largely on moral suasion and diplomatic pressure. The involvement of the ILO in the substantial problem of forced labour in Burma presented a mixed picture of the organization's effectiveness.[32] The new initiatives on child labour, another area of ILO concentration, have yet to bear fruit.[33] The ILO has yet, under its new leadership and equipped with its enhanced, post-Singapore mandate, to prove itself any more effective than it has been in the past. It therefore seems likely that pressure for WTO involvement in labour issues will continue, simply because of the greater power which the WTO has vis-à-vis recalcitrant national states.

---

[29] See generally I Kaul, I Grunberg, and M Stern, *Global Public Goods: International Cooperation in the 21st Century* (OUP, 1999).

[30] C McCrudden and A Davies, 'A Perspective on Trade and Labour Rights (2000) 3(1) JIEL 43, 60.

[31] C McCrudden, 'Property Rights and Labour Rights Revisited: International Investment Agreements and the "Social Clause" Debate' in I Irish (ed), *The Auto Pact: Investment, Labour and the WTO* (Kluwer, 2004) 300.

[32] F Maupain, 'Is the ILO Effective in Upholding Workers' Rights? Reflections on the Myanmar Experience' in P Alston (ed) *Labour Rights as Human Rights* (OUP, 2005).

[33] ILO Convention 182, Convention Concerning the Prohibition and Immediate Action for the Elimination of the Worst Forms of Child Labour (1999) <http://www.ilo.org/ilolex/english/convdisp1.htm>; ILO Recommendation 190, Recommendation Concerning the Prohibition and Immediate Action for the Elimination of the Worst Forms of Child Labour (1999) <http://www.ilo.org/ilolex/english/recdisp1.htm>.

In this scenario, requiring the WTO to address the status equality agenda itself as a principal actor is not seen as so extraordinary. For example, membership of the organization could be made conditional on a country's willingness to conform to minimum anti-discrimination standards. Or we could go further, requiring equal status requirements to be promoted through 'social clauses' in international trade, investment, and procurement agreements.[34] Such social clauses would involve the parties promising to comply with particular equality standards, or risk trade sanctions being imposed.[35] In this case, trade law would become the mechanism of better social standards. Many different arguments have been advanced in favour of incorporating social standards into an amended set of WTO agreements.[36] Such a link would defend the social achievements of developed countries from erosion, and facilitate further trade liberalization by reassuring voters in those countries. Externalities, such as the sense of outrage in many countries about the treatment of some workers abroad, would justify regulatory intervention, just as much as pollution crossing borders justifies regulation by the receiving country.[37] Promoting better social standards would be an act of solidarity with the disadvantaged in the developing world. An effective international regulatory structure may constrain the unilateral use of trade sanctions, and thus reduce the risk of covert protectionism.

It would be naive to think, however, that there is not considerable opposition to any linkage between international trade and other non-economic issues, such as social standards or human rights, particularly from developing countries. Many arguments have been advanced against an explicit linkage between the WTO regime and labour rights, for example.[38] Differences in rights between countries are seen to be a legitimate source of comparative advantage. Current high-standard countries had much lower labour standards when they were developing and it is therefore unfair that developing countries should be denied the same opportunities. In any event, standards rise with per capita income and liberal trade promotes higher growth. Trade adjustment measures are better than trade restrictions to help

---

[34] Some of the precedents for this are reviewed in P Waer, 'Social Clauses in International Trade: The Debate in the European Union' (1996) 30 Journal of World Trade 25, 27–8.

[35] The precise institutional mechanism for this merits careful consideration. For discussion, see P Stirling, 'The Use of Trade Sanctions as an Enforcement Mechanism for Basic Human Rights: A Proposal for Addition to the World Trade Organisation' (1996) 11 American University Journal of International Law and Policy 1; E de Wet, 'Labour Standards in the Globalised Economy: The Inclusion of a Social Clause in the General Agreement on Tariffs and Trade/World Trade Organisation' (1995) 17 Human Rights Quarterly 443..

[36] See eg R Kyloh, 'The Governance of Globalisation: ILO's Contribution' in R Kyloh (ed), *Mastering the Challenge of Globalisation: Towards a Trade Union Agenda* (ILO, 1998); de Wet (n 35 above).

[37] This issue (and the analogy between environment and labour concerns more generally) is explored in H Ward, 'Common but Differentiated Debates: Environment, Labour and the World Trade Organisation' (1996) 45 ICLQ 592.

[38] See eg J Bhagwati, 'The Agenda of the WTO', and TN Srinivasan, 'International Trade and Labour Standards from an Economic Perspective' both in P van Dijck and G Faber (eds), *Challenges to the New World Trade Organisation* (Kluwer, 1996); AA Warner, 'Globalisation and Human Rights: An Economic Model' (1999) 25 Brooklyn Journal of International Law 99.

those who lose out in globalization. The labour rights agenda risks being captured by protectionist elements.[39] A link to core labour rights would simply lead to demands for links to more and more social standards. Stressing labour standards increases north-south tensions because of the sensitivity in developing countries over the issue of national sovereignty. Incorporating labour rights into the WTO would increase the number and difficulty of trade disputes. The WTO must be protected as an institution. If it is not, the global trading system might be undermined. Finally, it would be inappropriate for a body with primary expertise in trade to have to interpret labour standards. Trade law, in short, should not be used as a sword to enforce labour rights.

Realistic alternatives: negotiation, opting out, and interpretation

Whatever the rights and wrongs of these conflicting approaches in political theory, deeper integration seems unlikely in political practice, at least in the short to medium term. In the absence of alternatives, the WTO is therefore destined to muddle through, coping with periodic shocks to the system that may or may not be sufficiently severe to lead to its break up. Are there alternatives? Rather than attempting to increase the depth of integration, some have argued that the better solution is to keep the WTO out of the way; that it is preferable to see the WTO as a potential barrier to social progress and one whose role should therefore be minimized.

Three arguments support this approach. An argument from subsidiarity is that decisions affecting individuals should be taken as close to the individual as possible.[40] Decision-making should be localized as much as possible, and procurement linkages should be unconstrained. A second argument based on the institutional incompetence of the decision-making bodies in the WTO leads to a view that the best one can hope for is that these bodies remove themselves from the scene, and remove international trade agreements from being barriers to national decision-making in the area. The problem is that such strong localization of procurement linkages has given rise to externalities that called for, and continue to call for, collective action transnationally. A third argument is more interesting. This argument is particularly associated with Robert Howse and Brian Langille who argue that the WTO is, effectively, stuck in a time warp, unable to break free of the ideological strait jacket of neo-liberalism to which it is committed. 'It is becoming the last and best spokesperson' for 'the increasingly discredited neo-liberal approach to development'.[41]

---

[39] For interesting empirical evidence on this point, see AB Krueger, 'Observations on International Labour Standards and Trade', National Bureau of Economic Research Working Paper 5632 (1996).

[40] V Marleau, 'Globalization, Decentralization and the Role of Subsidiarity in the Labour Setting', in JDR Craig and SM Lynk (eds), *Globalization and the Future of Labour Law* (Cambridge University Press, 2006) 108.

[41] R Howse, and B Langille with J Burda, 'The World Trade Organization and Labour Rights: Man Bites Dog', in VA Leary and D Warner (eds), *Social Issues, Globalisation and International Institutions: Labour Rights and the EU, ILO, OECD and WTO* (Brill Academic, 2005) 161.

There are several possible methods that appear to be available to those who wish to minimize its role. One method involves those states deciding to join the GPA attempting to protect procurement linkages by minimizing their commitments under the Agreement. States joining the GPA could protect procurement linkages by taking particular care to use the entry negotiations to ensure that (by negotiating the exclusion of particular sectors of the economy, or the exclusion of particular parts of government, or by taking advantage of the opportunity given to adopt policies in contracts that fall below the threshold) their linkages are not subject to being contested. Perhaps most importantly in practice, we see in the conclusion of bilateral procurement agreements the increasing inclusion in the country annexes of tailored exclusions to protect particular types of linkages.

Renegotiation

Is a more fundamental *multilateral* renegotiation of commitments between the existing parties the appropriate pragmatic response to some of the issues raised? There are opportunities for a more general clarification of the legality or illegality of such measures in the body of the GPA 1994 itself.[42] There are two linked issues commending revision. The first is the desirability of ensuring that these issues are settled by negotiation rather than by litigation, with the latter's attendant costs and tensions. There is, however, another reason that has become important, the failure of the GPA to make itself attractive to countries outside a relatively small group. It is true that the original small group of members is likely to become larger. However, very few developing states are likely to become members, and in part that seems to be because of a perception that the GPA would be too restrictive of their use of procurement for socio-economic goals.[43]

Any substantial general renegotiation of the text or substantial renegotiation of individual commitments by particular states would be politically complicated. There are several different sets of interests, each of which represents a broad coalition. There are the concerns of developing countries.[44] As Fenster has argued, given the diversity of interests and the variety of different types of measures that might be appropriate for different countries, 'any multilateral rules need to be framed sufficiently broadly to allow developing countries to choose the most suitable form. This will be a challenge. (. . .) The reality is so complex that discrimination is often not amenable to rules-based regulation.'[45] For developing countries, in particular, either of two extremes would be unacceptable: 'a very precise regime

---

[42] The French government, in 2006, encouraged the EU to renegotiate an exception for preferences for small businesses equivalent to that in the US annex, see 'Small Businesses: French Seek to Level the Public Procurement Playing Field', *European Report*, 13 July 2006.

[43] S Arrowsmith, *The Law of Public and Utilities Procurement* (2nd edn, Sweet and Maxwell, 2005) 769.

[44] See G Fenster, 'Multilateral Talks on Transparency in Government Procurement: Concerns for Developing Countries' (2003) 34(2) IDS Bulletin 63–81.   [45] ibid 73.

that might remove discrimination but at the cost of a heavy burden of compliance, and a looser regime that would leave developing countries as victims of opaque or discriminatory practices by other member states'.[46]

What would it take for such negotiations to work? Negotiations would need to be constructed in a way that ensures that both the social and the economic roles that procurement can play are adequately considered. As Thomas Cottier and his colleagues argue: 'Taking human rights seriously in trade negotiations [and the same applies to equal status issues] would require broader participation of different actors and assessments of the potential impact of global trade policies on the enjoyment of human rights.'[47] Those concerned with procurement linkages would participate directly in the debate at the international level and, perhaps more importantly, ensure that the formulation of policies at the international levels is seen by national governments as open to a much broader input from equality and human rights interests than we have seen has happened in the past.[48] There would also be a need for significantly increased policy coordination within governments. 'Problems faced on the international level between international organizations often merely reflect the fact that governments are equally fragmented and domestic policy making does not take into account trade and human rights concerns to the full extent.'[49]

This approach comes closest to what Shell has termed a 'trade stakeholders model'.[50] As developed and applied to the procurement context by John Linarelli:

... the trade stakeholders model values broad participation by domestic constituencies in trade policy at both the domestic and international levels, as an end in itself. It is a process-oriented model of deliberative democracy in which social justice is taken into account as a variable separate from economic efficiency. Domestic constituencies are important. Interest groups are cast in a positive light ... Interest groups in an open and transparent policymaking process serve the function of consolidating diverse societal interests.[51]

But we must beware of any naive belief that this would be easy. The extensive studies of attempts to mainstream gender in the European and global context have demonstrated the difficulty of participating from the point of view of the potential beneficiaries of linkage, among other pitfalls.[52] Given the extent to which

---

[46] ibid 76.   [47] Introduction, in Cottier *et al* (n 18 above) 10.

[48] cf argument by Larmarche in the Canadian context, L Lamarche *et al*, 'Retaining Employment Equity Measures in Trade Agreements' (Status of Women Canada, February 2005). For a more general argument on the potential for domestic politics and law to bring institutions of globalization under more democratic control, see AC Aman, *The Democracy Deficit: Taming Globalization Through Law Reform* (NYU Press, 2004).   [49] Introduction, in Cottier *et al* (n 18 above) 10.

[50] GR Shell, 'Trade Legalism and International Relations Theory: An Analysis of the World Trade Organization' (1995) 44 Duke Law Journal 829.

[51] J Linarelli, 'The WTO Transparency Agenda: Law, Economics and International Relations Theory' in S Arrowsmith and M Trybus (eds), *Public Procurement: The Continuing Revolution* (Kluwer, 2003) 256.

[52] See eg A Woodward, 'European Gender Mainstreaming: Promises and Pitfalls of Transformative Policy' (2003) 20(1) Review of Policy Research 65; MA Pollack and E Hafner-Burton, 'Mainstreaming Gender in the European Union' (2000) 7(3) JEPP 432; E Hafner-Burton

linkages are redistributive, we should also expect to come up against entrenched interests that will resist such participation.[53]

Opting out

Faced with these difficulties, we have seen that some countries have simply opted out of the GPA. 'Opting out' may occur in two somewhat different ways. One method of opting out involves decisions by states not to become parties to the GPA, at least in part because of their wish to preserve their procurement linkages. This is particularly the case, it would seem, in the countries of the developing world, which have, almost without exception, refused to become parties. The example that best illustrates the issues, because of the relatively greater amount of information available, is South Africa. Another opting-out strategy is less passive and more aggressive. It is to minimize any further role for the WTO in states with linkages by resisting the conclusion of any further agreements that might encroach on domestic policy space. The best example of this is the failure of the negotiations for a multilateral agreement on transparency in public procurement as part of the Doha Round of trade negotiations. The negotiations surrounding procurement were considered in detail above, concentrating on the approach that Malaysia adopted. The problem with each of these opting-out strategies is similar: that states are required to sacrifice whatever economic and political benefits might accrue from being part of a multilateral economic agreement.

Adjudication

It is unlikely that negotiations or opting out will resolve these issues in the near future.[54] In particular, therefore, the WTO adjudicatory institutions seem likely to be called on at some point to interpret the GPA in contexts where the appropriateness of linkages made by others will have to be scrutinized. The dispute panels and the Appellate Body may not be able to avoid dealing with such linkages directly.

In that case, the issue will be the appropriate amount of legal space that states will be given through interpretation of the existing GPA to pursue such social goals. There remain some considerable uncertainties regarding the admissibility of social policy measures under the GPA as it is currently drafted. The exact position of the WTO Appellate Body on many of the relevant issues is still unknown. Thus, it is

---

and MA Pollack, 'Mainstreaming Gender in Global Governance' (2002) 8(3) European Journal of International Relations 339; F Beveridge, S Nott, and K Stephen, 'Mainstreaming and the Engendering of Policy-Making: a Means to an End?' (2000) 7(3) JEPP 385.

[53] See, among others, A Lensihow, 'New Regulatory Approaches to "Greening" EU Policies' (2002) 8(1) European Law Journal 19, especially at 33–5.

[54] A Erridge and R Fee, 'Contract Compliance: National, Regional and Global Regimes' (1999) 27 Policy and Politics 199: prospects for the development of a global regime through the WTO are not favourable.

quite possible to argue that social policy measures will not violate Article III of the GPA as long as they do not protect domestic products, services, or suppliers but we cannot be certain that this will be the case. While Appellate Body jurisprudence has done much to clarify the meaning of the chapeau and the 'necessity' requirement in Article XX, it is practically impossible to answer the crucial question of how much room for equality concerns there is under the 'public morals' and 'public order' categories from existing case law. Where it is legally possible to do so, my argument has been that trade law should not be used as a sword to attack such policies, provided they are not protectionist.

There are two principal issues associated with taking the approach suggested. First, some would question the institutional capacity of the existing WTO adjudicatory mechanisms to undertake the analysis that would be necessary, given their membership and modus operandi. In particular, it might be said, delving into such complex issues is well beyond what the existing bodies were set up to do, which was primarily to handle issues of trade law and policy. However, not only does this criticism seem much less well directed at the Appellate Body than at the disputes panels, but there is also a potential solution: broadening the membership of the appropriate bodies, and modifying the procedures under which disputes panels and the Appellate Body operate. This might be done by widening participation in the proceedings further, and accepting advice from the ILO (in labour rights issues) and the UN Human Rights Commissioner (in broader human rights issues), thus allowing in a wider range of information and policy-relevant argument than has hitherto been usual.[55]

A second issue relates more to the legitimacy of the WTO adjudicatory institutions taking this approach. To what extent should the WTO adjudicatory bodies be second-guessing governments in issues of such delicate political judgement? This issue will be significantly influenced by the standard of review that the dispute panels and the Appellate Body apply to the actions of the states parties to the Agreement. The dream which some seem to have of a WTO innocent of involvement with non-trade issues has already been shattered in the context of environmental norms, and it may only be a matter of time before the same occurs in the context of equality and human rights issues. This raises interesting questions about the role of the WTO Appellate Body. How would it handle a case involving equality rights? Is the Appellate Body the appropriate forum to resolve such cases?[56] Some see the Appellate Body as a court in evolution, making policy trade-offs in the way that other courts regularly do, confident in its legitimacy to interpret the texts of trade agreements. Others would reject this approach, claiming that it fails to understand

---

[55] For discussions, see AK Schneider, 'Democracy and Dispute Resolution: Individual Rights in International Trade Organisations' (1998) 19 UP JIEL 587; S Charnovitz, 'Participation of Non-governmental Organisations in the World Trade Organisations' (1996) 17 UP JIEL 331.

[56] SP Croley and JH Jackson, 'WTO Dispute Procedures, Standard of Review, and Deference to National Governments' (1996) 90 AJIL 193, contains an interesting discussion of the appropriate role of an international dispute settlement body.

the institutional fragility of the dispute settlement process, and would urge caution, regarding the need for trade-offs as essentially a role for the political actors.

V. Equal Status Law and Social Policy

We turn now to our final theme: the relationship between procurement linkages and equal status law and policy. Five relatively distinct types of equality linkages have been identified in the course of the book: the use of procurement as a method of enforcing anti-discrimination law in the employment context; the use of procurement to advance a wider conception of distributive justice, particularly affirmative action in employment; the use of procurement as a method to help to stimulate increased entrepreneurial activity by disadvantaged groups defined by ethnicity or gender; the inclusion in procurement contracts of requirements to ensure fairness and equality when services are transferred from the public sector to the private sector; and the use of procurement as a means of putting pressure on companies operating in other countries to conform to equality norms. We saw that there was the difficult and important issue of what is meant by 'status equality' and the extent to which different (and conflicting) ideas of status equality operate in these different contexts. In particular, we saw that there was a significant difference between approaches aiming to achieve individual justice and approaches aiming to advance group justice. We saw that one important source of legal debate about the acceptability of procurement linkages arose from debates within equal status law and policy.

Little has been said so far, however, about the *effectiveness* of procurement linkages in delivering any of these goals. Here we encounter a significant problem. Although, in the course of the book, procurement linkages from several different jurisdictions have been examined, the extent to which there have been systematic empirical assessments of the effects of these procurement linkages, good or bad, varies considerably between these different jurisdictions, partly depending on whether the country in which the procurement linkages operate is a developing or a developed country (with research being more common in the latter), partly depending on how recent the introduction of procurement linkages were (with older established regimes being more likely to be subject to research), partly depending on how politically controversial the procurement linkages have proven to be (the more controversial, the more likelihood they will have been empirically investigated, with the exception of Malaysia), and partly depending on how politically liberal the country in which the procurement linkages operate is (with politically liberal states being more likely to have such research). The result is that there has been extensive independent empirical research carried out in the United States, some in Canada and South Africa, comparatively little in the European states, and practically none in Malaysia.

What are the aggregate results of the empirical research that has been carried out? As might be expected, the research findings present a mixed picture. On the one hand, research seems to indicate considerable beneficial effects resulting from linkage. Procurement linkages have had beneficial results in leading to improvements in the processes that firms use in handling equal status issues, particularly in leading to increased numbers adopting formal equal opportunities policies. The use of procurement linkages has contributed to increasing the representation of protected groups both in employment (using contract compliance type linkages) and in business (using set-aside type linkages). There is substantial evidence that, under certain conditions, linkage can, for example, produce change in the composition of employers' workforces to the benefit of the targeted group, both in terms of the numbers employed, and in terms of the occupational status of those employed in the organization generally.[57] On the other hand, there have been several problems associated with the operation of procurement linkages that have reduced the effectiveness of linkages, most notably where enforcement, monitoring, and compliance efforts have been inadequately funded and resourced, or previous political support has been withdrawn, or those administering the procurement linkages have seen them as 'secondary' and peripheral to their primary function.[58] Procurement linkages have also led, on occasions, to increased costs[59] and sometimes introduced undesirable side-effects, such as facilitating corruption. We now consider this research in each of the jurisdictions in which it is available.

United States empirical studies

Changes in proportion of employees in studies of contract compliance

Studies covering the period up to the mid-1970s tend to concentrate on the impact of the United States federal contract compliance programme on racial inequality, largely because, as we have seen, gender was not fully included in the programme until the early 1970s. Some of the studies considered increases in employment over the period, the effect of compliance reviews, and occupational advances. Other

---

[57] There is also (even less systematic) evidence that linking social conditions to the award of contracts can bring results internationally. It seems, for example, that American corporations reacted much more favourably to pressure to change the employment practices of their foreign-based subsidiaries in South Africa and Northern Ireland after US state and local contracts were linked to the corporations' acceptance of the Sullivan and MacBride Principles. See C McCrudden, 'Human Rights Codes for Transnational Corporations: What Can the Sullivan and MacBride Principles Tell Us?' (1999) 19 OJLS 167–201.

[58] In addition to the research presented below, see the recently completed study on the social aspects of construction which surveyed the application of nine ILO labour standards over a four-year period, with the objective of improving the conditions for construction workers. S Ladbury, AP Cotton, and M Jennings, *Implementing labour standards in construction: A sourcebook* (Water Engineering Development Centre (WEDC), Loughborough University, 2003).

[59] In addition to the above, there is some evidence that, in the past, the operation of the Priority Supplier Scheme in the UK led to some extra costs for departments, 'Cabinet Office, Management and Personnel Office, Government Purchasing: A Review of Government Contract and Procurement Procedures' (1984, HMSO) paras 9.13–9.14.

studies considered only some of these issues. This review of the literature will concentrate generally on the cross-sectional analyses using large scale data sets of large numbers of employers.[60]

Orley Ashenfelter and James Heckman,[61] in a study covering the period 1966–70, found that the annual rate of relevant growth for employment of black males was 0.82 percentage points higher among federal contractors than among non-contractors. Over the four-year period the growth in employment for black men compared to white men was 3.3 per cent greater in the federal contractor firms than in non-contractor firms. Another study covering the period 1967–79 indicated that black male employment in firms with government contracts increased by 5.6 per cent, and black female employment by 12.9 per cent, in firms with government contracts compared with firms without such contracts.[62] As regards occupational advance, the relative occupational position of black males advanced 2.48 per cent, and black females 9.19 per cent more rapidly in firms with government contracts. However, Morris Goldstein and Robert Smith[63], in a study covering the period 1970–72, found that black workers had only slightly improved their position among contractors' firms, although employment of black males tended to be higher in firms that had been subject to a compliance review. They found an insignificant increase in employment for black females and a decrease in employment for white females. Other studies were limited to particular geographical areas. James Heckman and Kenneth Wolpin,[64] in a study of the Chicago Metropolitan area covering the period 1970–73, found that in the short run, federal contractors employed 2.2 per cent more black males than identical non-contractor firms. They found a negative effect for both white females (2.3 per cent fewer white females than in non-contractor firms) and black females (0.6 per cent fewer black females than in non-contractors). Like Goldstein and Smith, they found that employment of black males tended to be higher in firms that had been subject to a compliance review.[65]

---

[60] For a case study of the operation of contract compliance in particular industries, see eg on the effect of the New York Plan, R Waldinger and T Bailey, 'The Continuing Significance of Race: Racial Conflict and Racial Discrimination in Construction' (1991) 19(3) Politics and Society 291.

[61] O Ashenfelter and J Heckman, 'Measuring the Effect of an Antidiscrimination Program' in O Ashenfelter and J Blum (eds), *Estimating the Labour Market Effects of Social Programs* (Princeton, 1976) 46–84.

[62] Discussed in RJ Flanagan, 'Actual versus potential impact of government antidiscrimination programs' (1976) 29(4) Industrial and Labor Relations Review 486, 497–8.

[63] M Goldstein and RS Smith, 'The Estimated Impact of the Antidiscrimination Program aimed at Federal Contractors' (1976) 29(4) Industrial and Labor Relations Review 523.

[64] JJ Heckman and KI Wolpin, 'Does the Contract Compliance Program Work? An analysis of the Chicago Data' (1976) 29(4) Industrial and Labor Relations Review 544.

[65] In an important study of the reasons for black economic progress in South Carolina in the mid-1960s, Heckman and Payner conclude that: 'Regression analyses of black employment reveal a structural shift in employment equations that cannot be accounted for by conventional measures of output or the growth in alternative opportunities. There is some evidence of greater black employment in counties that sold more goods to the U.S. government. Both the timing and the regression evidence suggest that government activity played an important role in integrating textiles.' JJ Heckman and BS Payner, 'Determining the Impact of Federal Antidiscrimination Policy on the Economic Status of Blacks: A Study of South Carolina' 79(1) American Economic Review 138, 173.

Commentators have pointed to several methodological problems and problems of interpretation of these studies.[66] Most of the studies compare the employment profiles of contractor and non-contractor firms. This comparison may be flawed for several reasons. The studies generally do not distinguish between different sectors of the economy or different regions, therefore only very general comparisons are possible. Affirmative action adopted by federal contractors may have a demonstration effect on non-contractors, leading them to adopt affirmative action in emulation. Non-contractor firms may also increase the hiring of the groups covered in order to improve their chances of gaining contracts. Either or both of these effects would lead to an underestimation of the impact of the contract compliance programme on a comparative basis. It is unclear to what extent the differences between firms merely reflect increased competition between firms for a limited number of qualified minorities and women, resulting in contractor firms hiring the protected groups from the non-contractor firms, without leading to an overall improvement of the group. Lastly, the indicators used for the strength of implementation of the programme, such as the number of compliance reviews, are relatively crude and unsophisticated.

Jonathan Leonard's studies of the period between 1974 and 1980 attempted to take some of these limitations in previous studies into account.[67] He found that between 1974 and 1980 black male and female employment shares increased significantly faster in contractor establishments than in non-contractor establishments. Even after controlling for establishment size, growth, region, industry, occupational and corporate structure, the employment of members of the covered groups grew significantly faster in contractor than in non-contractor establishments. Black male employment rates grew more among federal contractors than among non-contractors, with the annual rate of growth being 0.42 percentage points higher among the former than the latter. Black female employment increased 1.5 percentage points among federal contractors and 1.2 percentage points among non-contractors. Expressed as an annual growth rate, black male employment grew 0.62 per cent faster in the contractor sector, compared with 0.2 per cent slower for white males. In terms of the occupational advance of black males, Leonard found that black males' share of employment increased faster in

---

However, the authors were not concerned with separating the effect of contract compliance from the effect of other federal laws, and therefore the study is of limited usefulness as an indicator of the specific effect of that programme.

[66] See the useful summary by J Faundez, *Affirmative Action: International Perspectives* (ILO, 1994), drawing on C Brown, 'The Federal Attack on Labor Market Discrimination: The Mouse that Roared?' (1984) 5 Research in Labour Economics, 33 among others.

[67] JS Leonard, 'Antidiscrimination or Reverse Discrimination: The Impact of Changing Demographics, Title VII and Affirmative Action on Productivity' (1984) XIX(2) Journal of Human Resources 145; 'The Impact of Affirmative Action on Employment' (1984) 2(4) Journal of Labor Economics 439; 'The Impact of Affirmative Action Regulation and Equal Employment Law on Black Employment' (1990) 4(4) Journal of Economic Perspectives 47; 'Women and Affirmative Action' (1989) 3(1) Journal of Economic Perspectives 61.

contractor than in non-contractor firms in every occupation except labourers and white-collar trainees. The occupational index for black males had increased 2 per cent more among federal contractors than among non-contractors.

As regards the impact on women, Leonard found that, in 1974, 28 per cent of the average federal contractor workforce was composed of white women, while 39 per cent of the average non-contractor workforce was composed of white women. By 1980, employment of white women had increased by six-tenths of a percentage point among non-contractors compared to an increase of 1.2 percentage points among contractors; if white female employment share among contractors had only grown at the slower non-contractor rate, roughly 2 per cent fewer white females would have been employed among federal contractors in 1980. Noel Uri and J Wilson Mixon also examined the impact that contract compliance programmes had on the employment of women relative to men in the United States. Using time series data covering the period 1947–88, the results indicate that women in the 20 to 54 age group benefited in terms of greater stability of employment (ie less sensitivity to short-run variations in employment) over the period 1965–80, but they lost some of these gains over the period 1981–88.[68]

For Leonard, two factors increased the likelihood of some contractors being more affected by the pressure to undertake affirmative action than others. First, compliance reviews played a significant role. For black males, the employment impact of undergoing a compliance review was roughly twice that of not having been reviewed. The occupational advance of black males had also been greater in firms that had been subject to a compliance review. Among contractors that had been reviewed, the occupational index for black males had increased by 3 per cent. Second, contract compliance policies were far more successful at establishments in which employment was growing. However, contractor reviews appeared to have a negative effect on the employment of white females. Leonard explains this by the enforcement priority having been placed on race rather than gender during that period, with reviewed contractors substituting minority for white employment growth as a result. The effect of compliance activity also showed up in comparing advances made before 1980 and after 1980, when Leonard identified a marked scaling back of enforcement activity. In his review of these studies, Morley Gunderson concludes that 'affirmative action under the federal contract compliance program appears to have improved the labor market position of those groups to which it is directed, with stricter enforcement enhancing effectiveness'.[69] As Faye Crosby has pointed out, however, in her review of the empirical literature, 'Other scholars have been more optimistic than Leonard' about the effectiveness

[68] ND Uri and JW Mixon, 'Effects of US Affirmative Action Programs on Women's Employment' (1991) 13(3) Journal of Policy Modeling 367–82.

[69] M Gunderson, 'Male-Female Wage Differentials and Policy Responses' (1989) XXVII Journal of Economic Literature 46, 53.

of contract compliance even during the 1980s and 1990s,[70] citing the work of William Rogers and Spriggs.[71] They reported that differences in minorities' share of employment between contractor and non-contractor firms were comparable or even larger at the end of the period than at the beginning, although the share of women's employment had decreased slightly. Subsequent research does, however, at least appear to support Leonard's view regarding the effect of different regulatory regimes on the effectiveness of compliance reviews. 'Compliance reviews initiated in the 1970s were significantly more effective than those initiated in the 1980s or 1990s, and their effects persisted into the two latter periods. Employers who faced compliance reviews in the 1970s appear to have altered their behavior in ways that had lasting effects for white women, black women, and black men. Compliance reviews initiated in the 1980s had more limited effects.'[72]

Using the information from Leonard's report to the Department of Labor, the impact of the programme was assessed independently for the Office of Federal Contract Compliance Programs (OFCCP). The study found minority employment to have increased by 20.1 per cent and women's employment to have increased by 15.2 per cent between 1974 and 1980 in federal contractor workplaces, with a total employment growth of only 3 per cent. In non-contracting workplaces, the gains were a 12.3 per cent increase for minorities and a 2.2 per cent increase for women, with an 8.2 per cent total employment growth over that period.[73] Gains were even greater among contractors which had been reviewed by the OFCCP compared to those which had not. Minorities and women also tended to gain increased representation in higher level jobs in federal contractor companies than in non-contractor companies. Minority employment in skilled and white-collar positions in contractor establishments increased by 9.5 per cent from 1974 to 1980, while increasing by only 3.2 per cent in non-contractor establishments. Women's employment in higher level jobs in contractor establishments increased by 6.2 per cent while it increased by only 2.4 per cent in the non-contractor establishments.

Morley Gunderson rightly cautions against placing too much reliance on the data due to 'data problems and difficulties in disentangling the pure legislative effect from the myriad of other factors that have changed in the labour market for females over the same period...'[74] In their review, John Donohue and James

---

[70] FJ Crosby, *Affirmative Action is Dead; Long Live Affirmative Action* (Yale University Press, 2004) 103.

[71] See eg WM Rogers III and WE Spriggs, 'The Effect of Federal-Contractor Status on Racial Differences in Establishment-Level Employment Shares: 1979–1992' (1996) 86(2) American Economic Review 290.

[72] A Kalev and RW Dobbin, 'Enforcement of Civil Rights Law in Private Workplaces: The Effects of Compliance Reviews and Lawsuits Over Time' (December 2005), available at <http://www.wjh .harvard.edu/~dobbin/cv/working_papers/eeopractice2.pdf>.

[73] US Department of Labor, Office of Federal Contract Compliance Programmes, 'Employment Patterns of Minorities and Women in Federal Contractor and Noncontractor Establishments' (June 1984). See also DLR No 113, 10 June 1983, A-8.   [74] Gunderson (n 69 above) 54.

Heckman conclude that the studies demonstrate 'a positive correlation between black employment growth and contractor status...the presence of a governmental effect has been confirmed, although its precise nature is still uncertain'.[75] Nor is it clear how far policy changes initiated during the 1990s, requiring a more commercial approach to purchasing in the United States, have affected the implementation of contract compliance or, indeed, of set-asides.[76]

Different types of costs have been identified as potentially arising from the operation of contract compliance programmes. Of these, few have been tested empirically. There has, however, been some limited amount of research on *compliance* costs, ie the costs that arise for employers in conforming with the reporting requirements under the programmes and costs of compliance reviews. A Business Roundtable study estimated compliance costs at around 0.1 per cent of revenue for forty large federal contractors.[77] Leonard calculated that the 'direct administrative costs' were 'comparable in magnitude to the costs of giving each employee a New Year's turkey or two'.[78] Harry Holzman and David Neumark concluded, after a review of the empirical evidence available up to the late 1990s, that 'it seems fair to say that the direct administrative costs to contractors of administering Affirmative Action programs raise their compensation costs by roughly 1% on average'.[79]

United States set-aside programmes: are they successful and at what cost?

Relatively little larger-scale work appears to have been carried out to estimate the effect of federal set-aside programmes. The most significant piece of work was that carried out as part of the White House Review that resulted from the *Adarand* decision discussed in chapter 7 above. George Stephanopoulos and Christopher Edley, who carried out the Review, reported that between 1982 and 1991 federal contracts awarded to minority-owned firms increased by more than 125 per cent, whilst those awarded to firms owned by women increased by more than 200 per cent. There were important increases in particular federal departments; the Department of Defense increased its contracting with small disadvantaged businesses from 2.1 per cent of departmental contracting being awarded to such firms in 1985, to 5.5 per cent in 1994.[80] Most evidence of a positive correlation between set-asides and increases in minority-owned business participation in government contracting arises from studies conducted at the state and local levels. On the basis of a review of this evidence, Holzer and Neumark conclude that these programmes

    [75] JJ Donohue III and J Heckman, 'Continuous versus Episodic Change: The Impact of Civil Rights Policy on the Economic Status of Blacks' (1991) XXIX Journal of Economic Literature 1603, 1635.
    [76] SL Schooner, 'Commerical Purchasing: The Chasm Between the United States Government's Evolving Policy and Practice' in S Arrowsmith and M Trybus (eds), *Public Procurement: The Continuing Revolution* (Kluwer, 2003) 166–7.   [77] Crosby (n 70 above) 108.
    [78] ibid.
    [79] HJ Holzer and D Neumark, 'Assessing Affirmative Action', NBER Working Paper No W7323, August 1999, 54.
    [80] G Stephanopoulos and C Edley, 'Review of Federal Affirmative Action Programs: Report to the President' (Government Printing Office, 1995) chapter 9, p 5.

were 'responsible for the overall growth in government contracts with minorities and women',[81] whilst Faye Crosby concludes that the policy 'is generally thought to have helped minority businesses obtain contracts and clients'.[82]

Based on their study of the empirical research conducted up to the late 1990s, Holzer and Neumark point to several possible effects for which there is some credible evidence. First, with set-asides being concentrated in particular industries, such as construction, in which there were already significant numbers of existing minority firms, this may lead to further concentration of new minority firms in that industry, rather than encouraging such firms to establish in other industries. Second, there is no evidence to support the argument that set-asides prop up weak contractors. Third, there is credible evidence of fraud, by which they mean the establishment of a minority-owned front company to enable a larger white-owned company to succeed in obtaining the bid, but which closes once the contract is finished. But, overall, the evidence 'on the efficiency/performance effects . . . is limited'.[83]

In particular, they single out the lack of information on the effect of the programme in increasing the amount of the winning bid. Some evidence suggests that an affirmative action programme that used bid preferences for minority firms might lower the winning bid if it forced non-minority firms to bid more aggressively.[84] Since their review, Justin Marion has conducted research that examines this issue.[85] He examined the differences between the cost of the winning bids for California state highway construction contracts after Proposition 209 was put into effect banning set-asides, with the costs of the winning bids on federal highway construction contracts in California that continued to be subject to set-asides. After Proposition 209, the winning bid on state contracts fell by between 3.7 and 6.0 per cent compared to federal contracts. He suggests that this results primarily from differences in the quality of subcontractors employed.

Assessments of Canadian procurement linkages

Aboriginal business set-asides

There have been several reviews of the operation of Aboriginal business set asides in Canada, both under the Land Claims Agreements and under the Procurement Strategy for Aboriginal Business (PASB). As part of the five-year review of the implementation of the Nunavut Land Claims Agreement (ie, up to 1998), an independent review[86] found that progress had been made in the implementation

---

[81] Holzer and Neumark (n 79 above) 43.   [82] Crosby (n 70 above) 96.

[83] Holzer and Neumark (n 79 above) 65.

[84] A Corns and A Schotter, 'Can Affirmative Action Be Cost Effective? An Experimental Examination of Price Preference Auctions' (1999) 89(1) American Economic Review 291.

[85] J Marion, 'How Costly Is Affirmative Action? Government Contracting and California's Proposition 209' (September 2005).

[86] NL Vertes, DMH Connelly, and BAS Knott, 'Five year Review 1993 to 1996, Implementation of the Nunavut Land Claims Agreement: An Independent Review' (Nortext Multimedia Inc, October 1999).

of the obligations relating to procurement, but that implementation was not complete. Policies had been adopted by the federal government, 'but not applied to all branches' of the government.[87] The consultations required 'did not meet the requirements' of the Agreement, 'although both [sides] could have taken a more constructive approach'.[88] There was 'no current process for adapting purchasing practices to evolving Inuit capabilities'.[89] However, in contrast, territorial government contracting processes 'have been adapted adequately and respond to evolving Inuit capabilities'.[90]

The Department of Indian and Northern Affairs has published annual reviews of PSAB for each year up to 2003.[91] These show a mixed picture of the operation of the programme, in terms of the numbers and value of contracts awarded under PSAB.

	1997	1998	1999	2000	2001	2002	2003
Can $ value in millions	44.5	85.4	112.0	136.4	262.6	253.2	487.3
Number of contracts	3,233	8,741	11,118	9,066	16,521	13,732	8,156

A fuller evaluation was carried out by the Department's Audit and Evaluation Branch, with external assistance, and published in August 2000.[92] The report concluded that 'overall, the PSAB has been successful in meeting its stated objectives, and that a sound rationale for the strategy continues to exist'.[93] Both the number and value of contracts with Aboriginal firms 'have consistently increased over every year' in the life of the programme.[94] However, after 'a strong start, PSAB implementation and communication activities have slowed since the launch of the strategy',[95] resulting in a 'low level of knowledge among both government personnel and Aboriginal firms, and significant misunderstanding of the goals and operation of the program'.[96] The growth and development of Aboriginal contracting was 'not evenly distributed'.[97] 'A relatively small number of large contracts from a few departments accounts for most of the increase in contract value'.[98] Small and rural Aboriginal businesses appeared not to benefit to the same extent as larger firms in or near urban areas. There were not enough qualified Aboriginal firms.

There were, in addition, several effects of the programme, identified by federal procurement managers. Aboriginal firms with federal government contracting experience were now selling to other levels of government as well.[99] Entrepreneurial spirit was developing. Less positive effects were also noted: 'An extra

---

[87] ibid 3.   [88] ibid.   [89] ibid.   [90] ibid.

[91] See eg, 'Procurement Strategy for Aboriginal Business, Performance Report for 2000' (Indian and Northern Affairs, Canada, 2000). Reports are available at <http://www.ainc-inac.gc.ca/saea-psab/pub/index_e.html>.

[92] Department of Indian Affairs and Northern Development Corporate Services, Departmental Audit and Evaluation Branch, 'Evaluation of the Procurement Strategy for Aboriginal Business' (August 2002).   [93] ibid i.

[94] ibid iii.   [95] ibid ii.   [96] ibid.   [97] ibid iii.   [98] ibid.   [99] ibid 31.

step [had] been added to the procurement process for buyers, thereby slowing the process of creating orders and requests for proposals/tenders', although this was contested by others.[100] Some federal managers also indicated that 'privileged access to contracts may be inconsistent with the other principles of procurement, namely "best value" and "equal access". Some believe that they are paying a premium to do business with Aboriginal firms.'[101] A complaint from both federal procurement managers and from Aboriginal leaders was that 'shell' companies were reported to have been established to allow firms to circumvent requirements of the programme relating to what constituted an 'Aboriginal' business. This appeared to include Aboriginal firms and/or individuals 'fronting for non-Aboriginal firms; and Aboriginal firms buying service-based "finished products" complete with a management contract from non-Aboriginal firms and marking up the price for sale to the government'.[102] There were 'few incentives'[103] for federal purchasing personnel to apply the policy vigorously, 'nor are there penalties for failing to observe it. Some departments are ignoring their obligations under PSAB, with little or no accountability being demanded.'[104]

Effectiveness of the Canadian contract compliance programmes

An official evaluation of the Federal Contractors Program (FCP) was first concluded in 1992. By 1991, two companies that had signed certificates of commitment were found to be in non-compliance. As a result, the companies were not allowed to bid on further federal government contracts. Both companies subsequently submitted plans that met the requirements of the Program and the sanctions were removed.[105] There was little research on the effectiveness of the contract compliance experience between then and 2002, as research tended to concentrate on the effects of the Employment Equity Act 1986, rather than the FCP.[106] Carol Agócs noted in 2000 that 'little information is publicly available concerning results achieved under the [FCP]'.[107] A small-scale research project in 1999, which involved interviewing a selection of procurement officers and workplace equity officers in businesses subject to FCP, concluded that 'although the national scheme looks good on paper, it is under funded and therefore cannot possibly achieve what it sets out to do. The whole process is in need of simplification.'[108]

---

[100] ibid 31 and 36.   [101] ibid 16.   [102] ibid 38.   [103] ibid 48.   [104] ibid.
[105] Third Canadian Periodic Report to the Committee on the Elimination of Discrimination Against Women, CEDAW/C/CAN/3, 25 September 1992, 31, para 150.
[106] See eg, JD Leck and DM Saunders, 'Hiring Women: The Effects of Canada's Employment Equity Act' (1992), XVIII(2) Canadian Public Policy 203; C Agócs, 'Canada's employment equity legislation and policy, 1987–2000: The gap between policy and practice' (2002) 23(3) International Journal of Manpower 256.   [107] Agócs (n 106 above) 261.
[108] A Erridge and R Fee, 'The Impact of Contract Compliance Policies in Canada—Perspectives from Ontario' (2001) 1(1) Journal of Public Procurement 51, 67–8.

The major evaluation of FCP occurred in 2001–2 as part of a broader governmental process of evaluation of the federal employment equity obligations.[109] The evaluation was conducted for Evaluation and Data Development, Human Resources Development Canada, by SPR Associates of Toronto and Ottawa. The objectives of the evaluation were to measure progress made in FCP firms/organizations for the designated groups, and to assess the success of the programme in encouraging employers to comply with employment equity principles. Issues addressed by the evaluation included the adequacy of compliance, the effectiveness of delivery, the extent of employment equity activities by employers, and the extent of impacts on representation. Surveys of over 700 FCP employers and a comparison group of 1,000 non-FCP employers were conducted, interviews with over fifty stakeholders were undertaken, and ten case studies of FCP employers were completed.

Although it considered that the FCP had the potential to be effective, it was not proving to be so in its then current state.[110] Compared to non-FCP employers, in 1999 FCP employers indicated only slightly higher representation for Aboriginal people, and persons with disabilities as compared to non-FCP employers. Analysis of FCP employers' information indicated improvements in representation between 1995 and 1999 for persons with disabilities, visible minorities, and women. Overall, however, multivariate analyses comparing FCP and non-FCP employers indicated that while FCP had significant positive impacts on representation for persons with disabilities and Aboriginal persons in 1995, these effects had largely disappeared by 1999. On the more positive side, FCP appeared to have no significant impacts on contracting or the purchasing position of the federal government. Indeed, less than 5 per cent of employers reported that they were discouraged from bidding on Federal contracts because of FCP requirements. The potential for individual firms to gain from additional economic benefits resulting from FCP was confirmed in a preliminary way by the evaluation findings, in that a number of employers reporting increased representation of designated groups indicated that employment equity had had positive effects in areas such as productivity improvement and competitiveness. These evaluation findings, however, were not widespread. Cost did not appear to be a major factor, as those employers implementing employment equity reported only modest extra costs.

Leaving aside the *impact* of the programme, its overall *administration* was viewed as having considerable difficulties, and to have been hindered by declining programme capacity over the period 1995–2001. These programme delivery factors were thought, possibly, to explain the relatively weak implementation of

---

[109] 'Evaluation of the Federal Contractors Program, Evaluation and Data Development, Strategic Policy', Human Resources Development Canada, Final Report, SP-AH183-04-02E, April 2002.

[110] The following paragraphs are heavily based on and are adapted from the Executive Summary of the Evaluation Report.

employment equity measures by FCP employers. Changes in the administration of FCP had lowered the profile of the programme within the Department responsible for enforcing it since 1995 and reduced the resources devoted to its implementation. There had been significant staffing reductions in FCP in the period 1995–2000. Other resources, such as internal information systems, were found to be out of date, incomplete, and ineffective. Compliance reviews of individual FCP employers had fallen substantially from a four-year average of 152 (for 1992–95) to only 57, on average, for 1996–99. Programme information systems were found to be inadequate or not current enough to monitor activity, or progress, or to manage the FCP effectively.

It is not difficult to pick up a sense of frustration, of an opportunity not taken advantage of, particularly given the key finding of the evaluation that there was clear evidence that FCP had the capacity to impact in a substantial way on employers. Approximately 90 per cent of FCP employers indicated that they were only involved in any employment equity activities at all because of the FCP. This finding was a considerable improvement over the results of the 1992 evaluation. A related finding was that the effectiveness of the programme increased the more the elements of the programme were fully implemented by employers. Employers which had implemented a greater number of the FCP employment equity steps showed generally higher levels of representation for the designated groups. But only about 10 per cent of FCP employers had fully implemented FCP, and only about half of FCP employers had implemented half or more of the required employment equity measures.

United Kingdom procurement linkages

Contract compliance in the ILEA and the GLC during the 1980s

Empirical research was carried out by the ILEA Contract Compliance Equal Opportunities Unit on the effect of contract compliance as operated by the Greater London Council (GLC) and the Inner London Education Authority (ILEA) prior to the Local Government Act 1988 changes.[111] Research compared the equal opportunity practices of companies before the unit intervened, and those adopted after review. The statistical analysis was based on the 152 companies that were fully reviewed by the unit. The key finding was that the level of equal opportunities practice in those companies greatly improved following the review: 'Companies were between four and five times more likely to follow certain equal opportunities practices and procedures after a contract compliance review than they were before it.'

---

[111] Contract Compliance: a brief history (1990), summarised in 'Contract compliance assessed' (May/June 1990) 31 Equal Opportunities Review 26–8.

In addition, 'whereas only 2% originally mentioned equal opportunities in job advertisements, 80% did so after review by the unit'. The unit was more successful in persuading companies to adopt some policies compared with others:

In particular there were dramatic improvements in the proportions adopting an equal opportunities policy/statement; using non-discriminatory job application form(s); introducing disciplinary procedures for discrimination or harassment; putting an equal opportunities statement in job advertisements; and monitoring the workforce for equal opportunity purposes. In contrast the lowest level of action following the review occurred with respect to undertaking positive action initiatives.[112]

Adoption of race-related contract compliance policies under the British Local Government Act 1988

During the early 1990s in Britain, research consistently demonstrated the virtual absence of procurement linkages by British local authorities, and even where they were adopted, the almost complete lack of monitoring of any conditions that were included in contracts. Joe Charlesworth and Veronique Voruz, discussing research carried out in 1994, concluded that the use of the available powers under section 18, considered in detail in chapter 11 above, was 'limited' and that there was 'little enthusiasm' for such a policy within the local authorities surveyed.[113] They attribute this to lack of administrative back-up, with 'no centralized guidance giving consistency to the policy',[114] the few additional resources that had been allocated, and the absence of any 'specific locus of responsibility' within local authorities for enforcing requirements. In addition, however, there was a 'certain amount of confusion as to conformity with European Union law', and the low visibility of such policies attracted 'little pressure from the community in question'. 'If the local ethnic community is passive or very small, the policy will remain dormant, since otherwise its development will depend solely upon the initiative of council members or officers.'[115]

West Midlands common standard

We saw in chapters 11 and 13 above that six local authorities in the West Midlands, in England, developed a 'common standard' to assess whether a firm's policy on

---

[112] J Wrench and T Modood, 'The Effectiveness of Employment Equality Policies in Relation to Immigrants and Ethnic Minorities in the UK', International Migration Papers, 38, International Migration Branch (ILO, Geneva, June 2000) 48–9, citing (May/June 1990) 31 Equal Opportunities Review, and IRS Employment Trends 462, 19 April 1990.

[113] J Charlesworth and V Voruz, 'The Contract Compliance Policy: An Illustration of the Persistence of Racism as the Failure of Modernity' (1998) 7 Social and Legal Studies 193, 199.

[114] ibid.   [115] ibid 200.

race relations meets the legal requirements regarding racial equality.[116] Michael Orton and Peter Radcliffe have examined the scheme in detail and describe how the West Midlands standard:

... is based on what is described as the 'pre-qualification' stage. This relies on the councils having 'standing lists' of approved contractors. A standing list is a database of firms who have expressed interest in tendering for work from the council, and have been assessed by the council as being suitable to do so. Typically, a firm that contacts a council will be asked to complete a pre-qualification questionnaire probing such matters as the company's technical competence and financial soundness. Each of the councils involved in the West Midlands initiative has a standing list of several hundred companies.[117]

The councils' standing lists concern tenders below the EC threshold. The standard was originally introduced for building and construction in connection with the councils' approved lists. However, at least one of the councils has now started using the standard for service contracts as well.[118]

Orton and Ratcliffe found that the West Midlands common standard (WMCS) had 'a significant impact on encouraging firms to adopt' equal opportunities policies (EOP):

Some companies had never before had an EOP and the introduction of the WMCS meant that for the first time these companies were engaging with equalities' issues and addressing how to ensure their employment practices promoted equality of opportunity. In such cases, the impact of the WMCS was dramatic. Other companies had formerly relied on an equal opportunities statement expressing their commitment to the principle of equality.[119]

Of those companies that already had an EOP in place, 'WMCS had an impact in that it encouraged firms to review, update and revise policies, for example addressing areas of weakness such as the failure to monitor workforce composition.' With regard to policy implementation, 'the evaluation also found a broad range of generally positive responses. The research provided examples of companies making great progress on equal opportunities: for example, through the provision of training on equalities' issues, the development of more formalized recruitment practices and even the adoption of positive action strategies.' There were, however, 'isolated examples of companies which claimed to be taking no steps at all to implement their policy' but: 'Closer examination revealed that this was not quite true: they had, for example, circulated the new policy to staff and stated in job

---

[116] See M Orton and P Ratcliffe, 'New Labour Ambiguity, or Neo-Consistency? The Debate About Inequality in Employment and Contract Compliance' (2005) 34(2) Journal of Social Policy 255–72.   [117] ibid 261.
[118] European Commission, 'Study of the Use of Equality and Diversity Considerations in Public Procurement: Final Report' (December 2003).   [119] ibid 262–3.

advertisements that the company was an equal opportunities employer. For firms that had not previously engaged with equalities' issues, even such small steps represented clear progress.'

Supplier diversity in Britain

We saw in chapter 13 above, that, in May 2003, a review conducted by the Better Regulation Task Force and the Small Business Council recommended government measures to address obstacles that may prevent SMEs from gaining government contracts.[120] In parallel with this review, the Office of Government Commerce and the Department of Trade and Industry conducted two pilot projects, regarding the participation of Ethnic Minority Businesses (EMBs) and women in government contracts, one in the West Midlands, the other in Haringey, to run until the spring of 2005. In November 2004, the evaluation report on the West Midlands pilot was published.[121] Monder Ram and David Smallbone conclude, however, that: 'Supplier diversity programmes are currently in the very early stages of development in the UK, particularly those concerned with increasing the access of EMBs to public and private sector contracts. As a result, the number of EMBs that are participating appears very small and there is little hard evidence of significant, positive benefits for EMBs, as a result of these projects.'[122]

Mainstreaming: Northern Ireland pilot project

In Northern Ireland, we saw in chapter 13 above, that a pilot project for the utilisation of the unemployed in public contracts commenced in June 2003 for a two-year period. Those tendering for contracts included in the pilot project were required to submit an unemployment utilization plan as part of their bid. This would be taken into account at the award stage only if two or more tenders were considered to be equally qualified. In any event, the successful tenderer's plan would be incorporated into the contract conditions of the contract. The operation of the pilot project was monitored by an independent team from the University of Ulster.[123] Fifteen projects were started during the evaluation period, fewer than the planned twenty projects due to some projects being withdrawn and delays in project commencement. The monitoring of the project involved an initiation meeting with each project sponsor, the collection and analysis of tender documentation, including employment plans, and interviews with client contract

---

[120] Better Regulation Task Force and Small Business Council, 'Government: Supporter and Customer' (May 2003).

[121] Small Business Service and Office of Government Commerce, 'West Midlands SME Procurement Pilot: Final Project Evaluation Report: Management Summary' (November 2004).

[122] M Ram and D Smallbone, 'Supplier Diversity Initiatives and the Diversification of Ethnic Minority Businesses in the UK' (2003) 24(4) Policy Studies 187, 189, 200.

[123] A Erridge, R Fee, and S Hennigan, 'Pilot Project on Utilising the Unemployed in Public Contracts: Final Evaluation Report', University of Ulster at Jordanstown, School of Policy Studies, September 2005, available at <http://www.cpdni.gov.uk/unemployed_in_construction.pdf>.

managers and contractor project managers at the beginning, middle, and end of the contract. This schedule was subject to the completion of the project within the evaluation period. Throughout the two-year period of the pilot, unemployment in Northern Ireland was at its lowest level since records began. In fourteen of the fifteen projects all the winning tenderers submitted a plan with their bid (two did so retrospectively). One of the contracts failed to obtain any employment plans from tenderers due to their failure to include the guidance notes on the pilot in the tender documentation. A total of seventy-five employment plans were submitted across fourteen contracts, and in all but one case all plans submitted were deemed to be bona fide, which showed that tenderers took time and effort to prepare their plans to a professional standard. Up to the date of completion of the research (June 2005), fifty-one people had commenced employment on the pilot, of which forty-six were still in employment. Of these, thirty-two people were employed in the service sector and nineteen in the construction sector. Ninety per cent of contractors believed that the pilot did not lead to an increase in direct costs, while over 64 per cent of public bodies involved considered that the pilot did not result in any significant increase in workload.

Procurement linkages in the Netherlands

We saw earlier, in chapter 11 above, how linking public procurement in the Netherlands to equality issues was adopted in the 1980s by Dutch local authorities, but was rejected by Dutch central government. In 1999, however, the Dutch national government started a pilot project (Sociaal Bestek) on the use of contract compliance in the context of its labour market policy. The Ministry of Social Affairs commissioned new research on contract compliance, which reported on the use of contract compliance by regional and local governments.[124] The 1999 pilot was evaluated and a final report on the project was published in July 2003.[125] The research summarizes the evidence from these empirical studies. Wilthagen *et al* found that contract compliance as an instrument to social policy was mainly used by larger municipalities and mostly in the construction industry. Between 1994 and 1998, 17 per cent of all (569) Dutch local governments considered the use of contract compliance but only nine, mainly large municipalities, actually put contract compliance into practice. Those nine municipalities together applied contract compliance to a total of thirteen projects. The local public bodies that did not use this tool put forward several reasons for not doing so. Some stated that they had never thought of the possibility of contract compliance and others claimed that (the lack of) labour market participation of ethnic minorities was not a problem in their area.

---

124 Wilthagen *et al*, 'Onder sociale voorwaarden', Minsterie van Sociale Zaken en Werkgelegenheid (AWSB, The Netherlands School for Social and Economic Policy Research, 2000).
125 Regioplan, 'Evaluatie Sociaal Bestek—eindrapport' Amsterdam, March 2003.

As regards the use of government procurement in connection with the unemployed in the Netherlands, a study published in 2000 found that several of the bigger municipal governments used public procurement for social purposes, mainly to increase the labour participation of long-term unemployed.[126] The use of public procurement for social purposes was still mainly used in the building sector. The use of public procurement was being thought about, and being used, more often since 1994 than before then. During the time of the study, quite a few municipal governments were thinking of starting the use of public procurement for social purposes. The municipal governments that were already using contract compliance expected that they would use it more often in the future. The study makes clear that the use of procurement for these purposes gives rise to obligations not only on the contractor. At the same time a mutual responsibility arises for government and other organizations to reach the group that is being aimed at and to get potential employees out of this group ready for the job that will be offered to them by the supplier. Where this happens, the use of procurement to increase employment opportunities can achieve a positive result.

As regards the effect of Sociaal Bestek, there were initial difficulties in launching the pilot. The actual construction projects started later than expected. Hardly any job seekers could be found to participate. The pilot was formally ended in 2002 without any significant results. Only three construction projects actually worked under a public contract including a social clause. They only attracted five candidates from the unemployed pool who had not received training prior to the project due to lack of time. A few of them withdrew from the project at an early stage. The participants in the project and the national coordinator of the project mentioned two key factors that they held responsible for the failure of the pilot. First, the labour market conditions changed. In 1997, when the government decided on the pilot, there was a large pool of unemployed, but this changed during the pilot, and finally the pilot was operating in a tight labour market and the pool had narrowed down significantly. A second factor was the slow pace of implementation of the projects.

Drawing on both sets of research together, the research concluded that contract compliance was effectively applied by just a few public bodies in a small number of cases and only if certain conditions were being fulfilled. Little could be said about the effectiveness of the use of contract compliance by governments to stimulate the labour market participation of certain target groups. It identified, however, certain conditions as 'keys to success'. The inclusion of social clauses in public contracts is more suitable for local, small-scale, and short-term projects. It is essential to include in the contract executable and effective sanctions for non-compliance with the social clause. Field experts and experts on relevant initiatives should

---

[126] 'Onder Sociale Voorwaarden: toepassing van contract compliance door de gemeentelijke en provinciale overheid: randvoorwaarden, ervaringen en resultaten' (loosely translated as 'Under Social Conditions: use of contract compliance by municipal and provincial government: constraints, experiences and results') (Elsevier, 2001).

be employed to advise on contract compliance policy and legal limitations. Commitment and serious involvement of the parties is essential. Contract compliance policy should be connected with structural regional/local labour market policy. Sufficient preparation and planning time is essential to the successful implementation of the instrument. The public body involved must provide for a large pool of potential participants from target groups. Potential participants need to be properly trained and schooled before or during the project. Enough proper technical and social guidance for the participants before and during the project is important. A manager should be made responsible for the project and one department should be made responsible for contract compliance policy. Contract compliance policy should be formally documented internally and monitored by the finance department of the public body. Proper internal and external publicity of this policy is essential. Contract compliance is preferably initiated by economics ministries rather than by social ministries to increase the weight that this will have with trade and industry. Employer organizations, trade unions, field experts and organizations, employment agencies, and relevant social services should all be actively involved. All relevant parties should be engaged from the start and convinced of the benefits of contract compliance.

Critiques of the operation of preferential procurement in South Africa

The Regulations made under the Preferential Procurement Policy Framework Act (PPPFA) came into effect in 2001. Within two years, criticisms of the way in which it was being operated were made by most sections of South African political life. As we saw in Chapter 9 above, several criticisms of the *operation* of preferential procurement policies recurred during this period. Mostly, the criticisms related to policy incoherence, close-to-chaotic administration, corruption, and the absence of adequate monitoring of outcomes.

Policy incoherence and lack of joined-up government was a persistent theme, with various overlapping elements. Policy incoherence was also seen as arising because of the absence of centralized administration. This was exacerbated due to the plethora of separate and overlapping goals sought to be achieved under the legislation. The Act provided no means of applying policy (goals were set by officials without specific targets to be achieved).[127] PPPFA policies were not properly formulated and national targets were not set in respect of important policy objectives.[128] There was no uniformity in how different state organs applied the PPPFA, with resulting fragmented and inconsistent[129] interpretation of key concepts across

---

[127] Finance Select Committee, 'Preferential Procurement Policy Framework Act, Public Hearings', 8 September 2003, available at <http://www.pmg.org.za> (hereafter FSC PPPFA).
[128] National Treasury, 2003, Policy Strategy to Guide Uniformity in Procurement Reform Processes in Government (07-04/2003) (hereafter Treasury Policy Strategy), para 1.1.2.
[129] FSC PPPFA (n 127 above) 10 September 2003.

government.[130] Certain organs of state, for example, applied set-aside practices, instead of the prescribed preference points system.[131] Certain departmental policy directives were in conflict with the provisions of the PPPFA.[132] One result was criticism that one or other particular aim was being overemphasized at the cost of falling short with other aims. Business South Africa (BSA), for example, argued that the PPPFA placed too much emphasis on equity ownership, at the expense of capacity building and the promotion of local content. Nor was the PPPFA (or its Regulations) aligned with the Black Economic Empowerment (BEE) initiatives.[133] This caused confusion and, in certain instances, a disregard of the PPPFA and its associated Regulations.[134]

Administration of the legislation was inefficient and chaotic. The calculations required to award points were too many and too laborious.[135] The PPPFA and its supporting regulations were complex and therefore difficult to implement correctly.[136] Procurement practitioners were not adequately trained in the application of the PPPFA and its associated regulations.[137] There was limited expertise and knowledge in all spheres of government concerning how to implement and apply the Act.[138] There was inadequate oversight and accountability within government. A complainant could only go to the courts, leading to problems arising from delays due to litigation. Litigation was therefore constraining the process.[139]

Allegations of corruption were of different types. Some allegations were of straightforward corruption, 'usually linked to politically connected "business people" gaining access to government and municipal tenders to the exclusion of other competent black/women/disabled suppliers or service providers'.[140] Other, more common, allegations were of 'fronting', similar to the 'Ali-Baba' problem we have seen operating in the Malaysian context, in which established companies 'use blacks as fronts to gain access to tenders'.[141] The effect is that: 'No transfer of skills takes place under these circumstances and black entrepreneurship ends up not being developed in the long run.'[142] There was an absence of mechanisms to monitor fronting ('rent-a-black') adequately.[143] Fronting occurred, according to BSA, because there was a lack of capacity and skills.[144] There was a recurring difficulty

---

[130] ibid 8 September 2003.   [131] Treasury Policy Strategy (n 128 above) para 2.2.
[132] ibid.   [133] FSC PPPFA (n 127 above) 8 September 2003.
[134] Treasury Policy Strategy (n 128 above) para 1.1.2.
[135] FSC PPPFA (n 127 above) 8 September 2003.
[136] Treasury Policy Strategy (n 128 above) para 2.2.   [137] ibid.
[138] FSC PPPFA (n 127 above) 8 September 2003.
[139] Treasury Policy Strategy (n 128 above) para 2.2.
[140] LM Mbabane, 'Preferential Procurement in South Africa's Black Economic Empowerment Policy and its prospects for combating discrimination and reducing economic inequalities', Working Paper prepared for the 4th Session of the ILO workshop on equality, 'Public Procurements—How effective are they in combating discrimination?', ILO, Geneva, 23–24 May 2006, 8. See also T Lodge, 'Political Corruption in South Africa' (1998) 97 African Affairs 157, 182–4.
[141] Mbabane (n 140 above) 8. See also J Reed, 'Open to abuse? Why cronyism threatens to sour the South African dream', *Financial Times*, 18 April 2006, 13.
[142] Mbabane (n 140 above).   [143] FSC PPPFA (n 127 above) 8 September 2003.
[144] FSC PPPFA (n 127 above) 10 September 2003.

in securing the involvement of sufficient numbers of black entrepreneurs. Several reasons were advanced for this, including lack of access to capital, the presence of a 'low entrepreneurship culture in South Africa in general and among blacks and women in particular',[145] and the continuing effects of apartheid. There was inadequate provision for capacity building to enable disadvantaged enterprises to compete successfully for government contracts.[146]

Inadequate monitoring of the implementation of the legislation was also seen as a problem. The costs and outcomes of the PPPFA were not assessed adequately to evaluate the merits of the system. This was mainly due to the lack of a systematic and consistent collection of data throughout government,[147] but also because preferential procurement policies were not clearly formulated and targets were not set for the introduction of sunset and graduation provisions once targets had been achieved.[148] Indeed, some of the goals the Act aimed to achieve could not be measured.[149]

There appear to have been three major independent attempts at assessing the *effects* of the preferential procurement policy in South Africa. The first was a study of the analysis of contracts awarded by the Department of Public Works for the period 1 August 1996 to 31 June 1998, carried out by Sivi Gounden. This research concluded that there had been a significant increase in participation by the targeted groups in public works procurement following the introduction of the new policy, 'whilst incurring a nominal financial premium'.[150] The extent of such participation, however, varied across particular construction categories, 'with the most significant benefits observed in contracts above a R2 million threshold, where... participation as sub-contractors increased significantly'.[151] For contracts below R2 million, increases in participation, whilst 'noticeable', were not as significant as in the larger contracts. There was higher participation in general construction than in more specialized areas of construction, such as civil, electrical, and mechanical areas of construction. Although the financial costs were nominal, there were other indirect costs, in that contractors not subject to preferences 'performed better... as prime contractors in the general contracts subsector for the price range between R100,000 and R2 million' than contractors with preferences.[152] The latter also tended to start their contracts later, to submit their payment certificates later, and to have had greater difficulty in document management and managing variations during the construction phase. They also tended to produce lower quality work, and were more likely to use substandard materials.

A second, more extensive, empirical study 'to assess the effectiveness of TP [targeted procurement] as a preferential procurement instrument and to determine

---

[145] Mbabane (n 140 above) 9.   [146] Treasury Policy Strategy (n 128 above) para 2.2.

[147] ibid para 1.1.2.   [148] ibid para 2.2.

[149] FSC PPPFA (n 127 above) 8 September 2003.

[150] S Gounden, 'The Impact of the National Department of Public Works's Affirmative Procurement Policy on the Participation and Growth of Affirmable Business Entrerprises in the Construction Sector' (unpublished PhD thesis, 2000), available at <http://www.targetedprocurement .co.za/papers/SG/SGpapers.html> 9.4.   [151] ibid.

[152] ibid.

whether the anticipated socio-economic benefits it was designed to deliver are being realized'[153] was carried out on behalf of the South African Department of Public Works, the International Labour Office, and the Development Bank of Southern Africa during February 2002. The research was based on a review of the available literature, a limited analysis of projects, review of data collected by government for monitoring the effect of the policy, and interviews with stakeholders and contractors. The research found that in the absence of 'a suitable monitoring and evaluation mechanism' the effectiveness of targeted procurement as an instrument of social policy 'was hard to judge'.[154] Nevertheless, the research considered that targeted procurement had been 'largely successful' in attaining its stated goals.[155] The process had 'undoubtedly opened up the construction industry to emerging enterprises' and delivered 'socio-economic benefits to the target groups'.[156] It was 'accepted across all tiers of government and is mainstreamed into public sector project management procedures throughout the country'.[157] Nevertheless, 'an unsystematic and fragmented approach to implementation has more than likely reduced the potential benefits'.[158]

As regards the preparation and planning of targeted procurement within public bodies, the research found 'confusion in many quarters over policy goals and the choice of implementation methodologies, thus resulting in failures'.[159] The 'initial creativity' in operating targeted procurement, 'seems to be on the wane, with evidence of hesitancy to challenge established principles and seek improvements to expand and innovate'.[160] The contracting process was 'unduly complicated, particularly for target groups...who are not highly knowledgeable about contractual matters'.[161] The objectives of the programme were 'distorted by the problems of "fronting"'.[162] Breaking down large contracts into smaller parcels 'seems inefficient...and leads to an increased workload in the public sector and economic inefficiency in the execution of projects'.[163] The private sector was 'willing to accept the challenge' of implementing targeted procurement, but at a cost to the project, resulting in extra financial costs to the public sector. Specific target groups like women and disabled workers benefited less than other targeted groups. Monitoring of the programme focused mainly on contract award statistics 'and not on the long-term sustainability' of individual targeted business enterprises.[164] There were no 'uniform or coordinated monitoring and evaluation procedures' in place 'to measure the impacts and effectiveness of [targeted procurement] in the industry'. Risks were being borne too much by the private sector.

A third assessment of preferential procurement was carried out as a joint operation by the South African government and the World Bank in 2001–02, in the

---

[153] TE Manchidi and I Hammond, 'Targeted Procurement in the Republic of South Africa: An Independent Assessment' (ILO, 2002) 2.   [154] ibid 9.
[155] ibid.   [156] ibid.   [157] ibid.   [158] ibid.   [159] ibid 4.   [160] ibid.
[161] ibid.   [162] ibid 6.   [163] ibid.   [164] ibid 8.

context of a Country Procurement Assessment Review.[165] The assessment report was critical of the operation of the preference policy. It found that preferential procurement policies were 'not well formulated' by public bodies 'due to lack of national targets'. Benefiting from the preferences was largely a matter of self-assessment: qualification standards were 'insufficient or not adequately verified'. Bidders were 'seldom required to provide detailed information to verify their claims'. The system did not 'cater for capacity building of "disadvantaged enterprises" '. The cost and outcome of the preferential system were 'not adequately assessed to evaluate the merits of the system'. There were 'no significant quantitative data on the cost and outcome of the preferential system'.

The effects of the more recent changes, discussed in chapter 9 above, do not yet appear to have been subjected to rigorous empirical analysis, over an extended period. Preliminary research by Empowerdex indicated that in 2005, R300 billion was reported as the preferential procurement spend by Johannesburg Stock Exchange listed companies that provided information.[166] By 2005, 26 per cent of procurement spending was based on preferential procurement. This was a dramatic increase since the ending of apartheid, and even from before the introduction of the B-BBEE Act in 2003. In 1992, 1 per cent of procurement spending went to black suppliers in 1992, whilst the figure was 4 per cent in 2002. Nevertheless, this is substantially less than the 70 per cent compliance target set out in the Codes.

VI. In Conclusion...

Are procurement linkages worth it?

None of the benefits or disadvantages shown by these empirical studies is guaranteed or inevitable. Much depends on the context. What are we to make of this? Perhaps the best starting point may be the adage that 'the best is the enemy of the good'. Achieving social change through regulation is immensely complex and uncertain. There is no consensus on what makes for an effective regulatory scheme. The wise policy maker, therefore, will not want to put all her eggs in one basket, and will want instead to keep a range of tools available with which to attempt to achieve the desired changes in behaviour. Is procurement linkage a regulatory tool sufficiently valuable to be kept available in the armoury, when there are so many constraints? In making this assessment, we must be careful not to assume that the alternatives to the use of procurement linkages are necessarily better in being more effective in delivering results without unacceptable indirect

---

[165] World Bank, Report No 25751-SA, 'South Africa Country Procurement Assessment Report, Refining the Public Procurement System, Volume I: Summary of Findings and Recommendations', February 2003, <http://www-wds.worldbank.org/external/default/WDSContentServer/IW3P/IB/2003/05/13/000094946_03042504054534/Rendered/PDF/multi0page.pdf> para 4.7.

[166] Empowerdex, 'Guide to the Codes of Good Practice; An Empowerdex Guide' (2006) Part 1, p 2.

effects. It may be the case in particular jurisdictions with particular systems of government that this is true but we cannot assume so without empirical evidence comparing different systems of regulation.[167]

Empirical issues for the future

Practically all the theoretical arguments for and against procurement linkages set out in chapter 5 above can be tested empirically. Yet, in practice, empirical research testing the extent to which these theoretical arguments are accurate is in its infancy in many countries. There is a dearth of empirical information available on which to judge the effect of these linkages. Some of the questions that need to be addressed include: Does linkage increase the opportunity for, or have the effect of, excluding competitors? Does linkage make it more difficult for SMEs to tender successfully? Does linkage increase overall costs?[168] Does linkage lead to a reduction in transparency of the procurement process? Does linkage lead to greater bureaucratization of the procurement process? Does linkage increase the opportunities for corruption? Does procurement linkage lead to an evasion of democratic and constitutional control? Are policies on linkage serious or mere window-dressing? Are the adverse effects of procurement linkages proportionately greater for tenderers in one state than those in another? Is an approach based on award criteria more effective in practical terms than one based on contract conditions? What alternative measures are available to implement status equality policy and how effective are they in comparison to using procurement linkages? Do procurement linkages achieve the goals that those who adopt them say they want to achieve? In the context of arriving at policy on procurement linkages, there is a clear need for further empirical research of the phenomenon.

Engagement

Finally, it seems useful to address a concern often heard from those primarily interested in securing greater status equality. We have seen that some who are sceptical of the social use of procurement focus on the extent to which procurement professionals will be called on to be involved in the interpretation and application of

---

[167] For a somewhat similar defence of tax subsidies, see EA Zelinsky, 'James Madison and Public Choice at Gucci Gulch: A Procedural Defense of Tax Expenditures and Tax Institutions' (1993) 102 Yale Law Journal 1165.

[168] As we have seen from the case studies, the evidence is very mixed on this. See further, European Commission, 'A report on the functioning of public procurement markets in the EU: benefits from the application of EU directives and challenges for the future', 3 February 2004, available at <http://ec.europa.eu/internal_market/publicprocurement/docs/public-proc-market-final-report_en.pdf> 21, which reported that the analysis of prices reported by public authorities seems to suggest that introducing environmental clauses does not increase the prices actually paid for the supplies, services, or works, and that there is some evidence suggesting that the introduction of social clauses results in slightly higher prices actually being paid by authorities.

social norms with which they are unfamiliar. To the extent that these values are seen by these professionals to be exogenous to their prime concerns, some argue that the importance of such values will be underestimated; therefore, it is better not to try to integrate the social and the economic because otherwise the social will lose out. For equality professionals, then, there is a risk of the growing 'commodification' of equality, the issue with which I began the book. Is it better to stick to tried and tested methods of implementation where interpretation of equality is in the hands of equality activists and professionals? Is it worth running risks with linking procurement with social policy when there are alternative policy instruments available? The question of whether to use procurement to buy social justice raises an issue of importance that divides equality practitioners, involving a debate about the forums in which we should engage in political action to further equality. My own position, for what it is worth, is closer to that of Michael Ignatieff, who suggests that human rights (and by implication, equality) advocates should 'stop thinking of human rights as trumps and begin thinking of them as a language that creates the basis for deliberation'.[169] Engagements with procurement professionals, engagements with trade officials, engagements with corporations, are all part of this process of deliberation. It is a politics that 'must reconcile moral ends to concrete situations and must be prepared to make painful compromises not only between means and ends, but between ends themselves'.[170]

---

[169] M Ignatieff, 'Human Rights as Idolatry', in M Ignatieff (A Gutman (ed)), *Human Rights as Politics and Idolatry* (Princeton University Press, 2003) 53, 95.   [170] ibid 22.

Bibliography

Aaronson, S A, ' "Minding Our Business": What the United States Government Has Done and Can do to Ensure that U.S. Multinationals Act Responsibly in Foreign Markets' (2005) 59 Journal of Business Ethics 175

Abbas, S, 'Traditional Elements of the Malaysian Constitution' in Trindade, F A and Lee, H P (eds), *The Constitution of Malaysia: Further Perspectives and Developments* (OUP, 1986)

Abbott, F, 'Rule-Making in the WTO: Lessons from the Case of Bribery and Corruption' (2001) 4 JIEL 275

Abella, R S, *Equality in Employment: A Royal Commission Report* (Supply and Services Canada, 1984)

Ackermann, T G, 'Dis"ordre"ly Loopholes: TRIPS Patent Protection, GATT, and the ECJ' (1997) 32 Texas Journal of International Law 489

Adams, R J, and Singh, P, 'Early Experience with NAFTA's Labour Side Accord' (1997) 18(2) *Comparative Labor Law Journal* 161

Agócs, C, 'Canada's employment equity legislation and policy, 1987–2000' (2002) 23(3) International Journal of Manpower 256

—— and Burr, C, 'Employment Equity, Affirmative Action and Managing Diversity: Assessing the Differences' (1996) 17 (4–5) International Journal of Manpower 30

Allouche, J (ed), *Corporate Social Responsibility: Volume 1: Concept, Accountability and Reporting* (Palgrave Macmillan, 2006)

Allouche, J, de Bry, F, Huault, I, and Schmidt, G, 'The Institutionalization of CSR in France: the State Injunction' in Allouche, J (ed), *Corporate Social Responsibility: Volume 1: Concept, Accountability and Reporting* (Palgrave Macmillan, 2006) 284

Alston, P, 'Resisting the Merger and Acquisition of Human Rights by Trade Law: A Reply to Petersmann' (2002) 13 EJIL 815

—— (ed), *Labour Rights as Human Rights* (OUP, 2005)

—— (ed), *Non-State Actors and Human Rights* (OUP, 2005)

—— and Robinson, M (eds), *Human Rights and Development: Towards Mutual Reinforcement* (OUP, 2005)

Aman, A C, *The Democracy Deficit: Taming Globalization Through Law Reform* (NYU Press, 2004)

Amato, T A, 'Note: Labour Rights Conditionality: United States Trade Legislation and the International Trade Order' (1990) 65 NYU LR 79

Anderson, T H, *The Pursuit of Fairness: A History of Affirmative Action* (OUP, 2004)

Apprenticeship Task Force, 'Final Report: The Business Case for Apprenticeships' (Apprenticeship Task Force, July 2005)

Arnavas, D P, and Ruberry, W J, *Government Contract Guidebook* (2nd edn, Federal Publications Inc, 1994)

Arnold, W, 'Scandal Lets Malaysia Prove Its Mettle' *The New York Times*, 16 October 2002, sec W, p 1, col 4

Arnould, J, 'A Turning Point in the Use of Additional Award Criteria?: The Judgment of the European Court in the French Lycées Case' (2001) 10 PPLR NA13–14

——, 'Secondary Policies in Public Procurement: The innovations of the new directives' (2004) 13 PPLR 187

Arrowsmith, S, *Government Procurement and Judicial Review* (Carswell, 1988)

—— 'The Legality of "Secondary" Procurement Policies under the Treaty of Rome and the Works Directive' (1992) 1 PPLR 408

—— *A Guide to the Procurement Cases of the Court of Justice* (Earlsgate Press, 1992)

—— 'Restricted Awards Procedures under the Public Works Contracts Regulations 1991: A Commentary on General Building and Maintenance v Greenwich Borough Council' (1993) 4 PPLR CS92

—— *The Lawyer*, 27 September 1994, 25

—— 'Abolition of the United Kingdom's Procurement Preference Scheme for Disabled Workers' (1994) 3 PPLR CS225

—— 'Public Procurement as an Instrument of Policy and the Impact of Market Liberalisation' (1995) 111 LQR 235

—— 'The Community's Legal Framework on Public Procurement: "The Way Forward" at Last' (1999) 36 CMLR 13

—— 'Towards a Multilateral Agreement on Transparency in Government Procurement' (1997) 47 ICLQ 793

—— 'The European Commission's Proposals for New Directives on Public and Utilities Procurement' (2000) 9 PPLR NA 125

—— 'Reviewing the GPA: The Role and Development of the Plurilateral Agreement After Doha' (2002) 5(4) JIEL 761

—— 'The EC Procurement Directives, National Procurement Policies and Better Governance: The Case for a New Approach' (2002) 27 ELR 3

—— *Government Procurement in the WTO* (Kluwer Law International, 2003)

—— 'An Assessment of the New Legislative Package on Public Procurement' (2004) 41 CMLR 1

—— *The Law of Public and Utilities Procurement* (2nd edn, Sweet & Maxwell, 2005)

—— 'The Past and Future Evolution of EC Procurement Law: From Framework to Common Code' (2006) 35(3) Public Contracts Law Journal 337

—— and Davies, A (eds), *Public Procurement: Global Revolution* (Kluwer Law International, 1998)

—— Linarelli, J, and Wallace Jr, D (eds), *Regulating Public Procurement: National and International Perspectives* (Kluwer Law International, 2000)

—— and Trybus, M (eds), *Public Procurement: The Continuing Revolution* (Kluwer, 2003)

—— and Kunzlik, P (eds), *Social and Environmental Policies under the EC Procurement Rules: New Directives and New Directions* (provisional title) (Cambridge University Press, in press)

—— and Maund, C, 'CSR in the utilities sector and the implications of EC procurement policy: a framework for debate' in Arrowsmith, S, and Kunzlik, P (eds), *Social and Environmental Policies under the EC Procurement Rules: New Directives and New Directions* (provisional title) (Cambridge University Press, in press)

Arthurs, H, 'Who's Afraid of Globalization?' in Craig, J D R, and Lynk, S M (eds), *Globalization and the Future of Labour Law* (Cambridge University Press, 2006) 56

Ashenfelter, O, and Blum, J (eds), *Estimating the Labour Market Effects of Social Programs* (Princeton University Press, 1976)

—— and Heckman, J, 'Measuring the Effect of an Antidiscrimination Program' in Ashenfelter, O, and Blum, J (eds), *Estimating the Labour Market Effects of Social Programs* (Princeton University Press, 1976) 46

Atik, J, 'Identifying Antidemocratic Outcomes: Authenticity, Self-Sacrifice and International Trade' (1998) 19 UP JIEL 229

Australian Capital Territory, Government Procurement Board, 'Equal Employment Opportunity for Women in the Workplace: Procurement Circular' (December 2002)

Australian Government, Department of Finance and Administration, 'Commonwealth Procurement Guidelines and Best Practice Guidance' (February 2002)

—— Department of Finance and Administration, 'Guidance on Complying with Legislation and Government Policy in Procurement' (Financial Management Guidance No 10, January 2005), available at <http://www.finance.gov.au/procurement/complying_with_legislation.html>

—— Department of Foreign Affairs and Trade, 'WTO Agreement on Government Procurement: Review of Membership Implications' (AGPS, 1997)

—— Productivity Commission, 'Review of the Disability Discrimination Act 1992' (Report No 30, vol 1, 30 April 2004)

—— 'Unfinished Business: Equity for Women in Australian Workplaces: Final Report of the Regulatory Review of the Affirmative Action (Equal Employment Opportunity for Women) Act 1986' (June 1998)

Ayres, I, *Pervasive Prejudice?: Unconventional Evidence of Race and Gender Discrimination* (Chicago University Press, 2001)

—— and Vars, F E, 'When Does Private Discrimination Justify Public Affirmative Action' (1998) 98 Columbia Law Review 1577

—— and Crampton, P, 'How Affirmative Action at the FCC Auctions Decreased the Deficit' in Ayres, I, *Pervasive Prejudice?: Unconventional Evidence of Race and Gender Discrimination* (Chicago University Press, 2001) 315

Aziz, R, 'Doha Development Agenda: The Way Forward' in The Federal Trust, *Where Next for the WTO? After Cancun: Views, ideas and proposals by trade ministers* (Federal Trust, 2003) 31

Badcoe, P, 'Best Value—A New Approach in the UK' in Arrowsmith, S, and Trybus, M (eds), *Public Procurement: The Continuing Revolution* (Kluwer, 2003) 197

Bagilhole, B, 'Managing to be Fair: Implementing Equal Opportunities in a Local Authority' (1993) 19(2) Local Government Studies 163

Baldwin, R E, *Nontariff Distortions of International Trade* (Brookings Institution, 1979)

Ballestrero, M V, 'New Legislation in Italian Equality Law' (1992) 21 ILJ 152

Barnard, C, *EC Employment Law* (2nd edn, OUP, 2000)

—— 'Labour Market Integration: Lessons from the European Union' in Craig, J D R, and Lynk, S M, *Globalization and the Future of Labour Law* (Cambridge University Press, 2006) 225

Barnett, M N, and Finnemore, M, 'The Politics, Power and Pathologies of International Organizations' (1999) 53 International Organization 699

Barshefsky, C, Sutton, A, and Swindler, A, 'Developments in EC Procurement Under the 1992 Program' (1990) 4 BYU LR 1269

Bartels, L, 'Conditionality in GSP Programmes' in Cottier, T, Pauwelyn J, and Bürgi, E (eds), *Human Rights and International Trade* (OUP, 2006) 463

Baxi, U, *The Future of Human Rights* (OUP, 2002)

Bean, J J, *Beyond the Broker State: Federal Policies Towards Small Business, 1936–1961* (University of North Carolina Press, 2002)

Bell, D, *Faces at the Bottom of the Well: The Permanence of Racism* (Basic Books, 1992)

Bell, M, 'The New Article 13 EC Treaty: A Sound Basis for European Anti-Discrimination Law?' (1999) 6 Maas JEL 5

—— *Anti-discrimination Law and the European Union* (OUP, 2002)

—— and Waddington, L, 'The 1996 Intergovernmental Conference and the Prospects of a Non-discrimination Treaty Article' (1996) 25 ILJ 320

Bellamy, C W, and Child, G D, *Common Market Law of Competition* (3rd edn, Sweet & Maxwell, 1987)

Benedict, C, *Sekundärzwecke im Vergabeverfahren* (Springer, 2000)

Bercusson, B, *Fair Wages Resolutions* (Mansell, 1978)

—— and Bruun, N, 'Labour Law Aspects of Public Procurement in the EU' in Nielsen, R, and Treumer, S (eds), *The New EU Public Procurement Directives* (DJØF Publishing, 2005) 97

Bernstein, D E, 'Roots of the "Underclass": the Decline of Laissez-Faire Jurisprudence and the Rise of Racist Labor Legislation' (1991) 43 American University Law Review 85

—— *Only One Place of Redress: African-Americans, Labor Regulations, and the Courts from Reconstruction to the New Deal* (Duke University Press, 2001)

Bernstein, J, *The Living Wage Movement: What is it, Why is it, and What's Known about its Impact* (October 2003) available at <http://apps.atlantaga.gov/lwcfiles/12.pdf>

Besse, G, 'Mondalialisation des échanges et droits fondamentaux de l'homme au travail: quel progès possible aujourd'hui?' (1994) 11 Droit Social 841

Beveridge, F, Nott, S, and Stephen, K, 'Mainstreaming and the Engendering of Policy-Making: a Means to an End?' (2000) 7(3) JEPP 385

Bhagwati, J, 'The Agenda of the WTO' in van Dijck, P, and Faber, G (eds), *Challenges to the New World Trade Organisation* (Kluwer Law International, 1996) 27

—— and Hudec, R (eds), *Fair Trade and Harmonization* (MIT Press, 1996)

Bhala, R, 'Fighting Bad Guys with International Trade Law' (1997) 31 University of California Davis Law Review 1

Bichta, C, *Corporate Social Responsibility: A Role in Government Policy and Regulation?* (Centre for the Study of Regulated Industries, University of Bath School of Management, 2003)

Biggar, D, 'Background Note', in 'Procurement Markets' (1999) 1(4) OECD Journal of Competition Law and Policy 6

Bindman, G, 'The law, equal opportunity and affirmative action' (1980) VIII New Community 251

Binks, J, *Using Public Procurement to Drive Skills and Innovation: A Report for the Department of Trade and Industry* (Local Futures Group, March 2006)

Bisopoulos, A P, *Public Procurement and Public Works Contracting in the European Community with Special Reference to the UK and Greece* (PhD thesis, University of London, 1990)

Blackett, A, 'Whither Social Clause? Human Rights, Trade Theory and Treaty Interpretation' (1999) 31 Col HRLR 1

Blank, A, and Marceau, G, 'The History of the Government Procurement Negotiations Since 1945' (1996) 5 PPLR 77

Blumrosen, A W, *Modern Law: The Law Transmission System and Equal Employment Opportunity* (University of Wisconsin Press, 1993)

Bock, C, 'An Overview of Swiss Federal Procurement Policy' (1998) 7 PPLR CS134

Boehm, F, and Polanco, J, 'Corruption and Privatisation of Infrastructure in Developing Countries, Transparency International: Integrity Pact And Public Procurement Programme' (IP & PC Working Paper 1, November 2003) available at <http://www.transparency.org/integrity_pact/resources/working_papers/dnld/wk1_boehm_polanco.pdf>

Bolling, R W, *House Out of Order* (Dutton, 1966)

Bolton, P, 'The Use of Government Procurement as an Instrument of Policy' (2004) 121 South African Law Journal 619

—— *The Legal Regulation of Government Procurement in South Africa* (PhD thesis, 2005)

—— 'An Analysis of the Preferential Procurement Legislation in South Africa' in Arrowsmith, S, and Kunzlik, P (eds), *Social and Environmental Policies under the EC Procurement Rules: New Directives and New Directions* (provisional title) (Cambridge University Press, in press)

Bonfield, A, 'The Origin and Development of American Fair Employment Legislation' (1967) 52 Iowa Law Review 1043

Bourgeois, J H J, 'The Tokyo Round Agreements on Technical Barriers and on Government Procurement in International and EEC Perspective' (1982) 19 CMLR 5

Bouwer, M, de Jong, K, Jonk, M, Berman, T, Bersani, R, Lusser, H, Nissinen, A, Parikka, K, and Szuppinger P, *Green Public Procurement in Europe 2005—Status Overview* (Virage Milieu & Management bv, 2005)

Bovis, C H, 'Extra-territorial effects in the application of the EC Utilities Directive and the Public Procurement Trade War between US and EC' (1993) 4(2) Utilities Law Review 84

—— 'Public Procurement in the European Union: Lessons from the Past and Insights to the Future' (2005) 12(1) Col J Eur L 53

—— *Public Procurement in the European Union* (Palgrave Macmillan, 2005)

—— 'The New Public Procurement Regime: A Different Perspective on the Integration of Public Markets of the European Union' (2006) 12 EPL 73

Boyer, P, *Equality for All: Report of the Parliamentary Committee on Equality Rights* (Queen's Printer for Canada, 1985)

Boyle, R, 'Best Value?' (2000) 9 PPLR CS70

—— 'Disability Issues in Public Procurement' in Arrowsmith, S, and Kunzlik, P (eds), *Social and Environmental Policies under the EC Procurement Rules: New Directives and New Directions* (provisional title) (Cambridge University Press, in press)

Brandeis, E, 'Labor Legislation' in Commons, J R (ed), *History of Labor in the United States, 1896–1932, volume III* (Macmillan, 1935)

Brander, L, and Olsthoorn, X, *Three Scenarios for Green Public Procurement* (Institute for Environmental Studies, Vrije Universiteit, December 2003)

Bratton, W, McCahery, J, Picciotto, S, and Scott, C (eds), *International Regulatory Competition and Co-ordination* (OUP, 1996)

Brauer, C M, *John F. Kennedy and the Second Reconstruction* (Columbia University Press, 1979)

Braun, P, 'A Matter of Principle(s)—The Treatment of Contracts Falling Outside the Scope of the European Public Procurement Directives' (2000) 9 PPLR 39

Breining-Kaufman, C, 'The Legal Matrix of Human Rights and Trade Law: State Obligations versus Private Rights and Obligations' in Cottier, T, Pauwelyn, J, and Bürgi, E (eds), *Human Rights and International Trade* (OUP, 2005) 95

Brimmer, A F, and Terrell, H S, 'The economic potential of black capitalism: a paper presented before the 82nd meeting of the American Economic Association' (1969)

Brinkmann, G, 'Lawmaking under the Social Chapter of Maastricht' in Harlow, C, and Craig, P (eds) *Lawmaking in the European Union* (Aspen, 1998) 239

Bronckers, M, and Quick, R (eds), *New Directions in International Economic Law: Essays in Honour of John H. Jackson* (Springer, 2000)

Brown, C, 'The Federal Attack on Labor Market Discrimination: The Mouse that Roared?' (1984) 5 Research in Labor Economics 33

Budlong, S C, 'Article 130r(2) and the Permissibility of State Aids for Environmental Compliance in the EC' 30 Col JTL 431 (1992)

Burkhauser, R V, and Haveman, R H, *Disability and Work: The Economics of American Policy* (Johns Hopkins University Press, 1982)

Burstein, K, *The Right Road: A Report to the Under-Secretary General for Management on the Global Compact and the Practice of Administration in the United Nations* (United Nations, 2004)

Campbell, DC, 'US Firms and Black Labor in South Africa: Creating a Structure of Change' (1986) VII(1) Journal of Labor Research 1

Canadian Government, Department of Indian Affairs and Northern Development Corporate Services, Departmental Audit and Evaluation Branch, 'Evaluation of the Procurement Strategy for Aboriginal Business' (DIAND, August 2002)

—— Employment and Immigration Canada, 'Employment Equity: A guide for employers' (Employment and Immigration Canada, 1991)

—— Employment and Immigration Canada, 'Employment Equity: Federal Contractors Program: Questions and Answers' (Employment and Immigration Canada, 1987)

—— Employment and Immigration Canada, 'Federal Contractors Program: Information for Suppliers and Organizations' (Employment and Immigration Canada, 1991)

—— 'Federal Policy Guide, Aboriginal Self-Government: The Government of Canada's Approach to Implementation of the Inherent Right and the Negotiation of Aboriginal Self-Government' (1995)

—— Human Resources and Skills Development Canada, '2003 Annual Report: Employment Equity Act 2003' (Government of Canada, 2004)

—— Human Resources and Skills Development Canada, '2004 Annual Report: Employment Equity Act' (Government of Canada, 2005).

—— Human Resources Development Canada, 'Evaluation of the Federal Contractors Program, Evaluation and Data Development, Strategic Policy, Final Report' (SP-AH183-04-02E, April 2002)

—— Indian and Northern Affairs Canada, Procurement Strategy for Aboriginal Business, 'Performance Report for 2000' (Indian and Northern Affairs, Canada, 2000)

—— Minister of Supply and Services, 'The Canada-U.S. Free Trade Agreement and Government Procurement: An Assessment' (1989)

—— 'Report of the Royal Commission on Aboriginal Peoples', five volumes, available online at <http://www.inac.gc.ca/rcap/index.html>

—— 'Third Canadian Periodic Report to the Committee on the Elimination of Discrimination Against Women', UN, CEDAW/C/CAN/3, 25 September 1992

Canadian Parliament, Standing Committee on Human Resources Development and the Status of Persons with Disabilities, 'Promoting Equality in the Federal Jurisdiction: A Review of the Employment Equity Act: Committee Report' (Public Works Canada, June 2002) available at <http://www.parl.gc.ca/InfoComDoc/37/1/HUMA/Studies/Reports/HUMARP9-e.htm>

Cannon, T, *Corporate Responsibility* (Pearson Education, 1994)

Cao, F, 'China's Government Procurement Reform: From the Bidding Law to the Government Procurement Law' in Arrowsmith, S, and Trybus, M (eds), *Public Procurement: The Continuing Revolution* (Kluwer, 2003) 78

Caron, D D, 'The Structure and Pathologies of Local Selective Procurement Ordinances: A Study of the Apartheid-Era South Africa Ordinances' (2003) 21 Berkeley Journal of International Law 159

Carr, J, 'Background Paper on Contract Compliance in the UK' (January 1986)

—— 'New Roads to Equality: Contract Compliance for the UK' (Fabian Society Tract No 517, January 1987)

Carvajal, A, 'State and Local "Free Burma" Laws: The Case for Sub-national Trade Sanctions' (1998) 29 LPIB 257

Case, W, *Politics in Southeast Asia: Democracy or Less* (Routledge Curzon, 2002)

Chaney, P, and Fevre, R, 'An Absolute Duty: Equal Opportunities and the National Assembly for Wales—A Study of the Equality Policies of the Welsh Assembly Government and their Implementation: July 1999 to March 2002' (Institute of Welsh Affairs, June 2002)

Chang, H, 'An Economic Analysis of Trade Measures To Protect the Global Environment' (1995) 83 Georgia Law Journal 2131

Charlesworth, J, and Voruz, V, 'The Contract Compliance Policy: An Illustration of the Persistence of Racism as the Failure of Modernity' (1998) 7 Social and Legal Studies 193

Charnovitz, S, 'Fair Labor Standards and International Trade' (1986) 20 JWTL 61

—— 'Participation of Non-governmental Organisations in the World Trade Organisation' (1996) 17 UP JIEL 331

—— 'The Moral Exception in Trade Policy' (1998) 38 Virg JIL 689

—— 'The Law of Environmental "PPMs" in the WTO: Debunking the Myth of Illegality' (2002) 27 Yale JIL 59

Charpentier, L, 'Le dilemme de l'action positive' (European University Institute, Working Paper SPS No 93/6, EUI,1993)

Charro, P, 'Case Note, Case C-513/99, Concordia Bus Finland Oy Ab v. Helsingin kaupunki and HKL-Bussiliikenne' (2003) 40 CMLR 179

Chua, A, *World on Fire: How Exporting Free Market Democracy Breeds Ethnic Hatred and Global Instability* (new edn, Arrow, 2004)

Clark, B, 'New Developments in Compulsory Competitive Tendering and the Duty of Best Value' (1998) 7 PPLR CS85

Clark, S E, and Gaile, G L, 'Local Politics in a Global Era: Thinking Locally, Acting Globally' (1997) 551 Annals of the American Academy of Political and Social Science 28

Clay, G M, 'Executive (Ab)use of the Procurement Power: Chamber of Commerce v Reich' (1996) 84 Georgetown Law Journal 2573

Cleesattel, N, 'Government procurement in the Federal Republic of Germany' (1987) 21 GW JILE 59

Cleveland, S H, 'Norm Internalization and US Economic Sanctions' (2001) 26 Yale JIL 1

Cock, J, and Webster, E C, 'Environmental and Social Impact Assessments' in Griesgraber, J M, and Gunter, B G (eds), *The World Bank: Lending on a Global Scale* (Pluto, 1996) 81

Collins, E, *Contract Compliance: An Opportunity for Progress towards Equality in the 1990's?* (LLM thesis, Queen's University, Belfast, September 1990)

Collins, H, *Regulating Contracts* (OUP, 2005)

Colneric, N, 'Vorlagepflicht nach EG-Recht bei Normenkontrolle über Frauenquote' (1991) Der Betriebs-Berate (BB) S 1118

—— 'The Prohibition on Discrimination against Women under Community Law' (1992) 8(3) International Journal of Comparative Labour Law and Industrial Relations 191

Commission for Racial Equality 'Positive Action and Equal Opportunity in Employment' (CRE, 1985)

—— 'Principles of Practice for Contract Compliance' (CRE, September 1987)

—— 'Local Authority Contracts and Racial Equality' (CRE, 1989)

—— 'NHS Contracts and Racial Equality: A Guide' (CRE, 1991)

—— 'Racial Equality and Council Contractors' (CRE, 1995)

—— 'Racial Equality Means Quality: A Standard for Racial Equality for Local Government in England and Wales' (CRE, 1995)

—— 'CRE Code of Practice on the Duty to Promote Race Equality' (CRE, 2002)

—— 'The Duty to Promote Race Equality: Performance guidelines for government departments' (CRE, June 2002)

—— 'CRE Guidance on Equality and Procurement' (CRE, July 2003)

—— 'Public Procurement and Race Equality—Guidelines for Public Authorities' (CRE, 2003)

—— 'Race and Procurement in Local Government' (CRE, 2003)

—— 'Race Equality and Public Procurement' (CRE, 2003)

——/Schneider-Ross, 'Towards Racial Equality: An evaluation of the public duty to promote race equality and good race relations in England and Wales' (CRE, 2003)

Committee on the Administration of Justice, 'Mainstreaming Fairness: A summary of a consultation process around "Policy Appraisal and Fair Treatment"' (CAJ, June 1997)

Compa, L A, and Diamond, S F (eds), *Human Rights, Labour Rights, and International Trade* (University of Pennsylvania Press, 1996)

—— and Darricarrère, T H, 'Private Labor Rights Enforcement Through Corporate Codes of Conduct' in Compa L A, and Diamond, S F (eds), *Human Rights, Labour Rights and International Trade* (University of Pennsylvania Press, 1996) 181

Confederation of British Industry—Commission for Racial Equality, 'Public procurement and race equality—briefing for suppliers' (CRE/CBI, 2003)

Corns, A, and Schotter, A, 'Can Affirmative Action Be Cost Effective? An Experimental Examination of Price Preference Auctions' (1999) 89(1) American Economic Review 291

Cottier, T, Pauwelyn J, and Bürgi, E (eds), *Human Rights and International Trade* (OUP, 2005)

Council of Europe, Rapporteur Group on Equality Between Women and Men, Gender Mainstreaming, GR-EG (98) 1 (Council of Europe, March 26, 1998)

Cowe, R, and Porritt, J, *Government's Business: Enabling Corporate Responsibility* (Forum for the Future, 2002)

Craig, J D R, and Lynk, S M (eds), *Globalization and the Future of Labour Law* (Cambridge University Press, 2006)

Croley, S P, and Jackson, J H, 'WTO Dispute Procedures, Standard of Review, and Deference to National Governments' (1996) 90 AJIL 193

Crosby, F J, *Affirmative Action is Dead; Long Live Affirmative Action* (Yale University Press, 2004)

Curtin, D, 'Effective Sanctions and the Equal Treatment Directive: The von Colson and Harz Cases' (1985) 22 CMLR 505

—— *Irish Employment Equality Law* (Round Hall Press, 1989)

D'Hooghe, D, and Heijse, R, 'New Belgian Legislation on the Award of Public Procurement Contracts' (1997) 6 PPLR CS90

Daintith, T, 'Regulation by Contract: The New Prerogative' [1979] Current Legal Problems 41

—— 'The Executive Power Today: bargaining and economic control' in Jowell J, and Oliver D (eds), The Changing Constitution (OUP, 1985) 174

—— (ed), *Implementing EC Law in the United Kingdom: Structures for Indirect Rule* (Wiley Chancery Law, 1995)

Dashwood, A, and O'Leary, S (eds), *The Principle of Equal Treatment in EC Law* (Sweet & Maxwell, 1997)

Dauses, M A, 'The Protection of Fundamental Rights in the Community Legal Order' (1985) 10 ELR 398

Davies, A, 'Remedies for Enforcing the WTO Agreement on Government Procurement from the Perspective of the European Community: A Critical View' (1996–7) 20 World Competition 113

Davies, ACL, 'Using Contracts to Enforce Standards: The Case of Waiting Times in the National Health Service' in McCrudden, C, *Regulation and Deregulation* (OUP, 1999) 79

Davies, P, 'The Emergence of European Labour Law' in McCarthy, W (ed), *Legal Intervention in Industrial Relations* (Blackwell, 1992) 313

—— 'Market Integration and Social Policy in the Court of Justice' (1995) 24 ILJ 49

—— Lyon-Caen, A, Sciarra, S, and Simitis S (eds), *European Community Labour Law: Principles and Perspectives: Liber Amicorum Lord Wedderburn* (OUP, 1996)

Day, C, 'Buying green: the crucial role of public authorities' (2005) 10(2) Local Environment: The International Journal of Justice and Sustainability 201

de Búrca, G, 'The Role of Equality in European Community Law' in Dashwood, A, and O'Leary, S (eds), *The Principle of Equal Treatment in EC Law* (Sweet & Maxwell, 1997) 13

—— and Scott, J, 'The Impact of the WTO on EU Decision-Making', Harvard Jean Monnet Working Paper 06/00 (2000)

de George, R T, *Competing with Integrity in International Business* (OUP, 1993)

de Graaf, G, and King, M, 'Toward a More Global Government Procurement Market: The Expansion of the GATT Government Procurement Agreement in the Context of the Uruguay Round' (1995) 29(2) The International Lawyer 435

de Jonquières, G, 'WTO Set for Showdown on Labour Rights' *Financial Times*, 1 November 1999

de la Cuesta González, M, and Martinez, C V, 'Fostering Corporate Social Responsibility Through Public Initiative: From the EU to the Spanish Case' (2004) 55 Journal of Business Ethics 275

de Laubadère, A, Moderne, F, and Delvolvé, P, *Traité des Contrats Administratifs* (2ème éd, 2 vol, LGDJ, 1984)

de Mestral, A L C, 'The Impact of the GATT Agreement on Government Procurement in Canada' in Quinn, J, and Slayton, P (eds), *Non-Tariff Barriers After the Tokyo Round* (Institute for Research on Public Policy, 1982) 171 de Schutter, O, 'The Accountability of Multinationals for Human Rights Violations in European Law' in Alston, P (ed), *Non-State Actors and Human Rights* (OUP, 2005) 227

—— 'Transnational Corporations as Instruments of Human Development' in Alston, P, and Robinson, M (eds), *Human Rights and Development: Towards Mutual Reinforcement* (OUP, 2005) 403

De Simone, P, and Moses, W F, *A Guide to American State and Local Laws in South Africa* (IRRC, 1995)

de Sousa Santos, B, *Toward a New Legal Common Sense: Science and Politics in the Paradigmatic Transition* (Routledge, 1995)

de Wet, E, 'Labour Standards in the Globalised Economy: The Inclusion of a Social Clause in the General Agreement on Tariffs and Trade/World Trade Organisation' (1995) 17 Human Rights Quarterly 443

Deakin, S, 'Labour Law as Market Regulation' in Davies, P, Lyon-Caen, A, Sciarra, S, and Simitis S (eds), *European Community Labour Law: Principles and Perspectives: Liber Amicorum Lord Wedderburn* (OUP, 1996) 63

—— 'Social Rights in a Globalized Economy' in Alston, P (ed), *Labour Rights as Human Rights* (OUP, 2005) 55

Deinert, O, 'Posting of Workers to Germany—Previous Evolutions and New Influences Throughout EU Legislation Proposals' (2000) 16 International Journal of Comparative Labour Law and Industrial Relations 217

del Rosario, V O, 'Mainstreaming Gender Concerns: Aspects of Compliance, Resistance and Negotiation' (1995) 26(3) IDS Bulletin 102

Derfler, L, *Alexandre Millerand: The Socialist Years* (Mouton, 1977)

Dew, G, *Government and municipal contracts: fair wages movement: a brief history* (2nd edn, 1896) (available at: LSE Library, HD4/252, M(PAMPHLETS 174))

Didier, P, 'The Uruguay Round Government Procurement Agreement: Implementation in the European Union' in Hoekman, B M, and Mavroidis, P C (eds), *Law and Policy in Public Purchasing: The WTO Agreement on Government Procurement* (Studies in International Trade Policy, University of Michigan Press, 1997) 125

Digings, L, *Competitive Tendering and the European Communities: Public Procurement, CCT and Local Services* (Association of Metropolitan Authorities, 1991)

Diller, J, 'A Social Conscience in the Global Marketplace? Labour Dimensions of Codes of Conduct, Social Labelling and Investor Initiatives' (1999) 138 International Labour Review 99

Docksey, C, 'The European Community and the Promotion of Equality' in McCrudden, C (ed), *Women, Employment and European Equality Law* (Eclipse, 1987) 1

Dodds, R F, 'Offsets in Chinese Government Procurement: The Partially Open Door' (1995) 26 LPIB 1119

Donahue, J, *Disunited States* (Basic Books, 1997)

Donohue III, J J, and Heckman, J, 'Continuous versus Episodic Change: The Impact of Civil Rights Policy on the Economic Status of Blacks' (1991) XXIX Journal of Economic Literature 1603

Dormady, V A, 'Note, Women's Rights in International Law: A Prediction Concerning the Legal Impact of the United Nations' Fourth World Conference on Women' (1997) 30 Vanderbilt Journal of Transnational Law 97

Driesen, D, 'What is Free Trade?: The Real Issue Lurking Behind the Trade and Environment Debate' (2001) 41 Virg JIL 279

Dubray, J, 'Use of Public Procurement Policies in the United States to Combat Discrimination and to Promote Equal Employment Opportunities' (Working Paper prepared for the fourth session of the ILO workshop on equality, 'Public Procurements—How effective are they in combating discrimination?', ILO, Geneva, 23–24 May 2006)

duRivage, V, 'The OFCCP Under the Reagan Administration: Affirmative Action in Retreat' (1985) 36 Labor Law Journal 360

Earley, J, *Green Procurement in Trade Policy: Background Paper prepared for the Commission for Environmental Cooperation* (Commission for Environmental Cooperation, 2003) available at <http://www.cec.org>

Elliott, K A, 'Backing Illegal Sanctions' Journal of Commerce, 6 August 1997

Ellis, E, *European Community Sex Equality Law* (OUP, 1991)

Emancipatieraad, 'Advies over de nota positieve actieprogramma's voor vrouwen in arbeidssorganisaties, adv. nr. II/75/89; d.d. 21 maart 1989' in *Emancipatieraad, Positive Actie: Advies en onderzoe*k (Emancipatieraad, 1989)

—— 'Van Marge Naar Mainstream: Adviesgrief Onderzoek Over Het Mainstreamen Van Emancipatie, in Algemeen Beleid', adv. nr. IV/51/96, 1997 (Emancipatieraad, 1997)

Empowerdex, 'Guide to the Codes of Good Practice: An Empowerdex Guide' (Empowerdex, 2006)

Emsley, I, *The Malaysian Experience of Affirmative Action: Lessons for South Africa* (Human & Rousseau Tafelberg, 1996)

Epstein, R A, *Forbidden Grounds: The Case Against Employment Discrimination Laws* (Harvard University Press, 1992)

—— *Bargaining with the State* (Princeton University Press, 1993)

Equal Opportunities Commission for Northern Ireland, 'European Social Policy: Options for Union: Response to Green Paper' (EOCNI, March 1994)

—— 'Report on Formal Investigation into Competitive Tendering in Health and Education Services Northern Ireland' (EOCNI, 1996)

Equal Opportunities Commission, 'The Gender Impact of CCT in Local Government' (EOC, 1995)

—— 'Mainstreaming Gender in Local Government' (EOC, 1997)

—— 'The Sex Discrimination Legislation: Recommendations for Change' (EOC, June 1997)

Equal Opportunities Review, 'Equal opportunities and contract compliance' (1986) 8 Equal Opportunities Review 9

—— 'Local Government Bill would restrict contract compliance' (1987) 15 Equal Opportunities Review 24

—— 'The Local Government Act and contract compliance: an EOR guide' (1988) 19 Equal Opportunities Review 27

—— 'Contract compliance assessed' (1990) 31 Equal Opportunities Review 26

—— 'Party policies on equal opportunity' (1992) 42 Equal Opportunities Review 12

—— 'Equal Opportunities in the Health Service: a survey of NHS trusts' (1994) 53 Equal Opportunities Review 24

Equalities Review, 'Interim Report for Consultation' *Equalities Review*, March 2006

Equality Studies Centre, 'A Framework for Equality Proofing: A Paper Prepared for the National Economic and Social Forum' (April 1995)

Erdmenger, C (ed), *Buying into the Environment* (Greenleaf Publishing, 2003)

Erridge, A, and Fee, R, 'Contract Compliance: National, Regional and Global Regimes' (1999) 27 Policy and Politics 199

—— 'The Impact of Contract Compliance Policies in Canada—Perspectives from Ontario' (2001) 1(1) Journal of Public Procurement 51

—— and Hennigan, S, 'Pilot Project on Utilising the Unemployed in Public Contracts: Final Evaluation Report' (University of Ulster at Jordanstown, School of Policy Studies, September 2005)

Estivill, J, *Concepts and Strategies for Combating Social Exclusion* (ILO, 2003)

EuroCities, 'CARPE Guide to Responsible Procurement' (Eurocities, 2004)

European Commission, White Paper, 'Completing the Internal Market' (Office for Official Publications of the European Communities, Luxembourg, 1985)

—— 'EC Report on United States Trade Barriers and Unfair Practices' (European Commission, 1990)

—— 'Equal Opportunities for Women and Men in the European Union 1996' (1997)

—— 'Public Procurement in the EU: Special Sectoral Report No. 1' (1997)

—— 'Study of the Use of Equality and Diversity Considerations in Public Procurement: Final Report' (European Commission, December 2003)

—— 'A report on the functioning of public procurement markets in the EU: benefits from the application of EU directives and challenges for the future' (European Commission, 2004), available at <http://ec.europa.eu/internal_market/publicprocurement/docs/public-proc-market-final-report_en.pdf>

—— 'Buying Green! A handbook on environmental public procurement' (OOPEC, 2004)

—— 'The Cost of Non-Europe in Public Sector Procurement, in The Cost of Non-Europe, Basic Findings', vols 5A and 5B

—— Draft Council Recommendation on the Promotion of Positive Action for Women, COM(84)234 final (1984)

—— 'Reexamined proposal for a Council Directive amending Directive 77/62/EEC relating to the co-ordination of procedures on the award of public supply contracts and deleting certain provisions of Directive 80/767/EEC' COM(88)42 final/2

—— 'Public Procurement: Regional and Social Aspects' COM(89)400 final

—— 'Towards Sustainability: A European Community Programme of Policy and Action in Relation to the Environment and Sustainable Development' COM(92)23 final (1992)

—— 'White Paper on Growth, Competitiveness and Employment: The challenges and ways forward into the 21st Century', COM(93)7000

—— 'Proposal for a Council Decision on the Fourth Medium-term Community Action Programme on Equal Opportunities for Women and Men (1996–2000)' COM(95)381 final (1995)

—— 'Communication from the Commission and Council and the European Parliament, Integrating Gender Issues in Development Cooperation' COM(95)423 final (1995)

—— 'Commission Communication, Incorporating Equal Opportunities for Women and Men into All Community Policies and Activities' COM(96)67 final (1996)

—— 'Commission Communication on the consultation of management and labour on the prevention of sexual harassment at work' COM(1996)378

—— Communication of the Commission on Equality of Opportunity for People with Disabilities, COM (96) 406 final (1996)

—— 'Progress Report from the Commission on the Follow- up of the Communication, "Integrating Equal Opportunities for Women and Men in All Community Policies and Activities"' COM(98)122 final (1998)

—— 'Commission Communication, Incorporating equal opportunities for women and men into all Commission policies and activities' COM(2000)334

—— 'Towards a Community Framework Strategy on Gender Equality (2001–2005)' COM(2000)335 final (2000)

—— 'Communication from the Commission to the Council, the European Parliament, the Economic and Social Committee and the Committee of the Regions, Sixth environment action programme of the European Community: "Environment 2010: Our future, Our choice"' COM(2001)31 final

—— 'The European Union's Role in Promoting Human Rights and Democratisation in Third Countries' COM(2001)252 final (2001)

—— 'Commission interpretative communication on the Community law applicable to public procurement and the possibilities for integrating environmental considerations into public procurement' COM(2001)0274 final

—— Green Paper, 'Promoting a European Framework for Corporate Social Responsibility' COM(2001)366 final

—— 'Promoting Core Labour Standards and Improving Social Governance in the Context of Globalisation' COM(2001)416 final (2001)

—— 'Interpretative Communication of the Commission on the Community Law Applicable to Public Procurement and the Possibilities for Integrating Social Considerations into Public Procurement' COM(2001)566 final (2001)

—— 'Commission Communication, Implementing the Partnership for Growth and Jobs: Making Europe a Pole of Excellence on Corporate Social Responsibility' COM(2006)136

—— Communication from the European Communities, Positive Effects of Transparency in Government Procurement, WT/WGTGP/W/41 ¶10

—— DGV, Outline of various interesting positive action schemes for women run in the public and private sectors of the Member States of the European Communities, Doc V/872/86-E (European Commission, 1986)

European Fair Trade Association, 'Fair Procura: Making Public Authorities and Institutional Buyers Local Actors of Sustainable Development' (EFTA, 2005)

European Industrial Relations Reports, 'Law on positive action' (1991) 208 European Industrial Relations Reports 22

European Trade Union Confederation, 'Public Procurement: Social Clauses' (ETUC, January 1990)

Evenett, S J, 'Multilateral Disciplines and Government Procurement' in English, P, Hoekman, B M, and Matto, A (eds), *Development, Trade and the WTO* (WTO, 2002) 423

—— and Hoekman, B M, 'Transparency in Government Procurement: What Can We Expect from International Trade Agreements?' in Arrowsmith, S, and Trybus, M (eds), *Public Procurement: The Continuing Revolution* (Kluwer, 2003) 271

Ewing, K D, *Global Rights in Global Companies: Going for Gold at the UK Olympics* (Institute of Employment Rights, 2006).

Fair Employment Commission for Northern Ireland, 'Review of the Fair Employment Acts' (FEC, 1996)

Farrar, M M, *Principled Pragmatist: The Political Career of Alexandre Millerand* (Berg, 1991)

Faundez, J, *Affirmative Action: International Perspectives* (ILO, 1994)

Feddersen, C T, 'Focusing on Substantive Law in International Economic Relations: The Public Morals of GATT's Article XX(a) and "Conventional" Rules of Interpretation' (1998) 7 Minnesota Journal of Global Trade 75

Fee, R, and Erridge, A, 'Contract Compliance in Canada and Northern Ireland: A Comparative Analysis' (Paper presented to 8th International Annual IPSERA Conference, 1999)

—— Maxwell, P, and Erridge, A, 'Contracting for Services—a Double Jeopardy? An Analysis of Contract Compliance in the Context of European and UK Social and Public Procurement Policy' (1998) 13 Public Policy and Administration 79

Fenster, G, 'Multilateral Talks on Transparency in Government Procurement: Concerns for Developing Countries' (2003) 34(2) IDS Bulletin 63

Ferguson, R B, and Page, A C, 'Pay Restraint: The Legal Constraints' (1978) 127 New Law Journal 515

Ferman, L, *The Negro and Equal Employment Opportunities: A Review of Management Experiences in Twenty Companies* (Praeger, 1968)

Fernández Martín, J M, *The EC Public Procurement Rules: A Critical Analysis* (OUP, 1996)

Finger, J M, and Schuller, P, 'Implementation of Uruguay Commitments: The Development Challenge', World Bank Research Department, Policy Research Working Paper (World Bank, 1999)

Fiss, O, 'The fate of the idea whose time has come: Anti-discrimination Law in the Second Decade after Brown v. Board of Education' (1974) 41 University of Chicago Law Review 742

Fitzhugh, N (ed), *Problems and Opportunities Confronting Negroes in the Field of Business* (National Conference on Small Business, 1961)

Flanagan, R J, 'Actual versus potential impact of government antidiscrimination programs' (1976) 29(4) Industrial and Labor Relations Review 486

Fleming, H C, 'The federal executive and civil rights: 1961–1965' (1965) 94 Daedalus 921

Fletcher, A, *The Silent Sell-Out: Government Betrayal of Blacks to the Craft Unions* (Third Press, 1974)

Forbath, W E, *Law and the Shaping of the American Labor Movement* (Harvard University Press, 1991)

Ford, D, 'Public-sector procurement and corporate social responsibility' in Brown, C S (ed), *The Sustainable Enterprise: Profiting from Best Practice* (Kogan Page, London, 2005) 49

Fox, T, Ward, H, and Howard, B, *Public Sector Roles in Strengthening Corporate Social Responsibility: A Baseline Study* (World Bank, 2002)

Francioni, F, 'An International Bill of Rights: Why it Matters, How it Can be Used' (1997) 32 Texas International Law Journal 471

Frazer, T, 'The New Structural Funds, State Aids and Interventions on the Single Market' (1995) 20 ELR 3

Fredman, S, 'Transformation or Dilution: Fundamental Rights in the EU Social Space' (2006) 12 European Law Journal 41

—— and Morris, G S, *The State as Employer* (Mansell, 1989)

Freedland, M, 'Government by Contract and Public Law' [1994] Public Law 86

Funston, J, 'Malaysia's Tenth Elections: Status Quo, Reformasi, or Islamization?' (2000) 22(1) Contemporary Southeast Asia 23

Gaedtke, J-C, *Politische Auftragsvergabe und Welthandelsrecht* (Duncker und Humblot, 2006)

Gaeta, L, and Zoppoli, L (eds), *Il Dritto Diseguale: Commento Alla Legge 10 Aprille 1991, N. 125* (G Appichelli Editore, 1992)

Gaines, S, 'Processes and Production Methods: How to Produce Sound Policy for Environmental PPM-Based Trade Measures?' (2002) 27 Col J Env L 383

Ganguly, S, 'Ethnic Policies and Political Quiescence in Malaysia and Singapore' in Brown, M E, and Ganguly, S (eds), *Government Policies and Ethnic Relations in Asia and the Pacific* (MIT Press, 1997) 234

Gantt, P H, and Speck, W H, 'Domestic v. Foreign Trade Problems in Federal Government Contracting: Buy American Act and Executive Order' (1958) 7 Journal of Public Law 378

Ganz, G, 'Comment' [1978] Public Law 333

Garcia, F J, 'Trading Away the Human Rights Principle' (1999) 25 Brooklyn Journal of International Law 51

Garfinkel, H, *When Negroes March* (The Free Press, 1959)

Garten, J E, 'Destination Unknown' 76(3) *Foreign Affairs*, May–June 1997, 67

Garvey, S P, 'Freeing Prisoners' Labor' (1998) 50 Stanford Law Review 339

GATT, 'Practical Guide to the GATT Agreement on Government Procurement' (revised edn, February 1989)

Geroski, P, 'Procurement Policy as a Tool of Industrial Policy' (1990) 4(2) International Review of Applied Economics 182

Giesen, R, 'Posting: Social protection of worker vs fundamental freedoms?' (2003) 40 CMLR 143

Gjnnes, A D, 'Proposed New Norwegian Legislation on the Award of Public Procurement Contracts' (1997) 6 PPLR CS189

Glazer, N, *Affirmative Discrimination: Ethnic Inequality, and Public Policy* (Basic Books, 1975)

Glossop, P, 'Recent US Trade Restrictions Affecting Cuba, Iran and Libya—a View from Outside the US' (1997) 15 Journal of Energy and National Resources Law 212

Goetz, A M, 'The Politics of Integrating Gender to State Development Processes' (Occasional Paper No 2, United Nations Research Institute for Social Development, May 1995)

Goldman, C, 'An Introduction to the French Law of Government Procurement Contracts' (1987) 20 GW JILE 461

Goldstein, E, 'Doing Business Under the Agreement on Government Procurement: The Telecommunications Business—a Case in Point' (1980) 55 St. John's Law Review 63

Goldstein, M, and Smith, R S, 'The Estimated Impact of the Antidiscrimination Program Aimed at Federal Contractors' (1976) 29(4) Industrial and Labor Relations Review 523

Gomez, E T, *Political Business: Corporate Involvement of Malaysian Political Parties* (Centre for South-east Asian Studies, James Cook University of North Queensland, 1994)

—— 'Capital Development in Malaysia' in Yahaya, J *et al* (eds), *Sustaining Growth, Enhancing Distribution: The NEP and NDP Revisited* (Proceedings of CEDER Conference, 2003) 71

—— and Jomo, K S, *Malaysia's Political Economy* (Cambridge University Press, 1999)

Gounden, S, *The Impact of the National Department of Public Works's Affirmative Procurement Policy on the Participation and Growth of Affirmable Business Entrerprises in the Construction Sector* (PhD thesis, 2000), available at <http://www.targetedprocurement.co.za/papers/SG/SGpapers.html>

Grandi, M, and Pera, G (eds), *Commentario Breve Acco Statuto Dei Lavoratori* (CEDAM, 1985)

Gray, K R, 'The Nunavut Land Claims Agreement and the Future of the Eastern Arctic: The Uncharted Path to Effective Self-Government' (1994) 52 University of Toronto Faculty of Law Review 300

Greater London Council, 'Ethnic Minority/Contract Compliance Conference Report' (May 1984)

—— Contract Compliance Equal Opportunities Unit, 'Contracting for Equality: First Annual Report of the GLC-ILEA Contract Compliance Equal Opportunities Unit' (1985–86)

—— Contract Compliance Equal Opportunities Unit, 'The ILEA/GLC is one of the largest equal opportunities employers . . . but that's not enough . . . ' (nd)

—— Contract Compliance Equal Opportunities Unit, 'Contract Compliance and Trade Unions' (nd)

Greenwold, S, and Cox, A, 'The Legal and Structural Obstacles to Free Trade in the United States Procurement Market' (1993) 2 PPLR 237

Grier, J H, 'Recent Developments in International Trade Agreements Covering Government Procurement' (2006) 35 Public Contract Law Journal 385

Griesgraber, J M, and Gunter, B G, *The World Bank: Lending on a Global Scale* (Pluto, 1996)

Griller, S, 'International economic law as a means to further human rights?: selective purchasing under the WTO Agreement on Government Procurement' in Griller, S (ed), *International Economic Governance and Non-economic Concerns: New Challenges for the International Legal Order* (Springer, 2003) 267

Grossman, D A, 'Voluntary Affirmative Action Plans in Italy and the United States: Differing Notions of Gender Equality' (1993) 14 Comparative Labor Law Journal 1885

Gunderson, M, 'Male-Female Wage Differentials and Policy Responses' (1989) XXVII Journal of Economic Literature 46

Gurlit, E, 'Vergabe öffentlicher Aufträge als Instrument der Frauenförderung' in Koreuber, M, and Mager, U (eds), *Recht und Geschlecht* (Nomos Verlagsgesellschaft, 2004) 153

Haas, P M, 'Introduction, Epistemic Communities and International Policy Coordination' (1992) 46 International Organization 1

Haass, R (ed), *Economic Sanctions and American Diplomacy* (Council on Foreign Relations, 1998)

Hafner-Burton, E, and Pollack, M A, 'Mainstreaming Gender in Global Governance' (2002) 8(3) European Journal of International Relations 339

Halford, A, 'An Overview of E.C.-United States Trade Relations in the Area of Public Procurement' (1995) 4 PPLR 36

Hamann, R, 'Mining companies' role in sustainable development: the "why" and "how" of corporate social responsibility from a business perspective' (2003) 20(6) Development Southern Africa 237

Hanley, C, 'Avoiding the Issue: The Commission and Human Rights Conditionality in Public Procurement' (2002) 27(6) ELR 714

Hannah, P F, 'Government by Procurement' *The Business Lawyer*, July 1963, 997

Hanrahan, J D, *Government by Contract* (Norton, 1983)

Harden, I, *The Contracting State* (Open University Press, 1992)

Harding, A, *Law, Government and the Constitution in Malaysia* (Brill Academic, 1996)

Haringey SME Procurement Pilot: Community Benefit Clauses in Tenders and Contracts, 5 April 2005

Harlow, C, and Craig, P (eds), *Lawmaking in the European Union* (Aspen, 1998)

Hart, M, *Decision at Midnight: Inside the Canada-US Free-Trade Negotiations* (UBC Press, 1994)

Harvey, J C, *Civil Rights During the Kennedy Administration* (University and College Press of Mississippi, 1971)

Hay, C, and Marsh, D (eds), *Demystifying Globalization* (Macmillan, 2000)

Heath, A, 'Ethnic Minorities in the Labour Market', Report to the PIU (Cabinet Office, October 2001)

Heckman, J J, and Wolpin, K I, 'Does the Contract Compliance Program Work? An analysis of the Chicago Data' (1976) 29(4) Industrial and Labor Relations Review 544

—— and Payner, B S, 'Determining the Impact of Federal Antidiscrimination Policy on the Economic Status of Blacks: A Study of South Carolina' (1989) 79(1) American Economic Review 138

Hellman, J S, *et al*, 'Measuring Governance Corruption, and State Capture: How Firms and Bureaucrats Shape the Business Environment in Transition Economies' (EBRD and the World Bank: Policy Research Working Paper 2312 date), available at <http://www.worldbank.org/wbi/governance/pdf/measure.pdf>

Hemphill, T A, 'The White House Apparel Industry Partnership Agreement: Will Self Regulation Be Successful? (1999) 104(2) Business and Society Review 121

Henkin, L, *Foreign Affairs and the United States Constitution* (2nd edn, OUP, 2002)

Hepple, B, *Race, Jobs and the Law in Britain* (2nd edn, Penguin, 1970)

—— (ed), *The Making of Labour Law in Europe: A Comparative Study of Nine Countries up to 1945* (Mansell, 1986)

—— *European Social Dialogue* (Institute of Employment Rights, 1993)

—— *Labour Laws and Global Trade* (Hart, 2005)

—— and Szyszczak, E M, *Discrimination: the Limits of Law* (Mansell, 1992)

—— Coussey, M, and Choudhury, T, *Equality: A New Framework: Report of the Independent Review of the Enforcement of UK Anti-Discrimination Legislation* (Hart, 2000)

Hernandez, R C, 'Harminization [sic] of Procurement Policies and Practices of Public International Financial Institutions' (Presentation made at the High Level Forum on Harmonization, Rome, 24–25 February, 2003)

Herrmann, K K, 'Corporate Social Responsibility and Sustainable Development: The European Union Initiative as a Case Study' (2004) 11(2) Indiana Journal of Global Legal Studies 205

Hickling, R H, 'An Overview of Constitutional Changes in Malaysia: 1957–1977' in Suffian, T M, Lee, H P, and Trindade, F A (eds), *The Constitution of Malaysia: Its Development: 1957–1977* (OUP, 1978) 23

Higbee, J A, *Development and Administration of the New York Law against Discrimination* (University of Alabama Press, 1966)

Hill, H, 'Labor union control of job training: A critical analysis of apprenticeship outreach programs and the hometown plans' (Occasional paper—Institute for Urban Research, Howard University; Vol 2, No 1)

—— *Racism and Organized Labor* (NAACP, 1971)

Hjelmborg, S E, Jakobsen, P S, and Poulsen, S T, *Public Procurement Law: the EU directive on public contracts* (DJØF Publishing, 2006)

Hoekmann, B M, and Mavroidis, P C, 'The WTO's Agreement on Government Procurement: Expanding Disciplines, Declining Membership?' (1995) 4 PPLR 63

—— and —— (eds), *Law and Policy in Public Purchasing: The WTO Agreement on Government Procurement* (Studies in International Trade Policy, University of Michigan Press, 1997)

Hogan, G, and Morgan, D, *Administrative Law in Ireland* (2nd edn, Sweet & Maxwell, 1991)

Holzer, H J, and Neumark, D, 'Assessing Affirmative Action' (NBER Working Paper No W7323August 1999)

—— and —— 'What Does Affirmative Action Do?' *Industrial and Labor Relations Review*, January 2000

—— and ——, 'Equal Employment Opportunity and Affirmative Action' (Public Policy Institute of California Working Paper No 2002–07, December 2002)

Horowitz, D, *Ethnic Groups in Conflict* (University of California Press, 1985)

Horsch, R A, 'Eliminating Nontariff Barriers to International Trade: The MTN Agreement on Government Procurement' (1979) 12 New York Journal of International Law and Politics 315

Howenstein, E J, 'Contemporary Public Works Policy: An International Comparison of its Role in Economic Stabilization and Growth', OECD Archives, OECD 166, MS/S/65.214, 1965)

Howse, R, 'The World Trade Organisation and the Protection of Workers' Rights' (1999) 3 Journal of Small and Emerging Business Law 131

—— 'Human Rights in the WTO: Whose Rights, What Humanity? Comment on Petersmann' (2002) 13 EJIL 651

—— 'The Appellate Body Rulings in the Shrimp/Turtle Case: A New Legal Baseline for the Trade and Environment Debate' (2002) 27 Col J Env L 491

—— and Regan, D, 'The Product/Process Distinction—An Illusory Basis for Disciplining "Unilateralism" in Trade Policy' (2000) 11 EJIL 249

—— and Langille, B, with Burda, J, 'The World Trade Organization and Labour Rights: Man Bites Dog' in Leary, V A and Warner, D (eds), *Social Issues, Globalisation and International Institutions: Labour Rights and the EU, ILO, OECD and WTO* (Brill Academic, 2005) 157

Hudec, R, 'The Product-Process Distinction in GATT/WTO Jurisprudence' in Bronckers, M, and Quick, R (eds), *New Directions in International Economic Law: Essays in Honour of John H. Jackson* (Springer, 2000) 187

Hufbauer, G C, Elliott, K A, Cyrus, T, and Winston, E, 'US Economic Sanctions: Their Impact on Trade, Jobs, and Wages' (Working Paper, Institute for International Economics, 1997).

Human Rights and Equal Opportunity Commission, 'People with Disability in the Open Workplace: Final Report of the National Inquiry into Employment and Disability' (December, 2005)

Husserl, G, 'Public Policy and Ordre Public' (1938) 25 *Virginia* Law Review 27

Huthmacher, J J, *Senator Robert F Wagner and the Rise of Urban Liberalism* (Atheneum, 1968)

Hutson, N, 'Policy Appraisal and Fair Treatment in Northern Ireland: A Contribution to the Debate on Mainstreaming Equality' (SACHR Discussion Paper, November 1996)

Ignatieff, M, 'Human Rights as Idolatry' in Ignatieff, M, (Gutman, A (ed)), *Human Rights as Politics and Idolatry* (Princeton University Press, 2003) 53

Industrial Relations Review and Report, 'Contract compliance and equal opportunities' (1986) 381 Industrial Relations Review and Report 2

Institute of Personnel Management, *Contract Compliance: the U.K. Experience* (IPM, London, October 1987)

International Labour Conference, 19th Session, Report VI (Vol 1): Reduction of Hours of Work (ILO, 1935)

—— 31st Session, Report VI (b)(1): Wages: (b) Fair Wages Clauses in Public Contracts (ILO, 1947)

—— 31st Session, Wages: (b) Fair Wages Clauses in Public Contracts, Reports: VI(b)(1) and (2) and Supplement (ILO, 1948)

—— 72nd Session 1986, Equal Remuneration: General Survey by the Committee of Experts on the Application of Conventions and Recommendations (ILO, 1986)

—— 75th Session 1988, Equality in Employment and Occupation: General Survey by the Committee of Experts on the Application of Conventions and Recommendations (ILO, 1988)

International Labour Office, 'Public Works Policy' (Studies and reports, Series C No 19, ILO, 1935).

—— 'Report of the Director-General, Time for Equality at Work: Global Report under the Follow-up to the ILO Declaration on Fundamental Principles and Rights at Work' (International Labour Conference, 91st Session 2003, Report I(B) (ILO, 2003)

—— 'Unemployment and Public Works' (Studies and reports, Series C, No 15, ILO, 1931)

International Labour Organisation, 'Report of the Committee of Experts on the Application of Conventions and Recommendations' (ILO, Geneva, 1957)

—— 'The ILO, Standard Setting and Globalisation: Report of the Director-General (1997)', International Labour Conference, 85th Session (ILO, 1997) available at <http://www. ilo.org/public/english/10ilc/ilc85/dg-rep.htm>

—— 'Declaration on Fundamental Principles and Rights at Work' (ILO, 1998), International Labour Conference, 86th Session, available on the ILO website at <http://www .ilo.org/public/english/10ilc/8lc86/com-dtxt.htm>

—— 'Forced Labour in Myanmar (Burma): Report of the Commission of Inquiry appointed under article 26 of the Constitution of the International Labour Organisation to examine the observance by Myanmar of the Forced Labour Convention, 1930 (No. 29)' (ILO, 1998)

—— 'Report of the Director General to the ILO Conference in 2001' (ILO, 2001), available at <http://www.ilo.org/public/english/standards/relm/ilc/ilc89/pdf/rep-i-a.pdf>

Investor Research Responsibility Center, 'State and Local Selective Purchasing Laws As of September 1997' (IRRC, 1997)

—— 'US Business in Burma (Myanmar), Social Issues Service, 1998 Background Report E:2' (IRRC, 1998)

Jackson, J H, *The World Trading System: Law and Policy of International Economic Relations* (2nd edn, MIT Press, 1997)

Jackson, J, 'The Limits of International Trade: Workers' Protection, the Environment and Other Human Rights' (2000) 94 American Society of International Law Proceedings 222

Jain, M P, 'Administrative Law in Malaysia', in Hooker, M B (ed), *Malaysian Legal Essays* (Malayan Law Journal,1986) 213

—— *Administrative Law of Malaysia and Singapore* (Butterworths Asia, 1997)

Janik, M T, 'A US Perspective on the GATT Agreement on Government Procurement' (1987) 20(3) GW JILE 491

Jayasankaran, S, 'The New Way: Thinking Small', *Far Eastern Economic Review*, 6 November 2003, 14

—— 'Tycoons in Trouble', *Far Eastern Economic Review*, 15 January 2004, 50

Jayasuriya, K, 'Governance, Post-Washington Consensus and the New Anti-Politics' in Lindsey, T, and Dick, H (eds), *Corruption in Asia: Rethinking the Governance Paradigm* (Federation Press, 2002) 24

Jeanrenaud, C, 'Marchés publics et politique économique' in Jeanrenaud, C (ed), *Regional Impact of Public Procurement* (Saint-Saphorin, 1984) 151

Johnson, R A, 'Affirmative Action Policy in the United States: its impact on women' (1990) 18(2) Policy and Politics 77

Jones, M L, 'The GATT-MTN System and the European Community as International Frameworks for the Regulation of Economic Activity: The Removal of Barriers to Trade in Government Procurement' (1984) 8 Maryland Journal of International Law and Trade 53

Jørgensen, H B, and Jørgensen, P M P, Jungk, M, Cramer, A, *Strengthening Implementation of Corporate Social Responsibility in Global Supply Chains* (World Bank, IFC, October 2003)

Kalev, A and Johnson, R W, *Enforcement of Civil Rights Law in Private Workplaces: The Effects of Compliance Reviews and Lawsuits Over Time* (December 2005) available at <http://www.wjh.harvard.edu/~dobbin/cv/working_papers/eeopractice2.pdf>

Kaul, I, Grunberg, I, and Stern, M, *Global Public Goods: International Cooperation in the 21st Century* (OUP, 1999)

Keeping, J M, *The Inuvialuit Final Agreement* (Canadian Institute of Resources Law, October 1989)

Kellerson, H, 'The ILO Declaration of 1998 on Fundamental Principles and Rights: A Challenge for the Future' (1998) 137 International Labour Review 223

Kelly, M, 'Early Federal Regulation of Hours of Labor in the United States' (1950) 3 Industrial and Labor Relations Review 362

Kenan Institute, 'Promoting Global Corporate Social Responsibility: The Kenan Institute Study Group Consensus' (Kenan Institute, September 2003)

Kennedy, D M, *Freedom from Fear: the American People in Depression and War, 1929–1945* (OUP, 2001)

Kenner, J, *EU Employment Law: From Rome to Amsterdam and Beyond* (Hart, 2003)

Kersten, A E, *Race, Jobs, and the War: The FEPC in the Midwest 1941–1946* (University of Illinois Press, 2000)

Kesselman, L, *Social Politics of FEPC* (University of North Carolina Press, 1948)

Kessler, H H, *The Crippled and the Disabled: Rehabilitation of the Physically Handicapped in the United States* (Columbia University Press, 1935)

Khor, M, 'WTO "Singapore Issues": What's at Stake and Why it Matters' in TWN, *Briefings for Cancun*, No 3, available at <http://www.twnside.org.sg>

Kingsmill, D, 'Report on Women's Employment and Pay' (2001)

Klein, J M, *International Codes and Multinational Business: setting guidelines for international operations* (Quorum Books, 1985)

Kletz, P, and Pesqueux, Y, 'Globalization: Towards a Cross-National Model of Corporate Social Responsibility' in Allouche, J (ed), *Corporate Social Responsibility, volume 1* (Palgrave Macmillan, 2006) 99

Kling, M, *Die Zulässigkeit vergabefremder Regelungen* (Schriffenreihe des Forum Vergabe, 2000)

Kluger, R, *Simple Justice: The History of Brown v. Board of Education and Black America's Struggle for Equality* (Alfred A Knopf, 1976)

Knapp, U, 'Betriebliche Frauenförderpläne und Strukturpolitik', WSI Mitteilungen 11/1990, p 738

Kolehmainen, E, 'The Directive Concerning the Posting of Workers: Synchronization of the Functions of National Legal Systems' (1998) 20 Comparative Labor Law and Policy Journal 71

Koreuber, M, and Mager, U (eds), *Recht und Geschlecht* (Nomos Verlagsgesellschaft, 2004)

Krueger, A O, 'Observations on International Labour Standards and Trade' (National Bureau of Economic Research Working Paper 5632, 1996)

—— (ed), *The WTO as an International Organisation* (University of Chicago Press, 1998) 213

Krüger, K, Nielsen, R, and Bruun, N, *European Public Contracts in a Labour Law Perspective* (DJØF Publishing, 1998)

Krügner, M, 'The Principles of Equal Treatment and Transparency and the Commission Interpretative Communication on Concessions' (2003) 12 PPLR 181

Kulacoglu, V, 'An Overview of Developments within the WTO Since the Singapore Ministerial Conference' (Paper delivered to the Conference 'Public Procurement: Global Revolution', University of Wales, Aberystwth, 11–12 September 1997)

Kullmann, U, ' "Fair Labour Standards" in International Commodity Agreements' (1980) JWTL 527

Kunzlik, P, 'Environmental Issues in Public Procurement' in Arrowsmith, S, and Davies, A (eds), *Public Procurement: Global Revolution* (Kluwer Law International, 1998)

—— 'International Procurement Regimes and the Scope for the Inclusion of Environmental Factors in Public Procurement' (2003) 3(4) OECD Journal on Budgeting 107

—— ' "Green Procurement" Under the New Regime' in Nielsen, R, and Treumer, S (eds), *The New EU Public Procurement Directives* (DJØF Publishing, 2005) 117

—— 'The Procurement of "Green" Energy' in Arrowsmith, S, and Kunzlik, P (eds), *Social and Environmental Policies under the EC Procurement Rules: New Directives and New Directions* (provisional title) (Cambridge University Press, in press)

Kyloh, R, 'The Governance of Globalisation: ILO's Contribution' in Kyloh, R (ed), *Mastering the Challenge of Globalisation: Towards a Trade Union Agenda* (ILO, 1998)

La Noue, G, 'Split Visions: Minority Set-Asides' in Orlans, H, and O'Neill, J (eds), 'Affirmative Action Revisited' (1992) 523 Annals of the American Academy of Political and Social Science 104

Ladbury, S, Cotton, A P, and Jennings M, *Implementing labour standards in construction: A sourcebook* (Water Engineering Development Centre (WEDC), Loughborough University, 2003)

Laffont, J-J, and Tirole, J, *A Theory of Incentives in Procurement and Regulation* (MIT Press, 1993)

Laing, E A, 'Equal Access/Non-Discrimination and Legitimate Discrimination in International Economic Law' (1996) 14 Wisconsin International Law Journal 246

Lamarche, L *et al*, *Retaining Employment Equity Measures in Trade Agreements* (Status of Women Canada, February 2005)

Lamm, C, 'Vergaberecht in Deutschland' (1992) 2(3) Europäisches Vergaberecht 90

Landelijk Bureau Racismebestrijding, 'Positieve Actie Bedingen: Contract compliance in Nederland' (Landelijk Bureau Racismebestrijding, 1989)

Langille, B A, 'Eight Ways to Think about International Labour Standards' (1997) 31 Journal of World Trade 27

—— 'Globalization and the Just Society—Core Labour Rights, the FTAA, and Development' in Craig, J D R, and Lynk, S M (eds), *Globalization and the Future of Labour Law* (Cambridge University Press, 2006) 278

Laurence, S, 'Moderates, Municipal Reformers, and the Issue of Tariff Reform 1894–1934' in Saint, A (ed), *Politics and the People of London: The London County Council 1889–1965* (Hambledon Press, 2003) 94

Lawrence, R, 'Defenders of Smaller US Firms Force Strauss to Amend Negotiating Plans on Procurement Practices Code', *Journal of Commerce*, 29 March 1979, 171

Leary, V A, 'The Paradox of Workers' Rights as Human Rights' in Compa, L A, and Diamond, S F (eds), *Human Rights, Labour Rights, and International Trade* (University of Pennsylvania Press, 1996)

—— 'Workers' Rights and International Trade: The Social Clause (GATT, ILO, NAFTA, U.S. Laws' in Bhagwati, J, and Hudec, R (eds), *Fair Trade and Harmonization* (MIT Press 1996) 177

—— and Warner, D (eds), *Social Issues, Globalisation and International Institutions: Labour Rights and the EU, ILO, OECD and WTO* (Brill Academic, 2005)

Leck, J D, and Saunders, D M, 'Hiring Women: The Effects of Canada's Employment Equity Act' (1992) XVIII(2) Canadian Public Policy 203

Lee, E, 'Globalisation and Employment: Is the Anxiety Justified?' (1996) 135 International Labour Review 485

Leebron, D W, 'Linkages' (2002) 96 AJIL 5

Lefebvre, M-C, 'Evaluation of Women's Involvement in European Social Fund Cofinanced Measures in 1990' *Social Europe*, Supplement 2/93

Leimkuhler, W F, 'Enforcing Social and Economic Policy Through Government Contracts' [1980] *Annual Survey of American Law* 539

Leitman, M, 'A Federal Contract Compliance Program for Equal Employment Opportunities' in *Equality in Employment: A Royal Commission Report: Research Studies* (Canada Supply and Services, 1985) 183

Lelyveld, M S, 'Weld letter a new wrinkle on EU-Massachusetts spat' *Journal of Commerce*, 13 March 1997

—— 'Anti-sanctions Forces Win Key Vote' *Journal of Commerce*, 7 August 1998

Lemke, M, 'The Experience of Centralized Enforcement in Poland' in Arrowsmith, S, and Trybus, M (eds), *Public Procurement: The Continuing Revolution* (Kluwer, 2003) 108

Lensihow, A, 'New Regulatory Approaches to "Greening" EU Policies' (2002) 8(1) European Law Journal 19

Leonard, J S, 'Antidiscrimination or Reverse Discrimination: The Impact of Changing Demographics, Title VII and Affirmative Action on Productivity' (1984) XIX(2) Journal of Human Resources 145

—— 'The Impact of Affirmative Action on Employment' (1984) 2(4) Journal of Labor Economics 439

—— 'Women and Affirmative Action' (1989) 3(1) Journal of Economic Perspectives 61

—— 'The Impact of Affirmative Action Regulation and Equal Employment Law on Black Employment' (1990) 4(4) Journal of Economic Perspectives 47

Letchmiah, D, 'The Process of Public Sector Procurement Reform in South Africa' (1999) 8 PPLR 15

Levin-Waldman, O M, *Political Economy of the Living Wage: A Study of Four Cities* (ME Sharpe, 2004)

Levy, R A, 'An Equal Protection Analysis of the Davis-Bacon Act' (1995) Detroit College of Law Review 973

Likosky, M, *Infrastructures* (Cambridge University Press, 2006)

Linarelli, J, 'The WTO Transparency Agenda: Law, Economics and International Relations Theory' in Arrowsmith, S, and Trybus M (eds), *Public Procurement: The Continuing Revolution* (Kluwer, 2003) 256

Local Authorities Race Relations Information Exchange, 'Race Equality and the Contracting Process: Larrie Survey' (Larrie, June 1995)

Local Government Management Board, 'Equalities and the Contract Culture' (Local Government Management Board, 1995)

Lodge, T, 'Political Corruption in South Africa' (1998) 97 African Affairs 157

Loew, T, Ankele, K, Braun, S, and Clausen, J, *Significance of the CSR debate for sustainability and the requirements for companies* (Eigenverlag, 2004)

Loquet, P, 'L'utilisation de la clause du mieux-disant social dans les marchés publics: une simple affaire de volonté politique et d'ingénierie sociale' (1999) 9(10) Droit Social 759

Low, M, Matton, A, and Subramanian, A, 'Government Procurement in Services' (1996) 20 World Competition 5

MacFarlane, R, and Cook, M, *Achieving community benefits through procurement* (Joseph Rowntree Foundation, 2002)

Macklem, P, 'The Right to Bargain Collectively in International Law: Workers' Right, Human Right, International Right?' in Alston, P (ed), *Labour Rights as Human Rights* (OUP, 2005) 61

Macleod, S, and Lewis, D, 'Transnational Corporations: Power, Influence and Responsibility' (2004) 4(1) Global Social Policy 77

Macmorran, J L, *Municipal Public Works and Planning in Birmingham* (City of Birmingham Public Works Committee, 1973)

Macneil, I, 'Contracts: adjustment of long-term economic relations under classical, neoclassical and relational contract law' (1978) 72(6) Northwestern University Law Review 854

Madi, P M, *Black Economic Empowerment in the New South Africa: The Rights and the Wrongs* (Knowledge Resources, 1997)

Mahathir, M, *The Way Forward: Growth, Prosperity and Multiracial Harmony in Malaysia* (Weidenfeld and Nicolson, 1998)

Maindrault, M, 'Les aspects commerciaux des droits sociaux et des droits de l'homme au travail' (1994) 11 Droit Social 850

Malbon, J, 'The Australian-United States Free Trade Agreement: Trade Trumps Indigenous Interests' (2004) 111 Media International Australia (incorporating *Culture and Policy*) 34

Manchidi, T E, and Hammond, I, *Targeted Procurement in the Republic of South Africa: An Independent Assessment* (ILO, 2002)

Mandel, H, 'Note: In Pursuit of the Missing Link: International Worker Rights and International Trade' (1989) 27 Col JTL 443

Manpower Services Commission, 'Sheltered Employment Procurement and Consultancy Service', *Priority Suppliers Directory* (Summer 1984)

Marceau, G, 'WTO Dispute Settlement and Human Rights' (2002) 13(4) EJIL 753

Marecic, C J, 'Nunavut Territory: Aboriginal Governing in the Canadian Regime of Governance' (1999–2000) 24 American Indian Law Review 275

Marks, K, 'Judicial Independence' (1994) 68 Australian Law Journal 173

Marleau, V, 'Globalization, Decentralization and the Role of Subsidiarity in the Labour Setting' in Craig, J D R, and Lynk, S M (eds), *Globalization and the Future of Labour Law* (Cambridge University Press, 2006) 108

Marron, D B, 'Buying Green: Government Procurement as an Instrument of Environmental Policy' (1997) 25(3) Public Finance Review 285

Mastny, L, 'Purchasing Power: Harnessing Institutional Procurement for People and the Planet' (Worldwatch Paper 166, July 2003)

Matten, D, and Moon, J, '"Implicit" and "Explicit" CSR: A conceptual framework for understanding CSR in Europe' (No 29-2004 ICCSR Research Paper Series, 2004)

Mattoo, A, and Mavroidis, P C, 'Trade, Environment and the WTO: The Dispute Settlement Practice Relating to Article XX of GATT' in Petersmann, E-U (ed), *International Trade Law and the GATT/WTO Dispute Settlement System* (Kluwer, 1997)

Manupain, F, 'The Settlement of Disputes within the International Labour Office' (1999) 2 JIEL 273

—— 'Is the ILO effective in Upholding Workers' Rights? Reflections on the Myanmar Experience' in Alston, P (ed), *Labour Rights as Human Rights* (OUP, 2005)

Maxwell, R, 'Public Sector Purchasing: an economic weapon that the government must organise itself to use in pursuit of national industrial objectives' (A report to the Economic Group of the Parliamentary Labour Party, 1967)

Mayhew, L H, *Law and Equal Opportunity: A Study of the Massachusetts Commission against Discrimination* (Harvard University Press, 1968)

Mbabane, L M, 'Preferential Procurement in South Africa's Black Economic Empowerment Policy and its prospects for combating discrimination and reducing economic inequalities' (Working Paper prepared for the fourth session of the ILO workshop on equality, 'Public Procurements—How effective are they in combating discrimination?', ILO, Geneva, 23–24 May 2006)

McBarnett, D, 'Corporate Social Responsibility: Beyond Law, Through Law, For Law' in McBarnett, D, Voiculescu, D A, and Campbell, T (eds), *The New Corporate Responsibility and the Law* (Cambridge University Press, in press)

—— Voiculescu, D A, and Campbell, T (eds), *The New Corporate Responsibility and the Law* (Cambridge University Press, in press)

—— and Whelan, C, 'Challenging the Regulators: Strategies for Restricting Control', in McCrudden, C, *Regulation and Deregulation* (OUP, 1999) 67

McBeth, A, 'A Look at Corporate Code of Conduct Legislation' (2004) 33(3) Common Law World Review 222

McChesney, F S, *Money for Nothing: Politicians, Rent Extraction, and Political Extortion* (Harvard University Press, 1997)

McCorquodale, R, 'Women, development and corporate responsibility' in Rees, S, and Wright, S, *Human Rights, Corporate Responsibility: A Dialogue* (Pluto Press, 2000) 174

—— with Fairbrother, R, 'Globalization and Human Rights' (1999) 21 Human Rights Quarterly 735

McCourt, K, 'The New Edition of the "Green Book" Guide to Public Procurement in Ireland' (1994) 3 PPLR CS185

McCrudden, C, 'Law Enforcement by Regulatory Agency: the Case of Employment Discrimination in Northern Ireland' (1982) 45 MLR 617

——— 'The Commission for Racial Equality: Formal Investigations in the Shadow of Judicial Review' in Baldwin, R, and McCrudden, C (eds), *Regulation and Public Law* (Weidenfeld, 1987)

——— (ed), *Women, Employment and European Equality Law* (Eclipse, 1987)

——— 'The Fair Employment Bill in Parliament' in Hayes, J, and O'Higgins, P (eds), *Lessons from Northern Ireland* (SLS, 1991)

——— *Anti-Discrimination Law* (Ashgate, 1st edn, 1991; 2nd edn, 2004)

——— 'Affirmative Action and Fair Participation: Interpreting the Fair Employment Act 1989' (1992) ILJ 170

——— 'The Effectiveness of European Equality Law' (1993) 13 OJLS 320

——— *Equality in Law between Men and Women in the European Community: United Kingdom* (Martinus Nijhoff Publishers and Office for Official Publications of the European Communities, 1994)

——— 'Public Procurement and Equal Opportunities in the EC: a study of "contract compliance" in the Member States of the European Community and under European Community Law' (unpublished report for the European Commission, 1989)

——— 'The Constitutionality of Affirmative Action in the United States: A Note on Adarand Constructors Inc. v Pena' (1996) 1 International Journal of Discrimination and the Law 369

——— 'Mainstreaming Fairness? A discussion paper on "Policy Appraisal and Fair Treatment"' (CAJ, November 1996)

——— (ed), *Regulation and Deregulation: Policy and Practice* (OUP, 1998)

——— 'Merit Principles' (1998) 18 OJLS 543

——— 'Social Policy Issues in Public Procurement: A Legal Overview' in Arrowsmith, S, and Davies, A (eds), *Public Procurement: Global Revolution* (Kluwer Law International, 1998)

——— 'Benchmarks for Change: Mainstreaming Fairness in the Governance of Northern Ireland' (CAJ, 1998)

——— 'Social Policy and Economic Regulators: Some Issues for the Reform of Utility Regulation' in McCrudden, C (ed), *Regulation and Deregulation: Policy and Practice* (OUP, 1999) 275

——— 'Advice to a legislator on problems regarding the enforcement of anti-discrimination law and strategies to overcome them' in Loenen, T, and Rodrigues, P (eds), *Non-discrimination law: comparative perspectives* (Kluwer Law International, 1999) 295

——— 'Human Rights Codes for Transnational Corporations: What Can the Sullivan and MacBride Principles Tell Us?' (1999) 19 OJLS 167

——— 'International Economic Law and the Pursuit of Human Rights: A Framework for Discussion of the Legality of "Selective Purchasing" Laws under the WTO Government Procurement Agreement' (1999) 2(1) JIEL 3

——— 'Mainstreaming Equality in the Governance of Northern Ireland' (1999) 22 Fordham International Law Journal 1696

——— 'National Remedies for Racial Discrimination in European and International Law' in Fredman, S (ed), *Discrimination and Human Rights* (OUP, 2001) 251

McCrudden, C, 'Theorising European Equality Law' in Costello, C, and Barry, E (eds), *Equality in Diversity* (Irish Centre for European Law, 2003) 1

—— 'Using Public Procurement to Achieve Social Outcomes' (2004) 28 Natural Resources Forum 257

—— 'Equality and Non-Discrimination' in Feldman, D (ed), *English Public Law* (OUP 2004)

—— 'Property Rights and Labour Rights Revisited: International Investment Agreements and the "Social Clause" Debate' in Irish, M (ed), *The Auto Pact: Investment, Labour and the WTO* (Kluwer, 2004) 300

—— 'Integration of Social Policy into Sustainable Public Procurement: A Study for the United Nations, Department of Economic and Social Affairs' (unpublished, 2004)

—— 'Public Procurement: How effective is it in combating discrimination?' (May 2006, background paper prepared for the ILO workshop on equality, ILO, Geneva, 23–24 May 2006)

—— 'Buying Social Justice: Equality and Procurement' [2007] Current Legal Problems (in press)

—— 'Corporate Social Responsibility and Public Procurement' in McBarnet, D, Voiculescu, V, and Campbell, T (eds), *The New Corporate Accountability: Corporate Social Responsibility and the Law* (Cambridge University Press, in press)

—— 'EC Public Procurement Law and Equality Linkages: Foundations for Interpretation' in Arrowsmith, S, and Kunzlik, P (eds), *Social and Environmental Policies under the EC Procurement Rules: New Directives and New Directions* (provisional title) (Cambridge University Press, in press)

—— Smith, D J, and Brown, C, 'Groups versus Individuals: the Ambiguity behind the Race Relations Act' (1991) 12 Policy Studies

——, —— and ——, *Racial Justice at Work: The Enforcement of the Race Relations Act 1976 in Employment* (PSI, 1991) 26

—— and Black, J, 'Achieving Equality between Men and Women in Social Security: Some Issues of Costs and Problems of Implementation' in McCrudden, C (ed), *Equality Between Women and Men in Social Security* (Butterworths, 1994), 215

—— and Davies, A, 'A Perspective on Trade and Labour Rights' (2000) 3(1) JIEL 43

—— and Gross, S, 'WTO Government Procurement Rules and the Local Dynamics of Procurement Policies: A Malaysian Case Study' (2006) 17 EJIL 151

—— and Kountouros, H, 'Human Rights and European Equality Law' in Meenan, H (ed), *Equality Law for an Enlarged Europe: Towards a Greater Understanding of the Article 13 Directives* (Cambridge University Press, in press)

McGrew, A, 'The Globalization Debate: Putting the Advanced Capitalist State in Its Place' (1998) 12(3) Global Society 299

McLaughlin, E and Quirk, P, *Policy Aspects of Employment Equality in Northern Ireland* (SACHR, 1996)

Medjad, K, 'In Search of the "Hard Law": Judicial Activism and International Corporate Social Responsibility' in Allouche, J (ed), *Corporate Social Responsibility: Volume 1: Concept, Accountability and Reporting* (Palgrave Macmillan, 2006) 181

Mehmet, O, Mendes, E, and Sinding, R, *Towards a Fair Global Labour Market: Avoiding a New Slave Trade* (Routledge, 1999)

Meireles, M de C, *The World Bank Procurement Regulations: A Critical Analysis of the Enforcement Mechanism and of the Application of Secondary Policies in Financial Projects* (PhD thesis, University of Nottingham, 2006)

Menzel, H-J, 'Berücksichtigung sozialpolitischer Kriterien bei der öffentlichen auftragsvergabe' (1981) 6 Der Betrieb (DB) 303

Messerlin, P A, 'Agreement on Public Procurement' in OECD, *The New World Trading System: Readings* (OECD, 1995) 65

Michel, A, 'Positive action for the benefit of women: preliminary study' (Doc EG (86) 1, Council of Europe, 1986)

Miller, A S, 'Government Contracts and Social Control: A Preliminary Inquiry' (1955) 41 Virginia Law Review 27

Montgomery, D, *Beyond Equality: Labor and the Radical Republicans 1862–1872* (Alfred A Knopf, 1967)

Moon, J, 'Government as a Driver of Corporate Social Responsibility' (ICCSR Research Paper Series, No 20-2004, 2004)

Moorman, Y, 'Integration of Core ILO Labor Standards into the WTO' (2001) 39 Col JTL 555

More, G, 'The Principle of Equal Treatment: From Market Unifier to Fundamental Right?' in Craig, P, and de Búrca, G (eds), *The Evolution of EU Law* (OUP, 1999) 517

Morgan, J, and Niessen, J, 'Immigrant and Minority Businesses: Making the Policy Case' (2003) 4 European Journal of Migration and Law 329

Morris, P E, 'Legal Regulation of Contract Compliance: An Anglo-American Comparison' (1990) 19 Anglo-American Law Review 87

Moses, W F, *A Guide to American State and Local Laws on South Africa* (IRRC, 1993)

Muggenberg, C, 'The Government Procurement Chapter of NAFTA' (1993) 1 United States-Mexico Law Journal 295

Multi Development UK and Department for Social Development, 'People and Place: Victoria Square Scheme—Community and Business Opportunity Plan' (May 2006), available <http://at www.dsdni.gov.uk>

Mund, V A, *Government and Business* (Harper and Row, 1965)

Murphy, J L, *Gender Issues on World Bank Lending* (World Bank, 1995)

Murray, J, 'Corporate Codes of Conduct and Labour Standards' in Kyloh R (ed), *Mastering the Challenge of Globalisation: Towards a Trade Union Agenda* (ILO, 1998)

Muse, R L, 'A Public International Law Critique of the Extraterritorial Jurisdiction of the Helms-Burton Act (Cuban Liberty and Democratic Solidarity (Libertad) Act of 1996)' (1996–97) 30 GW JILE 207

Namibian Government, Department of Transport, 'Green Paper on Labour Based Works' (February 1997)

Nathan, R P, 'Jobs and Civil Rights: The role of the Federal Government in promoting equal opportunity in employment and training' (US Government Printing Office, 1969)

National Association of Manufacturers, 'A Catalog of New US Unilateral Economic Sanctions for Foreign Policy Purposes 1993–96' (NAM, 1997)

National Audit Office, 'Sustainable Procurement in Central Government' (September 2005)

National Economic and Social Forum, 'Equality Proofing Issues National Economic and Social Forum' (February 1996)

National Employment Panel, 'Report to Chancellor' (March 2005)

Nesiah, D, *Discrimination With Reason?: The Policy of Reservations in the United States, India and Malaysia* (OUP, 2004)

Netherlands Government, Ministry of Social Affairs and Employment, 'Meer Kansen Afdwinghen?' (March 1989)

Newcastle City Council, 'Can We Do Business? Racial Equality in a Competitive Environment' (1993)

—— 'Proposed Draft British Standard, Schedule of Requirements for Open Employment' (July 1993)

Nicholas, B, *The French Law of Contract* (2nd edn, OUP, 1992)

Nicholls, A, and Opal, C, *Fair Trade: Market-Driven Ethical Consumption* (Sage, 2004)

Nichols, P M, 'Corruption in the World Trade Organisation: Discerning the Limits of the World Trade Organisation's Authority' (1996) 28 NYU JILP 711

Niedzela, A, 'Recent Legislation on Public Procurement in Germany: Measures for Implementing the E.C. Procurement Rules' (1994) 3 PPLR CS44

Nielsen, H K, 'Public Procurement and International Labour Standards' (1995) 4 PPLR 94

Nielsen, R, and Szyszczak, E, *The Social Dimension of the European Union* (3rd edn, Handelshøjskolens Forlag, 1997)

—— and Treumer, S (eds), *The New EU Public Procurement Directives* (DJØF Publishing, 2005)

Noah, L, 'Administrative Arm-Twisting in the Shadow of Congressional Delegations of Authority' (1997) Wisconsin Law Review, 873

Noel, J, 'Étude relative à la possibilité d'introduire, par la voie légale, réglementaire ou administrative, une clause sociale dans les marchés publics des différents pouvoirs adjudicateurs en Belgique' 2000(1) Administration Publique 229

Nolan, C, *Jobs on the Block: The Use of Local Labour Training and Employment Schemes in the Construction Industry—a proposal for West Belfast* (West Belfast Economic Forum, August 1999)

Northern Ireland Government, 'Report and Recommendations of the Working Party on Discrimination in the Private Sector of Employment' (HMSO, 1973)

—— Department of Economic Development 'Equality of Opportunity in Employment in Northern Ireland' (1986)

—— Department of the Environment for Northern Ireland, 'Strategy for the Environment and the Economy in Northern Ireland' (March 1993)

—— Northern Ireland Procurement Review Implementation Team, 'A Review of Public Procurement: Findings and Recommendations' (Northern Ireland Department of Finance, February 2002)

—— Office of the First and Deputy First Minister, 'Review of Opportunities for Public Private Partnerships in Northern Ireland' (May 2002)

—— Office of the First and Deputy First Minister and the Department of Finance and Personnel, 'Working Together in Financing Our Future: Policy Framework for Public Private Partnerships in Northern Ireland' (February 2003)

Note, 'The Philadelphia Plan: A Study in the Dynamics of Executive Power' (1972) 39 University of Chicago Law Review 723

—— 'US Labor Practices in South Africa: Will a Mandatory Fair Employment Code Succeed Where the Sullivan Principles Have Failed?' (1983–4) 7 Fordham International Law Journal 358

—— 'State Buy American Laws in a World of Liberal Trade' (1992) 7 Connecticut Journal of International Law 311

—— 'To Compel or Encourage: Seeking Compliance with International Trade Agreements at the State Level' (1993) 2 Minnesota Journal of Global Trade 143

—— 'In Re Holocaust Victims' Assets Litigation: Do the US Courts Have Jurisdiction over the Lawsuits Filed by Holocaust Survivors Against the Swiss Banks?' (1997) Maryland Journal of International Law and Trade 251

—— 'The Iran and Libya Sanctions Act of 1996: A Thorn in the Side of the World Trading System' (1997) XXIII Brooklyn Journal of International Law 505

—— 'Linking Labour Standards and Trade Sanctions: An Analysis of their Current Relationship' (1998) 36 Col JTL 659

Nye, J S, Jr, *Soft Power: The Means to Success in World Politics* (Public Affairs, 2005)

O'Brien, G, 'Envisaged Change in the Procurement Regime: the Point of View of the European Commission' (Paper to the seminar on 'Legal Aspects of EC Public Procurement', Luxembourg, 29–30 October 1998)

O'Byrne, S K, 'Public Power and Private Obligation: an Analysis of the Government Contract' (1992) 14 Dalhousie Law Journal 485

O'Farrell, O, 'Gender Proofing and Structural Funds' (1995) 3 Equality News 6

Ochoa, C, 'Advancing the Language of Human Rights in Global Economic Order: An Analysis of a Discourse' (2003) 23 Boston College Third World Law Journal 57

OECD, *Greener Public Purchasing: Issues and Practical Solutions* (OECD, 2000)

—— 'The Size of Government Procurement Markets' (2002) 1(4) OECD Journal on Budgeting 16

—— *The Environmental Performance of Public Procurement: Issues of Policy Coherence* (OECD, 2003)

—— *The Environmental Performance of Public Performance: Issues of Policy Coherence* (OECD, 2003)

Ogus, A, 'Corrective Taxation as a Regulatory Instrument' in McCrudden, C (ed), *Regulation and Deregulation: Policy and Practice* (OUP, 1998) 15

Ong, P M, *Racial/Ethnic Inequality in the USA Labor Market: Empirical Patterns and Policy Options* (Performace and Innovation Unit, Cabinet Office, 2002)

Ontario Government, Ministry of Citizenship Office of the Employment Equity Commissioner, 'Opening Doors: A Report on the Employment Equity Consultations' (Queen's Printer for Ontario, 1992)

—— Ministry of Citizenship, Office of the Employment Equity Commissioner, 'Working Towards Equality: The Discussion Paper on Employment Equity Legislation' (Queen's Printer for Ontario, 1992)

Orton, M, and Ratcliffe, P, 'New Labour Ambiguity, or Neo-Consistency? The Debate About Inequality in Employment and Contract Compliance' (2005) 34(2) Journal of Social Policy 255

Osborne, R, Gallagher, A, and Cormack, R, with Shortall, S, 'The Implementation of the Policy Appraisal and Fair Treatment Guidelines in Northern Ireland' in McLaughlin, E, and Quirk, P, *Policy Aspects of Employment Equality in Northern Ireland* (SACHR, 1996)

Osterloh, L, 'Rechtsgutachten zu Fragen der Frauenförderung im Rahmen der öffentlichen Mittelvergabe' (June 1991)

—— 'Kurzgutachten über die Möglichkeiten der Frauenförderung im Rahmen der Vergabe öffentlicher Mittel, insbesondere in Form öffentlicher Aufträge' (October 1993)

Ostry, S, 'The World Trading System: In Dire Need of Reform' (2003) 109 Temple International and Comparative Law Journal 109

Othman, A H *et al*, 'Social Change and National Integration' in Yahaya, J *et al* (eds), *Sustaining Growth, Enhancing Distribution: The NEP and NDP Revisited* (Proceedings of CEDER Conference, 2003)

Paddon, M, 'Going Public in Europe: A Guide to the EC Public Procurement Directives' (Association of Metropolitan Authorities and the Local Government Management Board, July 1993)

Palmeter, D, and Mavroidis, P C, 'The WTO Legal System: Sources of Law' (1998) 92 AJIL 398

Panetta, L E, *Bring Us Together* (Lippincott, 1971)

Paternotte, M-P, 'Positive action in the public sector in Belgium' (1991) 3 Social Europe 112

Paulsen, G E, *A Living Wage for the Forgotten Man* (Susquehanna University Press, 1996)

Pauwelyn, J, 'Human Rights in WTO Dispute Settlement' in Cottier, T, Pauwelyn, J, and Bürgi, E (eds), *Human Rights and International Trade* (OUP, 2005) 214

Pedersen, E R, and Andersen, M, 'Safeguarding Corporate Social Responsibility (CSR) in Global Supply Chains: How Codes of Conduct are Managed in Buyer-Supplier Relationships' (2006) 3–4 Journal of Public Affairs 228

Pemberton, Jr, J de J (ed), *Equal employment opportunity: responsibilities, rights, remedies* (Practising Law Institute, 1975)

Penfold, G, and Reburn, P, 'Public procurement' in Woolman, S, Roux, J, Klaaren, J, Spitz, G, Steyn, D, Stein, A, and Chaskalson, M (eds), *Constitutional Law of South Africa* (loose leaf) (2nd edn, Juta Law, 2002)

Petersmann, E-U, *International and European Trade and Environmental Law After the Uruguay Round* (Kluwer, 1995)

—— 'Time for a United Nations "Global Compact" for Integrating Human Rights into the Law of International Organisations: Lessons from European Integration' (2002) 13 EJIL 621

Peterson, D J, 'The Trade Agreements Act of 1979: The Agreement on Government Procurement' (1980) 14 GW JILE 321

Pfarr, H M, and Eitel, L, 'Equal Opportunity Policies for Women in the Federal Republic of Germany' in Schmid, G, and Weitzel, R (eds), *Sex Discrimination and Equal Opportunity: The Labour Market and Employment Policy* (Gower, 1984) 155

Phillips, E, 'Positive Discrimination in Malaysia: A Cautionary Tale for the United Kingdom' in Hepple, B, and Szyszczak, E M, *Discrimination: the Limits of Law* (Mansell, 1992) 349

Pillay, S C K G, 'The Changing Faces of Administrative Law in Malaysia' (1999) 1 Malayan Law Journal cxl

Pipkin, C W, *The Idea of Social Justice: A Study of Legislation and Administration and the Labour Movement in England and France between 1900 and 1926* (Macmillan, 1927)

—— *Social Politics and Modern Democracies* (Macmillan, 1931)

Piselli, E, 'The Scope for Excluding Providers who have Committed Criminal Offences under the EU Procurement Directives' (2000) 9 PPLR 267

Pollack, M A, and Hafner-Burton, E, 'Mainstreaming Gender in the European Union' (2000) 7(3) Journal of European Public Policy 432

Pomeranz, M, 'Toward a New International Order in Government Procurement' (1979) 11 LPIB 1263

Potomac Institute, *Affirmative Action: The Unrealized Goal: A decade of opportunity* (The Potomac Institute, 1973)

Powell, A, 'Affirmative Action for Women in Australia' (A paper prepared for the International Labour Office) (ILO, September 1992)

Prechal, S, 'Equality of Treatment, Non-Discrimination and Social Policy: Achievements in Three Themes' (2004) 41 CMLR 533

President's Export Council, *Unilateral Economic Sanctions: A Review of Existing Sanctions and their Impacts on US Economic Interests with Recommendations for Policy and Process Improvement* (PEC, June 1997)

Preston McAfee, R, and McMillan, J, *Incentives in Government Contracting* (University of Toronto Press, 1998)

Price, D M, and Hannah, J P, 'The Constitutionality of United States State and Local Sanctions' (1998) 39 Harv ILJ 443

Priess, H-J and Pitschas, C, 'Recent German Public Procurement Case Law: Bodies Governed by Public Law and Social Criteria Unrelated to Public Procurement Rules' (1999) 8 PPLR CS120

—— and ——, 'Secondary Policy Criteria and Their Compatibility with EC and WTO Procurement Law: The Case of the German Scientology Declaration' (2000) 9 PPLR 171

—— and Graf von Merveldt, M, 'The Impact of the EC State Aid Rules on Secondary Policies in Public Procurement' in Arrowsmith, S, and Kunzlik, P (eds), *Social and Environmental Policies under the EC Procurement Rules: New Directives and New Directions* (provisional title) (Cambridge University Press, in press)

Quebec Government, 'Contract Compliance: One More Step Towards Employment Equity: Information for Organizations' (Government of Quebec, 1989)

Queensland Government, Department of Employment and Training, 'Indigenous Employment Policy for Queensland Government Building and Civil Construction Projects' (January 2004)

Quinn, J, and Slayton, P (eds), *Non-Tariff Barriers After the Tokyo Round* (Institute for Research on Public Policy, 1982)

Ram, M, and Smallbone, D, 'Supplier Diversity Initiatives and the Diversification of Ethnic Minority Businesses in the UK' (2003) 24(4) Policy Studies 187

Ramsey, L, 'The New Public Procurement Directives: A Partial Solution to the Problems of Procurement Compliance' (2006) 12 EPL 275

Raskin, C, *Equal Opportunity for Women: Affirmative Action: A Canadian Perspective* (ILO, unpublished, October 1992)

Razavi, S, and Miller, C, 'Gender Mainstreaming: A Study of Efforts by the UNDP, The World Bank and the ILO to Institutionalize Gender Issues' (Occasional Paper No 4, United Nations Research Institute for Social Development, August 1995)

Reed, M E, *Seedtime for the Modern Civil Rights Movement: The President's Committee on Fair Employment Practice, 1941–1946* (Louisiana State University Press, 1991)

Rees, T, *Mainstreaming Equality in the European Union* (Routledge, 1998)

Reich, A, *International Public Procurement Law: the Evolution of International Regimes on Public Purchasing* (Kluwer Law International, 1999)

Risik, P M, 'Federal Government Contract Clauses and Forms' (1954) 23 George Washington Law Review 125

Robarts, S, with Coote, A, and Ball, E, *Positive Action for Women: the next step* (NCCL 1981)

Robertson, D B, *Capital, Labor, and State: The Battle for American Labor Markets from the Civil War to the New Deal* (Rowman and Littlefield, 2000)

Robinson, J A, 'The Role of the Rules Committee in Arranging the Program of the U.S House of Representatives' (1959) 12(3) Western Political Quarterly 654

Rodman, K A, 'Think Globally, Punish Locally: Nonstate Actors, Multinational Corporations, and Human Rights Sanctions' (1998) 12 Ethics and International Affairs 19

Rodrik, D, 'Sense and Nonsense in the Globalisation Debate', *Foreign Policy* (Summer 1997) 19

Roessler, F, 'Domestic Policy Objectives and the Multilateral Trade Order: Lessons from the Past' in Krueger, A O (ed), *The WTO as an International Organisation* (University of Chicago Press, 1998) 213

Rogers III, W M, and Spriggs, W E, 'The Effect of Federal-Contractor Status on Racial Differences in Establishment-Level Employment Shares: 1979–1992' (1996) 86(2) American Economic Review 86

Romano, R, 'Public Pension Fund Activism in Corporate Government Reconsidered' (1993) 93 Columbia Law Review 795

Rosdahl, A, 'The Policy to Promote Social Responsibility of Enterprises in Denmark' (Paper prepared for the European Commission, DG EMPL Peer Review Programme, September, 2001)

Rubery, J, and Fagan C, 'Occupational Segregation of Women and Men in the European Community', *Social Europe*, Supplement 3/93, 112

Ruchames, L, *Race, Jobs and Politics: The Story of FEPC* (Columbia University Press, 1953)

Ruggie, J G, 'International Regimes, Transactions, and Change: Embedded Liberalism and the Postwar Economic Order' (1982) 36(2) International Organization 379

Runnymede Trust, Race Relations Bill Briefing Group, 'Brief No. 1, Government Contracts and their Role in Promoting Equal Opportunity in Employment' (nd)

Rustin, B, *Down the Line* (Quadrangle Books, 1971)

Rutherglen, R, 'After Affirmative Action: Conditons and Consequences of Ending Preferences in Employment' (1992) University of Illinois Law Review 339

Safire, W, *Before the Fall* (Tower Publications, 1975)

Santanillo, R, 'Klare Regeln für Ausschreibungen' (1991) 2(12) Europäisches Vergaberecht 93

Saunders, W, *History of the First London County Council, 1889–1890–1891* (National Press Agency Ltd, 1892)

Schlesinger Jr, A M, *Robert Kennedy and His Times* (Reissue edn, Ballantine Books, 1996)

Schmahmann, D R, Finch, J, and Chapman, T, 'Off the Precipice: Massachusetts Expands Its Foreign Policy Expedition from Burma to Indonesia' (1997) 30 Van JTL 1021

Schmid, G, and Weitzel, R (eds), *Sex Discrimination and Equal Opportunity: The Labour Market and Employment Policy* (Gower, 1984)

Schneider, A K, 'Democracy and Dispute Resolution: Individual Rights in International Trade Organisations' (1998) 19 UP JIEL 587

Schooner, S L, 'Commerical Purchasing: The Chasm Between the United States Government's Evolving Policy and Practice' in Arrowsmith, S, and Trybus, M (eds), *Public Procurement: The Continuing Revolution* (Kluwer, 2003) 166

Schwelb, S, 'The Influence of the Universal Declaration of Human Rights on International and National Law' (1959) 53 American Society of International Law Proceedings 217

Scott, C, and Macklem, P, 'Constitutional Ropes of Sand or Justiciable Guarantees? Social Rights in a New South African Constitution' (1992) 141 UP LR 1

Seddon, N, *Government Contracts: Federal, State and Local* (3rd rev edn, Federation Press, 2004)

Seidenfeld, M, 'An Apology for Administrative Law in "The Contracting State"' (2000) 28 Florida University Law Review 215

Selznick, P, *Law, Society and Industrial Justice* (Russell Sage Foundation, 1969)

Serdjenian, E, 'Inventory of Positive Action in Europe' *Women of Europe*, Supplement No 42 (1994)

Servais, J-M, 'The social clause in trade agreements: Wishful thinking or an instrument of social progress?' (1989) 128 International Labour Review 423

Shaffer, G, 'WTO Blue-Green Blues: The Impact of U.S. Domestic Politics on Trade-Labor, Trade-Environment Linkages for the WTO's Future' (2000) 24 Fordham International Law Journal 608

Shaw, J, 'Equal Opportunities for Women in the Federal Republic: Institutional Developments' (1990) 9 Equal Opportunities International 15

Shaw, J (ed), *Social Law and Policy in an Evolving European Law* (Hart, 2000)

Sheehan, M, and Tomlinson, M, 'Long-Term Unemployment in West Belfast' in McLaughlin, E, and Quirk, P, *Policy Aspects of Employment Equality in Northern Ireland, Volume iii Employment Equality in Northern Ireland* (SACHR, 1996)

Shell, G R, 'Trade Legalism and International Relations Theory: An Analysis of the World Trade Organization'(1995) 44 Duke Law Journal 829

Sheppard, C, 'Challenging Systemic Racism in Canada: Affirmative Action and Equity for Racialized Communities and Aboriginal Peoples' in Dubordieu, E (ed), *Race and Inequality: World Perspectives on Affirmative Action* (Ashgate, 2006)

Sheridan, L A, and Groves, H E, *The Constitution of Malaysia* (3rd edn, Malayan Law Journal,1979)

Shue, H, *Basic Rights: Subsistence, Affluence, and US Foreign Policy* (2nd edn, Princeton University Press, 1996)

Shuman, M H, 'GATTzilla v Communities' (1994) 27 Cornell International Law Journal 527

Sitkoff, H, *A New Deal for Blacks: The Emergence of Civil Rights as a National Issue, Volume 1: The Depression Decade* (OUP, 1978)

Slaughter, A M *et al*, 'International Law and International Relations Theory: A New Generation' (1998) 92 AJIL 367

Small Business Service and Office of Government Commerce, 'West Midlands SME Procurement Pilot: Final Project Evaluation Report: Management Summary' (November 2004)

Smith, B L R (ed), *The New Political Economy: The Public Use of the Private Sector* (Macmillan, 1975)

Smith, D, and Chambers, G, *Inequality in Northern Ireland* (OUP, 1991)

Smith, G, and Feldman, D, *Implementation Mechanisms for Codes of Conduct* (World Bank, IFC, November 2004)

Sobel, L A, *Job bias* (Facts on File, 1976)

Sohrab, J A, 'The Single European Market and Public Procurement' (1990) 10 OJLS 522 (1990)

South African Government, 'Public Sector Procurement Reform in South Africa: Interim Strategies: A 10-point Plan' (November 1995)

—— Department of Labour, 'Employment and Occupational Equality' (*Government Gazette*, Vol 373 No 17303, July 1996)

—— Ministry of Finance and the Ministry of Public Works, 'Green Paper on Public Sector Procurement Reform in South Africa: An Initiative of the Ministry of Finance and the Ministry of Public Works' (*Government Gazette*, Vol 382, No 17928, 14 April 1997)

South African Government, 'White Paper on Affirmative Action' (*Government Gazette*, Vol 394, No 18800, April 1998)

South African Government, National Treasury, 'Policy Strategy to Guide Uniformity in Procurement Reform Processes in Government' (07-04/2003, 2003)

—— Department of Trade and Industry, 'South Africa into the Future: The National Industrial Participation Programme' (DTI, nd), available at <http://www.dti.gov.za/uploads/offerings/files/127_46.pdf>

Southwick, J D, 'Binding the States: A Survey of State Law Conformance with the Standards of the GATT Procurement Code' (1992) 13 University of Pennsylvania Journal of International Business Law 57

Sowell, T, *Preferential Policies: An International Perspective* (William Morrow, 1990)

Spennemann, C, 'The WTO Agreement on Government Procurement—A Means of Furtherance of Human Rights?' [2001] Zeitschrift für Europarechtliche Studien 43

Spiesshofer, B, and Lang, M, 'The New German Public Procurement Law: Commentary and English Translation of the Text' (1999) 8 PPLR CS103

Spiro, P J, 'Note: State and Local Anti-South African Action as an Intrusion Upon the Federal Power in Foreign Affairs' (1986) 72 Virginia Law Review 813

Srinivasan, T N, 'International Trade and Labour Standards from an Economic Perspective' in van Dijck, P, and Faher, G (eds), *Challenges to the New World Trade Organisation* (Martinus Nijhoff/Kluwer, 1996) 219

Srivastava, V, 'India's Accession to the GPA: Identifying Costs and Benefits' (Paper presented to the World Bank, National Council of Applied Economic Research and World Trade Organization South Asia Workshop, New Delhi, 20–21 December 2003)

Stafford, DGSD, 'Malaysia's New Economic Policy and the Global Economy: The Evolution of Ethnic Accommodation' (1997) 10 Pacific Review 556

Standing Advisory Commission on Human Rights, 'Religious and Political Discrimination and Equality of Opportunity in Northern Ireland: Report on Fair Employment' (Cm 237, HMSO, 1987)

—— 'Employment Equality: Building for the Future' (Cm 3684, HMSO, 1997)

Stark, B, 'After/word(s): "Violations of Human Dignity" and Postmodern International Law' (2002) 27 Yale JIL 315

Stephanopoulos, G, and Edley, C, 'Review of Federal Affirmative Action Programs: Report to the President' (US GPO, 1995)

Stern, R, 'Labor Standards and Trade' in Bronckers, M, and Quick, R (eds), *New Directions in International Economic Law: Essays in Honour of John H. Jackson* (Springer, 2000) 425

Stirling, P, 'The Use of Trade Sanctions as an Enforcement Mechanism for Basic Human Rights: A Proposal for Addition to the World Trade Organisation' (1996) 11 American University Journal of International Law and Policy 1

Street, H, Howe, G, and Bindman, G, *Street Report on Anti-Discrimination Legislation* (Political and Economic Planning, 1967)

Strohs, M, 'Die Berücksichtigung vergabefremder Kriterien bei der Vergabe von Bauaufträgen durch die öffentliche Hand' (1988) 2 BauR 144

Sudhof, M, 'Rechtsgutachten zur Frage der Vereinbarkeit einer Kopplung der Vergabe öffentlicher Aufträge des Landes Hessen mit frauenfördernden Auftragsvergabebedingungen' (nd)

Sullivan, D F, *Civil Rights Programs of the Kennedy Administration* (University Microfilms International, 1986)

Sullivan, R, 'NGO expectations of companies and human rights' (2003) 3 Non-State Actors and International Law 303

Summers, L, 'A Trade Round that Works for People' *Financial Times*, 29 November 1999

Sundquist, J L, *Politics and policy: the Eisenhower, Kennedy, and Johnson Years* (Brookings Institution, 1968)

Swedish Government, National Integration Office and Lappalainen, P, 'Ingen diskriminering med skattemedel! Avtalsklausuler mot diskriminering vid offentlig upphandling' (2000:7)

Symposium, 'New York Law School Centre for International Law: States' Rights vs International Trade: The Massachusetts Law' (2000) 19 New York Law School Journal of International and Comparative Law 347

Symposium, 'The Emergence of Global Administrative Law' (2005) 68 Law and Comtemporary Problems Nos 3 and 4

Symposium, 'Whither Zschernig?' (2001) 46 Villanova Law Review 1259

Takase, C, 'Integrating Social Aspects in Public Procurement' (Paper prepared for 3rd Expert Meeting on Sustainable Public Procurement, New York, 15–17 June 2005)

Tarnopolsky, W S, and Pentney, W, *Discrimination and the Law: Including equality rights under the Charter* (2nd edn, Don Mills, 1985)

Tate, P, 'Breaking into the US markets' (1983) 29 Datamation 162

Taylor, A, 'Trade, Human Rights, and the WHO Framework Convention on Tobacco Control: Just What the Doctor Ordered?' in Cottier, T, Pauwelyn, J, and Bürgi, E (eds), *Human Rights and International Trade* (OUP, 2005) 322

Thomas, A, and Jain, H C, 'Employment Equity in Canada and South Africa: Progress and Propositions' (2004) 15 International Journal of Human Resource Management 36

Thompson, F, 'Black Economic Empowerment in South Africa: the role of parastatals and choices for the restructuring of the electricity industry' (Paper presented at the ICS/CAS International Conference 'Looking at South Africa Ten Years On', London, 10–12 September 2004)

Tiefer, C, 'The GATT Agreement on Government Procurement in Theory and Practice' (1997) 26 University of Baltimore Law Review 31

Tobler, C, 'Encore: "Women's Clauses" In Public Procurement Under Community Law' (2000) 25 ELR 618

—— 'Remedies and Sanctions in EC Non-Discrimination Law' (Office of Official Publications, 2005)

Tomalin, C, *Samuel Pepys: The Unequalled Self* (Penguin, new edn, 2003)

Tomasevski, K, *Development Aid and Human Rights Revisited* (Pinter, 1993)

Tomei, M, 'Affirmative Action for Racial Equality: Features, impact and challenges', ILO InFocus Programme, Working Paper 44 (ILO, May 2005)

Toth, A G, *The Oxford Encyclopaedia of European Community Law*, Vol 1 (OUP, 1990)

Tracey, C, 'Comment: An Argument for the Repeal of the Davis-Bacon Act' (2001) 5 Journal of Small and Emerging Business Law 285

Trachtman, J P, 'Unilateralism and Multilateralism in US Human Rights Laws Affecting International Trade' in Abbott, F M, Breining-Kaufman, C, and Cottier, T (eds), *International Trade and Human Rights: Foundations and Conceptual Issues* (University of Michigan Press, 2006) 357

Trades Union Congress, 'Race Relations Advisory Committee, Guidance Note on Contract Compliance and Equal Opportunities (May 1986)', reprinted in the *Report for 1985–6 of the Trades Union Congress, Women's Advisory Committee* (TUC, 1986)

TRB, 'Race unconscious' *The New Republic*, 16 December 1991, 4

Trebilcock, M J, and Howse, R, 'Trade Liberalisation and Regulatory Diversity: Reconciling Competitive Markets with Competitive Politics' (1998) 6 European Journal of Law and Economics 5

—— and Howse, R, *The Regulation of International Trade* (3rd edn, Routledge, 2004)

Treitel, G, 'Contract: General Rules' in Birks, P, *English Private Law, Volume II* (OUP, 2004)

Trepte, P-A, *Public Procurement in the EC* (CCH Editions, 1993)

—— *Regulating Procurement: Understanding the Ends and Means of Public Procurement Regulation* (OUP, 2004)

Tridimas, T, 'Equality' in Toth, A G (ed), *The Oxford Encyclopaedia of European Community Law, Volume 1* (OUP, 1990) 188

—— *The General Principles of EC Law* (OUP, 1999)

Trindade, F A, and Lee, H P (eds), *The Constitution of Malaysia: Further Perspectives and Developments* (OUP, 1986)

Twiggs, J E, *The Tokyo Round of Multilateral Trade Negotiations: A Case Study in Building Domestic Support for Diplomacy* (University Press of America, 1997)

Unison, 'Best Value and the Two-Tier Workforce in Local Government' (Unison, January 2002)

—— 'Contracting Out and the Two-Tier Workforce' (Unison, September 2000)

United Kingdom Government, Report of the Fair Wages Committee (Cd 4422, HC (1908) XXXIV, 551

—— 'Interim Report of the Committee on Re-Employment of Ex-Service Men' (1920) Vol XIX, 503, Cmnd 951

—— 'Interim Report of the King's Roll National Council on the employment of disabled ex-service men' (1923) Vol xii, 517, Cmnd 1919

—— Report of the Inter-departmental Committee on the Rehabilitation and Resettlement of Disabled Persons (Cmd 6415, HMSO, 1943)

—— Colonial Office, 'Report of the Federation of Malaya Constitutional Commission 1957', Colonial No 330 (HMSO, 1957)

—— White Paper, 'Racial Discrimination' (Cmnd 6234, HMSO, 1975)

—— White Paper, 'The Attack on Inflation' (Cmnd 6151, HMSO, 1975)

—— Department of Industry and the Central Office of Information, 'Government Contracts Preference Schemes' (Central Office of Information,1976)

—— Cabinet Office, Management and Personnel Office, 'Government Purchasing: A Multi-Departmental Review of Government Contract and Procurement Procedures' (Cabinet Office, 1984)

—— Cabinet Office, Management and Personnel Office, 'Government Purchasing: A Review of Government Contract and Procurement Procedures' (1984, HMSO)

—— 'Competition in the Provision of Local Authority Services' (Consultation Paper, February 1985)

—— Department of Economic Development, 'Equality of Opportunity in Northern Ireland: Future Strategy Options: A Consultative Paper' (HMSO,1986)

—— Department of Health and Social Security, 'The Priority Suppliers Scheme' (Department of Health and Social Security, 1988)

—— White Paper, 'Competing for Quality' (HMSO, 1991)

—— White Paper, 'Setting New Standards: A Strategy for Government Procurement' (Cm 2840, HMSO, 1995)

—— Department of the Environment, Transport and the Regions/Welsh Office, Consultation Paper, 'Compulsory Competitive Tendering: Changes to regulations and Guidance' (DETR/Welsh Office, July 1997)

—— Department of the Environment, Transport and the Regions, 'Modernising Local Government: Improving Local Services Through Best Value' (DETR, March 1998)

—— Department of the Environment, Transport and the Regions, 'Modern Local Government: In Touch With the People' (Cm 4013, HMSO, 1998)

—— Cabinet Office, Better Regulation Task Force, 'Anti-discrimination Legislation Review' (Cabinet Office, May 1999) available at <http://www.brc.gov.uk/downloads/pdf/antidisc.pdf>

—— Department of Finance and Personnel, 'A Strategic Review of Procurement Policy and of Purchasing Arrangements within the Northern Ireland Civil Service Departments, Final Executive Report' (Department of Finance and Personnel, December 1999)

—— Cabinet Office, Performance and Innovation Unit, 'Ethnic Minorities in the Labour Market' (Cabinet Office, 2002)

—— Cabinet Office, Strategy Unit, 'Ethnic Minorities in the Labour Market' (Cabinet Office, March, 2003)

—— Cabinet Office, Better Regulation Task Force and Small Business Council, 'Government: Supporter and Customer' (May 2003) available at http://www.brc.gov.uk/downloads/pdf/smeprocurement.pdf

—— Department of the Environment, Food and Rural Affairs, 'Changing Patterns: The UK Government Framework for Sustainable Consumption and Production' (DEFRA, September 2003)

—— Office of Government Commerce (OGC)/DEFRA, 'Joint Note On Environmental Issues' (OGC/DEFRA, October, 2003)

—— Office of the Deputy Prime Minister and the Local Government Association, National Procurement Strategy for Local Government in England (2003)

—— Department for Education and Skills and Office of Government Commerce, 'The policy and legal framework for using public procurement to enable contracted in staff to access basic skills training within government departments' (DfES/OGC, 2003)

—— Department of Finance and Personnel, 'The Northern Ireland Practical Guide to the Green Book' (2003 edn, Department of Finance and Personnel, 2003)

—— HM Treasury Guide, 'Appraisal and Evaluation in Central Government' (2003 edition)

—— Department of Trade and Industry, 'Five Year Programme: Building Wealth from Knowledge' (DTI, 2004)

—— Office of Government Commerce, 'Capturing Innovation: Nurturing Suppliers' Ideas in the Public Sector' (OGC, 2004)

—— Office of Deputy Prime Minister, Code of Practice on Workforce Matters (September 2005)

United Kingdom Government, Office of Government Commerce, Guidance on Fair and Ethical Trading (OGC, 2005)

—— HM Treasury, Cox review of creativity in business, 'Building on the UK's strengths' (2005)

United Kingdom Government, Office of Government Commerce and Department for Education and Skills, 'Approaches to support workforce skills through public procurement: The policy and legal framework' (2005)

—— Office of Government Commerce, Social issues in purchasing (OGC, 2006)

United Kingdom Parliament, House of Lords, Select Committee on the Sweating System, Fourth Report (HC 331, 1889)

—— House of Lords, Select Committee on the Sweating System, Final Report (HC 257, 1890)

—— Report of the Select Committee on Training and Employment of Disabled Ex-Service Men (1922) vol vi, 389, HC 170

—— House of Commons, Select Committee on Race Relations and Immigration, 'Organisation of Race Relations Administration, Report' (HMSO, 1975)

—— House of Commons, Treasury and Civil Service Committee, Sixth Report: The Role of the Civil Service: Interim Report, vol 2 Minutes of Evidence (HC 390-I, Session 1992–3, HMSO, 1993)

United Nations Development Programme (UNDP), 'Making Global Trade Work for the People' (UNDP, 2003)

United Nations High Commissioner for Human Rights, 'Analytical study of the High Commissioner for Human Rights on the fundamental principle of non-discrimination in the context of globalization', 15 January 2004, E/CN.4/2004/40

United States Civil Rights Commission, 'Federal Civil Rights Enforcement Effort' (USCRC, 1971)

—— 'The Federal Civil Rights Enforcement Effort—1974, vol 5, To Eliminate Employment Discrimination' (USCRC, July 1975)

United States Congress, House of Representatives, 'Hearings before the Subcommittee on General Oversight and Minority Enterprise of the Committee on Small Business, House of Representatives, Multinational Trade Negotiations', 96th Congress, First Session, 4 April 1979

—— Senate, International Trade Commission, 'Agreements Being Negotiated at the Multilateral Trade Negotiations in Geneva, Analysis of Non-tariff Agreements, Agreement on Government Procurement, A Report prepared at the request of the Committee on Finance', MTN Studies 6, Pt 3, United States Senate, 96th Congress, 1st Session, CP 96-27 (US GPO, 1979)

—— House of Representatives, Committee on Education and Labor, Sub-Committee on Employment Opportunities, 'Record of Oversight Hearings on Affirmative Action and the Federal Enforcement of Equal Opportunity Laws' (US GPO, 1981)

—— Senate, 'Hearings before the Subcommittee on International Trade of the Committee on Finance, Oversight on Government Procurement Code and Related Agreements', United States Senate, 97th Congress, 2nd Session, 9 June 1982

—— House of Representatives, Committee on Education and Labor, Sub-Committee on Employment Opportunities, 'Oversight Hearings on the OFCCP's proposed affirmative action regulations' (US GPO, 1983)

—— House of Representatives, Committee on Education and Labor, Sub-Committee on Employment Opportunities, 'Oversight Review of the Department of Labor's Office of Federal Contract Compliance Programs and Affirmative Action Programs' (US GPO, 1986)

—— House of Representatives, Committee on Education and Labour, 'A Report on the Investigation of the Civil Rights Enforcement Activities of the Office of Federal Contract Compliance Programs, U.S. Department of Labour' (1987).

United States General Accounting Office, 'The Equal Employment Opportunity Program for Federal Nonconstruction Contractors Can be Improved' (US Govt Print Off, 1975)

—— 'The International Agreement on Government Procurement: An Assessment of Its Commercial Value and US Government Implementation' (GAO/NSIAD-84-117, 16 July 1984)

—— 'International Procurement: Problems in Identifying Foreign Discrimination Against US Companies' (GAO/NSIAD-90-127, 5 April 1990)

United States, Department of Justice, Office of Legal Counsel, Memorandum to General Counsels (Department of Justice, June 28, 1995)

United States, Department of Labor, Office of Federal Contract Compliance Programmes, 'Employment Patterns of Minorities and Women in Federal Contractor and Noncontractor Establishments' (Department of Labor, June 1984)

Uri, N D, and Mixon, J W, 'Effects of US Affirmative Action Programs on Women's Employment' (1991) 13(3) Journal of Policy Modelling 367

Vaas, F J, 'Title VII: Legislative History' (1966) 7 Boston College Industrial & Commercial Law Review 431

van Calaster, G, 'Green Procurement and the WTO—Shades of Gray' (2003) 11(3) RECIEL 298

Van Cleve Jr, H R, 'The Use of Federal Procurement to Achieve National Goals' [1961] Wisconsin Law Review 566

van der Westhuizen, J, *Adapting to Globalization: Malaysia, South Africa, and the Challenges of Ethnic Redistribution with Growth* (Praeger, 2002)

van Dijck, P, and Faher, G (eds), *Challenges to the New World Trade Organisation* (Kluwer Law International, 1996)

Van Dyk, A, 'Recent Changes in the Canadian Government's Contracting Policy' (1998) 7 PPLR CS110

van Gervan, W, 'General Report to the 14th FIDE Congress' in FIDE, *L'Application dans les Etats Membres des Directives sur les Marchés Publics* (FIDE, 1990)

van Liemt, G, 'Minimum labour standards and international trade: Would a social clause work?' (1989) 128 International Labour Review 433

van Vleuten, C E, 'Contract Compliance 1: De situatie in de Verenigde Staten' (September/October 1989) 5 Nemesis, Tijdschrift voor Vrouw en Recht 169

—— *Contract Compliance in de Verenigde Statten, in Emancipatieraad, Positive Actie: Advies en onderzoek* (Emancipatieraad, 1989)

van Wezel Stone, K, 'Labour in the Global Economy: Four Approaches to Transnational Labour Regulation' in Bratton, W, McCahery, J, Picciotto, S, and Scott, C (eds), *International Regulatory Competition and Co-ordination* (OUP, 1996) 445

Vazquez-Fernandez, M, 'Outcome of the first equal opportunities plan in Spain (1988–90)' (1991) 3 Social Europe 115

Verbist, J, 'Government Procurement Law and Procedure of Belgium' (1987) 21 GW JILE 5

Verloo, M, 'Planning for Public Space: A Gender Impact Assessment Analysis' (Paper to the International Conference on Women and Public Policy: The Shifting Boundary Between the Public and Private Domains, 8–10 December 1994)

Vermulst E, and Driessen, B, 'The Choice of a Switch: The European Reaction to the Helms-Burton Act' (1998) 11 Leiden Journal of International Law 81

Vertes, N L, Connelly, D M H, and Knott, B A S, *Five year Review 1993 to 1996, Implementation of the Nunavut Land Claims Agreement: An Independent Review* (Nortext Multimedia, October 1999).

Verwilghen, M (ed), *Equality in Law between Men and Women in the European Community, vol II: National Reports* (Presses universitaires de Louvain, 1986)

—— *Access to Equality* (Presses universitaires de Louvain, 1993)

Vincent-Jones, P, 'Central-Local Relations under the Local Government Act 1999: A New Consensus?' (2000) 63 MLR 84

Vittoz, S, *New Deal Labor Policy and the American Industrial Economy* (University of North Carolina Press, 1987)

Vogel, D, *The Market for Virtue: The Potential and Limits of Corporate Social Responsibility* (Brookings Institution, 2005)

Vogel-Polsky, E, 'Study on Positive Action Programmes as Strategies to Integrate Female Workers and Other Hard-to-Place Groups into the Labour Market: Summary Report' (European Commission, V/30/83-EN, Doc Nr 34, November 1982)

—— 'Positive action programmes for women' (1985) 124 (3 and 4) International Labour Review 253, 385

—— 'Positive Action and the Constitutional and Legislative Hindrances to its Implementation in the Member States of the Council of Europe' (Council of Europe, EG (89) 1, 1989)

Waaldijk, K and Bonini-Beraldi, M (eds), 'Combating Sexual Orientation Discrimination in Employment: Legislation in Fifteen EU Member States: Report of the European Group of Experts on Combating Sexual Orientation Discrimination submitted to the European Commission' (November 2004)

Wachtel, H, 'Labour's Stake in the WTO' (March–April 1998) 37 The American Prospect 34

Waddington, L, *The Expanding Role of the Equality Principle in European Union Law* (EUI, 2003)

Waddock, S, 'Rhetoric, Reality and Relevance for Corporate Citizenship: Building a Bridge to Actionable Knowledge' in Allouche, J (ed), *Corporate Social Responsibility: Volume 1: Concept, Accountability and Reporting* (Palgrave Macmillan, 2006) 20

Waer, P, 'Social Clauses in International Trade: The Debate in the European Union' (1996) 30 Journal of World Trade 25

Waldinger, R, and Bailey, T, 'The Continuing Significance of Race: Racial Conflict and Racial Discrimination in Construction' (1991) 19(3) Politics and Society 291

Walker, C, 'Setting up a Public Procurement System: The Six Step Method' in Arrowsmith, S, and Trybus, M (eds), *Public Procurement: The Continuing Revolution* (Kluwer, 2003) 5

Ward, H, 'Common but Differentiated Debates: Environment, Labour and the World Trade Organisation' (1996) 45 ICLQ 592

Warner, M A A, 'Globalisation and Human Rights: An Economic Model' (1999) 25 Brooklyn Journal of International Law 99

Wasmeier, M, 'The Integration of Environmental Protection as a General Rule for Interpreting Community Law' (2001) 38 CMLR 159

Watermeyer, R B, Nevin, G Amod, and S Hallet, R A, 'An evaluation of projects within Soweto's contractor development programme' (1995, Second Quarter) SAICE Journal 17

—— 'Mobilising the Private Sector to Engage in Labour-Based Infrastructure Works: A South African Perspective' (Paper to Sixth Regional Seminar for Labour-Based Practitioners, 29 September–3 October 1997, Jinja, Uganda)

Webb, S, 'The Economics of Direct Employment, with an account of the fair wages policy' (Fabian Tract No 84, 1898)

—— and Webb, B, *The History of Trade Unionism, 1666–1920* (Longmans, Green, 1920)

Webster, T L, *Erskine May, A Treatise on the Law, Privileges, Proceedings and Usage of Parliament* (11th edn, William Clowes,1906)

Weiler, J H H, 'Fundamental Rights and Fundamental Boundaries: On the Conflict of Standards and Values in the Protection of Human Rights in the European Legal Space' in Weiler, J H H, *The Constitution of Europe* (Cambridge University Press, 1999) 102

—— *The Constitution of Europe* (Cambridge University Press, 1999)

Weiss, F, *Public Procurement in European Community Law* (Athlone Press, 1993)

Weissbrodt, D, and Kruger, M, 'Norms on the Responsibilities of Transnational Corporations and Business Enterprises with Regard to Human Rights' (2003) 97 AJIL 901

Weissenberg, P, 'Öffentliche Aufträge—Instrumente neutraler Beschaffung oder staatlicher Steuerung?' (1984) Der Betrieb (DB) 2285

Wendt, A, *Social Theory of International Politics* (Cambridge University Press, 1999)

West Midlands Forum, 'Racial Equality: Common Standards for Council Contracts' (West Midlands Forum, July 1998)

—— 'Common Standards for Equalities in Public Procurement' (2nd edn, West Midlands Forum, June 2005)

Westphal, T, 'Greening Procurement: An Attempt to Reduce Uncertainty' (1999) 8 PPLR 1

Whitton, S, 'On the pursuit of non-economical policies in the EU law of public contracts, with special focus on case law and forthcoming Dir 2004/18/EC' (University of Warwick, unpublished paper, 22 February 2005)

Williams, R, and Smellie, R, 'Public Purchasing: An Administrative Cinderella'(1985) 63 Public Administration 23

Williamson, O, *Markets and Hierarchies, Analysis and Antitrust Implications: A Study in the Economics of Internal Organization* (Free Press, 1983)

—— *The Economic Institutions of Capitalism* (Free Press, 1998)

Wilthagen, H, van het Kaar, van Lieshout en Luijendijk, 'Onder Sociale Voorwaarden: toepassing van contract compliance door de gemeentelijke en provinciale overheid: randvoorwaarden, ervaringen en resultaten' (Minsterie van Sociale Zaken en Werkgelegenheid/AWSB, The Netherlands School for Social and Economic Policy Research, 2000)

Winter, J A, 'Public Procurement' (1991) 28 CMLR 774

Witherspoon, J P, *Administrative Implementation of Civil Rights* (University of Texas Press, 1968)

Wolthers, A, *Rapport over DSB's ligestillingsarbejde 1987–1990* (DSB, 1990)

Women and Work Commission, 'Shaping a Fairer Future' (February 2006)

Woodham-Smith, C, *The Great Hunger: Ireland 1845–1849* (Penguin edition, 1991)

Woodward, A, 'European Gender Mainstreaming: Promises and Pitfalls of Transformative Policy' (2003) 20(1) Review of Policy Research 65

World Bank, 'South Africa Country Procurement Assessment Report, Refining the Public Procurement System, Volume I: Summary of Findings and Recommendations' (World Bank, Report No 25751-SA, February 2003) available at <http://www-wds.worldbank .org/external/default/WDSContentServer/IW3P/IB/2003/05/13/000094946_03042 504054534/Rendered/PDF/multi0page.pdf>

WTO, 'Singapore Ministerial Declaration (13 December 1996), WT/MIN(96)/DEC' (1997) 36 International Legal Materials 218 (1997)

—— 'Trade Policy Review: Malaysia—Report by the Government' (WTO, 1997)

—— 'Trade Policy Review: Malaysia' (WTO, WT/TPR/S/31, 3 November 1997)

—— Trade Policy Review—Republic of South Africa—Report by the Secretariat (WTO, WT/TPR/S/34, 06/04/1998)

—— 'Ministerial Declaration, Ministerial Conference, Fourth Session' (WTO, WT/MIN(01)DEC/W/1, 14 November 2001)

—— 'Trade Policy Review: Southern African Customs Union: report by the Secretariat, Annex: South Africa' (WTO, WT/TPR/S/114/ZAF, 24 March 2003)

Wrench, J, and Modood, T, 'The Effectiveness of Employment Equality Policies in Relation to Immigrants and Ethnic Minorities in the UK' (International Migration Papers, 38, International Migration Branch, ILO, June 2000)

Yeung, K, 'The Private Enforcement of Competition Law' in McCrudden, C (ed), *Regulation and Deregulation: Policy and Practice* (OUP, 1999) 37

Zadek, S, Lingayah, S, and Forstater, M, *Social Labels: Tools for Ethical Trade: Final Report* (European Commission, 1998)

Zappalà, G, 'Corporate Citizenship and the Role of Government: the Public Policy Case' (Information and Research Services, Department of the Parliamentary Library, Research Paper No 4, 2003)

Zelinsky, E A, 'James Madison and Public Choice at Gucci Gulch: A Procedural Defense of Tax Expenditures and Tax Institutions' (1993) 102 Yale Law Journal 1165

Index